GUNS ILLUSTRATED® 2011

EDITED BY

Dan Shideler

Published by

Gun Digest® Books, an imprint of F+W Media, Inc.
Krause Publications • 700 East State Street • Iola, WI 54990-0001
715-445-2214 • 888-457-2873
www.krausebooks.com

To order books or other products call toll-free 1-800-258-0929
or visit us online at www.krausebooks.com, www.gundigeststore.com
or www.Shop.Collect.com

CAUTION: Technical data presented here, particularly technical data on handloading and on firearms adjustment and alteration, inevitably reflects individual experience with particular equipment and components under specific circumstances the reader cannot duplicate exactly. Such data presentations therefore should be used for guidance only and with caution. Gun Digest Books accepts no responsibility for results obtained using these data.

ISSN 0072-9078

ISBN 13: 978-1-4402-1392-2
ISBN 10: 1-4402-1392-5

Designed by Dave Hauser and Patsy Howell
Cover design by Tom Nelsen

Edited by Dan Shideler

Printed in the United States of America

ABOUT THE COVER

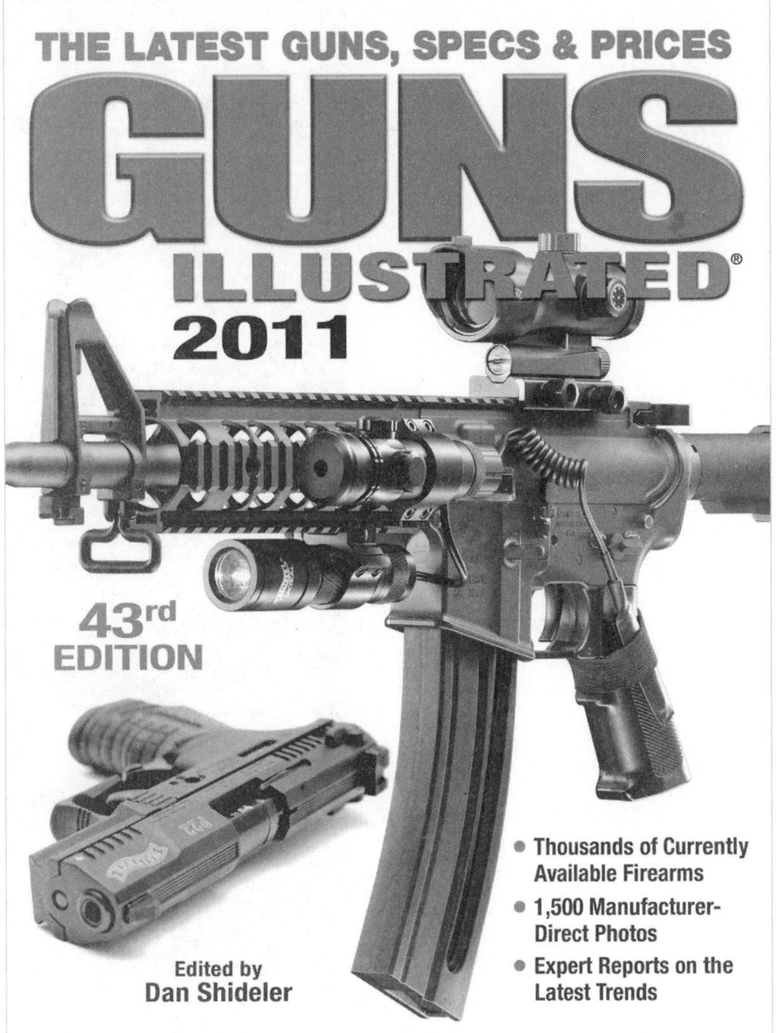

The recent centerfire ammunition shortage, painful though it was, yielded at least one benefit: a renewed appreciation for the .22 rimfire. The tricked-out Colt/Umarex M4 Carbine (top) combines two red-hot products – the AR-15 and the .22 Long Rifle round – into a package that offers economical practice and a whole lot of fun. Advertised as a "user-friendly adaptation of the larger P99," the hammer-fired Walther P22 (below) is a single/double-action semiauto that offers the look and feel of a centerfire combat pistol – but it, too, is chambered in .22 Long Rifle. With excellent-quality .22 LR ammo once again available in quantity, the Colt/Umarex M4 and the Walther P22 are bound to be crowd-pleasers.

CON

TENT

S

RIFLES

BY TOM TABOR

If it were possible to lay my hands on the old Savage Model 110 that I hunted with as a youth and place it next to one of the rifles I currently use today, on the surface few people would notice a great deal of difference. But while the basic firearm design concepts haven't changed significantly in recent decades, the gun manufacturers have without a doubt made significant inroads when it comes to accuracy, performance and dependability. I suppose that is why people such as I get so excited each year when the new models are brought out. No matter what shooting discipline we choose to participate in, we are eager to take advantage of anything that could result in improving our shooting performance. The following is just a sampling of some of the innovative rifles that are now available to world's sportsmen.

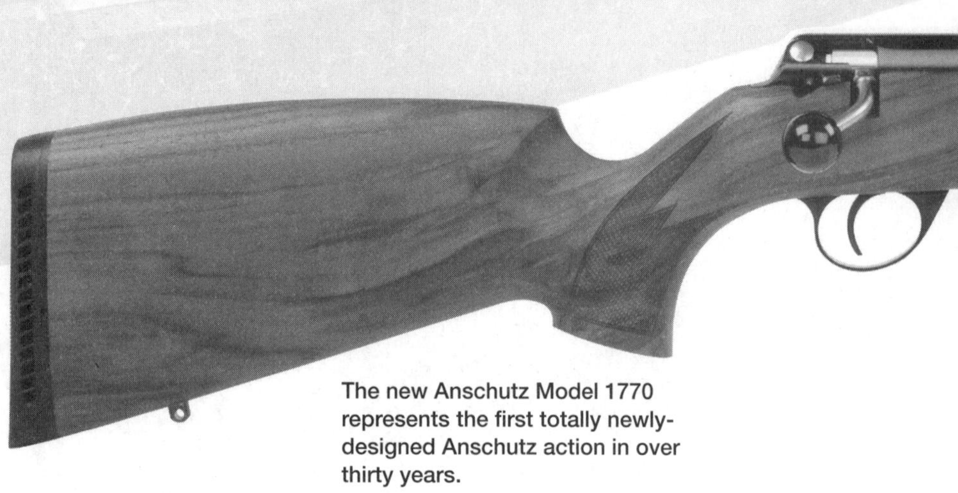

The new Anschutz Model 1770 represents the first totally newly-designed Anschutz action in over thirty years.

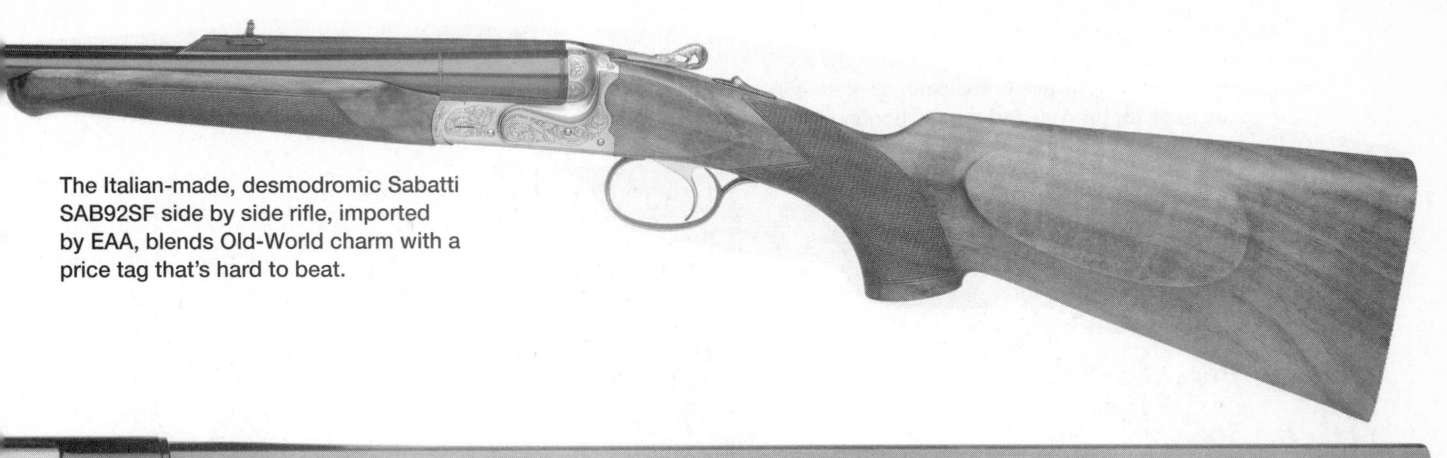

The Italian-made, desmodromic Sabatti SAB92SF side by side rifle, imported by EAA, blends Old-World charm with a price tag that's hard to beat.

Author shown with an Asian water buffalo taken in the Northern Territory of Australia with a custom rifle using a CZ action chambered for .500 Jeffrey.

ANSCHUTZ

The Model 1770 is the latest addition to Anschutz's hunting rifle line and is currently offered in only .223 Remington. This rifle represents the first time in over thirty years that Anschutz has introduced a totally new action. The design includes a six locking lug, a short 60-degree bolt lift and a single stage match trigger, which is set at the factory to 2.5-lbs. pull, but can be adjusted from 2 to 4.5 lbs. The German style Meister grade stock comes with an oil finish, semi-oval cheek piece, Schnabel forend and rosewood pistol grip cap. The stock is checkered at the pistol grip and forend. The medium weight barrel is cold hammer forged and 22 inches long. Overall length of the Model 1770 is 41.73 inches and the weight without a scope is 7.48 lbs. The MSRP for the new Model 1770 is $2,495.

BENELLI U.S.A.

Benelli is possibly best known for their semiautomatic shotguns, but recently the company has announced a new combat carbine rifle that is not only used and appreciated by the U.S. military forces but now can be the centerpiece of an effective home defense plan and in some cases for hunting and target shooting. The new MR1 fires the 5.56mm NATO (.223 Remington) and uses the ultra-reliable, battle-proven ARGO (Auto-Regulating Gas-Operated) system. This is the same system developed by Benelli for the M1014 and used for over a decade in multiple conflicts by the U.S. Marine Corps. The ARGO system incorporates a gas port located just forward of the chamber where the

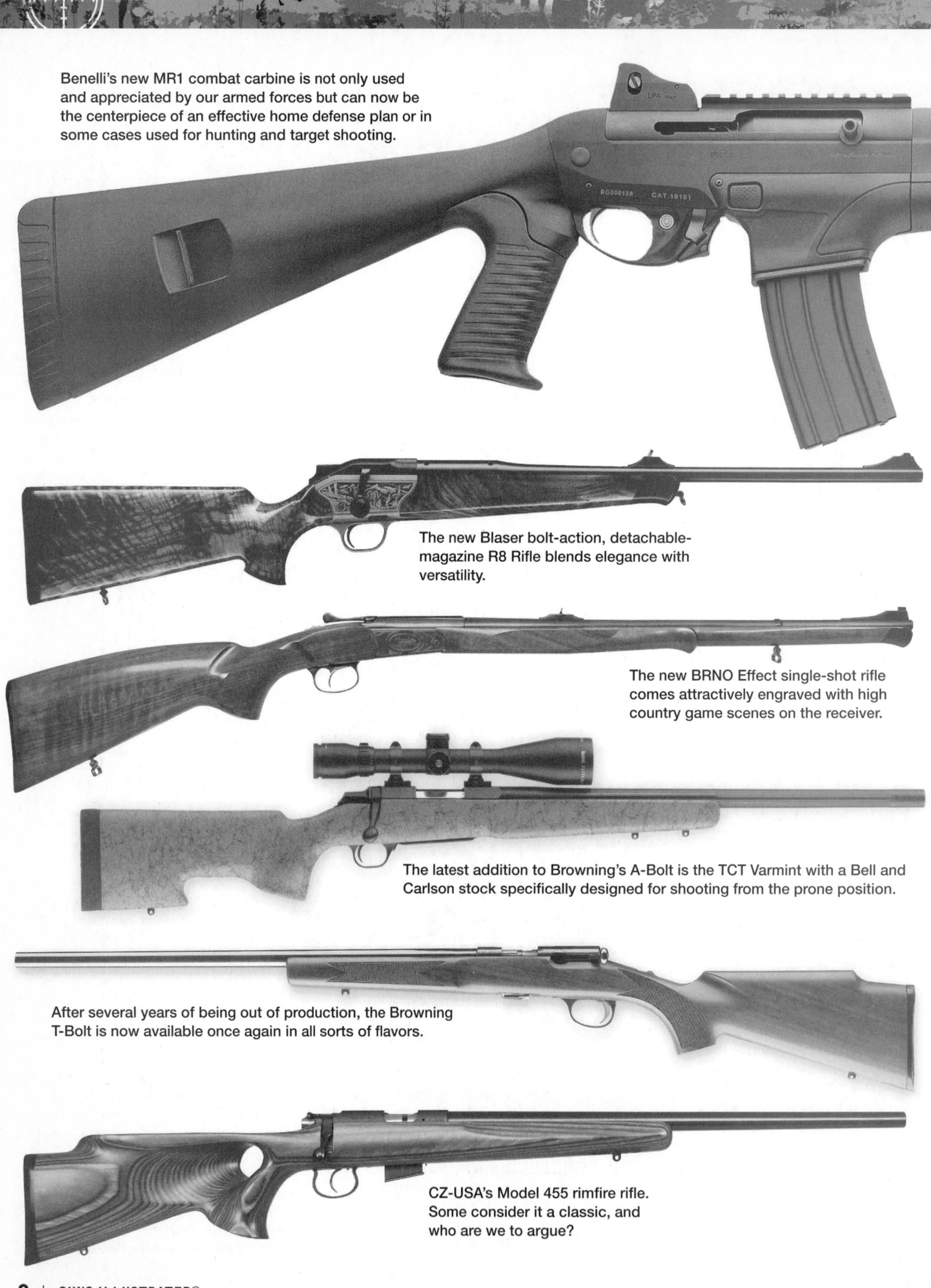

Benelli's new MR1 combat carbine is not only used and appreciated by our armed forces but can now be the centerpiece of an effective home defense plan or in some cases used for hunting and target shooting.

The new Blaser bolt-action, detachable-magazine R8 Rifle blends elegance with versatility.

The new BRNO Effect single-shot rifle comes attractively engraved with high country game scenes on the receiver.

The latest addition to Browning's A-Bolt is the TCT Varmint with a Bell and Carlson stock specifically designed for shooting from the prone position.

After several years of being out of production, the Browning T-Bolt is now available once again in all sorts of flavors.

CZ-USA's Model 455 rimfire rifle. Some consider it a classic, and who are we to argue?

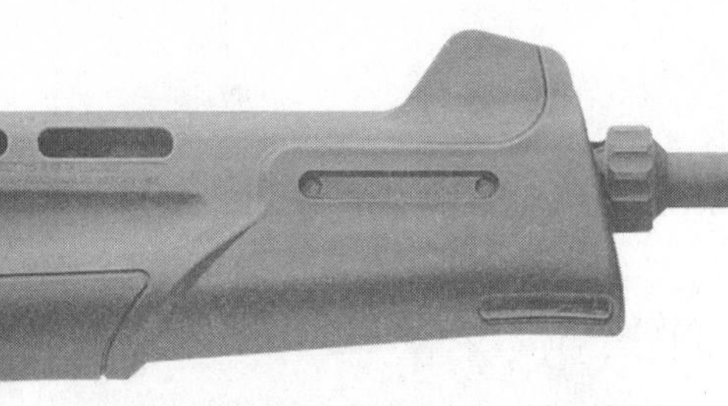

gases are hotter and cleaner, resulting in less fouling and more reliable cycling. The stainless steel, self-cleaning piston operates directly against the rotating bolt, thereby eliminating the need for complex linkages. The Picatinny rail allows mounting of both conventional and night-vision sights, while still retaining the capabilities of the metallic-sight. And, an optical Picatinny tri-rail forend kit is available that permits the mounting of a laser sight. The rifle comes from the factory equipped with a five-round magazine, but it will also accept any standard M16 magazines.

BLASER U.S.A.

For years Blaser has been recognized for their versatile interchangeable-barrel rifles, but the company has carried this trait one step further with their new Blaser bolt-action, detachable magazine R8 Rifle. The R8's magazine and trigger assembly have been merged together into a single compact module. The magazine buttons are positioned just above the trigger guard. For safety reasons, when you remove the magazine the R8 automatically de-cocks, keeping the cocking slide from engaging. The new Blaser Precision Trigger breaks at a trigger pull of 1-5/8 lbs. with an extremely short release time and does not rely on a spring to reset the trigger after firing. The desmodromic trigger mechanism offers reliability in extreme conditions such as freezing rain and blowing dust. [*Editor's Note: "desmodromic"? No, Tom didn't just make up that word. It refers to mechanisms that use different types of controls in order to function. Who knew? –DMS*] A wide variety of R8 models are available to select from, including even an individually engraved version.

BRNO

The new BRNO Effect single-shot rifle comes with a select walnut stock and is available in full-length style. The rifle weighs only a mere 6-pounds and comes engraved with high country game scenes on the receiver. It also comes with a single set trigger, automatic safety and iron sights and includes the scope base for mounting optics. Currently the Effect is available in .308 Winchester and .30-06 and carries a MSRP of $1,699.

BROWNING

Years ago, Browning's inventory consisted of only two guns: the Superposed and the Auto-5 shotguns, but today that line has been expanded to include approximately 300 flavors of shotguns alone, about 350 different models of rifles and around 30 different pistols. Included with that vast array of noteworthy firearms today is the T-Bolt™ .22 rifle. After dropping this innovative straight-pull design years ago, Browning decided to bring it back recently and now offers several different stock variations and finishes, including composites, sporters and target/varmint styles. The short-throw action makes the T-Bolt quick to load from the unique 10-round "Double Helix" magazine. MSRP for the T-Bolts range from $705 to $789.

Another Browning rifle that has experienced a great deal of success has been the A-Bolt. Like the T-Bolt, this rifle is offered in many different variations and styles including the recent TCT Varmint. (Sad to say, the "TCT" has nothing to do with the author's own initials.) This particular A-Bolt comes with a glass bedded receiver that is matte blued and drilled and tapped for a scope. The barrel is free-floating, 22 inches long and fluted and is also matt blued with a target crown. The composite stock is a hand-laid fiberglass Bell and Carlson that is specifically designed for shooting from the prone position and comes with aluminum bedded block for improved accuracy. Currently the TCT Varmint is available chambered for .223, .22-250 and .308 and weighs 10 lbs., 6 oz. MSRP is $1,299.

COOPER FIREARMS OF MONTANA

When compared to many other rifle manufacturers, Cooper Firearms of Montana isn't a large company, but over the last two decades they have earned a reputation for making rifles of exceptional high quality that possess unsurpassed tact-driving accuracy. Cooper changed ownership in 2009 and since that time the company has focused their attention on better customer relations, improved products and a shorter order turnaround time.

In the past the company has concentrated primarily on rimfire and the smaller centerfire chamberings that lend themselves for use by varmint hunters and predator hunters and for moderate-range target shooting. This has included both the normal production cartridges as well as a broad array of wildcats. This year the company entered a new era of production by offering a short-action repeater called the Model 54. This totally newly-designed rifle was specifically developed for the classic .243-.308 family of cartridges. Currently it is available in .22-250 Remington, .243 Winchester, .250 Savage, 7mm-08 Remington, .308 Winchester and .260 Remington, but the company plans to add to those choices in the near future. The Model 54 comes in a wide variety of stock configurations including several classic styles and varmint designs. All of the Model 54s come with fully adjustable single stage triggers of the Cooper design, Sako style machined extractors, plunger style ejectors machined from solid bar stock and the three front bolt locking lugs that Cooper has become known for. The basic MSRP for the Classic and Varmint Laminate is $1,695 and that of the Western Classic is $3,895. Because Coopers is essentially a custom shop, custom features can be added to any of their rifles. Prices for those are available upon request.

CZ-USA

The CZ 455 is a new generation of rimfire bolt-action rifles that will eventually consolidate all of the receivers currently used in the Model 452 line into a single platform. This combination, with CZ's new interchangeable barrel system, will allow the user to easily change the stock configuration as well as the caliber. The American Model is the first to see the benefits of this change, but other configurations will soon follow. The Model 455 comes with an adjustable trigger, hammer forged barrel and billet machined receiver and is available in .22 LR, .22 WMR and .17HMR. The MSRP for the American CZ 455 is $463 to $504.

EUROPEAN AMERICAN ARMORY - SABATTI

Quality double rifles often come with five-figure price tags. On the other hand, European American Armory (EAA) is importing a high-quality, Italian-made

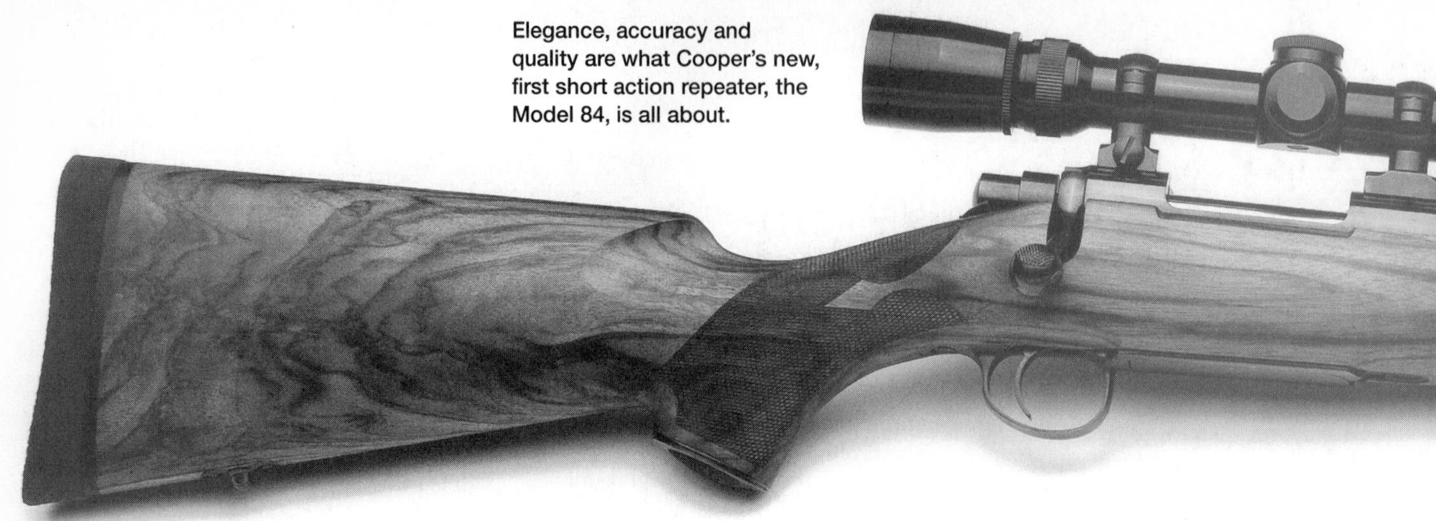
Elegance, accuracy and quality are what Cooper's new, first short action repeater, the Model 84, is all about.

double that not only carries an attractive price tag but it is chambered in a wide variety of cartridges, ranging from the tried-and-true .45-70 all the way up to the big .500 Nitro Express. [*Editor's Note: Yes, but is it desmodromic? –DMS*] The Sabatti SAB92SF comes with all the quality features and characteristics that are common in doubles today including a beavertail forend, European styled checkpiece, deep cut checkering, high grade walnut stock, tang mounted safety, chrome-moly barrels, very attractive full engraving and a chrome-steel receiver. For quick target acquisition, modern fiber optic sights have been added. MSRP on the Sabatti SAB92SF is just over $6,000. For more information you can visit http://www.ussginc.com/index.html, or contact EAA Corp. at 411 Hawk St., Rockledge, FL 32955 or at (321) 639-4842.

HI-POINT

Hi-Point Carbines may not be exactly what all shooters are looking for, but these lightweight, low-cost, very versatile rifles fills a nice niche in the firearm field that few others seem to be filling at this time. Currently the Hi-Point Carbine comes chambered in 9mm Luger or .40 S&W, which allows the shooters the benefits associated with using the same ammunition for both their rifle and sidearm. This makes these rifles an excellent choice for either law enforcement or for home defense applications. The robust all-weather black molded polymer skeletonized stock is both tough and lightweight. The forearm has a grabby surface that permits the shooter to wear gloves or shoot bare handed in all types of weather. The simple blow back design feeds the cartridges from the compact single stack 10-round magazine, which is interchangeable with those of the Hi-Point series semi-auto pistols of same caliber. The metal finish is a special high-durability black powder coat and the stock is a black molded polymer construction. The carbine comes equipped with both an upper and lower Picatinny rail, so you can hang no end of stuff off it if you want. Depending on caliber, the barrel length varies from 16-1/2 to 17 inches and the weight runs about 7 lbs. The Hi-Point Carbine's MSRP is remarkably low at only $249 to $299.

HOWA

Howa has extended its Howa/Hogue Model lineup recently to include the newly developed .375 Ruger powerhouse cartridge. It includes a Hogue Overmolded™ stock in either black or OD green color, a 20-inch #2 contour barrel, Hi-Vis #3 front and rear sights and is available in either blued or stainless.

KIMBER

Kimber has now added to their line of fine Model 84s with a brand new long action rifle, appropriately called the Model 84L. It comes in two styles: the Classic Select Grade and the Classic. The Classic Select Grade Model is available in .25-06 Remington, .270 Winchester and .30-06 Springfield. The stock is French walnut with an ebony forend tip. The Classic Model 84L is available in .270 Winchester and .30-06 Springfield and comes with a Claro walnut stock. The weight is the same for both the Classic Select and Select Grade at a mere 6 lbs., 2 oz. Both come with 24-inch barrels and are equipped with all-steel trigger guards and floorplates. MSRP for the Classic Select is $1,359 and $1,179 for the Classic.

MOSSBERG

Mossberg has recently released two new centerfire bolt action rifles in the company's Maverick Series: a Long-Action Rifle and a Super Bantam Short-Action Rifle. The standard features include such niceties as a free-floating button-rifled barrel, a recessed muzzle crown, factory installed Weaver-style two-piece scope bases and a 4+1 cartridge capacity. They are offered in four popular calibers. The long action model comes in either .30-06 Springfield or .270 Winchester and the short action Super Bantam comes in either .243 Winchester or .308 Winchester. Both come with a matte blued finish and a black synthetic stock, but in the case of the Super Bantam the stock is adjustable in order for it to grow as the youngster grows. Adding or removing inserts at the butt permits the stock to be lengthened or shortened as needed to fit the shooter.

NOSLER

Nosler has made a significant addition to their current Model 48 line of rifles with the introduction of the Model 48 Trophy Grade Rifle (TGR). The new TGR features a free-floating 24-inch chrome-moly barrel and a crisp 3-lb. Basix trigger. Targeting those hunters who face wet and inhospitable conditions, the TGR includes a custom aluminum bedded Bell & Carlson composite stock and the exterior metal surfaces are protected by a special application of Cerakote. The interior working parts have a corrosion-resistant coating of Micro-Slick, too. Nosler officials indicate that hunters can expect sub-MOA performance at 100 yards with the TGR. It is available in nine big game calibers, with the addition of two new choices in the Model

The Howa/Hogue Model lineup is now available chambered for .375 Ruger.

The utilitarian Hi-Point Carbine comes chambered in either 9mm Luger or .40 S&W.

The stylish Kimber 84L Classic Select Grade.

Mossberg's Super Bantam Short-Action Rifle comes with the ability of "growing" in stock length as the young shooter grows.

Ruger's 10-22 VLEH Target Tactical rifle.

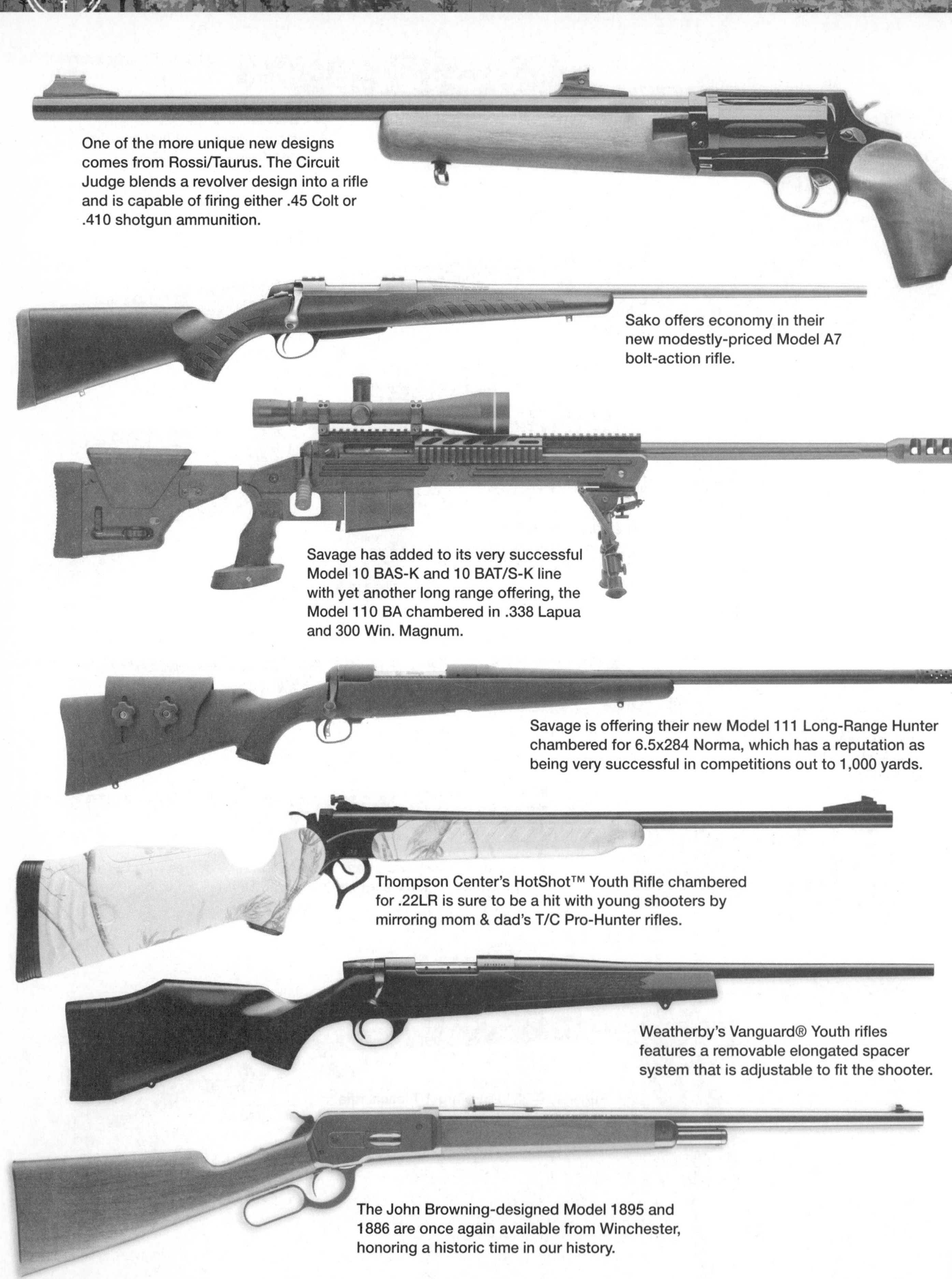

One of the more unique new designs comes from Rossi/Taurus. The Circuit Judge blends a revolver design into a rifle and is capable of firing either .45 Colt or .410 shotgun ammunition.

Sako offers economy in their new modestly-priced Model A7 bolt-action rifle.

Savage has added to its very successful Model 10 BAS-K and 10 BAT/S-K line with yet another long range offering, the Model 110 BA chambered in .338 Lapua and 300 Win. Magnum.

Savage is offering their new Model 111 Long-Range Hunter chambered for 6.5x284 Norma, which has a reputation as being very successful in competitions out to 1,000 yards.

Thompson Center's HotShot™ Youth Rifle chambered for .22LR is sure to be a hit with young shooters by mirroring mom & dad's T/C Pro-Hunter rifles.

Weatherby's Vanguard® Youth rifles features a removable elongated spacer system that is adjustable to fit the shooter.

The John Browning-designed Model 1895 and 1886 are once again available from Winchester, honoring a historic time in our history.

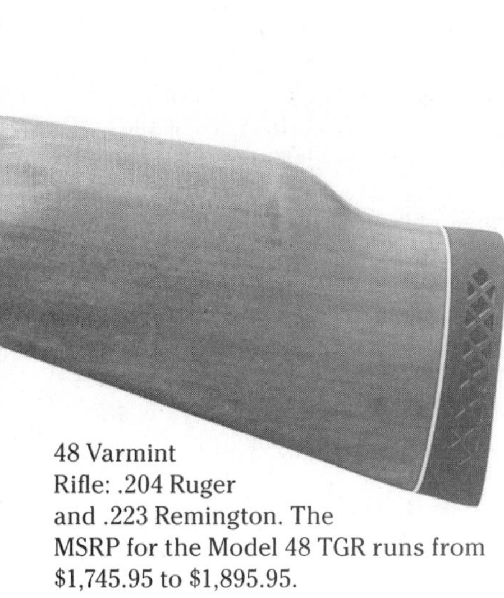

48 Varmint Rifle: .204 Ruger and .223 Remington. The MSRP for the Model 48 TGR runs from $1,745.95 to $1,895.95.

OLYMPIC ARMS, INC.

Olympic Arms continues to build top quality ARs in a wide variety of configurations. The usual 5.56mm, 6.8 SPC and .7.62x39 are available, as well as some pistol calibers. Unique to Olympic is the Model K8-MAG that is offered in .223, .243 and .25 WSSM. New for 2010 is a new cartridge developed by Olympic called the .300 Olympic Super Short Magnum (OSSM). This new hotrod produces ballistics exceeding those of the .30-06 out of a 22-inch barrel. Winchester .25 WSSM brass is easily necked-up to make the cases. Hornady makes the dies, Hodgdon will have load data available soon, and HSM supplies factory loaded ammo. Complete rifles, as well as uppers ready to go on your existing AR, are available. The complete rifle is called the "Gamestalker" and it's a real looker with its camo finish, ACE skelton-buttstock and ERGO Sure Grip. It comes with no sights, but its flattop design allows shooters to arrange it in any optics configuration that they see fit. The aluminum handguard is free-floated and the 22-inch stainless-steel barrel is of a lightweight hunting contour. Overall weight is a comfortable 7.5 lbs.

ROSSI/TAURUS

Possibly one of the most unique new rifles making its debut is the Rossi/Taurus Circuit Judge. [*Editor's note: The Circit Judge also pops up in our Shotguns section. –DMS*] The rifle combines the design of the Taurus revolvers with that of a long gun. This shotgun/rifle crossover offers the ability to shoot .410 2-1/2- or 3-inch magnum shotshells or .45 Colt ammunition in any order or combination without the need of changing barrels. The Circuit Judge is available in either a smooth bore or a rifled barrel version and comes with a blued finish, hardwood Monte Carlo style stock, single-action/double-action trigger, fiber-optic front sight, yoke detent, recoil pad, transfer bar and the Taurus Security System. The barrel measures 18.5 inches long, the overall firearm length is only 38 inches and total weight is only a mere 4.75 lbs. MSRP is $618.00.

RUGER

It wasn't long after Ruger appeared on the firearm/shooting scene in 1949 that shooters throughout the world began to appreciate the quality of the products that this company produces. Over the six-plus decades that followed, Ruger has established a reputation as a very progressive company that seemingly has the inherent ability to supply exactly the type of firearms that shooters are looking for. And there is no better example of this than a couple of newly released rimfires.

First there is the SR-2 that combines the visual features of an AR rifle with the fun and economy of shooting a .22 LR. The SR-22 uses a standard 10/22 action inside a top-quality, all-aluminum chassis that faithfully replicates the AR-platform dimensions between the sighting plane, buttstock height and the grip. It includes a Picatinny rail optic mount and a six-position telescoping M4-style buttstock on a mil-spec diameter tube, plus a Hogue Monogrip pistol grip. The round, mid-length handguard is mounted using a standard-thread AR-style barrel nut, which allows a vast array of rail-mounted sights and accessories to be used. The 15-1/8-inch barrel is precision-rifled and constructed of cold hammer forged alloy steel and comes capped with a SR-556/Mini-14 flash suppressor.

The second new addition to Ruger's rimfire rifles is the 10/22® VLEH Target Tactical rifle. This rifle offers many of the inherent features used in the Hawkeye® Tactical bolt-action rifle but in a semi-auto rimfire action. It builds on many of the features of the Ruger 10/22 Target Model, beginning with the same precision-rifled, cold hammer forged, spiral-finished barrel, but cut to the shorter length of 16-1/8 inches in order to reduce the weight and improve the handling. The .920-inch OD match-grade barrel is capped with a target crown to protect the rifling at the muzzle, and the barreled action is mounted in a non-slip, rugged Hogue OverMolded stock. The trigger of the 10/22® VLEH Target Tactical rifle is the same as used on the 10/22® Target Model and an adjustable bipod comes with each rifle. The rifle, minus the bipod, weighs 6-7/8 lbs.

SAKO

For the economy-minded shooter, Sako has merged many of the desirable Sako features into their Model A7 bolt-action rifle, yet kept the price down. The A7 comes in wide variety of the most popular calibers ranging from .243 up to the .300 Win. Mag. It is available in either blued or stainless steel and includes such features as a cold hammer forged match-grade barrel, single stage adjustable trigger (adjustable from 2 to 4 lbs. pull), detachable magazine, two-position safety with separate bolt release button, Weaver-style scope bases and a lightweight synthetic stock. Depending on caliber, the weight ranges from 6-3/8 to 6-5/8 lbs. with barrel lengths from 22-7/16 to 24-3/8 inches. Each rifle is guarantee to place five shots into a 1-inch group at 100 yards. MSRP for the blued model is from $850 to $900 and the stainless model runs from $950 to $1,000.

SAVAGE ARMS

In the last decade Savage Arms has substantially improved both the quality of their products and expanded their firearms lines. The company's newly developed AccuTrigger and AccuStock come stock on many of those products, and this has provided Savage with a significant edge over their competition. This year the company followed up their very successful 2009 release of the radical Model 10 BAS-K and 10 BAT/S-K tactical/target rifles with yet another: the Model 110 BA. Chambered for .338 Lapua and .300 Win. Mag., this considerably extends the range of these great precision rifles. The BA modular platform is built around an aluminum stock that features Savage's innovative three-dimensional bedding system. Buttstock and pistol grips are easily interchanged and a three-sided accessory rail adds versatility. The 110 BA features a five-round detachable magazine, high-efficiency muzzle brake and a Magpul PRS adjustable stock. MSRP is $2,267.

Another great addition at Savage is their new Model 111 Long-Range Hunter with a new chambering for 2010, the 6.5x284 Norma. The 6.5x284 Norma has been very successful in competition out to 1,000 yards and is a favorite of those who appreciate 26-calibers. The new Long-Range Hunter features a 26-inch fluted magnum sporter barrel, AccuTrigger, AccuStock with Karsten adjustable cheekpiece and a matte blued finish. MSRP is $934 to $972.

SMITH & WESSON

Smith & Wesson is best known for their high-quality handguns, but over the last few decades the company has very successfully moved into the rifle and shotgun market. Recently the company released a great new addition to their line of rifles, the .22LR-platform Model M&P 15-22, which mirrors the AR-style centerfire rifles. The M&P 15-22 comes with a 25-round detachable magazine and a six-position collapsible CAR stock that's capable of collapsing to an overall length of 30.5 inches or extending to 33.75 inches. The match-grade precision barrel is 16 inches long with a 1:16 twist. The weight is a moderate 5.5 lbs. and the sights are an adjustable A2-style post in the front and an adjustable dual aperture in the rear. In addition, the M&P 15-22 comes with a functioning charging handle, quad rail handguard, threaded barrel with an A1-style compensator, and lightweight, high strength polymer upper and lower receivers. They come from Smith and Wesson with a lifetime service policy and carry an MSRP of $569.

THOMPSON/CENTER ARMS

In the recent years Thompson/Center Arms (nowa Smith & Wesson company) has become a major player in the area of sporting firearms. Answering the calls of predator hunters, in January 2010 the company added yet one more member to their Venture family of rifles, the T/C Venture Predator. At the core of the T/C Venture Predator is its 22-inch precision barrel with 5R "offset" rifling and target grade crown. T/C guarantees these rifles to have MOA accuracy. Just a few of the many inherent favorable features include a trigger with an adjustable pull from 3.5 to 5 lbs, a nitrate-coated bolt with a 60-degree lift, a roller-burnished receiver (which helps to provide quick follow-up shots), and a classic styled composite stock with inlaid traction grip panels. The T/C Venture Predator comes from the factory with a drilled and tapped receiver and ships complete with Weaver-style scope bases already installed. Currently the rifle is available in .204, .22-250, .223 and .308 and comes with a single stack 3+1 detachable nylon box magazine. The Venture Predator is entirely made in the U.S. and is backed by Thompson/Center's lifetime warranty for a retail price from $549 to $599. Sounds like a helluva deal to us.

To be available in April of 2010 from T/C is the new .22LR HotShot Youth Rifle. Designed to mirror mom and dad's T/C Pro-Hunter, the HotShot includes many features that are favorable to a youngster, like an easy to operate break-open system, a weight of only 3 lbs. (!) and an overall length of 30-1/4 inches. With the rifle's single shot design and hammer block trigger, the HotShot will not fire until the hammer is cocked. It's available in three colors (black composite, Realtree AP camouflage and pink AP camouflage). The HotShot is made totally in the United States and is also backed by T/C's lifetime warrantee at an anticipated retail price ranging from $229 to $249 (again: !).

WEATHERBY

Weatherby has long been a supporter of our youth and the company's introduction of their new Vanguard® Youth Rifle further emphases that dedication of getting youngsters involved in shooting sports. The Vanguard Youth features a removable elongated spacer system that is adjustable to fit the shooter. Installing the spacers creates a longer length of the pull, allowing it be changed from 12-1/2 up to 13-5/8 inches. The rifle weighs only 6-1/2 lbs. and comes with a #1 contour 20-inch barrel. It's equipped with a black synthetic stock, fully adjustable trigger, a cold hammer forged barrel and the proven Vanguard short action. It has an injection molded Monte Carol style stock and is currently only available in a right-hand version. Available calibers include .223 Remington, .22-250 Remington, .243 Winchester, 7mm-08 Remington and the

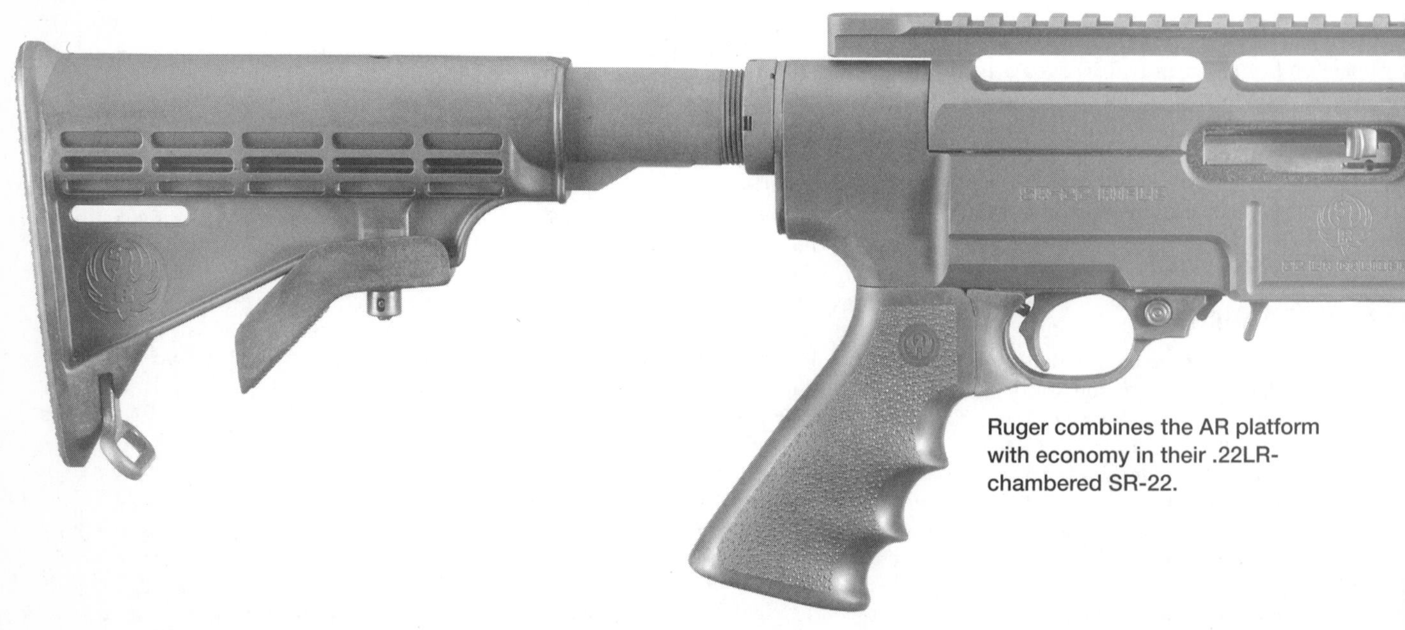
Ruger combines the AR platform with economy in their .22LR-chambered SR-22.

Olympic Arms' Model K8-MAG is now offered in a new cartridge developed by Olympic, the .300 Olympic Super Short Magnum (OSSM).

The latest addition to Nosler's line of fine rifles is the Model 48 Trophy Grade Rifle (TGR).

.308 Winchester. The Youth Vanguard Weatherby carries a MSRP of $529.00.

A number of shooters appealed to Weatherby, requesting that the company produce a detachable magazine rifle. Weatherby responded with a couple of new offerings in their Vanguard line: the Synthetic DBM (stands for detachable box magazine) and the Sporter DBM. The magazines are made of a durable polymer, which helps to reduce the overall weight of the rifles. The magazines hold three rounds and come with a unique cartridge counter for easy reference in the field. Other features of the Synthetic DBM include a black injection-molded composite Monte Carlo stock, matte black metalwork and a low-density recoil pad. The Sporter DBM has a raised-comb Monte Carlo walnut stock with a satin urethane finish, a rosewood forend and low-luster, matte-blued metalwork. Both rifles weigh 7 lbs. and are available in .25-06 Remington, .270 Winchester and .30-06 Springfield and come with a 24-inch #2 contour barrel, but, again, only in a right hand. configuration

WINCHESTER REPEATING ARMS

Winchester has expanded its line of rifles once again to include a couple of John Browning-designed models from our distant past: the Grade I Model 1895 and the extra light Model 1886. Both of these lever action models have deeply blued receivers and blued steel end caps and are equipped with straight buttplates. Both come with top tang safeties and adjustable buckhorn rear sights. The 1895 is available in .405 Winchester, .30-06 and .30-40 Krag, while the 1896 is available only in .45-70. The Grade I 1895 carries a MSRP of $1,179 and the Grade I 1896 is $1,269. Also new from Winchester is a takedown versison of the 16-inch-barrelled Model 1892 Trapper Carbine, a finely-machined little honey that's expected to be vailable in short, short, short supply sometime this year.

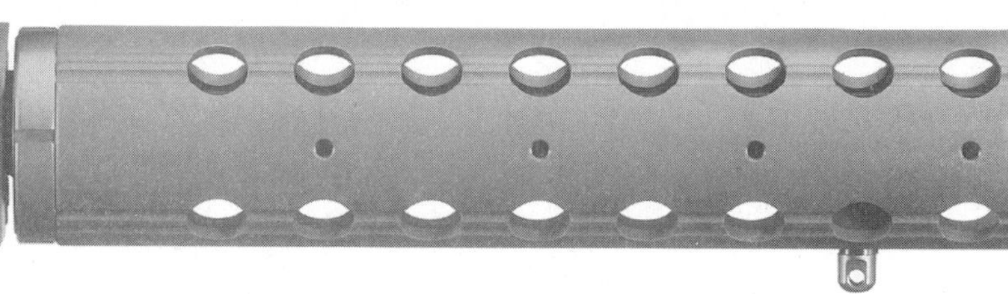

THE UNLIKELIEST SLEEPER of them all

BY DAN SHIDELER

Back around 1971, when I was just getting interested in guns and shooting, my older cousin Steve Shideler sent me a full-page ad he had clipped from the pages of Guns & Ammos magazine. In the margin of the ad he had penned a brief editorial comment: "HA HA HA!"

The ad showed two guns, the ugliest things I had ever seen. They looked like some sort of over-and-under rimfire rifle, but there wasn't a splinter of wood anywhere on them. Their stocks were made of wire. They apparently had two triggers. And they were headlined "Bronco. No nonsense, hard-working guns without the frills. "

Ah, yes, the Garcia Bronco! At the time, I dismissed the Bronco as just another one of those nutty phenomena that appeared with distressing regularity in those days, like Tiny Tim or George McGovern. Time heals all wounds, however, and today the ugly-duckling Bronco is a prime collectible. Don't believe me? Just try to find one!

The weird little gun best known as the Garcia Bronco appeared in a number of incarnations in the late 1960s and early to mid-1970s. To begin with, the name "Bronco" wasn't even unique to the skeleton-stock rifle. Garcia - a major sporting goods distributor - used the name "Bronco" pretty willy-nilly. In fact, if you wanted to spend a day in the Great Outdoors, you could outfit your Garcia Bronco spinning rod with a Garcia Bronco open-face reel. For good measure you could carry your Garcia Bronco recurve bow and strap on your Garcia Bronco quiver. And if squirrel season was in, you'd better take along your Garcia Bronco rifle.

The gun later known as the Bronco was first made in 1967 in Accokeek, Maryland, by Firearms International Corporation and wasn't labeled "Bronco" at all. It came in only one flavor: a 3-1/2 lb., 16-1/2-inch-barreled, solid-frame single-shot .22 rifle. When Garcia bought Firearms International in 1970, they added three more flavors: a single-shot .22 Magnum rifle with pretty much the same dimensions as the .22 LR version; a 4 lb. single-shot .410 shotgun with a somewhat heavier receiver and a 20-inch barrel; and a .22/.410 over-under combo gun with a 20-inch barrel. As Garcia maintained, the Broncos were indeed guns "without the frills." No truer words were ever spoken.

My first impressions of the Garcia Bronco were erroneous. The gun did not in fact have two triggers: what I had mistaken for a front trigger was in fact a cocking piece. On the single-shot version, what appeared to be the upper barrel was in fact a pivot rod that allowed the barrel to swing sideways for loading. And the stock wasn't wire at all but a zinc-alloy casting with a rod-stock insert.

If the truth be told, the Bronco was nothing more than an updated version of the old Hamilton Model 7 made from 1889 to 1901 by the Hamilton Rifle Company of Plymouth, Michigan. In the Hamilton Model 7, the barrel pivoted to the right away from a standing breech. You stuck a shell in the exposed chamber, swung the barrel to the left to close the action, cocked the striker, and touched 'er off. It was a simple, low-cost, virtually foolproof system. In fact, the system was so elemental and easy to manufacture that it later appeared in Hamilton's later Model 11 and in the Savage Model 101 single-shot revolver-that-wasn't-a-revolver.

The Hamilton Model 7 was a rather attractive little gun, what with its brilliant nickel plating. The appearance of the Bronco, however, fell somewhat short of brilliant. On the Firearms International models, the pot-metal frame and stock were painted with olive drab or bronze enamel (often incorrectly described as an anodized or powder-coated finish), while the post-1970 Garcia versions were finished in black crinkle paint. The Bronco differed in other details from the Hamilton, too. When the front "trigger" was squeezed back, it simultaneously cocked the coil spring-operated striker and retracted a locating pin that locked the swiveling barrel to the breech. You then swung the barrel to the left, exposing the chamber. A short plunger-style extractor on the right side of the barrel assembly popped out the empty. The safety was a plain, square trigger-locking pushbolt mounted just above the rear of the trigger guard.

The Bronco's rear sight was minimal or, as Garcia might put it, "without frills": a crescent-shaped stamping secured to a barrel lug with a common screw. The Bronco's sights were thus adjustable for both windage and elevation, often unin-

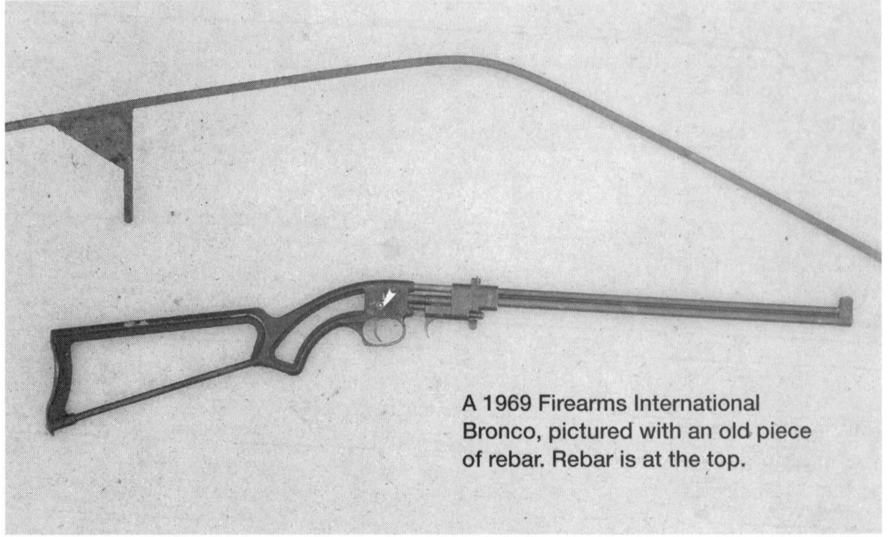

A 1969 Firearms International Bronco, pictured with an old piece of rebar. Rebar is at the top.

Bronco. No nonsense, hard-working guns without the frills.
The Bronco is a work gun. A sur-
vival gun. A camp gun. It's for the
man who cares more about how his
gun works than how it looks.
We didn't design the Bronco to be
pretty. We designed it to be rugged
and dependable, without a nickel's
worth of frills that would add something to the cost without adding
something to its function.
The Bronco is available in two
versions: a single-shot .22 with a
16½-inch barrel (it handles Short,
Long and Long Rifle cartridges),
and the new Bronco over and under
rifle/shotgun chambered for .22 and
.410 (up to 3-inch shells), with 20-
inch barrels. Both take down in seconds for travel or handy storage.
The sights on both the rifle and
the over/under are adjustable for
windage and elevation. In addition,
the rear sight on the over/under
serves as the barrel selector. Snap
the sight up to fire the rifle barrel,
down for the shotgun.
Broncos are built to work . . . and
work hard. We built them to spend
their lives jouncing in a jeep or
lashed to a backpack or tucked under a bush pilot's seat.
A Bronco is a perfect gun for a
backpacker or a trapper, for example. It weighs only 3 pounds in .22—
less than 4½ pounds in the .22/.410
over and under—so it can be carried all day long without fatigue.
A Bronco isn't expensive, so for a
farmer who wants to keep a gun
locked in the henhouse or the barn
against an over-ambitious varmint,
the Bronco is perfect. We know of
another farmer in Virginia who hangs
a Bronco from his tractor for wood-
chuck and crows, plus an occa-
sional rabbit for the pot. After a
couple of seasons of this, his Bronco
looks somewhat the worse for wear,
but it still shoots as well as ever, and
that's what he cares about.
And a lot of commercial and sport
fishermen are discovering that the
Bronco makes a great boat gun. It
has a crackle-finish, one-piece stock
and receiver, and the gun's flat,
compact shape makes mounting out
of the way, like up against a bulk-
head, a real cinch. A .410 rifled slug,
they've learned, is a powerful shark
repellent.
As a survival gun, the Bronco is
hard to beat. Its ruggedness, light
weight, ease of takedown and low
cost mean that it's likely to be with
you when an emergency arises. After all, a survival gun isn't going to
do you much good if you've left it
back at camp.
The same simplicity that makes it
so reliable makes Bronco a great
gun for a beginner, too. The Bronco
has a positive cam extractor, cross-
bolt safety, and ordnance steel barrels. It's a lot of gun for the money.
Bronco. It may not be much to
look at, at first. But the more you
get to know it, the better it looks.
The garcia Corporation
329 Alfred Av., Teaneck, N.J. 07666

The operative phrase here is "without the frills."

tentionally, at the same time. The front sight was a stubby, flat-topped post, protected by two ears like the front sight of an M1 carbine. On the combo version, the rear sight was a more substantial affair that also served as a barrel selector. Pulling the sight up selected the upper rifle barrel. Pushing it down selected the lower shotgun barrel.

For the first few years of its existence, the Bronco was a fixed-barrel rifle. After a few years, however, it morphed into a takedown version. To take down a Bronco, you swung a flimsy, stamped lever located on the right side of the receiver backward. This in turn rotated an integral cam inside the receiver, disengaging it from an oblique cut in the pivoting barrel extension. The whole barrel assembly then pulled off toward the front. That's the easy part. Reassembling the Bronco is a different matter entirely. In fact, I monkeyed with mine for perhaps 10 minutes, during which the barrel extension stubbornly refused to reseat itself in the receiver. After filling the atmosphere with a thick purple haze of profanity, I realized that the oblique cut had to be facing downward and the lever cam had to be in its full rearward position for the barrel extension to fully enter its recess. Swinging the lever forward relocked the whole works.

If you're trying to disassemble a Bronco, you'll quickly notice that there aren't many screws in sight. The gun is held together mostly by pins, all of which have to be laboriously driven out by hand. This may account for the fact that relatively few Broncos have survived: it was easier to throw them away when they broke rather than fool around with them.

Detailed serial number records for the Bronco haven't survived, but the guns can be approximately dated nevetheless. Firearms International models don't bear the Bronco name, and until 1969 they didn't have serial numbers, either. Serial-numbered, unnamed Firearms International models were made in 1969 and 1970. When Garcia bought Firearms International in 1970, they named the rifle the Bronco which, as we have seen, was a proprietary Garcia pet name. The combo gun was made in limited quantities in 1975 only, and the Bronco was dropped altogether that same year despite a failed attempt to remarket it as the "Bauer Rabbit."

Pete Dickey of the American Rifleman's technical staff maintains that the Bronco ultimately failed because of the Gun Control Act of 1968 and the transfer paperwork it mandated. Before GCA 1968, you could walk into a hardware store with cash in hand and walk out with a Bronco. After GCA 1968, you had to fill out forms to own a Bronco, and that hardly seemed worth the effort for a gun that retailed for under $20 for most of its life.

In my admittedly limited experience, the Bronco's chief fault, aside from its hideous sights, is that its pivoting barrel extension and locating pin inevitably gather their fair share of slop, resulting in a loose barrel-to-receiver fit. This doesn't help accuracy any, but my Bronco will still put five shots into three inches at 40 yards despite the fact that its bore looks like the colon of a goat that's been eating steel wool.

My friend Richard Clauss has what may well be the Rolls-Royce of customized Broncos. Richard filled the skeletonized buttstock of his .410 Bronco with hinged walnut inserts that conceal, as so many of Richard's buttstocks do, a reservoir of shells. The pistol grip is decked out with checkered walnut panels. Richard also installed a beautiful walnut forend that conceals an integral laser sight. It would be a horrible offense against aesthetic principles to call any Bronco beautiful, but there's no doubt that Richard's is an attractive little shotgun. The idea of adding wood to the Bronco also occurred to the Rau Arms Corporation of El Dorado, Kansas, who refined the Bronco concept to what is certainly its highest evolutionary factory form: the Wildcat Model 500. (The Wildcat will be the subject of the next of these mercifully brief columns.)

So far I haven't noticed anyone offering to trade their Model 70 collection for a Garcia Bronco. I suspect that to most serious gun fanciers, a Bronco isn't worth the calories it would burn to

The Bronco's receiver, cocking handle and barrel assembly. Ain't it purty?

throw one in the river. But there's apparently a handful of die-hard enthusiasts out there who are willing to pay $200 to $300 for a Bronco in pristine condition. The combo gun is a real collector's prize and may command a 25 to 50 percent premium.

As Garcia put it, the Bronco was "a work gun. A survival gun. A camp gun. It's for the man who cares more about how his gun works than how it looks." Admittedly, the Bronco looked horrible in its day. But to modern collectors, they look pretty good!

SHOTGUNS

BY JOHN HAVILAND

Ithaca's Mike Farrell his holding his company's Phoenix 12-gauge over-and-under that is in production after a year and some of final development.

Except for hunting pronghorn antelope at long-range, a shotgun in various forms of dress works fine for every type of hunting in North America. With one receiver a hunter can clamp on a rifled barrel to shoot slugs and hunt big game from deer and elk to bears and hogs. That barrel can be switched out for a smoothbore barrel that accepts various screw-in choke tubes to hunt feathered game from waterfowl and turkeys to grouse and quail and stay tuned up on clay targets all year. Many of us, though, are not quite so utilitarian and like a separate shotgun for each shooting game. Let's see what the shotgun companies have for both practical and particular shotgunners this year.

BENELLI

Last year Benelli built up the suspense to the unveiling of their Vinci shotgun with advertisements of fashion models running through the street, carrying an oblong parcel containing the shotgun and looking with concern over their shoulders like international secret agents were on their trail. Once Benelli opened the box in early spring I got my hands on a Vinci and I've been shooting it ever since.

The Vinci comes from the box in three pieces: barrel/receiver, trigger group/forearm and buttstock. The barrel/receiver mates with the trigger group/forearm and a turn of the forearm cap locks them together. The front of the buttstock locks into the rear of the trigger group/forearm and a clockwise partial turn of the buttstock fastens them. Once the gun is together its profile does have a rather bulbous belly forward of the trigger guard.

The Vinci action uses the In-Line Iner-

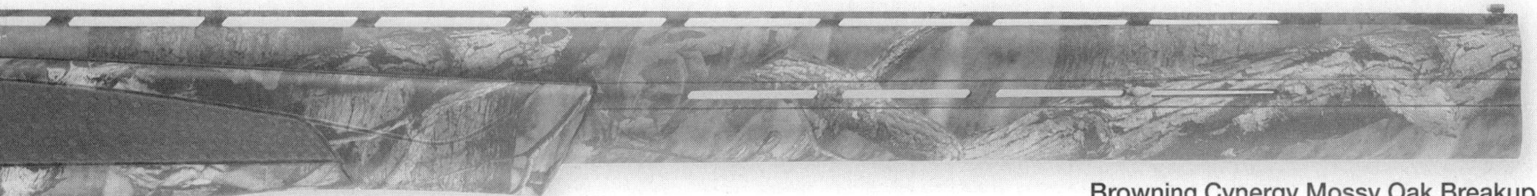

Browning Cynergy Mossy Oak Breakup.

tia Driven operating system. Its two-lug bolt is similar to other Benelli autoloaders. However, the bolt's rearward spring and guide rod compress against a plate inside the receiver, instead of extending into the stock like the Inertia Driven system in other autoloading Benellis. The In-Line Inertia Driven system cycles very reliably and the Vinci fired several hundred 1- and 1-1/8-oz. target loads without a single blip, leaving just a slight amount of grime inside of the action after all that shooting.

The Vinci's ComforTech Plus recoil reduction system is gentle on the shoulder and cheek when shooting that many target loads and hunting loads. The smooth insert on the comb allows the cheek to slide during recoil. Vertical rows of gel inserts in the buttstock allow the buttstock to flex and absorb recoil and a soft recoil pad caps it off. Several days in the duck swamps I shot the Vinci with Winchester Xtended Range Hi-Density waterfowl loads with 1-1/4 and 1-3/8 oz. of shot. The recoil was much less than with my old Benelli Super 90.

The Vinci weighs six lbs. 14 oz. with a 28-inch barrel. That's fairly light for a three-inch 12-gauge, so I carried it into the mountains for blue grouse and along the creek bottoms for ruffed grouse. I shot handloaded 1-1/8 oz. of 7½s for the grouse and if I do say so myself, I shot rather well with the gun.

This year the turkey version of the Vinci is available. It has a SteadyGrip vertical grip stock and 24-inch barrel, camouflaged muzzle to toe.

On the light and handy side, Benelli's Legacy autoloader is chambered in 28 gauge. The gun weighs five pounds with either a 24- or 26-inch barrel with a carbon fiber ventilated rib. Benelli states it is the lightest autoloader in the world. Its walnut stock and forearm are covered with WeatherCoat finish to protect the wood from the rain and snow. An acid-etched bird hunting scene covers the lower receiver and an Aircell recoil pad soaks up what little recoil the 28 gauge generates.

BERETTA

Shotgun companies continue to develop mechanical methods to reduce the brutal recoil of 12-gauge 3½-inch magnum shells. My solution is to simply not shoot shells the size of a Roman candle.

Beretta's autoloading A400 Xplor is for bird hunters who want a portable 3-inch 12-gauge shotgun, but with the option, if the silly notion ever overtakes them, to shoot 3-1/2-inch shells. The Xplor weighs 6.6 pounds, slightly less than Beretta's AL 391 3-inch 12-gauge. To reduce recoil, the Xplor uses the Kick-Off system that incorporates two hydraulic dampers in front of the recoil pad and a third inside the stock bolt to check the slam of the bolt against the rear of the receiver. In addition to lessening the sharp stab of recoil, that third damper reduces wear on the internal parts.

Often a 3-1/2-inch gun has a difficult time cycling target loads. An elastic band on the gas piston in the Xplor, though, prevents propellant gases from escaping from the gas valve so all the gas operates the action. The elastic band also scrubs gas residue off the inside of the cylinder. I shot Federal 1-1/8 oz. target loads one after another through an Xplor without a single hiccup. Recoil was only a slight jump of the

Gail Haviland struts her stuff with a Beretta Tx4 Storm autoloader 12-gauge.

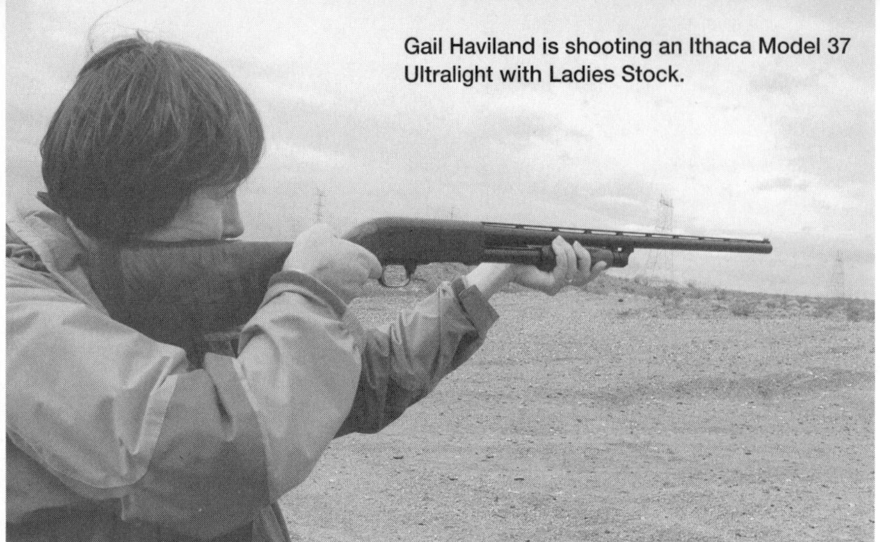
Gail Haviland is shooting an Ithaca Model 37 Ultralight with Ladies Stock.

gun in my hands. The silly notion to fire 3-1/2-inch shells in the gun momentarily overtook me. I came to my senses and fired just one. The recoil was *ouch!* there but no more than from other guns weighing a couple more pounds.

The Beretta Tx4 Storm autoloader is a home-defense 12-gauge. The Storm weighs slightly under 6-1/2 pounds with its 18-inch barrel ported at the muzzle. The length of pull of the buttstock can be adjusted with half-inch spacers. Rubber grip inlays on the synthetic stock and forearm ensure a firm grasp. An adjustable ghost ring sight mounts on a rail on the receiver top to aim in conjunction with a high front sight with protective ears.

My wife shot the Storm with buckshot loads at 25 yards. The paper target was a sieve when she finished shooting and I plan to stay on her good side.

BLASER

The over-and-under F3 SuperTrap uses interchangeable single or over-and-under 12-gauge barrels. The barrels are free-floating and adjustable to move pattern impact of each barrel. The tall rib is also vertically adjustable to fine tune pattern placement. A barrel weight system keeps the gun's weight the same whether one or two barrels is in the receiver. The stock is set with cast for left or right-handed shooters and the comb is adjustable for height.

The F3 frame is also available in 28 gauge with 28-inch Competition or 28-inch Game barrels. The Competition barrel features the identical weight, balance and rib as all the other F3 Competition barrels in 12 and 20-gauge. A variety of Briley choke tubes comes with each barrel.

BROWNING

The Maxus Hunter is a good looking version of the camouflage Maxus autoloader introduced last year. The Hunter wears a walnut stock and forearm and the nickel finish on its aluminum receiver is engraved with a mallard and a pheasant. The barrel is blued with a flat ventilated rib and comes with full, modified and improved cylinder Invector-Plus choke tubes.

The Maxus Sporting Carbon Fiber has a silver and carbon fiber finish on its receiver and stock and forearm and carbon fiber finish on its barrel. It comes with five screw-in choke tubes and an Inflex Technology recoil pad.

As always, there are new Citori over-and-unders.

The Citori 625 Feather Three Barrel Set comes in a leather-trimmed case with 26 or 28 inch lightweight profile barrels in 20 and 28-gauge and .410-bore. The aluminum receiver has a walnut forearm with a Schnabel tip.

Browning Maxus Sporting Carbon Fiber.

A leather case holds the Citori 625 Sporting Four Barrel Set with 30-inch barrels in 12, 20 and 28 gauge and .410. Each barrel set has five screw in choke tubes and a HiViz fiber optic front sight. The 12-gauge barrels have a tapered floating top rib. The 20, 28 and .410 have a ventilated top and side rib. The 12 and 20-gauge barrels are ported.

Remington 870 Express Tactical A-TACS Camo.

Remington 870 Super Mag Turkey-Predator Camo.

Remington 870 Bone Collector.

Browning Cynergy Classic Feather Combo.

Mossberg Slugger with LPA trigger.

Ithaca's Phoenix 12-gauge over-and-under. The gun has no soldered parts.

Blaser F3 Super Trap.

Browning Citori 625 four-barrel set.

Browning Citori Micro.

Browning Citori WHite Lightning.

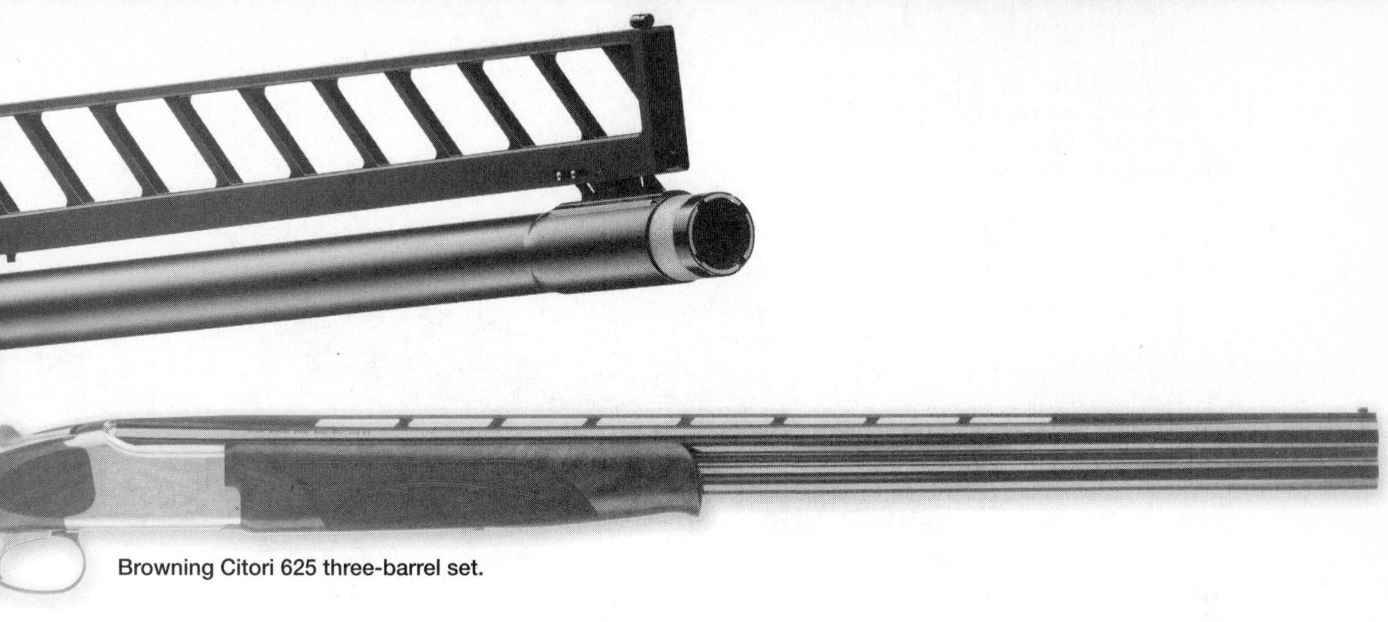

Browning Citori 625 three-barrel set.

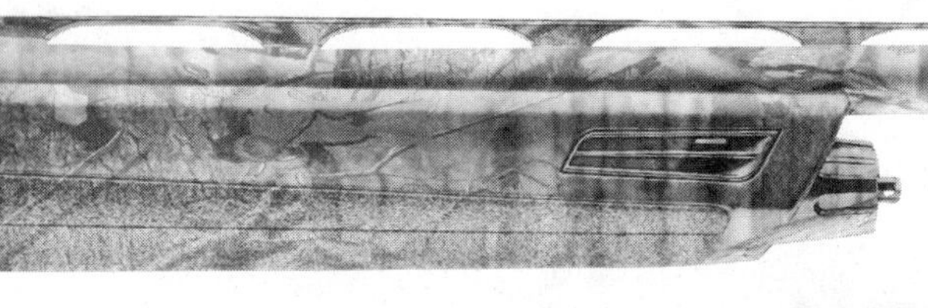

The Winchester SX3 All-Purpose.

The Citori 625 Sporting Golden Clays is chambered in 12 gauge with a 2-3/4-inch chamber. Its steel receiver is finished in silver nitride with gold engraving of a game bird transforming into a clay target. The stock has a gloss oil finish on high grade walnut with tight radius grip. Lengthened forcing cones go along with five choke tubes.

The Citori Lightning's steel receiver has a blued finish and engraving and a gloss finish on its walnut stock and forearm. The Lightning is chambered in 12, 20 and 28 gauge and .410 and comes with three choke tubes. The Citori White Lightning is pretty much the same gun with a silver nitride finish on the receiver.

The Citori Micro has a steel receiver. Its 24 or 26-inch barrels are chambered in three-inch 20 or 12-gauge. The stock is short with a 13-3/4-inch length of pull to match the slender forearm.

More than a few Browning guns are now stocked with a Dura-Touch Armor Coated composite stock and forearm covered with camouflage:

- *The Gold Light and National Wild Turkey Federation's Gold Light 10-Gauge are covered with Mossy Oak Break-Up Infinity.*
- *The 12-gauge 3 and 3½-inch Browning Pump Shotguns are also covered with Break-Up Infinity camo. The BPS Rifled Deer 12-gauge has a composite stock while the 20-gauge version has a wood stock. Both guns have 22-inch barrels and a cantilever base for mounting optics.*
- *The Cynergy over-and-under 12-gauge with a 3-1/2-inch chamber likewise has a composite stock covered with Mossy Oak Infinity or Duck Blind camo.*

Browning's Cynergy line of over-and-unders is starting to rival the number of its long-established Citori models. The Cynergy Classic Feather Combo has an aluminum receiver and comes with 27-inch barrels in 3-inch 20 gauge and 2-3/4-inch 28 gauge. Three choke tubes come with each barrel set and the whole package fits in a leather case. The Cynergy Classic Field has a steel receiver with a silver nitride finish. The 12 gauge model has engraved pheasants on the left side of the receiver and mallards on the right. The 20 and 28 gauges and .410 are engraved with quail and grouse. The Cynergy Classic Sporting with Adjustable Comb has all that plus ported barrels and ventilated top and side ribs.

The Winchester SX3 Comact.

Browning Citori 625
Sporting Golden Clays.

Mossberg Mini Super Bantam.

Benelli Vinci – just as it comes from the box.

The innovative Rossi Circuit Judge revolving shotgun.

Benelli Xplor. A fine-handling shotgun.

Mossberg Combo with LPA trigger.

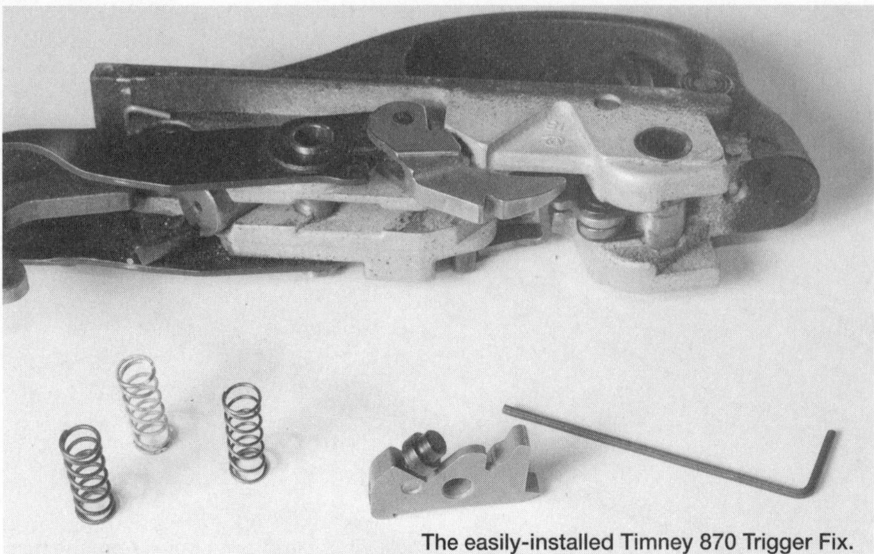
The easily-installed Timney 870 Trigger Fix.

bolt-action centerfire rifles. Now the trigger is available on its pump-action guns and is called the Lightning Pump Action (LPA) trigger. The LPA's pull can be adjusted from under three to seven pounds. The trigger is featured on the Mossberg 500, 535 and 835 Turkey, Slugster and Combo models.

The Just In Case Mossberg 500 pump breaks down into three pieces to store in soft case. To keep it compact, the gun has a synthetic pistol grip stock and 18-1/2-inch cylinder bore barrel. The grip attaches to the receiver with a slotted head bolt. Assembled, the gun measures only 28-3/4 inches in length and holds five rounds in the magazine and one up the spout. Such a compact package stores out of the way in a boat or truck, but is there just in case you need it.

ITHACA

Ithaca is putting its Ladies Stock on its Model 37 pump 20 gauges. The stock has a little less pitch on the butt, a bit more toe out and drop of the comb heel to fit a woman. The gun comes with a 14.25-inch length of pull, but Ithaca will cut the stock to any length requested when ordering a gun. Ithaca's Mike Farrell said, "I rejected the first four forearms they brought into my office because they were all too big." The forearm Farrell finally approved is just large enough to fill the hand, yet keep the fingers away from the barrel.

My wife, Gail, picked up a Model 37 Ultralight with a Ladies Stock to shoot a few clay targets thrown by Farrell. Being a typical male, I coached her on fixing her focus on the target and to bring the gun up to the target and fire. Farrell leaned over and said, "Why don't you just let her shoot." As fast as Farrell could push the release button on the electric trap, Gail dusted nine targets in a row with the little Ultralight 20-gauge.

As Gail kept shooting, I took the hint and walked over to look at Ithaca's Phoenix 12-gauge over-and-under that is in production after a year and some of final development. Ithaca starts with a 15-lb. length of steel to make the over-and-under's barrels. Two pounds of steel remain by the time the barrels are final machined. All that machining leaves behind integral dovetails at the muzzle that lock the barrels together and stanchions for the replaceable rib that is held in place with one screw. The breech end of the barrels are held with a tubular connector. "There is no solder on these barrels," Farrell said, "and they will never shoot loose or move or warp due to heat or just about anything else."

It was kind of noisy trying to talk with Farrell, as Gail was in the background, still busting targets with the Ultralight.

MOSSBERG

Mossberg has reduced the size of its Youth model pump and called it the 510 Mini. The .410and 20-gauge Mini both have 18½-inch barrels and a length of pull of 10-1/2 or 11-1/2 inches, 1-1/2 inches shorter than the standard Youth Bantam models. The forearm is also scaled down from the traditional youth size and is easy for short arms to reach.

Mossberg first put its adjustable Lightning Bolt Action triggers on all its

REMINGTON

Remington continues to add models to its Model 887 Nitro Mag with three new pumps.

The Nitro Mag Bone Collector Edition has a 26-inch barrel with a HiViz fiber optic front sight and is emblazoned with that TV show's whitetail skull logo. The gun has a 12-gauge 3½-inch chamber and its pump action insures it will cycle every type of shot and slug load.

The 887 Nitro Mag Combo is made for waterfowl and turkeys. A 22-inch barrel for turkeys has HiViz fiber-optic rifle sights and a Super Full Turkey Rem Choke tube. The 28-inch waterfowl barrel has a front HiViz fiber optic sight and an Extended Waterfowl choke tube.

The forearm on the Ithaca Model 37 Ultralight with Ladies Stock is just big enough for the hand to hold and keep the fingers away the barrel.

The Model 887 Nitro Mag Tactical has an 18-1/2-inch barrel with a clamped on rail for mounting a flashlight or other accessories. A tube extension increases magazine capacity to six rounds. At the muzzle are a HiViz fiber optic sight and an extended, ported tactical Rem choke. Sling swivel studs are built-in the stock and on the forearm.

The 870 Express Super Magnum Turkey/Waterfowl is covered with Mossy Oak Bottomland camo. Its 26-inch barrel is chambered for 3-1/2-inch shells and has includes Wingmaster HD Waterfowl and Turkey Extra Full Rem choke tubes. A HiViz fiber optic front sight and receiver drilled and tapped for an optic sight tops it off.

The 870 SPS Super Magnum Turkey/Predator is mounted with a TruGlo 30mm Red/Green Dot Scope. The ambidextrous ShurShot vertical grip stock has soft molded-in panels for a sure hold and its 20-inch barrel has a Wingmaster HD Turkey/Predator Rem choke tube.

A black padded sling and Wingmaster HD™ Turkey/Predator Rem Choke are included.

The Tactical A-Tacs Camo dresses the Model 870 Express Tactical A-Tacs. The Tactical has an 18-1/2-inch barrel with an extended, ported Tactical Rem choke. The SpeedFeed IV pistol grip stock provides a firm grip and a SuperCell recoil pad dampens recoil. A fully adjustable XS Ghost Ring Sight is mounted on a Picatinny rail on the receiver rail with white bead front sight. The gun holds seven rounds of 2-3/4-inch shells with the two-shot magazine extension.

The Model 11-87 has been banging away in the duck swamps and pheasant fields for decades. This year the 11-87 returns to its roots with the Sportsman Field wearing a satin-finished walnut stock and forearm with cut checkering. A nickel-plated bolt and gold-plated trigger accent the satin blue barrel and receiver. The 12-gauge model has a 28-inch barrel with a ventilated rib and modified choke tube. The 20-gauge has a 26-inch barrel.

In Remington-speak, the word "Super" means a 12-gauge 3-1/2-inch gun. Remington has several new Super 11-87s. The 11-87 Sportsman ShurShot Super Magnum Turkey has a ShurShot pistol-grip stock and is covered with Realtree APG HD camo. Its 23-inch barrel has fully adjustable TruGlo rifle sights and a Wingmaster Turkey choke tube. The 11-87 Sportsman Super Magnum comes with HiViz front fiber optic sight with interchangeable light pipes on its 28-inch barrel. The 11-87 Sportsman Super Magnum Waterfowl includes an Adjustable Length of Pull Kit to vary pull one inch. It also has a HiViz front fiber optic sight with interchangeable light pipes on its 28-inch barrel. All 11-87 Supers now have rubber overmolded grip panels on the stock and forearm, SuperCell recoil pad and a black padded sling.

ROSSI

Rossi's sister company, Taurus, has been backordered on its Judge .410/.45 Colt revolver ever since it was introduced several years ago. Rossi has run with the Judge and made a long gun out of it and called it the Circuit Judge. The revolving cylinder gun is available with an 18-1/2-inch smoothbore or a rifled barrel and weighs 4-3/4-pounds. The Circuit Judge has a blued finish and a hardwood stock with a Monte Carlo comb. A fiber optic front sight, recoil pad and transfer bar safety system finishes it.

TIMNEY TRIGGERS

The 870 Trigger Fix lightens the pull and removes the creep from the trigger on Remington 870 pumps. The Trigger Fix comes with a sear, light, medium, or heavy pull weight springs and a hex head wrench. I put in the new sear and a spring in my 870 in about fifteen minutes. I drifted out the two pins that hold the trigger assembly in the 870 and then the pin that holds the sear in place. Then I slipped in the new sear with the light spring and tapped the sear pin back in place. The original sear and spring in the trigger produced a pull with a lot of mush and a four pound pull. The new sear and spring reduced the pull to two pounds and removed all the creep. A few turns in of the adjustment screw increased the pull weight to 2-1/2 pounds, just right.

WEATHERBY

The Synthetic Youth 20 gauge semiauto weighs 5-3/4 pounds and has a 12-1/2 inch length of pull and a 24-inch barrel. That light weight is the result of an aluminum receiver and a synthetic stock and forearm. The barrel bore is chrome lined and comes with improved cylinder, modified and full choke tubes.

The PA-08 Synthetic pump shotgun has a black injection-molded stock and metal with matte black finish. Like its partner the Upland, with walnut stock and forearm, the Synthetic is a 12 gauge with a 3-inch chamber and a 26 or 28-inch barrel and a weight of 6-1/2 pounds. Improved cylinder, modified and full choke tubes are supplied.

The PA459 pump is a home defense shotgun. Its vertical rubber grip buttstock makes it quick to point and shoot. Its forearm incorporates a rail to clamp on accessories such as flashlight. A second rail is screwed on the receiver and is mounted with a ghost ring sight adjustable for windage and elevation. The blade front sight has a fiber optic pin. The 19-inch barrel is chrome lined and fitted with an extended and ported cylinder choke tube.

WINCHESTER

Winchester has several new variations of its Super X3 autoloader for big game and bird hunting and target shooting. The Super X3 All-Purpose Field 12-gauge has a 3-1/2-inch chamber. Its gas-operated Active Valve System cycles target to magnum shells in combination with full, modified and improved cylinder choke tubes in 26- or 28-inch barrels. Its stock is adjustable with two length of pull spacers and drop and cast adjustment shims, which are included. Mossy Oak Break-Up Infinity camo, with Dura-Touch Armor Coating, covers the entire gun. The Super X3 Compact Field 12- and 20-gauge models have 26 or 28-inch barrels with a 13-inch length of pull on the stock. A supplied spacer increases that length to 13-1/4-inches. Cast and drop shims are also included. The gun's chamber and bore are chrome-plated and the bolt, slide and carrier are nickel-plated. An Inflex Technology recoil pad helps dampen recoil.

The Super X3 Rifled Deer Cantilever has a 22-inch rifled barrel and is covered in Mossy Oak Breakup Infinity on the metal and composite stock.

The Super X3 Sporting Adjustable has a walnut stock with an adjustable comb. The Sporting 12-gauge has a 2-3/4-inch chamber, ambidextrous safety and Pachmayr Decelerator recoil pad. Five choke tubes are included.

The Super X3 Walnut Field 20-gauge weighs 6-1/2 pounds with a 28-inch barrel. The 12-gauge model weighs only 7 pounds. That light weight is the result of an aluminum receiver and magazine tuber and slender barrel with a trim forearm. A Pachmayr Decelerator recoil pad is installed and two stock spacers can lengthen pull.

THE VOLUNTEER ARMS/COMMANDO MARK 45 CARBINE

BY DAN SHIDELER

That's no Thompson! It's the Mark 45 Carbine by Volunteer Arms.

I've always had a thing for Thompson submachineguns. It's one of the few truly iconic firearms in the world, one that you can immediately identify only by its silhouette. Alas, I have a phobia of governmental red tape, so I don't care to own a genuine Thompson. But a semi-auto Thompson clone? That's more like it!

My latest acquisition along these lines is a Volunteer Enterprises Mark 45 carbine, and though it's certainly no Thompson, it does go a long way toward scratching an itch that goes back almost 40 years. Back in the days when dinosaurs ruled the earth and I was a kid, every year I eagerly awaited the day when dad would come home from work, take off his coat and hat and plunk down the new Gun Digest for his two sons to devour. It was better than Christmas.

It was from one of those mid-'60s Digests that I first got bitten by the Thompson-clone bug. Its catalog section included what had to be the coolest gun ever, one that had apparently been made to appeal to a seven-year-old kid in Fort Wayne, Indiana. It was called the Eagle, and it was a bastardized tommygun knockoff chambered in .45 ACP and 9mm Parabellum. I can close my eyes and still see the picture that appeared in the Digest four decades ago: it showed a gun with a Thompson M1 buttstock, a tubular receiver like that of an M3 Greasegun, a vertical foregrip like that of a 1921/28 Thompson and a carbine-length barrel.

The Spitfire Carbine by Spitfire Mfg. of Phoenix, one of the earliest pistol-caliber semi-auto carbines (PCSAC).

For a kid raised on comic books starring Sergeant Fury and His Howling Commandos, I spent untold hours figuring out some way to get dad to buy me an Eagle carbine. Alas, the gun appeared in the Digest for only one more year and then went bubbling away down the river of time. I know now that the Eagle was actually called the Eagle Apache Carbine and that it was made by the Eagle Gun Company, Inc., of Stratford, Connecticut. Moreover, it was the first of what gunsmith J. B. Wood calls "pick-sacks": Pistol Caliber Semi-Auto Carbines (PCSACs).

Another PCSAC appeared around the same time as the Eagle Apache. This was the .45 ACP Spitfire, made by Spitfire Mfg. of Phoenix, Arizona, and it was very similar to the Eagle Apache, at least to the untrained eye. Michael Winthrop of Hollywood, Florida, is an authority on these early PCSACs, and he summarizes the key differences between the Eagle Apache and the Spitfire thus:

"Subtle differences included the extractor (a flat style, as opposed to the Eagle's,which has a crescent shape clip to attach it to the bolt; the ejector, which on the Eagle is an extension of the disconnecter [whereas] on the Spitfire there is a separate tang welded to the bottom of the receiver tube which protrudes up into the channel under the bolt; the Spitfire's front sight is cast aluminum and the end of the barrel is turned down to a smaller diameter, whereas the Eagle has a machined front sight (probably from another surplus firearm) and the barrel is untouched. Lastly, the vertical hand grips are aluminum on both models but the Spitfire's has a smoother finish and is slightly smaller, more Thompson-looking."

So there you had the Spitfire and the Apache Eagle, both of which today have a dedicated cult following. But there was yet another entry in the late-'60s PCSAC Sweepstakes: the Volunteer Carbine made by Volunteer Arms of Knoxville, Tennessee. Michael Winthrop notes that the Volunteer, the lineal ancestor of the Volunteer Enterprises/Commando Arms Mark 45, was "a 95-percent copy of the Spitfire." Like the Eagle Apache and the Spitfire, the Volunteer used M1 Grease Gun magazines and shared the Apache's and Spitfire's tubular receiver and overall M1/Thompson appearance. Soon after the Volunteer was introduced, it was superseded by the Volunteer Mark II, which differed from its predecessor in the method by which its barrel was joined to its receiver.

The Eagle Apache, the Spitfire and the Volunteer/Volunteer Mark II had one supremely important feature in common:

they fired from an open bolt. An open bolt operates just as the term suggests: when the bolt is retracted to chamber the first cartridge, it stays in the open position until the trigger is pulled. Then the bolt slams forward, scoops up a cartridge from the magazine, fires it, and returns to the open position as the fired cartridge case is extracted and ejected. Guns using an open-bolt arrangement are sometimes known as "slam-fires," a descriptive term that usually refers to a type of malfunction, at least in genteel circles.

Over the years, quite a few commercial carbines were based on open-bolt designs, including the French Gevarm .22 of the 1960s and one or two early Marlin semi-auto rimfires. Open-bolt rifles picked up some unwanted baggage in the anti-gun late 1960s, however, and the BATF was not supportive of manufacturers who built such guns. What the BATF found so worrisome was the fact that with some minor modifications, most open-bolt designs could be rather easily converted to full-auto operation. Legally, such a modification could be made only by a properly-licensed manufacturer, and the BATF felt that open-bolt designs were just too tempting for some home gunsmiths to resist.

A federal ruling in 1968 spelled an end to the Spitfire. To quote our friends at the BATF:

It has been determined by tests and examination that the Spitfire Carbine is a weapon which is capable of automatically firing more than one shot without manual reloading and by a single function of the trigger, and therefore is a machinegun as defined by section 5848(2) of the Code. . . Accordingly, it is held that the Spitfire Carbine, manufactured by the Spitfire Manufacturing Co., Phoenix, Ariz., is a weapon which comes within the purview of the National Firearms Act.

The BATF's ruling made the Spitfire subject to all the administrative restrictions that ownership of such entails, including registration. Their market severely curtailed, Spitfire Mfg. bit the dust with only around 3,000 units produced. Probably for similar reasons, Eagle Arms also went out of businesss around the same time -- but Volunteer Enterprises did not.

Rather, Volunteer totally redesigned the Volunteer, replacing its tubular receiver with a square design that was modeled after that of the original Thompson. The change was the brainchild of an inventive gunsmith named Lee R. Frix.

The name of Lee R. Frix is not as well-known today as that of John M. Browning or Samuel Colt. In fact, all I have been able to discover about him is that he lived in Nashville, Tennessee, and was granted patent 3,695,143 on October 3, 1972, for "a firing mechanism for semiautomatic firearms including positive disconnect means."

Frix, who assigned the patent to Volunteer Enterprises, described his patentable invention this way: "[A] firing mechanism [in which the] disconnect comprises an elongated flat portion disposed in a plane substantially parallel to one side wall of said trigger housing and contiguous thereto, and a lateral projection intermediate the ends of said elongated portion and extending substantially horizontally therefrom across said cavity in said trigger housing." Well, now I get it!

Basically, Frix was saying that his patent covered a simple, semi-auto mechanism that incorporated a positive semi-auto disconnect. I would quote his patent application at length here, but there's no humane reason for me to subject you to further passages. Patent examiner Stephen C. Bentley, who heard Brix's application, certainly earned his pay on October 3, 1972.

Thus as early as 1972, Volunteer Enterprises owned a semi-auto design that was not likely to give the BATF any serious heartburn. Frix's design entered production as the Mark III carbine. Chambered in .45 ACP and firing from a closed bolt, the Mark III had a 16.5-inch barrel and was loosely styled after the Thompson M1. Unlike the M1, however, the Mark III's lower receiver incorporated an integral magazine well quite unlike that of the Thompson. As a result, the carbine could accept Thompson stick magazines but not the higher-capacity M1921/28-style drums. The overall resemblance to the Thompson was further emphasized by the Mark III's faux compensator, modeled after

One side of an original promotional brochure for the Commando Arms Mark 45 showing available accessories. Courtesy John Torelli of Jersey Small Arms Gunsmithing.

"For just plain plinking, it's a blast." Flip side of an original promotional brochure for the Commando Arms Mark 45. Courtesy John Torelli of Jersey Small Arms Gunsmithing.

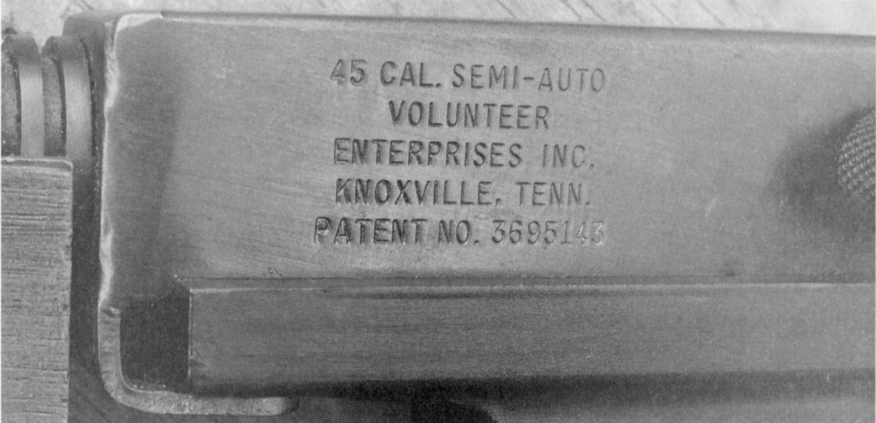

(top) Left receiver view showing the left-side bolt handle, the crossbolt safety, the funky pistol grip, the plastic lower receiver and the finned barrel shroud of the Mark 45.

(above) Rollmarks on the left receiver of the Mark 45.

the famous Cutts. (The Mark III's barrel was not vented, so the "compensator" could haven't have had much effect on muzzle climb except for adding a little weight.)

Oh, and one other thing: the Thompson's lower receiver was made of steel, while the Mark III's was made from plastic. Yes, plastic. Today's marketing potato-heads would undoubtedly call it "high-impact polymerized ABS" or something, but it was plastic -- a highly specialized thermoform plastic called polybutylene terephthalate, marketed by General Electric under the trade name "Valox." The Mark III wasn't the first production rifle to have a receiver fashioned partially of plastic -- I believe that distinction belongs to Remington's Nylon 66 .22 rifle of 1959 -- but you have to give credit to Volunteer Enterprises for having the chutzpah to tool up the mold. According to Michael Winthrop, the Mark III's plastic receiver was molded in Italy, where it was cheaper to do so. (In another cost-cutting measure, the Mark III was designed to use Thompson stick magazines, unlike its predecessors that used Grease Gun mags. Volunteer Arms got a good deal on war surplus Thompson magazines from a European supplier -- so good a deal that it made sense to redesign the receiver to accept the less-expensive tommygun magazines.)

The Mark III was superseded by the short-lived Mark IV, and I must confess that I've been unable so far to find out exactly what the differences were between the Mark III and Mark IV. The Mark IV in turn gave way to the Mark V, which is the same gun that we know today as the Mark 45 carbine. However, it seems that a company named Weatherby already owned rights to the "Mark V" name, so Volunteer Enterprises quickly rechristened its latest carbine as the Mark 45. The company even ginned up a 9mm Parabellum version of the Mark 45 called the Mark Nine.

It's not known precisely how many Mark 45s were made under the Volunteer Enterprises name, but it is known that around 1978 (some sources say 1982) the company changed its name to Commando Arms. I remember seeing the Mark 45 in the gun magazines of the period, and although I was married with a small daughter, I wanted one just as I had wanted the earlier Eagle carbine.

Thanks to my new friend John Torelli of Jersey Small Arms Gunsmithing of Millville, New Jersey (856-825-5766), I have been able to learn quite a bit about the Volunteer Enterprises/Commando Arms Mark 45 Carbine. As a promotional slick for the new gun explained, "This Mark 45 Carbine, originally designed for law enforcement use, is built to operate reliably in conditions in which other guns could fail. If not beautiful, it's practical, inexpensive and it works." Commando Arms further explained that the Mark 45 carbine was meant, not only for police, but for practically everybody who spent time outdoors: "For you four-wheelers, it's good security in your vehicle's gun rack. For farmers, guides and others in remote areas, the Mark 45 is often life insurance. For just plain plinking, it's a blast." Thus the Mark 45 carbine was one of the first centerfire rifles to be marketed as what we might call a Fun Gun, one whose primary application was just the good, clean fun of shooting.

Like the earlier Volunteers, the Mark 45 was loosely modeled after the Thompson, but any such resemblance was purely superficial. In addition to the fake Thompson-style compensator and squared receiver, the Mark 45 used what was apparently a reconditioned Thompson buttstock. Its pistol grip, however, was an oddly-proportioned, stubby affair only 2/3 as tall as the Thompson's. The fins on the Mark 45's barrel were a separately-machined shroud fitted over the barrel proper, and the bolt handle was situated on the left side of the receiver whereas the handles of the 1921/28 and M1/M1A1 Thompson were located on the top and right side, respectively. The 8-lb. Mark 45 also featured a loosely-fitted sliding crossbolt safety, quite unlike the Thompson's swinging lever safety.

Commando Arms offered the Mark 45 with an incredible number of accessories that would make many of today's manufacurers blush. For a retail price of around $150, you could get the basic Mark 45 carbine with a matte-blued or nickel-plated barrel and upper receiver and a 30-round stick magazine -- but that was just the beginning. You could also buy a vertical or horizontal foregrip and a sling swivel for the latter; a Weaver Quik-Point sight; a "heavy-gauge vinyl carrying case" or a fitted Packard Professional hard case; a web sling; and a variety of magazines. The magazines merit discussion.

Optional magazines for the Mark 45 included two half-length magazines of either five- or 15-round capacity; the standard 30-rounder; and a monstrous 90-round magazine that consisted of three staggered 30-round magazines spot-welded together! I can't imagine how the carbine would balance with either the right or left side of the 90-round magazine inserted, but it must have been a handful. All of the stick mags were made from modified mil-surplus Thompson magazines. The 30-round stick on my Mark 45, for example, is marked "S-W CO," one of the more commonly-encountered Thompson mags.

The Mark 45's front sight is integral with the faux compensator, which is pinned in place and therefore non-adjustable. The rear sight is a winged peep assembly allen-bolted to the receiver and adjustable for elevation only by bending it up and down. Such an arrangement hardly promotes match-grade accuracy, but let's be serious.

Operation of the Mark 45 is as simple as it gets: simply insert a magazine, retract the bolt, release it, move the safety to the FIRE posiiton and blaze away. Counterintuitively, the FIRE position for the safety is all the way to the right; moving it to the left puts it on SAFE. This takes some getting used to for anyone who was brought up on Remington products, as I was.

From what I can tell by my own carbine, the quality of the Mark 45 wasn't quite up to modern standards. The thin bluing is all right, I suppose, but the polymer receiver shows rather obvious mold flash marks. The trigger is an obscenity: a broad, stamped-metal blob with entirely too much play and overtravel. I've owned several capguns with better trigger pulls. The crossbolt safety is a loose fit in the lower receiver and its ends aren't even polished, displaying obvious pits and toolmarks. Oh, well! What do you expect for $150 retail?

To take down the Mark 45 for cleaning or repair, make sure the bolt is fully forward and remove the two Phillips screws that hold the buttstock to the receiver. Pull the stock free. Remove the slotted screw on the underside of the receiver and pull apart the upper and lower halves of the receiver. Then carefully remove the allen screw that secures the rear sight; this allows you to remove the recoil spring plug and the spring. Now slide the bolt rearward, aligning it with the takedown recess in the upper receiver, and slide the bolt out the rear of the receiver.

Commando Arms was in business in Knoxville until the mid-1980s, when it finally fizzled out and went gently into that good night. My Mark 45 bears a serial number in the 59,000 range, so Volunteer Enterprises/Commando Arms apparently made at least that many of them and probably a great many more. Commando Arms was succeeded by the short-lived Manchester Arms, an enterprise so obscure that most references don't even list it. Manchester Arms Company was located in Lenoir City, Tennessee, about 25 miles southwest of Knoxville, and they continued to manufacture the Mark 45 for a brief time. The company also made a pistol variant of the carbine with a truncated barrel and no buttstock. It too accepted the 90-round magazine, and I'd pay good money to see someone fire one like that.

The Manchester Arms pistol seems to be as rare these days as the much earlier Apache Eagle carbine, which is to say pretty rare, and even the Volunteer Enterprises/Commando Arms Mark 45 carbines aren't especially common. The value for one in Very Good or better condition is between $400 and $550 for the blued version, with the nickeled version bringing slightly more. This is downright cheap, though, compared to the earlier open-bolt Apache Eagle, which has skyrocketed in value. In October of 2008, for example, an Eagle Apache in Excellent condition sold for over $3,000 at an online gun auction.

Whether one is worth that kind of money is strictly up to you but speaking as a former kid, I find it awfully tempting.

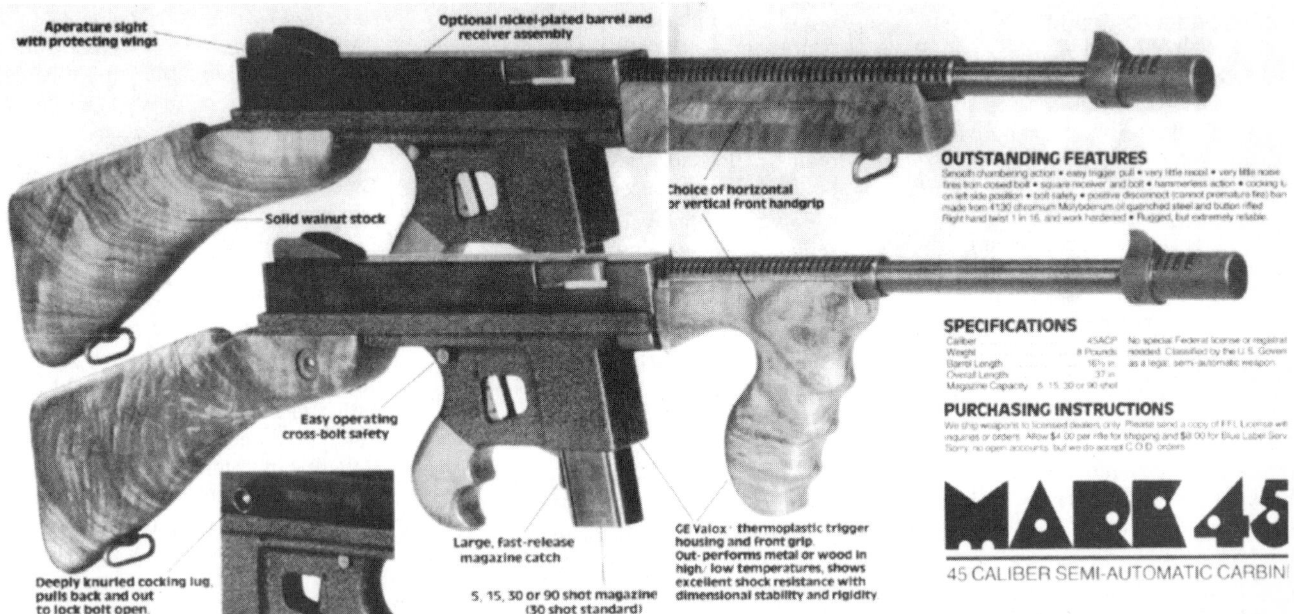

A thing of beauty is a joy forever. Courtesy John Torelli of Jersey Small Arms Gunsmithing.

SEMI-AUTO PISTOLS

BY JOHN MALLOY

The big news in the semiautomatic pistol world for 2011 is, of course, that the Colt/ Browning 1911 design has been in continuous — and growing — production for a full 100 years!

Few manufactured items of any kind are made continuously for a century. It is even rarer for a century-old item to be the leader in its field. This position, however, has been achieved by the Colt/Browning 1911 pistol design.

As the 1911's centennial approached, the venerable design gained, rather than lost, popularity. With the passing of the years, more and more companies added 1911s to their product lines. In the year 2010 alone, over half a dozen firms added their names to those offering a 1911. To celebrate the 100th anniversary, 1911 centennial commemoratives will be offered by a number of companies.

Not only has the original centerfire locked-breech 1911 design remained popular, but 22-caliber versions — blowback pistols styled after the 1911, and with many 1911 features — have been offered. Several new ones appear this year alone.

Even with the historical importance of the centennial, the news is not all 1911. The recent trend of very small 380-caliber pistols continues into this year. A number of new little .380s are added this year, offered by both major firms and smaller companies.

22-caliber pistols are always of interest, whether they look like 1911s or not. Several new .22 semiautomatic pistols appear this year. Also, more new conversion kits to allow larger-caliber pistols to handle .22 Long Rifle ammunition are being introduced. .22 pistols are regularly used for training, competition, hunting and recreational shooting.

Polymer-frame pistols remain strong sellers. Slowly gaining popularity over the years, polymers have become a mainstay in the world of autoloading pistols. A number of new polymer-frame guns, from a variety of companies, and in a variety of calibers, are being introduced.

Pistols varying greatly from traditional designs are being made, and the usefulness of carbines chambered for traditional autoloading pistol cartridges has been demonstrated. So, in this report, I'll continue to cover unconventional pistols and pistol-caliber carbines. There are a lot of very interesting things going on in the world of semiautomatic pistols. Let's take a look at what the companies are offering:

AKDAL

The Turkish-made Akdal pistols have found a home in America. They will be imported by American Tactical Imports. (See ATI.) Akdal pistols were introduced by ATI in January 2010. These pistols, first mentioned on these pages last year, are polymer-frame pistols in 9mm and .40 S&W, designed to compete in the Glock niche. These new pistols may be wearing new names when they reach the production stage.

AMERICAN CLASSIC

American Classic 1911 pistols are imported by Import Sports, a New Jersey company. The original 1911-A1 "Mil-Spec" version has been joined by enhanced American Classic II (full-size 5-inch) and Commander (4.25-inch) variants. Both of these pistols are available with either deep blue or new hard chrome finishes.

The new top-of-the-line Trophy Model is a full-size 5-inch gun available in hard chrome finish only. It has a number of enhancements, including adjustable Novak-type rear sight, dovetailed fiber-optic front sight, front and rear slide serrations, full-length guide rod and eight-round magazine.

ARMSCOR

Armscor is a Philippine manufacturing company with U. S. headquarters in Nevada. The company produces pistols patterned after the 1911 and CZ-75 pistols. In the United States, 1911-type guns are sold under the Rock Island Armory (RIA) name. With the current interest in 22-caliber 1911 pistols, a new RIA 22-caliber pistol was displayed at the 2010 SHOT Show. Of "open-top" slide design, the new .22 pistol has a fixed barrel. Production models were scheduled for summer of 2010.

ATI

American Tactical Imports, a relatively new player in the semiautomatic pistol field, seems to have a larger presence with the passing of time.

The line of ATI ported double-action pistols introduced last year, made by the Tisas firm in Turkey, is now in full production. These are striking-looking pistols, with true functional barrel porting, and also decorative porting on the sides of the slides.

There is also a new high-capacity 9mm with similar mechanism, but styled somewhat after the Browning Hi-Power 9mm pistol. It is designated the American Tactical HP9. The HP9 has a 5-inch barrel and carries an 18-round magazine. It is available in black, chrome and two-tone finishes.

And, if we have a pistol that favors the Hi-Power, why not one that looks a bit like the Beretta 92? ATI is also marketing a new 9mm AT92. The AT92 can be had in a full-size version with 4.9-inch barrel, and a compact with 4.3-inch barrel. Capacity is 15+1.

GSG (German Sporting Guns) firearms are also imported by ATI. So new it didn't get into the catalog is the GSG 1911 22-caliber pistol. Made as a .22 rimfire pistol, the frame and all other parts below the slide are all big-bore 1911. The .22 magazine is the same thickness as that of the original 45. ATI describes it as having "the same weight and feel of a 1911 pistol with many interchangeable parts."

And, now, as of January 21, 2010, ATI will also offer full-caliber 1911 pistols. A few prototypes on display at the 2010 SHOT Show were marked "American

Here is a look at a prototype Armscor Rock Island 22-caliber 1911 pistol. It has an open-top slide to reduce weight.

The largest of ATI's line of Turkish-designed double-action ported pistols is the .45 ACP Model C45.

American Tactical's HP9 pistol looks a bit like one might expect a double-action Hi-Power to look. The double-column magazine holds 18 rounds.

American Tactical Imports' Model 92 pistol has a familiar shape, similar to that of a Beretta 92.

In the United States, Philippine-made Armscor 1911 pistols are marketed under the Rock Island Armory name.

Tactical M1911 A1." A "Mil-Spec" 5-inch pistol will be one of the first variants offered. Pistols with rails, enhanced models, and short cone-barrel variants are also in the works. The popularity of the 1911 is stronger now than ever before, and now ATI will have a full line of 1911 pistols.

ATI also distributes the Guncrafter Industries 50-caliber conversion kit for Glock pistols. The kit consists of a complete top end and magazine, and fits Glock Models 20 and 21. When the kit is installed, the Glock can handle the powerful .50 GI cartridge, with 275- and 300-gr. bullets at 875 and 700 fps.

BERETTA

Beretta doesn't make a 1911, but they do have an anniversary. The Beretta 9mm pistol was adopted by the US military in 1985, so it has achieved its 25th year of service. Actually, the design dates back to 1975, when the Beretta Model 92 came into being. A variant of the 92 was adopted as the US service pistol on April 10, 1985, and became the M9. The commercial 25th Anniversary M9 pistol available to civilians is a close copy of the military M9, with military-style markings that are close to those of the actual military pistols. They have a unique M9 prefix to the serial numbers.

The Model 92 series has some new variants now. The most distinctive feature of the new 92A1 (9mm) and 96A1 (40) is the rail on the forward part of the frame. They also have higher-capacity magazines (17 rounds in 9mm, 12 in 40), and removable front sights. There are some internal modifications also, and — note this — the trigger guards are now rounded.

The PX4 Storm has a new variant in the series. A compact Storm is now between the full-size and sub-compact versions. The new Compact Storm has a 3.2-inch barrel, which gives it a 6.8-inch overall length and 5.2-inch height. It weighs about 27 ounces. Magazine capacity is 15 rounds in 9mm, and 12 rounds in .40 S&W.

The NEOS pistol now has a new carbine kit available. The kit has a grip frame that is moulded with a shoulder stock, and a longer barrel. These parts allow the conversion of the pistol into a handy carbine for informal shooting. Each kit comes with a warning against using the shoulder stock frame with the original pistol barrel.

BERSA

Acknowledging the presence of women in the shooting world is a good thing. A rather abstract way of doing this is to put colors generally related to the female sex on special pistols. In 2010, Bersa joined other companies by promoting the color pink. The Bersa Thunder 380 will now be available with optional pink grips.

A new line of Bersa polymer-frame concealed-carry pistols with a slim grip profile is in the works. Planned in 9mm (BP9cc) and .40 S&W (BP40cc), the new polymer-frame Bersas will weigh about 21 ounces, with 3.2-inch barrels. The new compact pistols look good. However, as of January 2010, the new pistols had not yet been approved by BATFE, so all I can do here is give you this advance notice.

BREN TEN

The Bren Ten is back! Really, the exact name, this time. In the last edition of this publication, recall that Vltor had already put into production an improved version of the original Bren Ten as the Vltor Fortis pistol. Since then, the company has acquired the rights to the name "Bren Ten." Pistols will now be marketed under the Bren Ten name. Bren Ten-marked pistols were planned for May 2010 availability. Standard, Vice and Special Forces variants are scheduled. They are made by Vltor and distributed by Sporting Products, LLC.

BROWNING

Browning doesn't have a 1911 in its line, but the Hi-Power, introduced in 1935, reached its 75th anniversary in 2010. Special Hi-Power pistols made during 2010 will have commemorative engraving on the top of the slide. Three variants were planned: a Standard model with walnut grips and fixed sights, a Standard model with walnut grips and adjustable sights, and a Mark III variant with composite grips with matte finish and fixed sights. The Hi-Power is available in 9mm and .40 S&W, but all the 75th Anniversary engraved versions will be in the original 9mm chambering only.

New lighter Buck Mark 22-caliber pistols have been added to Browning's rimfire pistol line. The pistols have fluted aluminum alloy barrels with steel sleeves. Available with 5.5-inch (28 ounces) or 7.5-inch (30 ounces) barrels, the guns are available with either matte grey or matte green finishes.

CANIK

A new line of Turkish-made pistols was introduced at the 2010 SHOT Show. Introduced as the Canik 55 series, the 9mm pistols are based on the CZ 75 double-action system. The basic "Standard" model is accompanied by the self-descriptive "Light" and "Compact" models. Variations from these offerings seem to be identified with sea-life names such as the Shark, the Piranha, the Stingray and the Dolphin. No importer had been named at the time of this writing.

CENTURY INTERNATIONAL ARMS

Century International Arms continues to offer its Arcus 9mm pistols (double-action versions of the Browning HP) and its line of Shooters Arms 45-caliber 1911 pistols, as well as other traditional semiauto pistols. This year, something a bit more unconventional is offered in the form of the Colefire Magnum pistol. The Colefire has the appearance of the Sterling 9mm submachinegun design but is a semiautomatic pistol chambered for the 7.62x25mm Tokarev cartridge. The unusual pistol uses a modified side-mounted Sten magazine that holds 25 rounds of ammunition. Why 7.62x25? Well, during the ammunition shortage that is still continuing at the time of this writing, surplus Tokarev ammo is one of the least expensive and most readily-available kinds of surplus pistol ammunition! The Colefire has a 4.5-inch barrel and is a bit over 13 inches long. It weighs well over four pounds, and should be easy to shoot for even long plinking sessions.

CHARLES DALY

A sad note. KBI, the parent company of Charles Daly and other firearms brands, went out of business on January 29, 2010. As of the time of this writing, arrangements were being made for another company to handle service for guns that had been offered by KBI. In its last year, KBI marketed handguns bearing the names Charles Daly and Jericho, as well as the new line of CD striker-fired pistols.

A company statement expressed hope that another firm will offer Charles Daly products in the future.

CHIAPPA

Introduced in prototype on these pages last year, the Chiappa 1911 22-caliber pistol is now a production item.

Styled after the popular 45-caliber 1911 pistol, the concept behind the Chiappa 1911 22 was to provide a 22-caliber semiauto pistol at a cost less than that of a conversion kit for a 45.

The black-finish production pistols fall into three categories, separated basically by sighting systems. The Standard Model 1911-22 has traditional fixed sights. The Tactical model has an angled rear sight that extends slightly to the rear of the rear sight dovetail. The Target model has a fully-adjustable rear sight. Other options are two-tone variants, which combine the black frame with a slide colored either tan or olive drab. All variants are supplied with double-diamond grips with the Chiappa logo in the middle. Barrels are 5 inches, weight is 32 ounces, and magazines hold 10 rounds of 22 Long Rifle ammunition. A sample target demonstrated by Chiappa showed impressive accuracy.

The Chiappa Model 1911-22 is distributed in America by MKS Supply. Essentially identical pistols, marked PUMA 1911-22, are also distributed by Legacy Sports International.

CIMARRON

For many years, Cimarron has been a leader in providing the superb replicas of historical rifles and revolvers favored by Cowboy Action shooters. Now, for the first time, the company will offer semiautomatic pistols.

Cimarron is working with Armscor to make a true 1911, representative of the period during which the "old west" was gradually becoming modernized. This transitional period is sometimes referred to as the "Wild Bunch" era, memorialized by motion pictures such as *The Wild Bunch*, *The Professionals*, and *Big Jake*.

A few prototypes were exhibited at the Cimarron display at the 2010 SHOT Show. They had true 1911 frames, without the recesses behind the trigger area. The slides were marked with the original patent dates to 1913 and carried the Cimarron name. Production versions will have, of course, double-diamond wood grips. A company representative said they were looking ahead to a 100-year commemorative version.

C.O. ARMS

New 1911-style pistols have recently been introduced by C.O. Arms, a company based in Millington, Tennessee. The Scorpion model is a full-size model with forged stainless-steel slide and frame. The Stinger variant has a short 3.25-inch

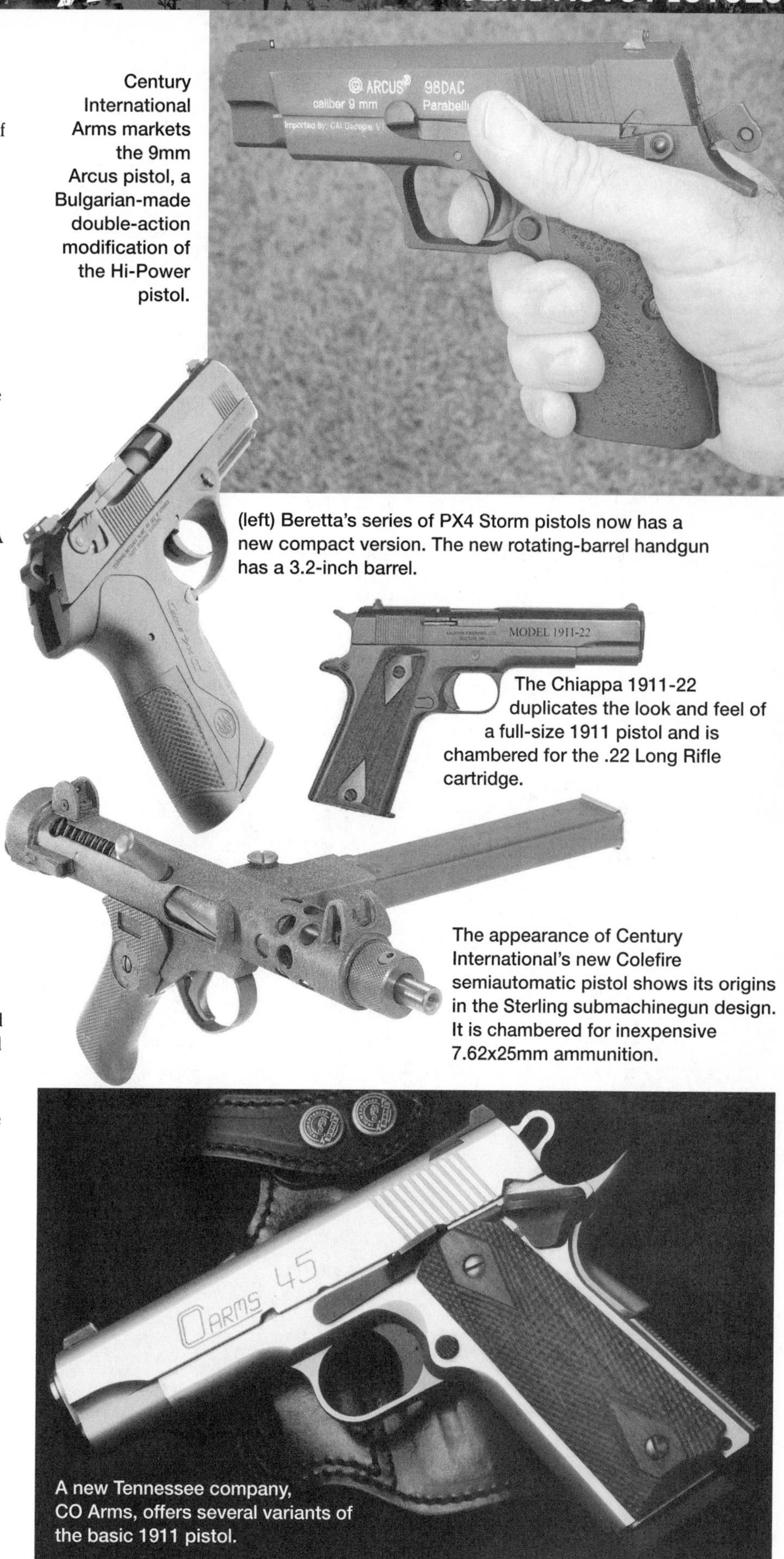

Century International Arms markets the 9mm Arcus pistol, a Bulgarian-made double-action modification of the Hi-Power pistol.

(left) Beretta's series of PX4 Storm pistols now has a new compact version. The new rotating-barrel handgun has a 3.2-inch barrel.

The Chiappa 1911-22 duplicates the look and feel of a full-size 1911 pistol and is chambered for the .22 Long Rifle cartridge.

The appearance of Century International's new Colefire semiautomatic pistol shows its origins in the Sterling submachinegun design. It is chambered for inexpensive 7.62x25mm ammunition.

A new Tennessee company, CO Arms, offers several variants of the basic 1911 pistol.

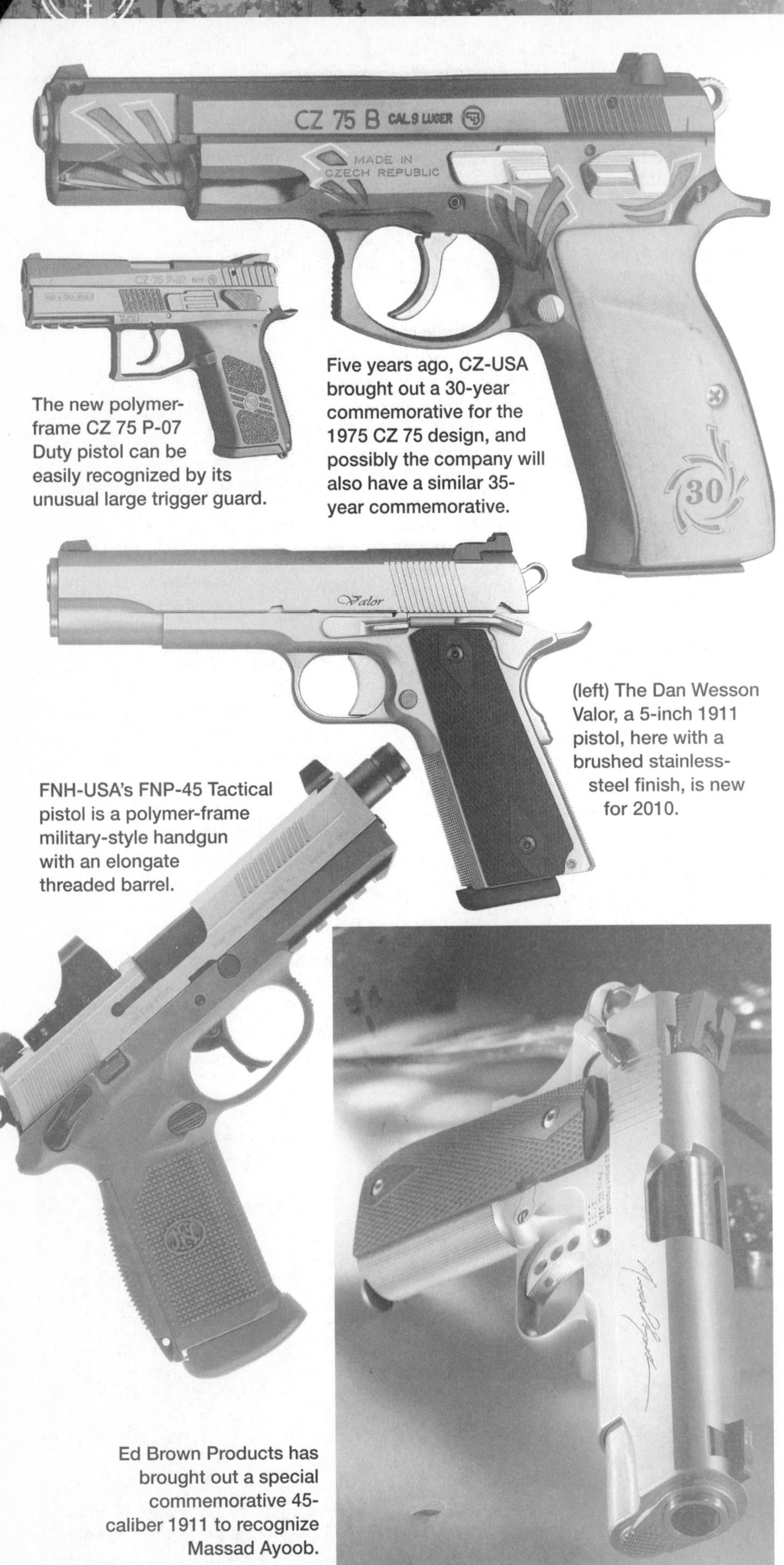

The new polymer-frame CZ 75 P-07 Duty pistol can be easily recognized by its unusual large trigger guard.

Five years ago, CZ-USA brought out a 30-year commemorative for the 1975 CZ 75 design, and possibly the company will also have a similar 35-year commemorative.

(left) The Dan Wesson Valor, a 5-inch 1911 pistol, here with a brushed stainless-steel finish, is new for 2010.

FNH-USA's FNP-45 Tactical pistol is a polymer-frame military-style handgun with an elongate threaded barrel.

Ed Brown Products has brought out a special commemorative 45-caliber 1911 to recognize Massad Ayoob.

barrel and slide, but has a full-size aluminum grip frame length, giving it 9+1 capacity. Caliber? .45 ACP, of course.

COBRA

Cobra Enterprises, a Utah company, offers personal-protection semiautomatic pistols in calibers from .32 ACP to .45 ACP. Small variations slip into the catalog with little fanfare. A new finish is now offered for their Patriot 45, a 19-ounce polymer-frame double-action-only (DAO) pistol. Previously available with the stainless-steel slide covered in a matte black finish, it is now offered in polished finish for those who like a bright slide on a two-tone pistol. The Patriot has one of the best DAO autopistol triggers I have tried — much like a good revolver double-action trigger.

COLT

Needless to say, Colt is taking the 100th anniversary of its Colt/Browning 1911 design seriously. All guns made during the year of 2011 will have special markings. The company is not just going to put a new roll-stamp on existing products, however. Colt has a number of new variants of the basic 1911 offered, in order to cover as many niches as possible.

The Colt Rail Gun, introduced on these pages last year as a stainless-steel pistol, is now also available with a blackened finish. The 9mm chambering, popular with many women, and with men who want a lower-recoiling pistol, is now offered in its small Defender (3-inch, stainless-steel carry pistol with white-dot sights) and New Agent (3-inch, blued carry pistol with trench sight system).

The New Agent 45 is now also available in a new double-action-only version. Colt is coming back into the double-action world with relatively little fanfare, as its Double Eagle offering of the past did not take the firearms world by storm. The full-size 5-inch Government Model is also available in a double-action-only variant. This variant is of additional interest because it is also put together with a lightweight aluminum-alloy frame.

In addition, the standard single-action Government Model is also now available with the lightweight frame. A number of shooters have expressed interest in a lighter full-size 5-inch Government Model as a good carry pistol. In some modes of carry, the forward weight distribution of the longer barrel actually allows easier carry, as well as slightly improved ballistics The reduced weight can make carry easier.

Colt also is making a pitch for parts sales via the internet. A customer can go to www.coltsmfg.com and order original-equipment spare parts and accessories direct from the factory, at what the company describes as "unbeatable prices."

COONAN

Coonan is back! Regular readers of this report will recall Coonan Arms as a manufacturer of modified 1911 pistols that would handle the .357 Magnum revolver cartridge. Some years ago, they had expanded the product line to include the .41 Magnum, but then financial problems caused the company to close. Now Coonan is back, with the guns in full production in .357 chambering. Standard 5-inch, and more compact 4-inch versions are offered. Will the .41 again be available? A company official said it is a possibility.

CZECHPOINT

Czechpoint, Inc. (easy to remember the name), operating from Knoxville, Tennessee, distributes firearms manufactured in the Czech Republic. Along with a number of rifles, Czechpoint also offers the .32 ACP Scorpion pistol. Recall that the original "Skorpion" was a tiny .32 ACP submachinegun developed by the Czechs for clandestine use while the country was under Communist control.

The newly-made Scorpion pistol is the same size as the original (10.6 inches long, 4.5-inch barrel, weight 39 ounces) but is semiautomatic only and has no provision for the wire shoulder stock of the original. The mechanism is straight blowback, and the gun is fed from either 10- or 20-round detachable magazines.

With each Scorpion pistol comes a hard case, one 10-round and two 20-round magazines, a magazine pouch, a holster, and — a nice touch — a CD with the owner's manual and the history of the gun. Grips can be one of four different styles of wood or plastic.

CZ-USA

The latest pistol to be imported by CZ-USA is the CZ 75 P-07 Duty, announced on these pages last year. It is a conventional double action, steel-slide, polymer-frame pistol. Barrel length is 3.7 inches. The overall dimensions are roughly 5x7 inches, placing the P-07 in the compact class. Weight is about 27 ounces. The capacity of this 9mm pistol is 16+1. Unlike the other CZ 75 variants, the P-07 is shipped as a decocker-only, but parts are available for an owner-installed conversion to permit cocked-and-locked operation. Perhaps the most noticeable feature of the P-07 is its unusual extra-large trigger guard, with a long vertical front portion. Because the front of the frame has a moulded accessory rail, it seems almost as if the trigger guard was designed as an index for an attached accessory. Originally introduced in 9mm, the P-07 will soon be available in .40 S&W, with 12+1 capacity.

A limited edition stainless-steel variant of the CZ 75 B (the B indicates the new firing-pin safety) was offered in early 2010. It is a full-size pistol with 4.7-inch barrel, in 9mm, with 16+1 capacity. The stainless pistol is fitted with an ambidextrous safety, which the standard CZ 75 B does not have.

The CZ Custom Shop offers several competition and target variants that do not appear in the general CZ lineup. Although the pistol dates back to 1975, I have not yet heard of a 35-year commemorative edition, but one may be in the works. The company brought out a special 30-year commemorative, and at this time, when commemoratives are in the air, we might yet see a 35th year pistol.

We are in a period of great interest in accessory rails on pistols. Relatively few shooters regularly use the rails for light or laser attachment, but the rails can be put to such use when desired. Now, CZ gives us another use. The company offers a bayonet suited to attachment on the rails! The bayonet also has a rail, so an additional accessory can be placed below the mounted bayonet. A real attention-catcher.

DAN WESSON

Dan Wesson (recall that the DW company is now under the ownership of CZ-USA) produces 1911-type pistols that extends CZ's line of double-action autoloaders. Two new models were introduced in early 2010. The Valor is a stainless-steel full-size 5-inch 1911, available in brushed stainless finish, or a matte black "Duty" finish. The new 45-caliber Valor has a match barrel with 1:16 twist, and features Heinie "straight eight" night sights.

Another introduction, the Dan Wesson Guardian pistol, is designed as a lighter "Commander-size" carry pistol. It comes in 9mm chambering, the only 9mm pistol in the Dan Wesson lineup. It is built on an aluminum-alloy frame, which has a "bobtail" treatment at the lower rear portion of the grip frame. The 29-ounce pistol has ambidextrous thumb safeties.

DETONICS

Since the beginning of its history, Detonics has always had the knack of coming up with features outside the mainstream. An innovation for its traditional small 45-caliber CombatMaster is putting the front sight on the barrel itself. This arrangement allows an interesting new way to index the slide and barrel together on the forward travel of the slide.

DIAMONDBACK

Florida has become a major player in the firearms industry, with a number of companies providing a wide range of firearms. The latest addition is Diamondback Firearms, of Cocoa, Florida. Their product is a small new 380-caliber locked-breech pocket pistol, the DB 380. The compact polymer-frame pistol is only 3/4-inch wide and weighs 8.8 ounces. It has a 2.8-inch barrel. Capacity is 6+1. Two 6-round magazines are available, one with a flush base and one with a finger-rest base. Trigger mechanism is double-action-only, with a reported 5-pound pull. The trigger activates a striker firing system. The three-dot sights are adjustable for windage on the rear sight. I am not sure how the company name was established; however, having grown up in Florida, I can attest to the fact that the state is home to some spectacular diamondback rattlesnakes. At the time of this writing, RSR, of Grand Prairie, Texas, is the exclusive distributor of the Diamondback DB380.

DOUBLESTAR

The DoubleStar .45 pistol was introduced on these pages two years ago and went into production last year. Now, a new "Combat Pistol" is being offered. The new gun offers the basic pistol with new options. The Combat Pistol offers Novak three-dot sights, a Novak 8-round magazine, and 25-lpi checkering and other features. Although relatively new to the 1911 world, DoubleStar will offer a 100-year commemorative variant.

ED BROWN

People who have made great contributions to the honorable use of handguns for sport, personal defense and law-enforcement purposes deserve to be recognized for what they do. In January 2010, Ed Brown Products announced that they would honor Massad Ayoob with a special Massad Ayoob Signature

Edition 1911. The limited edition pistol will be a 4.25-inch Commander-size pistol with bobtail frame and double-diamond grips. Made of stainless steel, the commemorative pistol weighs about 35 ounces. The sights are three-dot night sights. Ayoob specified that the trigger have a 4.5-pound pull and that the pistol be able to group jacketed-hollow-point ammunition into two inches or less at 25 yards. What makes the pistol special as a commemorative is a facsimile of Ayoob's signature on the right side of the slide. A copy of Ayoob's book, *The Gun Digest Book of Concealed Carry*, is included with each pistol.

Thinking ahead, Ed Brown announced that the company will put out a 100-year commemorative to acknowledge the unique record of the Colt/Browning1911 design during the past century.

EMF

Last year, EMF got back to its "Early and Modern Firearms" beginnings. They added, to their western-style guns, a line of 1911 pistols and a new polymer-frame 9mm pistol.

Now, the polymer-frame pistol, the FMK, is in full production. The 1911 line, made in Tennessee, has several variants, including the original 1911 A1, an enhanced Combat model, and a new Nightstalker 1911, in black with a rail. Slides are now marked "Hartford Model 1911."

This year, EMF has also added a line of pistol-caliber carbines. The new JR Carbine is a straight blowback, offered in 9mm, .40 S&W and .45 ACP. It looks a little bit like an AR-15, but is much simpler. However, it will accept many AR aftermarket items, and is loaded with rails that allow all sorts of additions. The construction is interesting, in that calibers can be changed with only a magazine well, bolt and barrel change. The carbine can be ordered with either right- or left-handed controls, and the bolt handle and ejection of empty cases can be on either side. The carbines are initially furnished with appropriate Glock magazines, but the magazine well is modular and can be adapted to other magazines. Looks as if a lot of thought has gone into this design.

FNH USA

A number of new pistols were introduced by FNH USA this year. Let's start with the largest first.

The FNP-45 Tactical pistol is a .45 ACP polymer-frame conventional double action arm that pretty obviously had its origin in FN's design program for military testing. The pistol is described as "completely ambidextrous," with decocker/safety, slide stop and magazine release operable from either side. The 5.3-inch barrel extends forward of the slide and is threaded. The flat dark earth frame has an accessory rail moulded into its forward portion. Interchangeable backstraps are furnished. The slide has high night sights front and rear. The top of the slide is cut and threaded for an electronic sight, and a plate is furnished to cover the mounting holes. The FNP-45 Tactical pistol comes with three 15-round magazines in a fitted Cordura nylon case.

The new FNX-40 and FNX-9 pistols are polymer-frame guns that have four interchangeable backstraps. Each FNX has a 4-inch barrel. The 40-caliber version weighs 24 ounces and uses a 15-round magazine. The 9mm weighs 22 ounces and uses a 17-round magazine. Each pistol comes with three magazines and a lockable hard case.

The Five-seveN pistol, chambered for the 5.7x28 cartridge, is now available with low-profile fixed combat sights, as well as the adjustable sights previously offered. The Five-seveN pistols are available in black, dark earth and olive drab. Magazines of 10- and 20-round capacity are available, and three magazines come with each pistol.

GIRSAN

Girsan, a Turkish manufacturer, has made 9mm pistols based on the open-slide Beretta 92 design. At the 2010 SHOT Show, Girsan displayed several new models of closed-slide 9mm pistols with front frame rails, including their MC 27 and MC 27E (a ported variant). The MC 21 is a .45 ACP pistol made with a similar configuration.

Of great interest to us here is a new line, the Girsan MC 1911. As you might have guessed, it is a full-size .45 ACP based on the Colt/Browning 1911 design. Prototypes displayed at the SHOT Show were of the general WWII 1911A1 configuration. Interestingly, at least one early prototype had a true 1911 frame, with no frame recesses behind the trigger. The MC 1911 S is the standard "Government Model" style, but with a forward frame rail.

I was told that an American firm would import the Girsan 1911s but could not get any definite details.

GLOCK

Glock has introduced the Generation 4 (generally referenced as Gen4) series of Glock pistols. The new features include three interchangeable grip backstrap options, a non-slip texture on the grip frame, a reversible magazine release, and a new dual recoil-spring system.

Each larger backstrap adds 2 millimeters to the linear distance between the trigger and the rear of the backstrap. The more-aggressive grip frame texture is a series of polymer pyramids (Glock calls them "polymids"); Models 17, 19, 22 and 23 are now available with this surface. Glock calls this the RTF, or "Rough Textured Frame." The reversible magazine catch is somewhat larger than former ones, and Glock apparently will provide information for shooters who want to make the change to left-hand operation. The new dual recoil springs are considered an "assembly." The first Gen4 pistol is the 40-caliber Model 22. The model number on the slide reads, "22Gen4." Other versions will obviously become available.

GSG

German Sporting Guns (GSG) has introduced a new 22-caliber 1911 pistol. The lower portion is completely 1911, with a fixed barrel and blowback operation of the slide up above. The GSG – 1911 will be handled by American Tactical Imports. (See ATI.)

GUNCRAFTER

Guncrafter Industries makes 1911-type pistols in their own proprietary .50 GI cartridge. This year, they offer a new Model 3, a Commander-style pistol with a 4.25-inch barrel and a "bobtail" frame treatment. Guncrafter offers a new load for the .50 GI with solid copper hollow-point bullets that open up into four "wings."

This year, Guncrafter offers — of all things — a standard .45 ACP 1911. The 1911 .45 went into the catalog before a name was chosen for it. It is known, for the time being, as the "no-name" pistol.

A conversion kit to convert the Glock Models 20 or 21 to .50 GI is offered. Such items are available through American Tactical Imports. (See ATI.)

HK

Heckler & Koch has offered their P30 pistol in 9mm chambering, and by January 2010, had also offered the basic pistol in .40 S&W. The 40-caliber version has a 13-round magazine and has a 3.85-

inch barrel. The longer 4.45-inch barrel available as an option for the 9mm is not offered for the 40-caliber P30.

HK feels that the P30 pistol holds up pretty well. On display at the 2010 SHOT Show was a 9mm P30 that had shot 75,000 rounds. Yes, there were nine stoppages, but the HK people are working to correct that.

HIGH STANDARD

The "Space Gun" is back! One of the most recognizable 22-caliber target pistols of all time, the long-barrel High Standard Olympic Trophy is back in production. Its long barrel, muzzle brake, and extra weight under the barrel gave it a distinctive appearance, and it was generally referred to as the "Space Gun." The rear sight was mounted on the barrel, not on the slide, to prevent misalignment. The Olympic Trophy was a winner on the firing line in decades past.

Now, it is back again, in an updated version. The frame is now stainless steel, with a black Teflon coating. Barrel lengths offered are 6.75, 8 and 10 inches. Optional weights are 2-ounce or 3-ounce. I was fortunate to have the new Olympic Trophy demonstrated to me by Bob Shea, who started working with High Standard way back in 1942, and who still serves as an advisor to the present organization.

Not enough nostalgia yet? High Standard plans were to reintroduce the affordable Dura-Matic 22-caliber plinking pistol of years past. The new Dura-Matic was scheduled for May 2010 introduction at the National Rifle Association (NRA) convention.

HI-POINT

Hi-Point continues to offer its line of affordable pistols and pistol-caliber carbines. Nothing new is being offered in the pistol line this year, but the carbines are wearing new stocks. Regular readers of this publication may recall that I sneaked a picture of prototype number 1 of the new stock design into this report last year. Now, they are standard. The new stocks have rails on the top of the receiver cover, rails under the forearm, and rails on the sides of the forearm. There is plenty of space to hang just about anything a shooter wants on the Hi-Point carbine now. A recoil-reducing butt pad is attached. Available in 9mm and .40 S&W, the carbines come with sling, swivels, scope base, adjustable aperture rear sight and trigger lock.

One of the new FNH polymer-frame guns with interchangeable backstraps, the 9mm FNX-9, here is shown with a black slide and a flat grip backstrap.

(right) Guncrafters Industries offers a kit to convert a Glock Model 20 or 21 to use the big-bore 50 GI cartridge.

A new 22-caliber 1911. The new .22 has been introduced by German Sporting Guns.

The High Standard Olympic Trophy, often called the "Space Gun," is back in production. Here, the reintroduced pistol is demonstrated by Bob Shea, who started working for High Standard in 1942. Shea knows these guns well.

A new small 380-caliber pistol, the I.O. Hellcat, has been introduced by I.O., Inc. Here is a peek at prototype X2.

Interstate Arms Corporation's new Regent 45 is a "Series '70" pistol, made for IAC by Tisas in Turkey.

(right) The new manual-safety version of the Kahr PM9 also has a loaded chamber indicator.

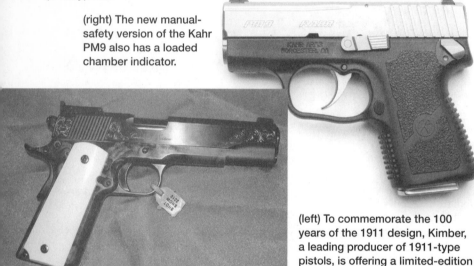

(left) To commemorate the 100 years of the 1911 design, Kimber, a leading producer of 1911-type pistols, is offering a limited-edition commemorative pistol.

(right) The new Kriss pistol. Well, all right, this is really the Kriss submachinegun with the stock removed. However, this is how the Kriss pistol will look, but it will be semiautomatic only.

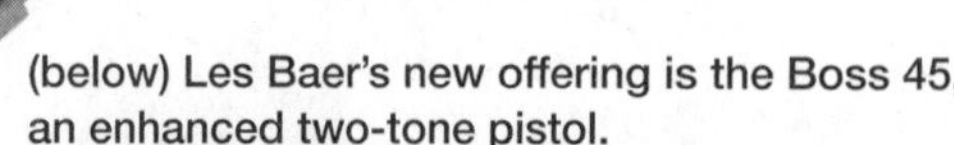

Legacy Sports International has expanded its Citadel 1911 line. The new .38 Super version is offered now, with several finish options.

(below) Les Baer's new offering is the Boss 45, an enhanced two-tone pistol.

Hi-Point firearms are backed by the company's no-questions-asked lifetime warranty. They are distributed by MKS Supply.

INTERSTATE ARMS

A new 1911! Interstate Arms Corp. (IAC) is offering the new Regent 1911 A1 "Series '70" pistol. The new pistol is manufactured for IAC by the Tisas firm in Turkey. The new pistol looks good, and production models are said to have a consistent 5.5-pound trigger pull. (See TISAS.)

ISSC

The 22-caliber Austrian ISSC pistol, first mentioned on these pages in the last edition of this publication, is now in production. Looking much like a hammer-fired Glock, the ISSC can be used as a training understudy for those using Glock pistols, as well as other uses. The new 22s now have an accessory rail. "ISSC – USA" will be the new markings on the pistols.

ITHACA

Ithaca Gun Company produced Model 1911A1 45-caliber pistols during World War II. Ithaca was the third-largest producer of 45s during that conflict, making close to 20% of the total pistols made. A total of about 369,000 were manufactured by Ithaca back then.

Now, Ithaca is back in the 1911 pistol business. For the 100th anniversary of the 1911 design, Ithaca is making a commemorative pistol, as close to WWII specifications as possible. The only changes in the slide markings are that Ithaca has changed its business location, and "Upper Sandusky, OH" appears in place of the original "Ithaca, NY." Ray Rozic, who worked on the development of the new Ithaca .45, explained that CNC machining allowed much closer clearances now. Made of 4140 certified steel, a prototype with .002-inch slide/frame clearance fired 1000 rounds in about an hour without problems.

The only other WWII manufacturer still making 1911 pistols is, of course, Colt. It is good to have Ithaca back.

IVER JOHNSON

It seemed as if the Iver Johnson 1911 pistols would be stuck in limbo, but they are now a production reality, in time for the 100th anniversary of the 1911 design. Both .45 ACP and 22-caliber pistols were scheduled for full production by mid-2010. A number of different variants, from basic GI style to deluxe enhanced guns, full-size and commander-size, are offered.

Iver Johnson also offers conversion kits to make any 45-caliber 1911 into a .22.

IO, INC.

IO, Inc., of Monroe, North Carolina, provider of many surplus items and US-made AK-style rifles, has introduced a new small US-made .380 pistol. A company representative noted that IO had seen the popularity of small 380-caliber pistols and had combined the best features of existing offerings and made improvements to make a new pistol. The Hellcat .380 is a polymer-frame double-action-only pistol with a 2.7-inch barrel. Weight is only 6.6 ounces. Size is 5.5 inches long by 3.6 inches high — it will almost, but not quite, hide under a common 3x5 index card. I did not get a chance to shoot one, but tried the trigger, and it was decent in double-action. Capacity is 6+1. Each pistol will come with two six-round magazines and an inside-the-pants holster.

KAHR

Kahr Arms has a new version of their PM9. Recall that the PM9 is a subcompact 9mm with black polymer frame and matte stainless slide. It has a 3-inch barrel, measures 5.3x4inches, and can use either six- or seven-round magazines. Weight is about 16 ounces.

The new variant has an external manual thumb safety, and also a loaded chamber indicator, one that rises above the top level of the slide. These new features allow sale of the PM9 in states (such as Massachusetts) where the standard model is prohibited. However, the standard model PM9 will remain in the company's product line.

Another new addition to the PM9 lineup is a variant that comes with a Crimson Trace laser sight.

The little P380, introduced here last year, has a new variant. The original small .380 had a black polymer frame and stainless slide. The new "black" variant has the stainless slide coated in black to produce a less-noticeable pistol for discrete carry.

KBI

A noted above, KBI is no longer in business, as of early 2010. (See Charles Daly.)

KEL-TEC

Kel-Tec's big news is their new PMR-30, a light 30-shot pistol chambered for the .22 Winchester Magnum Rimfire (.22 WMR) cartridge. It is a full-size pistol, measuring almost 6x8 inches, but is light, only 13.6 ounces unloaded (going only to 19.5 ounces fully loaded with 30 rounds). Barrel length is 4.3 inches, and Kel-Tec records a velocity of 1230 fps with a standard 40-grain .22 WMR load.

Kel-Tec harnesses the relatively high-pressure .22 WMR cartridge by what they call a "hybrid blowback/locked breech system." Apparently, a problem using the .22 Magnum in a blowback system is that the case begins to move out of the chamber while still under substantial pressure. Kel-Tec uses a fluted rearward-moving barrel that stays in contact with the breechblock during the time of highest pressure. This appears to be similar to the system used by the FN Five-seveN pistol, and the origin of the mechanism dates back to the French MAB Model R pistol of the 1950s.

The PMR-30 has slide and barrel made of 4140 steel, and the basic frame is 7075 aluminum. Other parts, including the magazine, are glass-reinforced nylon (Zytel). The magazine has an internal rib that separates the rims of the cartridges, avoiding rim-over-rim problems and aiding smooth feeding. The magazine has view holes, so that the shooter can tell how many rounds are loaded. The pistol has fiber-optic sights,\ and a surprisingly good trigger. Introduced at the January 2010 SHOT Show, the PMR-30 was expected to be available by mid-2010.

KIMBER

Kimber has built a good part of its reputation on its 1911 pistols, and you can bet that the firm is going to recognize the 100th anniversary of the 1911. The Centennial Edition comes from Kimber's Custom Shop. In .45 ACP (of course), the Centennial has a special casehardened finish by Turnbull Restoration. Engraved slides, true elephant ivory grips and other features make the Centennial special. Only 250 of the cased guns will be offered.

Also from the Custom Shop, a new line of carry pistols has been introduced. The fist thing that caught my eye about the Super Carry series was the rounded butt treatment – not really a "bobtail," but reminiscent of the smooth curve of the old Colt pocket pistols of 1903. The Super Carry Custom is a full-size 5-incher, the Pro has a 4-inch bushingless barrel, and the Ultra goes down to 3 inches, with a shorter grip frame. With aluminum frames, weights are 31, 28 and 25 ounces, respectively.

Kimber deserves praise for its support of the shooting sports. Setting aside a portion of sales of certain guns, the company has donated to the U.S. Shooting Team, to the time of this writing, a total of $675,000. Thank you, Kimber.

KRISS

Kriss firearms are offered by Transformational Defense Industries (TDI). Introduced here in this publication two years ago, the Kriss semiautomatic .45 ACP 16-inch carbine (an outgrowth of the earlier Kriss .45-caliber submachinegun) was joined last year by a 45-caliber "short-barrel rifle" and a 40-caliber carbine.

Now, in early 2010, the Kriss semiautomatic pistol has joined the family. The new pistol has a 5.5-inch barrel, and is, in essence, the short-barrel rifle without any provision for a stock. It is BATF-approved, but cannot be made available in some states or municipalities, perhaps because it has an unusual appearance.

LEGACY

In 2009, Legacy Sports International introduced its Citadel line of 45-caliber 1911 pistols, in full-size 5-inch and Concealed Carry 3.5-inch variants. The line expanded in 2010. The Citadel line now offers both versions with one-piece wraparound Hogue grips of various colors. In addition, finishes may now be matte black, brushed nickel or polished nickel. Brand new is the Citadel .38 Super, a full-size 5-incher. It can be had with black, brushed nickel or polished nickel finishes, all with double-diamond wood grips.

Joining the centerfire 1911 pistols is the new Puma 1911-22. Roughly the same size, and with similar operating characteristics, the Puma 22 Long Rifle pistol has a 5-inch barrel, a 10-round magazine and weighs 32 ounces. Made by Chiappa Firearms, it is mechanically the same pistol as the Chiappa 1911-22 marketed by MKS Supply. (See Chiappa.)

The polymer-frame 9mm BUL pistols introduced last year by Legacy have quietly slipped out of the catalog for 2010.

LES BAER

A .45 autoloader named after a car? Les Baer Custom admits that owner Les Baer is an aficionado of powerful automobiles as well as powerful handguns. The new "Boss 45" introduced this year harks back to the Ford Mustang Boss

429 of yesteryear.

The pistol has a chromed frame and blued slide, with grasping serrations only at the rear. An adjustable rear sight and red fiber-optic front sight allow accurate sighting. The Boss 45 is guaranteed to shoot 3-inch groups at 50 yards.

MAGNUM RESEARCH

Magnum Research now has a 1911! The Minnesota company will offer a full-size 5-inch and Commander-size 4.3-inch "Desert Eagle" 1911 pistols. A prototype Government-size pistol at the 2010 SHOT Show was marked "Desert Eagle 1911 G. / Magnum Research, Minn, MN." The Commander-size pistols will carry 1911 C. markings. The pistols will be enhanced models, with beavertail tang, ventilated hammer and trigger, lowered ejection port, and special sights. The new 1911s are reported to be manufactured by BUL in Israel.

The "Baby Desert Eagle" name has been applied to new additions to the Magnum Research line, polymer-frame "fast action" pistols. The new guns will be offered in 9mm and .40 S&W. Capacity of the 9mm is 15+1, the .40 is 12+1.

The little 380-caliber Micro Desert Eagle, introduced last year, now is offered in three finishes. The 14-ounce pistols will be available as blued, nickel or two-tone blue/nickel.

MASTERPIECE ARMS

Masterpiece Arms, of Braselton, Georgia, makes a line of "MAC-10" pistols and carbines in 9mm and .45 ACP. Both traditional top-cocking, and (new for 2010) side-cocking variants are offered. Pistols may have 3-, 6-, or 10-inch barrels, and the carbines carry 16-inch barrels. In addition to the new side-cocking option, two new calibers have now been introduced, going both lower and higher in power levels.

For those who like low recoil and low cost, the MPA 22T is offered in .22 Long Rifle. The new .22 is built on the 9mm frame and comes with a long 27-round magazine. With its unconventional looks, it may be the dream plinking pistol for some people.

For those who want more power than the .45 ACP offers, MPA now can offer pistols and carbines in .460 Rowland caliber. Both pistols and carbines come with muzzle brakes and have 30-round magazines.

PARA

The Para GI Expert (Product Code GI45) introduced last year as a lower-price "basic" 1911 with some updated features many shooters want, now has two additional variants. The same gun is now offered in a stainless-steel version (GI45S) with the same features. The additional new variant has the same finish as the original GI Expert, but is enhanced with a beavertail tang with a bump on the grip safety portion, an adjustable trigger, and fiber-optic front sight. This new gun gets the Product Code GI45ESP. Each GI Expert comes with two 8-round magazines.

RUGER

Ruger's first striker-fired centerfire pistol, the 9mm SR9, now has a compact variant. The new SR9c has shortened the barrel from the SR9's 4.14 inches to 3.5 inches. The grip frame has been shortened to accommodate a 10-round magazine, instead of the original 17-rounder. The SR9c has pared the weight of the original down from 26.5 ounces to 23.4 ounces.

Although the SR9c has a 10-shot magazine, there are options. The magazine comes with two interchangeable bases: one flush and one with a finger grip extension. Actually, the 17-round magazine can also be used with the compact pistol, and Ruger offers a grip extension adapter to fill in the extra space. The compact pistols ship with one 10-round and one 17-round magazine, the two bases and the extension for the longer magazine.

Many features of the larger SR9, such as three-dot sights and reversible backstrap, are also included with the compact version.

SIG-SAUER

A number of new things from SIG-Sauer this year. Let's start with the updates from items introduced last year.

The new 380-caliber P238, a pretty little thing in its original form, now can be had in seven different versions. All are mechanically the same, and all have black anodized frames. The differences are in different materials and colors of grips, and different color finishes on the slides and small parts. They make an attractive group.

The long-range P556 pistol introduced last year now has a 22-caliber understudy. The new P522 is roughly the same general size as the 223-caliber P556, but is chambered for the .22 Long Rifle cartridge. With a 10-inch barrel, the overall length is a bit over 20 inches, and weight is about 5.5 pounds. The P522 pistol comes with a 25-round magazine. A 10-round magazine is also available.

The modular P250 is an interesting design. A single frame containing the entire trigger and firing mechanism can be used with polymer grip frames of various sizes, and barrels and magazines for different calibers can be used. So, the owner of a P250 can have several different guns by switching parts. How to do this? Well, SIG has made it easier with its P250 2SUM kit. The kit contains a full-size P250, and also everything needed to convert it to a P250 subcompact. A lot better than having a pistol and ordering a bunch of extra parts to convert it.

New E2 (Enhanced Ergonomics) variants of the P226 and P229 are available. The new one-piece grip frame reduces the area of the backstrap, and reduces overall circumference. The modular grip snaps into place, eliminating screws. The E2 models also have a reduced-reach trigger and feature SIG's Short Reset Trigger (SRT) system. The company believes these characteristics will allow these 9mm pistols to better fit a wider range of shooters' hands.

SMITH & WESSON

S&W has had good success recycling old revolver names onto their new items. Following the reuse of Chief's Special and Military & Police, now we have totally new guns that bear the Bodyguard name. The company developed two small new handguns that would wear the Bodyguard designation — a laser-sighted .38 revolver and a laser-sighted .380 pistol. Both guns were designed from the start to have integral lasers. The revolver is interesting, but you'll read about it elsewhere. Let's take a look at the 380.

The little pistol is double-action-only, but has second-strike capability. It also has a manual safety. It is tilting-barrel recoil-operated and is not a blowback. The gun has a stainless-steel slide and barrel (coated with Melonite) and a polymer frame. The 6+1 pistol is hammer-fired, and weighs less than 12 ounces. The integral laser sighting system is part of the frame, and has ambidextrous controls. The laser has three positions—constant, pulse, and off. The new bodyguard pistols were introduced on January 19, 2010, and scheduled for May 1 production.

Incidentally, the original Bodyguard revolver will remain in production with a unique model number, a separate series from the new Bodyguard guns.

Smith & Wesson also has introduced a new "Pro-Series" line of pistols. According to a company representative, these guns will bridge the gap between standard production and Performance Center guns. Included are three M&P polymer-frame pistols and two SW1911 pistols. The M&P guns are in 9mm and .40, with enhancements in sights and trigger pulls. The 1911 guns include a 5-inch full-size variant in 9mm, and a 3-inch subcompact .45, with special sights and other features.

SPRINGFIELD

The Springfield XD(M) line, introduced on these pages in the last edition, now has two new additions. The XD(M)–3.8 is a new shorter-barrel variant in 9mm, with 19+1 capacity and .40 S&W, with 16+1 capacity. The 3.8 designation refers to the 3.8-inch length of the barrel. The XD(M)–4.5 features the new slip-resistant slide serrations. By the beginning of 2011, a new .45 ACP version of the XD(M) is planned to also be included in the Springfield line.

Every XD(M) comes with a case that contains the pistol, two magazines, a lock, paddle holster, magazine loader, double magazine pouch, and three interchangeable backstraps.

STI

STI International has an anniversary of its own. The Texas company is celebrating its 20th year and has produced an eyecatching 20th Anniversary pistol to commemorate the occasion. The special commemorative pistol is marked on the slide "20th Anniversary, 1990-2010." The grasping grooves on the slide include a distinct XX, the Roman numerals for 20.

The company has introduced its patented 2011 frame, a metal/polymer composite. STI claims the new frame is appropriate for the 100th anniversary of the 1911 design, taking it into a new century. The metal frame/polymer grip system allows lighter weight and a grip thickness hardly larger than the original. A number of STI guns are now using this frame.

The lightest pistol in STI's lineup is the Escort. At 22.8 ounces, the 3-inch .45 has a Commander-size frame.

STI pistols tend to be eyecatchers. One of the most striking pistols the firm offers is the Elektra. In several variants, the one most likely to attract attention is the Electra Pink version. With its

Magnum Research has entered the 1911 world. Here is the Desert Eagle 1911 G., a full-size .45.

(left) Masterpiece Arms has introduced a new 22-caliber version of its "MAC-10" style pistols. The 22 pistol comes with a 27-round magazine.

A compact version of the company's 9mm SR9 pistol, Ruger's new SR9c has a 3.5-inch barrel and shortened grip.

SIG SAUER's P522 is a 22-caliber unconventional pistol with a 10-inch barrel and a 25-round magazine.

The 380-caliber SIG SAUER P238 is now available in seven different finishes. This striking specimen has the "rainbow" metal finish.

STI has passed its 20-year anniversary, and has put out a special pistol to commemorate the event. Notice the Roman numeral XX, used to represent 20, in the slide grasping grooves.

pink grips and pink filling of the slide lettering, it seems appropriate for either a man or woman shooter.

STOEGER

The Stoeger Cougar pistol is now available in .45 ACP chambering. The new Cougar 45 is only slightly larger than the 9mm and 40-caliber versions previously offered. Designated Model 8045, the .45 has a 3.6-inch barrel.

Recall that the Cougar design was originally introduced by Beretta, a mid-sized pistol with a rotating-barrel locking system. A few years ago, Stoeger took the design over. Now, it is made in Turkey and imported by Stoeger.

The .45 that I examined had an all-black finish. However, the 9mm and .40 pistols in the Cougar line are now offered in several other finishes. They can be had as all silver with black grips, or with a silver frame and black slide and grips.

TACTICAL INNOVATIONS

Shown for the first time at the 2010 SHOT Show, the COHORT pistol is offered by Tactical Innovations. The new 22-caliber pistols are based on a modified Ruger 10/22 platform. Made in Idaho, the new pistols have aluminum receivers and a Ruger-style bolt. However, one can see a big difference right away—the action is rear-charging, with a bolt retraction system patterned after that of the AR-15. A rail allows any sighting system desired by the shooter.

Barrels are stainless steel, with various lengths and configurations. Threaded muzzles (with caps) are standard. A 25-round Tactical magazine is furnished with the Cohort pistol, and an AK-style magazine release is used. The laminated stocks come in a variety of colors. Matched with different colors of triggers and trigger housings, the Cohort can become a very colorful, and very individualized, gun.

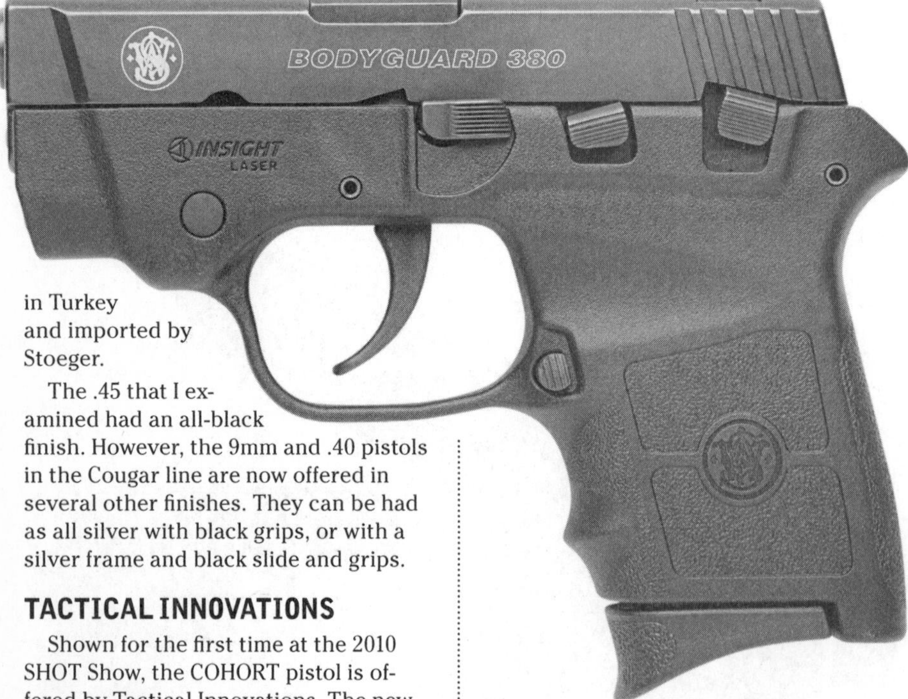

The Bodyguard .380 from Smith & Wesson has its controls on the left, but its double-action-only mechanism is suitable for use with either hand.

TAURUS

Taurus' new offerings were dominated by an amazing lineup of "Judge" .45/.410 revolvers, but you'll have to read about them elsewhere. Although overshadowed by the big revolvers, interesting semiauto pistols have been introduced by Taurus.

Carrying through on the renewed interest in small 380-caliber pistols that began last year, the Taurus 738 TCP is now a production item. The small 6+1 pistol weighs about 10 ounces (9 ounces in the Titanium version).

The 24/7 G2 series of polymer-frame pistols is the culmination of Taurus experience with the 24/7 series and the 800 series lines. The new 24/7 G2 offers a choice of single-action, conventional double-action, or double-action-only triggers. The double-actions offer "strike two" capability. Slide stops, decockers and manual safeties are ambidextrous. Calibers are now 9mm, .40 S&W, and .45 ACP. Along with the traditional 4.2-inch barrel, there are now a compact version with a 3.5-inch barrel and a long slide variant with a 5-inch barrel.

The 800 series now has a compact of

its own. The larger 4-inch 800 pistols have been scaled down to a compact size appropriate for a 3.5-inch barrel. The 809 compact is available in 9mm, .357 SIG, and .40 S&W.

The 700 "Slim" pistol series, introduced in the 9mm chambering, has gone both up and down. The slim single-column pistols are now available in both .380 and .40 S&W versions.

Taurus has had a hard time coming up with a satisfactory 22-caliber pistol for target, plinking and recreational shooting. Several worthy prototypes have been introduced over the years, but none made it to full production status. Now, the company thinks a new .22 on the 800 frame will do the trick. The Model 822 will be available with either 4.5- or 6-inch barrels. The hammer-fired guns will be conventional double action, and will have "strike two" capability. 822 pistols will have adjustable sights. A conversion kit, allowing any 800-series pistol to shoot .22 Long Rifle ammunition, will also be offered.

TISAS

The Turkish firm Tisas introduced a 45-caliber 1911-style pistol on these pages a few years ago. Now, the new 1911 is offered in the United States by Interstate Arms as the Regent pistol. (See Interstate Arms.)

USELTON

Uselton Arms, a maker of 1911-style pistols since 1999, planned for a special gun to commemorate the 100th year anniversary of the 1911 design. The result is a striking-looking handgun. The frame is case colored, and the slide is polished mirror bright. Engraved on the right side of the slide (and effectively using roman numerals) is this legend in a three-line display: MODEL 1911 / MCMXI-MMXI / COMMEMORATING 100 YEARS. The Uselton 100 Year Commemorative will be available in full-size Government Model, and also in compact Officers Model versions.

VLTOR

The pistol based on the Bren Ten design, and offered for the first time last year as the Vltor Fortis, is now available under the original Bren Ten name. (See Bren Ten.)

VOLQUARTSEN

Volquartsen Custom makes an amazing number of interesting 22-caliber pistols, most based on the original Ruger design. Last year, Volquartsen introduced a prototype of a new design of .22 target pistol, which they named the V-10X. The frame was CNC-machined from aluminum billet material, and the barrel was a taper fit into the aluminum frame. Finger grooves were machined into the frame, and followed the contour of the grips. The laminated wood grips themselves were available with either right or left thumb rest.

Now, a year later, the company also offers new variations with built-in muzzle brakes, and with rails mounted top and bottom for attaching various types of sights and accessories. Traditional open sights are, however, furnished with each pistol. Trigger is set at about 2 pounds and has pretravel and overtravel adjustments. Want a special color? The V-10X is available hard-anodized in black, silver, red, green, blue and purple.

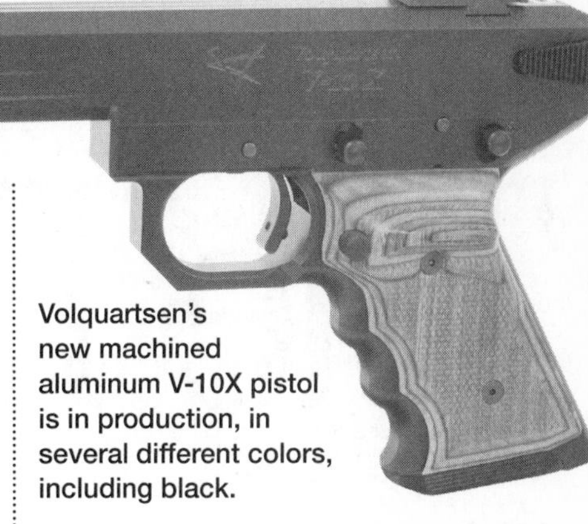

Volquartsen's new machined aluminum V-10X pistol is in production, in several different colors, including black.

WALTHER

The Walther PK380, introduced on these pages last year, is now a production item, and already has several new variants. The PK380, at 5.2x6.5 inches, is larger than the current offerings of small 380s, but is roughly the same size as Walther's P22, the firm's small 22-caliber pistol. The PK380 has a 3.7-inch barrel and weighs about 21 ounces.

Along with basic black, other variants now available are: a First Edition (serial numbers 1 through 2000 are reserved) which comes with an extra magazine and a nylon holster, a nickel slide version, and a black gun with an attached laser. All variants of the Walther PK380 use an eight-round single-column magazine.

WILSON

The Wilson Sentinel, a small steel-frame 9mm with a 3.6-inch barrel, was introduced last year in this publication. It quickly achieved a certain popularity, and its suitability as a lady's carry pistol was examined. The result was a new variant named appropriately, if somewhat tongue-in-cheek, Ms. Sentinel.

The Ms. Sentinel pistol was specifically designed to be carried equally well in a purse or in a holster. The configuration of some of the controls is subdued to avoid snagging. A round butt frame was used. A shortened trigger, better suited to smaller hands, was installed. To reduce weight, an aluminum frame and a fluted 3.5-inch barrel were used. The result, Wilson feels, is a 9mm pistol that will be a very good choice for a woman's protection pistol.

Tactical Innovations has just introduced the Cohort pistol, based on the Ruger 10/22 design, but with rear-charging operation.

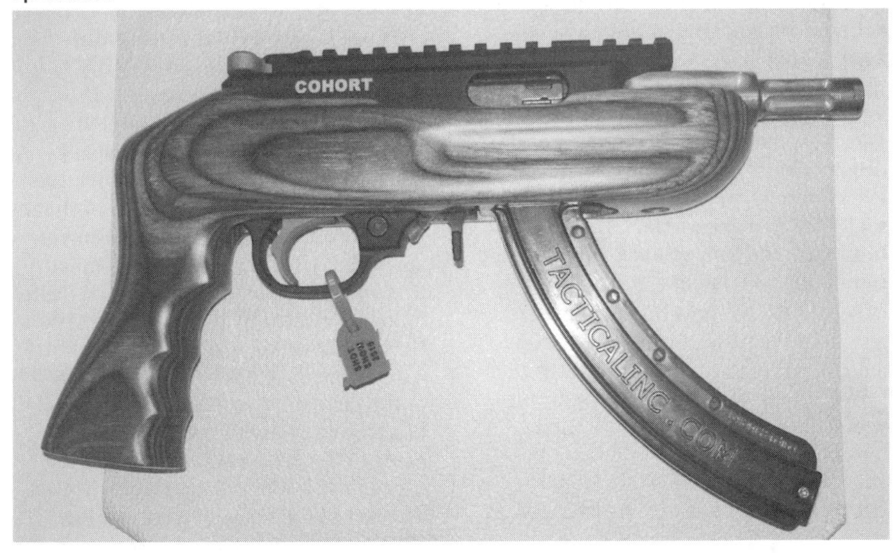

The Enforcer

BY **DAN SHIDELER**

Every now and then a gun is introduced for no good reason at all. Perhaps the best example of this is the 4.25mm Liliput semi-auto pistol made by August Menz in the 1920s. Barely larger than a box of matches, the Liliput served absolutely no useful purpose, except perhaps to show what could be accomplished if you had enough time on your hands.

But their total lack of usefulness hasn't kept some guns from becoming valuable collector's items. Although the Liliput is now a high-dollar collectible, other good-for-nothin' guns are still on the affordable side, at least for now. My favorite oddity of this sort is the Enforcer pistol. The Enforcer, derived from the M1 carbine, simply defies classification. It's not a C&R. It's not a modern re-creation. It's not a sporting arm. It's not a target gun. It's not a self-defense gun.

In fact, it's nothing more than a fun gun. And, by crackey, that's good enough for me!

The story of the Enforcer starts with the original United States Carbine, Caliber .30, M1. Of course, everyone knows – especially if they've seen the 1952 movie Carbine Williams starring Jimmy Stewart – that a convicted murderer named Marsh Williams invented the M1 after his release from prison. Everyone knows it; the problem is, it's not true.

Actually, Williams did invent the short-stroke gas piston that made the M1 carbine possible but that's about it. The M1 was mostly the work of Winchester's William Roemer and Fred Humeston, who took a mere 13 days in the spring of 1941 to bang together a prototype. All in all, around six million M1 carbines and their variants were produced between June of 1942 and August of 1945, when the big balloon went up over Hiroshima.

It's important to know who actually designed the M1 carbine, because that way you know precisely whose name to cuss. Probably no other US military rifle has been the target of such hostility as the M1 carbine. This isn't because the gun itself is lousy, because it isn't. It's because of the .30 Carbine cartridge, which is generally considered to be one step up from a Wham-O Rubber Band Gun in terms of stopping power. As a rifle cartridge, the .30 Carbine is indeeed puny, but by handgun standards it ain't half-bad. After all, the carbine was designed to replace the 1911A1 pistol among certain troops, and the slender little .30 Carbine has more than twice the muzzle energy of the big fat .45 ACP. All things considered, I'd rather be missed by a .30 Carbine bullet than hit by one. It's no .30-06, but it wasn't designed to be.

After the Korean War ended, zillions of M1 carbines flooded the surplus market. Even more were made from spare parts, Plainfield and Universal being the major producers of these built-up M1s. Somewhere along the line, Universal decided to "improve" the M1's design by incorporating two recoil springs into the action in place of the original's single spring. This ill-advised modification, and the other changes that it necessitated, left the Universal M1 clones as strange, chromosomally-damaged copies of the original. Most internal parts weren't even interchangeable with those of the real M1s. To make matters, the modifications gave the Universal carbines a toxic reputation as jammers.

So, Mr. Bones, how do you market a turkey? Well, Mr. Jones, you make a pistol out of it. At least that's what Universal did to some of their carbine wanna-bes. They whacked off their buttstocks and replaced them with shapeless little pistol grips. Then they cut the barrels back to 9-1/2 or 11-1/4 inches and did away with unnecessary frills like bolt hold-opens. Thus was born the Enforcer, a pistol like no other before or since.

Production of the Enforcer apparently began around 1972, more or less simultaneously by Plainfield and Universal. Some of the early models used US mil-spec parts. Some Enforcers even used the single recoil spring of the genuine M1 carbine and milled, not stamped, operating rods. This may be why some Enforcers fire and cycle as well as any M1 ever built, while others jam so consistently that they're basically bolt-operated manual repeaters.

Reliability aside, there's no doubt that the Enforcer looked intimidating. And so it was, considering its 15- and 30-round magazines. In the parlance of the '60s and '70s (and I should know), it was wicked, pronounced "wickkk-id!" I've had two Enforcers, one Plainfield and one Universal, and they certainly attracted attention wherever they went. I never took them to Maryland, California or Canada, which is probably just as well since they're illegal there and probably in a hundred other places, too.

There's quite a debate in certain circles about who made the best Enforcer: Universal, Plainfield, or Iver Johnson. The question is muddled because, although the three makers started out as separate companies, Iver Johnson eventually gobbled up both its competitors (Plainfield in 1975, Universal in 1983). General consensus holds that the Plainfield version was the best, followed closely by Iver Johnson with Universal coming in a very distant third. Aside from cosmetics (e.g., the shape of the pistol grip and a metal-vs.-wood handguard), they're pretty much the same thing, with quality ranging from purty durn good to unspeakably rotten. The last of the Enforcers left the Iver

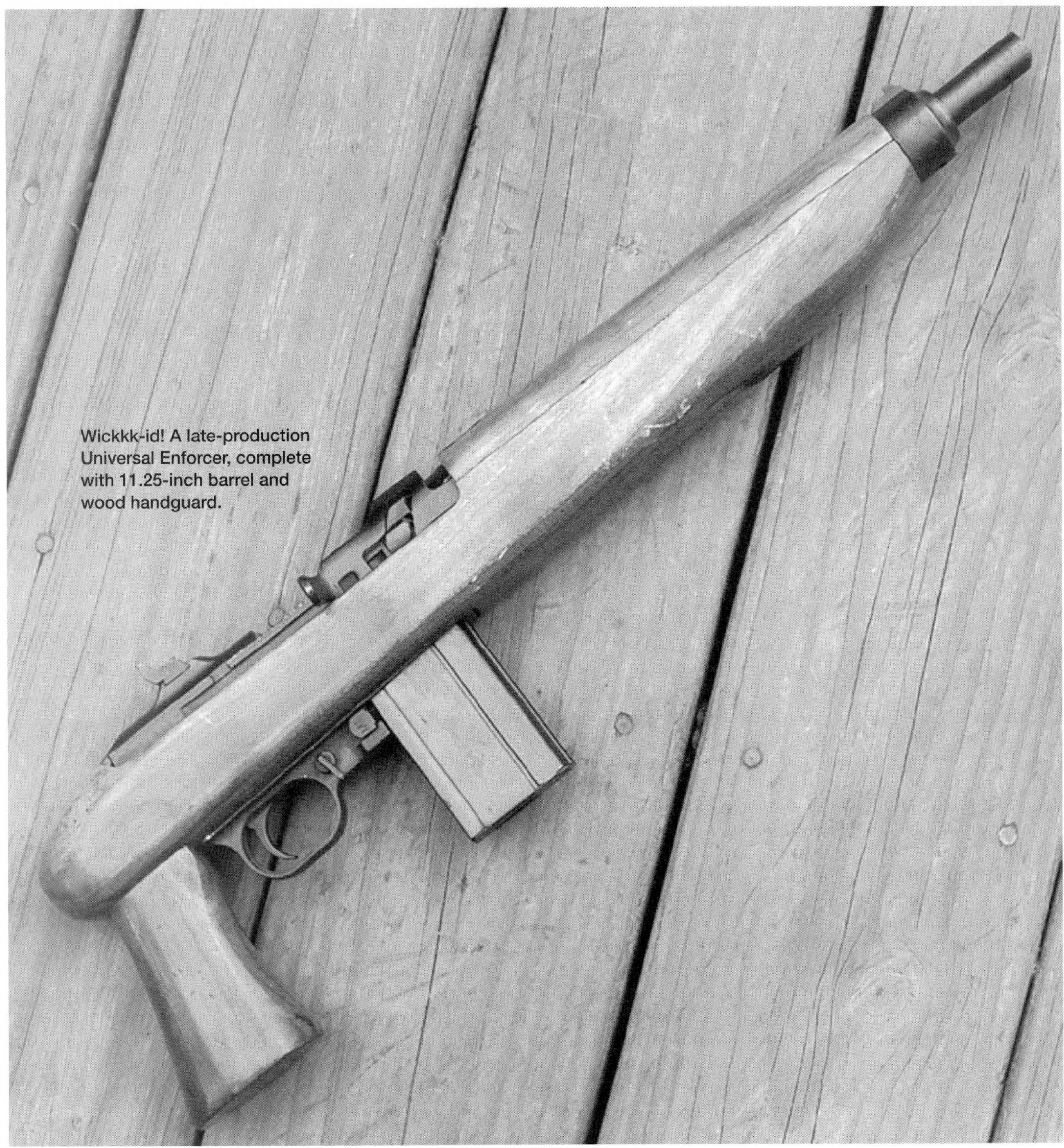

Wickkk-id! A late-production Universal Enforcer, complete with 11.25-inch barrel and wood handguard.

Johnson factory in 1986.

Plainfield's version was known variously as the Enforcer and the Super Enforcer. No, I don't know what the difference was, if there was a difference at all. Universal called its Enforcer the Model 3000 and offered it in blued, nickel-plated, and gold-plated versions. Gold-plating an Enforcer is like putting a crystal doorknob on an outhouse, but the effect must have been eye-catching to say the very least.

If you have an Enforcer stashed away somewhere, you might consider cashing it in for a handful of Ben Franklins. Five or so years ago you could find a decent Enforcer for about $250 (and if you look diligently in the right places, you still can). Today, an excellent Enforcer can run as high as $500 or even more. I have heard reports of a mint Plainfield Super Enforcer selling for $950 at auction. If true, this is a fluke of monstrous proportions.

My only explanation for the renewed interest in the Enforcer is that the kids who could only drool over them back in the '70s are now in a position to buy them. Thus demand creates value. I can't predict where the Enforcer will top out in terms of value, but I can tell you that mine's not for sale. It's wickkk-id!

The Mateba six-shot semiauto revolver in .44 Magnum, shown here with compensator. Photo courtesy J. C. Devine.

REVOLVERS

BY JEFF QUINN

The past year has certainly been an interesting one for gun owners. We have in our nation the finest selection of firearms available anywhere in the world, yet we also have politicians vowing to rip those guns from our possession. However, on most fronts, I think we're winning.

Just in the last few months, several new concealed-carry guns have hit the market, and more are on the way. I have seen prototypes of some very interesting and useful compact revolvers that should be available by the time this *Gun Digest* goes to press. While many choose a semiauto for concealed carry, the compact revolver still holds its own, with many knowledgeable citizens recognizing the advantages of a reliable revolver as a last-ditch fighting gun. While revolvers can break, it is a rare occurrence. I have never heard of a revolver having a failure to feed or having a cartridge case hang up halfway through ejection. Another plus is that a revolver does not leave your empty brass lying on the ground. Many of us choose revolvers for personal defense for these reasons, and while there are some good semiautos that are used for hunting, most handgun hunters choose either a revolver or a quality single-shot, for reasons of accuracy, power, and reliability.

Let's take a look at some of the better offerings of revolvers, derringers, and single-shot pistols that are available today. With modern revolvers now having capacities from five to twelve rounds in their cylinders, 2011 is a good year for those who choose to purchase and enjoy "Revolvers and Others."

AMERICAN WESTERN ARMS

AWA is best known for their line of 1873 single action revolvers, which are some excellent Colt replica sixguns. Offered in most popular chamberings and barrel lengths, the AWA line consists of their Classic revolvers, made very much like the sixguns of the late nineteenth

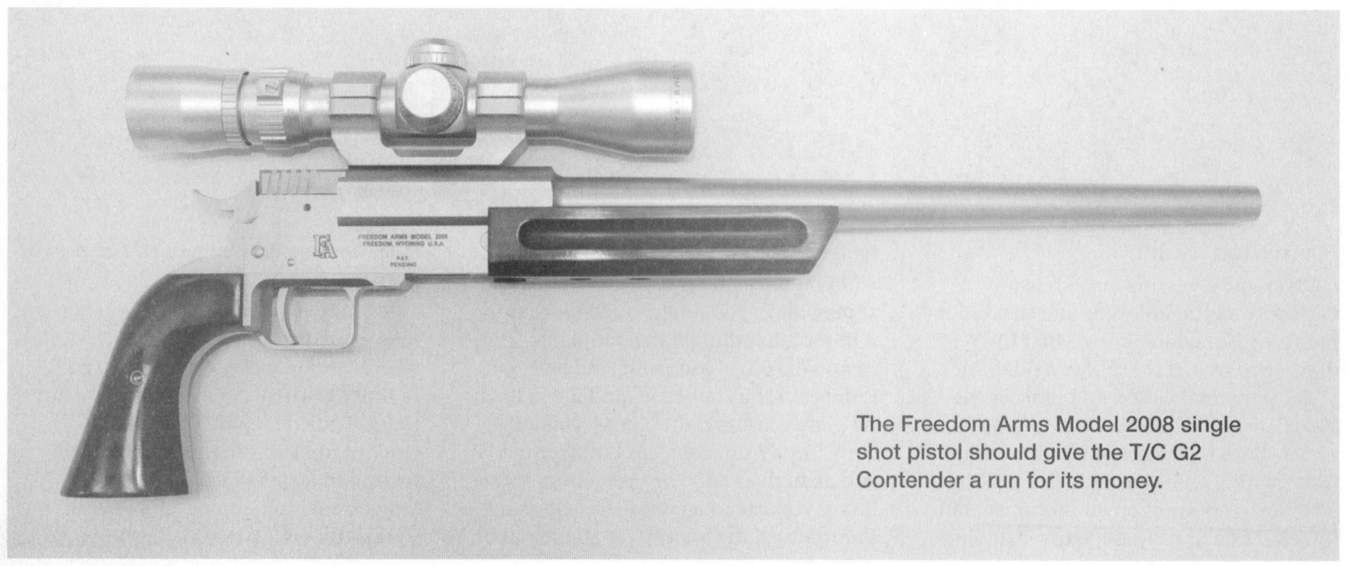

The Freedom Arms Model 2008 single shot pistol should give the T/C G2 Contender a run for its money.

One big honkin' single action revolver: the Magnum Research BFR .45-70.

AND OTHERS

Bond Arms Snake Slayer .45 Colt/.410 shotshell derringer. An extremely well-built derringer of the Remington pattern.

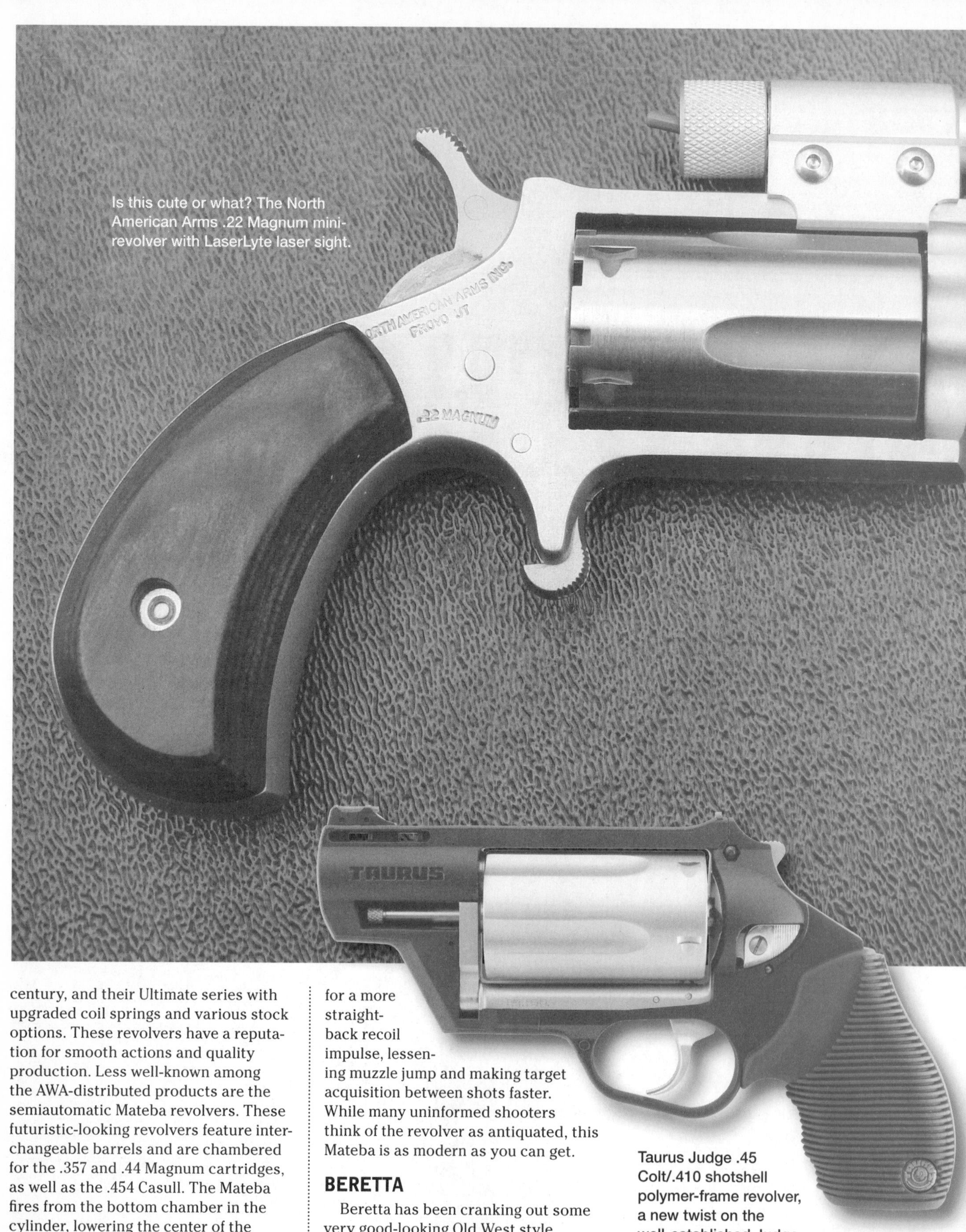

Is this cute or what? The North American Arms .22 Magnum mini-revolver with LaserLyte laser sight.

Taurus Judge .45 Colt/.410 shotshell polymer-frame revolver, a new twist on the well-established Judge lineup.

century, and their Ultimate series with upgraded coil springs and various stock options. These revolvers have a reputation for smooth actions and quality production. Less well-known among the AWA-distributed products are the semiautomatic Mateba revolvers. These futuristic-looking revolvers feature interchangeable barrels and are chambered for the .357 and .44 Magnum cartridges, as well as the .454 Casull. The Mateba fires from the bottom chamber in the cylinder, lowering the center of the recoil in relation to the shooter's hand, for a more straight-back recoil impulse, lessening muzzle jump and making target acquisition between shots faster. While many uninformed shooters think of the revolver as antiquated, this Mateba is as modern as you can get.

BERETTA

Beretta has been cranking out some very good-looking Old West style firearms for a few years now, since their

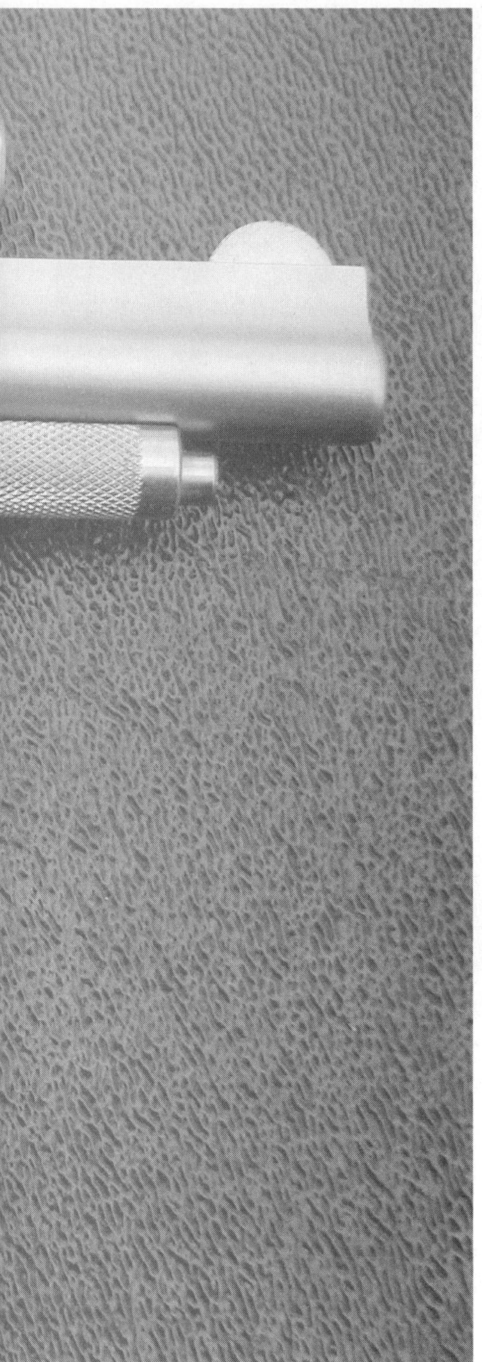

corporate acquisition of Uberti. Building on the quality firearms produced by Uberti, Beretta markets their Single Action Army replicas with some high-grade finishes such as a brilliant carbona-type blue, along with authentic-looking case coloring and an antique finish that makes the gun look like an original, well-worn gun from the late nineteenth century. Beretta adds a transfer bar safety system to their revolvers that allows the firearm to be carried fully loaded, with a live cartridge under the hammer – unlike the original style 1873 single action, which should be safely carried with an empty chamber under the hammer. Beretta offers not only the 1873 Single Action Army style but a modified Bisley style sixgun as well.

There is also the Stampede Marshall, which has a Thunderer-style birdshead grip frame. Beretta revolvers are chambered for either the .357 Magnum or .45 Colt cartridges.

BOND ARMS

Bond Arms has been producing high-quality two-shot derringers for several years now and have reached the apex in derringer design. Their derringers are often regarded as the best that money can buy, and Bond offers an extensive variety of chamberings, from .22 Long Rifle up through .45 Colt/.410 shotshell, covering many popular chamberings in between. Bond derringers are built primarily of stainless steel, and they exhibit first class craftsmanship and are built with quality materials. My personal favorite is the Snake Slayer. I have one that I carry often. Besides its intended use against venomous reptiles, it is also a fine personal defense arm for use against carjackers and other two-legged predators. Loaded with #000 buckshot or Winchester's new buck and birdshot load, it would be a very effective close-range defensive weapon. The Bond Arms derringers offer a lot of versatility, with the barrels being interchangeable, so one can switch calibers as needed. Bond Arms also offers some high quality

Author with Colt .45 SAA.

The eye-catching Cougar and Panther from Charter Arms.

leather holsters in which to carry your derringer. I particularly like the horizontal driving holster. It is ideal to wear while riding in a vehicle or on an ATV or motorcycle, placing the handgun within reach for a fast and comfortable draw.

CHARTER ARMS

Charter Arms has built their reputation upon providing very useful gun designs that are affordable for the common man. I have many times relied upon a Charter revolver for various needs, mostly a .38 Special riding in a boot or pocket for protection, and at other times packing their handy little .22LR Pathfinder as a trail gun while just bumming around in the woods. The Charter revolvers are available in blued steel or stainless, and recently they have added alloy frames to the lineup for those who want to carry the lightest possible package.

The latest innovation from Charter is the finishes that they apply to their alloy-frame guns. Made in a variety of colors, their pink finish has proven to be extremely popular with women in Charter's Pink Lady variation of their five-shot .38. They also have a couple of revolvers with a mottled finish. I refer to them unofficially as their "Cat" revolvers. The Cougar has a pink mottled finish, and the Panther a medium-dark bronze mottled finish. I have handled and shot both of these, and they are indeed good-shooting, lightweight revolvers. Both have exposed hammers and black synthetic grips, and they draw a crowd when brought out in public. Some love the finish while others hate it. No one seems to be neutral on these flashy new finishes from Charter Arms. Personally I like them, especially the bronze mottled finish.

Besides these, Charter still builds their legendary .44 Special Bulldog revolvers. These powerful belly guns fill a needed niche in the market as they have for the past few decades. The Bulldog is lightweight and easy to conceal yet carries five .44 Special cartridges in the cylinder. Recoil is stiff with heavy loads, but not really painful at all. These stainless revolvers are not much bigger than a compact .38 Special but pack a hefty punch. In addition to their popular .38 Special and .44 Special revolvers, Charter still has their rimfire Pathfinder line in .22 Long Rifle and .22 Magnum, along with revolvers chambered for the .32 H&R Magnum, .327 Federal Magnum, and .357 Magnum. Charter also makes a true left-handed snubnose revolver called the Southpaw. The Southpaw is a mirror image of their standard revolver design with the cylinder latch on the right side; the cylinder swings out to the right as well.

Also of interest to us here is the Charter Dixie Derringer. The Dixie is a five-shot .22 Long Rifle or .22 Magnum mini-revolver with a crossbolt safety. Construction is stainless steel throughout. Weighing in at just six ounces, the Dixie Derringer can hide just about anywhere and is pretty effective at close range, especially the .22 Magnum version.

CHIAPPA

Chiappa is a relatively new name in the firearms business but is the outgrowth of the well-established Armi Sport company. Chiappa has entered the market with several quality replica firearms, but the one of interest here is not a replica of an Old West gun at all but a thoroughly modern revolver. The Chiappa Rhino is a unique sixgun that fires its cartridges from the bottom barrel in the cylinder, resulting in a lower bore axis in relation to the shooter's hand, and greatly reduced muzzle jump upon firing. Much like the Mateba in design, the Rhino is more compact but does *not* share the Mateba's semiauto design. I have not yet been able to fire the new Rhino, but have seen and handled a few examples in various barrel lengths. It appears to be well-crafted of quality materials. The Rhino is chambered for the 357 Magnum cartridge. It certainly has a very unconventional appearance but feels really good in my hand. I have high hopes that it will work very well in reducing the muzzle jump and felt recoil of the .357 Magnum cartridge.

CIMARRON

For many years now, Mike Harvey and the gang at Cimarron Firearms in Fredericksburg, Texas, have been at the forefront of marketing quality replicas of Old West style rifles and handguns. Of concern here is their extensive line of authentically reproduced historic sixguns. Cimarron has not only 1873 Single Action Army replicas, but has also delved into other lesser-known but very historic firearms of the nineteenth century. Cimarron offers replicas of most of the major players in the cap and ball sixgun business of that era, such as the Walker, Dragoon, Army and Navy guns, as well as the Remington and even the Leech & Rigdon guns. Cimarron covers the transition from cap and ball to cartridge with their conversion revolvers and the 1872 Colt replica. The company also offers the Remington 1875 and 1890 cartridge revolvers, as well as a variety of the Smith & Wesson break-open sixguns such as the Russian and Schofield models.

Besides these authentic single action

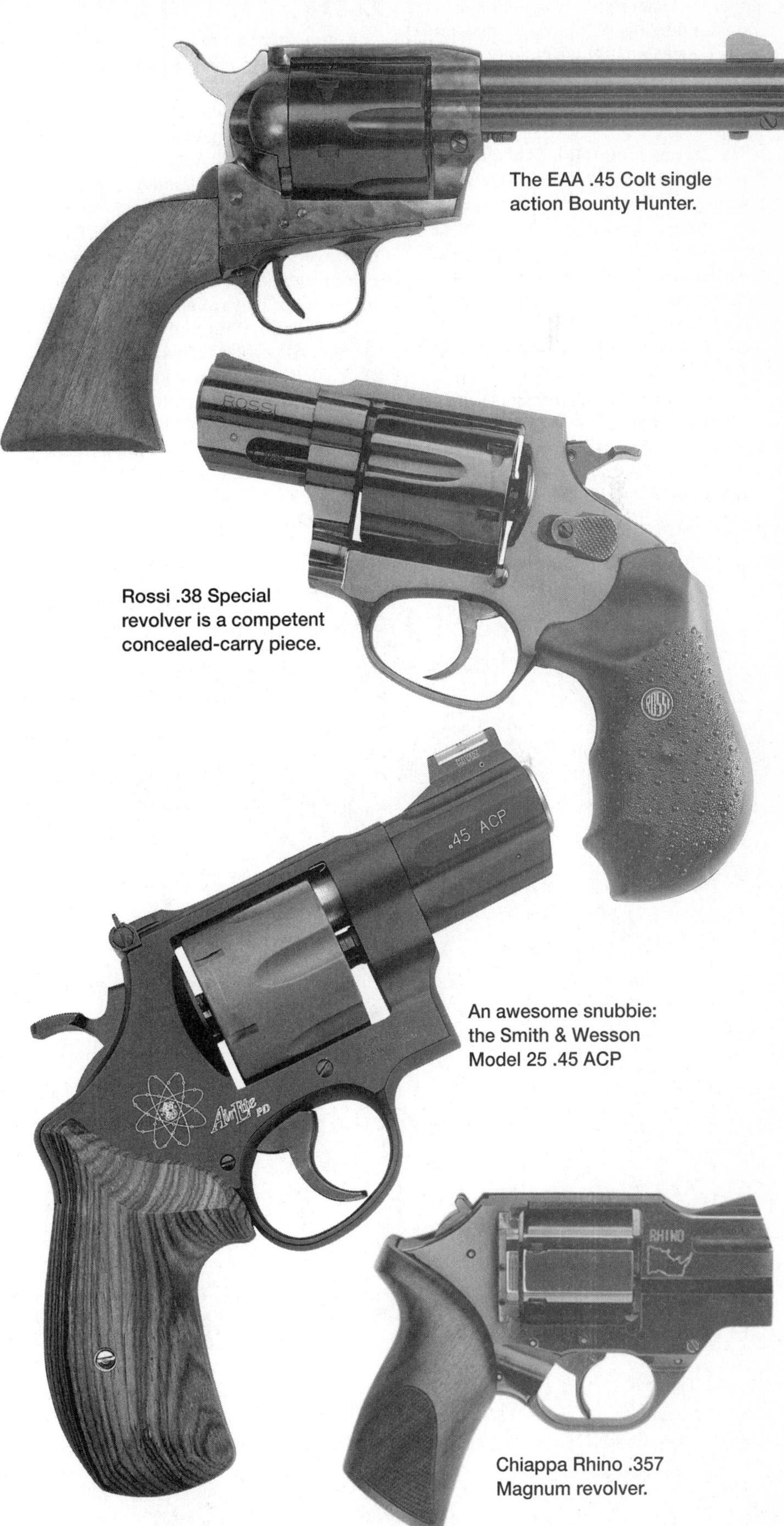

The EAA .45 Colt single action Bounty Hunter.

Rossi .38 Special revolver is a competent concealed-carry piece.

An awesome snubbie: the Smith & Wesson Model 25 .45 ACP

Chiappa Rhino .357 Magnum revolver.

replicas, Cimarron has a selection of two-shot derringers. They are small and easily concealed and are chambered for the .22 Long Rifle and Magnum rimfire cartridges, as well as the .32 H&R Magnum and the .38 Special.

The .22 Long Rifle and .22 Magnum Plinkerton revolvers are priced to get most anyone into the single action revolver game. These guns are built from a non-ferrous alloy but have steel-lined chambers and barrel, and they shoot surprisingly well. The Plinkerton would make a good understudy to Cimarron's centerfire sixguns, but it's also a handy and reliable plinker.

One new attention-getter from Cimarron is the so-called "Holy Smoker," modeled after Russell Crowe's revolver in the film *3:10 to Yuma*. It has a tastefully-rendered, gold-plated sterling silver crucifix on each grip panel.

COBRA

Cobra Firearms of Utah manufactures some small and reliable two-shot single action derringers. These compact derringers are made in .22 Long Rifle, .22 Magnum, .38 Special, 9mm Luger, .25 Auto, .32 Auto, .380 Auto, and .32 H&R Magnum. Their Titan model is built of stainless steel, and is offered in 9mm Luger and .45 Colt/.410 shotshell. These derringers are available in a variety of colors, and each sells at an affordable price. Brand new from Cobra this year is their Shadow +P-rated five-shot .38 Special revolver. This one has a concealed hammer and looks very much like a Smith & Wesson Model 642. It has a stainless cylinder and barrel with an aluminum frame for an overall a weight of fifteen ounces. I have not yet had the opportunity to fire one of these, but I have handled a couple of them, and they appear to be well-made from quality materials. I look forward to trying one out soon.

COLT

Colt has been producing revolvers for almost 175 years now. In fact, if it were not for Sam Colt, we might not have revolvers. His first successful revolver, the Paterson, set the stage for all revolvers that have followed. That design, while it worked pretty well, was delicate and underpowered, but it led to the big Colt Walker, which packed a lot of punch and set the Colt company on its way to success. Through the years, Colt has produced some very good revolver designs, but today has only one Colt revolver in its stable, that being the Single Action Army. The SAA is probably the most recognized handgun in the world, and is certainly the most copied

Ruger LCR polymer-framed .38 Special, one of the hottest revolvers on the market.

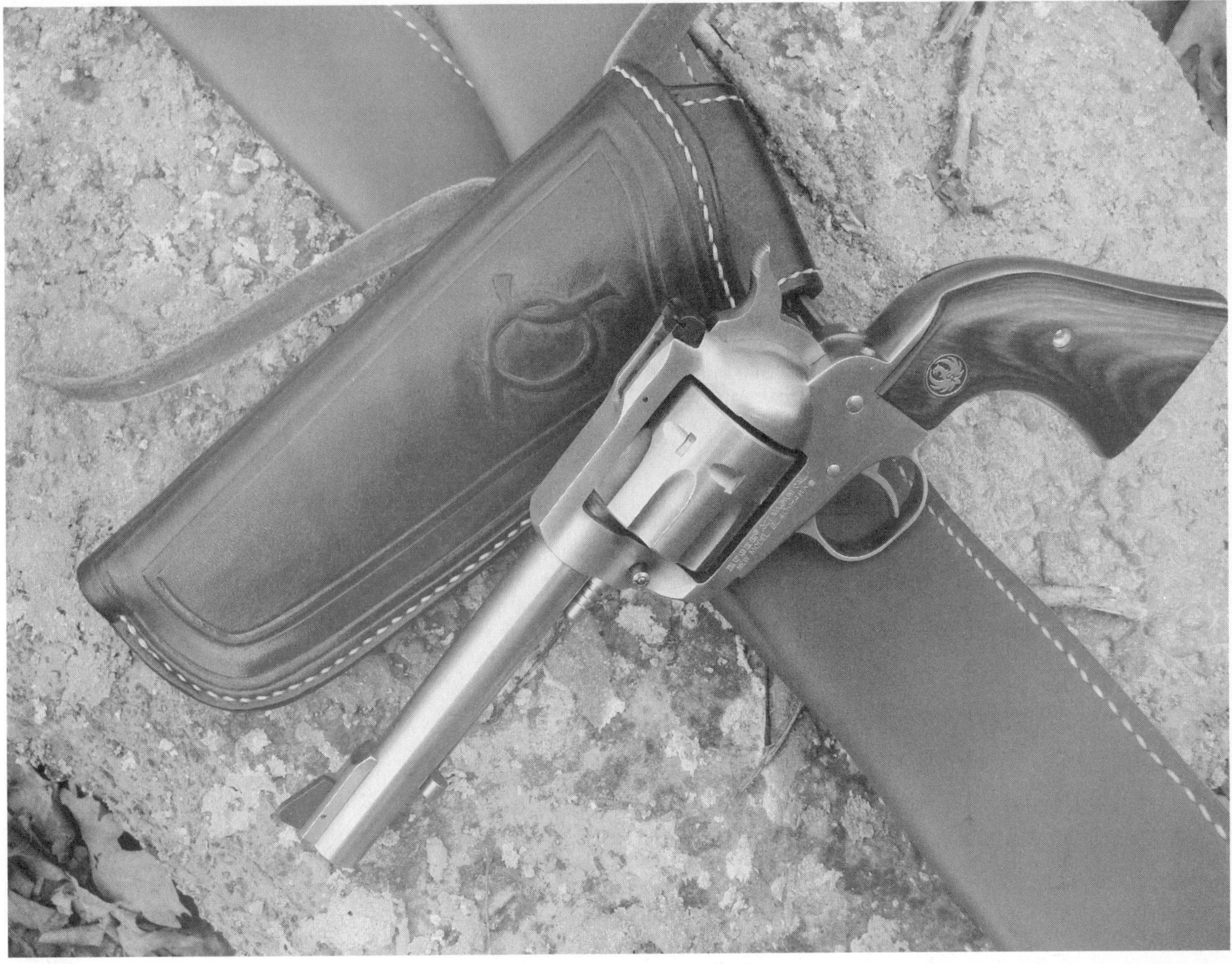

revolver design ever produced. Colt still produces the SAA, and the latest sixguns that they have been shipping for the past few years are as good as any that Colt has ever produced. Available in three barrel lengths (4.75, 5.5, and 7.5 inches), the Single Action Army is chambered in a choice of .357 Magnum, .44 WCF, .45 Colt, .38 Special, .32 WCF (.32-20) and .38 WCF (.38-40). The SAA is available in blued/case-hardened or nickel finishes. Through the Colt Custom Shop, many options are available such as non-standard barrel lengths and hand engraving.

EUROPEAN AMERICAN ARMORY

EAA Corp. has a line of Single Action Army replica revolvers called the Bounty Hunter. These sixguns are available chambered for the .22 Long Rifle and .22 Magnum cartridges, with an alloy frame and a choice of six or eight-shot cylinders. The available centerfire chamberings are the .357 and .44 Magnums and the .45 Colt. These sixguns are built with all-steel frames in a choice of nickeled, blued, or case-hardened finishes and have the traditional half-cock loading feature but include a modern transfer bar safety action that permits carrying them fully loaded, with a live round under the hammer without fear of firing if accidentally dropped.

The double-action Windicator revolvers are chambered for the .38 Special cartridge with an alloy frame, or the all-steel .357 Magnum version. Both revolvers have a synthetic rubber grip and a businesslike matte blue finish, with a choice of two- or four-inch barrel.

FREEDOM ARMS

Freedom Arms of Freedom, Wyoming, is best known for its fine, sturdy, and super-accurate revolvers. It is often said that a Freedom Arms revolver is built like a fine Swiss watch. I disagree. A Swiss watch has a lot of tiny, delicate parts, and can get screwed up beyond

Blackhawk Ruger eight-shot .327 Federal Magnum Blackhawk with Barranti Leather rig. The term "six-shooter" is obviously inadequate to describe it.

repair if dropped hard. The Freedom Arms revolver is tough. It is built to very close tolerances but can also take a lot of abuse. Chambered for such powerful cartridges as the .454 Casull and the .475 Linebaugh, the Freedom revolvers will withstand a lot more punishment than most shooters can endure. The Freedom Arms revolvers are meticulously fitted and finished to perfection. The chambers in the cylinder are precisely aligned with the bore, and every detail of these revolvers follows the same precise standard of quality.

The large-frame Model 83 is the flagship of the Freedom Arms line and is chambered for the aforementioned .454 Casull and .475 Linebaugh cartridges, in addition to the .357 Magnum and .500 Wyoming Express cartridges and the

.41 and .44 Magnums. It's available with fixed sights or rugged adjustable sights. The adjustable-sight guns also accept a variety of scope mounts.

The Model 97 is Freedom's compact frame single action revolver. Built to the same tight tolerances as the Model 83 revolvers, the Model 97 is a bit handier to carry all day and is chambered for the .17 HMR and .22 Long Rifle/Magnum rimfire cartridges, as well as the .327 Federal, .357 Magnum, .41 Magnum, .44 Special, and .45 Colt centerfire cartridges. In addition to these standard handgun cartridges, the Model 97 is also available in Freedom Arms' own .224-32 cartridge, which is a fast-stepping .22 centerfire based on the .327 Federal cartridge case.

First introduced to the public last year, the Freedom Arms Model 2008 Single Shot pistol is the first single shot handgun that ever stirred any interest in me. There have been several very good single shot pistols on the market for years, but the Freedom Arms is the only one that is built like a Freedom Arms revolver. I have fired a couple of these chambered in the 6.5x55 and 6.5 JDJ cartridges, as well as one chambered for the .375 Winchester cartridge. Current chamberings offered are the .223 Remington, 6.5 Swede, 7mm BR, 7mm-08, .308 Winchester, .357 Magnum, .357 Maximum, .338 Federal and .375 Winchester. Standard barrel lengths are 10,15, and 16 inches, depending on caliber, but non-standard lengths are available as well for a nominal cost.

What makes this single shot so comfortable to shoot is the single action revolver grip style. Shooting the pistol allows the gun to recoil comfortably, with no pain at all to the hands as is encountered with some single shot pistols. The barrels are interchangeable, with extra fitted barrels available from Freedom Arms, allowing the shooter to switch among any of the available barrel and caliber options all on one frame. The Model 2008 weighs in around four pounds, depending on barrel length and caliber. The barrel is drilled for a Freedom Arms scope mount, and the scope stays with the barrel, allowing the interchange of the barrels without affecting the sight adjustment. These new single shot pistols have handsome impregnated wood grips and forends and are shipping now.

LEGACY SPORTS

Legacy Sports is best known for their Howa and Puma rifles, but they also have made a big splash in the market last year with their Bounty Hunter Model 92 lever action pistol. The Bounty Hunter resembles a sawed-off Model 92 lever action rifle, but is built from the start as a pistol, so it needs no special NFA tax stamp for approval. It can be purchased just like any other pistol, and has become quite popular for its nostalgic appeal, as well as its reliable function and accuracy. Legacy also markets a couple of good holster rigs for this "mare's leg" pistol, made by Bob Mernickle exclusively for Legacy Sports. The holster and belt combo is a beautiful rig and makes a necessary addition to the Bounty Hunter, completing the nostalgic package.

Legacy also has their 1873 Colt replica sixgun called the Puma Westerner. These are reliable and well-built sixguns, chambered for the .357 Magnum, .44 WCF, and .45 Colt cartridges, with 4.75-, 5.5-, or 7.5- inch barrels. They are very high-quality Colt SAA replicas. These sixguns are offered with a blued and case-hardened finish with walnut grips, nickel finish with walnut grips, or with a stainless finish and white synthetic ivory grips. The Puma line also includes a very affordable single action replica chambered for the .22 Long Rifle or .22 Magnum cartridge that would make a good trainer for the larger bores, but will be a lot less costly to shoot.

MAGNUM RESEARCH

Magnum Research of Minneapolis, Minnesota, has been producing their quality BFR revolver for many years now. These robust single action revolvers are built for hunting the largest, most dangerous game on the planet. In addition to their venerable .454 Casull revolvers, the BFR is available in other high-performance calibers like the .460 and .500 Smith & Wesson Magnums, the .475 Linebaugh and .480 Ruger revolver cartridges, as well as the .30-30 Winchester, .444 Marlin, and .45-70 rifle cartridges. The BFR is also available chambered for the ever-popular .45 Colt/.410 shotshell combination, which offers a lot of versatility in a handgun.

NORTH AMERICAN ARMS

The North American Arms mini-revolvers are well-established in the market place, being in production for a long time now, but they seem more popular than ever. These little five-shot miniature revolvers are more often than not bought as a deep-concealment handgun. They're small enough to fit into most any pocket, and are handy enough to always be with you, no matter what the attire or climate. Chambered for the .22 Short, .22 Long Rifle, or .22 Magnum cartridges, these little jewels are easy to carry and surprisingly accurate within their intended range. The small sights and short sight radius makes hitting at a distance a challenge with most of them, but there is one model – the Pug – available with a really good set of high-visibility sights, and now LaserLyte makes a laser sight just for the NAA revolvers, adding to their usefulness and versatility.

ROSSI

Rossi has been producing reliable and affordable revolvers for decades. These double-action sixguns are available chambered for the .38 Special and .357 Magnum cartridges, in either blued steel or stainless finishes. Rossi was acquired by Taurus a few months ago, and all of

The oddly-named and somewhat angular Windicator .38 Special.

the Rossi revolvers are now produced by Taurus in Brazil. They are quality, reliable revolvers built for concealed carry or as a duty/hunting gun. Available with short barrels and fixed sights for concealment or longer barrels and adjustable sights for precision shooting, the Rossi line still means a quality product at an affordable price.

RUGER

Sturm, Ruger builds some of the strongest and most reliable revolvers available today. The company's Single-Six and Blackhawk lines are running strong, with the welcome addition of the New Model Flattop Blackhawk introduced a couple of years ago. Ruger now offers as a regular catalog item the Flattop .44 Special. This is a long-awaited .44 Special built on the frame that is sized like that of the original .357 Blackhawk. The .44 Special Flattop is also available in a Bisley model this year, with a blued finish, and also as a regular Flattop made of stainless steel. These new Flattop models have proven to be wildly popular among single action sixgun enthusiasts.

Ruger has also taken the .327 Federal cartridge that they introduced a couple of years ago in the SP-101 compact revolver and chambered it in the Blackhawk. This stainless Blackhawk has an eight-shot cylinder and is strong enough to exploit the full potential of the .327 Federal cartridge. This little cartridge really performs, offering high velocities and deep penetration. The Ruger's cylinder is long enough to handle the long 120- and 135-gr. .327 bullets (which actually measure from .312 to .313 inch diameter).

In their double action revolver line, Ruger also chambers the relatively new .327 Federal in their GP-100 revolver. This revolver is also built from stainless steel, wears a four-inch barrel, and has a seven-shot cylinder. Of course, Ruger still has the GP-100 in .357 Magnum. This is one of the strongest, most reliable, and most durable double action .357 Magnum sixguns ever built. Ruger got started in the double action revolver business with their excellent Six series guns back in 1971. My first handgun was a blued steel four-inch .357 Magnum Ruger Security-Six. I learned to shoot with that superb sixgun. It was strong, reliable, and just the right size and balance for a .357 Magnum revolver.

The Six series has given way now to the GP-100 series, and the GP is a worthy replacement, probably better in many ways than my old Security-Six. The GP-100 has proven itself already, selling in large numbers since its introduction in 1986. This year Lipsey's, a large Ruger distributor, has a special high-polish blued steel GP-100 that is the best-looking double action .357 Magnum to ever leave the Ruger factory. Moving up in size a bit is the Ruger Redhawk, chambered for the .44 Magnum and .45 Colt cartridges. The Redhawk is bull-strong and as reliable as an anvil. Though it has been around for over thirty years, I have never seen a worn-out Redhawk. They can withstand a lifetime of shooting and never miss a beat. At the top of the heap, at least in size, is the Super Redhawk, chambered for the .44 Magnum and the .454 Casull. The .454 can also chamber and fire .45 Colt cartridges – as long as the shooter takes care to scrub the chambers clean afterwards – and is a very versatile handgun. Built for hunting, the Super Redhawk comes supplied with scope mounts and is a superb choice for hunting large game with teeth and claws.

At the other end of the size scale, Ruger introduced their polymer-framed LCR five-shot .38 Special revolver last year, and it has been a runaway success. Ruger has sold many thousands of these little pocket revolvers the first year, and demand is still outpacing supply. Mine has proven to be strong, reliable, and accurate. Look for other additions to the Ruger defensive revolver line this year. They have some promising new handguns in the works.

SMITH & WESSON

Smith & Wesson has been in the revolver business for over 150 years. No longer producing any single action revolvers, with the one exception of their Performance Center engraved Model 3 Schofield, S&W is probably the most prolific producer of double action revolvers in the world. From the .22 Long Rifle up through the formidable .500 Smith & Wesson Magnum, if a revolver cartridge exists, chances are that S&W has at least one revolver chambered for it. The small J-frame five-shot .38 Special revolvers are some of the most popular self defense guns ever produced. The Model 642 is probably the best-selling revolver in the S&W line. It is a compact, reliable five-shot revolver with a concealed hammer and a lightweight frame. It's easily slipped into the pocket, where it rides comfortably, day in and day out, ready for action when needed. While not my first choice if headed for a fight, I often carry a lightweight .38 S&W in my pocket. It can just be placed there and

Smith & Wesson Performance Center .460 S&W Magnum revolver. This may be the largest production revolver currently built.

forgotten, but is always ready should a need arise.

Moving up in size, the S&W K&L frame revolvers (K = medium frame; L = "medium-plus") are the mainstay of the Smith & Wesson duty line. These revolvers have served well for generations of sixgun users, both for defense and for hunting. The larger N-frame guns are the epitome of what a Smith & Wesson revolver should be. The classic Models 27 and 29 are back in the lineup and are beautiful and functional examples of the timeless double action revolver. The N-frames are now available in snubbie configurations, something unimaginable even a decade ago. Large but well-balanced, these .357 and .44 Magnum sixguns define the double action revolver to many shooters; with their typically crisp single action trigger pulls and butter-smooth double action trigger pulls, they are reliable and accurate.

Moving up again in size to the S&W X-frame gun, we find the most powerful double action revolvers ever produced. The .460 and .500 S&W Magnums are at the upper limits of what most would ever consider possible in a hand-held revolver. Just thirty years ago, the .44 Magnum was considered to be the "most powerful handgun in the world, and would blow your head clean off," as Dirty Harry Callahan phrased it. The .44 Magnum now pales in comparison to the power of the .460 and .500 Magnums. Of course, even back when the Dirty Harry movies were made, that was not a true statement, but it made for good theatre. However, today there is no doubt that the big S&W Magnums are powerful enough to take any game animal on Earth.

On the other end of the scale in both size and power, Smith & Wesson has just introduced a small polymer-frame revolver. I have only briefly fired two examples of them, but both shot very well. The Bodyguard 38 is a five-shot .38 Special revolver with a built-in laser sight. The cylinder release is ambidextrous and rides at the top rear of the frame. Just to the right of that is the activation switch for the laser. I am a firm believer in laser sights for defensive weapons. At night, it is hard to see the regular notch and blade sights on a handgun. Tritium sight inserts are good, but in a conflict, your attention will be on the target. The laser sight places the dot on the target, making solid hits much more likely under stress. The built-in laser sight is a good idea. In addition to the integral laser on the Bodyguard, S&W also offers the excellent Crimson Trace Lasergrip on many of their defensive handguns, which is a welcome option.

TAURUS

Taurus USA has many different revolvers available for use for concealed carry, target shooting and hunting. From their small lightweight pocket revolvers up through their 454 Raging Bull, Taurus has a wide selection of revolvers from which to choose. Their small-frame snubnose revolvers are available chambered for the .22 Long Rifle, .22 Magnum, .32 H&R Magnum, .327 Federal, .38 Special, and .357 Magnum calibers. They are available in blued, nickel, or stainless finishes, mostly with fixed sights, but a couple of models have fully adjustable rear sights. Their duty-size four- and six-inch .357 Magnum revolvers are still in production, with a wide variety of models available. The Raging series of hunting handguns chamber powerful cartridges like the .44 Magnum and .454 Casull and are good choices for hunting big game.

Still probably the hottest-selling revolvers on the planet now are the many variations of the Taurus Judge. Folks have really taken to these versatile handguns. They are available in all-steel or lightweight versions, with two-, three-, or six-inch barrels, depending on model. Available chambered for the 2-1/2- or 3-inch .410 shotshell, both also chamber and fire the .45 Colt cartridge. These are formidable close-range defensive weapons, firing .45 Colt, .410 birdshot and .410 buckshot. They will also fire .410 slugs, but if a solid projectile is desired, the .45 Colt cartridge is a much better choice. I really like the personal defense loads that are now being sold by Winchester, Hornady, and Federal. These loads are tailor-made for the Judge series of handguns and are very effective for social work. New for this year is the Taurus Judge with a short barrel and a polymer frame, making for a relatively lightweight and compact package.

THOMPSON/CENTER

Thompson/Center is responsible for making the single shot hunting pistol popular. Starting with their Contender model decades ago, the T/C pistols have evolved into the Encore and Contender G2 designs, but both are just improvements and refinements of the original Contender pistol. The Contender is offered in just about any chambering that one would want, from .22 Long Rifle up through powerful rifle cartridges such as the .45-70 Government and all the magnum handgun cartridges, including the .460 and .500 S&W Magnums. Thompson/Center offers wooden and synthetic stocks and a variety of barrel lengths. The barrels are interchangeable within the same frame group, and these hand-rifles come pre-drilled for scope mounts to take full advantage of their power and accuracy potential.

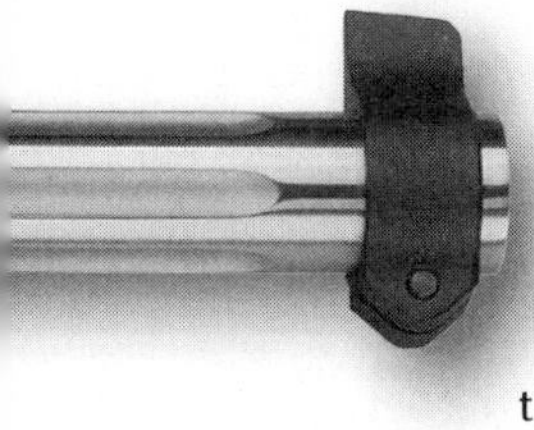

UBERTI

Uberti Firearms has been producing quality replicas of nineteenth century American firearms for decades now. While manufacturing replica rifles and handguns for other companies such as Beretta (Uberti's parent company) and Cimarron, Uberti also markets their own line of replica firearms. The Uberti Cattleman series replicates the Colt Single Action Army design and includes the brand-new Callahan Model that is chambered for the .44 Magnum cartridge, probably a first for an SAA clone. This Magnum is offered with original-style fixed sights or as a flattop style with adjustable target sights. In addition to the Callahan, Uberti offers this 1873 style sixgun in .45 Colt, .357 Magnum, and .44 WCF (.44-40) cartridges. Finish options run from a standard blued/case-hardened to nickel and even a bright charcoal blue finish.

The Uberti Stallion is a slightly scaled-down version of the Single Action Army and is chambered in a choice of six-shot .22 Long Rifle or .38 Special, or a ten-shot .22 Long Rifle. There are also Bisley and birdshead grip models available. Uberti also has fans of the old Remington revolvers covered with their Outlaw, Police, and Frontier models, replicating the 1875 and 1890 Remington revolvers. Uberti has several variations of the S&W top-break revolver, including the Number 3 Second model, as well as the Russian, in both nickel and blued finishes as well as fully hand engraved models. These are available in .38 Special, .44 Russian, and .45 Colt chamberings. Uberti has not forgotten the fans of the early cap and ball sixguns and offers authentic replicas of the Colt and Remington cap and ball revolvers.

U. S. FIRE ARMS

USFA of Hartford, Connecticut, builds some of the best 1873 style Single Action Army revolvers that money can buy, crafted to precisely replicate one of the finest sixguns ever designed but built on modern CNC machinery and hand-fitted by American craftsmen. I own a few of the USFA revolvers, and each one that I have owned and fired has been very accurate and well-fitted. USFA offers an extensive choice of calibers and options, from hand engraving to ivory or fancy walnut stocks. Caliber choices include .45 Colt, .22 Long Rifle, .32 WCF, .38 WCF, .44 WCF, .38 Special and .44 Special. Standard barrel lengths of 4.75, 5.5, and 7.5 inches are available, as well as non-standard custom shop lengths. Abbreviated barrel lengths are available on some models.

One very unique USFA sixgun that I love is their Snubnose model. This sixgun has a two-inch barrel, a modified Thunderer style grip, and is the ultimate single action big bore belly gun. Offered in blue or nickel, it wears a full-size rounded grip and for a touch of class, it has a lanyard loop on the butt. [*Editor's Note: The USFA Snubnose, as well as its big brother the Omnipotent, seem to be modeled after the Colt Model 1878 Double Action but are single action only. -DMS*] Another USFA that I love is their John Wayne "Red River D" sixgun. This gun replicates the Single Action Army revolver that John Wayne carried in most of his western movies, and it has his Red River D cattle brand tastefully applied to the gun. The John Wayne revolver has a special serial number range, simulated ivory grips, and a quality western holster and belt rig.

USFA now offers a slightly scaled down version of the SAA frame that is chambered for the .327 Federal cartridge. Called the Sparrowhawk, this eight-shot revolver wears a blued finish and a 7-1/2-inch barrel. It has a fully adjustable rear sight and a post front sight. The sights are just like the ones on their .357 Magnum Shooting Master revolver.

As I stated at the beginning of this piece, last year was certainly an interesting one for gun owners, and this next year looks to be exciting as well. Gun manufacturers are reporting all-time high sales numbers, as well as strong profits, all in this time of deep financial recession. As we cross into this second decade of this new millennium, revolver sales are still very strong. The semiauto fans have tried to put the nail into the coffin of the antiquated revolver for decades now, but it refuses to die. No need for such rivalry! While semiauto designs are more popular than ever, many shooters, hunters, and those who carry concealed still prefer the reliable, accurate, and easy-to-use revolver. At the same time, the derringer is still running strong, providing a compact, simple design with plenty of power for close-range performance. The single shot pistol is still very popular with hunters, offering rifle-like accuracy with rugged reliability and simplicity. 2011 is shaping up to be a banner year for gun sales of all types, with revolver sales continuing to be red-hot.

S&W 63: Smith & Wesson Model 63 .22 Long Rifle.

The H&R Vest Pocket

BY DAN SHIDELER

To me, revolvers are a thing of beauty and a joy forever. I can get just as tickled by an old Iver Johnson top-break .32 as I can by a Smith &Wesson Triple Lock .44 -- which just goes to show that my mother probably dropped me on my head when I was little.

A Forehand and Wadsworth? I'm your boy. A Whitneyville .22? Bring it on. An H&R .32 Vest Pocket? You betcha! In fact, I just bought my first H&R Vest Pocket .32, and it's one of the ugliest, oddest little revolvers I've ever owned -- so much so, in fact, that I just have to share it with you.

Most of us today probably wouldn't think of Harrington & Richardson as primarily a revolver manufacturer, but that's how they started. The company that would become known as H&R was founded in Worcester, Massachusetts, in 1871 when Gilbert H. Harrington teamed up with Frank Wesson, brother of the more famous Daniel B. Wesson, to form Wesson & Harrington, Inc. Among Wesson & Harrington's first offerings was a family of solid-frame, spur-trigger single-action rimfires that were named, in Smith & Wesson style, the Models 1, 2, and 3 revolvers. The Wesson & Harrington Model 1 was patented in 1871 but it's unknown how many of the Models 1, 2 and 3 were produced.

It's possible that Frank Wesson had little to do with the actual design of these revolvers; Harrington may have partnered with him because of the prestige of the Wesson name. At any rate, Wesson didn't hang around long and by 1877 Harrington had partnered with William A. Richardson to perfect a top-breaking, shell-ejecting revolver, a gun that H&R/Marlin now says was the first American gun of its type. (This is a tough claim to support, since H&R's First Model Hand Ejector appeared in 1886 and S&W's first break-open revolver hit the market as early as 1878.) Prior to the introduction of the First Model Hand Ejector, H&R's bread and butter had been a tremendous variety of solid-frame, removable-cylinder .32 and .38 revolvers. The double-action-only Vest Pocket .32 is one of these.

In the beginning, H&R revolvers weren't marked with the Harrington & Richardson name. Some were marked "Aetna"; others, including the Vest Pocket .32, were unmarked. In fact, the only markings on the Vest Pocket are "VEST POCKET"on the topstrap and ".32" on the barrel. The grips are of no help; they're just plain filagreed hard rubber. We can be pretty sure it's an H&R, however, because of the close resemblance it bears to a revolver illustrated in the 1888 - 1889 Great Western Gun Works Catalog.

The gun shown in the Great Western catalog is listed as the American Bulldog, which was a trade name used by H&R, Johnson & Bye, and a few other makers as well. You'll also find similar guns by H&R branded as Young America, Bicycle, Victor, and various other trade names. The general outline of the American Bulldog, however, is a dead ringer for that of the H&R Vest Pocket except for barrel length. If you squint a little and use your imagination, you can see that the American Bulldog is the same basic gun as the Vest Pocket.

Except, of course, for the Vest Pocket's stubby, absurd-looking 1" barrel. That tiny barrel throws the symmetry of the gun entirely out of whack, but the silly little thing does fit in a vest pocket. (I know. I tried it.) The H&R Vest Pocket has to have been one of the smallest centerfire revolvers ever produced. I for one have never seen a smaller one, not even a Belgian velodog.

The Great Western catalog lists the American Bulldog for sale "with either the ordinary old-style hammer, or with the patent safety hammer." And that's something noteworthy about my Vest Pocket. Even by nineteenth-century standards, it is primitive -- so primitive, in fact, that it's hard to believe it was ever offered to the public. It does not have a rebounding hammer. In other words, the gun's firing pin always rests at full-down position. This is hard to believe in today's safety-oriented, litigious world.

Here's how it works. To remove the cylinder, you depress the cylinder latch underneath the barrel and withdraw the cylinder pin. You then wiggle the cylinder out of the right side of the frame. Note that the firing pin still protrudes from the recoil shield! There is no way to retract the hammer as it doesn't have a spur.

Now you load the cylinder. If you load all five chambers, you will find, when you replace the cylinder, that a loaded cartridge now rests directly underneath the firing pin. Not good! As I say,

It pays to load only four .32 S&Ws in the H&R Vest Pocket .32. Hardly a man-stopper, but who wouldn't love a 125-year-old gun in this condition?

it's a little tough to imagine such a thing. The closest modern equivalent is to be found in the various .22 mini-revolvers, which are loaded in pretty much the same way as the H&R Vest Pocket. However, the mini-revolvers have safety notches between the chambers in the cylinder that provide a place for the firing pin to rest in and stay out of trouble. There are no such notches in the Vest Pocket's cylinder.

Sounds incredible, doesn't it? I had such a hard time believing it myself that I had the gun examined by three professional gunsmiths, all of whom disassembled it and agreed that the little thing had absolutely no provision for a safe hammer rest, or in fact for a safety of any sort.

I can only speculate that if you were the owner of an H&R Vest Pocket revolver, you loaded only four chambers and inserted the cylinder so the firing pin would rest over an empty one. With any luck, you'd discover this technique before you accidentally shot yourself in the gut.

H&R must have recognized the inherent weakness in this design, for the H&R Vest Pocket was soon upgraded to the "Vest Pocket, Safety Hammer," as alluded to in the great Western catalog copy. You can easily tell a Vest Pocket Safety Hammer revolver from the earlier Vest Pocket by looking at the gap between the face of the cylinder and the recoil shield, preferably while the gun is unloaded. If the firing pin protrudes into this gap, you have a Vest Pocket. If it doesn't, you have a Vest Pocket, Safety Hammer. Of course, you could save yourself all this trouble by reading the markings on the topstrap.

I actually carried my H&R Vest Pocket as a self-defense gun for a week or two, but then I stopped for two reasons: 1) it's so small I was afraid I might lose it in my pocket, and 2) it looks like a Hong Kong cap gun -- not likely to inspire fear in the criminal heart. And, truth to tell, I have some concerns about the long-term reliability of the gun.

The H&R Vest Pocket, like so many other economical (i.e., cheap) revolvers of the period, lacks a positive cylinder lock. At the moment of firing, there's nothing holding the cylinder in position except the pressure of the pawl. Once the trigger is released, the pawl returns to rest and the cylinder is free to rotate every whichaway. This system isn't entirely impractical -- the Colt Model 1878 used a similar design -- but it does promote wear on the hand under the pressure of repeated firing. A gun of this type will shoot loose, eventually, and there's not much you can do about it.

And then there's the whole aesthetics thing. I ask you, dear reader, is this not the ugliest revolver you've ever seen? The Japanese Type 26 revolver was ugly as a road-killed turtle, but the H&R Vest Pocket has it beat by a mile. Am I right?

I can't say for sure when my H&R Vest Pocket was made, but as a member of the Aetna/Young America/American Bulldog family -- and judging from from the style of the lettering on the topstrap – it probably left the factory around 1880, give or take a few years. It's hard to believe, but these tiny little guns are currently priced in the $150 to $200 range in Excellent or better condition – when you can find them, that is.

That's not exactly a steal by my standards, but if you like unusual revolvers, it's not too bad. At least I didn't think so.

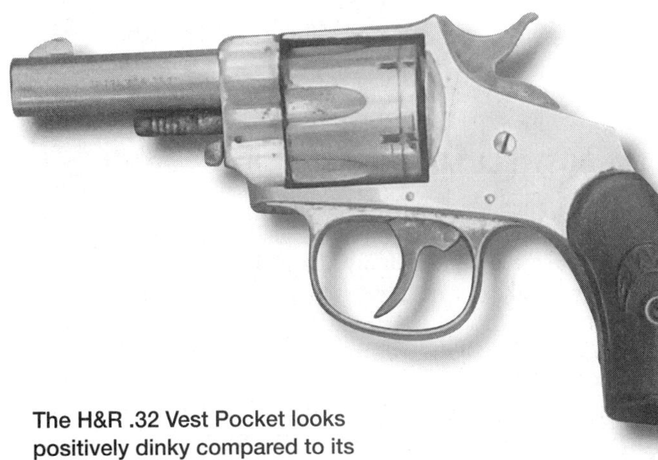

The H&R .32 Vest Pocket looks positively dinky compared to its contemporary, the Forehand & Wadsworth .32 Double Action at top, and the 1926-vintage Colt Police Positive at bottom.

With all due respect to my able Contributing Editors, I'd like to note a handful of new products that tripped my personal trigger during the last 12 months. You can read more about a few of them in other areas of this book, but this is my take.

EDITOR'S PICKS

BY **DAN SHIDELER**

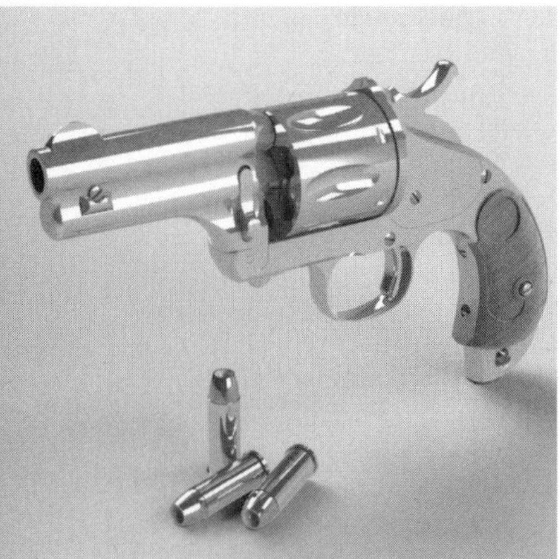

CAD rendering of the new Merwin, Hulbert .44 Pocket Army. Note the historically-correct skullpopper butt.

RETURN OF THE MERWIN, HULBERT

One of the biggest news items, at least in my worldview, is the return of the famous Merwin, Hulbert large-frame revolver. The original M,H revolvers were made by Hopkins & Allen beginning around 1876 and marketed under the Merwin, Hulbert name until around 1890; they were the fourth best-selling large revolver in the days of westward expansion, trailing Colt, S&W and Remington.

The best-known Merwin, Hulbert is probably the .44 Pocket Army, a chunky little spud chambered in .44-40 which, like all Merwin, Hulbert large-frame double-action centerfires, features a unique – you better believe it's unique! – pivoting barrel assembly that acts as a simultaneous cartridge extractor. If you've ever examined an original Merwin, Hulbert Pocket Army, you're not likely to forget the experience.

And now, thanks to computer-aided machining technology, the Merwin, Hulbert .44 Pocket Army is being remanufactured by Michael Blank's Merwin, Hulbert & Company right here in the USA. According to my contact at M,H& Co., the .44 Pocket Army is the first model to be released, followed by the Frontier Army 2nd Model and 3rd Model Double Action. M,H&Co. also tell me that they have added A-Square safari rifles and ammunition manufacturing to their production mix, with the august personage of Col. Art Alphin himself heading their R&D/New Product Development effort. Heady stuff indeed!

The new Merwin, Hulberts are expected to hit the market in 2010 with a base retail proce of $1250, not bad at all as such things go. You can learn more – and even pre-order your new Merwin, Hulbert – at the company's website, http://www.merwinhulbertco.com.

The Minie Ball Pipe by J.M. Boswell.

J.M. BOSWELL MINIE BALL PIPE

My long-time readers (both of them) know that I am an inveterate pipe smoker. I will now pause for 30 seconds so you can berate me and cite a litany of dreadful statistics that show that pipe smoking is not good for me.

Point taken – and disregarded. I don't ask much of a pipe: it should stay cool all the way through the smoke; it should break in quickly; it should draw smoothly even if I've packed it too tightly. That's why I prefer Boswell pipes, handmade by J.M. Boswell and his son Dan of Chambersburg, Pennsylvania. J.M. has been making handcrafted and custom pipes for 35 years, and I'd say he's just about perfected his art. For my money, they're among the Top Ten finest makes in the world.

I own several Boswells, but one of my favorites is his Minie Ball Pipe. The story goes that during the Civil War, soldiers

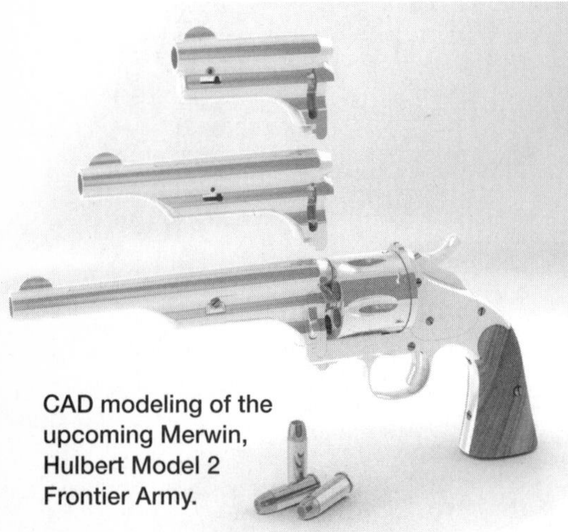

CAD modeling of the upcoming Merwin, Hulbert Model 2 Frontier Army.

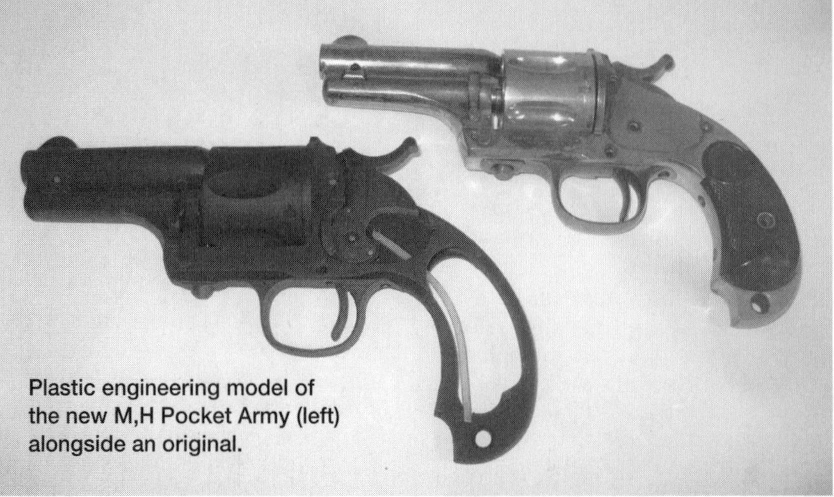

Plastic engineering model of the new M,H Pocket Army (left) alongside an original.

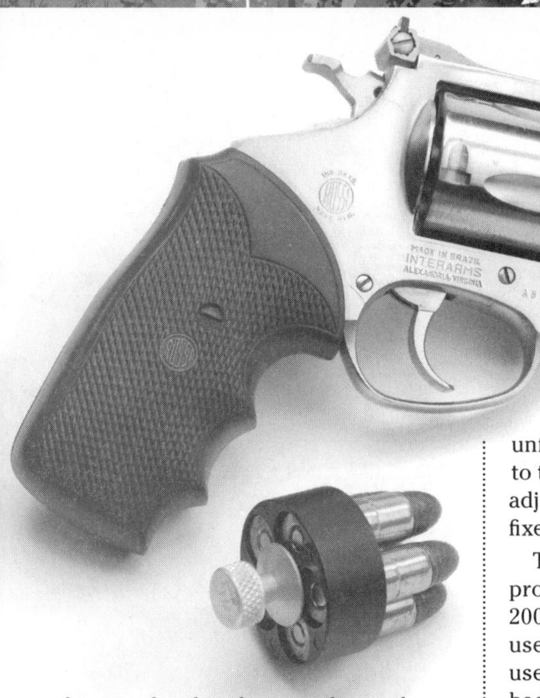

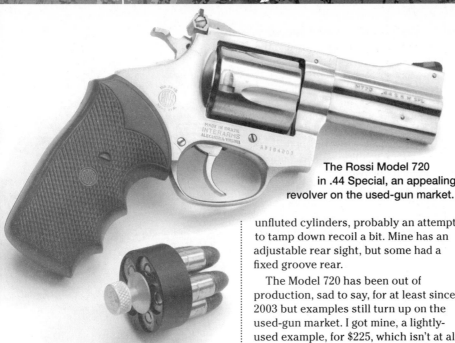

The Rossi Model 720 in .44 Special, an appealing revolver on the used-gun market.

who were hard up for a smoke used to bore a hole in the hollow base of a lead 58-caliber Minie Ball, insert a straw or reed, and puff away happily. I can't say I particularly like the sound of smoking a lead pipe, so I was delighted to learn that J.M. has improved on the concept by making his Minie Ball Pipe out of briar and fitting a vulcanite churchwarden stem to it. It makes for a delightful short smoke.

J.M.'s pipe is also quite a bit larger than a real Minie ball, and its grease grooves are not quite to scale. But as a smoking pipe it's as clean and cool as a good Dunhill, and that's saying plenty. If you're a pipe smoker or a Civil War reenactor, you'll want to try this pipe. Prices hover around $90, and that includes an ounce of your choice of the Boswells' excellent blends. For more information, visit boswellpipes.com.

ROSSI 720 .44 SPECIAL REVOLVER

Last summer I stumbled onto what I consider an excellent little revolver, the Rossi Model 720 five-shooter in .44 Special. I'm the first to admit that early Rossis may have left a bit to be desired, but later-production Rossis strike me as well-built guns. (Rossi is now owned by Taurus, don'tcha know.)

The Model 720 has a 3-inch barrel and a fluted cylinder and is made from stainless steel throughout. Dimensionally, it approximates a S&W K-frame, though S&W never offered a .44 in that medium frame size. Some Model 720s left the Rossi factory with 3.5-inch barrels and unfluted cylinders, probably an attempt to tamp down recoil a bit. Mine has an adjustable rear sight, but some had a fixed groove rear.

The Model 720 has been out of production, sad to say, for at least since 2003 but examples still turn up on the used-gun market. I got mine, a lightly-used example, for $225, which isn't at all bad for any steel-framed .44 Special. As you remember, the K-frame S&W Combat Magnum didn't really hold up well under the battering of full-house .357 loads, so I use the old 246-gr. pointed lead .44 Special load in my 720, or a 200-gr. Cowboy Action load. Recoil is gratifyingly stout, something like a .45 hardball out of a 1911.

.44 Special snubbies are a boutique item, with the market currently dominated by variations on the Charter Arms Bulldog. But if you for some reason want an adjustable-sight .44 carry gun with better than average fit and finish, don't automatically turn up your nose at a Rossi 720 at a good price. I used to, and I was just plain wrong.

DAISY MODEL 25 BB GUN

I have a soft spot for Daisy airguns, so I was happy learn that Daisy has brought back the hallowed Model 25 pump BB gun.

For those of you who came in late, the Model 25 was introduced way back when Hector was a pup, back in 1915. With a muzzle velocity of around 400 fps, it quickly gained a reputation as a hard-hitter. The grand old Model 25 had a run that lasted until 1979, with two commemorative editions being released in 1986 and 1994.

Now Daisy has brought back the Model 25 – not as a special-run promotional but as a legitimate production item. The "new" Model 25 is made offshore to Daisy's specifications and features all the goodies that we older kids remember: the scissors-jointed pump action (which can pinch the unwary fingertip), the 50-shot magazine tube, the flip-up peep rear sight with choice of U-notch or aperture. Daisy lists the Model 25's velocity as 350 fps, which is just about perfect for small birds, rodents, aluminum cans and all sorts of paper targets.

The Model 25's buttstock and pump handle are made of an attractively-stained oriental mystery wood and its receiver is roll-engraved.

The reintroduced Daisy Model 25 50-shot BB repeater – a legitimate classic.

I admit that after I tore open the carton and monkeyed around with the Model 25 for a few minutes, I immediately ordered another one to set aside unopened. It really is that cool.

The Model 25 lists at $74.99 on the Daisy website (daisy.com) but can be had for substantially less from a number of online retailers and possibly some brick-and-mortar shops, too. At full-boat retail, the Daisy Model 25 is still an exceptional bargain, even in these days of "serious" upscale airguns.

CHIAPPA ARMS 1911-22 PISTOL

The Chiappa 1911-22 was introduced in the fourth quarter of 2009, so these attractive rimfire pistols have been around long enough for me to form an opinion of them. I like them.

The 2-lb., 1-oz. 1911-22 is a straight blowback pistol chambered in .22 LR and patterned after the 1911. In fact, my hands have a hard time telling the difference. The Chiappa is built on an alloy aluminum frame with a steel barrel and has all its essential controls in the same place as its centerfire counterpart. Its rear sight is drift-adjustable, though I have heard of, but not seen, a version with a fully-adjustable rear sight. The 1911-22 has a key-activated lawyer safety on the rear right side of the slide and dispenses altogether with the "real" 1911's grip safety, so it's by no means a perfect rimfire clone of the 1911 or even the sainted Colt Ace. Close enough for me, though.

The 1911-22 is intended to provide the 1911 shooter with an economical rimfire pistol that's price-competitive with a .22 conversion barrel/slide assembly. With a street price of well under $300, it succeeds in that role rather well. *Gun Digest* Contribuing Editor Jeff Quinn reports one-hole groups from a good rest at 25 yards with his 1911-22; I haven't equalled that performance yet, but I have managed several 2.5-inch groups offhand at 25 yards. That's all I can reasonably expect, given my advancing years and receding abilities.

I have talked to a few shooters who have complained that the 1911-22 is prone to stovepipe jams. This was true in the case of mine, too, until 250 or 300 rounds slicked things up. It then proved remarkably reliable and jam-free. Just shows what a good cleaning every now and then and six boxes of ammunition can do. Some shooters have broken in their 1911-22s using ammo with a little more oomph, such as CCI Stingers, but I used good old Remington Thunderbolt and Federal American Eagle. What my 1911-22 really prefers, though – in terms of both accuracy and reliability – is Remington Golden Bullet hollowpoints.

The 1911-22's trigger takes some getting used to. It's creepy, and you have to get into the habit of releasing it fully so it can reset. The gun's finish is rather thin, and I suspect that a few hundred more trips into and out of the holster will strip the bluing (or blacking, rather) off the slide pretty thoroughly. Still, for an extremely affordable plinker or as a training stand-in for a "real" 1911, these are petty gripes.

The Chiappa 1911-22 comes in a lockable hard case with two 10-round polymer magazines and a surprisingly well-written user's manual. As near as I can tell, it's made of offshore components that are assembled in God's Country (Dayton, Ohio). Never head of Chiappa? Sure you have – it used to be known as Armi Sport. For more information, visit chiappafirearms.com.

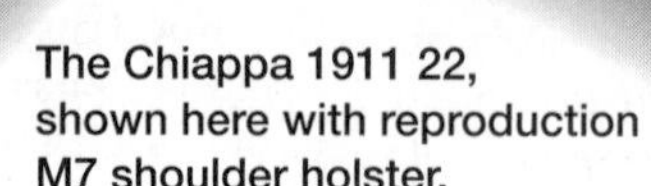

The Chiappa 1911 22, shown here with reproduction M7 shoulder holster.

The 50-caliber Shinsung Dragon Slayer PCP air rifle, shown with Leaper's scope and bipod.

SHINSUNG CAREER DRAGON SLAYER .50 AIR RIFLE

I'm either growing up or growing down, but I'm finally taking an active interest in air rifles. These are banner days for the airgun industry, and the hottest thing in an already-hot market is the pre-charged pneumatic (PCP) gun. In a PCP airgun, compressed air is held under extremely high pressure (up to 3,000 lbs.) in a tubelike reservoir usually located beneath the gun's barrel.

The ShinSung Career Dragon Slayer .50 is the Godzilla of PCP rifles, firing 200-gr. pellets at 600 fps, give or take. That's 160 ft-lbs. of energy, generally comparable to the old blackpowder loading of the .44 Russian revolver cartridge. Needless to say the Dragon Slayer .50 is capable of game a good deal larger than starlings or chipmunks.

The good folks at Pyramyd Air Gun Mall kindly lent me a Dragon Slayer .50 so I could see what this PCP fuss was all about. Contrary to my expectations, however, there's really nothing mysterious about operating this behemoth of an air rifle. You can charge the reservoir from a scuba tank or a heavy-duty hand pump that Pyramyd recommends. Living in the middle of Amish country, I didn't have a scuba tank handy and was rather put off by the array of fittings and adapters that might be needed to fill the reservoir in this manner, but the hand pump did the trick just fine, especially if you can pull a Tom Sawyer and trick someone else into doing it.

When the reservoir is full, cock the sidelever near the breech, insert the pellet, and seat it by closing the lever. You're now ready to go.

My Dragon Slayer had about a 5.5-lb. trigger pull with zero staginess, and considering that the rifle weighs around 11.5 lbs. when duded up with a Leapers 4-16x50AO scope and a bipod, you're not likely to have too many called fliers due to the jitters. My Dragon Slayer turned in consistent 2.25-inch groups at 50 yards with the swaged hollowpoint pellets supplied by Pyramyd and 3-inch groups with the solids. (When I opened the boxes, the pellets neither looked nor felt as though they weighed 200 grains, but my RCBS reloading scale says they did, right down to the half-grain.)

If you think that the Dragon Slayer is silent simply because it's an airgun, allow me to disabuse you. The Dragon Slayer sounded to me an awful lot like a Browning Baby or Colt Vest Pocket semiauto in .25 ACP being fired in a small room. That kind of report isn't going to deafen children or break windows, but it's quite noticeable.

Pyramyd Air retails the Dragon Slayer Combo (with scope, hard case, and bipod) for a cool $799. Add another $238 for the hand pump and you can see that owning the Mother of All Airguns entails quite an investment. The Dragon Slayer is a remarkably well-crafted airgun that shoots like there's no tomorrow, but I suppose my uses would be better served by the new Benjamin Marauder 25-caliber PCP airgun that's scheduled to appear as this edition of *Gun Digest* goes to press. Still, if the biggest and baddest is your cup of tea, you might want to pay an online visit to Pyramyd Air at pyramydair.com and check out the Dragon Slayer (and about a thousand other fascinating airguns).

200-gr. 50-cal. pellets for the Dragon Slayer, with a .357 Magnum for scale.

Ithaca's M66 Supersingle

BY DAN SHIDELER

To borrow a line from the old Lone Ranger radio show, return with me now to those thrilling days of yesteryear when I used to hunt groundhogs on the old Erie-Lackawanna railroad embankment heading west out of Fort Wayne toward Huntington, Indiana.

My perennial hunting buddy, my brother Dave, and I had honed our groundhog hunting to the level of a science, but one with the delicacy of a fine art. We'd walk the tracks, scoping out the grades and washouts and gullies and irrigation ditches for the telltale yellow splashes of sand and clay that told us that a groundhog had set up housekeeping nearby.

Dave would then produce a dog whistle from his pocket and give it a loud, piercing blow. As brilliant clouds of indigo buntings rose from the scrub brush, more often than not a hog would poke his head out of his hole, as if to ask who in the hell is making so much racket? Then we'd let him have it.

Even today, I grin when I read of varminters picking off groundhogs with carefully-placed shots at 300 yards. Back in our railroad days, Dave and I harvested bushels of them with such distinctly non-varmint guns as a Colt Model 1927 .45 Auto, an H&R Model 922 .22 revolver and a Marlin 336C in .35 Remington. Thanks to that two-dollar dog whistle, most of our shots were under 35 yards.

I particularly remember one unfortunate dirt-piggy who had the bad judgment to pop out of his hole on the dried clay bank of an irrigation ditch barely 25 yards away from Dave and me. I raised my shotgun to my shoulder and sent a 3" magnum charge of #4 lead shot right at his head. The shot patterned perfectly and sent up a round, absolutely symmetrical puff of

Ithaca M66 Super Single in .410 – ugly as sin, but what a shooter!

Rebounding hammer and automatic extractor come standard in the M66. Note the barrel wall thickness in this .410.

clay dust positioned like a halo around the groundhog's head. Lights out, piggy!

That was the single most entertaining gunshot I've ever taken. Even now, 30 years later, the memory of that dust cloud splashing up around that groundhog's head – as round and even as a smoke ring blown from my pipe – never fails to make me smile. My hair could be on fire and I could have a hornet up my nose, but the recollection of that perfect groundhog, that perfect pattern, would still make me grin.

I wish I still had the shotgun I was toting that day. It was a 12-ga. Ithaca Model 66 Supersingle. Most serious shotgunners would dismiss the Model 66 as a kid's gun or worse, but this kid has taken a lot of rabbits, one or two grouse and, yes, even plenty of groundhogs with the old M66.

As I write this I have a .410 Model 66 propped up in a corner of my office. It's an ugly little spud, with its lever hanging beneath its blocky receiver and oddly Western-style straight stock, but the little gun can shoot. I will bet you a case of Leinenkugel's Honey Weiss that I can take a Brenneke rifled slug load, pop it into the Model 66, and hit a can of pork and beans with it two times out of three at 35 yards, using only the brass bead front sight. Did I say a case? Hell, let's go two cases.

As shotguns go, the Ithaca M66 is an example of a type that isn't exactly flourishing anymore: the single-barrel break-open beginner's gun. Yes, I know that H&R, Baikal and Rossi still make such shotguns, God bless 'em, but part of me still longs for the day when the local K-Mart stocked Savage 94s and Winchester 37As and Ithaca Model 66s. Those were the days.

The Ithaca M66 is about as simple as you could get: it has a lock, a stock, and a barrel, and that's about it. With its painted aluminum receiver and matte barrel, it's a utility gun and not a showpiece. In fact, I can literally strike an Ohio Blue Tip match on the barrel of my .410 M66. Its finish is that raw.

The M66 has no positive safety, just a rebounding hammer. To load it, you flip the lever downward and the barrel drops, exposing the chamber. You insert the shell, snap the barrel shut and keep your thumb on the hammer in case something runs out or flies up in front of you. If it does, you cock the hammer and squeeze 'er off. If you can't make the shot, you very carefully lower the hammer and hope for better luck next time.

The stock on the M66 has what's called "impressed checkering." Note: That's "impressed," not "impressive." But it does the job and keeps the gun from squirming out of your hands on rainy days. And the M66 is one gun you don't mind taking out on a rainy day.

The M66 was offered in .410, 20-gauge, and 12-gauge, all with 3-inch chambers. Most of the M66s I find floating around out there are choked full, but a good number of the 12s and 20s have modified chokes.

Ithaca's "ugly gun" was manufactured from around 1963 to 1978. Interestingly, there's a possibility that the venerable Winchester Repeating Arms Company dallied with the idea of producing a Model 66 knockoff.

Wildwood, Inc., a gunshop in China Village, Maine, once posted on the GunsAmerica website a prototype shotgun described thus:

"AGAWAM ARMS 12GA SINGLE LEVER ACTION SINGLE SHOT 12GA PROTOTYPE TESTED BY WINCHESTER FOR POSSIBLE PRODUCTION, STAMPED X-2 BY WINCHESTER, LETTER OF AUTHENTICITY FROM ED ULRICH, RETIRED WINCHESTER CUSTOM SHOP."

The photo accompanying the listing shows a gun that looks suspiciously like an Ithaca M66. Ultimately Winchester opted not to produce the prototype gun, choosing instead to procure a simplified version of their old Model 37 single-shot shotgun from Cooey Arms of Coburg, Ontario, later a division of Winchester. The Cooey gun would later be marketed in the USA as the Winchester Model 37A or the Model 840.

The Ithaca Model 66 came in four basic flavors: the 12- or 20-gauge or .410 Standard Model, with plain stock and 24" bead-sighted barrel; the Youth Model, which was offered in 20 gauge and .410 only and sported a shortened stock with recoil pad; the Vent Rib Model, which was similar to the Standard Model but had a vent rib on its barrel; and the 20-gauge Model 66 Buck Buster, which featured a 22" smoothbore barrel with rifled sights.

I've had two Buck Busters, and each was very accurate with Foster and Brenneke slugs. I theorize that Ithaca gave Buck Buster barrels the same treatment they gave to their Model 37 Deerslayer barrels, which is to say a very thorough polishing. At any rate, M66 Buck Busters are not to be trifled with, especially if you're brown and hairy and have antlers growing out of your head.

Values for all of the M66 family run from about $150 to as high as $300 for examples in excellent condition. I know I'd pay that much for a really nice Buck Buster, and I'd kinda like to have a Vent Rib model, too. If Ithaca can supply the kid's gun, I can still supply the kid!

GUNS AND GEAR FOR WOMEN

BY GILA HAYES

When savvy shooting women shop for guns and gear, they ask two simple que stions:

1. Does it work?
2. Does it fit?

Feminized packaging may add eye appeal as illustrated by colored pistol frames, pink or pearl grips, color-laminated long-gun stocks, pink-o-flage clothing, brightly colored hearing protection and safety glasses and more. While female-oriented marketing campaigns may catch women's attention initially, ultimately how well guns and shooting equipment fit and function is the determining factor in a woman's long and successful experience with the gear.

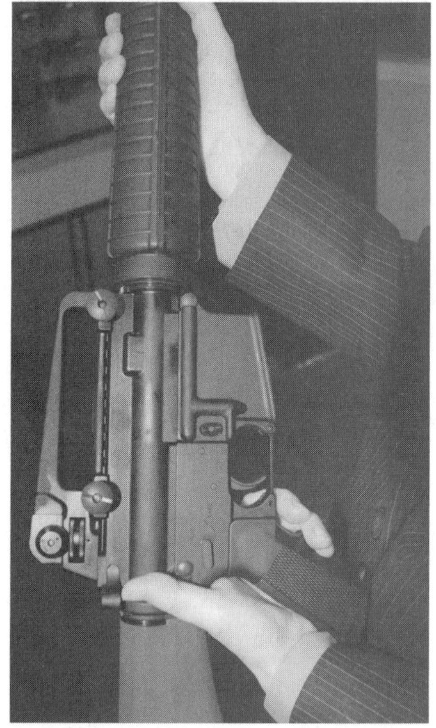

Stag Arms left-handed AR puts the controls under the lefty's thumb where they belong.

How well are gun and shooting gear manufacturers meeting the less glamorous requirement of reliability and functionality? Products displayed at the 2010 SHOT Show, the industry's premier convention where manufacturers show their wares to media and retailers, reveal a continued availability of woman-friendly designs, ranging from hunting and tactical clothing for ladies, to shotguns and rifles that

Jennie Van Tuyl's short, light DPMS Panther Arms AR15 is outfitted with an LE Entry Tactical Stock from Brownell's.

fit smaller shooters, pistols that fit small hands and accommodate women's more challenging concealment needs as well as a few holsters, and a lot of holster handbags.

Gone, we fervently hope, are the days when the woman braving the local gun shop was automatically pointed toward the fake pearl-gripped .25 caliber semiauto or, if its operation seemed too daunting, a double action revolver! Still, beginners of either gender are well served by a quality .22LR handgun or rifle, simply because it provides lots of trigger time with little recoil and does so with minimal expense. For years, Ruger's Mark II pistols ruled the market in .22 semiautos, while a great variety of kit guns from Smith & Wesson, Taurus and other revolver manufacturers, some of whom have come and gone and come back again, made choosing a beginner's revolver not an issue of availability, but one of deciding between all the options! HKS even makes speed loaders for .22s, making an introduction to speed loading drills possible!

Not all women are fond of the stiff, long trigger pull characteristic of the double action revolver, however. For these beginners, the plethora of .22LR caliber semiautomatic pistols provides the ability to practice all the steps to operate a full-sized self-defense pistol, again with the lighter recoil and cheaper ammunition. Options include traditional favorites like the Ruger Mark II, Browning Buck Mark, Smith & Wesson's .22 pistols, Beretta's pocket models as well as their Neos plus a variety of high-end competition pistols. With operations closer to those of full-sized handguns, Sig Sauer's Mosquito, full-sized CZs and EAAs in .22, Walther's P22 and conversion kits for 1911s and Glocks are also good choices for beginners for whom shooting skills will eventually address self-defense concerns.

While beginning shooters of either gender may prefer to start with a small caliber gun and its easy operating characteristics, with good training, both men and women graduate quickly to guns in reasonable defense calibers, if that is their reason for taking up shooting. These advancing shooters may still cherish their .22LR rifles and handguns for plinking, practicing, and pleasure, but with a bit of diligence, the pursuit of highly suitable revolvers, pistols, rifles and shotguns in more effective calibers yields a variety of choices.

HANDGUNS "FIT" FOR A QUEEN

The trend toward adjustable backstrap inserts makes fitting a pistol to small-handed shooters far easier than it was even five years ago, though sometimes the backstrap inserts seem merely a way to increase a medium-sized grip to sizes large and extra large! The latest and possibly most celebrated manufacturer to offer the adjustable grip option is Glock. In the smallest variation, Glock's fourth generation pistol's grip is about 1/8 inch smaller in circumference. It is currently available in Models 17 and 22, and Glock insiders predict the 4th Generation Model 19s and 23s should be out around May of 2010.

Walther's pistol options include the .22LR P22, the .380 PK380, and for concealed carry the very minimalist PPS in 9mm.

The large-gripped polymer-framed Glock has long been the subject of destructive grip recontouring and refinishing as shooters have struggled to slim down that ubiquitous handgun to improve trigger reach. For those for whom this size

Author admits to a yearning to own a SIG P238 with the Titanium rainbow-colored slide.

(top) STI's Elektra model is a carry-sized 9mm with pink grips indicating their marketing plan for sales to women. It also comes in black.

(above) Carol Rutherford of Woolstenhulme Designer Bags shows a nicely accessorized blue gun purse.

reduction makes a sufficient difference, the fourth generation of Glocks eliminates that after-market expense.

SIG-Sauer took a different route when they tackled the need for a more individualized pistol fit. Their Model 250 is extremely modular, allowing choices in caliber, frame size, barrel length and more. A one-piece polymer grip is available in compact and full size. For some, the backstrap to trigger reach will still be too long, and SIG's short trigger offers help.

Other models of handguns are perennial favorites with women, because from the very beginning, their grips were small enough for a good fit. Kahr Arms' many models in 9mm Parabellum, .40 and even .45 come immediately to mind in this class, as does Walther's model PPS, and more historically, the single column 1911 design in its many variations and calibers.

Of the latter, the popularity of models chambered in alternatives to the traditional .45 ACP cartridge continues to increase. In addition to expanding ammunition options for the small-hand-friendly 1911, this classic handgun type is served by a tremendous variety of after market options and accessories, including thin grip panels to further reduce bulk, night sights, high visibility sights, laser sights, triggers of varying lengths, grip safeties of varying geometry, extended, bobbed, minimalist and ambidextrous thumb safeties, modified magazine releases and more!

9mms and .40 S&W caliber 1911s are no longer rare, whether emblazoned with the logos of Kimber, Para Ordnance, STI, Springfield Armory, Taurus and even Colt's Manufacturing! Colt's, of course, marketed a 9mm Parabellum Commander now and again in the years after WWII, though in recent decades, they've become somewhat rare. Thus, at the 2010 SHOT Show, I was delighted to see a 9mm Colt Defender on display. The new Defender is a lightweight subcompact with an alloy frame, a 3-inch barrel, and the traditional single action semiautomatic manual of arms. In my opinion, the pistol just cried out for a pair of slim grip panels and a short trigger. Still, I predict it will prove a solid foundation for many a customized women's self defense pistol and I was glad to see it.

As we strive to customize and modify a handgun to fulfill individual needs and desires, we often begin to impinge on reliability. Unfortunately, the 1911 has long been subject to excessive gunsmithing, often to the detriment of its dependability. In addition, a common rule of thumb to bear in mind: the short-barreled concealment pistols are frequently finickier about ammunition, the strength of the shooter's grip during the firing cycle and other variations that interrupt the relationship and interaction between the recoil spring, the weight of the slide, and the pressure of the cartridge. A sometimes delicate balance is required to shuck out the empty case and feed in a fresh one. Sometimes the snubbiest semiautos use very stiff recoil springs, and while vital to reliability, this feature may make it challenging for some female shooters to manually cycle the action.

ITSY, BITSY, TEENY WEENY...UM, HANDGUN

Overall gun size is always a challenge when women gear up for self defense. Gun weight has been reduced – in my opinion, to unrealistic extremes – in the alloy framed revolvers. That's right, I'm no fan of the super light, 11- and 12-oz. snubbies, because with high-performance defense ammunition, they are simply beastly to shoot. A pistol's overall dimensions, however, contribute or detract considerably from whether or not women will find it a realistic choice for daily carry for self defense.

Pistols like the Defender, Springfield EMP, Glock 26 and 27, Springfield XD subcompact, Ruger's new subcompact SR9,

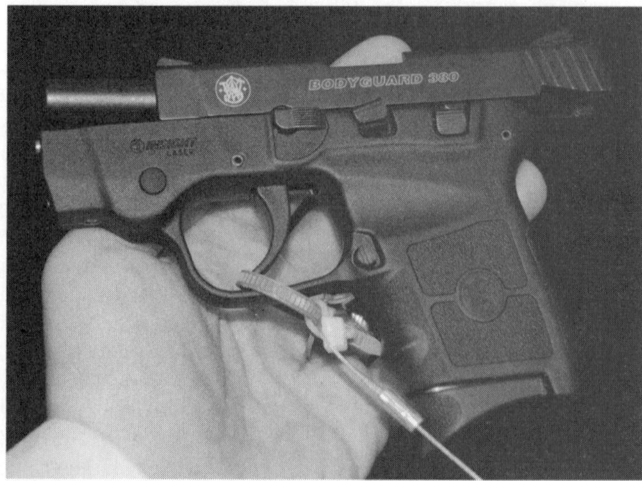

Smith & Wesson's tiny .380 Bodyguard semiautomatic.

Short stocks make these small-statured shotgunners smile! On the left, women's gun columnist Diane Walls holds her Remington 11-87 fit with custom-made Choate stock, while Rivendell Consulting owner Jennie Van Tuyl's Remington 1100 has a traditional wooden stock that is cut down considerably.

and many others of similar size are the preferred choices because they are just large enough to afford a good shooting grip, moderate recoil control, and a reasonable sight radius. But what to carry during hot summer days, at dress-up affairs, and under other circumstances when even those chopped-down variations are too big to conceal? In times like these, a .380 that men consider a backup, deep-concealment hideout or a pocket pistol is likely to become the primary defense gun for many a lady.

While these are the guns to which many default in challenging concealment conditions, they are poorly suited to the beginner who is learning the lessons of sight alignment, trigger control and gun manipulation like loading and malfunction clearing. Not only does the pistol's small, light size amplify even the .380 ACP's recoil, the miniaturized frame often compromises a strong grip somewhat, and the miniaturized controls and levers – when they are even present – can be slow and fumble-prone. Still, the genre continues to be among the most popular pistols a gun shop can stock.

It is ironic that concurrent with the worst .380 ACP ammo shortage in my memory, gun manufacturers have introduced more miniaturized .380 pistols than ever before. No longer does shooting a .380 mean lugging around a Beretta Cougar or Bersa Thunder, guns nearly as large as a 9mm Glock 26/27 and much bigger than a Kahr Arms PM9! Nowadays, the deep concealment .380s are half that size, with measurements of slightly more than 3-1/2 inches by 5 inches for the Ruger LCP and its ilk.

In 2001, North American Arms debuted their .380 Guardian, a slightly larger echo of their earlier .32 ACP all-steel micro pistol based on the venerable Seecamp design. Its continuing popularity gives shooters who worry about polymer's durability a valued option. Not long thereafter, Kel-Tec beefed up their madly popular polymer-framed .32 ACP semiauto to chamber .380 ACP ammo and the result was the P3AT. The eight ounce .380 has proven amazingly durable, though the sights are rudimentary. Both alternatives were the mainstays of the pocket pistol crowd until two years ago when Ruger reworked the Kel Tec design into their polymer-framed LCP.

That same year Kahr Arms introduced their P380, which just continues to become more and more popular. The simple, DAO mini is less than 5 inches long, and, at just under 4 inches, is a bit longer through the grip. Unlike most other pocket pistols, the Kahr P380 comes from the factory equipped with the manufacturer's conventional drift-adjustable bar-dot combat sights. Many years ago, the folks at NAA put a set of Novak pistol sights on my Guardian 380, achieving the same effect. Now Kahr Arms does it from the start.

This year, Smith & Wesson joined the pocket semiautomatic market in a big way with their Bodyguard line. A partially polymer revolver of J-frame size and a .380 mini semiauto were on display at the 2010 SHOT Show, attracting a lot of attention. Both are manufactured with integral lasers from Insight Technology.

The S&W Bodyguard 380 takes the double action semiauto pocket gun concept to a new level. While the forerunners – Seecamps, Guardians and Kel Tecs – cut back on bulk by eliminating operating levers like slide stops and thumb safeties, the Bodyguard 380 has

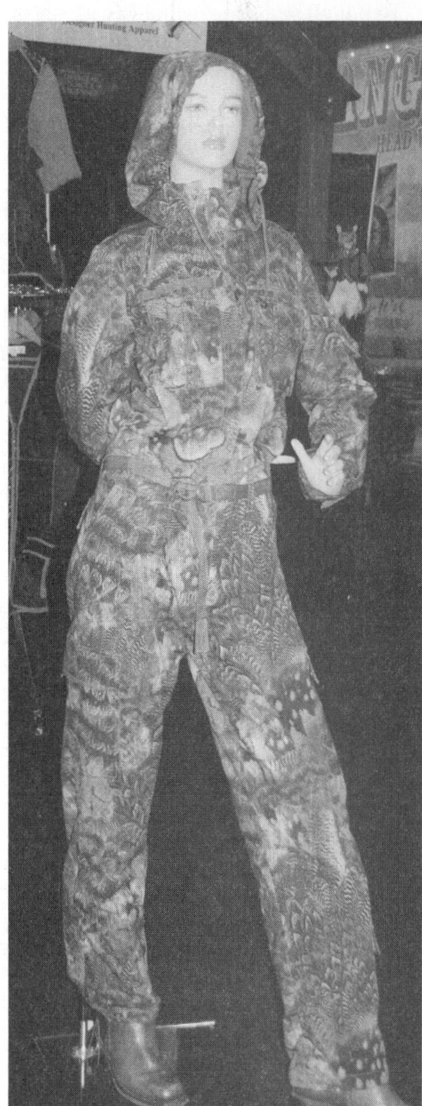

Outdoor gear like this camouflage by Foxy Huntress gives ladies a choice in hunting clothing.

a full complement of controls – a thumb safety, a slide lock, and a take down lever, all tucked in flush to frame. While unobtrusive, these controls make gun operation far more user-friendly. The .380 Bodyguard is just over 4 inches high, 5-1/4 inches long, and weighs just less than 12 ounces unloaded. It holds six cartridges, plus one in the chamber.

SIG-Sauer's P238, a redux of the old single action semiauto Colt .380s, caught my eye at SHOT Show last year, so in 2010 it was a delight to see several new variations, including one breath-takingly beautiful option with a rainbow Titanium finished slide equipped with SIGLITE® night sights atop a matte black frame and wearing pretty rosewood grips. The P238s weigh 15 ounces, and are just under 4 inches tall and 5-1/2 inches long, with a 2.7-inch barrel. Other finish options included a two-tone scheme, as well as an all matte black option. Interestingly enough, the single action trigger weight is set between 7-1/2 to 8-1/2 lbs., considerably heavier than the double action only LCR, Kel Tec or Bodyguard.

SO MANY PISTOLS, SO LITTLE TIME

Handgun selection, while vastly assisted by the plethora of models and variations marketed, can also become a confusing and potentially expensive adventure. Two questions – highlighted at this article's beginning – must guide handgun selection. First, is the handgun reliable? If unable to shoot and test reliability yourself, you will be dependent on anecdotal reports, though in the age of the Internet, such accounts probably outnumber the stars in the firmament. Certain handgun brands, however, like Glock pistols for example, are designed for reliability before any other consideration. The second question, of course, concerns fit. If you find a reliable gun that fits properly, search no further!

Before leaving the subject of handgun fit and function, I'd like to add that several decades ago, semiauto pistol reliability was suspect, patchy and unpredictable. The pistols were often ammunition-sensitive, and at worst, it was expected that a gunsmith's services were required to guarantee a reliable semiauto. If you wanted a totally reliable handgun, you simply bought a revolver! While we still occasionally run into pistols that won't function reliably, that hassle is far less prevalent nowadays.

At the same time, revolvers are a fine handgun choice for shooters of either gender, though ladies rankle at the suggestion that women find them more suitable owing to their simple operation! Really, skillful handgun operation results from full familiarity and training with the gun, regardless of its design. Still, the choice between revolver and semiautomatic asks how much strength is required to manually cycle a semiauto's slide versus the stiffness of the revolver's trigger pull. Both can be impediments to skill with a handgun, so we welcome the lighter springs of many 9mm handguns compared to the stiffer spring often required to keep a heavy-caliber pistol running, especially in the short-barreled concealment configurations. New approaches to revolver design have changed trigger geometry, but too often these innovations show up in the super lightweight polymer and alloy revolvers that are too light for much recoil absorption, so the recoil batters the shooter with each discharge, and practice is painful.

THE HOLSTER HASSLE

Gun fit issues pale in comparison to the thorny issue of holsters for women. Gun purses are available in profusion,

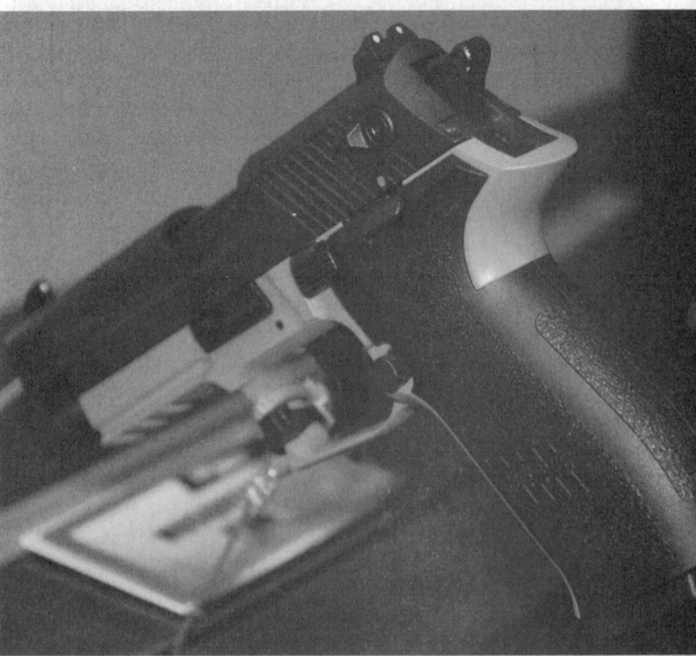

(top)Sig Sauer's P238 now comes in several options, including one with a Titanium rainbow colored slide.

(middle) Colt's 9mm Defender New Agent.

(bottom} Sig Sauer .22 LR Mosquito in a bold black and shocking pink design

THE MAGIC IS IN THE FIT

Given enough time and concentration, most shooters can coax accurate shots out of handguns, rifle or shotguns that do not fit them. While plinking at the range, a deliberate rate of fire – one shot every minute or two, for example – accommodates all manner of misfit gear. It is, instead, during high-intensity defense or duty training, or Heaven forbid, under the stress of a self defense emergency that ill-fit guns betray their unfortunate owners.

Instead of long seconds committed to getting the gun in just the right firing position, followed by a careful alignment of the sights or optics and slow, deliberate pressure applied to the trigger, under stress we find the gun extended toward target in an approximation of grip and stance, often fired while moving away from the threat or to cover. Trigger control must occur in an extremely compressed cycle, delivering multiple shots in a matter of seconds. Here, the shooter discovers that the compromised grip and shooting platform imposed by the ill-fitting gun interferes with accuracy, interrupts use of the sights (if there is even sufficient light to see and use them), and exaggerates muzzle flip and recoil. How much better it would be to solve gun fit problems at the time of the gun purchase!

HANDGUN FIT

With the pistol centered in the web of the hand, both the length of the fingers and the meatiness of the hand determine how well the trigger finger will be able to contact the face of the trigger. A mere tip of a trigger finger is a poor candidate for a smooth, straight-to-the-rear trigger pull, especially at speed.

A handgun that allows the crease of the trigger finger's first joint full contact with the face of the trigger while the gun is centered in the web of the hand gives the most natural pointing. Since babyhood, humans have locked out the arm and extended the index finger when emphatically pointing. A properly fitting handgun takes advantage of all those repetitions, and aiming it mimics that oft-repeated action.

When the pistol is too big, as is this big Glock Model 29 for these small hands, the mere tip of the finger on the trigger is insufficient for a smooth pull.

An extremely small-handed shooter or one mandated to use an overly-large gun accommodates by moving the backstrap toward or even beyond the ball of the thumb. A gun gripped thus naturally points somewhat to the right for a right-handed shooter and to the left for a lefty. A strong isosceles-style stance combined with a hard two-handed grip brings the natural aim back to center when poor fit thus compromises natural pointing. This is harder to maintain if circumstances throw the shooter into one-handed shooting, though responsibility for a child, calling for help on a phone or radio, or other concerns may result in one-handed shooting in a fast-breaking situation.

FITTING LONG GUNS

Classically, we've considered stock fit on shotguns acceptable if, when the butt is held in the crook of the elbow, the trigger finger has a good purchase on the trigger. It is still a good standard, though we see the value of an even somewhat shorter stock when the small-statured shooter operates the pump-action shotgun, or needs to be able to mount and fire the rifle or shotgun rapidly. The shorter the stock, the easier, as illustrated by special response teams in law enforcement's use of the collapsible AR stock.

For shotgunners, recoil control and subsequently accurate, rapid fire is considerably improved when a short stock accommodates quickly mounting the shotgun, attaining a repeatable cheek weld, and having a strong flex in both the shooting and support arm to hold the shotgun firmly against the pectoral muscle.

While we love the collapsible AR stocks for their easy adaptability for short shooters, many don't encourage a good cheek weld, a factor that deserves consideration when setting up a rifle for a woman.

SPECIALTY NICHE

In a world where gun stores with high-volume sales tend to stock products purchased by the majority of their customers, who are men, it can be a challenge for a smaller shooter to locate a good selection from which to choose. An industry that actively pursues the woman's market must surely be heartened by small businesses like the newly-opened Rivendell Sales & Consulting, a one-woman operation focused on custom orders for women who need personalized attention to detail to be sure they get a gun that fits.

Owner Jennie Van Tuyl was getting her new business started at the 2010 SHOT Show, meeting not only with resources to help with the businesses' operation, but identifying guns most likely to fit her customers.

It takes some extra effort to pull all the details together, but with determination and creativity, women can find a nice selection of pistols, shotguns and rifles that work reliably and fit them well.

When this small-handed shooter centers the tang of a Springfield EMP pistol in the web of her hand, the trigger finger has good contact with the trigger.

Great fit and the left-handed option will sell this Remington rifle to a number of female shooters.

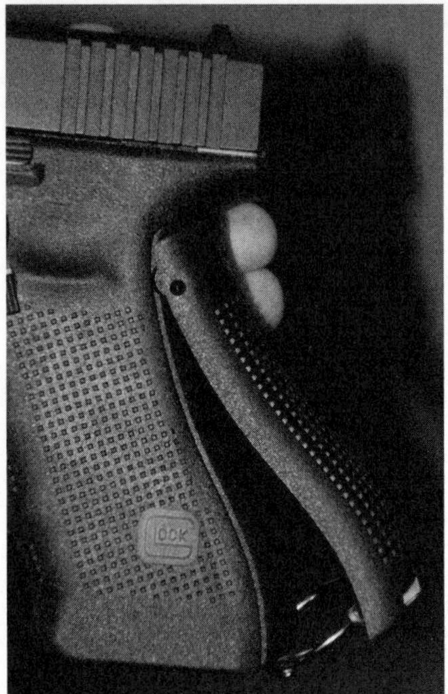

Glock's 4th generation pistol and the insert used to adjust grip size.

however, and some of them show considerable thought and ingenuity, with more and more designed by women who habitually carry guns for self defense. Galco has long been the leader, and Lisa Des Camps deserves a nod of appreciation for her guiding hand in developing a line of stylish and functional gun purses. The other big player in fashionable gun purses is Coronado.

Several start-ups that are bringing in more options in fashionable gun purses are Gun Tote'n Mamas and Designer Concealed Carry, with a variety of big, brightly colored bags with built-in holsters for concealed handgun carry.

For range work requiring belt holsters, Blade Tech's women's dropped and offset belt holster works well. Kramer Handgun Leather led the way in dropped and offset designs, and Kramer's women's belt scabbard continues to relieve holster discomfort for short-waisted women. Other alternatives include several of C. Rusty Sherrick's holsters, FIST holsters, and Del Fatti Leather's SLP/F model designed to be worn forward of the strong side hip. Its muzzle forward rake reminds me of one of the first women's holsters I saw, Mitch Rosen's Nancy Special, designed for short-barreled guns, and also using the muzzle forward orientation to get the grips away from the ribcage.

Another alternative that works extremely well is one-on-one work with smaller holster makers who are happy to work up a custom holster solution for women. Sometimes – as in the case of *Concealed Carry Magazine* editor Kathy Jackson's experience with Ted Blocker Holsters of Tigard, Oregon – a couple of small but vital modifications yielded an extremely comfortable IWB holster worn in front of the strong side hip. Ladies who want to cash in on Kathy's success need only call this holster maker and ask for the LFI-OZC.

Up-and-coming holster maker John Ralston of 5-Shot Leather provided the same kind of service when he made a deeply canted IWB the author wears behind the strong side hip. Minimal in design, the Ralston holster is a take off on his stock item, the Inside Burton Scabbard.

Both the Blocker and Ralston holsters are comfortably carried on contour cut belts from the makers of the holsters, and the contoured belts go far to increase the comfort of holsters worn for long hours at a time.

THE BIG WORLD OF LONG GUNS

If the backstrap to trigger measurement is the key to good handgun fit, on rifles and shotguns the critical element is the length of pull, measured from trigger face to the end of the stock. Women who like to shoot shotguns and rifles get help with stock fit from the so-called youth models, as well as variable length "collapsible" tactical stocks, or they find relief in replacement stocks in shorter lengths of pull. Fortunately the prevalence of 12- and 13-inch length of pull stocks, often in the mis-named "youth models," are a common variant among all the reputable shotgun and rifle lines.

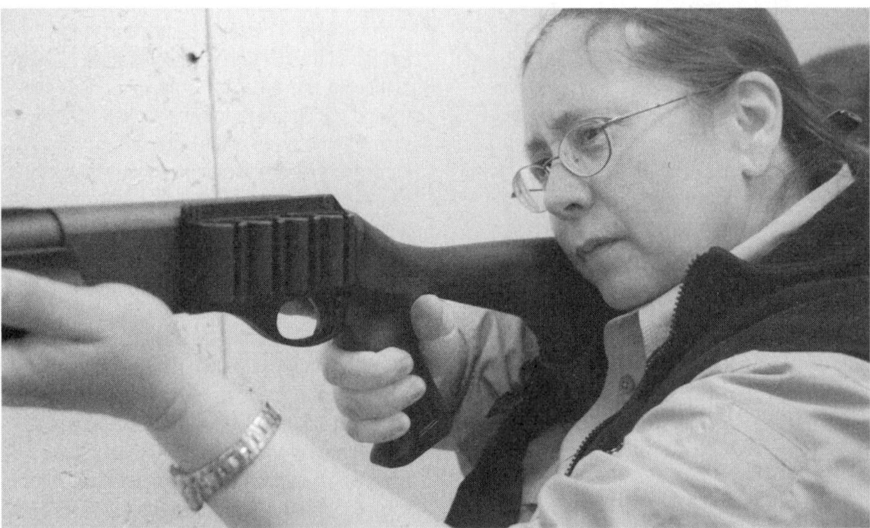

(above) Diane Walls likes the control her custom Choate pistol grip gives her Remington 11-87.

(left) Jennie Van Tuyl chose the Rock River Arms LE Entry Tactical Stock to tailor her DPMS Panther Arms AR-15 rifle to her shorter stature.

When fitting rifles and shotguns to women, another factor can complicate gun selection. Women have higher incidences of cross-eye dominance than do men. The easiest cure is to shoot the rifle or shotgun from the shoulder corresponding to the dominant eye, which in the case of cross-dominance is usually the left side. Consider the plight of the woman eager to join her friends at the shotgun or rifle range, If left-eye dominant, she faces the further challenge of operating a gun designed for right-handed shooters with her less dexterous hand!

With shotguns, we value features like Mossberg's tang-mounted safety that make the gun more ambidextrous. With semiautomatic rifles, innovations like Stag Arms' fully left-handed AR-15 are welcome indeed. With nearly all of the AR-15s sold optimized for right-handed shooters, we are particularly appreciative of Stag Arms fully adapted left hand AR-15! Though lefties can make do with the standard right-handed semiauto rifles, how nice it would be to have the "fire" and "safe" switch under the thumb where it is most ergonomic.

In bolt rifles, Remington, Savage, Browning and Ruger have a variety of excellent options for both short hunters and left handed ones, as well. The Ruger M77 Hawkeye comes in lefty and righty configurations, as well as models with the standard 13-1/2-inch length of pull and a compact version with a 12-1/2-inch LOP. A half dozen caliber choices run the gamut from .223 Rem. to .308 Win.

Kramer Handgun Leather was one of the first to make what became their wildly successful Women's Dropped and Offset holster, shown here with a S&W M640.

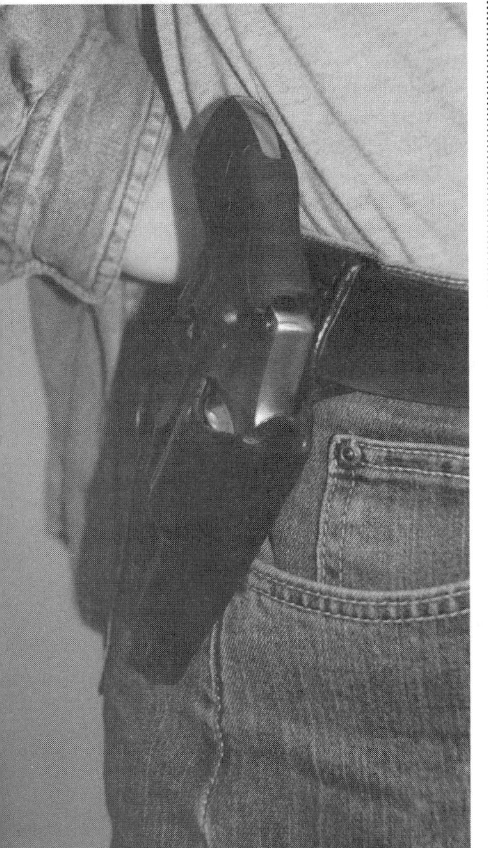

WHAT TO WEAR

Speaking of hunting, women's outdoor clothing has long been one area in which smaller manufacturers have excelled, with the options ranging from moderately reworked men's outdoor wear, to some very feminine fashions for outdoor wear. Smaller gloves, boots and socks, functional jackets, vests, trousers and even coveralls are marketed to female outdoors enthusiasts. At the 2010 SHOT Show, a feminine Henley short sleeved shirt that had its own protective recoil pad sewn into the shoulder area particularly charmed me.

There's probably a market for both pink, cutsie outdoorswoman clothing and toys, but for my money, I am considerably more heartened by clothing and products made to meet women's specific needs – proper fit for the smaller frame, true functionality like weather proofing and comfort – than I am by sheer, lacy pink camouflage negligees! [*Editor's Note: There is probably room for opinion on this point. -DMS*]

EOTAC, Fernando Coelho's tactical clothing company, has just added a line of women's tactical trousers for female shooters, competitors and the more serious needs of women in law enforcement. Featuring a shorter rise than EOTAC's men's tactical trousers, but still fitting through the seat and thigh, the pants are available in four colors of light weight rip stop fabric. Coelho predicted that future variations would include more fabric choices, shorts and maybe even capris!

(top) Foxy Huntress' shooting shirt in women's sizes and styles makes shotgunning more fun.

(right) Tina Coelho of EOTAC shows their tactical trousers specifically designed for women.

(left) Good fit comes first on these Wiley-X safety glasses; the pink accent color may attract the female customer.

H&R's Forgotten Tacklebox Guns

The quintessential tacklebox gun: The H&R Model 732 snubbie chambered in .32 S&W.

BY DAN SHIDELER

In the gun literature of the '50s and '60s, I find numerous references to "tacklebox guns." That's the kind of phrase you skate right past without giving it a second thought, but now that I've got you trapped there in your chair, I ask you, sir: what exactly is a tacklebox gun, anyway?

Good question. In the spirit of scientific inquiry I'll waddle out to the garage and check my own tackleboxes.

Okay. I'll start with this big double-hung monster labeled "TOP WATER." After unlatching the hasps and lifting the lid, I find three Jitterbugs; two old Smithwick Devil's Horses; 11 – wow! 11! – wood-bodied South Bend Nip-I-Didees and four smaller Spin-I-Didees; two Heddon Crazy Crawlers; 23 Rapala Floaters, ranging from tiny #5s to mammoth #17s, several of them painfully scarred by pike teeth; and two old Fred Arbogast Hula Poppers with their skirts missing. Not bad!

And what have we here? Why, it's a corroded bottle of Uncle Josh pork rinds, one of which has somehow escaped from its jar and welded itself to a Johnson Silver Minnow! And here's a leaky bottle of what may have been salmon eggs. How'd they get in here? No matter. I can't pry them loose anyway. Ewwwww.

But wait! There it is, hiding under a spool of 10-lb. Stren: a Harrington & Richardson Model 732 revolver. No doubt about it, pardner: that there's a tacklebox gun.

What's a gun doing in a tacklebox, anyway? Beats me. In all my fishing excursions, I've never had to draw down on a rogue bluegill or fend off a sex-crazed trout. Once, in northern Michigan, I did see a guy shoot a dogfish off his hook rather than touch it, but I personally need a tacklebox gun like I need a sixpack of Chanel #5. Once again, however, we see the yawning gulf between "need" and "want." I may not need a tacklebox gun, but I sure do want a tacklebox gun.

Nobody makes tacklebox guns any more. Properly applied, the term refers to an inexpensive, short-barreled (4-inch maximum), solid-frame revolver with fixed sights that was chambered for .22 rimfire or .32 centerfire. H&R's top-break models such as the justly-famous Model 999 Sportsman or the Model 925 Defender can't really be considered tacklebox guns because their fit and finish made them much too nice to stick in a tacklebox.

A real tacklebox gun has fixed sights, usually a blade front paired with a hog-wallow groove milled into the topstrap. Some models from the 1980s have a drift-adjustable rear sight dovetailed into the topstrap, but that's about as fancy as they get. The purpose of a tacklebox gun, as best I can figure, is to shoot a snake, or to defend oneself from a class of miscreant that my father loosely categorized as "Red-Headed Ridge-Runners," or to blast open a stubborn can of Van Camp pork-'n'-beans. Who needs target sights?

Before the war, lots of makers – H&R, Iver Johnson, Forehand & Wadsworth, Hopkins & Allen, Howard Arms and about a zillion others – made inexpensive, small-frame revolvers, but these seem to have been intended more for the coat pocket or the nightstand drawer than the tacklebox. Many such H&R revolvers were sold through the Sears, Roebuck Wish Book, priced as low as $1.75 apiece (add 20 cents for postage) and advertised as "STRICTLY FIRST CLASS IN EVERY RESPECT." Uh huh.

The Golden Age of the Tacklebox Gun lasted from 1950 to around 1990, coinciding with the post-war boom in anything related to the outdoor sports. It was the glorious era of George Leonard Herter, Old Town Canoes, Nimrod pipe lighters, Winchester Staynless shotgun shells – and tacklebox guns.

Harrington & Richardson was the king of tacklebox gunmakers. Iver Johnson gave them a run for their money, but H&R concentrated on tacklebox guns with an admirable singleness of purpose. Today, these sturdy little revolvers are universally ignored by collectors. As a result, they're usually dirt cheap, an attribute not without merit. In addition, they're virtually indestructible and they go bang when you want them to, usually in the general direction they're pointed. Most importantly, they're not so precious that you'd be heartbroken if they ended up at the bottom of the Tippecanoe River. What's not to like?

H&R's tacklebox guns subdivide into two types: those with swing-out cylinders and those with removable cylinders. Both types can be fired in single- or double-action mode. The swing-out revolvers were the Cadillacs of the H&R tacklebox line, if such a thing can be said without my being sued for slander by General Motors. The cylinders of these guns lock at only one point: the spring-loaded extractor rod engages a recess in the recoil shield. And that's it. No lug up front with an additional lock, a la Smith and Wesson; no thumb latch on the sideplate or anywhere else. To swing out the cylinder, you pull forward on the spring-loaded extractor rod and swing the cylinder out of the frame. A swift bop on the extractor head pops out all empty shells simultaneously.

H&R's removable-cylinder tacklebox guns come in two flavors. The first, and most common, features a removable cylinder pin. You press a spring-loaded detent on the frame, pull the cylinder pin entirely free of the gun and roll the cylinder out into your waiting hand (and hopefully not into Lake Wawasee). Then you laboriously stab out each empty case with the cylinder pin.

The second flavor features a snap-out cylinder. In this design, the cylinder, cylinder pin and extractor are all comprised in a single assembly. Pressing the detent lets you snap out the whole works through a cut-out on the left side of the frame, after which you extract all empties simultaneously with one thrust of the extractor. Although H&R advertised their snap-out revolvers for at least 20 years, I haven't seen more than a handful of them on the used-gun market in my life. Possibly too many cylinders snapped out permanently and now sleep with the fishes: "Snap! Splash! Aw, *#*&*!!" It appears that the snap-out models were produced concurrently with the removable-cylinder pin models before being discontinued altogether in the mid-1960s.

H&R tacklebox guns usually incorporate two features that you wouldn't expect to find on a price-point revolver. The first is H&R's patented "safety rim," a raised edge running around the rear face of the cylinder and enclosing the chambers. The safety rim was intended to protect the shooter from the effects of a case head separation, a fairly common occurrence with the rimfire ammunition of the day. (In my shooting life I've experienced only one case head failure, and trust me, once is enough.)

The second remarkable feature is H&R's transfer bar safety. This feature first appeared, not on the Ruger New Model Blackhawk of the 1970s, but on pre-war Iver Johnson revolvers. Advertised under the memorable tagline "Why It's Safe to Hammer the Hammer," the IJ transfer bar interposed a steel wedge between the hammer and the frame-mounted firing that transferred the hammer blow to the firing pin but only if the trigger were held all the way back. I don't know whether H&R purchased rights for the transfer bar from Iver Johnson, but most if not all H&R tacklebox guns have one nevertheless.

H&R's "safety rim" cylinder incorporated a raised edge that enclosed the cartridge rims and offered some degree of protection against a pierced primer or case head failure.

Assembling a model-by-model chronology of H&R's tacklebox guns is a bit difficult because some models seemingly drifted in and out of the product line willy-nilly. Features such as grip material seem to have varied according to whatever H&R had on hand. And things really got muddled during the company's final years when it was known as H&R 1871, Inc., and New England Firearms (NEF) simultaneously.

All in all, H&R built tacklebox guns under one name or another from around 1950 to 1998. When Marlin bought the assets of H&R 1871/NEF in November of 2000, manufacture of H&R revolvers ceased altogether. Here's a run-down of H&R's tacklebox guns, courtesy of the 13th edition of Modern Gun Values (Krause Publications), which I had the great pleasure of editing:

SWING-OUT-CYLINDER MODELS

H&R Model 732: A bulky little six-shooter chambered in .32 S&W/.32 S&W Long. Blued finish with checkered plastic grips and a 2-1/2- or 4-inch barrel. Introduced 1958 and dropped in 1985.

H&R Model 733: Identical to the Model 732 but in chrome finish with white plastic grips.

H&R Model 900: An economy-grade nine-shooter chambered for .22 rimfire. 2-1/2-,4- and 6-inch barrels with blued finish and plastic grips. Introduced 1962 and dropped one year later.

H&R Model 901: Similar to Model 900 but with chrome finish and white plastic grips.

Model 929 Sidekick: This was H&R's first swing-out cylinder model. Introduced in 1956, it merited mention in the editorial section of the 1956 Gun Digest, one of the very few times that august publication deigned to do so. Barrels were 2-1/2-, 4 and 6 inches. Blued finish with checkered plastic grips. Discontinued 1985.

New England Firearms Model R73: Based on the older Model 732, this was a 3-inch-barreled five-shooter chambered in .32 H&R Magnum. Blue or nickel finish with hardwood grips. Introduced in 1988 and dropped in 1999. The scarcest of H&R's tacklebox guns.

New England Firearms Model R92: The last incarnation of the Model 929. A .22 rimfire nine-shooter with blue or nickel finish and hardwood grips. Introduced in 1988 and dropped in 1999.

REMOVABLE-CYLINDER MODELS

H&R Model 532: A five-shooter chambered in .32 H&R Magnum. Blued finish with hardwood grips. Introduced 1984 and dropped one year later. A remarkably difficult gun to find.

H&R Model 622: H&R's plain vanilla tacklebox gun. A .22 rimfire six-shooter with blued finish and plastic grips. 2-1/2-, 4- and 6-inch barrels; introduced in 1957 and dropped in 1963.

H&R Model 623: Similar to the Model 622 but in chrome finish with white plastic grips.

H&R Model 632 Guardsman: A .32 S&W Short or Long six-shooter with 2-1/2- or 4-inch barrel and blued finish with black plastic grips. Centerfire version of the Model 622. Introduced around 1950 and discontinued around 1957.

H&R Model 733 Guardsman: Similar to the Model 732 but with chrome finish and white plastic grips.

H&R Model 922: Similar to the Model 622 but with a nine-shot cylinder and 4-, 6- or 10-inch barrel (the latter being called the "Trapper Model"). Introduced as early as 1919 and reintroduced around 1950 without the 10-inch barrel option. Wood (early production) or reddish-brown or black plastic grips. Discontinued in 1985.

H&R Model 923: Similar to Model 922 but with nickel or chrome finish and black or white plastic grips (walnut on early models).

When Marlin acquired H&R 1871/New England Firearms in November of 2000, they dropped all handgun models permanently. The only lasting reminder of the tacklebox gun is, oddly enough, the .32 H&R Magnum cartridge, an excellent little number that was first chambered in H&R's Model 532.

Most H&R tacklebox guns can be had for under $200, even in Excellent or Mint in Box condition. The few models chambered for .32 H&R Magnum may go as high as $275. At these prices, I'm tempted to buy as many of these little boogers as I can find. If I run out of places to store them, I suppose I can always buy more tackleboxes.

The numbers and varieties of muzzleloading guns offered to American consumers continue to evolve. Some companies have reduced or eliminated traditional muzzleloaders to concentrate on newer muzzleloader or cartridge guns. Nonetheless, CVA has upgraded their entire line of muzzleloaders, Dixie Gun Works is importing two new Davide Pedersoli guns, Pedersoli continues to introduce new guns, Thompson/Center Arms has a new drop-barrel in-line and Traditions has new lightweight rifles and a hunter's pistol.

Although Knight Rifles has discontinued gun production and is looking for a buyer, the company maintains a repair and accessory sales office in Ohio. Some Knight guns were offered through Sportsman's Warehouse at discounted prices, and these guns sold out within days.

Navy Arms Co. no longer sells muzzleloading guns, and CVA and Thompson/Center have almost completely discontinued their side-lock rifles and smoothbores. However, there is still moderate interest in replica military smoothbores and shotguns.

WHY USE SMOOTHBORES?

Smoothbore muzzleloaders are a mystery to many shooters who hunt with in-line rifles. Users of the newer muzzleloaders often don't understand how an unrifled gun can shoot accurately enough to kill anything but small game with birdshot.

I don't shoot everything with smoothbore guns; I also hunt with muzzleloading rifles and pistols. I have taken ducks, geese, swan, quail, dove, guinea fowl, pheasant, squirrels, rabbits, deer, hogs, bison and a blue wildebeest with smoothbores. If there is something that I have not shot with a smoothbore, it is only because I haven't gotten around to it.

Smoothbore guns come in and out of the market. Some of those that I describe have not been made for decades. With the demise of Knight Rifles the most advanced muzzleloading smoothbore ever made, the TK-2000, is out of production. The bright side is that Davide Pedersoli and others still offer traditional military and sporting muzzleloaders for reenactors and hunters.

At present, Davide Pedersoli has a variety of sporting and military smoothbore guns that are sold by several importers; MDM has a 209-primed break-action shotgun; and Thompson/Center Arms' Custom Shop sells a muzzleloading turkey barrel for Encore-frame guns.

One source of original guns, a few of which are sound enough to be shot, is Atlanta Cutlery, who imported thousands of muzzleloaders from the Royal Arsenal of Nepal. Many were made in India or Nepal and are smoothbore versions of English-designed rifles, including the Brunswick and Enfield patterns.

Author with Earnst Dyason and buffalo.

MUZZLELOADERS

BY **WM. HOVEY SMITH**

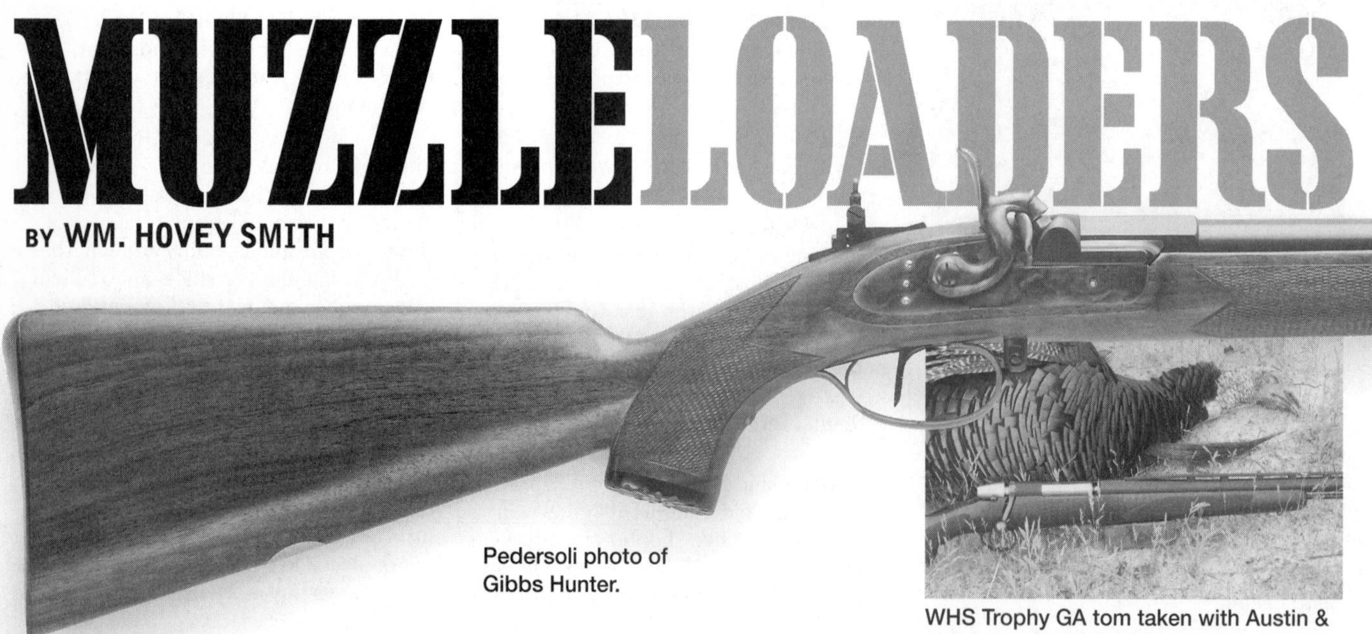

Pedersoli photo of Gibbs Hunter.

WHS Trophy GA tom taken with Austin & Halleck muzzleloading shotgun.

SMOOTHBORE GUNS, LOADS AND GAME TAKEN

Gun	System	Powder	Shot	Gauge	SG	P	D	G	S	Tk	BG
Tanegashima	Match	50[1]	½	.50	X						
Bess	Flint	100/95	1¼	11	X		X		X		X**
Mortimer	Flint	25 FFFg	1	12	X		X	X			
		50FFg	1-1/8	12	X		X	X			
Brunswick[3]	Perc.	80	1 1/8	14	X	X				X	
1842 Musket[4]	Perc.	100	1¼	11	X		X	X	X		X**
T/C Mountain	Perc.	100	1¼	12	X		X	X	X	X	
D.P. Slug	Perc.	100	1¼	12	X		X		X		X**
Austin&Halleck[2]	209	85 T7	1 3/8	12	X	X	X	X	X	X	
TK-2000[2]	209	120	1½	12	X	X	X	X	X		

Abbreviations: T7=Triple Seven, SG=Small game, P=Pheasant, D=Ducks, G=Geese, S=Swan, Tk=Turkey, BG=Big Game

Notes:

1) Powder is GOEX FFg black powder unless otherwise designated.

2) With the Austin & Halleck and TK-2000 I use 1-1/4-ounce by volume of HeviShot for waterfowl or the approximately equivalent 1-3/8-oz of lead shot for turkey.

3) Atlanta Cutlery sells guns only as collector's items. Many are unsafe to shoot. Only exceptional guns that have been shot with proof charges should be used.

4) Powder charges are increased for round ball loads used on big game.

A JAPANESE MATCHLOCK

Tanegashima, or Tagie for short, is a Japanese matchlock that I recommend to anyone who wants the maximum hunting experience but does not want to clean much game. I have not been lucky enough to have a deer in front if it when it was inclined to shoot.

With a patched .50-caliber round ball and a load of 85 grains of FFg black powder, this gun will shoot 4-inch groups at 50 yards once its numerous eccentricities are mastered. Matchlocks, this one included, also sometimes fire spontaneously. This is the heaviest charge that I can use in this gun with a degree of comfort.

BROWN BESS MUSKET

Bess, a .75-caliber flintlock musket, was imported from Japan by Dixie Gun Works and is now made by Davide Pedersoli. This "Indian Gun" variation of the Brown Bess musket has a shortened browned barrel, robust lock and is .75-caliber or 11 gauge. The instant I saw it, I thought that this gun had the potential of being a serious waterfowler. This proved to be correct, and it has taken a variety of game. One accomplishment was killing the first "flintlocked" swan in living memory at Lake Mattamuskeet, North Carolina.

Bess has also taken two deer with single shots. Shooting round ball with a gun that has no rear sight takes skill in that the face must be positioned in exactly the same spot on the stock for consistent results.

A FLINTLOCK FOWLER

Davide Pedersoli's Mortimer 12-gauge fowler was a difficult gun to figure out. It had a very tight barrel, making it difficult to load standard 12-gauge plastic wads, and I once tipped over a johnboat in freezing water trying to reload it. The best-shooting load was a duplex load employing 25 grains of FFFg followed by 50 grains FFg and 1-1/8-ounces of shot – a 16-gauge load. If you overload this gun it will shoot a hollow-centered pattern that you could throw a goose through.

With conventional paper and fiber wads I have used it to take dove, quail and small game and have employed bismuth loads for ducks. Bismuth shot in this gun will kill close-range waterfowl, but I prefer HeviShot loads contained in plastic shot cups which enabled me to successfully use this gun on snow geese.

BRITISH 1842 PERCUSSION MUSKET

As might be supposed for the percussion version of the British Brown Bess,

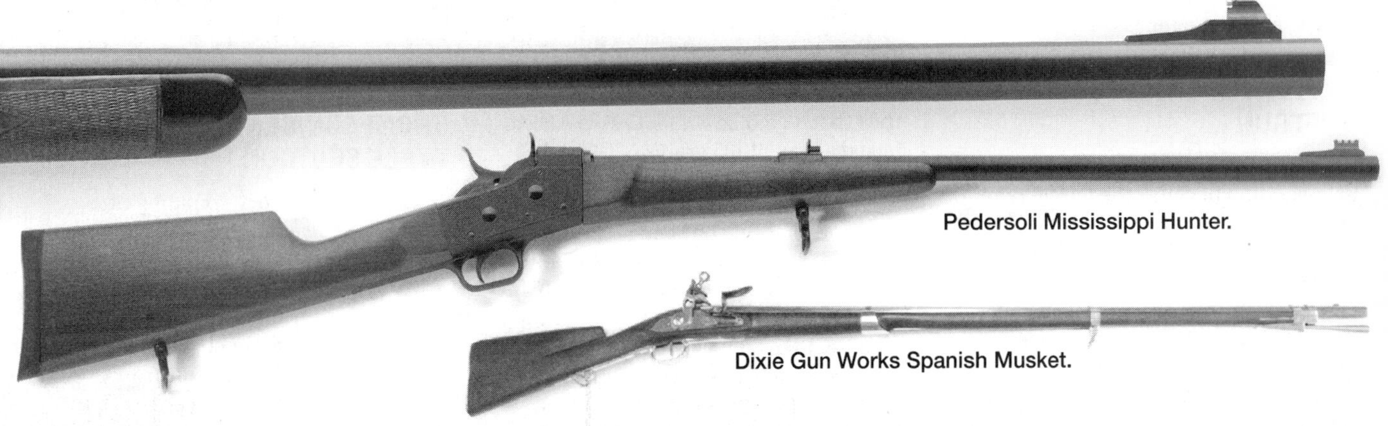

Pedersoli Mississippi Hunter.

Dixie Gun Works Spanish Musket.

the 1842 can use the same loads. My best work with this gun was on decoying geese near Wisconsin's Horicon Marsh. In this instance the big birds were coming in close. Shooting a cylinder-bored gun was advantageous compared to the others who where shooting silver-dollar-sized patterns at 15 yards from their tightly-choked semiautos.

This gun was made around 1850 for the British East India Co. by Wilkinson Sword. Although it had some rust pits on the outside of the barrel, it was in good condition compared to similar guns sold by Atlanta Cutlery. I re-proofed the gun before using it using proof charges from Dixie Gun Works' catalogue.

BRUNSWICK SMOOTHBORE

This relic was in poor condition when received. I replaced a spring and restored it to shooting condition because I wanted to shoot a 69-caliber, or 14-gauge, gun. The 14 was popular as a muzzleloading gauge but dropped out of favor when cartridge guns came along. I first took it on a preserve hunt for pheasant, where it did well, and then killed a turkey with it. Having done these hunts, I disabled it and gave it to a friend as a wall hanger. My conclusion was that the muzzleloading 14-gauge killed well and was economical in its use of powder and shot.

Wads for 14-gauge guns are available from Dixie Gun Works These wads can also be used in replica 69-caliber muskets to convert these into usable shotguns for hunting upland game. Should you already own a replica musket in this caliber, there is no reason why it cannot be used as a hunting gun.

I do not recommend the "buck and ball" military loads for deer. If you hit with the 69-caliber ball you won't need the three .30-caliber buckshot. If you hit with only the buckshot, that will likely only wound the deer.

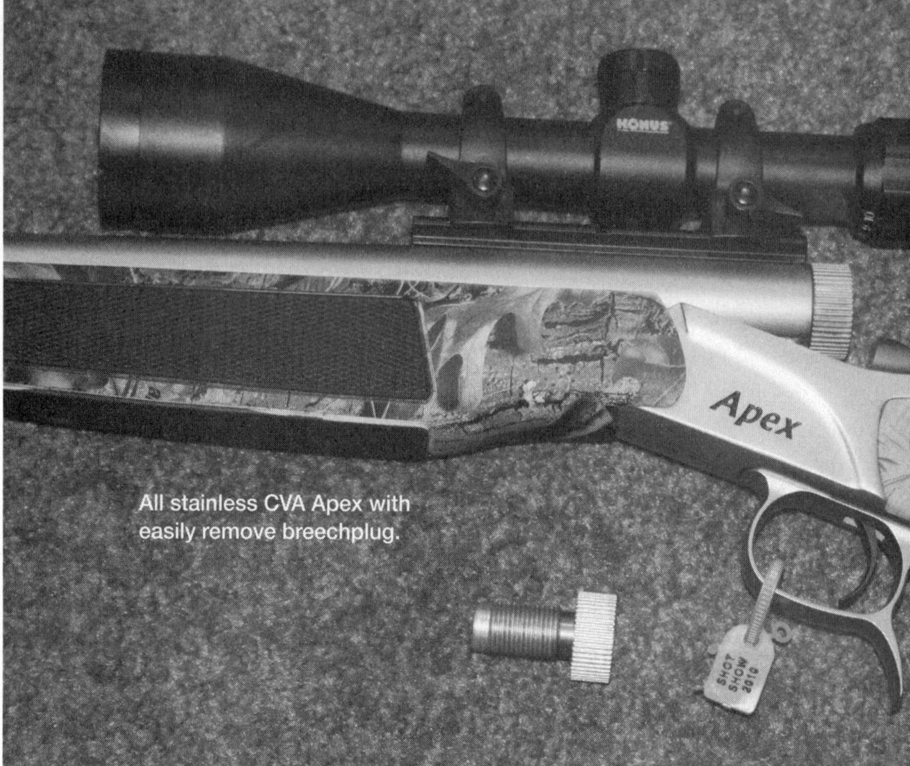

All stainless CVA Apex with easily remove breechplug.

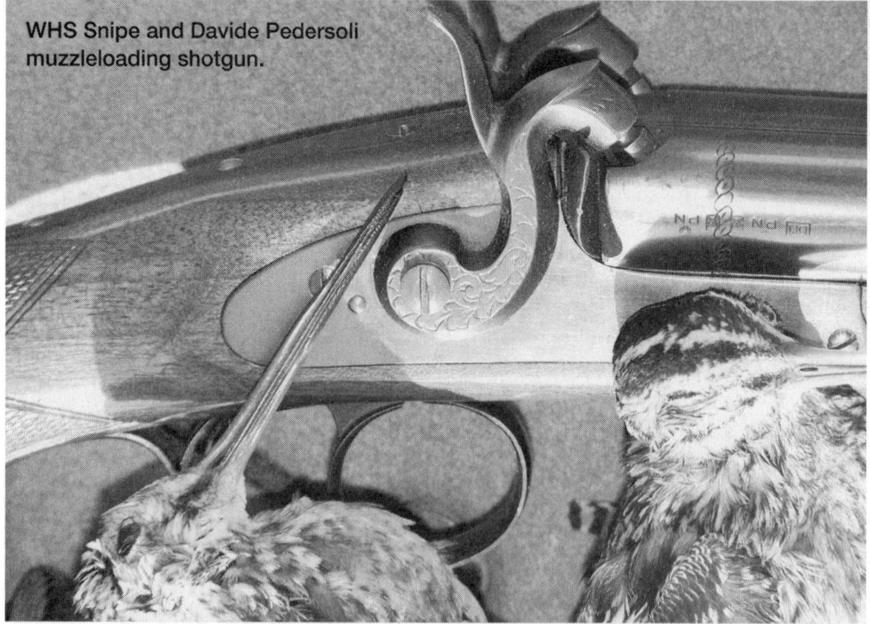
WHS Snipe and Davide Pedersoli muzzleloading shotgun.

DAVIDE PEDERSOLI SLUG SHOTGUN

I chose to purchase Davide Pedersoli's slug-shotgun because the flip-up rear sight and cylinder-bored barrels offered the potential of using it as a shotgun and double-barreled round-ball gun.

Experimenting with both patched round balls and balls contained in plastic Winchester 1-1/4-ounce Red Wads, I found that both did well. I chose the plastic-wadded load to take deer in the U.S. and a blue wildebeest in Africa. I used a load of 135 grains of GOEX FFg in the U.S. and a 155-gr. charge of WANO black powder in Africa. With the WANO load and shooting offhand at 35 yards, I put a left and right within two inches of the bull which is good shooting with any double gun, rifled or not.

In Georgia, I often use this as a ball and shot gun with one barrel loaded with shot and the other with a round ball. This way I am ready for anything.

THOMPSON/CENTER MOUNTAIN RIFLE SHOTGUN

This contradictory-sounding title results because this gun was the shotgun version of the now-discontinued T/C Mountain Rifle. This gun was made in when the advantages of musket-cap ignition were re-appreciated, but before the use of 209 primers in muzzleloading guns. This gun was meant to be a lightweight muzzleloader for mountain

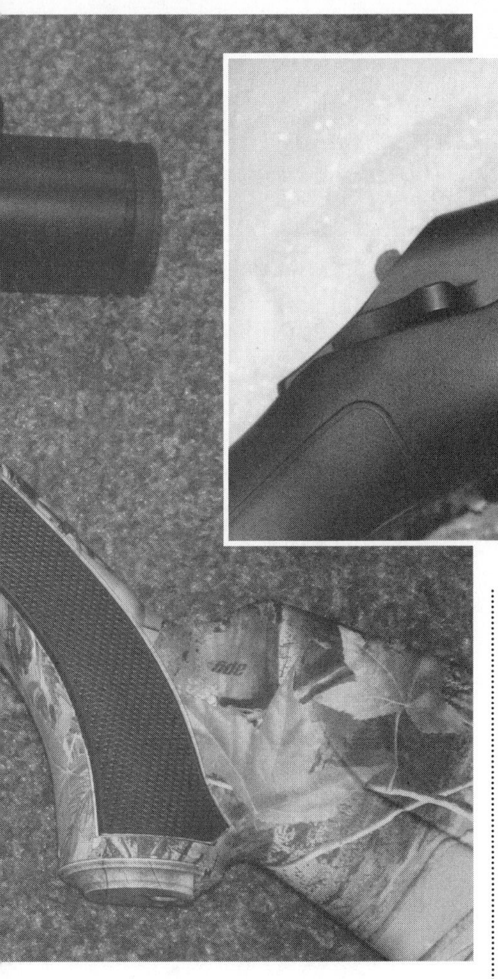

use. As a shotgun, it was too light until I increased its weight with some lead shot and beeswax poured into the buttstock.

This was also the first muzzleloader that I experimented with that had interchangeable chokes. I would have liked a longer barrel, but did fine with the gun using it for small game, ducks, geese, swan and turkey.

AUSTIN & HALLECK 12-GAUGE BOLT ACTION

I had three problems with this now-discontinued gun. The first one was that it weighted only 6 pounds. This was too light for a shotgun to take 1-1/4-ounce waterfowl loads. I loaded its butt with lead shot and beeswax and installed a solid steel ramrod. This helped make the gun much more shooter-friendly. Another problem occurred because the machined projection on the end of the firing pin was too small reliably fire the 209 primers. This was complicated by a coil spring that weakened over time and failed to fire on the gun's first swan hunt. I ordered another firing pin

Barrel shroud lock in Thompson Centers Impact

and strengthened the spring by putting washers on the firing pin spindle.

With these modifications, it worked fine on a Canadian snow goose hunt, Nebraska pheasant hunt and North Carolina brant hunt. The firing pin must be carefully adjusted to ensure that it will fire the 209 primer.

KNIGHT TK-2000

Without question, the best use of the Knight TK-2000 is to scope it and use it as a turkey gun. With its capability of shooting loads containing up to 2-1/2-ounces of shot and producing tight patterns, this muzzleloader is as capable a turkey slayer as any cartridge shotgun. This capability comes at the costs of considerable recoil which may be acceptable for one or two shots at a turkey, but not for waterfowling.

The heavy shot charges pattern low, and I had to use the adjustable iron sights to compensate. I did some serious killing on wild-flushing pheasants in West Virginia with 1-1/2-ounce loads of lead #5s and 120 grains of GOEX FFg. I still had iron sights on the gun when I took it for its swan hunt. When a good swan flew nearby I had trouble finding its head in my sights. I had to stand with one leg on the seat and shoot over the back of the blind.

The bird fell with the shot, and I also fell from my unstable perch. The gun knocked my glasses off, cut my nose and the recoil kicked me to the other side of the blind. The charge caught the swan in the head and there were over 20 hits in the bird's head and neck at about 40 yards.

Based on this experience, I removed the rear sight and reduced the load to 120 grains of FFg equivalent and 1¼-ounces of shot.

HUNTING WITH A POOR MAN'S DOUBLE RIFLE

Many double rifles in African calibers are priced at $10,000 and up. When I saw Traditions' no-longer-made Rex over/under .50 caliber rifle, I immediately thought of Africa. The gun's 12-pound weight made it heavier than a deer rifle needed to be, but I reasoned that this weight could soak up the recoil from a black-powder load that was potent enough for Cape buffalo.

This proved to be the correct. I worked up a load of 150 grains of Hodgdon's White Hot pellets and PowerBelt's 530-grain steel-tipped Dangerous Game Bullet that developed 1,316 fps and 2,038 ft./lbs. of muzzle energy. I used as few of the discontinued steel-pointed bullets as possible to zeroed the scope at 50 yards while shooting the fixed barrel. The second, adjustable, barrel shot this heavy bullet 3-inches high.

Another difficulty was that the gun sometimes doubled with this load. This meant that I could only shoot one barrel before opening the gun and priming the second barrel. My plan was to fire the top barrel first and carry a priming tool in my left hand to slap a primer into the lower barrel when needed. The result was that I was carrying two single-shots rather than achieving the rapid left-right shots offered by a double gun.

The hunt offered additional difficulties. Earnst Dyason, of Spear Safari, could fit me in for a South African hunt the first week in April. This was at the

Boutet Empire pistol 45 caliber smoothbore.

end of the rainy season on a property that was very thickly vegetated.

On the third day of the hunt we cut fresh tracks of a lone "Dugga Boy." After tracking through sometimes head-high brush and weeds we found him at about 20 yards. We waited until he offered the clearest possible shot at its shoulder. I aimed as low as I could see and fired. The bullet penetrated the near-side shoulder, passed through the ribs and broke the off-side leg. Despite this injury, the buffalo ran. After multiple encounters, the buffalo charged and Dyason stopped it with a brain shot at 4-5 yards.

When the buffalo was butchered, the bullet had performed well, but hit too high in the chest cavity to intersect the lungs. I now know more about shooting Cape buffalo than I did, and I mentally replayed my shot on every other buffalo that I saw.

Close up of action and ghost sights Gibbs .72 caliber Hunter.

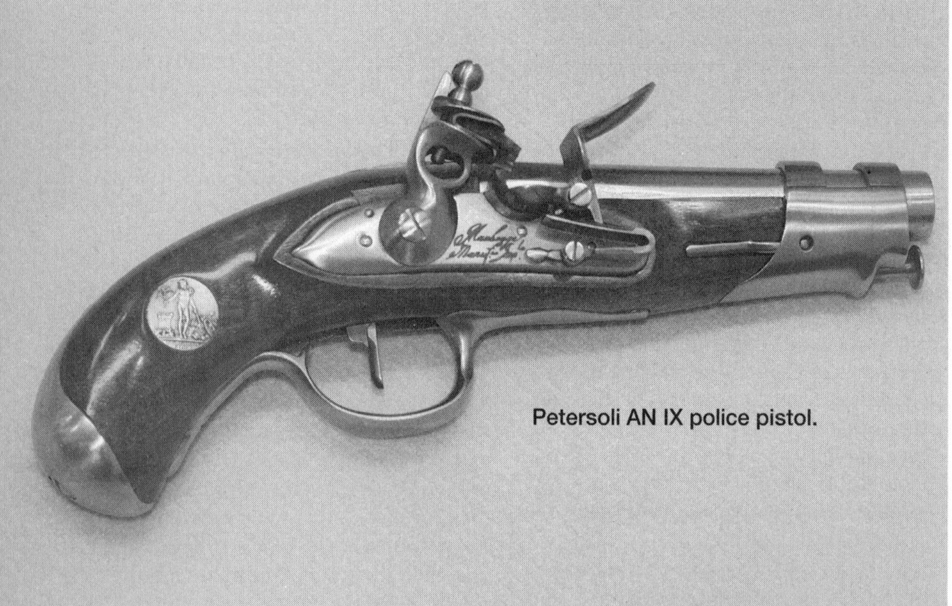

Petersoli AN IX police pistol.

Dyason and I also stalked ostrich. I used the same 150-grain charge, but with the .444-grain PowerBelt bullet. The huge bird took over 2,000 pounds of muzzle energy and stayed on its feet. Another shot was needed to kill it. The bullets expanded to about .70-caliber and remained in the animal. This copper plated lead bullet would have been too soft to offer sufficient penetration on Cape buffalo. This experience confirmed PowerBelt's Michael McMichael's observation that these bullets did not offer deep penetration on buffalo-sized animals.

GOOD OLD BOY HUNT

An adjunct to my buffalo hunt was a hunt in the Cape Province that was arranged by WhiteSmoke Forum (www.whitesmoke.co.za) moderator Willem O'Kelly. A few days before my arrival the first shipment of Bobbiejanbutts (baboon butt) smoothbores had been received from India's Delhi Gun Works, and forum members were eager to try them out.

These guns were replicas of the long-barreled flintlock smoothbores that the Dutch settlers used in South Africa from the late 1600s-1870s and most resemble America's Hudson River Fowlers. With the assistance of many individuals, I was hosted on a farm owned by Johan von Rensburg and participated in some "buckskinning" Afrikaans style.

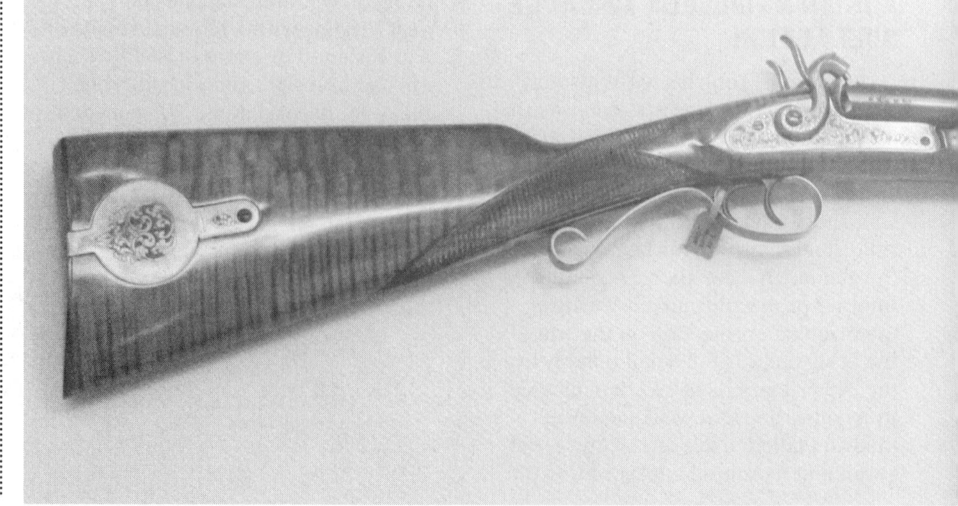

(above) South African hunters in period dress with their replica smoothbores.
(left) Exposed ignition in Thompson Centers NorthWest Explorer.

Although no big game was taken by the smoothbores on this trip, they did gather some springhairs and rabbits with their new guns using loads of pink Sannadex power, a South African-made black-powder substitute.

New Guns

CVA

Almost every gun in the CVA line received an upgrade for 2010. The Apex, Accura, and Optima are now all stainless steel guns. They, along with the other drop-barrel guns in the line, are now fitted with the new QRBP (Quick Release Breech Plug), to allow easer than ever cleaning and unloading.

The bolt-action Elkhorn Pro has an exposed nipple for musket and #11 caps for use in those states that require exposed ignition while the least expensive gun in the line, the Buckhorn at under $200, has 209-ignition in a simple striker-fired gun. CVA's best-selling gun, the Wolf break-action, is still priced at under $250 and also comes with the new QDBP system.

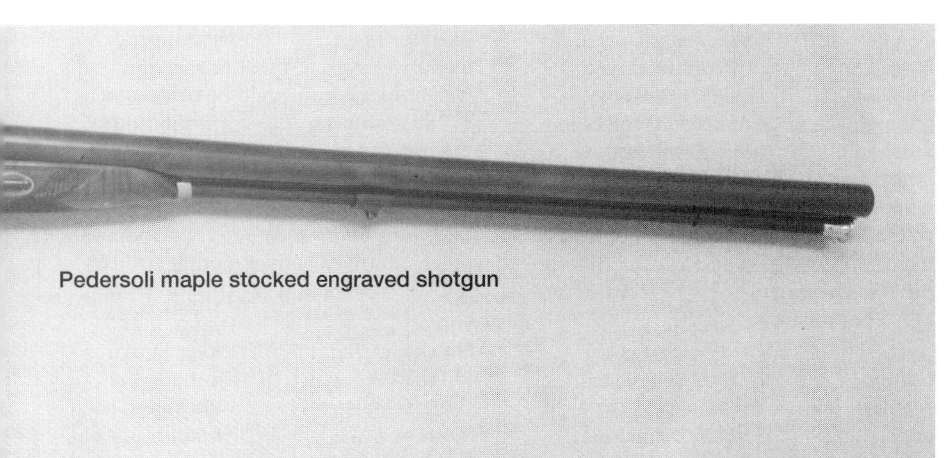

Pedersoli maple stocked engraved shotgun

DAVIDE PEDERSOLI

This Italian gunmakers' muzzleloading and black-powder cartridge guns are marketed through various outlets, including Cabela's, Dixie Gun Works, Traditions and others. Three new guns attracted my attention. These were a maple-stocked 12-gauge "Old English" muzzleloading double shotgun with engraving and browned barrels ($1,718); the commemorative Gendarme AN IX flintlock pistol in 15.2mm caliber ($694); and a half-magazine round-barreled 1886 Winchester lever action. The '86 will be available in June for about $1,600.

Other new guns included the White Hawk, which is a falling-barrel "parlor rifle" that shoots lead BBs or .177 pellets powered by 209 primers ($300) and a Derringer Guardian which also uses 209 primers ($220). One model of the Guardian also fires .177-size projectiles. Another new pistol is an elegant replica of a .45-caliber smoothbore flintlock pistol made by Nicholas-Noel Boutet, who was gunmaker to Napoleon and had his workshop at Versailles ($1,180).

Additional models were also offered of the company's replica Sharps and Winchester single-shot cartridge guns. Expanded offerings were also made in the Mississippi Hunter rolling block which is now chambered in .22LR ($754), .357 Magnum, .38-55, .45 Colt and .45-70 ($888).

This year the company also launched an on-line magazine, "Pedersoli No. 1," which will feature articles about muzzleloading events, guns and hunting – including some by the author. Free subscriptions are available at www.davide-pedersoli.com.

DIXIE GUN WORKS

Two new muzzleloaders are being offered by Dixie. The most unusual is the Gibbs African Hunter rifle with a .72-caliber rifled barrel, ghost-ring adjustable sights with a 1:75 round-ball twist that will sell for about $1,640. The recommended load for this gun is a 100-grain charge of FFg black powder and a patched round ball and bullet (Pedersoli mold U309-720). I prefer to use about 150 grains of FFg and a hard-lead 12-gauge ball for African plains game and larger bores for bigger animals.

The African Hunter does not come with a ramrod, which detracts from its utility as a hunting gun. Installing a heavy steel ramrod would improve this gun's over-all usefulness and the added weight would enhance the user's ability to more comfortably shoot heavier loads.

Dixie also introduced a .69-caliber Spanish Musket for reenactors who wanted a gun that resembled those used in Spanish-America about the time of the Revolutionary War. This gun uses a 1-inch flint and a .680 patched round ball. It has a recommended retail price of $1,400.

(top) Traditions Vortek rifle with easy remove breech plug.

(above) Traditions new Vortek 50-caliber pistol.

THOMPSON/CENTER ARMS

A new design of break-action muzzleloader, the Impact, was introduced by Thompson/Center Arms. With a competitive price of $249 for the blued-finished model, this gun will appeal to many hunters. The barrel is closed by a manually retracted barrel shroud, reminding me of the locking mechanism used by Remington and Valmet, among others. The gun is polymer stocked and at 6.5 pounds is very light.

The gun also has an adjustable buttstock and uses the same trigger as the more-expensive Omega ($330-$550) and Triumph ($430-$650). The Impact would be an ideal beginner's rifle. Initially, loads as low as 55 grains of FFg and a patched round ball could be used for targets and turkey hunting. As a youngster grew, the loads, length and weight of the gun could be increased to 100 grains and 240-grain saboted bullets. For maximum performance with heavier loads, the gun needs to have some additional weight added to the buttstock and a solid steel ramrod, both of which are easy user modifications.

As does CVA and Traditions, Thompson/Center also has a version of its Omega, called the NorthWest Explorer ($327-$407), which has a cut-away section of the barrel to provide an exposed ignition and a 1:48-inch twist for full-caliber bullets. These modifications make this gun legal to use in Washington, Oregon and Idaho.

TRADITIONS

Traditions continues to carry a number of side-lock flintlock and percussion rifles in its line. Three new additions to the Vortek line include the Ultralight and Northwest Edition rifles and a pistol.

The Vortek .50-caliber muzzleloading rifles have drop-out triggers, CeraKote finishes and Accelerator Breech Plugs. The Northwest edition has the rear of the barrel milled out to expose the primer. These guns weigh 6.25 pounds and have 28-inch barrels. Both rifles sell for between $439-$499, depending on options.

The pistol version is also a .50-caliber break-barreled gun, but with a 13-inch barrel and CeraKote finish for $369. Although I have not shot this gun, I am impressed by how it feels, by the quality of its iron sights and by its general design. I would prefer a few more inches of barrel and a steel ramrod, but this pistol has all appearances of being a winner.

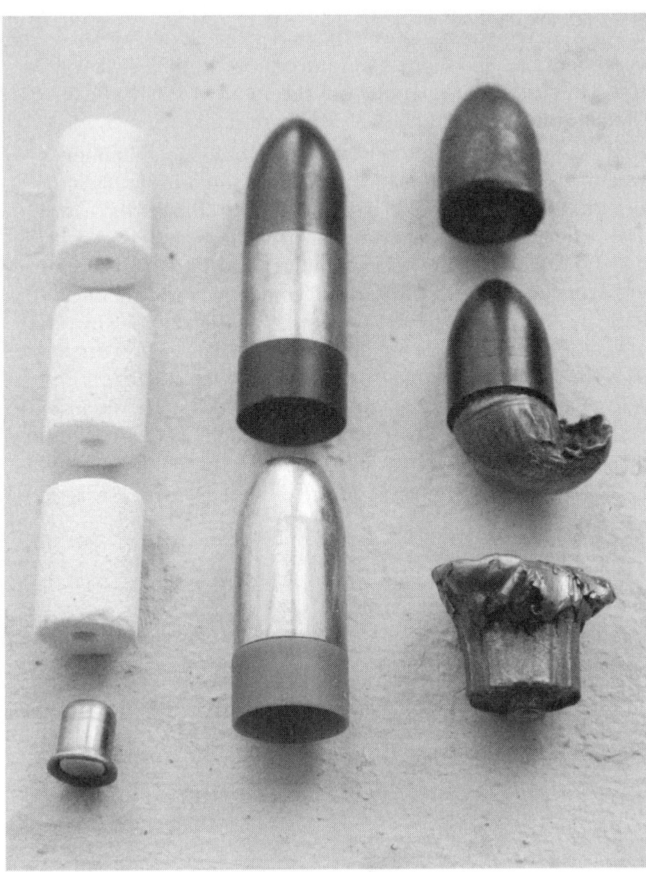

PowerBelt bullets and Hodgdon WhiteHot pellets.

Powders, Bullets and Accessories

Alliant, the maker of Red Dot powder, will be launching Black Dot powder, which is advertised as a cleaner burning, virtually non-corrosive black-powder substitute. This powder may be used in muzzleloaders (including flintlocks) and in cartridges loaded by Cowboy Action shooters.

Muzzleloading shooters going to South Africa will find this country's home-grown Sannadex to be acceptable in both flintlock and percussion guns, although there are apparent problems in batch-to-batch uniformity. If you ever have occasion to use it, allow some range time to determine what charge corresponds to your gun's black-powder load.

Sannadex Powder on Giraffe skull.

IMR's White Hot pellets worked very well in the Traditions's double that I used and in other guns. This powder has a low residue and cleans up easily with soap and water.

Both Thompson/Center Arms and Traditions now offer low-cost saboted lead bullets for use in sighting in. Thompson/Center calls its bullets Cheap Shot Sabots and Traditions has named their sighting-in bullets Plinkers ($9.99 for 20). Both are 240-gr. hollow-pointed lead bullets which are also effective close-range deer and wild hog killers.

Gavin Margrate is a fine craftsman who produces black-powder accessories sold under the Bushbuck Trading label. Besides offering hand-made brass cappers, flask and shot bags, he also makes powder horns using horns from African antelopes. Should you like a powder horn made from an antelope that you shot, he can produce a custom horn and/or bag to make a unique African trophy. His telephone numbers are 0444-883-1113 or 082-469-3236, or he may also be contacted by E-mail at plumcrazy@absamail.co.za.

New Book

X-treme Muzzleloading: Fur, Fowl and Dangerous Game with Muzzleloading Rifles, Smoothbores and Pistols is now available (about $20, AuthorHouse, Amazon.com and others). Based on a lifetime of hunting with many muzzleloading guns in North America, Europe and Africa, this book describes the author's sometime zany, sometimes dangerous experiences with these front-loading guns.

BIG? YES! BORING? NO!

BY DAN SHIDELER

The lever-action rifle has been in continuous production longer than any other type of American firearm. The Hunt Rocket Ball and Volitional Repeater of 1848 paved the way for the Volcanic lever-actions and, in turn , the Henry; the Spencer; Winchester 's Models 1866, 1873, 1876, 1892, 1894, 1895, 88, etc.; the Marlins; the Savage 1898 and 1899; the Stevens 425; and, finally, the most highly-evolved lever-action of them all, the BLR (Browning Lever Rifle) Model 81.

Between the Hunt and the today's ultra-Modern BLR Lightweight came a number of lever-actions that, well, just didn't live up to their potential. We're not talking pre-'64 Winchesters here. That market has matured, and the high prices that those great old guns command have discouraged many entry-level collectors who, naturally, have turned their attention elsewhere. And many of them have looked to Winchester's Big Bore and XTR lever-actions as tomorrow's hot collectible.

What's a "Big Bore"? Contrary to what you might think, it's not necessarily a .444, .450, or .45-70. As applied to collectible lever-actions, the term "Big Bore" actually refers to a trio of medium-bore cartridges chambered in the Winchester 94 that never quite got off the ground: the .307 Winchester, the .356 Winchester, and the .375 Winchester. These cartridges were "Big Bores" only in comparison to the dinky ol' 30-30, but Winchester's marketing department must have thought that calling them Big Bores would help them hold their heads up alongside Marlin's .444 and .45-70.

The first of the new "Big Bore" cartridges was the .375 Winchester. Rolled out in 1978, the .375 was a slightly beefier knock-off of the old .38-55 Winchester. The ".375" designation may have struck a chord among those who confused it with the old .375 H&H stomper, but in truth the .375 Winchester was a ballistic dead-ringer for Marlin's 336 chambered in .35 Remington. That made it a perfectly competent woods load and, besides, it gave Winchester something to put up against the Marlin that didn't have the hated word "Remington" in its name. The .375 found its home in a redesigned version of the Winchester Model 1894, the '94 Big Bore."

Two years later, Winchester really got in the game with the .307 Winchester. Introduced in 1982, the .307 was a rimmed .308 Winchester loaded with 150- and 180-gr. roundnose bullets. Cartridge capacity was actually a bit less than that of the .308 Winchester because the .307's bullet had to be seated a skoosh deeper in the cartridge case to function in the tried-and-true Model 94 action. But even so, the .307 was a barn-burner, retaining about as much energy at 200 yards as the .30-30 did at 100 yards.

1982 also witnessed the birth of the third member of the Big Bore family, the .356 Winchester. Depending on how you look at it, the .356 Winchester was either a necked-up .307 or a rimmed version of the .358 Winchester introduced in 1955. Either way, the .356 blew a 200-gr. bullet out the spout at 400 fps faster than Marlin's Model 336 in .35 Remington.

My editor hits me in the head with a ball-peen hammer whenever I commit an inaccuracy, so I should probably mention that the .307 and .356 weren't literally "Big Bores" at all. That title is properly reserved only for the .375. Between 1978 and 1982, Winchester was reorganized as United States Repeating Arms Company (USRAC), and someone at USRAC decided that the "Big Bore" tag was not entirely satisfactory. Thus the new .307 and .356 were chambered in the so-called Winchester 94 XTR, "XTR" being an acronym for "Extended Range." The XTR designation was also applied to the 94 chambered in 7-30 Waters, which is a collectible in its own right. (Most collectors, however, refer to all of the .307/.356/.375 guns as "Big Bores.")

Call it what you will, 94 Big Bore or XTR or Angle Eject, the

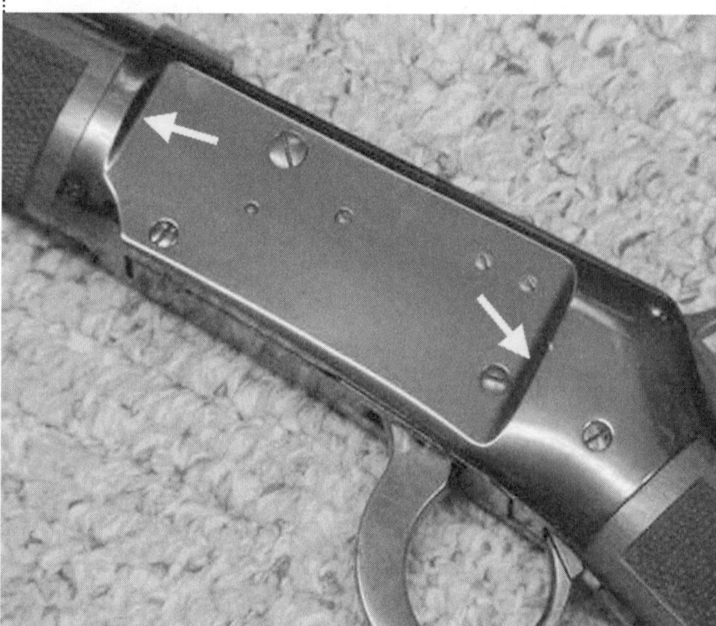

The receiver of the Winchester 94 Big Bore/XTR/Angle Eject was thicker and much stronger front and rear (arrows) than that of the standard Model 94. Photo courtesy Country Mile Enterprises (www.cmeguns.com).

The 94 Big Bore XTR .375 appeared in the 1980 Gun Digest at a princely suggested retail of $220.

CENTERFIRE RIFLES—LEVER ACTION

Savage Model 99-358 Lever Action Rifle
Similar to Model 99 CD except has straight-grip stock, no checkering, chambered for 358 Win., 6-shot rotary magazine with cartridge counter, no Monte Carlo, weight 7 lbs., removable ramp front sight, folding leaf rear. Has vent. recoil pad, swivel studs. Introduced 1977. .... **$256.66**

WESTERN FIELD 79 LEVER ACTION CARBINE
Caliber: 30-30, 6-shot magazine.
Barrel: 20".
Weight: 7½ lbs. **Length:** 38½" over-all.
Stock: Walnut finished hardwood.
Sights: Ramp front, adj. rear.
Features: Trigger moves with lever on opening, cross-bolt hammer-block safety. Solid top receiver with side ejection. Scope not included. Ward article No. 10772.
Price: Standard Model **$139.99**

WINCHESTER MODEL 94 BIG BORE XTR
Caliber: 375 Win., 6-shot magazine.
Barrel: 20".
Weight: 6½ lbs. **Length:** 37¾" over-all.
Stock: American walnut with fine cut checkering, warm rich color. Satin finish.
Sights: Hooded ramp front, semi-buckhorn rear adjustable for w. & e.
Features: All external metal parts have Winchester's new deep blue high polish finish. Stock measurements are: 13⅝" x 1⅜" x 2½". Rifling twist 1 in 12". Rubber recoil pad fitted to buttstock. Introduced 1978.
Price: **$220.00**

WINCHESTER 94 LEVER ACTION CARBINE
Caliber: 30-30, (12" twist). 6-shot tubular mag.
Barrel: 20"
Weight: 6½ lbs. **Length:** 37¾" over-all
Stock: Walnut straight grip stock and fore-end (13"x1¾"x2½").
Sights: Bead front sight on ramp with removable cover; open rear. Tapped for receiver sights.
Features: Solid frame, top ejection, half-cock hammer safety.
Price: **$153.00**

Winchester Model 94XTR Carbine
Same as standard Model 94 except has high-grade finish on stock and fore-end with cut checkering on both. Metal has highly polished deep blue finish.
Price: **$172.00**

Winchester 94 Antique Carbine
Same as M94 except: color case-hardened and scroll-engraved receiver, brass-plated loading gate and saddle ring. 30-30 only **$164.00**

Winchester Legendary Frontiersmen Commemorative
Similar to standard Model 94 except has engraved antique silver-finished receiver; scenes typical of the old frontier are engraved on both sides. Barrel, finger lever, hammer and trigger are polished deep blue. Butt and fore-end are of semi-fancy walnut with deep cut checkering, satin finish. Buttstock has a special nickel-silver medallion depicting a buckskin-clad frontiersman in hand-to-hand combat with an American Indian. Fore-end tip is silver-plated, curved steel buttplate is blued.
Price: **$425.00**

CAUTION: PRICES CHANGE. CHECK AT GUNSHOP.

34TH EDITION, 1980 325

redesigned gun rectified a notorious weakness of the original Model 1894: an open-topped receiver that couldn't take the pounding of anything heavier than the .30-30 and that wouldn't accept scope mounts. The Big Bore/XTR/Angle Eject corrected this failing with a thick, brawny receiver incorporating an ejection port that hurled empties not out the top but off to the side, kinda-sorta. The design worked, and it finally gave USRAC something that would compete with Marlin's solid-topped 336.

The standard 94 Big Bore featured a 20-inch barrel and walnut stock and forearm. They were attractive rifles, as are all Model 94s. But they didn't succeed in the marketplace, probably because the cartridges just weren't a good fit with the basic 94 design, at least as far as the .307 and .356 were concerned. A 20-inch lever-action is a woods rifle, plain and simple, and the logic of chambering a woods rifle for a hot-rodded cartridge apparently escaped most potential buyers. I'm one of them. If we set the extreme limit of a woods rifle at, say 150 yards -- in my stomping grounds of northern Michigan, 50 yards is more like it -- the truth was that the .30-30 and .35 Remington have things pretty well sewn up. In the case of the .375, the modernized .38-55 really wasn't an improvement over the .35, and the .444 left it eating dust. In 1989, USRAC called it quits and quietly deep-sixed the Big Bores. (Marlin also experimented with the .356 in a version of the 336 lever-action called the Model 336 ER -- another strong sleeper -- but that's a story for another day.)

Winchester played fast and loose with the Big Bore/XTR designation. A Deluxe version (the "Winchester 94 XTR Deluxe") was offered in 1987 and 1988, but this fancy little gun was chambered not in a high-performance cartridge but in the plain old .30-30. Winchester's .444 Timber Carbine was also known for a year or so as the "94 Big Bore Timber," but to collectors, the term "Big Bore" will always refer only to the .307/.356/.375 flavors.

Two or three years ago, you could pick up a Winchester 94 Big Bore in excellent condition for $275 to $325. That situation is changing. Excellent examples are now bringing upwards of $750. Yet it's surprising how many of these guns are floating around out there, some in NOS (new old stock) condition. The .375 is most frequently encountered, the .307 and .356 less so. My bet is that the .307 will appreciate more rapidly than its brethren.

If you're looking for a good deal on a 94 Big Bore, I wouldn't expect to find one on the internet, of course. On the web, you're competing with tens of thousands of other bargain-hunters, many of whom also recognize the collectibility of the Big Bores. No, the best way to find an affordable Big Bore is to check the pages of Gun Digest Magazine regularly and to do as I do: prowl the racks of the hundreds of gun stores and gun shows scattered throughout the Eastern and Great Lakes regions. It's a tough job, but. . . .

When you find a Big Bore, grab it. The value of these ill-fated but unarguably neat rifles has nowhere to go but up!

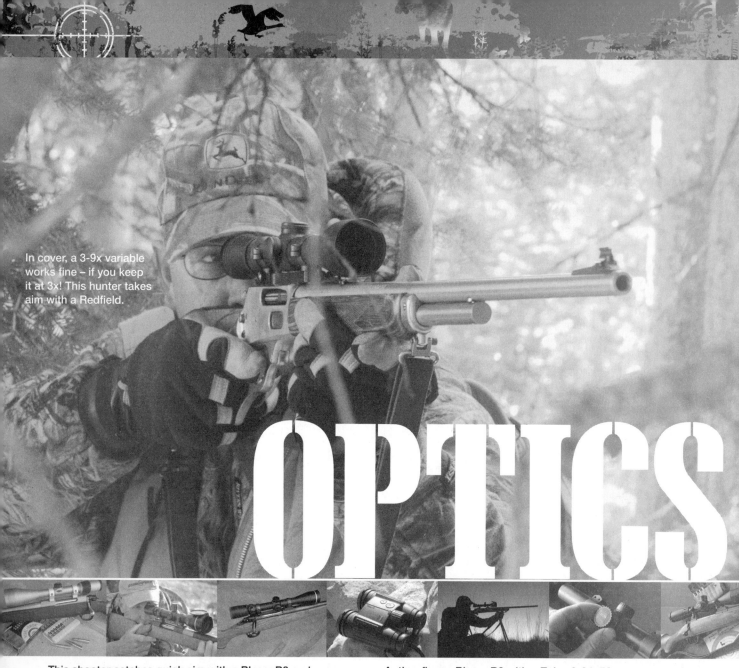

In cover, a 3-9x variable works fine – if you keep it at 3x! This hunter takes aim with a Redfield.

OPTICS

This shooter catches quick aim with a Blaser R8 and a new Zeiss Compact Point red dot sight.

Author fires a Blaser R8 with a Zeiss 6-24x56 scope, one of three new Victory Diavaris this year.

BY **WAYNE VAN ZWOLL**

Yes, I found plenty of new hardware at January's SHOT (Shooting, Hunting and Outdoor Trade) show. The Las Vegas Convention Center, SHOT's traditional home, was, alas, not available. Hundreds of exhibitors converged on the town's Venetian and Palazzo Hotel complex and the rat-runs of conference rooms opened to add square feet to the refurbished Sands Convention Center. "Plenty of traffic.... Better than I expected.... Needed more space" pretty much summed it up. The recession has surely influenced the choices of hunters and shooters; but it has hardly kept them home. They're buying rifles, ammo and optics. Dealers and distributors are writing orders. Product lines continue to grow – especially those that deliver value for the dollar.

An upbeat SHOT Show can trigger irrational exuberance – the marketing of products with no real utility. Alas, such items appear even in somber times. In this report I'll try to winnow that chaff and separate the worthy from the merely recent.

AIMPOINT

Since its start in 1974, Aimpoint has worked to offer the best red dot sights. Early on, that was easy, because red dot sights were then new. In fact, Gunnar Sandberg's first "single-point sight" had no optical tunnel. You couldn't look through this sight; you looked into the tube with one eye while your other registered a dot superimposed on the target. Sandberg refined the device and founded Aimpoint to produce it. Hunters liked the illuminated dot, suspended in a wide field they could see from almost any place behind the sight. The front lens of a modern Aimpoint is a compound glass that corrects for parallax – unlike most red dot sights, whose reflective paths shift with eye position. Aimpoint's doublet brings the dot to your eye in a line parallel with the sight's optical axis, so you hit where you see the dot, even when your eye is off-axis. A 1x Aimpoint gives you unlimited eye relief too. Advanced circuitry on the newest models reduces power demand. Batteries last up to 50,000 hours with a mid-level brightness setting.

The lightest of Aimpoint's 9000 series weighs just 6.5 ounces. Each windage and elevation click moves point of impact 13mm at 100 meters. The newest Hunter series comprises four models: long and short tubes, 34mm and 30mm in diameter. They all feature 1x images, 2-minute dots, half-minute clicks. A 12-position dial lets you fine-tune dot intensity – low for dim light, high under sunny skies. One CR-2032 battery lasts five years if you never turn the sight off! Hunter sights are waterproof. Fully multi-coated lenses (43mm up front on the 30mm sight, 47mm on the 34mm tube) deliver a sharp image, and as with all Aimpoints, the internal design gives you unlimited eye relief with zero parallax. Sturdy enough for military use, Aimpoints have been adopted by armed forces in the U.S. and France. They serve sportsmen in forty countries. One of every ten moose hunters using optical sights in Sweden carries an Aimpoint. I've killed moose with these optics in dark timber, then shot golf-ball-size groups on paper at 100 yards. The company's line includes a Micro H1, ideal for bows and handguns. (Aimpoint.com.)

ALPEN

A young optics company, Alpen has surprised everyone over the last few years with "great buy" credits from such venerable sources as *Outdoor Life*. While 2010 brings only a few new products to the catalog, many established optics in the Alpen line deserve another look. In short-summary fashion, then:

The Rainier 20-60x80 spotting scope accommodates a camera adapter for photography at long range. AR riflescopes for air guns were designed to endure double-shuffle recoil. Carriage-class Rainier binoculars now come in 8x32 and 10x32 versions that are 20 percent lighter than the 42mm originals but still wear BAK4 lenses, phase-corrected coatings, a locking diopter dial and twist-out eyecups. The AlpenPro Porro series includes an 8x30 that's ideal for the woods. Alpen's energetic

Author took this Montana rifle with a 1.5-5x Leupold to Africa, shot game from 12 to 250 yards.

This Weaver Grand Slam scope, one in a big stable of fine variables, tops a Tikka T3 rifle.

Vickie Gardner is busy "scrambling to fill back-orders from 2009!" Why? "Alpen offers great value; the riflescopes and binoculars truly are great buys."

Also, some 2009 introductions were premature; stock didn't arrive until late in the year. Wings binoculars, for example. Choose 8x42 or 10x42, with ED glass as an option. The 8x42 has impressed me in the field; so has a new Apex rifle-scope on a bolt-gun in the rack. The four Apex sights just cataloged include three with turret-mounted parallax dial and new bullet-drop-compensating reticle. "We've also upgraded our 20-60x80 spotting scope with a fine-focus knob," says Vickie. Shift focus quickly with the standard dial, then refine the image with this new adjustment. (Alpenoutdoors.com.)

BARRETT

While Barrett is known for its 50-caliber rifles, it also markets an optic that helps shooters hit at long range. The Barrett Optical Ranging System – BORS – is a sight attachment, a 13-ounce device you pair with a scope. It incorporates a small ranging computer powered by a CR-123 lithium battery. There's a liquid crystal display with a four-button keypad. Factory-installed cartridge tables tailored to your loads enable the computer to deliver precise holds for long-distance shooting. The BORS includes an elevation knob and a knob adapter. A set of steel rings mounts the unit to any M1913 rail and are secured with hex nuts that endure the beating from Barrett rifles in .50 BMG. Press the 6-o'clock power button, and you're ready to engineer a shot. The screen shows your zero or sight-in range and indicates any cant (tipping of the rifle), which at long range can cause you to miss. To determine range, you specify target size, then move the horizontal wire of your reticle from top to bottom on the target. The range appears in yards or meters. Now you can use the elevation knob to dial the range. The BORS unit must know your load, of course. You provided that data earlier; the unit stores it as a ballistics table. It can hold up to 100 tables for instant access. At the end of this process – which takes longer to explain than to do – you can hold dead-on at any range. The BORS automatically compensates for vertical shot angles. You can adjust the scope for up to 90 degrees of inclination and declination, in increments of 2 degrees. Temperature and barometric pressure come on-screen when you press the 9-o'clock button. If the battery dies, you can use the scope as if the electronics were not there. Paired with a Leupold Mark 4 LR/Tactical 4.5-14x50 scope, the BORS unit on my Barrett rifle shrugs off the .50's blast and recoil. (Barrettrifles.com.)

BURRIS

When variables started to gain traction with hunters, the 3-9x became the logical leader. Not only did 3x afford fast sighting; 9x was all you needed for any big game – and even coyotes at long range. The three-times power range seemed adequate. As shooters chased power, though, four-times magnification appeared, in 3-12x and 4-16x 30mm scopes. Burris was among the first with six-times magnification. Its 2-12x scope is surely versatile! Like the Euro Diamond and Black Diamond lines, both Six Series sights (40mm and 50mm up front) feature 30mm tubes and 4 inches of eye relief. Signature Select and Fullfield II models have 1-inch tubes. The Fullfield II 6x40 and 3-9x40 have impressed me as fine values – also the 2-7x35. Burris Ballisic Plex and Ballistic Mil-Dot reticles are available in the Euro Diamond and Black Diamond scopes, and the Signature Select and Fullfield II lines. Illuminated reticles define the Fullfield II LRS scopes, which have flat battery housings on the turret. Fullfield 30s (3-9x40 and 3.5-10x50) feature 30mm tubes at affordable prices. The biggest news at Burris in 2010 is the Eliminator, a programmable laser range-finding scope. You enter the ballistic path of your cartridge (drop figures at 500 yards, with a 100- or 200-yard zero) to get instant reads for correct hold when you see game. The sight (at its core a 4-12x42 LaserScope) tells you the exact distance. You get accurate data to 800 yards on reflective objects, 550 on deer and elk. At 26 ounces, the Eliminator is heavy, but not burdensome.

If long shooting isn't a priority, compact scopes should be. Burris' 1-inch Timberline series, from 4x20 to 4.5-14x32 AO, fills this slot. The firm recently improved its 1.6-ounce reflex-style red dot sight: FastFire II is now waterproof. Battery-saver mode extends the life of the lithium CR2032 battery to five years. FastFire mounts

Oldie but goodie: This Swarovski Habicht variable complements an Ultra Light rifle in .30-06.

In thickets, you want low magnification. Author has a 1.5-5x Leupold on this Montana rifle.

fit popular lever rifles; a mounting plate slipped between receiver and buttstock on repeating shotguns gives you Speed-Bead. I tried this sight on a Remington 1100; the clay targets suffered that day! The company also lists a 1x, 5-ounce tube-style red dot sight, the 135. Like many optics firms, Burris has grown its tactical line. Fullfield II Tactical scopes and Fullfield TAC30 variables (3-9x40, 3.5-10x50 and 4.5-14x42) have been joined by a 3x AR-332 prism sight, and an AR-Tripler, which you place on a pivot mount behind a red dot sight for extra magnification. Binoculars and spotting scopes complete the extensive Burris line. (Burrisoptics.com.)

BUSHNELL

Last year the Elite 6500-series rifle-scopes – 2.5-16x42, 2.5-16x50 and 4.5-30x50 – introduced Bushnell fans to nearly-seven-times magnification, the broadest range in the industry. (I've since seen a scope with 10-times magnification. It wasn't a Bushnell, and at the top third of its range the image was noticeably soft.) The 6500 Elite still impresses me, now with the DOA (Dead On Accurate) reticle. It has the spaced bars common to many reticles. Minute-of-angle dots mark intersections with the bottom wire. DOA can also be ordered on Elite 3200 and Trophy sights. The Elite 4200 employs standard and lighted reticles. In this series, the 3-9x40, 2.5-10x40 and 4-16x40 appeal to me. I've found the images sharp and bright; you can also mount these scopes low. Target knobs and side-focus dials appear on selected Elite scopes, like the 6-24x40. For hunters on a budget, Bushnell has up-graded the Trophy series. Trophy XLT scopes feature fully multi-coated lenses, fast-focus eyepiece, even flip-up lens caps. I like the 2-6x32, but there are alternatives, up to 6-18x50. Bushnell's 4-12x laser range-finding rifle-scope complements a long line of hand-held laser instruments.

For 2010, ED Prime glass and Rain-Guard HD coatings improve Bushnell's top-end Elite 8x42 and 10x42 binoculars. A step down in price, you'll find new Legend 8x36 and 10x36 binoculars. At 21 ounces, these roof-prism glasses are an ideal size for the trail. My pick: the 8x36, with its 4 1/2mm exit pupil. It has many Elite features, including ED glass and RainGuard. An Excursion spotting scope, with folded light path, comes in 15-45x60 and 20-60x80 versions. And there's a new15-45x spotting scope compact enough to slip into a backpack. Dual-speed focus on this Legend HD allows for coarse and fine focusing, quickly. Bushnell's most field-worthy laser range-finder may be the Scout 1000 with ARC, technology that takes shot angle into account so you get corrected distance for accurate shooting at steep vertical angles. Single-button control makes this 6 1/2-ounce range-finder easy to use with one hand. In bow mode, it reads between 5 and 100 yards. Rifle mode sets it for 100 to 800 yards. (Bushnell.com.)

CABELA'S

Because it does not make riflescopes, Cabela's markets those from other firms – branded items from Leupold, Nikon, Swarovski, Zeiss and other well-known manufacturers and imported optics – with its own Cabela's label. Its manufacturers also produce for "name" companies in optics. They own the best of machines and technology and negotiate modest labor costs. Cabela's enjoys an economy of scale that contributes to low prices, so it's no surprise that these optics are exceptionally good buys. The Alaska Guide series of rifle-scopes includes fixed-powers as well as eleven variables. Most useful for big game and varmint hunters are the 3-9x, 4-12x AO and 6.5-20x AO scopes, all with 40mm objectives and 1-inch tubes. They list for less than $400. A 4x Cabela's scope helped me take a mountain goat and a moose in British Columbia. If you're feeling the cruel pinch of want these days, consider the Pine Ridge line; it's less expensive still. There's also a series of Cabela's tactical scopes with inter-changeable turrets and left-side parallax knobs. The 2-7x32, 3-9x40, 3-12x40 and 6-18x40 start at less than $100, with fully multi-coated lenses, fast-focus eyepieces and adjustable objectives. A new Lever-Action scope features a reticle proportioned to help you determine and hold for distances that impose significant bullet drop. Five inches of eye relief help you aim fast. Cost: $100. Cabela's lists similar scopes for shotguns and muzzleloaders. (Cabelas.com.)

DOCTER

World War II brought big changes in

Author takes a bead with a Magnum Research rifle and Greybull-modified Leupold scope.

This Leupold 4.5-14x50 VX-3 has been modified for long shooting by GreyBull Precision.

the staid and respected German optics industry. Long after the ripples of that conflict subsided, new names attached themselves to old companies. In 1991 the Carl Zeiss Jena factory in Thuringia, Germany, began producing Docter optics. In 2006 Merkel USA became the U.S. importer. Docter Optic has since wooed hunters Stateside with rifle-scopes featuring 1-inch tubes and rear-plane reticles. The 3-9x40, 3-10x40, 4.5-14x40 AO and 8-25x50 AO Docter Sport scopes boast features of more expensive sights. Docter's line also includes 1-inch 6x42 and 8x56 fixed-power Classic models, plus 30mm Classic variables: 1-4x24, 1.5-6x42, 2.5-8x48 and 3-12x5 with fast-focus eyepieces, resettable windage/elevation dials and lighted reticles. In the Unipoint series, the electronically controlled rear-plane dot stays a constant size, while the first-plane main reticle varies with magnification (and stays in constant relationship with the target). Doctor catalogs three magnesium/alloy-frame binoculars: 8x42, 10x42 and a bright 8x58. They're of roof-prism design with center focus and four-layer achromatic front lenses. A central diopter dial with vernier scale ensures precise focus to just 3 feet! (Merkel-usa.com and docter-germany.com.)

GREYBULL PRECISION

Ballistic performance has many measures. Most venerated among hunters is reach – long-range accuracy and payload. Extending reach is, after all, a fundamental purpose for firearms. One shooter who has made long reach a mission is John Burns, a Wyoming gun-builder who, with Coloradans Scott Downs and Don Ward, runs GreyBull Precision. They fashion mid-weight hunting rifles for hunters who expect to shoot far.

Optics are a key component of GreyBull rifles. The firm contracts with Leupold to install Greybull's own reticle in Leupold's 4.5-14x VX III sight. It's essentially a Duplex with a few fine horizontal lines for range estimation, and one-minute tics to help you shade for wind. The elevation dial is meant to move; each is cut for a specific load and marked so you can quickly dial the distance and hold center. Adjusting windage dials, most hunters agree, is unwise. Wind changes speed and direction, and you can get lost correcting yourself off zero. So GreyBull scope dials have numbers scribed above distance marks. They show minutes of adjustment needed in a 10-mph crosswind. Testing these scopes, I've found yardage and windage marks spot on. Of course, a laser range-finder is all but necessary to get accurate distance reads. I enjoyed the opportunity to test the Greybull scope on a Greybull rifle, and both performed magnificently. (Greybullprecision.com.)

LEICA

Best known for its superlative Ultravid binoculars and Geovid range-finding binoculars, Leica now offers 8+12x42 and 10+15x50 Duovid glasses. These aren't "zoom" or variable binoculars. Such mechanisms are too heavy and bulky for binoculars, and those that have appeared from less prestigious firms show substandard images. The Duovid is an "either-or" instrument. Switch from 8x to 12x (or 10x to 15x) for a close-up view. At 37 and 44 ounces, Duovids aren't light. But they're relatively compact and certainly more portable than spotting scopes. Optical quality is excellent – so too that of the Geovid, now with 42mm objectives as well as light-gobbling 56s. Geovids have been up-graded with the HD fluorite glass of Leica's Ultravid HD binoculars. These fluorite lenses enhance brightness and resolution and can reduce overall weight. All four Geovids (8x42, 10x42, 8x56 and 12x56) have alloy frames and deliver accurate range reads to 1,200 yards. The Ultravid has replaced the time-honored Trinovid binocular. The line includes 8x20 and 10x25 compact models, and full-size roof-prism glasses from 8x32 to 12x50. HD versions feature fluorite in every lens, proprietary AquaDura coating on exposed glass.

The big news at Leica this year is two new riflescopes, the company's first under its own label. The 2.5-10x42 and 3.5-14x42 feature 30mm tubes, rear-plane reticles and AquaDura lens coating to shed water. This hydrophobic compound (also featured on Leica binoculars) beads water and makes lens cleaning easy. At 15 and 17 ounces, these rifle-scopes are lightweight. They're also good-looking and have plenty of free tube for mounting. Four inches of eye relief make the new scopes a logical choice for hard-kicking rifles. (Leica-sportoptics.com.)

Nikon's ProStaff scope and T/C's new Venture rifle are bargain-priced but perform at higher levels.

AR-style rifles have become the rage. AR-specific scopes like this Bushnell have followed.

LEUPOLD

Last year Leupold quietly bought the Redfield name. It is now producing a new line of Redfield riflescopes and binoculars. Hard to believe! During my youth, the two firms were fierce competitors. They represented, with Bausch & Lomb, the best of American-made hunting optics. The new Redfields are made at Leupold's Beaverton, Oregon, facility. Starting at $160, they're priced to sell! Choose from 2-7x33, 3-9x40, 3-9x50 and 4-12x40 "Revolution" scopes, all with fully multi-coated optics and finger-adjustable dials. Leupold VP Andy York joined me on an elk hunt last fall, to initiate the Redfield line. Alas, neither of us killed an elk; but Andy assures me the Redfield name had nothing to do with our luck! I like the 3-9x40's classic profile, sharp images, generous eye relief. The satin finish complements any rifle. Three knurled rings on the eyepiece are signature Redfield – as distinctive as Leupold's gold ring. Subdued red logos grace the turret and objective bell. A 4-Plex reticle (remember, it's not a Duplex unless it's a Leupold!) and a range-finding "Accu-Range" reticle are both standard. The latter is a plex with a circle at the field's center. At 4x, I found the circle subtends one foot at 100 yards. There's a dot on the bottom wire for precise aim to around 400 yards with most cartridges. These affordable 1-inch scopes should appeal to any hunter. Mount them in low rings, like the one-piece, lightweight Talleys I prefer.

Though it's hard to trump the new Redfield series for value, shooters who insist on the best optics still have many choices at Leupold. Two years ago, Leupold introduced its top-end VX-7 scopes. The low-profile VX-7L, with a concave belly up front, followed (3.5-14x56 and 4.5-18x56, complementing the VX-7 in 1.5-6x24, 2.5-10x45 and 3.5-14x50). These sights have European-style eyepieces and "lift and lock" SpeedDial turret knobs. Xtended Twilight glass features scratch-resistant DiamondCoat 2 lens coating. The power ring is matched to a "Ballistic Aiming System" so you can tailor magnification and reticle to the target and distance. Nitrogen was replaced by argon/krypton gas to better prevent fogging.

The VX-7 is still top-of-the-line. But it's being crowded by the VX-3 series introduced last year to replace the Vari-X III. Nearly 40 models are listed. Cryogenically treated stainless adjustments move 1/4, 1/8 and 1/10 m.o.a. per click in standard, competition and target/varmint versions. An improved spring system ensures precise erector movement. The fast-focus eyepiece has a rubber ring. These features also appear on the new FX-3 6x42, 6x42 AO, 12x40 AO and two scopes designed for metallic silhouette shooting: a 25x40 AO and 30x40 AO. Choose from 18 reticle options for the VX-3 and FX-3 series, and five finishes for the 1-inch and 30mm 6061-T6 aircraft alloy tubes.

To accommodate the AR-10 and AR-15 platforms, there's a new Mark AR series: 1.5-4x20, 3-9x40, 4-12x40, 6-18x40. The Mark 4 tactical line includes an ER/T M1 4.5-14x50 sight with front-plane reticle. As in European scopes, this reticle stays in constant relationship to the target throughout the magnification span, so you can range a target at any power. The smallest of Leupold's scopes – FX II 2.5x20 Ultralight – remains one of my favorites. It sits tight to the receiver in extra-low rings, slides easily into scabbards, weighs just 7-1/2 ounces and has all the power you need for big game to 200 yards. For bolt rifles with longer reach, I prefer the 4x33 and 6x36 FX IIs.

Long shooting at small targets calls for the 6.5-20x40 Long Range VX-3 – and other sights in the LR stable. New pocket range-finders, the RX-1000 and RX-1000 TBS, boast better light transmission – three times what you get from some others, according to Leupold. In open country last fall, I downed an elk far away with a VX-3 4.5-14x. The extra magnification helped. (Leupold.com.)

MEOPTA

Having produced high-quality optics for 77 years, Meopta has announced a line of 1-inch rifle-scopes specifically for the American market. The MeoPro sights, in 3-9x42, 4-12x50 and 6-18x50, have handsome profiles and plenty of free tube, with compact eyepieces that allow for the forward mounting I prefer. The 6-18x50 features a turret-mounted parallax dial. "MB550 Ion Assisted" lens coatings sound as if they belong in a science-fiction movie; in truth, they're excellent coatings that boost light transmission to the highest levels.

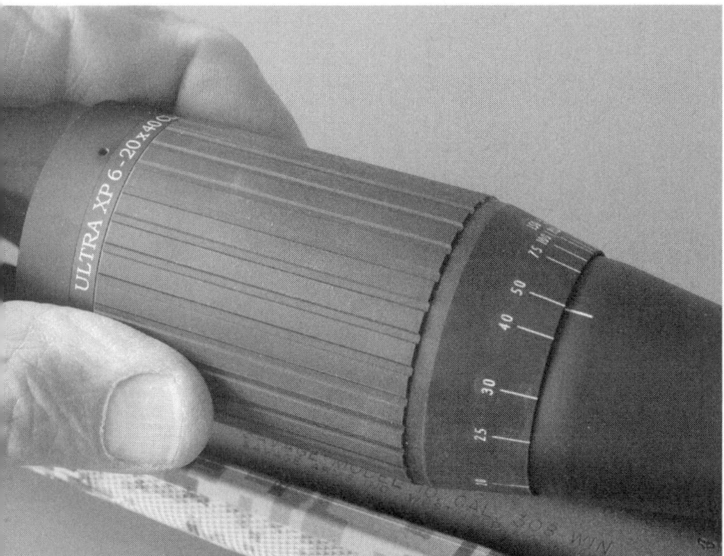

Author fitted this Clearidge 6-20x40 AO to a Savage M10 rifle in .308. Low cost. Good optics.

This T/C Venture wears a new Nitrex scope. ATK owns Nitrex, now under the Weaver label.

These scopes complement three new binoculars: 6.5x32, 8x42 and 10x42. That 6.5x, with its wide field and great depth of focus, is just what hunters need in cover – and has plenty of power for most hunting in the mountains. The Czech-made Meopta lines still include 30mm MeoStar variable rifle-scopes. The newest R1 series comprises seven scopes, from 1-4x22 to 4-16x44. There's also a 7x56 fixed-power. Four MeoStar binoculars include 20-ounce 8x32 and 10x32 glasses. Meostar S1 spotting scopes (75mm objective) come with standard or APO glass, straight or angled eyepiece, and 30x, 30x wide-angle or 20-60x zoom eyepiece. There's a collapsible 75mm scope, too. (Meopta.com.)

NIGHTFORCE

The name isn't descriptive. Nightforce has nothing to do with infrared imaging. This optics firm specializes in high-quality rifle-scopes for precision shooting. Since 1993, more world records in long-range Benchrest events have been set with Nightforce scopes than with any other. They're a top choice among 1,000-yard and 50-caliber marksmen. The 8-32x56 and 12-42x56 Precision Benchrest models have resettable dials with 1/8-minute clicks, as well as glass-etched illuminated reticles. Their four-times magnification range is shared by the NXS series, from the 3.5-15x50 and 3.5-15x56 NSX to the 5.5-22x50 and 5.5-22x56, the 8-32x56 and 12-42x56. Compact scopes for big game hunting recently joined that roster. The 1-4x24 and a 2.5-10x24 sights and, now, a 2.5-10x32 weigh just over a pound with the 30mm bronze alloy tubes common to Nightforce scopes. Like all but the Precision Benchrest models, the new 2.5-10x has a turret-mounted focus/parallax dial. (The 8-32x56 and 12-42x56 bench scopes wear front-sleeve parallax rings.) A new 3.5-15x50 F1 with first-plane reticle caters to hunters who want the reticle to stay in constant relationship to the target throughout the power range. Nightforce rifle-scopes endure the toughest tests in the industry. Each sight must remain leak- and fog-proof after submersion in 100 feet of water for 24 hours, freezing in a box at a minus 80° F, then heating within an hour to 250° F. Every scope gets pounded in a device that delivers 1,250 Gs, backward and forward. Lens coatings must pass mil-spec abrasion tests.

Nightforce now offers eleven illuminated reticle options. They're distinctive and appealing because they cover so little of the field. The firm also markets accessories for competitive and tactical shooters. Mil radian windage and elevation knobs deliver .1 mil per click. Long-range shooters can specify a turret with 1-minute elevation and half-minute windage graduations, for big changes in yardage with short dial movement. A "zero-stop" turret has an elevation dial that can be set to return to any of 400 detents in its adjustment range. One-piece steel scope bases have a recoil lug to ensure the mount doesn't move. Five heights of steel rings let you install the scope in just the right location. Unimount, machined from 7075-T6 alloy, has titanium crossbolts and a 20-minute taper for long shooting. Nightforce's Ballistic Program for Windows, and the abbreviated version for Pocket PCs, helps you determine bullet arc at distance. The company assembles its carriage-class optics at its plant in Idaho. (Nightforceoptics.com.)

NIKON

While Nikon's optics line has grown this year, the company's biggest news may be its ballistics program, which you can access free from Nikon's website. Plug in a cartridge, the bullet type and velocity to get down-range speed and energy data instantly. Specify zero range, and you'll see the bullet's arc. Or work backward to find the sight-in range that gives you longest point-blank distance. Nikon has programmed in dozens of popular centerfire rounds. Manipulations are so simple even a cave man can do them. How does Nikon benefit? "We get a chance to show you how our optics help you hit," explains C.J. Davis. "Beyond that, it's just good business to do what we can for the industry and for our customers." Having played a little with the program, I can endorse it. While I've no interest in anything that extends my time at a computer screen, Nikon's ballistics program threatens to do just that!

As for hardware, Nikon riflescopes now include an M-223 series for AR shooters. The 1-4x20, 2-8x32 and 3-12x42 can be used on other rifles, of course; but BDC reticles for the 2-8x and 3-12x M-223 are tailored for popular AR-15

Zeiss Varipoint scopes feature a lighted rear-plane reticle, controlled by a left-hand turret dial.

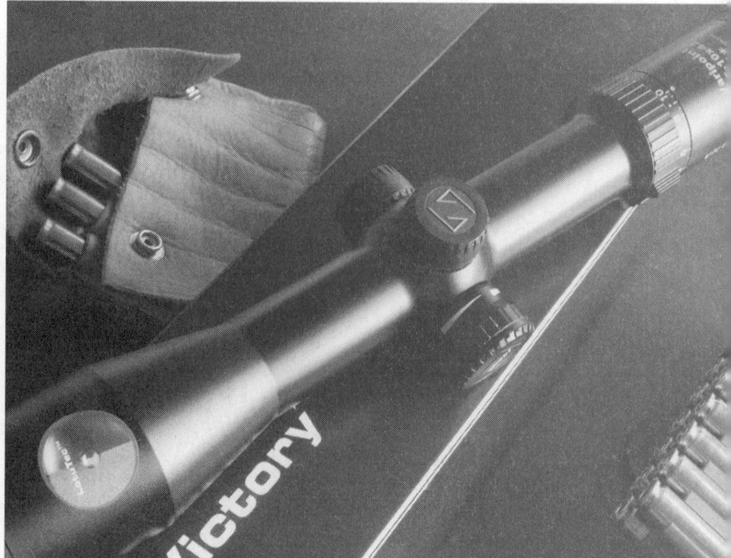

Among Author's favorite scopes is the Zeiss Victory 2.5-10x42, available with Varipoint reticle.

loads. The Monarch line remains Nikon's flagship, with its "African" and "Long Range" subsets. The 1-4x20 has a 1-inch tube; the 1.1-4x24, available with an illuminated reticle, is a 30mm sight. Both provide four inches of eye relief for fast aim and "recoil space." They feature German #4 reticles and half-minute click adjustments. The African scopes round out a line tilted to high-power optics by the 2008 debut of an 8-32x50ED SF with 1/8-minute adjustments. The 5-20x44 affords great reach in a sight of reasonable size. For all-around hunting, the 2.5-10x42 is hard to beat.

The 4-16x50SF and 2-8x32, recent additions, pretty much cover the rest of the field. I've found Monarch optics to equal the brightest in the industry. The "Gold" and "X" series have 30mm tubes. "Coyote Special" rifle-scopes introduced last year (a 3-9x40 and a 4.5-14x40) still sell well. They feature BDC reticles and camouflage finish. A reflection-fighting screen hides the front lens. The Omega 1.65-5x36 scope for muzzleloaders is also a hit, as is the 1.65-5x36 SlugHunter. Both have a generous five inches of eye relief and BDC reticles suited to the trajectories of the most common bullets. Omega's parallax setting is 100 yards, that of the SlugHunter 75. The value-oriented ProStaff stable has a new entry for 2010: this 4-12x40 is an excellent scope that gives you bright images, a useful power range and a svelte tube that complements trim rifles. Nikon also lists two new range-finders this year, one for archers, the other for riflemen. There are new 42mm models in the mid-priced Monarch ATB binocular line. Nikon's top-end EDG binoculars (7x42, 8x42, 10x42, 8x32, 10x32) with open-bridge design and a locking diopter are good glasses made better with ED lenses. Ditto the EDG Fieldscope, 85mm or 65mm. Its zoom eyepieces (16-48x and 20-60x) interchange with Nikon fixed-power eyepieces. (Nikonhunting.com.)

PENTAX

In 2010, Pentax is taking on the recession with a new series of value-priced rifle-scopes it calls the GameSeeker II line. There are six models, from the yeoman 3-9x40 to a 4-16x50 and a light-grabbing 2.5-10x56. They feature one-piece, 1-inch alloy tubes, fully multi-coated optics and finger-adjustable windage and elevation dials. Choose from a standard plex reticle or the Precision Plex BDC. GameSeeker scopes are priced from around $100, which should make them popular. Last year, Pentax added a 3-15x50 GameSeeker to that stable. Five-times magnification offers more versatility than you'll likely need for big game. I chose instead a 3-9x32 for a moose hunt. That 12-ounce sight was perfect for my Ruger carbine in .300 RCM. Its high level of resolution helped me shoot a bull when I picked out a sliver of antler deep in shadowed timber. You can choose from eight 1-inch variable GameSeekers, plus 4x32 and 6x42 fixed-power sights. The 30mm Lightseeker 30 series comprises 3-10x40, 4-16x50, 6-24x50 and 8.5-32x50 scopes. Pioneer II models, 3-9x40 and 4.5-14x42, feature 1-inch tubes, fully multi-coated optics. Among Pentax spotting scopes, the compact PF-63 Zoom with fixed 20-50x eyepiece is particularly well suited to hunting, while the PF-80ED and PF-100ED excel when weight doesn't matter. Interchangeable eyepieces include 32x, 46x and 20-60x options for the 37-ounce PF-65ED, which also accepts a Pentax PF-CA35 camera adapter for 35mm SLRs.

Pentax binoculars include a7x50 Marine model with built-in compass on a liquid bearing for fast dampening. Waterproof, with twist-up eye-cups and a click-stop diopter ring, the rubber-armored 7x50 has all the best features of the Pentax roof-prism DCF roof prism binoculars. These come in 8x, 10x and 12.5x, with 32mm to 50mm objectives, with phase-corrected prisms in alloy and polycarbonate shells. A Porro prism PCF line includes 8x40, 10x50, 12x50 and 20x60 binoculars. Among my favorite hunting glasses is an unlikely choice: the Pentax 9x28 BCF LV. Despite its modest exit pupil, this binocular gives me bright images, and at 13 ounces it's eminently portable. I like the twist-out eyecups, click-stop diopter. The surface is easy to grip. Other good choices for the trail: 8x36 and 10x36 DCF NV roof-prism glasses. (Pentaxsportoptics.com.)

SCHMIDT & BENDER

Long revered for excellence in rifle-scopes, Schmidt & Bender has hewed mainly to the European traditions of big tubes and first-plane reticles. Last year S&B announced its first 1-inch riflescope for the American market. The 16-ounce 2.5-10x40 Summit has a rear-plane

Kimber's 84L delivered excellent groups with a Leupold VX-3. A handsome outfit too!

Leupold has re-introduced the Redfield brand, with binoculars and rifle-scopes built in Oregon.

reticle. Optically, it seems to me the equivalent of higher-priced Classic and top-end Zenith lines. It has the right power range and profile for at least 99 percent of all big game hunting! Recent changes in S&B administration have not shifted its main focus. A small company by most standards, S&B still caters to people who want the very best in optical sights. Its roots lie in the hunting field, but it has brought innovation to the tactical table too. Three years ago a S&B 3-12x was adopted by the U.S. Marine Corps for its 30- and 50-caliber sniper rifles. Its 34mm Police/Marksman scopes rank among the most sophisticated LE sights around. Lighted mil dot reticles, as on S&B's 4-16x42 P/M II, come with 11-setting turret-mounted rheostats. The automatic shutoff saves battery while the previous setting automatically engages when you hit the illumination switch again. A side-mounted parallax adjustment hides the battery cage. Windows on windage and elevation knobs show you where the reticle is in its adjustment range. Flash-dot reticles incorporate a beam-splitter to illuminate a dead-center dot, which vanishes at a touch if you desire just the black reticle. The Police/Marksman line now comprises 17 scopes with 30mm and 34mm tubes. The latest is a 5-25x56 PM II with locking turrets.

For hunting, I've come to favor S&B's 3-12x42 Classic, a versatile, durable, good-looking 30mm scope that delivers brilliant, tack-sharp images. I like the 6x42 and 10x42 fixed-power Classics as well, available with 1-inch and 30mm chassis. The Zenith series comprises four 30mm variables: 1.1-4x24, 1.5-6x42 (a great hunting sight!), 2.5-10x56, 3-12x50. They wear the P/M's "Posicon" windage and elevation dials. (Schmidt-bender.de or scopes@cyberportal.net [the website of its U.S. importer].)

SHEPHERD

The advantages and disadvantages of front- and rear-plane scope reticles are clear. A front-plane reticle grows in apparent size as you dial up the power but stays the same size in relation to the target. It does not move out of the optical center of the scope, and as a range-finding device it gives you the same picture no matter what the magnification. But at long range, where targets appear small and you want precise aim, the reticle can obscure the aiming point. Up close, when you power down for quick shots in thickets, the reticle shrinks, becoming hard to see quickly. A second-plane reticle stays the same apparent size throughout the power range, so it won't hide distant targets at high magnification, and it won't vanish when you turn down the power to find game quickly up close. But because its dimensional relationship to the target changes with every change in magnification, range-finding becomes a task best limited to one power setting.

Shepherd scopes offer both reticles. You get an aiming reticle that doesn't change size and a range-finding reticle that varies in dimension with power changes. Superimposed, the front- and rear-plane reticles appear as one. The former comprises a stack of circles of decreasing diameter. To determine yardage, match a deer-size (18-inch) target with one of the circles. Correct holdover is factored in because the circles are placed to compensate for bullet drop. A trio of range-finding reticles suit the trajectories of popular cartridges. Vertical and horizontal scales are marked in minutes of angle so you can compensate for wind. The 6-18x M556 Shepherd is specially designed for AR-style rifles. I've used these sights; they work as advertised. An amigo has a 6-18x that he says "is really unfair to coyotes." (Shepherdscopes.com.)

SIGHTRON

Magnesium is 33 percent lighter than aluminum, so hunters should appreciate Sightron's SIIIMS line of binoculars. New for 2010, it includes 8x32, 10x32, 8x42 and 10x42 roof-prism, magnesium-frame glasses scaling 20 to 25 ounces. The 8x32 is my choice. All feature phase-corrected, multi-coated optics and twist-up eye-cups. The company is also listing a new ESD – Electronic Sighting Device. It's a 33mm red dot sight with a 5-minute dot. Choose from eight intensity levels. Recession got you? Sightron's S1 scopes are bargain-priced but feature multi-coated front and rear lenses. Pick from a broad selection of reticles, finishes and power ranges. SII and SIII series are up-grades. Like its competition, Sightron is now offering a range-compensating reticle with dots spaced out on the lower wire. Several high-power variables have joined the Sightron family this

Author bears down offhand with a Weatherby Vanguard rifle and Bushnell Elite 6500 scope.

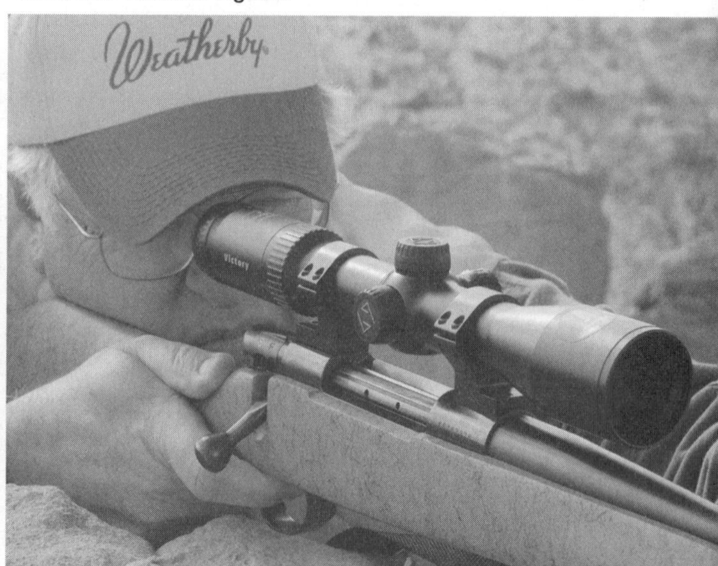

Dave Anderson's Weatherby rifle sports a Zeiss Victory scope. Some now feature FL glass.

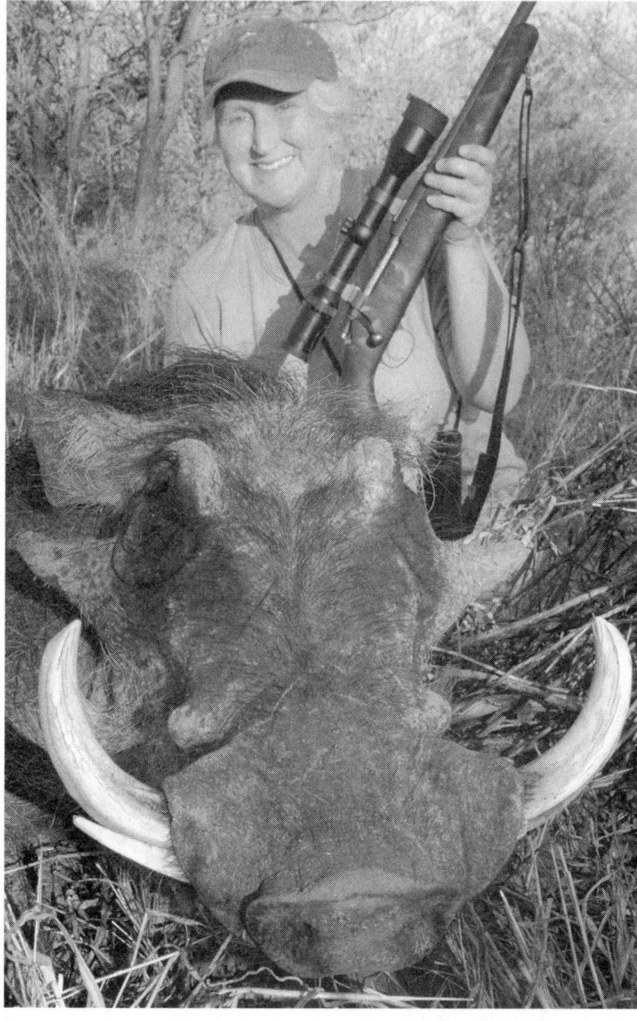
A Swarovski variable on an Ultra Light rifle helped Dori Riggs collect this fine warthog.

year. A new SIII Tactical Fixed Power line comprises 10x, 16x, and 20x scopes with 42mm objectives, 30mm tubes.

All told, the 2010 catalog lists more than 50 scopes in SI, SII and SIII series. Long Range models feature 30mm tubes, turret-mounted parallax dials and reticles that include a mil dot and an illuminated German #4A. Target knobs are tall for easy access. From the 3.5-10x44 to the 8-32x56, these scopes feature fully multi-coated optics in one-piece tubes, with resettable ExacTrack windage and elevation adjustments and a fast-focus eyepiece. External lenses wear "Zact-7," a seven-layer coating to reduce light loss. A hydrophobic wash disperses raindrops. Eye relief approaches four inches. An SII 1.25-5x20 Dangerous Game sight with over six inches of clear tube has replaced the 2.5x20 that has served me well on hard-kicking rifles. High-power variables and 36x benchrest sights have front-end parallax sleeves. I like the dot reticle in these scopes, also available on the 5-20x42. Sightron's Hunter Holdover reticle for hunting scopes incorporates a couple of simple hash marks on the lower wire. Specify it on 3-9x42, 3-12x42 and 45.5-14x42 SIIs, and on the 3-9x40 SI. In my experience, Sightron scopes deliver great value for the dollar. (Sightron.com.)

STEINER

Aggressively pursuing hunting markets after decades of service to military units the world over, Steiner introduced last year the 21-ounce Wildlife Pro 8x30 binocular, its first center-focus Porro-prism glass in twenty years. For 2010, the firm has announced a laser range-finding binocular. The 10x50 LRF can reportedly range reflective targets to 1,600 yards, and with 1-yard accuracy to 500. The digital display comes up quickly; a scan mode helps you range moving targets. The LRF has HD glass and weighs 46 ounces. Also new from Steiner: 8x56 and 10x56 Predator C5 binoculars. While at 40 and 43 ounces these aren't as portable as smaller Steiners, they give you brilliant images in poor light. The 7mm and nearly-6mm exit pupils are all the average eye can use in the deepest shadow. I find these glasses very bright. The newest center-focus versions wear a thin rubber armor for a slim profile. Still the flagship of Steiner's line is the Peregrine XP. This center-focus, open-bridge binocular

Zeiss introduced its range-finding binocular a couple of years ago. It's a marvelous instrument!

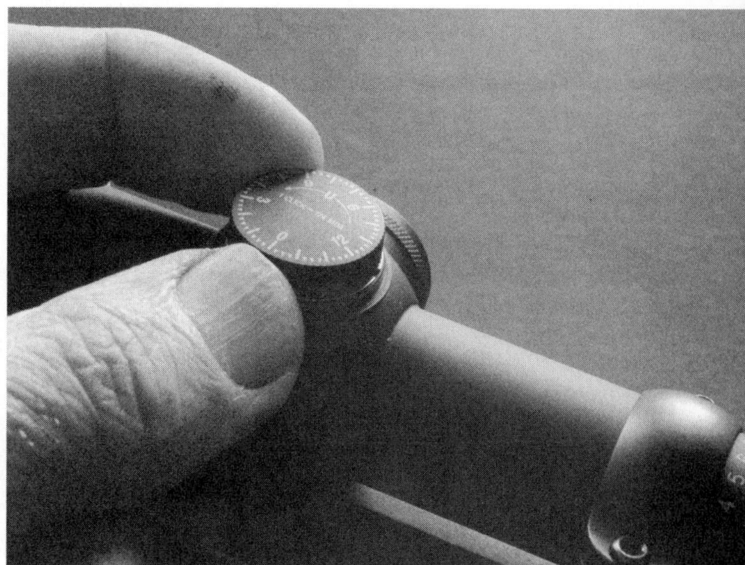
Modestly priced, new Redfield rifle-scopes have finger-friendly dials, very good optics.

focuses as close as 6-1/2 feet. The large 30mm eyepieces have twist-up eyecups and flexible wings that fold back to prevent external fogging from face moisture. Outside lens surfaces feature a hydrophobic "NANO Protection." It beads water so you can see clearly in rain and snow. The Peregrine XP (8x44 and 10x44) is waterproof and lightweight, with a rugged magnesium frame. It comes with neoprene hood and a clever Click-Loc strap. The Peregrine XP has earned the NRA's coveted Golden Bullseye Award for excellence. (Steiner-binoculars.com.)

SWAROVSKI

After a decade of vigorous new-product development, Swarovski is tweaking its EL binocular. The Traveler 8x32 and 10x32 are the company's best hunting binos in casual dress. I like the open-hinge design. Swarovski has expanded its Z6 rifle-scope line to include 2.5-15x56 and 2.5-15x44 sights. They afford you the lowest practical magnification plus enough power to pester prairie dogs in the off-season. I've used the 1.7-10x42 afield, have only good things to say about it. The newest Z6 is a 2.5-15x56. As with other 30mm Z6 models, an illuminated reticle is an option. The switch, atop the eyepiece, has an automatic shutoff and two memory locations, one for daytime and one for night use. Turn the switch and the reticle delivers illumination for prevailing conditions. The 1-6x24 Z6 has the broadest power range of any "dangerous game" sight. At 4-3/4 inches, its eye relief is most generous.

Author killed this leopard in tall grass at 12 yards. Credit a Leupold 1.5-5x20 for the quick shot!

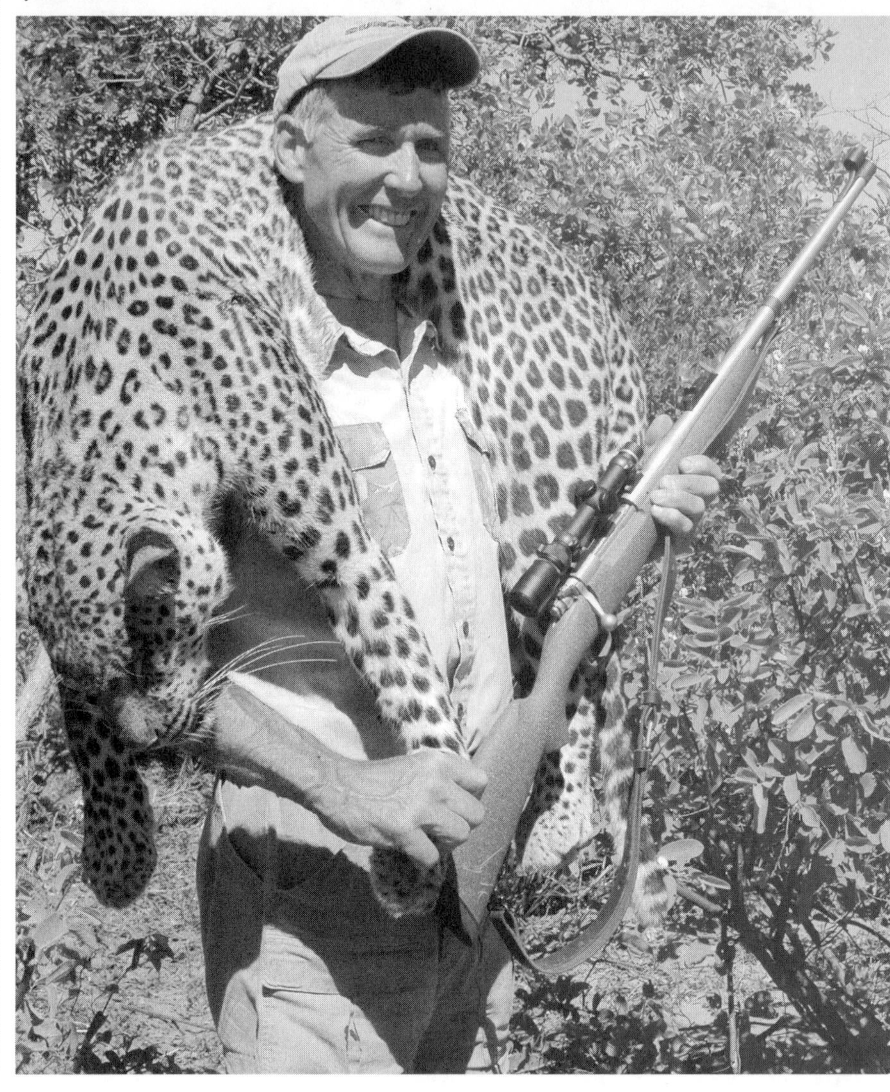

Nightforce specializes in high-power riflescopes. But hunting models have recently appeared.

Bright glass (here in a Leupold) can salvage a hunt when your only shot comes in dim light!

Swarovski's Z5 rifle-scopes offer five-times magnification in one-inch tubes. A 3-15x42 may be the perfect scope for shooters who want the greatest versatility in a relatively lightweight scope. Swarovski borrowed from subsidiary Kahles to produce a Ballistic Turret capable of storing several zero settings. You set those zeroes with ballistics tables or by live firing. Change load and zero; then return to your original in a wink. The Ballistic Turret is an option on selected Swarovski scopes. A simpler way to hit long-range targets is with the BR reticle. Its ladder-type bottom wire has 10 hash-marks. BR is available in three AV models and 1.7-10x42 and 2-12x50 Z6 sights. (Swarovskioptik.com.)

TRIJICON

The ACOG (Advanced Combat Optical Gunsight) established Trijicon as a leading innovator in rifle optics. More than half a million have been sold. But the ACOG's application is primarily military. The AccuPoint is Trijicon's flagship hunting optic, a scope with two sources of reticle illumination. The fiber optic window in the ocular bell, and tritium in the reticle itself, yield a bright aiming point without batteries. An adjustable cover lets you trim light from the fiber optic coil and tune reticle brightness. Last year AccuPoint came up with plex and crosswire-and-dot reticles, as alternatives to its original super-fast delta. Lost in the lumination hype, however, has been the quality of Trijicon optics. "It's definitely top-drawer," Trijicon's Andrew Chilkewicz reminds me. I agree. Trijicon's fully multi-coated glass gives you brilliant, razor-edged images. And if you've shied from lighted reticles, this is the brand to try first. Choose a delta in amber, red or green, a dot in amber or green. Combine it with a black crosswire if you like. I prefer the crosswire and amber dot. My pick among Trijicon scopes is the 3-9x40. After decades in the field, it's still in my view the most practical for all-around big game hunting. But you can also opt for a 1.25-4x24 or a 2.5-10x56 with 1-inch tube. A 1-4x24 and a powerful 5-20x50 have 30mm tubes. For fast shooting in 'pole thickets, Trijicon markets reflex sights with lighted dots of various sizes. The RMR (Ruggedized Miniature Reflex) can be had with a light-emitting diode that automatically adjusts to incident light. It has an alloy housing, the Trijicon RedDot sight a nylon-polymer frame. Either can be paired with the ACOG. A battery-free RMR uses tritium and fiber optics only; the electronic version is powered by a 17,000-hour lithium battery. (Trijicon.com.)

TRUGLO

Luminescent shotgun beads and rifle-sight inserts, with tritium and fiber-optic elements, brought TruGlo early success. Now the firm offers red dot sights and rifle-scopes too. Waterproof and compatible with any Weaver-style mount, the red dot sights come in reflex (open) configuration or 1-inch and 30mm and 40mm tubes. Dual-Color (red and green) Multi-Reticles come standard in some models. All versions of the tube sight have unlimited eye relief, multi-coated lenses, click-stop windage/elevation adjustments, an 11-level rheostat to control reticle brightness. Reflex red dot sights weigh as little as 2 ounces, carry a 4-minute dot with manual and light-sensitive automatic brightness modes. TruGlo markets several series of rifle-scopes, topped by the Maxus XLE in 1.5-6x44, 3-9x44 and 3.5-10x50. The Infinity 4-16x44 and 6-24x44 have adjustable objectives. To make long-range hits easier across a variety of loads, each comes with three replaceable BDC elevation knobs. Tru-Brite Xtreme Illuminated rifle-scopes feature dual-color plex and range-finding reticles. Pick a 3-9x44, 3-12x44 or 4-16x50. Muzzleloader versions are available. The 4x32 Compact scope for rimfires and shotguns, 4x32 and 1.5-5x32 illuminated sights for crossbows round out TruGlo's stable of 1-inch scopes. TruGlo line of illuminated iron sights includes a fiber optic AR-15 gas block front sight with protected green bead. (Truglo.com.)

VORTEX

New Razor scopes from Vortex reflect the growing interest in tactical sights. The 1.4-4x24 has a 30mm tube, the 5-20x50 a 35mm tube. Both scopes deliver brilliant images from extra-low-dispersion lenses. Lighted, etched-glass reticles lie in the first focal plane. A zero-stop mechanism in the elevation dial prevents it from spinning past sight-in setting, for fast return to zero. Vortex matches turrets with reticles; and you can specify mil-dot graduations,

Author banged this gong repeatedly from 540 yards with a Leupold/Greybull scope on a .243.

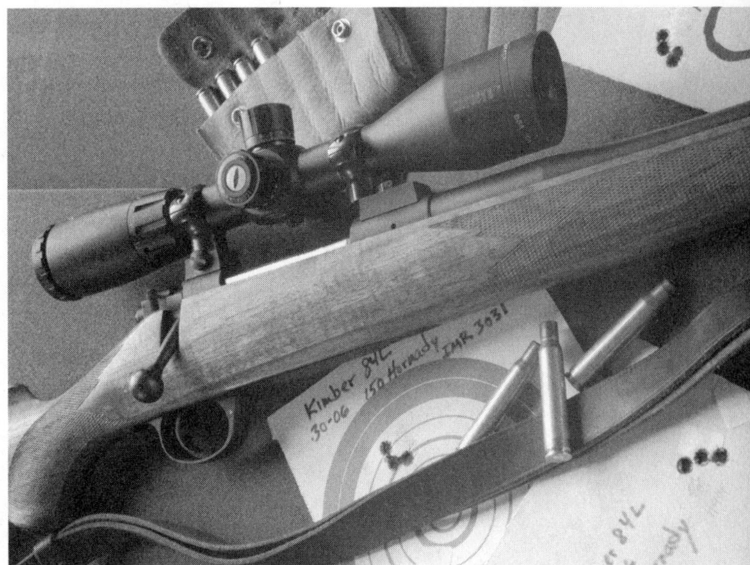

A BSA Catseye scope on a Kimber 84L in .30-06 produced these groups (and filled a deer tag).

or minutes of angle. More practical for most hunters are Vortex Vipers. Also available in tactical guise, they come in six versions and five power ranges. I prefer the 3-9x40 (14 ounces) and 4-12x40 (17 ounces). Choose from six reticles, including dot, BDC and mil-dot. The Viper line features both 30mm and 1-inch tubes. More affordable Vortex Diamondbacks have 1-inch tubes only, as do entry-level Crossfires. All boast fully multi-coated optics.

The widest selection in the Vortex family comes under the Crossfire banner. That line includes 2-7x32 and 4x32 sights for rimfires, a 2x20 handgun scope and a 3x32 for crossbows. As with the Vipers, you get tall target knobs (and 30mm tubes) on the most powerful scopes. Specify a mil dot or illuminated mil dot reticle on the 6-24x50 AO. Vortex also lists a red dot sight, the Strikefire, with fully multi-coated lenses. Choose red or green dot to suit conditions. The sight has a 30mm tube and weighs 7.2 ounces. It has unlimited eye relief, comes with a 2x optical doubler. The new, shorter Sparc red dot sight weighs just 5 ounces and features a one-piece, multi-height base, a 2-minute dot. Like the Strikefire, it is parallax-free beyond 50 yards and comes with a doubler. Fully multi-coated optics of course. In spotting scopes Vortex catalogs two Nomad models, both with your choice of straight or angled eyepiece. The 20-60x80 and the budget-priced 20-60x60 accept adapters for most pocket-size digital cameras. At the top end, there's the Razor HD spotting scope with apochromatic lenses and an 85mm objective. It weighs 66 ounces with an angled 20-60x eyepiece. The die-cast magnesium alloy body is argon-gas purged. It has coarse and fine focusing wheels. (Vortex.com.)

WEAVER

Eight decades after Bill Weaver's 330 led a trend away from iron sights, Weaver is re-introducing the 330's progeny, the iconic steel-tube K4. More than any other scope, the K4 confirmed the value of optical sights for my generation of hunters. The new version has a Dual-X reticle that doesn't move off-center in the field when you adjust windage and elevation! While the K4 may be all you need on that '06, Weaver offers more for 2010. The Super Slam series now includes a 1-5x24 Dangerous Game sight with heavy Dual-X that should excel in thickets. Besides the Grand Slam, Classic V, Classic K and T-series scopes, there's now a Buck Commander line, with 2.5-10x42, 3-12x50 and 4-16x42 models. Prices start at just $280, retail. For close shooting, Weaver offers a red/green dot sight with five brightness settings. It has a 30mm tube, an integral Weaver-style base. Tactical sights will probably proliferate, as the shooting public is not that of Bill Weaver's day. Thus, the firm announced in 2009 a 4-20x50 Tactical scope with 30mm tube, front-plane mil dot reticle and side-focus parallax dial. But you can still buy a K-series fixed-power hunting scope (one of the most-overlooked bargains in rifle sights). Among target scopes, I like the T-24. It offers a 1/2-minute or 1/8-minute dot reticle. Target adjustments on dual-spring supports ensure repeatable changes.

New Classic binoculars have been added to Weaver's line this year: 8x32, 8x36 (my pick), 8x42, 10x42. ATK, parent company to several shooting-industry brands, counts Nitrex as well as Weaver in its family. Early in 2010, Nitrex became part of the Weaver fold, although the lines remain separate. Nitrex TR One scopes (similar to Weaver's Grand Slam) are joined by TR Two (Super Slam) scopes with additional reticles: glass-etched EBX (ballistic), dot and illuminated. These sights boast five-times magnification – 2.5-10x42 to 4-20x50 – and turret parallax dials. Pull-up, resettable windage and elevation knobs need no caps. The TR One series includes a new 4-15x50 AO scope. (Weaveroptics.com, Nitrexoptics.com.)

ZEISS

Brisk sales of Conquest rifle-scopes several years after their introduction confirm their appeal to shooters keen for value. I like the 4x32; if you must have a variable, the 2-8x32 and 3-9x40 make sense. The 4.5-14x44 milks the reach of hot-rod cartridges but looks good on lightweight hunting rifles. Like the 6.5-20x50, it features a turret-mounted parallax dial. By the way, Zeiss has just cut the list price on its 3-9x40 Conquest from $499 to $399! While there's little new in the Conquest stable for 2010, the top-rung Victory series boasts an up-grade of the 6-24x72, a 34mm scope

The finger-friendly dial on Author's BSA Catseye scope delivers predictable, repeatable clicks.

The new Redfield 3-9x40 seems a great match for this Marlin 1895 rifle in .338 Marlin Express.

Author shot this elk with a Magnum Research rifle in 6.5 Creedmoor, Leupold/GreyBull sight.

introduced in 2005 but now with quarter-minute clicks and FL glass. Two new Victory scopes also incorporate fluorite lenses. I used a 6-24x56 recently, on a super-accurate Blaser R8 in .300 Winchester. At 600 yards, prone, it was no trick to reduce a plastic pail to splinters. The 4-16x50 is better suited to hunting rifles, and should be on your short list if you expect long shooting. But for all-around hunting there's no better sight than the Victory 2.5-10x42. With four other Victory scopes, it's available with Varipoint, an illuminated dot in the second focal plane complementing a black first-plane reticle. So the main reticle stays in constant relationship to the target (for easy ranging), while the dot subtends a tiny area even at high power. A left-side turret knob controls dot brightness on the 1.1-4x24 Victory. The 2.5-10x42T*, 2.5-10x50T*, 3-12x56T* feature automatic brightness control.

Zeiss has just introduced a Compact Point red dot sight. Its 3.5-minute dot has five brightness levels. Weight: less than 3 ounces with two 3V lithium batteries. The 8x45 and 10x45 T* RF binoculars introduced last year have proven themselves afield, with a laser range-finding unit that requires no "third eye" emitter but delivers 1,300-yard range on reflective targets. This unit is fast – you get a read in about a second – and the LED self-compensates for brightness. The binocular itself has peerless optics, with a rain-repellent LotuTec coating on ocular and objective lenses. You can program the RF with computer data to get holdover for six standard bullet trajectories. Zeiss still sets the bar for laser-ranging scopes, too, with its 3-12x56 Diarange. The Zeiss PhotoScope is a 20-60x80 DiaScope spotting scope with a 7-megapixel digital camera built in. The 15-45x power range affords you the equivalent of a 600-1800mm zoom in a 35mm camera – plus a 68-degree field at 15x, which Zeiss claims is 40 percent wider than normal. The camera uses a 7.4-volt lithium ion battery and SD card to deliver images in standard file formats. PhotoScope 85T* FL weighs 6-1/2 pounds. And yes, it does produce images that qualify for full-page prints! (Zeiss.com/sports.)

Author found this BSA scope a worthy hunting sight, despite its low price. Rifle: a Kimber 84L.

S&W's big Model 58 in .41 Magnum still makes for quite a handful.

S&W Model 58

BY DAN SHIDELER

I have just received a letter from Local #417 of the Brotherhood of Independent Gunwriters & Septic Tank Pumpers (BIGSTP) informing me that my membership in BIGSTP would be terminated if I didn't write something – anything – about the Smith & Wesson Model 58 in .41 Magnum.

You see, every gunwriter is obligated to write something about the Model 58. It's a rite of passage, like kissing your first girl or mixing your first dry martini. But what can I possibly say about the Model 58 that hasn't been said before?

By now, of course, everyone knows the story of the Model 58: how it was introduced in 1964 as the perfect cop gun, the revolver that would pacify the nastiest felon like a 20-lb. sledgehammer coming down on a cockroach. Model 58s are fairly scarce these days, so you might assume that the big revolver fell somewhat short of its stated goal. And you'd be right.

The Model 58 was born during a period of civil unrest, when American police were first realizing that their fuddy-duddy old .38 Special revolvers just weren't cutting it anymore. Even the .357 Magnum was criticized as being a little on the iffy side. Back then, in a time when a nutcase from the Symbionese Liberation

Army (remember them?) might be hiding behind every shrub, it was only natural to want a sidearm that had some oomph.

The logic behind the N-framed, fixed-sight Model 58 and its .41 Magnum chambering was that something in between the "underpowered" .357 Magnum and the overpowered .44 Magnum was needed for police use. Personally, I don't consider the .357 underpowered. When I worked in the funeral industry 25 years ago, I had occasion to offer my professional services to two ex-criminals (one a rapist, the other a bank robber who made it to the bottom of the FBI's "Ten Most Wanted" list) who were on the receiving end of a couple of .357 loads. At the time I met them, neither of these two gentlemen was in any condition to complain about how underpowered the .357 Magnum was.

I do agree, however, that the .44 Magnum is probably overpowered for police use. I've seen a .44 shoot lengthways through a deer, so I imagine that overpenetration could be a bit of a problem unless you could line up four or five bad guys in a row before squeezing off a shot. But rather than load up the .357 or load down the .44, Remington and Smith & Wesson came up with an in-betweener, the .41 Remington Magnum. Surely it would become the last word in law enforcement ordnance if it were chambered in the right gun.

As far as S&W was concerned, the right gun was the Model 58. In many ways it was a throwback to the big .44 and .45 Hand Ejectors of the early twentieth century: a massive, service-gripped N-frame with a fixed blade front sight and a non-adjustable rear sight milled into the topstrap. Why monkey with adjustable sights on a gun intended for up-close use? And to top it off, the Model 58 would feature a four-inch barrel that could be drawn from a holster in the blink of an eye.

Short barrels on magnums look good on paper, but only on paper. I've done a lot of shooting with S&W N-frames, and the sight of a four-inch barrel on one still gives me the willies. (My hair is now permanently parted on the right side, thanks to a four-inch Model 29 .44 Magnum that I persisted in shooting one afternoon a few years ago.)

S&W and Remington anticipated that recoil and blast might be a problem with the Model 58, so they cooperatively introduced two .41 Magnum loads for the big new revolver: a 210-gr. lead-bullet version with a muzzle velocity of around 1150 fps and a 210-gr. jacketed version at around 1400 fps. As might be expected, however, sooner or later the high-velocity jacketed load intended for the Model 58's longer-barreled, adjustable-sighted counterpart, the Model 57, ended up in the Model 58. When police tried the new Model 58 with full-house jacketed loads, the noise and muzzle blast were so ferocious that even old-school troopers found it a bit much. Nevertheless, the Model 58 hung on in S&W's lineup until 1977, when the semi-auto revolution finally deep-sixed it for good. Total production was around 23,000 units, or about 1750 units per year on average.

So what's it like to shoot a Model 58? Actually, it's not that different from shooting a Model 29 in .44 Magnum. Recoil and blast are perceptibly less, but not enough to make much of a difference. Target reacquisition is a tad bit faster, perhaps, but when you touch one off, there's no doubt that you're shooting a big, hairy revolver. I'd feel well-turned-out with a Model 58 on my hip this deer season, which is exactly where mine will be come next November.

The Model 58's fixed sights aren't as much of a handicap as you might think. With that four-inch barrel, the effect of barrel time in raising point of impact is negligible, so lead loads and jacketed loads all shoot pretty much to the same point of aim. I wouldn't compete in a tournament with a Model 58, perhaps, but I'm sure that anything I want to shoot with a Model 58 within 30 yards or so is going to end up with a .41-caliber hole in it.

Part of the appeal of the Model 58 is that it was made during a period when S&W's quality was absolutely second to none. Bluing was as deep and glossy as a freshly-opened can of black enamel paint; cylinder chambers were counterbored; barrels were pinned into place. Now that my hair is gray, I suppose I qualify as an old-timer. As such, I can say without fear of reprisal that I prefer Smith & Wesson's older, forged-and-milled revolvers of the '60s and '70s to today's MIM or stainless-steel ones. There's no doubt that S&W today makes the finest double-action revolvers generally available, but a nice Bangor Punta-era S&W really takes my breath away.

Today, Model 58s are among the most collectible S&W N-frames, with Excellent-condition examples starting for around $600 and peaking at over a grand for boxed examples. Heady stuff! But then again, all N-frames are escalating rapidly in value. Shockingly so, in my opinion. Even the humblest of the N-frames, the matte-finished Model 28 Highway Patrolman -- which sold for as little as $250 only a year or two ago -- now goes for upwards of $500 for a nice one. It's worth it, too, in my opinion.

In general, .41 Magnums do pretty well on the used-gun market -- if you can find the right buyer. Marlin's early Model 1894 -- the 1980s version, not the 1890s version -- chambered in .41 is eagerly sought-after by Marlin fans, and Ruger's Redhawk in .41 Magnum is increasingly collectible, too. I've seen some examples sell for upwards of $600, which doesn't really surprise me because there's something appealing about such a massively over-engineered revolver with a .41-caliber hole in its barrel. (The .357 Redhawk is a nice find, too.)

What does the future hold for the .41 Magnum? Not much, I think. Ammunition will no doubt continue to be manufactured for the foreseeable future -- too many guns out there for it to be dropped -- but I wouldn't look for too many more new loads. After all, there really isn't anything the .41 can do that the .44 can't do even better. Even if you somehow whipped up a 275-grain super-hot load for the .41, it would still play second-fiddle to the 300-grain .44 Magnum load, and recoil and blast would be almost as fierce.

As for police use, the .41 Magnum is as dead as Jacob Marley. Modern .40 S&W loads approximate the original .41 Magnum police load, and they're available in super-capacity autopistols as well. I don't know of any active-duty police officers who carry revolvers nowadays, no matter how powerful they are. As for sporting use, I can't imagine why you would take a .41 Magnum deer-hunting if you had a .44 Magnum close at hand.

Unless you prefer the unusual, of course. Unless you like the off-beat. Unless you're exactly like me.

AIRGUNS

BY **TOM CACECI**

The 2010 SHOT Show had many new products of interest to anyone using an airgun. Modern airguns are serious, high-performance tools for target competition or sport hunting. New technology and production methods have created air weapons that are affordable, easy to use, and typically free from most of the restrictions imposed on firearms. At the same time, they're powerful enough to use effectively in pest control operations or serious small game hunting. What's out there today isn't a "kid's BB gun" any more.

AIR ARMS from the United Kingdom has introduced the EV-Z MARK IV rifle for target work. It has an adjustable palm rest and a poplar stock that can be finished in a wide variety of colors to suit the taste of the buyer.

BEEMAN, another UK manufacturer no stranger to US airgunners, has introduced the dual-caliber ELITE X-2 rifle with interchangeable barrels.

BELTFED is a brand-new name in the airgun world, with a product that is unique. Everyone loves full-auto fire: while BB guns and softair guns simulate it, this company's .22 is a CO^2-powered pellet gun, firing actual pellets at the astonishing rate of 12 shots per second or 720 rounds per minute. As the name implies, it's belt fed: the belt is enclosed in a drum-type housing that gives the Beltfed the look of a "Tommy Gun" to go with its performance. Power is provided by a large CO^2 reservoir that connects to a tank adapter. Magazine capacity is up to 125 rounds, and velocities are comparable to other CO^2 powered guns. No word yet on when this product will be on dealer shelves.

BSA is one of the best-known brands of airguns in the world, usually associated with pump-pneumatic and break-barrel rifles, but they have introduced a new line of PCP (precharged pneumatic) rifles to the American market this year. The Ultra Tactical

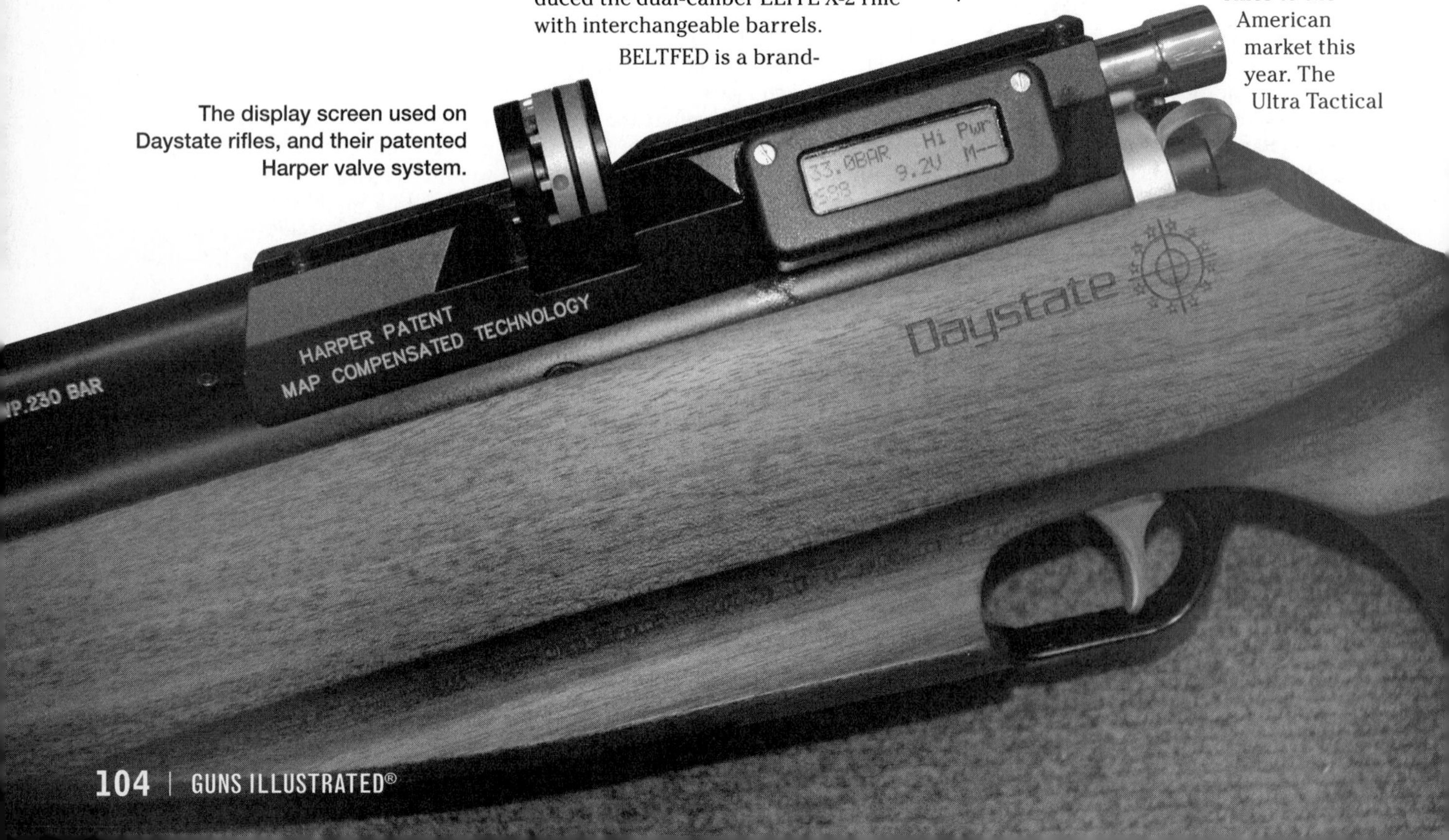

The display screen used on Daystate rifles, and their patented Harper valve system.

lowest priced PCP rifles on the market, no doubt making it even more attractive to new airgun enthusiasts.

CROSMAN, America's most famous airgun manufacturer, displayed many new products, and an entirely new technology for break-barrel guns, the Nitro Piston Magnum power plant in their Trail NPXL series rifles, available in .177, .22, and now .25 calibers. The Nitro Piston mechanism replaces the conventional spring of the typical break-barrel gun. The heart of the Nitro Piston is a gas-filled cylinder, which offers numerous advantages compared to a spring. Crosman claims it is 70% quieter than a conventional spring, requires less cocking force to achieve the same level of power, and most importantly, can be cocked well in advance of shooting. In a spring-powered rifle, cocking too far in advance of the shot will result in the spring taking a "set" and the result is

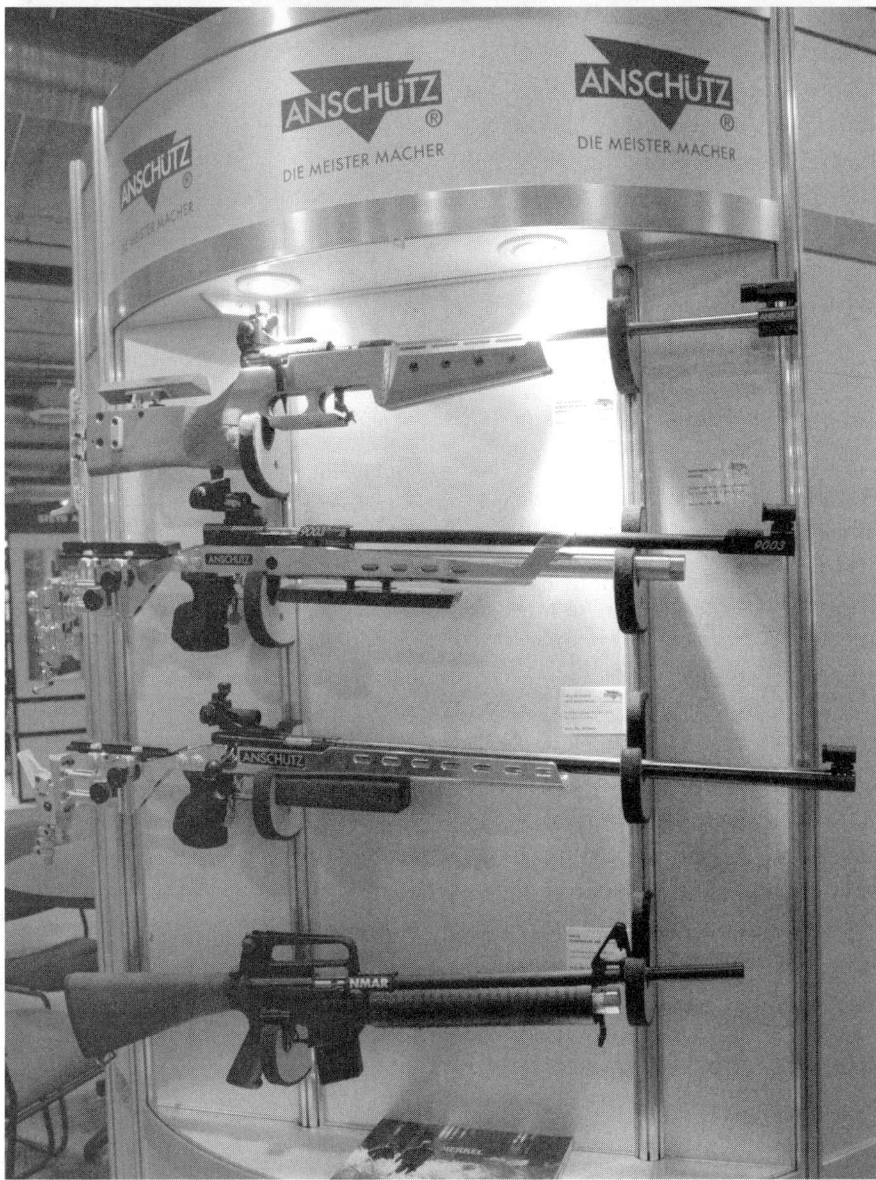

(top) Alan George, General manager of Air Arms, holds their EV-2 Mark IV rifle, a target gun with adjustable palm rest and a poplar stock that can be finished in many different colors.

(above) Dani Navikas of Beeman Precision Airguns displays the X12.5, a 1250 FPS rifle in their line.

(left) Anschutz is a major name in shooting, and have a line of airguns to complement their firearms, which have long dominated the field of biathlon competition. Anschutz expects the use of airguns in biathlon to continue to grow, as they permit younger shooters to enter the sport.

Top to bottom: The Air Wolf MCT, the Air Ranger, the Huntsman Midas Grade, and the Mk 4 from Daystate.

diminished power: not so with the Nitro Piston system. The gas cylinder is also unaffected by outside temperature so that velocities are consistent from shot to shot. Another advantage is a reduction in recoil compared to spring power.

Following up on the success of their BENJAMIN Discovery and Marauder series, Crosman has brought out a .25 caliber version of the Marauder, their top-of-the-line PCP rifle. The new Marauder operates at 2500 PSI, moving a heavy .25 caliber pellet at 850+ fps, generating 45 foot-pounds of muzzle energy, a significant increase over the .22 caliber version introduced last year. It has a "choked" (tapered bore) barrel to enhance accuracy and uniformity of velocity, will run on CO^2 as well as air (the so-called "Dual Fuel" option), and a built in pressure gauge. The handsome hardwood stock is checkered, and a two-stage, adjustable trigger is standard equipment. The .25 Marauder is intended for the varmint hunter and pest control airgunner who needs high levels

Crosman introduced the Silhouette, a PCP handgun for target shooting.

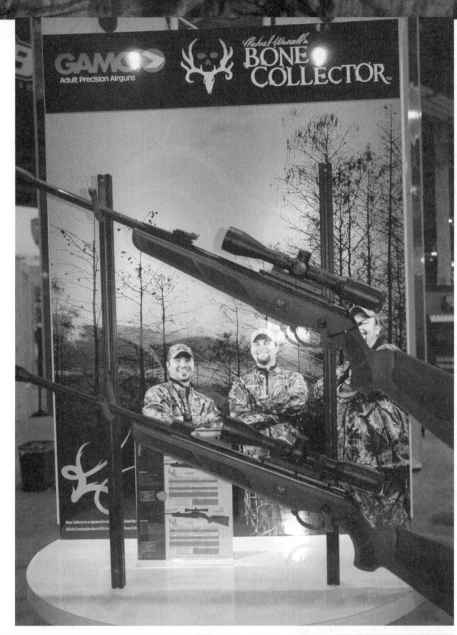

of power; the big pellet is more effective, with superior knock-down power for larger animals.

Crosman hasn't neglected the air-powered handgunners, either. They have introduced two new PCP pistols, the Silhouette and a one-hand version of the Marauder. The Silhouette is offered in .177, the Marauder pistol in .22. The 10-shot Marauder pistol utilizes the same internal technology and sophisticated trigger system that the rifle version does, and Crosman offers a detachable shoulder stock as an optional accessory. The smaller-caliber Silhouette has a barrel made by Lothar Walther and Crosman claims it will shoot quarter-inch groups at 30 meters. Velocity of the Silhouette is approximately 450 fps. It meets both International Handgun Metallic Silhouette Association and NRA standards for competition.

Crosman Corporation also has partnered with REMINGTON (which also owns Marlin) to produce new branded products. The MARLIN Cowboy is a traditionally-styled lever-action BB gun with an "Old West" look and feel that will appeal to kids. It has numerous safety features that guns of a previous era lacked, though: notably an anti-snap-back system to prevent the cocking lever from pinching hands if it's accidentally released. With a velocity of 350 fps, the Marlin Cowboy is an ideal entry point into shooting for young people.

A Remington-brand break-barrel rifle using Crosman's Nitro Piston technology will be available with a number of features to appeal to the small game hunter: a synthetic all-weather stock with a ventilated butt plate, enhanced trigger, and a Crosman CenterPoint 3-9x40 scope.

Crosman is also producing airsoft guns under the BUSHMASTER brand, with applications to gaming and law enforcement training. The Bushmaster Predator and Carbon 15 airsoft guns are very realistic electrically-driven rifles suited to law enforcement training scenarios. The Game Face airsoft line has also been expanded to include three very realistic models marketed to the gamers.

(top) Named for the Outdoor Channel's TV series, the "Bone Collector" is new from Gamo.

(left) The Hatsan rifles feature the "Quattro Trigger" for improved pull and crisper let-off than is typical of break-barrel rifles.

{above} Hatsan also has an extensive line of conventional spring-pistol break-barrel designs.

{below} The prototype for Cometa's new value-priced PCP rifle, which is slated to enter the US market in the Spring of 2010.

Crosman has introduced Verdict Marker Pellets for use in all airsoft guns. These are coated with a chalk-like substance that leaves a mark when it impacts a player at 60 fps or more – a feature especially useful in law enforcement training activities, where there must be confirmation of a hit. The Verdict pellets are seamless and environmentally friendly, as they are biodegradable. Biodegradable pellets are also sold under the Game Face label.

Located in the UK, DAYSTATE is one of the world's premier manufacturers. They are offering rifles on the cutting edge of airgun technology that incorporate proven systems and first-class workmanship. This year they have introduced the Air Wolf MCT, a PCP rifle, available in both .177 and .22 caliber. In the UK, air rifles are limited by law to energy levels of 12 foot-pounds or less, but the Air Wolf is intended for the American market and is far more powerful, producing muzzle energy of 17

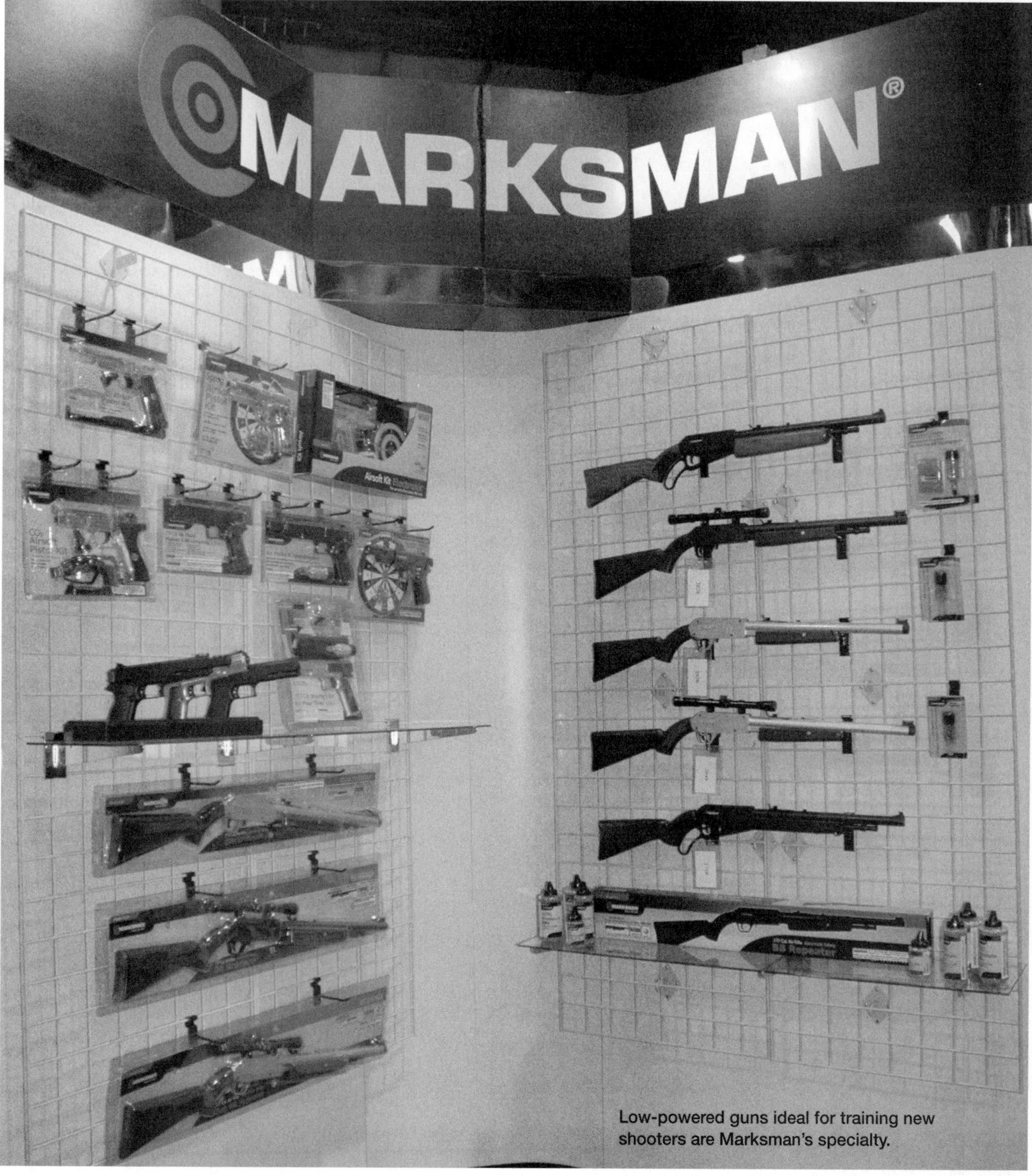

Low-powered guns ideal for training new shooters are Marksman's specialty.

foot-pounds and 40 foot-pounds depending on which caliber is chosen. The Air Wolf uses a patented Harper "slingshot" valve, designed to reduce the "hammer bounce" usually associated with PCP rifles and to permit very high power levels thanks to the use of what Daystate calls "Map Compensated Technology" (MCT) system. The Air Wolf is a very high-tech rifle, designed with the needs of the airgun hunter and field target shooter in mind.

The Air Wolf MCT is a 10-shot repeater with a 230-Bar (3335 PSI) air tank that can provide up to 70 shots at 40 foot-pounds and as many as 400 at 12 foot-pounds before a refill is needed. MCT uses an on-board computer to monitor the firing cycle on a micro-second basis, feeding the information back into the main firing valve control system to produce consistent velocity from one shot to the next, by adjusting the valve output and lock time. Continual regulation of the power output results in a flat power curve as well as absolutely controlled air release. No air is "wasted" by

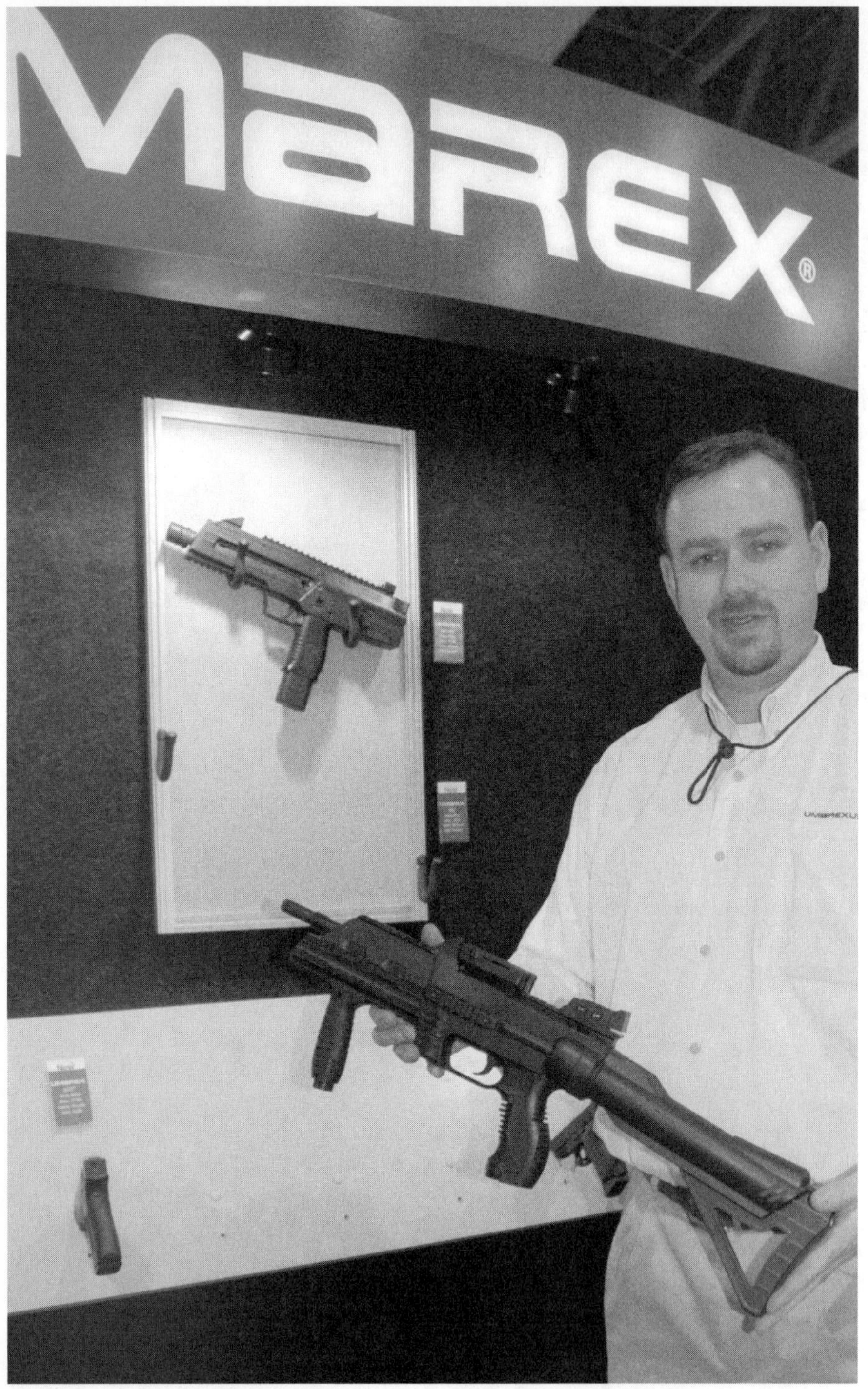

Justin Biddle, Marketing Manager for Umarex USA, displays the new "EBOS" (Electronic Burst of Steel) CO2-powered full-auto BB gun.

this very precise, computer-controlled air regulation, producing more shots per tank. An LCD display screen shows the rifle's status continually.

The on-board computer also permits the shooter to choose one of eight distinct firing modes and to choose one of two pre-programmed power levels. Another version (cataloged as the Air Wolf MVT) permits the shooter can select the level of velocity and power desired. The Air Wolf is available in a left-hand model, as well as in rifle or carbine length. Other features include a sound moderator system, adjustable electronic trigger, and a keyed safety "Power Isolator" switch.

The MCT technology is also used in Daystate's MK4 iS-S and ST rifles, also available in rifle or carbine length. The MK4 series guns are fully programmable, and equipped with handsome walnut stocks, with the option of conventional (S) or thumbhole (ST) styles.

Also on display was the latest version of Daystate's famous Huntsman rifle, the Huntsman Midas LE Grade. This beautifully upgraded Huntsman is to be made in very limited quantities: only 100 will be produced for worldwide distribution. The number to be sent to the USA has not yet been determined. Airguns of Arizona, Daystate's importer, said they have ordered 25 of the Midas grade rifles but don't have a delivery date yet.

GAMO, one of the world's leading manufacturers, has several new break-barrel guns and high-tech pellets that provide a new level of performance. Chief among these is the Gamo Bone Collector, a break-barrel rifle designed in collaboration with Michael Waddell and Travis "T Bone" Turner of the Outdoor Channels TV series of that name. The Bone Collector rifles are a limited release, with a special Hunter Green synthetic stock handsomely accented with grey rubber inserts. The Bone Collector logo is emblazoned on each side of the stock. Bone Collectors are available in both .177 and .22, with muzzle velocities of up to 1250 and 950 fps respectively using Gamo's new PBA pellets (see below). The rifles are fitted with integral sound suppressors and a special 3-9x40 scope as well as open sights.

Gamo's new products also include the a new series, the SOCOM Tactical, Carbine, and Extreme guns. These all utilize an advanced power plant to drive pellets up to an amazing 1600 fps in the Extreme. The SOCOM Tactical, offered in .177, has an adjustable cheekpiece on its synthetic stock, a molded fore-end and a palm swell. It is fitted with a scope as well as open sights and includes as well a fully adjustable laser and light for night use. The SOCOM Carbine in .177 is a fast-handling high-powered rifle fitted with a scope only; it too has an adjustable stock. The SOCOM Extreme has taken the break-barrel rifle to a new level, with a completely redesigned power plant that has been tuned for maximum velocity with the PBA .177 pellets. The composite bull barrel reduces cocking force and the near vertical pistol grip assures excellent control. The 3-9x40 scope provided includes red, green, and blue illuminated reticles.

For hunters, Gamo has brought out the Rocket series, designed for high performance at moderate price. In .177, they generate velocities of 1250+ fps, and are fitted with 4x32 scopes from the factory. Stock options include black or camouflage synthetic. The light weight and high performance of these sporting guns make them ideal for the small game airgun hunter.

In keeping with the current trend towards big bores in airguns, Gamo has introduced their Hunter Extreme "Cannon" Big Bore in .25 caliber. This scoped rifle has a high-grade beech stock and a 3-9x40 scope, and claims 1000 fps with PBA ammunition. It's Gamo's ultimate product for hunting and varmint control.

High velocity is the key to airgun utility: the slogan of the airgunner is "Speed Kills," and Gamo has taken steps to produce special pellets with lower weight for enhanced ballistic performance. The heart of this new pellet technology is the Platinum Ballistic Alloy (PBA) introduced in 2005 and incorporated into several new pellet designs. PBA is lighter than lead, offering the potential for up to 30% higher speeds. Pellets made from PBA are available in several styles, including a domed all-PBA version, and two specially-tipped varieties. PBA pellets are made in .177, .22, and .25 and are suitable for use in all makes of guns.

In addition to the domed version, Gamo has brought out the tipped Blue Flame and Glow Fire pellets. The Blue Flame is made in .177 using the PBA alloy; the Glow Fire is a lead pellet. Both are made in .177 at this time. Both the Blue Flame and Glow Fire pellets incorporate a polymer tip, for reduced weight and higher velocities. The Blue Flame's tip initiate expansion on impact, coupling high velocity and high terminal energy for use on small and medium sized game. The Glow Fire lead pellet is intended for the night hunter: its polymer tip literally glows in the dark after exposure to light, to facilitate loading a rifle at night.

STOEGER is a new name in the airgun field, though not to American shooters. They are importing an attractively-priced line of break-barrel guns made in China. The Stoeger X-Series rifles run from the X-5 to the X-20, the numbers indicating top velocity levels. The X-5 is rated at 800 fps, the X-10 and X-20 at 1200 fps and the X-50 at 1500 fps (all ratings listed are with alloy pellets).

All the X-Series rifles are in .177 caliber, and have an ambidextrous safety catch, adjustable rear sights, and an adjustable two-stage trigger. Stock options include wood, black synthetic, and Advantage Timber HD camouflage. The X-10 and X-20 can be fitted with an optional scope sight. This range of airguns is expected to cover the needs of new shooters, youths, and small game hunting.

UMAREX has teamed up with Ruger to produce a youth-oriented spring-air gun carrying the Ruger brand name. The Ruger Explorer Youth rifle is light, moderately powered, and sized to smaller shooters; it incorporates several safety features that make it ideal for training new shooters. The Explorer weighs less than 4-1/2 pounds and is only 37 inches long, sized to fit smaller frames. Its synthetic thumbhole stock is ambidextrous; the power plant drives a pellet at under 500 fps and requires a cocking effort of

Walther of Germany makes a line of precision target air rifles as well as their famous firearms.

Produced by Crosman, this traditional Western-style Marlin BB gun is sure to be a hit with youngsters.

16-1/2 pounds, half the normal amount. Importantly, the Explorer is equipped with a trigger barrel-safety system to prevent the barrel from slamming closed if the trigger is pulled while it's open, eliminating the chance of a finger injury. Very competitively priced, and with a "name" label, it should appeal to new shooters and their parents or coaches.

Umarex has also teamed up with BROWNING and has expanded their line of pistols with the Browning Model 800 Mag spring-air handgun in .22 caliber, complementing the .177 model already in the line. Like the .177 version, the Model 800 has an ergonomic ambidextrous grip and recoilless action which reduces the amount of recoil produced by the movement of the spring piston. It attains a velocity of 600 fps in .22 caliber, and to reduce cocking effort, includes a cocking assist handle. Other features of the Model 800 Mag include an automatic safety, fiber optic sights, and a synthetic ergonomic pistol grip.

Umarex also makes CO^2 powered guns, with licensed branding from other famous companies. New this year is the MP5K-PDW in their HK-branded line, a tactical-style rifle shooting BBs at 400 fps. The COLT Defender is yet another CO^2-powered BB gun, a close copy of the scaled-down M1911-style Colt product. The Umarex copy has double-action-only lockwork and a maximum speed of 440 fps from its 4.3-inch barrel.

Umarex sells CO^2-powered guns under its own name as well, and has several new entries into this fun-shooting segment of the market. The tactical style Electronic Burst of Steel (EBOS) semi-automatic has an electronic trigger to control gas release, and three modes of operation: single shot, a four-shot burst, and an eight-shot burst. In single-fire mode this gun generates 540 fps with BBs and boasts tactical railing, a removable forearm grip, and an adjustable rear sight. Power is provided by an 88-gram CO^2 capsule concealed in the gun's grip.

Also out under the Umarex brand is another tactical style BB gun, the Steel Storm, featuring a six-shot burst mode, a 300-shot reservoir, and tactical railing for mounting accessories. The Steel Storm uses a pair of 12-gram CO^2 capsules and can generate speeds up to 430 fps in single-shot mode.

Realism is part of the fun of shooting BB guns, and Umarex caters to that need with their new High Power Pistol (HPP), which routes some of the CO^2 propellant into a circuit to "blow back" the slide, producing a very realistic recoil feel. This is an invaluable training feature. Despite using gas to simulate recoil, the HPP moves a BB out at a very respectable 410 fps.

Umarex's entry into the "ultra-fast pellet" competition is the new RWS Hypermax alloy pellet, in .22 caliber.

Predator International is importing the Polymag pellets, in various calibers: this one is not for 155mm howitzer, it's a display of their polymer-tipped product!

Sunny Sun of Xisico USA, with the bamboo-stocked Model 206.

This follows on the very successful .177 version and is intended for use in all brands of .22 caliber guns.

It's no secret that China is one of the largest sources of airguns. Given their enormous domestic market and their power in export sales, neither is it a surprise that new players and new companies come into the game every year. XISICO AIRGUNS is now competing in the USA, with a break-barrel rifle and pistol as new products.

The Model 206 break-barrel gun made by this company has a stock made from bamboo. Bamboo is an excellent stock material, thanks to its density and hardness: the arrangement of the fibers in this woody material give it extraordinary strength in compression. Bamboo is also capable of being worked almost like metal to facilitate inletting and precision fit. The companion piece to the Model 206 is a break-barrel pistol with a Picatinny rail and an automatic safety feature.

Xisico has an under-lever rifle, the Model 46U with a quick-release lever lock, an auto safety, and a pellet speed of 1000 fps.

They are also producing and exporting their first CO^2 powered gun, the Model 60C. The model designation is obvious when you look at it: it bears a startling external resemblance to the famous Marlin Model 60 autoloading .22 rifle! This too has an automatic safety and it boats an adjustable trigger.

Turkey has recently emerged as source of economically-priced, high-value firearms, and their industry is turning its attention to the airgun market as well. ARMED is producing two break-barrel guns, the Model 6 and the Model 6W, the latter having a wood stock. To date there is no importer bringing Armed guns to the USA but they hope to be selling here in the next year.

HATSAN, a Turkish company better known in the USA for its line of shotguns, is now producing break barrel rifles. The Hatsan Model 88 features a specially designed Quattro Trigger system for improved pull; and also a power plant with an integral recoil reduction system. The mechanically identical Model 88 TH has a thumbhole stock.

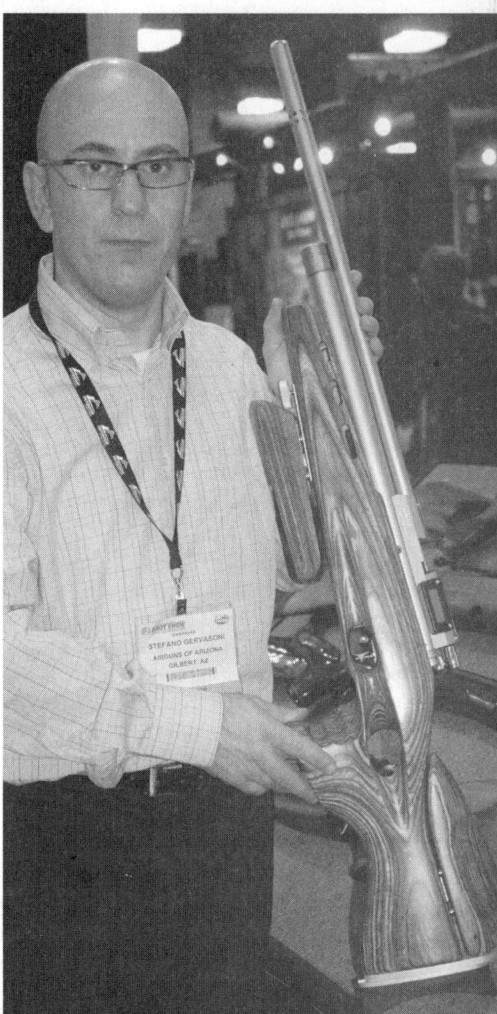

Stefan Gervasoni, Export Manager for Daystate in the UK, holds the Grand Prix, their top-of-the-line rifle for field target shooting.

Remington's Amazing Model 552 Speedmaster

BY **DAN SHIDELER**

22 Short, Long or Long Rifle. The Model 552 will gobble them all up and beg for more.

I type the same way I play piano – badly, and with two fingers. But today I'm using only one finger to type this because my left hand is holding a palmful of .22 Shorts.

There's something about a .22 Short that just makes me giggle. How tiny it is, how oddly proportioned, like a miniature howitzer shell. And when I see one with a hollowpoint, that dinky little hollowpoint that couldn't possibly expand unless it hit the grille of a '55 Buick Roadmaster – well, I just lose all my composure and practically wet myself.

I love the .22 Short – and the Long, and the Long Rifle. Nowadays the high-performance .22 and .17 rimfires get all the attention, but there was a time, laddie, when there were only three rimfires worth mentioning: the .22 Short, the .22 Long, and the .22 Long Rifle. Remember when every .22 bolt-action, pump or lever gun was marked on its barrel ".22 S – L – LR"? I wonder how many kids today wouldn't even know what the S and the L stood for.

In my day, sonny, you could walk into a Guarantee Auto hardware store with a $5 bill and come out with enough .22 Shorts or Longs to keep a kid occupied for an entire month. You'd buy the Long Rifles for serious work like rabbit hunting, but for perforating cans the Shorts and Longs did just fine. As a matter of fact, the high-velocity Shorts didn't do a half-bad job on rabbits, either. You bought Longs if they were on sale, but that was about it.

Over the course of the last 35 years, I've accumulated several coffee cans of mixed .22 rimfire ammunition: Shorts (thousands of them), Longs (just a few of those), Long Rifles, birdshot, Kleanbore, Wildcat, C-I-L, Peters, Stingers, Mohawk, Yellow Jackets, you name it. Wouldn't it be nice to have a rifle – a semiauto, maybe – that would shoot all of it?

Well, I do. It's a Remington 552 Speedmaster, one of the greatest .22s ever made.

In the pantheon of great .22 semiautos, the Remington 552 Speedmaster is right up there with the Marlin Model 60 and the Ruger 10/22. Yet the 552 has a singular advantage over the Marlin and the Ruger: it'll gobble up Shorts, Longs and Long Rifles with nary a hiccup. To me, what with my considerable inventory of oddball .22 rimfire ammunition, this is a very big deal indeed.

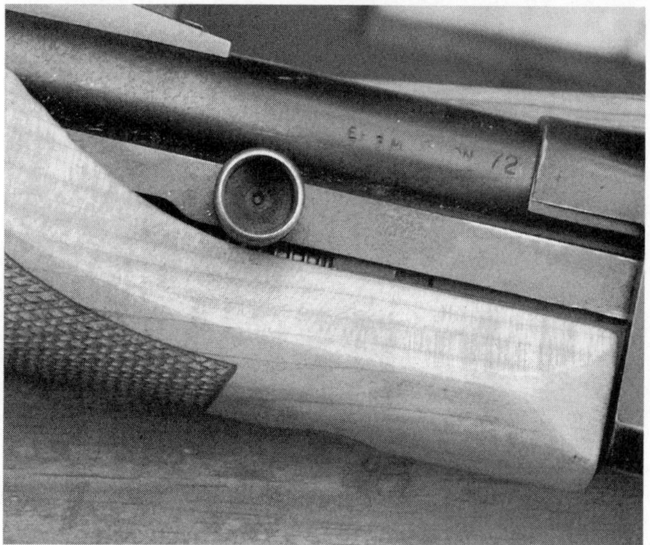
The 552's bolt handle is on the left side of the receiver. Watch your thumb!

The Model 552 Speedmaster was introduced in 1957, which means that it celebrated its Golden Anniversary in 2007. It took the place of the Model 550 in Remington's lineup, though the two competing models were produced simultaneously for a time. (According to Remington, the Model 550-1 was made right up until 1970, though I certainly don't remember seeing any of them new on dealers' shelves as late as that.)

Introduced in 1941, the Model 550 was the first American semi-auto to fire .22 Shorts, Longs and Long Rifles interchangeably. It did this through a floating-chamber design that has been attributed to Marsh "Carbine" Williams. In Williams' design, the 550's chamber contained a floating front end that allowed lower-powered cartridges to amplify their back-thrust against the bolt face and thus cycle the action.

If there was ever a practical problem with the Model 550, I have yet to read about it or experience it. The only deficiencies of the 550 were that 1) it was relatively expensive to manufacture, and 2) it looked a little clunky, as many '50s-vintage .22 rifles did. When Remington introduced the Model 552 Speedmaster in 1957, however, it solved both problems at once, giving us a rifle that still looks great and performs perfectly 50 years later.

The Model 552 dispensed with its predecessor's floating chamber design in favor of a lightweight, buffered bolt that a .22 Short would cycle and a .22 Long Rifle wouldn't batter to pieces. Shorts, Longs, Long Rifles -- as Henry Stebbins says of the Model 552 in Rifles: A Modern Encyclopedia, "You can mix 'em up, but you can't screw 'em up."

My 1970s-vintage Speedmaster will shoot any combination of .22 S - L - LR that you can dump into it, but apparently the earliest models were a bit glitchy in this respect. Writing in the 1958 edition of Gun Digest, a noticeably cranky Bob Wallack gave the Model 552 a mixed review after he loaded its magazine with alternating Short, Long and Long Rifle cartridges:

"Functionally the gun is excellent in all respects," Wallack says. "[But] in my first try I found that the 552 does not handle mixed ammunition 100%, in fact I got a couple of jams by trying the stunt. . . .Remington should stop the publicity about this feature."

Maybe Wallack got a bad one, or maybe Remington didn't have all the bugs ironed out of its first-run guns. All I can say is that my two Model 552s have flawlessly digested any mix of ammo I could fit into their tubular magazines with the exception of .22 CB and BB caps and Aguila's primer-only .22 Colibri squirters. These subloads can be fired in the 552, of course, but you have to operate the bolt handle manually, and that gives iffy results as far as ejection is concerned.

Speaking of ejection, there's no mistaking the 552 for anything else because of the shell deflector stuck on the right side of the receiver. Some may think it ugly, but there's no question that it performs its job admirably. Fired shell cases fly well in front of the shooter and generally land in a tidy pile. I for one don't think the deflector is ugly, any more than I think the beauty mark on Elizabeth Taylor's cheek is ugly. (If you don't know what I'm talking about, watch Cleopatra sometime. Wow.)

Let's talk about the Model 552's bolt handle for a minute. When I took my latest 552 out for a test-drive, I unthinkingly adopted an elbow-on-hip, cradle-the-receiver schuetzen posture to see how I could do offhand at 50 yards. At the first shot, that little bolt handle, which is mounted on the left side of the receiver, came racing back fast enough to remove a sizeable chunk of the pad of my left thumb. I mean a chunk big enough to bait a trotline with.That meant no hitch-hiking for a while, but I decided not to hold it against the rifle. (My thumb, that is.)

The Model 552 is no target gun. Its barrel is rifled for the standard 36- or 40-grain .22 Long Rifle load, and indeed some 552s are capable of 1.5-inch 50-yard groups with such ammunition. But load up a tubeful of Shorts and the situation changes. The Short's 29-grain bullet is way overstabilized by the 552's rifling, and 50-yard groups open up considerably. For serious target shooters this is a real deal-killer, but for guys like me it's copasetic. If the Lord had wanted us to risk everything on one shot, He wouldn't have given us 20-round tubular magazines.

In 1957, the Model 552 Speedmaster had a suggested retail price of $52.25. That made the 552 a fairly expensive .22. The comparable Savage Model 6 retailed for $42.75; the Stevens Model 87 for $37.95; the Mossberg 98 for $43.95. But the Browning .22 Autoloading Rifle carried a sticker price of $69.50, and Winchester's legendary Model 63 sold for a whopping $79.45. (Who thought up those prices, anyway? Seventy-nine dollars and forty-five cents?!)

Today a new Model 552 will set you back around $400, definitely on the salty side. But if $200 of that is for the basic gun, the other $200 has got to be for style. In my opinion, the 552 Speedmaster looks every bit as good today as it did back in 1957. As I've suggested, I may be the only person left on the planet who shoots .22 Shorts anymore, and when I want to plink tin cans by the caseload, there's nothing like a Model 552 and a few boxes of Shorts to land me smack-dab on Cloud 9.

According to Remington, the Model 552 was made in two grades: the 552A Standard and the 552BDL. The BDL had fancier wood, nicer checkering, and a somewhat finer finish. Three variations were cataloged: the .22 Short-only 552GS Gallery Special; the 552C Carbine; and the 552 150th Anniversary Edition. All are considered collectible, at least as far as Model 552s go. Me, I'd love to have one of each.

If you run across a Model 552 at a good price, my advice is to buy it. You probably won't regret it, and you might just rediscover how much fun the .22 Short can be.

HANDLOADING

BY **LARRY STERETT**

With the increased prices of factory loaded ammunition, interest in handloading should also increase – and apparently it has, judging from the recent backorder situations at many manufacturers of reloading tools and components. The major cost of a loaded cartridge is the brass case, and if the case can be reloaded five to ten times, or more, the cost per round decreases, after the cost of the reloading equipment is recouped. Plus, you can tailor your loads for varmint hunting, big game hunting, target shooting, tactical shooting or whatever the need. (Trapshooters often reload several thousand rounds of their favorite load each year in order to reduce the cost of shells needed for practice.) The equipment covered in this update doesn't cover everything available, but it should provide an idea as to what is currently available and what's new.

DATA

Reloaders need reliable reloading data. Thankfully, such data for factory, obsolete, and even wildcat cartridges is all over the place.

The hardbound volumes of data, such as those by Barnes, Hornady, Lee, Nosler, Speer, and others, or the large, softbound volumes of Lyman, Accurate Arms, etc., are enormously valuable. Their only downside is the lapse time between new editions. A recent trend is toward a smaller paper-bound manual or magazine-size volume of data issued yearly, often by powder manufacturers or distributors. One of the most informative, the *Hodgdon Annual,* is issued by the Hodgdon Powder Company and published by *Shooting Times.*

The latest *Hodgdon Annual* features one less than a dozen excellent articles on reloading by well-known writers,

The Hornady Auto Charge is a sophisticated digital powder measure. Note the drain plug on the right side.

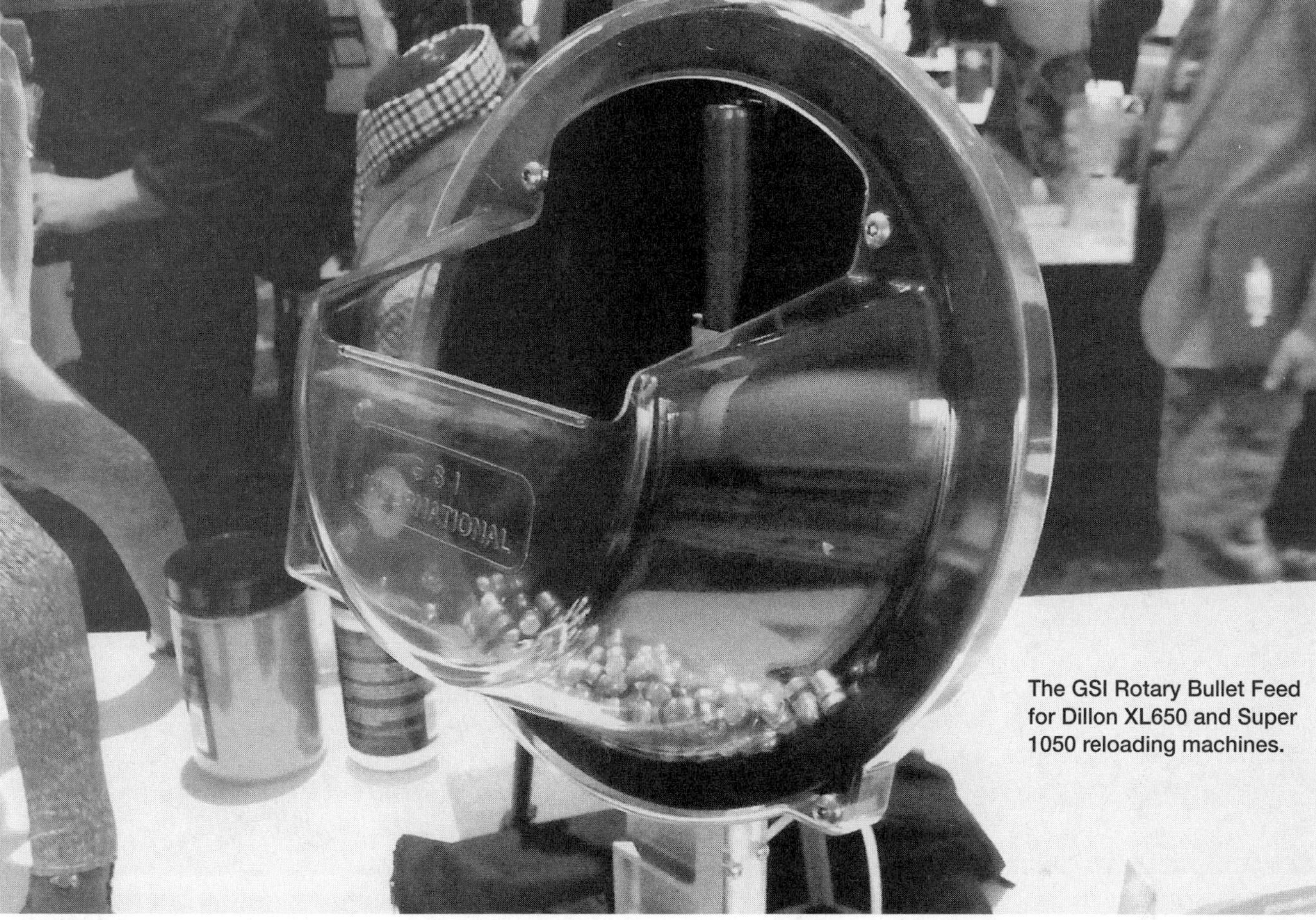

The GSI Rotary Bullet Feed for Dillon XL650 and Super 1050 reloading machines.

plus the latest loading data for 135 rifle cartridges, from the .17 Ackley Hornet to the .50 BMG, and 72 handgun cartridges from the .22 Remington Jet to the .500 S&W Magnum. In addition there are a few other valuable features, including a table of Relative Burn Rates for powders, rated from the fastest (Norma R1) to the slowest (Vihtavouri 20N29); a table of Powder Usage for various pistol, rifle and shotgun powders; a description of many of the powders currently on the market; and a legend of the abbreviations used in the manual. (Data is provided for ten different 6.5mm cartridges, including two of the newest, the 6.5 Grendel and the 6.5 Creedmoor, but not for the older 6.5mm Remington Magnum.)

No loading data for shotshells is provided in this manual, but for each of the rifle or handgun cartridges, load data is provided as follows, for specified bullets (the bullet being listed by weight, brand name, bullet type, diameter and overall loaded cartridge length): powder, grains, velocity (instrumental) and pressure (CUP) for both starting loads and maximum loads. Other data provided for the loads for a specific cartridge include the case used (Federal, Hornady, Remington, Sierra, Winchester, etc.), trim length, primer brand (type and size), barrel length and rate of twist. It doesn't get much better or more complete than this.

Lyman Products will have a new *Cast Bullet Handbook* available by the time you read this. This is the fourth edition and the first new one in thirty years. The entire Lyman line of pistol and rifle bullet moulds will be chronicled, along with data for some moulds by other manufacturers whose bullet designs will be of interest to reloaders of cast bullets. A number of new cartridges since the third edition will be featured, such as the .327 Federal, along with some new black powder loads for a number of the popular older cartridges, especially those regaining status among Cowboy Action. A number of authoritative "how to" articles are also featured.

LYMAN PRODUCTS

Other new Lyman products for handloaders include a Big Dipper Casting Furnace, Big Dipper Casting Kit, Cast Iron Lead Pot, Magnum Inertia Bullet Puller, and a Universal Case Prep Accessory Kit. The Big Dipper Furnace has a 10-lb. capacity, features heavy-duty aluminum construction with a stable non-tipping design, and operates on 115 volts. Heat-up time is rapid, with control to +/- 10 degrees. (The Casting Kit contains the BD furnace, a casting dipper, ingot mould, Super Moly Bullet Lube and the *Lyman Reloading and Cast Bullet Guide* – everything needed to get started in casting bullets, except for a bullet mould of the required size.) The Cast Iron Lead Pot has a 10-lb. lead capacity and is flat-bottomed to reduce tipping. A heat source, such as an electric hotplate, is needed to melt the lead and keep it hot. (With the older iron pot I used to use a tripod, similar to what plumbers used at one time, over a single gas flame; it worked.)

To salvage the components when you make a reloading flub, the new Magnum Inertia Bullet Puller will be handy. With a full size handle for comfort, the Puller features a head design capable of handling case sizes from the FN 5.7x28mm to the largest magnum. Insert cartridge, secure cap, strike puller on a solid sur-

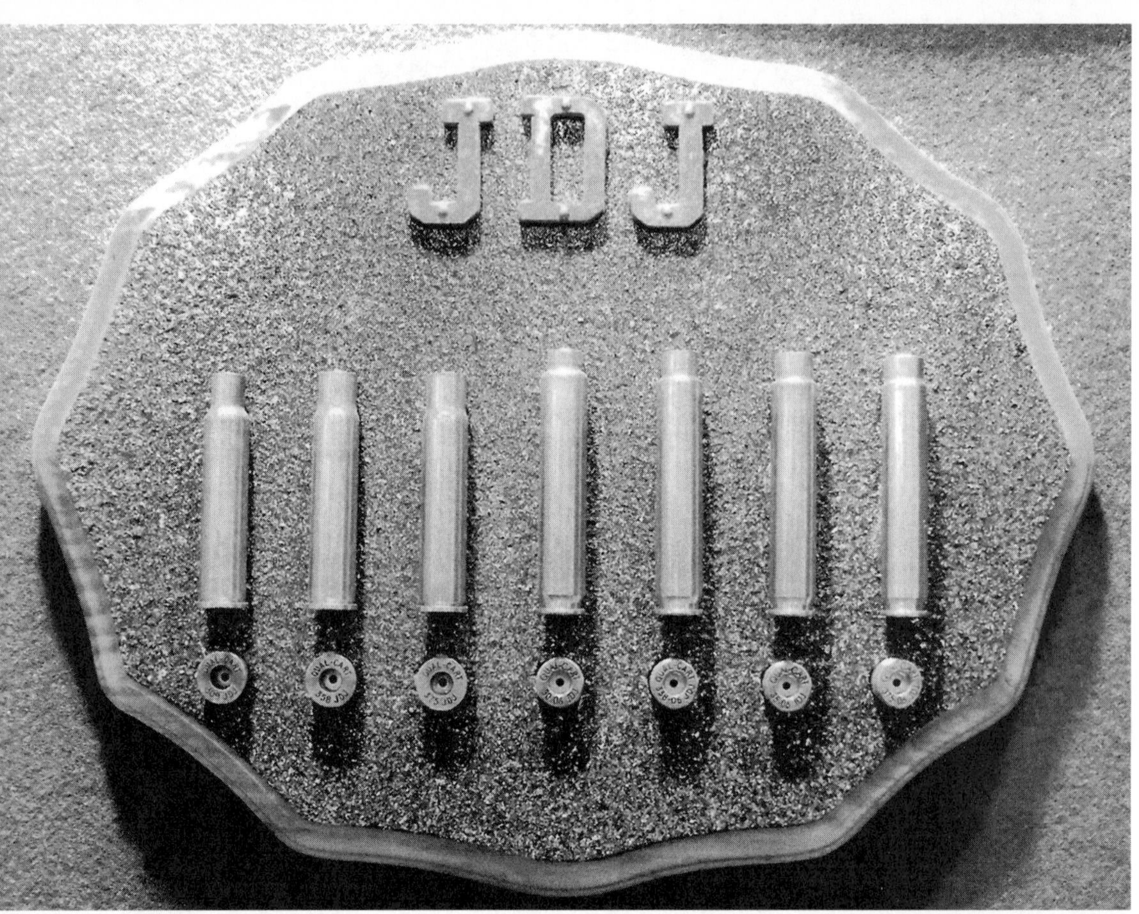

SOME OF THE QUALITY CARTRIDGE UNPRIMED CASES FOR THE J. D. JONES LINE OF WILDCAT CARTRIDGES.

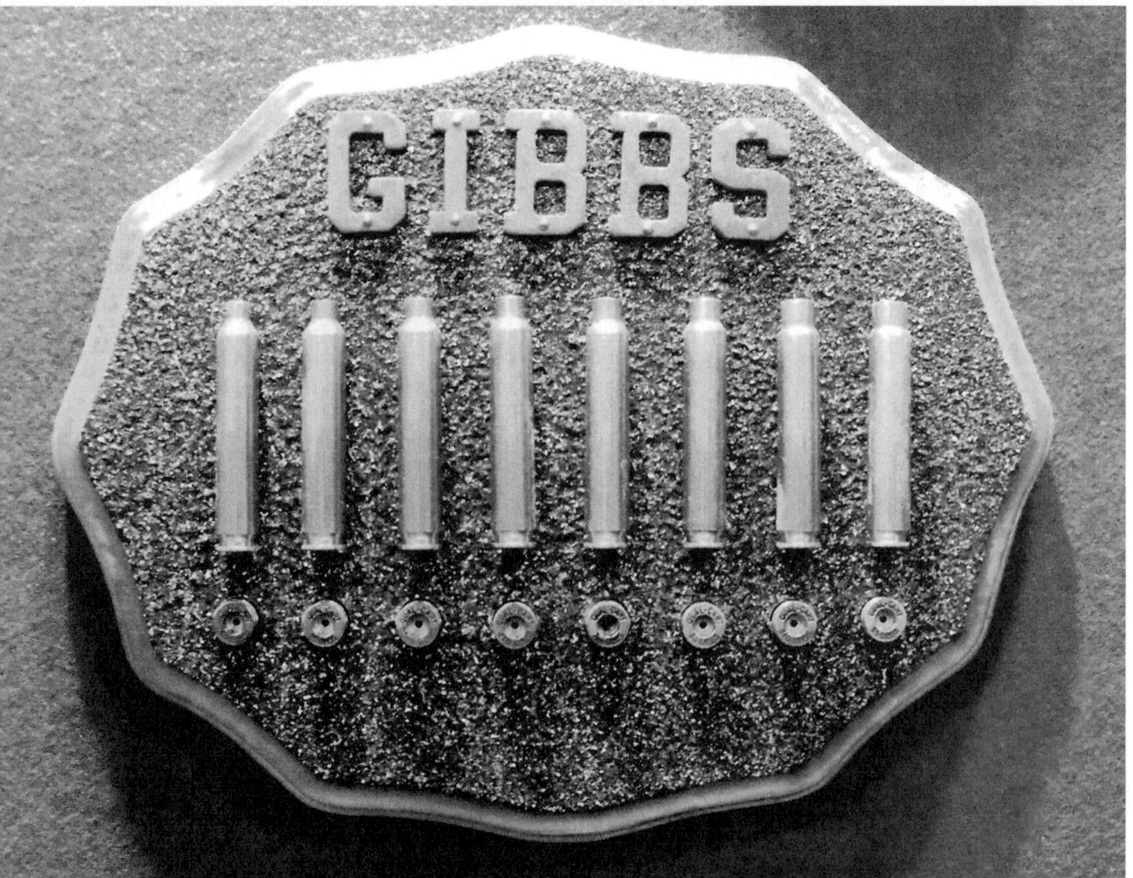

QUALITY CARTRIDGE UNPRIMED CASES FOR THE COMPLETE GIBBS SHARP SHOULDER, SHORT NECK, LINE OF CARTRIDGES.

ACKLEY CARTRIDGES, REGULAR AND IMPROVED, RANGED FROM .17 CALIBER TO .475 AND POSSIBLY HIGHER. THESE ARE A FEW OF THE UNPRIMED ACKLEY CASES AVAILABLE FROM QUALITY CARTRIDGE.

OBSOLETE CARTRIDGES COME IN ALL SIZES. THESE UNPRIMED CASES BY QUALITY CARTRIDGE REPRESENT ONLY A FEW OF THE MANY AVAILABLE.

Hornady's digital Sonic Cleaner literally blasts the dirt and carbon buildup from inside and outside the cartridge case.

face. (A 6x6-inch square, inch-thick plate of cold-rolled steel works very well as a surface on which to strike the Puller.) Then unscrew the cap and remove the bullet, powder and case. Depending on the cartridge, bullet seating depth, and crimp tightness, two or more strikes may be necessary, but it will eventully remove the bullet.

The Universal Case Prep Accessory Kit features eight small tools to fine-tune trimmed cartridge cases prior to reloading. Packaged in a folding zippered storage pouch are a pair each of primer pocket reamers (small and large), primer pocket cleaners, primer pocket uniformers, and inside and outside deburring tools to eliminate the sharp edges on a trimmed case mouth. A new Carbide Cutter Head for the Lyman Case Trimmer and a new Universal Carbide Case Trimmer are available. (The Carbide head holds its sharp edge much longer than the regular steel trimmer head.)

GSI INTERNATIONAL

If you reload using one of the Dillon XL 650 or RL 1050 or Super 1050 reloading machines, GSI International has a new Rotary Bullet Feed to speed up the reloading process. The Conversion Units contain all parts necessary for feeding one caliber of bullet, including the feed ring, bullet column, feed wheel, seat stems, bushing and GSI toolhead assembly. (XL 650 users will need to move some items from their regular toolhead to the GSI toolhead, such as the sizing die, powder die and system, powder check, if used, and the crimp die.) The GSI toolhead for the 1050, with the Bullet Feed Mechanism integrated into the left side, replaces the standard 1050 toolhead. The new system includes a new casefeed post and bracket which mount directly into existing machine holes. Also included are a camming plate for the bullet feeder's index lever and a gas spring to handle the added weight of the bullet and feeder. The 1050 Rotary system includes the GSI toolhead with feed mechanism, extended case feed post with brackets, clear plastic feed tub, an indexer camming plate, and gas spring with locating block. Items to be moved from the standard 1050 toolhead include the case feed cam, primer pushrod, ratchet cam, fasteners, sizing die, powder die and system, powder checker (if used), and the crimp die.

The GSI Rotary Bullet Feeder uses a small DC electric motor to rotate the feed ring counterclockwise. (For the USA, the 110 VAC input becomes, via a transformer, a 12 VDC output.) The feed rings are caliber specific, and many popular calibers such as 9mm, .40 S&W, .45 ACP, .223 Remington, etc., are currently available.

REDDING RELOADING EQUIPMENT

Redding Reloading Equipment has a number of new die sets available, plus some new calibers in the regular die sets. (The G-R Carbide Push-Thru Base Sizing Die to resize the base section of fired .40 S&W cases were mentioned last year, and it's a excellent die for reloaders of large quantities of .40 S&W ammunition using once-fired brass.) Now available in the regular Series D die sets for bottleneck case are full length and neck-sizing dies for the .260 Remington Improved (40°), 6.5 Creedmoor, .370 Sako Magnum, and .458 SOCOM cartridges. (Individual dies and Deluxe sets are available, but no trim and form dies for these cartridges.) Redding has new National Match Die Sets available for the .223 Remington, .308 Winchester, and .30-06 Springfield cartridges. These three-die sets, which list for over a pair of C-notes, include a full length sizing die, competition bullet seating die, and a taper crimp die. (Taper crimp dies are available for handgun cartridges that headspace on the case mouth, and for the following additional rifle cartridges: 6.5 Grendel, 6.8 Remington SPC, .30-30 Winchester, 7.62x39mm, .300 Winchester Magnum, and .300 Remington Ultra Magnum.)

Benchrest shooters and any other handloader interested in obtaining maximum accuracy from their handloads can now obtain an "Instant Indicator" Headspace and Bullet Comparator for two additional cartridges, the .204 Ruger and .338 Lapua Magnum. (The Instant Indicator, with or without the dial indicator, is currently available for 34 different rifle cartridges. It can be used on any family of cartridges that have the same shoulder angle.) It is supplied with the proper bore diameter bushing, surface contactor, shoulder contactor, headspace gauge, and complete instructions. Its use permits the sorting of bullets and sized cases for uniformity – uniformity of shoulder bump, bullet seating depth, trimmed case uniformity, and comparison of fired cases to sized cases for headspace differences. It can even be used to sort cases fired in different rifles, determine when cases need trimmed, and sort loaded ammunition for uniformity.

Any handloader with a loading press and a set of dies, but lacking other essentials, might check out the Redding Versa Pak Reloading Kit. It contains all the other items, powder measure, case trimmer, case lube and pad, powder funnel, powder scale, etc. that simplify the handloading process, including a new Hodgdon reloading manual and a DVD titled "Advanced Handloading Beyond the Basics."

RCBS

Bullet pullers and feeders seem to be the hot items at present for reloading equipment manufacturers. RCBS has a new Pow'r Pull kit and two two Bullet Feeder kits for their progressive presses. The Pow'r Pull features a rugged one-piece body, plus cap, and comes with three chucks to accommodate cases heads from the 5.7x28mm to the Winchester WSM and Remington RUM families. (By the way, NEVER attempt to pull bullets from rimfire cartridges using an inertia bullet puller.)

The RCBS Bullet Feeder kits are available in two sizes, one for 22- or 30-caliber rifle cartridges, and one for handgun calibers from 9mm to .45 ACP. The Feeders operate on 110 VAC, with adapters for United Kingdom, Australian, and continental European use included. Designed to fit onto most 7/8"x14 threaded progressive presses, the Feeders orient the bullets to drop into the feed mechanism, but are for jacketed or FMJ bullets only and not for use with lead bullets, cast or swaged. Hopper capacities are approximately 250 (22-caliber) or 100 (30-caliber) bullets for the rifle caliber feeder and 200 for the handgun caliber feeder. The Feeders carry a two-year warranty and are said to increase the loading rate by as much as 50%.

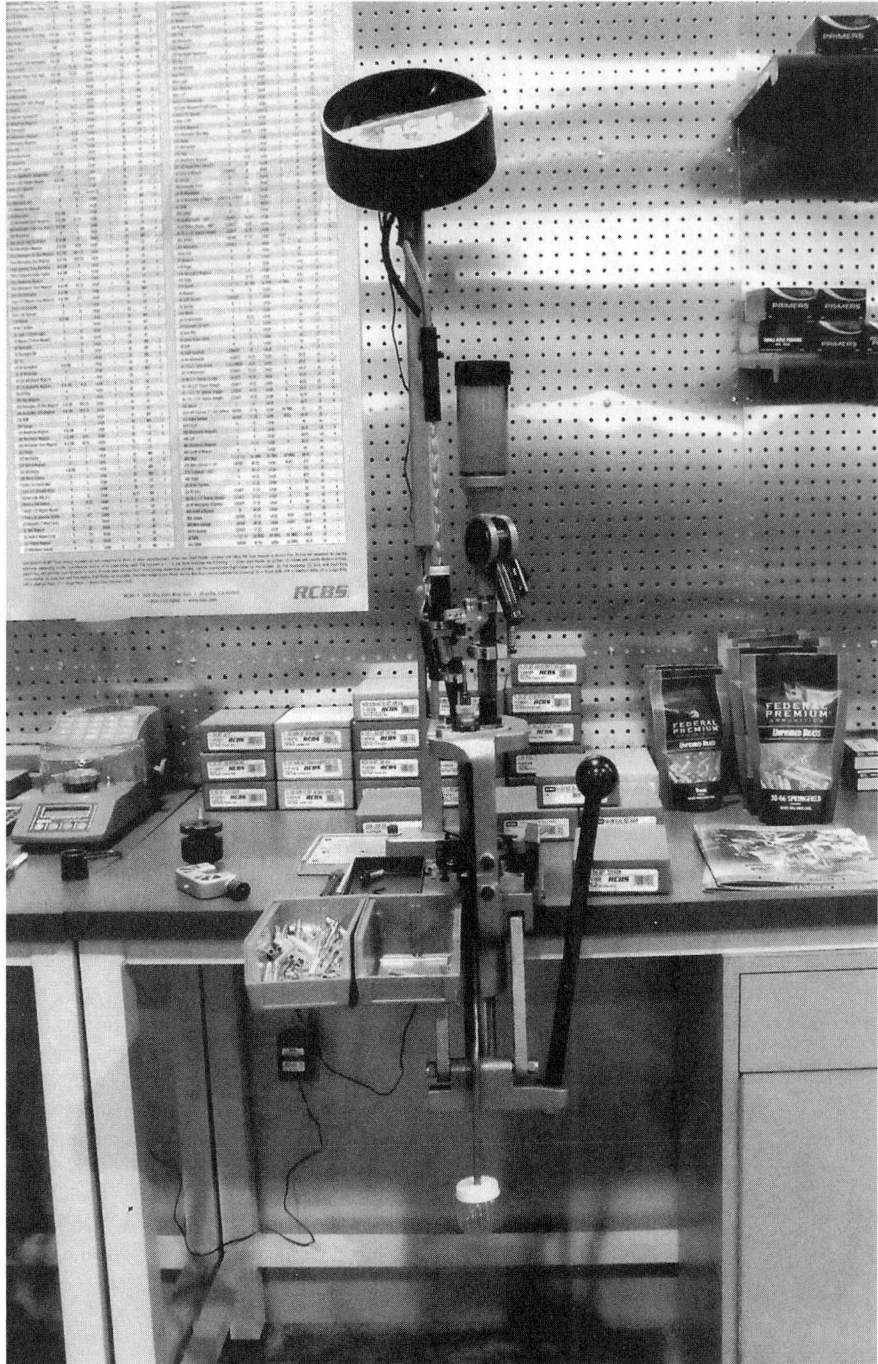

The RCBS Bullet Feeder set up on the RCBS progressive loading press. It feeds the bullets, base down, directly into the feeding tube, ready to be dropped into the case mouth.

Keeping loading presses, dies, etc., cleaned and lubed is a necessity for both successful and long-term operation. RCBS has a couple of Die/Press Lube Kits: one kit for loading dies and a

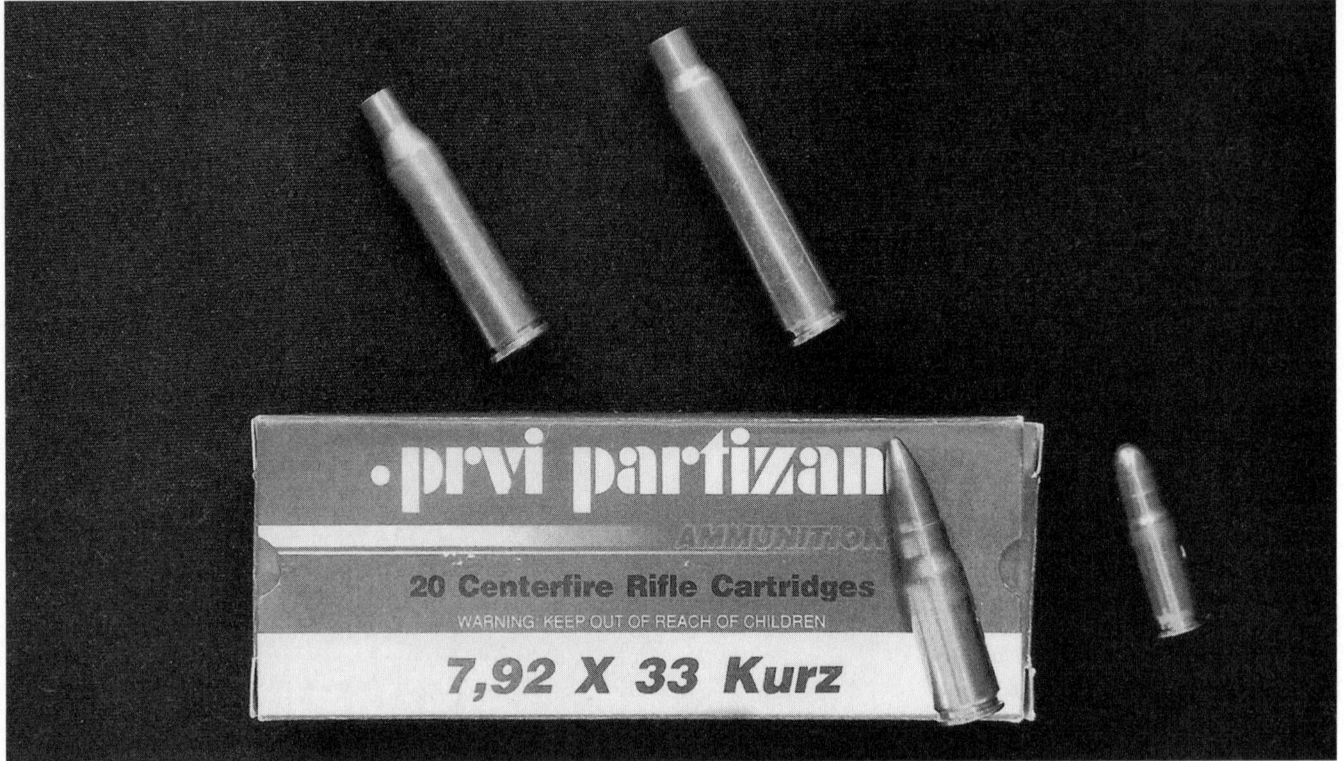

Unprimed brass and a couple of loaded cartridges from TR&Z USA. Left to right: 6.5x51R; 7.7x58mm Japanese; 7.92x33mm Kurz; and 7.63mm Mauser.

separate one for loading presses. These kits contain the necessary chemicals and brushes to permit proper cleaning and ensure equipment longevity.

RCBS has added six new calibers to their loading die lineup. These include the .30 T/C and .338 Marlin Express to the Group A line, and 6.5 Creedmoor, .30 Remington AR, .338 Norma Magnum, and .416 Ruger to the Group D line. Full-length die sets and neck sizer dies are available, but no trim dies at present. Not exactly new, but for those handloaders of the really big bore, RCBS has die sets for the .416 Barrett, .460 Steyr, and .50 BMG cartridges, in addition to a Safari Series line covering seven calibers from the .404 Jeffery to the .505 Gibbs. If what you need isn't available, RCBS does have a listing of nearly 650 "special order" die sets. (Note that the firm no longer produces one-of-a-kind custom die sets.)

HORNADY

In addition to having some new cartridge loads available, plus a couple of new cartridges for U. S. shooter, Hornady Manufacturing has several new components and a couple of great equipment items for handloaders. The Lock-n-Load Power Case Prep Center was introduced last year. Combining a power trimmer with primer pocket uniformer, cleaner, reamer, flash hole deburring tool, case mouth chamfer and deburring tools, etc. , the Case Prep Center takes up little space on the reloading bench. The two new Hornady tools include the Lock-n-Load Auto Charge and the Sonic Cleaner.

The Auto Charge has a scale capacity of 1,000 grains and will weigh accurately to within 0.1 grains. Finished in Hornady red with a clear plastic hopper, the machine features an easy-to-use keypad with backlit display, manual and automatic dispensing options, plus trickle function, overcharge protection, and several other unique features. A side-mounted clean-out spout or drain makes emptying the hopper a real breeze. An electric Hornady powder scale with a 1,000-grain capacity should be available about the time you read this.

Sonic parts cleaners have been available and in use by the automotive industry and others for a good many years. Now Hornady has a Lock-n-Load Sonic Case Cleaner. The new Cleaning unit can hold up to one hundred .308-size cases, or two hundred cases of .223 size. Coupled with a unique cleaning solution called One-Shot Sonic Cleaner, available in one-quart containers, this device, which features a digital timer, uses ultrasonic action to literally blast away carbon and dirt building up from the outside, inside, and even the primer pocket areas of the cases. (The cleaner can also be used on small parts.) No tumbling, no vibrating, just put in the One-Shot, place the dirty cartridge into the solution, set the digital timer, and the Sonic Cleaner will take care of the rest.

In addition to the the new Auto Charge and Sonic Cleaner for handloaders, Hornady will have unprimed brass available in 6.5 Grendel, .338 Marlin Express and 9.2 x62mm, with the same available as Lock-n-Load Modified "Series A " cases for the O.A.L. Gauges. Custom Grade, Series I two-die sets are available for the 6.5 Grendel, and a number of new FTX seating stems are available for use in seating dies. These FTX stems are available in five calibers, from .30 to .50, and for bullet weights up to 300 grains.

One handy item to have on the loading bench is the Die Maintenance Kit. This Kit includes spare decap pins, zip spindles, retaining rings, Sure-Loc ring, a decap retainer, and an Allen wrench. Another handy new items is the Universal Shellholder Extenstion. It isn't needed often, but it's worth its weight in gold when it is.

For the really dedicated handloader who wants to form a large number of standard cases into an improved design, without having to fireform, Hornady has the answer: a Hydraulic Form Die Kit. It's available in two basic sizes: for cases under 2.60 inches or less in length and for cases 2.601 to 2.999 inches in length. Prices are under $200. Custom dies are also available (form, size, seat, trim, etc.) as a single die, or up to a four-die set, depending on the cartridge.

It's not new reloading equipment, but new to the Hornady line is the 5.45x39mm loaded with a 60-gr. V-MAX in the Varmint Express line. No loading dies, yet. Another item, not related to handloading *per se*, is the Hornady Cartridge Introduction Board. Featured in a shadow box display are 21 the of the SAMMI cartridges which the Hornady firm has introduced since 1988, from the rimfire to the big bores.

SIERRA

Sierra, The Bulletsmiths, has a new laminated countermat that illustrates the entire Sierra line of bullets, including the Long Range Specialty Bullets, from .22 to .338. Other non-bullet items of interest to the handloader include four reloading videos, VHS or DVD, plus an advanced video, "Beyond the Basics." Handloaders wanting to check out exterior ballicstics can do so on the Sierra Infinity, Version 6, Computer Software. This software, which is available in CD-ROM format only, has the entire 5th Edition of the *Sierra Rifle and Handgun Reloading Manual* integrated into it. An Infinity Mobile program is also available for handheld computers, using the Windows Mobile Operating Sysem, Versions 5.0 and above.

NOSLER

Nosler has several new bullets for handloaders, including some lead-free BT (Ballistic Tip) .204, .224, and .243 designs for varmint shooters. Designed to perform best at high velocity (a minimum of 1600 fps is recommended with no upper limit), these bullets feature a fragmenting copper core. Nosler now has new unprimed brass for the 6.5x55mm Mauser, .300 WSM and .375 H & H Magnum cartridges, and custom loaded ammunition for the last two cartridges.

A new, expanded (848 pages) *Nosler Reloading Guide, No. 6,* features loading data for 117 cartridges. Each cartridge section begins with an introduction by a different well-known industry name or writer, relating personal experiences, advice, or anecdotes. "Comments From The Lab" are presented for many of the cartridges. Written by the Nosler ballistics team, they provide advice and insight for working up safe, effective and accurate loads. Load data for each cartridge is presented in a graphic format with easy-to-read bar graphs giving the reader a quick comparison of load velocities for each bullet weight. These graphs also permit a comparison between powders, making powder selection for a specific cartridge easier and faster than before. (Starting, intermediate and maximum loads for each powder listed are provided for each cartridge.)

MISCELLANEOUS NEAT STUFF

Not a loading manual, but a valuable reference for handloaders is *Ammo & Ballistics 4*, published by **Safari Press**. This large 438-page softbound volume provides ballistics data for over 160 centerfire cartridges of interest to handloaders, and similar data for some rimfire cartridges. Over 2400 factory loads for handguns and rifles are documented, and case dimensions are provided for most of the cartridges, including some for which dimensions are not easily found elsewhere. (Not that the dimensions for the .500 A-Square, .577 Tyrannosaur, or .700 Nitro Express are needed frequently.) This volume also contains some useful miscellaneous information, including a "How to Use This Book," along with four short feature articles, including one on handgun hunting and another on the great .470 Nitro Express cartridge.

Foster Products has a new 3-in-1 Carbide Case Mouth Cutter for either the original manually-operated case trimmer or the power case trimmer. It slides over the cutter shaft and secures in place with one set screw. The 3-in-1 feature comes from the fact the new cutter will perform three functions simultaneously in one pass. It trims the case to length, chamfers the inside case mouth to an angle of 14° and the outside of the case mouth to an angle of 30° — 3-in1. Three caliber choices (.224, .243, and .308) are currently available, with additional calibers to be added later. The cutter blades are made from U. S.-manufactured carbide steel, and if used exclusively on brass cases, should never need sharpening.

Barnes has more than twenty new bullets available, including a 300-gr. Tipped Triple-Shock X bullet for the .458 SOCOM

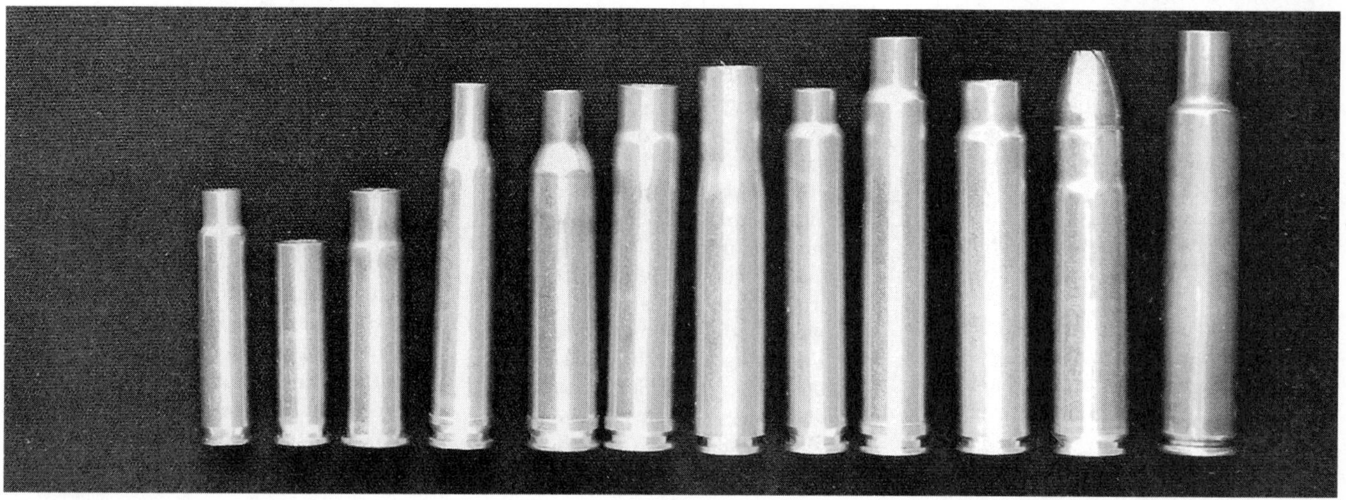

Some Quality Cartridge unprimed brass cases, left to right: 6/5mm TCU; .351 Winchester Self Loading (SL); 357 Herrett; .240 H & H Magnum; .270 Ackley Magnum; .416 Taylor; .425 Westley Richards; .30 Gibbs; .358 STA; .416 ACC-REL; .500 Cyrus; and .366 DGW.

cartridge and four Barnes Buster Bullets for non-deflecting deep penetration, three for big-bore handguns and a 400-gr. for the 45-70 Gov't.

Barnes also has two clubs handloaders can join (www.bcarnesbullets.com). One, Club X, is free, while the Copper Club has a minimal annual fee. Club X members can view selected loads from the Barnes Ballistics Lab, peek at the latest products, receive an online newsletter, receive handloading tips, and even enter drawings for prices. The Copper Club members receive five gift packages, have access to all load data being developed for *Barnes Reloading Manual No. 5*, enrollment in Barnes University, and more.

Frankford Arsenal has new 20-round slip-top boxes to house handloaded cartridges in the .222 Remington size range, from the .17 Remington to the .222 Remington Magnum. These boxes are available in choice of blue or gray coloring. Another great Frankford box for container for handloads is the Ammo Vault. Available in two sizes to fit most cartridges, the Vault is constructed of impact-resistant material which will not break if dropped. A rubber molded bottom cushions the cartridges, and foam inserts hold the cartridges securely. Overall height adjustment accommodates different cartridges, and the two sections of the vault lock together to keep the lid from falling off. (Simply squeeze where it states "Press Here" and pull to separate the two halves and access the cartridges.) The RMD size Ammo Vault accommodates rounds from .222 Remington up to .35 Whelen size, while the RLG Vaults handle the Magnums — Remington, Weatherby, Winchester, etc. — and cartridges to the .50-110 Winchester or similar sizes.

Loading trays are a necessity for handloading and Frankford Arsenal has a Universal Loading Tray capable of handling most rifle case calibers from .17 to .458 and handgun caliber cases from 9mm to .500 Smith & Wesson. Unique stepped cavities accommodate several different size brass cases Handgun caliber holes are on one side, and the rifle case caliber holes are on the reverse side. The trays measure 11-1/4 inches long, by 5-1/2 inches wide and measure 1-1/4 inches deep. Capacity is 50 cases, either side. For handloaders with preference for loading trays to fit a specific cartridge case, Frankford has a dozen "Perfect Fit" trays to fit most cases from the .25 ACP to the .500 Nitro Express. Except for the .500 Nitro tray, which has a 45-case capacity, the trays hold .50 cases.

Sinclair International features drop tubes for powder measures, R.F.D. Culver-style powder measures, neck sorting tools, flash hole cleaners, and a host of other products for handloaders. Sinclair manufactures some products and is a source for others, such as Forster, Lyman, RCBS, Redding, and Wilson. (Wilson manufactures stainless steel straight line neck sizing and bullet seating dies, while Sinclair produces an arbor press which works well with the Wilson dies and is small enough to take to the range.) Sinclair's Custom Press is C-type press machined from solid aluminum alloy. Capable of handling cases up to the .308 size, the press features a one-inch ram with a snap-in shellholder slot and is also small enough to take to the range.

Any handloader using Redding dies will appreciate the Sinclair Lock Ring Pliers. These machined aluminum split pliers clamp around the locking rings and lock nut on the Redding dies and make loosening a jammed ring easy. And the pliers do not damage the locking rings.

Western Powders Inc. publishes two Load Guides, one for Accurate powders and one for Ramshot powder. The latest editions are 3.4 and 4.4, respectively, and both feature new data for the 7.62 x39mm, 6.5x47mm Lapua, and the .308 Marlin cartridges. No dimensional drawings are in these guides, but they do include good loading data with a listing of bullet weight, make, type, starting load, maximum load, velocities, maximum load pressure, and cartridge overall length (COL). Other pertinent information includes test barrel length and rate of twist, primer used, and bullet diameter.

The Accurate guide provides loading data for twenty handgun cartridges from the 5.7x28mm FN to the .500 Maximum, and seventy rifle cartridges from the .17 Remington Fireball to the .550 Magnum. Loads for lead bullets are provided for some of the cartridges. In addition, a few loads are provided for Blackhorn 209 powder users in their muzzleloaders and for 22 cartridges used frequently by Cowboy Action Shooters. These CAS cartridges range from the .32 H & R Magnum to the .50-90. Some notes are provided for specific cartridges, such as using Dacron filler with the load for the .45-120 SS cartridge.

The Ramshot Guide includes loading data for two dozen handgun cartridges from the FN 5.7x28mm to the .500 Maximum, and 71 rifle cartridges from the .17 Remington Fireball to the .550 Magnum. The data is provided in the same manner in both guides but not all cartridges in production today are included. (Data for the .416 Remington Magnum cartridge is provided in both guides, for example, but no data is provided for the .416 Ruger or .416 Rigby cartridges.)The same Buckhorn 209 data is included in this guide, but there are loads for five popular CAS handgun cartridges using regular Ramshot powder and lead cast or swaged bullets.

Another handy reference volume for handloaders is the *Ammo Encyclopedia, 2nd Edition*, from **Blue Book Publications**. This 840-page softbound volume resembles one of older Sears, Roebuck & Co. catalogs in size. It does not feature loading data, but it does contain dimensioned drawings of cartridges from the .17 Remington Fireball to the .700 Nitro Express in the centerfire sporting rifle section, and additional cartridges under other chapter headings. (This tome contains 62 chapters, with cartridges — current, obsolete, sporting, military, proprietary, wildcats, rimfire, shotshells, etc. — featured in chapters 40 through 54. There are even a few cartridges listed as "Too New to Include....") Data for each cartridge includes alternate names and/or calibers, history, description, ballistics, current manufacturer if still in production, and comments, along with a dimensioned drawing. Dimensions are provided for most, but not all, cartridges. For example, the 5.8x42mm Chinese cartridge has dimensions provided, but the 5.8x21mm Chinese cartridge does not.

This volume provides information on primer, propellant, cartridge case, and bullet manufacturing, ballistics, history, formulas and much more. The case dimensions are all much of the same type, but not always to the same scale. In the first edition, not all cartridge drawings were of the same type and some computer-generated drawings were rather crude. In this edition it is much easier to compare cartridges, and there are nearly 600 handgun, rifle, and shotshell cartridges featured.

Shotshell handloaders should check out **Ballistic Products Inc.** (BPI).This firm, which has been in business since 1974, advertises it has "Everything for Shotgunners." It offers calls, books, choke tubes, and even more important to handloaders, loading presses, accessories and shotshell reloading components. At last count the firm had sixteen different reloading manuals, each devoted to a specific topic, such as "The Sixteen Gauge Manual," "The Mighty 10 Gauge," "Handloading Steel Shotshells," and "Handloading Hevi-Shot." Some of these manuals have gone through several revisions so the contained information is up-to-date.

Need a roll crimper, wads for reloading 8-gauge, 24- or 32-gauge shells? BPI has them. Roll crimpers for use in a drill press are available in six gauges, from 28 to 8, plus .410 (no 14-, 24-, or 32-gauge roll crimpers). Wads are available in the usual gauges, plus also for the small gauges, such as the 24, 28, and 32. BPI even has all-brass hulls for these smaller gauges, including the 32 but not the 14. To package those reloaded shotshells, especially if you purchase any once-fired hulls, BPI has new factory-style boxes in 5-, 10- and 25-round sizes. Constructed of select-grade heavy card stock, these boxes will outlast many factory boxes.

Handloaders looking for a new powder measure might check out the JDS Quick Measure (www.quick-measure.com) produced by **Johnson Design Specialities.** This measure is said to charge 100 cases in less than four minutes and not cut any powder. It may not be a beauty to behold, but efficiency is the key word, and if it works well, color, shape, etc., shouldn't matter.

If you handload for any unusual wildcat or obsolete cartridges for which your brass supply is running low, or are looking for suitable brass, the Hollywood, Maryland, firm of **Quality Cartridges** (http:/www.qual-cart.com) might jut have what you need. This firm loads for over 200 different cartridges, and has brass with the correct head-stamps on the cases. The firm does not sell single cases but in minimums of 20 rounds or more. The firm even has brass for some of the old smallbore English cartridges such as the .240 Holland & Holland (note that this is not the larger, and later, .244 H&H Magnum) and the .242 Vickers. Among the wildcat cases available, or loaded cartridges, are most of the Ackley line; the sharp-shoulder Gibbs; the Mashburn; and the list goes on. If you're loading for one of the early Winchester Self-Loading rifles and need .32 WSL, .35 WSL, .351 WSL, or .401 WSL cases, try Quality.

There are times when the ultimate handloader can make use of a small lathe. (Most handloaders have a bit of experimenter in them, resulting in all sorts of wildcat cartridges and other related oddities.) **Sherline Products** (www.sherline.com) has two lathes, the Model 4000 (inch) and Model 4400 (inch), which operate on regular 100-240 VAC lines. Sherline also has several models, including metric sizes, in place of inch (English) measurements. The 4000 lathe has eight inches between centers, while the 4400 has 17 inches between centers. The Model 4000 weighs less than 24 pounds, which means it can fit easily onto most loading benches. Accessories are available including digital readouts, vertical mills, tool posts, stereo micsroscope, zero handwheels, live center, and more. Reducing the rim diameter or thickness on a cartridge case becomes a simple task, as does making a rimless case or a rebated-rim case out of a rimmed case. Capable of machining most materials from plastic to stainless steel, the Sherline lathe can even be used to produce small parts, although most work would probably center around cartridge case, bullets or possibly loading dies.

Wolfe Publishing Company has a new (5th) edition of *Propellant Profiles*. Featuring detailed descriptions of most of the current and discontinued powder, this 452-page volume is probably the most comprehensive book of its type available on the market today. It also includes some recommended loads and tips for improving your reloading procedures.

The Big Three (Federal, Remington, and Winchester) all offer unprimed brass cases for the most popular cartridges they manufacture, but for the obsolete and some of the less popular calibers brass for reloading may be difficult to locate. **Graf & Sons** (grafs.com), **Huntington Die Specialities** (www.huntingtons.com), and **Quality Cartridges** (www.qual-cart.com) are excellent places to start looking. For obsolete military caliber brass and some others, **TR&Z USA** Trading Corporation (www.ppu-usa.com) has some great new brass from Serbia. (The firm also had loaded ammunition in most calibers.) Looking for .22 Jet (remember this revolver cartridge?) or 7.63mm Mauser (not 7.62mm Tokarev) brass and/or cartridges? TR&Z USA has them, and even .30 (7.65mm) Luger, along with the more popular 9mm Luger, .40 S&W, .45 ACP, etc. In the rifle line there are the 6.5x52mm Carcano, 6.5x55mm Swedish, 7.54x54mm French, 7.5x55mm Swiss, 8x50mm Lebel, 7.63x53mm Argentine, and 8x56mm Mannlicher, and for those who happened to obtain one of the new semi-auto MP-44s, 7.9x33mm Kurz, commonly called the 8mm Kurz. The firm also has 9.3x62mm Mauser brass and cartridges in addition to many of the regular American calibers. (No unprimed 5.45x39mm brass or cartridges yet.)

Annual reloading manuals, such as this one by the Hodgdon Powder Company, provide the most up-to-date handloading data.

Handloaders who are building their own wildcat rifle, and need or want to do their loading dies at the same time, can obtain 7/8"x14 tpi die blanks, in 12L-14 or 416 stainless steel, from **Newlon Precision** (www.newlonprecision.com). Available as body forming, sizing, and/or bullet seating dies, and ready to ream, with pilot holes from .17 to .338 caliber, these dies use standard Redding or Wilson bushings.

The Smith & Wesson First Model .32 Hand Ejector

BY **DAN SHIDELER**

This doggy old First Model .32 Hand Ejector looks every bit of its 100-plus years, but it still speaks right up with a cylinderful of .32 S&W Short, .32 S&W Long or .32 Colt New Police.

It just amazes me how some classic guns obstinately refuse to become collectible. I can think of no better example than Smith & Wesson's First Model .32 Hand Ejector, aka Model of 1896. This gun isn't a hot collectible, and for the life of me I can't figure out why.

These days, any gun with the Colt name is an automatic collectible. Part of this is no doubt due to the on-again, off-again status of the Colt company itself. Any day, it seems, Colt's Manufacturing Company, LLC will breathe its last and go to the Big Reloading Press in the Sky. Yet Smith & Wessons lag far behind Colts in general collectibility.

Put down that rotten tomato and hear me out. I know that Triple Locks and most other N-frames are very hot these days. I know that the old S&W large-frame top-break single- and double-actions are collector's gold. I know that a real rarity like the S&W .320 Revolving Rifle will command thousands upon thousands of dollars. But when a shootable, fully-functional example of a S&W First Model .32 Hand Ejector can be had for under $200, something's way out of whack somewhere.

The First Model .32 Hand Ejector was a truly significant firearm. For one thing, it was S&W's first solid-frame, swing-out revolver. For another, it was an important transitional model between S&W's black powder top-break revolvers and its classic double-actions. For yet another, it introduced the .32 S&W Long cartridge, possible the best-natured centerfire cartridge of all time. For still another – and most significantly -- its design was truly timeless, being the basis for virtually every S&W and Taurus revolver introduced between 1896 and today, including the ultra-modern .460 and .500 S&W Magnum X-frames.

So although I am certainly in the oppressed minority on this one – hey, maybe I qualify for a government grant! -- I maintain that the S&W First Model .32 Hand Ejector is the fifth most significant American handgun of all time, right after the Colt Paterson .36 percussion revolver, the Colt Model P/1873 Single Action Army, the Colt 1911, and the Colt 1889 Double Action. As such, it should be the bonnie darling of American collectors. But it's not.

Prior to the First Model .32 Hand Ejector, S&W's products had been pretty much confined to two-piece-frame revolvers: the itty-bitty Models 1, 1-1/2 and 2 rimfire tip-ups; the First, Second and Third Model large-frame .44 and .45 top-breaks; the various .32- and .38-caliber top-breaks; and the huge .44-caliber Frontiers, Double Actions and Favorites. As varied as they were, these revolvers all had one thing in common: a hinged frame that was nowhere near as strong as Colt's solid-frame guns.

I'm not throwing stones at these early Smiths. In my opinion, they're the epitome of the mid-Victorian American revolver. I jist love 'n' ad-marr them, as we say here in Indiana. But they all became yesterday's news in 1889 when Colt rolled out its first solid-frame, swing-out-cylinder double action. The Colt Model 1889 – and its immediate descendants, the Model 1892, Model 1895, New Model Pocket and New Model Police -- totally redefined the concept of the revolver and set every other existing American handgun on the road to obsolescence.

Don't believe me? When Theodore Roosevelt, our most gun-wise President, served as Police Commissioner of New York City in 1895 and 1896, he decided to standardize the sidearm of New York's Finest. He chose the Colt New Model Police .32 double action, believing it to be the most advanced revolver available. No big-bore Colt or S&W single action for Teddy but a solid-frame .32 Colt double action with a swing-out cylinder.

Roosevelt apparently had a thing for Colt swing-out double actions. When he went charging up San Juan Hill on July 1, 1898, he was carrying a Colt Model 1895 .38 Long Colt double action, and he sent at least one Spaniard to his eternal rest with it. As a volunteer and an officer, Roosevelt could have carried any sidearm he liked, and he chose a Colt .38 double action.

Where were Smith & Wesson all this time? They were fat, dumb and happy, like a child who's eaten too much cheesecake. In 1871 they had received a massive contract from Russia's Grand Duke Alexis for their #3 .44 Russian top-break, a deal that was pretty much the Mother of All Defense Contracts. It wasn't until Colt shocked them awake in 1889 that Smith & Wesson decided that they'd better get cracking and come up with a solid-frame double-action of their own. They did and in doing so changed their destiny forever.

The First Model .32 Hand Ejector, Model of 1896 was covered under a bevy of patents, the most important of which covered the revolver's double-action lockwork and swing-out cylinder design. In fact, the company was so proud, or so protective, of its patents that it took the unique step of roll-marking them not on the gun's barrel or rib, but on the outside of its cylinder. I have not yet chased down each of the patents pertaining to the Model 1896, but I won't have any trouble remembering their issue dates. There they are, plain as day:

"SMITH & WESSON
SPRINGFIELD MASS.
USA PATENTED
JULY 1. 84.
APRIL 9. 89.
MARCH 27. 94. MAY 29. 94.
MAY 21. 95. JULY 16. 95."

That's a mouthful to put on such a tiny cylinder. With all these patents being displayed so prominently, it's safe to assume that Smith & Wesson knew they had a winner on their hands. And they did. Even today, more than a century later, it remains a winner.

The First Model .32 Hand Ejector differed a bit from the later Hand Ejectors that we all know and love. Its cylinder locks up at two points, at its rear and on its top. There's no barrel lug to secure the extractor rod up front. It doesn't even have a cylinder latch on its left sideplate; you unlatch the cylinder by pulling forward on the spring-loaded extractor rod. Finally, its cylinder bolts not at the bottom, as a function of the lockwork, but at the top of the frame.

This last feature was a carryover from the earlier S&W top-break double actions. It is simple and ingenious. A spring-loaded bar – the cylinder bolt proper -- is set lengthwise into the top strap and hinged at its front. When the hammer is cocked, either in single or double action, a cam on the top of the hammer lifts the spring-loaded bolt

Here we see the hinged cylinder bolt in the top strap just beginning to rise, freeing the cylinder for indexing.

The S&W Model 1896 introduced the .32 S&W Long (left) but also fired the .32 S&W (center) and the .32 Colt New Police (right).

clear of the cylinder's bolt cut, releasing it only when the cylinder has cycled fully. The bolt is then released to its fully downward position, locking itself into the cylinder bolt cut.

The Model 1896 got its Hand Ejector name from its method of ejecting (or more properly extracting) fired cartridges. Just pull forward on the cylinder pin, swing out the cylinder, pop the Ejector rod briskly with your Hand (get it?) and all six empties would come flying out all at once. This procedure isn't quite as fast as that of the various S&W top-breaks with their automatic ejectors, but when paired with the Model 1896's solid-frame design it made for quite an admirable little revolver. At any rate so thought the Jersey City, N.J. Police Department, which bought 169 of them in 1896 in what was Smith & Wesson's first sale to a law enforcement agency.

No doubt about it, the Model 1896 was a new breed of cat for Smith & Wesson. All that was lacking was a cartridge with a little more oomph than the .32 Long – which made its debut in the Model 1896 – and that was just down the road with the .38 Hand Ejector Model of 1899 chambered in .38 Special. Yet the inside-lubricated .32 S&W Long wasn't a bad cartridge by the standards of the day. Colt recognized this fact and ditched its outside-lubricated .32 Short and Long Colt chamberings, introducing a flat-pointed knockoff of the .32 S&W Long that they called the .32 Colt New Police. (Yes, the .32 Colt New Police is interchangeable with the .32 S&W Long. The .32 Short and Long Colt are not.)

The First Model .32 Hand Ejector was manufactured from 1896 until 1903, when it was superseded by the .32 Hand Ejector, Second Model, Model of 1903. The Model of 1903 had all the features we've come to associate with Hand Ejectors: a barrel lug that provided an additional cylinder lock; a cylinder latch thumbpiece on the left sideplate; and a lockwork-activated cylinder bolt that operated from the bottom, not the top, of the frame recess.

The Model 1896 was built on the obsolete S&W "I" frame, which is a tad smaller than today's "J" frame. The revolver was available with 3-1/4-, 4-1/4-, and 6-inch barrels, with the 3-1/4-incher seeming to be the most common. Finishes were blue or nickel and grips were plain black hard rubber. A target model with adjustable sights was offered but is very scarce. For more information on this very first Hand Ejector, or any other Hand Ejector, I can recommend no better reference than Nahas' and Supica's Standard Catalog of Smith & Wesson.

Nahas and Supica say that a Model 1896 in Excellent condition is worth around $550. I've not yet found one in Excellent condition. My 1896 is in somewhat less than Excellent condition, its nickel plating being severely eroded. Now back in the days when I was product manager of the country's oldest maker of band instruments, we determined that sulphur compounds rapidly oxidize nickel finishes. We also found that sulphur is present in substances you'd never suspect such as pencil erasers, adhesives, natural gas and certain grades of coal. I suppose the lesson here is that, to keep your nickel-plated guns as tarnish- and corrosion-free as possible, keep them away from sulphur-bearing compounds. Don't store them near a gas furnace or in a coal bin lest they end up looking like my poor old 1896.

Whoever owned my 1896 must have given it a sulphur bath every Saturday night. Its finish is at best cloudy and bubbled; at worst, it's non-existent. Still, its grips are sound, if worn, and it functions perfectly. I try not to get too attached to any particular gun, but I have to admit that there's something about my 1896 that pops my cork. It'll never win Best of Show, but it goes bang six times pretty quickly if I want it to.

It cost me $150. In my eyes, that's absurdly low for a gun of such historical significance. But rather than argue that the Model 1896 should be more collectible, and thus more expensive, I think I'll just make the most of the situation and buy every 1896 I come across. That'll mean no beer or pipe tobacco for a couple of weeks every month, but that's a sacrifice I'm willing to make.

GUNSMITHING PRODUCTS

BY KEVIN MURAMATSU

"There's nothing new under the sun." Maybe so, but there seems to always a bigger hammer, nicer house, faster car, more expensive rifle, or higher capacity pistol.

Gunsmithtown is like that. Many companies come out with something new, like parts or sights for just one or few firearms, and then spend the next two years expanding the line to cover all the common models. This is a good thing, as a well-intentioned and -manufactured product should be applied to the limits of its applicability. The original idea is expanded until it is improved, flatteringly copied, or, sometimes, outright stolen. Then maybe something new comes along, but frequently it is really the same thing but looks a bit different to meet someone else's idea of perfection. Those are two of the great things about freedom: free enterprise and free markets. If someone wants something, someone else will make it. [*Editor's Note: . . .and, most likely, someone else will rip it off. -DMS*]

A perfect example of this phenomenon is the vast assortment of aftermarket parts and upgrades for the AR-15 series of rifles, particularly pistol grips and handguards. Many of these items are effectively user installable, many are not, and even the easy ones are often taken to a smith to install anyway.

On the flip side of the coin are even cooler, and unfortunately, less common examples. New tools that only a gunsmith could (or even should) appreciate can be seen in the pages of catalogs from places like Brownells. A sear polishing jig means nothing and is worth nothing to the average American, but it can be the centerpiece of a gunsmith's source of income. An AR-15 action wrench just looks like a weird metal stick to my cousin, but to the armorer's eyes it is a tool of indispensable value.

Every year we are blessed with a small new assortment of those unique tools, a few not so unique but still very useful tools, and an absolute glut of new parts to meet some dude's pseudoscientific value assessment for "the best of the best."

There are always new cleaning utensils and liquids every year, so we shall begin by discussing a few of those new residents in Gunsmithtown.

THE TOOLS OF CLEANING

The boys at **Battenfeld Technologies** have developed two little handy accessories. The first is called a Patch Trap. A "why didn't anyone think of that sooner" tool, it simply straps onto the muzzle and catches patches and splatter as they are pushed out of the bore. Gunsmiths have been taping or rubber banding water bottles for years onto rifle muzzles, but this little inexpensive doohickey replaces that system with a little elegance and a lot of sanitary thinking. It reduces clean up times and dimes involved in wiping solvent and crud off the floor, bench, and face.

In conjunction with the trap, they have also developed a little tool called a Rapid Bore Guide to replace the third hand that you weren't born with. Taking a standard bore guide (which everyone with a brain ought to be using to clean a rifle) they have added a little attachment to make it easier to center a patch on a jag while pushing the rod through the bore guide into the barrel, using only two hands. The leading attachment grasps the patch perpendicularly to the bore, and you just shove the rod and jag through the attachment into the bore, taking the patch with it. Now this isn't

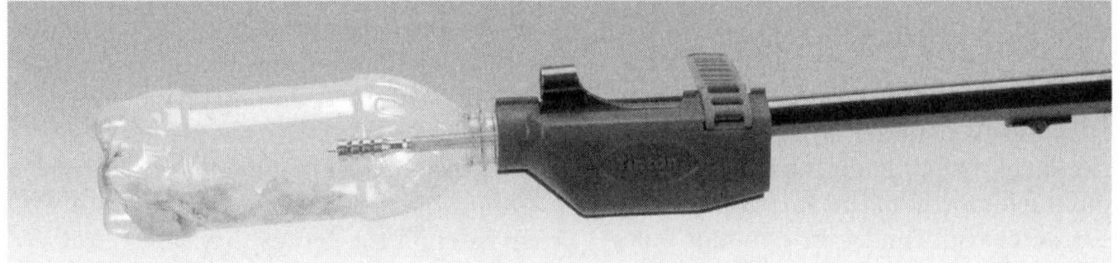

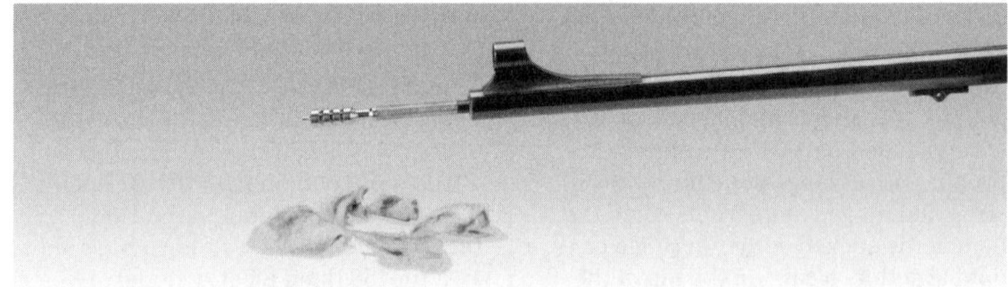

Tipton Patch Trap. Catch it or clean it up. Your choice. (Photo courtesy Battenfeld Tech.)

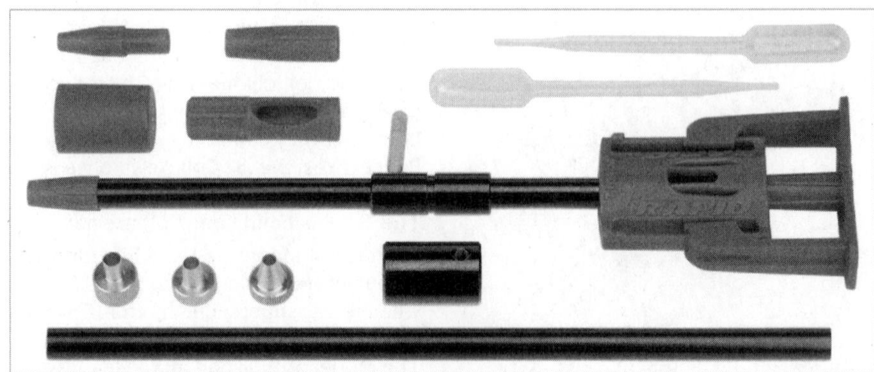

The Tipton Rapid jag/patch assist is like a third hand with seven fingers. (Photo courtesy Battenfeld Tech.)

a difficult task without this tool, but it does quicken it up, and in combination with the bore guide keeps the patch on the jag as it goes through the receiver, where you have no opposable thumb to hold it on, and where the patch can often fall off. Oil or solvent can also be efficiently applied while the patch is being held.

An interesting, related developmental thread has resulted in tri-lobed cleaning patches from **Rigel Products** known as Triangle Patches. We all know that normal, square patches work well, but the surface area of the patches is not maximized, because the patches form folds that are not used effectively. These lobed patches, when pushed down the bore, offer similar amounts of surface area for cleaning but wrap around the brush better without jamming in the bore. This effectively grants the user a patch that hits the bore with more effective surface area and thus shortens the time used in bore cleaning and reduces the number of patches used.

The same outfit also makes bore brushes of two diameters called Jag Brushes. The smaller diameter frontal bristles hold the patch while the standard diameter brushes at the rear scrape away crud.

THE GOOPINESS OF CLEANING

A cursory look at the new cleaners and oils on the market reveals a trend transitioning to the synthetic. A great representative of this movement is from good old **Brownells**. Friction Defense Xtreme gun oil has a huge operating range; from -100°F to +550°F. Any oil with additives like Teflon, being suspensions rather than solutions, generally settle, needing to be shaken prior to use to resuspend the small particles or nodules composing the additives. An unsung benefit to this stuff is that it does not come out of suspension like other lubricants. Thus there's little need to vigorously shake the bottle prior to application, and anything that comes out today will be as good as the stuff that came out yesterday after sitting on the shelf.

...AND FROM THE BROWN CORNER...

Brownells also has a neat new bluing tank accessory that will reduce pain. Hot bluing salts hurt when they splash and burn a hole clear through your hand. The Bluing Shield is meant to act

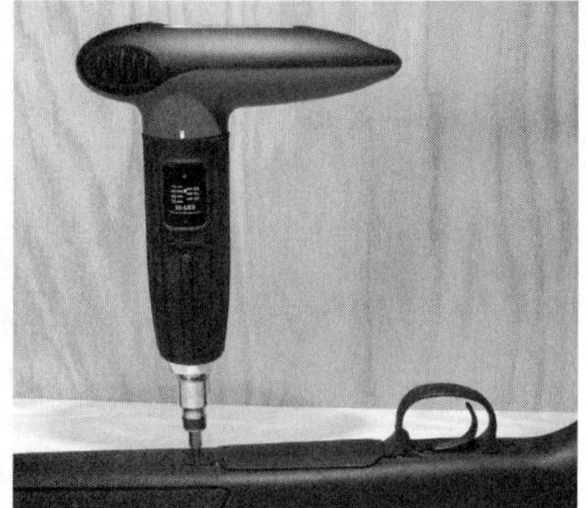

Brownells' new torque handle. Hefty and tough. Here, it is seen magically turning a Remington action screw all by itself.

as a splash guard when adding hot salts to the hot tanks, thus keeping your skin intact by blocking any possible splash during these occasions. It is sized to fit the Brownells bluing tanks perfectly.

Welcomed is the Brownells Adjustable Torque Handle. From as little as five inch/pounds to well over seventy inch/pounds it is suitable for scope bases and rings, action screws, and anything else you could think of to torque. It is heavy and well made, and very ergonomic and easy to adjust, using the standard Brownells Magna-Tip inserts.

Brownells is also selling a four-inch Magna-Tip extension for the screwdriver sets. Sometimes the long driver handle is just not quite long enough, and for many of those times, this extension should calm the troubled storms of frustration caused by a driver being just a little bit too short.

TOOLS, TOOLS GALORE

Score High Gunsmithing has a wonderful new tool to assist in bedding an action into a stock. Complementing their excellent adjustable pillar stock drilling jig and Pro Bed 2000 epoxy are their stock bedding blocks. These units are available for Remington 700 short and long actions, ADLs and BDLs, and replace the trigger guard and bottom metal during the bedding process, preventing damage or stuck-on compound on the trigger guards. The blocks come off the stock quickly and easily, with no cracking, and if release agent is used, do so every time.

A pocket-sized contraption called The Gun Tool has been produced by **Avid Design**. Essentially a folding pocket gunsmith toolbox, it can be easily carried in a range bag and contains some very useful items. Torx and hex head drivers, replaceable magnetic bits retained in a compartment, a choke tube wrench and scope adjustment blade, punch, and a small knife are all housed within its walls. Keep it in the range bag with a small hammer and any gunsmith worth his lathe should be able to fix three-quarters of the problems at the range and make despondent shooters there happy indeed.

Used in other fields such as camping and government activities are the products from the company known as **Loksak**. I've found that these tough waterproof, airproof, extreme temperature-resistant bags are excellent choices for long term storage of firearms. I have cleaned up for storage many antique or collectable firearms, and the idea of a flexible container with these properties is very appealing to me. Combined with active moisture fighters like the

The Avid Gun Tool is a pocket toolbox. Notable are the hex driver bits in the back that insert in the end.

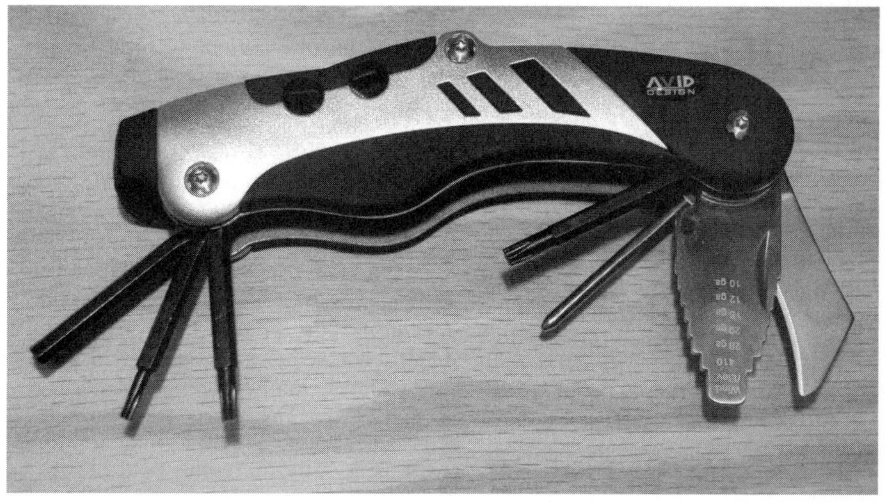

vapor releasing Inhibitor VCI Pro Chips from **Van Patten Industries**, or even plain old desiccant packs, a gunsmith or gun owner can keep an old valuable heirloom safe and sound, not worrying about ambient moisture causing harm to the collection or keepsake. They are just now breaking into the firearms storage arena, and the bags come in many sizes and are surprisingly affordable. The glory days of cosmoline are over.

Not even available or even properly named as this column is written is a very useful upgrade to the Hawkeye borescope from **Gradient Lens Corporation**. The Hawkeye uses a small eyepiece and tube, and with the use of proprietary gradient lens technology, it allows the gunsmith to peer down the bore of a firearm with crystal clarity. Useful for determining bore condition and finding imperfections or damage, looking through the little eyepiece can nevertheless be somewhat straining, and only one person can see it at a time. Fortunately, any existing Hawkeye borescope can now be upgraded with video technology. It allows the user to run the scope down the bore and display the image in video form on a computer monitor. This is incredibly useful. Customers often look upon the gunsmith with suspicion, never believing that they, of all people, could damage their bores, crowns, or chambers with poor practices. It never quite clicks that there may be a series of pits in the bore too small to see clearly from the muzzle or heavy copper fouling in the grooves that is affecting accuracy.

This upgrade not only displays in video for a present customer, but also records the video so that the relatively computer-competent smith can save it to use as evidence of a problem. It should be easy to foresee the arguments reduced, the solutions more quickly reached, and the incredible reduction in eye strain made possible by this product.

The last entry in the general tools is from **Manson Precision Reamers**. A new revolver tooling reamer set is sure to make revolversmiths' lives more convenient. This set is designed to pilot off the shaft of the reamer itself, with some spring tension at the muzzle end pulling the reamer forward, while the hand turns the T-handle beyond the muzzle. This allows truly concentric cutting with minimized chatter. One reamer cuts the forcing cone, another trues and squares the rear of the barrel, and the third chamfers the corner between the two.

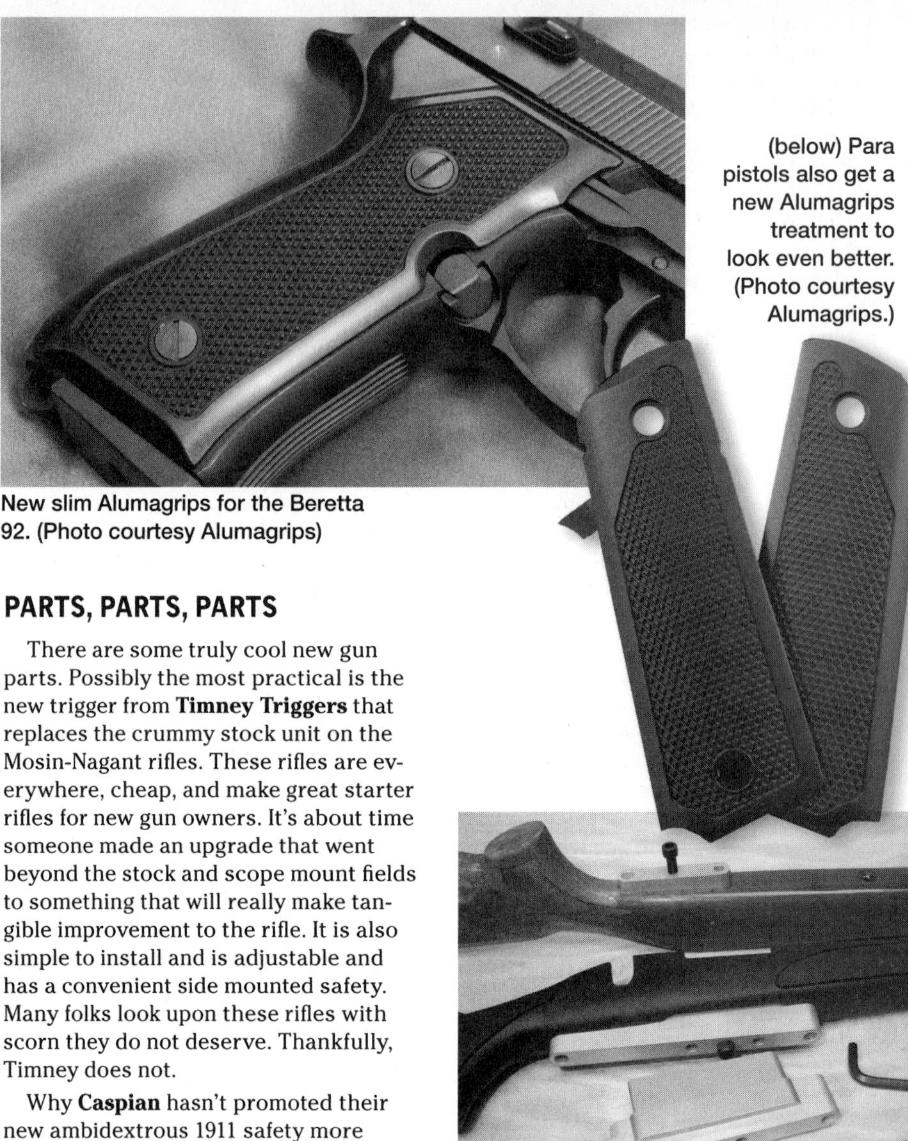

New slim Alumagrips for the Beretta 92. (Photo courtesy Alumagrips)

(below) Para pistols also get a new Alumagrips treatment to look even better. (Photo courtesy Alumagrips.)

(above) The Score High Gunsmithing Bedding Block set in an ADL stock at the top and BDL stock in the middle.

PARTS, PARTS, PARTS

There are some truly cool new gun parts. Possibly the most practical is the new trigger from **Timney Triggers** that replaces the crummy stock unit on the Mosin-Nagant rifles. These rifles are everywhere, cheap, and make great starter rifles for new gun owners. It's about time someone made an upgrade that went beyond the stock and scope mount fields to something that will really make tangible improvement to the rifle. It is also simple to install and is adjustable and has a convenient side mounted safety. Many folks look upon these rifles with scorn they do not deserve. Thankfully, Timney does not.

Why **Caspian** hasn't promoted their new ambidextrous 1911 safety more energetically is puzzling. It utilizes an oversized sear pin with a dovetail on the end to retain the right side piece. This means that the little tab (while still present), and corresponding cut-out in the right grip panel is unnecessary, and that the right side piece stays tightly onto the frame. Furthermore, the joint between the two safety pieces uses not the usual tongue-in-groove, but a square peg and hole, and the connection is actually inside the right frame wall rather than in the middle. These features result in a much smoother, well-fit, better-feeling upgrade to the standard ambi safety.

Alumagrips has continued their line of aluminum pistol grips. Added to the pot are units for Beretta 92 pistols and Para double stack 1911 pistols. Both are slim line to minimize the width of the pistol grips. The beauty of these grips, as was true of the previous incarnations of them, is the incredibly textured

(right) Dave Manson's reamer set for revolvers is a new, innovative, convenient way to work on your revolver's forcing cone. (Photo courtesy Manson Precision Reamers.)

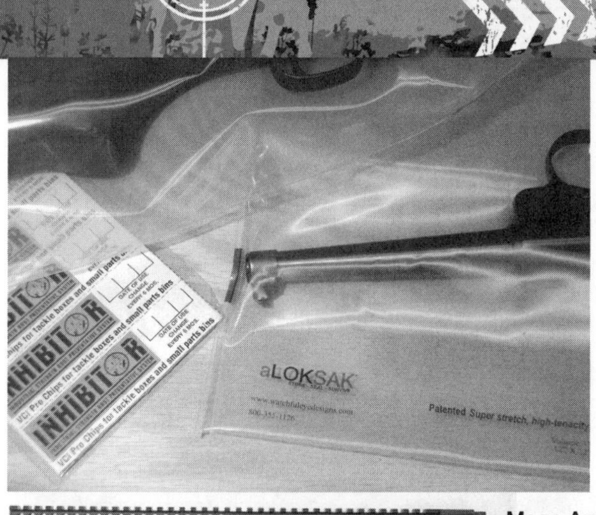

A great way to store guns for long periods, the Loksak bags combined with Inhibitor chips will keep your guns rust free for an extended time in the back of your closet or under your lawn.

Mega Arms' MTS monolithic single rail upper receiver, seen here on matching lower. A quad rail is also available for those needing to hang Christmas ornaments. (Photo courtesy Mega Arms.)

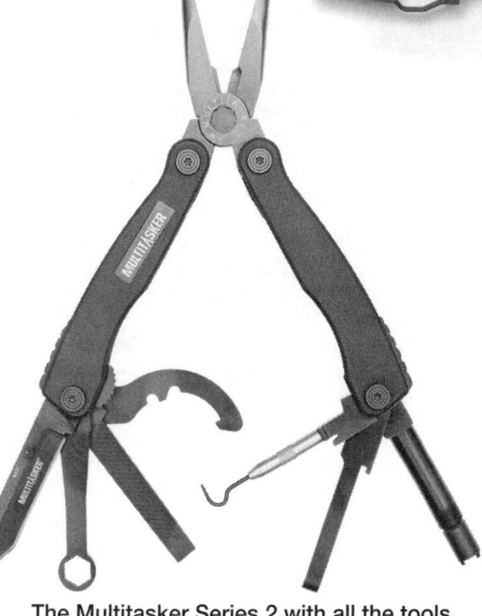

The Multitasker Series 2 with all the tools necessary to field repair the AR15 in a high quality package. (Photo courtesy Multitasker.)

checkering surfaces, providing a firm slip-resistant grip for even wet hands. The best part is that they look quite smart and definitely liven up the appearance of the handgun.

On a similar note, **Hogue** has expanded past the rubbery grips that they have been well known for and has introduced a line of grips made from G10. Varied checking patterns cut into these types of grips really take advantage of the appearance, setting off the laminated layers of multicolored material. This Extreme series also includes Damascus style steel, Titanium, and exotic wood insert grips as well.

Cylinder & Slide is producing replacement parts for the old Colt .380 (Type M) pistol. A quality replacement sear and hammer should work well in the old classics when the originals wear out and make great additions to the current line of parts for these collectables.

The last general part covered here is more of a representation of a positive trend than a note on a specific new part. The Winchester Model 70 allen-headed action screws from **NECG**, available from Brownells, are evidence of a growing drift toward non-traditional screw heads. This is the 21st century and there is no excuse to remain with flat heads and Phillips heads in screws. Let's get with the program. When we have hex heads, and even better, Torx headed screws available, then let us fully transition over. Hex heads, and Torx even more so, are much more difficult to bugger up; they prevent skipping and sliding off (which causes many blemishes on guns using flat headed screws); and they have a far higher torque resistance. Best of all, they look a heck of a lot cooler. A few companies such as Remington have been using hex-headed action screws for some time now and the rest of the pack needs to jump on the bandwagon forthwith. Sure, Torx or hex heads are a few pennies more expensive. But chances are an awful lot of people would be pleased to pay those few pennies to get a better screw or bolt.

AR STUFF

Continuing to lead the pack of new gunsmithing products are those for the AR-15. Still very hot sellers, the accessories related to the AR craze continue on *ad infinitum*. Can't complain, though.

Joining the oodles of upper and lower receivers on the market, sold stripped for home-building pleasure, is the **Mega Arms** MTS upper receiver. This Monolithic Tactical System (monolithic meaning that the upper receiver and handguard are one solid machined unit) will fit any milspec lower receiver. Being one solid unit aids in stiffening what would normally be the upper/handguard interface, making the rifle more consistently accurate by removing a stress point where the handguard, barrel, and receiver meet. Enhancing that even further is that the barrel remains free-floated. The MTS uses standard off-the-shelf barrels, and with a proprietary barrel nut and wrench it's simple for anyone, from the old time gunsmith to the hobby builder, to construct a nice rifle. A really snappy-looking AR can be build using this product, available in quad rail or single top rail models, combined with the corresponding matching lower that Mega has been producing for several years. Both pieces are machined from a large billet of 7075 aluminum. Together, this is one of the most cosmetically attractive arrangements in the AR world and it is clear that Mega is into good looks.

In the "convenient tools to have" category are two by **Multitasker**. A leatherman-style folding model called a Series 2 has a pair of pliers and several more AR specific tools enclosed within it, such as a carbine stock wrench, front sight tool, and cleaning pick. The Ultralight model is much smaller, the size of a Swiss army knife, with the same specialty tools, but minus the pliers, knife, and file. They will just disappear into your pocket, and if you are a AR busy gunsmith, they'll serve you well with those impromptu repairs at the range.

THE HAMILTON NO. 7

BY DAN SHIDELER

The original Hamilton No. 7 (bottom) was the inspiration for the later, and much sturdier, Firearms International/Garcia Bronco.

Some time back I told you about two single-shot rifles that, were they paintings, would certainly be described as minimalist: the Firearms International/Garcia Bronco and the Rau Arms Wildcat. Both the Bronco and the Wildcat were skeleton-stocked, pivoting-breech .22 rimfires that owed their design to a long-forgotten boys' rifle, the Hamilton No. 7.

Thanks to an inquiry from a reader whom I'll call Mr. Lincoln, I've been fortunate enough to get my hands on an original Hamilton No. 7. It's a fascinating little rifle, a memento of an equally fascinating era when young boys regularly shot rifles and no one gave it a second thought.

If you've never seen a Hamilton No. 7, you're not alone. If you have seen one, you're not likely to forget it. Probably more people were introduced to the No. 7 by the old Sears, Roebuck Consumer Guide, better known simply as the "Wish Book," than by any other route. For example, on page 373 of Sears, Roebuck's "Catalog No. 110" published in the fall of 1900, we find the following tucked into a sixteenth of a page in the upper right column:

"Our $2.00 Rifle – A Rare Bargain, and Perfectly Safe," the copywriter crowed. "Worth $3.50 / No. 34669 / Our new 22-Caliber Rifle. Uses 22-caliber short rim fire cartridges, including smokeless. Is absolutely safe. Total length, 32 inches. Length of barrel, 8 inches, brass lined, with steel jacket. The rifling is absolutely perfect, as fine as the highest priced rifles. Bead front and peep rear sights. All parts interchangeable. Entirely nickel plated. We recommend and guarantee these rifles. Our special price $2.00." [EDITOR NOTE: BOLD TYPE IN ORIGINAL]

That brief thumbnail description is just about as accurate as anything I could write, but is it just my imagination or does the writer sound a bit defensive? "A Real Bargain – And Perfectly Safe." "Worth $3.50." "Is absolutely safe." Farmer Brown, reading his Wish Book in the outhouse under the flickering light of a kerosene lamp 106 years ago, might be forgiven if he had his doubts about No. 34669. After all, two inches below this entry was one for the Quackenbush Junior .22 Safety Rifle, priced at $3.95. How could a two-buck gun made of bent wire be perfectly safe? And what kind of rifle has an 8-inch barrel, anyway?

Say hello to the Hamilton No. 7, Farmer Brown. Sears, Roebuck didn't mention the rifle by name, probably because the Hamilton Rifle Company of Plymouth, Mich., wouldn't permit it. After all, Hamilton had other retailers, too, probably none of whom would appreciate being undercut by Sears, Roebuck, the Wal-Mart of its day. But as the accompanying engraving clearly shows, the Sears, Roebuck No. 34669 was none other than the Hamilton No. 7, the very first product of the new Hamilton Rifle Company.

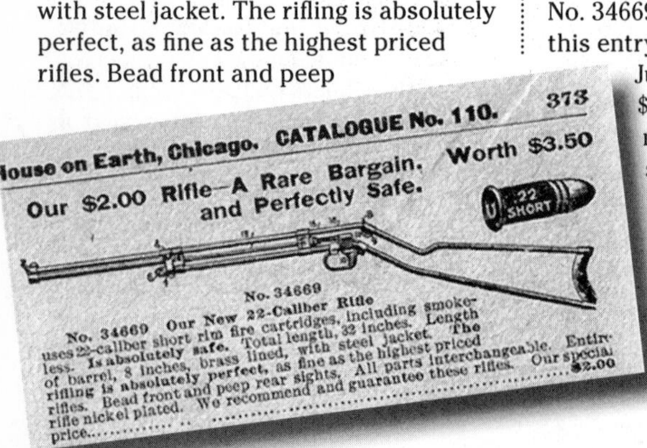

House on Earth, Chicago. CATALOGUE No. 110. 373

Our $2.00 Rifle—A Rare Bargain, and Perfectly Safe. Worth $3.50

No. 34669 Our New 22-Caliber Rifle

No. 34669 Our New 22-Caliber Rifle uses 22-caliber short rim fire cartridges, including smokeless. Is absolutely safe. Total length, 32 inches. Length of barrel, 8 inches, brass lined, with steel jacket. The rifling is absolutely perfect, as fine as the highest priced rifles. Bead front and peep rear sights. All parts interchangeable. Entire rifle nickel plated. We recommend and guarantee these rifles. Our special price........ $2.00

The Hamilton No. 7 as it appeared in the 1900 Sears, Roebuck catalog.

The Hamilton Rifle Co. may be the least-documented American rifle manufacturer. Information concerning it is usually found in bits and pieces over a wide variety of printed and electronic sources. One of the most helpful resources I have found is a website maintained by a fellow named Jim Ringbauer; its web address is http://home.comcast.net/%7Ejimringbauer/HamiltonRiflesindex.html. I recommend his site highly to anyone having an interest in Hamilton rifles.

According to Mr. Ringbauer, Clarence Hamilton of Plymouth, Mich., founded a windmill manufacturing concern, the descriptively-named Plymouth Iron Windmill Company, in 1882. Before

Believe it or not, the actual barrel of the No. 7 is only 8 inches long! The small ring-shaped assembly by the chamber mouth is the extractor.

the company folded about 16 years later, Hamilton entered a partnership with a buddy of his who had patented an all-metal air rifle. The two began producing the air rifle, which surprised everyone by becoming more popular than the company's windmills! In 1898, Hamilton sold out his share of the windmill concern as well as the air rifle company, the latter of which would go on to enduring fame as the Daisy Air Rifle Company. Hamilton's son Coello, a tool and die maker, joined what was left of his father's business, and the Hamilton Rifle Company was born.

Clarence Hamilton died two years later, but the company he founded would persist until 1945. The Hamilton Rifle Company would eventually manufacture 14 different models of rimfire rifles. The No. 7 was its first. (I have no idea what happened to Models No. 1 through No. 6. Possibly the numbering system started with the earlier Plymouth air rifles.)

The Hamilton Rifle Company marketed their products through several innovative channels and not just through the Sears, Roebuck catalog. According to Mr. Ringbauer, Hamilton rifles were often given away as a premium for selling so much costume jewelry or other door-to-door items, much as the early Daisy air rifles were given away for free if you bought a new windmill. Mr. Ringbauer relates that some feed manufacturers secreted Hamilton rifles in sacks of their product: "If you were lucky enough to buy the right sack, you got a free rifle." Sounds better than Cracker Jack!

All in all, 44,700 No. 7s were made from 1899 to 1901, of which Mr. Ringbauer estimates 99.9 percent have since gone to "Rifle Heaven." Perhaps this is why it took me 46 long years to see my first Hamilton No. 7. It's an interesting little gun.

The No. 7's stock, frame and receiver are made of four or more heavy steel wires or rods, anchored at the aft end by a cast-brass buttplate and at the fore by a pair of collar-shaped brass castings. (The skeleton stock apparently didn't thrill everyone, for the No. 7 morphed into the No. 11 after only two years. The No. 11 was basically a No. 7 with the skeleton stock filled by a metal panel, just as the Rau Wildcat was basically a Bronco with the stock filled by a walnut insert.)

As in the Bronco and Wildcat, the upper frontmost of these wires is a pivot rod, below which the 8-inch barrel is mounted. The barrel is locked in battery by a spring-loaded detent. To open the action and expose the chamber, you simply twist the barrel clockwise. A spring-steel extractor is inlet into the chamber; pulling it backward extracts the fired case. The entire gun, with the exception of the trigger, rear sight and firing pin spring, is nickel-plated.

The No. 7's front sight is a thin blade mounted onto a figure-8-shaped cast-brass collar that holds together the pivot rod and the barrel. The rear peep sight is a flimsy sheet-metal flange, wrapped around the upper buttstock wire and secured with a common screw and nut.

To fire the No. 7, you open the action, insert a shell and snap the action shut. You cock it by pulling back on a knurled circular boss mounted on a rod located just above the trigger and powered by an exposed coil spring. This is the firing pin, at 9 inches in length possibly the longest firing pin ever to grace a cartridge firearm. Once the firing pin is pulled all the way back, it engages a sear on the trigger. The gun is now ready to fire. There is no safety. If you decided not to fire a loaded No. 7, you

Manufacturer and model names are cast into the nickel-plated, cast brass buttplate.

had to grab the knurled boss securely, hold it in position, pivot the barrel to expose the chamber, and operate the extractor. Alternately, you could use the knurled boss to lower the firing pin oh-so-gently. Frankly, I'd rather just fire it in the mud.

If you have a sound No. 7, you should NOT fire modern .22 Shorts in it. Let me make that clearer: DO NOT FIRE MODERN .22 SHORT AMMUNITION IN A HAMILTON NO. 7. Remember, that little chamber is just a thin steel chamber surrounded by a brass casting. Frankly, in my opinion even CCI's .22 Short CB ammo has a little too much oomph for a Hamilton rifle. RWS .22 BB caps – which are powered only by the rimfire primer – appear to be safe in my No. 7, as are Aguila Super Colibris, though the latter's .22 Long dimensions make extraction a little difficult.

But let's be serious. There doesn't seem to be a compelling reason to shoot a Hamilton #7, not when so many totally safe rifles are just begging to be fired. I fired mine a few times, partly to be able to write this story and partly to be able to say that I have done it. But now that I've done it, up on the wall it goes.

Values for Hamilton No. 7s are a little hard to ascertain since they come on the market so infrequently. Other Hamiltons, such as the later No. 15 and No. 27, are a bit less scarce and typically command prices in the $150 to $300 range, based as always on condition. There appears to be no such thing as a Hamilton No. 7 in Mint or even Excellent condition; boys' rifles then were treated no better than boys' bicycles are today, and we all know what that means.

So here's to the Hamilton No. 7, a remarkable artifact of a by-gone day when boys were boys and men were men. But there's still a lot of boy in this man, and I'm happy I have a Hamilton No. 7 to remind me of it.

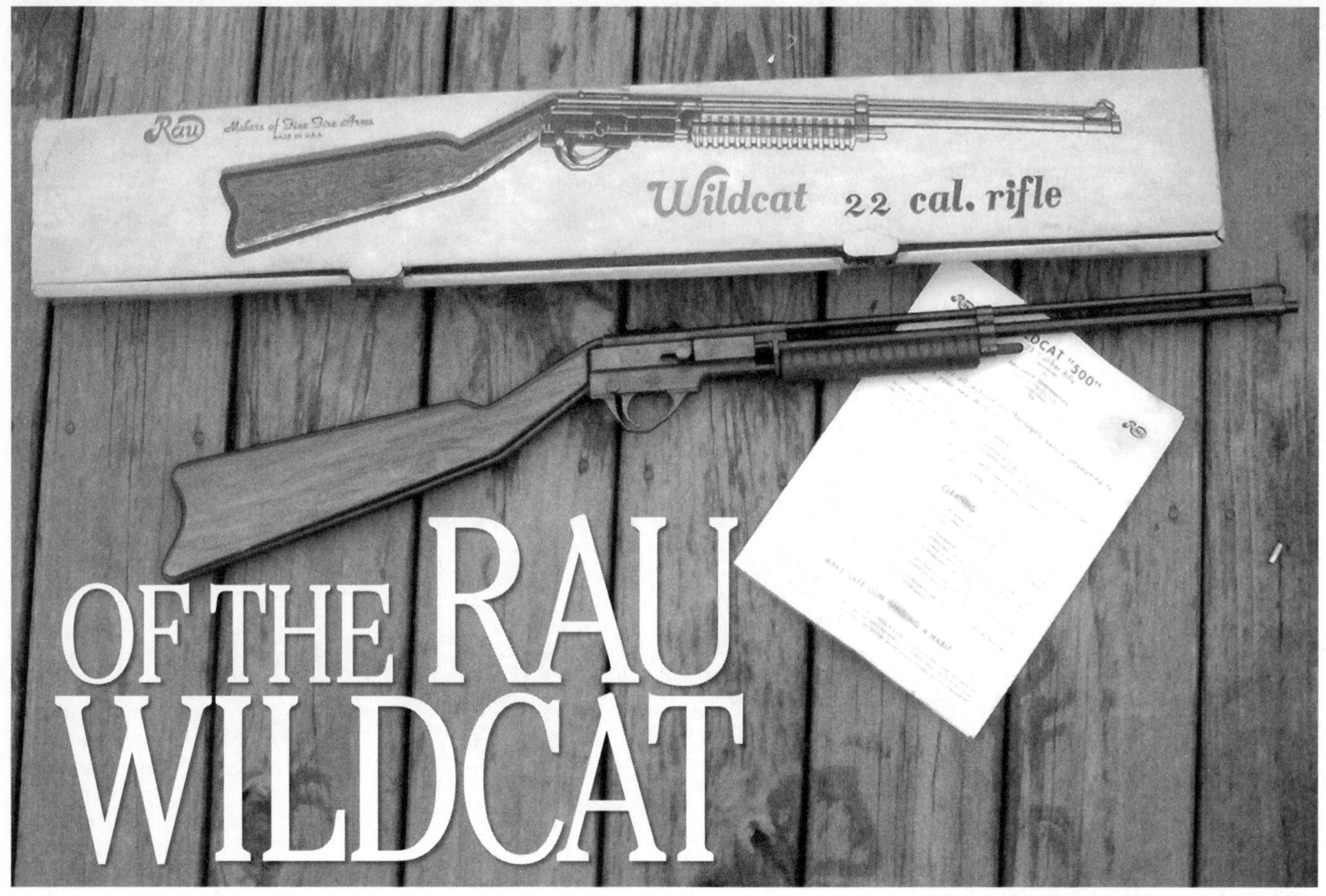

OF THE RAU WILDCAT

A new-in-box Rau Wildcat, complete with owner's manual.

BY **DAN SHIDELER**

Once upon a time, I told you about the Garcia Bronco, a laughably flimsy .22 rifle that looked like it was built on the sly in the Pendleton State Reformatory's metal shop.

When you start poking around a particular gun's history, you never know where you'll turn up. In this case, I turned up at the shop of Richard Clauss in Garrett, Indiana. As you might recall, Richard had customized a Bronco and washed away virtually all of its hideous ugliness.

As I sat there by Richard's bench admiring his handiwork, I saw a little light bulb flash above his head. "Hey!" he said. "Maybe you've seen one of these things before. . . ." After a few moments of burrowing through his secret archives he emerged carrying an oblong cardboard box. He plunked it down in front of me.

The box was two-color spot-printed with the legend "Rau / Makers of Fine Fire Arms / Made in U. S. A. / Wildcat .22 cal. Rifle / Rau Arms Corporation / 220 Metcalf Road / El Dorado, Kansas 67042." Next to the legend was a line drawing of something that I first took for an old Vulcan or Timberwolf pump-action carbine. As I opened the box I found that it was neither.

What I saw nestled there, along with its original owner's manual, looked like the monstrous mutant offspring of a Garcia Bronco and a Winchester Model 62 pump. It was all there: the Bronco's skeleton stock, slabby little receiver and pivoting barrel extension. But hanging beneath the barrel was a corncob forend that looked for all the world like an old Winchester .22 pump handle.

As I looked more closely, however, I realized that this was no pump repeater. It was a pivoting-barrel single-shot .22. What I had taken as a pump handle was simply the operating handle for the extractor. It was close to a Bronco, all right, yet it wasn't. For one thing, its skeletonized buttstock was heavy-gauge wire, not a zinc casting, and it was filled with a boardlike, walnut-stained panel. Whereas the Garcia's cocking handle looked like a second trigger, the Wildcat's was a more conventional serrated knob on the right side of the receiver. And unlike the Bronco, in which you unlocked the action by pulling back on the trigger-like handle, the Wildcat's barrel was locked shut simply by a spring-loaded ball detent.

I skimmed through the Wildcat's yellowing four-panel owner's manual. "Manufactured by RAU ARMS CORPORATION," it proclaimed, disproving my suspicion that it was merely a duded-up Bronco. Its description of the Wildcat's operating instructions was admirably succint:

The Wildcat "500" .22 rifle is equipped with a swing-out type action.

To load, pull Operating Handle to rear of Action. Push safety from left to right. Your rifle is now in "safe" position. Place shell in chamber. Close Action and return safety to the left position. Your rifle is now ready to fire.

To eject the fired case, turn forearm counter-clockwise to open. Pull forearm one-quarter inch toward action.

Your Wildcat "500" may be used with .22 caliber short, long or long-rifle ammunition.

On the second page, the following statement caught my eye: At all times, treat your rifle as the precision instrument that it actually is. Then followed some cleaning instructions, an exploded view, and a blank warranty card.

Wow! This was no cheap gun at all - it was a precision instrument! My so-called gun collection is noticeably short on precision instruments, so I asked Richard if he'd sell it to me. He glanced up as though suspecting a joke, and then allowed that he might be persuaded to part with it. I left with it tucked under my arm.

Everyone who writes about guns harbors secret hopes that he will someday discover a model that no one has ever written about. I hurried home with the Wildcat and checked my reference books. Nothing there about the Wildcat! And then, durn the luck, I checked the internet and found that a handful of folks know quite a bit about the Wildcat.

My children accuse me of living in front of my computer. My response is, "You call this living?" (I do venture outside occasionally, mostly on cloudy days when the black helicopters can't get me.) So after wading hip-deep into the wunnerful World-Wide Web, I found a nice little website maintained by a fellow named A. K. Church. Mr. Church offered quite a bit of background on the Wildcat, and his readers supplied even more. With the help of Mr. Church and his kind contributors, we can sketch the history of the Rau Wildcat:

The Rau Arms Corporation was founded in El Dorado, Kansas, on September 11, 1969. (If you think that El Dorado was just some anonymous dot on the map, think again: Almon Stowger invented the first dial telephone in El Dorado in 1899. So there.) According to a former employee, Harold Rau was a Florida retiree who developed an itch to get into the gun business. Borrowing heavily from certain features of several Hamilton rifles and the Garcia Bronco, he designed what was intended to be a light target rifle for women and children.

The name of the rifle, the Wildcat, isn't surprising. Kansas State University, home of the Wildcats, is only about 100 miles from El Dorado. The Wildcat came in two models: the Wildcat 500 (blued with mahogany stock) and the Model 600 Deluxe (chrome plated with walnut stock). The rifles' actions and receivers were actually built in Oklahoma City, Oklahoma, with final assembly taking place in El Dorado. It isn't clear how many Wildcats were made; mine is Number 547. Known serial numbers range close to 3,000 - Model 500s had an "A" prefix; Model 600s, a "D" prefix -- so it's a safe bet that production reached at least that many.

Harold Rau seems to have backed out of the business in August of 1970, selling the company to Precision Industries (aka Mountain Arms) of Ozark, Missouri. Rau Arms was formally delisted as a Kansas corporation on December 15, 1970, and the factory at 220 Metcalf Road was emptied out sometime in 1971. Precision Industries/Mountain Arms continued producing Wildcats under the Rau Arms name from 1971 to 1975, at which time the rifle became known as the Mountain Arms Wildcat.

Mountain Arms seems not to have been a well-documented enterprise, but thanks to our friends at the ATF, we can tell precisely how many Mountain Arms Wildcats were made before the company fizzled out altogether in 1978:

YEAR	NUMBER PRODUCED
1975	496
1976	1,782
1977	3,649
1978	316
TOTAL:	6,243

Mountain Arms was way ahead of its time, if not in firearms design, then certainly in marketing strategy. They arranged for Wildcats to be sold through Woolworth (Woolco), the original five-and-dime and the Wal-Mart of that era. Each Woolco (in the Southwest, anyway) received six Wildcats. Pricing them at $29.95, Woolco intended to stack 'em deep and sell 'em cheap, but they apparently languished on the shelves.

Mountain Arms introduced a number of changes to the Wildcat including a takedown model and plastic stock inserts. Production seems to have been a rather hit-or-miss affair, at least as the company was winding down, because some Mountain Arms Wildcats have been reported as being new in the box but missing stock inserts or other parts.

Few Wildcats, either Rau Arms or Mountain Arms varieties, enter the used-gun market, so it's a bit hard to assign value to them. Pristine Rau Arms specimens have brought as much as $350 at auction, but that's largely a matter of finding the right buyer. It's safe to say, however, that Wildcats are prime sleepers. After all, 1000% appreciation ain't half-bad, even adjusted for inflation!

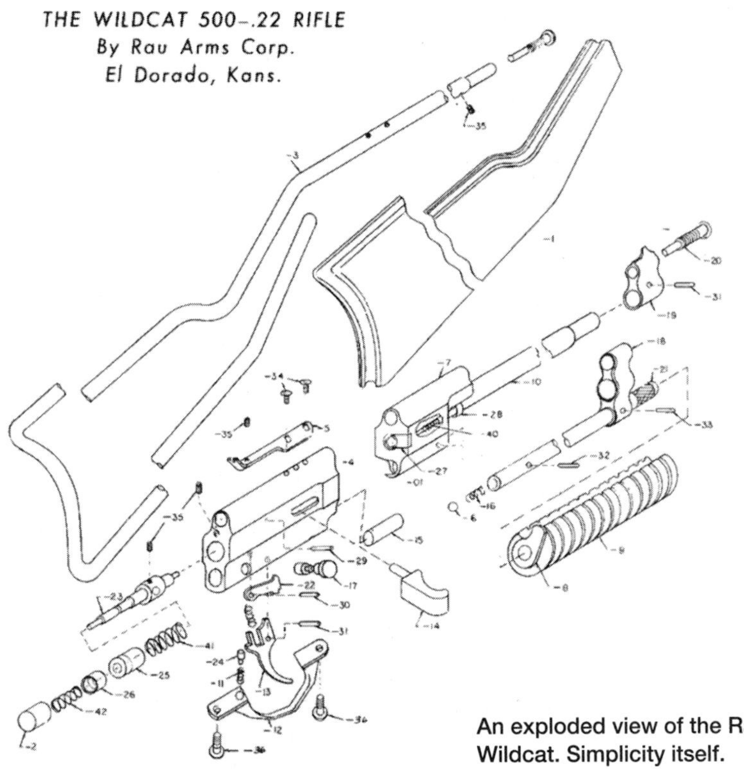

An exploded view of the Rau Wildcat. Simplicity itself.

AMMUNITION, BALLISTICS AND COMPONENTS

BY **HOLT BODINSON**

BY HOLT BODINSON

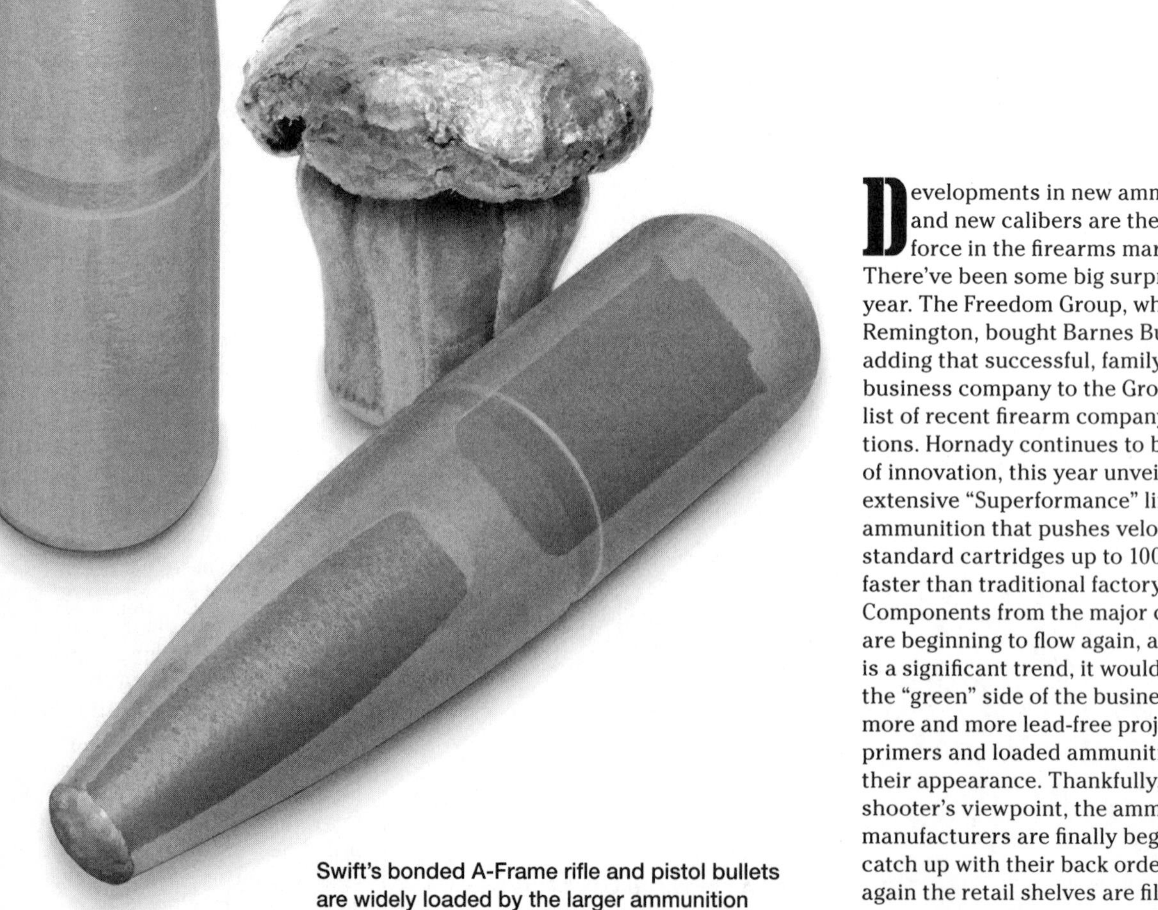

Swift's bonded A-Frame rifle and pistol bullets are widely loaded by the larger ammunition manufacturers.

Developments in new ammunition and new calibers are the driving force in the firearms market today. There've been some big surprises this year. The Freedom Group, which owns Remington, bought Barnes Bullets, adding that successful, family-owned business company to the Group's long list of recent firearm company acquisitions. Hornady continues to be a hotbed of innovation, this year unveiling its extensive "Superformance" line of rifle ammunition that pushes velocities of standard cartridges up to 100-200 fps faster than traditional factory loads. Components from the major companies are beginning to flow again, and if there is a significant trend, it would be toward the "green" side of the business with more and more lead-free projectiles, primers and loaded ammunition making their appearance. Thankfully, from a shooter's viewpoint, the ammunition manufacturers are finally beginning to catch up with their back orders so once again the retail shelves are filling up with ammunition and components.

Aguila predicts that the 5mm Remington Rimfire Magnum will be chambered commercially this year.

AGUILA

Introduced in 1970, the modern-looking, bottlenecked 5mm Remington Rimfire Magnum (RRM) arrived loaded with potential. Here was a fast, varmint cartridge capable of propelling a 38-grain, 0.2045-inch diameter hollowpoint bullet to 2,100 fps. Chambered in Remington's 5-pound, plinker-grade Models 591 and 592, the 5mm RRM fell flat on its face.

In 2008, Aguila revived the little 5mm with a 30-gr. JHP at 2,300 fps, and the firearms world was abuzz wondering which company would be the first to chamber the round in a quality firearm. It didn't happen in 2008 or 2009, but something's up in 2010 because Aguila gave me a wink and a nod at the SHOT Show. They're coming out with an additional jacketed soft-point loading with similar ballistics for the 5mm RRM this year. Something's up. Stay tuned.

ALLIANT POWDER

Having introduced five new spherical handloading powders this past year, Alliant is getting into the substitute black powder business. They will be marketing a very successful existing BP substitute, BlackMag Xp, under the label "Black Dot." Black Dot is compatible with all ignition systems, contains no sulfur and is non-corrosive and non-fouling. With an indefinite shelf life, Black Dot is also moisture resistant. A smaller -grained form of Black Dot, know as "Flash" under the BlackMag label, may also be marketed as a priming powder for flintlocks. Alliant is also introducing a new shotgun powder designed specifically for reduced recoil loads (7/8- 1 1/8 oz.) in the 12-gauge. Called "Extra-Light" it is a clean-burning propellant with sufficient density so that normal wads and cases can be used for reloading. Data on Black Dot and Extra-Light is available at www.alliantpowder.com.

BALLISTIC PRODUCTS

Ballistic Products, the source for everything related to shotgun ammunition and components, is teaming up this year with RIO Ammunition, reportedly the world's largest manufacturer of shotshells. RIO, a Spanish firm dating back to 1896, has established an American manufacturing facility in McEwen, Tennessee, and will be focusing its marketing efforts on the independent dealer. RIO manufactures all the components for its shotshells: powders, primers, hulls, wads and shot. Under their business arrangement, Ballistic Products will be the source of RIO components as well as loaded shotshells. See Ballistic Products' wide line of components, tooling, literature, just about everything you need as a shotgunner, at www.ballisticproducts.com.

Craig Sanborn's black powder substitute, Black Mag Xp, will be marketed by Alliant under the "Black Dot" label.

BARNES BULLETS

The big story at Barnes this year is that they have been bought by the Freedom Group and are now part of the family of companies that includes Remington, Marlin, Dakota Arms, Parker Gun, Bushmaster, DPMS Panther Arms, H&R, L.C. Smith and others. The Freedom Group is now the largest manufacturer of commercial arms and ammunition in the USA. Building on the success of their "Tipped Triple-Shock X Bullet" that combines the accuracy and controlled expansion of the conventional Triple-Shock X with a polymer tip, there are seven new offerings in 2011 ranging from a .264 (100-gr.) to a .458 (300-gr.), the latter designed specifically for the SOCOM cartridge. The standard TSX line is upgraded with a .224 (50-gr.), a .338 (285-gr.) and a .375 (350-gr.). The Barnes tactical lines get a facelift with the addition of a TAC-X .308 (110-gr.) and a .338 (285-gr.). The tactical pistol line (TAC-XP) sees the addition of a 9mm (95-gr.) while the TAC-RRLP (Tactical Reduced Ricochet Limited Penetration) group gets a 6.8 SPC (85-gr.). For updated bullet specifications go to www.barnesbullets.com and www.barnesbullets.com/mle.

Barnes new Triple-Shock X bullet in .375 caliber (350-gr.) should be a terrific big game load.

BERGER BULLETS

As we went to press, Berger announced that it was working on a .338 (250-300-gr.) hunting bullet with an extremely high ballistic coefficient in the range of 0.85-0.86. The rest of the line remains unchanged while production catches up with demand. See www.bergerbullets.com.

BERRY'S MANUFACTURING

Berry's offers an extensive line of copper-plated lead handgun bullets at very attractive prices. An upgraded line of competition bullets is being developed with thicker copper-plated jacket to insure flawless feeding in autoloaders. The heaver plated additions include a 9mm (124-gr.) hollow base, a .40 S&W (190-gr.) and a .45 ACP in either 185 or 200 grains. See Berry's full line of plated, non-plated and "cowboy" bullets at www.berrysmfg.com.

(above) Black Hills' .223 Rem ammunition featuring a 62-gr. Barnes TSX bullet at 3,100 fps is a devastating hunting or tactical load.

(below) Black Hills' .260 Rem. Gold Line target load features Lapua's sensational 139-gr. Scenar match bullet.

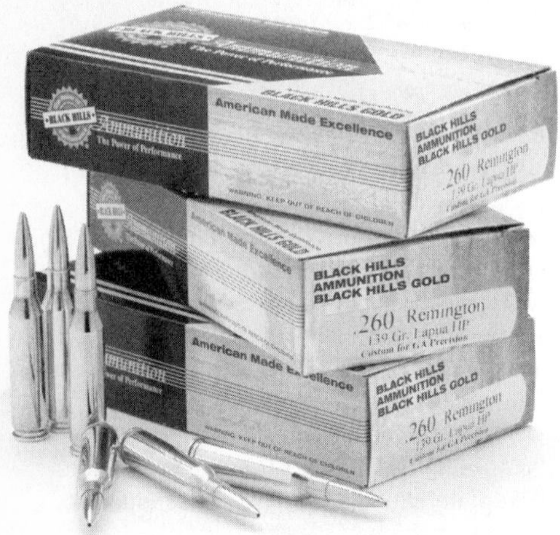

BLACK HILLS AMMUNITION

Consistently providing some of the most accurate ammunition on the market, Black Hills is offering three new loadings this year. At the top of the list is what could be considered the most efficient and effective .223 load on the market – a 62-gr. Barnes TSX bullet at 3,100 fps from a 24-inch barrel. The monolithic 62-gr. TSX expands immediately on impact to .45 caliber but continues to penetrate without loss of bullet weight. In the .223, it's a devastating hunting or tactical load. In the Gold Line, the .260 Rem. case is being loaded with Lapua's match bullet, the 139-gr. Scenar, for long range target and tactical use. Black Hills is the only company currently loading the .338 Norma Magnum. The .338 Norma Magnum with a 300-gr. Sierra MatchKing at 2,725 fps produces the same or better ballistics than the .338 Lapua. The Norma case is both shorter and more efficient than the Lapua version, and long .338 projectiles with high ballistic coefficients can be loaded in the Norma case without intruding into the powder column. Expect to see more use of the excellent .338 Norma Magnum as a long range target and tactical round once loaded ammunition and components become more available. www.black-hills.com.

BRENNEKE USA

Long known for their advanced hunting shotgun slug designs, Brenneke is introducing two new tactical slug loadings for the 12 ga. 2 3/4-inch. The first is a reduced recoil slug weighing 438 grains with a velocity of 1,256 fps. Called the "Tactical Home Defense" slug load, it is designed to deliver maximum stopping power without over-penetration or projectile deformation. The second tactical slug load is known as the "Special Forces Short Magnum." Featuring a hardened 525-gr. slug at 1,418 fps, the SFSM is designed for maximum penetration without deformation and is quite capable of plowing through vehicles, doors and walls. In independent tests, the SFSM penetrated 34.9 inches of FBI-spec ballistic gelatin while its nearest competitor was stopped at 26 inches. See the interesting test data and graphic photos of these new tactical loads at www.brennekeusa.com.

CCI

CCI's rimfires have gone green! For the small game hunter, the popular .17 HMR now comes packed with a 16-gr. TNT Green bullet at 2,500 fps. For 22 LR fans, CCI is offering a "Short Range Green" lead-free plinking round featuring a 21-gr. copper/polymer mix bullet at 1,650 fps. It's great to see the rimfire line getting ahead of the non-lead curve. See the details at www.cci-ammunition.com.

CENTURY INTERNATIONAL ARMS

Century is in unique position to ferret out great ammunition deals from across the globe. They offer a variety of military and standard rifle and pistol calibers under their "Hotshot" brand at bargain basement prices. What caught my eye this year were offerings for H&K's weird experimental round, the petite 4.3x45mm, as well as the 9mm Flobert Long loaded with #9 and #10 shot, the 9mm Browning Long and the 9mm Largo. Stock up on these exceedingly hard-to-find rounds before they're gone forever. www.centuryarms.com.

FEDERAL PREMIUM

Introduced several years ago, Federal's proprietary "FliteControl" wad has a proven track record of delivering exceptionally uniform and dense shot patterns. This year the FliteControl wad technology coupled with FliteStopper shot is being introduced in two specialized loads. The first, labeled Black Cloud Snow Goose FS Steel, is designed specifically to reach up there in the clouds where the snow geese fly. In a 3-inch 12-gauge loading, the new shell packs 1-1/8 oz. of FliteStopper steel BBs or #2s at 1,635 fps. The second new shell, labeled Prairie Storm FS Lead, is designed to fold tough and wiry late season pheasants at extended ranges. The dual shot load consists of 30% nickel-plated FliteStopper lead shot and 70% copper-plated hard lead shot. Available in the 2-3/4/12-ga. (1-1/4 oz at 1,500 fps) and 3-inch 12-ga. (1-5/8 oz. at 1,350 fps) and 3-inch 20-gauge (1-1/4 oz. at 1,300 fps), Prairie Storm is loaded with #4, #5 or #6 shot.

With the Taurus Judge revolver now available with a 3-inch cylinder, Federal has generated two new 3-inch .410 loads for the Judge. One features five pellets of #000 buck at 960 fps and the other, nine pellets of #4 buck at 1,100 fps. Two interesting new loads featuring the Barnes Triple-Shock X bullet are a 110-gr. loading for the .30-'06 sporting a sizzling muzzle velocity of 3,400 fps and a 50-gr. load in the .22-250 Rem. at 3,750 fps. Going green receives some attention in the varmint line with Speer TNT Green bullets being loaded in the .22 Hornet (30-gr. at 3,150 fps) and the .204 Ruger (32-gr. at 4,030 fps). Target shooters should be pleased with three new loadings in the Gold Medal match line with 93-gr. and 123-gr. Sierra MatchKings being loaded in the 6.5x55 at 2,625 fps and 2,750 fps respectively plus a 250-gr. MatchKing for the long range .338 Lapua Magnum at 2,950 fps.

Handgun hunters will hail the addition of Swift A-Frame bullets in the .357 Mag., .41 Rem. Mag., .44 Rem. Mag., .454 Casull, .460 S&W and .500 S&W. Federal has done an outstanding job of feeding the big game hunting market with great loadings in all the classic American, British and metric calibers. This year those lines are being improved with the additional loading of Barnes Banded Solids and Triple Shock X bullets as well as Swift A-Frames. Finally, Federal is making a major effort to bring on line a host of new handloading components including Trophy Bonded Bear Claw and Sledgehammer Solid bullets. See the complete catalog at www.federalpremium.com.

Federal intends to supply a variety of fresh handloading components to the marketplace.

(above) Federal's Prairie Storm FS Lead ammunition is designed to fold tough and wiry pheasants.

(below) Federal's Black Cloud Snow Goose ammunition is designed to deliver a deadly pattern to the high-flying birds.

FIOCCHI

With "ballistics to be determined," Fiocchi is fielding two new cartridges this year: a 28-ga. 3-inch and the 7mm Penna, a handgun cartridge designed for IPSC that will be chambered initially by STI. Fiocchi is highly focused on their new non-toxic lines that include rifle, pistol and shotgun ammunition. Fiocchi's answer is a proprietary "Tundra" composite composed of a mixture of Tungsten-Iron-Fluoropolymer. Fiocchi claims that their Tundra shot is softer than Bismuth, 115% heavier than lead and safe for all chokes and older pre-steel barrels. As a bullet core material, it will appear in new loadings for the .223, .308 Win., .30-'06 and 9x19 EMB. By mid-year, Fiocchi will finally be offering a new line of paper hulled target loads for the 12-gauge. Still available for those classic British doubles in the 2-1/2-inch 24- and 32-gauges are high antimony lead field loads. See their latest lineup at www.fiocchiusa.com.

GRAF & SONS

Working with Hornady, Graf virtually revived old military cartridges like the 6.5 Carcano loaded with a proper 0.268-inch diameter bullet and the 8x56 Hungarian Mannlicher with its odd 0.330-inch bullet. When you need hard-to-find reloading components NOW, Graf usually has them on the shelf. The company is a great source for surplus ammunition and ammunition loaded by all of the European makers. See their online catalog at www.grafs.com.

HODGDON

Burning up the benchrest and varmint hunting circuits is Hodgdon's new small bore powder, IMR 8208 XBR. IMR 8208 XBR is a small grain propellant that is part of Hodgdon's "Extreme" family of powders that are uniquely insensitive to variations of temperature. The new powder is proving ideal in the centerfire .22s and compact-case cartridges up through .30 caliber. In the 6mm PPC, it's winning all the matches. Hodgdon has just released its new 5000+ loads reloading manual that does a good job of covering test reports on IMR 8208 XBR. The easy way to keep track of Hodgdon loading data and its three powder subsidiaries is through the web at www.hodgdon.com, www.goexpowder.com, www.imrpowder.com and www.wwpowder.com.

HORNADY

Hornady shook up the sporting ammunition industry this year with the introduction of their "Superperformance" line that carries the bragging tagline, "The new standard by which all ammunition will be judged." The secret is in the powder formulation that permits standard loading procedures to achieve velocities 100-200 fps faster than conventional factory loads without increases in pressure, recoil or pricing. The Superperformance line currently covers 18 centerfire rifle cartridges ranging from the .243 Win. to the .458 Win. Magnum. Superperformance cartridges are loaded with either the SST or Hornady's new non-toxic monolithic game bullet made from gilding metal, called the "GMX." In fact, the GMX bullets and the equally revolutionary Flex Tip (FTX) bullets are being offered this year in a variety of calibers as handloading components. Responding to the need for "green" varmint ammunition, Hornady is loading its non-leaded NTX bullets in the .17 Mach 2, .17 HMR, .22 WMR, .204 Ruger and .223 Rem. NXT bullets are also being offered as handloading components.

Giving the AK and AKM shooters some real game loads, Hornady is loading V-Max bullets in the 5.6x39mm and the 7.62x39mm cartridges. The 6.5 Grendel and 6.5 Creedmoor get upgraded with a variety of new bullets, and the Critical Defense ammunition line is expanded with the addition of a .357 Mag. (125-gr.) FTX, .40 S&W (165-gr.) FTX and .45 ACP (185-gr.) FTX. See the complete Hornady catalog at www.hornady.com.

LAPUA

This year Lapua is producing two new precision-drawn cases for handloaders: the .22-250 Rem. and the .308 Win. Palma, which takes a small rifle primer. The full Lapua story is at www.lapua.com.

LIGHTFIELD

Known for its outstanding shotgun slug loads, Lightfield has expanded into the field of less lethal law enforcement and home defense ammunition. This year the focus is on home defense rounds in 12-gauge, 20-gauge and .410. Lightfield's proprietary rubber/polymer balls, buckshot and spiny star projectiles will be loaded to a different specification for home defense use. The home defense rounds are designed for close-quarter engagements while avoiding the possibility of collateral damage. www.lightfieldslugs.com.

Norma's new monolithic solids feature a flat meplat to insure deep, straight-line penetration.

NORMA

Based on necked-up .300 Norma Magnum brass, the .338 Norma Magnum is finally making its debut but initially as component brass only. You'll have to load the exceptional cartridge yourself or go to www.black-hills.com for custom ammunition. This year Norma is teaming up with Blaser to develop a complete Blaser family of big game cartridges based on the .404 Jeffery case. The proprietary Blaser line will include cartridges in 7mm, .300, .338 and .375 calibers, and Blaser insisted that the new line deliver velocity/energy values superior to the 7mm Rem. Mag., .300 Win. Mag., .338 Win. Mag and the .375 H&H. Blaser fans will have something to look forward to! Famous for its African PH line of big bore cartridges, Norma has introduced a new monolithic flat-meplat solid that is plated with a black synthetic to reduce pressure and fouling. The improved solid is being loaded across the African PH line from the mild mannered 9.3x62 to the booming .505 Gibbs. Finally, through an improved production process, Norma is "double-press heading" its brass to obtain maximum strength in their cases. See Norma's extensive lines of hunting and match ammunition at www.norma.cc.

Going green, Nosler is introducing a new line of lead-free Ballistic Tips for varmint calibers.

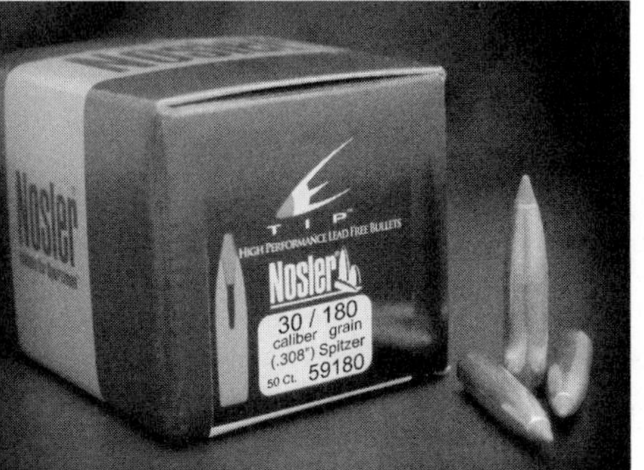

(below) Nosler's Trophy Grade hunting ammunition is match quality all the way.

NOSLER

There's a lot of "green" at the Nosler store this year. Leading the charge is a new line of lead-free Ballistic Tip varmint bullets including a .204-inch (32-gr.), .224-inch (35- and 40-gr.) and a 6mm (55-gr.). The big game E-Tip line, which is proving to be quite accurate, is being expanded with the addition of a .257 (100-gr.), a 7mm (140-gr.) and an 8mm (180-gr.). Over in the Nosler/Winchester Combined Technology corner are nine new offerings: a .204 (32-gr.), a 6mm (95-gr.), a .257 (115-gr.), two .270s (130- and 150-gr.), two 7mms (140- and 150-gr.), an 8mm (180-gr.) and – surprise! – a 300-gr. RN bullet for the .45/70. Over in the match bullet category, there are two new precision bullets: a 6.8mm (115-gr.) and a .308 (190-gr.).

Calling it "The World's Finest Manufactured Ammunition," Nosler will be expanding its Trophy Grade Ammunition line with the loads for the .223, .22-250, 6.5x55, 7mm Rem. Mag., .308 Win. and .300 Rem. Ultra Mag. See their catalog and the company store at www.nosler.com.

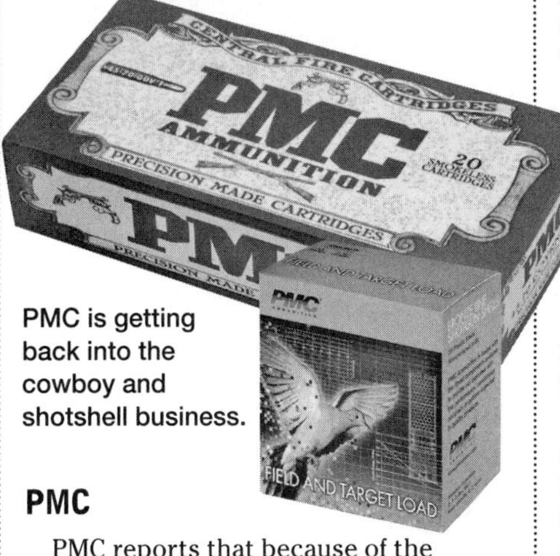

PMC is getting back into the cowboy and shotshell business.

PMC

PMC reports that because of the insatiable demand for rifle and handgun ammunition in 2009, they were forced to put new introductions on hold until later this year. Plans call for bringing back their shotshell and cowboy lines and introducing new frangible, tactical and target loads. Stay tuned at www.pmcammo.com

Remington's Copper Solid big game bullets have developed an enviable reputation for performance in the field.

REMINGTON

Big Green is upping the power factor of their lightweight R-15 AR platform rifle for big game with a new .30 Remington AR load featuring a 150-gr. Core-Lokt PSP at 2,575 fps. Again, the "green fever" is catching, so Remington is adding its polymer-tipped Premier Copper-Solid bullets to the .30-30 (150-gr.), .30-'06 (165-gr.), .300 Win. Mag. (165-gr.) and .300 Ultra Mag. (165-gr.). Among the more unique offerings this year in the "Remington Rifle" ammunition line are the .338 Marlin Express with a 250-gr. SP at 2,189 fps and .450 Bushmaster with a 260-gr. AccuTip at 2,180 fps.

Remington is releasing its Premier Core-Lokt Ultra Bonded bullet line as reloading components.

Recognizing the increasing popularity of the Taurus Judge revolver, Remington has loaded four Heavy Density #00 buck in a 2-1/2-inch .410 shell. With a velocity of 1,300 fps, it's a wicked little buckshot load. Labeled the "Disintegrator CTF," Remington is loading a highly frangible bullet composed of sintered copper and tin in the 9mm +P, .38 Special +P, .40 S&W and .45 Auto. While not announced yet, Remington engineers have developed 3-inch and 3-1/2-inch 12-gauge shotshells capable of delivering 1-1/8 to

1-3/8 oz. of steel shot at the unheard-of velocity of 1,700 fps. Be looking for this revolutionary shotshell in the second half of the year. Maybe the best news is that Remington components will once again be available in quantity including primers, bulk-packed rifle and pistol brass and bullets as well as Premier Core-Lokt Ultra Bonded, Core-Lokt and Premier AccuTip bullets. See Big Green's excellent website and catalog at www.remington.com.

RIO AMMUNITION

This old and respected Spanish firm is one of the largest manufacturers, if not the largest, of shotshells in the world and has recently finished an ultra-modern North American production facility in McEwan, Tennessee. Rio's a vertically integrated company manufacturing all the components that go into a shotshell itself and thus can assure a high degree of quality control and consistency of product. Currently its marketing focus is the independent sporting dealer rather than the large box stores. With a full line-up of game and target loads and with its latest affiliation with Ballistic Products, it's a product line well worth looking for. www.rioammo.com

SIERRA

Sierra reports they've had a hard time just keeping up with demand this year, much less introducing any new products. See the bulletsmiths at www.sierrabullets.com.

SPEER

"Deepcurl" is the moniker for Speer's latest lines of electro-chemically bonded rifle and pistol bullets. The rifle lineup extends from 6mm through .338-caliber while the handgun hunter gets every caliber from .38 through .475 and .500. Responding to the increasing popularity of the .204 Ruger, Speer is introducing a 32-gr. TNT Green bullet and a conventional 39-gr. TNT HP for the little 20-caliber.

Encapsulating a lead core in a FMJ is an ingenious technique to control lead. Speer's electro-chemical plating process gives the company an advantage since the end product is uniformly and completely bonded in a jacket. New this year is an expansion of the TMJ encapsulated rifle bullet line with offerings in .22, 6mm, .270, 7mm and .30 caliber. The justifiably famous Gold Dot bullet line is expanding with the addition of Gold Dot HP's for the .327 Federal Magnum (100-gr.) and the .380 Auto (90-gr.). See the whole component list at www.speer-bullets.com.

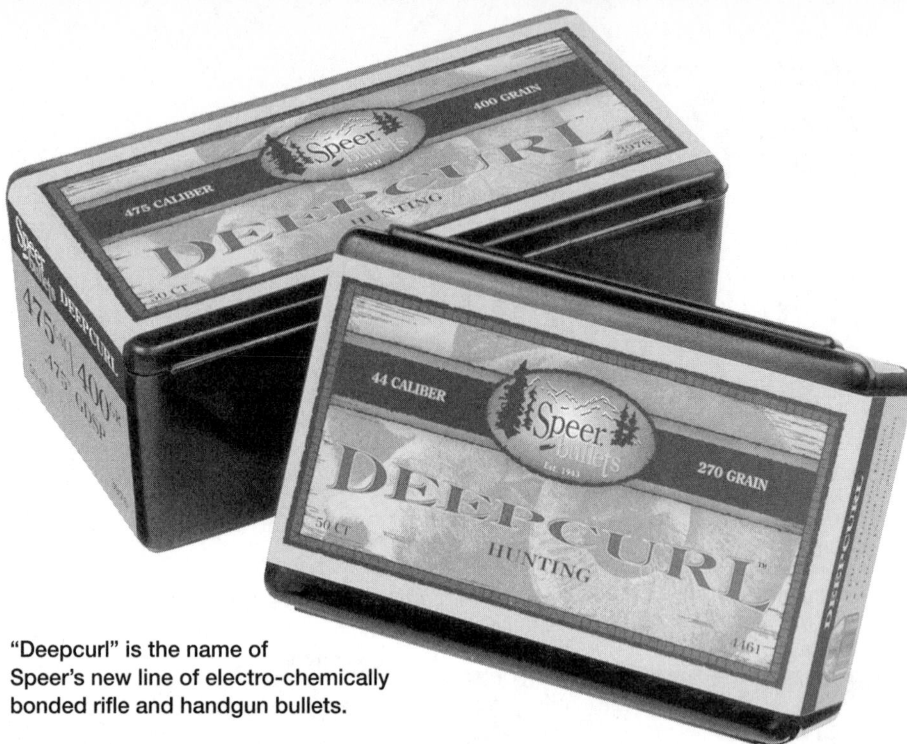

"Deepcurl" is the name of Speer's new line of electro-chemically bonded rifle and handgun bullets.

SWIFT BULLET COMPANY

Swift's A-Frame bullets have quite a reputation in the big game fields of the world for controlled expansion and weight retention. For calibers like the .505 Gibbs, .500 Jeffery, .500 Nitro or .50 Alaskan, Swift is introducing 535- and 570-gr. A-Frame bullets in .505-inch and .510-inch diameters. The A-Frame pistol bullet line is growing this year with the addition of a .357 caliber (180-gr.), a .41 caliber (210-gr.) and a .50 caliber (325-gr.). See them all at www.swiftbullets.com.

WINCHESTER AMMUNITION

Winchester has reinvented the classic buck-and-ball load as a personal defense shell.

Called the Supreme Elite PDX1 12, the 12-gauge 2-3/4-inch shell packs 3 pellets of #00 plated buckshot over a 1-ounce Power Point slug. Call it a Hammer Load! The other shotshell is designed for the Taurus Judge revolver to overcome the problem of the rifling engaging the shot wad/shot column and throwing it down and to the right. The new Supreme Elite PDX1 410/2 1/2" shell comes loaded with three flat "Defense Disk" projectiles and 12 plated BBs. It's a variation of the buck-and-ball concept and should prove lethal at short distances.

Winchester's Bonded PDX1 handgun ammunition line has been expanded to include the .380 Auto and .45 Colt. Winchester, too, has come down with the green fever with the addition of lead-free Ballistic Silvertips in the .223 Rem. (35-gr.) and .22-250 Rem. (35-gr.) plus a .22 LR round loaded with a 26-gr. tin truncated HP bullet. Winchester's patented Dual Bond big game bullet delivering double-caliber expansion and 100% weight retention is now loaded in the .45-70 Gov't (375-gr.) and the .44 Magnum (240-gr.).

Marking 200 years since Oliver Winchester's birth, Winchester's collector's series of commemorative ammunition packaged in vintage boxes celebrates the .22 LR, .30-30 and .45 Colt this year. Finally, the Super-X Power Max Bonded centerfire rifle line, designed specifically for whitetail deer hunting, has been expanded to include the .243 Win. (100-gr.), 7mm Rem. Mag. (150-gr.), 7mm WSM (150-gr.), .30-'06 (180-gr.), .300 WSM (180-gr.) and the .300 Win. Mag. (180-gr.). See all these products and Winchester's new web-based Ballistic Calculator at www.winchester.com.

WOLF

No new cartridges or loads this year, but Wolf will be importing a complete line of rifle, pistol and shotgun primers at very attractive prices. www.wolfammo.com.

WOODLEIGH

Woodleigh has developed a radically new homogeneous, "hydrostatically stabilized" hollowpoint big game bullet. Machined from a copper alloy, the bullet is perfectly cylindrical from its base to the beginning of its short, hollow, cone-shaped nose. Woodleigh claims the new design delivers incredible straight-line penetration with massive wound cavitation. The new bullet is available in calibers ranging from .30 to .577, including all the classic British double rifle calibers. www.woodleighbullets.com.au.

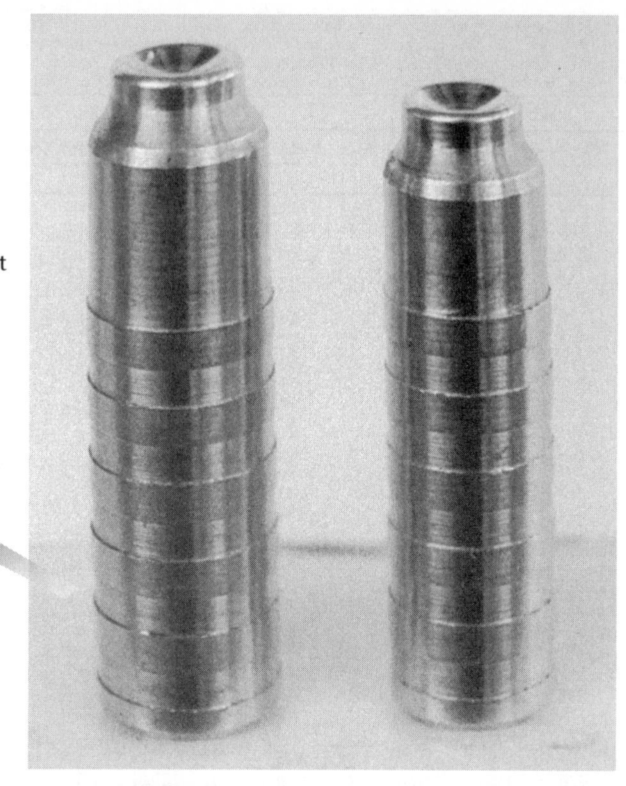

(left) Woodleigh's "hydrostatically stablized" big game bullet has proven as effective as it is unusual.

Norma has designed a proprietary line of Blaser brand magnums based on the .404 Jeffery case.

Many manufacturers do not supply suggested retail prices. Others did not get their pricing to us before press time. All pricing can vary dependent on the exact brand and style of ammo selected and/or the retail outlet from which you make your purchase. Pricing has been rounded to the nearest dollar and represents our best estimate of average pricing. An * after the cartridge means these loads are available with Nosler Partition or Swift A-Frame bullets. Listed pricing may or may not reflect this bullet type. ** = these are packed 50 to box, all others are 20 to box. Wea. Mag.= Weatherby Magnum. Spfd. = Springfield. A-Sq. = A-Square. N.E.=Nitro Express.

Cartridge	Bullet Wgt. Grs.	VELOCITY (fps)					ENERGY (ft. lbs.)					TRAJ. (in.)				Est. Price/box
		Muzzle	100 yds.	200 yds.	300 yds.	400 yds.	Muzzle	100 yds.	200 yds.	300 yds.	400 yds.	100 yds.	200 yds.	300 yds.	400 yds.	
17, 22																
17 Remington Fireball	20	4000	3380	2840	2360	1930	710	507	358	247	165	1.6	1.5	-2.8	-13.5	NA
17 Remington Fireball	25	3850	3280	2780	2330	1925	823	597	429	301	206	0.9	0.0	-5.4	NA	NA
17 Remington	25	4040	3284	2644	2086	1606	906	599	388	242	143	+2.0	+1.7	-4.0	-17.0	$17
204 Ruger (Fed)	32 Green	4030	3320	2710	2170	1710	1155	780	520	335	205	0.9	0.0	-5.7	-19.1	NA
204 Ruger	32	4225	3632	3114	2652	2234	1268	937	689	500	355	.6	0.0	-4.2	-13.4	NA
204 Ruger	40	3900	3451	3046	2677	2336	1351	1058	824	636	485	.7	0.0	-4.5	-13.9	NA
204 Ruger	45	3625	3188	2792	2428	2093	1313	1015	778	589	438	1.0	0.0	-5.5	-16.9	NA
221 Fireball	50	2800	2137	1580	1180	988	870	507	277	155	109	+0.0	-7.0	-28.0	0.0	$14
22 Hornet (Fed)	30 Green	3150	2150	1390	990	830	660	310	130	65	45	0.0	-6.6	-32.7	NA	NA
22 Hornet	34	3050	2132	1415	1017	852	700	343	151	78	55	+0.0	-6.6	-15.5	-29.9	NA
22 Hornet	35	3100	2278	1601	1135	929	747	403	199	100	67	+2.75	0.0	-16.9	-60.4	NA
22 Hornet	45	2690	2042	1502	1128	948	723	417	225	127	90	+0.0	-7.7	-31.0	0.0	$27**
218 Bee	46	2760	2102	1550	1155	961	788	451	245	136	94	+0.0	-7.2	-29.0	0.0	$46**
222 Remington	40	3600	3117	2673	2269	1911	1151	863	634	457	324	+1.07	0.0	-6.13	-18.9	NA
222 Remington	50	3140	2602	2123	1700	1350	1094	752	500	321	202	+2.0	-0.4	-11.0	-33.0	$11
222 Remington	55	3020	2562	2147	1773	1451	1114	801	563	384	257	+2.0	-0.4	-11.0	-33.0	$12
22 PPC	52	3400	2930	2510	2130	NA	1335	990	730	525	NA	+2.0	1.4	-5.0	0.0	NA
223 Remington	40	3650	3010	2450	1950	1530	1185	805	535	340	265	+2.0	+1.0	-6.0	-22.0	$14
223 Remington	40	3800	3305	2845	2424	2044	1282	970	719	522	371	0.84	0.0	-5.34	-16.6	NA
223 Remington (Rem)	45 Green	3550	2911	2355	1865	1451	1259	847	554	347	210	2.5	2.3	-4.3	-21.1	NA
223 Remington	50	3300	2874	2484	2130	1809	1209	917	685	504	363	1.37	0.0	-7.05	-21.8	NA
223 Remington	52/53	3330	2882	2477	2106	1770	1305	978	722	522	369	+2.0	+0.6	-6.5	-21.5	$14
223 Remington (Win)	55 Green	3240	2747	2304	1905	1554	1282	921	648	443	295	1.9	0.0	-8.5	-26.7	NA
223 Remington	55	3240	2748	2305	1906	1556	1282	922	649	444	296	+2.0	-0.2	-9.0	-27.0	$12
223 Remington	60	3100	2712	2355	2026	1726	1280	979	739	547	397	+2.0	+0.2	-8.0	-24.7	$16
223 Remington	64	3020	2621	2256	1920	1619	1296	977	723	524	373	+2.0	-0.2	-9.3	-23.0	$14
223 Remington	69	3000	2720	2460	2210	1980	1380	1135	925	750	600	+2.0	+0.8	-5.8	-17.5	$15
223 Remington	75	2790	2554	2330	2119	1926	1296	1086	904	747	617	2.37	0.0	-8.75	-25.1	NA
223 Remington	77	2750	2584	2354	2169	1992	1293	1110	948	804	679	1.93	0.0	-8.2	-23.8	NA
223 WSSM	55	3850	3438	3064	2721	2402	1810	1444	1147	904	704	0.7	0.0	-4.4	-13.6	NA
223 WSSM	64	3600	3144	2732	2356	2011	1841	1404	1061	789	574	1.0	0.0	-5.7	-17.7	NA
222 Rem. Mag.	55	3240	2748	2305	1906	1556	1282	922	649	444	296	+2.0	-0.2	-9.0	-27.0	$14
225 Winchester	55	3570	3066	2616	2208	1838	1556	1148	836	595	412	+2.0	+1.0	-5.0	-20.0	$19
224 Wea. Mag.	55	3650	3192	2780	2403	2057	1627	1244	943	705	516	+2.0	+1.2	-4.0	-17.0	$32
22-250 Rem.	40	4000	3320	2720	2200	1740	1420	980	660	430	265	+2.0	+1.8	-3.0	-16.0	$14
22-250 Rem.	45 Green	4000	3293	2690	2159	1696	1598	1084	723	466	287	1.7	1.7	-3.2	-15.7	NA
22-250 Rem.	50	3725	3264	2641	2455	2103	1540	1183	896	669	491	0.89	0.0	-5.23	-16.3	NA
22-250 Rem.	52/55	3680	3137	2656	2222	1832	1654	1201	861	603	410	+2.0	+1.3	-4.0	-17.0	$13
22-250 Rem.	60	3600	3195	2826	2485	2169	1727	1360	1064	823	627	+2.0	+2.0	-2.4	-12.3	$19
220 Swift	40	4200	3678	3190	2739	2329	1566	1201	904	666	482	+0.51	0.0	-4.0	-12.9	NA
220 Swift	50	3780	3158	2617	2135	1710	1586	1107	760	506	325	+2.0	+1.4	-4.4	-17.9	$20
220 Swift	50	3850	3396	2970	2576	2215	1645	1280	979	736	545	0.74	0.0	-4.84	-15.1	NA
220 Swift	55	3800	3370	2990	2630	2310	1765	1390	1090	850	650	0.8	0.0	-4.7	-14.4	NA
220 Swift	55	3650	3194	2772	2384	2035	1627	1246	939	694	506	+2.0	+2.0	-2.6	-13.4	$19
220 Swift	60	3600	3199	2824	2475	2156	1727	1364	1063	816	619	+2.0	+1.6	-4.1	-13.1	$19
22 Savage H.P.	71	2790	2340	1930	1570	1280	1225	860	585	390	190	+2.0	-1.0	-10.4	-35.7	NA
6mm (24)																
6mm BR Rem.	100	2550	2310	2083	1870	1671	1444	1185	963	776	620	+2.5	-0.6	-11.8	0.0	$22
6mm Norma BR	107	2822	2667	2517	2372	2229	1893	1690	1506	1337	1181	+1.73	0.0	-7.24	-20.6	NA
6mm PPC	70	3140	2750	2400	2070	NA	1535	1175	895	665	NA	+2.0	+1.4	-5.0	0.0	NA
243 Winchester	55	4025	3597	3209	2853	2525	1978	1579	1257	994	779	+0.6	0.0	-4.0	-12.2	NA
243 Winchester	60	3600	3110	2660	2260	1890	1725	1285	945	680	475	+2.0	+1.8	-3.3	-15.5	$17
243 Winchester	70	3400	3040	2700	2390	2100	1795	1435	1135	890	685	1.1	0.0	-5.9	-18.0	NA
243 Winchester	75/80	3350	2955	2593	2259	1951	1993	1551	1194	906	676	+2.0	+0.9	-5.0	-19.0	$16
243 W. Superformance	80	3425	3080	2760	2463	2184	2083	1684	1353	1077	847	1.1	0.0	-5.7	-17.1	NA
243 Winchester	85	3320	3070	2830	2600	2380	2080	1770	1510	1280	1070	+2.0	+1.2	-4.0	-14.0	$18
243 Winchester	90	3120	2871	2635	2411	2199	1946	1647	1388	1162	966	1.4	0.0	-6.4	-18.8	NA
243 Winchester*	100	2960	2697	2449	2215	1993	1945	1615	1332	1089	882	+2.5	+1.2	-6.0	-20.0	$16
243 Winchester	105	2920	2689	2470	2261	2062	1988	1686	1422	1192	992	+2.5	+1.6	-5.0	-18.4	$21
243 Light Mag.	100	3100	2839	2592	2358	2138	2133	1790	1491	1235	1014	+1.5	0.0	-6.8	-19.8	NA
243 WSSM	55	4060	3628	3237	2880	2550	2013	1607	1280	1013	794	0.6	0.0	-3.9	-12.0	NA
243 WSSM	95	3250	3000	2763	2538	2325	2258	1898	1610	1359	1140	1.2	0.0	-5.7	-16.9	NA
243 WSSM	100	3110	2838	2583	2341	2112	2147	1789	1481	1217	991	1.4	0.0	-6.6	-19.7	NA
6mm Remington	80	3470	3064	2694	2352	2036	2139	1667	1289	982	736	+2.0	+1.1	-5.0	-17.0	$16
6mm R. Superformance	95	3235	2955	2692	2443	3309	2207	1841	1528	1259	1028	1.2	0.0	-6.1	-18.0	NA
6mm Remington	100	3100	2829	2573	2332	2104	2133	1777	1470	1207	983	+2.5	+1.6	-5.0	-17.0	$16
6mm Remington	105	3060	2822	2596	2381	2177	2105	1788	1512	1270	1059	+2.5	+1.1	-3.3	-15.0	$21
6mm Rem. Light Mag.	100	3250	2997	2756	2528	2311	2345	1995	1687	1418	1186	1.59	0.0	-6.33	-18.3	NA
6.17(.243) Spitfire	100	3350	3122	2905	2698	2501	2493	2164	1874	1617	1389	2.4	3.2	0.0	-8.0	NA
240 Wea. Mag.	87	3500	3202	2924	2663	2416	2366	1980	1651	1370	1127	+2.0	+2.0	-2.0	-12.0	$32
240 Wea. Mag.	100	3395	3106	2835	2581	2339	2559	2142	1785	1478	1215	+2.5	+2.8	-2.0	-11.0	$43

Cartridge	Bullet Wgt. Grs.	VELOCITY (fps)					ENERGY (ft. lbs.)					TRAJ. (in.)				Est. Price/box
		Muzzle	100 yds.	200 yds.	300 yds.	400 yds.	Muzzle	100 yds.	200 yds.	300 yds.	400 yds.	100 yds.	200 yds.	300 yds.	400 yds.	
25-20 Win.	86	1460	1194	1030	931	858	407	272	203	165	141	0.0	-23.5	0.0	0.0	**$32****
25-35 Win.	117	2230	1866	1545	1282	1097	1292	904	620	427	313	+2.5	-4.2	-26.0	0.0	**$24**
250 Savage	100	2820	2504	2210	1936	1684	1765	1392	1084	832	630	+2.5	+0.4	-9.0	-28.0	**$17**
257 Roberts	100	2980	2661	2363	2085	1827	1972	1572	1240	965	741	+2.5	-0.8	-5.2	-21.6	**$20**
257 Roberts+P	117	2780	2411	2071	1761	1488	2009	1511	1115	806	576	+2.5	-0.2	-10.2	-32.6	**$18**
257 R. Superformance	117	2946	2705	2478	2265	2057	2253	1901	1595	1329	1099	1.1	0.0	-5.7	-17.1	**NA**
257 Roberts+P	120	2780	2560	2360	2160	1970	2060	1750	1480	1240	1030	+2.5	+1.2	-6.4	-23.6	**$22**
257 Roberts	122	2600	2331	2078	1842	1625	1831	1472	1169	919	715	+2.5	0.0	-10.6	-31.4	**$21**
25-06 Rem.	87	3440	2995	2591	2222	1884	2286	1733	1297	954	686	+2.0	+1.1	-2.5	-14.4	**$17**
25-06 Rem.	90	3440	3043	2680	2344	2034	2364	1850	1435	1098	827	+2.0	+1.8	-3.3	-15.6	**$17**
25-06 Rem.	100	3230	2893	2580	2287	2014	2316	1858	1478	1161	901	+2.0	+0.8	-5.7	-18.9	**$17**
25-06 Rem.	117	2990	2770	2570	2370	2190	2320	2000	1715	1465	1246	+2.5	+1.0	-7.9	-26.6	**$19**
25-06 R. Superformance	117	3110	2861	2626	2403	2191	2512	2127	1792	1500	1246	1.4	0.0	-6.4	-18.9	**NA**
25-06 Rem.*	120	2990	2730	2484	2252	2032	2382	1985	1644	1351	1100	+2.5	+1.2	-5.3	-19.6	**$17**
25-06 Rem.	122	2930	2706	2492	2289	2095	2325	1983	1683	1419	1189	+2.5	+1.8	-4.5	-17.5	**$23**
25 WSSM	85	3470	3156	2863	2589	2331	2273	1880	1548	1266	1026	1.0	0.0	-5.2	-15.7	**NA**
25 WSSM	115	3060	284	2639	2442	2254	2392	2066	1778	1523	1398	1.4	0.0	-6.4	-18.6	**NA**
25 WSSM	120	2990	2717	2459	2216	1987	2383	1967	1612	1309	1053	1.6	0.0	-7.4	-21.8	**NA**
257 Wea. Mag.	87	3825	3456	3118	2805	2513	2826	2308	1870	1520	1220	+2.0	+2.7	-0.3	-7.6	**$32**
257 Wea. Mag.	100	3555	3237	2941	2665	2404	2806	2326	1920	1576	1283	+2.5	+3.2	0.0	-8.0	**$32**
257 Scramjet	100	3745	3450	3173	2912	2666	3114	2643	2235	1883	1578	+2.1	+2.77	0.0	-6.93	**NA**
6.5																
6.5x47 Lapua	123	2887	NA	2554	NA	2244	2285	NA	1788	NA	1380	NA	4.53	0.0	-10.7	**NA**
6.5x50mm Jap.	139	2360	2160	1970	1790	1620	1720	1440	1195	985	810	+2.5	-1.0	-13.5	0.0	**NA**
6.5x50mm Jap.	156	2070	1830	1610	1430	1260	1475	1155	900	695	550	+2.5	-4.0	-23.8	0.0	**NA**
6.5x52mm Car.	139	2580	2360	2160	1970	1790	2045	1725	1440	1195	985	+2.5	0.0	-9.9	-29.0	**NA**
6.5x52mm Car.	156	2430	2170	1930	1700	1500	2045	1630	1285	1005	780	+2.5	-1.0	-13.9	0.0	**NA**
6.5x52mm Carcano	160	2250	1963	1700	1467	1271	1798	1369	1027	764	574	+3.8	0.0	-15.9	-48.1	**NA**
6.5x55mm Swe.	93	2625	2350	2090	1850	1630	1425	1140	905	705	550	2.4	0.0	-10.3	-31.1	**NA**
6.5x55mm Swe.	123	2750	2570	2400	2240	2080	2065	1810	1580	1370	1185	1.9	0.0	-7.9	-22.9	**NA**
6.5x55mm Swe.	140	2550	NA	NA	NA	NA	2020	NA	NA	NA	NA	0.0	0.0	0.0	0.0	**$18**
6.5x55mm Swe.*	139/140	2850	2640	2440	2250	2070	2525	2170	1855	1575	1330	+2.5	+1.6	-5.4	-18.9	**$18**
6.5x55mm Swe.	156	2650	2370	2110	1870	1650	2425	1950	1550	1215	945	+2.5	0.0	-10.3	-30.6	**NA**
260 Remington	125	2875	2669	2473	2285	2105	2294	1977	1697	1449	1230	1.71	0.0	-7.4	-21.4	**NA**
260 Remington	140	2750	2544	2347	2158	1979	2351	2011	1712	1448	1217	+2.2	0.0	-8.6	-24.6	**NA**
6.5 Creedmoor	120	3020	2815	2619	2430	2251	2430	2111	1827	1574	1350	1.4	0.0	-6.5	-18.9	**NA**
6.5 C. Superformance	129	2950	2756	2570	2392	2221	2492	2175	1892	1639	1417	1.5	0.0	-6.8	-19.7	**NA**
6.5 Creedmoor	140	2820	2654	2494	2339	2190	2472	2179	1915	1679	1467	1.7	0.0	-7.2	-20.6	**NA**
6.5-284 Norma	142	3025	2890	2758	2631	2507	2886	2634	2400	2183	1982	1.13	0.0	-5.7	-16.4	**NA**
6.71 (264) Phantom	120	3150	2929	2718	2517	2325	2645	2286	1969	1698	1440	+1.3	0.0	-6.0	-17.5	**NA**
6.5 Rem. Mag.	120	3210	2905	2621	2353	2102	2745	2248	1830	1475	1177	+2.5	+1.7	-4.1	-16.3	**Disc.**
264 Win. Mag.	140	3030	2782	2548	2326	2114	2854	2406	2018	1682	1389	+2.5	+1.4	-5.1	-18.0	**$24**
6.71 (264) Blackbird	140	3480	3261	3053	2855	2665	3766	3307	2899	2534	2208	+2.4	+3.1	0.0	-7.4	**NA**
6.8mm Rem.	115	2775	2472	2190	1926	1683	1966	1561	1224	947	723	+2.1	0.0	-3.7	-9.4	**NA**
27																
270 Winchester	100	3430	3021	2649	2305	1988	2612	2027	1557	1179	877	+2.0	+1.0	-4.9	-17.5	**$17**
270 Win. (Rem.)	115	2710	2482	2265	2059	NA	1875	1485	1161	896	NA	0.0	4.8	-17.3	0.0	**NA**
270 Winchester	130	3060	2776	2510	2259	2022	2702	2225	1818	1472	1180	+2.5	+1.4	-5.3	-18.2	**$17**
270 Win. Supreme	130	3150	2881	2628	2388	2161	2865	2396	1993	1646	1348	1.3	0.0	-6.4	-18.9	**NA**
270 W. Superformance	130	3200	2984	2788	2582	2393	2955	2570	2228	1924	1653	1.2	0.0	-5.7	-16.7	**NA**
270 Winchester	135	3000	2780	2570	2369	2178	2697	2315	1979	1682	1421	+2.5	+1.4	-6.0	-17.6	**$23**
270 Winchester*	140	2940	2700	2480	2260	2060	2685	2270	1905	1590	1315	+2.5	+1.8	-4.6	-17.9	**$20**
270 Winchester*	150	2850	2585	2336	2100	1879	2705	2226	1817	1468	1175	+2.5	+1.2	-6.5	-22.0	**$17**
270 Win. Supreme	150	2930	2693	2468	2254	2051	2860	2416	2030	1693	1402	1.7	0.0	-7.4	-21.6	**NA**
270 WSM	130	3275	3041	2820	2609	2408	3096	2669	2295	1564	1673	1.1	0.0	-5.5	-16.1	**NA**
270 WSM	140	3125	2865	2619	2386	2165	3035	2559	2132	1769	1457	1.4	0.0	-6.5	-19.0	**NA**
270 WSM	150	3120	2923	2734	2554	2380	3242	2845	2490	2172	1886	1.3	0.0	-5.9	-17.2	**NA**
270 Wea. Mag.	100	3760	3380	3033	2712	2412	3139	2537	2042	1633	1292	+2.0	+2.4	-1.2	-10.1	**$32**
270 Wea. Mag.	130	3375	3119	2878	2649	2432	3287	2808	2390	2026	1707	+2.5	-2.9	-0.9	-9.9	**$32**
270 Wea. Mag.*	150	3245	3036	2837	2647	2465	3507	3070	2681	2334	2023	+2.5	+2.6	-1.8	-11.4	**$47**
7mm																
7mm BR	140	2216	2012	1821	1643	1481	1525	1259	1031	839	681	+2.0	-3.7	-20.0	0.0	**$23**
7mm Mauser*	139/140	2660	2435	2221	2018	1827	2199	1843	1533	1266	1037	+2.5	0.0	-9.6	-27.7	**$17**
7mm Mauser	145	2690	2442	2206	1985	1777	2334	1920	1568	1268	1017	+2.5	+0.1	-9.6	-28.3	**$18**
7mm Mauser	154	2690	2490	2300	2120	1940	2475	2120	1810	1530	1285	+2.5	+0.8	-7.5	-23.5	**$17**
7mm Mauser	175	2440	2137	1857	1603	1382	2313	1774	1340	998	742	+2.5	-1.7	-16.1	0.0	**$17**

Cartridge	Bullet Wgt. Grs.	VELOCITY (fps)					ENERGY (ft. lbs.)					TRAJ. (in.)				Est. Price/box
		Muzzle	100 yds.	200 yds.	300 yds.	400 yds.	Muzzle	100 yds.	200 yds.	300 yds.	400 yds.	100 yds.	200 yds.	300 yds.	400 yds.	
7x30 Waters	120	2700	2300	1930	1600	1330	1940	1405	990	685	470	+2.5	-0.2	-12.3	0.0	$18
7mm-08 Rem.	120	3000	2725	2467	2223	1992	2398	1979	1621	1316	1058	+2.0	0.0	-7.6	-22.3	$18
7mm-08 Rem.*	140	2860	2625	2402	2189	1988	2542	2142	1793	1490	1228	+2.5	+0.8	-6.9	-21.9	$18
7mm-08 Rem.	154	2715	2510	2315	2128	1950	2520	2155	1832	1548	1300	+2.5	+1.0	-7.0	-22.7	$23
7-08 R. Superformance	139	2950	2857	2571	2393	2222	2686	2345	2040	1768	1524	1.5	0.0	-6.8	-19.7	NA
7x64mm Bren.	140	Not Yet Announced														$17
7x64mm Bren.	154	2820	2610	2420	2230	2050	2720	2335	1995	1695	1430	+2.5	+1.4	-5.7	-19.9	NA
7x64mm Bren.*	160	2850	2669	2495	2327	2166	2885	2530	2211	1924	1667	+2.5	+1.6	-4.8	-17.8	$24
7x64mm Bren.	175	Not Yet Announced														$17
284 Winchester	150	2860	2595	2344	2108	1886	2724	2243	1830	1480	1185	+2.5	+0.8	-7.3	-23.2	$24
280 R. Superformance	139	3090	2890	2699	2516	2341	2946	2578	2249	1954	1691	1.3	0.0	-6.1	-17.7	NA
280 Remington	140	3000	2758	2528	2309	2102	2797	2363	1986	1657	1373	+2.5	+1.4	-5.2	-18.3	$17
280 Remington*	150	2890	2624	2373	2135	1912	2781	2293	1875	1518	1217	+2.5	+0.8	-7.1	-22.6	$17
280 Remington	160	2840	2637	2442	2556	2078	2866	2471	2120	1809	1535	+2.5	+0.8	-6.7	-21.0	$20
280 Remington	165	2820	2510	2220	1950	1701	2913	2308	1805	1393	1060	+2.5	+0.4	-8.8	-26.5	$17
7x61mm S&H Sup.	154	3060	2720	2400	2100	1820	3200	2520	1965	1505	1135	+2.5	+1.8	-5.0	-19.8	NA
7mm Dakota	160	3200	3001	2811	2630	2455	3637	3200	2808	2456	2140	+2.1	+1.9	-2.8	-12.5	NA
7mm Rem. Mag. (Rem.)	140	2710	2482	2265	2059	NA	2283	1915	1595	1318	NA	0.0	-4.5	-1.57	0.0	NA
7mm Rem. Mag.*	139/140	3150	2930	2710	2510	2320	3085	2660	2290	1960	1670	+2.5	+2.4	-2.4	-12.7	$21
7 R.M. Superformance	139	3240	3033	2836	2648	2467	3239	2839	2482	2163	1877	1.1	0.0	-5.5	-15.9	NA
7mm Rem. Mag.	150/154	3110	2830	2568	2320	2085	3221	2667	2196	1792	1448	+2.5	+1.6	-4.6	-16.5	$21
7mm Rem. Mag.*	160/162	2950	2730	2520	2320	2120	3090	2650	2250	1910	1600	+2.5	+1.8	-4.4	-17.8	$34
7 R.M. Superformance	154	3100	2914	2736	2565	2401	3286	2904	2560	2250	1970	1.3	0.0	-5.9	-17.2	NA
7mm Rem. Mag.	165	2900	2699	2507	2324	2147	3081	2669	2303	1978	1689	+2.5	+1.2	-5.9	-19.0	$28
7mm Rem Mag.	175	2860	2645	2440	2244	2057	3178	2718	2313	1956	1644	+2.5	+1.0	-6.5	-20.7	$21
7mm Rem. SA ULTRA MAG	140	3175	2934	2707	2490	2283	3033	2676	2277	1927	1620	1.3	0.0	-6	-17.7	NA
7mm Rem. SA ULTRA MAG	150	3110	2828	2563	2313	2077	3221	2663	2188	1782	1437	2.5	2.1	-3.6	-15.8	NA
7mm Rem. SA ULTRA MAG	160	2960	2762	2572	2390	2215	3112	2709	2350	2029	1743	2.6	2.2	-3.6	-15.4	NA
7mm Rem. WSM	140	3225	3008	2801	2603	2414	3233	2812	2438	2106	1812	1.2	0.0	-5.6	-16.4	NA
7mm Rem. WSM	160	2990	2744	2512	2081	1883	3176	2675	2241	1864	1538	1.6	0.0	-7.1	-20.8	NA
7mm Wea. Mag.	140	3225	2970	2729	2501	2283	3233	2741	2315	1943	1621	+2.5	+2.0	-3.2	-14.0	$35
7mm Wea. Mag.	154	3260	3023	2799	2586	2382	3539	3044	2609	2227	1890	+2.5	+2.8	-1.5	-10.8	$32
7mm Wea. Mag.*	160	3200	3004	2816	2637	2464	3637	3205	2817	2469	2156	+2.5	+2.7	-1.5	-10.6	$47
7mm Wea. Mag.	165	2950	2747	2553	2367	2189	3188	2765	2388	2053	1756	+2.5	+1.8	-4.2	-16.4	$43
7mm Wea. Mag.	175	2910	2693	2486	2288	2098	3293	2818	2401	2033	1711	+2.5	+1.2	-5.9	-19.4	$35
7.21(.284) Tomahawk	140	3300	3118	2943	2774	2612	3386	3022	2693	2393	2122	2.3	3.2	0.0	-7.7	NA
7mm STW	140	3325	3064	2818	2585	2364	3436	2918	2468	2077	1737	+2.3	+1.8	-3.0	-13.1	NA
7mm STW Supreme	160	3150	2894	2652	2422	2204	3526	2976	2499	2085	1727	1.3	0.0	-6.3	-18.5	NA
7mm Rem. Ultra Mag.	140	3425	3184	2956	2740	2534	3646	3151	2715	2333	1995	1.7	1.6	-2.6	-11.4	NA
7mm Firehawk	140	3625	3373	3135	2909	2695	4084	3536	3054	2631	2258	+2.2	+2.9	0.0	-7.03	NA
30																
7.21 (.284) Firebird	140	3750	3522	3306	3101	2905	4372	3857	3399	2990	2625	1.6	2.4	0.0	-6.0	NA
30 Carbine	110	1990	1567	1236	1035	923	977	600	373	262	208	0.0	-13.5	0.0	0.0	$28**
303 Savage	190	1890	1612	1327	1183	1055	1507	1096	794	591	469	+2.5	-7.6	0.0	0.0	$24
30 Remington	170	2120	1822	1555	1328	1153	1696	1253	913	666	502	+2.5	-4.7	-26.3	0.0	$20
7.62x39mm Rus.	123/125	2300	2030	1780	1550	1350	1445	1125	860	655	500	+2.5	-2.0	-17.5	0.0	$13
30-30 Win.	55	3400	2693	2085	1570	1187	1412	886	521	301	172	+2.0	0.0	-10.2	-35.0	$18
30-30 Win.	125	2570	2090	1660	1320	1080	1830	1210	770	480	320	-2.0	-2.6	-19.9	0.0	$13
30-30 Win.	150	2390	2040	1723	1447	1225	1902	1386	989	697	499	0.0	-7.5	-27.0	-63.0	NA
30-30 Win. Supreme	150	2480	2095	1747	1446	1209	2049	1462	1017	697	487	0.0	-6.5	-24.5	0.0	NA
30-30 Win.	160	2300	1997	1719	1473	1268	1879	1416	1050	771	571	+2.5	-2.9	-20.2	0.0	$18
30-30 Win. Lever Evolution	160	2400	2150	1916	1699	NA	2046	1643	1304	1025	NA	3.0	0.2	-12.1	NA	NA
30-30 PMC Cowboy	170	1300	1198	1121			638	474				0.0	-27.0	0.0	0.0	NA
30-30 Win.*	170	2200	1895	1619	1381	1191	1827	1355	989	720	535	+2.5	-5.8	-23.6	0.0	$13
300 Savage	150	2630	2354	2094	1853	1631	2303	1845	1462	1143	886	+2.5	-0.4	-10.1	-30.7	$17
300 Savage	180	2350	2137	1935	1754	1570	2207	1825	1496	1217	985	+2.5	-1.6	-15.2	0.0	$17
30-40 Krag	180	2430	2213	2007	1813	1632	2360	1957	1610	1314	1064	+2.5	-1.4	-13.8	0.0	$18
7.65x53mm Arg.	180	2590	2390	2200	2010	1830	2685	2280	1925	1615	1345	+2.5	0.0	-27.6	0.0	NA
7.5x53mm Argentine	150	2785	2519	2269	2032	1814	2583	2113	1714	1376	1096	+2.0	0.0	-8.8	-25.5	NA
308 Marlin Express	160	2660	2430	2226	2026	1836	2513	2111	1761	1457	1197	3.0	1.7	-6.7	-23.5	NA
307 Winchester	150	2760	2321	1924	1575	1289	2530	1795	1233	826	554	+2.5	-1.5	-13.6	0.0	Disc.
307 Winchester	180	2510	2179	1874	1599	1362	2519	1898	1404	1022	742	+2.5	-1.6	-15.6	0.0	$20
7.5x55 Swiss	180	2650	2450	2250	2060	1880	2805	2390	2020	1700	1415	+2.5	+0.6	-8.1	-24.9	NA
7.5x55mm Swiss	165	2720	2515	2319	2132	1954	2710	2317	1970	1665	1398	+2.0	0.0	-8.5	-24.6	NA
30 Remington AR	123/125	2800	2465	2154	1867	1606	2176	1686	1288	967	716	2.1	0.0	-9.7	-29.4	NA

Cartridge	Bullet Wgt. Grs.	VELOCITY (fps)					ENERGY (ft. lbs.)					TRAJ. (in.)				Est. Price/box
		Muzzle	100 yds.	200 yds.	300 yds.	400 yds.	Muzzle	100 yds.	200 yds.	300 yds.	400 yds.	100 yds.	200 yds.	300 yds.	400 yds.	
308 Winchester	55	3770	3215	2726	2286	1888	1735	1262	907	638	435	-2.0	+1.4	-3.8	-15.8	**$22**
308 Winchester	150	2820	2533	2263	2009	1774	2648	2137	1705	1344	1048	+2.5	+0.4	-8.5	-26.1	**$17**
308 W. Superformance	150	3000	2772	2555	2348	1962	2997	2558	2173	1836	1540	1.5	0.0	-6.9	-20.0	**NA**
308 Winchester	165	2700	2440	2194	1963	1748	2670	2180	1763	1411	1199	+2.5	0.0	-9.7	-28.5	**$20**
308 Winchester	168	2680	2493	2314	2143	1979	2678	2318	1998	1713	1460	+2.5	0.0	-8.9	-25.3	**$18**
308 Win. (Fed.)	170	2000	1740	1510	NA	NA	1510	1145	860	NA	NA	0.0	0.0	0.0	0.0	**NA**
308 Winchester	178	2620	2415	2220	2034	1857	2713	2306	1948	1635	1363	+2.5	0.0	-9.6	-27.6	**$23**
308 Winchester*	180	2620	2393	2178	1974	1782	2743	2288	1896	1557	1269	+2.5	-0.2	-10.2	-28.5	**$17**
30-06 Spfd.	55	4080	3485	2965	2502	2083	2033	1483	1074	764	530	+2.0	+1.9	-2.1	-11.7	**$22**
30-06 Spfd. (Rem.)	125	2660	2335	2034	1757	NA	1964	1513	1148	856	NA	0.0	-5.2	-18.9	0.0	**NA**
30-06 Spfd.	125	3140	2780	2447	2138	1853	2736	2145	1662	1279	953	+2.0	+1.0	-6.2	-21.0	**$17**
30-06 Spfd.	150	2910	2617	2342	2083	1853	2820	2281	1827	1445	1135	+2.5	+0.8	-7.2	-23.4	**$17**
30-06 Superformance	150	3080	2848	2617	2417	2216	3159	2700	2298	1945	1636	1.4	0.0	-6.4	-18.9	**NA**
30-06 Spfd.	152	2910	2654	2413	2184	1968	2858	2378	1965	1610	1307	+2.5	+1.0	-6.6	-21.3	**$23**
30-06 Spfd.*	165	2800	2534	2283	2047	1825	2872	2352	1909	1534	1220	+2.5	+0.4	-8.4	-25.5	**$17**
30-06 Spfd.	168	2710	2522	2346	2169	2003	2739	2372	2045	1754	1497	+2.5	+0.4	-8.0	-23.5	**$18**
30-06 Spfd. (Fed.)	170	2000	1740	1510	NA	NA	1510	1145	860	NA	NA	0.0	0.0	0.0	0.0	**NA**
30-06 Spfd.	178	2720	2511	2311	2121	1939	2924	2491	2111	1777	1486	+2.5	+0.4	-8.2	-24.6	**$23**
30-06 Spfd.*	180	2700	2469	2250	2042	1846	2913	2436	2023	1666	1362	-2.5	0.0	-9.3	-27.0	**$17**
30-06 Superformance	180	2820	2630	2447	2272	2104	3178	2764	2393	2063	1769	1.8	0.0	-7.6	-21.9	**NA**
30-06 Spfd.	220	2410	2130	1870	1632	1422	2837	2216	1708	1301	988	+2.5	-1.7	-18.0	0.0	**$17**
30-06 Light Mag.	150	3100	2815	2548	2295	2058	3200	2639	2161	1755	1410	+1.4	0.0	-6.8	-20.3	**NA**
30-06 Light Mag.	180	2880	2676	2480	2293	2114	3316	2862	2459	2102	1786	+1.7	0.0	-7.3	-21.3	**NA**
30-06 High Energy	180	2880	2690	2500	2320	2150	3315	2880	2495	2150	1845	+1.7	0.0	-7.2	-21.0	**NA**
30 T/C Superformance	150	3000	2772	2555	2348	2151	2997	2558	2173	1836	1540	1.5	0.0	-6.9	-20.0	**NA**
30 T/C Superformance	165	2850	2644	2447	2258	2078	2975	2560	2193	1868	1582	1.7	0.0	-7.6	-22.0	**NA**
300 Rem SA Ultra Mag	150	3200	2901	2622	2359	2112	3410	2803	2290	1854	1485	1.3	0.0	-6.4	-19.1	**NA**
300 Rem SA Ultra Mag	165	3075	2792	2527	2276	2040	3464	2856	2339	1898	1525	1.5	0.0	-7	-20.7	**NA**
300 Rem SA Ultra Mag	180	2960	2761	2571	2389	2214	3501	3047	2642	2280	1959	2.6	2.2	-3.6	-15.4	**NA**
7.82 (308) Patriot	150	3250	2999	2762	2537	2323	3519	2997	2542	2145	1798	+1.2	0.0	-5.8	-16.9	**NA**
300 RCM Superformance	150	3310	3065	2833	2613	2404	3648	3128	2673	2274	1924	1.1	0.0	-5.4	-16.0	**NA**
300 RCM Superformance	165	3185	2964	2753	2552	2360	3716	3217	2776	2386	2040	1.2	0.0	-5.8	-17.0	**NA**
300 RCM Superformance	180	3040	2840	2649	2466	2290	3693	3223	2804	2430	2096	1.4	0.0	-6.4	-18.5	**NA**
300 WSM	150	3300	3061	2834	2619	2414	3628	3121	2676	2285	1941	1.1	0.0	-5.4	-15.9	**NA**
300 WSM	180	2970	2741	2524	2317	2120	3526	3005	2547	2147	1797	1.6	0.0	-7.0	-20.5	**NA**
300 WSM	180	3010	2923	2734	2554	2380	3242	2845	2490	2172	1886	1.3	0	-5.9	-17.2	**NA**
308 Norma Mag.	180	3020	2820	2630	2440	2270	3645	3175	2755	2385	2050	+2.5	+2.0	-3.5	-14.8	**NA**
300 Dakota	200	3000	2824	2656	2493	2336	3996	3542	3131	2760	2423	+2.2	+1.5	-4.0	-15.2	**NA**
300 H&H Magnum*	180	2880	2640	2412	2196	1990	3315	2785	2325	1927	1583	+2.5	+0.8	-6.8	-21.7	**$24**
300 H&H Magnum	220	2550	2267	2002	1757	NA	3167	2510	1958	1508	NA	-2.5	-0.4	-12.0	0.0	**NA**
300 Win. Mag.	150	3290	2951	2636	2342	2068	3605	2900	2314	1827	1424	+2.5	+1.9	-3.8	-15.8	**$22**
300 WM Superformance	150	3400	3150	2914	2690	2477	3850	3304	2817	2409	2043	1.0	0.0	-5.1	-15.0	**NA**
300 Win. Mag.	165	3100	2877	2665	2462	2269	3522	3033	2603	2221	1897	+2.5	+2.4	-3.0	-16.9	**$24**
300 Win. Mag.	178	2900	2760	2568	2375	2191	3509	3030	2606	2230	1897	+2.5	+1.4	-5.0	-17.6	**$29**
300 Win. Mag.*	180	2960	2745	2540	2344	2157	3501	3011	2578	2196	1859	+2.5	+1.2	-5.5	-18.5	**$22**
300 WM Light Mag.	180	3100	2879	2668	2467	2275	3840	3313	2845	2431	2068	+1.39	0.0	-6.45	-18.7	**NA**
300 WM Superformance	180	3130	2927	2732	2546	2366	3917	3424	2983	2589	2238	1.3	0.0	-5.9	-17.3	**NA**
300 Win. Mag.	190	2885	1691	2506	2327	2156	3511	3055	2648	2285	1961	+2.5	+1.2	-5.7	-19.0	**$26**
300 Win. Mag.*	200	2825	2595	2376	2167	1970	3545	2991	2508	2086	1742	-2.5	+1.6	-4.7	-17.2	**$36**
300 Win. Mag.	220	2680	2448	2228	2020	1823	3508	2927	2424	1993	1623	+2.5	0.0	-9.5	-27.5	**$23**
300 Rem. Ultra Mag.	150	3450	3208	2980	2762	2556	3964	3427	2956	2541	2175	1.7	1.5	-2.6	-11.2	**NA**
300 Rem. Ultra Mag.	150	2910	2686	2473	2279	2077	2820	2403	2037	1716	1436	1.7	0.0	-7.4	-21.5	**NA**
300 Rem. Ultra Mag.	180	3250	3037	2834	2640	2454	4221	3686	3201	2786	2407	2.4	0.0	-3.0	-12.7	**NA**
300 Rem. Ultra Mag.	180	2960	2774	2505	2294	2093	3501	2971	2508	2103	1751	2.7	2.2	-3.8	-16.4	**NA**
300 Rem. Ultra Mag.	200	3032	2791	2562	2345	2138	4083	3459	2916	2442	2030	1.5	0.0	-6.8	-19.9	**NA**
300 Wea. Mag.	100	3900	3441	3038	2652	2305	3714	2891	2239	1717	1297	+2.0	+2.6	-0.6	-8.7	**$32**
300 Wea. Mag.	150	3600	3307	3033	2776	2533	4316	3642	3064	2566	2137	+2.5	+3.2	0.0	-8.1	**$32**
300 Wea. Mag.	165	3450	3210	3000	2792	2593	4360	3796	3297	2855	2464	+2.5	+3.2	0.0	-7.8	**NA**
300 Wea. Mag.	178	3120	2902	2695	2497	2308	3847	3329	2870	2464	2104	+2.5	-1.7	-3.6	-14.7	**$43**
300 Wea. Mag.	180	3330	3110	2910	2710	2520	4430	3875	3375	2935	2540	+1.0	0.0	-5.2	-15.1	**NA**
300 Wea. Mag.	190	3030	2830	2638	2455	2279	3873	3378	2936	2542	2190	+2.5	+1.6	-4.3	-16.0	**$38**
300 Wea. Mag.	220	2850	2541	2283	1964	1736	3967	3155	2480	1922	1471	+2.5	+0.4	-8.5	-26.4	**$35**
300 Warbird	180	3400	3180	2971	2772	2582	4620	4042	3528	3071	2664	+2.59	+3.25	0.0	-7.95	**NA**
300 Pegasus	180	3500	3319	3145	2978	2817	4896	4401	3953	3544	3172	+2.28	+2.89	0.0	-6.79	**NA**
31																
32-20 Win.	100	1210	1021	913	834	769	325	231	185	154	131	0.0	-32.3	0.0	0.0	**$23****

Cartridge	Bullet Wgt. Grs.	VELOCITY (fps)					ENERGY (ft. lbs.)					TRAJ. (in.)				Est. Price/box
		Muzzle	100 yds.	200 yds.	300 yds.	400 yds.	Muzzle	100 yds.	200 yds.	300 yds.	400 yds.	100 yds.	200 yds.	300 yds.	400 yds.	
303 British	180	2460	2124	1817	1542	1311	2418	1803	1319	950	687	+2.5	-1.8	-16.8	0.0	**$18**
303 Light Mag.	150	2830	2570	2325	2094	1884	2667	2199	1800	1461	1185	+2.0	0.0	-8.4	-24.6	**NA**
7.62x54mm Rus.	146	2950	2730	2520	2320	NA	2820	2415	2055	1740	NA	+2.5	+2.0	-4.4	-17.7	**NA**
7.62x54mm Rus.	180	2580	2370	2180	2000	1820	2650	2250	1900	1590	1100	+2.5	0.0	-9.8	-28.5	**NA**
7.7x58mm Jap.	150	2640	2399	2170	1954	1752	2321	1916	1568	1271	1022	+2.3	0.0	-9.7	-28.5	**NA**
7.7x58mm Jap.	180	2500	2300	2100	1920	1750	2490	2105	1770	1475	1225	+2.5	0.0	-10.4	-30.2	**NA**
8x56 R	205	2400	2188	1987	1797	1621	2621	2178	1796	1470	1196	+2.9	0.0	-11.7	-34.3	**NA**
8mm																
8x57mm JS Mau.	165	2850	2520	2210	1930	1670	2965	2330	1795	1360	1015	+2.5	+1.0	-7.7	0.0	**NA**
32 Win. Special	165	2410	2145	1897	1669	NA	2128	1685	1318	1020	NA	2.0	0.0	- 13.0	-19.9	**NA**
32 Win. Special	170	2250	1921	1626	1372	1175	1911	1393	998	710	521	+2.5	-3.5	-22.9	0.0	**$14**
8mm Mauser	170	2360	1969	1622	1333	1123	2102	1464	993	671	476	+2.5	-3.1	-22.2	0.0	**$18**
325 WSM	180	3060	2841	2632	2432	2242	3743	3226	2769	2365	2009	+1.4	0.0	-6.4	-18.7	**NA**
325 WSM	200	2950	2753	2565	2384	2210	3866	3367	2922	2524	2170	+1.5	0.0	-6.8	-19.8	**NA**
325 WSM	220	2840	2605	2382	2169	1968	3941	3316	2772	2300	1893	+1.8	0.0	-8.0	-23.3	**NA**
8mm Rem. Mag.	185	3080	2761	2464	2186	1927	3896	3131	2494	1963	1525	+2.5	+1.4	-5.5	-19.7	**$30**
8mm Rem. Mag.	220	2830	2581	2346	2123	1913	3912	3254	2688	2201	1787	+2.5	+0.6	-7.6	-23.5	**Disc.**
33																
338 Federal	180	2830	2590	2350	2130	1930	3200	2670	2215	1820	1480	1.8	0.0	-8.2	-23.9	**NA**
338 Marlin Express	200	2565	2365	2174	1992	1820	2922	2484	2099	1762	1471	3.0	1.2	-7.9	-25.9	**NA**
338 Federal	185	2750	2550	2350	2160	1980	3105	2660	2265	1920	1615	1.9	0.0	-8.3	-24.1	**NA**
338 Federal	210	2630	2410	2200	2010	1820	3225	2710	2265	1880	1545	2.3	0.0	-9.4	-27.3	**NA**
338-06	200	2750	2553	2364	2184	2011	3358	2894	2482	2118	1796	+1.9	0.0	-8.22	-23.6	**NA**
330 Dakota	250	2900	2719	2545	2378	2217	4668	4103	3595	3138	2727	+2.3	+1.3	-5.0	-17.5	**NA**
338 Lapua	250	2963	2795	2640	2493	NA	4842	4341	3881	3458	NA	+1.9	0.0	-7.9	0.0	**NA**
338 RCM Superformance	185	2980	2755	2542	2338	2143	3647	3118	2653	2242	1887	1.5	0.0	-6.9	-20.3	**NA**
338 RCM Superformance	200	2950	2744	2547	2358	2177	3846	3342	2879	2468	2104	1.6	0.0	-6.9	-20.1	**NA**
338 RCM Superformance	225	2750	2575	2407	2245	2089	3778	3313	2894	2518	2180	1.9	0.0	-7.9	-22.7	**NA**
338 WM Superformance	185	3080	2850	2632	2424	2226	3896	3337	2845	2413	2034	1.4	0.0	-6.4	-18.8	**NA**
338 Win. Mag.*	210	2830	2590	2370	2150	1940	3735	3130	2610	2155	1760	+2.5	+1.4	-6.0	-20.9	**$33**
338 Win. Mag.*	225	2785	2517	2266	2029	1808	3871	3165	2565	2057	1633	+2.5	+0.4	-8.5	-25.9	**$27**
338 WM Superformance	225	2840	2758	2582	2414	2252	4318	3798	3331	2911	2533	1.5	0.0	-6.8	-19.5	**NA**
338 Win. Mag.	230	2780	2573	2375	2186	2005	3948	3382	2881	2441	2054	+2.5	+1.2	-6.3	-21.0	**$40**
338 Win. Mag.*	250	2660	2456	2261	2075	1898	3927	3348	2837	2389	1999	+2.5	+0.2	-9.0	-26.2	**$27**
338 Ultra Mag.	250	2860	2645	2440	2244	2057	4540	3882	3303	2794	2347	1.7	0.0	-7.6	-22.1	**NA**
8.59(.338) Galaxy	200	3100	2899	2707	2524	2347	4269	3734	3256	2829	2446	3	3.8	0.0	-9.3	**NA**
340 Wea. Mag.*	210	3250	2991	2746	2515	2295	4924	4170	3516	2948	2455	+2.5	+1.9	-1.8	-11.8	**$56**
340 Wea. Mag.*	250	3000	2806	2621	2443	2272	4995	4371	3812	3311	2864	+2.5	+2.0	-3.5	-14.8	**$56**
338 A-Square	250	3120	2799	2500	2220	1958	5403	4348	3469	2736	2128	+2.5	+2.7	-1.5	-10.5	**NA**
338-378 Wea. Mag.	225	3180	2974	2778	2591	2410	5052	4420	3856	3353	2902	3.1	3.8	0.0	-8.9	**NA**
338 Titan	225	3230	3010	2800	2600	2409	5211	4524	3916	3377	2898	+3.07	+3.8	0.0	-8.95	**NA**
338 Excalibur	200	3600	3361	3134	2920	2715	5755	5015	4363	3785	3274	+2.23	+2.87	0.0	-6.99	**NA**
338 Excalibur	250	3250	2922	2618	2333	2066	5863	4740	3804	3021	2370	+1.3	0.0	-6.35	-19.2	**NA**
34, 35																
348 Winchester	200	2520	2215	1931	1672	1443	2820	2178	1656	1241	925	+2.5	-1.4	-14.7	0.0	**$42**
357 Magnum	158	1830	1427	1138	980	883	1175	715	454	337	274	0.0	-16.2	-33.1	0.0	**$25****
35 Remington	150	2300	1874	1506	1218	1039	1762	1169	755	494	359	+2.5	-4.1	-26.3	0.0	**$16**
35 Remington	200	2080	1698	1376	1140	1001	1921	1280	841	577	445	+2.5	-6.3	-17.1	-33.6	**$16**
35 Rem. Lever Evolution	200	2225	1963	1721	1503	NA	2198	1711	1315	1003	NA	3.0	-1.3	-17.5	NA	**NA**
356 Winchester	200	2460	2114	1797	1517	1284	2688	1985	1434	1022	732	+2.5	-1.8	-15.1	0.0	**$31**
356 Winchester	250	2160	1911	1682	1476	1299	2591	2028	1571	1210	937	+2.5	-3.7	-22.2	0.0	**$31**
358 Winchester	200	2490	2171	1876	1619	1379	2753	2093	1563	1151	844	+2.5	-1.6	-15.6	0.0	**$31**
358 STA	275	2850	2562	2292	2039	NA	4958	4009	3208	2539	NA	+1.9	0.0	-8.6	0.0	**NA**
350 Rem. Mag.	200	2710	2410	2130	1870	1631	3261	2579	2014	1553	1181	+2.5	-0.2	-10.0	-30.1	**$33**
35 Whelen	200	2675	2378	2100	1842	1606	3177	2510	1958	1506	1145	+2.5	-0.2	-10.3	-31.1	**$20**
35 Whelen	225	2500	2300	2110	1930	1770	3120	2650	2235	1870	1560	+2.6	0.0	-10.2	-29.9	**NA**
35 Whelen	250	2400	2197	2005	1823	1652	3197	2680	2230	1844	1515	+2.5	-1.2	-13.7	0.0	**$20**
358 Norma Mag.	250	2800	2510	2230	1970	1730	4350	3480	2750	2145	1655	+2.5	+1.0	-7.6	-25.2	**NA**
358 STA	275	2850	2562	229*2	2039	1764	4959	4009	3208	2539	1899	+1.9	0.0	-8.58	-26.1	**NA**
9.3mm																
9.3x57mm Mau.	286	2070	1810	1590	1390	1110	2710	2090	1600	1220	955	+2.5	-2.6	-22.5	0.0	**NA**
9.3x62mm Mau.	286	2360	2089	1844	1623	NA	3538	2771	2157	1670	1260	+2.5	-1.6	-21.0	0.0	**NA**
370 Sako Mag.	286	3550	2370	2200	2040	2880	4130	3570	3075	2630	2240	2.4	0.0	-9.5	-27.2	**NA**
9.3x64mm	286	2700	2505	2318	2139	1968	4629	3984	3411	2906	2460	+2.5	+2.7	-4.5	-19.2	**NA**
9.3x74Rmm	286	2360	2136	1924	1727	1545	3536	2896	2351	1893	1516	0.0	-6.1	-21.7	-49.0	**NA**
375																

Cartridge	Bullet Wgt. Grs.	VELOCITY (fps)					ENERGY (ft. lbs.)					TRAJ. (in.)				Est. Price/box
		Muzzle	100 yds.	200 yds.	300 yds.	400 yds.	Muzzle	100 yds.	200 yds.	300 yds.	400 yds.	100 yds.	200 yds.	300 yds.	400 yds.	
375 Winchester	200	2200	1841	1526	1268	1089	2150	1506	1034	714	527	+2.5	-4.0	-26.2	0.0	**$27**
375 Winchester	250	1900	1647	1424	1239	1103	2005	1506	1126	852	676	+2.5	-6.9	-33.3	0.0	**$27**
376 Steyr	225	2600	2331	2078	1842	1625	3377	2714	2157	1694	1319	2.5	0.0	-10.6	-31.4	**NA**
376 Steyr	270	2600	2372	2156	1951	1759	4052	3373	2787	2283	1855	2.3	0.0	-9.9	-28.9	**NA**
375 Dakota	300	2600	2316	2051	1804	1579	4502	3573	2800	2167	1661	+2.4	0.0	-11.0	-32.7	**NA**
375 N.E. 2-1/2"	270	2000	1740	1507	1310	NA	2398	1815	1362	1026	NA	+2.5	-6.0	-30.0	0.0	**NA**
375 Flanged	300	2450	2150	1886	1640	NA	3998	3102	2369	1790	NA	+2.5	-2.4	-17.0	0.0	**NA**
375 Ruger	270	2840	2600	2372	2156	1951	4835	4052	3373	2786	2283	1.8	0.0	-8.0	-23.6	**NA**
375 Ruger	300	2660	2344	2050	1780	1536	4713	3660	2800	2110	1572	2.4	0.0	-10.8	-32.6	**NA**
375 H&H Magnum	250	2670	2450	2240	2040	1850	3955	3335	2790	2315	1905	+2.5	-0.4	-10.2	-28.4	**NA**
375 H&H Magnum	270	2690	2420	2166	1928	1707	4337	3510	2812	2228	1747	+2.5	0.0	-10.0	-29.4	**$28**
375 H&H Magnum*	300	2530	2245	1979	1733	1512	4263	3357	2608	2001	1523	+2.5	-1.0	-10.5	-33.6	**$28**
375 H&H Hvy. Mag.	270	2870	2628	2399	2182	1976	4937	4141	3451	2150	1845	+1.7	0.0	-7.2	-21.0	**NA**
375 H&H Hvy. Mag.	300	2705	2386	2090	1816	1568	4873	3793	2908	2195	1637	+2.3	0.0	-10.4	-31.4	**NA**
375 Rem. Ultra Mag.	270	2900	2558	2241	1947	1678	5041	3922	3010	2272	1689	1.9	2.7	-8.9	-27.0	**NA**
375 Rem. Ultra Mag.	300	2760	2505	2263	2035	1822	5073	4178	3412	2759	2210	2.0	0.0	-8.8	-26.1	**NA**
375 Wea. Mag.	300	2700	2420	2157	1911	1685	4856	3901	3100	2432	1891	+2.5	-.04	-10.7	0.0	**NA**
378 Wea. Mag.	270	3180	2976	2781	2594	2415	6062	5308	4635	4034	3495	+2.5	+2.6	-1.8	-11.3	**$71**
378 Wea. Mag.	300	2929	2576	2252	1952	1680	5698	4419	3379	2538	1881	+2.5	+1.2	-7.0	-24.5	**$77**
375 A-Square	300	2920	2626	2351	2093	1850	5679	4594	3681	2917	2281	+2.5	+1.4	-6.0	-21.0	**NA**
38-40 Win.	180	1160	999	901	827	764	538	399	324	273	233	0.0	-33.9	0.0	0.0	**$42****
40, 41																
400 A-Square DPM	400	2400	2146	1909	1689	NA	5116	2092	3236	2533	NA	2.98	0.0	-10.0	NA	**NA**
400 A-Square DPM	170	2980	2463	2001	1598	NA	3352	2289	1512	964	NA	2.16	0.0	-11.1	NA	**NA**
408 CheyTac	419	2850	2752	2657	2562	2470	7551	7048	6565	6108	5675	-1.02	0.0	1.9	4.2	**NA**
405 Win.	300	2200	1851	1545	1296		3224	2282	1589	1119		4.6	0.0	-19.5	0.0	**NA**
450/400-3"	400	2050	1815	1595	1402	NA	3732	2924	2259	1746	NA	0.0	NA	-33.4	NA	**NA**
416 Ruger	400	2400	2151	1917	1700	NA	5116	4109	3264	2568	NA	0.0	-6.0	-21.6	0.0	**NA**
416 Dakota	400	2450	2294	2143	1998	1859	5330	4671	4077	3544	3068	+2.5	-0.2	-10.5	-29.4	**NA**
416 Taylor	400	2350	2117	1896	1693	NA	4905	3980	3194	2547	NA	+2.5	-1.2	15.0	0.0	**NA**
416 Hoffman	400	2380	2145	1923	1718	1529	5031	4087	3285	2620	2077	+2.5	-1.0	-14.1	0.0	**NA**
416 Rigby	350	2600	2449	2303	2162	2026	5253	4661	4122	3632	3189	+2.5	-1.8	-10.2	-26.0	**NA**
416 Rigby	400	2370	2210	2050	1900	NA	4990	4315	3720	3185	NA	+2.5	-0.7	-12.1	0.0	**NA**
416 Rigby	410	2370	2110	1870	1640	NA	5115	4050	3165	2455	NA	+2.5	-2.4	-17.3	0.0	**$110**
416 Rem. Mag.*	350	2520	2270	2034	1814	1611	4935	4004	3216	2557	2017	+2.5	-0.8	-12.6	-35.0	**$82**
416 Wea. Mag.*	400	2700	2397	2115	1852	1613	6474	5104	3971	3047	2310	+2.5	0.0	-10.1	-30.4	**$96**
10.57 (416) Meteor	400	2730	2532	2342	2161	1987	6621	5695	4874	4147	3508	+1.9	0.0	-8.3	-24.0	**NA**
404 Jeffrey	400	2150	1924	1716	1525	NA	4105	3289	2614	2064	NA	+2.5	-4.0	-22.1	0.0	**NA**
425, 44																
425 Express	400	2400	2160	1934	1725	NA	5115	4145	3322	2641	NA	+2.5	-1.0	-14.0	0.0	**NA**
44-40 Win.	200	1190	1006	900	822	756	629	449	360	300	254	0.0	-33.3	0.0	0.0	**$36****
44 Rem. Mag.	210	1920	1477	1155	982	880	1719	1017	622	450	361	0.0	-17.6	0.0	0.0	**$14**
44 Rem. Mag.	240	1760	1380	1114	970	878	1650	1015	661	501	411	0.0	-17.6	0.0	0.0	**$13**
444 Marlin	240	2350	1815	1377	1087	941	2942	1753	1001	630	472	+2.5	-15.1	-31.0	0.0	**$22**
444 Marlin	265	2120	1733	1405	1160	1012	2644	1768	1162	791	603	+2.5	-6.0	-32.2	0.0	**Disc.**
444 Marlin Light Mag	265	2335	1913	1551	1266		3208	2153	1415	943		2.0	-4.9	-26.5	0.0	**NA**
444 Mar. Lever Evolution	265	2325	1971	1652	1380	NA	3180	2285	1606	1120	NA	3.0	-1.4	-18.6	NA	**NA**
45																
45-70 Govt.	300	1810	1497	1244	1073	969	2182	1492	1031	767	625	0.0	-14.8	0.0	0.0	**$21**
45-70 Govt. Supreme	300	1880	1558	1292	1103	988	2355	1616	1112	811	651	0.0	-12.9	-46.0	-105.0	**NA**
45-70 Lever Evolution	325	2050	1729	1450	1225	NA	3032	2158	1516	1083	NA	3.0	-4.1	-27.8	NA	**NA**
45-70 Govt. CorBon	350	1800	1526	1296			2519	1810	1307			0.0	-14.6	0.0	0.0	**NA**
45-70 Govt.	405	1330	1168	1055	977	918	1590	1227	1001	858	758	0.0	-24.6	0.0	0.0	**$21**
45-70 Govt. PMC Cowboy	405	1550	1193				1639	1280				0.0	-23.9	0.0	0.0	**NA**
45-70 Govt. Garrett	415	1850					3150					3.0	-7.0	0.0	0.0	**NA**
45-70 Govt. Garrett	530	1550	1343	1178	1062	982	2828	2123	1633	1327	1135	0.0	-17.8	0.0	0.0	**NA**
450 Bushmaster	250	2200	1831	1508	1480	1073	2686	1860	1262	864	639	0.0	-9.0	-33.5	0.0	**NA**
450 Marlin	350	2100	1774	1488	1254	1089	3427	2446	1720	1222	922	0.0	-9.7	-35.2	0.0	**NA**
450 Mar. Lever Evolution	325	2225	1887	1585	1331	NA	3572	2569	1813	1278	NA	3.0	-2.2	-21.3	NA	**NA**
458 Win. Magnum	350	2470	1990	1570	1250	1060	4740	3065	1915	1205	870	+2.5	-2.5	-21.6	0.0	**$43**
458 Win. Magnum	400	2380	2170	1960	1770	NA	5030	4165	3415	2785	NA	+2.5	-0.4	-13.4	0.0	**$73**
458 Win. Magnum	465	2220	1999	1791	1601	NA	5088	4127	3312	2646	NA	+2.5	-2.0	-17.7	0.0	**NA**
458 Win. Magnum	500	2040	1823	1623	1442	1237	4620	3689	2924	2308	1839	+2.5	-3.5	-22.0	0.0	**$61**
458 Win. Magnum	510	2040	1770	1527	1319	1157	4712	3547	2640	1970	1516	+2.5	-4.1	-25.0	0.0	**$41**

Cartridge	Bullet Wgt. Grs.	VELOCITY (fps)					ENERGY (ft. lbs.)					TRAJ. (in.)				Est. Price/box
		Muzzle	100 yds.	200 yds.	300 yds.	400 yds.	Muzzle	100 yds.	200 yds.	300 yds.	400 yds.	100 yds.	200 yds.	300 yds.	400 yds.	
450 N.E. 3-1/4"	465	2190	1970	1765	1577	NA	4952	4009	3216	2567	NA	+2.5	-3.0	-20.0	0.0	NA
450 N.E. 3-1/4"	500	2150	1920	1708	1514	NA	5132	4093	3238	2544	NA	+2.5	-4.0	-22.9	0.0	NA
450 No. 2	465	2190	1970	1765	1577	NA	4952	4009	3216	2567	NA	+2.5	-3.0	-20.0	0.0	NA
450 No. 2	500	2150	1920	1708	1514	NA	5132	4093	3238	2544	NA	+2.5	-4.0	-22.9	0.0	NA
458 Lott	465	2380	2150	1932	1730	NA	5848	4773	3855	3091	NA	+2.5	-1.0	-14.0	0.0	NA
458 Lott	500	2300	2062	1838	1633	NA	5873	4719	3748	2960	NA	+2.5	-1.6	-16.4	0.0	NA
450 Ackley Mag.	465	2400	2169	1950	1747	NA	5947	4857	3927	3150	NA	+2.5	-1.0	-13.7	0.0	NA
450 Ackley Mag.	500	2320	2081	1855	1649	NA	5975	4085	3820	3018	NA	+2.5	-1.2	-15.0	0.0	NA
460 Short A-Sq.	500	2420	2175	1943	1729	NA	6501	5250	4193	3319	NA	+2.5	-0.8	-12.8	0.0	NA
460 Wea. Mag.	500	2700	2404	2128	1869	1635	8092	6416	5026	3878	2969	+2.5	+0.6	-8.9	-28.0	$72
475																
500/465 N.E.	480	2150	1917	1703	1507	NA	4926	3917	3089	2419	NA	+2.5	-4.0	-22.2	0.0	NA
470 Rigby	500	2150	1940	1740	1560	NA	5130	4170	3360	2695	NA	+2.5	-2.8	-19.4	0.0	NA
470 Nitro Ex.	480	2190	1954	1735	1536	NA	5111	4070	3210	2515	NA	+2.5	-3.5	-20.8	0.0	NA
470 Nitro Ex.	500	2150	1890	1650	1440	1270	5130	3965	3040	2310	1790	+2.5	-4.3	-24.0	0.0	$177
475 No. 2	500	2200	1955	1728	1522	NA	5375	4243	3316	2573	NA	+2.5	-3.2	-20.9	0.0	NA
50, 58																
505 Gibbs	525	2300	2063	1840	1637	NA	6166	4922	3948	3122	NA	+2.5	-3.0	-18.0	0.0	NA
500 N.E.-3"	570	2150	1928	1722	1533	NA	5850	4703	3752	2975	NA	+2.5	-3.7	-22.0	0.0	NA
500 N.E.-3"	600	2150	1927	1721	1531	NA	6158	4947	3944	3124	NA	+2.5	-4.0	-22.0	0.0	NA
495 A-Square	570	2350	2117	1896	1693	NA	5850	4703	3752	2975	NA	+2.5	-1.0	-14.5	0.0	NA
495 A-Square	600	2280	2050	1833	1635	NA	6925	5598	4478	3562	NA	+2.5	-2.0	-17.0	0.0	NA
500 A-Square	600	2380	2144	1922	1766	NA	7546	6126	4920	3922	NA	+2.5	-3.0	-17.0	0.0	NA
500 A-Square	707	2250	2040	1841	1567	NA	7947	6530	5318	4311	NA	+2.5	-2.0	-17.0	0.0	NA
500 BMG PMC	660	3080	2854	2639	2444	2248	13688		500 yd. zero			+3.1	+3.9	+4.7	+2.8	NA
577 Nitro Ex.	750	2050	1793	1562	1360	NA	6990	5356	4065	3079	NA	+2.5	-5.0	-26.0	0.0	NA
577 Tyrannosaur	750	2400	2141	1898	1675	NA	9591	7633	5996	4671	NA	+3.0	0.0	-12.9	0.0	NA
600, 700																
600 N.E.	900	1950	1680	1452	NA	NA	7596	5634	4212	NA	NA	+5.6	0.0	0.0	0.0	NA
700 N.E.	1200	1900	1676	1472	NA	NA	9618	7480	5774	NA	NA	+5.7	0.0	0.0	0.0	NA

Notes: Blanks are available in 32 S&W, 38 S&W and 38 Special. "V" after barrel length indicates test barrel was vented to produce ballistics similar to a revolver with a normal barrel-to-cylinder gap. Ammo prices are per 50 rounds except when marked with an ** which signifies a 20 round box; *** signifies a 25-round box. Not all loads are available from all ammo manufacturers. Listed loads are those made by Remington, Winchester, Federal, and others. DISC. is a discontinued load. Prices are rounded to the nearest whole dollar and will vary with brand and retail outlet. † = new bullet weight this year; "c" indicates a change in data.

Cartridge	Bullet Wgt. Grs.	VELOCITY (fps)			ENERGY (ft. lbs.)			Mid-Range Traj. (in.)		Bbl. Lgth. (in).	Est. Price/ box
		Muzzle	50 yds.	100 yds.	Muzzle	50 yds.	100 yds.	50 yds.	100 yds.		
22, 25											
221 Rem. Fireball	50	2650	2380	2130	780	630	505	0.2	0.8	10.5"	**$15**
25 Automatic	35	900	813	742	63	51	43	NA	NA	2"	**$18**
25 Automatic	45	815	730	655	65	55	40	1.8	7.7	2"	**$21**
25 Automatic	50	760	705	660	65	55	50	2.0	8.7	2"	**$17**
30											
7.5mm Swiss	107	1010	NA	NA	240	NA	NA	NA	NA	NA	**NEW**
7.62mmTokarev	87	1390	NA	NA	365	NA	NA	0.6	NA	4.5"	**NA**
7.62 Nagant	97	790	NA	NA	134	NA	NA	NA	NA	NA	**NEW**
7.63 Mauser	88	1440	NA	NA	405	NA	NA	NA	NA	NA	**NEW**
30 Luger	93†	1220	1110	1040	305	255	225	0.9	3.5	4.5"	**$34**
30 Carbine	110	1790	1600	1430	785	625	500	0.4	1.7	10"	**$28**
30-357 AeT	123	1992	NA	NA	1084	NA	NA	NA	NA	10"	**NA**
32											
32 S&W	88	680	645	610	90	80	75	2.5	10.5	3"	**$17**
32 S&W Long	98	705	670	635	115	100	90	2.3	10.5	4"	**$17**
32 Short Colt	80	745	665	590	100	80	60	2.2	9.9	4"	**$19**
32 H&R Magnum	85	1100	1020	930	230	195	165	1.0	4.3	4.5"	**$21**
32 H&R Magnum	95	1030	940	900	225	190	170	1.1	4.7	4.5"	**$19**
327 Federal Magnum	85	1400	1220	1090	370	280	225	NA	NA	4-V	**NA**
327 Federal Magnum	100	1500	1320	1180	500	390	310	-0.2	-4.50	4-V	**NA**
32 Automatic	60	970	895	835	125	105	95	1.3	5.4	4"	**$22**
32 Automatic	60	1000	917	849	133	112	96			4"	**NA**
32 Automatic	65	950	890	830	130	115	100	1.3	5.6	NA	**NA**
32 Automatic	71	905	855	810	130	115	95	1.4	5.8	4"	**$19**
8mm Lebel Pistol	111	850	NA	NA	180	NA	NA	NA	NA	NA	**NEW**
8mm Steyr	112	1080	NA	NA	290	NA	NA	NA	NA	NA	**NEW**
8mm Gasser	126	850	NA	NA	200	NA	NA	NA	NA	NA	**NEW**
9mm, 38											
380 Automatic	60	1130	960	NA	170	120	NA	1.0	NA	NA	**NA**
380 Automatic	85/88	990	920	870	190	165	145	1.2	5.1	4"	**$20**
380 Automatic	90	1000	890	800	200	160	130	1.2	5.5	3.75"	**$10**
380 Automatic	95/100	955	865	785	190	160	130	1.4	5.9	4"	**$20**
38 Super Auto +P	115	1300	1145	1040	430	335	275	0.7	3.3	5"	**$26**
38 Super Auto +P	125/130	1215	1100	1015	425	350	300	0.8	3.6	5"	**$26**
38 Super Auto +P	147	1100	1050	1000	395	355	325	0.9	4.0	5"	**NA**
9x18mm Makarov	95	1000	NA	NA	NA	NA	NA	NA	NA	NA	**NEW**
9x18mm Ultra	100	1050	NA	NA	240	NA	NA	NA	NA	NA	**NEW**
9x21	124	1150	1050	980	365	305	265	NA	NA	4	**NA**
9x23mm Largo	124	1190	1055	966	390	306	257	0.7	3.7	4"	**NA**
9x23mm Win.	125	1450	1249	1103	583	433	338	0.6	2.8	NA	**NA**
9mm Steyr	115	1180	NA	NA	350	NA	NA	NA	NA	NA	**NEW**
9mm Luger	88	1500	1190	1010	440	275	200	0.6	3.1	4"	**$24**
9mm Luger	90	1360	1112	978	370	247	191	NA	NA	4"	**$26**
9mm Luger	95	1300	1140	1010	350	275	215	0.8	3.4	4"	**NA**
9mm Luger	100	1180	1080	NA	305	255	NA	0.9	NA	4"	**NA**
9mm Luger	115	1155	1045	970	340	280	240	0.9	3.9	4"	**$21**
9mm Luger	123/125	1110	1030	970	340	290	260	1.0	4.0	4"	**$23**
9mm Luger	140	935	890	850	270	245	225	1.3	5.5	4"	**$23**
9mm Luger	147	990	940	900	320	290	265	1.1	4.9	4"	**$26**
9mm Luger +P	90	1475	NA	NA	437	NA	NA	NA	NA	NA	**NA**
9mm Luger +P	115	1250	1113	1019	399	316	265	0.8	3.5	4"	**$27**
9mm Federal	115	1280	1130	1040	420	330	280	0.7	3.3	4"V	**$24**
9mm Luger Vector	115	1155	1047	971	341	280	241	NA	NA	4"	**NA**
9mm Luger +P	124	1180	1089	1021	384	327	287	0.8	3.8	4"	**NA**
38											
38 S&W	146	685	650	620	150	135	125	2.4	10.0	4"	**$19**
38 Short Colt	125	730	685	645	150	130	115	2.2	9.4	6"	**$19**
39 Special	100	950	900	NA	200	180	NA	1.3	NA	4"V	**NA**
38 Special	110	945	895	850	220	195	175	1.3	5.4	4"V	**$23**
38 Special	110	945	895	850	220	195	175	1.3	5.4	4"V	**$23**
38 Special	130	775	745	710	175	160	120	1.9	7.9	4"V	**$22**

Notes: Blanks are available in 32 S&W, 38 S&W and 38 Special. "V" after barrel length indicates test barrel was vented to produce ballistics similar to a revolver with a normal barrel-to-cylinder gap. Ammo prices are per 50 rounds except when marked with an ** which signifies a 20 round box; *** signifies a 25-round box. Not all loads are available from all ammo manufacturers. Listed loads are those made by Remington, Winchester, Federal, and others. DISC. is a discontinued load. Prices are rounded to the nearest whole dollar and will vary with brand and retail outlet. † = new bullet weight this year; "c" indicates a change in data.

Cartridge	Bullet Wgt. Grs.	VELOCITY (fps)			ENERGY (ft. lbs.)			Mid-Range Traj. (in.)		Bbl. Lgth. (in).	Est. Price/ box
		Muzzle	50 yds.	100 yds.	Muzzle	50 yds.	100 yds.	50 yds.	100 yds.		
38 Special Cowboy	140	800	767	735	199	183	168			7.5" V	NA
38 (Multi-Ball)	140	830	730	505	215	130	80	2.0	10.6	4"V	$10**
38 Special	148	710	635	565	165	130	105	2.4	10.6	4"V	$17
38 Special	158	755	725	690	200	185	170	2.0	8.3	4"V	$18
38 Special +P	95	1175	1045	960	290	230	195	0.9	3.9	4"V	$23
38 Special +P	110	995	925	870	240	210	185	1.2	5.1	4"V	$23
38 Special +P	125	975	929	885	264	238	218	1	5.2	4"	NA
38 Special +P	125	945	900	860	250	225	205	1.3	5.4	4"V	#23
38 Special +P	129	945	910	870	255	235	215	1.3	5.3	4"V	$11
38 Special +P	130	925	887	852	247	227	210	1.3	5.50	4"V	NA
38 Special +P	147/150(c)	884	NA	NA	264	NA	NA	NA	NA	4"V	$27
38 Special +P	158	890	855	825	280	255	240	1.4	6.0	4"V	$20
357											
357 SIG	115	1520	NA	NA	593	NA	NA	NA	NA	NA	NA
357 SIG	124	1450	NA	NA	578	NA	NA	NA	NA	NA	NA
357 SIG	125	1350	1190	1080	510	395	325	0.7	3.1	4"	NA
357 SIG	150	1130	1030	970	420	355	310	0.9	4.0	NA	NA
356 TSW	115	1520	NA	NA	593	NA	NA	NA	NA	NA	NA
356 TSW	124	1450	NA	NA	578	NA	NA	NA	NA	NA	NA
356 TSW	135	1280	1120	1010	490	375	310	0.8	3.5	NA	NA
356 TSW	147	1220	1120	1040	485	410	355	0.8	3.5	5"	NA
357 Mag., Super Clean	105	1650									NA
357 Magnum	110	1295	1095	975	410	290	230	0.8	3.5	4"V	$25
357 (Med.Vel.)	125	1220	1075	985	415	315	270	0.8	3.7	4"V	$25
357 Magnum	125	1450	1240	1090	585	425	330	0.6	2.8	4"V	$25
357 (Multi-Ball)	140	1155	830	665	420	215	135	1.2	6.4	4"V	$11**
357 Magnum	140	1360	1195	1075	575	445	360	0.7	3.0	4"V	$25
357 Magnum FlexTip	140	1440	1274	1143	644	504	406	NA	NA	NA	NA
357 Magnum	145	1290	1155	1060	535	430	360	0.8	3.5	4"V	$26
357 Magnum	150/158	1235	1105	1015	535	430	360	0.8	3.5	4"V	$25
357 Mag. Cowboy	158	800	761	725	225	203	185				NA
357 Magnum	165	1290	1189	1108	610	518	450	0.7	3.1	8-3/8"	NA
357 Magnum	180	1145	1055	985	525	445	390	0.9	3.9	4"V	$25
357 Magnum	180	1180	1088	1020	557	473	416	0.8	3.6	8"V	NA
357 Mag. CorBon F.A.	180	1650	1512	1386	1088	913	767	1.66	0.0		NA
357 Mag. CorBon	200	1200	1123	1061	640	560	500	3.19	0.0		NA
357 Rem. Maximum	158	1825	1590	1380	1170	885	670	0.4	1.7	10.5"	$14**
40, 10mm											
40 S&W	135	1140	1070	NA	390	345	NA	0.9	NA	4"	NA
40 S&W	155	1140	1026	958	447	362	309	0.9	4.1	4"	$14***
40 S&W	165	1150	NA	NA	485	NA	NA	NA	NA	4"	$18***
40 S&W	180	985	936	893	388	350	319	1.4	5.0	4"	$14***
40 S&W	180	1015	960	914	412	368	334	1.3	4.5	4"	NA
400 Cor-Bon	135	1450	NA	NA	630	NA	NA	NA	NA	5"	NA
10mm Automatic	155	1125	1046	986	436	377	335	0.9	3.9	5"	$26
10mm Automatic	170	1340	1165	1145	680	510	415	0.7	3.2	5"	$31
10mm Automatic	175	1290	1140	1035	650	505	420	0.7	3.3	5.5"	$11**
10mm Auto. (FBI)	180	950	905	865	361	327	299	1.5	5.4	4"	$16**
10mm Automatic	180	1030	970	920	425	375	340	1.1	4.7	5"	$16**
10mm Auto H.V.	180†	1240	1124	1037	618	504	430	0.8	3.4	5"	$27
10mm Automatic	200	1160	1070	1010	495	510	430	0.9	3.8	5"	$14**
10.4mm Italian	177	950	NA	NA	360	NA	NA	NA	NA	NA	NEW
41 Action Exp.	180	1000	947	903	400	359	326	0.5	4.2	5"	$13**
41 Rem. Magnum	170	1420	1165	1015	760	515	390	0.7	3.2	4"V	$33
41 Rem. Magnum	175	1250	1120	1030	605	490	410	0.8	3.4	4"V	$14**
41 (Med. Vel.)	210	965	900	840	435	375	330	1.3	5.4	4"V	$30
41 Rem. Magnum	210	1300	1160	1060	790	630	535	0.7	3.2	4"V	$33
41 Rem. Magnum	240	1250	1151	1075	833	706	616	0.8	3.3	6.5V	NA
44											
44 S&W Russian	247	780	NA	NA	335	NA	NA	NA	NA	NA	NA
44 S&W Special	180	980	NA	NA	383	NA	NA	NA	NA	6.5"	NA
44 S&W Special	180	1000	935	882	400	350	311	NA	NA	7.5"V	NA
44 S&W Special	200†	875	825	780	340	302	270	1.2	6.0	6"	$13**
44 S&W Special	200	1035	940	865	475	390	335	1.1	4.9	6.5"	$13**

Notes: Blanks are available in 32 S&W, 38 S&W and 38 Special. "V" after barrel length indicates test barrel was vented to produce ballistics similar to a revolver with a normal barrel-to-cylinder gap. Ammo prices are per 50 rounds except when marked with an ** which signifies a 20 round box; *** signifies a 25-round box. Not all loads are available from all ammo manufacturers. Listed loads are those made by Remington, Winchester, Federal, and others. DISC. is a discontinued load. Prices are rounded to the nearest whole dollar and will vary with brand and retail outlet. † = new bullet weight this year; "c" indicates a change in data.

Cartridge	Bullet Wgt. Grs.	VELOCITY (fps)			ENERGY (ft. lbs.)			Mid-Range Traj. (in.)		Bbl. Lgth. (in).	Est. Price/ box
		Muzzle	50 yds.	100 yds.	Muzzle	50 yds.	100 yds.	50 yds.	100 yds.		
44 S&W Special	240/246	755	725	695	310	285	265	2.0	8.3	6.5"	**$26**
44-40 Win. Cowboy	225	750	723	695	281	261	242				**NA**
44 Rem. Magnum	180	1610	1365	1175	1035	745	550	0.5	2.3	4"V	**$18****
44 Rem. Magnum	200	1400	1192	1053	870	630	492	0.6	NA	6.5"	**$20**
44 Rem. Magnum	210	1495	1310	1165	1040	805	635	0.6	2.5	6.5"	**$18****
44 Rem. Mag. FlexTip	225	1410	1240	1111	993	768	617	NA	NA	NA	**NA**
44 (Med. Vel.)	240	1000	945	900	535	475	435	1.1	4.8	6.5"	**$17**
44 R.M. (Jacketed)	240	1180	1080	1010	740	625	545	0.9	3.7	4"V	**$18****
44 R.M. (Lead)	240	1350	1185	1070	970	750	610	0.7	3.1	4"V	**$29**
44 Rem. Magnum	250	1180	1100	1040	775	670	600	0.8	3.6	6.5"V	**$21**
44 Rem. Magnum	250	1250	1148	1070	867	732	635	0.8	3.3	6.5"V	**NA**
44 Rem. Magnum	275	1235	1142	1070	931	797	699	0.8	3.3	6.5"	**NA**
44 Rem. Magnum	300	1200	1100	1026	959	806	702	NA	NA	7.5"	**$17**
44 Rem. Magnum	330	1385	1297	1220	1406	1234	1090	1.83	0.00	NA	**NA**
440 CorBon	260	1700	1544	1403	1669	1377	1136	1.58	NA	10"	**NA**
45, 50											
450 Short Colt/450 Revolver	226	830	NA	NA	350	NA	NA	NA	NA	NA	**NEW**
45 S&W Schofield	180	730	NA	NA	213	NA	NA	NA	NA	NA	**NA**
45 S&W Schofield	230	730	NA	NA	272	NA	NA	NA	NA	NA	**NA**
45 G.A.P.	185	1090	970	890	490	385	320	1.0	4.7	5"	**NA**
45 G.A.P.	230	880	842	NA	396	363	NA	NA	NA	NA	**NA**
45 Automatic	165	1030	930	NA	385	315	NA	1.2	NA	5"	**NA**
45 Automatic	185	1000	940	890	410	360	325	1.1	4.9	5"	**$28**
45 Auto. (Match)	185	770	705	650	245	204	175	2.0	8.7	5"	**$28**
45 Auto. (Match)	200	940	890	840	392	352	312	2.0	8.6	5"	**$20**
45 Automatic	200	975	917	860	421	372	328	1.4	5.0	5"	**$18**
45 Automatic	230	830	800	675	355	325	300	1.6	6.8	5"	**$27**
45 Automatic	230	880	846	816	396	366	340	1.5	6.1	5"	**NA**
45 Automatic +P	165	1250	NA	NA	573	NA	NA	NA	NA	NA	**NA**
45 Automatic +P	185	1140	1040	970	535	445	385	0.9	4.0	5"	**$31**
45 Automatic +P	200	1055	982	925	494	428	380	NA	NA	5"	**NA**
45 Super	185	1300	1190	1108	694	582	504	NA	NA	5"	**NA**
45 Win. Magnum	230	1400	1230	1105	1000	775	635	0.6	2.8	5"	**$14****
45 Win. Magnum	260	1250	1137	1053	902	746	640	0.8	3.3	5"	**$16****
45 Win. Mag. CorBon	320	1150	1080	1025	940	830	747	3.47			**NA**
455 Webley MKII	262	850	NA	NA	420	NA	NA	NA	NA	NA	**NA**
45 Colt	200	1000	938	889	444	391	351	1.3	4.8	5.5"	**$21**
45 Colt	225	960	890	830	460	395	345	1.3	5.5	5.5"	**$22**
45 Colt + P CorBon	265	1350	1225	1126	1073	884	746	2.65	0.0		**NA**
45 Colt + P CorBon	300	1300	1197	1114	1126	956	827	2.78	0.0		**NA**
45 Colt	250/255	860	820	780	410	375	340	1.6	6.6	5.5"	**$27**
454 Casull	250	1300	1151	1047	938	735	608	0.7	3.2	7.5"V	**NA**
454 Casull	260	1800	1577	1381	1871	1436	1101	0.4	1.8	7.5"V	**NA**
454 Casull	300	1625	1451	1308	1759	1413	1141	0.5	2.0	7.5"V	**NA**
454 Casull CorBon	360	1500	1387	1286	1800	1640	1323	2.01	0.0		**NA**
460 S&W	200	2300	2042	1801	2350	1851	1441	0	-1.60	NA	**NA**
460 S&W	260	2000	1788	1592	2309	1845	1464	NA	NA	7.5"V	**NA**
460 S&W	250	1450	1267	1127	1167	891	705	NA	NA	8.375-V	**NA**
460 S&W	250	1900	1640	1412	2004	1494	1106	0	-2.75	NA	**NA**
460 S&W	300	1750	1510	1300	2040	1510	1125	NA	NA	8.4-V	**NA**
460 S&W	395	1550	1389	1249	2108	1691	1369	0	-4.00	NA	**NA**
475 Linebaugh	400	1350	1217	1119	1618	1315	1112	NA	NA	NA	**NA**
480 Ruger	325	1350	1191	1076	1315	1023	835	2.6	0.0	7.5"	**NA**
50 Action Exp.	325	1400	1209	1075	1414	1055	835	0.2	2.3	6"	**$24****
500 S&W	275	1665	1392	1183	1693	1184	854	1.5	NA	8.375	**NA**
500 S&W	325	1800	1560	1350	2340	1755	1315	NA	NA	8.4-V	**NA**
500 S&W	350	1400	1231	1106	1523	1178	951	NA	NA	10"	**NA**
500 S&W	400	1675	1472	1299	2493	1926	1499	1.3	NA	8.375	**NA**
500 S&W	440	1625	1367	1169	2581	1825	1337	1.6	NA	8.375	**NA**
500 S&W	500	1425	1281	1164	2254	1823	1505	NA	NA	10"	**NA**

Note: The actual ballistics obtained with your firearm can vary considerably from the advertised ballistics.
Also, ballistics can vary from lot to lot with the same brand and type load.

Cartridge	Bullet Wt. Grs.	Velocity (fps) 22-1/2" Bbl.		Energy (ft. lbs.) 22-1/2" Bbl.		Mid-Range Traj. (in.)	Muzzle Velocity
		Muzzle	100 yds.	Muzzle	100 yds.	100 yds.	6" Bbl.
17 Aguila	20	1850	1267	NA	NA	NA	NA
17 Hornady Mach 2	17	2100	1530	166	88	0.7	NA
17 HMR TNT Green	16	2500	1642	222	96	NA	NA
17 HMR	17	2550	1902	245	136	NA	NA
17 HMR	20	2375	1776	250	140	NA	NA
5mm Rem. Rimfire Mag.	30	2300	1669	352	188	NA	24
22 Short Blank	—	—	—	—	—	—	—
22 Short CB	29	727	610	33	24	NA	706
22 Short Target	29	830	695	44	31	6.8	786
22 Short HP	27	1164	920	81	50	4.3	1077
22 Colibri	20	375	183	6	1	NA	NA
22 Super Colibri	20	500	441	11	9	NA	NA
22 Long CB	29	727	610	33	24	NA	706
22 Long HV	29	1180	946	90	57	4.1	1031
22 LR Pistol Match	40	1070	890	100	70	4.6	940
22 LR Shrt. Range Green	21	1650	912	127	NA	NA	NA
22 LR Sub Sonic HP	38	1050	901	93	69	4.7	NA
22 LR Standard Velocity	40	1070	890	100	70	4.6	940
22 LR AutoMatch	40	1200	990	130	85	NA	NA
22 LR HV	40	1255	1016	140	92	3.6	1060
22 LR Silhoutte	42	1220	1003	139	94	3.6	1025
22 SSS	60	950	802	120	86	NA	NA
22 LR HV HP	40	1280	1001	146	89	3.5	1085
22 Velocitor GDHP	40	1435	0	0	0	NA	NA
22 LR Hyper HP	32/33/34	1500	1075	165	85	2.8	NA
22 LR Expediter	32	1640	NA	191	NA	NA	NA
22 LR Stinger HP	32	1640	1132	191	91	2.6	1395
22 LR Lead Free	30	1650	NA	181	NA	NA	NA
22 LR Hyper Vel	30	1750	1191	204	93	NA	NA
22 LR Shot #12	31	950	NA	NA	NA	NA	NA
22 WRF LFN	45	1300	1015	169	103	3	NA
22 Win. Mag. Lead Free	28	2200	NA	301	NA	NA	NA
22 Win. Mag.	30	2200	1373	322	127	1.4	1610
22 Win. Mag. V-Max BT	33	2000	1495	293	164	0.60	NA
22 Win. Mag. JHP	34	2120	1435	338	155	1.4	NA
22 Win. Mag. JHP	40	1910	1326	324	156	1.7	1480
22 Win. Mag. FMJ	40	1910	1326	324	156	1.7	1480
22 Win. Mag. Dyna Point	45	1550	1147	240	131	2.60	NA
22 Win. Mag. JHP	50	1650	1280	300	180	1.3	NA
22 Win. Mag. Shot #11	52	1000	—	NA	—	—	NA

NOTES: * = 10 rounds per box. ** = 5 rounds per box. Pricing variations and number of rounds per box can occur with type and brand of ammunition. Listed pricing is the average nominal cost for load style and box quantity shown. Not every brand is available in all shot size variations. Some manufacturers do not provide suggested list prices. All prices rounded to nearest whole dollar. The price you pay will vary dependent upon outlet of purchase. # = new load spec this year; "C" indicates a change in data.

10 Gauge 3-1/2" Magnum

Dram Equiv.	Shot Ozs.	Load Style	Shot Sizes	Brands	Avg. Price/ box	Velocity (fps)
4-1/2	2-1/4	premium	BB, 2, 4, 5, 6	Win., Fed., Rem.	$33	1205
Max	2	premium	4, 5, 6	Fed., Win.	NA	1300
4-1/4	2	high velocity	BB, 2, 4	Rem.	$22	1210
Max	18 pellets	premium	00 buck	Fed., Win.	$7**	1100
Max	1-7/8	Bismuth	BB, 2, 4	Bis.	NA	1225
Max	1-3/4	high density	BB, 2	Rem.	NA	1300
4-1/4	1-3/4	steel	TT, T, BBB, BB, 1, 2, 3	Win., Rem.	$27	1260
Mag	1-5/8	steel	T, BBB, BB, 2	Win.	$27	1285
Max	1-5/8	Bismuth	BB, 2, 4	Bismuth	NA	1375
Max	1-1/2	steel	T, BBB, BB, 1, 2, 3	Fed.	NA	1450
Max	1-3/8	steel	T, BBB, BB, 1, 2, 3	Fed., Rem.	NA	1500
Max	1-3/8	steel	T, BBB, BB, 2	Fed., Win.	NA	1450
Max	1-3/4	slug, rifled	slug	Fed.	NA	1280
Max	24 pellets	Buckshot	1 Buck	Fed.	NA	1100
Max	54 pellets	Super-X	4 Buck	Win.	NA	1150

12 Gauge 3-1/2" Magnum

Dram Equiv.	Shot Ozs.	Load Style	Shot Sizes	Brands	Avg. Price/ box	Velocity (fps)
Max	2-1/4	premium	4, 5, 6	Fed., Rem., Win.	$13*	1150
Max	2	Lead	4, 5, 6	Fed.	NA	1300
Max	2	Copper plated turkey	4, 5	Rem.	NA	1300
Max	18 pellets	premium	00 buck	Fed., Win., Rem.	$7**	1100
Max	1-7/8	Wingmaster HD	4, 6	Rem.	NA	1225
Max	1-7/8	heavyweight	5, 6	Fed.	NA	1300
Max	1-3/4	high density	BB, 2, 4, 6	Rem.		1300
Max	1-7/8	Bismuth	BB, 2, 4	Bis.	NA	1225
Max	1-5/8	Hevi-shot	T	Hevi-shot	NA	1350
Max	1-5/8	Wingmaster HD	T	Rem.	NA	1350
Max	1-5/8	high density	BB, 2	Fed.	NA	1450
Max	1-3/8	Heavyweight	2, 4, 6	Fed.	NA	1450
Max	1-3/8	steel	T, BBB, BB, 2, 4	Fed., Win., Rem.	NA	1450
Max	1-1/2	FS steel	BBB, BB, 2	Fed.	NA	1500
Max	1-1/2	Supreme H-V	BBB, BB, 2, 3	Win.	NA	1475
Max	1-3/8	H-speed steel	BB, 2	Rem.	NA	1550
Max	1-1/4	Steel	BB, 2	Win.	NA	1625
Max	24 pellets	Premium	1 Buck	Fed.	NA	1100
Max	54 pellets	Super-X	4 Buck	Win.	NA	1050

12 Gauge 3" Magnum

Dram Equiv.	Shot Ozs.	Load Style	Shot Sizes	Brands	Avg. Price/ box	Velocity (fps)
4	2	premium	BB, 2, 4, 5, 6	Win., Fed., Rem.	$9*	1175
4	1-7/8	premium	BB, 2, 4, 6	Win., Fed., Rem.	$19	1210
4	1-7/8	duplex	4x6	Rem.	$9*	1210
Max	1-3/4	turkey	4, 5, 6	Fed., Fio., Win., Rem.	NA	1300
Max	1-3/4	high density	BB, 2, 4	Rem.	NA	1450
Max	1-5/8	high density	BB, 2	Fed.	NA	1450
Max	1-5/8	Wingmaster HD	4, 6	Rem.	NA	1227
Max	1-5/8	high velocity	4, 5, 6	Fed.	NA	1350
4	1-5/8	premium	2, 4, 5, 6	Win., Fed., Rem.	$18	1290
Max	1-1/2	Wingmaster HD	T	Rem.	NA	1300
Max	1-1/2	Hevi-shot	T	Hevi-shot	NA	1300
Max	1-1/2	high density	BB, 2, 4	Rem.	NA	1300
Max	1-5/8	Bismuth	BB, 2, 4, 5, 6	Bis.	NA	1250
4	24 pellets	buffered	1 buck	Win., Fed., Rem.	$5**	1040
4	15 pellets	buffered	00 buck	Win., Fed., Rem.	$6**	1210
4	10 pellets	buffered	000 buck	Win., Fed., Rem.	$6**	1225
4	41 pellets	buffered	4 buck	Win., Fed., Rem.	$6**	1210
Max	1-3/8	heavyweight	5, 6	Fed.	NA	1300
Max	1-3/8	high density	B, 2, 4, 6	Rem. Win.	NA	1450

12 Gauge 3" Magnum *(cont.)*

Dram Equiv.	Shot Ozs.	Load Style	Shot Sizes	Brands	Avg. Price/ box	Velocity (fps)
Max	1-3/8	slug	slug	Bren.	NA	1476
Max	1-1/4	slug, rifled	slug	Fed.	NA	1600
Max	1-3/16	saboted slug	copper slug	Rem.	NA	1500
Max	7/8	slug, rifled	slug	Rem.	NA	1875
Max	1-1/8	low recoil	BB	Fed.	NA	850
Max	1-1/8	steel	BB, 2, 3, 4	Fed., Win., Rem.	NA	1550
Max	1-1/16	high density	2, 4	Win.	NA	1400
Max	1	steel	4, 6	Fed.	NA	1330
Max	1-3/8	buckhammer	slug	Rem.	NA	1500
Max	1	slug, rifled	slug, magnum	Win., Rem.	$5**	1760
Max	1	saboted slug	slug	Rem., Win., Fed.	$10**	1550
Max	385 grs.	partition gold	slug	Win.	NA	2000
Max	1-1/8	Rackmaster	slug	Win.	NA	1700
Max	300 grs.	XP3	slug	Win.	NA	2100
3-5/8	1-3/8	steel	BBB, BB, 1, 2, 3, 4	Win., Fed., Rem.	$19	1275
Max	1-1/8	snow goose FS	BB, 2	Fed.	NA	1635
Max	1-1/8	steel	BB, 2, 4	Rem.	NA	1500
Max	1-1/8	steel	T, BBB, BB, 2, 4, 5, 6	Fed., Win.	NA	1450
Max	1-1/8	steel	BB, 2	Fed.	NA	1400
4	1-1/4	steel	T, BBB, BB, 1, 2, 3, 4, 6	Win., Fed., Rem.	$18	1400
Max	1-1/4	FS steel	BBB, BB, 2	Fed.	NA	1450

12 Gauge 2-3/4"

Dram Equiv.	Shot Ozs.	Load Style	Shot Sizes	Brands	Avg. Price/ box	Velocity (fps)
Max	1-5/8	magnum	4, 5, 6	Win., Fed.	$8*	1250
Max	1-3/8	lead	4, 5, 6	Fiocchi	NA	1485
Max	1-3/8	turkey	4, 5, 6	Fio.	NA	1250
Max	1-3/8	steel	4, 5, 6	Fed.	NA	1400
Max	1-3/8	Bismuth	BB, 2, 4, 5, 6	Bis.	NA	1300
3-3/4	1-1/2	magnum	BB, 2, 4, 5, 6	Win., Fed., Rem.	$16	1260
Max	1-1/4	Supreme H-V	4, 5, 6, 7-1/2	Win. Rem.	NA	1400
3-3/4	1-1/4	high velocity	BB, 2, 4, 5, 6, 7-1/2, 8, 9	Win., Fed., Rem., Fio.	$13	1330
Max	1-1/4	high density	B, 2, 4	Win.	NA	1450
Max	1-1/4	high density	4, 6	Rem.	NA	1325
3-1/4	1-1/4	standard velocity	6, 7-1/2, 8, 9	Win., Fed., Rem., Fio.	$11	1220
Max	1-1/8	Hevi-shot	5	Hevi-shot	NA	1350
3-1/4	1-1/8	standard velocity	4, 6, 7-1/2, 8, 9	Win., Fed., Rem., Fio.	$9	1255
Max	1-1/8	steel	2, 4	Rem.	NA	1390
Max	1	steel	BB, 2	Fed.	NA	1450
3-1/4	1	standard velocity	6, 7-1/2, 8	Rem., Fed., Fio., Win.	$6	1290
3-1/4	1-1/4	target	7-1/2, 8, 9	Win., Fed., Rem.	$10	1220
3	1-1/8	spreader	7-1/2, 8, 8-1/2, 9	Fio.	NA	1200
3	1-1/8	target	7-1/2, 8, 9, 7-1/2x8	Win., Fed., Rem., Fio.	$7	1200
2-3/4	1-1/8	target	7-1/2, 8, 8-1/2, 9, 7-1/2x8	Win., Fed., Rem., Fio.	$7	1145
2-3/4	1-1/8	low recoil	7-1/2, 8	Rem.	NA	1145
2-1/2	26 grams	low recoil	8	Win.	NA	980
2-1/4	1-1/8	target	7-1/2, 8, 8-1/2, 9	Rem., Fed.	$7	1080
Max	1	spreader	7-1/2, 8, 8-1/2, 9	Fio.	NA	1300
3-1/4	28 grams (1 oz)	target	7-1/2, 8, 9	Win., Fed., Rem., Fio.	$8	1290
3	1	target	7-1/2, 8, 8-1/2, 9	Win., Fio.	NA	1235
2-3/4	1	target	7-1/2, 8, 8-1/2, 9	Fed., Rem., Fio.	NA	1180
3-1/4	24 grams	target	7-1/2, 8, 9	Fed., Win., Fio.	NA	1325
3	7/8	light	8	Fio.	NA	1200
3-3/4	8 pellets	buffered	000 buck	Win., Fed., Rem.	$4**	1325

NOTES: * = 10 rounds per box. ** = 5 rounds per box. Pricing variations and number of rounds per box can occur with type and brand of ammunition. Listed pricing is the average nominal cost for load style and box quantity shown. Not every brand is available in all shot size variations. Some manufacturers do not provide suggested list prices. All prices rounded to nearest whole dollar. The price you pay will vary dependent upon outlet of purchase. # = new load spec this year; "C" indicates a change in data.

12 Gauge 2-3/4" *(cont.)*

Dram Equiv.	Shot Ozs.	Load Style	Shot Sizes	Brands	Avg. Price/ box	Velocity (fps)
4	12 pellets	premium	00 buck	Win., Fed., Rem.	$5**	1290
3-3/4	9 pellets	buffered	00 buck	Win., Fed., Rem., Fio.	$19	1325
3-3/4	12 pellets	buffered	0 buck	Win., Fed., Rem.	$4**	1275
4	20 pellets	buffered	1 buck	Win., Fed., Rem.	$4**	1075
3-3/4	16 pellets	buffered	1 buck	Win., Fed., Rem.	$4**	1250
4	34 pellets	premium	4 buck	Fed., Rem.	$5**	1250
3-3/4	27 pellets	buffered	4 buck	Win., Fed., Rem., Fio.	$4**	1325
		PDX1	1 oz. slug, 3-00 buck	Win.	NA	1150
Max	1	saboted slug	slug	Win., Fed., Rem.	$10**	1450
Max	1-1/4	slug, rifled	slug	Fed.	NA	1520
Max	1-1/4	slug	slug	Lightfield		1440
Max	1-1/4	saboted slug	attached sabot	Rem.	NA	1550
Max	1	slug, rifled	slug, magnum	Rem., Fio.	$5**	1680
Max	1	slug, rifled	slug	Win., Fed., Rem.	$4**	1610
Max	1	sabot slug	slug	Sauvestre		1640
Max	7/8	slug, rifled	slug	Rem.	NA	1800
Max	400	plat. tip	sabot slug	Win.	NA	1700
Max	385 grains	Partition Gold Slug	slug	Win.	NA	1900
Max	385 grains	Core-Lokt bonded	sabot slug	Rem.	NA	1900
Max	325 grains	Barnes Sabot	slug	Fed.	NA	1900
Max	300 grains	SST Slug	sabot slug	Hornady	NA	2050
3	1-1/8	steel target	6-1/2, 7	Rem.	NA	1200
2-3/4	1-1/8	steel target	7	Rem.	NA	1145
3	1#	steel	7	Win.	$11	1235
3-1/2	1-1/4	steel	T, BBB, BB, 1, 2, 3, 4, 5, 6	Win., Fed., Rem.	$18	1275
3-3/4	1-1/8	steel	BB, 1, 2, 3, 4, 5, 6	Win., Fed., Rem., Fio.	$16	1365
3-3/4	1	steel	2, 3, 4, 5, 6, 7	Win., Fed., Rem., Fio.	$13	1390
Max	7/8	steel	7	Fio.	NA	1440

16 Gauge 2-3/4"

Dram Equiv.	Shot Ozs.	Load Style	Shot Sizes	Brands	Avg. Price/ box	Velocity (fps)
3-1/4	1-1/4	magnum	2, 4, 6	Fed., Rem.	$16	1260
3-1/4	1-1/8	high velocity	4, 6, 7-1/2	Win., Fed., Rem., Fio.	$12	1295
Max	1-1/8	Bismuth	4, 5	Bis.	NA	1200
2-3/4	1-1/8	standard velocity	6, 7-1/2, 8	Fed., Rem., Fio.	$9	1185
2-1/2	1	dove	6, 7-1/2, 8, 9	Fio., Win.	NA	1165
2-3/4	1		6, 7-1/2, 8	Fio.	NA	1200
Max	15/16	steel	2, 4	Fed., Rem.	NA	1300
Max	7/8	steel	2, 4	Win.	$16	1300
3	12 pellets	buffered	1 buck	Win., Fed., Rem.	$4**	1225
Max	4/5	slug, rifled	slug	Win., Fed., Rem.	$4**	1570
Max	.92	sabot slug	slug	Sauvestre	NA	1560

20 Gauge 3" Magnum

Dram Equiv.	Shot Ozs.	Load Style	Shot Sizes	Brands	Avg. Price/ box	Velocity (fps)
3	1-1/4	premium	2, 4, 5, 6, 7-1/2	Win., Fed., Rem.	$15	1185
Max	1-1/4	Wingmaster HD	4, 6	Rem.	NA	1185
3	1-1/4	turkey	4, 6	Fio.	NA	1200
Max	1-1/4	Hevi-shot	2, 4, 6	Hevi-shot	NA	1250
Max	1-1/8	high density	4, 6	Rem.	NA	1300
Max	18 pellets	buck shot	2 buck	Fed.	NA	1200
Max	24 pellets	buffered	3 buck	Win.	$5**	1150
2-3/4	20 pellets	buck	3 buck	Rem.	$4**	1200
3-1/4	1	steel	1, 2, 3, 4, 5, 6	Win., Fed., Rem.	$15	1330
Max	7/8	steel	2, 4	Win.	NA	1300

20 Gauge 3" Magnum *(cont.)*

Dram Equiv.	Shot Ozs.	Load Style	Shot Sizes	Brands	Avg. Price/ box	Velocity (fps)
Max	1-1/16	high density	2, 4	Win.	NA	1400
Max	1-1/16	Bismuth	2, 4, 5, 6	Bismuth	NA	1250
Mag	5/8	saboted slug	275 gr.	Fed.	NA	1900

20 Gauge 2-3/4"

Dram Equiv.	Shot Ozs.	Load Style	Shot Sizes	Brands	Avg. Price/ box	Velocity (fps)
2-3/4	1-1/8	magnum	4, 6, 7-1/2	Win., Fed., Rem.	$14	1175
2-3/4	1	high velocity	4, 5, 6, 7-1/2, 8, 9	Win., Fed., Rem., Fio.	$12	1220
Max	1	Bismuth	4, 6	Bis.	NA	1200
Max	1	Hevi-shot	5	Hevi-shot	NA	1250
Max	1	Supreme H-V	4, 6, 7-1/2	Win. Rem.	NA	1300
Max	7/8	Steel	2, 3, 4	Fio.	NA	1500
2-1/2	1	standard velocity	6, 7-1/2, 8	Win., Rem., Fed., Fio.	$6	1165
2-1/2	7/8	clays	8	Rem.	NA	1200
2-1/2	7/8	promotional	6, 7-1/2, 8	Win., Rem., Fio.	$6	1210
2-1/2	1	target	8, 9	Win., Rem.	$8	1165
Max	7/8	clays	7-1/2, 8	Win.	NA	1275
2-1/2	7/8	target	8, 9	Win., Fed., Rem.	$8	1200
Max	3/4	steel	2, 4	Rem.	NA	1425
2-1/2	7/8	steel - target	7	Rem.	NA	1200
Max	1	buckhammer	slug	Rem.	NA	1500
Max	5/8	Saboted Slug	Copper Slug	Rem.	NA	1500
Max	20 pellets	buffered	3 buck	Win., Fed.	$4	1200
Max	5/8	slug, saboted	slug	Win.,	$9**	1400
2-3/4	5/8	slug, rifled	slug	Rem.	$4**	1580
Max	3/4	saboted slug	copper slug	Fed., Rem.	NA	1450
Max	3/4	slug, rifled	slug	Win., Fed., Rem., Fio.	$4**	1570
Max	.9	sabot slug	slug	Sauvestre		1480
Max	260 grains	Partition Gold Slug	slug	Win.	NA	1900
Max	260 grains	Core-Lokt Ultra	slug	Rem.	NA	1900
Max	260 grains	saboted slug	platinum tip	Win.	NA	1700
Max	3/4	steel	2, 3, 4, 6	Win., Fed., Rem.	$14	1425
Max	250 grains	SST slug	slug	Hornady	NA	1800
Max	1/2	rifled, slug	slug	Rem.	NA	1800

28 Gauge 3"

Dram Equiv.	Shot Ozs.	Load Style	Shot Sizes	Brands	Avg. Price/ box	Velocity (fps)
Max	7/8	tundra tungsten	4, 5, 6	Fiocchi	NA	TBD

28 Gauge 2-3/4"

Dram Equiv.	Shot Ozs.	Load Style	Shot Sizes	Brands	Avg. Price/ box	Velocity (fps)
2	1	high velocity	6, 7-1/2, 8	Win.	$12	1125
2-1/4	3/4	high velocity	6, 7-1/2, 8, 9	Win., Fed., Rem., Fio.	$11	1295
2	3/4	target	8, 9	Win., Fed., Rem.	$9	1200
Max	3/4	sporting clays	7-1/2, 8-1/2	Win.	NA	1300
Max	5/8	Bismuth	4, 6	Bis.	NA	1250
Max	5/8	steel	6, 7	NA	NA	1300

410 Bore 3"

Dram Equiv.	Shot Ozs.	Load Style	Shot Sizes	Brands	Avg. Price/ box	Velocity (fps)
Max	11/16	high velocity	4, 5, 6, 7-1/2, 8, 9	Win., Fed., Rem., Fio.	$10	1135
Max	9/16	Bismuth	4	Bis.	NA	1175
Max	3/8	steel	6	NA	NA	1400
		judge	5 pellets 000 Buck	Fed.	NA	960
		judge	9 pellets #4 Buck	Fed.	NA	1100

410 Bore 2-1/2"

Dram Equiv.	Shot Ozs.	Load Style	Shot Sizes	Brands	Avg. Price/ box	Velocity (fps)
Max	1/2	high velocity	4, 6, 7-1/2	Win., Fed., Rem.	$9	1245
Max	1/5	slug, rifled	slug	Win., Fed., Rem.	$4**	1815
1-1/2	1/2	target	8, 8-1/2, 9	Win., Fed., Rem., Fio.	$8	1200
Max	1/2	sporting clays	7-1/2, 8, 8-1/2	Win.	NA	1300
Max		Buckshot	5-000 Buck	Win.	NA	1135
		judge	12-bb's, 3 disks	Win.	NA	TBD

2011 Guns Illustrated

Catalog of Arms & Accessories

Prices given are believed to be accurate at time of publication however, many factors affect retail pricing so exact prices are not possible.

ACCU-TEK AT-380 II 380 ACP PISTOL
Caliber: 380 ACP, 6-shot magazine. **Barrel:** 2.8". **Weight:** 23.5 oz. **Length:** 6.125" overall. **Grips:** Textured black composition. **Sights:** Blade front, rear adjustable for windage. **Features:** Made from 17-4 stainless steel, has an exposed hammer, manual firing-pin safety block and trigger disconnect. Magazine release located on the bottom of the grip. American made, lifetime warranty. Comes with two 6-round stainless steel magazines and a California-approved cable lock. Introduced 2006. Made in U.S.A. by Excel Industries.
Price: Satin stainless **$262.00**

AMERICAN CLASSIC 1911-A1
1911-style semiauto pistol chambered in .45 ACP. Features include Series 90 lockwork, 7+1 capacity, walnut grips, 5-inch barrel, blued or hard-chromed steel frame, checkered wood grips, drift adjustable sights.
Price: . . . . **N/A**

AMERICAN CLASSIC COMMANDER
1911-style semiauto pistol chambered in .45 ACP. Features include 7+1 capacity, checkered mahogany grips, 4.25-inch barrel, blued or hard-chromed steel frame, drift adjustable sights.
Price: . . . . **N/A**

ARMALITE AR-24 PISTOL
Caliber: 9mm Para., 10- or 15-shot magazine. **Barrel:** 4.671", 6 groove, right-hand cut rifling. **Weight:** 34.9 oz. **Length:** 8.27" overall. **Grips:** Black polymer. **Sights:** Dovetail front, fixed rear, 3-dot luminous design. **Features:** Machined slide, frame and barrel. Serrations on forestrap and backstrap, external thumb safety and internal firing pin box, half cock. Two 15-round magazines, pistol case, pistol lock, manual and cleaning brushes. Manganese phosphate finish. Compact comes with two 13-round magazines, 3.89" barrel, weighs 33.4 oz. Made in U.S.A. by ArmaLite.
Price: AR-24 Full Size. **$550.00**
Price: AR-24K Compact **$550.00**

ARMSCOR/ROCK ISLAND ARMORY 1911A1-45 FS GI
1911-style semiauto pistol chambered in .45 ACP (8 rounds), 9mm Parabellum, .38 Super (9 rounds). Features include checkered plastic or hardwood grips, 5-inch barrel, parkerized steel frame and slide, drift adjustable sights.
Price: . . . . **N/A**

ARMSCOR/ROCK ISLAND ARMORY 1911A1-45 CS GI
1911-style Officer's-size semiauto pistol chambered in .45 ACP. Features plain hardwood grips, 3.5-inch barrel, parkerized steel frame and slide, drift adjustable sights.
Price: . . . . **N/A**

AUTO-ORDNANCE TA5 SEMI-AUTO PISTOL
Caliber: 45 ACP, 30-round stick magazine (standard), 50- or 100-round drum magazine optional. **Barrel:** 10.5", finned. **Weight:** 6.5 lbs. **Length:** 25" overall. **Features:** Semi-auto pistol patterned after Thompson Model 1927 semi-auto carbine. Horizontal vertical foregrip, aluminum receiver, top cocking knob, grooved walnut pistolgrip.
Price: **$1,143.00**

AUTO-ORDNANCE 1911A1 AUTOMATIC PISTOL
Caliber: 45 ACP, 7-shot magazine. **Barrel:** 5". **Weight:** 39 oz.

Length: 8.5" overall. **Grips:** Brown checkered plastic with medallion. **Sights:** Blade front, rear drift-adjustable for windage. **Features:** Same specs as 1911A1 military guns-parts interchangeable. Frame and slide blued; each radius has non-glare finish. Introduced 2002. Made in U.S.A. by Kahr Arms.
Price: 1911PKZSE Parkerized, plastic grips **$627.00**
Price: 1911PKZSEW Parkerized **$662.00**
Price: 1911PKZMA Parkerized, Mass. Compliant (2008). **$627.00**

BAER H.C. 40 AUTO PISTOL
Caliber: 40 S&W, 18-shot magazine. **Barrel:** 5". **Weight:** 37 oz. **Length:** 8.5" overall. **Grips:** Wood. **Sights:** Low-mount adjustable rear sight with hidden rear leaf, dovetail front sight. **Features:** Double-stack Caspian frame, beavertail grip safety, ambidextrous thumb safety, 40 S&W match barrel with supported chamber, match stainless steel barrel bushing, lowered and flared ejection port, extended ejector, match trigger fitted, integral mag well, bead blast blue finish on lower, polished sides on slide. Introduced 2008. Made in U.S.A. by Les Baer Custom, Inc.
Price: **$2,960.00**

BAER 1911 CUSTOM CARRY AUTO PISTOL
Caliber: 45 ACP, 7- or 10-shot magazine. **Barrel:** 5". **Weight:** 37 oz. **Length:** 8.5" overall. **Grips:** Checkered walnut. **Sights:** Baer improved ramp-style dovetailed front, Novak low-mount rear. **Features:** Baer forged NM frame, slide and barrel with stainless bushing. Baer speed trigger with 4-lb. pull. Partial listing shown. Made in U.S.A. by Les Baer Custom, Inc.
Price: Custom Carry 5", blued **$1,995.00**
Price: Custom Carry 5", stainless **$2,120.00**
Price: Custom Carry 4" Commanche length, blued **$1,995.00**
Price: Custom Carry 4" Commanche length, stainless **$2,120.00**

BAER 1911 ULTIMATE RECON PISTOL
Caliber: 45 ACP, 7- or 10-shot magazine. **Barrel:** 5". **Weight:** 37 oz. **Length:** 8.5" overall. **Grips:** Checkered cocobolo. **Sights:** Baer improved ramp-style dovetailed front, Novak low-mount rear. **Features:** NM Caspian frame, slide and barrel with stainless bushing. Baer speed trigger with 4-lb. pull. Includes integral Picatinny rail and Sure-Fire X-200 light. Made in U.S.A. by Les Baer Custom, Inc. Introduced 2006.
Price: Bead blast blued **$3,070.00**
Price: Bead blast chrome **$3,390.00**

BAER 1911 PREMIER II AUTO PISTOL
Caliber: 38 Super, 400 Cor-Bon, 45 ACP, 7- or 10-shot magazine. **Barrel:** 5". Weight: 37 oz. **Length:** 8.5" overall. **Grips:** Checkered rosewood, double diamond pattern. **Sights:** Baer dovetailed front, low-mount Bo-Mar rear with hidden leaf. **Features:** Baer NM forged steel frame and barrel with stainless bushing, deluxe Commander

Prices given are believed to be accurate at time of publication however, many factors affect retail pricing so exact prices are not possible.

hammer and sear, beavertail grip safety with pad, extended ambidextrous safety; flat mainspring housing; 30 lpi checkered front strap. Made in U.S.A. by Les Baer Custom, Inc.
Price: 5" 45 ACP **$1,790.00**
Price: 5" 400 Cor-Bon **$1,890.00**
Price: 5" 38 Super **$2,070.00**
Price: 6" 45 ACP, 400 Cor-Bon, 38 Super, from. **$1,990.00**
Price: Super-Tac, 45 ACP, 400 Cor-Bon, 38 Super, from . . **$2,280.00**

BAER 1911 S.R.P. PISTOL
Caliber: 45 ACP. **Barrel:** 5". **Weight:** 37 oz. **Length:** 8.5" overall. **Grips:** Checkered walnut. **Sights:** Trijicon night sights. **Features:** Similar to the F.B.I. contract gun except uses Baer forged steel frame. Has Baer match barrel with supported chamber, complete tactical action. Has Baer Ultra Coat finish. Introduced 1996. Made in U.S.A. by Les Baer Custom, Inc.
Price: Government or Commanche length **$2,590.00**

BAER 1911 STINGER PISTOL
Caliber: 45 ACP, 7-round magazine. **Barrel:** 5". **Weight:** 34 oz. **Length:** 8.5" overall. **Grips:** Checkered cocobolo. **Sights:** Baer dovetailed front, low-mount Bo-Mar rear with hidden leaf. **Features:** Baer NM frame. Baer Commanche slide, Officer's style grip frame, beveled mag well. Made in U.S.A. by Les Baer Custom, Inc.
Price: Blued **$1,890.00**
Price: Stainless **$1,970.00**

BAER 1911 PROWLER III PISTOL
Caliber: 45 ACP, 8-round magazine. **Barrel:** 5". **Weight:** 34 oz. **Length:** 8.5" overall. **Grips:** Checkered cocobolo. **Sights:** Baer dovetailed front, low-mount Bo-Mar rear with hidden leaf. **Features:** Similar to Premier II with tapered cone stub weight, rounded corners. Made in U.S.A. by Les Baer Custom, Inc.
Price: Blued **$2,580.00**

BERETTA MODEL 92FS PISTOL
Caliber: 9mm Para., 10-shot magazine. **Barrel:** 4.9". **Weight:** 34 oz. **Length:** 8.5" overall. **Grips:** Checkered black plastic. **Sights:** Blade front, rear adjustable for windage. Tritium night sights available. **Features:** Double action. Extractor acts as chamber loaded indicator, squared trigger guard, grooved front and backstraps, inertia firing pin. Matte or blued finish. Introduced 1977. Made in U.S.A.
Price: With plastic grips **$650.00**

BERETTA MODEL 80 CHEETAH SERIES DA PISTOLS
Caliber: 380 ACP, 10-shot magazine (M84); 8-shot (M85); 22 LR, 7-shot (M87). **Barrel:** 3.82". **Weight:** About 23 oz. (M84/85); 20.8 oz. (M87). **Length:** 6.8" overall. **Grips:** Glossy black plastic (wood optional at extra cost). **Sights:** Fixed front, drift-adjustable rear. **Features:** Double action, quick takedown, convenient magazine release. Introduced 1977. Made in U.S.A.
Price: Model 84 Cheetah, plastic grips **$650.00**

BERETTA MODEL 21 BOBCAT PISTOL
Caliber: 22 LR or 25 ACP. Both double action. **Barrel:** 2.4". **Weight:** 11.5 oz.; 11.8 oz. **Length:** 4.9" overall. **Grips:** Plastic. **Features:** Available in nickel, matte, engraved or blue finish. Introduced in 1985.
Price: Bobcat, 22 or 25, blue . . **$335.00**
Price: Bobcat, 22, Inox **$420.00**
Price: Bobcat, 22 or 25, matte **$335.00**

BERETTA MODEL 3032 TOMCAT PISTOL
Caliber: 32 ACP, 7-shot magazine. **Barrel:** 2.45". **Weight:** 14.5 oz. **Length:** 5" overall. **Grips:** Checkered black plastic. **Sights:** Blade front, drift-adjustable rear. **Features:** Double action with exposed hammer; tip-up barrel for direct loading/unloading; thumb safety; polished or matte blue finish. Made in U.S.A. Introduced 1996.
Price: Matte **$435.00**
Price: Inox **$555.00**

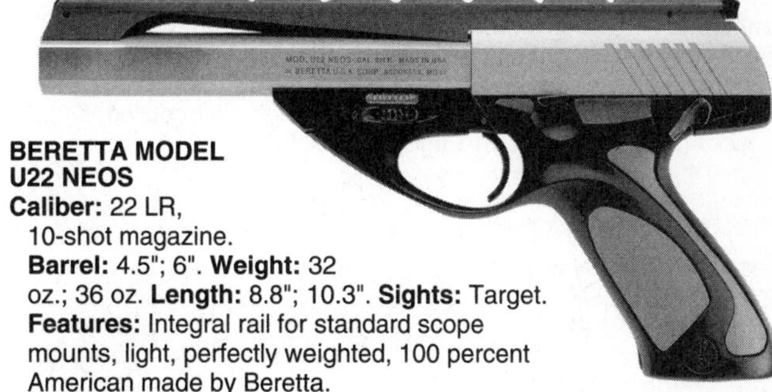

BERETTA MODEL U22 NEOS
Caliber: 22 LR, 10-shot magazine. **Barrel:** 4.5"; 6". **Weight:** 32 oz.; 36 oz. **Length:** 8.8"; 10.3". **Sights:** Target. **Features:** Integral rail for standard scope mounts, light, perfectly weighted, 100 percent American made by Beretta.
Price: **$250.00**
Price: Inox **$350.00**

BERETTA MODEL PX4 STORM
Caliber: 9mm Para., 40 S&W. Capacity: 17 (9mm Para.); 14 (40 S&W). **Barrel:** 4". **Weight:** 27.5 oz. **Grips:** Black checkered w/3 interchangeable backstraps. **Sights:** 3-dot system coated in Superluminova; removable front and rear sights. **Features:** DA/SA, manual safety/hammer decocking lever (ambi) and automatic firing pin block safety. Picatinny rail. Comes with two magazines (17/10 in 9mm Para. and 14/10 in 40 S&W). Removable hammer unit. American made by Beretta. Introduced 2005.
Price: **$600.00**
Price: 45 ACP **$650.00**

BERETTA MODEL PX4 STORM SUB-COMPACT
Caliber: 9mm, 40 S&W. Capacity: 13 (9mm); 10 (40 S&W). **Barrel:** 3". **Weight:** 26.1 oz. **Length:** 6.2" overall. **Grips:** NA. **Sights:** NA. **Features:** Ambidextrous manual safety lever, interchangeable backstraps included, lock breech and tilt barrel system, stainless steel barrel, Picatinny rail.
Price: **$600.00**

BERETTA MODEL M9
Caliber: 9mm Para. Capacity: 15. **Barrel:** 4.9". **Weight:** 32.2-35.3 oz. **Grips:** Plastic. **Sights:** Dot and post, low profile, windage adjustable rear. **Features:** DA/SA, forged aluminum alloy frame, delayed locking-bolt system, manual safety doubles as decocking lever, combat-style trigger guard, loaded chamber indicator. Comes with two magazines (15/10). American made by Beretta. Introduced 2005.
Price: **$650.00**

BERETTA MODEL M9A1
Caliber: 9mm Para. Capacity: 15. **Barrel:** 4.9". **Weight:** 32.2-35.3 oz. **Grips:** Plastic. **Sights:** Dot and post, low profile, windage adjustable rear. **Features:** Same as M9, but also includes integral Mil-Std-1913 Picatinny rail, has checkered frontstrap and backstrap. Comes with two magazines (15/10). American made by Beretta. Introduced 2005.
Price: **$750.00**

BERSA THUNDER 45 ULTRA COMPACT PISTOL
Caliber: 45 ACP. **Barrel:** 3.6". **Weight:** 27 oz. **Length:** 6.7" overall. **Grips:** Anatomically designed polymer. **Sights:** White outline rear. **Features:** Double action; firing pin safeties, integral locking system. Available in matte, satin nickel, gold, or duo-tone. Introduced 2003. Imported from Argentina by Eagle Imports, Inc.
Price: Thunder 45, matte blue **$402.00**
Price: Thunder 45, stainless **$480.00**
Price: Thunder 45, satin nickel **$445.00**

BERSA THUNDER 380 SERIES PISTOLS
Caliber: 380 ACP, 7 rounds **Barrel:** 3.5". **Weight:** 23 oz. **Length:** 6.6" overall. **Features:** Otherwise similar to Thunder 45 Ultra Compact. 380 DLX has 9-round capacity. 380 Concealed Carry has 8 round capacity. Imported from Argentina by Eagle Imports, Inc.
Price: Thunder 380 Matte **$310.00**
Price: Thunder 380 Satin Nickel **$336.00**
Price: Thunder 380 Blue DLX **$332.00**
Price: Thunder 380 Matte CC (2006) **$315.00**

BERSA THUNDER 9 ULTRA COMPACT/40 SERIES PISTOLS
Caliber: 9mm Para., 40 S&W. **Barrel:** 3.5". **Weight:** 24.5 oz. **Length:** 6.6" overall. **Features:** Otherwise similar to Thunder 45 Ultra Compact. 9mm Para. High Capacity model has 17-round capacity. 40 High Capacity model has 13-round capacity. Imported from Argentina by Eagle Imports, Inc.
Price: Thunder 9mm Para. Matte **$402.00**
Price: Thunder 40 High Capacity Satin Nickel **$419.00**

BROWNING HI POWER 9MM AUTOMATIC PISTOL
Caliber: 9mm Para., 13-round magazine; 40 S&W, 10-round magazine. **Barrel:** 4-5/8". **Weight:** 32 to 39 oz. **Length:** 7.75" overall. **Metal Finishes:** Blued (Standard); black-epoxy/silver-chrome (Practical); black-epoxy (Mark III). **Grips:** Molded (Mark III); wraparound Pachmayr (Practical); or walnut grips (Standard). **Sights:** Fixed (Practical, Mark III, Standard); low-mount adjustable rear (Standard). Cable lock supplied. **Features:** External hammer with half-cock and thumb safeties. Fixed rear sight model available. Commander-style (Practical) or spur-type hammer, single action. Includes gun lock. Imported from Belgium by Browning.
Price: Mark III **$979.00**
Price: Standard, fixed sights, from **$999.00**
Price: SMark III, Digital green (2009) **$985.00**

BROWNING BUCK MARK PISTOLS
Common Features: Caliber: 22 LR, 10-shot magazine. **Action:** Blowback semi-auto. **Trigger:** Wide grooved style. **Sights:** Ramp front, Browning Pro-Target rear adjustable for windage and elevation.

Grips: Cocobolo, target-style (Hunter, 5.5 Target, 5.5 Field); polymer (Camper, Camper Stainless, Micro Nickel, Standard, STD Stainless); checkered walnut (Challenge); laminated (Plus and Plus Nickel); laminated rosewood (Bullseye Target, FLD Plus); rubber (Bullseye Standard). **Metal finishes:** Matte blue (Hunter, Camper, Challenge, Plus, Bullseye Target, Bullseye Standard, 5.5 Target, 5.5 Field, FLD Plus); matte stainless (Camper Stainless, STD Stainless, Micro Standard); nickel-plated (Micro Nickel, Plus Nickel, and Nickel). **Features:** Machined aluminum frame. Includes gun lock. Introduced 1985. Hunter, Camper Stainless, STD Stainless, 5.5 Target, 5.5 Field all introduced 2005. Multiple variations, as noted below. Made in U.S.A. From Browning.
Price: Hunter, 7.25" heavy barrel, 38 oz., Truglo sight **$429.00**
Price: Camper, 5.5" heavy barrel, 34 oz. **$329.00**
Price: FLD Camper Stainless URX, 5.5" tapered bull barrel, 34 oz. **$359.00**
Price: Standard URX, 5.5" flat-side bull barrel, 34 oz. **$399.00**
Price: Standard Stainless URX, 5.5" flat-side bull barrel, 34 oz. **$439.00**
Price: Micro Standard URX, 4" flat-side bull barrel, 32 oz. ... **$399.00**
Price: Micro Standard Stainless URX, 4" flat-side bull barrel, 32 oz. **$439.00**
Price: Challenge, 5.5" lightweight taper barrel, 25 oz. **$399.00**
Price: Contour 5.5 URX, 5.5" barrel, 36 oz. **$469.00**
Price: Contour 7.25 URX, 7.25", 39 oz. **$479.00**
Price: Contour Lite 5.5 URX, 5.5" barrel, 28 oz., adj. sights . **$519.00**
Price: Contour Lite 7.25 URX, 7.25" barrel, 30 oz., adj. sights **$529.00**
Price: Bullseye URX, 7.25" fluted bull barrel, 36 oz. **$549.00**
Price: Bullseye Target Stainless, 7.25" fluted bull barrel, 36 oz. **$719.00**
Price: 5.5 Target, 5.5" round bull barrel, target sights, 35.5 oz. **$579.00**
Price: 5.5 Field, 5.5" round bull barrel, 35 oz. **$579.00**
Price: Plus Stainless UDX (2007)...................... **$509.00**
Price: Plus UDX (2007)............................ **$469.00**
Price: FLD Plus Rosewood UDX (2007)................. **$469.00**
Price: Stainless Camper, 5.5" tapered bull barrel (2008) **$379.00**
Price: Practical URX Fiber-Optic, 5.5" barrel (2009) **$379.00**
Price: Lite Splash 5.5 URX **$489.00**
Price: Lite Splash 7.25 URX **$509.00**

BUSHMASTER CARBON 15 .223 PISTOL
Caliber: 5.56/223, 30-round. **Barrel:** 7.25" stainless steel. **Weight:** 2.88 lbs. **Length:** 20" overall. **Grips:** Pistol grip, Hogue overmolded unit for ergonomic comfort. **Sights:** A2-type front with dual-aperture

slip-up rear. **Features:** AR-style semi-auto pistol with carbon composite receiver, shortenend handguard, full-length optics rail.
Price: . . . . N/A
Price: Type 97 pistol, without handguard $1,055.00

CHARLES DALY ENHANCED 1911 PISTOLS
Caliber: 45 ACP. **Barrel:** 5". **Weight:** 38 oz. **Length:** 8.75" overall. **Grips:** Checkered double diamond hardwood. **Sights:** Dovetailed front and dovetailed snag-free low profile rear sights, 3-dot system. **Features:** Extended high-rise beavertail grip safety, combat trigger, combat hammer, beveled magazine well, flared and lowered ejection port. Field Grade models are satin-finished blued steel. EMS series includes an ambidextrous safety, 4" barrel, 8-shot magazine. ECS series has a contoured left hand safety, 3.5" barrel, 6-shot magazine. Two magazines, lockable carrying case. Introduced 1998. Empire series are stainless versions. Imported from the Philippines by K.B.I., Inc.
Price: EFS, blued, 39.5 oz., 5" barrel $649.00
Price: EMS, blued, 37 oz., 4" barrel $649.00
Price: ECS, blued, 34.5 oz., 3.5" barrel $649.00

CHARLES DALY M-5 POLYMER-FRAMED HI-CAP 1911 PISTOL
Caliber: 9mm Para., 12-round magazine; 40 S&W 17-round magazine; 45 ACP, 13-round magazine. **Barrel:** 5". **Weight:** 33.5 oz. **Length:** 8.5" overall. **Grips:** Checkered polymer. **Sights:** Blade front, adjustable low-profile rear. **Features:** Stainless steel beaver-tail grip safety, rounded trigger-guard, tapered bull barrel, full-length guide rod, matte blue finish on frame and slide. 40 S&W models in M-5 Govt. 1911, M-5 Commander, and M-5 IPSC introduced 2006; M-5 Ultra X Compact in 9mm Para. and 45 ACP introduced 2006; M-5 IPSC .45 ACP introduced 2006. Made in Israel by BUL, imported by K.B.I., Inc.
Price: M-5 Govt. 1911, 40 S&W/45 ACP, matte blue $749.00
Price: M-5 Commander, 40 S&W/45 ACP, matte blue $749.00
Price: M-5 Ultra X Compact, 9mm Para., 3.1" barrel, 7" OAL, 28 oz. $749.00
Price: M-5 Ultra X Compact, 45 ACP, 3.1" barrel, 7" OAL, 28 oz. $749.00

CHIAPPA 1911-22
1911-style semiauto pistol chambered in .22 LR. Features include alloy frame; steel barrel; matte blue-black or bright nickel finish, walnut-like grips, two 10-round magazines, fixed sights. Straight blowback action.
Price: $295.00

COBRA ENTERPRISES FS32, FS380 AUTO PISTOL
Caliber: 32 ACP, 380 ACP, 7-shot magazine. **Barrel:** 3.5". **Weight:** 2.1 lbs. **Length:** 6-3/8" overall. **Grips:** Black composition. **Sights:** Fixed. **Features:** Choice of bright chrome, satin nickel or black finish. Introduced 2002. Made in U.S.A. by Cobra Enterprises of Utah, Inc.
Price: $165.00

COBRA ENTERPRISES PATRIOT 45 PISTOL
Caliber: 45 ACP, 6, 7, or 10-shot magazine. **Barrel:** 3.3". **Weight:** 20 oz. **Length:** 6" overall. **Grips:** Black polymer. **Sights:** Rear adjustable. **Features:** Stainless steel or black melonite slide with

load indicator; Semi-auto locked breech, DAO. Made in U.S.A. by Cobra Enterprises of Utah, Inc.
Price: $380.00

COBRA ENTERPRISES CA32, CA380 PISTOL
Caliber: 32 ACP, 380 ACP. **Barrel:** 2.8". **Weight:** 22 oz. **Length:** 5.4". **Grips:** Black molded synthetic. **Sights:** Fixed. **Features:** Choice of black, satin nickel, or chrome finish. Made in U.S.A. by Cobra Enterprises of Utah, Inc.
Price: $157.00

COLT MODEL 1991 MODEL O AUTO PISTOL
Caliber: 45 ACP, 7-shot magazine. **Barrel:** 5". **Weight:** 38 oz. **Length:** 8.5" overall. **Grips:** Checkered black composition. **Sights:** Ramped blade front, fixed square notch rear, high profile. **Features:** Matte finish. Continuation of serial number range used on original G.I. 1911A1 guns. Comes with one magazine and molded carrying case. Introduced 1991.
Price: Blue $786.00
Price: Stainless $839.00

COLT XSE SERIES MODEL O AUTO PISTOLS
Caliber: 45 ACP, 8-shot magazine. **Barrel:** 4.25", 5". **Grips:** Checkered, double diamond rosewood. **Sights:** Drift-adjustable 3-dot combat. **Features:** Brushed stainless finish; adjustable, two-cut aluminum trigger; extended ambidextrous thumb safety; upswept beavertail with palm swell; elongated slot hammer. Introduced 1999. From Colt's Mfg. Co., Inc.
Price: XSE Government (5" bbl.) $944.00
Price: XSE Government (4.25" bbl.) $944.00

COLT XSE LIGHTWEIGHT COMMANDER AUTO PISTOL

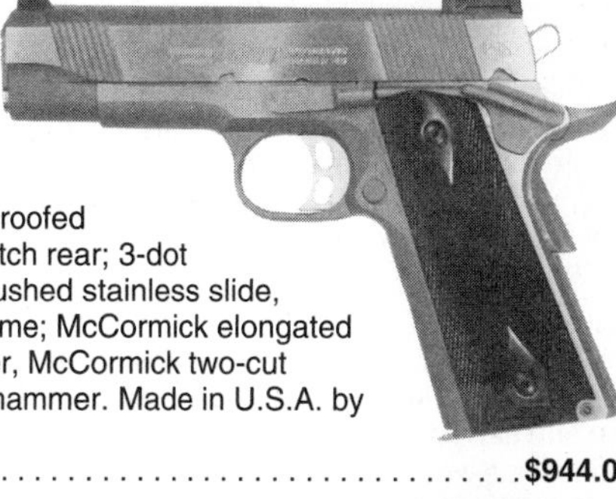

Caliber: 45 ACP, 8-shot. **Barrel:** 4.25". **Weight:** 26 oz. **Length:** 7.75" overall. **Grips:** Double diamond checkered rosewood. **Sights:** Fixed, glare-proofed blade front, square notch rear; 3-dot system. **Features:** Brushed stainless slide, nickeled aluminum frame; McCormick elongated slot enhanced hammer, McCormick two-cut adjustable aluminum hammer. Made in U.S.A. by Colt's Mfg. Co., Inc.
Price: Stainless $944.00

COLT DEFENDER

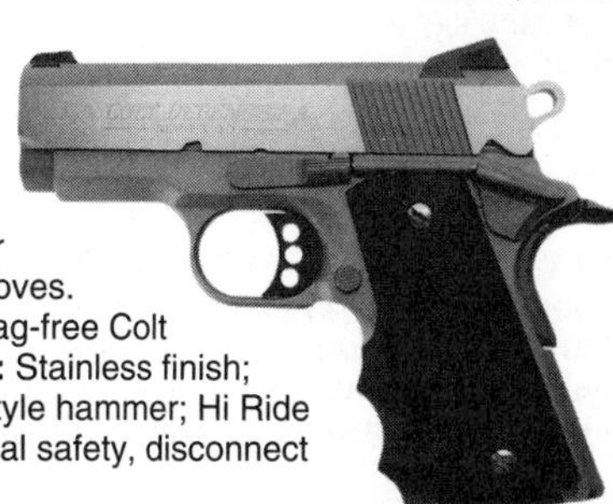

Caliber: 45 ACP, 7-shot magazine. **Barrel:** 3". **Weight:** 22-1/2 oz. **Length:** 6.75" overall. **Grips:** Pebble-finish rubber wraparound with finger grooves. **Sights:** White dot front, snag-free Colt competition rear. **Features:** Stainless finish; aluminum frame; combat-style hammer; Hi Ride grip safety, extended manual safety, disconnect

safety. Introduced 1998. Made in U.S.A. by Colt's Mfg. Co., Inc.
Price: 07000D, stainless **$885.00**

COLT SERIES 70
Caliber: 45 ACP.
Barrel: 5".
Weight: NA.
Length: NA.
Grips: Rosewood with double diamond checkering pattern.
Sights: Fixed. **Features:** Custom replica of the Original Series 70 pistol with a Series 70 firing system, original rollmarks. Introduced 2002. Made in U.S.A. by Colt's Mfg. Co., Inc.
Price: Blued **$919.00**
Price: Stainless **$950.00**

COLT 38 SUPER
Caliber: 38 Super. **Barrel:** 5". **Weight:** NA. **Length:** 8.5" **Grips:** Checkered rubber (stainless and blue models); wood with double diamond checkering pattern (bright stainless model). **Sights:** 3-dot. **Features:** Beveled magazine well, standard thumb safety and service-style grip safety. Introduced 2003. Made in U.S.A. by Colt's Mfg. Co., Inc.
Price: Blued **$837.00**
Price: Stainless **$866.00**
Price: Bright Stainless **$1,090.00**

COLT 1918 WWI REPLICA
Caliber: 45 ACP, 2 7-round magazines. **Barrel:** 5". **Weight:** 38 oz. **Length:** 8.5". **Grips:** Checkered walnut with double diamond checkering pattern. **Sights:** Tapered blade front sight, U-shaped rear notch. **Features:** Reproduction based on original 1911 blueprints. Original rollmarks and inspector marks. Smooth mainspring housing with lanyard loop, WWI-style manual thumb and grip safety, black oxide finish. Introduced 2007. Made in U.S.A. by Colt's Mfg. Co., Inc.
Price: Blued **$990.00**

COLT RAIL GUN
Caliber: 45 ACP (8+1). **Barrel:** NA. **Weight:** NA. **Length:** NA. **Grips:** Rosewood double diamond. **Sights:** White dot front and Novak rear. **Features:** 1911-style semi-auto. Stainless steel frame and slide, front and rear slide serrations, skeletonized trigger, integral; accessory rail, Smith & Alexander upswept beavertail grip palm swell safety, tactical thumb safety, National Match barrel.
Price: . . . . **TO BE ANNOUNCED**

COLT NEW AGENT
Caliber: 45 ACP (7+1). **Barrel:** 3". **Weight:** 25 oz. **Length:** 6.75" overall. **Grips:** Double diamond slim fit. **Sights:** Snag free trench style. **Features:** Semi-auto pistol with blued finish and enhanced black anodized aluminum receiver. Skeletonized aluminum trigger, series 80 firing system, front strap serrations, beveled magazine well.
Price: **$885.00**

COLT DEFENDER PISTOL
1911-style semiauto pistol chambered in .45 ACP and 9mm Parabellum. Features include Series 90 lockwork, 7+1 (.45) or 8+1 (9mm) capacity, wraparound rubber grips, 3-inch barrel, beveled magazine well, aluminum alloy frame with stainless steel slide, white dot carry sights.
Price: **$939.00**

COLT NEW AGENT PISTOL
Similar to Colt Defender but with steel frame and fixed sights.
Price: **$939.00**

COLT SPECIAL COMBAT GOVERNMENT CARRY MODEL
Caliber: 45 ACP (8+1), 38 Super (9+1). **Barrel:** 5". **Weight:** NA. **Length:** NA. **Grips:** Black/silver synthetic. **Sights:** Novak front and rear night. **Features:** 1911-style semi-auto. Skeletonized three-hole trigger, slotted hammer, Smith & Alexander upswept beavertail grip palm swell safety and extended magazine well, Wilson tactical ambidextrous safety. Available in blued, hard chrome, or blue/satin nickel finish, depending on chambering.
Price: **$1,676.00**

CZ 75 B AUTO PISTOL
Caliber: 9mm Para., 40 S&W, 10-shot magazine. **Barrel:** 4.7". **Weight:** 34.3 oz. **Length:** 8.1" overall. **Grips:** High impact checkered plastic. **Sights:** Square post front, rear adjustable for windage; 3-dot system. **Features:** Single action/double action design; firing pin block safety; choice of black polymer, matte or high-polish blue finishes. All-steel frame. B-SA is a single action with a drop-free magazine. Imported from the Czech Republic by CZ-USA.
Price: 75 B, black polymer, 16-shot magazine **$597.00**
Price: 75 B, dual-tone or satin nickel **$617.00**
Price: 40 S&W, black polymer, 12-shot magazine **$615.00**
Price: 40 S&W, glossy blue, dual-tone, satin nickel **$669.00**
Price: 75 B-SA, 9mm Para./40 S&W, single action **$609.00**

CZ 75 BD Decocker
Similar to the CZ 75B except has a decocking lever in place of the safety lever. All other specifications are the same. Introduced 1999. Imported from the Czech Republic by CZ-USA.
Price: 9mm Para., black polymer **$609.00**

CZ 75 B Compact Auto Pistol
Similar to the CZ 75 B except has 14-shot magazine in 9mm Para., 3.9" barrel and weighs 32 oz. Has removable front sight, non-glare ribbed slide top. Trigger guard is squared and serrated; combat hammer. Introduced 1993. Imported from the Czech Republic by CZ-USA.
Price: 9mm Para., black polymer **$631.00**
Price: 9mm Para., dual tone or satin nickel **$651.00**
Price: 9mm Para. D PCR Compact, alloy frame **$651.00**

CZ 75 Champion Pistol
Similar to the CZ 75 B except has a longer frame and slide, rubber grip to accommodate new heavy-duty magazine. Ambidextrous thumb safety, extended magazine release; three-port compensator. Blued slide and stain nickel frame finish. Introduced 2005. Imported from the Czech Republic by CZ-USA.
Price: 40 S&W, 12-shot mag. **$1,739.00**

CZ 75 Tactical Sport
Similar to the CZ 75 B except the CZ 75 TS is a competition ready pistol designed for IPSC standard division (USPSA limited division). Fixed target sights, tuned single-action operation, lightweight polymer match trigger with adjustments for take-up and overtravel, competition hammer, extended magazine catch, ambidextrous manual safety, checkered walnut grips, polymer magazine well, two tone finish. Introduced 2005. Imported from the Czech Republic by CZ-USA.
Price: 9mm Para., 20-shot mag. **$1,338.00**
Price: 40 S&W, 16-shot mag. **$1,338.00**

CZ 75 SP-01 Pistol
Similar to NATO-approved CZ 75 Compact P-01 model. Features an integral 1913 accessory rail on the dust cover, rubber grip panels, black polycoat finish, extended beavertail, new grip geometry with checkering on front and back straps, and double or single action operation. Introduced 2005. The Shadow variant designed as an IPSC "production" division competition firearm. Includes competition hammer, competition rear sight and fiber-optic front sight, modified slide release, lighter recoil and main spring for use with "minor power

Prices given are believed to be accurate at time of publication however, many factors affect retail pricing so exact prices are not possible.

factor" competition ammunition. Includes polycoat finish and slim walnut grips. Finished by CZ Custom Shop. Imported from the Czech Republic by CZ-USA.
Price: SP-01 9mm Para., black polymer, 19+1 . . . . **$850.00**

CZ 75 SP-01 Phantom
Similar to the CZ 75 B. 9mm Luger, 19-round magazine, weighs 26 oz. and features a polymer frame with accessory rail, and a forged steel slide with a weight-saving scalloped profile. Two interchangeable grip inserts are included to accommodate users with different-sized hands.
Price: **$695.00**

CZ 85 B/85 Combat Auto Pistol

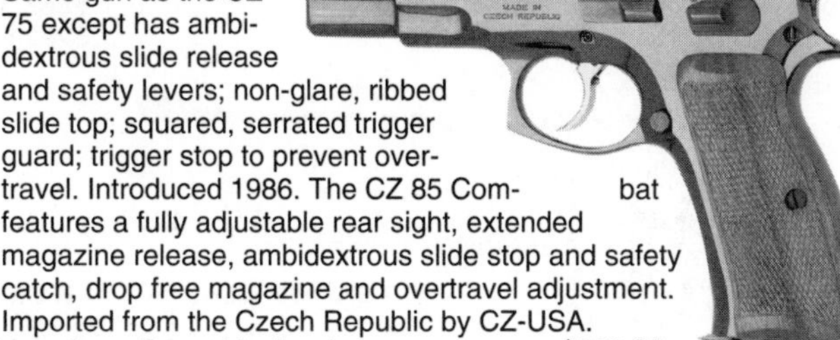

Same gun as the CZ 75 except has ambidextrous slide release and safety levers; non-glare, ribbed slide top; squared, serrated trigger guard; trigger stop to prevent overtravel. Introduced 1986. The CZ 85 Combat features a fully adjustable rear sight, extended magazine release, ambidextrous slide stop and safety catch, drop free magazine and overtravel adjustment. Imported from the Czech Republic by CZ-USA.
Price: 9mm Para., black polymer **$628.00**
Price: Combat, black polymer **$702.00**
Price: Combat, dual-tone, satin nickel **$732.00**

CZ 75 KADET AUTO PISTOL
Caliber: 22 LR, 10-shot magazine. **Barrel:** 4.88". **Weight:** 36 oz. **Grips:** High impact checkered plastic. **Sights:** Blade front, fully adjustable rear. **Features:** Single action/double action mechanism; all-steel construction. Introduced 1999. Kadet conversion kit consists of barrel, slide, adjustable sights, and magazine to convert the centerfire 75 to rimfire. Imported from the Czech Republic by CZ-USA.
Price: Black polymer **$689.00**
Price: Kadet conversion kit **$412.00**

CZ 83 DOUBLE-ACTION PISTOL
Caliber: 32 ACP, 380 ACP, 12-shot magazine. **Barrel:** 3.8". **Weight:** 26.2 oz. **Length:** 6.8" overall. **Grips:** High impact checkered plastic. **Sights:** Removable square post front, rear adjustable for windage; 3-dot system. **Features:** Single action/double action; ambidextrous magazine release and safety. Blue finish; non-glare ribbed slide top. Imported from the Czech Republic by CZ-USA.
Price: Glossy blue, 32 ACP or 380 ACP **$495.00**
Price: Satin Nickel **$522.00**

CZ 97 B AUTO PISTOL
Caliber: 45 ACP, 10-shot magazine. **Barrel:** 4.85". **Weight:** 40 oz. **Length:** 8.34" overall. **Grips:** Checkered walnut. **Sights:** Fixed. **Features:** Single action/double action; full-length slide rails; screw-in barrel bushing; linkless barrel; all-steel construction; chamber loaded indicator; dual transfer bars. Introduced 1999. Imported from the Czech Republic by CZ-USA.
Price: Black polymer **$779.00**
Price: Glossy blue **$799.00**

CZ 97 BD Decocker
Similar to the CZ 97 B except has a decocking lever in place of the safety lever. Tritium night sights. Rubber grips. All other specifications are the same. Introduced 1999. Imported from the Czech Republic by CZ-USA.
Price: 9mm Para., black polymer **$874.00**

CZ 2075 RAMI/RAMI P AUTO PISTOL
Caliber: 9mm Para., 40 S&W. **Barrel:** 3". **Weight:** 25 oz. **Length:** 6.5" overall. **Grips:** Rubber. **Sights:** Blade front with dot, white outline rear drift adjustable for windage. **Features:** Single-action/double-action; alloy or polymer frame, steel slide; has laser sight mount. Imported from the Czech Republic by CZ-USA.
Price: 9mm Para., alloy frame, 10 and 14-shot magazines . . . **$671.00**
Price: 40 S&W, alloy frame, 8-shot magazine **$671.00**
Price: RAMI P, polymer frame, 9mm Para., 40 S&W **$612.00**

CZ P-01 AUTO PISTOL
Caliber: 9mm Para., 14-shot magazine. **Barrel:** 3.85". **Weight:** 27 oz. **Length:** 7.2" overall. **Grips:** Checkered rubber. **Sights:** Blade front with dot, white outline rear drift adjustable for windage. **Features:** Based on the CZ 75, except with forged aircraft-grade aluminum alloy frame. Hammer forged barrel, decocker, firing-pin block, M3 rail, dual slide serrations, squared trigger guard, re-contoured trigger, lanyard loop on butt. Serrated front and back strap. Introduced 2006. Imported from the Czech Republic by CZ-USA.
Price: CZ P-01 . . . . **$672.00**

DAN WESSON FIREARMS POINTMAN SEVEN AUTO PISTOL
Caliber: 10mm, 40 S&W, 45 ACP. **Barrel:** 5". **Grips:** Diamond checkered cocobolo. **Sights:** Bo-Mar style adjustable target sight. **Weight:** 38 oz. **Features:** Stainless-steel frame and serrated slide. Series 70-style 1911, stainless-steel frame, forged stainless-steel slide. One-piece match-grade barrel and bushing. 20-LPI checkered mainspring housing, front and rear slide cocking serrations, beveled magwell, dehorned by hand. Lowered and flared ejection port, Ed Brown slide stop and memory groove grip safety, tactical extended thumb safety. Commander-style match hammer, match grade sear, aluminum trigger with stainless bow, Wolff springs. Introduced 2000. Made in U.S.A. by Dan Wesson Firearms, distributed by CZ-USA.
Price: 45 ACP, 7+1 . . . . **$1,158.00**
Price: 10mm, 8+1 . . . . **$1,191.00**
Price: 40 S&W, stainless **$1,189.00**
Price: 45 ACP, Desert Tan **$1,269.00**

Dan Wesson Commander Classic Bobtail Auto Pistols
Similar to Pointman Seven, a Commander-sized frame with 4.25" barrel. Available with stainless finish, fixed night sights. Introduced 2005. Made in U.S.A. by Dan Wesson Firearms, distributed by CZ-USA.
Price: 45 ACP, 7+1, 33 oz. **$1,191.00**
Price: 10mm, 8+1, 33 oz., stainless **$1,224.00**
Price: 10mm, 33 oz. two-tone **$1,530.00**

DAN WESSON DW RZ-10 AUTO PISTOL
Caliber: 10mm, 9-shot. **Barrel:** 5". **Grips:** Diamond checkered cocobolo. **Sights:** Bo-Mar style adjustable target sight. **Weight:** 38.3 oz. **Length:** 8.8" overall. **Features:** Stainless-steel frame and serrated slide. Series 70-style 1911, stainless-steel frame, forged stainless-steel slide. Commander-style match hammer. Reintroduced 2005. Made in U.S.A. by Dan Wesson Firearms, distributed by CZ-USA.
Price: 10mm, 8+1 . . . . **$1,191.00**

Dan Wesson DW RZ-10 Sportsman
Similar to the RZ-10 Auto except with 8-shot magazine. Weighs 36 oz., length is 8.8" overall.
Price: **$1,448.00**

Dan Wesson DW RZ-45 Heritage
Similar to the RZ-10 Auto except in 45 ACP with 7-shot magazine. Weighs 36 oz., length is 8.8" overall.
Price: 10mm, 8+1 . . . . **$1,141.00**

DESERT EAGLE MARK XIX PISTOL

Caliber: 357 Mag., 9-shot; 44 Mag., 8-shot; 50 AE, 7-shot. **Barrel:** 6", 10", interchangeable. **Weight:** 357 Mag.-62 oz.; 44 Mag.-69 oz.; 50 AE-72 oz. **Length:** 10.25" overall (6" bbl.). **Grips:** Polymer; rubber available. **Sights:** Blade on ramp front, combat-style rear. Adjustable available. **Features:** Interchangeable barrels; rotating three-lug bolt; ambidextrous safety; adjustable trigger. Military epoxy finish. Satin, bright nickel, chrome, brushed, matte or black-oxide finishes available. 10" barrel extra. Imported from Israel by Magnum Research, Inc.

Price: Black-6, 6" barrel **$1,475.00**
Price: Black-10, 10" barrel **$1,575.00**
Price: Component System Package, 3 barrels, carrying case, from **$2,801.00**

DESERT BABY MICRO DESERT EAGLE PISTOL

Caliber: 380 ACP, 6-rounds. **Barrel:** 2.22". **Weight:** 14 oz. **Length:** 4.52" overall. **Grips:** NA. **Sights:** Fixed low-profile. **Features:** Small-frame DAO pocket pistol. Steel slide, aluminum alloy frame, nickel-teflon finish.

Price: **$535.00**

DESERT BABY EAGLE PISTOLS

Caliber: 9mm Para., 40 S&W, 45 ACP, 10- or 15-round magazines. **Barrel:** 3.64", 3.93", 4.52". **Weight:** 26.8 to 39.8 oz. **Length:** 7.25" to 8.25" overall. **Grips:** Polymer. **Sights:** Drift-adjustable rear, blade front. **Features:** Steel frame and slide; slide safety; decocker. Reintroduced in 1999. Imported from Israel by Magnum Research, Inc.

Price: **$619.00**

EAA WITNESS FULL SIZE AUTO PISTOL

Caliber: 9mm Para., 38 Super, 18-shot magazine; 40 S&W, 10mm, 15-shot magazine; 45 ACP, 10-shot magazine. **Barrel:** 4.50". **Weight:** 35.33 oz. **Length:** 8.10" overall. **Grips:** Checkered rubber. **Sights:** Undercut blade front, open rear adjustable for windage. **Features:** Double-action/single-action trigger system; round trigger guard; frame-mounted safety. Introduced 1991. Polymer frame introduced 2005. Imported from Italy by European American Armory.

Price: 9mm Para., 38 Super, 10mm, 40 S&W, 45 ACP, full-size steel frame, Wonder finish **$514.00**
Price: 45/22 22 LR, full-size steel frame, blued **$472.00**
Price: 9mm Para., 40 S&W, 45 ACP, full-size polymer frame . **$472.00**

EAA WITNESS COMPACT AUTO PISTOL

Caliber: 9mm Para., 40 S&W, 10mm, 12-shot magazine; 45 ACP, 8-shot magazine. **Barrel:** 3.6". **Weight:** 30 oz. **Length:** 7.3" overall. Otherwise similar to Full Size Witness. Polymer frame introduced 2005. Imported from Italy by European American Armory.

Price: 9mm Para., 10mm, 40 S&W, 45 ACP, steel frame, Wonder finish **$514.00**
Price: 9mm Para., 40 S&W, 45 ACP, polymer frame **$472.00**

EAA WITNESS-P CARRY AUTO PISTOL

Caliber: 10mm, 15-shot magazine; 45 ACP, 10-shot magazine. **Barrel:** 3.6". **Weight:** 27 oz. **Length:** 7.5" overall. Otherwise similar to Full Size Witness. Polymer frame introduced 2005. Imported from Italy by European American Armory.

Price: 10mm, 45 ACP, polymer frame, from **$598.00**

EAA ZASTAVA EZ PISTOL

Caliber: 9mm Para., 15-shot magazine; 40 S&W, 11-shot magazine; 45 ACP, 10-shot magazine. **Barrel:** 3.5" or 4." **Weight:** 30-33 oz. **Length:** 7.25" to 7.5" overall. **Features:** Ambidextrous decocker, slide release and magazine release; three dot sight system, aluminum frame, steel slide, accessory rail, full-length claw extractor, loaded chamber indicator. M88 compact has 3.6" barrel, weighs 28 oz. Introduced 2008. Imported by European American Armory.

Price: 9mm Para. or 40 S&W, blued **$547.00**
Price: 9mm Para. or 40 S&W, chromed **$587.00**
Price: 45 ACP, chromed **$587.00**
Price: M88, from **$292.00**

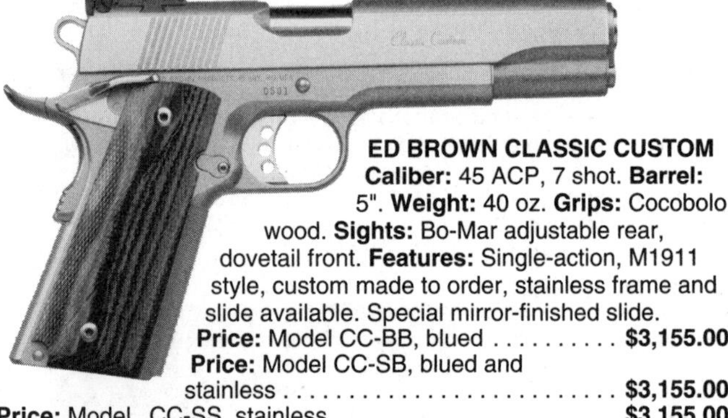

ED BROWN CLASSIC CUSTOM

Caliber: 45 ACP, 7 shot. **Barrel:** 5". **Weight:** 40 oz. **Grips:** Cocobolo wood. **Sights:** Bo-Mar adjustable rear, dovetail front. **Features:** Single-action, M1911 style, custom made to order, stainless frame and slide available. Special mirror-finished slide.

Price: Model CC-BB, blued **$3,155.00**
Price: Model CC-SB, blued and stainless **$3,155.00**
Price: Model CC-SS, stainless **$3,155.00**

ED BROWN KOBRA AND KOBRA CARRY

Caliber: 45 ACP, 7-shot magazine. **Barrel:** 5" (Kobra); 4.25" (Kobra Carry). **Weight:** 39 oz. (Kobra); 34 oz. (Kobra Carry). **Grips:** Hogue exotic wood. **Sights:** Ramp, front; fixed Novak low-mount night sights, rear. **Features:** Has snakeskin pattern serrations on forestrap and mainspring housing, dehorned edges, beavertail grip safety.

Price: Kobra K-BB, blued **$2,195.00**
Price: Kobra K-SB, stainless and blued **$2,195.00**
Price: Kobra K-SS, stainless **$2,195.00**
Price: Kobra Carry blued, blued/stainless, or stainless from **$2,445.00**

Ed Brown Executive Pistols

Similar to other Ed Brown products, but with 25-lpi checkered frame and mainspring housing.

Price: Elite blued, blued/stainless, or stainless, from **$2,395.00**
Price: Carry blued, blued/stainless, or stainless, from **$2,645.00**
Price: Target blued, blued/stainless, or stainless (2006) from **$2,595.00**

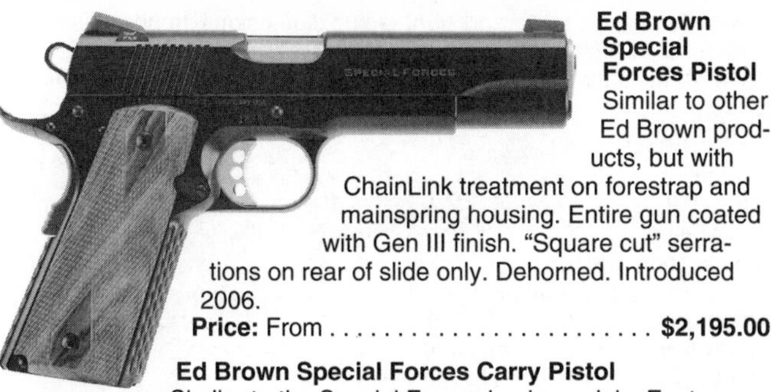

Ed Brown Special Forces Pistol
Similar to other Ed Brown products, but with ChainLink treatment on forestrap and mainspring housing. Entire gun coated with Gen III finish. "Square cut" serrations on rear of slide only. Dehorned. Introduced 2006.
Price: From **$2,195.00**

Ed Brown Special Forces Carry Pistol
Similar to the Special Forces basic models. Features a 4.25" Commander model slide, single stack commander Bobtail frame. Weighs approx. 35 oz. Fixed dovetail 3-dot night sights with high visibility white outlines.
Price: From **$2,445.00**

EXCEL ARMS ACCELERATOR MP-17/MP-22 PISTOLS
Caliber: 17 HMR, 22 WMR, 9-shot magazine. **Barrel:** 8.5" bull barrel. **Weight:** 54 oz. **Length:** 12.875" overall. **Grips:** Textured black composition. **Sights:** Fully adjustable target sights. **Features:** Made from 17-4 stainless steel, comes with aluminum rib, integral Weaver base, internal hammer, firing-pin block. American made, lifetime warranty. Comes with two 9-round stainless steel magazines and a California-approved cable lock. 22 WMR Introduced 2006. Made in U.S.A. by Excel Arms.
Price: **$433.00**
Price: Camo finishes (2008) **$520.00**

FIRESTORM AUTO PISTOLS
Caliber: 22 LR, 32 ACP, 10-shot magazine; 380 ACP, 7-shot magazine; 9mm Para., 40 S&W, 10-shot magazine; 45 ACP, 7-shot magazine. **Barrel:** 3.5". **Weight:** From 23 oz. **Length:** From 6.6" overall. **Grips:** Rubber. **Sights:** 3-dot. **Features:** Double action. Distributed by SGS Importers International.
Price: 22 LR, matte or duotone, from **$309.95**
Price: 380, matte or duotone, from **$311.95**
Price: Mini Firestorm 9mm Para., matte, duotone, nickel, from **$395.00**
Price: Mini Firestorm 40 S&W, matte, duotone, nickel, from . . **$395.00**
Price: Mini Firestorm 45 ACP, matte, duotone, chrome, from **$402.00**

GLOCK 17/17C AUTO PISTOL
Caliber: 9mm Para., 17/19/33-shot magazines. **Barrel:** 4.49". **Weight:** 22.04 oz. (without magazine). **Length:** 7.32" overall. **Grips:** Black polymer. **Sights:** Dot on front blade, white outline rear adjustable for windage. **Features:** Polymer frame, steel slide; double-action trigger with "Safe Action" system; mechanical firing pin safety, drop safety; simple takedown without tools; locked breech, recoil operated action. ILS designation refers to Internal Locking System. Adopted by Austrian armed forces 1983. NATO approved 1984. Imported from Austria by Glock, Inc.
Price: Fixed sight **$690.00**

GLOCK 17 GEN4
Similar to Model G17 but with multiple backstrap system allowing three options: a short frame version, medium frame or large frame; reversible, enlarged magazine release catch; dual recoil spring assembly; new Rough Textured Frame (RTF) surface designed to enhance grip traction.
Price: . . . . **N/A**

GLOCK 19/19C AUTO PISTOL
Caliber: 9mm Para., 15/17/19/33-shot magazines. **Barrel:** 4.02". **Weight:** 20.99 oz. (without magazine). **Length:** 6.85" overall. Compact version of Glock 17. Pricing the same as Model 17. Imported from Austria by Glock, Inc.
Price: Fixed sight **$699.00**
Price: 19C Compensated (fixed sight) **$675.00**

GLOCK 20/20C 10MM AUTO PISTOL
Caliber: 10mm, 15-shot magazines. **Barrel:** 4.6". **Weight:** 27.68 oz. (without magazine). **Length:** 7.59" overall. **Features:** Otherwise similar to Model 17. Imported from Austria by Glock, Inc. Introduced 1990.
Price: Fixed sight, from **$700.00**

GLOCK MODEL 20 SF SHORT FRAME PISTOL
Caliber: 10mm. **Barrel:** 4.61" with hexagonal rifling. **Weight:** 27.51 oz. **Length:** 8.07" overall. **Sights:** Fixed. **Features:** Otherwise similar to Model 20 but with short-frame design, extended sight radius.
Price: **$664.00**

GLOCK 21/21C AUTO PISTOL
Caliber: 45 ACP, 13-shot magazines. **Barrel:** 4.6". **Weight:** 26.28 oz. (without magazine). **Length:** 7.59" overall. **Features:** Otherwise similar to Model 17. Imported from Austria by Glock, Inc. Introduced 1991. SF version has tactical rail, smaller diameter grip, 10-round magazine capacity. Introduced 2007.
Price: Fixed sight, from **$700.00**

GLOCK 22/22C AUTO PISTOL
Caliber: 40 S&W, 15/17-shot magazines. **Barrel:** 4.49". **Weight:** 22.92 oz. (without magazine). **Length:** 7.32" overall. **Features:** Otherwise similar to Model 17, including pricing. Imported from Austria by Glock, Inc. Introduced 1990.
Price: Fixed sight, from **$641.00**

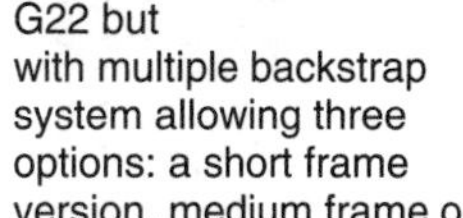

GLOCK 22 GEN4
Similar to Model G22 but with multiple backstrap system allowing three options: a short frame version, medium frame or large frame; reversible, enlarged magazine release catch; dual recoil spring assembly; new Rough Textured Frame (RTF) surface designed to enhance grip traction.
Price: . . . . **N/A**

GLOCK 23/23C AUTO PISTOL
Caliber: 40 S&W, 13/15/17-shot magazines. **Barrel:** 4.02". **Weight:** 21.16 oz. (without magazine). **Length:** 6.85" overall. **Features:** Otherwise similar to Model 22, including pricing. Compact version of Glock 22. Imported from Austria by Glock, Inc. Introduced 1990.
Price: Fixed sight **$641.00**
Price: 23C Compensated (fixed sight) **$694.00**

GLOCK 26 AUTO PISTOL
Caliber: 9mm Para. 10/12/15/17/19/33-shot magazines. **Barrel:** 3.46". **Weight:** 19.75 oz. **Length:** 6.29" overall. Subcompact version of Glock 17. Pricing the same as Model 17. Imported from Austria by Glock, Inc.
Price: Fixed sight **$690.00**

GLOCK 27 AUTO PISTOL
Caliber: 40 S&W, 9/11/13/15/17-shot magazines. **Barrel:** 3.46". **Weight:** 19.75 oz. (without magazine). **Length:** 6.29" overall. **Features:** Otherwise similar to Model 22, including pricing. Subcompact version of Glock 22. Imported from Austria by Glock, Inc. Introduced 1996.
Price: Fixed sight **$750.00**

GLOCK 29 AUTO PISTOL
Caliber: 10mm, 10/15-shot magazines. **Barrel:** 3.78". **Weight:** 24.69 oz. (without magazine). **Length:** 6.77" overall. **Features:** Otherwise similar to Model 20, including pricing. Subcompact version of Glock 20. Imported from Austria by Glock, Inc. Introduced 1997.
Price: Fixed sight **$672.00**

GLOCK MODEL 29 SF SHORT FRAME PISTOL
Caliber: 10mm. **Barrel:** 3.78" with hexagonal rifling. **Weight:** 24.52 oz. **Length:** 6.97" overall. **Sights:** Fixed. **Features:** Otherwise similar to Model 29 but with short-frame design, extended sight radius.
Price: **$660.00**

GLOCK 30 AUTO PISTOL
Caliber: 45 ACP, 9/10/13-shot magazines. **Barrel:** 3.78". **Weight:** 23.99 oz. (without magazine). **Length:** 6.77" overall. **Features:** Otherwise similar to Model 21, including pricing. Subcompact version of Glock 21. Imported from Austria by Glock, Inc. Introduced 1997. SF version has tactical rail, octagonal rifled barrel with a 1:15.75 rate of twist, smaller diameter grip, 10-round magazine capacity. Introduced 2008
Price: Fixed sight **$700.00**

GLOCK 31/31C AUTO PISTOL
Caliber: 357 Auto, 15/17-shot magazines. **Barrel:** 4.49". **Weight:** 23.28 oz. (without magazine). **Length:** 7.32" overall. **Features:** Otherwise similar to Model 17. Imported from Austria by Glock, Inc.
Price: Fixed sight, from **$641.00**

GLOCK 32/32C AUTO PISTOL
Caliber: 357 Auto, 13/15/17-shot magazines. **Barrel:** 4.02". **Weight:** 21.52 oz. (without magazine). **Length:** 6.85" overall. **Features:** Otherwise similar to Model 31. Compact. Imported from Austria by Glock, Inc.
Price: Fixed sight **$669.00**

GLOCK 33 AUTO PISTOL
Caliber: 357 Auto, 9/11/13/15/17-shot magazines. **Barrel:** 3.46". **Weight:** 19.75 oz. (without magazine). **Length:** 6.29" overall. **Features:** Otherwise similar to Model 31. Subcompact. Imported from Austria by Glock, Inc.
Price: Fixed sight, from **$641.00**

GLOCK 34 AUTO PISTOL
Caliber: 9mm Para. 17/19/33-shot magazines. **Barrel:** 5.32". **Weight:** 22.9 oz. **Length:** 8.15" overall. Competition version of Glock 17 with extended barrel, slide, and sight radius dimensions. Imported from Austria by Glock, Inc.
Price: Adjustable sight, from **$648.00**

GLOCK 35 AUTO PISTOL
Caliber: 40 S&W, 15/17-shot magazines. **Barrel:** 5.32". **Weight:** 24.52 oz. (without magazine). **Length:** 8.15" overall. **Features:** Otherwise similar to Model 22. Competition version of Glock 22 with extended barrel, slide, and sight radius dimensions. Imported from Austria by Glock, Inc. Introduced 1996.
Price: Adjustable sight **$648.00**

GLOCK 36 AUTO PISTOL
Caliber: 45 ACP, 6-shot magazines. **Barrel:** 3.78". **Weight:** 20.11 oz. (without magazine). **Length:** 6.77" overall. **Features:** Single-stack magazine, slimmer grip than Glock 21/30. Subcompact. Imported from Austria by Glock, Inc. Introduced 1997.
Price: Adjustable sight **$616.00**

GLOCK 37 AUTO PISTOL
Caliber: 45 GAP, 10-shot magazines. **Barrel:** 4.49". **Weight:** 25.95 oz. (without magazine). **Length:** 7.32" overall. **Features:** Otherwise similar to Model 17. Imported from Austria by Glock, Inc. Introduced 2005.
Price: Fixed sight, from **$562.00**

GLOCK 38 AUTO PISTOL
Caliber: 45 GAP, 8/10-shot magazines. **Barrel:** 4.02". **Weight:** 24.16 oz. (without magazine). **Length:** 6.85" overall. **Features:** Otherwise similar to Model 37. Compact. Imported from Austria by Glock, Inc.
Price: Fixed sight **$614.00**

GLOCK 39 AUTO PISTOL
Caliber: 45 GAP, 6/8/10-shot magazines. **Barrel:** 3.46". **Weight:** 19.33 oz. (without magazine). **Length:** 6.3" overall. **Features:** Otherwise similar to Model 37. Subcompact. Imported from Austria by Glock, Inc.
Price: Fixed sight . . **$614.00**

GLOCK MODEL G17/G22/G19/G23 RTF
Similar to Models G17, G22, G19 and G23 but with rough textured frame.
Price: . . . . **N/A**

HECKLER & KOCH USP AUTO PISTOL
Caliber: 9mm Para., 15-shot magazine; 40 S&W, 13-shot magazine; 45 ACP, 12-shot magazine. **Barrel:** 4.25-4.41". **Weight:** 1.65 lbs. **Length:** 7.64-7.87" overall. **Grips:** Non-slip stippled black polymer. **Sights:** Blade front, rear adjustable for windage. **Features:** New HK design with polymer frame, modified Browning action with recoil reduction system, single control lever. Special "hostile environment" finish on all metal parts. Available in SA/DA, DAO, left- and right-hand versions. Introduced 1993. 45 ACP Introduced 1995. Imported from Germany by Heckler & Koch, Inc.
Price: USP 45 . . . . **$919.00**
Price: USP 40 and USP 9mm **$859.00**

HECKLER & KOCH USP COMPACT AUTO PISTOL
Caliber: 9mm Para., 13-shot magazine; 40 S&W and .357 SIG, 12-shot magazine; 45 ACP, 8-shot magazine. Similar to the USP except the 9mm Para., 357 SIG, and 40 S&W have 3.58" barrels, measure

6.81" overall, and weigh 1.47 lbs. (9mm Para.). Introduced 1996. 45 ACP measures 7.09" overall. Introduced 1998. Imported from Germany by Heckler & Koch, Inc.

Price: USP Compact 45 . . . . . $959.00
Price: USP Compact 9mm Para., 40 S&W $879.00

HECKLER & KOCH USP45 TACTICAL PISTOL

Caliber: 40 S&W, 13-shot magazine; 45 ACP, 12-shot magazine. **Barrel:** 4.90-5.09". **Weight:** 1.9 lbs. **Length:** 8.64" overall. **Grips:** Non-slip stippled polymer. **Sights:** Blade front, fully adjustable target rear. **Features:** Has extended threaded barrel with rubber O-ring; adjustable trigger; extended magazine floorplate; adjustable trigger stop; polymer frame. Introduced 1998. Imported from Germany by Heckler & Koch, Inc.

Price: USP Tactical 45 . . . . $1,239.00
Price: USP Tactical 40 . . . . $1,179.00

HECKLER & KOCH USP COMPACT TACTICAL PISTOL

Caliber: 45 ACP, 8-shot magazine. Similar to the USP Tactical except measures 7.72" overall, weighs 1.72 lbs. Introduced 2006. Imported from Germany by Heckler & Koch, Inc.

Price: USP Compact Tactical $1,179.00

HECKLER & KOCH MARK 23 SPECIAL OPERATIONS PISTOL

Caliber: 45 ACP, 12-shot magazine. **Barrel:** 5.87". **Weight:** 2.42 lbs. **Length:** 9.65" overall. **Grips:** Integral with frame; black polymer. **Sights:** Blade front, rear drift adjustable for windage; 3-dot. **Features:** Civilian version of the SOCOM pistol. Polymer frame; double action; exposed hammer; short recoil, modified Browning action. Introduced 1996. Imported from Germany by Heckler & Koch, Inc.

Price: $2,139.00

HECKLER & KOCH P2000 AUTO PISTOL

Caliber: 9mm Para., 13-shot magazine; 40 S&W and .357 SIG, 12-shot magazine. **Barrel:** 3.62". **Weight:** 1.5 lbs. **Length:** 7" overall. **Grips:** Interchangeable panels. **Sights:** Fixed Patridge style, drift adjustable for windage, standard 3-dot. **Features:** Incorporates features of HK USP Compact pistol, including Law Enforcement Modification (LEM) trigger, double-action hammer system, ambidextrous magazine release, dual slide-release levers, accessory mounting rails, recurved, hook trigger guard, fiber-reinforced polymer frame, modular grip with exchangeable back straps, nitro-carburized finish, lock-out safety device. Introduced 2003. Imported from Germany by Heckler & Koch, Inc.

Price: $879.00
Price: P2000 LEM DAO, 357 SIG, intr. 2006 . . . . $879.00
Price: P2000 SA/DA, 357 SIG, intr. 2006 . . . . $879.00

HECKLER & KOCH P2000 SK AUTO PISTOL

Caliber: 9mm Para., 10-shot magazine; 40 S&W and .357 SIG, 9-shot magazine. **Barrel:** 3.27". **Weight:** 1.3 lbs. **Length:** 6.42" overall. **Sights:** Fixed Patridge style, drift adjustable. **Features:** Standard accessory rails, ambidextrous slide release, polymer frame, polygonal bore profile. Smaller version of P2000. Introduced 2005. Imported from Germany by Heckler & Koch, Inc.

Price: $919.00

HI-POINT FIREARMS MODEL 9MM COMPACT PISTOL

Caliber: 9mm Para., 8-shot magazine. **Barrel:** 3.5". **Weight:** 25 oz. **Length:** 6.75" overall. **Grips:** Textured plastic. **Sights:** Combat-style adjustable 3-dot system; low profile. **Features:** Single-action design; frame-mounted magazine release; polymer frame. Scratch-resistant matte finish. Introduced 1993. Comps are similar except they have a 4" barrel with muzzle brake/compensator. Compensator is slotted for laser or flashlight mounting. Introduced 1998. Made in U.S.A. by MKS Supply, Inc.

Price: C-9 9mm $155.00

Hi-Point Firearms Model 380 Polymer Pistol

Similar to the 9mm Compact model except chambered for 380 ACP, 8-shot magazine, adjustable 3-dot sights. Weighs 25 oz. Polymer frame. Action locks open after last shot. Includes 10-shot and 8-shot magazine; trigger lock. Introduced 1998. Comps are similar except they have a 4" barrel with muzzle compensator. Introduced 2001. Made in U.S.A. by MKS Supply, Inc.

Price: CF-380 . . . . $135.00

HI-POINT FIREARMS 40SW/POLY AND 45 AUTO PISTOLS

Caliber: 40 S&W, 8-shot magazine; 45 ACP (9-shot). **Barrel:** 4.5". **Weight:** 32 oz. **Length:** 7.72" overall. **Sights:** Adjustable 3-dot. **Features:** Polymer frames, last round lock-open, grip mounted magazine release, magazine disconnect safety, integrated accessory rail, trigger lock. Introduced 2002. Made in U.S.A. by MKS Supply, Inc.

Price: 40SW-B $186.00
Price: 45 ACP $186.00

HIGH STANDARD VICTOR 22 PISTOL

Caliber: 22 Long Rifle (10 rounds) or .22 Short (5 rounds). **Barrel:** 4.5"-5.5". **Weight:** 45 oz.-46 oz. **Length:** 8.5"-9.5" overall. **Grips:** Freestyle wood. **Sights:** Frame mounted, adjustable. **Features:** Semi-auto with drilled and tapped barrel, tu-tone or blued finish.

Price: $845.00

High Standard 10X Custom 22 Pistol

Similar to the Victor model but with precision fitting, black wood grips, 5.5" barrel only. High Standard Universal Mount, 10-shot magazine, barrel drilled and tapped, certificate of authenticity. Overall length is 9.5". Weighs 44 oz. to 46 oz. From High Standard Custom Shop.

Price: $1,095.00

HIGH STANDARD SUPERMATIC TROPHY 22 PISTOL

Caliber: 22 Long Rifle (10 rounds) or .22 Short (5 rounds/Citation version), not interchangable. **Barrel:** 5.5", 7.25". **Weight:** 44 oz., 46 oz. **Length:** 9.5", 11.25" overall. **Grips:** Wood. **Sights:** Adjustable. **Features:** Semi-auto with drilled and tapped barrel, tu-tone or blued finish with gold accents.

Price: 5.5" $845.00

High Standard Olympic Military 22 Pistol

Similar to the Supermatic Trophy model but in 22 Short only with 5.5" bull barrel, five-round magazine, aluminum alloy frame, adjustable sights. Overall length is 9.5", weighs 42 oz.

Price: $875.00

High Standard Supermatic Citation Series 22 Pistol

Similar to the Supermatic Trophy model but with heavier trigger pull, 10" barrel, and nickel accents. 22 Short conversion unit available. Overall length 14.5", weighs 52 oz.

Price: $895.00

HIGH STANDARD SUPERMATIC TOURNAMENT 22 PISTOL

Caliber: 22 LR. **Barrel:** 5.5" bull barrel. **Weight:** 44 oz. **Length:** 9.5" overall. **Features:** Limited edition; similar to High Standard Victor

model but with rear sight mounted directly to slide.
Price: **$835.00**

HIGH STANDARD SPORT KING 22 PISTOL
Caliber: 22 LR. **Barrel:** 4.5" or 6.75" tapered barrel. **Weight:** 40 oz. to 42 oz. **Length:** 8.5" to 10.75". **Features:** Sport version of High Standard Supermatic. Two-tone finish, fixed sights.
Price: **$725.00**

HI-STANDARD SPACE GUN
Semiauto pistol chambered in .22 LR. Recreation of famed competition "Space Gun" from 1960s. Features include 6.75- 8- or 10-inch barrel; 10-round magazine; adjustable sights; barrel weight; adjustable muzzle brake; blue-black finish with gold highlights.
Price: **$1095.00**

KAHR K SERIES AUTO PISTOLS
Caliber: K9: 9mm Para., 7-shot; K40: 40 S&W, 6-shot magazine. **Barrel:** 3.5". **Weight:** 25 oz. **Length:** 6" overall. **Grips:** Wraparound textured soft polymer. **Sights:** Blade front, rear drift adjustable for windage; bar-dot combat style. **Features:** Trigger-cocking double-action mechanism with passive firing pin block. Made of 4140 ordnance steel with matte black finish. Contact maker for complete price list. Introduced 1994. Made in U.S.A. by Kahr Arms.
Price: K9093C K9, matte stainless steel **$855.00**
Price: K9093NC K9, matte stainless steel w/tritium night sights **$985.00**
Price: K9094C K9 matte blackened stainless steel **$891.00**
Price: K9098 K9 Elite 2003, stainless steel **$932.00**
Price: K4043 K40, matte stainless steel **$855.00**
Price: K4043N K40, matte stainless steel w/tritium night sights **$985.00**
Price: K4044 K40, matte blackened stainless steel **$891.00**
Price: K4048 K40 Elite 2003, stainless steel **$932.00**

Kahr MK Series Micro Pistols
Similar to the K9/K40 except is 5.35" overall, 4" high, with a 3.08" barrel. Weighs 23.1 oz. Has snag-free bar-dot sights, polished feed ramp, dual recoil spring system, DA-only trigger. Comes with 5-round flush baseplate and 6-shot grip extension magazine. Introduced 1998. Made in U.S.A. by Kahr Arms.
Price: M9093 MK9, matte stainless steel .. **$855.00**
Price: M9093N MK9, matte stainless steel, tritium night sights **$958.00**
Price: M9098 MK9 Elite 2003, stainless steel **$932.00**
Price: M4043 MK40, matte stainless steel **$855.00**
Price: M4043N MK40, matte stainless steel, tritium night sights **$958.00**
Price: M4048 MK40 Elite 2003, stainless steel **$932.00**

KAHR P SERIES PISTOLS
Caliber: 380 ACP, 9x19, 40 S&W, 45 ACP. Similar to K9/K40 steel frame pistol except has polymer frame, matte stainless steel slide. Barrel length 3.5"; overall length 5.8"; weighs 17 oz. Includes two 7-shot magazines, hard polymer case, trigger lock. Introduced 2000. Made in U.S.A. by Kahr Arms.
Price: KP9093 9mm Para. **$739.00**
Price: KP4043 40 S&W **$739.00**
Price: KP4543 45 ACP **$805.00**
Price: KP3833 380 ACP (2008) **$649.00**

KAHR PM SERIES PISTOLS
Caliber: 9x19, 40 S&W, 45 ACP. Similar to P-Series pistols except has smaller polymer frame (Polymer Micro). Barrel length 3.08"; overall length 5.35"; weighs 17 oz. Includes two 7-shot magazines, hard polymer case, trigger lock. Introduced 2000. Made in U.S.A. by Kahr Arms.
Price: PM9093 PM9 .... **$786.00**
Price: PM4043 PM40 .... **$786.00**
Price: PM4543 (2007) **$855.00**

KAHR T SERIES PISTOLS
Caliber: T9: 9mm Para., 8-shot magazine; T40: 40 S&W, 7-shot magazine. **Barrel:** 4". **Weight:** 28.1-29.1 oz. **Length:** 6.5" overall. **Grips:** Checkered Hogue Pau Ferro wood grips. **Sights:** Rear: Novak low profile 2-dot tritium night sight, front tritium night sight. **Features:** Similar to other Kahr makes, but with longer slide and barrel upper, longer butt. Trigger cocking DAO; lock breech; "Browning-type" recoil lug; passive striker block; no magazine disconnect. Comes with two magazines. Introduced 2004. Made in U.S.A. by Kahr Arms.
Price: KT9093 T9 matte stainless steel **$831.00**
Price: KT9093-NOVAK T9, "Tactical 9," Novak night sight ... **$968.00**
Price: KT4043 40 S&W.............................. **$831.00**

KAHR TP SERIES PISTOLS
Caliber: TP9: 9mm Para., 7-shot magazine; TP40: 40 S&W, 6-shot magazine. Barrel: 4". **Weight:** 19.1-20.1 oz. **Length:** 6.5-6.7" overall. **Grips:** Textured polymer. Similar to T-series guns, but with polymer frame, matte stainless slide. Comes with two magazines. TP40s introduced 2006. Made in U.S.A. by Kahr Arms.
Price: TP9093 TP9 .... **$697.00**
Price: TP9093-Novak TP9 (Novak night sights) **$838.00**
Price: TP4043 TP40 .... **$697.00**
Price: TP4043-Novak (Novak night sights) . **$838.00**
Price: TP4543 (2007) **$697.00**
Price: TP4543-Novak (4.04 barrel, Novak night sights) **$838.00**

KAHR CW SERIES PISTOL
Caliber: 9mm Para., 7-shot magazine; 40 S&W and 45 ACP, 6-shot magazine. **Barrel:** 3.5-3.64". **Weight:** 17.7-18.7 oz. **Length:** 5.9-6.36" overall. **Grips:** Textured polymer. Similar to P-Series, but CW Series have conventional rifling, metal-injection-molded slide stop lever, no front dovetail cut, one magazine. CW40 introduced 2006. Made in U.S.A. by Kahr Arms.
Price: CW9093 CW9 .... **$549.00**
Price: CW4043 CW40 .... **$549.00**
Price: CW4543 45 ACP (2008) **$606.00**

KAHR P380
Very small double action only semiauto pistol chambered in .380 ACP. Features include 2.5-inch Lothar Walther barrel; black polymer frame with stainless steel slide; drift adjustable white bar/dot combat/sights; optional tritium sights; two 6+1 magazines. Overall length 4.9 inches, weight 10 oz. without magazine.
Price: Standard sights **$649.00**

KEL-TEC P-11 AUTO PISTOL
Caliber: 9mm Para., 10-shot magazine. **Barrel:** 3.1". **Weight:** 14 oz. **Length:** 5.6" overall. **Grips:** Checkered black polymer. **Sights:** Blade front, rear adjustable for windage. **Features:** Ordnance steel slide, aluminum frame. Double-action-only trigger mechanism. Introduced 1995. Made in U.S.A. by Kel-Tec CNC Industries, Inc.
Price: From **$333.00**

KEL-TEC PF-9 PISTOL
Caliber: 9mm Para.; 7 rounds. **Weight:** 12.7 oz. **Sights:** Rear sight adjustable for windage and elevation. **Barrel Length:** 3.1". **Length:** 5.85". **Features:** Barrel, locking system, slide stop, assembly pin, front sight, recoil springs and guide rod adapted from P-11. Trigger system with integral hammer block and the extraction system adapted from P-3AT. MIL-STD-1913 Picatinny rail. Made in U.S.A. by Kel-Tec CNC Industries, Inc.
Price: From **$333.00**

KEL-TEC P-32 AUTO PISTOL
Caliber: 32 ACP, 7-shot magazine. **Barrel:** 2.68". **Weight:** 6.6 oz. **Length:** 5.07" overall. **Grips:** Checkered composite. **Sights:** Fixed. **Features:** Double-action-only mechanism with 6-lb. pull; internal slide stop. Textured composite grip/frame. Now available in 380 ACP. Made in U.S.A. by Kel-Tec CNC Industries, Inc.
Price: From **$318.00**

KEL-TEC P-3AT PISTOL
Caliber: 380 ACP; 7-rounds. **Weight:** 7.2 oz. **Length:** 5.2". **Features:** Lightest 380 ACP made; aluminum frame, steel barrel.
Price: From **$324.00**

KEL-TEC PLR-16 PISTOL
Caliber: 5.56mm NATO; 10-round magazine. **Weight:** 51 oz. **Sights:** Rear sight adjustable for windage, front sight is M-16 blade. **Barrel Length:** 9.2". **Length:** 18.5". **Features:** Muzzle is threaded 1/2"-28 to accept standard attachments such as a muzzle brake. Except for the barrel, bolt, sights, and mechanism, the PLR-16 pistol is made of high-impact glass fiber reinforced polymer. Gas-operated semi-auto. Conventional gas-piston operation with M-16 breech locking system. MIL-STD-1913 Picatinny rail. Made in U.S.A. by Kel-Tec CNC Industries, Inc.
Price: Blued **$665.00**

Kel-Tec PLR-22 Pistol
Semi-auto pistol chambered in 22 LR; based on centerfire PLR-16 by same maker. Blowback action, 26-round magazine. Open sights and picatinny rail for mounting accessories; threaded muzzle. Overall length is 18.5", weighs 40 oz.
Price: **$390.00**

KIMBER CUSTOM II AUTO PISTOL
Caliber: 45 ACP. **Barrel:** 5". **Weight:** 38 oz. **Length:** 8.7" overall. **Grips:** Checkered black rubber, walnut, rosewood. **Sights:** Dovetailed front and rear, Kimber low profile adj. or fixed sights. **Features:** Slide, frame and barrel machined from steel or stainless steel. Match grade barrel, chamber and trigger group. Extended thumb safety, beveled magazine well, beveled front and rear slide serrations, high ride beavertail grip safety, checkered flat mainspring housing, kidney cut under trigger guard, high cut grip, match grade stainless steel barrel bushing, polished breech face, Commander-style hammer, lowered and flared ejection port, Wolff springs, bead blasted black oxide or matte stainless finish. Introduced in 1996. Made in U.S.A. by Kimber Mfg., Inc.
Price: Custom II **$828.00**
Price: Custom II Walnut (double-diamond walnut grips) **$872.00**

Kimber Stainless II Auto Pistols
Similar to Custom II except has stainless steel frame. 9mm Para. chambering and 45 ACP with night sights introduced 2008. Also chambered in 38 Super. Target version also chambered in 10mm.
Price: Stainless II 45 ACP **$964.00**
Price: Stainless II 9mm Para. (2008) **$983.00**
Price: Stainless II 45 ACP w/night sights (2008) **$1,092.00**
Price: Stainless II Target 45 ACP (stainless, adj. sight) **$942.00**

Kimber Pro Carry II Auto Pistol
Similar to Custom II, has aluminum frame, 4" bull barrel fitted directly to the slide without bushing. Introduced 1998. Made in U.S.A. by Kimber Mfg., Inc.
Price: Pro Carry II, 45 ACP **$888.00**
Price: Pro Carry II, 9mm **$929.00**
Price: Pro Carry II w/night sights **$997.00**

Kimber Compact Stainless II Auto Pistol
Similar to Pro Carry II except has stainless steel frame, 4-inch bbl., grip is .400" shorter than standard, no front serrations. Weighs 34 oz. 45 ACP only. Introduced in 1998. Made in U.S.A. by Kimber Mfg., Inc.
Price: **$1,009.00**

Kimber Ultra Carry II Auto Pistol
Lightweight aluminum frame, 3" match grade bull barrel fitted to slide without bushing. Grips .4" shorter. Low effort recoil. Weighs 25 oz. Introduced in 1999. Made in U.S.A. by Kimber Mfg., Inc.
Price: Stainless Ultra Carry II 45 ACP . . . **$980.00**
Price: Stainless Ultra Carry II 9mm Para. (2008) **$1,021.00**
Price: Stainless Ultra Carry II 45 ACP with night sights (2008) **$1,089.00**

Kimber Gold Match II Auto Pistol
Similar to Custom II models. Includes stainless steel barrel with match grade chamber and barrel bushing, ambidextrous thumb safety, adjustable sight, premium aluminum trigger, hand-checkered double diamond rosewood grips. Barrel hand-fitted for target accuracy. Made in U.S.A. by Kimber Mfg., Inc.
Price: Gold Match II **$1,345.00**
Price: Gold Match Stainless II 45 ACP **$1,519.00**
Price: Gold Match Stainless II 9mm Para. (2008) **$1,563.00**

Kimber Team Match II Auto Pistol
Similar to Gold Match II. Identical to pistol used by U.S.A. Shooting Rapid Fire Pistol Team, available in 45 ACP and 38 Super. Standard

features include 30 lines-per-inch front strap extended and beveled magazine well, red, white and blue Team logo grips. Introduced 2008.

Price: 45 ACP **$1,539.00**
Price: 9mm **$1,546.00**

Kimber CDP II Series Auto Pistol
Similar to Custom II, but designed for concealed carry. Aluminum frame. Standard features include stainless steel slide, fixed Meprolight tritium 3-dot (green) dovetail-mounted night sights, match grade barrel and chamber, 30 LPI front strap checkering, two-tone finish, ambidextrous thumb safety, hand-checkered double diamond rosewood grips. Introduced in 2000. Made in U.S.A. by Kimber Mfg., Inc.

Price: Ultra CDP II 9mm Para. (2008) **$1,359.00**
Price: Ultra CDP II 45 ACP **$1,318.00**
Price: Compact CDP II 45 ACP **$1,318.00**
Price: Pro CDP II 45 ACP. **$1,318.00**
Price: Custom CDP II (5" barrel, full length grip) **$1,318.00**

Kimber Eclipse II Series Auto Pistol
Similar to Custom II and other stainless Kimber pistols. Stainless slide and frame, black oxide, two-tone finish. Gray/black laminated grips. 30 lpi front strap checkering. All models have night sights; Target versions have Meprolight adjustable Bar/Dot version. Made in U.S.A. by Kimber Mfg., Inc.

Price: Eclipse Ultra II (3" barrel, short grip) **$1,236.00**
Price: Eclipse Pro II (4" barrel, full length grip) **$1,236.00**
Price: Eclipse Pro Target II (4" barrel, full length grip, adjustable sight) **$1,236.00**
Price: Eclipse Custom II 10mm **$1,291.00**
Price: Eclipse Target II (5" barrel, full length grip, adjustable sight) **$1,345.00**

KIMBER TACTICAL ENTRY II PISTOL
Caliber: 45 ACP, 7-round magazine. **Barrel:** 5". **Weight:** 40 oz. **Length:** 8.7" overall. **Features:** 1911-style semi auto with checkered frontstrap, extended magazine well, night sights, heavy steel frame, tactical rail.
Price: **$1,428.00**

KIMBER TACTICAL CUSTOM HD II PISTOL
Caliber: 45 ACP, 7-round magazine. **Barrel:** 5" match-grade. **Weight:** 39 oz. **Length:** 8.7" overall. **Features:** 1911-style semi auto with night sights, heavy steel frame.
Price: **$1,333.00**

KIMBER SIS AUTO PISTOL
Caliber: 45 ACP, 7-round magazine. **Barrel:** 3", ramped match grade. **Weight:** 31 oz. **Grips:** Stippled black laminate logo grips. **Sights:** SIS fixed tritium Night Sight with cocking shoulder. **Features:** Named for LAPD Special Investigation Section. Stainless-steel slides, frames and serrated mainspring housings. Flat top slide, solid trigger, SIS-pattern slide serrations, gray KimPro II finish, black small parts. Bumped and grooved beavertail grip safety, Kimber Service Melt on slide and frame edges, ambidextrous thumb safety, stainless steel KimPro Tac-Mag magazine. Rounded mainspring housing and frame on Ultra version. Introduced 2007. Made in U.S.A. by Kimber Mfg., Inc.

Price: SIS Ultra (2008) **$1,427.00**
Price: SIS Pro (2008) **$1,427.00**
Price: SIS Custom **$1,427.00**
Price: Custom/RL **$1,522.00**

KIMBER SUPER CARRY PRO
1911-syle semiauto pistol chambered in .45 ACP. Features include 8-round magazine; ambidextrous thumb safety; carry melt profiling; full length guide rod; aluminum frame with stainless slide; satin silver finish; super carry serrations; 4-inch barrel; micarta laminated grips; tritium night sights.
Price: **$1,530.00**

KIMBER CENTENNIAL EDITION 1911
Highly artistic 1911-style semiauto pistol chambered in .45 ACP. Features include color case-hardened steel frame; extended thumb safety; charcoal-blue finished steel slide; 5-inch match grade barrel; special serial number; solid smooth ivory grips; nitre blue pins; adjustable sights; presentation case. Edition limited to 250 units. Finished by Doug Turnbull Restoration.
Price: **$4,352.00**

KIMBER ULTRA CDP II
Compact 1911-syle semiauto pistol chambered in .45 ACP. Features include 7-round magazine; ambidextrous thumb safety; carry melt profiling; full length guide rod; aluminum frame with stainless slide; satin silver finish; checkered frontstrap; 3-inch barrel; rosewood double diamond Crimson Trace lasergrips grips; tritium 3-dot night sights.
Price: **$1,603.00**

KIMBER STAINLESS ULTRA TLE II
1911-syle semiauto pistol chambered in .45 ACP. Features include 7-round magazine; full length guide rod; aluminum frame with stainless slide; satin silver finish; checkered frontstrap; 3-inch barrel; tactical gray double diamond grips; tritium 3-dot night sights.
Price: **$1,210.00**

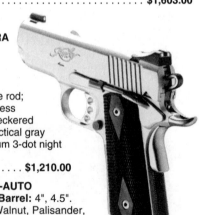

KORTH USA PISTOL SEMI-AUTO
Caliber: 9mm Para., 9x21. **Barrel:** 4", 4.5". **Weight:** 39.9 oz. **Grips:** Walnut, Palisander, Amboinia, Ivory. **Sights:** Fully adjustable. **Features:** DA/SA, 2 models available with either rounded or combat-style trigger guard, recoil-operated, locking block system, forged steel. Available finishes: High polish blue plasma, high polish or matted silver plasma, gray pickled

Prices given are believed to be accurate at time of publication however, many factors affect retail pricing so exact prices are not possible.

finish, or high polish blue. "Schalldampfer Modell" has special threaded 4.5" barrel and thread protector for a suppressor, many deluxe options available, 10-shot mag. From Korth USA.
Price: From **$15,000.00**

MAGNUM RESEARCH MICRO DESERT EAGLE PISTOL
Double action only semiauto pistol chambered in .380. Features include steel slide, aluminum allow frame, black polymer grips, nickel silver or blue anodized frame, 6-round capacity, fixed sights, 2.2-inch barrel. Weight less than 14 oz.
Price: **$535.00**

MAGNUM RESEARCH DESERT EAGLE MAGNUM PISTOL
Enormous gas-operated semiauto pistol chambered in .50 AE, .44 Magnum, .357 Magnum. Features include 6- or 10-inch barrel, adjustable sights, variety of finishes. Now made in the USA.
Price: . . . . **$1,650.00 to $2,156.00.**

MOSSBERG INTERNATIONAL MODELS 702 AND 802 PLINKSTER PISTOLS
Semiauto (702) or bolt action (802) pistols chambered in .22 LR. Features include black synthetic or laminated wood stock, 10-inch blued barrel, ergonomic grips, 10-shot detachable box magazine.
Price: . . . . **N/A**

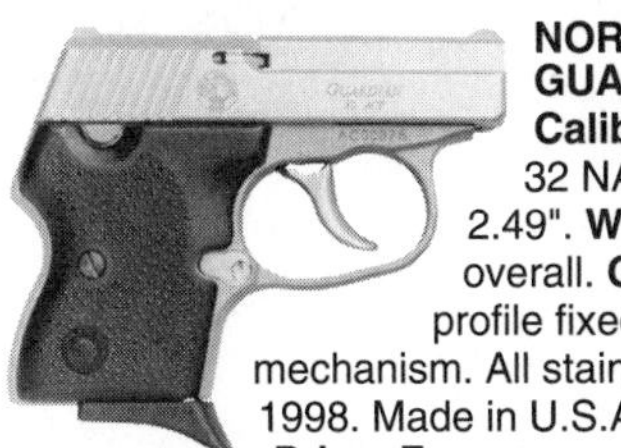

NORTH AMERICAN ARMS GUARDIAN DAO PISTOL
Caliber: 25 NAA, 32 ACP, 380 ACP, 32 NAA, 6-shot magazine. **Barrel:** 2.49". **Weight:** 20.8 oz. **Length:** 4.75" overall. **Grips:** Black polymer. **Sights:** Low profile fixed. **Features:** Double-action only mechanism. All stainless steel construction. Introduced 1998. Made in U.S.A. by North American Arms.
Price: From **$402.00**

OLYMPIC ARMS MATCHMASTER 5 1911 PISTOL
Caliber: 45 ACP, 7-shot magazine. **Barrel:** 5" stainless steel. **Weight:** 40 oz. **Length:** 8.75" overall. **Grips:** Smooth walnut with laser-etched scorpion icon. **Sights:** Ramped blade, LPA adjustable rear. **Features:** Matched frame and slide, fitted and head-spaced barrel, complete ramp and throat jobs, lowered and widened ejection port, beveled mag well, hand-stoned-to-match hammer and sear, lightweight long-shoe over-travel adjusted trigger, shaped and tensioned extractor, extended thumb safety, wide beavertail grip safety and full-length guide rod. Made in U.S.A. by Olympic Arms, Inc.
Price: **$903.00**

OLYMPIC ARMS MATCHMASTER 6 1911 PISTOL
Caliber: 45 ACP, 7-shot magazine. **Barrel:** 6" stainless steel. **Weight:** 44 oz. **Length:** 9.75" overall. **Grips:** Smooth walnut with laser-etched scorpion icon. **Sights:** Ramped blade, LPA adjustable rear. **Features:** Matched frame and slide, fitted and head-spaced barrel, complete ramp and throat jobs, lowered and widened ejection port, beveled mag well, hand-stoned-to-match hammer and sear, lightweight long-shoe over-travel adjusted trigger, shaped and tensioned extractor, extended thumb safety, wide beavertail grip safety and full length guide rod. Made in U.S.A. by Olympic Arms, Inc.
Price: **$973.00**

OLYMPIC ARMS ENFORCER 1911 PISTOL
Caliber: 45 ACP, 6-shot magazine. **Barrel:** 4" bull stainless steel. **Weight:** 35 oz. **Length:** 7.75" overall. **Grips:** Smooth walnut with etched black widow spider icon. **Sights:** Ramped blade front, LPA adjustable rear. **Features:** Compact Enforcer frame. Bushingless bull barrel with triplex counter-wound self-contained recoil system. Matched frame and slide, fitted and head-spaced barrel, complete ramp and throat jobs, lowered and widened ejection port, beveled mag well, hand-stoned-to-match hammer and sear, lightweight longshoe over-travel adjusted trigger, shaped and tensioned extractor, extended thumb safety, wide beavertail grip safety and full length guide rod. Made in U.S.A. by Olympic Arms.
Price: **$1,033.50**

OLYMPIC ARMS COHORT PISTOL
Caliber: 45 ACP, 7-shot magazine. **Barrel:** 4" bull stainless steel. **Weight:** 36 oz. **Length:** 7.75" overall. **Grips:** Fully checkered walnut. **Sights:** Ramped blade front, LPA adjustable rear. **Features:** Full size 1911 frame. Bushingless bull barrel with triplex counter-wound self-contained recoil system. Matched frame and slide, fitted and head-spaced barrel, complete ramp and throat jobs, lowered and widened ejection port, beveled mag well, hand-stoned-to-match hammer and sear, lightweight long-shoe over-travel adjusted trigger, shaped and tensioned extractor, extended thumb safety, wide beavertail grip safety and full length guide rod. Made in U.S.A. by Olympic Arms.
Price: **$973.70**

OLYMPIC ARMS BIG DEUCE PISTOL
Caliber: 45 ACP, 7-shot magazine. **Barrel:** 6" stainless steel. **Weight:** 44 oz. **Length:** 9.75" overall. **Grips:** Double diamond checkered exotic cocobolo wood. **Sights:** Ramped blade front, LPA adjustable rear. **Features:** Carbon steel parkerized slide with satin bead blast finish full size frame. Matched frame and slide, fitted and head-spaced barrel, complete ramp and throat jobs, lowered and widened

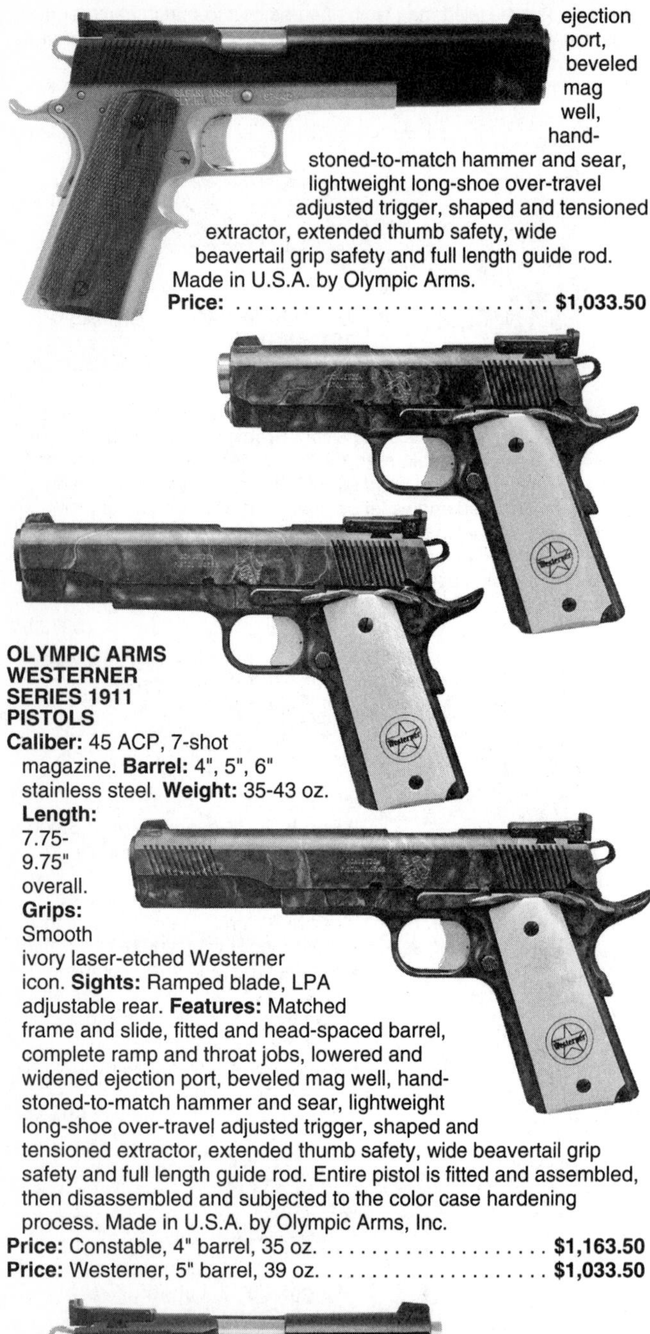

ejection port, beveled mag well, hand-stoned-to-match hammer and sear, lightweight long-shoe over-travel adjusted trigger, shaped and tensioned extractor, extended thumb safety, wide beavertail grip safety and full length guide rod. Made in U.S.A. by Olympic Arms.
Price: **$1,033.50**

OLYMPIC ARMS WESTERNER SERIES 1911 PISTOLS

Caliber: 45 ACP, 7-shot magazine. **Barrel:** 4", 5", 6" stainless steel. **Weight:** 35-43 oz. **Length:** 7.75-9.75" overall. **Grips:** Smooth ivory laser-etched Westerner icon. **Sights:** Ramped blade, LPA adjustable rear. **Features:** Matched frame and slide, fitted and head-spaced barrel, complete ramp and throat jobs, lowered and widened ejection port, beveled mag well, hand-stoned-to-match hammer and sear, lightweight long-shoe over-travel adjusted trigger, shaped and tensioned extractor, extended thumb safety, wide beavertail grip safety and full length guide rod. Entire pistol is fitted and assembled, then disassembled and subjected to the color case hardening process. Made in U.S.A. by Olympic Arms, Inc.
Price: Constable, 4" barrel, 35 oz. **$1,163.50**
Price: Westerner, 5" barrel, 39 oz. **$1,033.50**
Price: Trail Boss, 6" barrel, 43 oz. **$1,103.70**

OLYMPIC ARMS SCHUETZEN PISTOL WORKS 1911 PISTOLS

Caliber: 45 ACP, 7-shot magazine. **Barrel:** 4", 5.2", bull stainless steel. **Weight:** 35-38 oz. **Length:** 7.75-8.75" overall. **Grips:** Double diamond checkered exotic cocobolo wood. **Sights:** Ramped blade, LPA adjustable rear. **Features:** Carbon steel parkerized slide with satin bead blast finish full size frame. Matched frame and slide, fitted and head-spaced barrel, complete ramp and throat jobs, lowered and widened ejection port, beveled mag well, hand-stoned-to-match hammer and sear, lightweight long-shoe over-travel adjusted trigger, shaped and tensioned extractor, extended thumb safety, wide beavertail grip safety and full length guide rod. Custom made by Olympic Arms Schuetzen Pistol Works. Parts are hand selected and fitted by expert pistolsmiths. Several no-cost options to choose from. Made in U.S.A. by Olympic Arms Schuetzen Pistol Works.
Price: Journeyman, 4" bull barrel, 35 oz. **$1,293.50**
Price: Street Deuce, 5.2" bull barrel, 38 oz. **$1,293.50**

OLYMPIC ARMS OA-93 AR PISTOL

Caliber: 5.56 NATO. **Barrel:** 6.5" button-rifled stainless steel. **Weight:** 4.46 lbs. **Length:** 17" overall. **Sights:** None. **Features:** Olympic Arms integrated recoil system on the upper receiver eliminates the buttstock, flat top upper, free floating tubular match handguard, threaded muzzle with flash suppressor. Made in U.S.A. by Olympic Arms, Inc.
Price: **$1,202.50**

OLYMPIC ARMS K23P AR PISTOL

Caliber: 5.56 NATO. **Barrel:** 6.5" button-rifled chrome-moly steel. **Length:** 22.25" overall. **Weight:** 5.12 lbs. **Sights:** Adjustable A2 rear, elevation adjustable front post. **Features:** A2 upper with rear sight, free floating tubular match handguard, threaded muzzle with flash suppressor, receiver extension tube with foam cover, no bayonet lug. Made in U.S.A. by Olympic Arms, Inc. Introduced 2007.
Price: **$973.70**

OLYMPIC ARMS K23P-A3-TC AR PISTOL

Caliber: 5.56 NATO. **Barrel:** 6.5" button-rifled chrome-moly steel. **Length:** 22.25" overall. **Weight:** 5.12 lbs. **Sights:** Adjustable A2 rear, elevation adjustable front post. **Features:** Flat-top upper with detachable carry handle, free floating FIRSH rail handguard, threaded muzzle with flash suppressor, receiver extension tube with foam cover, no bayonet lug. Made in U.S.A. by Olympic Arms, Inc. Introduced 2007.
Price: **$1,118.20**

OLYMPIC ARMS WHITNEY WOLVERINE PISTOL

Caliber: 22 LR, 10-shot magazine. **Barrel:** 4.625" stainless steel. **Weight:** 19.2 oz. **Length:** 9" overall. **Grips:** Black checkered with fire/safe markings. **Sights:** Ramped blade front, dovetail rear. **Features:** Polymer frame with natural ergonomics and ventilated rib. Barrel with 6-groove 1x16 twist rate. All metal magazine shell. Made in U.S.A. by Olympic Arms.
Price: **$291.00**

PARA USA PXT 1911 SINGLE-ACTION SINGLE-STACK AUTO PISTOLS

Caliber: 38 Super, 9mm Para., 45 ACP. **Barrel:** 3.5", 4.25", 5". **Weight:** 28-40 oz. **Length:** 7.1-8.5" overall. **Grips:** Checkered cocobolo, textured composition, Mother of Pearl synthetic. **Sights:** Blade front, low-profile Novak Extreme Duty adjustable rear. High visibility 3-dot system. **Features:** Available with alloy, steel or stainless steel frames. Skeletonized trigger, spurred hammer. Manual thumb, grip and firing pin lock safeties. Full-length guide rod. PXT designates new Para Power Extractor throughout the line. Introduced 2004. Made in U.S.A. by Para USA.
Price: 1911 SSP 9mm Para. (2008) **$959.00**
Price: 1911 SSP 45 ACP (2008) **$959.00**

 Prices given are believed to be accurate at time of publication however, many factors affect retail pricing so exact prices are not possible.

PARA USA PXT 1911 SINGLE-ACTION HIGH-CAPACITY AUTO PISTOLS

Caliber: 9mm Para., 45 ACP, 10/14/18-shot magazines. **Barrel:** 3", 5". **Weight:** 34-40 oz. **Length:** 7.1-8.5" overall. **Grips:** Textured composition. **Sights:** Blade front, low-profile Novak Extreme Duty adjustable rear or fixed sights. High visibility 3-dot system. **Features:** Available with alloy, steel or stainless steel frames. Skeletonized match trigger, spurred hammer, flared ejection port. Manual thumb, grip and firing pin lock safeties. Full-length guide rod. Introduced 2004. Made in U.S.A. by Para USA.

Price: PXT P14-45 Gun Rights (2008), 14+1, 5" barrel **$1,149.00**
Price: P14-45 (2008), 14+1, 5" barrel **$919.00**

Para USA PXT Limited Pistols

Similar to the PXT-Series pistols except with full-length recoil guide system; fully adjustable rear sight; tuned trigger with over-travel stop; beavertail grip safety; competition hammer; front and rear slide serrations; ambidextrous safety; lowered ejection port; ramped match-grade barrel; dove-tailed front sight. Introduced 2004. Made in U.S.A. by Para USA.

Price: Todd Jarrett 40 S&W, 16+1, stainless **$1,729.00**

Para USA LDA Single-Stack Auto Pistols

Similar to LDA-series with double-action trigger mechanism. Cocobolo and polymer grips. Available in 45 ACP. Introduced 1999. Made in U.S.A. by Para USA.

Price: SSP, 8+1, 5" barrel **$899.00**

Para USA LDA Hi-Capacity Auto Pistols

Similar to LDA-series with double-action trigger mechanism. Polymer grips. Available in 9mm Para., 40 S&W, 45 ACP. Introduced 1999. Made in U.S.A. by Para USA.

Price: High-Cap 45, 14+1 .... **$1,279.00**

PARA USA WARTHOG

Caliber: 9mm Para., 45 ACP, 6, 10, or 12-shot magazines. **Barrel:** 3". **Weight:** 24 to 31.5 oz. **Length:** 6.5". **Grips:** Varies by model. **Features:** Single action. Big Hawg (2008) is full-size .45 ACP on lightweight alloy frame, 14+1, match grade ramped barrel, Power extractor, three white-dot fixed sights. Made in U.S.A. by Para USA.

Price: Slim Hawg (2006) single stack .45 ACP, stainless, 6+1 .... **$1,099.00**
Price: Nite Hawg .45 ACP, black finish, 10+1 .... **$1,099.00**
Price: Warthog .45 ACP, Regal finish, 10+1 ....**$959.00**
Price: Warthog Stainless **$1,069.00**
Price: Big Hawg (2008)...............................**$959.00**

PHOENIX ARMS HP22, HP25 AUTO PISTOLS

Caliber: 22 LR, 10-shot (HP22), 25 ACP, 10-shot (HP25). **Barrel:** 3". **Weight:** 20 oz. **Length:** 5.5" overall. **Grips:** Checkered composition. **Sights:** Blade front, adjustable rear. **Features:** Single action, exposed hammer; manual hold-open; button magazine release. Available in satin nickel, matte blue finish. Introduced 1993. Made in U.S.A. by Phoenix Arms.

Price: With gun lock **$130.00**
Price: HP Range kit with 5" bbl., locking case and accessories (1 Mag) **$171.00**
Price: HP Deluxe Range kit with 3" and 5" bbls., 2 mags, case **$210.00**

PICUDA .17 MACH-2 GRAPHITE PISTOL

Caliber: 17 HM2, 22 LR, 10-shot magazine. **Barrel:** 10" graphite barrel, "French grey" anodizing. **Weight:** 3.2 pounds. **Length:** 20.5" overall. **Grips:** Barracuda nutmeg laminated pistol stock. **Sights:** None, integral scope base. **Features:** MLP-1722 receiver, target trigger, match bolt kit. Introduced 2008. Made in U.S.A. by Magnum Research, Inc.

Price: **$699.00**

ROCK RIVER ARMS BASIC CARRY AUTO PISTOL

Caliber: 45 ACP. **Barrel:** NA. **Weight:** NA. **Length:** NA. **Grips:** Rosewood, checkered. **Sights:** dovetail front sight, Heinie rear sight. **Features:** NM frame with 20-, 25- or 30-LPI checkered front strap, 5-inch slide with double serrations, lowered and flared ejection port, throated NM Kart barrel with NM bushing, match Commander hammer and match sear, aluminum speed trigger, dehorned, Parkerized finish, one magazine, accuracy guarantee. 3.5 lb. Trigger pull. Introduced 2006. RRA Service Auto 9mm has forged NM frame with beveled mag well, fixed target rear sight and dovetail front sight, KKM match 1:32 twist 9mm Para. barrel with supported ramp. Guaranteed to shoot 1-inch groups at 25 yards with quality 9mm Para. 115-124 grain match ammunition. Intr. 2008. Made in U.S.A. From Rock River Arms.

Price: Basic Carry PS2700......................... **$1,600.00**
Price: Limited Match PS2400....................... **$2,185.00**
Price: RRA Service Auto 9mm Para. PS2715 .... **$1,790.00**

ROCK RIVER ARMS LAR-15/LAR-9 PISTOLS

Caliber: .223/5.56mm NATO chamber 4-shot magazine. **Barrel:** 7", 10.5" Wilson chrome moly, 1:9 twist, A2 flash hider, 1/2-28 thread. **Weight:** 5.1 lbs. (7" barrel), 5.5 lbs. (10.5" barrel). **Length:** 23" overall. Stock: Hogue rubber grip. **Sights:** A2 front. **Features:** Forged A2 or A4 upper, single stage trigger, aluminum free-float tube, one magazine. Similar 9mm Para. LAR-9 also available. From Rock River Arms, Inc.

Price: LAR-15 7" A2 AR2115 ....**$955.00**
Price: LAR-15 10.5" A4 AR2120........................**$945.00**
Price: LAR-9 7" A2 9MM2115....................... **$1,125.00**

ROHRBAUGH R9 SEMI-AUTO PISTOL

Caliber: 9mm Parabellum, 380 ACP. **Barrel:** 2.9". **Weight:** 12.8 oz. **Length:** 5.2" overall. **Features:** Very small double-action-only semi-auto pocket pistol. Stainless steel slide with matte black aluminum frame. Available with or without sights. Available with all-black (Stealth) and partial Diamond Black (Stealth Elite) finish.

Price: **$1,149.00**

RUGER SR9 AUTOLOADING PISTOL

Caliber: 9mm Para. **Barrel:** 4.14". **Weight:** 26.25, 26.5 oz. **Grips:** Glass-filled nylon in two color options—black or OD Green, w/flat or arched reversible backstrap. **Sights:** Adjustable 3-dot, built-in Picatinny-style rail. **Features:** Semi-DA, 6 configurations, striker-fired, through-hardened stainless steel slide, brushed or blackened stainless slide with black grip frame or blackened stainless slide with OD Green grip frame, ambi manual 1911-style safety, ambi mag release, mag disconnect, loaded chamber indicator, Ruger camblock design to absorb recoil, two 10 or 17-shot mags. Intr. 2008. Made in U.S.A. by Sturm, Ruger & Co.

Price: SR9 (17-Round), SR9-10 (SS) **$525.00**
Price: KBSR9 (17-Round), KBSR9-10 (Blackened SS) **$565.00**
Price: KODBSR9 (17-Round), KODBSR9-10 (OD Green Grip) **$565.00**

RUGER SR9C COMPACT PISTOL

Compact double action only semiauto pistol chambered in 9mm Parabellum. Features include 1911-style ambidextrous manual safety; internal trigger bar interlock and striker blocker; trigger safety; magazine disconnector; loaded chamber indicator; two magazines, one 10-round and the other 17-round; 3.5-inch barrel; 3-dot sights; accessory rail; brushed stainless or blackened allow finish. Weight 23.40 oz.

Price: **$525.00**

RUGER LCP

Caliber: .380 ACP. **Barrel:** 2.75" **Weight:** 9.4 oz. **Grips:** Glass-filled nylon. **Sights:** Fixed. **Features:** SA, one configuration, ultra-light compact carry pistol in Ruger's smallest pistol frame, through-hardened stainless steel slide, blued finish, lock breach design, 6-shot mag. Intr. 2008. Made in U.S.A. by Sturm, Ruger & Co.

Price: LCP. **$347.00**

RUGER P90 MANUAL SAFETY MODEL AUTOLOADING PISTOL

Caliber: 45 ACP, 8-shot magazine. **Barrel:** 4.50". **Weight:** 33.5 oz. **Length:** 7.75" overall. **Grips:** Grooved black synthetic composition. **Sights:** Square post front, square notch rear adjustable for windage, both with white dot. **Features:** Double action; ambidextrous slide-mounted safety-levers. Stainless steel only. Introduced 1991.

Price: KP90 with extra mag, loader, case and gunlock **$617.00**
Price: P90 (blue) **$574.00**

Ruger KP944 Autoloading Pistol

Sized midway between full-size P-Series and compact KP94. 4.2" barrel, 7.5" overall length, weighs about 34 oz. KP94 manual safety model. Slide gripping grooves roll over top of slide. KP94 has ambidextrous safety-levers; Stainless slide, barrel, alloy frame. Also blue. Includes hard case and lock, spare magazine. Introduced 1994. Made in U.S.A. by Sturm, Ruger & Co.

Price: P944, blue, manual safety, .40 cal. . . . **$541.00**
Price: KP944 (40-caliber) (manual safety-stainless) **$628.00**

RUGER P95 AUTOLOADING PISTOL

Caliber: 9mm, 15-shot magazine. **Barrel:** 3.9". **Weight:** 30 oz. **Length:** 7.25" overall. **Grips:** Grooved; integral with frame. **Sights:** Blade front, rear drift adjustable for windage; 3-dot system. **Features:** Molded polymer grip frame, stainless steel or chrome-moly slide. Suitable for +P+ ammunition. Safety model, decocker. Introduced 1996. Made in U.S.A. by Sturm, Ruger & Co. Comes with lockable plastic case, spare magazine, loader and lock, Picatinny rails.

Price: KP95PR15 safety model, stainless steel **$424.00**
Price: P95PR15 safety model, blued finish **$395.00**
Price: P95PR 10-round model, blued finish **$393.00**
Price: KP95PR 10-round model, stainless steel **$424.00**

RUGER 22 CHARGER PISTOL

Caliber: .22 LR. **Barrel:** 10". **Weight:** 3.5 lbs (w/out bi-pod). Stock: Black Laminate. **Sights:** None. **Features:** Rimfire Autoloading, one configuration, 10/22 action, adjustable bi-pod, new mag release for easier removal, precision-rifled barrel, black matte finish, combination Weaver-style and tip-off scope mount, 10-shot mag. Intr. 2008. Made in U.S.A. by Sturm, Ruger & Co.

Price: CHR22-10. . . . . **$380.00**

RUGER MARK III STANDARD AUTOLOADING PISTOL

Caliber: 22 LR, 10-shot magazine. **Barrel:** 4.5", 4.75", 5.5", 6", or 6-7/8". **Weight:** 33 oz. (4.75" bbl.). **Length:** 9" (4.75" bbl.). **Grips:** Checkered composition grip panels. **Sights:** Fixed, fiber-optic front, fixed rear. **Features:** Updated design of original Standard Auto and Mark II series. Hunter models have lighter barrels. Target models have cocobolo grips; bull, target, competition, and hunter barrels; and adjustable sights. Introduced 2005.

Price: MKIII4, MKIII6 (blued) **$352.00**
Price: MKIII512 (blued bull barrel) **$417.00**
Price: KMKIII512 (stainless bull barrel) **$527.00**
Price: MKIII678 (blued) **$417.00**
Price: KMKIII678GC (stainless slabside barrel) **$606.00**
Price: KMKIII678H (stainless fluted barrel) **$620.00**
Price: KMKIII45HCL (Crimson Trace Laser Grips, intr. 2008) . **$787.00**
Price: KMKIII454 (2009) **$620.00**

Ruger 22/45 Mark III Pistol

Similar to other 22 Mark III autos except has Zytel grip frame that matches angle and magazine latch of Model 1911 45 ACP pistol. Available in 4" standard, 4.5", 5.5", 6-7/8" bull barrels. Comes with extra magazine, plastic case, lock. Introduced 1992. Hunter introduced 2006.

Price: P4MKIII, 4" bull barrel, adjustable sights **$380.00**
Price: P45GCMKIII, 4.5" bull barrel, fixed sights **$380.00**
Price: P512MKIII (5.5" bull blued barrel, adj. sights) **$380.00**
Price: KP512MKIII (5.5" stainless bull barrel, adj. sights **$475.00**
Price: Hunter KP45HMKIII 4.5" barrel (2007), KP678HMKIII, 6-7/8" stainless fluted bull barrel, adj. sights **$562.00**

Prices given are believed to be accurate at time of publication however, many factors affect retail pricing so exact prices are not possible.

SABRE DEFENCE SPHINX PISTOLS

Caliber: 9mm Para., 45 ACP., 10-shot magazine. **Barrel:** 4.43". **Weight:** 39.15 oz. **Length:** 8.27" overall. **Grips:** Textured polymer. **Sights:** Fixed Trijicon Night Sights. **Features:** CNC engineered from stainless steel billet; grip frame in stainless steel, titanium or high-strength aluminum. Integrated accessory rail, high-cut beavertail, decocking lever. Made in Switzerland. Imported by Sabre Defence Industries.

Price: 45 ACP (2007) **$2,990.00**
Price: 9mm Para. Standard, titanium w/decocker **$2,700.00**

SEECAMP LWS 32/380 STAINLESS DA AUTO

Caliber: 32 ACP, 380 ACP Win. Silvertip, 6-shot magazine. **Barrel:** 2", integral with frame. **Weight:** 10.5 oz. **Length:** 4-1/8" overall. **Grips:** Glass-filled nylon. **Sights:** Smooth, no-snag, contoured slide and barrel top. **Features:** Aircraft quality 17-4 PH stainless steel. Inertia-operated firing pin. Hammer fired double-action-only. Hammer automatically follows slide down to safety rest position after each shot, no manual safety needed. Magazine safety disconnector. Polished stainless. Introduced 1985. From L.W. Seecamp.

Price: 32 . . . . **$446.25**
Price: 380 . . . . **$795.00**

SIG SAUER 250 COMPACT AUTO PISTOL

Caliber: 9mm Para. (16-round magazine), 357 SIG, 40 S&W and 45 ACP. **Barrel:** NA. **Weight:** 24.6 oz. **Length:** 7.2" overall. **Grips:** Interchangeable polymer. **Sights:** Siglite night sights. **Features:** Modular design allows for immediate change in caliber and size; subcompact, compact and full. Six different grip combinations for each size. Introduced 2008. From Sig Sauer, Inc.

Price: P250 . . . . **$750.00**

SIG SAUER 1911 PISTOLS

Caliber: 45 ACP, 8-shot magazine. **Barrel:** 5". **Weight:** 40.3 oz. **Length:** 8.65" overall. **Grips:** Checkered wood grips. **Sights:** Novak night sights. Blade front, drift adjustable rear for windage. **Features:** Single-action 1911. Hand-fitted dehorned stainless-steel frame and slide; match-grade barrel, hammer/sear set and trigger; 25-lpi front strap checkering, 20-lpi mainspring housing checkering. Beavertail grip safety with speed bump, extended thumb safety, firing pin safety and hammer intercept notch. Introduced 2005. XO series has contrast sights, Ergo Grip XT textured polymer grips. Target line features adjustable target night sights, match barrel, custom wood grips, non-railed frame in stainless or Nitron finishes. TTT series is two-tone 1911 with Nitron slide and black controls on stainless frame. Includes burled maple grips, adjustable combat night sights. STX line available from Sig Sauer Custom Shop; two-tone 1911, non-railed, Nitron slide, stainless frame, burled maple grips. Polished cocking serrations, flat-top slide, magwell. Carry line has Novak night sights, lanyard attachment point, gray diamondwood or rosewood grips, 8+1 capacity. Compact series has 6+1 capacity, 7.7" OAL, 4.25" barrel, slim-profile wood grips, weighs 30.3 oz. RCS line (Compact SAS) is Customs Shop version with anti-snag dehorning. Stainless or Nitron finish, Novak night sights, slim-profile gray diamondwood or rosewood grips. 6+1 capacity. 1911 C3 (2008) is a 6+1 compact .45

ACP, rosewood custom wood grips, two-tone and Nitron finishes. Weighs about 30 ounces unloaded, lightweight alloy frame. Length is 7.7". From SIG SAUER, Inc.

Price: Nitron **$1,200.00**
Price: Stainless. **$1,170.00**
Price: XO Black **$1,005.00**
Price: Target Nitron (2006) **$1,230.00**
Price: TTT (2006) **$1,290.00**
Price: STX (2006) **$1,455.00**
Price: Carry Nitron (2006). **$1,200.00**
Price: Compact Nitron. **$1,200.00**
Price: RCS Nitron **$1,305.00**
Price: C3 (2008) **$1,200.00**
Price: Platinum Elite **$1,275.00**
Price: Blackwater (2009) **$1,290.00**

SIG SAUER P220 AUTO PISTOLS

Caliber: 45 ACP, (7- or 8-shot magazine). **Barrel:** 4.4". **Weight:** 27.8 oz. **Length:** 7.8" overall. **Grips:** Checkered black plastic. **Sights:** Blade front, drift adjustable rear for windage. Optional Siglite night sights. **Features:** Double action. Stainless-steel slide, Nitron finish, alloy frame, M1913 Picatinny rail; safety system of decocking lever, automatic firing pin safety block, safety intercept notch, and trigger bar disconnector. Squared combat-type trigger guard. Slide stays open after last shot. Introduced 1976. P220 SAS Anti-Snag has dehorned stainless steel slide, front Siglite Night Sight, rounded trigger guard, dust cover, Custom Shop wood grips. Equinox line is Custom Shop product with Nitron stainless-steel slide with a black hard-anodized alloy frame, brush-polished flats and nickel accents. Truglo tritium fiber-optic front sight, rear Siglite night sight, gray laminated wood grips with checkering and stippling. From SIG SAUER, Inc.

Price: P220 Two-Tone, matte-stainless slide, black alloy frame. **$1,110.00**
Price: P220 Elite Stainless (2008) **$1,350.00**
Price: P220 Two-Tone SAO, single action (2006), from . . . **$1,086.00**
Price: P220 DAK (2006) **$853.00**
Price: P220 Equinox (2006) **$1,200.00**
Price: P220 Elite Dark (2009). **$1,200.00**
Price: P220 Elite Dark, threaded barrel (2009) **$1,305.00**

SIG SAUER P220 CARRY AUTO PISTOLS

Caliber: 45 ACP, 8-shot magazine. **Barrel:** 3.9". **Weight:** NA. **Length:** 7.1" overall. **Grips:** Checkered black plastic. **Sights:** Blade front, drift adjustable rear for windage. Optional Siglite night sights. **Features:** Similar to full-size P220, except is "Commander" size. Single stack, DA/SA operation, Nitron finish, Picatinny rail, and either post and dot contrast or 3-dot Siglite night sights. Introduced 2005. Many

variations availble. From SIG SAUER, Inc.
Price: P220 Carry, from . . . . **$975.00**; w/night sights **$1,050.00**
Price: P220 Carry Elite Stainless (2008) **$1,350.00**

SIG SAUER P229 DA Auto Pistol
Similar to the P220 except chambered for 9mm Para. (10- or 15-round magazines), 40 S&W, 357 SIG (10- or 12-round magazines). Has 3.86" barrel, 7.1" overall length and 3.35" height. Weight is 32.4 oz. Introduced 1991. Snap-on modular grips. Frame made in Germany, stainless steel slide assembly made in U.S.; pistol assembled in U.S. Many variations available. From SIG SAUER, Inc.
Price: P229, from . . . . **$975.00**; w/night sights **$1,050.00**
Price: P229 Platinum Elite (2008) **$1,275.00**

SIG SAUER P226 Pistols
Similar to the P220 pistol except has 4.4" barrel, measures 7.7" overall, weighs 34 oz. Chambered in 9mm, 357 SIG, or 40 S&W. X-Five series has factory tuned single-action trigger, 5" slide and bar- rel, ergonomic wood grips with beavertail, ambidextrous thumb safety and stainless slide and frame with magwell, low-profile adjustable target sights, front cocking serrations and a 25-meter factory test target. Many variations available. Snap-on modular grips. From SIG SAUER, Inc.
Price: P226, from **$975.00**
Price: P226 Blackwater Tactical (2009) **$1,300.00**

SIG SAUER SP2022 PISTOLS
Caliber: 9mm Para., 357 SIG, 40 S&W, 10-, 12-, or 15-shot magazines. **Barrel:** 3.9". **Weight:** 30.2 oz. **Length:** 7.4" overall. **Grips:** Composite and rubberized one-piece. **Sights:** Blade front, rear adjustable for windage. Optional Siglite night sights. **Features:** Polymer frame, stainless steel slide; integral frame accessory rail; replaceable steel frame rails; left- or right-handed magazine release, two interchangeable grips. From SIG SAUER, Inc.
Price: SP2009, Nitron finish **$613.00**

SIG SAUER P232 PERSONAL SIZE PISTOL
Caliber: 380 ACP, 7-shot. **Barrel:** 3.6". **Weight:** 17.6-22.4 oz. **Length:** 6.6" overall. **Grips:** Checkered black composite. **Sights:** Blade front, rear adjustable for windage. **Features:** Double action/single action or DAO. Blow-back operation, stationary barrel. Introduced 1997. From SIG SAUER, Inc.
Price: P232, from **$660.00**

SIG SAUER P238 PISTOL
Ultra-cool 1911-styled single action semiauto pistol chambered for .380 Auto. Features include 2.7-inch barrel; 6-round magazine; Siglite night sights or laser sights, polymer or wood grips; alloy frame; stainless slide; stainless, two-tone, rainbow or black nitride finish. Weight: 15.2 oz.
Price: **$643.00**

SIG SAUER P239 PISTOL
Caliber: 9mm Para., 8-shot, 357 SIG 40 S&W, 7-shot magazine. **Barrel:** 3.6". **Weight:** 25.2 oz. **Length:** 6.6" overall. **Grips:** Checkered black composite. **Sights:** Blade front, rear adjustable for windage. Optional Siglite night sights. **Features:** SA/DA or DAO; blackened stainless steel slide, aluminum alloy frame. Introduced 1996. Made in U.S.A. by SIG SAUER, Inc.
Price: P239, from **$840.00**

SIG SAUER MOSQUITO PISTOL
Caliber: 22 LR, 10-shot magazine. **Barrel:** 3.9". **Weight:** 24.6 oz. **Length:** 7.2" overall. **Grips:** Checkered black composite. **Sights:** Blade front, rear adjustable for windage. **Features:** Blowback operated, fixed barrel, polymer frame, slide-mounted ambidextrous safety. Introduced 2005. Made in U.S.A. by SIG SAUER, Inc.
Price: Mosquito, from **$375.00**

SIG SAUER P522 PISTOL
Semiauto blowback pistol chambered in .22 LR. Pistol version of SIG522 rifle. Features include a 10-inch barrel; lightweight polymer lower receiver with pistol grip; ambi mag catch; aluminum upper; faux gas valve; birdcage; 25-round magazine; quad rail or "clean" handguard; optics rail.
Price: . . . . **$572.00 to $643.00**

SMITH & WESSON M&P AUTO PISTOLS
Caliber: 9mm Para., 40 S&W, 357 Auto. **Barrel:** 4.25". **Weight:** 24.25 oz. **Length:** 7.5" overall. **Grips:** One-piece Xenoy, wraparound with straight backstrap. **Sights:** Ramp dovetail mount front; tritium sights optional; Novak Lo-mount Carry rear. **Features:** Zytel polymer frame, embedded stainless steel chassis; stainless steel slide and barrel, stainless steel structural components, black Melonite finish, reversible magazine catch, 3 interchangeable palmswell grip sizes, universal rail, sear deactivation lever, internal lock system, magazine disconnect. Ships with 2 magazines. Internal lock models available. Overall height: 5.5"; width: 1.2"; sight radius: 6.4". Introduced November 2005. 45 ACP version introduced 2007, 10+1 or 14+1 capacity. **Barrel:** 4.5". **Length:** 8.05". **Weight:** 29.6 ounces. **Features:** Picatinny-style equipment rail; black or bi-tone, dark-earth-brown frame. Bi-tone M&P45 includes ambidextrous,

 Prices given are believed to be accurate at time of publication however, many factors affect retail pricing so exact prices are not possible.

frame-mounted thumb safety, take down tool with lanyard attachment. Compact 9mm Para./357 SIG/40 S&W versions introduced 2007. Compacts have 3.5" barrel, OAL 6.7". 10+1 or 12+1 capacity. **Weight:** 21.7 ounces. **Features:** Picatinny-style equipment rail. Made in U.S.A. by Smith & Wesson.

Price: Full Size, from **$719.00**
Price: Compacts, from **$719.00**
Price: Midsize, from **$758.00**
Price: Crimson Trace Lasergrip models, from . . **$988.00**
Price: Thumb-safety M&P models, from **$719.00**

SMITH & WESSON PRO SERIES MODEL M&P40

Striker-fired DAO semiauto pistol chambered in .40 S&W. Features include 4.25- or 5-inch barrel, matte black polymer frame and stainless steel slide, tactical rail, Novak front and rear sights or two-dot night sights, polymer grips, 15+1 capacity.

Price: **$830.00**

Smith & Wesson Pro Series Model M&P9

Similar to M&P40 but chambered in 9mm Parabellum. Capacity 17+1, 4.25-inch barrel, two-dot night sights.

Price: **$830.00**

SMITH & WESSON MODEL 908 AUTO PISTOL

Caliber: 9mm Para., 8-shot magazine. **Barrel:** 3.5". **Weight:** 24 oz. **Length:** 6-13/16". **Grips:** One-piece Xenoy, wraparound with straight backstrap. **Sights:** Post front, fixed rear, 3-dot system. **Features:** Aluminum alloy frame, matte blue carbon steel slide; bobbed hammer; smooth trigger. Introduced 1996. Made in U.S.A. by Smith & Wesson.

Price: Model 908, black matte finish **$679.00**
Price: Model 908S, stainless matte finish **$679.00**
Price: Model 908S Carry Combo, with holster **$703.00**

SMITH & WESSON MODEL 4013TSW AUTO

Caliber: 40 S&W, 9-shot magazine. **Barrel:** 3.5". **Weight:** 26.8 oz. **Length:** 6 3/4" overall. **Grips:** Xenoy one-piece wraparound. **Sights:** Novak 3-dot system. **Features:** Traditional double-action system; stainless slide, alloy frame; fixed barrel bushing; ambidextrous decocker; reversible magazine catch, equipment rail. Introduced 1997. Made in U.S.A. by Smith & Wesson.

Price: Model 4013TSW **$1,027.00**

SMITH & WESSON MODEL 910 DA AUTO PISTOL

Caliber: 9mm Para., 10-shot magazine. **Barrel:** 4". **Weight:** 28 oz. **Length:** 7-3/8" overall. **Grips:** One-piece Xenoy, wraparound with straight backstrap. **Sights:** Post front with white dot, fixed 2-dot rear. **Features:** Alloy frame, blue carbon steel slide. Slide-mounted decocking lever. Introduced 1995.

Price: **$648.00**

SMITH & WESSON MODEL 3913 TRADITIONAL DOUBLE ACTIONS

Caliber: 9mm Para., 8-shot magazine. **Barrel:** 3.5". **Weight:** 24.8 oz. **Length:** 6.75" overall. **Grips:** One-piece Delrin wraparound, textured surface. **Sights:** Post front with white dot, Novak LoMount Carry with two dots. **Features:** TSW has aluminum alloy frame, stainless slide. Bobbed hammer with no half-cock notch; smooth .304" trigger with rounded edges. Straight backstrap. Equipment rail. Extra magazine included. Introduced 1989. The 3913-LS Ladysmith has frame that is upswept at the front, rounded trigger guard. Comes in frosted stainless steel with matching gray grips. Grips are ergonomically correct for a woman's hand. Novak LoMount Carry rear sight adjustable for windage. Extra magazine included. Introduced 1990.

Price: 3913TSW **$924.00**
Price: 3913-LS **$909.00**

SMITH & WESSON MODEL SW1911 PISTOLS

Caliber: 45 ACP, 8 rounds; 9mm, 11 rounds. **Barrel:** 5". **Weight:** 39 oz. **Length:** 8.7". **Grips:** Wood or rubber. **Sights:** Novak Lo-Mount Carry, white dot front. **Features:** Large stainless frame and slide with matte finish, single-side external safety. No. 108284 has adjustable target rear sight, ambidextrous safety levers, 20-lpi checkered front strap, comes with two 8-round magazines. DK model (Doug Koenig) also has oversized magazine well, Doug Koenig speed hammer, flat competition speed trigger with overtravel stop, rosewood grips with Smith & Wesson silver medallions, oversized magazine well, special serial number run. No. 108295 has olive drab Crimson Trace lasergrips. No. 108299 has carbon-steel frame and slide with polished flats on slide, standard GI recoil guide, laminated double-diamond walnut grips with silver Smith & Wesson medallions, adjustable target sights. Tactical Rail No. 108293 has a Picatinny rail, black Melonite finish, Novak Lo-Mount Carry Sights, scandium alloy frame. Tactical Rail Stainless introduced 2006. SW1911PD gun is Commander size, scandium-alloy frame, 4.25" barrel, 8" OAL, 28.0 oz., non-reflective black matte finish. Gunsite edition has scandium alloy frame, beveled edges, solid match aluminum trigger, Herrett's logoed tactical oval walnut stocks, special serial number run, brass bead Novak front sight. SC model has 4.25" barrel, scandium alloy frame, stainless-steel slide, non-reflective matte finish.

Price: From **$1,130.00**
Price: Crimson Trace Laser Grips **$1,493.00**

SMITH & WESSON MODEL 1911 SUB-COMPACT PRO SERIES

Caliber: 45 ACP, 7 + 1-shot magazine. **Barrel:** 3". **Weight:** 24 oz. **Length:** 6-7/8". **Grips:** Fully stippled synthetic. **Sights:** Dovetail white dot front, fixed white 2-dot rear. **Features:** Scandium frame with stainless steel slide, matte black finish throughout. Oversized external extractor, 3-hole curved trigger with overtravel stop, full-length guide rod, and cable lock. Introduced 2009.

Price: **$1,304.00**

SMITH & WESSON ENHANCED SIGMA SERIES DAO PISTOLS

Caliber: 9mm Para., 40 S&W; 10-, 16-shot magazine. **Barrel:** 4". **Weight:** 24.7 oz. **Length:** 7.25" overall. **Grips:** Integral. **Sights:** White dot front, fixed rear; 3-dot system. Tritium night sights available. **Features:** Ergonomic polymer frame; low barrel centerline; internal striker firing system; corrosion-resistant slide; Teflon-filled,

electroless-nickel coated magazine, equipment rail. Introduced 1994. Made in U.S.A. by Smith & Wesson.
Price: From **$482.00**

SMITH & WESSON MODEL CS9 CHIEF'S SPECIAL AUTO
Caliber: 9mm Para., 7-shot magazine. **Barrel:** 3". **Weight:** 20.8 oz. **Length:** 6.25" overall. **Grips:** Hogue wraparound rubber. **Sights:** White dot front, fixed 2-dot rear. **Features:** Traditional double-action trigger mechanism. Alloy frame, stainless slide. Ambidextrous safety. Introduced 1999. Made in U.S.A. by Smith & Wesson.
Price: Stainless **$782.00**

SMITH & WESSON MODEL CS45 CHIEF'S SPECIAL AUTO
Caliber: 45 ACP, 6-shot magazine. **Weight:** 23.9 oz. **Features:** Introduced 1999. Made in U.S.A. by Smith & Wesson.
Price: From **$787.00**

SPRINGFIELD ARMORY EMP ENHANCED MICRO PISTOL
Caliber: 9mm Para., 40 S&W; 9-round magazine. **Barrel:** 3" stainless steel match grade, fully supported ramp, bull. **Weight:** 26 oz. **Length:** 6.5" overall. **Grips:** Thinline cocobolo hardwood. **Sights:** Fixed low profile combat rear, dovetail front, 3-dot tritium. **Features:** Two 9-round stainless steel magazines with slam pads, long aluminum match-grade trigger adjusted to 5 to 6 lbs., forged aluminum alloy frame, black hardcoat anodized; dual spring full-length guide rod, forged satin-finish stainless steel slide. Introduced 2007. From Springfield Armory.
Price: 9mm Para. Compact Bi-Tone **$1,329.00**
Price: 40 S&W Compact Bi-Tone (2008) **$1,329.00**

SPRINGFIELD ARMORY XD POLYMER AUTO PISTOLS
Caliber: 9mm Para., 40 S&W, 45 ACP. **Barrel:** 3", 4", 5". **Weight:** 20.5-31 oz. **Length:** 6.26-8" overall. **Grips:** Textured polymer. **Sights:** Varies by model; Fixed sights are dovetail front and rear steel 3-dot units. **Features:** Three sizes in X-Treme Duty (XD) line: Sub-Compact (3" barrel), Service (4" barrel), Tactical (5" barrel). Three ported models available. Ergonomic polymer frame, hammer-forged barrel, no-tool disassembly, ambidextrous magazine release, visual/tactile loaded chamber indicator, visual/tactile striker status indicator, grip safety, XD gear system included. Introduced 2004. XD 45 introduced 2006. Compact line introduced 2007. Compacts ship with one extended magazine (13) and one compact magazine (10). From Springfield Armory.
Price: Sub-Compact OD Green 9mm Para./40 S&W, fixed sights **$543.00**
Price: Compact 45 ACP, 4" barrel, Bi-Tone finish (2008) **$589.00**
Price: Compact 45 ACP, 4" barrel, OD green frame, stainless slide (2008) **$653.00**
Price: Service Black 9mm Para./40 S&W, fixed sights **$543.00**
Price: Service Dark Earth 45 ACP, fixed sights **$571.00**

Price: Service Black 45 ACP, external thumb safety (2008) **$571.00**
Price: V-10 Ported Black 9mm Para./40 S&W **$573.00**
Price: Tactical Black 45 ACP, fixed sights **$616.00**
Price: Service Bi-Tone 40 S&W, Trijicon night sights (2008) .. **$695.00**

SPRINGFIELD ARMORY GI 45 1911A1 AUTO PISTOLS
Caliber: 45 ACP; 6-, 7-, 13-shot magazines. **Barrel:** 3", 4", 5". **Weight:** 28-36 oz. **Length:** 5.5-8.5" overall. **Grips:** Checkered double-diamond walnut, "U.S" logo. **Sights:** Fixed GI style. **Features:** Similar to WWII GI-issue 45s at hammer, beavertail, mainspring housing. From Springfield Armory.
Price: GI .45 4" Champion Lightweight, 7+1, 28 oz. **$619.00**
Price: GI .45 5" High Capacity, 13+1, 36 oz. **$676.00**
Price: GI .45 5" OD Green, 7+1, 36 oz. **$619.00**
Price: GI .45 3" Micro Compact, 6+1, 32 oz. **$667.00**

SPRINGFIELD ARMORY MIL-SPEC 1911A1 AUTO PISTOLS
Caliber: 38 Super, 9-shot magazines; 45 ACP, 7-shot magazines. **Barrel:** 5". **Weight:** 35.6-39 oz. **Length:** 8.5-8.625" overall. **Features:** Similar to GI 45s. From Springfield Armory.
Price: Mil-Spec Parkerized, 7+1, 35.6 oz. **$715.00**
Price: Mil-Spec Stainless Steel, 7+1, 36 oz. **$784.00**
Price: Mil-Spec 38 Super, 9+1, 39 oz. **$775.00**

Springfield Armory Custom Loaded Champion 1911A1 Pistol
Similar to standard 1911A1, slide and barrel are 4". 7.5" OAL. Available in 45 ACP only. Novak Night Sights. Delta hammer and cocobolo grips. Parkerized or stainless. Introduced 1989.
Price: Stainless, 34 oz. **$1,031.00**
Price: Lightweight, 28 oz. **$989.00**

Springfield Armory Custom Loaded Ultra Compact Pistol
Similar to 1911A1 Compact, shorter slide, 3.5" barrel, 6+1, 7" OAL. Beavertail grip safety, beveled magazine well, fixed sights. Videki speed trigger, flared ejection port, stainless steel frame, blued slide, match grade barrel, rubber grips. Introduced 1996. From Springfield Armory.
Price: Stainless Steel **$1,031.00**

SPRINGFIELD ARMORY CUSTOM LOADED MICRO-COMPACT 1911A1 PISTOL
Caliber: 45 ACP, 6+1 capacity. **Barrel:** 3" 1:16 LH. **Weight:** 24-32 oz. **Length:** 4.7". **Grips:** Slimline cocobolo. **Sights:** Novak LoMount

 Prices given are believed to be accurate at time of publication however, many factors affect retail pricing so exact prices are not possible.

tritium. Dovetail front. **Features:** Aluminum hard-coat anodized alloy frame, forged steel slide, forged barrel, ambi-thumb safety, Extreme Carry Bevel dehorning. Lockable plastic case, 2 magazines.
Price: Lightweight Bi-Tone **$992.00**

SPRINGFIELD ARMORY CUSTOM LOADED LONG SLIDE 1911A1 PISTOL
Caliber: 45 ACP, 7+1 capacity. **Barrel:** 6" 1:16 LH. **Weight:** 41 oz. **Length:** 9.5". **Grips:** Slimline cocobolo. **Sights:** Dovetail front; fully adjustable target rear. **Features:** Longer sight radius, 7.9".
Price: Bi-Tone Operator w/light rail **$1,189.00**

Springfield Armory Tactical Response Loaded Pistols
Similar to 1911A1 except 45 ACP only, checkered front strap and main-spring housing, Novak Night Sight combat rear sight and matching dove-tailed front sight, tuned, polished extractor, oversize barrel link; lightweight speed trigger and combat action job, match barrel and bushing, extended ambidextrous thumb safety and fitted beavertail grip safety. Checkered cocobolo wood grips, comes with two Wilson 7-shot magazines. Frame is engraved "Tactical" both sides of frame with "TRP." Introduced 1998. TRP-Pro Model meets FBI specifications for SWAT Hostage Rescue Team. From Springfield Armory.
Price: 45 TRP Service Model, black Armory Kote finish, fixed Trijicon night sights **$1,741.00**

SPRINGFIELD ARMORY XDM-3.8
Double action only semiauto pistol chambered in 9mm Parabellum (19+1) and .40 S&W (16+1). Features include 3.8-inch steel full-ramp barrel; dovetail front and rear 3-dot sights (tritium and fiber-optics sights available); polymer frame; stainless steel slide with slip-resistant slide serrations; loaded chamber indicator; grip safety. Black, bi-tone or stainless steel finish. Overall length 7 inches, weight 27.5 oz. (9mm). Also available with 4.5-inch barrel as Model XDM-4.5.
Price: . . . . **N/A**

STI LIMITED EDITION STI 20TH ANNIVERSARY PISTOL
1911-style semiauto pistol chambered in 9x19, .38 Super, .40 S&W, and .45 ACP to commemorate STI's 20th anniversary. Features include ambidextrous thumb safeties and knuckle relief high-rise beavertail grip safety; gold TiN (or Titanium Nitride) coating; full length steel bar stock slide with custom serrations specific to this model; 5-inch fully ramped and supported bull barrel; STI adjustable rear sight and a Dawson fiber optic front sight. STI will only build 200 of these pistols and the serial numbers reflect this (1 of 200, 2 of 200, etc.).
Price: . . . . **N/A**

STI DUTY ONE PISTOL
1911-style semiauto pistol chambered in .45 ACP. Features include government size frame with integral tactical rail and 30 lpi checkered frontstrap; milled tactical rail on the dust cover of the frame; ambidextrous thumb safeties; high rise beavertail grip safety; lowered and flared ejection port; fixed rear sight; front and rear cocking serrations; 5-inch fully supported STI International ramped bull barrel.
Price: . . . . **N/A**

STI APEIRO PISTOL
1911-style semiauto pistol chambered in 9x19, .40 S&W, and .45 ACP. Features include Schuemann "Island" barrel; patented modular steel frame with polymer grip; high capacity double-stack magazine; stainless steel ambidextrous thumb safeties and knuckle relief high-rise beavertail grip safety; unique sabertooth rear cocking serrations; 5-inch fully ramped, fully supported "island" bull barrel, with the sight milled in to allow faster recovery to point of aim; custom engraving on the polished sides of the (blued) stainless steel slide; stainless steel magwell; STI adjustable rear sight and Dawson fiber optic front sight; blued frame.
Price: . . . . **N/A**

STI EAGLE PISTOL
1911-style semiauto pistol chambered in .45 ACP, 9mm, .40 S&W. Features include modular steel frame with polymer grip; high capacity doule-stack magazines; scalloped slide with front and rear cocking serrations; dovetail front sight and STI adjustable rear sight; stainless steel STI hi-ride grip safety and stainless steel STI ambi-thumb safety; 5- or 6-inch STI stainless steel fully supported, ramped bull barrel or the traditional bushing barrel; blued or stainless finish.
Price: . . . . **N/A**

STI ECLIPSE PISTOL
Compact 1911-tyle semiauto pistol chambered in 9x19, .40 S&W, and .45 ACP. Features include 3-inch slide with rear cocking serrations, oversized ejection port; 2-dot tritium night sights recessed into the slide; high-capacity polymer grip; single sided blued thumb safety; bobbed, high-rise, blued, knuckle relief beavertail grip safety; 3-inch barrel.
Price: . . . . **N/A**

STI ESCORT PISTOL
Similar to STI Eclipse but with aluminum allow frame and chambered in .45 ACP only.
Price: . . . . **N/A**

TAURUS MODEL 800 SERIES
Caliber: 9mm Para., 40 S&W, 45 ACP. **Barrel:** 4". **Weight:** 32 oz. **Length:** 8.25". **Grips:** Checkered. **Sights:** Novak. **Features:** DA/SA. Blue and Stainless Steel finish. Introduced in 2007. Imported from Brazil by Taurus International.
Price: 809B, 9mm Para., Blue, 17+1 . . . . **$623.00**

TAURUS MODEL 1911
Caliber: 45 ACP, 8+1 capacity. **Barrel:** 5". **Weight:** 33 oz. **Length:** 8.5". **Grips:** Checkered black. **Sights:** Heinie straight 8. **Features:** SA. Blue, stainless steel, duotone blue, and blue/gray finish.

Prices given are believed to be accurate at time of publication however, many factors affect retail pricing so exact prices are not possible.

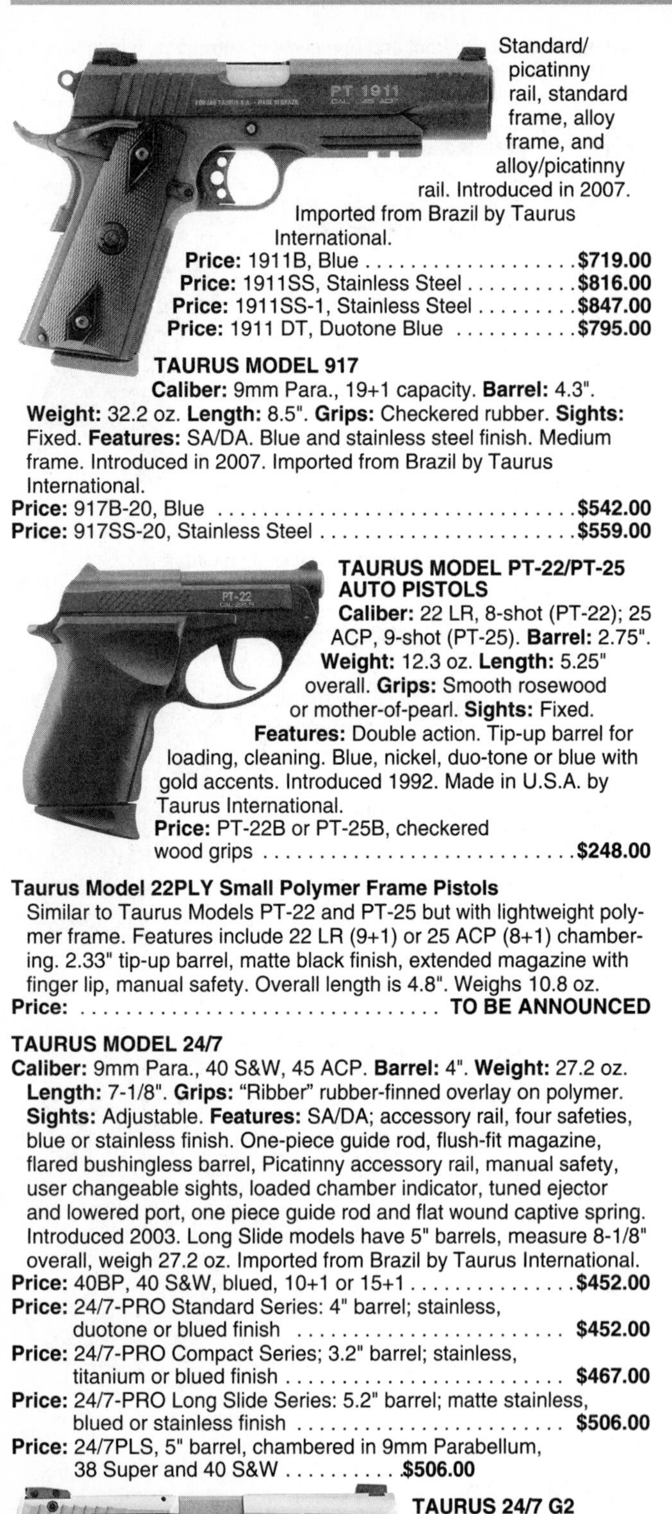

Standard/ picatinny rail, standard frame, alloy frame, and alloy/picatinny rail. Introduced in 2007. Imported from Brazil by Taurus International.

Price: 1911B, Blue **$719.00**
Price: 1911SS, Stainless Steel **$816.00**
Price: 1911SS-1, Stainless Steel **$847.00**
Price: 1911 DT, Duotone Blue **$795.00**

TAURUS MODEL 917

Caliber: 9mm Para., 19+1 capacity. **Barrel:** 4.3". **Weight:** 32.2 oz. **Length:** 8.5". **Grips:** Checkered rubber. **Sights:** Fixed. **Features:** SA/DA. Blue and stainless steel finish. Medium frame. Introduced in 2007. Imported from Brazil by Taurus International.

Price: 917B-20, Blue **$542.00**
Price: 917SS-20, Stainless Steel **$559.00**

TAURUS MODEL PT-22/PT-25 AUTO PISTOLS

Caliber: 22 LR, 8-shot (PT-22); 25 ACP, 9-shot (PT-25). **Barrel:** 2.75". **Weight:** 12.3 oz. **Length:** 5.25" overall. **Grips:** Smooth rosewood or mother-of-pearl. **Sights:** Fixed. **Features:** Double action. Tip-up barrel for loading, cleaning. Blue, nickel, duo-tone or blue with gold accents. Introduced 1992. Made in U.S.A. by Taurus International.

Price: PT-22B or PT-25B, checkered wood grips **$248.00**

Taurus Model 22PLY Small Polymer Frame Pistols

Similar to Taurus Models PT-22 and PT-25 but with lightweight polymer frame. Features include 22 LR (9+1) or 25 ACP (8+1) chambering. 2.33" tip-up barrel, matte black finish, extended magazine with finger lip, manual safety. Overall length is 4.8". Weighs 10.8 oz.

Price: . . . . **TO BE ANNOUNCED**

TAURUS MODEL 24/7

Caliber: 9mm Para., 40 S&W, 45 ACP. **Barrel:** 4". **Weight:** 27.2 oz. **Length:** 7-1/8". **Grips:** "Ribber" rubber-finned overlay on polymer. **Sights:** Adjustable. **Features:** SA/DA; accessory rail, four safeties, blue or stainless finish. One-piece guide rod, flush-fit magazine, flared bushingless barrel, Picatinny accessory rail, manual safety, user changeable sights, loaded chamber indicator, tuned ejector and lowered port, one piece guide rod and flat wound captive spring. Introduced 2003. Long Slide models have 5" barrels, measure 8-1/8" overall, weigh 27.2 oz. Imported from Brazil by Taurus International.

Price: 40BP, 40 S&W, blued, 10+1 or 15+1 . . . . **$452.00**
Price: 24/7-PRO Standard Series: 4" barrel; stainless, duotone or blued finish **$452.00**
Price: 24/7-PRO Compact Series; 3.2" barrel; stainless, titanium or blued finish **$467.00**
Price: 24/7-PRO Long Slide Series: 5.2" barrel; matte stainless, blued or stainless finish **$506.00**
Price: 24/7PLS, 5" barrel, chambered in 9mm Parabellum, 38 Super and 40 S&W **$506.00**

TAURUS 24/7 G2

Double/single action semiauto pistol chambered in 9mm Parabellum (15+1), .40 S&W (13+1), and .45 ACP (10+1). Features include blued or stainless finish; "Strike Two" capability; new trigger safety; low-profile adjustable rear sights for windage and elevation; ambidextrous magazine release; 4.2-inch barrel; Picatinny rail; polymer frame; polymer grip with metallic inserts and three interchangeable backstraps. Also offered in compact model with shorter grip frame and 3.5-inch barrel.

Price: . . . . **N/A**

Taurus Model 2045 Large Frame Pistol

Similar to Taurus Model 24/7 but chambered in 45 ACP only. Features include polymer frame, blued or matte stainless steel slide, 4.2" barrel, ambidextrous "memory pads" to promote safe finger position during loading, ambi three-position safety/decocker. Picatinny rail system, fixed sights. Overall length is 7.34". Weighs 31.5 oz.

Price: **$577.00**

TAURUS MODEL 58 PISTOL

Caliber: 380 ACP (19+1). **Barrel:** 3.25. **Weight:** 18.7 oz. **Length:** 6.125" overall. **Grips:** Polymer. **Sights:** Fixed. **Features:** SA/DA semi-auto. Scaled-down version of the full-size Model 92; steel slide, alloy frame, frame-mounted ambi safety, blued or stainless finish, and extended magazine.

Price: 58HCB **$602.00**
Price: 58HCSS **$617.00**

TAURUS MODEL 92 AUTO PISTOL

Caliber: 9mm Para., 10- or 17-shot mags. **Barrel:** 5". **Weight:** 34 oz. **Length:** 8.5" overall. **Grips:** Checkered rubber, rosewood, mother-of-pearl. **Sights:** Fixed notch rear. 3-dot sight system. Also offered with micrometer-click adjustable night sights. **Features:** Double action, ambidextrous 3-way hammer drop safety, allows cocked & locked carry. Blue, stainless steel, blue with gold highlights, stainless steel with gold highlights, forged aluminum frame, integral key-lock. .22 LR conversion kit available. Imported from Brazil by Taurus International.

Price: 92B **$542.00**
Price: 92SS **$559.00**

Taurus Model 99 Auto Pistol

Similar to Model 92, fully adjustable rear sight.

Price: 99B **$559.00**

Taurus Model 90-Two Semi-Auto Pistol

Similar to Model 92 but with one-piece wraparound grips, automatic disassembly latch, internal recoil buffer, addition slide serrations, picatinny rail with removable cover, 10- and 17-round magazine (9mm) or 10- and 12-round magazines (40 S&W). Overall length is 8.5". Weight is 32.5 oz.

Price: **$725.00**

TAURUS MODEL 100/101 AUTO PISTOL

Caliber: 40 S&W, 10- or 11-shot mags. **Barrel:** 5". **Weight:** 34 oz. **Length:** 8.5". **Grips:** Checkered rubber, rosewood, mother-of-pearl. **Sights:** 3-dot fixed or adjustable; night sights available. **Features:** Single/double action with three-position safety/decocker. Reintroduced in 2001. Imported by Taurus International.

Price: 100B **$542.00**

TAURUS MODEL 111 MILLENNIUM PRO AUTO PISTOL

Caliber: 9mm Para., 10- or 12-shot mags. **Barrel:** 3.25". **Weight:** 18.7 oz. **Length:** 6-1/8" overall. **Grips:** Checkered polymer. **Sights:** 3-dot fixed; night sights available. Low profile, 3-dot combat. **Features:** Double action only, polymer frame, matte stainless or blue steel slide, manual safety, integral key-lock. Deluxe models with wood grip inserts.

Price: 111BP, 111BP-12. . . . . **$419.00**
Price: 111PTi titanium slide **$592.00**

TAURUS 132 MILLENNIUM PRO AUTO PISTOL

Caliber: 32 ACP, 10-shot mag. **Barrel:** 3.25". **Weight:** 18.7 oz. **Grips:** Polymer. **Sights:** 3-dot fixed; night sights available. **Features:** Double-action-only, polymer frame, matte stainless or blue steel slide, manual safety, integral key-lock action. Introduced 2001.

Price: 132BP. **$419.00**

Prices given are believed to be accurate at time of publication however, many factors affect retail pricing so exact prices are not possible.

TAURUS 138 MILLENNIUM PRO SERIES
Caliber: 380 ACP, 10- or 12-shot mags. **Barrel:** 3.25". **Weight:** 18.7 oz. **Grips:** Polymer. **Sights:** Fixed 3-dot fixed. **Features:** Double-action-only, polymer frame, matte stainless or blue steel slide, manual safety, integral key-lock.
Price: 138BP **$419.00**

TAURUS 140 MILLENNIUM PRO AUTO PISTOL
Caliber: 40 S&W, 10-shot mag. **Barrel:** 3.25". **Weight:** 18.7 oz. **Grips:** Checkered polymer. **Sights:** 3-dot fixed; night sights available. **Features:** Double action only; matte stainless or blue steel slide, black polymer frame, manual safety, integral key-lock action. From Taurus International.
Price: 140BP **$436.00**

TAURUS 145 MILLENNIUM PRO AUTO PISTOL
Caliber: 45 ACP, 10-shot mag. **Barrel:** 3.27". **Weight:** 23 oz. Stock: Checkered polymer. **Sights:** 3-dot fixed; night sights available. **Features:** Double-action only, matte stainless or blue steel slide, black polymer frame, manual safety, integral key-lock. Compact model is 6+1 with a 3.25" barrel, weighs 20.8 oz. From Taurus International.
Price: 145BP, blued **$436.00**
Price: 145SSP, stainless, ... **$453.00**

Taurus Model 609Ti-Pro
Similar to other Millennium Pro models but with titanium slide. Chambered in 9mm Parabellum. Weighs 19.7 oz. Overall length is 6.125". Features include 13+1 capacity, 3.25" barrel, checkered polymer grips, and Heinie Straight-8 sights.
Price: **$608.00**

TAURUS SLIM 700 SERIES
Compact double/single action semiauto pistol chambered in 9mm Parabellum (7+1), .40 S&W (6+1), and .380 ACP (7+1). Features include polymer frame; blue or stainless slide; single action/double action trigger pull; low-profile fixed sights. Weight 19 oz., length 6.24 inches, width less than an inch.
Price: . . . . **N/A**

TAURUS MODEL 738 TCP COMPACT PISTOL
Caliber: 380 ACP, 6+1 (standard magazine) or 8+1 (extended magazine). **Barrel:** 3.3". **Weight:** 9 oz. (titanium slide) to 10.2 oz. **Length:** 5.19". **Sights:** Low-profile fixed. **Features:** Lightweight DAO semi-auto with polymer frame; blued (738B), stainless (738SS) or titanium (738Ti) slide; concealed hammer; ambi safety; loaded chamber indicator.
Price: . . . . **$623.00 to $686.00**

TAURUS 800 SERIES COMPACT
Compact double/single action semiauto pistol chambered in 9mm (12+1), .357 SIG (10+1) and .40 cal (10+1). Features include 3.5-inch barrel; external hammer; loaded chamber indicator; polymer frame; blued or stainless slide.
Price: . . . . **N/A**

TAURUS 822
Compact double/single action semiauto pistol chambered in .22 LR (10+1). Features include ambidextrous magazine release; external hammer; checkered grip; adjustable sights; 4.5-inch or 6-inch barrel; loaded chamber indicator; and Picatinny rail. Centerfire-to-rimfire conversion kit also available.
Price: . . . . **N/A**

TAURUS MODEL 911B AUTO PISTOL
Caliber: 9mm Para., 10-shot mag. **Barrel:** 4". **Weight:** 28.2 oz. **Length:** 7" overall. **Grips:** Checkered rubber, rosewood, mother-of-pearl. **Sights:** Fixed, 3-dot blue or stainless; night sights optional. **Features:** Double action, semi-auto ambidextrous 3-way hammer drop safety, allows cocked & locked carry. Blue, stainless steel, blue with gold highlights, or stainless steel with gold highlights, forged aluminum frame, integral key-lock.
Price: From **$584.00**

TAURUS MODEL 940B AUTO PISTOL
Caliber: 40 S&W, 10-shot mag. **Barrel:** 3-5/8". **Weight:** 28.2 oz. **Length:** 7" overall. **Grips:** Checkered rubber, rosewood or mother-of-pearl. **Sights:** Fixed, 3-dot blue or stainless; night sights optional. **Features:** Double action, semi-auto ambidextrous 3-way hammer drop safety, allows cocked & locked carry. Blue, stainless steel, blue with gold highlights, or stainless steel with gold highlights, forged aluminum frame, integral key-lock.
Price: From **$584.00**

TAURUS MODEL 945B/38S SERIES
Caliber: 45 ACP, 8-shot mag. **Barrel:** 4.25". **Weight:** 28.2/29.5 oz. **Length:** 7.48" overall. **Grips:** Checkered rubber, rosewood or mother-of-pearl. **Sights:** Fixed, 3-dot; night sights optional. **Features:** Double-action with ambidextrous 3-way hammer drop safety allows cocked & locked carry. Forged aluminum frame, 945C has ported barrel/slide. Blue, stainless, blue with gold highlights, stainless with gold highlights, integral key-lock. Introduced 1995. 38 Super line based on 945 frame introduced 2005. 38S series is 10+1, 30 oz., 7.5" overall. Imported by Taurus International.
Price: From **$625.00**

THOMPSON CUSTOM 1911A1 AUTOMATIC PISTOL
Caliber: 45 ACP, 7-shot magazine. **Barrel:** 4.3". **Weight:** 34 oz. **Length:** 8" overall. **Grips:** Checkered laminate grips with a Thompson bullet logo inlay. **Sights:** Front and rear sights are black with serrations and are dovetailed into the slide. **Features:** Machined from 420 stainless steel, matte finish. Thompson bullet logo on slide. Flared ejection port, angled front and rear serrations on slide, 20-lpi checkered mainspring housing and frontstrap. Adjustable trigger, combat hammer, stainless steel full-length recoil guide rod, extended beavertail grip safety; extended magazine release; checkered slide-stop lever. Made in U.S.A. by Kahr Arms.
Price: 1911TC, 5", 39 oz., 8.5" overall, stainless frame **$813.00**

THOMPSON TA5 1927A-1 LIGHTWEIGHT DELUXE PISTOL
Caliber: 45 ACP, 50-round drum magazine. **Barrel:** 10.5" 1:16 right-hand twist. **Weight:** 94.5 oz. **Length:** 23.3" overall. **Grips:** Walnut, horizontal foregrip **Sights:** Blade front, open rear adjustable. **Features:** Based on Thompson machine gun design. Introduced 2008. Made in U.S.A. by Kahr Arms.
Price: TA5 (2008) **$1,237.00**

U.S. FIRE ARMS 1910 COMMERCIAL MODEL AUTOMATIC PISTOL

Caliber: 45 ACP, 7-shot magazine. **Barrel:** 5". **Weight:** NA. **Length:** NA. **Grips:** Browning original wide design, full checkered diamond walnut grips. **Sights:** Fixed. **Features:** High polish Armory Blue, fire blue appointments, 1905

Prices given are believed to be accurate at time of publication however, many factors affect retail pricing so exact prices are not possible.

patent dates, grip safety, small contoured checkered thumb safety and round 1905 fire blue hammer with hand cut checkering. Introduced 2006. Made in U.S.A. by United States Fire Arms Mfg. Co.
Price: **$1,895.00**

U.S. FIRE ARMS 1911 MILITARY MODEL AUTOMATIC PISTOL
Caliber: 45 ACP, 7-shot magazine. **Barrel:** 5". **Weight:** NA. **Length:** NA. **Grips:** Browning original wide design, full checkered diamond walnut grips. **Sights:** Fixed. **Features:** Military polish Armory Blue, fire blue appointments, 1905 patent dates, grip safety, small contoured checkered thumb safety and round 1905 fire blue hammer with hand cut checkering. Introduced 2006. Made in U.S.A. by United States Fire Arms Mfg. Co.
Price: **$1,895.00**

U.S. FIRE ARMS SUPER 38 AUTOMATIC PISTOL
Caliber: 38 Auto, 9-shot magazine. **Barrel:** 5". **Weight:** NA. **Length:** NA. **Grips:** Browning original wide design, full checkered diamond walnut grips. **Sights:** Fixed. **Features:** Armory blue, fire blue appointments, 1913 patent date, grip safety, small contoured checkered thumb safety and spur 1911 hammer with hand cut checkering. Supplied with two Super 38 Auto. mags. Super .38 roll mark on base. Introduced 2006. Made in U.S.A. by United States Fire Arms Mfg. Co.
Price: **$1,895.00**

U.S. FIRE ARMS ACE .22 LONG RIFLE AUTOMATIC PISTOL
Caliber: 22 LR, 10-shot magazine. **Barrel:** 5". **Weight:** NA. **Length:** NA. **Grips:** Browning original wide design, full checkered diamond walnut grips. **Sights:** Fixed. **Features:** Armory blue commercial finish, fire blue appointments, 1913 patent date, grip safety, small contoured checkered thumb safety and spur 1911 hammer with hand cut checkering. Supplied with two magazines. Ace roll mark on base. Introduced 2006. Made in U.S.A. by United States Fire Arms Mfg. Co.
Price: **$1,995.00**

WALTHER PPS PISTOL
Caliber: 9mm Para., 40 S&W. 6-, 7-, 8-shot magazines for 9mm Para.; 5-, 6-, 7-shot magazines for 40 S&W. **Barrel:** 3.2". **Weight:** 19.4 oz. **Length:** 6.3" overall. Stocks: Stippled black polymer. **Sights:** Picatinny-style accessory rail, 3-dot low-profile contoured sight. **Features:** PPS-"Polizeipistole Schmal," or Police Pistol Slim. Measures 1.04 inches wide. Ships with 6- and 7-round magazines. Striker-fired action, flat slide stop lever, alternate backstrap sizes. QuickSafe feature decocks striker assembly when backstrap is removed. Loaded chamber indicator. First Edition model, limited to 1,000 units, has anthracite grey finish, aluminum gun case. Introduced 2008. Made in U.S.A. by Smith & Wesson.
Price: **$713.00**
Price: First Edition. **$665.00**

WALTHER PPK/S AMERICAN AUTO PISTOL
Caliber: 32 ACP, 380 ACP, 7-shot magazine. **Barrel:** 3.27". **Weight:** 23-1/2 oz. Length: 6.1" overall. Stocks: Checkered plastic. **Sights:** Fixed, white markings. **Features:** Double action; manual safety blocks firing pin and drops hammer; chamber loaded indicator on 32 and 380; extra finger rest magazine provided. Made in the United States. Introduced 1980. Made in U.S.A. by Smith & Wesson.
Price: **$605.00**

WALTHER P99 AUTO PISTOL
Caliber: 9mm Para., 9x21, 40 S&W, 10-shot magazine. **Barrel:** 4". **Weight:** 25 oz. Length: 7" overall. **Grips:** Textured polymer. **Sights:** Blade front (comes with three interchangeable blades for elevation adjustment), micrometer rear adjustable for windage. **Features:** Double-action mechanism with trigger safety, decock safety, internal striker safety; chamber loaded indicator; ambidextrous magazine release levers; polymer frame with interchangeable backstrap inserts. Comes with two magazines. Introduced 1997. Made in U.S.A. by Smith & Wesson.
Price: From **$799.00**

WALTHER P99AS NIGHT SIGHT DEFENSE KIT
Striker-fired DAO semiauto pistol similar to Walther P99AS but with front and rear tritium sights. Chambered in .40 S&W (12 rounds) or 9mm Parabellum (15 rounds). Features include polymer frame and grip, decocker button, 4-inch (9mm) or 4.17-inch (.40) stainless steel barrel, integral weaver-style accessory rail, black Tenifer finish overall.
Price: . . . . **N/A**

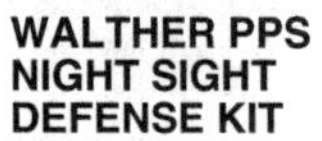

WALTHER PPS NIGHT SIGHT DEFENSE KIT

Striker-fired compact DAO semiauto pistol similar to Walther PPS but with front and rear tritium sights. Chambered in .40 S&W (6 rounds) or 9mm Parabellum (7 rounds). Features include polymer frame and grip, decocker button, loaded chamber indicator, 3.2-inch stainless steel barrel, integral weaver-style accessory rail, black Tenifer finish overall.
Price: . . . . **N/A**

WALTHER P22 PISTOL

Caliber: 22 LR. **Barrel:** 3.4", 5". **Weight:** 19.6 oz. (3.4"), 20.3 oz. (5"). **Length:** 6.26", 7.83". **Grips:** NA. **Sights:** Interchangeable white dot, front, 2-dot adjustable, rear. **Features:** A rimfire version of the Walther P99 pistol, available in nickel slide with black frame, or green frame with black slide versions. Made in U.S.A. by Smith & Wesson.
Price: From **$362.00**

WILSON COMBAT ELITE PROFESSIONAL
Caliber: 9mm Para., 38 Super, 40 S&W; 45 ACP, 8-shot magazine. **Barrel:** Compensated 4.1" hand-fit, heavy flanged cone match grade. **Weight:** 36.2 oz. Length: 7.7" overall. **Grips:** Cocobolo. **Sights:** Combat Tactical yellow rear tritium inserts, brighter green tritium front insert. **Features:** High-cut front strap, 30-lpi checkering on front strap and flat mainspring housing, High-Ride Beavertail grip safety. Dehorned, ambidextrous thumb safety, extended ejector, skeletonized ultralight hammer, ultralight trigger, Armor-Tuff finish on frame and slide. Introduced 1997. Made in U.S.A. by Wilson Combat.
Price: From **$2,600.00**

BAER 1911 ULTIMATE MASTER COMBAT PISTOL
Caliber: 38 Super, 400 Cor-Bon 45 ACP (others available), 10-shot magazine. **Barrel:** 5", 6"; Baer NM. **Weight:** 37 oz. **Length:** 8.5" overall. **Grips:** Checkered cocobolo. **Sights:** Baer dovetail front, low-mount Bo-Mar rear with hidden leaf. **Features:** Full-house competition gun. Baer forged NM blued steel frame and double serrated slide; Baer triple port, tapered cone compensator; fitted slide to frame; lowered, flared ejection port; Baer reverse recoil plug; full-length guide rod; recoil buff; beveled magazine well; Baer Commander hammer, sear; Baer extended ambidextrous safety, extended ejector, checkered slide stop, beavertail grip safety with pad, extended magazine release button; Baer speed trigger. Made in U.S.A. by Les Baer Custom, Inc.
Price: 45 ACP Compensated **$2,790.00**
Price: 38 Super Compensated **$2,940.00**

BAER 1911 NATIONAL MATCH HARDBALL PISTOL
Caliber: 45 ACP, 7-shot magazine. **Barrel:** 5". **Weight:** 37 oz. Length: 8.5" overall. **Grips:** Checkered walnut. **Sights:** Baer dovetail front with under-cut post, low-mount Bo-Mar rear with hidden leaf. **Features:** Baer NM forged steel frame, double serrated slide and barrel with stainless bushing; slide fitted to frame; Baer match trigger with 4-lb. pull; polished feed ramp, throated barrel; checkered front strap, arched mainspring housing; Baer beveled magazine well; lowered, flared ejection port; tuned extractor; Baer extended ejector, checkered slide stop; recoil buff. Made in U.S.A. by Les Baer Custom, Inc.
Price: **$1,890.00**

Baer 1911 Bullseye Wadcutter Pistol
Similar to National Match Hardball except designed for wadcutter loads only. Polished feed ramp and barrel throat; Bo-Mar rib on slide; full length recoil rod; Baer speed trigger with 3-1/2-lb. pull; Baer deluxe hammer and sear; Baer beavertail grip safety with pad; flat mainspring housing checkered 20 lpi. Blue finish; checkered walnut grips. Made in U.S.A. by Les Baer Custom, Inc.
Price: From **$1,890.00**

BF CLASSIC PISTOL
Caliber: Customer orders chamberings. **Barrel:** 8-15" Heavy Match Grade with 11-degree target crown. **Weight:** Approx 3.9 lbs. **Length:** From 16" overall. **Grips:** Thumbrest target style. **Sights:** Bo-Mar/Bond ScopeRib I Combo with hooded post front adjustable for height and width, rear notch available in .032", .062", .080" and .100" widths; 1/2-MOA clicks. **Features:** Hand fitted and headspaced, drilled and tapped for scope mount. Etched receiver; gold-colored trigger. Introduced 1988. Made in U.S.A. by E. Arthur Brown Co. Inc.
Price: **$699.00**

COLT GOLD CUP TROPHY PISTOL
Caliber: 45 ACP, 8-shot + 1 magazine. **Barrel:** 5". **Weight:** NA. **Length:** 8.5". **Grips:** Checkered rubber composite with silver-plated medallion. **Sights:** (O5070X) Dovetail front, Champion rear; (O5870CS) Patridge Target Style front, Champion rear. **Features:** Adjustable aluminum trigger, Beavertail grip safety, full length recoil spring and target recoil spring, available in blued finish and stainless steel.
Price: O5070X **$1,022.00**
Price: O5870CS **$1,071.00**

COLT SPECIAL COMBAT GOVERNMENT
Caliber: 45 ACP, 38 Super. **Barrel:** 5". **Weight:** 39 oz. Length: 8.5". **Grips:** Rosewood w/double diamond checkering pattern. **Sights:** Clark dovetail, front; Bo-Mar adjustable, rear. **Features:** A competition-ready pistol with enhancements such as skeletonized trigger, upswept grip safety, custom tuned action, polished feed ramp. Blue or satin nickel finish. Introduced 2003. Made in U.S.A. by Colt's Mfg. Co.
Price: **$1,676.00**

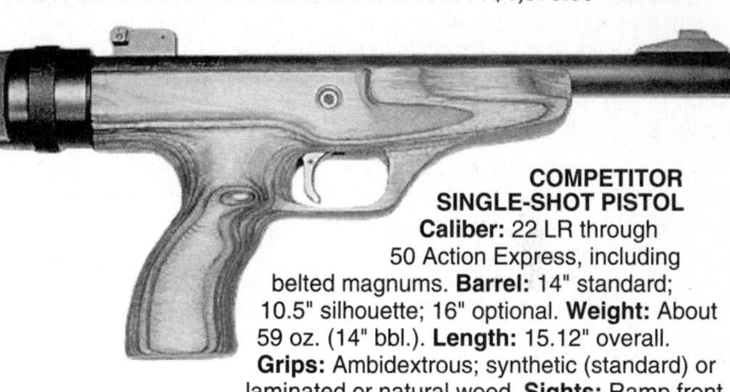

COMPETITOR SINGLE-SHOT PISTOL
Caliber: 22 LR through 50 Action Express, including belted magnums. **Barrel:** 14" standard; 10.5" silhouette; 16" optional. **Weight:** About 59 oz. (14" bbl.). **Length:** 15.12" overall. **Grips:** Ambidextrous; synthetic (standard) or laminated or natural wood. **Sights:** Ramp front, adjustable rear. **Features:** Rotary cannon-type action cocks on opening; cammed ejector; interchangeable barrels, ejectors. Adjustable single stage trigger, sliding thumb safety and trigger safety. Matte blue finish. Introduced 1988. From Competitor Corp., Inc.
Price: 14", standard calibers, synthetic grip **$660.00**

CZ 75 CHAMPION COMPETITION PISTOL
Caliber: 9mm Para., 40 S&W, 16-shot mag. **Barrel:** 4.4". **Weight:** 2.5 lbs. **Length:** 9.4" overall. **Grips:** Black rubber. **Sights:** Blade front, fully adjustable rear. **Features:** Single-action trigger mechanism; three-port compensator (40 S&W, 9mm Para. have two port) full-length guide rod; extended magazine release; ambidextrous safety; flared magazine well; fully adjustable match trigger. Introduced 1999. Imported from the Czech Republic by CZ-USA.
Price: Dual-tone finish **$1,691.00**

EAA WITNESS ELITE GOLD TEAM AUTO
Caliber: 9mm Para., 9x21, 38 Super, 40 S&W, 45 ACP. **Barrel:** 5.1". **Weight:** 44 oz. **Length:** 10.5" overall. **Grips:** Checkered walnut, competition-style. **Sights:** Square post front, fully adjustable rear. **Features:** Triple-chamber cone compensator; competition SA trigger; extended safety and magazine release; competition hammer; beveled magazine well; beavertail grip. Hand-fitted major components. Hard chrome finish. Match-grade barrel. From E.A.A. Custom Shop. Introduced 1992. Limited designed for IPSC Limited Class competition. Features include full-length dust-cover frame, funneled magazine well, interchangeable front sights. Stock (2005) designed for IPSC Production Class competition. Match introduced 2006. Made in Italy, imported by European American Armory.

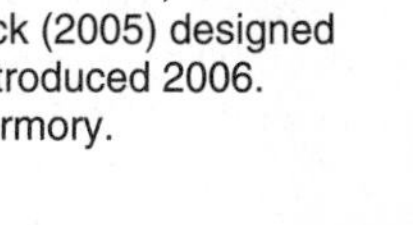

Price: Gold Team **$1,902.00**
Price: Limited, 4.5" barrel, 18+1 capacity **$1,219.00**
Price: Stock, 4.5" barrel, hard-chrome finish **$930.00**
Price: Match, 4.75" barrel, two-tone finish **$632.00**

FREEDOM ARMS MODEL 83 22 FIELD GRADE SILHOUETTE CLASS
Caliber: 22 LR, 5-shot cylinder. **Barrel:** 10". **Weight:** 63 oz. **Length:** 15.5" overall. **Grips:** Black micarta. **Sights:** Removable Patridge front blade; Iron Sight Gun Works silhouette rear, click adjustable for windage and elevation (optional adj. front sight and hood). **Features:** Stainless steel, matte finish, manual sliding-bar safety system; dual firing pins, lightened hammer for fast lock time, pre-set trigger stop. Introduced 1991. Made in U.S.A. by Freedom Arms.
Price: Silhouette Class **$1,860.00**

FREEDOM ARMS MODEL 83 CENTERFIRE SILHOUETTE MODELS
Caliber: 357 Mag., 41 Mag., 44 Mag.; 5-shot cylinder. **Barrel:** 10", 9" (357 Mag. only). **Weight:** 63 oz. (41 Mag.). **Length:** 15.5", 14.5" (357 only). **Grips:** Pachmayr Presentation. **Sights:** Iron Sight Gun Works silhouette rear sight, replaceable adjustable front sight blade with hood. **Features:** Stainless steel, matte finish, manual sliding-bar safety system. Made in U.S.A. by Freedom Arms.
Price: Silhouette Models, from **$1,741.65**

HAMMERLI SP 20 TARGET PISTOL
Caliber: 22 LR, 32 S&W. **Barrel:** 4.6". **Weight:** 34.6-41.8 oz. **Length:** 11.8" overall. **Grips:** Anatomically shaped synthetic Hi-Grip available in five sizes. **Sights:** Integral front in three widths, adjustable rear with changeable notch widths. **Features:** Extremely low-level sight line; anatomically shaped trigger; adjustable JPS buffer system for different recoil characteristics. Receiver available in red, blue, gold, violet or black. Introduced 1998. Imported from Switzerland by Larry's Guns of Maine.
Price: Hammerli 22 LR **$1,539.00**

HIGH STANDARD SUPERMATIC TROPHY TARGET PISTOL
Caliber: 22 LR, 9-shot mag. **Barrel:** 5.5" bull or 7.25" fluted. **Weight:** 44-46 oz. **Length:** 9.5-11.25" overall. **Stock:** Checkered hardwood with thumbrest. **Sights:** Undercut ramp front, frame-mounted micro-click rear adjustable for windage and elevation; drilled and tapped for scope mounting. **Features:** Gold-plated trigger, slide lock, safety-lever and magazine release; stippled front grip and backstrap; adjustable trigger and sear. Barrel weights optional. From High Standard Manufacturing Co., Inc.
Price: 5.5" barrel, adjustable sights **$795.00**
Price: 7.25", adjustable sights **$845.00**

HIGH STANDARD VICTOR TARGET PISTOL
Caliber: 22 LR, 10-shot magazine. **Barrel:** 4.5" or 5.5" polished blue; push-button takedown. **Weight:** 46 oz. **Length:** 9.5" overall. **Stock:** Checkered walnut with thumbrest. **Sights:** Undercut ramp front, micro-click rear adjustable for windage and elevation. Also available

with scope mount, rings, no sights. **Features:** Stainless steel frame. Full-length vent rib. Gold-plated trigger, slide lock, safety-lever and magazine release; stippled front grip and backstrap; polished blue slide; adjustable trigger and sear. Comes with barrel weight. From High Standard Manufacturing Co., Inc.
Price: 4.5" or 5.5" barrel, vented sight rib, universal scope base **$795.00**

KIMBER SUPER MATCH II
Caliber: 45 ACP, 8-shot magazine. **Barrel:** 5". **Weight:** 38 oz. **Length:** 8.7" overall. **Grips:** Rosewood double diamond. **Sights:** Blade front, Kimber fully adjustable rear. **Features:** Guaranteed shoot 1" group at 25 yards. Stainless steel frame, black KimPro slide; two-piece magazine well; premium aluminum match-grade trigger; 30 lpi front strap checkering; stainless match-grade barrel; ambidextrous safety; special Custom Shop markings. Introduced 1999. Made in U.S.A. by Kimber Mfg., Inc.
Price: **$2,225.00**

KIMBER RIMFIRE TARGET
Caliber: 22 LR, 10-shot magazine. **Barrel:** 5". **Weight:** 23 oz. **Length:** 8.7" overall. **Grips:** Rosewood, Kimber logo, double diamond checkering, or black synthetic double diamond. **Sights:** Blade front, Kimber fully adjustable rear. **Features:** Bumped beavertail grip safety, extended thumb safety, extended magazine release button. Serrated flat top slide with flutes, machined aluminum slide and frame, matte black or satin silver finishes, 30 lines-per-inch checkering on frontstrap and under trigger guard; aluminum trigger, test target, accuracy guarantee. No slide lock-open after firing the last round in the magazine. Introduced 1999. Made in U.S.A. by Kimber Mfg., Inc.
Price: **$833.00**

RUGER MARK III TARGET MODEL AUTOLOADING PISTOL
Caliber: 22 LR, 10-shot magazine. **Barrel:** 5.5" to 6-7/8". **Weight:** 41 to 45 oz. **Length:** 9.75" to 11-1/8" overall. **Grips:** Checkered cocobolo/laminate. **Sights:** .125" blade front, micro-click rear, adjustable for windage and elevation, loaded chamber indicator; integral lock, magazine disconnect. Plastic case with lock included. Mark II series introduced 1982, discontinued 2004. Mark III introduced 2005.
Price: MKIII512 (bull barrel, blued) **$417.00**
Price: KMKIII512 (bull barrel, stainless) **$527.00**
Price: MKIII678 (blued Target barrel, 6-7/8") **$417.00**
Price: KMKIII678GC (stainless slabside barrel) **$606.00**
Price: KMKIII678H (stainless fluted barrel) **$620.00**
Price: KMKIII45HCL (Crimson Trace Laser Grips, intr. 2008) . **$787.00**
Price: KMKIII45H (2009) **$620.00**

SMITH & WESSON MODEL 41 TARGET
Caliber: 22 LR, 10-shot clip. **Barrel:** 5.5", 7". **Weight:** 41 oz. (5.5" barrel). **Length:** 10.5" overall (5.5" barrel). **Grips:** Checkered walnut with modified thumbrest, usable with either hand. **Sights:** 1/8"

Patridge on ramp base; micro-click rear adjustable for windage and elevation. **Features:** 3/8" wide, grooved trigger; adjustable trigger stop drilled and tapped.
Price: S&W Bright Blue, either barrel **$1,288.00**

SMITH & WESSON MODEL 22A PISTOLS
Caliber: 22 LR, 10-shot magazine. **Barrel:** 4", 5.5" bull. **Weight:** 28-39 oz. **Length:** 9.5" overall. **Grips:** Dymondwood with ambidextrous thumbrests and flared bottom or rubber soft touch with thumbrest. **Sights:** Patridge front, fully adjustable rear. **Features:** Sight bridge with Weaver-style integral optics mount; alloy frame, stainless barrel and slide; blue/black finish. Introduced 1997. The 22S is similar to the Model 22A except has stainless steel frame. Introduced 1997. Made in U.S.A. by Smith & Wesson.
Price: from **$308.00**
Price: Realtree APG camo finish (2008).................. **$356.00**

SPRINGFIELD ARMORY LEATHAM LEGEND TGO SERIES PISTOLS
Three models of 5" barrel, 45 ACP 1911 pistols built for serious competition. TGO 1 has deluxe low mount Bo-Mar rear sight, Dawson fiber optics front sight, 3.5 lb. trigger pull.
Price: TGO 1 .... **$3,095.00**

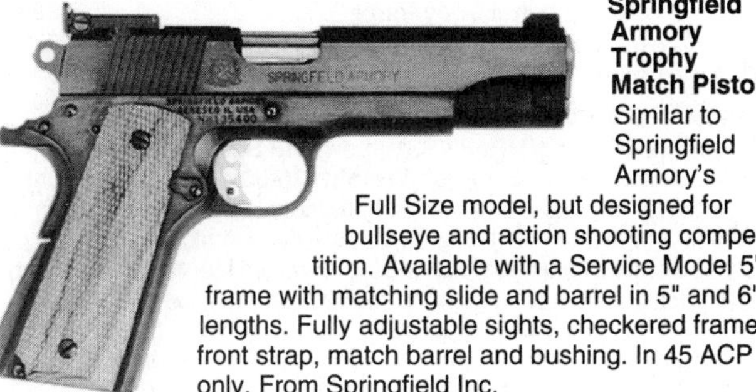

Springfield Armory Trophy Match Pistol
Similar to Springfield Armory's Full Size model, but designed for bullseye and action shooting competition. Available with a Service Model 5" frame with matching slide and barrel in 5" and 6" lengths. Fully adjustable sights, checkered frame front strap, match barrel and bushing. In 45 ACP only. From Springfield Inc.
Price: **$1,573.00**

STI EAGLE 5.0, 6.0 PISTOL
Caliber: 9mm Para., 9x21, 38 & 40 Super, 40 S&W, 10mm, 45 ACP, 10-shot magazine. **Barrel:** 5", 6" bull. **Weight:** 34.5 oz. **Length:** 8.62" overall. **Grips:** Checkered polymer. **Sights:** STI front, Novak or Heinie rear. **Features:** Standard frames plus 7 others; adjustable match trigger; skeletonized hammer; extended grip safety with locator pad. Introduced 1994. Made in U.S.A. by STI International.
Price: .... (5.0 Eagle) **$1,940.12,** (6.0 Eagle), **$1,049.98**

STI EXECUTIVE PISTOL
Caliber: 40 S&W. **Barrel:** 5" bull. **Weight:** 39 oz. **Length:** 8-5/8". **Grips:** Gray polymer. **Sights:** Dawson fiber optic, front; STI adjustable rear. **Features:** Stainless mag. well, front and rear serrations on slide. Made in U.S.A. by STI.
Price: **$2,464.00**

STI TROJAN
Caliber: 9mm Para., 38 Super, 40 S&W, 45 ACP. **Barrel:** 5", 6". **Weight:** 36 oz. **Length:** 8.5". **Grips:** Rosewood. **Sights:** STI front with STI adjustable rear. **Features:** Stippled front strap, flat top slide, one-piece steel guide rod.
Price: (Trojan 5") **$1,110.00**
Price: (Trojan 6", not available in 38 Super) **$1,419.60**

CHARTER ARMS BULLDOG REVOLVER
Caliber: 44 Special. **Barrel:** 2.5". **Weight:** NA. **Sights:** Blade front, notch rear. **Features:** 6-round cylinder, soft-rubber pancake-style grips, shrouded ejector rod, wide trigger and hammer spur. American made by Charter Arms, distributed by MKS Supply.
Price: Blued **$455.00**
Price: Stainless **$465.00**
Price: Target Bulldog, 4" barrel, 23 oz. **$459.00**

CHARTER ARMS OFF DUTY REVOLVER
Caliber: 38 Spec. **Barrel:** 2". **Weight:** 12.5 oz. **Sights:** Blade front, notch rear. **Features:** 5-round cylinder, aluminum casting, DAO. American made by Charter Arms, distributed by MKS Supply.
Price: Aluminum **$438.00**

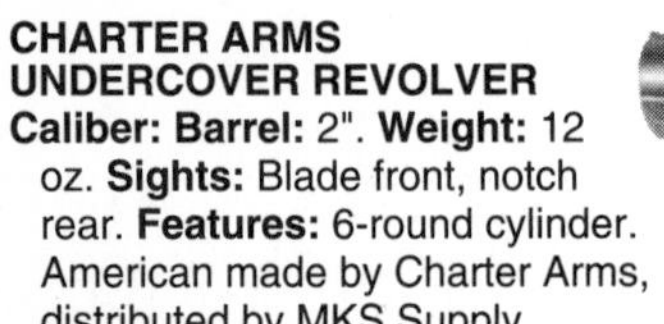

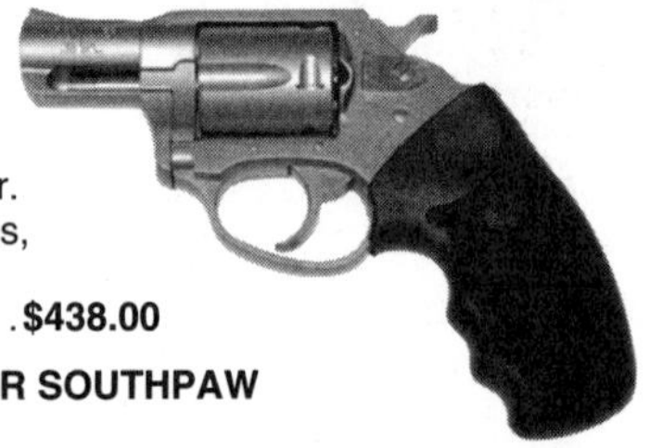

CHARTER ARMS UNDERCOVER REVOLVER
Caliber: Barrel: 2". **Weight:** 12 oz. **Sights:** Blade front, notch rear. **Features:** 6-round cylinder. American made by Charter Arms, distributed by MKS Supply.
Price: Blued **$438.00**

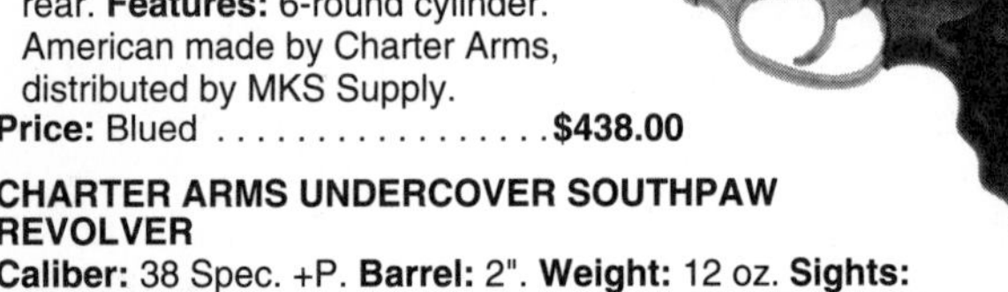

CHARTER ARMS UNDERCOVER SOUTHPAW REVOLVER
Caliber: 38 Spec. +P. **Barrel:** 2". **Weight:** 12 oz. **Sights:** NA. **Features:** Cylinder release is on the right side and the cylinder opens to the right side. Exposed hammer for both single and double-action firing. 5-round cylinder. American made by Charter Arms, distributed by MKS Supply.
Price: Blued **$469.00**

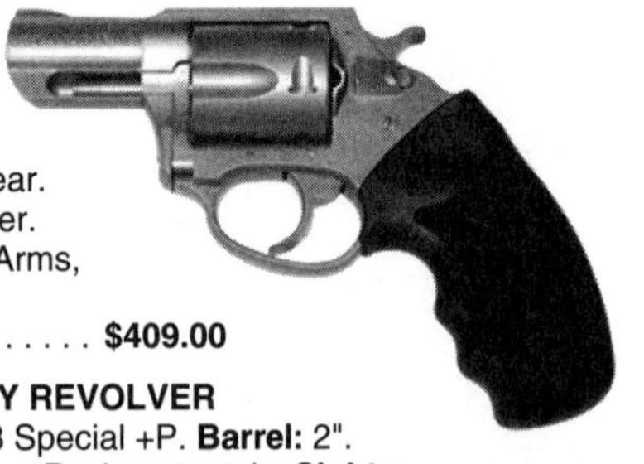

CHARTER ARMS MAG PUG REVOLVER
Caliber: 357 Mag. **Barrel:** 2.2". **Weight:** 23 oz. **Sights:** Blade front, notch rear. **Features:** Five-round cylinder. American made by Charter Arms, distributed by MKS Supply.
Price: Blued or stainless **$409.00**

CHARTER ARMS PINK LADY REVOLVER
Caliber: 32 H&R Magnum, 38 Special +P. **Barrel:** 2". **Weight:** 12 oz. **Grips:** Rubber Pachmayr-style. **Sights:** Fixed. **Features:** Snubnose, five-round cylinder. Pink anodized aluminum alloy frame.
Price: **$438.00**
Price: Lavender Lady, lavender frame **$438.00**
Price: Goldfinger, gold anodized frame, matte black barrel and cylinder assembly **$438.00**

CHARTER ARMS SOUTHPAW REVOLVER
Caliber: 38 Special +P. **Barrel:** 2". **Weight:** 12 oz. **Grips:** Rubber Pachmayr-style. **Sights:** NA. **Features:** Snubnose, five-round cylinder, matte black aluminum alloy frame with stainless steel cylinder. Cylinder latch and crane assembly are on right side of frame for convenience to left-hand shooters.
Price: **$469.00**

CHIAPPA RHINO
Ugly-as-hell revolver chambered in .357 Magnum. Features include 2-, 4-, 5- or 6-inch barrel; fixed or adjustable sights; visible hammer or hammerless design. Weight 24 to 33 oz. Walnut or synthetic grips with black frame; hexagonal-shaped cylinder. Unique design fires from bottom chamber of cylinder.
Price: .... **N/A**

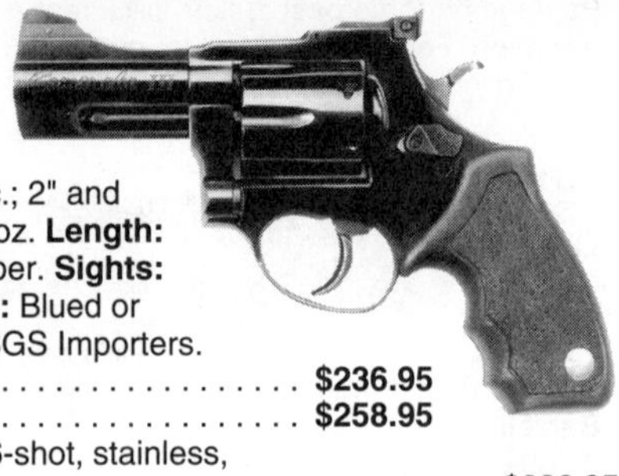

COMANCHE I, II, III DA REVOLVERS
Caliber: 22 LR, 9 shot. 38 Spec., 6 shot. 357 Mag, 6 shot. **Barrel:** 6", 22 LR; 2" and 4", 38 Spec.; 2" and 3", 357 Mag. **Weight:** 39 oz. **Length:** 10.8" overall. **Grips:** Rubber. **Sights:** Adjustable rear. **Features:** Blued or stainless. Distributed by SGS Importers.
Price: I Blue **$236.95**
Price: I Alloy **$258.95**
Price: II 38 Spec., 3" bbl., 6-shot, stainless, intr. 2006 .... **$236.95**
Price: II 38 Spec., 4" bbl., 6-shot, stainless **$219.95**
Price: III 357 Mag, 3" bbl., 6-shot, blue **$253.95**
Price: III 357 Mag. 4" bbl., 6-shot, blue **$274.95**

EAA WINDICATOR REVOLVERS
Caliber: 38 Spec., 6-shot; 357 Mag., 6-shot. **Barrel:** 2", 4". **Weight:** 30 oz. (4"). **Length:** 8.5" overall (4" bbl.). **Grips:** Rubber with finger grooves. **Sights:** Blade front, fixed or adjustable on rimfires; fixed only on 32, 38. **Features:** Swing-out cylinder; hammer block safety; blue finish. Introduced 1991. Imported from Germany by European American Armory.
Price: 38 Spec. 2" barrel, alloy frame **$277.00**
Price: 38 Spec. 4" barrel, alloy frame **$292.00**
Price: 357 Mag, 2" barrel, steel frame **$292.00**
Price: 357 Mag, 4" barrel, steel frame **$311.00**

KORTH USA REVOLVERS
Caliber: 22 LR, 22 WMR, 32 S&W Long, 38 Spec., 357 Mag., 9mm Para. **Barrel:** 3", 4", 5.25", 6". **Weight:** 36-52 oz. Grips, Combat, Sport: Walnut, Palisander, Amboinia, Ivory. Grips, Target: German Walnut, matte with oil finish, adjustable ergonomic competition style. **Sights:** Adjustable Patridge (Sport) or Baughman (Combat), interchangeable and adjustable rear w/Patridge front (Target) in blue and matte. **Features:** DA/SA, 3 models, over 50 configurations, externally adjustable trigger stop and weight, interchangeable cylinder, removable wide-milled trigger shoe on Target model. Deluxe models are highly engraved editions. Available finishes include high polish blue finish, plasma coated in high polish or matted silver, gold, blue, or charcoal. Many deluxe options available. 6-shot. From Korth USA.
Price: From.................................... **$8,000.00**
Price: Deluxe Editions, from **$12,000.00**

ROSSI R461/R462
Caliber: .357 Mag. **Barrel:** 2". **Weight:** 26-35 oz. **Grips:** Rubber. **Sights:** Fixed. **Features:** DA/SA, +P rated frame, blue carbon or high polish stainless steel, patented Taurus Security System, 6-shot.
Price: From.................................... **$352.00**

ROSSI MODEL R351/ R352/R851 REVOLVERS
Caliber: .38 Spec. **Barrel:** 2" (R35), 4" (R851). **Weight:** 24-32 oz. **Grips:** Rubber. **Sights:** Fixed (R35), Fully Adjustable (R851). **Features:** DA/SA, 3 models available, +P rated frame, blue carbon or high polish stainless steel, patented Taurus Security System, 5-shot (R35) 6-shot (R851).
Price: From............ **$352.00**

ROSSI MODEL R971/R972 REVOLVERS
Caliber: 357 Mag. +P, 6-shot. **Barrel:** 4", 6". **Weight:** 32 oz. **Length:** 8.5" or 10.5" overall. **Grips:** Rubber. **Sights:** Blade front, adjustable rear. **Features:** Single/double action. Patented key-lock Taurus Security System; forged steel frame. Introduced 2001. Made in Brazil by Amadeo Rossi. Imported by BrazTech/Taurus.

Prices given are believed to be accurate at time of publication however, many factors affect retail pricing so exact prices are not possible.

Price: Model R971 (blued finish, 4" bbl.) **$406.00**
Price: Model R972 (stainless steel finish, 6" bbl.) **$460.00**

Rossi Model 851
Similar to Model R971/R972, chambered for 38 Spec. +P. Blued finish, 4" barrel. Introduced 2001. Made in Brazil by Amadeo Rossi. From BrazTech/Taurus.
Price: **$352.00**

RUGER GP-100 REVOLVERS
Caliber: 327 Federal, 38 Spec. +P, 357 Mag., 6-shot. **Barrel:** 3" full shroud, 4" full shroud, 6" full shroud. **Weight:** 3" full shroud-36 oz., 4" full shroud-38 oz. **Sights:** Fixed; adjustable on 4" full shroud, all 6" barrels. **Grips:** Ruger Santoprene Cushioned Grip with Goncalo Alves inserts. **Features:** Uses action, frame features of both the Security-Six and Redhawk revolvers. Full length, short ejector shroud. Satin blue and stainless steel.
Price: GP-141 (357, 4" full shroud, adj. sights, blue) **$616.00**
Price: GP-161 (357, 6" full shroud, adj. sights, blue), 46 oz. . . **$616.00**
Price: KGP-141 (357, 4" full shroud, adj. sights, stainless) . . . **$680.00**
Price: KGP-161 (357, 6" full shroud, adj. sights, stainless) 46 oz. **$680.00**
Price: KGPF-331 (357, 3" full shroud, stainless) **$659.00**

RUGER SP-101 REVOLVERS
Caliber: 327 Federal, 6-shot; 38 Spec. +P, 357 Mag., 5-shot. **Barrel:** 2.25", 3-1/16". **Weight:** (38 & 357 mag models) 2.25"-25 oz.; 3-1/16"-27 oz. **Sights:** Adjustable on 327, fixed on others. **Grips:** Ruger Cushioned Grip with inserts. **Features:** Compact, small frame, double-action revolver. Full-length ejector shroud. Stainless steel only. Introduced 1988.
Price: KSP-321X (2.25", 357 Mag.) **$589.00**
Price: KSP-331X (3-1/16", 357 Mag.) **$589.00**
Price: KSP-821X (2.25", 38 Spec.) **$589.00**
Price: KSP-32731X (3-1/16", 327 Federal, intr. 2008) **$589.00**
Price: KSP-321X-LG (Crimson Trace Laser Grips, intr. 2008) . **$839.00**

Ruger SP-101 Double-Action-Only Revolver
Similar to standard SP-101 except double-action-only with no single-action sear notch. Spurless hammer, floating firing pin and transfer bar safety system. Available with 2.25" barrel in 357 Mag. Weighs 25 oz., overall length 7". Natural brushed satin, high-polish stainless steel. Introduced 1993.
Price: KSP321XL (357 Mag.) **$589.00**
Price: KSP321XL-LG (357 Mag., Crimson Trace Laser Grips, intr. 2008) **$839.00**

RUGER REDHAWK
Caliber: 44 Rem. Mag., 45 Colt, 6-shot. **Barrel:** 4", 5.5", 7.5". **Weight:** About 54 oz. (7.5" bbl.). **Length:** 13" overall (7.5" barrel). **Grips:** Square butt cushioned grip panels. **Sights:** Interchangeable Patridge-type front, rear adjustable for windage and elevation. **Features:** Stainless steel, brushed satin finish, blued ordnance steel. 9.5" sight radius. Introduced 1979.
Price: KRH-44, stainless, 7.5" barrel **$861.00**
Price: KRH-44R, stainless 7.5" barrel w/scope mount **$915.00**
Price: KRH-445, stainless 5.5" barrel **$861.00**
Price: KRH-444, stainless 4" barrel (2007) **$861.00**
Price: KRH-45-4, Hogue Monogrip, 45 Colt (2008) **$861.00**

RUGER SUPER REDHAWK REVOLVER
Caliber: 44 Rem. Mag., 45 Colt, 454 Casull, 480 Ruger, 5 or 6-shot. **Barrel:** 2.5", 5.5", 7.5", 9.5". **Weight:** About 54 oz. (7.5" bbl.). **Length:** 13" overall (7.5" barrel). **Grips:** Hogue Tamer Monogrip. **Features:** Similar to standard Redhawk except has heavy extended frame with Ruger Integral Scope Mounting System on wide topstrap. Wide hammer spur lowered for better scope clearance. Incorporates mechanical design features and improvements of GP-100. Ramp front sight base has Redhawk-style Interchangeable Insert sight blades, adjustable rear sight. Satin stainless steel and low-glare stainless finishes. Introduced 1987.
Price: KSRH-2454, 2.5" 454 Casull/45 Colt, Hogue Tamer Monogrip, Alaskan Model **$992.00**
Price: KSRH-7, 7.5" 44 Mag, Ruger grip **$915.00**
Price: KSRH-7454, 7.5" 45 Colt/454 Casull **$992.00**
Price: KSRH-9, 9" 44 Mag, Ruger grip **$915.00**
Price: KSRH-9480-5, 9.5", 480 Ruger, intr. 2008 . . . . **$963.00**
Price: KSRH-2, 2.5" 44 Mag, Alaskan Model, intr. 2008 . . . . . **$992.00**

SMITH & WESSON MODEL 14 CLASSIC
Caliber: 38 Spec. +P, 6-shot. Barrel: 6". Weight: 35 oz. Length: 11.5". Grips: Wood. Sights: Pinned Patridge front, micro adjustable rear. Features: Recreation of the vintage Model 14 revolver. Carbon steel frame and cylinder with blued finish.
Price: **$995.00**
Price: Model 14 150253, nickel finish **$1,074.00**

SMITH & WESSON M&P REVOLVERS

Caliber: 38 Spec., 357 Mag., 5 rounds (Centennial), 8 rounds (large frame). **Barrel:** 1.87" (Centennial), 5" (large frame). **Weight:** 13.3 oz. (Centennial), 36.3 oz. (large frame). **Length:** 6.31" overall (small frame), 10.5" (large frame). **Grips:** Synthetic. **Sights:** Integral U-Notch rear, XS Sights 24/7 Tritium Night. **Features:** Scandium alloy frame, stainless steel cylinder, matte black finish. Made in U.S.A. by Smith & Wesson.

Price: M&P 340, double action **$869.00**
Price: M&P 340CT, Crimson Trace Lasergrips........... **$1,122.00**
Price: M&P R8 large frame.......................... **$1,311.00**

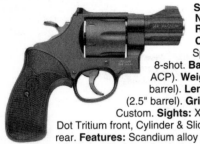

SMITH & WESSON NIGHT GUARD REVOLVERS

Caliber: 357 Mag., 38 Spec. +P, 5-, 6-, 7-, 8-shot. **Barrel:** 2.5 or 2.75" (45 ACP). **Weight:** 24.2 oz. (2.5" barrel). **Length:** 7.325" overall (2.5" barrel). **Grips:** Pachmayr Compac Custom. **Sights:** XS Sight 24/7 Standard Dot Tritium front, Cylinder & Slide Extreme Duty fixed rear. **Features:** Scandium alloy frame, stainless PVD cylinder, matte black finish. Introduced 2008. Made in U.S.A. by Smith & Wesson.

Price: Model 310, 10mm/40 S&W (interchangeable), 2.75" barrel, large-frame snubnose **$1,153.00**
Price: Model 315, 38 Special +P, 2.5" barrel, medium-frame snubnose **$995.00**
Price: Model 325, 45 ACP, 2.75" barrel, large-frame snubnose **$1,153.00**
Price: Model 327, 38/357, 2.5" barrel, large-frame snubnose **$1,153.00**
Price: Model 329, 44 Magnum/38 Special (interchangeable), 2.5" barrel, large-frame snubnose **$1,153.00**
Price: Model 357, 41 Magnum, 2.75" barrel, large-frame snubnose **$1,153.00**
Price: Model 386, 357 Magnum/44 Special +P (interchangeable), 2.5" barrel, medium-frame snubnose............. **$1,074.00**
Price: Model 396, 44 Special, 2.5" barrel, medium-frame snubnose **$1,074.00**

SMITH & WESSON J-FRAME REVOLVERS

The smallest S&W wheelguns come in a variety of chamberings, barrel lengths, and materials, as noted in the individual model listings.

SMITH & WESSON 60LS/642LS LADYSMITH REVOLVERS

Caliber: .38 Spec. +P, 357 Mag., 5-shot. **Barrel:** 1-7/8" (642LS); 2-1/8" (60LS) **Weight:** 14.5 oz. (642LS); 21.5 oz. (60LS); **Length:** 6.6" overall (60LS); . **Grips:** Wood. **Sights:** Black blade, serrated ramp front, fixed notch rear. **Features:** 60LS model has a Chiefs Special-style frame. 642LS has Centennial-style frame, frosted matte finish, smooth combat wood grips. Introduced 1996. Comes in a fitted carry/storage case. Introduced 1989. Made in U.S.A. by Smith & Wesson.

Price: From **$782.00**

SMITH & WESSON MODEL 63

Caliber: 22 LR, 8-shot. **Barrel:** 5". **Weight:** 28.8 oz. **Length:** 9.5" overall. **Grips:** Black rubber. **Sights:** Black ramp front sight, adjustable black blade rear sight. **Features:** Stainless steel construction throughout. Made in U.S.A. by Smith & Wesson.

Price: **$845.00**

SMITH & WESSON MODEL 442/637/638/642 AIRWEIGHT REVOLVERS

Caliber: 38 Spec. +P, 5-shot. **Barrel:** 1-7/8", 2-1/2". **Weight:** 15 oz. (37, 442); 20 oz. (3); 21.5 oz.; **Length:** 6-3/8" overall. **Grips:** Soft rubber. **Sights:** Fixed, serrated ramp front, square notch rear. **Features:** Aluminum-alloy frames. Models 37, 637; Chiefs Special-style frame with exposed hammer. Introduced 1996. Models 442, 642; Centennial-style frame, enclosed hammer. Model 638, Bodyguard style, shrouded hammer. Comes in a fitted carry/storage case. Introduced 1989. Made in U.S.A. by Smith & Wesson.

Price: From **$600.00**

SMITH & WESSON MODELS 637 CT/638 CT/642 CT

Similar to Models 637, 638 and 642 but with Crimson Trace Laser Grips.

Price: **$920.00**

SMITH & WESSON MODEL 60 CHIEF'S SPECIAL

Caliber: 357 Mag., 38 Spec. +P, 5-shot. **Barrel:** 2-1/8", 3" or 5". **Weight:** 22.5 oz. (2-1/8" barrel). **Length:** 6-5/8" overall (2-1/8" barrel). **Grips:** Rounded butt synthetic grips. **Sights:** Fixed, serrated ramp front, square notch rear. **Features:** Stainless steel construction, satin finish, internal lock. Introduced 1965. The 5"-barrel model has target semi-lug barrel, rosewood grip, red ramp front sight, adjustable rear sight. Made in U.S.A. by Smith & Wesson.

Price: 2-1/8" barrel, intr. 2005 ....**$798.00**
Price: 3" barrel, 7.5" OAL, 24 oz. **$830.00**

SMITH & WESSON MODEL 317 AIRLITE REVOLVERS

Caliber: 22 LR, 8-shot. **Barrel:** 1-7/8", 3". **Weight:** 10.5 oz. **Length:** 6.25" overall (1-7/8" barrel). **Grips:** Rubber. **Sights:** Serrated ramp front, fixed notch rear. **Features:** Aluminum alloy, carbon and stainless steels, Chiefs Special-style frame with exposed hammer. Smooth combat trigger. Clear Cote finish. Introduced 1997. Made in U.S.A. by Smith & Wesson.

Price: Model 317, 1-7/8" barrel **$766.00**
Price: Model 317 w/HiViz front sight, 3" barrel, 7.25 OAL **$830.00**

SMITH & WESSON MODEL 340/340PD AIRLITE SC CENTENNIAL

Caliber: 357 Mag., 38 Spec. +P, 5-shot. **Barrel:** 1-7/8". **Weight:** 12 oz. **Length:** 6-3/8" overall (1-7/8" barrel). **Grips:** Rounded butt rubber. **Sights:** Black blade front, rear notch **Features:** Centennial-style frame, enclosed hammer. Internal lock. Matte silver finish. Scandium alloy frame, titanium cylinder, stainless steel barrel liner. Made in U.S.A. by Smith & Wesson.

Price: Model 340 .... **$1,051.00**
Price: Model 340PD **$1,122.00**

SMITH & WESSON MODEL 351PD REVOLVER

Caliber: 22 Mag., 7-shot. **Barrel:** 1-7/8". **Weight:** 10.6 oz. **Length:** 6.25" overall (1-7/8" barrel). **Sights:** HiViz front sight, rear notch. **Grips:** Wood. **Features:** Seven-shot, aluminum-alloy frame. Chiefs Special-style frame with exposed hammer. Nonreflective matte-black finish. Internal lock. Made in U.S.A. by Smith & Wesson.

Price: **$830.00**

SMITH & WESSON MODEL 360/360PD AIRLITE CHIEF'S SPECIAL

Caliber: 357 Mag., 38 Spec. +P, 5-shot. **Barrel:** 1-7/8". **Weight:** 12 oz. **Length:** 6-3/8" overall (1-7/8" barrel). **Grips:** Rounded butt rubber. **Sights:** Black blade front, fixed rear notch.

Prices given are believed to be accurate at time of publication however, many factors affect retail pricing so exact prices are not possible.

Features: Chief's Special-style frame with exposed hammer. Internal lock. Scandium alloy frame, titanium cylinder, stainless steel barrel. Made in U.S.A. by Smith & Wesson.
Price: 360PD **$988.00**

SMITH & WESSON MODEL M&P360
Single/double-action J-frame revolver chambered in .357 Magnum. Features include 3-inch barrel, 5-round cylinder, fixed XS tritium sights, scandium frame, stainless steel cylinder, matte black finish, synthetic grips.
Price: **$980.00**

SMITH & WESSON MODEL 438
Caliber: 38 Spec. +P, 5-shot. **Barrel:** 1-7/8". **Weight:** 15.1 oz. **Length:** 6.31" overall. **Grips:** Synthetic. **Sights:** Fixed front and rear. **Features:** Aluminum alloy frame, stainless steel cylinder. Matte black finish throughout. Made in U.S.A. by Smith & Wesson.
Price: **$624.00**

SMITH & WESSON MODEL 632 POWERPORT PRO SERIES
Caliber: 327 Mag., 6-shot. **Barrel:** 3". **Weight:** 24.5 oz. **Length:** 7.5". **Grips:** Synthetic. **Sights:** Pinned serrated ramp front, adjustable rear. **Features:** Full-lug ported barrel with full-length extractor. Stainless steel frame and cylinder. Introduced 2009.
Price: **$980.00**

SMITH & WESSON MODEL 640 CENTENNIAL DA ONLY
Caliber: 357 Mag., 38 Spec. +P, 5-shot. **Barrel:** 2-1/8". **Weight:** 23 oz. **Length:** 6.75" overall. **Grips:** Uncle Mike's Boot grip. **Sights:** Serrated ramp front, fixed notch rear. **Features:** Stainless steel. Fully concealed hammer, snag-proof smooth edges. Internal lock. Introduced 1995 in 357 Mag.
Price: **$798.00**

SMITH & WESSON MODEL 649 BODYGUARD REVOLVER
Caliber: 357 Mag., 38 Spec. +P, 5-shot. **Barrel:** 2-1/8". **Weight:** 23 oz. **Length:** 6-5/8" overall. **Grips:** Uncle Mike's Combat. **Sights:** Black pinned ramp front, fixed notch rear. **Features:** Stainless steel construction, satin finish. Internal lock. Bodyguard style, shrouded hammer. Made in U.S.A. by Smith & Wesson.
Price: **$798.00**

SMITH & WESSON MODEL 442/642/640/632 PRO SERIES REVOLVERS
Double action only J-frame with concealed hammers chambered in .38 Special +P (442 & 642), .357 Magnum (640) or .327 Federal (632). Features include 5-round cylinder, matte stainless steel frame, fixed sights or dovetail night sights (632, 640), synthetic grips, cylinder cut for moon clips (442, 642, 640).
Price: . . . . **$640.00 (standard) to $916.00 (night sights)**

SMITH & WESSON K-FRAME/L-FRAME REVOLVERS
These mid-size S&W wheelguns come in a variety of chamberings, barrel lengths, and materials, as noted in individual model listings.

SMITH & WESSON MODEL 10 CLASSIC
Single/double action K frame revolver chambered in .38 Special. Features include bright blue steel frame and cylinder, checkered wood grips, 4-inch barrel, adjustable patridge-style sights.
Price: **$814.00**

SMITH & WESSON MODEL 48 CLASSIC
Single/double action K frame revolver chambered in .22 Magnum Rimfire (.22 WMR). Features include bright blue steel frame and cylinder, checkered wood grips, 4- or 6-inch barrel, adjustable patridge-style sights.
Price: . . . . **$1,043.00 to $1,082.00**

SMITH & WESSON MODEL 10 REVOLVER
Caliber: 38 Spec. +P, 6-shot. **Barrel:** 4". **Weight:** 36 oz. **Length:** 8-7/8" overall. **Grips:** Soft rubber; square butt. **Sights:** Fixed; black blade front, square notch rear. Blued carbon steel frame.
Price: Blue **$758.00**

SMITH & WESSON MODEL 64/67 REVOLVERS
Caliber: 38 Spec. +P, 6-shot. **Barrel:** 3". **Weight:** 33 oz. **Length:** 8-7/8" overall. **Grips:** Soft rubber. **Sights:** Fixed, 1/8" serrated ramp front, square notch rear. Model 67 (**Weight:** 36 oz. **Length:** 8-7/8") similar to Model 64 except for adjustable sights. **Features:** Satin finished stainless steel, square butt.
Price: From **$758.00**

SMITH & WESSON MODEL 617 REVOLVERS
Caliber: 22 LR, 6- or 10-shot. **Barrel:** 4". **Weight:** 41 oz. (4" barrel). **Length:** 9-1/8" (4" barrel). **Grips:** Soft rubber. **Sights:** Patridge front, adjustable rear. Drilled and tapped for scope mount. **Features:** Stainless steel with satin finish; 4" has .312" smooth trigger, .375" semi-target hammer; 6" has either .312" combat or .400" serrated trigger, .375" semi-target or .500" target hammer; 8-3/8" with .400" serrated trigger, .500" target hammer. Introduced 1990.
Price: From **$916.00**

SMITH & WESSON MODELS 620 REVOLVERS
Caliber: 38 Spec. +P; 357 Mag., 7 rounds. **Barrel:** 4". **Weight:** 37.5 oz. **Length:** 9.5". **Grips:** Rubber. **Sights:** Integral front blade, fixed rear notch on the 619; adjustable white-outline target style rear, red ramp front on 620. **Features:** Replaces Models 65 and 66. Two-piece semi-lug barrel. Satin stainless frame and cylinder. Made in U.S.A. by Smith & Wesson.
Price: . . . . **$893.00** . . . .

SMITH & WESSON MODEL 386 XL HUNTER
Single/double action L-frame revolver chambered in .357 Magnum. Features include 6-inch full-lug barrel, 7-round cylinder, Hi-Viz fiber optic front sight, adjustable rear sight, scandium frame, stainless steel cylinder, black matte finish, synthetic grips.
Price: **$1,019.00**

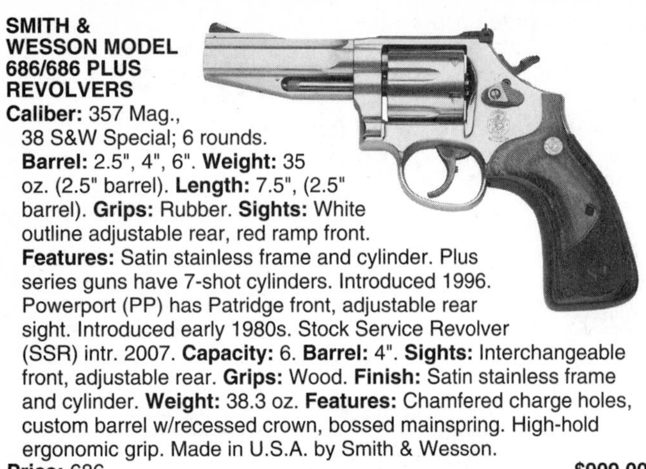

SMITH & WESSON MODEL 686/686 PLUS REVOLVERS

Caliber: 357 Mag., 38 S&W Special; 6 rounds. **Barrel:** 2.5", 4", 6". **Weight:** 35 oz. (2.5" barrel). **Length:** 7.5", (2.5" barrel). **Grips:** Rubber. **Sights:** White outline adjustable rear, red ramp front. **Features:** Satin stainless frame and cylinder. Plus series guns have 7-shot cylinders. Introduced 1996. Powerport (PP) has Patridge front, adjustable rear sight. Introduced early 1980s. Stock Service Revolver (SSR) intr. 2007. **Capacity:** 6. **Barrel:** 4". **Sights:** Interchangeable front, adjustable rear. **Grips:** Wood. **Finish:** Satin stainless frame and cylinder. **Weight:** 38.3 oz. **Features:** Chamfered charge holes, custom barrel w/recessed crown, bossed mainspring. High-hold ergonomic grip. Made in U.S.A. by Smith & Wesson.

Price: 686 . . . . **$909.00**
Price: Plus, 7 rounds **$932.00**
Price: PP, 6" barrel, 6 rounds, 11-3/8" OAL **$877.00**
Price: SSR **$1,059.00**

SMITH & WESSON MODEL 686 PLUS PRO SERIES

Single/double-action L-frame revolver chambered in .357 Magnum. Features include 5-inch barrel with tapered underlug, 7-round cylinder, satin stainless steel frame and cylinder, synthetic grips, interchangeable and adjustable sights.

Price: **$1,059.00**

SMITH & WESSON N-FRAME REVOLVERS

These large-frame S&W wheelguns come in a variety of chamberings, barrel lengths, and materials, as noted in the individual model listings.

SMITH & WESSON MODEL 21

Caliber: 44 Special, 6-round. Barrel: 4" tapered. **Weight:** NA. **Length:** NA. **Grips:** Smooth wood. **Sights:** Pinned half-moon service front; service rear. **Features:** Carbon steel frame, blued finish.

Price: **$924.00**

SMITH & WESSON MODEL 29 CLASSIC

Caliber: 44 Mag, 6-round. **Barrel:** 6.5". **Weight:** 48.5 oz. **Length:** 12". **Grips:** Altamont service walnut. **Sights:** Adjustable white-outline rear, red ramp front. **Features:** Carbon steel frame, polished-blued or nickel finish. Has integral key lock safety feature to prevent accidental discharges. Alo available with 3" barrel. Original Model 29 made famous by "Dirty Harry" character created in 1971 by Clint Eastwood.

Price: **$1240.00**

SMITH & WESSON MODEL 329PD AIRLITE REVOLVERS

Caliber: 44 Spec., 44 Mag., 6-round. **Barrel:** 4". **Weight:** 26 oz. **Length:** 9.5". **Grips:** Wood. **Sights:** Adj. rear, HiViz orange-dot front. **Features:** Scandium alloy frame, blue/black finish.

Price: From **$1,264.00**

SMITH & WESSON MODEL 625/625JM REVOLVERS

Caliber: 45 ACP, 6-shot. **Barrel:** 4", 5". **Weight:** 43 oz. (4" barrel). **Length:** 9-3/8" overall (4" barrel). **Grips:** Soft rubber; wood optional. **Sights:** Patridge front on ramp, S&W micrometer click rear adjustable for windage and elevation. **Features:** Stainless steel construction with .400" semi-target hammer, .312" smooth combat trigger; full lug barrel. Glass beaded finish. Introduced 1989. "Jerry Miculek" Professional (JM) Series has .265"-wide grooved trigger, special wooden Miculek Grip, five full moon clips, gold bead Patridge front sight on interchangeable front sight base, bead blast finish. Unique serial number run. Mountain Gun has 4" tapered barrel, drilled and tapped, Hogue Rubber Monogrip, pinned black ramp front sight, micrometer click-adjustable rear sight, satin stainless frame and barrel, weighs 39.5 oz.

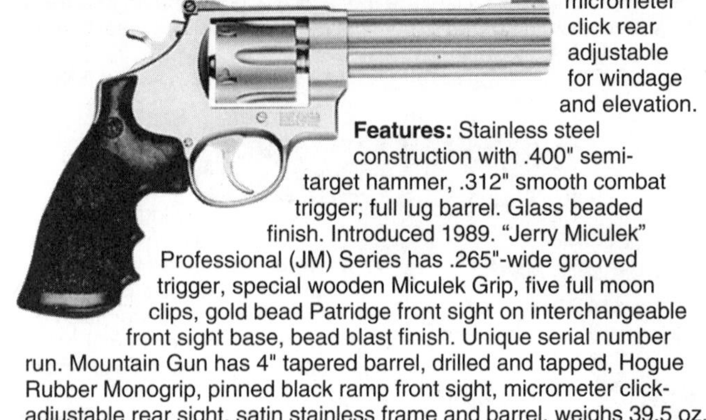

Price: 625JM **$1,074.00**

SMITH & WESSON MODEL 629 REVOLVERS

Caliber: 44 Magnum, 44 S&W Special, 6-shot. **Barrel:** 4", 5", 6.5". **Weight:** 41.5 oz. (4" bbl.). **Length:** 9-5/8" overall (4" bbl.). **Grips:** Soft rubber; wood optional. **Sights:** 1/8" red ramp front, white outline rear, internal lock, adjustable for windage and elevation. Classic similar to standard Model 629, except Classic has full-lug 5" barrel, chamfered front of cylinder, interchangeable red ramp front sight with adjustable white outline rear, Hogue grips with S&W monogram, drilled and tapped for scope mounting. Factory accurizing and endurance packages. Introduced 1990. Classic Power Port has Patridge front sight and adjustable rear sight. Model 629CT has 5" barrel, Crimson Trace Hoghunter Lasergrips, 10.5" OAL, 45.5 oz. weight. Introduced 2006.

Price: From **$1,035.00**

SMITH & WESSON MODEL 329 XL HUNTER

Similar to Model 386 XL Hunter but built on large N-frame and chambered in .44 Magnum. Other features include 6-round cylinder and 6.5-barrel.

Price: **$1,138.00**

SMITH & WESSON X-FRAME REVOLVERS

These extra-large X-frame S&W wheelguns come in a variety of chamberings, barrel lengths, and materials, as noted in individual model listings.

SMITH & WESSON MODEL S&W500 (163565)

Caliber: 500 S&W Mag., 5 rounds. **Barrel:** 6.5". **Weight:** 60.7 oz. **Length:** 12.875". **Grips:** Synthetic. **Sights:** Red Ramp front sights, adjustable white outline rear. **Features:** Similar to other S&W500 models but with integral compensator and half-length ejector shroud. Made in U.S.A. by Smith & Wesson.

Price: From **$1,375.00**

SMITH & WESSON MODEL 460V REVOLVERS

Caliber: 460 S&W Mag., 5-shot. Also chambers 454 Casull, 45 Colt. **Barrel:** 8-3/8" gain-twist rifling. **Weight:** 62.5 oz. **Length:** 11.25". **Grips:** Rubber. **Sights:** Adj. rear, red ramp front. **Features:** Satin stainless steel frame and cylinder, interchangeable compensator. 460XVR (X-treme Velocity Revolver) has black blade front sight with interchangeable green Hi-Viz tubes, adjustable rear sight. 7.5"-barrel version has Lothar-Walther barrel, 360-degree recoil compensator, tuned Performance Center action, pinned sear, integral Weaver base, non-glare surfaces, scope mount accessory kit for mounting full-size scopes, flashed-chromed hammer and trigger, Performance Center gun rug and shoulder sling. Interchangeable Hi-Viz green dot

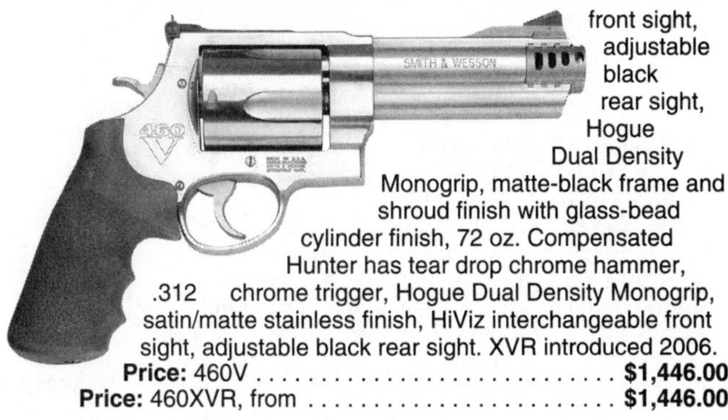

front sight, adjustable black rear sight, Hogue Dual Density Monogrip, matte-black frame and shroud finish with glass-bead cylinder finish, 72 oz. Compensated Hunter has tear drop chrome hammer, .312 chrome trigger, Hogue Dual Density Monogrip, satin/matte stainless finish, HiViz interchangeable front sight, adjustable black rear sight. XVR introduced 2006.

Price: 460V **$1,446.00**
Price: 460XVR, from **$1,446.00**

SMITH & WESSON MODEL 500 REVOLVERS

Caliber: 500 S&W Mag., 5 rounds. **Barrel:** 4", 8-3/8". **Weight:** 72.5 oz. **Length:** 15" (8-3/8" barrel). **Grips:** Hogue Sorbothane Rubber. **Sights:** Interchangeable blade, front, adjustable rear. **Features:** Recoil compensator, ball detent cylinder latch, internal lock. 6.5"-barrel model has orange-ramp dovetail Millett front sight, adjustable black rear sight, Hogue Dual Density Monogrip, .312" chrome trigger with over-travel stop, chrome tear-drop hammer, glassbead finish. 10.5"-barrel model has red ramp front sight, adjustable rear sight, .312 chrome trigger with overtravel stop, chrome tear drop hammer with pinned sear, hunting sling. Compensated Hunter has .400 orange ramp dovetail front sight, adjustable black blade rear sight, Hogue Dual Density Monogrip, glassbead finish w/black clear coat. Made in U.S.A. by Smith & Wesson.

Price: From **$1,375.00**

SUPER SIX CLASSIC BISON BULL

Caliber: 45-80 Government, 6-shot. **Barrel:** 10" octagonal with 1:14 twist. **Weight:** 6 lbs. **Length:** 17.5"overall. **Grips:** NA. **Sights:** Ramp front sight with dovetailed blade, click-adjustable rear. **Features:** Manganese bronze frame. Integral scope mount, manual crossbolt safety.

Price: . . . . **Appx. $1,100.00**

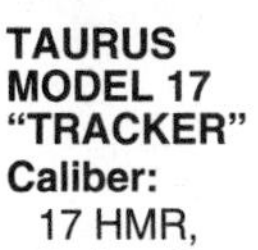

TAURUS MODEL 17 "TRACKER"

Caliber: 17 HMR, 7-shot. **Barrel:** 6.5". **Weight:** 45.8 oz. **Grips:** Rubber. **Sights:** Adjustable. **Features:** Double action, matte stainless, integral key-lock.

Price: From **$453.00**

TAURUS MODEL 44 REVOLVER

Caliber: 44 Mag., 6-shot. **Barrel:** 4", 6.5", 8-3/8". **Weight:** 44-3/4 oz. **Grips:** Rubber. **Sights:** Adjustable. **Features:** Double-action. Integral key-lock. Introduced 1994. New Model 44S12 has 12" vent rib barrel. Imported from Brazil by Taurus International Manufacturing, Inc.

Price: From. **$633.00**

TAURUS MODEL 65 REVOLVER

Caliber: 357 Mag., 6-shot. **Barrel:** 4". **Weight:** 38 oz. **Length:** 10.5" overall. **Grips:** Soft rubber. **Sights:** Fixed. **Features:** Double action, integral key-lock. Seven models for 2006 Imported by Taurus International.

Price: From **$419.00**

Taurus Model 66 Revolver

Similar to Model 65, 4" or 6" barrel, 7-shot cylinder, adjustable rear sight. Integral key-lock action. Imported by Taurus International.

Price: From **$469.00**

TAURUS MODEL 82 HEAVY BARREL REVOLVER

Caliber: 38 Spec., 6-shot. **Barrel:** 4", heavy. **Weight:** 36.5 oz. **Length:** 9-1/4" overall (4" bbl.). **Grips:** Soft black rubber. **Sights:** Serrated ramp front, square notch rear. **Features:** Double action, solid rib, integral key-lock. Imported by Taurus International.

Price: From **$403.00**

TAURUS MODEL 85 REVOLVER

Caliber: 38 Spec., 5-shot. **Barrel:** 2". **Weight:** 17-24.5 oz., titanium 13.5-15.4 oz. **Grips:** Rubber, rosewood or mother-of-pearl. **Sights:** Ramp front, square notch rear. **Features:** Blue, matte stainless, blue with gold accents, stainless with gold accents; rated for +P ammo. Integral keylock. Some models have titantium frame. Introduced 1980. Imported by Taurus International.

Price: From **$403.00**

TAURUS PROTECTOR POLYMER

Single/double action revolver chambered in .38 Special +P. Features include 5-round cylinder; polymer frame; faux wood rubber-feel grips; fixed sights; shrouded hammer with cocking spur; blued finish; 2.5-inch barrel. Weight 18.2 oz.

Price: . . . . **N/A**

Taurus 851 & 651 Revolvers

Small frame SA/DA revolvers similar to Taurus Model 85 but with Centennial-style concealed-hammer frame. Chambered in 38 Special +P (Model 851) or 357 Magnum (Model 651). Features include five-shot cylinder; 2" barrel; fixed sights; blue, matte blue, titanium or stainless finish; Taurus security lock. Overall length is 6.5". Weighs 15.5 oz. (titanium) to 25 oz. (blued and stainless).

Price: From **$411.00**

TAURUS MODEL 94 REVOLVER

Caliber: 22 LR, 9-shot cylinder; 22 Mag, 8-shot cylinder **Barrel:** 2", 4", 5". **Weight:** 18.5-27.5 oz. **Grips:** Soft black rubber. **Sights:** Serrated ramp front, click-adjustable rear. **Features:** Double action, integral key-lock. Introduced 1989. Imported by Taurus International.

Price: From **$369.00**

TAURUS MODEL 4510 JUDGE

Caliber: 3" .410/45 LC, 2.5" .410/45 LC. **Barrel:** 3", 6.5" (blued finish). **Weight:** 35.2 oz., 22.4 oz. **Length:** 7.5". **Grips:** Ribber. **Sights:** Fiber Optic. **Features:** DA/SA. Matte Stainless and Ultra-Lite Stainless finish. Introduced in 2007. Imported from Brazil by Taurus International.

Price: 4510T TrackerSS Matte Stainless **$569.00**
Price: 4510TKR-3B Judge **$558.00**
Price: 4510TKR-SSR, ported barrel, tactical rail **$608.00**

TAURUS JUDGE PUBLIC DEFENDER POLYMER

Single/double action revolver chambered in .45 Colt/.410 (2-1/2). Features include 5-round cylinder; polymer frame; Ribber rubber-feel grips; fiber-optic front sight; adjustable rear sight; blued or

stainless cylinder; shrouded hammer with cocking spur; blued finish; 2.5-inch barrel. Weight 27 oz.
Price: . . . . **N/A**

TAURUS JUDGE PUBLIC DEFENDER ULTRA-LITE
Single/double action revolver chambered in .45 Colt/.410 (2-1/2). Features include 5-round cylinder; lightweight aluminum frame; Ribber rubber-feel grips; fiber-optic front sight; adjustable rear sight; blued or stainless cylinder; shrouded hammer with cocking spur; blued finish; 2.5-inch barrel. Weight 20.7 oz.
Price: . . . . **N/A**

TAURUS RAGING JUDGE MAGNUM
Single/double action revolver chambered for .454 Casull, .45 Colt, 2.5-inch and 3-inch .410. Features include 3- or 6-inch barrel; fixed sights with fiber-optic front; blued or stainless steel finish; vent rib for scope mounting (6-inch only); cushioned Raging Bull grips.
Price: . . . . **N/A**

TAURUS RAGING JUDGE MAGNUM ULTRA-LITE
Single/double action revolver chambered for .454 Casull, .45 Colt, 2.5-inch and 3-inch .410. Features include 3- or 6-inch barrel; aluminum alloy frame; fixed sights with fiber-optic front; blued or stainless steel finish; cushioned Raging Bull grips. Weight: 41.4 oz. (3-inch barrel).
Price: . . . . **N/A**

TAURUS RAGING BULL MODEL 416
Caliber: 41 Magnum, 6-shot. **Barrel:** 6.5". **Weight:** 61.9 oz. **Grips:** Rubber. **Sights:** Adjustable. **Features:** Double-action, ported, ventilated rib, matte stainless, integral key-lock.
Price: **$706.00**

TAURUS MODEL 425 TRACKER REVOLVERS
Caliber: 357 Mag., 7-shot; 41 Mag., 5-shot. **Barrel:** 4" and 6". **Weight:** 28.8-40 oz. (titanium) 24.3-28. (6"). **Grips:** Rubber. **Sights:** Fixed front, adjustable rear. **Features:** Double-action stainless steel, Shadow Gray or Total Titanium; vent rib (steel models only); integral key-lock action. Imported by Taurus International.
Price: From. **$569.00**

TAURUS MODEL 444 ULTRA-LIGHT
Caliber: 44 Mag, 5-shot. **Barrel:** 4". **Weight:** 28.3 oz. **Length:** 9.8"overall. **Grips:** Cushioned inset rubber. **Sights:** Fixed red-fiber optic front, adjustable rear. **Features:** UltraLite titanium blue finish, titanium/alloy frame built on Raging Bull design. Smooth trigger shoe, 1.760" wide, 6.280" tall. Barrel rate of twist 1:16", 6 grooves. Introduced 2005. Imported by Taurus International.
Price: **$666.00**

TAURUS MODEL 416/444/454 RAGING BULL REVOLVERS
Caliber: 41 Mag., 44 Mag., 454 Casull. **Barrel:** 2.25" (454 Casull only), 5", 6.5", 8-3/8". **Weight:** 53-63 oz. **Length:** 12" overall (6.5" barrel). **Grips:** Soft black rubber. **Sights:** Patridge front, adjustable rear. **Features:** Double-action, ventilated rib, ported, integral key-lock. Introduced 1997. Imported by Taurus International.
Price: From **$641.00**

TAURUS MODEL 605 REVOLVER
Caliber: 357 Mag., 5-shot. **Barrel:** 2". **Weight:** 24 oz. **Grips:** Rubber. **Sights:** Fixed. **Features:** Double-action, blue or stainless or titanium, concealed hammer models DAO, porting optional, integral key-lock. Introduced 1995. Imported by Taurus International.
Price: From **$403.00**

TAURUS MODEL 608 REVOLVER
Caliber: 357 Mag. 38 Spec., 8-shot. **Barrel:** 4", 6.5", 8-3/8". **Weight:** 44-57 oz. **Length:** 9-3/8" overall. **Grips:** Soft black rubber. **Sights:** Adjustable. **Features:** Double-action, integral key-lock action. Available in blue or stainless. Introduced 1995. Imported by Taurus International.
Price: From. **$584.00**

TAURUS MODEL 617 REVOLVER
Caliber: 357 Mag., 7-shot. **Barrel:** 2". **Weight:** 28.3 oz. **Length:** 6.75" overall. **Grips:** Soft black rubber. **Sights:** Fixed. **Features:** Double-action, blue, Shadow Gray, bright spectrum blue or matte stainless steel, integral key-lock. Available with porting, concealed hammer. Introduced 1998. Imported by Taurus International.
Price: **$436.00**

TAURUS MODEL 650 CIA REVOLVER
Caliber: 357 Mag., 5-shot. **Barrel:** 2". **Weight:** 24.5 oz. **Grips:** Rubber. **Sights:** Ramp front, square notch rear. **Features:** Double-action only, blue or matte stainless steel, integral key-lock, internal hammer. Introduced 2001. From Taurus International.
Price: From **$411.00**

TAURUS MODEL 651 PROTECTOR REVOLVER
Caliber: 357 Mag., 5-shot. **Barrel:** 2". **Weight:** 17-24.5 oz. **Grips:** Rubber. **Sights:** Fixed. **Features:** Concealed single-action/double-action design. Shrouded cockable hammer, blue, matte stainless, Shadow Gray, Total Titanium, integral key-lock. Made in Brazil. Imported by Taurus International Manufacturing, Inc.
Price: From **$411.00**

Taurus Model 731 Revolver
Similar to the Taurus Model 605, except in .32 Magnum.
Price: **$469.00**

TAURUS MODEL 817 ULTRA-LITE REVOLVER
Caliber: 38 Spec., 7-shot. **Barrel:** 2". **Weight:** 21 oz. **Length:** 6.5" overall. **Grips:** Soft rubber. **Sights:** Fixed. **Features:** Double-action, integral key-lock. Rated for +P ammo. Introduced 1999. Imported from Brazil by Taurus International.
Price: From **$436.00**

TAURUS MODEL 850 CIA REVOLVER
Caliber: 38 Spec., 5-shot. **Barrel:** 2". **Weight:** 17-24.5 oz. **Grips:** Rubber, mother-of-pearl. **Sights:** Ramp front, square notch rear. **Features:** Double-action only, blue or matte stainless steel, rated for +P ammo, integral key-lock, internal hammer. Introduced 2001. From Taurus International.
Price: From **$411.00**

TAURUS MODEL 941 REVOLVER
Caliber: 22 LR (Mod. 94), 22 WMR (Mod. 941), 8-shot. **Barrel:** 2", 4", 5". **Weight:** 27.5 oz. (4" barrel). **Grips:** Soft black rubber. **Sights:** Serrated ramp front, rear adjustable. **Features:** Double-action, integral key-lock. Introduced 1992. Imported by Taurus International.
Price: From **$386.00**

TAURUS MODEL 970/971 TRACKER REVOLVERS
Caliber: 22 LR (Model 970), 22 Magnum (Model 971); 7-shot. **Barrel:** 6". **Weight:** 53.6 oz. **Grips:** Rubber. **Sights:** Adjustable. **Features:** Double barrel, heavy barrel with ventilated rib; matte stainless finish, integral key-lock. Introduced 2001. From Taurus International.
Price: **$453.00**
Price: Model 17SS6, chambered in 17 HMR **$453.00**

BERETTA STAMPEDE SINGLE-ACTION REVOLVER

Caliber: 357 Mag, 45 Colt, 6-shot. **Barrel:** 4.75", 5.5", 7.5", blued. **Weight:** 36.8 oz. (4.75" barrel). **Length:** 9.5" overall (4.75" barrel). **Grips:** Wood, walnut, black polymer. **Sights:** Blade front, notch rear. **Features:** Transfer-bar safety. Introduced 2003. Stampede Inox (2004) is stainless steel with black polymer grips. Compact Stampede Marshall (2004) has birdshead-style walnut grips, 3.5" barrel, color-case-hardened frame, blued barrel and cylinder. Manufactured for Beretta by Uberti.

Price: Nickel, 45 Colt **$630.00**
Price: Blued, 45 Colt, 357 Mag, 4.75", 5-1/2" **$575.00**
Price: Deluxe, 45 Colt, 357 Mag. 4.75", 5-1/2" **$675.00**
Price: Marshall, 45 Colt, 357 Mag. 3.5" **$575.00**
Price: Bisley nickel, 4.75", 5.5" **$775.00**
Price: Bisley, 4.75", 5.5" **$675.00**
Price: Stampede Deluxe, 45 Colt 7.5" **$775.00**
Price: Stampede Blued, 45 Colt 7.5" **$575.00**
Price: Marshall Old West, 45 Colt 3.5" **$650.00**

CHARTER ARMS DIXIE DERRINGER

Caliber: 22 LR, 22 Magnum, 22 LR/Magnum convertible. **Barrel:** 1-1/8". **Weight:** 6 oz. **Grips:** NA. **Sights:** NA. **Features:** Single-action minigun, five-round cylinder, hammer block safety, stainless steel construction.

Price: **$469.00**

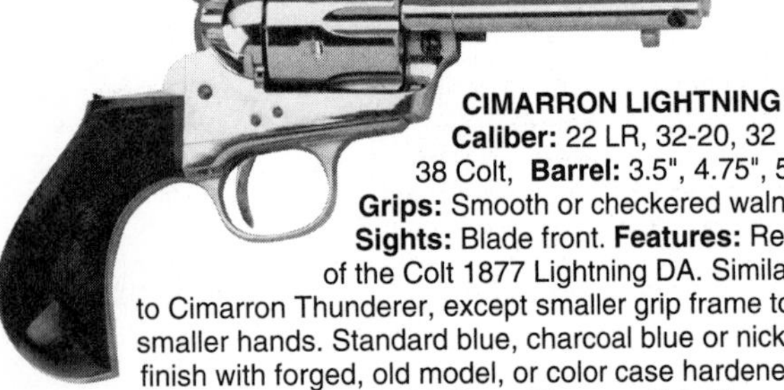

CIMARRON LIGHTNING SA

Caliber: 22 LR, 32-20, 32 H&R, 38 Colt, **Barrel:** 3.5", 4.75", 5.5". **Grips:** Smooth or checkered walnut. **Sights:** Blade front. **Features:** Replica of the Colt 1877 Lightning DA. Similar to Cimarron Thunderer, except smaller grip frame to fit smaller hands. Standard blue, charcoal blue or nickel finish with forged, old model, or color case hardened frame. Introduced 2001. From Cimarron F.A. Co.

Price: From **$480.70**

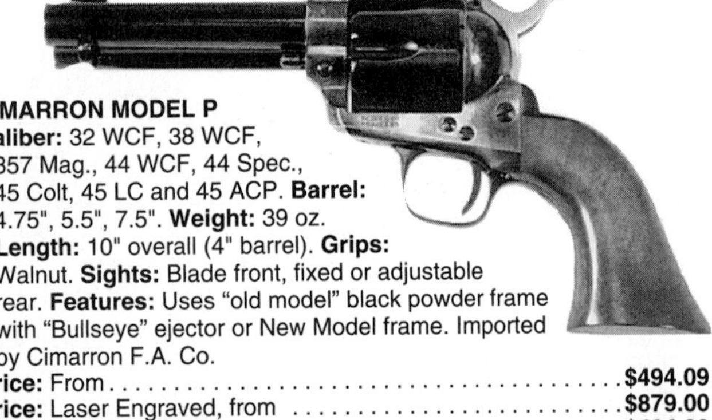

CIMARRON MODEL P

Caliber: 32 WCF, 38 WCF, 357 Mag., 44 WCF, 44 Spec., 45 Colt, 45 LC and 45 ACP. **Barrel:** 4.75", 5.5", 7.5". **Weight:** 39 oz. **Length:** 10" overall (4" barrel). **Grips:** Walnut. **Sights:** Blade front, fixed or adjustable rear. **Features:** Uses "old model" black powder frame with "Bullseye" ejector or New Model frame. Imported by Cimarron F.A. Co.

Price: From **$494.09**
Price: Laser Engraved, from **$879.00**
Price: New Sheriff, from **$494.09**

Cimarron Bisley Model Single-Action Revolvers

Similar to 1873 Model P, special grip frame and trigger guard, knurled wide-spur hammer, curved trigger. Available in 357 Mag., 44 WCF, 44 Spl., 45 Colt. Introduced 1999. Imported by Cimarron F.A. Co.

Price: From **$574.43**

CIMARRON MODEL "P" JR.

Caliber: 32-20, 32 H&R, **Barrel:** 3.5", 4.75", 5.5". **Grips:** Checkered walnut. **Sights:** Blade front. **Features:** Styled after 1873 Colt Peacemaker, except 20 percent smaller. Blue finish with color case-hardened frame; Cowboy action. Introduced 2001. From Cimarron F.A. Co.

Price: **$400.36**

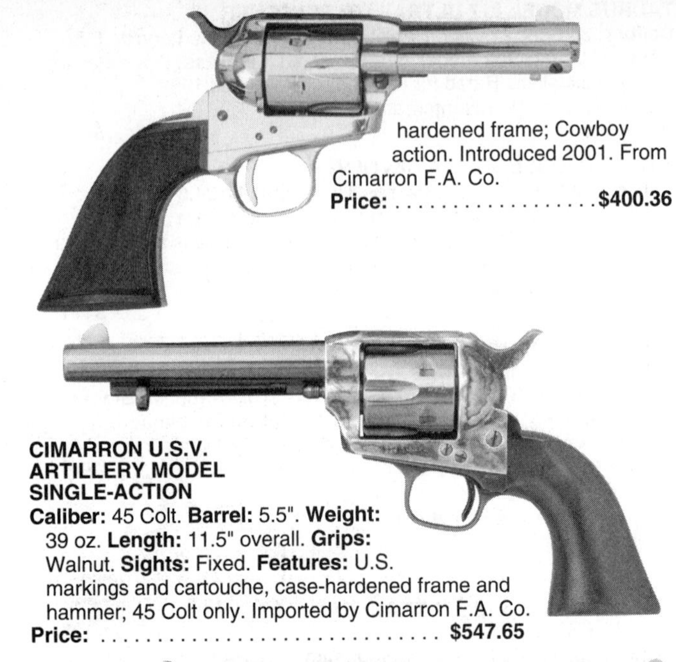

CIMARRON U.S.V. ARTILLERY MODEL SINGLE-ACTION

Caliber: 45 Colt. **Barrel:** 5.5". **Weight:** 39 oz. **Length:** 11.5" overall. **Grips:** Walnut. **Sights:** Fixed. **Features:** U.S. markings and cartouche, case-hardened frame and hammer; 45 Colt only. Imported by Cimarron F.A. Co.

Price: **$547.65**

CIMARRON 1872 OPEN TOP REVOLVER

Caliber: 38, 44 Special, 44 Colt, 44 Russian, 45 LC, 45 S&W Schofield. **Barrel:** 5.5" and 7.5". **Grips:** Walnut. **Sights:** Blade front, fixed rear. **Features:** Replica of first cartridge-firing revolver. Blue, charcoal blue, nickel or Original finish; Navy-style brass or steel Army-style frame. Introduced 2001 by Cimarron F.A. Co.

Price: **$467.31**

CIMARRON THUNDERER REVOLVER

Caliber: 357 Mag., 44 WCF, 45 Colt, 6-shot. **Barrel:** 3.5", 4.75", with ejector. **Weight:** 38 oz. (3.5" barrel). **Grips:** Smooth or checkered walnut. **Sights:** Blade front, notch rear. **Features:** Thunderer grip. Introduced 1993. Imported by Cimarron F.A. Co.

Price: Stainless **$534.26**

COLT SINGLE-ACTION ARMY REVOLVER

Caliber: 357 Mag., 38 Spec., .32/20, 44-40, 45 Colt, 6-shot. **Barrel:** 4.75", 5.5", 7.5". **Weight:** 40 oz. (4.75" barrel). **Length:** 10.25" overall (4.75" barrel). **Grips:** Black Eagle composite. **Sights:** Blade front, notch rear. **Features:** Available in full nickel finish with nickel grip medallions, or Royal Blue with color case-hardened frame. Reintroduced 1992. Sheriff's Model and Frontier Six introduced 2008, available in nickel in 2010.

Price: P1540, 32-20, 4.75" barrel, color case-hardened/blued finish **$1,290.00**
Price: P1656, 357 Mag., 5.5" barrel, nickel finish **$1,490.00**
Price: P1876, 45 LC, 7.5" barrel, nickel finish **$1,490.00**
Price: P2830S SAA Sheriff's, 3" barrel, 45 LC (2008) **$1,290.00**
Price: P2950FSS Frontier Six Shooter, 5.5" barrel, 44-40 (2008) **$1,350.00**

Prices given are believed to be accurate at time of publication however, many factors affect retail pricing so exact prices are not possible.

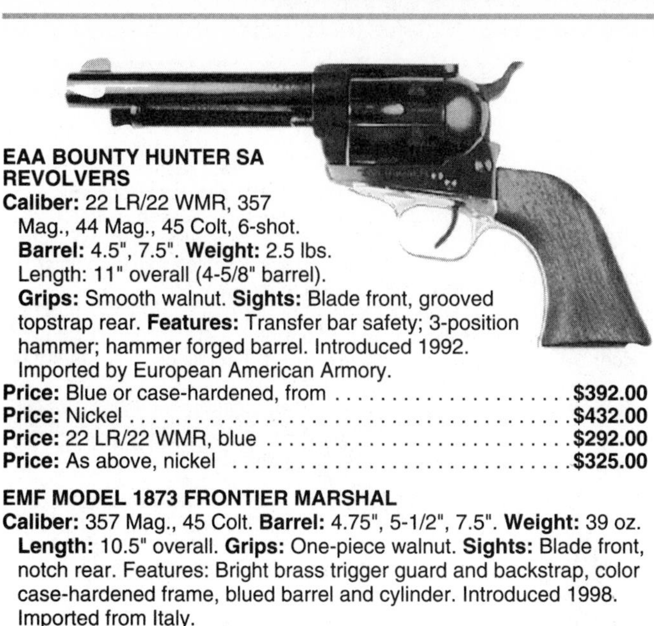

EAA BOUNTY HUNTER SA REVOLVERS

Caliber: 22 LR/22 WMR, 357 Mag., 44 Mag., 45 Colt, 6-shot. **Barrel:** 4.5", 7.5". **Weight:** 2.5 lbs. Length: 11" overall (4-5/8" barrel). **Grips:** Smooth walnut. **Sights:** Blade front, grooved topstrap rear. **Features:** Transfer bar safety; 3-position hammer; hammer forged barrel. Introduced 1992. Imported by European American Armory.

Price: Blue or case-hardened, from **$392.00**
Price: Nickel **$432.00**
Price: 22 LR/22 WMR, blue **$292.00**
Price: As above, nickel **$325.00**

EMF MODEL 1873 FRONTIER MARSHAL

Caliber: 357 Mag., 45 Colt. **Barrel:** 4.75", 5-1/2", 7.5". **Weight:** 39 oz. **Length:** 10.5" overall. **Grips:** One-piece walnut. **Sights:** Blade front, notch rear. Features: Bright brass trigger guard and backstrap, color case-hardened frame, blued barrel and cylinder. Introduced 1998. Imported from Italy.

Price: **$485.00**

EMF HARTFORD SINGLE-ACTION REVOLVERS

Caliber: 357 Mag., 32-20, 38-40, 44-40, 44 Spec., 45 Colt. **Barrel:** 4.75", 5.5", 7.5". **Weight:** 45 oz. **Length:** 13" overall (7.5" barrel). **Grips:** Smooth walnut. **Sights:** Blade front, fixed rear. **Features:** Identical to the original Colts. All major parts serial numbered using original Colt-style lettering, numbering. Bullseye ejector head and color case-hardening on old model frame and hammer. Introduced 1990. Imported by E.M.F. Co.

Price: Old Model **$489.90**
Price: Case-hardened New Model frame **$489.90**

EMF Great Western II Express Single-Action Revolver

Same as the regular model except uses grip of the Colt Lightning revolver. Barrel lengths of 4.75". Introduced 2006. Imported by E.M.F. Co.

Price: Stainless, Ultra Ivory grips **$715.00**
Price: Walnut grips **$690.00**

EMF 1875 OUTLAW REVOLVER

Caliber: 357 Mag., 44-40, 45 Colt. **Barrel:** 7.5", 9.5". **Weight:** 46 oz. **Length:** 13.5" overall. **Grips:** Smooth walnut. **Sights:** Blade front, fixed groove rear. **Features:** Authentic copy of 1875 Remington with firing pin in hammer; color case-hardened frame, blue cylinder, barrel, steel backstrap and trigger guard. Also available in nickel, factory engraved. Imported by E.M.F. Co.

Price: All calibers **$479.90**
Price: Laser Engraved **$684.90**

EMF 1890 Police Revolver

Similar to the 1875 Outlaw except has 5.5" barrel, weighs 40 oz., with 12.5" overall length. Has lanyard ring in butt. No web under barrel. Calibers: 45 Colt. Imported by E.M.F. Co.

Price: **$489.90**

EMF 1873 GREAT WESTERN II

Caliber: .357, 45 LC, 44/40. **Barrel:** 4 3/4", 5.5", 7.5". **Weight:** 36 oz. **Length:** 11" (5.5"). **Grips:** Walnut. **Sights:** Blade front, notch rear. **Features:** Authentic reproduction of the original 2nd generation Colt single-action revolver. Standard and bone case hardening. Coil hammer spring. Hammer-forged barrel.

Price: 1873 Californian **$520.00**
Price: 1873 Custom series, bone or nickel, ivory-like grips . . **$689.90**
Price: 1873 Stainless steel, ivory-like grips **$589.90**

FREEDOM ARMS MODEL 83 PREMIER GRADE REVOLVER

Caliber: 357 Mag., 41 Mag., 44 Mag., 454 Casull, 475 Linebaugh, 500 Wyo. Exp., 5-shot. **Barrel:** 4.75", 6", 7.5", 9" (357 Mag. only), 10" (except 357 Mag. and 500 Wyo. Exp. **Weight:** 53 oz. (7.5" bbl. In 454 Casull). **Length:** 13" (7.5" bbl.). **Grips:** Impregnated hardwood. **Sights:** Adjustable rear with replaceable front sight. Fixed rear notch and front blade. **Features:** Stainless steel construction with brushed finish; manual sliding safety bar. Micarta grips optional. 500 Wyo. Exp. Introduced 2006. Lifetime warranty. Made in U.S.A. by Freedom Arms, Inc.

Price: From **$2,099.00**

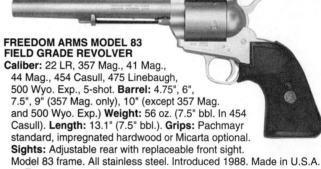

FREEDOM ARMS MODEL 83 FIELD GRADE REVOLVER

Caliber: 22 LR, 357 Mag., 41 Mag., 44 Mag., 454 Casull, 475 Linebaugh, 500 Wyo. Exp., 5-shot. **Barrel:** 4.75", 6", 7.5", 9" (357 Mag. only), 10" (except 357 Mag. and 500 Wyo. Exp.) **Weight:** 56 oz. (7.5" bbl. In 454 Casull). **Length:** 13.1" (7.5" bbl.). **Grips:** Pachmayr standard, impregnated hardwood or Micarta optional. **Sights:** Adjustable rear with replaceable front sight. Model 83 frame. All stainless steel. Introduced 1988. Made in U.S.A. by Freedom Arms Inc.

Price: From **$1,623.00**

FREEDOM ARMS MODEL 97 PREMIER GRADE REVOLVER

Caliber: 17 HMR, 22 LR, 32 H&R, 357 Mag., 6-shot; 41 Mag., 44 Special, 45 Colt, 5-shot. **Barrel:** 4.25", 5.5", 7.5", 10" (17 HMR, 22 LR & 32 H&R). **Weight:** 40 oz. (5.5" 357 Mag.). **Length:** 10.75" (5.5" bbl.). **Grips:** Impregnated hardwood; Micarta optional. **Sights:** Adjustable rear, replaceable blade front. Fixed rear notch and front blade. **Features:** Stainless steel construction, brushed finish, automatic transfer bar safety system. Introduced in 1997. Lifetime warranty. Made in U.S.A. by Freedom Arms.

Price: From **$1,772.00**

HERITAGE ROUGH RIDER REVOLVER

Caliber: 17 HMR, 17 LR, 32 H&R, 32 S&W, 32 S&W Long, 357 Mag,

44-40, 45 LC, 22 LR, 22 LR/22 WMR combo, 6-shot. **Barrel:** 2.75", 3.5", 4.75", 5.5", 6.5", 7.5", 9". **Weight:** 31 to 38 oz. **Length:** NA. **Grips:** Exotic cocobolo laminated wood or mother-of-pearl; bird's-head models offered. **Sights:** Blade front, fixed rear. Adjustable sight on 4", 6" and 9" models. **Features:** Hammer block safety. Transfer bar with Big Bores. High polish blue, black satin, silver satin, case-hardened and stainless finish. Introduced 1993. Made in U.S.A. by Heritage Mfg., Inc.
Price: From **$169.95**

MAGNUM RESEARCH BFR SINGLE-ACTION REVOLVER

(Long cylinder) **Caliber:** 30/30, 45/70 Government, 444 Marlin, 460 S&W, 45 LC/410, 450 Marlin, .500 S&W. **Barrel:** 7.5", 10". **Weight:** 4 lbs., 4.36 lbs. **Length:** 15", 17.5". ***(Short cylinder)*** **Caliber:** 50 AE, 454 Casull, 22 Hornet, BFR 480/475. **Barrel:** 6.5", 7.5", 10". **Weight:** 3.2 lbs, 3.5 lbs., 4.36 lbs. (10"). **Length:** 12.75 (6"), 13.75", 16.25". **Sights:** All have fully adjustable rear, black blade ramp front. **Features:** Stainless steel construction, rubber grips, all 5-shot capacity. Barrels are stress-relieved and cut rifled. Made in U.S.A. From Magnum Research, Inc.
Price: From **$929.00**

NAVY ARMS BISLEY MODEL SINGLE-ACTION REVOLVER

Caliber: 44-40 or 45 Colt, 6-shot cylinder. **Barrel:** 4.75", 5.5", 7.5". **Weight:** 40 oz. **Length:** 12.5" overall (7.5" barrel). **Grips:** Smooth walnut. **Sights:** Blade front, notch rear. **Features:** Replica of Colt's Bisley Model. Polished blue finish, color case-hardened frame. Introduced 1997. Imported by Navy Arms.
Price: **$503.00**

NAVY ARMS 1873 GUNFIGHTER SINGLE-ACTION REVOLVER

Caliber: 357 Mag., 44-40, 45 Colt, 6-shot cylinder. **Barrel:** 4.75", 5.5", 7.5". **Weight:** 37 oz. **Length:** 10.25" overall (4.75" barrel). **Grips:** Checkered black polymer. **Sights:** Blade front, notch rear. **Features:** Blued with color case-hardened receiver, trigger and hammer; German Silver backstrap and triggerguard. American made Wolff trigger and mainsprings installed. Introduced 2005. Imported by Navy Arms.
Price: **$545.00**

NAVY ARMS 1875 SCHOFIELD REVOLVER

Caliber: 44-40, 45 Colt, 6-shot cylinder. **Barrel:** 3.5", 5", 7". **Weight:** 39 oz. **Length:** 10.75" overall (5" barrel). **Grips:** Smooth walnut.

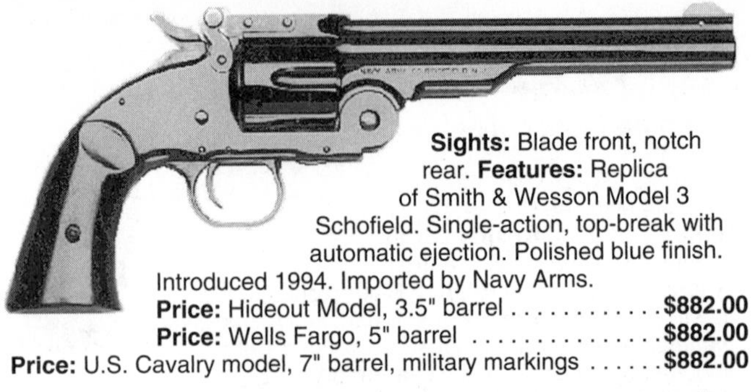

Sights: Blade front, notch rear. **Features:** Replica of Smith & Wesson Model 3 Schofield. Single-action, top-break with automatic ejection. Polished blue finish. Introduced 1994. Imported by Navy Arms.
Price: Hideout Model, 3.5" barrel **$882.00**
Price: Wells Fargo, 5" barrel **$882.00**
Price: U.S. Cavalry model, 7" barrel, military markings **$882.00**

NAVY ARMS FOUNDER'S MODEL SCHOFIELD REVOLVER

Caliber: 45 Colt, 38 Spl., 6-shot cylinder. **Barrel:** 7.5". **Weight:** 41 oz. **Length:** 13.75". **Grips:** Deluxe hand-rubbed walnut with cartouching. **Sights:** Blade front, notch rear. **Features:** Charcoal blued with bone color case-hardened receiver, trigger, hammer and backstrap. Limited production "VF" serial number prefix. Introduced 2005. Imported by Navy Arms.
Price: **$924.00**

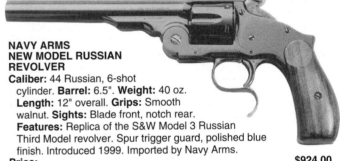

NAVY ARMS NEW MODEL RUSSIAN REVOLVER

Caliber: 44 Russian, 6-shot cylinder. **Barrel:** 6.5". **Weight:** 40 oz. **Length:** 12" overall. **Grips:** Smooth walnut. **Sights:** Blade front, notch rear. **Features:** Replica of the S&W Model 3 Russian Third Model revolver. Spur trigger guard, polished blue finish. Introduced 1999. Imported by Navy Arms.
Price: **$924.00**

NAVY ARMS SCOUT SMALL FRAME SINGLE-ACTION REVOLVER

Caliber: 38 Spec., 6-shot cylinder. **Barrel:** 4.75", 5.5". **Weight:** 37 oz. **Length:** 10.75" overall (5.5" barrel). **Grips:** Checkered black polymer. **Sights:** Blade front, notch rear. **Features:** Blued with color case-hardened receiver, trigger and hammer; German silver backstrap and triggerguard. Introduced 2005. Imported by Navy Arms.
Price: **$545.00**

NORTH AMERICAN ARMS MINI REVOLVERS

Caliber: 22 Short, 22 LR, 22 WMR, 5-shot. **Barrel:** 1-1/8", 1-5/8". **Weight:** 4 to 6.6 oz. **Length:** 3-5/8" to 6-1/8" overall. **Grips:** Laminated wood. **Sights:** Blade front, notch fixed rear. **Features:** All stainless steel construction. Polished satin and matte finish. Engraved models available. From North American Arms.
Price: 22 Short, 22 LR **$229.00**

NORTH AMERICAN ARMS MINI-MASTER

Caliber: 22 LR, 22 WMR, 5-shot cylinder. **Barrel:** 4". **Weight:** 10.7 oz. **Length:** 7.75" overall. **Grips:** Checkered hard black rubber. **Sights:** Blade front,

white outline rear adjustable for elevation, or fixed. **Features:** Heavy vented barrel; full-size grips. Non-fluted cylinder. Introduced 1989.
Price: Fixed sight **$284.00**
Price: Adjustable sight **$314.00**

North American Arms Black Widow Revolver
Similar to Mini-Master, 2" heavy vent barrel. Built on 22 WMR frame. Non-fluted cylinder, black rubber grips. Available with Millett Low Profile fixed sights or Millett sight adjustable for elevation only. Overall length 5-7/8", weighs 8.8 oz. From North American Arms.
Price: Adjustable sight, 22 LR or 22 WMR . . . **$299.00**
Price: Fixed sight, 22 LR or 22 WMR **$269.00**

NORTH AMERICAN ARMS "THE EARL" SINGLE-ACTION REVOLVER
Caliber: 22 Magnum with 22 LR accessory cylinder, 5-shot cylinder. **Barrel:** 4" octagonal. **Weight:** 6.8 oz. **Length:** 7-3/4" overall. **Grips:** Wood. **Sights:** Barleycorn front and fixed notch rear. **Features:** Single-action mini-revolver patterned after 1858-style Remington percussion revolver. Includes a spur trigger and a faux loading lever that serves as cylinder pin release.
Price: . . . . **$289.00** (22 Magnum only); **$324.00** (convertible)

RUGER NEW MODEL SINGLE SIX & NEW MODEL .32 H&R SINGLE SIX REVOLVERS
Caliber: 17 HMR, 22 LR, 22 Mag. **Barrel:** 4-5/8", 5.5", 6.5", 7.5", 9.5". 6-shot. **Grips:** Rosewood, black laminate. **Sights:** Adjustable or fixed. **Features:** Blued or stainless metalwork, short grips available, convertible models available. Introduced 2003 in 17 HMR.
Price: 17 HMR (blued) **$519.00**
Price: 22 LR/22 Mag., from **$506.00**

RUGER NEW MODEL BLACKHAWK/BLACKHAWK CONVERTIBLE
Caliber: 30 Carbine, 327 Federal, 357 Mag./38 Spec., 41 Mag., 44 Special, 45 Colt, 6-shot. **Barrel:** 4-5/8", 5.5", 6.5", 7.5" (30 carbine and 45 Colt). **Weight:** 36 to 45 oz. Lengths: 10-3/8" to 13.5". **Grips:** Rosewood or black checkered. **Sights:** 1/8" ramp front, micro-click rear adjustable for windage and elevation. **Features:** Rosewood grips, Ruger transfer bar safety system, independent firing pin, hardened chrome-moly steel frame, music wire springs throughout. Case and lock included. Convertibles come with extra cylinder.
Price: 30 Carbine, 7.5" (BN31, blued) **$541.00**
Price: 357 Mag. (blued or satin stainless), from **$541.00**
Price: 41 Mag. (blued) **$541.00**
Price: 45 Colt (blued or satin stainless), from **$541.00**
Price: 357 Mag./9mm Para. Convertible (BN34XL, BN36XL) . **$617.00**
Price: 45 Colt/45 ACP Convertible (BN44X, BN455XL) **$617.00**

Ruger Bisley Single-Action Revolver
Similar to standard Blackhawk, hammer is lower with smoothly curved, deeply checkered wide spur. The trigger is strongly curved with wide smooth surface. Longer grip frame. Adjustable rear sight, ramp-style front. Unfluted cylinder and roll engraving, adjustable sights. Chambered for 44 Mag. and 45 Colt; 7.5" barrel; overall length 13.5"; weighs 48-51 oz. Plastic lockable case. Orig. fluted cylinder introduced 1985; discontinued 1991. Unfluted cylinder introduced 1986.
Price: RB-44W (44 Mag), RB45W (45 Colt) **$683.00**

RUGER NEW MODEL SUPER BLACKHAWK
Caliber: 44 Mag., 6-shot. Also fires 44 Spec. **Barrel:** 4-5/8", 5.5", 7.5", 10.5" bull. **Weight:** 45-55 oz. **Length:** 10.5" to 16.5" overall. **Grips:** Rosewood. **Sights:** 1/8" ramp front, micro-click rear adjustable for windage and elevation. **Features:** Ruger transfer bar safety system, fluted or unfluted cylinder, steel grip and cylinder frame, round or square back trigger guard, wide serrated trigger, wide spur hammer. With case and lock.
Price: Blue, 4-5/8", 5.5", 7.5" (S-458N, S-45N, S-47N) **$650.00**
Price: Blue, 10.5" bull barrel (S-411N) **$667.00**
Price: Stainless, 4-5/8", 5.5", 7.5" (KS-458N, KS-45N, KS-47N) **$667.00**
Price: Stainless, 10.5" bull barrel (KS-411N) **$694.00**
Price: Super Blackhawk 50th Anniversary: Gold highlights, ornamentation; commemorates 50-year anniversary of Super Blackhawk **$729.00**

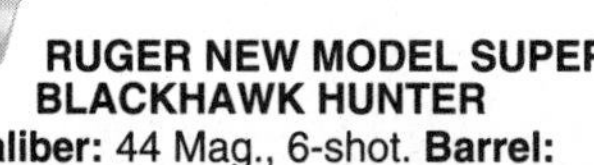

RUGER NEW MODEL SUPER BLACKHAWK HUNTER
Caliber: 44 Mag., 6-shot. **Barrel:** 7.5", full-length solid rib, unfluted cylinder. **Weight:** 52 oz. **Length:** 13-5/8". **Grips:** Black laminated wood. **Sights:** Adjustable rear, replaceable front blade. **Features:** Reintroduced Ultimate SA revolver. Includes instruction manual, high-impact case, set 1" medium scope rings, gun lock, ejector rod as standard.
Price: Hunter model, satin stainless, 7.5" (KS-47NHNN) **$781.00**
Price: Hunter model, Bisley frame, satin stainless 7.5" (KS-47NHB) **$781.00**

RUGER NEW VAQUERO SINGLE-ACTION REVOLVER
Caliber: 357 Mag., 45 Colt, 6-shot. **Barrel:** 4-5/8", 5.5", 7.5". **Weight:** 39-45 oz. **Length:** 10.5" overall (4-5/8" barrel). **Grips:** Rubber with Ruger medallion. **Sights:** Fixed blade front, fixed notch rear. **Features:** Transfer bar safety system and loading gate interlock. Blued model color case-hardened finish on frame, rest polished and blued. Engraved model available. Gloss stainless. Introduced 2005.
Price: 357 Mag., blued or stainless **$659.00**
Price: 45 Colt, blued or stainless **$659.00**
Price: 357 Mag., 45 Colt, ivory grips, 45 oz. (2009) **$729.00**

Ruger New Model Bisley Vaquero
Similar to New Vaquero but with Bisley-style hammer and grip frame. Chambered in 357 and 45 Colt. Features include a 5.5" barrel, simulated ivory grips, fixed sights, six-shot cylinder. Overall length is 11.12", weighs 45 oz.
Price: **$729.00**

RUGER NEW BEARCAT SINGLE-ACTION
Caliber: 22 LR, 6-shot. **Barrel:** 4". **Weight:** 24 oz. **Length:** 9" overall. **Grips:** Smooth rosewood with Ruger medallion. **Sights:** Blade front, fixed notch rear. **Features:** Reintroduction of the Ruger Bearcat with slightly lengthened frame, Ruger transfer bar safety system.

Available in blue only. Rosewood grips. Introduced 1996 (blued), 2003 (stainless). With case and lock.

Price: SBC-4, blued **$501.00**
Price: KSBC-4, satin stainless . **$540.00**

STI TEXICAN SINGLE-ACTION REVOLVER

Caliber: 45 Colt, 6-shot. **Barrel:** 5.5", 4140 chrome-moly steel by Green Mountain Barrels. 1:16 twist, air gauged to .0002". Chamber to bore alignment less than .001". Forcing cone angle, 3 degrees. **Weight:** 36 oz. **Length:** 11". **Grips:** "No crack" polymer. **Sights:** Blade front, fixed notch rear. **Features:** Parts made by ultra-high speed or electron discharge machined processes from chrome-moly steel forgings or bar stock. Competition sights, springs, triggers and hammers. Frames, loading gates, and hammers are color case hardened by Turnbull Restoration. Frame, back strap, loading gate, trigger guard, cylinders made of 4140 re-sulphurized Maxell 3.5 steel. Hammer firing pin (no transfer bar). S.A.S.S. approved. Introduced 2008. Made in U.S.A. by STI International.

Price: 5.5" barrel **$1,299.99**

TAURUS SINGLE-ACTION GAUCHO REVOLVERS

Caliber: 38 Spl, 357 Mag, 44-40, 45 Colt, 6-shot. **Barrel:** 4.75", 5.5", 7.5", 12". **Weight:** 36.7-37.7 oz. **Length:** 13". **Grips:** Checkered black polymer. **Sights:** Blade front, fixed notch rear. **Features:** Integral transfer bar; blue, blue with case hardened frame, matte stainless and the hand polished "Sundance" stainless finish. Removable cylinder, half-cock notch. Introduced 2005. Imported from Brazil by Taurus International.

Price: S/A-357-B, 357 Mag., Sundance blue finish, 5.5" barrel **$520.00**
Price: S/A-357-S/S7, 357 Mag., polished stainless, 7.5" barrel **$536.00**
Price: S/A-45-B7 . . . . **$520.00**

UBERTI 1851-1860 CONVERSION REVOLVERS

Caliber: 38 Spec., 45 Colt, 6-shot engraved cylinder. **Barrel:** 4.75", 5.5", 7.5", 8" **Weight:** 2.6 lbs. (5.5" bbl.). **Length:** 13" overall (5.5" bbl.). **Grips:** Walnut. **Features:** Brass backstrap, trigger guard; color case-hardened frame, blued barrel, cylinder. Introduced 2007. Imported from Italy by Stoeger Industries.

Price: 1851 Navy **$519.00**
Price: 1860 Army **$549.00**

UBERTI 1871-1872 OPEN TOP REVOLVERS

Caliber: 38 Spec., 45 Colt, 6-shot engraved cylinder. **Barrel:** 4.75", 5.5", 7.5". **Weight:** 2.6 lbs. (5.5" bbl.). **Length:** 13" overall (5.5" bbl.). **Grips:** Walnut. **Features:** Blued backstrap, trigger guard; color case-hardened frame, blued barrel, cylinder. Introduced 2007. Imported from Italy by Stoeger Industries.

Price: **$499.00**

UBERTI 1873 CATTLEMAN SINGLE-ACTION

Caliber: 45 Colt; 6-shot fluted cylinder. **Barrel:** 4.75", 5.5", 7.5". **Weight:** 2.3 lbs. (5.5" bbl.). **Length:** 11" overall (5.5" bbl.). **Grips:** Styles: Frisco (pearl styled); Desperado (buffalo horn styled); Chisholm (checkered walnut); Gunfighter (black checkered), Cody (ivory styled), one-piece walnut. **Sights:** Blade front, groove rear. **Features:** Steel or brass backstrap, trigger guard; color case-hardened frame, blued barrel, cylinder. NM designates New Model plunger style frame; OM designates Old Model screw cylinder pin retainer. Imported from Italy by Stoeger Industries.

Price: 1873 Cattleman Frisco **$789.00**
Price: 1873 Cattleman Desperado (2006) **$789.00**
Price: 1873 Cattleman Chisholm (2006) **$539.00**
Price: 1873 Cattleman NM, blued 4.75" barrel **$479.00**
Price: 1873 Cattleman NM, Nickel finish, 7.5" barrel **$609.00**
Price: 1873 Cattleman Cody. **$789.00**

UBERTI 1873 CATTLEMAN BIRD'S HEAD SINGLE ACTION

Caliber: 357 Mag., 45 Colt; 6-shot fluted cylinder **Barrel:** 3.5", 4", 4.75", 5.5". **Weight:** 2.3 lbs. (5.5" bbl.). **Length:** 10.9" overall (5.5" bbl.). **Grips:** One-piece walnut. **Sights:** Blade front, groove rear. **Features:** Steel or brass backstrap, trigger guard; color case-hardened frame, blued barrel, cylinder. Imported from Italy by Stoeger Industries.

Price: 1873 Cattleman Bird's Head OM 3.5" barrel **$539.00**

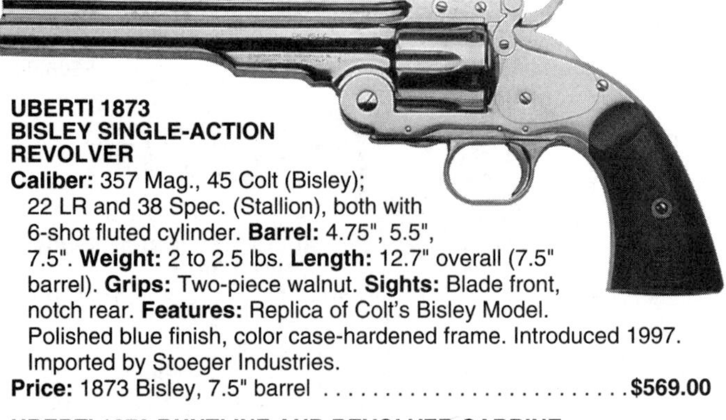

UBERTI 1873 BISLEY SINGLE-ACTION REVOLVER

Caliber: 357 Mag., 45 Colt (Bisley); 22 LR and 38 Spec. (Stallion), both with 6-shot fluted cylinder. **Barrel:** 4.75", 5.5", 7.5". **Weight:** 2 to 2.5 lbs. **Length:** 12.7" overall (7.5" barrel). **Grips:** Two-piece walnut. **Sights:** Blade front, notch rear. **Features:** Replica of Colt's Bisley Model. Polished blue finish, color case-hardened frame. Introduced 1997. Imported by Stoeger Industries.

Price: 1873 Bisley, 7.5" barrel **$569.00**

UBERTI 1873 BUNTLINE AND REVOLVER CARBINE SINGLE-ACTION

Caliber: 357 Mag., 44-40, 45 Colt; 6-shot fluted cylinder **Barrel:** 18". **Length:** 22.9" to 34". **Grips:** Walnut pistol grip or rifle stock. **Sights:** Fixed or adjustable. **Features:** Imported from Italy by Stoeger Industries.

Price: 1873 Revolver Carbine, 18" barrel, 34" OAL **$729.00**
Price: 1873 Catttleman Buntline Target, 18" barrel, 22.9" OAL **$639.00**

UBERTI OUTLAW, FRONTIER, AND POLICE REVOLVERS

Caliber: 45 Colt, 6-shot fluted cylinder. **Barrel:** 5.5", 7.5". **Weight:** 2.5 to 2.8 lbs. **Length:** 10.8" to 13.6" overall. **Grips:** Two-piece smooth walnut. **Sights:** Blade front, notch rear. **Features:** Cartridge version of 1858 Remington percussion revolver. Nickel and blued finishes. Imported by Stoeger Industries.

Price: 1875 Outlaw nickel finish **$629.00**
Price: 1875 Frontier, blued finish **$539.00**
Price: 1890 Police, blued finish **$549.00**

UBERTI 1870 SCHOFIELD-STYLE TOP BREAK REVOLVER

Caliber: 38, 44 Russian, 44-40, 45 Colt, 6-shot cylinder. **Barrel:** 3.5", 5", 7". **Weight:** 2.4 lbs. (5" barrel) **Length:** 10.8" overall (5" barrel).

Grips: Two-piece smooth walnut or pearl. **Sights:** Blade front, notch rear. **Features:** Replica of Smith & Wesson Model 3 Schofield. Single-action, top break with automatic ejection. Polished blue finish (first model). Introduced 1994. Imported by Stoeger Industries.
Price: No. 3-2nd Model, nickel finish **$1,369.00**

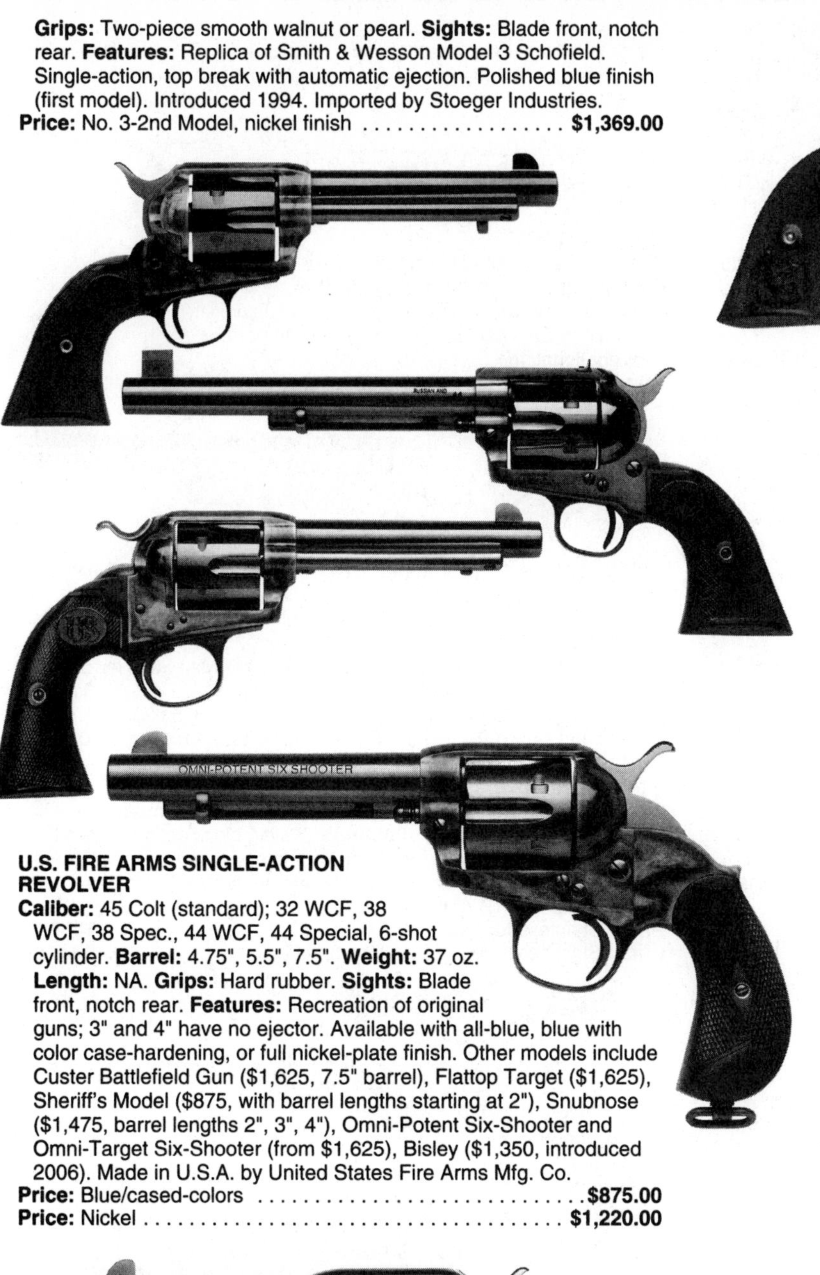

U.S. FIRE ARMS U.S. PRE-WAR
Caliber: 45 Colt (standard); 32 WCF, 38 WCF, 38 Spec., 44 WCF, 44 Special. **Barrel:** 4.75", 5.5", 7.5". **Grips:** Hard rubber. **Features:** Armory bone case/Armory blue finish standard, cross-pin or black powder frame. Introduced 2002. Made in U.S.A. by United States Firearms Mfg. Co.
Price: **$1,270.00**

U.S. FIRE ARMS SINGLE-ACTION REVOLVER
Caliber: 45 Colt (standard); 32 WCF, 38 WCF, 38 Spec., 44 WCF, 44 Special, 6-shot cylinder. **Barrel:** 4.75", 5.5", 7.5". **Weight:** 37 oz. **Length:** NA. **Grips:** Hard rubber. **Sights:** Blade front, notch rear. **Features:** Recreation of original guns; 3" and 4" have no ejector. Available with all-blue, blue with color case-hardening, or full nickel-plate finish. Other models include Custer Battlefield Gun ($1,625, 7.5" barrel), Flattop Target ($1,625), Sheriff's Model ($875, with barrel lengths starting at 2"), Snubnose ($1,475, barrel lengths 2", 3", 4"), Omni-Potent Six-Shooter and Omni-Target Six-Shooter (from $1,625), Bisley ($1,350, introduced 2006). Made in U.S.A. by United States Fire Arms Mfg. Co.
Price: Blue/cased-colors **$875.00**
Price: Nickel **$1,220.00**

U.S. FIRE ARMS RODEO COWBOY ACTION REVOLVER
Caliber: 45 Colt, **Barrel:** 4.75", 5.5". **Grips:** Rubber. **Features:** Historically correct Armory bone case hammer, blue satin finish, transfer bar safety system, correct solid firing pin. Entry level basic cowboy SASS gun. Other models include the Gunslinger ($1,145). 2006 version includes brown-rubber stocks.
Price: **$550.00**
Price: New Rodeo 2 (2007) **$605.00**

BOND ARMS TEXAS DEFENDER DERRINGER
Caliber: From 22 LR to 45 LC/410 shotshells. **Barrel:** 3". **Weight:** 20 oz. **Length:** 5". **Grips:** Rosewood. **Sights:** Blade front, fixed rear. **Features:** Interchangeable barrels, stainless steel firing pins, cross-bolt safety, automatic extractor for rimmed calibers. Stainless steel construction, brushed finish. Right or left hand.
Price: **$399.00**
Price: Interchangeable barrels, 22 LR thru 45 LC, 3" . . **$139.00**
Price: Interchangeable barrels, 45 LC, 3.5" . **$159.00 to $189.00**

BOND ARMS RANGER
Caliber: 45 LC/.410 shotshells. **Barrel:** 4.25". **Weight:** 23.5 oz. **Length:** 6.25". **Features:** Similar to Snake Slayer except no trigger guard. Intr. 2008. From Bond Arms.
Price: **$649.00**

BOND ARMS CENTURY 2000 DEFENDER
Caliber: 45 LC/.410 shotshells. **Barrel:** 3.5". **Weight:** 21 oz. **Length:** 5.5". **Features:** Similar to Defender series.
Price: **$420.00**

BOND ARMS COWBOY DEFENDER
Caliber: From 22 LR to 45 LC/.410 shotshells. **Barrel:** 3". **Weight:** 19 oz. **Length:** 5.5". **Features:** Similar to Defender series. No trigger guard.
Price: **$399.00**

BOND ARMS SNAKE SLAYER
Caliber: 45 LC/.410 shotshell (2.5" or 3"). **Barrel:** 3.5". **Weight:** 21 oz. **Length:** 5.5". **Grips:** Extended rosewood. **Sights:** Blade front, fixed rear. **Features:** Single-action; interchangeable barrels; stainless steel firing pin. Introduced 2005.
Price: **$469.00**

BOND ARMS SNAKE SLAYER IV
Caliber: 45 LC/410 shotshell (2.5" or 3"). **Barrel:** 4.25". **Weight:** 22 oz. **Length:** 6.25". **Grips:** Extended rosewood. **Sights:** Blade front, fixed rear. **Features:** Single-action; interchangeable barrels; stainless steel firing pin. Introduced 2006.
Price: **$499.00**

CHARTER ARMS DIXIE DERRINGERS
Caliber: 22 LR, 22 WMR. **Barrel:** 1.125". **Weight:** 6 oz. **Length:** 4" overall. **Grips:** Black polymer **Sights:** Blade front, fixed notch rear. **Features:** Stainless finish. Introduced 2006. Made in U.S.A. by Charter Arms, distributed by MKS Supply.
Price: **$215.00**

COBRA BIG BORE DERRINGERS
Caliber: 22 WMR, 32 H&R Mag., 38 Spec., 9mm Para., 380 ACP. **Barrel:** 2.75". **Weight:** 14 oz. **Length:** 4.65" overall. **Grips:** Textured black or white synthetic or laminated rosewood. **Sights:** Blade front, fixed notch rear. **Features:** Alloy frame, steel-lined barrels, steel breech block. Plunger-type safety with integral hammer block. Black, chrome or satin finish. Introduced 2002. Made in U.S.A. by Cobra Enterprises of Utah, Inc.
Price: **$165.00**

COBRA STANDARD SERIES DERRINGERS
Caliber: 22 LR, 22 WMR, 25 ACP, 32 ACP. **Barrel:** 2.4". **Weight:** 9.5 oz. Length: 4" overall. **Grips:** Laminated wood or pearl. **Sights:** Blade front, fixed notch rear. **Features:** Choice of black powder coat, satin nickel or chrome finish. Introduced 2002. Made in U.S.A. by Cobra Enterprises of Utah, Inc.
Price: **$145.00**

COBRA LONG-BORE DERRINGERS
Caliber: 22 WMR, 38 Spec., 9mm Para. **Barrel:** 3.5". **Weight:** 16 oz. **Length:** 5.4" overall. **Grips:** Black or white synthetic or rosewood. **Sights:** Fixed. **Features:** Chrome, satin nickel, or black Teflon finish. Introduced 2002. Made in U.S.A. by Cobra Enterprises of Utah, Inc.
Price: **$165.00**

COMANCHE SUPER SINGLE-SHOT PISTOL
Caliber: 45 LC, .410 **Barrel:** 10". **Sights:** Adjustable. **Features:** Blue finish, not available for sale in CA, MA. Distributed by SGS Importers International, Inc.
Price: **$200.00**

MAXIMUM SINGLE-SHOT PISTOL
Caliber: 22 LR, 22 Hornet, 22 BR, 22 PPC, 223 Rem., 22-250, 6mm BR, 6mm PPC, 243, 250 Savage, 6.5mm-35M, 270 MAX, 270 Win., 7mm TCU, 7mm BR, 7mm-35, 7mm INT-R, 7mm-08, 7mm Rocket, 7mm Super-Mag., 30 Herrett, 30 Carbine, 30-30, 308 Win., 30x39, 32-20, 350 Rem. Mag., 357 Mag., 357 Maximum, 358 Win., 375 H&H, 44 Mag., 454 Casull. **Barrel:** 8.75", 10.5", 14". **Weight:** 61 oz. (10.5" bbl.); 78 oz. (14" bbl.). **Length:** 15", 18.5" overall (with 10.5" and 14" bbl., respectively). **Grips:** Smooth walnut stocks and forend. Also available with 17" finger groove grip. **Sights:** Ramp front, fully adjustable open rear. **Features:** Falling block action; drilled and tapped for M.O.A. scope mounts; integral grip frame/receiver; adjustable trigger; Douglas barrel (interchangeable). Introduced 1983. Made in U.S.A. by M.O.A. Corp.
Price: Stainless receiver, blue barrel **$839.00**
Price: Stainless receiver, stainless barrel **$937.00**

THOMPSON/CENTER ENCORE PISTOL
Caliber: 22-250, 223, 204 Ruger, 6.8 Rem., 260 Rem., 7mm-08, 243, 308, 270, 30-06, 375 JDJ, 204 Ruger, 44 Mag., 454 Casull, 480 Ruger, 444 Marlin single shot, 450 Marlin with muzzle tamer, no sights. **Barrel:** 12", 15", tapered round. **Weight:** NA. **Length:** 21" overall with 12" barrel. **Grips:** American walnut with finger grooves, walnut forend. **Sights:** Blade on ramp front, adjustable rear, or none. **Features:** Interchangeable barrels; action opens by squeezing the trigger guard; drilled and tapped for scope mounting; blue finish. Announced 1996. Made in U.S.A. by Thompson/Center Arms.
Price: **$615.00**

Thompson/Center G2 Contender Pistol
A second generation Contender pistol maintaining the same barrel interchangeability with older Contender barrels and their corresponding forends (ex- cept Herrett forend). The G2 frame will not accept old-style grips due to the change in grip angle. Incorporates an automatic hammer block safety with built-in interlock. Features include trigger adjustable for overtravel, adjustable rear sight; ramp front sight blade, blued steel finish.
Price: **$600.00**

Prices given are believed to be accurate at time of publication however, many factors affect retail pricing so exact prices are not possible.

ARMALITE M15A2 CARBINE
Caliber: 223 Rem., 30-round magazine. **Barrel:** 16" heavy chrome lined; 1:9" twist. **Weight:** 7 lbs. **Length:** 35-11/16" overall. **Stock:** Green or black composition. **Sights:** Standard A2. **Features:** Upper and lower receivers have push-type pivot pin; hard coat anodized; A2-style forward assist; M16A2-type raised fence around magazine release button. Made in U.S.A. by ArmaLite, Inc.
Price: Green **$1,150.00**
Price: Black. **$1,150.00**

ARMALITE AR-10A4 SPECIAL PURPOSE RIFLE
Caliber: 308 Win., 10- and 20-round magazine. **Barrel:** 20" chrome-lined, 1:11.25" twist. **Weight:** 9.6 lbs. **Length:** 41" overall. **Stock:** Green or black composition. **Sights:** Detachable handle, front sight, or scope mount available; comes with international style flattop receiver with Picatinny rail. **Features:** Forged upper receiver with case deflector. Receivers are hard-coat anodized. Introduced 1995. Made in U.S.A. by ArmaLite, Inc.
Price: Green **$1,557.00**
Price: Black. **$1,557.00**

ArmaLite AR-10A2
Utilizing the same 20" double-lapped, heavy barrel as the ArmaLite AR10A4 Special Purpose Rifle. Offered in 308 Win. only. Made in U.S.A. by ArmaLite, Inc.
Price: AR-10A2 rifle or carbine **$1,561.00**

ARMALITE AR-10B RIFLE
Caliber: 308 Win. **Barrel:** 20" chrome lined. **Weight:** 9.5 lbs. **Length:** 41". **Stock:** Synthetic. **Sights:** Rear sight adjustable for windage, small and large apertures. **Features:** Early-style AR-10. Lower and upper receivers made of forged aircraft alloy. Brown Sudanese-style furniture, elevation scale window. Charging handle in carry handle. Made in U.S.A. by Armalite.
Price: **$1,699.00**

ARSENAL, INC. SLR-107F
Caliber: 7.62x39mm. **Barrel:** 16.25". **Weight:** 7.3 lbs. **Stock:** Left-side folding polymer stock. **Sights:** Adjustable rear. **Features:** Stamped receiver, 24mm flash hider, bayonet lug, accessory lug, stainless steel heat shield, two-stage trigger. Introduced 2008. Made in U.S.A. by Arsenal, Inc.
Price: SLR-107FR, includes scope rail **$1,035.00**

ARSENAL, INC. SLR-107CR
Caliber: 7.62x39mm. **Barrel:** 16.25". **Weight:** 6.9 lbs. **Stock:** Left-side folding polymer stock. **Sights:** Adjustable rear. **Features:** Stamped receiver, front sight block/gas block combination, 500-meter rear sight, cleaning rod, stainless steel heat shield, scope rail, and removable muzzle attachment. Introduced 2007. Made in U.S.A. by Arsenal, Inc.
Price: SLR-107CR **$1,200.00**

ARSENAL, INC. SLR-106CR
Caliber: 5.56 NATO. **Barrel:** 16.25", Steyr chrome-lined barrel, 1:7 twist rate. **Weight:** 6.9 lbs. **Stock:** Black polymer folding stock with cutout for scope rail. Stainless-steel heatshield handguard. **Sights:** 500-meter rear sight and rear sight block calibrated for 5.56 NATO. Warsaw Pact scope rail. **Features:** Uses Arsenal, Bulgaria, Mil-Spec receiver, two-stage trigger, hammer and disconnector. Polymer magazines in 5- and 10-round capacity in black and green, with Arsenal logo. Others are 30-round black waffles, 20- and 30-round versions in clear/smoke waffle, featuring the "10" in a double-circle logo of Arsenal, Bulgaria. Ships with 5-round magazine, sling, cleaning kit in a tube, 16" cleaning rod, oil bottle. Introduced 2007. Made in U.S.A. by Arsenal, Inc.
Price: SLR-106CR **$1,200.00**

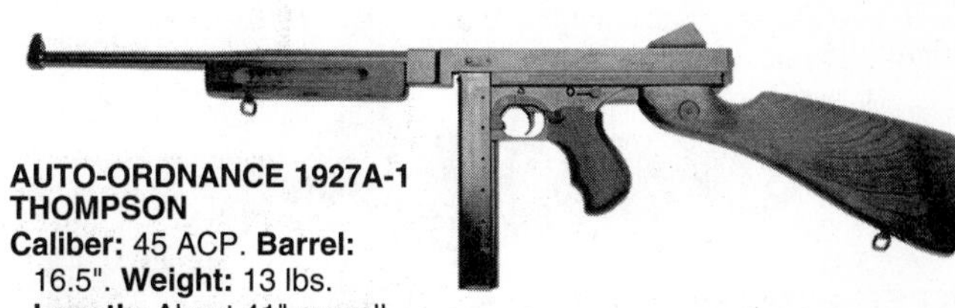

AUTO-ORDNANCE 1927A-1 THOMPSON
Caliber: 45 ACP. **Barrel:** 16.5". **Weight:** 13 lbs. **Length:** About 41" overall (Deluxe). **Stock:** Walnut stock and vertical forend. **Sights:** Blade front, open rear adjustable for windage. **Features:** Recreation of Thompson Model 1927. Semi-auto only. Deluxe model has finned barrel, adjustable rear sight and compensator; Standard model has plain barrel and military sight. From Auto-Ordnance Corp.
Price: Deluxe **$1,420.00**
Price: Lightweight model (9.5 lbs.) **$1,145.00**

Auto-Ordnance Thompson M1/M1-C
Similar to the 1927 A-1 except is in the M-1 configuration with side cocking knob, horizontal forend, smooth unfinned barrel, sling swivels on butt and forend. Matte-black finish. Introduced 1985.
Price: M1 semi-auto carbine. **$1,334.00**
Price: M1-C lightweight semi-auto **$1,065.00**

Auto-Ordnance 1927 A-1 Commando
Similar to the 1927 A-1 except has Parkerized finish, black-finish wood butt, pistol grip, horizontal forend. Comes with black nylon sling. Introduced 1998. Made in U.S.A. by Auto-Ordnance Corp.
Price: T1-C **$1,393.00**

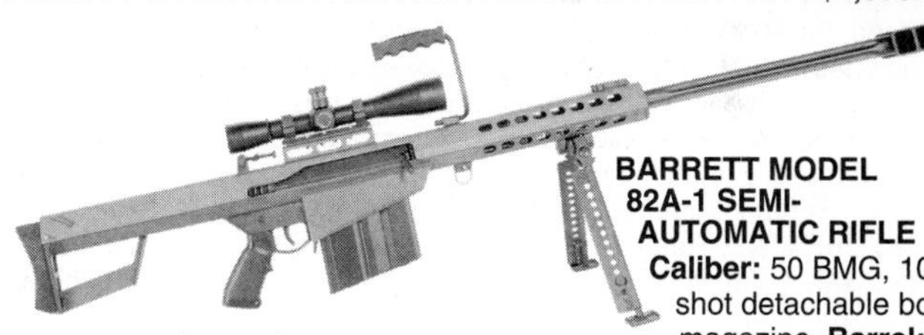

BARRETT MODEL 82A-1 SEMI-AUTOMATIC RIFLE
Caliber: 50 BMG, 10-shot detachable box magazine. **Barrel:** 29". **Weight:** 28.5 lbs. **Length:** 57" overall. **Stock:** Composition with energy-absorbing recoil pad. **Sights:** Scope optional. **Features:** Semi-automatic, recoil operated with recoiling barrel. Three-lug locking bolt; muzzle brake. Adjustable bipod. Introduced 1985. Made in U.S.A. by Barrett Firearms.
Price: From **$8,900.00**

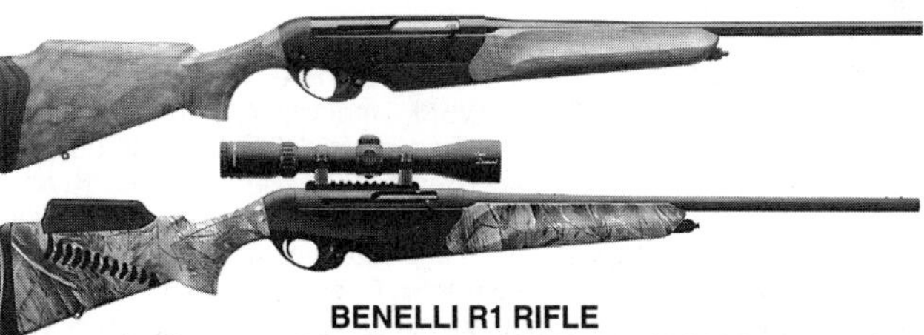

BENELLI R1 RIFLE
Caliber: 300 Win. Mag., 300 WSM, 270 WSM (24" barrel); 30-06 Spfl., 308 Win. (22" barrel); 300 Win. Mag., 30-06 Spfl., (20" barrel). **Weight:** 7.1 lbs. **Length:** 43.75" to 45.75". **Stock:** Select satin walnut or synthetic. **Sights:** None. **Features:** Auto-regulating gas-operated system, three-lug rotary bolt, interchangeable barrels, optional recoil pads. Introduced 2003. Imported from Italy by Benelli USA.
Price: Synthetic with ComforTech gel recoil pad **$1,549.00**
Price: Satin walnut **$1,379.00**
Price: APG HD camo, 30-06 (2008) **$1,689.00**

BENELLI MR1 RIFLE
Gas-operated semiauto rifle chambered in 5.56 NATO. Features include 16-inch 1:9 hard chrome-lined barrel, synthetic stock with pistol grip, rotating bolt, military-style aperture sights with picatinny rail. Comes equipped with 5-round detachable magazine but accepts M16 magazines.
Price: **$1299.00**

BERETTA CX4/PX4 STORM CARBINE
Caliber: 9mm Para., 40 S&W, 45 ACP. **Weight:** 5.75 lbs. **Barrel Length:** 16.6", chrome lined, rate of twist 1:16 (40 S&W) or 1:10 (9mm Para.). **Length:** NA. **Stock:** Black synthetic. **Sights:** NA. **Features:** Introduced 2005. Imported from Italy by Beretta USA.
Price: **$900.00**

BROWNING BAR SAFARI AND SAFARI W/BOSS SEMI-AUTO RIFLES
Caliber: Safari: 243 Win., 25-06 Rem., 270 Win., 7mm Rem. Mag.., 30-06 Spfl., 308 Win., 300 Win. Mag., 338 Win. Mag. Safari w/BOSS: 270 Win., 7mm Rem. Mag., 30-06 Spfl., 300 Win. Mag., 338 Win. Mag., plus 270 WSM, 7mm WSM, 300 WSM. **Barrel:** 22-24" round tapered. **Weight:** 7.4-8.2 lbs. **Length:** 43-45" overall. **Stock:** French walnut pistol grip stock and forend, hand checkered. **Sights:** No sights. **Features:** Has new bolt release lever; removable trigger assembly with larger trigger guard; redesigned gas and buffer systems. Detachable 4-round box magazine. Scroll-engraved receiver is tapped for scope mounting. BOSS barrel vibration modulator and muzzle brake system available. Mark II Safari introduced 1993. Imported from Belgium by Browning.
Price: BAR MK II Safari, from **$1,109.00**
Price: BAR Safari w/BOSS, from **$1,229.00**

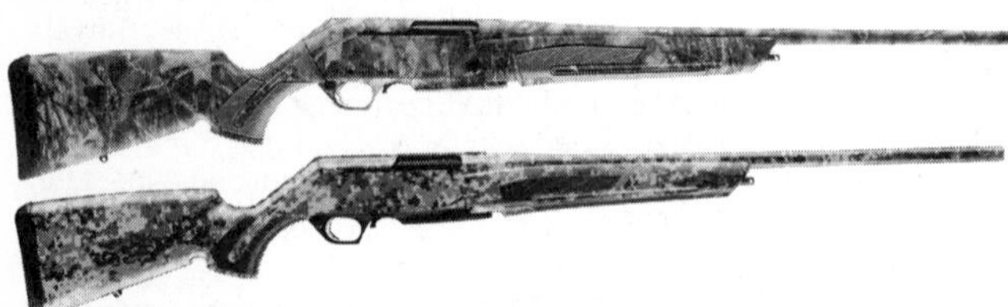

BROWNING BAR SHORTTRAC/LONGTRAC AUTO RIFLES
Caliber: (ShortTrac models) 270 WSM, 7mm WSM, 300 WSM, 243 Win., 308 Win., 325 WSM; (LongTrac models) 270 Win., 30-06 Spfl., 7mm Rem. Mag., 300 Win. Mag. **Barrel:** 23". **Weight:** 6 lbs. 10 oz. to 7 lbs. 4 oz. **Length:** 41.5" to 44". **Stock:** Satin-finish walnut, pistol-grip, fluted forend. **Sights:** Adj. rear, bead front standard, no sights on BOSS models (optional). **Features:** Designed to handle new WSM chamberings. Gas-operated, blued finish, rotary bolt design (LongTrac models).
Price: BAR ShortTrac, 243 Win., 308 Win. from **$1,079.00**
Price: BAR ShortTrac Left-Hand, intr. 2007, from **$1,129.00**
Price: BAR ShortTrac Mossy Oak New Break-up .... **$1,249.00 to $1,349.00**
Price: BAR LongTrac Left Hand, 270 Win., 30-06 Spfl., from **$1,129.00**
Price: BAR LongTrac, from......................... **$1,079.00**
Price: BAR LongTrac Mossy Oak Break Up, intr. 2007, from **$1,249.00**
Price: Bar LongTrac, Digital Green camo (2009) .... **$1,247.00 to $1,347.00**

BROWNING BAR STALKER AUTO RIFLES
Caliber: 243 Win., 308 Win., 270 Win., 30-06 Spfl., 270 WSM, 7mm WSM, 300 WSM, 300 Win. Mag., 338 Win. Mag. **Barrel:** 20-24". **Weight:** 7.1-7.75 LBS. **Length:** 41-45" overall. **Stock:** Black composite stock and forearm. **Sights:** Hooded front and adjustable rear. **Features:** Gas-operated action with seven-lug rotary bolt; dual action bars; 2-, 3- or 4-shot magazine (depending on cartridge). Introduced 2001. Imported by Browning.
Price: BAR ShortTrac or LongTrac Stalker, from **$1,119.00**
Price: BAR Lightweight Stalker, from **$1,099.00**

BUSHMASTER SUPERLIGHT CARBINES
Caliber: 223 Rem., 30-shot magazine. **Barrel:** 16", heavy; 1:9" twist. **Weight:** 6.25 lbs. **Length:** 31.25-34.5" overall. **Stock:** 6-position telestock or Stubby (7.25" length). **Sights:** Fully adjustable M16A2 sight system. **Features:** Adapted from original G.I. pencil-barrel profile. Chrome-lined barrel with manganese phosphate finish. "Shorty" handguards. Has forged aluminum receivers with pushpin. Made in U.S.A. by Bushmaster Firearms, Inc.
Price: From **$1, 250.00**

Bushmaster XM15 E2S Dissipator Carbine
Similar to the XM15 E2S Shorty carbine except has full-length "Dissipator" handguards. Weighs 7.6 lbs.; 34.75" overall; forged aluminum receivers with push-pin style takedown. Made in U.S.A. by Bushmaster Firearms, Inc.
Price: From.................................... **$1,240.00**

Bushmaster XM15 E25 AK Shorty Carbine
Similar to the XM15 E2S Shorty except has 14.5" barrel with an AK muzzle brake permanently attached giving 16" barrel length. Weighs 7.3 lbs. Introduced 1999. Made in U.S.A. by Bushmaster Firearms, Inc.
Price: From.................................... **$1,215.00**

Bushmaster M4 Post-Ban Carbine
Similar to the XM15 E2S except has 14.5" barrel with Mini Y compensator, and fixed telestock. MR configuration has fixed carry handle.
Price: **$1,190.00**

BUSHMASTER VARMINTER RIFLE
Caliber: 223 Rem., 5-shot. **Barrel:** 24", 1:9" twist, fluted, heavy, stainless. **Weight:** 8.75 lbs. **Length:** 42.25". **Stock:** Rubberized pistol grip. **Sights:** 1/2" scope risers. **Features:** Gas-operated, semi-auto, two-stage trigger, slotted free floater forend, lockable hard case.
Price: **$1,360.00**
Price: Bushmaster Predator: 20" 1:8 barrel, 223 Rem. **$1,245.00**
Price: Bushmaster Stainless Varmint Special: Same as Varminter but with 24" stainless barrel **$1,277.00**

BUSHMASTER 6.8 SPC CARBINE
Caliber: 6.8 SPC, 26-shot mag. **Barrel:** 16" M4 profile. **Weight:** 6.57 lbs. **Length:** 32.75" overall. **Features:** Semi-auto AR-style with Izzy muzzle brake, six-position telestock. Available in A2 (fixed carry handle) or A3 (removable carry handle) configuration.
Price: **$1,500.00**

BUSHMASTER ORC CARBINE
Caliber: 5.56/223. **Barrel:** 16" M4 profile. **Weight:** 6 lbs. **Length:** 32.5" overall. **Features:** AR-style carbine with chrome-lined barrel,

Prices given are believed to be accurate at time of publication however, many factors affect retail pricing so exact prices are not possible.

fixed carry handle, receiver-length picatinny optics rail, heavy oval M4-style handguards.
Price: **$1,085.00**

BUSHMASTER 11.5" BARREL CARBINE
Caliber: 5.56/223, 30-shot mag. **Barrel:** 11.5". **Weight:** 6.46 lbs. or 6.81 lbs. **Length:** 31.625" overall. **Features:** AR-style carbine with chrome-lined barrel with permanently attached BATF-approved 5.5" flash suppressor, fixed or removable carry handle, optional optics rail.
Price: **$1,215.00**

BUSHMASTER HEAVY-BARRELED CARBINE
Caliber: 5.56/223. **Barrel:** 16". **Weight:** 6.93 lbs. to 7.28 lbs. **Length:** 32.5" overall. **Features:** AR-style carbine with chrome-lined heavy profile vanadium steel barrel, fixed or removable carry handle, six-position telestock.
Price: **$1,215.00**

BUSHMASTER MODULAR CARBINE
Caliber: 5.56/223, 30-shot mag. **Barrel:** 16". **Weight:** 7.3 lbs. **Length:** 36.25" overall. **Features:** AR-style carbine with chrome-lined chrome-moly vanadium steel barrel, skeleton stock or six-position telestock, clamp-on front sight and detachable flip-up dual aperature rear.
Price: **$1,745.00**

BUSHMASTER CARBON 15 TOP LOADER RIFLE
Caliber: 5.56/223, internal 10-shot mag. **Barrel:** 16" chrome-lined M4 profile. **Weight:** 5.8 lbs. **Length:** 32.75" overall. **Features:** AR-style carbine with standard A2 front sight, dual aperture rear sight, receiver-length optics rail, lightweight carbon fiber receiver, six-position telestock. Will not accept detachable box magazines.
Price: **$1,070.00**

BUSHMASTER CARBON 15 FLAT-TOP CARBINE
Caliber: 5.56/223, 30-shot mag. **Barrel:** 16" M4 profile. **Weight:** 5.77 lbs. **Length:** 32.75" overall. **Features:** AR-style carbine Izzy flash suppressor, AR-type front sight, dual aperture flip, lightweight carbon composite receiver with receiver-length optics rail.
Price: **$1,155.00**
Price: Carbon 15 9mm, chambered in 9mm Parabellum . . . **$1,025.00**

BUSHMASTER 450 RIFLE AND CARBINE
Caliber: 450 Bushmaster. **Barrel:** 20" (rifle), 16" (carbine), five-round mag. **Weight:** 8.3 lbs. (rifle), 8.1 lbs. (carbine). **Length:** 39.5" overall (rifle), 35.25" overall (carbine). **Features:** AR-style with chrome-lined chrome-moly barrel, synthetic stock, Izzy muzzle brake.
Price: **$1,350.00**

BUSHMASTER GAS PISTON RIFLE
Caliber: 223, 30-shot mag. **Barrel:** 16". **Weight:** 7.46 lbs. **Length:** 32.5" overall. **Features:** Semi-auto AR-style with telescoping stock, carry handle, piston assembly rather than direct gas impingement.
Price: **$1,795.00**

BUSHMASTER TARGET RIFLE
Caliber: 5.56/223, 30-shot mag. **Barrel:** 20" or 24" heavy or standard. **Weight:** 8.43 lbs. to 9.29 lbs. **Length:** 39.5" or 43.5" overall. **Features:** Semi-auto AR-style with chrome-lined or stainless steel 1:9 barrel, fixed or removable carry handle, manganese phosphate finish.
Price: **$1,195.00**

BUSHMASTER M4A3 TYPE CARBINE
Caliber: 5.56/223, 30-shot mag. **Barrel:** 16". **Weight:** 6.22 to 6.7 lbs. **Length:** 31" to 32.5" overall. **Features:** AR-style carbine with chrome-moly vanadium steel barrel, Izzy-type flash-hider, six-position telestock, various sight options, standard or multi-rail handguard, fixed or removable carry handle.
Price: **$1,270.00**
Price: Patrolman's Carbine: Standard mil-style sights **$1,270.00**
Price: State Compliance Carbine: Compliant with various state regulations **$1,270.00**

CENTURY INTERNATIONAL AES-10 HI-CAP RIFLE
Caliber: 7.62x39mm. 30-shot magazine. **Barrel:** 23.2". **Weight:** NA. **Length:** 41.5" overall. **Stock:** Wood grip, forend. **Sights:** Fixed-notch rear, windage-adjustable post front. **Features:** RPK-style, accepts standard double-stack AK-type mags. Side-mounted scope mount, integral carry handle, bipod. Imported by Century Arms Int'l.
Price: AES-10, from **$450.00**

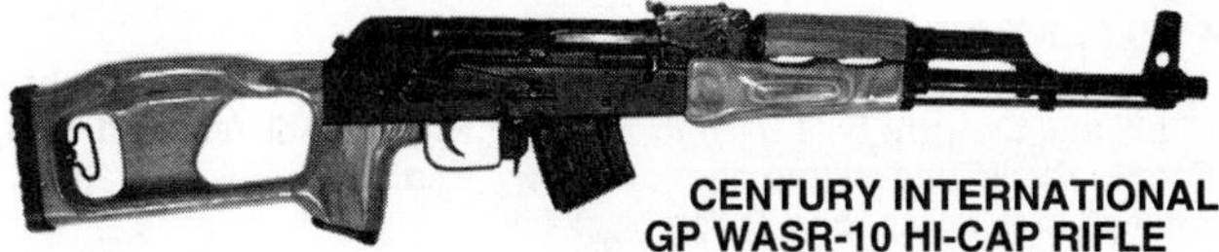

CENTURY INTERNATIONAL GP WASR-10 HI-CAP RIFLE
Caliber: 7.62x39mm. 30-shot magazine. **Barrel:** 16.25", 1:10 right-hand twist. **Weight:** 7.2 lbs. **Length:** 34.25" overall. **Stock:** Wood laminate or composite, grip, forend. **Sights:** Fixed-notch rear, windage-adjustable post front. **Features:** Two 30-rd. detachable box magazines, cleaning kit, bayonet. Version of AKM rifle; U.S.-parts added for BATFE compliance. Threaded muzzle, folding stock, bayonet lug, compensator, Dragunov stock available. Made in Romania by Cugir Arsenal. Imported by Century Arms Int'l.
Price: GP WASR-10, from **$350.00**

CENTURY INTERNATIONAL WASR-2 HI-CAP RIFLE
Caliber: 5.45x39mm. 30-shot magazine. **Barrel:** 16.25". **Weight:** 7.5 lbs. **Length:** 34.25" overall. Stocks: Wood laminate. **Sights:** Fixed-notch rear, windage-adjustable post front. **Features:** 1 30-rd. detachable box magazine, cleaning kit, sling. WASR-3 HI-CAP chambered in 223 Rem. Imported by Century Arms Int'l.
Price: GP WASR-2/3, from **$250.00**

CENTURY INTERNATIONAL M70AB2 SPORTER RIFLE
Caliber: 7.62x39mm. 30-shot magazine. **Barrel:** 16.25". **Weight:** 7.5 lbs. **Length:** 34.25" overall. Stocks: Metal grip, wood forend. **Sights:** Fixed-notch rear, windage-adjustable post front. **Features:** 2 30-rd. double-stack magazine, cleaning kit, compensator, bayonet lug and bayonet. Paratrooper-style Kalashnikov with under-folding stock. Imported by Century Arms Int'l.
Price: M70AB2, from **$480.00**

COLT MATCH TARGET MODEL RIFLE
Caliber: 223 Rem., 5-shot magazine. **Barrel:** 16.1" or 20". **Weight:** 7.1 to 8.5 lbs. **Length:** 34.5" to 39" overall. **Stock:** Composition stock, grip, forend. **Sights:** Post front, rear adjustable for windage and elevation. **Features:** 5-round detachable box magazine, flash suppressor, sling swivels. Forward bolt assist included. Introduced 1991. Made in U.S.A. by Colt's Mfg. Co., Inc.
Price: Match Target HBAR MT6601 . . . . **$1,182.00**

Colt Match Target M4
Similar to above but with carbine-length barrel.
Price: . . . . **NA**

DPMS PANTHER ARMS AR-15 RIFLES
Caliber: 223 Rem., 7.62x39. **Barrel:** 16" to 24". **Weight:** 7.75 to 11.75 lbs. **Length:** 34.5" to 42.25" overall. **Stock:** Black Zytel composite. **Sights:** Square front post, adjustable A2 rear. **Features:** Steel or stainless steel heavy or bull barrel; hardcoat anodized receiver; aluminum free-float tube handguard; many options. From DPMS Panther Arms.

Price: Panther Bull Twenty (20" stainless bull bbl.) **$920.00**
Price: Arctic Panther **$1,099.00**
Price: Panther Classic **$799.00**
Price: Panther Bull Sweet Sixteen (16" stainless bull bbl.) . . . **$885.00**
Price: DCM Panther (20" stainless heavy bbl., n.m. sights) **$1,099.00**
Price: Panther 7.62x39 (20" steel heavy bbl.) **$859.00**

DPMS PANTHER ARMS CLASSIC AUTO RIFLE
Caliber: 5.56x45mm. **Barrel:** Heavy 16" to 20" w/flash hider. **Weight:** 7 to 9 lbs. **Length:** 34-11/16" to 38-7/16". **Sights:** Adj. rear and front. **Stock:** Black Zytel w/trap door assembly. **Features:** Gas operated rotating bolt, mil spec or Teflon black finish.
Price: Panther A2 Tactical 16" **$814.00**
Price: Panther Lite 16 . . . . **$725.00**
Price: Panther Carbine **$799.00**
Price: Panther The Agency Rifle **$1,999.00**

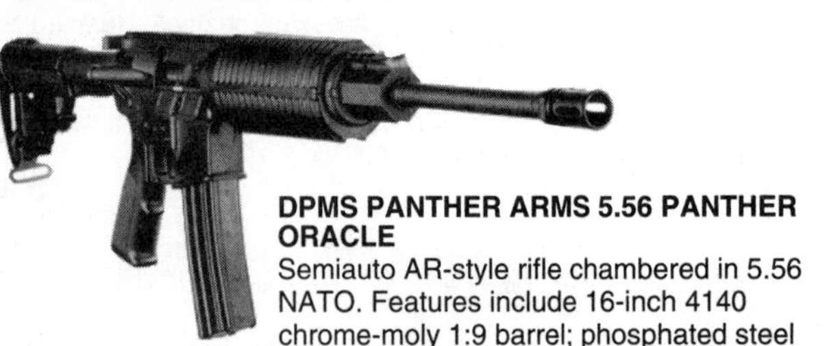

DPMS PANTHER ARMS 5.56 PANTHER ORACLE
Semiauto AR-style rifle chambered in 5.56 NATO. Features include 16-inch 4140 chrome-moly 1:9 barrel; phosphated steel bolt; oval GlacierGuard handguard; flattop upper with Picatinny rail; aluminum lower; two 30-round magazines; Pardus 6-position telescoping stock. Also available on larger platform in .308 Winchester/7.62 NATO.
Price: **$759.00**

DPMS PANTHER ARMS PANTHER 3G1
Semiauto AR-style rifle chambered in 5.56 NATO. Features include 18-inch 416 stainless 1:9 barrel; phosphated steel bolt; VTAC modular handguard; flattop upper with Picatinny rail; aluminum lower; two 30-round magazines; Magpul CTR adjustable stock.
Price: **$1,499.00**

DPMS PANTHER ARMS PRAIRIE PANTHER
Semiauto AR-style rifle chambered in 5.56 NATO. Features include 20-inch 416 stainless fluted heavy 1:8 barrel; phosphated steel bolt; free-floated carbon fiber handguard; flattop upper with Picatinny rail; aluminum lower; two 30-round magazines; skeletonized Zytel stock; finished in King's Desert Shadow camo overall.
Price: **$1,249.00**

DPMS PANTHER ARMS PANTHER RAPTR
Semiauto AR-style rifle chambered in 5.56 NATO. Features include 16-inch 4140 chrome-moly 1:9 barrel; phosphated steel bolt; ERGO Z-Rail 4-rail handguard; front vertical grip; standard A2 sights; aluminum lower; four 30-round magazines.
Price: **$1,649.00**

DPMS PANTHER ARMS PANTHER REPR
Semiauto AR-style rifle chambered in .308 Win./7.62 NATO. Features include 18-inch 416 stainless steel 1:10 barrel; phosphated steel bolt; 4-rail free-floated handguard; no sights; aluminum lower; two 19-round magazines; Coyote Brown camo finish overall.
Price: **$2,549.00**

DPMS PANTHER ARMS PANTHER 308 MK12
Semiauto AR-style rifle chambered in .308 Win./7.62 NATO. Features include 16-inch 4140 chrome-moly heavy 1:10 barrel; phosphated steel bolt; 4-rail free-floated handguard; flip-up front and rear sights; aluminum lower; two 19-round magazines; matte black finish overall; Magpul CTR adjustable stock.
Price: **$2,549.00**

DSA Z4 GTC CARBINE WITH C.R.O.S.
Caliber: 5.56 NATO **Barrel:** 16" 1:9 twist M4 profile fluted chrome lined heavy barrel with threaded Vortec flash hider. **Weight:** 7.6 lbs. **Stock:** 6 position collapsible M4 stock, Predator P4X free float tactical rail. **Sights:** Chrome lined Picatinny gas block w/removable front sight. **Features:** The Corrosion Resistant Operating System incorporates the new P.O.F. Gas Trap System with removable gas plug eliminates problematic features of standard AR gas system, Forged 7075T6 DSA lower receiver. Introduced 2006. Made in U.S.A. by DSA, Inc.
Price: **$1,800.00**

DSA CQB MRP, STANDARD MRP
Caliber: 5.56 NATO **Barrel:** 16" or 18" 1:7 twist chrome-lined or stainless steel barrel with A2 flash hider **Stock:** 6 position collapsible M4 stock. **Features:** LMT 1/2" MRP upper receiver with 20.5" Standard quad rail or 16.5" CQB quad rail, LMT-enhanced bolt with dual extractor springs, free float barrel, quick change barrel system, forged 7075T6 DSA lower receiver. EOTech and vertical grip additional. Introduced 2006. Made in U.S.A. by DSA, Inc.
Price: CQB MRP w/16" chrome-lined barrel **$2,420.00**
Price: CQB MRP w/16" stainless steel barrel **$2,540.00**
Price: Standard MRP w/16" chrome-lined barrel **$2,620.00**
Price: Standard MRP w/16" or 18" stainless steel barrel . . . **$2,740.00**

DSA STD CARBINE
Caliber: 5.56 NATO. **Barrel:** 16" 1:9 twist D4 w/A2 flash hider. **Weight:** 6.25 lbs. **Length:** 31". **Stock:** A2 buttstock, D4 handguard w/heatshield. **Sights:** Forged A2 front sight with lug. **Features:** Forged 7075T6 DSA lower receiver, forged A2 or flattop upper receiver. Introduced 2006. Made in U.S.A. by DSA, Inc.
Price: A2 or Flattop STD Carbine **$1,025.00**
Price: With LMT SOPMOD stock **$1,267.00**

DSA 1R CARBINE
Caliber: 5.56 NATO. **Barrel:** 16" 1:9 twist D4 w/A2 flash hider. **Weight:** 6.25 lbs. **Length:** Variable. **Stock:** 6 position collapsible M4 stock, D4 handguard w/heatshield. **Sights:** Forged A2 front sight with lug. **Features:** Forged 7075T6 DSA lower receiver, forged A2 or

flattop upper receiver. Introduced 2006. Made in U.S.A. by DSA, Inc.
Price: A2 or Flattop 1R Carbine **$1,055.00**
Price: With VLTOR ModStock **$1,175.00**

DSA XM CARBINE
Caliber: 5.56 NATO. **Barrel:** 11.5" 1:9 twist D4 with 5.5" permanently attached flash hider. **Weight:** 6.25 lbs. **Length:** Variable. **Stock:** Collapsible, Handguard w/heatshield. **Sights:** Forged A2 front sight with lug. **Features:** Forged 7075T6 DSA lower receiver, forged A2 upper receiver. Introduced 2006. Made in U.S.A. by DSA, Inc.
Price: **$1,055.00**

DSA STANDARD
Caliber: 5.56 NATO. **Barrel:** 20" 1:9 twist heavy barrel w/A2 flash hider. **Weight:** 6.25 lbs. **Length:** 38-7/16". **Stock:** A2 buttstock, A2 handguard w/heatshield. **Sights:** Forged A2 front sight with lug. **Features:** Forged 7075T6 DSA lower receiver, forged A2 or flattop upper receiver. Introduced 2006. Made in U.S.A. by DSA, Inc.
Price: A2 or Flattop Standard **$1,025.00**

DSA DCM RIFLE
Caliber: 223 Wylde Chamber. **Barrel:** 20" 1:8 twist chrome moly match grade Badger Barrel. **Weight:** 10 lbs. **Length:** 39.5". **Stock:** DCM freefloat handguard system, A2 buttstock. **Sights:** Forged A2 front sight with lug. **Features:** NM two stage trigger, NM rear sight, forged 7075T6 DSA lower receiver, forged A2 upper receiver. Introduced 2006. Made in U.S.A. by DSA, Inc.
Price: **$1,520.00**

DSA S1
Caliber: 223 Rem. Match Chamber. **Barrel:** 16", 20" or 24" 1:8 twist stainless steel bull barrel. **Weight:** 8.0, 9.5 and 10 lbs. **Length:** 34.25", 38.25" and 42.25". **Stock:** A2 buttstock with free float aluminum handguard. **Sights:** Picatinny gas block sight base. **Features:** Forged 7075T6 DSA lower receiver, Match two stage trigger, forged flattop upper receiver, fluted barrel optional. Introduced 2006. Made in U.S.A. by DSA, Inc.
Price: **$1,155.00**

DSA SA58 CONGO, PARA CONGO
Caliber: 308 Win. **Barrel:** 18" w/short Belgian short flash hider. **Weight:** 8.6 lbs. (Congo); 9.85 lbs. (Para Congo). **Length:** 39.75" **Stock:** Synthetic w/military grade furniture (Congo); Synthetic with non-folding steel para stock (Para Congo). **Sights:** Elevation adjustable protected post front sight, windage adjustable rear peep (Congo); Belgian type Para Flip Rear (Para Congo). **Features:** Fully-adjustable gas system, high-grade steel upper receiver with carry handle. Made in U.S.A. by DSA, Inc.
Price: Congo. **$1,850.00**
Price: Para Congo **$2,095.00**

DSA SA58 GRAY WOLF
Caliber: 308 Win. **Barrel:** 21" match-grade bull w/target crown. **Weight:** 13 lbs. **Length:** 41.75". **Stock:** Synthetic. **Sights:** Elevation-adjustable post front sight, windage-adjustable match rear peep. **Features:** Fully-adjustable gas system, high-grade steel upper receiver, Picatinny scope mount, DuraCoat finish. Made in U.S.A. by DSA, Inc.
Price: **$2,120.00**

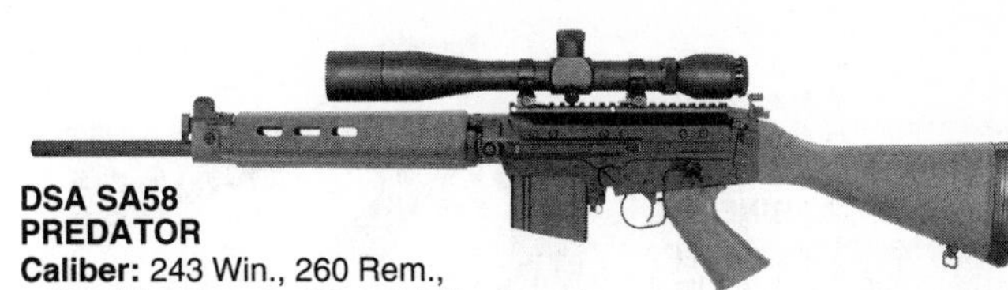

DSA SA58 PREDATOR
Caliber: 243 Win., 260 Rem., 308 Win. **Barrel:** 16" and 19" w/target crown. **Weight:** 9 to 9.3 lbs. **Length:** 36.25" to 39.25". **Stock:** Green synthetic. **Sights:** Elevation-adjustable post front; windage-adjustable match rear peep. **Features:** Fully-adjustable gas system, high-grade steel upper receiver, Picatinny scope mount, DuraCoat solid and camo finishes. Made in U.S.A. by DSA, Inc.
Price: 243 Win., 260 Rem. **$1,695.00**
Price: 308 Win. **$1,640.00**

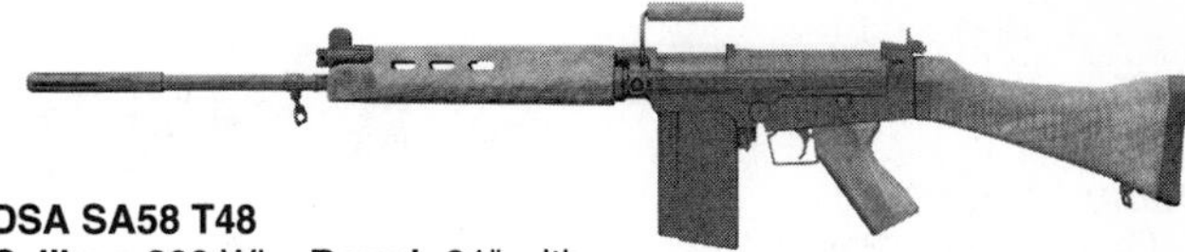

DSA SA58 T48
Caliber: 308 Win. **Barrel:** 21" with Browning long flash hider. **Weight:** 9.3 lbs. **Length:** 44.5". **Stock:** European walnut. **Sights:** Elevation-adjustable post front, windage adjustable rear peep. **Features:** Gas-operated semi-auto with fully adjustable gas system, high grade steel upper receiver with carry handle. DuraCoat finishes. Made in U.S.A. by DSA, Inc.
Price: **$1,995.00**

DSA SA58 G1
Caliber: 308 Win. **Barrel:** 21" with quick-detach flash hider. **Weight:** 10.65 lbs. **Length:** 44". **Stock:** Steel bipod cut handguard with hardwood stock and synthetic pistol grip. **Sights:** Elevation-adjustable post front, windage adjustable rear peep. **Features:** Gas-operated semi-auto with fully adjustable gas system, high grade steel upper receiver with carry handle, original GI steel lower receiver with GI bipod. DuraCoat finishes. Made in U.S.A. by DSA, Inc.
Price: **$1,850.00**

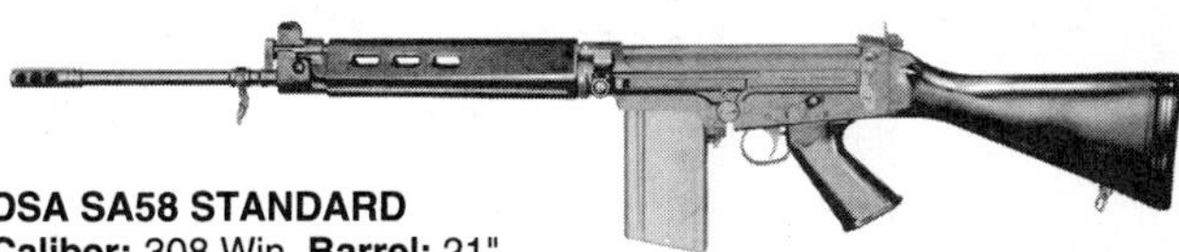

DSA SA58 STANDARD
Caliber: 308 Win. **Barrel:** 21" bipod cut w/threaded flash hider. **Weight:** 8.75 lbs. **Length:** 43". **Stock:** Synthetic, X-Series or optional folding para stock. **Sights:** Elevation-adjustable post front, windage-adjustable rear peep. **Features:** Fully adjustable short gas system, high grade steel or 416 stainless upper receiver. Made in U.S.A. by DSA, Inc.
Price: High-grade steel. **$1,595.00**
Price: Folding para stock **$1,845.00**

DSA SA58 CARBINE
Caliber: 308 Win. **Barrel:** 16.25" bipod cut w/threaded flash hider. **Weight:** 8.35 lbs. **Length:** 37.5". **Stock:** Synthetic, X-Series or optional folding para stock. **Sights:** Elevation-adjustable post front, windage-adjustable rear peep. **Features:** Fully adjustable short gas system, high grade steel or 416 stainless upper receiver. Made in U.S.A. by DSA, Inc.
Price: High-grade steel. **$1,595.00**
Price: Stainless steel **$1,850.00**

DSA SA58 TACTICAL CARBINE
Caliber: 308 Win. **Barrel:** 16.25" fluted with A2 flash hider. **Weight:** 8.25 lbs. **Length:** 36.5". **Stock:** Synthetic, X-Series or optional folding para stock. **Sights:** Elevation-adjustable post front, windage-adjustable match rear peep. **Features:** Shortened fully adjustable short gas system, high grade steel or 416 stainless upper receiver. Made in U.S.A. by DSA, Inc.
Price: High-grade steel **$1,595.00**
Price: Stainless steel **$1,850.00**

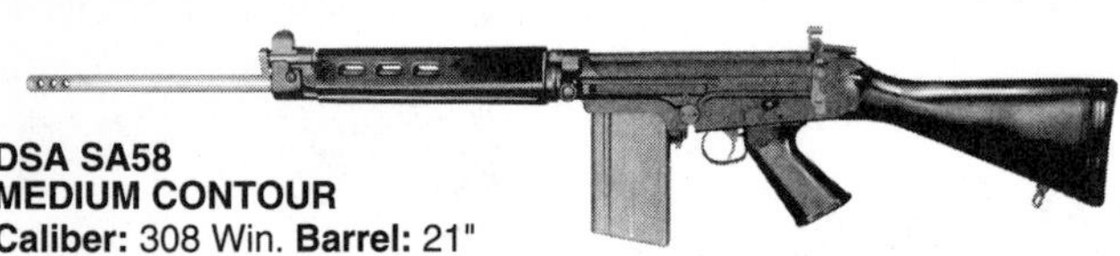

DSA SA58 MEDIUM CONTOUR
Caliber: 308 Win. **Barrel:** 21" w/threaded flash hider. **Weight:** 9.75 lbs. **Length:** 43". **Stock:** Synthetic military grade. **Sights:** Elevation-adjustable post front, windage-adjustable match rear peep. **Features:** Gas-operated semi-auto with fully adjustable gas system, high grade steel receiver. Made in U.S.A. by DSA, Inc.
Price: **$1,595.00**

DSA SA58 BULL BARREL RIFLE
Caliber: 308 Win. **Barrel:** 21". **Weight:** 11.1 lbs. **Length:** 41.5". **Stock:** Synthetic, free floating handguard. **Sights:** Elevation-adjustable windage-adjustable post front, match rear peep. **Features:** Gas-operated semi-auto with fully adjustable gas system, high grade steel or stainless upper receiver. Made in U.S.A. by DSA, Inc.
Price: **$1,745.00**
Price: Stainless steel **$1,995.00**

DSA SA58 MINI OSW
Caliber: 308 Win. **Barrel:** 11" or 13" w/A2 flash hider. **Weight:** 9 to 9.35 lbs. **Length:** 32.75" to 35". **Stock:** Fiberglass reinforced short synthetic handguard, para folding stock and synthetic pistol grip. **Sights:** Adjustable post front, para rear sight. **Features:** Semi-auto or select fire with fully adjustable short gas system, optional FAL rail handguard, SureFire Vertical Foregrip System, EOTech HOLOgraphic Sight and ITC cheekrest. Made in U.S.A. by DSA, Inc.
Price: **$1,845.00**

EXCEL ARMS ACCELERATOR RIFLES
Caliber: 17 HMR, 22 WMR, 17M2, 22 LR, 9-shot magazine. **Barrel:** 18" fluted stainless steel bull barrel. **Weight:** 8 lbs. **Length:** 32.5" overall. Grips: Textured black polymer. **Sights:** Fully adjustable target sights. **Features:** Made from 17-4 stainless steel, aluminum shroud w/Weaver rail, manual safety, firing-pin block, last-round bolt-hold-open feature. Four packages with various equipment available. American made, lifetime warranty. Comes with one 9-round stainless steel magazine and a California-approved cable lock. Introduced 2006. Made in U.S.A. by Excel Arms.
Price: MR-17 17 HMR. **$488.00**
Price: MR-22 22 WMR **$523.00**

HECKLER & KOCH USC CARBINE
Caliber: 45 ACP, 10-shot magazine. **Barrel:** 16". **Weight:** 8.6 lb. **Length:** 35.4" overall. **Stock:** Skeletonized polymer thumbhole. **Sights:** Blade front with integral hood, fully adjustable diopter. **Features:** Based on German UMP submachine gun. Blowback operation; almost entirely constructed of carbon fiber-reinforced polymer. Free-floating heavy target barrel. Introduced 2000. From H&K.
Price: **$1,249.00**

HI-POINT 9MM CARBINE
Caliber: 9mm Para., 40 S&W, 10-shot magazine. **Barrel:** 16.5" (17.5" for 40 S&W). **Weight:** 4.5 lbs. **Length:** 31.5" overall. **Stock:** Black polymer, camouflage. **Sights:** Protected post front, aperture rear. Integral scope mount. **Features:** Grip-mounted magazine release. Black or chrome finish. Sling swivels. Available with laser or red dot sights. Introduced 1996. Made in U.S.A. by MKS Supply, Inc.
Price: 995-B (black) **$220.00**
Price: 995-CMO (camo) **$235.00**

LES BAER CUSTOM ULTIMATE AR 223 RIFLES
Caliber: 223. **Barrel:** 18", 20", 22", 24". **Weight:** 7.75 to 9.75 lb. **Length:** NA. **Stock:** Black synthetic. **Sights:** None furnished; Picatinny-style flattop rail for scope mounting. **Features:** Forged receiver; Ultra single-stage trigger (Jewell two-stage trigger optional); titanium firing pin; Versa-Pod bipod; chromed National Match carrier; stainless steel, hand-lapped and cryo-treated barrel; guaranteed to shoot 1/2 or 3/4 MOA, depending on model. Made in U.S.A. by Les Baer Custom Inc.
Price: Super Varmint Model **$2,390.00**
Price: Super Match Model (introduced 2006) **$2,490.00**
Price: M4 Flattop model **$2,360.00**
Price: Police Special 16" (2008) **$1,690.00**
Price: IPSC Action Model **$2,640.00**

LR 300 RIFLES
Caliber: 5.56 NATO, 30-shot magazine. **Barrel:** 16.5"; 1:9" twist. **Weight:** 7.4-7.8 lbs. **Length:** NA. **Stock:** Folding. **Sights:** YHM flip front and rear. **Features:** Flattop receive, full length top picatinny rail. Phantom flash hider, multi sling mount points, field strips with no tools. Made in U.S.A. from Z-M Weapons.

Price: AXL, AXLT **$2,139.00**
Price: NXL **$2,208.00**

MERKEL MODEL SR1 SEMI-AUTOMATIC RIFLE
Caliber: 308 Win., 300 Win Mag. **Features:** Streamlined profile, checkered walnut stock and forend, 19.7- (308) or 20-8" (300 SM) barrel, two- or five-shot detachable box magazine. Adjustable front and rear iron sights with Weaver-style optics rail included. Imported from Germany by Merkel USA.
Price: **$1,595.00**

OLYMPIC ARMS K9, K10, K40, K45 PISTOL-CALIBER AR15 CARBINES
Caliber: 9mm Para., 10mm, 40 S&W, 45 ACP; 32/10-shot modified magazines. **Barrel:** 16" button rifled stainless steel, 1x16 twist rate. **Weight:** 6.73 lbs. **Length:** 31.625" overall. **Stock:** A2 grip, M4 6-point collapsible stock. **Features:** A2 upper with adjustable rear sight, elevation adjustable front post, bayonet lug, sling swivel, threaded muzzle, flash suppressor, carbine length handguards. Made in U.S.A. by Olympic Arms, Inc.
Price: K9GL, 9mm Para., Glock lower **$1,092.00**
Price: K10, 10mm, modified 10-round Uzi magazine **$1,006.20**
Price: K40, 40 S&W, modified 10-round Uzi magazine **$1,006.20**
Price: K45, 45 ACP, modified 10-round Uzi magazine. **$1,006.20**

OLYMPIC ARMS K3B SERIES AR15 CARBINES
Caliber: 5.56 NATO, 30-shot magazines. **Barrel:** 16" button rifled chrome-moly steel, 1x9 twist rate. **Weight:** 5-7 lbs. **Length:** 31.75" overall. **Stock:** A2 grip, M4 6-point collapsible buttstock. **Features:** A2 upper with adjustable rear sight, elevation adjustable front post, bayonet lug, sling swivel, threaded muzzle, flash suppressor, carbine length handguards. Made in U.S.A. by Olympic Arms, Inc.
Price: K3B base model, A2 upper. **$815.00**
Price: K3B-M4 M4 contoured barrel & handguards **$1,038.70**
Price: K3B-M4-A3-TC A3 upper, M4 barrel, FIRSH rail handguard. **$1,246.70**
Price: K3B-CAR 11.5" barrel with 5.5" permanent flash suppressor **$968.50**
Price: K3B-FAR 16" featherweight contoured barrel **$1,006.20**

OLYMPIC ARMS PLINKER PLUS AR15 MODELS
Caliber: 5.56 NATO, 30-shot magazine. Barrel 16" or 20" button-rifled chrome-moly steel, 1x9 twist. **Weight:** 7.5-8.5 lbs. **Length:** 35.5"-39.5" overall. **Stock:** A2 grip, A2 buttstock with trapdoor. **Sights:** A1 windage rear, elevation-adjustable front post. **Features:** A1 upper, fiberlite handguards, bayonet lug, threaded muzzle and flash suppressor. Made in U.S.A. by Olympic Arms, Inc.
Price: Plinker Plus. **$713.70**
Price: Plinker Plus 20 . . . . **$843.70**

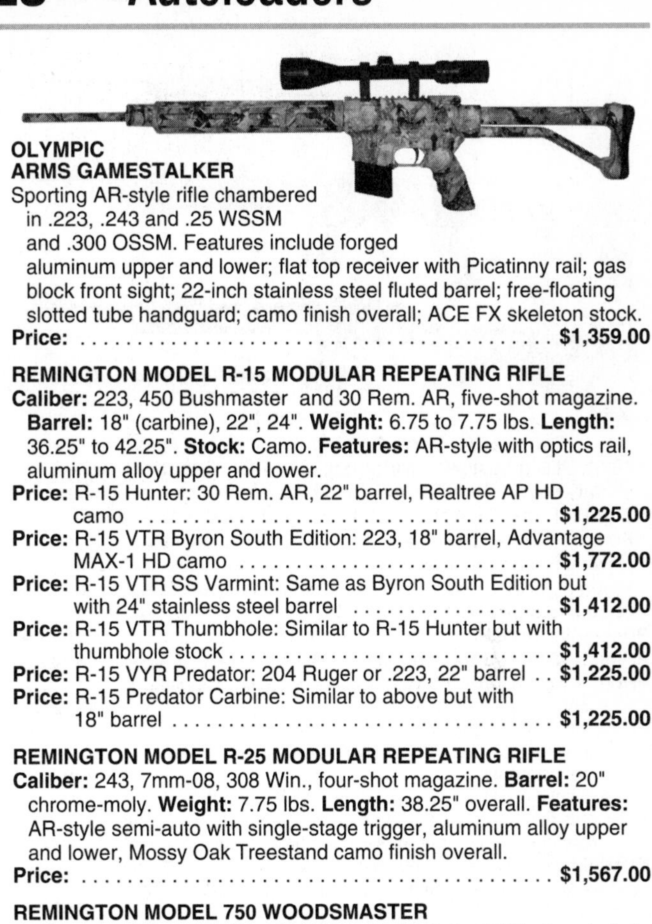

OLYMPIC ARMS GAMESTALKER
Sporting AR-style rifle chambered in .223, .243 and .25 WSSM and .300 OSSM. Features include forged aluminum upper and lower; flat top receiver with Picatinny rail; gas block front sight; 22-inch stainless steel fluted barrel; free-floating slotted tube handguard; camo finish overall; ACE FX skeleton stock.
Price: **$1,359.00**

REMINGTON MODEL R-15 MODULAR REPEATING RIFLE
Caliber: 223, 450 Bushmaster and 30 Rem. AR, five-shot magazine. **Barrel:** 18" (carbine), 22", 24". **Weight:** 6.75 to 7.75 lbs. **Length:** 36.25" to 42.25". **Stock:** Camo. **Features:** AR-style with optics rail, aluminum alloy upper and lower.
Price: R-15 Hunter: 30 Rem. AR, 22" barrel, Realtree AP HD camo **$1,225.00**
Price: R-15 VTR Byron South Edition: 223, 18" barrel, Advantage MAX-1 HD camo **$1,772.00**
Price: R-15 VTR SS Varmint: Same as Byron South Edition but with 24" stainless steel barrel **$1,412.00**
Price: R-15 VTR Thumbhole: Similar to R-15 Hunter but with thumbhole stock **$1,412.00**
Price: R-15 VYR Predator: 204 Ruger or .223, 22" barrel . . **$1,225.00**
Price: R-15 Predator Carbine: Similar to above but with 18" barrel **$1,225.00**

REMINGTON MODEL R-25 MODULAR REPEATING RIFLE
Caliber: 243, 7mm-08, 308 Win., four-shot magazine. **Barrel:** 20" chrome-moly. **Weight:** 7.75 lbs. **Length:** 38.25" overall. **Features:** AR-style semi-auto with single-stage trigger, aluminum alloy upper and lower, Mossy Oak Treestand camo finish overall.
Price: **$1,567.00**

REMINGTON MODEL 750 WOODSMASTER
Caliber: 243 Win., 270 Win., 308 Win., 30-06 Spfl., 35 Whelen. 4-shot magazine. **Barrel:** 22" round tapered. **Weight:** 7.5 lbs. **Length:** 42.6" overall. **Stock:** Restyled American walnut forend and stock with machine-cut checkering. Satin finish. **Sights:** Gold bead front sight on ramp; step rear sight with windage adjustable. **Features:** Replaced wood-stocked Model 7400 line introduced 1981. Gas action, SuperCell recoil pad. Positive cross-bolt safety. Carbine chambered in 308 Win., 30-06 Spfl., 35 Whelen. Receiver tapped for scope mount. Introduced 2006. Made in U.S.A. by Remington Arms Co.
Price: 750 Woodsmaster **$879.00**
Price: 750 Woodsmaster Carbine (18.5" bbl.) **$879.00**
Price: 750 Synthetic stock (2007). **$773.00**

ROCK RIVER ARMS STANDARD A2 RIFLE
Caliber: 45 ACP. **Barrel:** NA. **Weight:** 8.2 lbs. **Length:** NA. **Stock:** Thermoplastic. **Sights:** Standard AR-15 style sights. **Features:** Two-stage, national match trigger; optional muzzle brake. Pro-Series Government package includes side-mount sling swivel, chrome-lined 1:9 twist barrel, mil-spec forged lower receiver, Hogue rubber grip, NM two-stage trigger, 6-position tactical CAR stock, Surefire M73 quad rail handguard, other features. Made in U.S.A. From Rock River Arms.
Price: Standard A2 AR1280 . . . . **$945.00**
Price: Pro-Series Government Package GOVT1001 (2008) **$2,290.00**
Price: Elite Comp AR1270 (2008). **$1,145.00**

RUGER SR-556
AR-style semiauto rifle chambered in 5.56 NATO. Feature include two-stage piston; quad rail handguard; Troy Industries sights; black synthetic fixed or telescoping buttstock; 16.12-inch 1:9 steel barrel with birdcage; 10- or 30-round detachable box magazine; black matte finish overall.
Price: **$1,995.00**

RUGER MINI-14 RANCH RIFLE AUTOLOADING RIFLE

Caliber: 223 Rem., 5-shot detachable box magazine. **Barrel:** 18.5". Rifling twist 1:9". **Weight:** 6.75 to 7 lbs. **Length:** 37.25" overall. **Stock:** American hardwood, steel reinforced, or synthetic. **Sights:** Protected blade front, fully adjustable Ghost Ring rear. **Features:** Fixed piston gas-operated, positive primary extraction. New buffer system, redesigned ejector system. Ruger S100RM scope rings included on Ranch Rifle. Heavier barrels added in 2008, 20-round magazine added in 1009.

Price: Mini-14/5, Ranch Rifle, blued, scope rings **$855.00**
Price: K-Mini-14/5, Ranch Rifle, stainless, scope rings **$921.00**
Price: K-Mini-6.8/5P, All-Weather Ranch Rifle, stainless, synthetic stock (2008) **$921.00**
Price: Mini-14 Target Rifle: laminated thumbhole stock, heavy crowned 22" stainless steel barrel, other refinements **$1,066.00**
Price: Mini-14 ATI Stock: Tactical version of Mini-14 but with six-position collapsible stock or folding stock, grooved pistol grip. multiple picatinny optics/accessory rails . . . **$872.00**
Price: Mini-14 Tactical Rifle: Similar to Mini-14 but with 16-21" barrel with flash hider, black synthetic stock, adjustable sights **$894.00**

Ruger NRA Mini-14 Rifle

Similar to the Mini-14 Ranch Rifle except comes with two 20-round magazines and special Black Hogue OverMolded stock with NRA gold-tone medallion in grip cap. Special serial number sequence (NRA8XXXXX). For 2008 only.

Price: M-14/20C-NRA. **$1,035.00**
Price: M-14/5C-NRA (5-round magazines). **$1,035.00**

Ruger Mini Thirty Rifle

Similar to the Mini-14 Ranch Rifle except modified to chamber the 7.62x39 Russian service round. **Weight:** 6.75 lbs. Has 6-groove barrel with 1:10" twist, Ruger Integral Scope Mount bases and protected blade front, fully adjustable Ghost Ring rear. Detachable 5-shot staggered box magazine. Available 2010 with two 30-round magazines. Stainless w/synthetic stock. Introduced 1987.

Price: Stainless, scope rings **$921.00**

SABRE DEFENCE SABRE RIFLES

Caliber: 5.56 NATO, 6.5 Grendel, 30-shot magazines. **Barrel:** 20" 410 stainless steel, 1x8 twist rate; or 18" vanadium alloy, chrome-lined barrel with Sabre Gill-Brake. **Weight:** 6.77 lbs. **Length:** 31.75" overall. **Stock:** SOCOM 3-position stock with Samson M-EX handguards. **Sights:** Flip-up front and rear sights. **Features:** Fluted barrel, Harris bipod, and two-stage match trigger, Ergo Grips; upper and matched lower CNC machined from 7075-T6 forgings. SOCOM adjustable stock, Samson tactical handguards, M4 contour barrels available in 14.5" and 16" are made of MIL-B-11595 vanadium alloy and chrome lined. Introduced 2002. From Sabre Defence Industries.

Price: 6.5 Grendel, from **$1,409.00**
Price: Competition Extreme, 20" barrel, from **$2,189.00**
Price: Competition Deluxe, from **$2,299.00**
Price: Competition Special, 5.56mm, 18" barrel, from **$1,899.00**
Price: SPR Carbine, from **$2,499.00**
Price: M4 Tactical, from **$1,969.00**
Price: M4 Carbine, 14.5" barrel, from **$1,399.00**
Price: M4 Flat-top Carbine, 16" barrel, from **$1,349.00**
Price: M5 Flat-top, 16" barrel, from **$1,399.00**
Price: M5 Tactical, 14.5" barrel, from **$2,099.00**
Price: M5 Carbine, from **$1,309.00**
Price: Precision Marksman, 20" barrel, from **$2,499.00**
Price: A4 Rifle, 20" barrel, from **$1,349.00**
Price: A3 National Match, 20" barrel **$1,699.00**
Price: Heavy Bench Target, 24" barrel, from **$1,889.00**
Price: Varmint, 20" barrel **$1,709.00**

SIG 556 AUTOLOADING RIFLE

Caliber: 223 Rem., 30-shot detachable box magazine. **Barrel:** 16". Rifling twist 1:9". **Weight:** 6.8 lbs. **Length:** 36.5" overall. **Stock:** Polymer, folding style. **Sights:** Flip-up front combat sight, adjustable for windage and elevation. **Features:** Based on SG 550 series rifle. Two-position adjustable gas piston operating rod system, accepts standard AR magazines. Polymer forearm, three integrated Picatinny rails, forward mount for right- or left-side sling attachment. Aircraft-grade aluminum alloy trigger housing, hard-coat anodized finish; two-stage trigger, ambidextrous safety, 30-round polymer magazine, battery compartments, pistol-grip rubber-padded watertight adjustable butt stock with sling-attachment points. SIG 556 SWAT model has flat-top Picatinny railed receiver, tactical quad rail. SIG 556 HOLO sight options include front combat sight, flip-up rear sight, and red-dot style holographic sighting system with four illuminated reticle patterns. DMR features a 24" military grade cold hammer-forged heavy contour barrel, 5.56mm NATO, target crown. Imported by Sig Sauer, Inc.

Price: SIG 556 . . . . **$2,099.00**

Price: SIG 556 HOLO (2008) **$1,832.00**
Price: SIG 556 DMR (2008) **$2,400.00**
Price: SIG 556 SWAT **$2,000.00**
Price: SIG 556 SCM **$1,838.00**

SIG-SAUER SIG516 GAS PISTON RIFLE

AR-style rifle chambered in 5.56 NATO. Features include 14.5-, 16-, 18- or 20-inch chrome-lined barrel; free-floating, aluminum quad rail fore-end with four M1913 Picatinny rails; threaded muzzle with a standard (0.5x28TPI) pattern; aluminum upper and lower receiver is machined; black anodized finish; 30-round magazine; flattop upper; various configurations available.
Price: . . . . **N/A**

SIG-SAUER SIG716 TACTICAL PATROL RIFLE

AR-10 type rifle chambered in 7.62 NATO/.308 Winchester. Features include gas-piston operation with 3 round-position (4-position optional) gas valve; 16-, 18- or 20-inch chrome-lined barrel with threaded muzzle and nitride finish; free-floating aluminum quad rail fore-end with four M1913 Picatinny rails; telescroping buttstock; lower receiver is machined from a 7075-T6 Aircraft grade aluminum forging; upper receiver, machined from 7075-T6 aircraft grade aluminum with integral M1913 Picatinny rail.
Price: . . . . **N/A**

SMITH & WESSON M&P15 RIFLES

Caliber: 5.56mm NATO/223, 30-shot steel magazine. **Barrel:** 16", 1:9 **Weight:** 6.74 lbs., w/o magazine. **Length:** 32-35" overall. **Stock:** Black synthetic. **Sights:** Adjustable post front sight, adjustable dual aperture rear sight. **Features:** 6-position telescopic stock, thermo-set M4 handguard. 14.75" sight radius. 7-lbs. (approx.) trigger pull. 7075 T6 aluminum upper, 4140 steel barrel. Chromed barrel bore, gas key, bolt carrier. Hard-coat black-anodized receiver and barrel finish. Introduced 2006. Made in U.S.A. by Smith & Wesson.
Price: M&P15 No. 811000 . . . . **$1,406.00**
Price: M&P15T No. 811001, free float modular rail forend . **$1,888.00**
Price: M&P15A No. 811002, folding battle rear sight **$1,422.00**
Price: M&P15A No. 811013, optics ready compliant (2008). **$1,169.00**

SMITH & WESSON MODEL M&P15VTAC VIKING TACTICS MODEL

Caliber: 223 Remington/5.56 NATO, 30-round magazine. **Barrel:** 16". **Weight:** 6.5 lbs. **Length:** 35" extended, 32" collapsed, overall. **Features:** Six-position CAR stock. Surefire flash-hider and G2 light with VTAC light mount; VTAC/JP handguard; JP single-stage match trigger and speed hammer; three adjustable picatinny rails; VTAC padded two-point adjustable sling.
Price: **$2,196.00**

SMITH & WESSON M&P15PC CAMO

Caliber: 223 Rem/5.56 NATO, A2 configuration, 10-round mag. **Barrel:** 20" stainless with 1:8 twist. **Weight:** 8.2 lbs. **Length:** 38.5" overall. **Features:** AR-style, no sights but integral front and rear optics rails. Two-stage trigger, aluminum lower. Finished in Realtree Advantage Max-1 camo.
Price: **$2,046.00**

Smith & Wesson M&p15 Piston Rifle

Similar to AR-derived M&P15 but with gas piston. Chambered in 5.56 NATO. Features include adjustable gas port, optional Troy quad mount handguard, chromed bore/gas key/bolt carrier/chamber, 6-position telescoping or MagPul MOE stock, flattop or folding MBUS sights, aluminum receiver, alloy upper and lower, black anodized finish, 30-round magazine, 16-inch barrel with birdcage.
Price Standard handguard. **$1,531.00**
Price: Troy quad mount handguard **$1,692.00**

SPRINGFIELD ARMORY M1A RIFLE

Caliber: 7.62mm NATO (308), 5- or 10-shot box magazine. **Barrel:** 25-1/16" with flash suppressor, 22" without suppressor. **Weight:** 9.75 lbs. **Length:** 44.25" overall. **Stock:** American walnut with walnut-colored heat-resistant fiberglass handguard. Matching walnut handguard available. Also available with fiberglass stock. **Sights:** Military, square blade front, full click-adjustable aperture rear. **Features:** Commercial equivalent of the U.S. M-14 service rifle with no provision for automatic firing. From Springfield Armory
Price: SOCOM 16. . . . . **$1,855.00**
Price: SOCOM II, from **$2,090.00**
Price: Scout Squad, from **$1,726.00**
Price: Standard M1A, from **$1,608.00**
Price: Loaded Standard, from **$1,759.00**
Price: National Match, from **$2,249.00**
Price: Super Match (heavy premium barrel) about **$2,818.00**
Price: Tactical, from **$3,780.00**

STI SPORTING COMPETITION RIFLE

AR-style semiauto rifle chambered in 5.56 NATO. Features include 16-inch 410 stainless 1:8 barrel; mid-length gas system; Nordic Tactical Compensator and JP Trigger group; custom STI Valkyrie hand guard and gas block; flat-top design with picatinny rail; anodized finish with black Teflon coating. Also available in Tactical configuration.
Price: . . . . **N/A**

STONER SR-15 M-5 RIFLE

Caliber: 223. **Barrel:** 20". **Weight:** 7.6 lbs. **Length:** 38" overall. **Stock:** Black synthetic. **Sights:** Post front, fully adjustable rear (300-meter sight). **Features:** Modular weapon system; two-stage trigger. Black finish. Introduced 1998. Made in U.S.A. by Knight's Mfg.
Price: **$1,695.00**

STONER SR-25 CARBINE

Caliber: 7.62 NATO, 10-shot steel magazine. **Barrel:** 16" free-floating **Weight:** 7.75 lbs. **Length:** 35.75" overall. **Stock:** Black synthetic. **Sights:** Integral Weaver-style rail. Scope rings, iron sights optional. **Features:** Shortened, non-slip handguard; removable carrying handle. Matte black finish. Introduced 1995. Made in U.S.A. by Knight's Mfg. Co.
Price: **$3,345.00**

WILSON COMBAT TACTICAL RIFLES

Caliber: 5.56mm NATO, accepts all M-16/AR-15 Style Magazines, includes one 20-round magazine. **Barrel:** 16.25", 1:9 twist, match-grade fluted. **Weight:** 6.9 lbs. **Length:** 36.25" overall. **Stock:** Fixed or collapsible. **Features:** Free-float ventilated aluminum quad-rail handguard, Mil-Spec parkerized barrel and steel components, anodized receiver, precision CNC-machined upper and lower receivers, 7075 T6 aluminum forgings. Single stage JP Trigger/Hammer Group, Wilson Combat Tactical Muzzle Brake, nylon tactical rifle case. M-4T version has flat-top receiver for mounting optics, OD green furniture, 16.25" match-grade M-4 style barrel. SS-15 Super Sniper Tactical Rifle has 1-in-8 twist, heavy 20" match-grade fluted stainless steel barrel. Made in U.S.A by Wilson Combat.
Price: UT-15 Tactical Carbine. **$1,785.00**
Price: M4-TP Tactical Carbine **$1,575.00**
Price: SS-15P Super Sniper. **$1,795.00**

WINCHESTER SUPER X RIFLE

Caliber: 270 WSM, 30-06 Spfl., 300 Win. Mag., 300 WSM, 4-shot steel magazine. **Barrel:** 22", 24", 1:10", blued. **Weight:** 7.25 lbs. **Length:** up to 41-3/8". **Stock:** Walnut, 14-1/8"x 7/8"x 1.25". **Sights:** None. **Features:** Gas operated, removable trigger assembly, detachable box magazine, drilled and tapped, alloy receiver, enlarged trigger guard, crossbolt safety. Reintroduced 2008. Made in U.S.A. by Winchester Repeating Arms.
Price: Super X Rifle, from. **$949.00**

BERETTA 1873 RENEGADE SHORT LEVER-ACTION RIFLE
Caliber: 45 Colt, 357 Magnum. **Barrel:** 20" round or 24-1/2" octagonal. **Features:** Blued finish, checkered walnut buttstock and forend, adjustable rear sight and fixed blade front, ten-round tubular magazine.
Price: $1,350.00

BERETTA GOLD RUSH SLIDE-ACTION RIFLE AND CARBINE
Caliber: 357 Magnum, 45 Colt. **Barrel:** 20" round or 24-1/2"octagonal. **Features:** External replica of old Colt Lightning Magazine Rifle. Case-hardened receiver, walnut buttstock and forend, crescent buttplate, 13-round (rifle) or 10-round (carbine) magazine. Available as Standard Carbine, Standard Rifle, or Deluxe Rifle.
Price: Standard Carbine $1,375.00
Price: Standard Rifle $1,425.00
Price: Deluxe Rifle $11,950.00

BIG HORN ARMORY MODEL 89 RIFLE AND CARBINE
Lever action rifle or carbine chambered for .500 S&W Magnum. Features include 22-or 18-inch barrel; walnut or maple stocks with pistol grip; aperture rear and blade front sights; recoil pad; sling swivels; enlarged lever loop; magazine capacity 5 (rifle) or 7 (carbine) rounds.
Price: $1,889.00

BROWNING BLR RIFLES
Action: Lever action with rotating bolt head, multiple-lug breech bolt with recessed bolt face, side ejection. Rack-and-pinion lever. Flush-mounted detachable magazines, with 4+1 capacity for magnum cartridges, 5+1 for standard rounds. **Barrel:** Button-rifled chrome-moly steel with crowned muzzle. **Stock:** Buttstocks and forends are American walnut with grip and forend checkering. Recoil pad installed. Trigger: Wide-groove design, trigger travels with lever. Half-cock hammer safety; fold-down hammer. **Sights:** Gold bead on ramp front; low-profile square-notch adjustable rear. **Features:** Blued barrel and receiver, high-gloss wood finish. Receivers are drilled and tapped for scope mounts, swivel studs included. Action lock provided. Introduced 1996. Imported from Japan by Browning.

BROWNING BLR LIGHTWEIGHT W/PISTOL GRIP, SHORT AND LONG ACTION; LIGHTWEIGHT '81, SHORT AND LONG ACTION
Calibers: Short Action, 20" Barrel: 22-250 Rem., 243 Win., 7mm-08 Rem., 308 Win., 358, 450 Marlin. Calibers: Short Action, 22" Barrel: 270 WSM, 7mm WSM, 300 WSM, 325 WSM. Calibers: Long Action 22" Barrel: 270 Win., 30-06. Calibers: Long Action 24" Barrel: 7mm Rem. Mag., 300 Win. Mag. **Weight:** 6.5-7.75 lbs. **Length:** 40-45" overall. **Stock:** New checkered pistol grip and Schnabel forearm. Lightweight '81 differs from Pistol Grip models with a Western-style straight grip stock and banded forearm. Lightweight w/Pistol Grip Short Action and Long Action introduced 2005. Model '81 Lightning Long Action introduced 1996.
Price: Lightweight w/Pistol Grip Short Action, from $879.00
Price: Lightweight w/Pistol Grip Long Action $929.00
Price: Lightweight '81 Short Action $839.00
Price: Lightweight '81 Long Action $889.00
Price: Lightweight '81 Takedown Short Action, intr. 2007, from $949.00
Price: Lightweight '81 Takedown Long Action, intr. 2007, from $999.00

CHARLES DALY MODEL 1892 LEVER-ACTION RIFLES
Caliber: 45 Colt; 5-shot magazine with removable plug. **Barrel:** 24.25" octagonal. **Weight:** 6.8 lbs. **Length:** 42" overall. **Stock:** Two-piece American walnut, oil finish. **Sights:** Post front, adjustable open rear. **Features:** Color case-hardened receiver, lever, buttplate, forend cap. Introduced 2007. Imported from Italy by K.B.I., Inc.
Price: 1892 Rifle $1,094.00
Price: Take Down Rifle $1,249.00

CIMARRON 1860 HENRY RIFLE CIVIL WAR MODEL
Caliber: 44 WCF, 45 LC; 12-shot magazine. **Barrel:** 24" (rifle). **Weight:** 9.5 lbs. **Length:** 43" overall (rifle). **Stock:** European walnut. **Sights:** Bead front, open adjustable rear. **Features:** Brass receiver and buttplate. Uses original Henry loading system. Copy of the original rifle. Charcoal blue finish optional. Introduced 1991. Imported by Cimarron F.A. Co.
Price: From $1,444.78

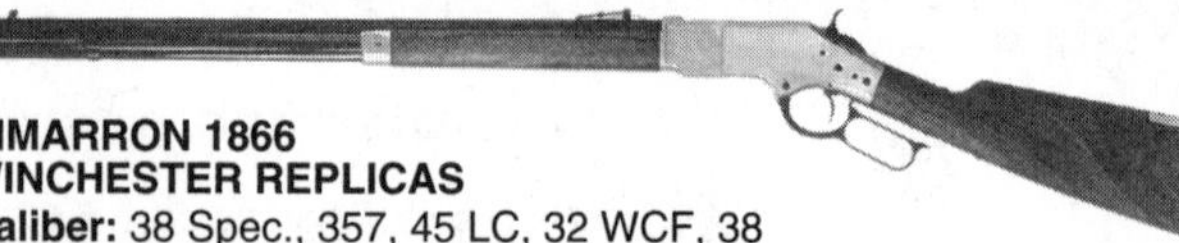

CIMARRON 1866 WINCHESTER REPLICAS
Caliber: 38 Spec., 357, 45 LC, 32 WCF, 38 WCF, 44 WCF. **Barrel:** 24" (rifle), 20" (short rifle), 19" (carbine), 16" (trapper). **Weight:** 9 lbs. **Length:** 43" overall (rifle). **Stock:** European walnut. **Sights:** Bead front, open adjustable rear. **Features:** Solid brass receiver, buttplate, forend cap. Octagonal barrel. Copy of the original Winchester '66 rifle. Introduced 1991. Imported by Cimarron F.A. Co.
Price: 1866 Sporting Rifle, 24" barrel, from $1,096.64
Price: 1866 Short Rifle, 20" barrel, from $1,096.64
Price: 1866 Carbine, 19" barrel, from $1,123.42
Price: 1866 Trapper, 16" barrel, from $1,069.86

CIMARRON 1873 SHORT RIFLE
Caliber: 357 Mag., 38 Spec., 32 WCF, 38 WCF, 44 Spec., 44 WCF, 45 Colt. **Barrel:** 20" tapered octagon. **Weight:** 7.5 lbs. **Length:** 39" overall. **Stock:** Walnut. **Sights:** Bead front, adjustable semi-buckhorn rear. **Features:** Has half "button" magazine. Original-type markings, including caliber, on barrel and elevator and "Kings" patent. From Cimarron F.A. Co.
Price: $1,203.76

Cimarron 1873 Deluxe Sporting Rifle
Similar to the 1873 Short Rifle except has 24" barrel with half-magazine.
Price: $1,324.70

CIMARRON 1873 LONG RANGE RIFLE
Caliber: 44 WCF, 45 Colt. **Barrel:** 30", octagonal. **Weight:** 8.5 lbs. **Length:** 48" overall. **Stock:** Walnut. **Sights:** Blade front, semi-buckhorn ramp rear. Tang sight optional. **Features:** Color case-hardened frame; choice of modern blue-black or charcoal blue for other parts. Barrel marked "Kings Improvement." From Cimarron F.A. Co.
Price: $1,284.10

DIXIE ENGRAVED 1873 SPORTING RIFLE
Caliber: 44-40, 13-shot magazine. **Barrel:** 24.25", tapered octagon. **Weight:** 8.25 lbs. **Length:** 43.25" overall. **Stock:** Walnut. **Sights:** Blade front, adjustable rear. **Features:** Engraved frame polished bright (casehardened on plain). Replica of Winchester 1873. Made in Italy. From Dixie Gun Works.
Price: Plain, blued rifle in .44/40, .45 LC, .32/20, .38/40. . . . $ 1,050.00

DIXIE 1873 DELUXE SPORTING RIFLE
Caliber: .44-40, .45 LC, .32-20 and .38-40, 13-shot magazine. **Barrel:** 24.25", tapered octagon. **Weight:** 8.25 lbs. **Length:** 43.25" overall. **Stock:** Walnut. Checkered pistol grip buttstock and forearm. **Sights:** Blade front, adjustable rear. **Features:** Color casehardened frame. Engraved frame polished bright. Replica of Winchester 1873. Made in Italy. From Dixie Gun Works.
Price: . . . . $ 1,050.00 to $ 1,100.00

DIXIE LIGHTNING RIFLE AND CARBINE
Caliber: .44-40 or .45 LC, 10-shot magazine. **Barrel:** 26" round or octagon, 1:16" or 1:36" twist. **Weight:** 7.25 lbs. **Length:** 43" overall. **Stock:** Walnut. **Sights:** Blade front, open adjustable rear. **Features:** Checkered forearm, blued steel furniture. Made by Pedersoli in Italy. Imported by Dixie Gun Works.
Price: $1,095.00
Price: Carbine $1,225.00

EMF 1860 HENRY RIFLE

Caliber: 44-40 or 45 Colt. **Barrel:** 24". **Weight:** About 9 lbs. **Length:** About 43.75" overall. **Stock:** Oil-stained American walnut. **Sights:** Blade front, rear adjustable for elevation. **Features:** Reproduction of the original Henry rifle with brass frame and buttplate, rest blued. Imported by EMF.

Price: Brass frame **$1,149.90**
Price: Casehardened frame **$1,229.90**

EMF 1866 YELLOWBOY LEVER ACTIONS

Caliber: 38 Spec., 44-40, 45 LC. **Barrel:** 19" (carbine), 24" (rifle). **Weight:** 9 lbs. **Length:** 43" overall (rifle). **Stock:** European walnut. **Sights:** Bead front, open adjustable rear. **Features:** Solid brass frame, blued barrel, lever, hammer, buttplate. Imported from Italy by EMF.

Price: Rifle **$1,044.90**
Price: Border Rifle, Short **$969.90**

EMF MODEL 1873 LEVER-ACTION RIFLE

Caliber: 32/20, 357 Mag., 38/40, 44-40, 45 Colt. **Barrel:** 18", 20", 24", 30". **Weight:** 8 lbs. **Length:** 43.25" overall. **Stock:** European walnut. **Sights:** Bead front, rear adjustable for windage and elevation. **Features:** Color case-hardened frame (blue on carbine). Imported by EMF.

Price: **$1,099.90**

EMF MODEL 1873 REVOLVER CARBINE

Caliber: 357 Mag., 45 Colt. **Barrel:** 18". **Weight:** 4 lbs., 8 oz. **Length:** 43-3/4" overall. **Stock:** One-piece walnut. **Sights:** Blade front, notch rear. **Features:** Color case-hardened frame, blue barrel, backstrap and trigger guard. Introduced 1998. Imported from Italy by EMF.

Price: Standard. . . . . **$979.90 to $1,040.00**

HENRY BIG BOY LEVER-ACTION CARBINE

Caliber: 357 Magnum, 44 Magnum, 45 Colt, 10-shot tubular magazine. **Barrel:** 20" octagonal, 1:38 right-hand twist. **Weight:** 8.68 lbs. **Length:** 38.5" overall. **Stock:** Straight-grip American walnut, brass buttplate. **Sights:** Marbles full adjustable semi-buckhorn rear, brass bead front. **Features:** Brasslite receiver not tapped for scope mount. Made in U.S.A. by Henry Repeating Arms.

Price: H006 44 Magnum, walnut, blued barrel **$899.95**
Price: H006DD Deluxe 44 Magnum, engraved receiver. . . . **$1,995.95**

Henry .30/30 Lever-Action Carbine

Same as the Big Boy except has straight grip American walnut, 30-30 only, 6-shot. Receivers are drilled and tapped for scope mount. Made in U.S.A. by Henry Repeating Arms.

Price: H009 Blued receiver, round barrel **$749.95**
Price: H009B Brass receiver, octagonal barrel. **$969.95**

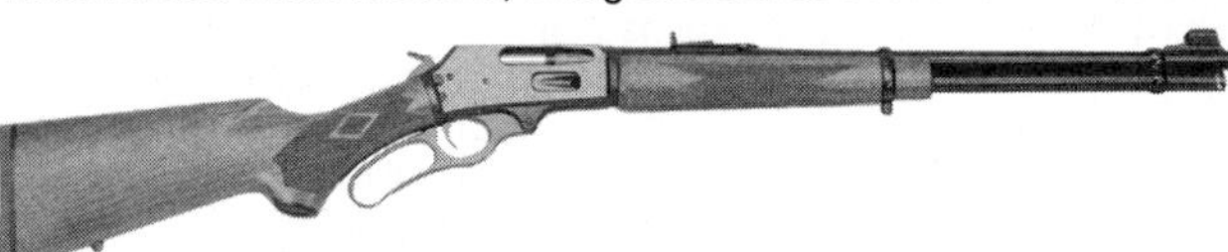

MARLIN MODEL 336C LEVER-ACTION CARBINE

Caliber: 30-30 or 35 Rem., 6-shot tubular magazine. **Barrel:** 20" Micro-Groove. **Weight:** 7 lbs. **Length:** 38.5" overall. **Stock:** Checkered American black walnut, capped pistol grip. Mar-Shield finish; rubber buttpad; swivel studs. **Sights:** Ramp front with Wide-Scan hood, semi-buckhorn folding rear adjustable for windage and elevation. **Features:** Hammer-block safety. Receiver tapped for scope mount, offset hammer spur; top of receiver sandblasted to prevent glare. Includes safety lock.

Price: **$530.00**

Marlin Model 336SS Lever-Action Carbine

Same as the 336C except receiver, barrel and other major parts are machined from stainless steel. 30-30 only, 6-shot; receiver tapped for scope. Includes safety lock.

Price: **$650.00**

Marlin Model 336W Lever-Action Rifle

Similar to the Model 336C except has walnut-finished, cut-checkered Maine birch stock; blued steel barrel band has integral sling swivel; no front sight hood; comes with padded nylon sling; hard rubber buttplate. Introduced 1998. Includes safety lock. Made in U.S.A. by Marlin.

Price: **$452.00**
Price: With 4x scope and mount **$495.00**

MARLIN 336BL

Lever action rifle chambered for .30-30. Features include 6-shot full length tubular magazine; 18-inch blued barrel with Micro-Groove rifling (12 grooves); big-loop finger lever; side ejection; blued steel receiver; hammer block safety; brown laminated hardwood pistol-grip stock with fluted comb; cut checkering; deluxe recoil pad; blued swivel studs.

Price: . . . . **N/A**

MARLIN 336 DELUXE

Lever action rifle chambered in .30-30. Features include 6-shot tubular magazine; side ejection; solid top receiver; highly polished deep blue finish; hammer block safety; #1 grade full fancy American black walnut stock and forend; 20-inch barrel with Micro-Groove rifling (12 grooves); adjustable semi-buckhorn folding rear, ramp front sight with brass bead and Wide-Scan™ hood. Solid top receiver tapped for scope mount; offset hammer spur (right or left hand) for scope use.

Price: . . . . **N/A**

Marlin Model XLR Lever-Action Rifles

Similar to Model 336C except has an 24" stainless barrel with Ballard-type cut rifling, stainless steel receiver and other parts, laminated hardwood stock with pistol grip, nickel-plated swivel studs. Chambered for 30-30 Win. with Hornady spire-pointed Flex-Tip cartridges. Includes safety lock. Introduced 2006. Similar models chambered for 308 Marlin Express introduced in 2007

Price: Model 336XLR **$816.00**

MARLIN MODEL 338MXLR

Caliber: 338 Marlin Express. **Barrel:** 24" stainless steel. **Weight:** 7.5 lbs. **Length:** 42.5" overall. **Features:** Stainless steel receiver, lever and magazine tube. Black/gray laminated checkered stock and forend. Hooded ramp front sight and adjustable semi-buckhorn rear; drilled and tapped for scope mounts. Receiver-mounted crossbolt safety.

Price: Model 338MXLR **$806.00**
Price: Model 308MXLR: 308 Marlin Express **$806.00**
Price: Model 338MX: Similar to Model 338MXLR but with blued metal and walnut stock and forend **$611.00**
Price: Model 308MX: 308 Marlin Express **$611.00**

MARLIN MODEL 444 LEVER-ACTION SPORTER

Caliber: 444 Marlin, 5-shot tubular magazine. **Barrel:** 22" deep cut Ballard rifling. **Weight:** 7.5 lbs. **Length:** 40.5" overall. **Stock:** Checkered American black walnut, capped pistol grip, rubber rifle buttpad. Mar-Shield finish; swivel studs. **Sights:** Hooded ramp front, folding semi-buckhorn rear adjustable for windage and elevation. **Features:** Hammer-block safety. Receiver tapped for scope mount; offset hammer spur. Includes safety lock.

Price: **$619.00**

Marlin Model 444XLR Lever-Action Rifle

Similar to Model 444 except has an 24" stainless barrel with Ballard-type cut rifling, stainless steel receiver and other parts, laminated hardwood stock with pistol grip, nickel-plated swivel studs. Chambered for 444 Marlin with Hornady Evolution spire-pointed Flex-Tip cartridges. Includes safety lock. Introduced 2006.

Price: (Model 444XLR) **$816.00**

MARLIN MODEL 1894 LEVER-ACTION CARBINE
Caliber: 44 Spec./44 Mag., 10-shot tubular magazine. **Barrel:** 20" Ballard-type rifling. **Weight:** 6 lbs. **Length:** 37.5" overall. **Stock:** Checkered American black walnut, straight grip and forend. Mar-Shield finish. Rubber rifle buttpad; swivel studs. **Sights:** Wide-Scan hooded ramp front, semi-buckhorn folding rear adjustable for windage and elevation. **Features:** Hammer-block safety. Receiver tapped for scope mount, offset hammer spur, solid top receiver sand blasted to prevent glare. Includes safety lock.
Price: **$576.00**

Marlin Model 1894C Carbine
Similar to the standard Model 1894 except chambered for 38 Spec./357 Mag. with full-length 9-shot magazine, 18.5" barrel, hammer-block safety, hooded front sight. Introduced 1983. Includes safety lock.
Price: **$576.00**

MARLIN MODEL 1894 COWBOY
Caliber: 357 Mag., 44 Mag., 45 Colt, 10-shot magazine. **Barrel:** 20" tapered octagon, deep cut rifling. **Weight:** 7.5 lbs. **Length:** 41.5" overall. **Stock:** Straight grip American black walnut, hard rubber buttplate, Mar-Shield finish. **Sights:** Marble carbine front, adjustable Marble semi-buckhorn rear. **Features:** Squared finger lever; straight grip stock; blued steel forend tip. Designed for Cowboy Shooting events. Introduced 1996. Includes safety lock. Made in U.S.A. by Marlin.
Price: **$822.00**

Marlin Model 1894SS
Similar to Model 1894 except has stainless steel barrel, receiver, lever, guard plate, magazine tube and loading plate. Nickel-plated swivel studs.
Price: **$704.00**

MARLIN 1894 DELUXE
Lever action rifle chambered in .44 Magnum/.44 Special. Features include 10-shot tubular magazine; squared finger lever; side ejection; richly polished deep blued metal surfaces; solid top receiver; hammer block safety; #1 grade fancy American black walnut straight-grip stock and forend; cut checkering; rubber rifle butt pad; Mar-Shield finish; blued steel fore-end cap: swivel studs; deep-cut Ballard-type rifling (6 grooves).
Price: .... **N/A**

MARLIN 1894CSS
Lever action rifle chambered in .357 Magnum/.38 Special. Features include 9-shot tubular magazine; stainless steel receiver, barrel, lever, trigger and hammer; squared finger lever; side ejection; solid top receiver; hammer block safety; American black walnut straight-grip stock and forend; cut checkering; rubber rifle butt pad; Mar-Shield finish.
Price: .... **N/A**

MARLIN MODEL 1895 LEVER-ACTION RIFLE
Caliber: 45-70 Govt., 4-shot tubular magazine. **Barrel:** 22" round. **Weight:** 7.5 lbs. **Length:** 40.5" overall. **Stock:** Checkered American black walnut, full pistol grip. Mar-Shield finish; rubber buttpad; quick detachable swivel studs. **Sights:** Bead front with Wide-Scan hood, semi-buckhorn folding rear adjustable for windage and elevation. **Features:** Hammer-block safety. Solid receiver tapped for scope mounts or receiver sights; offset hammer spur. Includes safety lock.
Price: **$619.00**

Marlin Model 1895G Guide Gun Lever-Action Rifle
Similar to Model 1895 with deep-cut Ballard-type rifling; straight-grip walnut stock. Overall length is 37", weighs 7 lbs. Introduced 1998. Includes safety lock. Made in U.S.A. by Marlin.
Price: **$630.00**

Marlin Model 1895GS Guide Gun
Similar to Model 1895G except receiver, barrel and most metal parts are machined from stainless steel. Chambered for 45-70 Govt., 4-shot, 18.5" barrel. Overall length is 37", weighs 7 lbs. Introduced 2001. Includes safety lock. Made in U.S.A. by Marlin.
Price: **$752.00**

Marlin Model 1895 SBLR
Similar to Model 1895GS Guide Gun but with stainless steel barrel (18.5"), receiver, large loop lever and magazine tube. Black/gray laminated buttstock and forend, XS ghost ring rear sight, hooded ramp front sight, receiver/barrel-mounted top rail for mounting accessory optics. Chambered in 45-70 Government. Overall length is 42.5", weighs 7.5 lbs.
Price: **$979.00**

Marlin Model 1895 Cowboy Lever-Action Rifle
Similar to Model 1895 except has 26" tapered octagon barrel with Ballard-type rifling, Marble carbine front sight and Marble adjustable semi-buckhorn rear sight. Receiver tapped for scope or receiver sight. Overall length is 44.5", weighs about 8 lbs. Introduced 2001. Includes safety lock. Made in U.S.A. by Marlin.
Price: **$785.00**

Marlin Model 1895XLR Lever-Action Rifle
Similar to Model 1895 except has an 24" stainless barrel with Ballard-type cut rifling, stainless steel receiver and other parts, laminated hardwood stock with pistol grip, nickel-plated swivel studs. Chambered for 45-70 Govt. Government with Hornady Evolution spire-pointed Flex-Tip cartridges. Includes safety lock. Introduced 2006.
Price: (Model 1895MXLR) **$816.00**

Marlin Model 1895M Lever-Action Rifle
Similar to Model 1895G except has an 18.5" barrel with Ballard-type cut rifling. Chambered for 450 Marlin. Includes safety lock.
Price: (Model 1895M) **$678.00**

Marlin Model 1895MXLR Lever-Action Rifle
Similar to Model 1895M except has an 24" stainless barrel with Ballard-type cut rifling, stainless steel receiver and other parts, laminated hardwood stock with pistol grip, nickel-plated swivel studs. Chambered for 450 Marlin with Hornady Evolution spire-pointed Flex-Tip cartridges. Includes safety lock. Introduced 2006.
Price: (Model 1895MXLR) **$874.00**

MARLIN 1895GBL
Lever action rifle chambered in .45-70 Government. Features include 6-shot, full-length tubular magazine; 18-1/2-inch barrel with deep-cut Ballard-type rifling (6 grooves); big-loop finger lever; side ejection; solid-top receiver; deeply blued metal surfaces; hammer block safety; pistol-grip two tone brown laminate stock with cut checkering; ventilated recoil pad; Mar-Shield finish, swivel studs.
Price: .... **N/A**

MOSSBERG 464 LEVER ACTION RIFLE
Caliber: 30-30 Win., 6-shot tubular magazine. **Barrel:** 20" round. **Weight:** 6.7 lbs. **Length:** 38.5" overall. **Stock:** Hardwood with straight or pistol grip, quick detachable swivel studs. **Sights:** Folding rear sight, adjustable for windage and elevation. **Features:** Blued receiver and barrel, receiver drilled and tapped, two-position top-tang safety. Available with straight grip or semi-pistol grip. Introduced 2008. From O.F. Mossberg & Sons, Inc.
Price: **$497.00**

 Prices given are believed to be accurate at time of publication however, many factors affect retail pricing so exact prices are not possible.

NAVY ARMS 1874 SHARPS #2 CREEDMORE RIFLE

Caliber: .45-70 Govt. **Barrel:** 30" octagon. **Weight:** 10 lbs. **Length:** 48" overall. **Sights:** Soule target grade rear tang sight, front globe with 12 inserts. **Features:** Highly polished nickel receiver and action, double-set triggers. From Navy Arms.

Price: Model SCR072 (2008) **$1,816.00**

NAVY ARMS MILITARY HENRY RIFLE

Caliber: 44-40 or 45 Colt, 12-shot magazine. **Barrel:** 24.25". **Weight:** 9 lbs., 4 oz. **Stock:** European walnut. **Sights:** Blade front, adjustable ladder-type rear. **Features:** Brass frame, buttplate, rest blued. Replica of the model used by cavalry units in the Civil War. Has full-length magazine tube, sling swivels; no forend. Imported from Italy by Navy Arms.

Price: **$1,199.00**

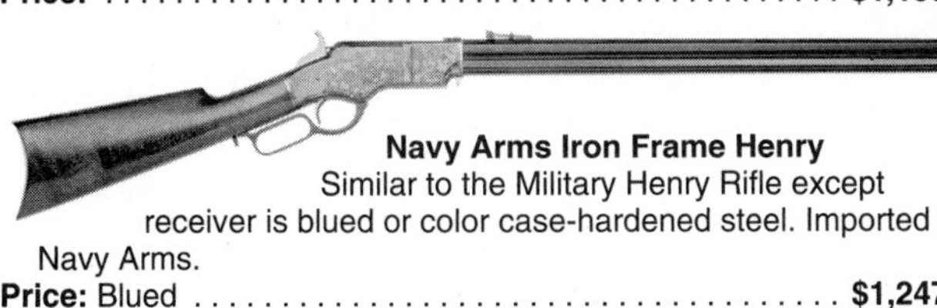

Navy Arms Iron Frame Henry

Similar to the Military Henry Rifle except receiver is blued or color case-hardened steel. Imported by Navy Arms.

Price: Blued **$1,247.00**

NAVY ARMS 1866 YELLOW BOY RIFLE

Caliber: 38 Spec., 44-40, 45 Colt, 12-shot magazine. **Barrel:** 20" or 24", full octagon. **Weight:** 8.5 lbs. **Length:** 42.5" overall. **Stock:** Walnut. **Sights:** Blade front, adjustable ladder-type rear. **Features:** Brass frame, forend tip, buttplate, blued barrel, lever, hammer. Introduced 1991. Imported from Italy by Navy Arms.

Price: Yellow Boy Rifle, 24.25" barrel **$915.00**

Price: Yellow Boy Carbine, 19" barrel **$882.00**

NAVY ARMS 1873 WINCHESTER-STYLE RIFLE

Caliber: 357 Mag., 44-40, 45 Colt, 12-shot magazine. **Barrel:** 24.25". **Weight:** 8.25 lbs. **Length:** 43" overall. **Stock:** European walnut. **Sights:** Blade front, buckhorn rear. **Features:** Color case-hardened frame, rest blued. Full-octagon barrel. Imported by Navy Arms.

Price: **$1,047.00**

Price: 1873 Carbine, 19" barrel **$1,024.00**

Price: 1873 Sporting Rifle (octagonal bbl., checkered walnut stock and forend) **$1,183.00**

Price: 1873 Border Model, 20" octagon barrel **$1,047.00**

Price: 1873 Deluxe Border Model **$1,183.00**

PUMA MODEL 92 RIFLES AND CARBINES

Caliber: 17 HMR (XP and Scout models, only; intr. 2008), 38 Spec./357 Mag., 44 Mag., 45 Colt, 454 Casull, 480 Ruger (.44-40 in 20" octagonal barrel). **Barrel:** 16" and 20" round; 20" and 24" octagonal. 1:30" rate of twist (exc. 17 HMR is 1:9"). **Weight:** 7.7 lbs. **Stock:** Walnut stained hardwood. **Sights:** Blade front, V rear, buckhorn sights sold separately. **Features:** Finishes available in blue/blue, blue/case colored and stainless/stainless with matching crescent butt plates. .454 and .480 calibers have rubber recoil pads. Full-length magazines, thumb safety. Large lever loop or HiViz sights available on select models. Magazine capacity is 12 rounds with 24" bbl.; 10 rounds with 20" barrel; 8 rounds in 16" barrel. Introduced in 2002. Scout includes long-eye-relief scope, rail, elevated cheekpiece, intr. 2008. XP chambered in 17 HMR, 38 Spec./357 Mag. and 44 Mag., loads through magazine tube or loading gate, intr. 2008. Imported from Brazil by Legacy Sports International.

Price: From **$959.00**

Price: Scout Model, w/2.5x32 Nikko-Stirling Nighteater scope, intr. 2008, from **$739.00**

Price: XP Model, tube feed magazine, intr. 2008, from **$613.00**

REMINGTON MODEL 7600/7615 PUMP ACTION

Caliber: 243 Win., 270 Win., 30-06 Spfl., 308; 223 Rem. (7615 only). **Barrel:** 22" round tapered. **Weight:** 7.5 lbs. **Length:** 42.6" overall. **Stock:** Cut-checkered walnut pistol grip and forend, Monte Carlo with full cheekpiece. Satin or high-gloss finish. Also, black synthetic. **Sights:** Gold bead front sight on matted ramp, open step adjustable sporting rear. **Features:** Redesigned and improved version of the Model 760. Detachable 4-shot clip. Cross-bolt safety. Receiver tapped for scope mount. Introduced 1981. Model 7615 Tactical chambered in 223 Rem. **Features:** Knoxx SpecOps NRS (Non Recoil Suppressing) adjustable stock, parkerized finish, 10-round detachable magazine box, sling swivel studs. Introduced 2007.

Price:7600 Wood **$792.00**

Price:7600 Synthetic. **$665.00**

Price: 7615 Ranch Carbine **$955.00**

Price: 7615 Camo Hunter. **$1,009.00**

Price: 7615 Tactical 223 Rem., 16.5" barrel, 10-rd. magazine (2008). **$932.00**

ROSSI R92 LEVER-ACTION CARBINE

Caliber: 38 Special/357 Mag, 44 Mag., 44-40 Win., 45 Colt, 454 Casull. **Barrel:** 16" or 20" with round barrel, 20" or 24" with octagon barrel. **Weight:** 4.8 lbs. to 7 lbs. **Length:** 34" to 41.5". **Features:** Blued or stainless finish. Various options available in selected chamberings (large lever loop, fiber optic sights, cheekpiece, etc.).

Price: From **$499.00**

TAURUS THUNDERBOLT PUMP ACTION

Caliber: 38/.357, 45 Long Colt, 12 or 14 rounds. **Barrel:** 26" blue or polished stainless. **Weight:** 8.1 lbs. **Length:** 43" overall. **Stock:** Hardwood stock and forend. Gloss finish. **Sights:** Longhorn adjustable rear. Introduced 2004. Imported from Brazil by Taurus International.

Price: C45BR (blued) **$705.00**

Price: C45SSR (stainless) **$813.00**

TRISTAR SHARPS 1874 SPORTING RIFLE

Caliber: 45-70 Govt. **Barrel:** 28", 32", 34" octagonal. **Weight:** 9.75 lbs. **Length:** 44.5" overall. **Stock:** Walnut. **Sights:** Dovetail front, adjustable rear. **Features:** Cut checkering, case colored frame finish.

Price: **$1,099.00**

UBERTI 1873 SPORTING RIFLE

Caliber: 357 Mag., 44-40, 45 Colt. **Barrel:** 19" to 24.25". **Weight:** Up to 8.2 lbs. **Length:** Up to 43.3" overall. **Stock:** Walnut, straight grip and pistol grip. **Sights:** Blade front adjustable for windage, open rear adjustable for elevation. **Features:** Color case-hardened frame, blued barrel, hammer, lever, buttplate, brass elevator. Imported by Stoeger Industries.

Price: 1873 Carbine, 19" round barrel **$1,199.00**

Price: 1873 Short Rifle, 20" octagonal barrel **$1,249.00**

Price: 1873 Special Sporting Rifle, 24.25" octagonal barrel **$1,379.00**

UBERTI 1866 YELLOWBOY CARBINE, SHORT RIFLE, RIFLE

Caliber: 38 Spec., 44-40, 45 Colt. **Barrel:** 24.25", octagonal. **Weight:** 8.2 lbs. **Length:** 43.25" overall. **Stock:** Walnut. **Sights:** Blade front adjustable for windage, rear adjustable for elevation. **Features:** Frame, buttplate, forend cap of polished brass, balance charcoal blued. Imported by Stoeger Industries.

Price: 1866 Yellowboy Carbine, 19" round barrel. **$1,079.00**

Price: 1866 Yellowboy Short Rifle, 20" octagonal barrel . . . **$1,129.00**

Price: 1866 Yellowboy Rifle, 24.25" octagonal barrel **$1,129.00**

UBERTI 1860 HENRY RIFLE

Caliber: 44-40, 45 Colt. **Barrel:** 24.25", half-octagon. **Weight:** 9.2 lbs. **Length:** 43.75" overall. **Stock:** American walnut. **Sights:** Blade front, rear adjustable for elevation. Imported by Stoeger Industries.

Price: 1860 Henry Trapper, 18.5" barrel, brass frame **$1,329.00**

Price: 1860 Henry Rifle Iron Frame, 24.25" barrel **$1,419.00**

UBERTI LIGHTNING RIFLE
Caliber: 357 Mag., 45 Colt, 10+1. **Barrel:** 20" to 24.25". **Stock:** Walnut. Finish: Blue or case-hardened. Introduced 2006. Imported by Stoeger Industries.
Price: 1875 Lightning Rifle, 24.25" barrel **$1,259.00**
Price: 1875 Lightning Short Rifle, 20" barrel **$1,259.00**
Price: 1875 Lightning Carbine, 20" barrel **$1,179.00**

UBERTI SPRINGFIELD TRAPDOOR RIFLE
Caliber: 4-70, single shot. **Barrel:** 22" or 32.5". **Stock:** Walnut. Finish: Blue and case-hardened. Introduced 2006. Imported by Stoeger Industries.
Price: Springfield Trapdoor Carbine, 22" barrel **$1,429.00**
Price: Springfield Trapdoor Army, 32.5" barrel **$1,669.00**

U.S. FIRE ARMS STANDARD LIGHTNING MAGAZINE RIFLE
Caliber: 45 Colt, 44 WCF, 44 Spec., 38 WCF, 15-shot. **Barrel:** 26". **Stock:** Oiled walnut. Finish: High polish blue. Nickel finish also available. Introduced 2002. Made in U.S.A. by United States Fire-Arms Manufacturing Co.
Price: Round barrel. **$1,480.00**
Price: Octagonal barrel, checkered forend **$1,750.00**
Price: Half-round barrel, checkered forend **$1,995.00**
Price: Premium Carbine, 20" round barrel **$1,480.00**
Price: Baby Carbine, 20" special taper barrel **$1,995.00**
Price: Deluxe Lightning **$2,559.00**

WINCHESTER MODEL 1895 SAFARI CENTENNIAL HIGH GRADE
Caliber: 405 Win. **Barrel:** 24" blued round, four-round box mag. **Weight:** 8 lbs. **Length:** NA. **Features:** Patterned after original Winchester Model 1895. Commemorates Theodore Roosevelt's 1909 African safari. Checkered walnut forend and buttstock with inlaid "TR" medallion, engraved and silvered receiver.
Price: **$1,749.00**
Price: Custom Grade: Jeweled hammer, fancier wood and angraving, gold-filled highlights and numerous accessories. Production limited to 100 sets **$3,649.00**

WINCHESTER MODEL 1894 CUSTOM GRADE
Lever-action rifle chambered in .30-30. Features include 24-inch half-round, half octagon deeply blued barrel; buckhorn rear sight with Marble's gold bead front sight; Grade IV/V walnut stock and forend with a rich, high gloss finish; deep scroll engraving on both sides of the blued receiver. Commemorates the 200th anniversary of Oliver F. Winchester's birth. An early Winchester Repeating Arms crest graces the left side of the receiver, with the right side bearing the words, "Two Hundred Years, Oliver F. Winchester," and the dates, "1810 — 2010," in gold. The barrel is deeply polished, with the signature of Oliver F. Winchester in gold on the top of the bolt. Sold individually in limited quantities and in 500 sets with the High Grade.
Price (single rifle): **$1,959.00**

WINCHESTER MODEL 1894 HIGH GRADE
Lever-action rifle chambered in .30-30. Features include 24-inch half-round, half octagon deeply blued barrel; buckhorn rear sight with Marble's gold bead front sight; silver nitride receiver; Grade II/III high gloss walnut stock and forend with a rich, high gloss finish; delicate scroll work, with Oliver F. Winchester's signature in gold on top of the bolt. The left side of receiver bears an early Winchester Repeating Arms crest; on right side are the words, "Two Hundred Years, Oliver F. Winchester," and the dates, "1810 — 2010." Sold individually in limited quantities and in 500 sets with the Custom Grade.
Price (single rifle): **$1,469.00**

BARRETT MODEL 95 BOLT-ACTION RIFLE

Caliber: 50 BMG, 5-shot magazine. **Barrel:** 29". **Weight:** 23.5 lbs. **Length:** 45" overall. **Stock:** Energy-absorbing recoil pad. **Sights:** Scope optional. **Features:** Bolt-action, bullpup design. Disassembles without tools; extendable bipod legs; match-grade barrel; muzzle brake. Introduced 1995. Made in U.S.A. by Barrett Firearms Mfg., Inc.

Price: From **$6,500.00**

BLASER R93 BOLT-ACTION RIFLE

Caliber: 22-250 Rem., 243 Win., 6.5x55, 270 Win., 7x57, 7mm-08 Rem., 308 Win., 30-06 Spfl., 257 Wby. Mag., 7mm Rem. Mag., 300 Win. Mag., 300 Wby. Mag., 338 Win. Mag., 375 H&H, 416 Rem. Mag. **Barrel:** 22" (standard calibers), 26" (magnum). **Weight:** 7 lbs. **Length:** 40" overall (22" barrel). **Stock:** Two-piece European walnut. **Sights:** None furnished; drilled and tapped for scope mounting. **Features:** Straight pull-back bolt action with thumb-activated safety slide/cocking mechanism; interchangeable barrels and bolt heads. Introduced 1994. Imported from Germany by Blaser USA.

Price: R93 Prestige, wood grade 3. **$3,275.00**
Price: R93 Luxus **$4,460.00**
Price: R93 Professional **$2,950.00**
Price: R93 Grand Luxe **$8,163.00**
Price: R93 Attache **$6,175.00**

BROWNING A-BOLT RIFLES

Common Features: Short-throw (60") fluted bolt, three locking lugs, plunger-type ejector; adjustable trigger is grooved. Chrome-plated trigger sear. Hinged floorplate, detachable box magazine. Slide tang safety. Receivers are drilled and tapped for scope mounts, swivel studs included. Barrel is free-floating and glass-bedded, recessed muzzle. Safety is top-tang sliding button. Engraving available for bolt sleeve or rifle body. Introduced 1985. Imported from Japan by Browning.

BROWNING A-BOLT HUNTER

Calibers: 22" Barrel: 223 Rem., 22-250 Rem., 243 Win., 270 Win., 30-06 Spfl., 7mm-08 Rem., 308 Win. **Barrel:** 270 WSM, 7mm WSM, 300 WSM, 325 WSM (intr. 2005). **Calibers:** 24" Barrel: 25-06 Rem. **Calibers:** 26" Barrel: 7mm Rem. Mag., 300 Win. Mag., 338 Win. Mag. **Weight:** 6.25-7.2 lbs. **Length:** 41.25-46.5" overall. **Stock:** Sporter-style walnut; checkered grip and forend. **Metal Finish:** Low-luster blueing.

Price: Hunter, left-hand, from **$819.00**

BROWNING A-BOLT HUNTER FLD

Caliber: 23" Barrel: 270 WSM, 7mm WSM, 300 WSM, 325 WSM (intr. 2005). **Weight:** 6.6 lbs. **Length:** 42.75" overall. **Features:** FLD has low-luster blueing and select Monte Carlo stock with right-hand palm swell, double-border checkering. Otherwise similar to A-Bolt Hunter.

Price: FLD. **$899.00**

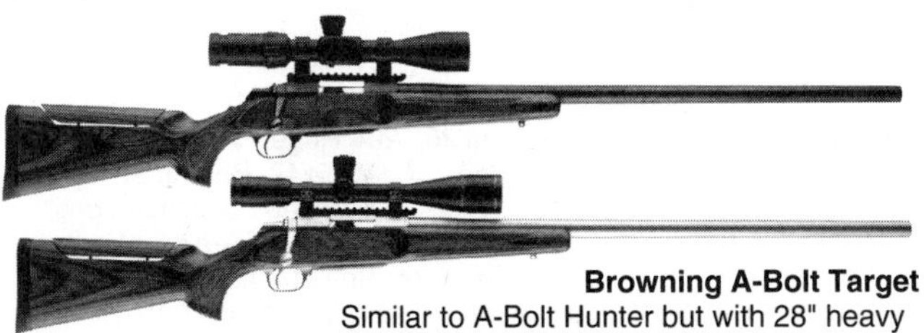

Browning A-Bolt Target

Similar to A-Bolt Hunter but with 28" heavy bull blued barrel, blued receiver, satin finish gray laminated stock with adjustable comb and semi-beavertail forend. Chambered in 223, 308 Winchester and 300 WSM. Available also with stainless receiver and barrel.

Price: From **$1,269.00**
Price: Stainless, from **$1,489.00**

BROWNING A-BOLT MOUNTAIN TI

Caliber: 223 WSSM, 243 WSSM, 25 WSSM (all added 2005); 270 WSM, 7mm WSM, 300 WSM. **Barrel:** 22" or 23". **Weight:** 5.25-5.5 lbs. **Length:** 41.25-42.75" overall. **Stock:** Lightweight fiberglass Bell & Carlson model in Mossy-Oak New Break Up camo. Metal Finish: Stainless barrel, titanium receiver. **Features:** Pachmayr Decelerator recoil pad. Introduced 1999.

Price: From. **$1,819.00**

BROWNING A-BOLT MICRO HUNTER AND MICRO HUNTER LEFT-HAND

Calibers: 20" Barrel: 22-250 Rem., 243 Win., 308 Win., 7mm-08. 22" Barrel: 22 Hornet, 270 WSM, 7mm WSM, 300 WSM, 325 WSM (2005). **Weight:** 6.25-6.4 lbs. **Length:** 39.5-41.5" overall. **Features:** Classic walnut stock with 13.3" LOP. Otherwise similar to A-Bolt Hunter.

Price: Micro Hunter, from **$759.00**
Price: Micro Hunter left-hand, from **$799.00**

BROWNING A-BOLT MEDALLION

Calibers: 22" Barrel: 223 Rem., 22-250 Rem., 243 Win., 308 Win., 270 Win., 280 Rem., 30-06.; 23" Barrel: 270 WSM, 7mm WSM, 300 WSM, 325 WSM (intr. 2005); 24" Barrel: 25-06 Rem.; 26" Barrel: 7mm Rem. Mag., 300 Win. Mag., 338 Win. Mag., 375 H&H. **Weight:** 6.25-7.1 lbs. **Length:** 41.25-46.5" overall. **Stock:** Select walnut stock, glossy finish, rosewood grip and forend caps, checkered grip and forend. Metal Finish: Engraved high-polish blued receiver.

Price: Medallion, from. **$909.00**
Price: Medallion WSM **$959.00**
Price: Medallion w/BOSS, intr. 1987, from **$1,009.00**

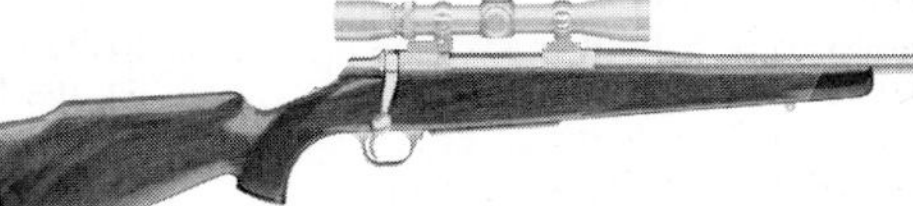

BROWNING A-BOLT WHITE GOLD MEDALLION, RMEF WHITE GOLD, WHITE GOLD MEDALLION W/BOSS

Calibers: 22" Barrel: 270 Win., 30-06. Calibers: 23" Barrel: 270 WSM, 7mm WSM, 300 WSM, 325 WSM (intr. 2005). Calibers: 26" Barrel: 7mm Rem. Mag., 300 Win. Mag. **Weight:** 6.4-7.7 lbs. **Length:** 42.75-46.5" overall. **Stock:** select walnut stock with brass spacers between rubber recoil pad and between the rosewood gripcap and forend tip; gold-filled barrel inscription; palm-swell pistol grip, Monte Carlo comb, 22 lpi checkering with double borders. **Metal Finish:** Engraved high-polish stainless receiver and barrel. BOSS version chambered in 270 Win. and 30-06 (22" barrel) and 7mm Rem. Mag. and 300 Win. Mag. (26" barrel). Introduced 1988. RMEF version has engraved gripcap, continental cheekpiece; gold engraved, stainless receiver and bbl. Introduced 2004.

Price: White Gold Medallion, from **$1,309.00**
Price: Rocky Mt. Elk Foundation White Gold, 325 WSM, intr. 2007 . . . . **$1,399.00**

BROWNING A-BOLT STAINLESS STALKER, STAINLESS STALKER LEFT-HAND

Calibers: 22" Barrel: 223 Rem., 243 Win., 270 Win., 280 Rem., 7mm-08 Rem., 30-06 Spfl., 308 Win. Calibers: 23" Barrel: 270 WSM, 7mm WSM, 300 WSM, 325 WSM (intr. 2005). Calibers: 24" Barrel: 25-06 Rem. Calibers: 26" Barrel: 7mm Rem. Mag., 300 Win. Mag., 338 Win. Mag., 375 H&H. **Weight:** 6.1-7.2 lbs. **Length:** 40.9-46.5" overall. **Features:** Similar to the A-Bolt Hunter model except receiver and barrel are made of stainless steel; other exposed metal surfaces are finished silver-gray matte. Graphite-fiberglass composite textured

stock. No sights are furnished, except on 375 H&H, which comes with open sights. Introduced 1987.
Price: Stainless Stalker left-hand, from **$1,029.00**
Price: Stainless Stalker w/Boss, from.................. **$1,119.00**

BROWNING A-BOLT COMPOSITE STALKER
Calibers: 22 Barrel: 270 Win., 30-06 Sprg.; 23" Barrel: 270 WSM, 7mm WSM, 300 WSM, 325 WSM; 24" Barrel: 25-06 Rem.; 26" Barrel: 7mm Rem. Mag., 300 Win. Mag., 338 Win. Mag. **Weight:** 6.6-7.3 lbs. **Length:** 42.5-46.5" overall. **Features:** Similar to the A-Bolt Stainless Stalker except has black composite stock with textured finish and matte-blued finish on all exposed metal surfaces except bolt sleeve. No sights are furnished.
Price: Composite Stalker w/BOSS, from **$869.00**
Price: Stainless Stalker **$1,009.00**
Price: Stainless Stalker w/Boss, from.................. **$1,079.00**

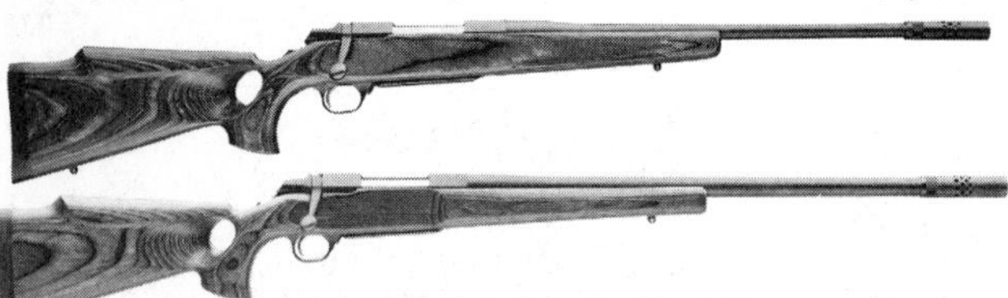

BROWNING A-BOLT ECLIPSE HUNTER W/ BOSS, M-1000 ECLIPSE W/BOSS, M-1000 ECLIPSE WSM, STAINLESS M-1000 ECLIPSE WSM
Calibers: 22" Barrel: 270 Win., 30-06. Calibers: 26" Barrel: 7mm Rem. Mag., 300 Win. Mag., 270 WSM, 7mm WSM, 300 WSM. **Weight:** 7.5-9.9 lbs. **Length:** 42.75-46.5" overall. **Features:** All models have gray/black laminated thumbhole stock. Introduced 1996. Two versions have BOSS barrel vibration modulator and muzzle brake. Hunter has sporter-weight barrel. M-1000 Eclipses have long actions and heavy target barrels, adjustable triggers, bench-style forends, 3-shot magazines. Introduced 1997.
Price: Eclipse Hunter w/BOSS, from **$1,259.00**
Price: M-1000 Eclipse, from **$1,169.00**
Price: M-1000 Eclipse w/BOSS, from **$1,259.00**
Price: Stainless M-1000 Eclipse WSM, from **$1,399.00**
Price: Stainless M-1000 Eclipse w/BOSS, from **$1,489.00**

BROWNING X-BOLT HUNTER
Calibers: 223, 22-250, 243 Win., 25-06 Rem., 270 Win., 270 WSM, 280 Rem., 30-06 Spfl., 300 Win. Mag., 300 WSM, 308 Win., 325 WSM, 338 Win. Mag., 375 H&H Mag., 7mm Rem. Mag., 7mm WSM, 7mm-08 Rem. **Barrels:** 22", 23", 24", 26", varies by model. Matte blued or stainless free-floated barrel, recessed muzzle crown. **Weight:** 6.3-7 lbs. **Stock:** Hunter and Medallion models have wood stocks; Composite Stalker and Stainless Stalker models have composite stocks. Inflex Technology recoil pad. **Sights:** None, drilled and tapped receiver, X-Lock scope mounts. **Features:** Adjustable three-lever Feather Trigger system, polished hard-chromed steel components, factory pre-set at 3.5 lbs., alloy trigger housing. Bolt unlock button, detachable rotary magazine, 60-degree bolt lift, three locking lugs, top-tang safety, sling swivel studs. Medallion has metal engraving, gloss finish walnut stock, rosewood fore-end grip and pistol grip cap. Introduced 2008. From Browning.

Browning X-Bolt Micro Hunter
Similar to Browning X-Bolt Hunter but with compact dimensions (13-15/16 length of pull, 41-1/4 overall length).
Price: Standard chamberings **$839.00**
Price: Magnum **$869.00**

Browning X-Bolt Varmint Stalker
Similar to Browning X-Bolt Stalker but with medium-heavy free-floated barrel, target crown, composite stock. Chamberings available: 223, 22-250, 243 Winchester and 308 Winchester only.
Price: **$1,019.00**

Browning X-Bolt RMEF White Gold
Similar to X-Bolt Medallion but with gold-engraved matte stainless finish and Rocky Mountain Elk Foundation grip cap. Chambered in 325 WSM only.
Price: **$1,399.00**

Browning X-Bolt RMEF Special Hunter
Similar to above but with matte blued finish without gold highlights.
Price: **$919.00**

BUSHMASTER BA50 BOLT-ACTION RIFLE
Caliber: 50 Browning BMG. **Barrel:** 30" (rifle), 22" (carbine), 10-round mag. **Weight:** 30 lbs. (rifle), 27 lbs. (carbine). **Length:** 58" overall (rifle), 50" overall (carbine). **Features:** Free-floated Lother Walther barrel with muzzle brake, Magpul PRS adjustable stock.
Price: **$4,895.00**

CARBON ONE BOLT-ACTION RIFLE
Caliber: 22-250 to 375 H&H. **Barrel:** Up to 28". **Weight:** 5.5 to 7.25 lbs. **Length:** Varies. **Stock:** Synthetic or wood. **Sights:** None furnished. **Features:** Choice of Remington, Browning or Winchester action with free-floated Christensen graphite/epoxy/steel barrel, trigger pull tuned to 3 to 3.5 lbs. Made in U.S.A. by Christensen Arms.
Price: Carbon One Hunter Rifle, 6.5 to 7 lbs............. **$1,775.00**
Price: Carbon One Custom, 5.5 to 6.5 lbs., Shilen trigger . . **$3,900.00**
Price: Carbon Extreme **$2,450.00**

CENTURY INTERNATIONAL M70 SPORTER DOUBLE-TRIGGER BOLT ACTION RIFLE
Caliber: 22-250 Rem., 270 Win., 300 Win. Mag, 308 Win., 24" barrel. **Weight:** 7.95 lbs. **Length:** 44.5". **Sights:** Flip-up U-notch rear sight, hooded blade front sight. **Features:** Mauser M98-type action; 5-rd fixed box magazine. 22-250 has hinged floorplate. Monte Carlo stock, oil finish. Adjustable trigger on double-trigger models. 300 Win. Mag. Has 3-rd. fixed box magazine. 308 Win. holds 5 rounds. 300 and 308 have buttpads. Manufactured by Zastava in Yugoslavia, imported by Century International.
Price: M70 Sporter Double-Trigger......................**$500.00**
Price: M70 Sporter Double-Trigger 22-250 ....**$475.00**
Price: M70 Sporter Single-Trigger .300 Win. Mag. **$475.00**
Price: M70 Sporter Single/Double Trigger 308 Win. **$500.00**

CHEYTAC M-200
Caliber: 408 CheyTac, 7-round magazine. **Barrel:** 30". **Length:** 55", stock extended. **Weight:** 27 lbs. (steel barrel); 24 lbs. (carbon fiber barrel). **Stock:** Retractable. **Sights:** None, scope rail provided. **Features:** CNC-machined receiver, attachable Picatinny rail M-1913, detachable barrel, integral bipod, 3.5-lb. trigger pull, muzzle brake. Made in U.S. by CheyTac, LLC.
Price: **$13,795.00**

COOPER MODEL 21 BOLT-ACTION RIFLE
Caliber: 17 Rem., 19-223, Tactical 20, .204 Ruger, 222 Rem, 222 Rem. Mag., 223 Rem, 223 Rem A.I., 6x45, 6x47. **Barrel:** 22" or 24" in Classic configurations, 24"-26" in Varminter configurations. **Weight:** 6.5-8.0 lbs., depending on type. **Stock:** AA-AAA select claro walnut, 20 lpi checkering. **Sights:** None furnished. **Features:** Three front locking-lug bolt-action single shot. Action: 7.75" long, Sako extractor. Button ejector. Fully adjustable single-stage trigger.

Options include wood upgrades, case-color metalwork, barrel fluting, custom LOP, and many others.
Price: From **$1,395.00**

COOPER MODEL 22 BOLT-ACTION RIFLE
Caliber: 22-250 Rem., 22-250 Rem. AI, 25-06 Rem., 25-06 Rem. AI, 243 Win., 243 Win. AI, 220 Swift, 250/3000 AI, 257 Roberts, 257 Roberts AI, 7mm-08 Rem., 6mm Rem., 260 Rem., 6 x 284, 6.5 x 284, 22 BR, 6mm BR, 308 Win. **Barrel:** 24" or 26" stainless match in Classic configurations. 24" or 26" in Varminter configurations. **Weight:** 7.5 to 8.0 lbs. depending on type. **Stock:** AA-AAA select claro walnut, 20 lpi checkering. **Sights:** None furnished. **Features:** Three front locking-lug bolt-action single shot. Action: 8.25" long, Sako style extractor. Button ejector. Fully adjustable single-stage trigger. Options include wood upgrades, case-color metalwork, barrel fluting, custom LOP, and many others.
Price: From **$1,495.00**

COOPER MODEL 38 BOLT-ACTION RIFLE
Caliber: 17 Squirrel, 17 He Bee, 17 Ackley Hornet, 17 Mach IV, 19 Calhoon, 20 VarTarg, 221 Fireball, 22 Hornet, 22 K-Hornet, 22 Squirrel, 218 Bee, 218 Mashburn Bee. **Barrel:** 22" or 24" in Classic configurations, 24" or 26" in Varminter configurations. **Weight:** 6.5-8.0 lbs. depending on type. **Stock:** AA-AAA select claro walnut, 20 lpi checkering. **Sights:** None furnished. **Features:** Three front locking-lug bolt-action single shot. Action: 7" long, Sako style extractor. Button ejector. Fully adjustable single-stage trigger. Options include wood upgrades, case-color metalwork, barrel fluting, custom LOP, and many others.
Price: From **$1,395.00**

CZ 527 LUX BOLT-ACTION RIFLE
Caliber: 204 Ruger, 22 Hornet, 222 Rem., 223 Rem., detachable 5-shot magazine. **Barrel:** 23.5"; standard or heavy barrel. **Weight:** 6 lbs., 1 oz. **Length:** 42.5" overall. **Stock:** European walnut with Monte Carlo. **Sights:** Hooded front, open adjustable rear. **Features:** Improved mini-Mauser action with non-rotating claw extractor; single set trigger; grooved receiver. Imported from the Czech Republic by CZ-USA.
Price: Brown laminate stock **$718.00**
Price: Model FS, full-length stock, cheekpiece **$827.00**

CZ 527 American Bolt-Action Rifle
Similar to the CZ 527 Lux except has classic-style stock with 18 lpi checkering; free-floating barrel; recessed target crown on barrel. No sights furnished. Introduced 1999. Imported from the Czech Republic by CZUSA.
Price: From **$751.00**

CZ 550 AMERICAN CLASSIC BOLT-ACTION RIFLE
Caliber: 22-250 Rem., 243 Win., 6.5x55, 7x57, 7x64, 308 Win., 9.3x62, 270 Win., 30-06. **Barrel:** free-floating barrel; recessed target crown. **Weight:** 7.48 lbs. **Length:** 44.68" overall. **Stock:** American classic-style stock with 18 lpi checkering or FS (Mannlicher). **Sights:** No sights furnished. **Features:** Improved Mauser-style action with claw extractor, fixed ejector, square bridge dovetailed receiver; single set trigger. Introduced 1999. Imported from the Czech Republic by CZ-USA.
Price: FS (full stock) **$894.00**
Price: American, from **$827.00**

CZ 550 Safari Magnum/American Safari Magnum Bolt-Action Rifles
Similar to CZ 550 American Classic. Chambered for 375 H&H Mag., 416 Rigby, 458 Win. Mag., 458 Lott. Overall length is 46.5"; barrel length 25"; weighs 9.4 lbs., 9.9 lbs (American). Hooded front sight, express rear with one standing, two folding leaves. Imported from the Czech Republic by CZ-USA.
Price: **$1,179.00**
Price: American **$1,261.00**
Price: American Kevlar **$1,714.00**

CZ 550 Varmint Bolt-Action Rifle
Similar to CZ 550 American Classic. Chambered for 308 Win. and 22-250. Kevlar, laminated stocks. Overall length is 46.7"; barrel length 25.6"; weighs 9.1 lbs. Imported from the Czech Republic by CZ-USA.
Price: **$841.00**
Price: Kevlar **$1,037.00**
Price: Laminated **$966.00**

CZ 550 Magnum H.E.T. Bolt-Action Rifle
Similar to CZ 550 American Classic. Chambered for 338 Lapua, 300 Win. Mag., 300 RUM. Overall length is 52"; barrel length 28"; weighs 14 lbs. Adjustable sights, satin blued barrel. Imported from the Czech Republic by CZ-USA.
Price: **$3,673.00**

CZ 550 Ultimate Hunting Bolt-Action Rifle
Similar to CZ 550 American Classic. Chambered for 300 Win Mag. Overall length is 44.7"; barrel length 23.6"; weighs 7.7 lbs. Imported from the Czech Republic by CZ-USA.
Price: **$4,242.00**

CZ 750 SNIPER RIFLE
Caliber: 308 Winchester, 10-shot magazine. **Barrel:** 26". **Weight:** 11.9 lbs. **Length:** 48" overall. **Stock:** Polymer thumbhole. **Sights:** None furnished; permanently attached Weaver rail for scope mounting. **Features:** 60-degree bolt throw; oversized trigger guard and bolt handle for use with gloves; full-length equipment rail on forend; fully adjustable trigger. Introduced 2001. Imported from the Czech Republic by CZ-USA.
Price: **$2,404.00**

DAKOTA 76 TRAVELER TAKEDOWN RIFLE
Caliber: 257 Roberts, 25-06 Rem., 7x57, 270 Win., 280 Rem., 30-06 Spfl., 338-06, 35 Whelen (standard length); 7mm Rem. Mag., 300 Win. Mag., 338 Win. Mag., 416 Taylor, 458 Win. Mag. (short magnums); 7mm, 300, 330, 375 Dakota Magnums. **Barrel:** 23". **Weight:** 7.5 lbs. **Length:** 43.5" overall. **Stock:** Medium fancy-grade walnut in classic style. Checkered grip and forend; solid buttpad. **Sights:** None furnished; drilled and tapped for scope mounts. **Features:** Threadless disassembly. Uses modified Model 76 design with many features of the Model 70 Winchester. Left-hand model also available. Introduced 1989. African chambered for 338 Lapua Mag., 404 Jeffery, 416 Rigby, 416 Dakota, 450 Dakota, 4-round magazine, select wood, two stock cross-bolts. 24" barrel, weighs 9-10 lbs. Ramp front sight, standing leaf rear. Introduced 1989.Made in U.S.A. by Dakota Arms, Inc.
Price: Classic **$6,095.00**
Price: Safari **$7,895.00**
Price: African **$9,495.00**

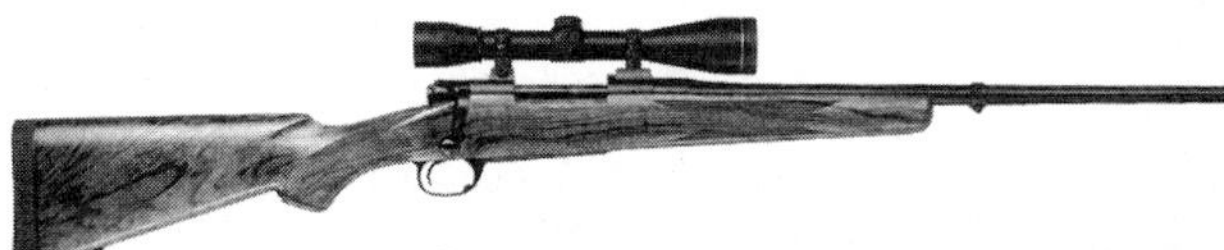

DAKOTA 76 CLASSIC BOLT-ACTION RIFLE
Caliber: 257 Roberts, 270 Win., 280 Rem., 30-06 Spfl., 7mm Rem. Mag., 338 Win. Mag., 300 Win. Mag., 375 H&H, 458 Win. Mag. **Barrel:** 23". **Weight:** 7.5 lbs. **Length:** 43.5" overall. **Stock:** Medium fancy grade walnut in classic style. Checkered pistol grip and forend; solid buttpad. **Sights:** None furnished; drilled and tapped for scope mounts. **Features:** Has many features of the original Winchester Model 70. One-piece rail trigger guard assembly; steel gripcap. Model 70-style trigger. Many options available. Left-hand rifle available at same price. Introduced 1988. From Dakota Arms, Inc.
Price: From **$4,595.00**

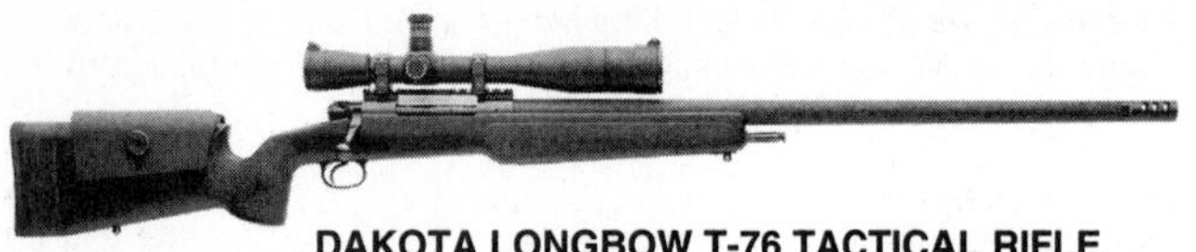

DAKOTA LONGBOW T-76 TACTICAL RIFLE

Caliber: 300 Dakota Magnum, 330 Dakota Magnum, 338 Lapua Magnum. **Barrel:** 28", .950" at muzzle **Weight:** 13.7 lbs. **Length:** 50" to 52" overall. **Stock:** Ambidextrous McMillan A-2 fiberglass, black or olive green color; adjustable cheekpiece and buttplate. **Sights:** None furnished. Comes with Picatinny one-piece optical rail. **Features:** Uses the Dakota 76 action with controlled-round feed; three-position firing pin block safety, claw extractor; Model 70-style trigger. Comes with bipod, case tool kit. Introduced 1997. Made in U.S.A. by Dakota Arms, Inc.

Price: **$4,795.00**

DAKOTA MODEL 97 BOLT-ACTION RIFLE

Caliber: 22-250 to 330. **Barrel:** 22" to 24". **Weight:** 6.1 to 6.5 lbs. **Length:** 43" overall. **Stock:** Fiberglass. **Sights:** Optional. **Features:** Matte blue finish, black stock. Right-hand action only. Introduced 1998. Made in U.S.A. by Dakota Arms, Inc.

Price: From **$3,395.00**

DAKOTA PREDATOR RIFLE

Caliber: 17 VarTarg, 17 Rem., 17 Tactical, 20 VarTarg, 20 Tactical, .20 PPC, 204 Ruger, 221 Rem Fireball, 222 Remington, 22 PPC, 223 Rem., 6mm PPC, 6.5 Grendel. **Barrel:** 22" match grade stainless;. **Weight:** NA. **Length:** NA. **Stock:** Special select walnut, sporter-style stock, 23 lpi checkering on forend and grip. **Sights:** None furnished. Drilled and tapped for scope mounting. **Features:** 13-5/8" LOP, 1/2" black presentation pad, 11" recessed target crown. Serious Predator includes XXX walnut varmint style stock w/semi-beavertail forend, stainless receiver. All-Weather Predator includes varmint style composite stock w/semi-beavertail forend, stainless receiver. Introduced 2007. Made in U.S.A. by Dakota Arms, Inc.

Price: Classic **$4,295.00**
Price: Serious **$3,295.00**
Price: All-Weather. **$1,995.00**

DSA DS-MP1

Caliber: 308 Win. match chamber. **Barrel:** 22", 1:10 twist, hand-lapped stainless-steel match-grade Badger Barrel with recessed target crown. **Weight:** 11.5 lbs. **Length:** 41.75". **Stock:** Black McMillan A5 pillar bedded in Marine-Tex with 13.5" length of pull. **Sights:** Tactical Picatinny rail. **Features:** Action, action threads and action bolt locking shoulder completely trued, Badger Ordnance precision ground heavy recoil lug, machined steel Picatinny rail sight mount, trued action threads, action bolt locking shoulder, bolt face and lugs, 2.5-lb. trigger pull, barrel and action finished in Black DuraCoat, guaranteed to shoot 1/2 MOA at 100 yards with match-grade ammo. Introduced 2006. Made in U.S.A. by DSA, Inc.

Price: **$2,800.00**

EAA/ZASTAVA M-93 BLACK ARROW RIFLE

Caliber: 50 BMG. **Barrel:** 36". **Weight:** 7 to 8.5 lbs. **Length:** 60". **Stock:** Synthetic. **Sights:** Scope rail and iron sights. **Features: Features:** Mauser action, developed in early 1990s by Zastava Arms Factory. Fluted heavy barrel with recoil reducing muzzle brake, self-leveling and adjustable folding integral bipod, back up iron sights, heavy duty carry handle, detachable 5 round box magazine, and quick detachable scope mount. Imported by EAA. Imported from Russia by EAA Corp.

Price: **$6,986.25**

ED BROWN HUNTING SERIES RIFLES

Caliber: Many calibers available. **Barrel:** 24" (Savanna, Express, Varmint); 23-24" (Damara); 22" (Compact Varmint). **Weight:** 8 to 8.5 lbs. (Savanna); 6.2 to 6.9 lbs. (Damara); 9 lbs. (Express); 10 lbs. (Varmint), 8.75 lbs. (Compact Varmint). **Stock:** Fully glass-bedded McMillan fiberglass sporter. **Sights:** None furnished. Talley scope mounts utilizing heavy-duty 8-40 screws. **Features:** Custom action with machined steel trigger guard and hinged floor plate.

Price: Savanna. **$3,895.00**
Price: Damara . . . . **$3,995.00 to $4,095.00**
Price: Express **$4,995.00**
Price: Varmint & Compact Varmint. **$3,895.00**

ED BROWN MODEL 704 BUSHVELD

Caliber: 338 Win. Mag., 375 H&H, 416 Rem. Mag., 458 Win. Mag., 458 Lott and all Ed Brown Savanna long action calibers. **Barrel:** 24" medium or heavy weight. **Weight:** 8.25 lbs. **Stock:** Fully bedded McMillan fiberglass with Monte Carlo style cheekpiece, Pachmayr Decelerator recoil pad. **Sights:** None furnished. Talley scope mounts utilizing heavy-duty 8-40 screws. **Features:** Stainless steel barrel, additional calibers: iron sights.

Price: From **$2,995.00**

ED BROWN MODEL 704 EXPRESS

Caliber: 375 H&H, 416 Rem, 458 Lott, other calibers available. **Barrel:** 24" #4 Stainless barrel with black Gen III coating for superior rust protection. **Weight:** 9 lbs. Stocks: Hand-bedded McMillan fiberglass stock. Monte Carlo style with cheek piece and full 1" thick Pachmayr Decel recoil pad. **Sights:** Adjustable iron sights. **Features:** Ed Brown controlled feed action. A special dropped box magazine ensures feeding and allows a full four-round capacity in the magazine, plus one in the chamber. Barrel band is standard for lower profile when carrying the rifle through heavy brush.

Price: From **$3,695.00**

HOWA M-1500 RANCHLAND COMPACT

Caliber: 223 Rem., 22-250 Rem., 243 Win., 308 Win. and 7mm-08. **Barrel:** 20" #1 contour, blued finish. **Weight:** 7 lbs. **Stock:** Hogue Overmolded in black, OD green, Coyote Sand colors. 13.87" LOP. **Sights:** None furnished; drilled and tapped for scope mounting. **Features:** Three-position safety, hinged floor plate, adjustable trigger, forged one-piece bolt, M-16 style extractor, forged flat-bottom receiver. Also available with Nikko-Stirling Nighteater 3-9x42 riflescope. Introduced in 2008. Imported from Japan by Legacy Sports International.

Price: Rifle Only, (2008) **$479.00**
Price: Rifle with 3-9x42 Nighteater scope (2008) **$599.00**

HOWA M-1500 THUMBHOLE SPORTER

Caliber: 204, 223 Rem., 22-250 Rem., 243 Win., 6.5x55 (2008) 25-06 Rem., 270 Win., 7mm Rem. Mag., 308 Win., 30-06 Spfl., 300 Win. Mag., 338 Win. Mag., 375 Ruger. Similar to Camo Lightning except stock. **Weight:** 7.6 to 7.7 lbs. **Stock:** S&K laminated wood in nutmeg (brown/black) or pepper (grey/black) colors, raised comb with forward taper, flared pistol grip and scalloped thumbhole. **Sights:** None furnished; drilled and tapped for scope mounting. **Features:** Three-position safety, hinged floor plate, adjustable trigger, forged one-piece bolt, M-16 style extractor, forged flat-bottom receiver. Introduced in 2001. Imported from Japan by Legacy Sports International.

Price: Blue/Nutmeg, standard calibers . . . . **$649.00 to $669.00**
Price: Stainless/Pepper, standard calibers . . . . **$749.00 to $769.00**

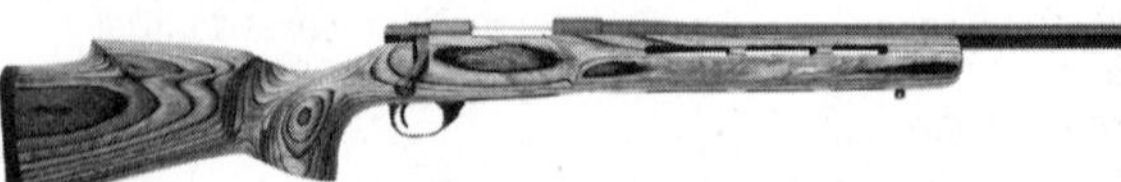

HOWA M-1500 VARMINTER SUPREME AND THUMBHOLE VARMINTER SUPREME

Caliber: 204, 223 Rem., 22-250 Rem., 243 Win., 308 Win. **Stock:** Varminter Supreme: Laminated wood in nutmeg (brown), pepper (grey) colors, raised comb and rollover cheekpiece, full pistol grip with palm-filling swell and broad beavertail forend with six vents for barrel cooling. Thumbhole Varminter Supreme similar, adds a high, straight comb, more vertical pistol grip. **Sights:** None furnished; drilled and tapped for scope mounting. **Features:** Three-position safety, hinged floor plate, adjustable trigger, forged one-piece bolt, M-16 style extractor, forged flat-bottom receiver, hammer forged bull barrel and recessed muzzle crown; overall length, 43.75", 9.7 lbs. Introduced 2001. Barreled actions imported by Legacy Sports International; stocks by S&K Gunstocks.

Price: Varminter Supreme, Blue/Nutmeg **$679.00**
Price: Varminter Supreme, Stainless/Pepper. **$779.00**

Price: Thumbhole Varminter Supreme, Blue/Nutmeg. **$679.00**
Price: Thumbhole Varminter Supreme, Stainless/Pepper **$779.00**

HOWA CAMO LIGHTNING M-1500

Caliber: 204, 223 Rem., 22-250 Rem., 243 Win., 25-06 Rem., 270 Win., 308 Win., 30-06 Spfl., 300 Win. Mag., 338 Win. Mag., 7mm Rem. Mag. **Barrel:** 22" standard calibers; 24" magnum calibers; #2 and #6 contour; blue and stainless. **Weight:** 7.6 to 9.3 lbs. **Length:** 42" to 44.5" overall. **Stock:** Synthetic with molded cheek piece, checkered grip and forend. **Sights:** None furnished; drilled and tapped for scope mounting. **Features:** Three-position safety, hinged floor plate, adjustable trigger, forged one-piece bolt, M-16 style extractor, forged flat bottom receiver. Introduced in 1993. Barreled actions imported by Legacy Sports International.

Price: Blue, #2 barrel, standard calibers. **$377.00**
Price: Stainless, #2 barrel, standard calibers **$479.00**
Price: Blue, #2 barrel, magnum calibers. **$390.00**
Price: Stainless, #2 barrel, magnum calibers **$498.00**
Price: Blue, #6 barrel, standard calibers. **$425.00**
Price: Stainless, #6 barrel, standard calibers **$498.00**

HOWA/HOGUE M-1500

Caliber: 204, 223 Rem., 22-250 Rem., 243 Win., 6.5x5 (2008), 25-06 Rem., 270 Win., 308 Win., 30-06 Spfl., 300 Win. Mag., 338 Win. Mag., 7mm Rem. Mag., 375 Ruger (2008). **Barrel:** Howa barreled action; stainless or blued, 22" #2 contour. **Weight:** 7.4 to 7.6 lbs. **Stock:** Hogue Overmolded, black, or OD green; ambidextrous palm swells. **Sights:** None furnished; drilled and tapped for scope mounting. **Length:** 42" to 44.5" overall. **Features:** Three-position safety, hinged floor plate, adjustable trigger, forged one-piece bolt, M-16 style extractor, forged flat bottom receiver, aluminum pillar bedding and free-floated barrels. Introduced in 2006. Available w/3-10x42 Nikko-Stirling Nighteater scope, rings, bases (2008). from Imported from Japan by Legacy Sports International.

Price: Blued, rifle only. . . . . **$479.00 to $499.00**
Price: Blue, rifle with scope package (2008). . . . . . **$599.00 to $619.00**
Price: Stainless, rifle only . . . . **$625.00 to $675.00**

HOWA/HOGUE M-1500 COMPACT HEAVY BARREL VARMINTER

Chambered in 223 Rem., 308 Win., has 20" #6 contour heavy barrel, recessed muzzle crown. **Stock:** Hogue Overmolded, black, or OD green; ambidextrous palm swells. **Sights:** None furnished; drilled and tapped for scope mounting. **Length:** 44.0" overall. **Features:** Three-position safety, hinged floor plate, adjustable trigger, forged one-piece bolt, M-16 style extractor, forged flat bottom receiver, aluminum pillar bedding and free-floated barrels. **Weight:** 9.3 lbs. Introduced 2008. Imported from Japan by Legacy Sports International.

Price: From **$559.00**

HOWA/AXIOM M-1500

Caliber: 204, 223 Rem., 22-250 Rem., 243 Win., 6.5x55 (2008), 25-06 Rem. (2008), 270 Win., 308 Win., 30-06 Spfl., 7mm Rem, 300 Win. Mag., 338 Win. Mag., 375 Ruger standard barrel; 204, 223 Rem., 243 Win. and 308 Win. heavy barrel. **Barrel:** Howa barreled action, 22" contour standard barrel, 20" #6 contour heavy barrel, and 24" #6 contour heavy barrel. **Weight:** 8.6-10 lbs. **Stock:** Knoxx Industries Axiom V/S synthetic, black or camo. Adjustable length of pull from 11.5" to 15.5". **Sights:** None furnished; drilled and tapped for scope mounting. **Features:** Three-position safety, adjustable trigger, hinged floor plate, forged receiver with large recoil lug, forged one-piece bolt with dual locking lugs Introduced in 2007. Standard-barrel scope packages come with 3-10x42 Nikko-Stirling Nighteater scope, rings, bases (2008). Heavy barrels come with 4-16x44 Nikko-Stirling scope. Imported from Japan by Legacy Sports International.

Price: Axiom Standard Barrel, black stock, from **$699.00**
Price: Axiom 20" and 24" Varminter, black or camo stock, from **$799.00**
Price: Axiom 20" and 24" Varminter, camo stock w/scope (2008), from **$819.00**

HOWA M-1500 ULTRALIGHT 2-N-1 YOUTH

Caliber: 223 Rem., 22-250 Rem., 243 Win., 308 Win., 7mm-08. **Barrel:** 20" #1 contour, blued. **Weight:** 6.8 lbs. **Length:** 39.25" overall. **Stock:** Hogue Overmolded in black, 12.5" LOP. Also includes adult-size Hogue Overmolded in OD green. **Sights:** None furnished; drilled and tapped for scope mounting. **Features:** Bolt and receiver milled to reduce weight, three-position safety, hinged floor plate, adjustable trigger, forged one-piece bolt, M-16 style extractor, forged flat-bottom receiver. Scope package includes 3-9x42 Nikko-Stirling riflescope with bases and rings. Imported from Japan by Legacy Sports International.

Price: Blue, Youth Rifle. **$539.00**
Price: w/Scope package (2008) **$589.00**

H-S PRECISION PRO-SERIES BOLT-ACTION RIFLES

Caliber: 30 chamberings, 3- or 4-round magazine. **Barrel:** 20", 22", 24" or 26", sporter contour Pro-Series 10X match-grade stainless steel barrel. Optional muzzle brake on 30 cal. or smaller. **Weight:** 7.5 lbs. **Length:** NA. **Stock:** Pro-Series synthetic stock with full-length bedding block chassis system, sporter style. **Sights:** None; drilled and tapped for bases. **Features:** Accuracy guarantee: up to 30 caliber, 1/2 minute of angle (3 shots at 100 yards), test target supplied. Stainless steel action, stainless steel floorplate with detachable magazine, matte black Teflon finish. Made in U.S.A. by H-S Precision, Inc.

Price: SPR **$2,680.00**
Price: SPL Lightweight (2008) **$2,825.00**

KEL-TEC RFB

Caliber: 7.62 NATO (308 Win.). **Barrels:** 18" to 32". **Weight:** 11.3 lbs. (unloaded). **Length:** 40" overall. **Features:** Gas-operated semi-auto bullpup-style, forward-ejecting. Fully ambidextrous controls, adjustable trigger mechanism, no open sights, four-sided picatinny forend. Accepts standard FAL-type magazines. Production of the RFB has been delayed due to redesign but was expected to begin first quarter 2009.

Price: **$1,800.00**

KENNY JARRETT BOLT-ACTION RIFLE

Caliber: 223 Rem., 243 Improved, 243 Catbird, 7mm-08 Improved, 280 Remington, .280 Ackley Improved, 7mm Rem. Mag., 284 Jarrett, 30-06 Springfield, 300 Win. Mag., .300 Jarrett, 323 Jarrett, 338 Jarrett, 375 H&H, 416 Rem., 450 Rigby., other modern cartridges. **Barrel:** NA. **Weight:** NA. **Length:** NA. **Stock:** NA. **Features:** Tri-Lock receiver. Talley rings and bases. Accuracy guarantees and custom loaded ammunition.

Price: Signature Series. **$7,640.00**
Price: Wind Walker **$7,380.00**
Price: Original Beanfield (customer's receiver) **$5,380.00**
Price: Professional Hunter **$10,400.00**
Price: SA/Custom **$6,630.00**

KIMBER MODEL 8400 BOLT-ACTION RIFLE

Caliber: 25-06 Rem., 270 Win., 7mm, 30-06 Spfl., 300 Win. Mag., 338 Win. Mag., or 325 WSM, 4 shot. **Barrel:** 24". **Weight:** 6 lbs. 3 oz. to 6 lbs 10 oz. **Length:** 43.25". **Stock:** Claro walnut or Kevlar-reinforced fiberglass. **Sights:** None; drilled and tapped for bases. **Features:** Mauser claw extractor, two-position wing safety, action bedded on aluminum pillars and fiberglass, free-floated barrel, match grade adjustable trigger set at 4 lbs., matte or polished blue or matte stainless finish. Introduced 2003. Sonora model (2008) has brown laminated stock, hand-rubbed oil finish, chambered in 25-06 Rem., 30-06 Spfl., and 300 Win. Mag. Weighs 8.5 lbs., measures 44.50" overall length. Front swivel stud only for bipod. Stainless steel bull barrel, 24" satin stainless steel finish. Made in U.S.A. by Kimber Mfg. Inc.

Price: Classic **$1,172.00**
Price: Classic Select Grade, French walnut stock (2008). . . **$1,359.00**
Price: SuperAmerica, AAA walnut stock. **$2,240.00**
Price: Sonora **$1,359.00**
Price: Police Tactical, synthetic stock, fluted barrel (300 Win. Mag only) **$2,575.00**

Kimber Model 8400 Caprivi Bolt-Action Rifle

Similar to 8400 bolt rifle, but chambered for .375 H&H and 458 Lott, 4-shot magazine. Stock is Claro walnut or Kevlar-reinforced fiberglass. Features twin steel crossbolts in stock, AA French walnut, pancake cheekpiece, 24 lines-per-inch wrap-around checkering, ebony forend tip, hand-rubbed oil finish, barrel-mounted sling swivel stud, 3-leaf express sights, Howell-type rear sling swivel stud and a Pachmayr Decelerator recoil pad in traditional orange color. Introduced 2008. Made in U.S.A. by Kimber Mfg. Inc.

Price: **$3,196.00**

Kimber Model 8400 Talkeetna Bolt-Action Rifle

Similar to 8400 bolt rifle, but chambered for .375 H&H, 4-shot magazine. Weighs 8 lbs, overall length is 44.5". Stock is synthetic. Features free-floating match grade barrel with tapered match grade chamber and target crown, three-position wing safety acts directly on the cocking piece for greatest security, and Pacmayr Decelerator. Made in U.S.A. by Kimber Mfg. Inc.

Price: **$2,108.00**

KIMBER MODEL 84M BOLT-ACTION RIFLE

Caliber: 22-250 Rem., 204 Ruger, 223 Rem., 243 Win., 260 Rem., 7mm-08 Rem., 308 Win., 5-shot. **Barrel:** 22", 24", 26". **Weight:** 5 lbs., 10 oz. to 10 lbs. **Length:** 41" to 45". **Stock:** Claro walnut, checkered with steel gripcap; synthetic or gray laminate. **Sights:** None; drilled and tapped for bases. **Features:** Mauser claw extractor, three-position wing safety, action bedded on aluminum pillars, free-floated barrel, match-grade trigger set at 4 lbs., matte blue finish. Includes cable lock. Introduced 2001. Montana (2008) has synthetic stock, Pachmayr Decelerator recoil pad, stainless steel 22" sporter barrel. Made in U.S.A. by Kimber Mfg. Inc.

Price: Classic (243 Win., 260, 7mm-08 Rem., 308) **$1,114.00**
Price: Varmint (22-250) **$1,224.00**
Price: Montana **$1,276.00**
Price: Classic Stainless, matte stainless steel receiver and barrel (243 Win., 7mm-08, 308 Win.) **$1,156.00**

KIMBER MODEL 84L CLASSIC RIFLE

Bolt action rifle chambered in .270 Win. and .30-06. Features include 24-inch sightless matte blue sporter barrel; hand-rubbed A-grade walnut stock with 20 lpi panel checkering; pillar and glass bedding; Mauser claw extractor; 3-position M70-style safety; 5-round magazine; adjustable trigger.

Price: **$1,172.00**

KIMBER MODEL 8400 PATROL RIFLE

Bolt action tactical rifle chambered in .308 Win. Features include 20-inch 1:12 fluted sightless matte blue heavy barrel; black epoxy-coated laminated wood stock with 20 lpi panel checkering; pillar and glass bedding; Mauser claw extractor; 3-position M70-style safety; 5-round magazine; adjustable trigger.

Price: **$1,476.00**

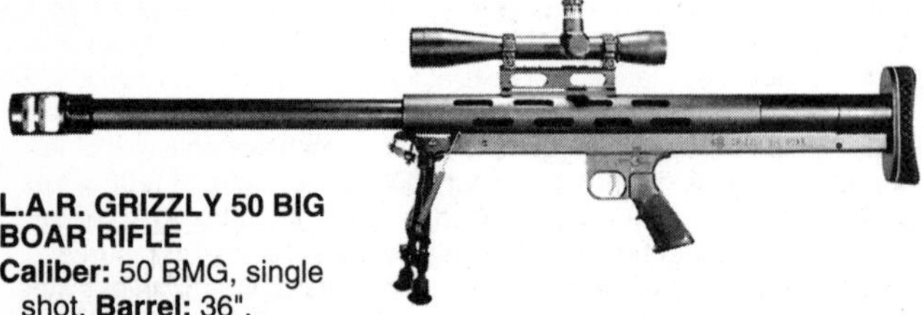

L.A.R. GRIZZLY 50 BIG BOAR RIFLE

Caliber: 50 BMG, single shot. **Barrel:** 36". **Weight:** 30.4 lbs. **Length:** 45.5" overall. **Stock:** Integral. Ventilated rubber recoil pad. **Sights:** None furnished; scope mount. **Features:** Bolt-action bullpup design, thumb and bolt stop safety. All-steel construction. Introduced 1994. Made in U.S.A. by L.A.R. Mfg., Inc.

Price: From **$2,350.00**

MAGNUM RESEARCH MOUNTAIN EAGLE MAGNUMLITE RIFLES

Caliber: .22-250, .223, .224, .243, .257, 7mm Rem. Mag., 7mm WSM, .280, .300 Win. Mag., .300 WSM, .30-06, 3-shot magazine. **Barrel:** 24" sport taper graphite; 26" bull barrel graphite. **Weight:** 7.1-9.2 lbs. **Length:** 44.5-48.25" overall (adjustable on Tactical model). **Stock:** Hogue OverMolded synthetic, H-S Precision Tactical synthetic, H-S

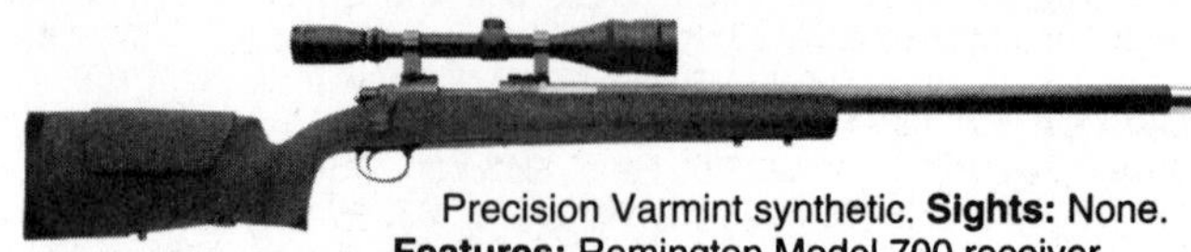

Precision Varmint synthetic. **Sights:** None. **Features:** Remington Model 700 receiver. Introduced in 2001. From Magnum Research, Inc.

Price: MLR3006ST24 Hogue stock **$2,295.00**
Price: MLR7MMBST24 Hogue stock **$2,295.00**
Price: MLRT22250 H-S Tactical stock, 26" bull barrel **$2,400.00**
Price: MLRT300WI Tactical **$2,400.00**

MARLIN XL7 BOLT ACTION RIFLE

Caliber: 25-06 Rem. 270 Win., 30-06 Spfl., 4-shot magazine. **Barrel:** 22" 1:10" right-hand twist, recessed barrel crown. **Weight:** 6.5 lbs. **Length:** 42.5" overall. **Stock:** Black synthetic or Realtree APG-HD camo, Soft-Tech recoil pad, pillar bedded. **Sights:** None. **Features:** Pro-Fire trigger is user adjustable down to 2.5 lbs. Fluted bolt, steel sling swivel studs, high polished blued steel, checkered bolt handle, molded checkering, one-piece scope base. Introduced in 2008. From Marlin Firearms, Inc.

Price: Black Synthetic. **$326.00**
Price: Camouflaged **$356.00**

Marlin XS7 Short-Action Bolt-Action Rifle

Similar to Model XL7 but chambered in 7mm-08, 243 Winchester and 308 Winchester.

Price: . . . . **NA**
Price: XS7Y Youth **$341.00**
Price: XS7C Camo, Realtree APG HD camo stock **$341.00**
Price: XS7S Stainless. . . . . **NA**

MERKEL KR1 BOLT-ACTION RIFLE

Caliber: 223 Rem., 243 Rem., 6.5x55, 7mm-08, 308 Win., 270 Win., 30-06, 9.3x62, 7mm Rem. Mag., 300 Win. Mag., 270 WSM, 300 WSM, 338 Win. Mag. **Features:** Short lock, short bolt movement, take-down design with interchangeable barrel assemblies, three-position safety, detachable box magazine, fine trigger with set feature, checkered walnut pistol-grip semi-schnable stock. Adjustable iron sights with quick release mounts. Imported from Germany by Merkel USA.

Price: **$1,995.00**
Price: Model KR1 Stutzen Antique: 20.8" barrel, case-colored receiver, Mannlicher-style stock **$3,395.00**

MOSSBERG 100 ATR BOLT-ACTION RIFLE

Caliber: 243 Win. (2006), 270 Win., 308 Win. (2006), 30-06 Spfl., 4-round magazine. **Barrel:** 22", 1:10 twist, free-floating, button-rifled, recessed muzzle crown. **Weight:** 6.7 to 7.75 lbs. **Length:** 42"-42.75" overall. **Stock:** Black synthetic, walnut, Mossy Oak New Break Up camo, Realtree AP camo. **Sights:** Factory-installed Weaver-style scope bases; scoped combos include 3x9 factory-mounted, bore-sighted scopes. **Features:** Marinecote and matte blue metal finishes, free gun lock, side lever safety. Introduced 2005. Night Train (2008)comes with Picatinny rail and factory-mounted 4-16x50mm variable scope. From O.F. Mossberg & Sons, Inc.

Price: Short-Action 243 Win., wood stock, matte blue, from. . . **$424.00**
Price: Long-Action 270 Win., Mossy Oak New Break Up camo, matte blue, from **$424.00**
Price: Scoped Combo 30-06 Spfl., Walnut-Dura-Wood stock, Marinecote finish, from **$481.00**
Price: Bantam Short Action 308 Win., 20" barrel **$471.00**
Price: Night Train Short-Action Scoped Combo (2008) **$567.00**

MOSSBERG 4X4 BOLT-ACTION RIFLE

Caliber: 25-06 Rem, 270 Win., 30-06 Spfl., 7mm Rem. Mag., .300 Win. Mag., .338 Win. Mag., detachable box magazine, 4 rounds

Prices given are believed to be accurate at time of publication however, many factors affect retail pricing so exact prices are not possible.

standard, 3 rounds magnum. **Barrel:** 24", 1:10 twist, free-floating, button-rifled, recessed muzzle crown. **Weight:** 7+ lbs. **Length:** 42" overall. **Stock:** Skeletonized synthetic laminate (2008); black synthetic, laminated, select American black walnut. **Sights:** Factory-installed Weaver-style scope bases. **Features:** Marinecote and matte blue metal finishes, free gun lock, side lever safety. Scoped combos include factory-mounted, bore-sighted 3-9x40mm variable. Introduced 2007. From O.F. Mossberg & Sons, Inc.

Price: 25-06 Rem., walnut stock, matte blue, from **$505.00**
Price: 300 Win. Mag., synthetic laminate stock (2008), from . . **$505.00**
Price: 4X4 Classic Stock Synthetic: Black synthetic stock and Marinecote metal surfaces **$654.00**
Price: 4X4 Scoped Combo: Matte blue finish and 3x9 scope **$654.00**
Price: 4X4 Classic Walnut Stock: Checkered walnut stock . . **$654.00**

REMINGTON MODEL 700 CDL CLASSIC DELUXE RIFLE

Caliber: 223 Rem., 243 Win., 25-06 Rem., 270 Win., 7mm-08 Rem., 280 Remington, 7mm Rem. Mag., 7mm Rem. Ultra Mag., 30-06 Spfl., 300 Rem. Ultra Mag., 300 Win. Mag., 35 Whelen. **Barrel:** 24" or 26" round tapered. **Weight:** 7.4 to 7.6 lbs. **Length:** 43.6" to 46.5" overall. **Stock:** Straight-comb American walnut stock, satin finish, checkering, right-handed cheek piece, black fore-end tip and grip cap, sling swivel studs. **Sights:** None. **Features:** Satin blued finish, jeweled bolt body, drilled and tapped for scope mounts. Hinged-floorplate magazine capacity: 4, standard calibers; 3, magnum calibers. SuperCell recoil pad, cylindrical receiver, integral extractor. Introduced 2004. CDL SF (stainless fluted) chambered for 260 Rem., 257 Wby. Mag., 270 Win., 270 WSM, 7mm-08 Rem., 7mm Rem. Mag., 30-06 Spfl., 300 WSM. Left-hand versions introduced 2008 in six calibers. Made in U.S. by Remington Arms Co., Inc.

Price: Standard Calibers: 24" barrel **$959.00**
Price: Magnum Calibers: 26" barrel **$987.00**
Price: CDL SF (2007), from **$1,100.00**
Price: CDL LH (2008), from **$987.00**
Price: CDL High Polish Blued (2008), from **$959.00**
Price: CDL SF (2009), 257 Roberts . . . . **NA**

REMINGTON MODEL 700 BDL RIFLE

Caliber: 243 Win., 270 Win., 7mm Rem. Mag. 30-06 Spfl., 300 Rem Ultra Mag. **Barrel:** 22, 24, 26" round tapered. **Weight:** 7.25-7.4 lbs. **Length:** 41.6-46.5" overall. **Stock:** Walnut. Gloss-finish pistol grip stock with skip-line checkering, black forend tip and gripcap with white line spacers. Quick-release floorplate. **Sights:** Gold bead ramp front; hooded ramp, removable step-adjustable rear with windage screw. **Features:** Side safety, receiver tapped for scope mounts, matte receiver top, quick detachable swivels.

Price: 243 Win., 270 Win., 30-06 . . . . **$927.00**
Price: 7mm Rem. Mag. 300 Rem Ultra Mag. **$955.00**

REMINGTON MODEL 700 SPS RIFLES

Caliber: 17 Rem. Fireball, 204 Ruger, 22-250 Rem., 6.8 Rem SPC, 223 Rem., 243 Win., 270 Win. 270 WSM, 7mm-08 Rem., 7mm Rem. Mag., 7mm Rem. Ultra Mag., 30-06 Spfl., 308 Win., 300 WSM, 300 Win. Mag., 300 Rem. Ultra Mag. **Barrel:** 20", 24" or 26" carbon steel. **Weight:** 7 to 7.6 lbs. **Length:** 39.6" to 46.5" overall. **Stock:** Black synthetic, sling swivel studs, SuperCell recoil pad. **Sights:** None. Introduced 2005. SPS Stainless replaces Model 700 BDL Stainless Synthetic. **Barrel:** Bead-blasted 416 stainless steel. **Features:** Plated internal fire control component. SPS DM features detachable box magazine. Buckmaster Edition versions feature Realtree Hardwoods HD camouflage and Buckmasters logo engraved on floorplate. SPS Varmint includes X-Mark Pro trigger, 26" heavy contour barrel, vented beavertail forend, dual front sling swivel studs. Made in U.S. by Remington Arms Co., Inc.

Price: SPS, from **$639.00**
Price: SPS DM (2005) **$672.00**
Price: SPS Youth, 20" barrel (2007) 243 Win., 7mm-08. . . . . . **$604.00**
Price: SPS Varmint (2007) **$665.00**
Price: SPS Stainless, (2005), from **$732.00**
Price: SPS Buckmasters Youth (2008), 243 Win. **$707.00**
Price: SPS Youth LH (2008), 243 Win., 7mm-08 . . . . **$620.00**
Price: SPS Varmint LH (2008) **$692.00**
Price: SPS Synthetic Left-Hand . . . . **NA**

REMINGTON 700 SPS TACTICAL

Bolt action rifle chambered in .223 and .308 Win. Features include 20-inch heavy-contour tactical-style barrel; dual-point pillar bedding; black synthetic stock with Hogue overmoldings; semi-beavertail fore-end; X-Mark Pro adjustable trigger system; satin black oxide metal finish; hinged floorplate magazine; SuperCell recoil pad.

Price **$734.00**

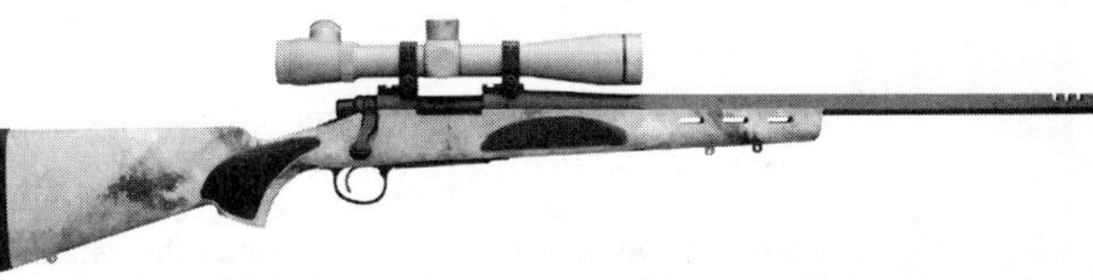

REMINGTON 700 VTR A-TACS CAMO WITH SCOPE

Bolt action rifle chambered in .223 and .308 Win. Features include ATACS camo finish overall; triangular contour 22-inch barrel has an integral muzzle brake; black overmold grips; 1:9 (.223 caliber) 0r 1:12 (.308) twist; factory-mounted scope.

Price: . . . . **NA**

REMINGTON MODEL 700 MOUNTAIN LSS RIFLES

Caliber: 270 Win., 280 Rem., 7mm-08 Rem., 30-06. **Barrel:** 22" satin stainless steel. **Weight:** 6.6 lbs. **Length:** 41.6" to 42.5" overall. **Stock:** Brown laminated, sling swivel studs, SuperCell recoil pad, black forend tip. **Sights:** None. **Barrel:** Bead-blasted 416 stainless steel, lightweight contour. Made in U.S. by Remington Arms Co., Inc.

Price: **$1,052.00**

REMINGTON MODEL 700 ALASKAN TI

Caliber: 25-06 Rem., 270 Win., 270 WSM, 280 Rem., 7mm-08 Rem., 7mm Rem. Mag., 30-06 Spfl., 300 WSM, 300 Win. Mag. **Barrel:** 24" round tapered. **Weight:** 6 lbs. **Length:** 43.6" to 44.5" overall. **Stock:** Bell & Carlson carbon-fiber synthetic, sling swivel studs, SuperCell gel recoil pad. **Sights:** None. **Features:** Formerly Model 700 Titanium, introduced 2001. Titanium receiver, spiral-cut fluted bolt, skeletonized bolt handle, X-Mark Pro trigger, satin stainless finish. Drilled and tapped for scope mounts. Hinged-floorplate magazine capacity: 4, standard calibers; 3, magnum calibers. Introduced 2007. Made in U.S. by Remington Arms Co., Inc.

Price: From **$2,225.00**

REMINGTON MODEL 700 VLS/VLSS TH RIFLES

Caliber: 204 Ruger, 223 Rem., 22-250 Rem., 243 Win., 308 Win. **Barrel:** 26" heavy contour barrel (0.820" muzzle O.D.), concave target-style barrel crown **Weight:** 9.4 lbs. **Length:** 45.75" overall. **Stock:** Brown laminated stock, satin finish, with beavertail forend, gripcap, rubber buttpad. **Sights:** None. **Features:** Introduced 1995. VLSS TH (varmint laminate stock stainless) thumbhole model introduced 2007. Made in U.S. by Remington Arms Co., Inc.

Price: VLS. $979.00
Price: VL SS TH $1,085.00

REMINGTON MODEL 700 VSSF-II/SENDERO SF II RIFLES

Caliber: 17 Rem. Fireball, 204 Ruger, 220 Swift, 223 Rem., 22-250 Rem., 308 Win. **Barrel:** satin blued 26" heavy contour (0.820" muzzle O.D.). VSSF has satin-finish stainless barreled action with 26" fluted barrel. **Weight:** 8.5 lbs. **Length:** 45.75" overall. **Stock:** H.S. Precision composite reinforced with aramid fibers, black (VSSF-II) Contoured beavertail fore-end with ambidextrous finger grooves, palm swell, and twin front tactical-style swivel studs. **Sights:** None. **Features:** Aluminum bedding block, drilled and tapped for scope mounts, hinged floorplate magazines. Introduced 1994. Sendero model is similar to VSSF-II except chambered for 264 Win. Mag, 7mm Rem. Mag., 7mm Rem. Ultra Mag., 300 Win. Mag., 300 Rem. Ultra Mag. Polished stainless barrel. Introduced 1996. Made in U.S. by Remington Arms Co., Inc.

Price: VSSF-II. $1,332.00
Price: Sendero SF II $1,359.00

REMINGTON MODEL 700 XCR RIFLE

Caliber: 25-06 Rem., 270 Win., 270 WSM, 7mm-08 Rem., 7mm Rem. Mag., 7mm Rem Ultra Mag., 30-06 Spfl., 300 WSM, 300 Win. Mag., 300 Rem. Ultra Mag., 338 Rem. Ultra Mag., 338 Win. Mag., 375 H&H Mag., 375 Rem. Ultra Mag. **Barrel:** 24" standard caliber; 26" magnum. **Weight:** 7.4 to 7.6 lbs. **Length:** 43.6" to 46.5" overall. **Stock:** Black synthetic, SuperCell recoil pad, rubber overmolded grip and forend. **Sights:** None. **Features:** XCR (Xtreme Conditions Rifle) includes TriNyte Corrosion Control System; drilled and tapped for scope mounts. 375 H&H Mag., 375 Rem. Ultra Mag. chamberings come with iron sights. Introduced 2005. XCR Tactical model introduced 2007. **Features:** Bell & Carlson OD green tactical stock, beavertail forend, recessed thumbhook behind pistol grip, TriNyte coating over stainless steel barrel, LTR fluting. Chambered in 223 Rem., 300 Win. Mag., 308 Win. 700XCR Left Hand introduced 2008 in 270 Win., 7mm Rem. Mag., 30-06 Spfl., 300 Rem Ultra Mag. Made in U.S. by Remington Arms Co., Inc.

Price: From $1,065.00
Price: XCR Tactical (2007). $1,407.00
Price: XCR Left Hand (2008) $1,092.00
Price: XCR Compact Tactical (2008), 223 Rem., 308 Win. . $1,434.00

Remington Model 700 XCR Camo RMEF

Similar to Model 700 XCR but with stainless barrel and receiver, AP HD camo stock, TriNyte coating overall, 7mm Remington Ultra Mag chambering.

Price: $1,199.00

REMINGTON 700 XCR II

Bolt action rifle chambered in .25-06 Remington, .270 Win, .280 Remington, 7mm Remington Mag., 7mm Remington Ultra Mag., .300 WSM, .300 Win Mag., .300 Remington Ultra Mag, .338 Win. Mag., .338 Remington Ultra Mag, .375 H&H, .375 Remington Ultra Mag., .30-06 Springfield. Features include black TriNyte corrosion control system coating; coated stainless steel barrel and receiver; olive drab green Hogue overmolded synthetic stock; SuperCell recoil pad; X-Mark Pro Trigger System; 2- or 26-inch barrel, depending on chambering.

Price: $970.00

REMINGTON 700 XCR II - BONE COLLECTOR EDITION

Similar to Remington 700 XCR II but with Realtree AP HD camo stock.

Price: $1,063.00

REMINGTON 700 XHR EXTREME HUNTING RIFLE

Caliber: 243 Win., 25-06, 270 Win., 7mm-08, 7mm Rem. Mag., 300 Win. Mag, 7mm Rem. Ultra Mag. **Barrel:** 24", 25", or 26" triangular magnum-contour counterbored. **Weight:** 7-1/4 to 7-5/8 lbs. **Length:** 41-5/8 to 46-1/2 overall. **Features:** Adjustable trigger, synthetic stock finished in Realtree AG HD camo, satin black oxide finish on exposed metal surfaces, hinged floorplate, SuperCell recoil pad.

Price: . . . . $879.00 to $927.00

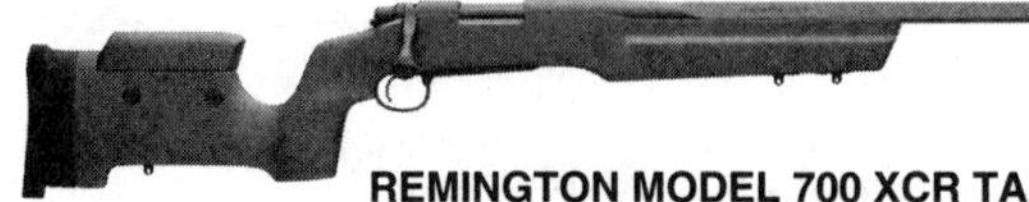

REMINGTON MODEL 700 XCR TARGET TACTICAL RIFLE

Caliber: 308 Win. Barrel: 26" triangular counterbored, 1:11-1/2 rifling. **Weight:** 11.75 lbs. **Length:** 45-3/4" overall. **Features:** Textured green Bell & Carlson varmint/tactical stock with adjustable comb and length of pull, adjustable trigger, satin black oxide finish on exposed metal surfaces, hinged floorplate, SuperCell recoil pad, matte blue on exposed metal surfaces.

Price: $1,407.00

REMINGTON MODEL 700 VTR VARMINT/TACTICAL RIFLE

Caliber: 17 Rem. Fireball, 204 Ruger, 22-250, 223 Rem., 243 Win., 308 Win. **Barrel:** 22" triangular counterbored. **Weight:** 7.5 lbs. **Length:** 41-5/8" overall. **Features:** Olive drab overmolded or Digital Tiger TSP Desert Camo stock with vented semi-beavertail forend, tactical-style dual swivel mounts for bipod, matte blue on exposed metal surfaces.

Price: $1,972.00
Price: VTR Desert Recon, Digital Desert Camo stock, 223 and 308 Win. only $1,972.00

REMINGTON MODEL 700 VARMINT SF RIFLE

Caliber: 17 Rem. Fireball, 204 Ruger, 22-250, 223, 220 Swift. **Barrel:** 26" stainless steel fluted. **Weight:** 8.5 lbs. **Length:** 45.75". **Features:** Synthetic stock with ventilated forend, stainless steel/triggerguard/floorplate, dual tactical swivels for bipod attachment.

Price: $825.00

REMINGTON MODEL 770 BOLT-ACTION RIFLE

Caliber: 243 Win., 270 Win., 7mm Rem. Mag., 7mm-08 Rem., 308 Win., 30-06 Spfl., 300 Win. Mag. **Barrel:** 22" or 24", button rifled. **Weight:** 8.5 lbs. **Length:** 42.5" to 44.5" overall. **Stock:** Black synthetic. **Sights:** Bushnell Sharpshooter 3-9x scope mounted and bore-sighted. **Features:** Upgrade of Model 710 introduced 2001. Unique action locks bolt directly into barrel; 60-degree bolt throw; 4-shot dual-stack magazine; all-steel receiver. Introduced 2007. Made in U.S.A. by Remington Arms Co.

Price: $460.00
Price: Youth, 243 Win. $460.00
Price: Stainless Camo (2008), stainless barrel, nickel-plated bolt, Realtree camo stock. $540.00

Prices given are believed to be accurate at time of publication however, many factors affect retail pricing so exact prices are not possible.

REMINGTON MODEL SEVEN CDL/CDL MAGNUM

Caliber: 17 Rem. Fireball, 243 Win., 260 Rem., 270 WSM, 7mm-08 Rem., 308 Win., 300 WSM, 350 Rem. Mag. **Barrel:** 20"; 22" magnum. **Weight:** 6.5 to 7.4 lbs. **Length:** 39.25" to 41.25" overall. **Stock:** American walnut, SuperCell recoil pad, satin finished. **Sights:** None. **Features:** Satin finished carbon steel barrel and action, 3- or 4-round magazine, hinged magazine floorplate. Furnished with iron sights and sling swivel studs, drilled and tapped for scope mounts. CDL versions introduced 2007. Made in U.S.A. by Remington Arms Co.

Price: CDL **$959.00**
Price: CDL Magnum **$1,01200**
Price: Predator (2008) **$825.00**
Price: 25th Anniversary (2008), 7mm-08 . . . . **$969.00**

REMINGTON MODEL 798/799 BOLT-ACTION RIFLES

Caliber: 243 Win., 270 Win., 7mm Rem. Mag., 308 Win., .30-06 Spfl., .300 Win. Mag., .375 H&H Mag., .458 Win. Mag. **Barrel:** 20" to 26". **Weight:** 7.75 lbs. **Length:** 39.5" to 42.5" overall. **Stock:** Brown or green laminated, 1-inch rubber butt pad. **Sights:** None. Receiver drilled and tapped for standard Mauser 98 (long- and short-action) scope mounts. **Features:** Model 98 Mauser action (square-bridge Mauser 98). Claw extractor, sporter style 2-position safety, solid steel hinged floorplate magazine. Introduced 2006. Made in U.S.A. by Remington Arms Co.

Price: Model 798 SPS, black synthetic stock (2008), from **$527.00**
Price: Model 798 Satin Walnut Stock (2008), from. **$648.00**
Price: Model 798 Safari Grade (2008), from. **$1,141.00**
Price: Model 799, from **$648.00**

REMINGTON 40-XB TACTICAL

Bolt action rifle chambered in .308 Winchester. Features include stainless steel bolt with Teflon coating; hinged floorplate; adjustable trigger; 27-1/4-inch tri-fluted 1:14 barrel; H-S precision pro series tactical stock, black color with dark green spiderweb; two front swivel studs; one rear swivel stud; vertical pistol grip.

Price: . . . . **NA**

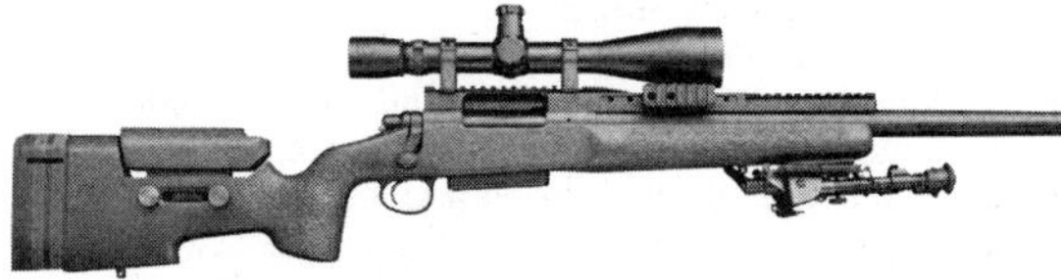

REMINGTON 40-XS TACTICAL - 338LM SYSTEM

Bolt action rifle chambered in .338 Lapua Magnum. Features include 416 stainless steel Model 40-X 24-inch 1:12 barreled action; black polymer coating; McMillan A3 series stock with adjustable length of pull and adjustable comb; adjustable trigger and Sunny Hill heavy duty, all-steel trigger guard; Harris bi-pod with quick adjust swivel lock Leupold Mark IV 3.5-10x40mm long range M1 scope with Mil Dot reticle; Badger Ordnance all-steel Picatinny scope rail and rings.

Price: . . . . **NA**

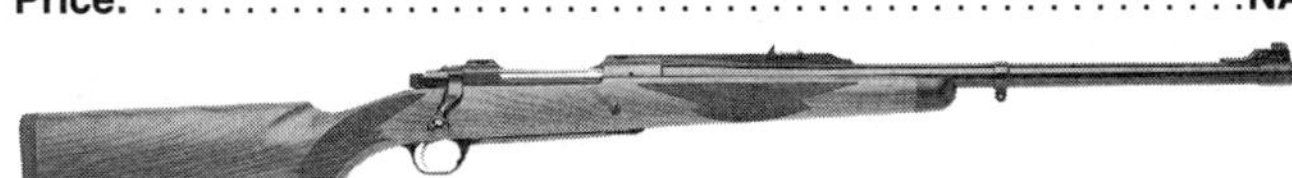

RUGER MAGNUM RIFLE

Caliber: 375 H&H, 416 Rigby, 458 Lott. **Barrel:** 23". **Weight:** 9.5 to 10.25 lbs. **Length:** 44". **Stock:** AAA Premium Grade Circassian walnut with live-rubber recoil pad, metal gripcap, and studs for mounting sling swivels. **Sights:** Blade, front; V-notch rear express sights (one stationary, two folding) drift-adjustable for windage. **Features:** Floorplate latch secures the hinged floorplate against accidental dumping of cartridges; one-piece bolt has a non-rotating Mauser-type controlled-feed extractor; fixed-blade ejector.

Price: M77RSM MKII **$2,334.00**

RUGER COMPACT MAGNUMS

Caliber: .338 RCM, .300 RCM; 3-shot magazine. **Barrel:** 20". **Weight:** 6.75 lbs. **Length:** 39.5-40" overall. **Stock:** American walnut and black synthetic; stainless steel and Hawkeye Matte blued finishes. **Sights:** Adjustable Williams "U" notch rear sight and brass bead front sight. **Features:** Based on a shortened .375 Ruger case, the .300 and .338 RCMs match the .300 and .338 Win. Mag. in performance; RCM stock is 1/2 inch shorter than standard M77 Hawkeye stock; LC6 trigger; steel floor plate engraved with Ruger logo and "Ruger Compact Magnum"; Red Eagle recoil pad; Mauser-type controlled feeding; claw extractor; 3-position safety; hammer-forged steel barrels; Ruger scope rings. Walnut stock includes extensive cut-checkering and rounded profiles. Intr. 2008. Made in U.S.A. by Sturm, Ruger & Co.

Price: HM77RCM (walnut/Hawkeye matte blued) **$995.00**
Price: HKM77PRCM (synthetic/SS) **$995.00**

RUGER 77/22 BOLT-ACTION RIFLE

Caliber: 22 Hornet, 6-shot rotary magazine. **Barrel:** 20" or 24". **Weight:** About 6.25 to 7.5 lbs. **Length:** 39.5" to 43.5" overall. **Stock:** Checkered American walnut, black rubber buttpad; brown laminate. **Sights:** None. **Features:** Same basic features as rimfire model except slightly lengthened receiver. Uses Ruger rotary magazine. Three-position safety. Comes with 1" Ruger scope rings. Introduced 1994.

Price: 77/22-RH (rings only, no sights). **$754.00**
Price: K77/22-VHZ Varmint, laminated stock, no sights **$836.00**

RUGER M77 HAWKEYE RIFLES

Caliber: 204 Ruger, 223 Rem., 22-250 Rem., 243 Win., 257 Roberts, 25-06 Rem., 270 Win., 280 Rem., 7mm/08, 7mm Rem. Mag., 308 Win., 30-06 Spfl., 300 Win. Mag., 338 Win. Mag., 338 Federal, 358 Win. Mag., 416 Ruger, 375 Ruger, 300 Ruger Compact Magnum, 338 Ruger Compact Magnum; 4-shot magazine, except 3-shot magazine for magnums; 5-shot magazine for 204 Ruger and 223 Rem. **Barrel:** 22", 24". **Weight:** 6.75 to 8.25 lbs. **Length:** 42-44.4" overall. **Stock:** American walnut. **Sights:** None furnished. Receiver has Ruger integral scope mount base, Ruger 1" rings. **Features:** Includes Ruger LC6 trigger, new red rubber recoil pad, Mauser-type controlled feeding, claw extractor, 3-position safety, hammer-forged steel barrels, Ruger scope rings. Walnut stock includes wrap-around cut checkering on the forearm and, more rounded contours on stock and top of pistol grips. Matte stainless version features synthetic stock. Hawkeye Alaskan and African chambered in 375 Ruger. Alaskan features matte-black finish, 20" barrel, Hogue OverMolded synthetic stock. African has 23" blued barrel, checkered walnut stock, left-handed model. 375's have windage-adjustable shallow "V" notch rear sight, white bead front sights. Introduced 2007. Left-hand models available 2008.

Price: Standard, right- and left-hand. **$803.00**
Price: All-Weather. **$803.00**
Price: Laminate, left-hand **$862.00**
Price: Ultra Light. **$862.00**

Price: All-Weather Ultra Light **$803.00**
Price: Compact **$803.00**
Price: Laminate Compact **$862.00**
Price: Compact Magnum **$899.00**
Price: African **$1,079.00**
Price: Alaskan **$1,079.00**
Price: Sporter **$862.00**
Price: Tactical **$1,138.00**
Price: Predator **$935.00**
Price: International **$939.00**

RUGER M77VT TARGET RIFLE

Caliber: 22-250 Rem., 223 Rem., 204 Ruger, 243 Win., 25-06 Rem., 308 Win. **Barrel:** 26" heavy stainless steel with target grey finish. **Weight:** 9 to 9.75 lbs. **Length:** Approx. 45.75" to 46.75" overall. **Stock:** Laminated American hardwood with beavertail forend, steel swivel studs; no checkering or gripcap. **Sights:** Integral scope mount bases in receiver. **Features:** Ruger diagonal bedding system. Ruger steel 1" scope rings supplied. Fully adjustable trigger. Steel floorplate and trigger guard. New version introduced 1992.
Price: KM77VT MKII **$935.00**

SAKO A7 AMERICAN BOLT-ACTION RIFLE

Caliber: 22-250, 243 Win., 25-06, 260 Rem., 270 Win., 270 WSM, 300 WSM, 30-06, 300 WM, 308 Win., 338 Federall, 7mm Rem. Mag., 7mm-08. **Barrel:** 22-7/16" standard, 24-3/8" magnum. **Weight:** 6 lbs. 3 oz. to 6 lbs. 13 oz. **Length:** 42-5/16" to 44-5/16" overall. **Features:** Blued or stainless barrel and receiver, black composite stock with sling swivels and recoil pad, two-position safety, adjustable trigger, detachable 3+1 box magazine.
Price: From . . . . **$850.00** (blued); **$950.00** (stainless)

SAKO TRG-22 AND TRG-42 TACTICAL RIFLES

Bolt action rifles chambered in .308 Winchester (TRG-22) or .338 Lapua Magnum (TRG-42). Features include target grade Cr-Mo or stainless barrels with muzzle brake; three locking lugs; 60° bolt throw; adjustable two-stage target trigger; adjustable or folding synthetic stock; receiver-mounted integral 17mm axial optics rails with recoil stop-slots; tactical scope mount for modern three turret tactical scopes (30 and 34 mm tube diameter); optional bipod.
Price: . . . . **$2,850.00 to $4,400.00**

SAKO MODEL 85 BOLT-ACTION RIFLES

Caliber: 22-250 Rem., 243 Win., 25-06 Rem., 260, 6.5x55mm, 270 Win., 270 WSM, 7mm-08 Rem., 308 Win., 30-06; 7mm WSM, 300 WSM, 338 Federal. **Barrel:** 22.4", 22.9", 24.4". **Weight:** 7.75 lbs. **Length:** NA. **Stock:** Polymer, laminated or high-grade walnut, straight comb, shadow-line cheekpiece. **Sights:** None furnished. **Features:** Controlled-round feeding, adjustable trigger, matte stainless or nonreflective satin blue. Quad model is polymer/stainless with four interchangeable barrels in 22 LR, 22 WMR 17 HMR and 17 Mach 2; 50-degree bolt-lift, ambidextrous palm-swell, adjustable butt-pad. Introduced 2006. Imported from Finland by Beretta USA.
Price: Sako 85 Hunter, walnut/blued **$1,700.00**
Price: Sako 85 Grey Wolf, laminated/stainless **$1,575.00**
Price: Sako 85 Quad, polymer/stainless **$925.00**
Price: Sako 85 Quad Combo, four barrels **$2,175.00**

Sako 85 Finnlight

Similar to Model 85 but chambered in 243 Win., 25-06, 260 Rem., 270 Win., 270 WSM, 300 WSM, 30-06, 300 WM, 308 Win., 6.5x55mm, 7mm Rem Mag., 7mm-08. Weighs 6 lbs., 3 oz. to 6 lbs. 13 oz. Stainless steel barrel and receiver, black synthetic stock.
Price: **$1,600.00**

SAKO 75 HUNTER BOLT-ACTION RIFLE

Caliber: 223 Rem., 22-250 Rem., 243 Win., 25-06 Rem., 260, 270 Win., 270 WSM, 280 Rem., 300 Win. Mag., 30-06; 7mm-08 Rem., 308 Win., 270 Wby. Mag., 7mm Rem. Mag., 7mm STW, 7mm Wby. Mag., 300 Wby. Mag., 338 Win. Mag., 340 Wby. Mag., 375 H&H. **Barrel:** 22", standard calibers; 24", 26" magnum calibers. **Weight:** About 6 lbs. **Length:** NA. **Stock:** European walnut with matte lacquer finish. **Sights:** None furnished; dovetail scope mount rails. **Features:** New design with three locking lugs and a mechanical ejector, key locks firing pin and bolt, cold hammer-forged barrel is free-floating, two-position safety, hinged floorplate or detachable magazine that can be loaded from the top, short 70-degree bolt lift. Five action lengths. Introduced 1997. Imported from Finland by Beretta USA.
Price: From **$1,375.00**

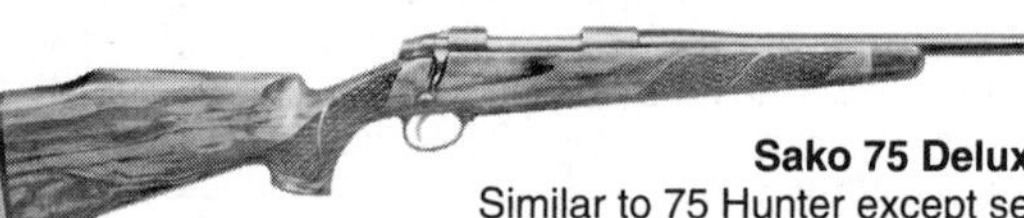

Sako 75 Deluxe Rifle

Similar to 75 Hunter except select wood rosewood gripcap and forend tip. Available in 17 Rem., 222, 223 Rem., 25-06 Rem., 243 Win., 7mm-08 Rem., 308 Win., 25-06 Rem., 270 Win., 280 Rem., 30-06; 270 Wby. Mag., 7mm Rem. Mag., 7mm STW, 7mm Wby. Mag., 300 Win. Mag., 300 Wby. Mag., 338 Win. Mag., 340 Wby. Mag., 375 H&H, 416 Rem. Mag. Introduced 1997. Imported from Finland by Beretta USA.
Price: From **$2,175.00**

Sako 75 Varmint Rifle

Similar to Model 75 Hunter except chambered only for 17 Rem., 222 Rem., 223 Rem., 22-250 Rem., 22 PPC and 6mm PPC, 24" heavy barrel with recessed crown; set trigger; beavertail forend. Introduced 1998. Imported from Finland by Beretta USA.
Price: **$1,850.00**

SAVAGE EDGE BOLT ACTION RIFLE

Entry-level bolt-action repeating rifle chambered in .223, .22-250, .243 Win., 7mm-08, .308 Win., .25-06, .270 Win., and .30-06. Features include 22-inch matte black barrel, synthetic black stock, 4-round capacity; detachable box magazine, drilled and tapped for scope mounts. Also available in camo finish (Edge Camo); XP variation (with 3x9 scope); and Camo XP (with camo finish and scope).
Price: . . . . **$329.00 to $424.00**

SAVAGE MODEL 25 BOLT ACTION RIFLES

Caliber: 204 Ruger, 223 Rem., 4-shot magazine. **Barrel:** 24", medium-contour fluted barrel with recessed target crown, free-floating sleeved barrel, dual pillar bedding. **Weight:** 8.25 lbs. **Length:** 43.75" overall. **Stock:** Brown laminate with beavertail-style forend. **Sights:** Weaver-style bases installed. **Features:** Diameter-specific action built around the 223 Rem. bolthead dimension. Three locking lugs, 60-degree bolt lift, AccuTrigger adjustable from 2.5 to 3.25 lbs. Model 25 Classic Sporter has satin lacquer American walnut with contrasting forend tip, wraparound checkering, 22" blued barrel. **Weight:** 7.15 lbs. **Length:** 41.75". Introduced 2008. Made in U.S.A. by Savage Arms, Inc.
Price: Model 25 Lightweight Varminter **$641.00**
Price: Model 25 Lightweight Varminter Thumbhole **$691.00**
Price: Model 25 Classic Sporter **$672.00**

SAVAGE CLASSIC SERIES MODEL 14/114 RIFLES

Caliber: 204 Ruger, 223 Rem., 22-250 Rem., 243 Win., 7mm-08 Rem., 308 Win., 270 WSM, 300 WSM (short action Model 14), 2- or 4-shot magazine; 270 Win., 7mm Rem. Mag., 30-06 Spfl., 300 Win. Mag. (long action Model 114), 3- or 4-shot magazine. **Barrel:** 22" or 24". **Weight:** 7 to 7.5 lbs. **Length:** 41.75" to 43.75" overall (Model 14); 43.25" to 45.25" overall (Model 114). **Stock:** Satin lacquer American walnut with ebony forend, wraparound checkering, Monte Carlo Comb

Prices given are believed to be accurate at time of publication however, many factors affect retail pricing so exact prices are not possible.

and cheekpiece. **Sights:** None furnished. Receiver drilled and tapped for scope mounting. **Features:** AccuTrigger, high luster blued barreled action, hinged floorplate. From Savage Arms, Inc.

Price: Model 14 or 114 Classic, from **$826.00**
Price: Model 14 or 114 American Classic, detachable box magazine, from. **$779.00**
Price: Model 14 or 114 Euro Classic, oil finish, from **$875.00**
Price: Model 14 Left Hand, 250 Savage and 300 Savage only **$779.00**

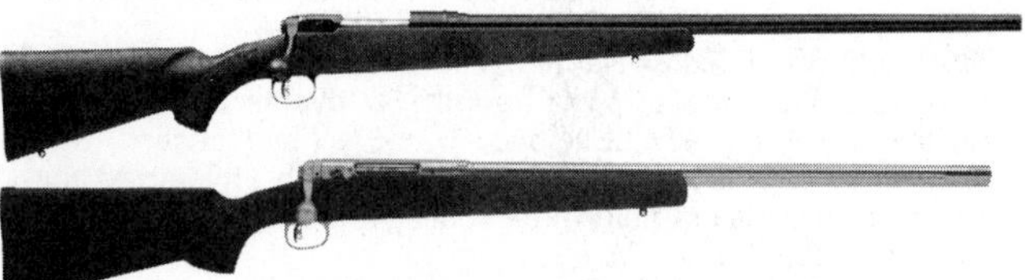

SAVAGE MODEL 12 SERIES VARMINT RIFLES

Caliber: 204 Ruger, 223 Rem., 22-250 Rem. 4-shot magazine. **Barrel:** 26" stainless barreled action, heavy fluted, free-floating and button-rifled barrel. **Weight:** 10 lbs. **Length:** 46.25" overall. **Stock:** Dual pillar bedded, low profile, laminated stock with extra-wide beavertail forend. **Sights:** None furnished; drilled and tapped for scope mounting. **Features:** Recessed target-style muzzle. AccuTrigger, oversized bolt handle, detachable box magazine, swivel studs. Model 112BVSS has heavy target-style prone laminated stock with high comb, Wundhammer palm swell, internal box magazine. Model 12FVSS has black synthetic stock, additional chamberings in 308 Win., 270 WSM, 300 WSM. Model 12FV has blued receiver. Model 12BTCSS has brown laminate vented thumbhole stock. Made in U.S.A. by Savage Arms, Inc.

Price: Model 12 Varminter, from. **$991.00**
Price: Model 12BVSS. **$899.00**
Price: Model 12FVSS, from **$815.00**
Price: Model 12FV **$658.00**
Price: Model 12BTCSS (2008) **$1,041.00**
Price: Model 12 Long Range (2008). **$1,239.00**
Price: Model 12 LRPV, single-shot only with right bolt/left port or left load/right eject receiver **$1,273.00**

SAVAGE MODEL 16/116 WEATHER WARRIORS

Caliber: 204 Ruger, 223 Rem., 22-250 Rem., 243 Win., 7mm-08 Rem., 308 Win., 270 WSM, 7mm WSM, 300 WSM (short action Model 16), 2- or 4-shot magazine; 270 Win., 7mm Rem. Mag., 30-06 Spfl., 300 Win. Mag., 338 Win. Mag. (long action Model 114), 3- or 4-shot magazine. **Barrel:** 22", 24"; stainless steel with matte finish, free-floated barrel. **Weight:** 6.5 to 6.75 lbs. **Length:** 41.75" to 43.75" overall (Model 16); 42.5" to 44.5" overall (Model 116). **Stock:** Graphite/fiberglass filled composite. **Sights:** None furnished; drilled and tapped for scope mounting. **Features:** Quick-detachable swivel studs; laser-etched bolt. Left-hand models available. Model 116FSS introduced 1991; 116FSAK introduced 1994. Made in U.S.A. by Savage Arms, Inc.

Price: Model 16FHSS or 116FHSS, hinged floorplate magazine, from. **$755.00**
Price: Model 16FLHSS or 116FLHSS, left hand models, from. **$755.00**
Price: Model 16FSS or 116FSS, internal box magazine, from . **$678.00**
Price: Model 16FCSS or 116FCSS, detachable box magazine, from. **$755.00**
Price: Model 16FHSAK or 116FHSAK, adjustable muzzle brake. **$822.00**

SAVAGE MODEL 10GXP3, 110GXP3 PACKAGE GUNS

Caliber: 223 Rem., 22-250 Rem., 243 Win., 7mm-08 Rem., 308 Win., 300 WSM (10GXP3). 25-06 Rem., 270 Win., 30-06 Spfl., 7mm Rem. Mag., 300 Win. Mag., 300 Rem. Ultra Mag. (110GXP3). **Barrel:** 22" 24", 26". **Weight:** 7.5 lbs. average. **Length:** 43" to 47". **Stock:** Walnut Monte Carlo with checkering. **Sights:** 3-9x40mm scope, mounted & bore sighted. **Features:** Blued, free floating and button rifled, internal box magazines, swivel studs, leather sling. Left-hand available.

Price: AccuTrigger, from. **$669.00**

SAVAGE MODEL 11FXP3, 111FXP3, 111FCXP3, 11FYXP3 (YOUTH) PACKAGE GUNS

Caliber: 223 Rem., 22-250 Rem., 243 Win., 308 Win., 300 WSM (11FXP3). 270 Win., 30-06 Spfl., 25-06 Rem., 7mm Rem. Mag., 300 Win. Mag., 338 Win. Mag., 300 Rem. Ultra Mag. (11FCXPE & 111FXP3). **Barrel:** 22" to 26". **Weight:** 6.5 lbs. **Length:** 41" to 47". **Stock:** Synthetic checkering, dual pillar bed. **Sights:** 3-9X40mm scope, mounted & bore sighted. **Features:** Blued, free floating and button rifled, Top loading internal box mag (except 111FXCP3 has detachable box magazine). Nylon sling and swivel studs. Some left-hand available.

Price: Model 11FXP3, from. **$640.00**
Price: Model 111FCXP3 . . . . **$519.00**
Price: Model 11FYXP3, 243 Win., 12.5" pull (youth) **$519.00**
Price: Model 11FLYXP3 Youth: Left-handed configuration of Model 11FYXP3 Youth **$640.00**

SAVAGE MODEL 16FXP3, 116FXP3 SS ACTION PACKAGE GUNS

Caliber: 223 Rem., 243 Win., 6.5x.284, 308 Win., 300 WSM, 270 Win., 30-06 Spfl., 7mm Rem. Mag., 300 Win. Mag., 338 Win. Mag., 375 H&H, 7mm S&W, 7mm Rem. Ultra Mag., 300 Rem. Ultra Mag. **Barrel:** 22", 24", 26". **Weight:** 6.75 lbs. average. **Length:** 41" to 46". **Stock:** Synthetic checkering, dual pillar bed. **Sights:** 3-9X40mm scope, mounted & bore sighted. **Features:** Free floating and button rifled. Internal box magazine, nylon sling and swivel studs.

Price: From **$736.00**

SAVAGE MODEL 11/111 HUNTER SERIES BOLT ACTIONS

Caliber: 223 Rem., 22-250 Rem., 243 Win., 7mm-08 Rem., 308 Win., 270 WSM, 7mm WSM, 300 WSM (short action Model 11), 2- or 4-shot magazine; 25-06 Rem., 270 Win., 7mm Rem. Mag., 30-06 Spfl., 300 Win. Mag., (long action Model 111), 3- or 4-shot magazine. **Barrel:** 22" or 24"; blued free-floated barrel. **Weight:** 6.5 to 6.75 lbs. **Length:** 41.75" to 43.75" overall (Model 11); 42.5" to 44.5" overall (Model 111). **Stock:** Graphite/fiberglass filled composite or hardwood. **Sights:** Ramp front, open fully adjustable rear; drilled and tapped for scope mounting. **Features:** Three-position top tang safety, double front locking lugs. Introduced 1994. Made in U.S.A. by Savage Arms, Inc.

Price: Model 11FL or 111FL **$564.00**
Price: Model 11FL or 111FL, left hand models, from **$564.00**
Price: Model 11FCNS or 111FCNS, detachable box magazine, from. **$591.00**
Price: Model 11FLNS or 111FLNS **$564.00**
Price: Model 11G or 111G, hardwood stock, from **$582.00**
Price: Model 11BTH or 111BTH, laminate thumbhole stock (2008) **$779.00**
Price: Model 11FNS Model FLNS **$591.00**
Price: Model 11FHNS or 111FHNS. **$656.00**
Price: Model 11FYCAK Youth **$691.00**
Price: Model 11GNS or 111GNS **$618.00**
Price: Model 11GLNS or 111GLSN **$618.00**
Price: Model 11GCNS or 111GCNS **$659.00**
Price: Model 11/111 Long-Range Hunter . . . . **$934 .00**

SAVAGE MODEL 10 BAS LAW ENFORCEMENT BOLT-ACTION RIFLE

Caliber: 380 Win. **Barrel:** 24" fluted heavy with muzzle brake. **Weight:** 13.4 lbs. **Length:** NA.

Features: Bolt-action repeater based on Model 10 action but with M4-style collapsible buttstock, pistolgrip with palm swell, all-aluminum Accustock, picatinny rail for mounting optics.
Price: $1,852.00
Price: 10 BAT/S, multi-adjustable buttstock $1,991.00

SAVAGE MODEL 10FP/110FP LAW ENFORCEMENT SERIES RIFLES

Caliber: 223 Rem., 308 Win. (Model 10), 4-shot magazine; 25-06 Rem., 300 Win. Mag., (Model 110), 3- or 4-shot magazine. **Barrel:** 24"; matte blued free-floated heavy barrel and action. **Weight:** 6.5 to 6.75 lbs. **Length:** 41.75" to 43.75" overall (Model 10); 42.5" to 44.5" overall (Model 110). **Stock:** Black graphite/fiberglass composition, pillar-bedded, positive checkering. **Sights:** None furnished. Receiver drilled and tapped for scope mounting. **Features:** Black matte finish on all metal parts. Double swivel studs on the forend for sling and/or bipod mount. Right- or left-hand. Model 110FP introduced 1990. Model 10FP introduced 1998. Model 10FCPXP has HS Precision black synthetic tactical stock with molded alloy bedding system, Leupold 3.5-10x40mm black matte scope with Mil Dot reticle, Farrell Picatinny Rail Base, flip-open lens covers, 1.25" sling with QD swivels, Harris bipod, Storm heavy duty case. Made in U.S.A. by Savage Arms, Inc.
Price: Model 10FP, 10FLP (left hand), 110FP $649.00
Price: Model 10FP folding Choate stock.......... $896.00
Price: Model 10FCP McMillan, McMillan fiberglass tactical stock $1,178.00
Price: Model 10FCP-HS HS Precision, HS Precision tactical stock $984.00
Price: Model 10FPXP-HS Precision $2,715.00
Price: Model 10FCP $866.00
Price: Model 10FLCP, left-hand model, standard stock or Accu-Stock $866.00
Price: Model 110FCP $866.00
Price: Model 10 Precision Carbine, 20" medium contour barrel, synthetic camo Accu-Stock, 223/308 .... $829.00
Price: Model 10 FCM Scout $646.00

Savage Model 110-50th Anniversary Rifle

Same action as 110-series rifles, except offered in 300 Savage, limited edition of 1,000 rifles. Has high-luster blued barrel and action, unique checkering pattern, high-grade hinged floorplate, scroll pattern on receiver, 24-karat gold-plated double barrel bands, 24-karat gold-plated AccuTrigger, embossed recoil pad. Introduced 2008. Made in U.S.A. from Savage Arms, Inc.
Price: Model 110 50th Anniversary.......... $1,724.00

SAVAGE 110 BA LAW ENFORCEMENT RIFLE

Bolt action rifle chambered .300 Win. Mag. And .338 Lapua Mag. Features include aluminum stock that features Savage's innovative three-dimensional bedding system; interchangeable buttstocks and pistol grips; three-sided accessory rail; 5-round detachable magazine; high-efficiency muzzlebrake; Magpul PRS adjustable stock; 26-inch carbon steel barrel.
Price: $2,267.00

SAVAGE MODEL 10 PREDATOR SERIES

Caliber: 223, 22-250, 243, 204 Ruger. **Barrel:** 22", medium-contour. **Weight:** 7.25 lbs. **Length:** 43"overall. **Stock:** Synthetic with rounded forend and oversized bolt handle. **Features:** Entirely covered in either Mossy Oak Brush or Realtree Hardwoods Snow pattern camo. Also features AccuTrigger, AccuStock, detachable box magazine.
Price: $806.00

Savage Model 10XP Predator Hunting Bolt-Action Rifle Package

Similar to Model 10 but chambered in 223, 204, 22-250 or 243 Win. Includes 4-12x40 scope, 22" barrel, AccuTrigger, choice of Realtree Snow or Mossy Oak Brush camo overall.
Price: $839.00

SAVAGE MODEL 12 PRECISION TARGET SERIES BENCHREST RIFLE

Caliber: 308 Win, 6.5x284 Norman, 6mm Norma BR. **Barrel:** 29" ultra-heavy. **Weight:** 12.75 lbs. **Length:** 50" overall. **Stock:** Gray laminate. Features: New Left-Load, Right-Eject target action, Target AccuTrigger adjustable from approx 6 oz to 2.5 lbs, oversized bolt handle, stainless extra-heavy free-floating and button-rifled barrel.
Price: $1,375.00

Savage Model 12 Precision Target Palma Rifle

Similar to Model 12 Benchrest but in 308 Palma only, 30" barrel, multi-adjustable stock, weighs 13.3 lbs.
Price: $1,798.00

Savage Model 12 F Class Target Rifle

Similar to Model 12 Benchrest but in 6.5x284 Norma, 6 Norma BR, 30" barrel, weighs 11.5 lbs.
Price: $1,341.00

Savage Model 12 F/TR Target Rifle

Similar to Model 12 Benchrest but in 308 Win. only, 30" barrel, weighs 12.65 lbs.
Price: $1,265.00

SMITH & WESSON I-BOLT RIFLES

Caliber: 25-06 Rem., 270 Win., 30-06 Win. (4-round magazine), 7mm Rem. Mag., 300 Win. Mag. (3-round magazine). **Barrel:** 23", 1:10" right-hand twist, 1:9" right-hand twist for 7mm Mag. Thompson/Center barrel. Blued and stainless. **Weight:** 6.75 lbs. **Stock:** Black synthetic, Realtree AP camo, walnut. Length of pull, 13-5/8", drop at comb, 7/8". Monte Carlo cheekpiece. **Sights:** Adjustable post front sight, adjustable dual aperture rear sight. **Features:** Adjustable Tru-Set Trigger. Introduced 2008. Made in U.S.A. by Smith & Wesson.
Price: Black synthetic stock, weather shield finish $588.00
Price: Camo stock, weather shield finish $658.00

STEVENS MODEL 200 BOLT-ACTION RIFLES

Caliber: 223, 22-250, 243, 7mm-08, 308 Win. (short action) or 25-06, 270 Win., 30-06, 7mm Rem. Mag., 300 Win Mag. Barrel: 22" (short action) or 24" (long action blued). **Weight:** 6.5 lbs. **Length:** 41.75" overall. **Stock:** Black synthetic or camo. **SIghts:** None. **Features:** Free-floating and button-rifled barrel, top loading internal box magazine, swivel studs.
Price: .... **$399.00** (standard); **$439.00** (camo)
Price: Model 200XP Long or Short Action Package Rifle with 4x12 scope.......... $449.00
Price: Model 200XP Camo, camo stock $499.00

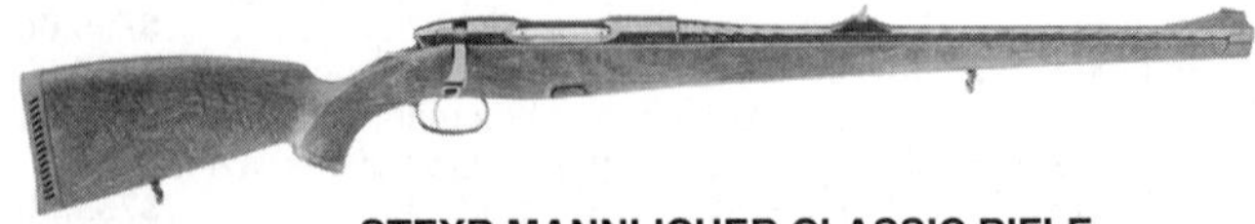

STEYR MANNLICHER CLASSIC RIFLE

Caliber: 222 Rem., 223 Rem., 243 Win., 25-06 Rem., 308 Win., 6.5x55, 6.5x57, 270 Win., 270 WSM, 7x64 Brenneke, 7mm-08 Rem., 7.5x55, 30-06 Spfl., 9.3x62, 6.5x68, 7mm Rem. Mag., 300 WSM, 300 Win. Mag., 8x68S, 4-shot magazine. **Barrel:** 23.6" standard; 26" magnum; 20" full stock standard calibers. **Weight:** 7 lbs. **Length:** 40.1" overall. **Stock:** Hand-checkered fancy European oiled walnut with standard forend. **Sights:** Ramp front adjustable for elevation, V-notch rear adjustable for windage. **Features:** Single adjustable trigger; 3-position roller safety with "safe-bolt" setting; drilled and tapped for Steyr factory scope mounts. Introduced 1997. Imported from Austria by Steyr Arms, Inc.
Price: Half stock, standard calibers $3,799.00
Price: Full stock, standard calibers.......... $4,199.00

Prices given are believed to be accurate at time of publication however, many factors affect retail pricing so exact prices are not possible.

Steyr Pro Hunter Rifle

Similar to the Classic Rifle except has ABS synthetic stock with adjustable butt spacers, straight comb without cheekpiece, palm swell, Pachmayr 1" swivels. Special 10-round magazine conversion kit available. Introduced 1997. Imported from Austria by Steyr Arms, Inc.

Price: From **$1,500.00**

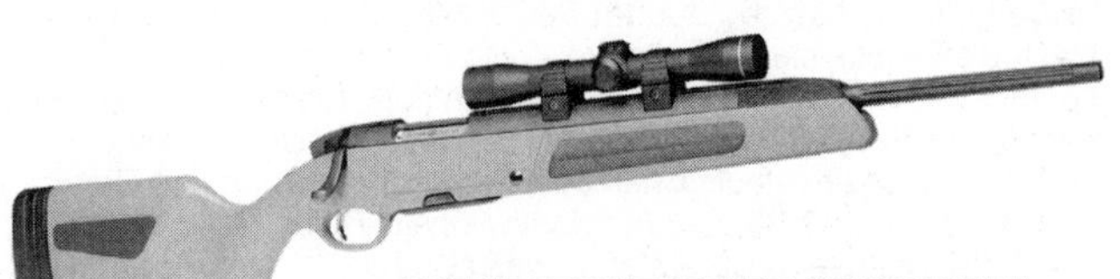

STEYR SCOUT BOLT-ACTION RIFLE

Caliber: 308 Win., 5-shot magazine. **Barrel:** 19", fluted. **Weight:** NA. **Length:** NA. **Stock:** Gray Zytel. **Sights:** Pop-up front & rear, Leupold M8 2.5x28 IER scope on Picatinny optic rail with Steyr mounts. **Features:** luggage case, scout sling, two stock spacers, two magazines. Introduced 1998. Imported from Austria by Steyr Arms, Inc.

Price: From **$2,199.00**

STEYR SSG 69 PII BOLT-ACTION RIFLE

Caliber: 22-250 Rem., 243 Win., 308 Win., detachable 5-shot rotary magazine. **Barrel:** 26". **Weight:** 8.5 lbs. **Length:** 44.5" overall. **Stock:** Black ABS Cycolac with spacers for length of pull adjustment. **Sights:** Hooded ramp front adjustable for elevation, V-notch rear adjustable for windage. **Features:** Sliding safety; NATO rail for bipod; 1" swivels; Parkerized finish; single or double-set triggers. Imported from Austria by Steyr Arms, Inc.

Price: **$1,889.00**

THOMPSON/CENTER ICON BOLT-ACTION RIFLE

Caliber: 22-250 Rem., 243 Win., 308 Win., 30TC, 3-round box magazine. **Barrel:** 24", button rifled. **Weight:** 7.5 lbs. **Length:** 44.5" overall. **Stock:** Walnut, 20-lpi grip and forend cut checkering with ribbon detail. **Sights:** None; integral Weaver style scope mounts. **Features:** Interchangeable bolt handle, 60-degree bolt lift, Interlok Bedding System, 3-lug bolt with T-Slot extractor, cocking indicator, adjustable trigger, preset to 3 to 3.5 lbs of pull. Introduced 2007. From Thompson/Center Arms.

Price: **$1,025.00**

Thompson/Center ICON Precision Hunter Rifle

Similar to the basic ICON model. Available in 204 Ruger, 223 Rem., 22-250 Rem., 243 Win. and 308 Win. 22" heavy barrel, blued finish, varminter-style stock. Introduced 2009.

Price: **$1,149.00**

THOMPSON/CENTER VENTURE BOLT-ACTION RIFLE

Caliber: 270 Win., 7mm Rem. Mag., 30-06 Springfield, 300 Win. Mag., 3-round magazine. **Barrel:** 24". **Weight:** NA. **Length:** NA. **Stock:** Composite. **Sights:** NA. **Features:** Nitride fat bolt design, externally adjustable trigger, two-position safety, textured grip. Introduced 2009.

Price: **$489.00**

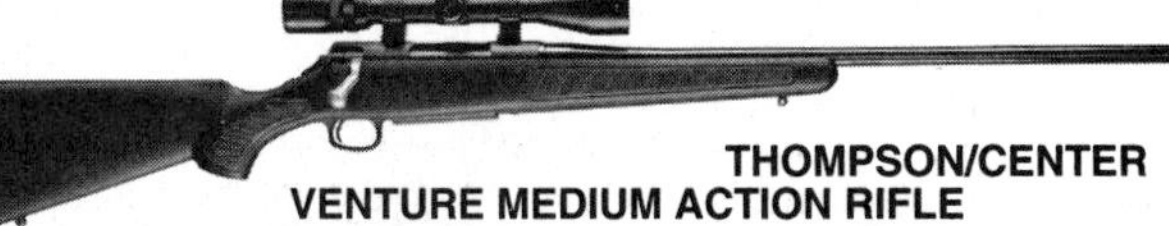

THOMPSON/CENTER VENTURE MEDIUM ACTION RIFLE

Bolt action rifle chambered in .204, .22-250, .223, .243, 7mm-08, .308 and 30TC. Features include a 24-inch crowned medium weight barrel, classic styled composite stock with inlaid traction grip panels, adjustable 3.5 to 5 pound trigger along with a drilled and tapped receiver (bases included). 3+1 detachable nylon box magazine. **Weight:** 7 lbs. **Length**: 43.5 inches.

Price: **$499.00**

THOMPSON/CENTER VENTURE PREDATOR PDX RIFLE

Bolt action rifle chambered in .204, .22-250, .223, .243, .308. Similar to Venture Medium action but with heavy, deep-fluted 22-inch barrel and Max-1 camo finish overall. **Weight:** 8 lbs. **Length:** 41.5 inches.

Price: . . . . **$549.00 to $599.00**

TIKKA T3 HUNTER

Caliber: 223 Rem., 22-250 Rem., 243 Win., 308 Win., 25-06 Rem., 270 Win., 30-06 Spfl., 300 Win. Mag., 338 Win. Mag., 270 WSM, 300 WSM, 6.5x55 Swedish Mauser, 7mm Rem. Mag. **Stock:** Walnut. **Sights:** None furnished. **Barrel:** 22-7/16", 24-3/8". **Features:** Detachable magazine, aluminum scope rings. Introduced 2005. Imported from Finland by Beretta USA.

Price: **$675.00**

Tikka T3 Stainless Synthetic

Similar to the T3 Hunter except stainless steel, synthetic stock. Available in 243 Win., 2506, 270 Win., 308 Win., 30-06 Spfl., 270 WSM, 300 WSM, 7mm Rem. Mag., 300 Win. Mag., 338 Win. Mag. Introduced 2005. Imported from Finland by Beretta USA.

Price: **$700.00**

Tikka T3 Lite Bolt-Action Rifle

Similar to the T3 Hunter, available in 223 Rem., 22-250 Rem., 308 Win., 243 Win., 25-06 Rem., 270 Win., 270 WSM, 30-06 Sprg., 300 Win Mag., 300 WSM, 338 Federal, 338 Win Mag., 7mm Rem. Mag., 7mm-08 Rem. Barrel lengths vary from 22-7/16" to 24-3/8". Made in Finland by Sako. Imported by Beretta USA.

Price: **$695.00**
Price: Stainless steel synthetic **$600.00**
Price: Stainless steel synthetic, left-hand **$700.00**

Tikka T3 Varmint/Super Varmint Rifle

Similar to the T3 Hunter, available in 223 Rem., 22-250 Rem., 308 Win. Length is 23-3/8" (Super Varmint). Made in Finland by Sako. Imported by Beretta USA.

Price: **$900.00**
Price: Super Varmint **$1,425.00**

ULTRA LIGHT ARMS BOLT-ACTION RIFLES

Caliber: 17 Rem. to 416 Rigby. **Barrel:** Douglas, length to order. **Weight:** 4.75 to 7.5 lbs. **Length:** Varies. **Stock:** Kevlar graphite composite, variety of finishes. **Sights:** None furnished; drilled and tapped for scope mounts. **Features:** Timney trigger, hand-lapped action, button-rifled barrel, hand-bedded action, recoil pad, sling-swivel studs, optional Jewell trigger. Made in U.S.A. by New Ultra Light Arms.

Price: Model 20 (short action). **$3,000.00**
Price: Model 24 (long action) **$3,100.00**
Price: Model 28 (magnum action) **$3,400.00**
Price: Model 40 (300 Wby. Mag., 416 Rigby) **$3,400.00**
Price: Left-hand models, add **$100.00**

WEATHERBY MARK V BOLT-ACTION RIFLES

Caliber: Deluxe version comes in all Weatherby calibers plus 243 Win., 270 Win., 7mm-08 Rem., 30-06 Spfl., 308 Win. **Barrel:** 24", 26", 28". **Weight:** 6.75 to 10 lbs. **Length:** 44" to 48.75" overall. **Stock:** Walnut, Monte Carlo with cheekpiece; high luster finish; checkered pistol grip and forend; recoil pad. **Sights:** None furnished. **Features:** 4 models with Mark V action and wood stocks; other common elements include cocking indicator; adjustable trigger; hinged floorplate, thumb safety; quick detachable sling swivels. Ultramark has hand-selected exhibition-grade walnut stock, maplewood/ebony spacers, 20-lpi checkering. Chambered for 257 and 300 Wby Mags. Lazermark same as Mark V Deluxe except stock

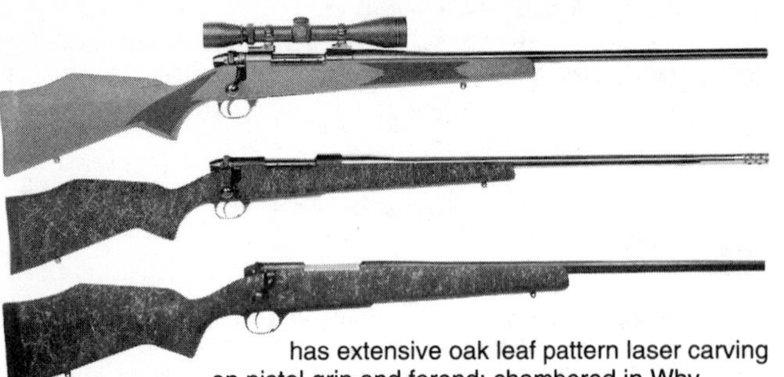

has extensive oak leaf pattern laser carving on pistol grip and forend; chambered in Wby. Magnums—257, 270 Win., 7mm., 300, 340, with 26" barrel. Introduced 1981. Sporter is same as the Mark V Deluxe without the embellishments. Metal has low-luster blue, stock is Claro walnut with matte finish, Monte Carlo comb, recoil pad. Chambered for these Wby. Mags: 257, 270 Win., 7mm, 300, 340. Other chamberings: 7mm Rem. Mag., 300 Win. Introduced 1993. Six Mark V models come with synthetic stocks. Ultra Lightweight rifles weigh 5.75 to 6.75 lbs.; 24", 26" fluted stainless barrels with recessed target crown; Bell & Carlson stock with CNC-machined aluminum bedding plate and tan "spider web" finish, skeletonized handle and sleeve. Available in 243 Win., Wby. Mag., 25-06 Rem., 270 Win., 7mm-08 Rem., 7mm Rem. Mag., 280 Rem, 308 Win., 30-06 Spfl., 300 Win. Mag. Wby. Mag chamberings: 240, 257, 270 Win., 7mm, 300. Introduced 1998. Accumark uses Mark V action with heavy-contour 26" and 28" stainless barrels with black oxidized flutes, muzzle diameter of .705". No sights, drilled and tapped for scope mounting. Stock is composite with matte gel-coat finish, full length aluminum bedding Hasblock. Weighs 8.5 lbs. Chambered for these Wby. Mags: 240 (2007), 257, 270, 7mm, 300, 340, 338-378, 30-378. Other chamberings: 22-250 (2007), 243 Win. (2007), 25-06 Rem. (2007), 270 Win. (2007), 308 Win.(2007), 7mm Rem. Mag., 300 Win. Mag. Introduced 1996. SVM (Super VarmintMaster) has 26" fluted stainless barrel, spiderweb-pattern tan laminated synthetic stock, fully adjustable trigger. Chambered for 223 Rem., 22-250 Rem., 243. Mark V Synthetic has lightweight injection-molded synthetic stock with raised Monte Carlo comb, checkered grip and forend, custom floorplate release. Weighs 6.5-8.5 lbs., 24-28" barrels. Available in 22-250 Rem., 243 Win., 25-06 Rem., 270 Win., 7mm-08 Rem., 7mm Rem., Mag, 280 Rem., 308 Win., 30-06 Spfl., 308 Win., 300 Win. Mag., 375 H&H Mag, and these Wby. Magnums: 240, 257, 270 Win., 7mm, 300, 30-378, 338-378, 340. Introduced 1997. Fibermark composites are similar to other Mark V models except has black Kevlar and fiberglass composite stock and bead-bead-blast blue or stainless finish. Chambered for 9 standard and magnum calibers. Introduced 1983; reintroduced 2001. SVR comes with 22" button-rifled chrome-moly barrel, .739 muzzle diameter. Composite stock w/bedding block, gray spiderweb pattern. Made in U.S.A. From Weatherby.

Price: Mark V Deluxe **$2,199.00**
Price: Mark V Ultramark **$2,979.00**
Price: Mark V Lazermark **$2,479.00**
Price: Mark V Sporter **$1,499.00**
Price: Mark V SVM **$1,959.00**
Price: Mark V Ultra Lightweight **$1,879.00**
Price: Mark V Ultra Lightweight LH. **$1,911.00**
Price: Mark V Accumark **$1,879.00**
Price: Mark V Synthetic **$1,209.00**
Price: Mark V Fibermark Composite. **$1,449.00**
Price: Mark V SVR Special Varmint Rifle **$1,259.00**

WEATHERBY VANGUARD BOLT-ACTION RIFLES

Caliber: 257, 300 Wby Mags; 223 Rem., 22-250 Rem., 243 Win., 25-06 Rem. (2007), 270 Win., 270 WSM, 7mm Rem. Mag., 308 Win., 30-06 Spfl., 300 Win. Mag., 300 WSM, 338 Win. Mag. **Barrel:** 24" barreled action, matte black. **Weight:** 7.5 to 8.75 lbs. **Length:** 44" to 46-3/4" overall. **Stock:** Raised comb, Monte Carlo, injection-molded composite stock. **Sights:** None furnished. **Features:** One-piece forged, fluted bolt body with three gas ports, forged and machined receiver, adjustable trigger, factory accuracy guarantee. Vanguard Stainless has 410-Series stainless steel barrel and action, bead blasted matte metal finish. Vanguard Deluxe has raised comb, semi-fancy grade Monte Carlo walnut stock with maplewood spacers, rosewood forend and grip cap, polished action with high-gloss-blued metalwork. Vanguard Synthetic Package includes Vanguard Synthetic rifle with Bushnell Banner 3-9x40mm scope mounted and boresighted, Leupold Rifleman rings and bases, Uncle Mikes nylon sling, and Plano PRO-MAX injection-molded case. Sporter has Monte Carlo walnut stock with satin urethane finish, fineline diamond point checkering, contrasting rosewood forend tip, matte-blued metalwork. Sporter SS metalwork is 410 Series bead-blasted stainless steel. Vanguard Youth/Compact has 20" No. 1 contour barrel, short action, scaled-down non-reflective matte black hardwood stock with 12.5" length of pull and full-size, injection-molded composite stock. Chambered for 223 Rem., 22-250 Rem., 243 Win., 7mm-08 Rem., 308 Win. Weighs 6.75 lbs.; OAL 38.9". Sub-MOA Matte and Sub-MOA Stainless models have pillar-bedded Fiberguard composite stock (Aramid, graphite unidirectional fibers and fiberglass) with 24" barreled action; matte black metalwork, Pachmayr Decelerator recoil pad. Sub-MOA Stainless metalwork is 410 Series bead-blasted stainless steel. Sub-MOA Varmint guaranteed to shoot 3-shot group of .99" or less when used with specified Weatherby factory or premium (non-Weatherby calibers) ammunition. Hand-laminated, tan Monte Carlo composite stock with black spiderwebbing; CNC-machined aluminum bedding block, 22" No. 3 contour barrel, recessed target crown. Varmint Special has tan injection-molded Monte Carlo composite stock, pebble grain finish, black spiderwebbing. 22" No. 3 contour barrel (.740 muzzle dia.), bead blasted matte black finish, recessed target crown. Made in U.S.A. From Weatherby.

Price: Vanguard Synthetic **$399.00**
Price: Vanguard Stainless **$709.00**
Price: Vanguard Deluxe, 7mm Rem. Mag., 300 Win. Mag. (2007) **$989.00**
Price: Vanguard Synthetic Package, 25-06 Rem. (2007) **$552.00**
Price: Vanguard Sporter **$689.00**
Price: Vanguard Sporter SS **$869.00**
Price: Vanguard Youth/Compact **$649.00**
Price: Vanguard Sub-MOA Matte, 25-06 Rem. (2007) **$929.00**
Price: Vanguard Sub-MOA Stainless, 270 WSM **$1,079.00**
Price: Vanguard Sub-MOA Varmint, 204 Ruger (2007) **$1,009.00**

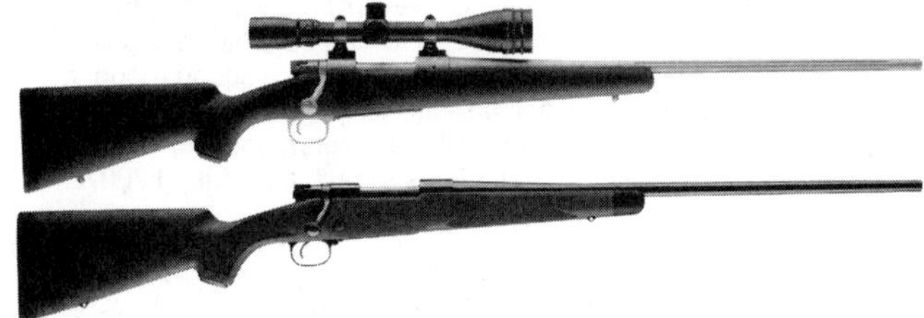

WINCHESTER MODEL 70 BOLT-ACTION RIFLES

Caliber: Varies by model. **Barrel:** Blued, or free-floating, fluted stainless hammer-forged barrel, 22", 24", 26". Recessed target crown. **Weight:** 6.75 to 7.25 lbs. **Length:** 41 to 45.75 " overall. **Stock:** Walnut (three models) or Bell and Carlson composite; textured charcoal-grey matte finish, Pachmayr Decelerator recoil pad. **Sights:** None. **Features:** Claw extractor, three-position safety, M.O.A. three-lever trigger system, factory-set at 3.75 lbs. Super Grade features fancy grade walnut stock, contrasting black fore-end tip and pistol grip cap, and sculpted shadowline cheekpiece. Featherweight Deluxe has angled-comb walnut stock, Schnabel fore-end, satin finish, cut checkering. Sporter Deluxe has satin-finished walnut stock, cut checkering, sculpted cheekpiece. Extreme Weather SS has composite stock, drop @ comb, 0.5"; drop @ heel, 0.5". Introduced 2008. Made in U.SA. from Winchester Repeating Arms.

Price: Extreme Weather SS, 270 Win., 270 WSM, 30-06 Spfl., 300 Win. Mag., 300 WSM, 308 Win., 325 WSM, 243 Winchester, 7mm WSM, from. **$1,069.00**
Price: Super Grade, 30-06 Sprg., 300 Win. Mag., 270 WSM, 300 WSM, 270 Winchester, from. **$1,139.00**
Price: Featherweight Deluxe, 243 Win., 270 Win., 270 WSM, 30-06 Spfl., 300 Win. Mag., 300 WSM, 308 Win., 325 WSM, 7mm-08 Rem., from **$999.00**
Price: Sporter Deluxe, 270 Win., 270 WSM, 30-06 Spfl., 300 Win. Mag., 300 WSM, 325 WSM, from **$999.00**

WINCHESTER MODEL 70 COYOTE LIGHT

Caliber: 22-250, 243 Winchester, 308 Winchester, 270 WSM, 300 WSM and 325 WSM, five-shot magazine (3-shot in 270 WSM, 300

 Prices given are believed to be accurate at time of publication however, many factors affect retail pricing so exact prices are not possible.

WSM and 325 WSM). **Barrel:** 22" fluted stainless barrel (24" in 270 WSM, 300 WSM and 325 WSM). **Weight:** 7.5 lbs. **Length:** NA. **Features:** Composite Bell and Carlson stock, Pachmayr Decelerator pad. Controlled round feeding. No sights but drilled and tapped for mounts.

Price: **$1,099.00**

WINCHESTER MODEL 70 FEATHERWEIGHT

Caliber: 22-250, 243, 7mm-08, 308, 270 WSM, 7mm WSM, 300 WSM, 325 WSM, 25-06, 270, 30-06, 7mm Rem. Mag., 300 Win. Mag., 338 Win. Mag. Capacity 5 rounds (short action) or 3 rounds (long action). **Barrel:** 22" blued barrel (24" in magnum chamberings). **Weight:** 6-1/2 to 7-1/4 lbs. **Length:** NA. **Features:** Satin-finished checkered Grade I walnut stock, controlled round feeding. Pachmayr Decelerator pad. No sights but drilled and tapped for scope mounts.

Price: Short action **$799.00**
Price: Long action and magnum) **$839.00**

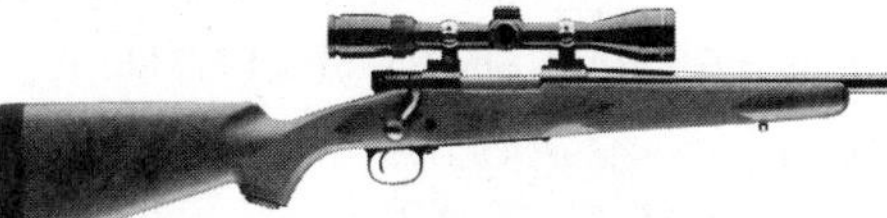

WINCHESTER MODEL 70 SPORTER

Caliber: 270 WSM, 7mm WSM, 300 WSM, 325 WSM, 25-06, 270, 30-06, 7mm Rem. Mag., 300 Win. Mag., 338 Win. Mag. Capacity 5 rounds (short action) or 3 rounds (long action). Barrel: 22", 24" or 26" blued. Weight: 6-1/2 to 7-1/4 lbs. Length: NA. Features: Satin-finished checkered Grade I walnut stock with sculpted cheekpiece, controlled round feeding. Pachmayr Decelerator pad. No sights but drilled and tapped for scope mounts.

Price: Short action **$799.00**
Price: Long action and magnum) **$839.00**

WINCHESTER MODEL 70 ULTIMATE SHADOW

Caliber: 243, 308, 270 WSM, 7mm WSM, 300 WSM, 325 WSM, 270, 30-06, 7mm Rem. Mag., 300 Win. Mag. Capacity 5 rounds (short action) or 3 rounds (long action). **Barrel:** 22" matte stainless (24" or 26" in magnum chamberings). **Weight:** 6-1/2 to 7-1/4 lbs. **Length:** NA. **Features:** Synthetic stock with WinSorb recoil pad, controlled round feeding. Pachmayr Decelerator pad. No sights but drilled and tapped for scope mounts.

Price: Standard. **$739.00**
Price: Magnum **$769.00**

ARMALITE AR-50 RIFLE
Caliber: 50 BMG **Barrel:** 31". **Weight:** 33.2 lbs. **Length:** 59.5" **Stock:** Synthetic. **Sights:** None furnished. **Features:** A single-shot bolt-action rifle designed for long-range shooting. Available in left-hand model. Made in U.S.A. by Armalite.
Price: **$3,359.00**

BALLARD 1875 1 1/2 HUNTER RIFLE
Caliber: NA. **Barrel:** 26-30". **Weight:** NA **Length:** NA. **Stock:** Hand-selected classic American walnut. **Sights:** Blade front, Rocky Mountain rear. **Features:** Color case-hardened receiver, breechblock and lever. Many options available. Made in U.S.A. by Ballard Rifle & Cartridge Co.
Price: **$3,250.00**

BALLARD 1875 #3 GALLERY SINGLE SHOT RIFLE
Caliber: NA. **Barrel:** 24-28" octagonal with tulip. **Weight:** NA. **Length:** NA. **Stock:** Hand-selected classic American walnut. **Sights:** Blade front, Rocky Mountain rear. **Features:** Color case-hardened receiver, breechblock and lever. Many options available. Made in U.S.A. by Ballard Rifle & Cartridge Co.
Price: **$3,300.00**

BALLARD 1875 #4 PERFECTION RIFLE
Caliber: 22 LR, 32-40, 38-55, 40-65, 40-70, 45-70 Govt., 45-90, 45-110, 50-70, 50-90. **Barrel:** 30" or 32" octagon, standard or heavyweight. **Weight:** 10.5 lbs. (standard) or 11.75 lbs. (heavyweight bbl.). **Length:** NA. **Stock:** Smooth walnut. **Sights:** Blade front, Rocky Mountain rear. **Features:** Rifle or shotgun-style buttstock, straight grip action, single or double-set trigger, "S" or right lever, hand polished and lapped Badger barrel. Made in U.S.A. by Ballard Rifle & Cartridge Co.
Price: **$3,950.00**

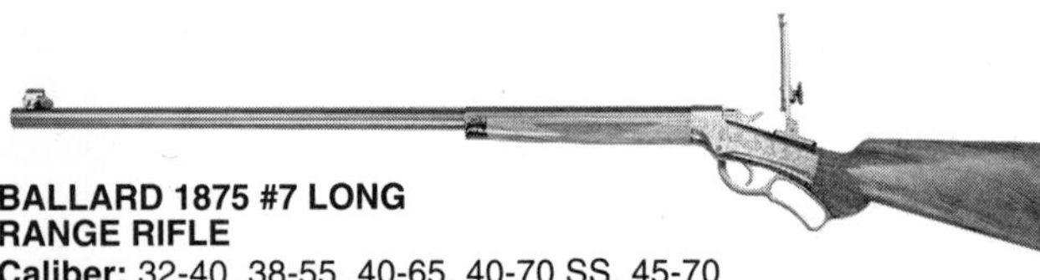

BALLARD 1875 #7 LONG RANGE RIFLE
Caliber: 32-40, 38-55, 40-65, 40-70 SS, 45-70 Govt., 45-90, 45-110. **Barrel:** 32", 34" half-octagon. **Weight:** 11.75 lbs. **Length:** NA. **Stock:** Walnut; checkered pistol grip shotgun butt, ebony forend cap. **Sights:** Globe front. **Features:** Designed for shooting up to 1000 yards. Standard or heavy barrel; single or double-set trigger; hard rubber or steel buttplate. Introduced 1999. Made in U.S.A. by Ballard Rifle & Cartridge Co.
Price: From **$3,600.00**

BALLARD 1875 #8 UNION HILL RIFLE
Caliber: 22 LR, 32-40, 38-55, 40-65 Win., 40-70 SS. **Barrel:** 30" half-octagon. **Weight:** About 10.5 lbs. **Length:** NA. **Stock:** Walnut; pistol grip butt with cheekpiece. **Sights:** Globe front. **Features:** Designed for 200-yard offhand shooting. Standard or heavy barrel; double-set triggers; full loop lever; hook Schuetzen buttplate. Introduced 1999. Made in U.S.A. by Ballard Rifle & Cartridge Co.
Price: From **$4,175.00**

BALLARD MODEL 1885 LOW WALL SINGLE SHOT RIFLE
Caliber: NA. **Barrel:** 24-28". **Weight:** NA. **Length:** NA. **Stock:** Hand-selected classic American walnut. **Sights:** Blade front, sporting rear. **Features:** Color case hardened receiver, breech block and lever. Many options available. Made in U.S.A. by Ballard Rifle & Cartridge Co.
Price: **$3,300.00**

BALLARD MODEL 1885 HIGH WALL STANDARD SPORTING SINGLE SHOT RIFLE
Caliber: 17 Bee, 22 Hornet, 218 Bee, 219 Don Wasp, 219 Zipper, 22 Hi-Power, 225 Win., 25-20 WCF, 25-35 WCF, 25 Krag, 7mmx57R, 30-30, 30-40 Krag, 303 British, 33 WCF, 348 WCF, 35 WCF, 35-30/30, 9.3x74R, 405 WCF, 50-110 WCF, 500 Express, 577 Express. **Barrel:** Lengths to 34". **Weight:** NA. **Length:** NA. **Stock:** Straight-grain American walnut. **Sights:** Buckhorn or flattop rear, blade front. **Features:** Faithful copy of original Model 1885 High Wall; parts interchange with original rifles; variety of options available. Introduced 2000. Made in U.S.A. by Ballard Rifle & Cartridge Co.
Price: **$3,300.00**

BALLARD MODEL 1885 HIGH WALL SPECIAL SPORTING SINGLE SHOT RIFLE
Caliber: NA. **Barrel:** 28-30" octagonal. **Weight:** NA. **Length:** NA. **Stock:** Hand-selected classic American walnut. **Sights:** Blade front, sporting rear. **Features:** Color case hardened receiver, breech block and lever. Many options available. Made in U.S.A. by Ballard Rifle & Cartridge Co.
Price: **$3,600.00**

BARRETT MODEL 99 SINGLE SHOT RIFLE
Caliber: 50 BMG. **Barrel:** 33". **Weight:** 25 lbs. **Length:** 50.4" overall. **Stock:** Anodized aluminum with energy-absorbing recoil pad. **Sights:** None furnished; integral M1913 scope rail. **Features:** Bolt action; detachable bipod; match-grade barrel with high-efficiency muzzle brake. Introduced 1999. Made in U.S.A. by Barrett Firearms.
Price: From **$4,000.00**

BROWN MODEL 97D SINGLE SHOT RIFLE
Caliber: 17 Ackley Hornet through 45-70 Govt. **Barrel:** Up to 26", air gauged match grade. **Weight:** About 5 lbs., 11 oz. **Stock:** Sporter style with pistol grip, cheekpiece and Schnabel forend. **Sights:** None furnished; drilled and tapped for scope mounting. **Features:** Falling block action gives rigid barrel-receiver matting; polished blue/black finish. Hand-fitted action. Many options. Made in U.S.A. by E. Arthur Brown Co., Inc.
Price: From **$999.00**

BROWNING MODEL 1885 HIGH WALL SINGLE SHOT RIFLE
Caliber: 22-250 Rem., 30-06 Spfl., 270 Win., 7mm Rem. Mag., 454 Casull, 45-70 Govt. **Barrel:** 28". **Weight:** 8 lbs., 12 oz. **Length:** 43.5" overall. **Stock:** Walnut with straight grip, Schnabel forend. **Sights:** None furnished; drilled and tapped for scope mounting. **Features:** Replica of J.M. Browning's high-wall falling block rifle. Octagon barrel with recessed muzzle. Imported from Japan by Browning. Introduced 1985.
Price: **$1,260.00**

C. SHARPS ARMS MODEL 1875 TARGET & SPORTING RIFLE
Caliber: 38-55, 40-65, 40-70 Straight or Bottlenecks, 45-70, 45-90. Barrel: 30" heavy taperred round. Weight: 11 lbs. Length: NA. Stock: American walnut. Sights: Globe with post front sight. Features: Long Range Vernier tang sight with windage adjustments. Pistol grip stock with cheek rest; checkered steel buttplate. Introduced 1991. From C. Sharps Arms Co.
Price: Without sights **$1,325.00**
Price: With blade front & Buckhorn rear barrel sights **$1,420.00**
Price: With standard Tang & Globe w/post & ball front sights **$1,615.00**
Price: With deluxe vernier Tang & Globe w/spirit level & aperture sights **$1,730.00**
Price: With single set trigger, add **$125.00**

C. Sharps Arms 1875 Classic Sharps
Similar to New Model 1875 Sporting Rifle except 26", 28" or 30" full octagon barrel, crescent buttplate with toe plate, Hartford-style forend with cast German silver nose cap. Blade front sight, Rocky Mountain buckhorn rear. Weighs 10 lbs. Introduced 1987. From C. Sharps Arms Co.
Price: **$1,670.00**

C. SHARPS ARMS 1874 BRIDGEPORT SPORTING RIFLE
Caliber: 38-55 TO 50-3.25. **Barrel:** 26", 28", 30" tapered octagon. **Weight:** 10.5 lbs. **Length:** 47". **Stock:** American black walnut; shotgun butt with checkered steel buttplate; straight grip, heavy forend with Schnabel tip. **Sights:** Blade front, buckhorn rear. Drilled and tapped for tang sight. **Features:** Double-set triggers. Made in U.S.A. by C. Sharps Arms.
Price: **$1,895.00**

C. SHARPS ARMS NEW MODEL 1885 HIGHWALL RIFLE
Caliber: 22 LR, 22 Hornet, 219 Zipper, 25-35 WCF, 32-40 WCF, 38-55 WCF, 40-65, 30-40 Krag, 40-50 ST or BN, 40-70 ST or BN, 40-90 ST or BN, 45-70 Govt. 2-1/10" ST, 45-90 2-4/10" ST, 45-100 2-6/10" ST, 45-110 2-7/8" ST, 45-120 3-1/4" ST. **Barrel:** 26", 28", 30", tapered full octagon. **Weight:** About 9 lbs., 4 oz. **Length:** 47" overall. **Stock:** Oil-finished American walnut; Schnabel-style forend. **Sights:** Blade front, buckhorn rear. Drilled and tapped for optional tang sight. **Features:** Single trigger; octagonal receiver top; checkered steel buttplate; color case-hardened receiver and buttplate, blued barrel. Many options available. Made in U.S.A. by C. Sharps Arms Co.
Price: From **$1,750.00**

C. SHARPS ARMS CUSTOM NEW MODEL 1877 LONG RANGE TARGET RIFLE
Caliber: 44-90 Sharps/Rem., 45-70 Govt., 45-90, 45-100 Sharps. **Barrel:** 32", 34" tapered round with Rigby flat. **Weight:** About 10 lbs. **Stock:** Walnut checkered. Pistol grip/forend. **Sights:** Classic long range with windage. **Features:** Custom production only.
Price: From $7,250.00

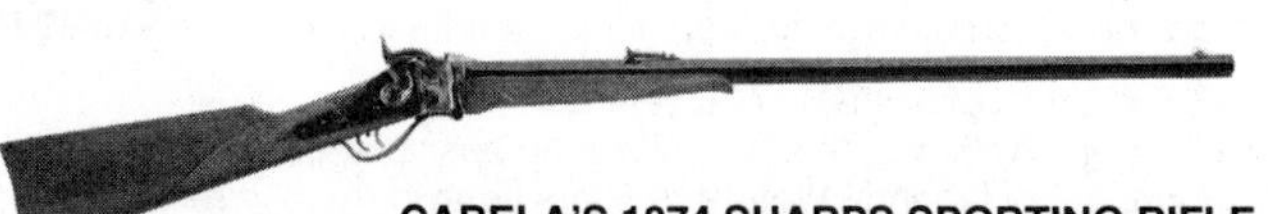

CABELA'S 1874 SHARPS SPORTING RIFLE
Caliber: 45-70. **Barrel:** 32", tapered octabon. **Weight:** 10.5 lbs. **Length:** 49.25" overall. **Stock:** Checkered walnut. **Sights:** Blade front, open adjustable rear. **Features:** Color case-hardened receiver and hammer, rest blued. Introduced 1995. Imported by Cabela's.
Price: 45-70 . . . . . . $1,399.99
Price: Quigley Sharps, 45-70 Govt., 45-120, 45-110 . . . . . . $1,699.99

CIMARRON BILLY DIXON 1874 SHARPS SPORTING RIFLE
Caliber: 40-40, 50-90, 50-70, 45-70 Govt. **Barrel:** 32" tapered octagonal. **Weight:** NA. **Length:** NA. **Stock:** European walnut. **Sights:** Blade front, Creedmoor rear. **Features:** Color case-hardened frame, blued barrel. Hand-checkered grip and forend; hand-rubbed oil finish. Introduced 1999. Imported by Cimarron F.A. Co.
Price: From $1,987.70

CIMARRON QUIGLEY MODEL 1874 SHARPS SPORTING RIFLE
Caliber: 45-110, 50-70, 50-40, 45-70 Govt., 45-90, 45-120. **Barrel:** 34" octagonal. **Weight:** NA. **Length:** NA. **Stock:** Checkered walnut. **Sights:** Blade front, adjustable rear. **Features:** Blued finish; double-set triggers. From Cimarron F.A. Co.
Price: From $2,156.70

CIMARRON SILHOUETTE MODEL 1874 SHARPS SPORTING RIFLE
Caliber: 45-70 Govt. **Barrel:** 32" octagonal. **Weight:** NA. **Length:** NA. **Stock:** Walnut. **Sights:** Blade front, adjustable rear. **Features:** Pistol-grip stock with shotgun-style buttplate; cut-rifled barrel. From Cimarron F.A. Co.
Price: $1,597.70

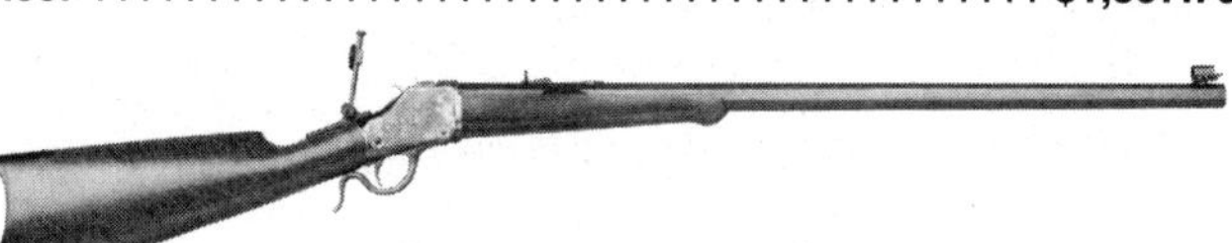

CIMARRON MODEL 1885 HIGH WALL RIFLE
Caliber: 38-55, 40-65, 45-70 Govt., 45-90, 45-120, 30-40 Krag, 348 Winchester. **Barrel:** 30" octagonal. **Weight:** NA. **Length:** NA. **Stock:** European walnut. **Sights:** Bead front, semi-buckhorn rear. **Features:** Replica of the Winchester 1885 High Wall rifle. Color case-hardened receiver and lever, blued barrel. Curved buttplate. Optional double-set triggers. Introduced 1999. Imported by Cimarron F.A. Co.
Price: From $1,002.91
Price: With pistol grip, from $1,136.81

DAKOTA MODEL 10 SINGLE SHOT RIFLE
Caliber: Most rimmed and rimless commercial calibers. **Barrel:** 23". **Weight:** 6 lbs. **Length:** 39.5" overall. **Stock:** Medium fancy grade walnut in classic style. Checkered grip and forend. **Sights:** None furnished. Drilled and tapped for scope mounting. **Features:** Falling block action with underlever. Top tang safety. Removable trigger plate for conversion to single set trigger. Introduced 1990. Made in U.S.A. by Dakota Arms.
Price: From $4,695.00
Price: Action only $1,875.00
Price: Magnum action only $1,875.00

EMF PREMIER 1874 SHARPS RIFLE
Caliber: 45/70, 45/110, 45/120. **Barrel:** 32", 34". **Weight:** 11-13 lbs. **Length:** 49", 51" overall. **Stock:** Pistol grip, European walnut. **Sights:** Blade front, adjustable rear. **Features:** Superb quality reproductions of the 1874 Sharps Sporting Rifles; casehardened locks; double-set triggers; blue barrels. Imported from Pedersoli by EMF.
Price: Business Rifle $1,199.90
Price: "Quigley", Patchbox, heavy barrel $1,799.90
Price: Silhouette, pistol-grip $1,499.90
Price: Super Deluxe Hand Engraved $3,500.00

HARRINGTON & RICHARDSON ULTRA VARMINT/ULTRA HUNTER RIFLES
Caliber: 204 Ruger, 22 WMR, 22-250 Rem., 223 Rem., 243 Win., 25-06 Rem., 30-06. **Barrel:** 22" to 26" heavy taper. **Weight:** About 7.5 lbs. **Stock:** Laminated birch with Monte Carlo comb or skeletonized polymer. **Sights:** None furnished. Drilled and tapped for scope mounting. **Features:** Break-open action with side-lever release, positive ejection. Scope mount. Blued receiver and barrel. Swivel studs. Introduced 1993. Ultra Hunter introduced 1995. From H&R 1871, Inc.
Price: Ultra Varmint Fluted, 24" bull barrel, polymer stock $406.00
Price: Ultra Hunter Rifle, 26" bull barrel in 25-06 Rem., laminated stock $357.00
Price: Ultra Varmint Rifle, 22" bull barrel in 223 Rem., laminated stock $357.00

HARRINGTON & RICHARDSON/NEW ENGLAND FIREARMS STAINLESS ULTRA HUNTER WITH THUMBHOLE STOCK
Caliber: 45-70 Govt. **Barrel:** 24". **Weight:** 8 lbs. **Length:** 40". **Features:** Stainless steel barrel and receiver with scope mount rail, hammer extension, cinnamon laminate thumbhole stock.
Price: $439.00

HARRINGTON & RICHARDSON/NEW ENGLAND FIREARMS HANDI-RIFLE/SLUG GUN COMBOS
Chamber: 44 Mag./12-ga. rifled slug and 357 Mag./20-ga. rifled slug. **Barrel:** Rifle barrel 22" for both calibers; shotgun barrels 28" (12 ga.) and 40" (20 ga.) fully rifled. **Weight:** 7-8 lbs. **Length:** 38" overall (both rifle chamberings). **Features:** Single-shot break-open rifle/shotgun combos (one rifle barrel, one shotgun barrel per combo). Rifle barrels are not interchangeable; shotgun barrels are interchangeable. Stock is black matte high-density polymer with sling swivel studs, molded checkering and recoil pad. No iron sights; scope rail included.
Price: $362.00

HARRINGTON & RICHARDSON CR-45LC
Caliber: 45 Colt. Barrel: 20". Weight: 6.25 lbs. Length: 34"overall. Features: Single-shot break-open carbine. Cut-checkered American black walnut with case-colored crescent steel buttplate, open sights, case-colored receiver.
Price: $407.00

HARRINGTON & RICHARDSON BUFFALO CLASSIC RIFLE
Caliber: 45-70 Govt. **Barrel:** 32" heavy. **Weight:** 8 lbs. **Length:** 46" overall. **Stock:** Cut-checkered American black walnut. **Sights:**

Williams receiver sight; Lyman target front sight with 8 aperture inserts. **Features:** Color case-hardened Handi-Rifle action with exposed hammer; color case-hardened crescent buttplate; 19th century checkering pattern. Introduced 1995. Made in U.S.A. by H&R 1871, Inc.

Price: Buffalo Classic Rifle **$449.00**

KRIEGHOFF HUBERTUS SINGLE-SHOT RIFLE

Caliber: 222, 243 Win., 270 Win., 308 Win., 30-06 Spfl., 5.6x50R Mag., 5.6x52R, 6x62R Freres, 6.5x57R, 6.5x65R, 7x57R, 7x65R, 8x57JRS, 8x75RS, 9.3x74R, 7mm Rem. Mag., 300 Win. Mag. **Barrel:** 23.5". **Weight:** 6.5 lbs. **Length:** 40.5. **Stock:** High-grade walnut. **Sights:** Blade front, open rear. **Features:** Break-open loading with manual cocking lever on top tang; takedown; extractor; Schnabel forearm; many options. Imported from Germany by Krieghoff International Inc.

Price: Hubertus single shot, from **$5,995.00**
Price: Hubertus, magnum calibers **$6,995.00**

MEACHAM HIGHWALL SILHOUETTE OR SCHUETZEN RIFLE

Caliber: any rimmed cartridge. **Barrel:** 26-34". **Weight:** 8-15 lbs. **Sights:** none. Tang drilled for Win. base, 3/8 dovetail slot front. **Stock:** Fancy eastern walnut with cheekpiece; ebony insert in forearm tip. **Features:** Exact copy of 1885 Winchester. With most Winchester factory options available, including double set triggers. Introduced 1994. Made in U.S.A. by Meacham T&H Inc.

Price: From **$4,999.00**

MERKEL K1 MODEL LIGHTWEIGHT STALKING RIFLE

Caliber: 243 Win., 270 Win., 7x57R, 308 Win., 30-06 Spfl., 7mm Rem. Mag., 300 Win. Mag., 9.3x74R. **Barrel:** 23.6". **Weight:** 5.6 lbs. unscoped. **Stock:** Satin-finished walnut, fluted and checkered; sling-swivel studs. **Sights:** None (scope base furnished). **Features:** Franz Jager single-shot break-open action, cocking/uncocking slide-type safety, matte silver receiver, selectable trigger pull weights, integrated, quick detach 1" or 30mm optic mounts (optic not included). Imported from Germany by Merkel USA.

Price: Jagd Stutzen Carbine **$3,795.00**

MERKEL K-2 CUSTOM SINGLE-SHOT "WEIMAR" STALKING RIFLE

Caliber: 308 Win., 30-06 Spfl., 7mm Rem. Mag., 300 Win. Mag. **Features:** Franz Jager single-shot break-open action, cocking. uncocking slide safety, deep relief engraved hunting scenes on silvered receiver, octagin barrel, deluxe walnut stock. Includes front and reare adjustable iron sights, scope rings. Imported from Germany by Merkel USA.

Price: Jagd Stutzen Carbine **$15,595.00**

NAVY ARMS 1874 SHARPS "QUIGLEY" RIFLE

Caliber: .45-70 Govt. **Barrel:** 34" octagon. **Weight:** 10 lbs. **Length:** 50" overall. Grips: Walnut checkered at wrist and forend. **Sights:** High blade front, full buckhorn rear. **Features:** Color case-hardened receiver, trigger, military patchbox, hammer and lever. Double-set triggers, German silver gripcap. Reproduction of rifle from "Quigley Down Under" movie.

Price: Model SQR045 (20087) **$2,026.00**

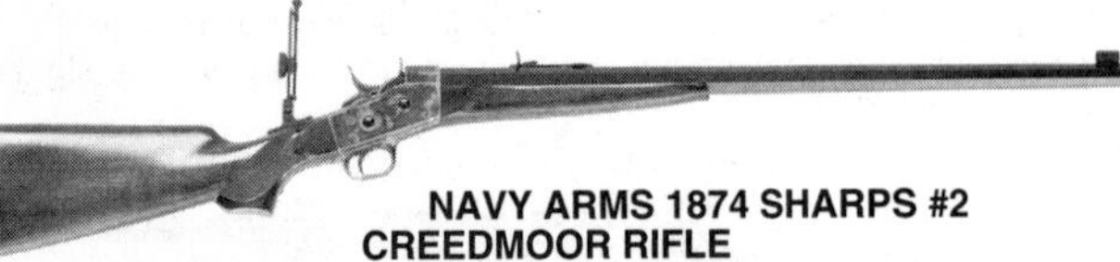

NAVY ARMS 1874 SHARPS #2 CREEDMOOR RIFLE

Caliber: 45/70. **Barrel:** 30" tapered round. **Stock:** Walnut. **Sights:** Front globe, "soule" tang rear. **Features:** Nickel receiver and action. Lightweight sporting rifle.

Price: **$1,816.00**

Navy Arms Sharps Sporting Rifle

Same as the Navy Arms Sharps Plains Rifle except has pistol grip stock. Introduced 1997. Imported by Navy Arms.

Price: 45-70 Govt. only **$1,711.00**
Price: #2 Sporting with case-hardened receiver **$1,739.00**
Price: #2 Silhouette with full octagonal barrel **$1,739.00**

NAVY ARMS 1885 HIGH WALL RIFLE

Caliber: 45-70 Govt.; others available on special order. **Barrel:** 28" round, 30" octagonal. **Weight:** 9.5 lbs. **Length:** 45.5" overall (30" barrel). **Stock:** Walnut. **Sights:** Blade front, vernier tang-mounted peep rear. **Features:** Replica of Winchester's High Wall designed by Browning. Color case-hardened receiver, blued barrel. Introduced 1998. Imported by Navy Arms.

Price: 28", round barrel, target sights **$1,120.00**
Price: 30" octagonal barrel, target sights **$1,212.00**

NAVY ARMS 1873 SPRINGFIELD CAVALRY CARBINE

Caliber: 45-70 Govt. **Barrel:** 22". **Weight:** 7 lbs. **Length:** 40.5" overall. **Stock:** Walnut. **Sights:** Blade front, military ladder rear. **Features:** Blued lockplate and barrel; color case-hardened breechblock; saddle ring with bar. Replica of 7th Cavalry gun. Officer's Model Trapdoor has single-set trigger, bone case-hardened buttplate, trigger guard and breechblock. Deluxe walnut stock hand-checkered at the wrist and forend. German silver forend cap and rod tip. Adjustable rear peep target sight. Authentic flip-up 'Beech' front target sight. Imported by Navy Arms.

Price: Model STC073 . . . . **$1,261.00**
Price: Officer's Model Trapdoor (2008). **$1,648.00**

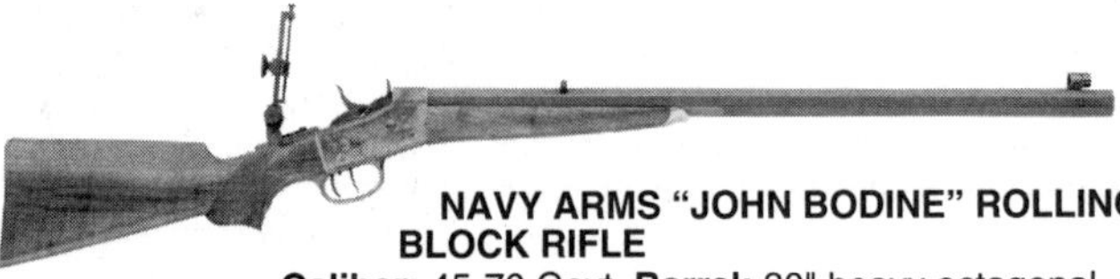

NAVY ARMS "JOHN BODINE" ROLLING BLOCK RIFLE

Caliber: 45-70 Govt. **Barrel:** 30" heavy octagonal. **Stock:** Walnut. **Sights:** Globe front, "soule" tang rear. **Features:** Double-set triggers.

Price: **$1,928.00**
Price: (#2 with deluxe nickel finished receiver) **$1,928.00**

NAVY ARMS 1874 SHARPS NO. 3 LONG RANGE RIFLE

Caliber: 45-70 Govt. **Barrel:** 34" octagon. **Weight:** 10 lbs., 14 oz. **Length:** 51.2". **Stock:** Deluxe walnut. **Sights:** Globe target front and match grade rear tang. **Features:** Shotgun buttplate, German silver forend cap, color case hardened receiver. Imported by Navy Arms.

Price: **$2,432.00**

NEW ENGLAND FIREARMS HANDI-RIFLE

Caliber: 204 Ruger, 22 Hornet, 223 Rem., 243 Win., 30-30, 270 Win., 280 Rem., 7mm-08 Rem., 308 Win., 7.62x39 Russian, 30-06 Spfl., 357 Mag., 35 Whelen, 44 Mag., 45-70 Govt., 500 S&W. **Barrel:** From 20" to 26", blued or stainless. **Weight:** 5.5 to 7 lbs. **Stock:** Walnut-finished hardwood or synthetic. **Sights:** Vary by model, but most have ramp front, folding rear, or are drilled and tapped for scope mount. **Features:** Break-open action with side-lever release. Swivel

Prices given are believed to be accurate at time of publication however, many factors affect retail pricing so exact prices are not possible.

studs on all models. Blue finish. Introduced 1989. From H&R 1871, Inc.

Price: Various cartridges. **$292.00**
Price: 7.62x39 Russian, 35 Whelen, intr. 2006 . . . . **$292.00**
Price: Youth, 37" OAL, 11.75" LOP, 6.75 lbs. **$292.00**
Price: Handi-Rifle/Pardner combo, 20 ga. synthetic, intr. 2006 . . . . **$325.00**
Price: Handi-Rifle/Pardner Superlight, 20 ga., 5.5 lbs., intr. 2006 . . . . **$325.00**
Price: Synthetic **$302.00**
Price: Stainless **$364.00**
Price: Superlight, 20" barrel, 35.25" OAL, 5.5 lbs. **$302.00**

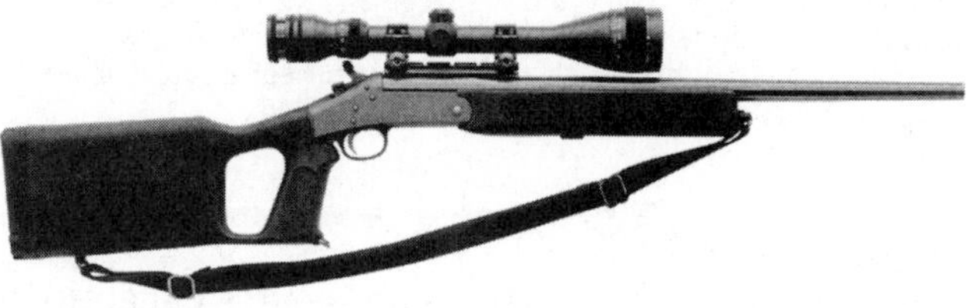

NEW ENGLAND FIREARMS SURVIVOR RIFLE
Caliber: 223 Rem., 308 Win., .410 shotgun, 45 Colt, single shot. **Barrel:** 20" to 22". **Weight:** 6 lbs. **Length:** 34.5" to 36" overall. **Stock:** Black polymer, thumbhole design. **Sights:** None furnished; scope mount provided. **Features:** Receiver drilled and tapped for scope mounting. Stock and forend have storage compartments for ammo, etc.; comes with integral swivels and black nylon sling. Introduced 1996. Made in U.S.A. by H&R 1871, Inc.
Price: Blue or nickel finish. **$304.00**

NEW ENGLAND FIREARMS SPORTSTER/VERSA PACK RIFLE
Caliber: 17M2, 17 HMR, 22 LR, 22 WMR, .410 bore single shot. **Barrel:** 20" to 22". **Weight:** 5.4 to 7 lbs. **Length:** 33" to 38.25" overall. **Stock:** Black polymer. **Sights:** Adjustable rear, ramp front. **Features:** Receiver drilled and tapped for scope mounting. Made in U.S.A. by H&R 1871, Inc.
Price: Sportster 17M2, 17 HMR **$193.00**
Price: Sportster **$161.00**
Price: Sportster Youth **$161.00**

REMINGTON MODEL SPR18 SINGLE SHOT RIFLES
Caliber: 223 Rem., 243 Win., 270 Win., .30-06 Spfl., 308 Win., 7.62x39mm. **Barrel:** 23.5" chrome-lined hammer forged, all steel receiver, spiral-cut fluting. **Weight:** 6.75 lbs. **Stock:** Walnut stock and fore-end, swivel studs. **Sights:** adjustable, with 11mm scope rail. **Length:** 39.75" overall. **Features:** Made in U.S. by Remington Arms Co., Inc.
Price: Blued/walnut (2008) **$277.00**
Price: Nickel/walnut (2008). **$326.00**

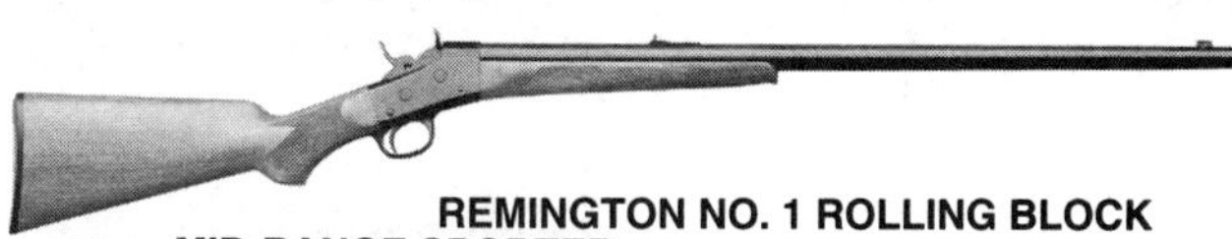

REMINGTON NO. 1 ROLLING BLOCK MID-RANGE SPORTER
Caliber: 45-70 Govt. **Barrel:** 30" round. **Weight:** 8.75 lbs. **Length:** 46.5" overall. **Stock:** American walnut with checkered pistol grip and forend. **Sights:** Beaded blade front, adjustable center-notch buckhorn rear. **Features:** Recreation of the original. Polished blue metal finish. Many options available. Introduced 1998. Made in U.S.A. by Remington.
Price: **$2,927.00**
Price: Silhouette model with single-set trigger, heavy barrel **$3,366.00**

ROSSI SINGLE-SHOT RIFLES
Caliber: 17, 223 Rem., 243 Win., 270 Win., .30-06, 308 Win., 7.62x39, 22-250. **Barrel:** 22" (Youth), 23". **Weight:** 6.25-7 lbs. Stocks: Wood, Black Synthetic (Youth). **Sights:** Adjustable sights, drilled and tapped for scope. **Features:** Single-shot break open, 13 models available, positive ejection, internal transfer bar mechanism, manual external safety, trigger block system, Taurus Security System, Matte blue finish, youth models available.
Price: **$238.00**

ROSSI MATCHED PAIRS
Gauge/Caliber: 12, 20, .410, 22 Mag, 22 LR, 17 HMR, 223 Rem, 243 Win., 270 Win., .30-06, 308Win., .50 (black powder). **Barrel:** 23", 28". **Weight:** 5-6.3 lbs. Stocks: Wood or black synthetic. **Sights:** Bead front on shotgun barrel, fully adjustable front and rear on rifle barrel, drilled and tapped for scope, fully adjustable fiber optic sights (black powder). **Features:** Single-shot break open, 27 models available, internal transfer bar mechanism, manual external safety, blue finish, trigger block system, Taurus Security System, youth models available.
Price: Rimfire/Shotgun, from. **$178.00**
Price: Centerfire/Shotgun **$299.00**
Price: Black Powder Matched Pair, from **$262.00**

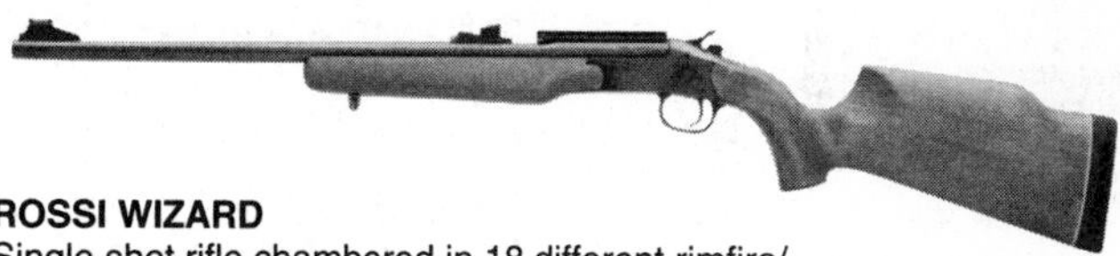

ROSSI WIZARD
Single shot rifle chambered in 18 different rimfire/centerfire/shotshell/muzzleloading configurations. Featured include drop-barrel action; quick, toolless barrel interchangeability; fiber optic front sight; adjustable rear sight with barrel-mounted optics rail; hardwood or camo Monte Carlo stock.
Price: . . . . **NA**

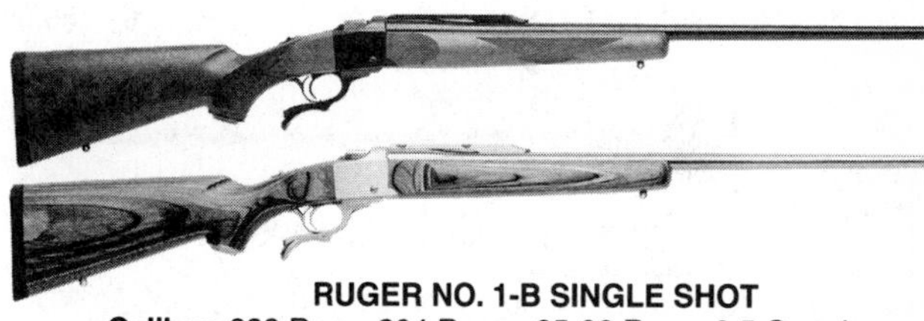

RUGER NO. 1-B SINGLE SHOT
Caliber: 223 Rem., 204 Ruger, 25-06 Rem., 6.5 Creedmore, 270 Win., 30-06 Spfl., 7mm Rem. Mag., 300 Win. Mag., 308 Win. **Barrel:** 26" round tapered with quarter-rib; with Ruger 1" rings. **Weight:** 8.25 lbs. **Length:** 42.25" overall. **Stock:** Walnut, two-piece, checkered pistol grip and semi-beavertail forend. **Sights:** None, 1" scope rings supplied for integral mounts. **Features:** Under-lever, hammerless falling block design has auto ejector, top tang safety.
Price: 1-B **$1,093.00**
Price: K1-B-BBZ stainless steel, laminated stock 25-06 Rem., 7mm Rem. Mag., 270, 300 Win. Mag., 243 Win., 30-06 . . . . **$1,186.00**

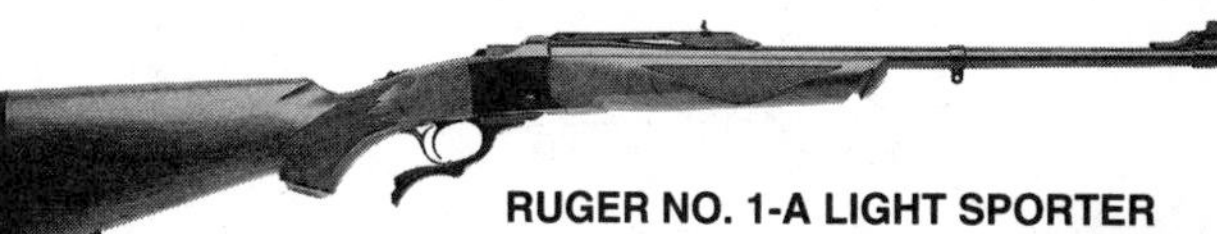

RUGER NO. 1-A LIGHT SPORTER
Caliber: 243 Win., 270 Win., 7x57, 30-06, 300 Ruger Compact Magnum. **Weight:** 7.25 lbs. Similar to the No. 1-B Standard Rifle except has lightweight 22" barrel, Alexander Henry-style forend, adjustable folding leaf rear sight on quarter-rib, dovetailed ramp front with gold bead.
Price: No. 1A. **$1,147.00**

Ruger No. 1-V Varminter
Similar to the No. 1-B Standard Rifle except has 24" heavy barrel. Semi-beavertail forend, barrel ribbed for target scope block, with 1" Ruger scope rings. Calibers 204 Ruger (26" barrel), 22-250 Rem., 223 Rem., 25-06 Rem. Weight about 9 lbs.
Price: No. 1-V **$1,147.00**

Ruger No. 1 RSI International
Similar to the No. 1-B Standard Rifle except has lightweight 20" barrel, full-length International-style forend with loop sling swivel, adjustable folding leaf rear sight on quarter-rib, ramp front with gold bead. Calibers 30-06 Spfl., 270 and 7x57. Weight is about 7.25 lbs.
Price: No. 1 RSI **$1,186.00**

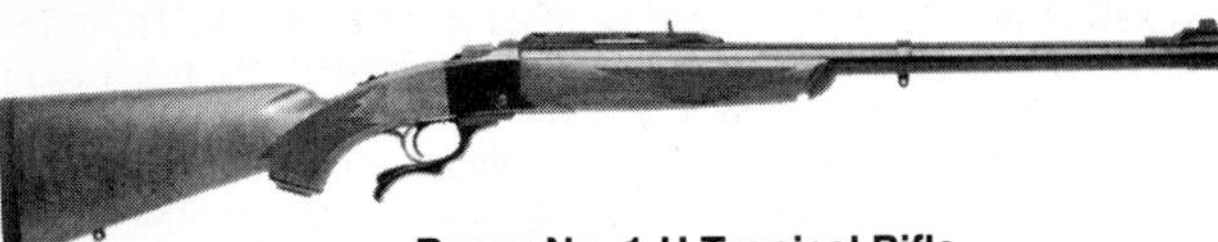

Ruger No. 1-H Tropical Rifle
Similar to the No. 1-B Standard Rifle except has Alexander Henry forend, adjustable folding leaf rear sight on quarter-rib, ramp front with dovetail gold bead, 24" heavy barrel. Calibers 375 H&H, 416 Rigby, 458 Lott, 405 Win., 450/400 Nitro Express 3" (weighs about 9 lbs.), 416 Ruger.
Price: No. 1H **$1,147.00**

Ruger No. 1-S Medium Sporter
Similar to the No. 1-B Standard Rifle except has Alexander Henry-style forend, adjustable folding leaf rear sight on quarter-rib, ramp front sight base and dovetail-type gold bead front sight. Calibers include 9.3x74R, 45-70 Govt. with 22" barrel, 300 H&H Mag, 338 Ruger Compact Magnum, 375 Ruger, 460 S&W Magnum, 480 Ruger/475 Linebaugh. Weighs about 7.25 lbs.
Price: No. 1-S **$1,147.00**
Price: K1-S-BBZ, S/S, 45-70 Govt. **$1,186.00**

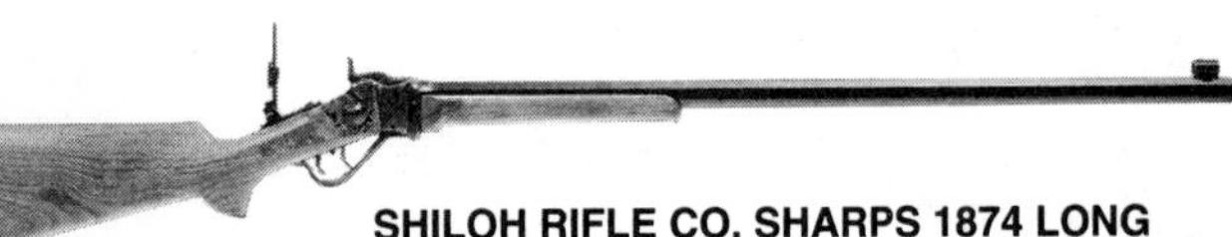

SHILOH RIFLE CO. SHARPS 1874 LONG RANGE EXPRESS
Caliber: 40-50 BN, 40-70 BN, 40-90 BN, 45-70 Govt. ST, 45-90 ST, 45-110 ST, 50-70 ST, 50-90 ST, 38-55, 40-70 ST, 40-90 ST. **Barrel:** 34" tapered octagon. **Weight:** 10.5 lbs. **Length:** 51" overall. **Stock:** Oil-finished walnut (upgrades available) with pistol grip, shotgun-style butt, traditional cheek rest, Schnabel forend. **Sights:** Customer's choice. **Features:** Re-creation of the Model 1874 Sharps rifle. Double-set triggers. Made in U.S.A. by Shiloh Rifle Mfg. Co.
Price: **$1,902.00**
Price: Sporter Rifle No. 1 (similar to above except with 30" barrel, blade front, buckhorn rear sight) **$1,902.00**
Price: Sporter Rifle No. 3 (similar to No. 1 except straight-grip stock, standard wood) **$1,800.00**

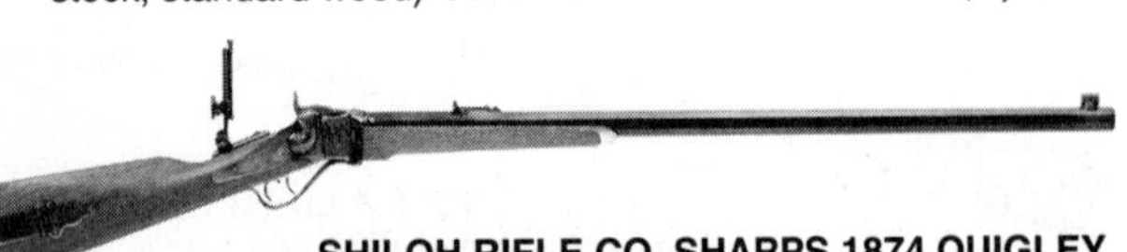

SHILOH RIFLE CO. SHARPS 1874 QUIGLEY
Caliber: 45-70 Govt., 45-110. **Barrel:** 34" heavy octagon. **Stock:** Military-style with patch box, standard grade American walnut. **Sights:** Semi buckhorn, interchangeable front and midrange vernier tang sight with windage. **Features:** Gold inlay initials, pewter tip, Hartford collar, case color or antique finish. Double-set triggers.
Price: **$3,298.00**

SHILOH RIFLE CO. SHARPS 1874 SADDLE RIFLE
Caliber: 38-55, 40-50 BN, 40-65 Win., 40-70 BN, 40-70 ST, 40-90 BN, 40-90 ST, 44-77 BN, 44-90 BN, 45-70 Govt. ST, 45-90 ST, 45-100 ST, 45-110 ST, 45-120 ST, 50-70 ST, 50-90 ST. **Barrel:** 26" full or half octagon. **Stock:** Semi fancy American walnut. Shotgun style with cheekrest. **Sights:** Buckhorn and blade. **Features:** Double-set trigger, numerous custom features can be added.
Price: **$1,852.00**

SHILOH RIFLE CO. SHARPS 1874 MONTANA ROUGHRIDER
Caliber: 38-55, 40-50 BN, 40-65 Win., 40-70 BN, 40-70 ST, 40-90 BN, 40-90 ST, 44-77 BN, 44-90 BN, 45-70 Govt. ST, 45-90 ST, 45-100 ST, 45-110 ST, 45-120 ST, 50-70 ST, 50-90 ST. **Barrel:** 30" full or half octagon. **Stock:** American walnut in shotgun or military style. **Sights:** Buckhorn and blade. **Features:** Double-set triggers, numerous custom features can be added.
Price: **$1,902.00**

SHILOH RIFLE CO. SHARPS CREEDMOOR TARGET
Caliber: 38-55, 40-50 BN, 40-65 Win., 40-70 BN, 40-70 ST, 40-90 BN, 40-90 ST, 44-77 BN, 44-90 BN, 45-70 Govt. ST, 45-90 ST, 45-100 ST, 45-110 ST, 45-120 ST, 50-70 ST, 50-90 ST. **Barrel:** 32", half round-half octagon. **Stock:** Extra fancy American walnut. Shotgun style with pistol grip. **Sights:** Customer's choice. **Features:** Single trigger, AA finish on stock, polished barrel and screws, pewter tip.
Price: **$2,743.00**

THOMPSON/CENTER ENCORE RIFLE
Caliber: 22-250 Rem., 223 Rem., 243 Win., 204 Ruger, 6.8 Rem. Spec., 25-06 Rem., 270 Win., 7mm-08 Rem., 308 Win., 30-06 Spfl., 7mm Rem. Mag., 300 Win. Mag. **Barrel:** 24", 26". **Weight:** 6 lbs., 12 oz. (24" barrel). **Length:** 38.5" (24" barrel). **Stock:** American walnut. Monte Carlo style; Schnabel forend or black composite. **Sights:** Ramp-style white bead front, fully adjustable leaf-type rear. **Features:** Interchangeable barrels; action opens by squeezing trigger guard; drilled and tapped for T/C scope mounts; polished blue finish. Introduced 1996. Made in U.S.A. by Thompson/Center Arms.
Price: . . . . **$604.00 to $663.00**
Price: Extra barrels **$277.00**

Thompson/Center Stainless Encore Rifle
Similar to blued Encore except stainless steel with blued sights, black composite stock and forend. Available in 22-250 Rem., 223 Rem., 7mm-08 Rem., 30-06 Spfl., 308 Win. Introduced 1999. Made in U.S.A. by Thompson/Center Arms.
Price: . . . . **$680.00 to $738.00**

THOMPSON/CENTER ENCORE "KATAHDIN" CARBINE
Caliber: 45-70 Govt., 450 Marlin. **Barrel:** 18" with muzzle tamer. **Stock:** Composite.
Price: **$619.00**

Thompson/Center G2 Contender Rifle
Similar to the G2 Contender pistol, but in a compact rifle format. Weighs 5.5 lbs. Features interchangeable 23" barrels, chambered for 17 HMR, 22 LR, 223 Rem., 30/30 Win. and 45/70 Govt.; plus a 45 cal. muzzleloading barrel. All of the 16.25"

and 21" barrels made for the old-style Contender will fit. Introduced 2003. Made in U.S.A. by Thompson/Center Arms.
Price: ....$622.00 to $637.00

THOMPSON/CENTER ENCORE PROHUNTER PREDATOR RIFLE

Contender-style break-action single shot rifle chambered in .204 Ruger, .223 Remington, .22-250 and .308 Winchester. Features include 28-inch deep-fluted interchangeable barrel, composite buttstock and forend with non-slip inserts in cheekpiece, pistol grip and forend. Max 1 camo finish overall. Overall length: 42.5 inches. Weight: 7-3/4 lbs.
Price: $799.00

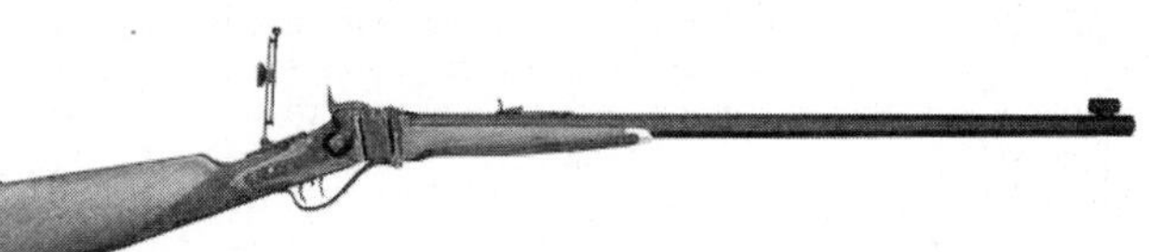

TRADITIONS 1874 SHARPS DELUXE RIFLE

Caliber: 45-70 Govt. **Barrel:** 32" octagonal; 1:18" twist. **Weight:** 11.67 lbs. **Length:** 48.8" overall. **Stock:** Checkered walnut with German silver nose cap and steel buttplate. **Sights:** Globe front, adjustable Creedmore rear with 12 inserts. **Features:** Color case-hardened receiver; double-set triggers. Introduced 2001. Imported from Pedersoli by Traditions.
Price: $1,545.00

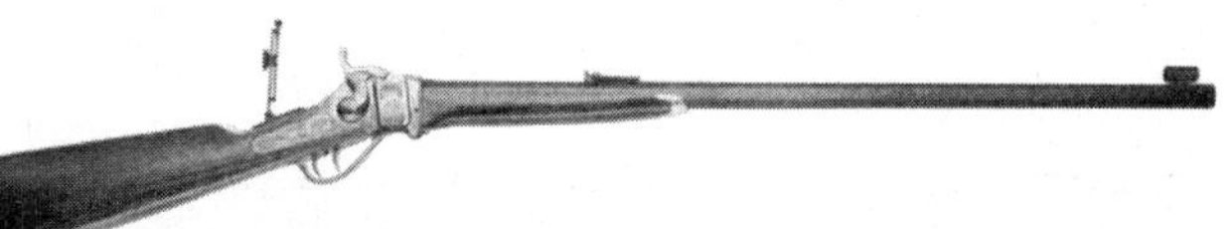

Traditions 1874 Sharps Sporting Deluxe Rifle

Similar to Sharps Deluxe but custom silver engraved receiver, European walnut stock and forend, satin finish, set trigger, fully adjustable.
Price: $2,796.00

Traditions 1874 Sharps Standard Rifle

Similar to 1874 Sharps Deluxe except has blade front and adjustable buckhorn-style rear sight. Weighs 10.67 pounds. Introduced 2001. Imported from Pedersoli by Traditions.
Price: $1,324.00

TRADITIONS ROLLING BLOCK SPORTING RIFLE

Caliber: 45-70 Govt. **Barrel:** 30" octagonal; 1:18" twist. **Weight:** 11.67 lbs. **Length:** 46.7" overall. **Stock:** Walnut. **Sights:** Blade front, adjustable rear. **Features:** Antique silver, color case-hardened receiver, drilled and tapped for tang/globe sights; brass buttplate and trigger guard. Introduced 2001. Imported from Pedersoli by Traditions.
Price: $1,029.00

UBERTI 1874 SHARPS SPORTING RIFLE

Caliber: 45-70 Govt. **Barrel:** 30", 32", 34" octagonal. **Weight:** 10.57 lbs. with 32" barrel. **Length:** 48.9" with 32" barrel. **Stock:** Walnut. **Sights:** Dovetail front, Vernier tang rear. **Features:** Cut checkering, case-colored finish on frame, buttplate, and lever. Imported by Stoeger Industries.
Price: Standard Sharps (2006), 30" barrel $1,459.00
Price: Special Sharps (2006) 32" barrel $1,729.00
Price: Deluxe Sharps (2006) 34" barrel $2,749.00
Price: Down Under Sharps (2006) 34" barrel $2,249.00
Price: Long Range Sharps (2006) 34" barrel $2,279.00
Price: Buffalo Hunters Sharps, 32" barrel $2,219.00
Price: Calvary Carbine Sharps, 22" barrel $1,569.00
Price: Sharps Extra Deluxe, 32" barrel (2009) $4,199.00
Price: Sharps Hunter, 28" barrel $1,459.00

UBERTI 1885 HIGH-WALL SINGLE-SHOT RIFLES

Caliber: 45-70 Govt., 45-90, 45-120 single shot. **Barrel:** 28" to 23". **Weight:** 9.3 to 9.9 lbs. **Length:** 44.5" to 47" overall. **Stock:** Walnut stock and forend. **Sights:** Blade front, fully adjustable open rear.

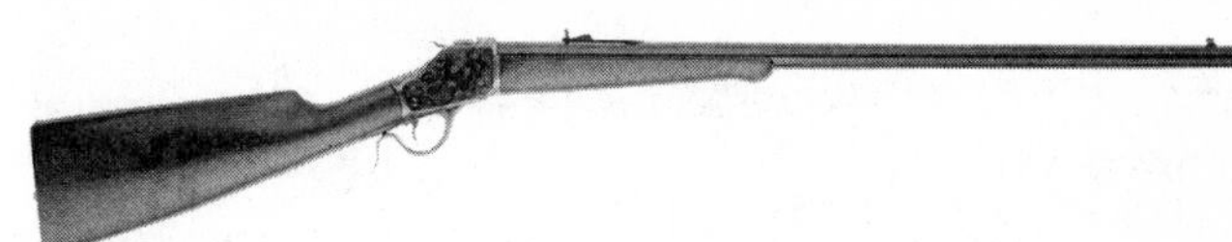

Features: Based on Winchester High-Wall design by John Browning. Color case-hardened frame and lever, blued barrel and buttplate. Imported by Stoeger Industries.
Price: 1885 High-Wall, 28" round barrel.................. $969.00
Price: 1885 High-Wall Sporting, 30" octagonal barrel $1,029.00
Price: 1885 High-Wall Special Sporting, 32" octagonal barrel $1,179.00

BERETTA EXPRESS SSO O/U DOUBLE RIFLES

Caliber: 375 H&H, 458 Win. Mag., 9.3x74R. **Barrel:** 25.5". **Weight:** 11 lbs. **Stock:** European walnut with hand-checkered grip and forend. **Sights:** Blade front on ramp, open V-notch rear. **Features:** Sidelock action with color case-hardened receiver (gold inlays on SSO6 Gold). Ejectors, double triggers, recoil pad. Introduced 1990. Imported from Italy by Beretta U.S.A.

Price: SSO6 . . . . **$21,000.00**
Price: SSO6 Gold **$23,500.00**

BERETTA MODEL 455 SXS EXPRESS RIFLE

Caliber: 375 H&H, 458 Win. Mag., 470 NE, 500 NE 3", 416 Rigby. **Barrel:** 23.5" or 25.5". **Weight:** 11 lbs. **Stock:** European walnut with hand-checkered grip and forend. **Sights:** Blade front, folding leaf V-notch rear. **Features:** Sidelock action with easily removable sideplates; color case-hardened finish (455), custom big game or floral motif engraving (455EELL). Double triggers, recoil pad. Introduced 1990. Imported from Italy by Beretta U.S.A.

Price: Model 455. . . . . **$36,000.00**
Price: Model 455EELL **$47,000.00**

CZ 584 SOLO COMBINATION GUN

Caliber/Gauge: 7x57R; 12, 2-3/4" chamber. **Barrel:** 24.4". **Weight:** 7.37 lbs. **Length:** 45.25" overall. **Stock:** Circassian walnut. **Sights:** Blade front, open rear adjustable for windage. **Features:** Kersten-style double lump locking system; double-trigger Blitz-type mechanism with drop safety and adjustable set trigger for the rifle barrel; auto safety, dual extractors; receiver dovetailed for scope mounting. Imported from the Czech Republic by CZ-USA.

Price: **$851.00**

CZ 589 STOPPER OVER/UNDER GUN

Caliber: 458 Win. Magnum. Barrels: 21.7". **Weight:** 9.3 lbs. **Length:** 37.7" overall. **Stock:** Turkish walnut with sling swivels. **Sights:** Blade front, fixed rear. **Features:** Kersten-style action; Blitz-type double trigger; hammer-forged, blued barrels; satin-nickel, engraved receiver. Introduced 2001. Imported from the Czech Republic by CZ USA.

Price: **$2,999.00**
Price: Fully engraved model **$3,999.00**

DAKOTA DOUBLE RIFLE

Caliber: 470 Nitro Express, 500 Nitro Express. **Barrel:** 25". **Stock:** Exhibition-grade walnut. **Sights:** Express-style. **Features:** Round action; selective ejectors; recoil pad; Americase. From Dakota Arms Inc.

Price: **$25,000.00**

GARBI EXPRESS DOUBLE RIFLE

Caliber: 7x65R, 9.3x74R, 375 H&H. **Barrel:** 24.75". **Weight:** 7.75 to 8.5 lbs. **Length:** 41.5" overall. **Stock:** Turkish walnut. **Sights:** Quarter-rib with express sight. **Features:** Side-by-side double; H&H-pattern sidelock ejector with reinforced action, chopper lump barrels of Boehler steel; double triggers; fine scroll and rosette engraving, or full coverage ornamental; coin-finished action. Introduced 1997. Imported from Spain by Wm. Larkin Moore.

Price: **$25,000.00**

HOENIG ROTARY ROUND ACTION DOUBLE RIFLE

Caliber: Most popular calibers from 225 Win. to 9.3x74R. **Barrel:** 22" to 26". **Stock:** English Walnut; to customer specs. **Sights:** Swivel hood front with button release (extra bead stored in trap door gripcap), express-style rear on quarter-rib adjustable for windage and elevation; scope mount. **Features:** Round action opens by rotating barrels, pulling forward. Inertia extractor system, rotary safety blocks strikers. Single lever quick-detachable scope mount. Simple takedown without removing forend. Introduced 1997. Made in U.S.A. by George Hoenig.

Price: **$19,980.00**

HOENIG ROTARY ROUND ACTION COMBINATION

Caliber: 28 ga. **Barrel:** 26". **Weight:** 7 lbs. **Stock:** English Walnut to customer specs. **Sights:** Front ramp with button release blades. Foldable aperture tang sight windage and elevation adjustable. Quarter-rib with scope mount. **Features:** Round action opens by rotating barrels, pulling forward. Inertia extractor; rotary safety blocks strikers. Simple takedown without removing forend. Made in U.S.A. by George Hoenig.

Price: **$25,000.00**

KRIEGHOFF CLASSIC DOUBLE RIFLE

Caliber: 7x57R, 7x65R, 308 Win., 30-06 Spfl., 8x57 JRS, 8x75RS, 9.3x74R, 375NE, 500/416NE, 470NE, 500NE. **Barrel:** 23.5". **Weight:** 7.3 to 8 lbs; 10-11 lbs. Big 5. **Stock:** High grade European walnut. Standard model has conventional rounded cheekpiece, Bavaria model has Bavarian-style cheekpiece. **Sights:** Bead front with removable, adjustable wedge (375 H&H and below), standing leaf rear on quarter-rib. **Features:** Boxlock action; double triggers; short opening angle for fast loading; quiet extractors; sliding, self-adjusting wedge for secure bolting; Purdey-style barrel extension; horizontal firing pin placement. Many options available. Introduced 1997. Imported from Germany by Krieghoff International.

Price: With small Arabesque engraving **$8,950.00**
Price: With engraved sideplates **$12,300.00**
Price: For extra barrels **$5,450.00**
Price: Extra 20-ga., 28" shotshell barrels **$3,950.00**

Krieghoff Classic Big Five Double Rifle

Similar to the standard Classic except available in 375 Flanged Mag. N.E., 500/416 NE, 470 NE, 500 NE. Has hinged front trigger, non-removable muzzle wedge (models larger than 375 caliber), Universal Trigger System, Combi Cocking Device, steel trigger guard, specially weighted stock bolt for weight and balance. Many options available. Introduced 1997. Imported from Germany by Krieghoff International. Imperial Model introduced 2006.

Price: **$11,450.00**
Price: With engraved sideplates **$14,800.00**

LEBEAU-COURALLY EXPRESS RIFLE SXS

Caliber: 7x65R, 8x57JRS, 9.3x74R, 375 H&H, 470 N.E. **Barrel:** 24" to 26". **Weight:** 7.75 to 10.5 lbs. **Stock:** Fancy French walnut with cheekpiece. **Sights:** Bead on ramp front, standing left express rear on quarter-rib. **Features:** Holland & Holland-type sidelock with automatic ejectors; double triggers. Built to order only. Imported from Belgium by Wm. Larkin Moore.

Price: **$50,000.00**

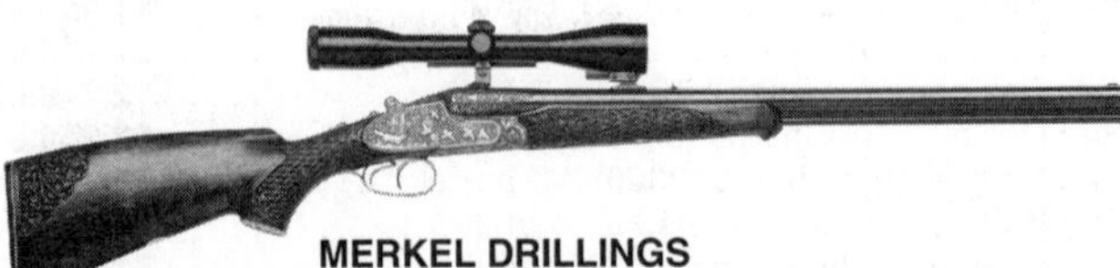

MERKEL DRILLINGS

Caliber/Gauge: 12, 20, 3" chambers, 16, 2-3/4" chambers; 22 Hornet, 5.6x50R Mag., 5.6x52R, 222 Rem., 243 Win., 6.5x55, 6.5x57R, 7x57R, 7x65R, 308 Win., 30-06 Spfl., 8x57JRS, 9.3x74R, 375 H&H. **Barrel:** 25.6". **Weight:** 7.9 to 8.4 lbs. depending upon caliber. **Stock:** Oil-finished walnut with pistol grip; cheekpiece on 12-, 16-gauge. **Sights:** Blade front, fixed rear. **Features:** Double barrel locking lug with Greener cross bolt; scroll-engraved, case-hardened receiver; automatic trigger safety; Blitz action; double triggers. Imported from Germany by Merkel USA.

Price: Model 96K (manually cocked rifle system), from **$8,495.00**
Price: Model 96K engraved (hunting series on receiver) ... **$9,795.00**

MERKEL BOXLOCK DOUBLE RIFLES

Caliber: 5.6x52R, 243 Winchester, 6.5x55, 6.5x57R, 7x57R, 7x65R, 308 Win., 30-06 Springfield, 8x57 IRS, 9.3x74R. **Barrel:** 23.6". **Weight:** 7.7 oz. **Length:** NA. **Stock:** Walnut, oil finished, pistol grip. **Sights:** Fixed 100 meter. **Features:** Anson & Deely boxlock action with cocking indicators, double triggers, engraved color case-hardened receiver. Introduced 1995. Imported from Germany by Merkel USA.

Price: Model 140-2, from **$11,995.00**
Price: Model 141 Small Frame SXS Rifle; built on smaller frame, chambered for 7mm Mauser, 30-06, or 9.3x74R **$8,195.00**
Price: Model 141 Engraved; fine hand-engraved hunting scenes on silvered receiver **$9,495.00**

RIZZINI EXPRESS 90L DOUBLE RIFLE

Caliber: 30-06 Spfl., 7x65R, 9.3x74R. **Barrel:** 24". **Weight:** 7.5 lbs. **Length:** 40" overall. **Stock:** Select European walnut with satin oil finish; English-style cheekpiece. **Sights:** Ramp front, quarter-rib with express sight. **Features:** Color case-hardened boxlock action; automatic ejectors; single selective trigger; polished blue barrels. Extra 20 gauge shotgun barrels available. Imported for Italy by Wm. Larkin Moore.

Price: With case **$3,850.00**

AMERICAN TACTICAL IMPORTS GSG-522

Semiauto tactical rifle chambered in .22 LR. Features include 16.25-inch barrel; black finish overall; polymer forend and buttstock; backup iron sights; receiver-mounted Picaatinny rail; 10-round magazine. Several other rifle and carbine versions available.

Price: **$475.00**

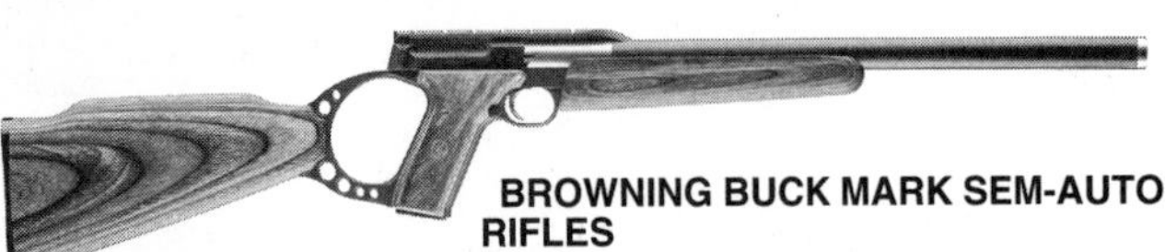

BROWNING BUCK MARK SEM-AUTO RIFLES

Caliber: 22 LR, 10+1. Action: A rifle version of the Buck Mark Pistol; straight blowback action; machined aluminum receiver with integral rail scope mount; manual thumb safety. **Barrel:** Recessed crowns. **Stock:** Stock and forearm with full pistol grip. **Features:** Action lock provided. Introduced 2001. Four model name variations for 2006, as noted below. **Sights:** FLD Target, FLD Carbon, and Target models have integrated scope rails. Sporter has Truglo/Marble fiber optic sights. Imported from Japan by Browning.

Price: FLD Target, 5.5 lbs., bull barrel, laminated stock. **$659.00**
Price: Target, 5.4 lbs., blued bull barrel, wood stock **$639.00**
Price: Sporter, 4.4 lbs., blued sporter barrel w/sights **$639.00**

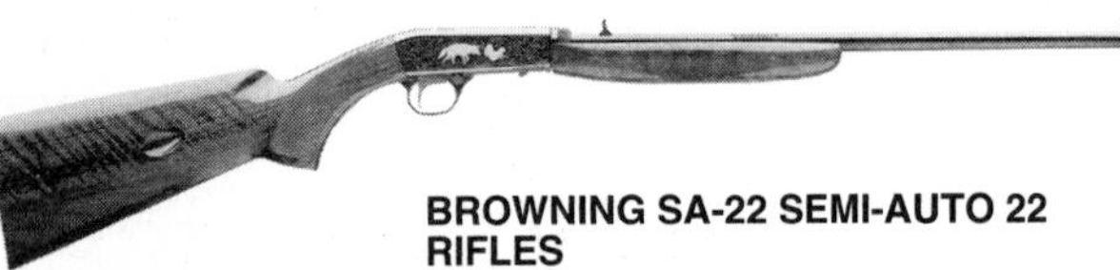

BROWNING SA-22 SEMI-AUTO 22 RIFLES

Caliber: 22 LR, 11+1. **Barrel:** 16.25". **Weight:** 5.2 lbs. **Length:** 37" overall. **Stock:** Checkered select walnut with pistol grip and semi-beavertail forend. **Sights:** Gold bead front, folding leaf rear. **Features:** Engraved receiver with polished blue finish; cross-bolt safety; tubular magazine in buttstock; easy takedown for carrying or storage. The Grade VI is available with either grayed or blued receiver with extensive engraving with gold-plated animals: right side pictures a fox and squirrel in a woodland scene; left side shows a beagle chasing a rabbit. On top is a portrait of the beagle. Stock and forend are of high-grade walnut with a double-bordered cut checkering design. Introduced 1987. Imported from Japan by Browning.

Price: Grade I, scroll-engraved blued receiver **$619.00**
Price: Grade VI BL, gold-plated engraved blued receiver . . **$1,329.00**

CZ 513 RIFLE

Caliber: 22 LR, 5-shot magazine. **Barrel:** 20.9". **Weight:** 5.7 lbs. **Length:** 39" overall. **Stock:** Beechwood. **Sights:** Tangent iron. **Features:** Simplified version of the CZ 452, no checkering on stock, simple non-adjustable trigger. Imported from the Czech Republic by CZ-USA.

Price: **$328.00**

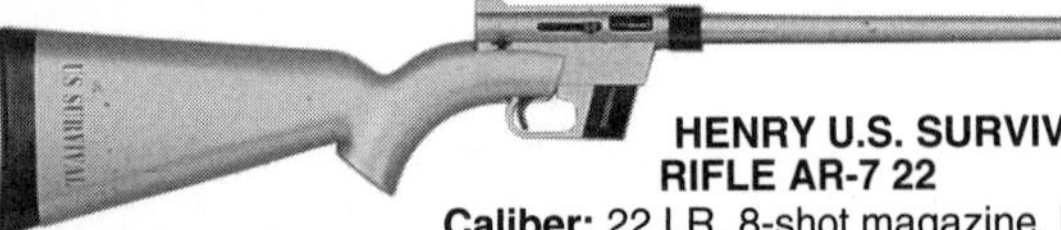

HENRY U.S. SURVIVAL RIFLE AR-7 22

Caliber: 22 LR, 8-shot magazine. **Barrel:** 16" steel lined. **Weight:** 2.25 lbs. **Stock:** ABS plastic. **Sights:** Blade front on ramp, aperture rear. **Features:** Takedown design stores barrel and action in hollow stock. Light enough to float. Silver, black or camo finish. Comes with two magazines. Introduced 1998. From Henry Repeating Arms Co.

Price: H002S Silver finish **$245.00**
Price: H002B Black finish **$245.00**
Price: H002C Camo finish **$310.00**

KEL-TEC SU-22CA

Caliber: 22 LR. **Features:** Blowback action, cross bolt safety, adjustable front and rear sights with integral picatinny rail. Threaded muzzle, 26-round magazine.

Price: . . . . **Appx. $400.00**

MAGNUM RESEARCH MAGNUMLITE RIFLES

Caliber: 22 WMR, 17 HMR, 22 LR 17M2, 10-shot magazine. **Barrel:** 17" graphite. **Weight:** 4.45 lbs. **Length:** 35.5" overall. **Stock:** Hogue OverMolded synthetic or walnut. **Sights:** Integral scope base. **Features:** Magnum Lite graphite barrel, French grey anodizing, match bolt, target trigger. 22 LR/17M2 rifles use factory Ruger 10/22 magazines. 4-5 lbs. average trigger pull. Graphite carbon-fiber barrel weighs approx. 13.04 ounces in 22 LR, 1:16 twist. Introduced: 2007. From Magnum Research, Inc.

Price: MLR22H 22 LR. **$640.00**

MARLIN MODEL 60 AUTO RIFLE

Caliber: 22 LR, 14-shot tubular magazine. **Barrel:** 19" round tapered. **Weight:** About 5.5 lbs. **Length:** 37.5" overall. **Stock:** Press-checkered, walnut-finished Maine birch with Monte Carlo, full pistol grip; Mar-Shield finish. **Sights:** Ramp front, open adjustable rear. **Features:** Matted receiver is grooved for scope mount. Manual bolt hold-open; automatic last-shot bolt hold-open. Model 60C is similar except has hardwood Monte Carlo stock with Mossy Oak Break-Up camouflage pattern. From Marlin.

Price: **$179.00**
Price: With 4x scope **$186.00**
Price: Model 60C camo **$211.00**

Marlin Model 60SS Self-Loading Rifle

Same as the Model 60 except breech bolt, barrel and outer magazine tube are made of stainless steel; most other parts are either nickel-plated or coated to match the stainless finish. Monte Carlo stock is of black/gray Maine birch laminate, and has nickel-plated swivel studs, rubber buttpad. Introduced 1993. From Marlin.

Price: **$283.00**

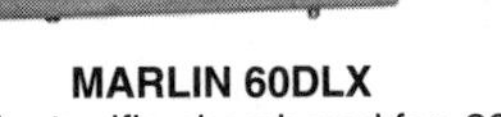

MARLIN 60DLX

Semiauto rifle chambered for .22 LR. Features include 14-shot tubular magazine; side ejection; manual and automatic last-shot bolt hold-opens; receiver top with serrrated, non-glare finish; cross-bolt safety; steel charging handle; Monte Carlo American walnut-finished hardwood; full pistol grip; tough Mar-Shield finish; 19-inch barrel with Micro-Groove® rifling. Limited availability.

Price: . . . . **NA**

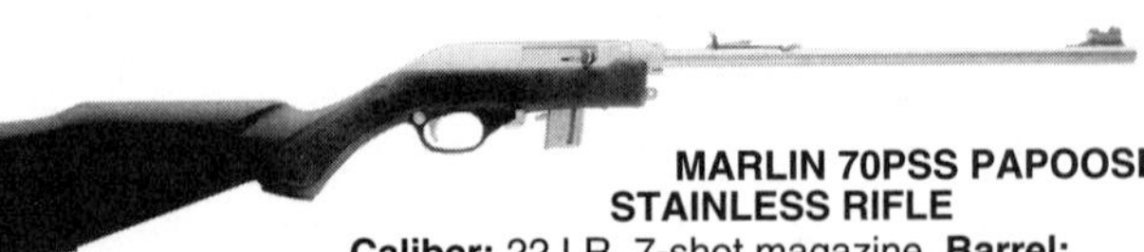

MARLIN 70PSS PAPOOSE STAINLESS RIFLE

Caliber: 22 LR, 7-shot magazine. **Barrel:** 16.25" stainless steel, Micro-Groove rifling. **Weight:** 3.25 lbs. **Length:** 35.25" overall. **Stock:** Black fiberglass-filled synthetic with abbreviated forend, nickel-plated swivel studs, molded-in checkering. **Sights:** Ramp front with orange post, cut-away Wide Scan hood; adjustable open rear. Receiver grooved for scope mounting. **Features:** Takedown barrel; cross-bolt safety; manual bolt hold-open; last shot bolt hold-open; comes with padded carrying case. Introduced 1986. Made in U.S.A. by Marlin.

Price: **$284.00**

MARLIN MODEL 795 AUTO RIFLE

Caliber: 22. **Barrel:** 18" with 16-groove Micro-Groove rifling. Ramp front sight, adjustable rear. Receiver grooved for scope mount. **Stock:** Black synthetic, hardwood, synthetic thumbhole, solid pink, pink camo, or Mossy Oak New Break-up camo finish. **Features:** 10-round magazine, last shot hold-open feature. Introduced 1997. SS is similar to Model 795 except stainless steel barrel. Most other parts nickel-plated. Adjustable folding semi-buckhorn rear sights, ramp

Prices given are believed to be accurate at time of publication however, many factors affect retail pricing so exact prices are not possible.

front high-visibility post and removable cutaway wide scan hood. Made in U.S.A. by Marlin Firearms Co.

Price: 795 . . . . **$157.00**
Price: 795SS **$227.00**

MOSSBERG MODEL 702 PLINKSTER AUTO RIFLE

Caliber: 22 LR, 10-round detachable magazine. **Barrel:** 18" free-floating. **Weight:** 4.1 to 4.6 lbs. **Sights:** Adjustable rifle. Receiver grooved for scope mount. **Stock:** Solid pink or pink marble finish synthetic. **Features:** Ergonomically placed magazine release and safety buttons, crossbolt safety, free gun lock. Made in U.S.A. by O.F. Mossberg & Sons, Inc.

Price: Pink Plinkster (2008) **$199.00**

MOSSBERG MODEL 702 PLINKSTER AUTOLOADING RIFLE WITH MUZZLE BRAKE

Semiauto rifle chambered in .22 LR. Features include a black synthetic stock with Schnabel, 10-round detachable box magazine, 21-inch matte blue barrel with muzzle brake, receiver grooved for scope mount.

Price: **$271.00**

REMINGTON MODEL 552 BDL DELUXE SPEEDMASTER RIFLE

Caliber: 22 S (20), L (17) or LR (15) tubular magazine. **Barrel:** 21" round tapered. **Weight:** 5.75 lbs. **Length:** 40" overall. **Stock:** Walnut. Checkered grip and forend. **Sights:** Big game. **Features:** Positive cross-bolt safety, receiver grooved for tip-off mount.

Price: **$593.00**
Price: Smoothbore model (2007) **$633.00**

REMINGTON 597 AUTO RIFLE

Caliber: 22 LR, 10-shot clip; 22 WMR, 8-shot clip. **Barrel:** 20". **Weight:** 5.5 lbs. **Length:** 40" overall. **Stock:** Black synthetic. **Sights:** Big game. **Features:** Matte black finish, nickel-plated bolt. Receiver is grooved and drilled and tapped for scope mounts. Introduced 1997. Made in U.S.A. by Remington.

Price: Synthetic Scope Combo (2007) **$239.00**
Price: Model 597 Magnum **$492.00**
Price: Model 597 w/Mossy Oak Blaze Pink or Orange, 22 LR (2008) **$260.00**
Price: Model 597 Stainless TVP, 22 LR (2008) **$552.00**
Price: Model 597 TVP: Skeletonized laminated stock with undercut forend, optics rail **$552.00**
Price: Model 597 FLX: Similar to Model 597, Blaze/Pink camo but with FLX Digital Camo stock **$260.00**

REMINGTON 597 VTR - QUAD RAIL

Semiauto rifle chambered in .22 LR, styled to resemble AR. Features include matte blued finished and black synthetic stock; 16-inch barrel; Pardus A2-style collapsible pistol-grip stock; quad-rail free-floated tube; 10-round magazine.

Price: **$618.00**

REMINGTON 597 VTR A-2 FIXED STOCK

Similar to Remington 597 VTR - Quad Rail but with fixed A2-style stock and standard handguard with quad rail.

Price: **$618.00**

REMINGTON 597 VTR COLLAPSIBLE STOCK

Similar to 597 VTR A-2 Fixed Stock but with Pardus A2-style collapsible pistol-grip stock.

Price: **$618.00**

REMINGTON 597 VTR A-TACS CAMO

Semiauto rifle chambered in .22 LR, styled to resemble AR. Features include ATACS camo finish overall; 16-inch barrel; Pardus A2-style collapsible pistol-grip stock; round handguard without rails; receiver-mounted optics rail; 10-round magazine.

Price: **$618.00**

RUGER 10/22 AUTOLOADING CARBINE

Caliber: 22 LR, 10-shot rotary magazine. **Barrel:** 18.5" round tapered. **Weight:** 5 lbs. **Length:** 37.25" overall. **Stock:** American hardwood with pistol grip and barrel band or synthetic. **Sights:** Brass bead front, folding leaf rear adjustable for elevation. **Features:** Detachable rotary magazine fits flush into stock, cross-bolt safety, receiver tapped and grooved for scope blocks or tip-off mount. Scope base adaptor furnished with each rifle.

Price: Model 10/22-RB (black matte) **$269.00**
Price: Model 10/22-CRR Compact RB (black matte), 2006 . . . **$307.00**

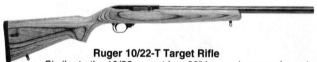

Ruger 10/22 Deluxe Sporter

Same as 10/22 Carbine except walnut stock with hand checkered pistol grip and forend; straight buttplate, no barrel band, has sling swivels.

Price: Model 10/22-DSP **$355.00**

Ruger 10/22-T Target Rifle

Similar to the 10/22 except has 20" heavy, hammer-forged barrel with tight chamber dimensions, improved trigger pull, laminated hardwood stock dimensioned for optical sights. No iron sights supplied. Introduced 1996. Made in U.S.A. by Sturm, Ruger & Co.

Price: 10/22-T **$485.00**
Price: K10/22-T, stainless steel **$533.00**

Ruger K10/22-RPF All-Weather Rifle

Similar to the stainless K10/22/RB except has black composite stock of thermoplastic polyester resin reinforced with fiberglass; checkered grip and forend. Brushed satin, natural metal finish with clear hard-coat finish. Weighs 5 lbs., measures 37" overall. Introduced 1997. From Sturm, Ruger & Co.

Price: **$318.00**

RUGER 10/22VLEH TARGET TACTICAL RIFLE

Semiauto rimfire rifle chambered in .22 LR. Features include precision-rifled, cold hammer-forged, spiral-finished 16-1/8-inch crowned match barrel; Hogue® OverMolded® stock; 10/22T target trigger; precision-adjustable bipod for steady shooting from the bench; 10-round rotary magazine. Weight: 6-7/8 lbs.

Price: **$555.00**

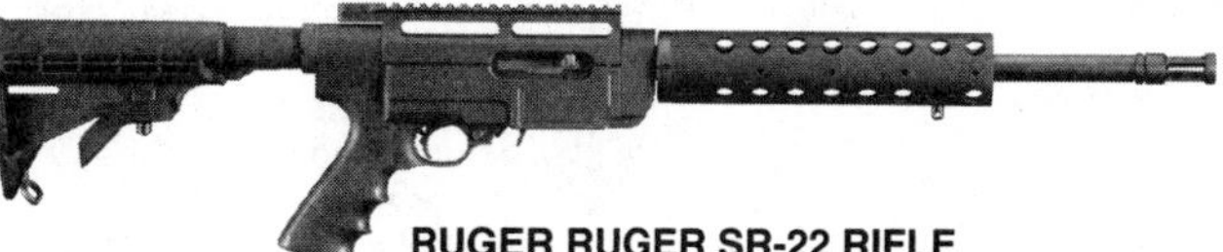

RUGER RUGER SR-22 RIFLE

AR-style semiauto rifle chambered in .22 LR, based on 0/22 action. Features include all-aluminum chassis replicating the AR-platform dimensions between the sighting plane, buttstock height, and grip; Picatinny rail optic mount includes a six-position, telescoping M4-style buttstock (on a Mil-Spec diameter tube); Hogue Monogrip pistol grip; buttstocks and grips interchangeable with any AR-style compatible option; round, mid-

length handguard mounted on a standard-thread AR-style barrel nut; precision-rifled, cold hammer forged 16-1/8-inch alloy steel barrel capped with an SR-556/Mini-14 flash suppressor.
Price: . . . . .NA

SAVAGE MODEL 64G AUTO RIFLE
Caliber: 22 LR, 10-shot magazine. **Barrel:** 20", 21". **Weight:** 5.5 lbs. **Length:** 40", 41". **Stock:** Walnut-finished hardwood with Monte Carlo-type comb, checkered grip and forend. **Sights:** Bead front, open adjustable rear. Receiver grooved for scope mounting. **Features:** Thumb-operated rotating safety. Blue finish. Side ejection, bolt hold-open device. Introduced 1990. Made in Canada, from Savage Arms.
Price: . . . . .From $187.00

SAVAGE BRJ SERIES SEMIAUTO RIMFIRE RIFLES
Similar to Mark II, Model 93 and Model 93R17 semiauto rifles but feature spiral fluting pattern on a heavy barrel, blued finish and Royal Jacaranda wood laminate stock.
Price: Mark II BRJ – .22 LR) **$456.00**
Price: Model 93 BRJ – .22 Mag. **$464.00**
Price: Model 93 R17 BRJ – .17 HMR $464 . . . . **$464.00**

SAVAGE TACTICAL SEMIAUTO RIMFIRE RIFLES
Similar to Savage Model BRJ series semiauto rifles but feature heavy barrel, matte finish and a tactical-style wood stock.
Price: Mark II TR – .22 LR) **$469.00**
Price: Mark II TRR – .22 LR with three-way accessory rail) . **$539.00**
Price: Model 93R17 TR – .17 HMR **$477.00**
Price: Model 93R17 TRR – .17 HMR with three-way accessory rail) **$536.00**

SMITH & WESSON M&P15-22
.22 LR rimfire verson of AR-derived M&P tactical autoloader. Features include blowback action, 15.5- or 16-inch barrel, 6-position telescoping or fixed stock, quad mount picatinny rails, plain barrel or compensator, alloy upper and lower, matte black finish, 10- or 25-round magazine.
Price: $589.00

THOMPSON/CENTER 22 LR CLASSIC RIFLE
Caliber: 22 LR, 8-shot magazine. **Barrel:** 22" match-grade. **Weight:** 5.5 pounds. **Length:** 39.5" overall. **Stock:** Satin-finished American walnut with Monte Carlo-type comb and pistol gripcap, swivel studs. **Sights:** Ramp-style front and fully adjustable rear, both with fiber optics. **Features:** All-steel receiver drilled and tapped for scope mounting; barrel threaded to receiver; thumb-operated safety; trigger guard safety lock included. New 22 Classic Benchmark TGT target rifle variant has 18" heavy barrel, brown laminated target stock, blued with matte finish, 10-shot magazine and no sights; drilled and tapped.
Price: T/C 22 LR Classic (blue) $396.00
Price: T/C 22 LR Classic Benchmark . . . . . $505.00 . . . .

UMAREX COLT TACTICAL RIMFIRE M4 OPS CARBINE
Blowback semiauto rife chambered in .22 LR, styled to resemble Colt M16. Features include 16.2.2-inch barrel; front sight adjustable for elevation; adjustable rear sight; alloy lower; adjustable telestock; flattop receiver with removable carry handle; 10- or 30-round detachable magazine.
Price: $599.00

UMAREX COLT TACTICAL RIMFIRE M4 CARBINE
Blowback semiauto rifle chambered in .22 LR, styled to resemble Colt M4. Features include 16.2-inch barrel; front sight adjustable for elevation; adjustable rear sight; alloy lower; adjustable telestock; flattop receiver with optics rail; 10- or 30-round detachable magazine.
Price: **$640.00**

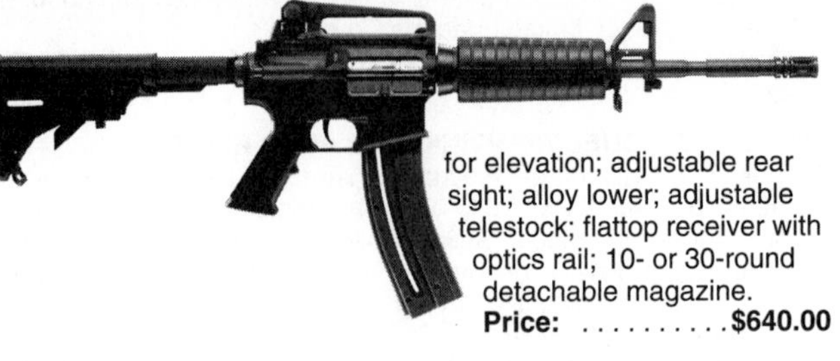

UMAREX COLT TACTICAL RIMFIRE M16 RIFLE
Blowback semiauto rifle chambered in .22 LR, styled to resemble Colt M16. Features include 21.2-inch barrel; front sight adjustable for elevation; adjustable rear sight; alloy lower; fixed stock; flattop receiver; removable carry handle; 10- or 30-round detachable magazine.
Price: $599.00

UMAREX COLT TACTICAL RIMFIRE M16 SPR RIFLE
Blowback semiauto rifle chambered in .22 LR, styled to resemble Colt M16 SPR. Features include 21.2-inch barrel; front sight adjustable for elevation; adjustable rear sight; alloy lower; fixed stock; flattop receiver with optics rail; removable carry handle; 10- or 30-round detachable magazine.
Price: $670.00

UMAREX H&K 416-22
Blowback semiauto rife chambered in .22 LR, styled to resemble H&K 416. Features include metal upper and lower receivers; RIS – rail interface system; retractable stock; pistol grip with storage compartment; on-rail sights; rear sight adjustable for wind and elevation; 16.1-inch barrel; 10- or 20-round magazine. Also available in pistol version with 9-inch barrel.
Price: $675.00

UMAREX H&K MP5 A5
Blowback semiauto rifle chambered in .22 LR, styled to resemble H&K MP5. Features include metal receiver; compensator; bolt catch; NAVY pistol grip; on-rail sights; rear sight adjustable for wind and elevation; 16.1-inch barrel; 10- or 25-round magazine. Also available in pistol version with 9-inch barrel. Also available with SD-type forend.
Price: $525.00

BROWNING BL-22 RIFLES

Action: Short-throw lever action, side ejection. Rack-and-pinion lever. Tubular magazines, with 15+1 capacity for 22 LR. **Barrel:** Recessed muzzle. **Stock:** Walnut, two-piece straight grip Western style. Trigger: Half-cock hammer safety; fold-down hammer. **Sights:** Bead post front, folding-leaf rear. Steel receiver grooved for scope mount. **Weight:** 5-5.4 lbs. **Length:** 36.75-40.75" overall. **Features:** Action lock provided. Introduced 1996. FLD Grade II Octagon has octagonal 24" barrel, silver nitride receiver with scroll engraving, gold-colored trigger. FLD Grade I has satin-nickel receiver, blued trigger, no stock checkering. FLD Grade II has satin-nickel receivers with scroll engraving; gold-colored trigger, cut checkering. Both introduced 2005. Grade I has blued receiver and trigger, no stock checkering. Grade II has gold-colored trigger, cut checkering, blued receiver with scroll engraving. Imported from Japan by Browning.

Price: BL-22 Grade I/II, from. **$529.00**
Price: BL-22 FLD Grade I/II, from **$569.00**
Price: BL-22 FLD, Grade II Octagon **$839.00**

HENRY LEVER-ACTION RIFLES

Caliber: 22 Long Rifle (15 shot), 22 Magnum (11 shots), 17 HMR (11 shots). **Barrel:** 18.25" round. **Weight:** 5.5 to 5.75 lbs. **Length:** 34" overall (22 LR). **Stock:** Walnut. **Sights:** Hooded blade front, open adjustable rear. **Features:** Polished blue finish; full-length tubular magazine; side ejection; receiver grooved for scope mounting. Introduced 1997. Made in U.S.A. by Henry Repeating Arms Co.

Price: H001 Carbine 22 LR. **$325.00**
Price: H001L Carbine 22 LR, Large Loop Lever. **$340.00**
Price: H001Y Youth model (33" overall, 11-round 22 LR) **$325.00**
Price: H001M 22 Magnum, 19.25" octagonal barrel, deluxe walnut stock **$475.00**
Price: H001V 17 HMR, 20" octagonal barrel, Williams Fire Sights **$549.95**

Henry Lever Octagon Frontier Model

Same as Lever rifles except chambered in 17 HMR, 22 Short/22 Long/22 LR, 22 Magnum; 20" octagonal barrel **Sights:** Marbles full adjustable semi-buckhorn rear, brass bead front. Weighs 6.25 lbs. Made in U.S.A. by Henry Repeating Arms Co.

Price: H001T Lever Octagon **$425.00**
Price: H001TM Lever Octagon 22 Magnum **$539.95**

HENRY GOLDEN BOY 22 LEVER-ACTION RIFLE

Caliber: 17 HMR, 22 LR (16-shot), 22 Magnum. **Barrel:** 20" octagonal. **Weight:** 6.25 lbs. **Length:** 38" overall. **Stock:** American walnut. **Sights:** Blade front, open rear. **Features:** Brasslite receiver, brass buttplate, blued barrel and lever. Introduced 1998. Made in U.S.A. from Henry Repeating Arms Co.

Price: H004 22 LR **$515.00**
Price: H004M 22 Magnum **$595.00**
Price: H004V 17 HMR **$615.00**
Price: H004DD 22 LR Deluxe, engraved receiver **$1,200.00**

HENRY PUMP-ACTION 22 PUMP RIFLE

Caliber: 22 LR, 15-shot. **Barrel:** 18.25". **Weight:** 5.5 lbs. **Length:** NA. **Stock:** American walnut. **Sights:** Bead on ramp front, open adjustable rear. **Features:** Polished blue finish; receiver grooved for scope mount; grooved slide handle; two barrel bands. Introduced 1998. Made in U.S.A. from Henry Repeating Arms Co.

Price: H003T 22 LR **$515.00**
Price: H003TM 22 Magnum **$595.00**

MARLIN MODEL 39A GOLDEN LEVER-ACTION RIFLE

Caliber: 22, S (26), L (21), LR (19), tubular magazine. **Barrel:** 24" Micro-Groove. **Weight:** 6.5 lbs. **Length:** 40" overall. **Stock:** Checkered American black walnut; Mar-Shield finish. Swivel studs; rubber buttpad. **Sights:** Bead ramp front with detachable Wide-Scan hood, folding rear semi-buckhorn adjustable for windage and elevation. **Features:** Hammer block safety; rebounding hammer. Takedown action, receiver tapped for scope mount (supplied), offset hammer spur, gold-colored steel trigger. From Marlin Firearms.

Price: **$593.00**

MOSSBERG MODEL 464 RIMFIRE LEVER-ACTION RIFLE

Caliber: 22 LR. **Barrel:** 20" round blued. **Weight:** 5.6 lbs. **Length:** 35-3/4" overall. **Features:** Adjustable sights, straight grip stock, 124-shot tubular magazine, plain hardwood straight stock and forend.

Price: . . . . **NA; apparently not yet in production**

REMINGTON 572 BDL DELUXE FIELDMASTER PUMP RIFLE

Caliber: 22 S (20), L (17) or LR (15), tubular magazine. **Barrel:** 21" round tapered. **Weight:** 5.5 lbs. **Length:** 40" overall. **Stock:** Walnut with checkered pistol grip and slide handle. **Sights:** Big game. **Features:** Cross-bolt safety; removing inner magazine tube converts rifle to single shot; receiver grooved for tip-off scope mount.

Price: **$607.00**

RUGER MODEL 96 LEVER-ACTION RIFLE

Caliber: 22 WMR, 9 rounds; 17 HMR, 9 rounds. **Barrel:** 18.5". **Weight:** 5.25 lbs. **Length:** 37-3/8" overall. **Stock:** Hardwood. **Sights:** Gold bead front, folding leaf rear. **Features:** Sliding cross button safety, visible cocking indicator; short-throw lever action. Introduced 1996. Made in U.S.A. by Sturm, Ruger & Co.

Price: 96/22M, 22 WMR or 17 HMR **$451.00**

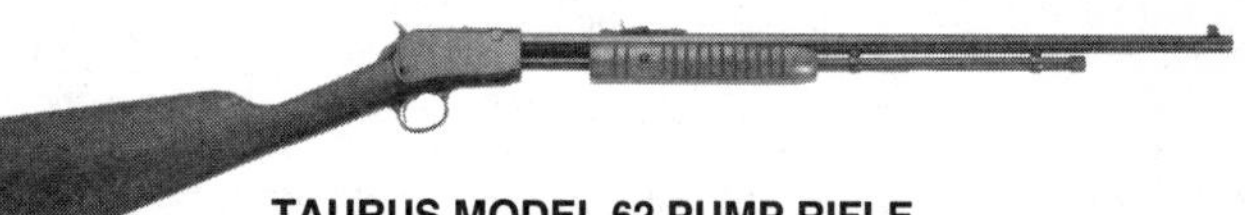

TAURUS MODEL 62 PUMP RIFLE

Caliber: 22 LR, 12- or 13-shot. **Barrel:** 16.5" or 23" round. **Weight:** 72 oz. to 80 oz. **Length:** 39" overall. **Stock:** Premium hardwood. **Sights:** Adjustable rear, bead blade front, optional tang. **Features:** Blue, case hardened or stainless, bolt-mounted safety, pump action, manual firing pin block, integral security lock system. Imported from Brazil by Taurus International.

Price: From **$299.00**

Taurus Model 72 Pump Rifle

Same as Model 62 except chambered in 22 Magnum or 17 HMR; 16.5" barrel holds 10-12 shots, 23" barrel holds 11-13 shots. Weighs 72 oz. to 80 oz. Introduced 2001. Imported from Brazil by Taurus International.

Price: From **$329.00**

ANSCHUTZ 1416D/1516D CLASSIC RIFLES

Caliber: 22 LR (1416D888), 22 WMR (1516D), 5-shot clip. **Barrel:** 22.5". **Weight:** 6 lbs. **Length:** 41" overall. **Stock:** European hardwood with walnut finish; classic style with straight comb, checkered pistol grip and forend. **Sights:** Hooded ramp front, folding leaf rear. **Features:** Uses Match 64 action. Adjustable single-stage trigger. Receiver grooved for scope mounting. Imported from Germany by Merkel USA.

Price: 1416D KL, 22 LR **$899.00**
Price: 1416D KL Classic left-hand **$949.00**
Price: 1516D KL, 22 WMR **$919.00**

ANSCHUTZ 1710D CUSTOM RIFLE

Caliber: 22 LR, 5-shot clip. **Barrel:** 24.25". **Weight:** 7-3/8 lbs. **Length:** 42.5" overall. **Stock:** Select European walnut. **Sights:** Hooded ramp front, folding leaf rear; drilled and tapped for scope mounting. **Features:** Match 54 action with adjustable single-stage trigger; roll-over Monte Carlo cheekpiece, slim forend with Schnabel tip, Wundhammer palm swell on pistol grip, rosewood gripcap with white diamond insert; skip-line checkering on grip and forend. Introduced 1988. Imported from Germany by Merkel USA.

Price: $1,649.00

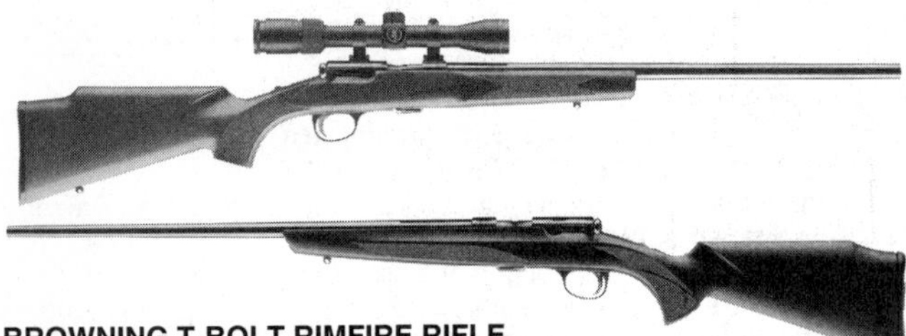

BROWNING T-BOLT RIMFIRE RIFLE

Caliber: 22 LR, 10-round rotary box Double Helix magazine. **Barrel:** 22", free-floating, semi-match chamber, target muzzle crown. **Weight:** 4.8 lbs. **Length:** 40.1" overall. **Stock:** Walnut, satin finish, cut checkering, synthetic buttplate. **Sights:** None. **Features:** Straight-pull bolt-action, three-lever trigger adjustable for pull weight, dual action screws, sling swivel studs. Crossbolt lockup, enlarged bolt handle, one-piece dual extractor with integral spring and red cocking indicator band, gold-tone trigger. Top-tang, thumb-operated two-position safety, drilled and tapped for scope mounts. Varmint model has raised Monte Carlo comb, heavy barrel, wide forearm. Introduced 2006. Imported from Japan by Browning. Left-hand models added in 2009.

Price: Sporter **$679.00**
Price: Sporter, left-hand, from **$689.00**
Price: Sporter, 17 HMR, 22 Mag., intr. 2008. . . . . **$709.00**
Price: Target/Varmint, intr. 2007 . . . . **$709.00**
Price: Composite Target/Varmint, intr. 2008 . . . . **$709.00**
Price: Composite Target/Varmint left-hand, from **$689.00**
Price: Composite Sporter, 17 HMR, 22 Mag., intr. 2008 . . . . . **$709.00**
Price: Composite Sporter left-hand, from **$689.00**

BUSHMASTER DCM-XR COMPETITION RIFLE

Caliber: 223 Rem, 10-shot mag. (2). **Barrel:** Heavy 1"-diameter free-floating match. **Weight:** 13.5 lbs. **Length:** 38.5" overall. **Features:** Fitted bolt, aperture rear sight that accepts four different inserts, choice of two front sight blades, two-stage competition trigger, weighted buttstock. Available in pre-and post-ban configurations.

Price: From . . . . **NA**

BUSHMASTER PIT VIPER 3-GUN COMPETITION RIFLE

Caliber: 5.56/223 Rem, 20-shot mag. (2). **Barrel:** Lapped/crowned 18" A2-profile 1:8. **Weight:** 7.5 lbs. **Length:** 38" overall. **Features:** AR-style semi-auto rifle designed for three-gun competition. Hybrid chambering to accept mil-spec ammunition, titanium nitride-coated bolt, free-floating handguard with two 3" rails and two 4" rails, JR tactical sight.

Price: From . . . . **NA**

COOPER MODEL 57-M BOLT-ACTION RIFLE

Caliber: 22 LR, 22 WMR, 17 HMR, 17 Mach 2. **Barrel:** 22" or 24" stainless steel or 4140 match grade. **Weight:** 6.5-7.5 lbs. **Stock:** AA-

AAA select Claro walnut, 22 lpi hand checkering. **Sights:** None furnished. **Features:** Three rear locking lug, repeating bolt-action with 5-shot magazine. for 22 LR and 17M2; 4-shot magazine for 22 WMR and 17 HMR. Fully adjustable trigger. Left-hand models add $150 to base rifle price. 1/4"-group rimfire accuracy guarantee at 50 yards; 0.5"-group centerfire accuracy guarantee at 100 yards. Options include wood upgrades, case-color metalwork, barrel fluting, custom LOP, and many others.

Price: Classic **$1,400.00**
Price: LVT **$1,595.00**
Price: Custom Classic **$2,395.00**
Price: Western Classic **$3,295.00**
Price: TRP-3 (22 LR only, benchrest style) **$1,395.00**
Price: Jackson Squirrel Rifle **$1,595.00**
Price: Jackson Hunter (synthetic) **$1,495.00**

CZ 452 LUX BOLT-ACTION RIFLE

Caliber: 22 LR, 22 WMR, 5-shot detachable magazine. **Barrel:** 24.8". **Weight:** 6.6 lbs. **Length:** 42.63" overall. **Stock:** Walnut with checkered pistol grip. **Sights:** Hooded front, fully adjustable tangent rear. **Features:** All-steel construction, adjustable trigger, polished blue finish. Imported from the Czech Republic by CZ-USA.

Price: 22 LR, 22 WMR **$427.00**

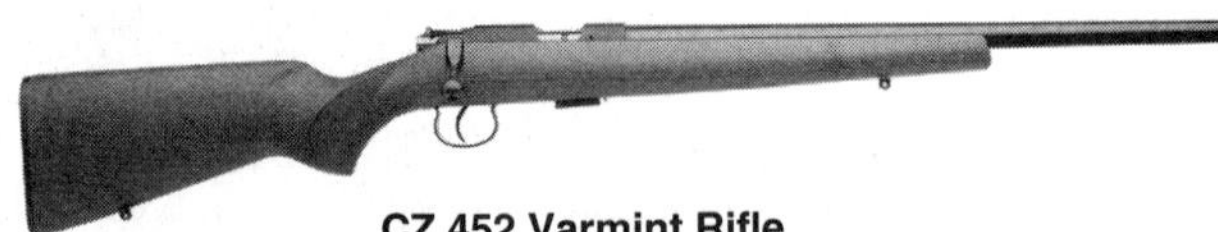

CZ 452 Varmint Rifle

Similar to the Lux model except has heavy 20.8" barrel; stock has beavertail forend; weighs 7 lbs.; no sights furnished. Available in 22 LR, 22 WMR, 17HMR, 17M2. Imported from the Czech Republic by CZ-USA.

Price: From **$497.00**

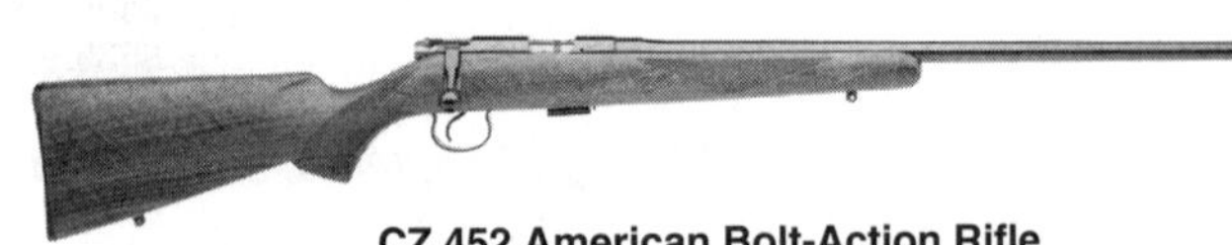

CZ 452 American Bolt-Action Rifle

Similar to the CZ 452 M 2E Lux except has classic-style stock of Circassian walnut; 22.5" free-floating barrel with recessed target crown; receiver dovetail for scope mounting. No open sights furnished. Introduced 1999. Imported from the Czech Republic by CZ-USA.

Price: 22 LR, 22 WMR **$463.00**

DAVEY CRICKETT SINGLE SHOT RIFLE

Caliber: 22 LR, 22 WMR, single shot. **Barrel:** 16-1/8". **Weight:** About 2.5 lbs. **Length:** 30" overall. **Stock:** American walnut. **Sights:** Post on ramp front, peep rear adjustable for windage and elevation. **Features:** Drilled and tapped for scope mounting using special Chipmunk base ($13.95). Engraved model also available. Made in U.S.A. Introduced 1982. Formerly Chipmunk model. From Keystone Sporting Arms.

Price: From **$220.00**

HENRY ACU-BOLT RIFLE

Caliber: 22, 22 Mag., 17 HMR; single shot. **Barrel:** 20". **Weight:** 4.15 lbs. **Length:** 36". **Stock:** One-piece fiberglass synthetic. **Sights:** Scope mount and 4x scope included. **Features:** Stainless barrel and receiver, bolt-action.

Price: H007 22 LR **$399.95**

HENRY "MINI" BOLT ACTION 22 RIFLE

Caliber: 22 LR, single shot youth gun. **Barrel:** 16" stainless, 8-groove rifling. **Weight:** 3.25 lbs. **Length:** 30", LOP 11.5". **Stock:** Synthetic, pistol grip, wraparound checkering and beavertail forearm. **Sights:** William Fire sights. **Features:** One-piece bolt configuration manually operated safety.

Price: H005 22 LR, black fiberglass stock **$249.95**
Price: H005S 22 LR, orange fiberglass stock **$249.95**

MARLIN MODEL 917 BOLT-ACTION RIFLES

Caliber: 17 HMR, 4- and 7-shot clip. **Barrel:** 22". **Weight:** 6 lbs., stainless 7 lbs. **Length:** 41". **Stock:** Checkered walnut Monte Carlo SS, laminated black/grey. **Sights:** No sights but receiver grooved. **Features:** Swivel studs, positive thumb safety, red cocking indicator, safety lock, SS 1" brushed aluminum scope rings.

Price: 917 . . . . **$240.00**
Price: 917VS Stainless steel barrel **$287.00**
Price: 917VT Laminated thumbhole stock (2008), from **$382.00**
Price: 917VST, stainless-finish metal, gray/black laminated thumbhole stock **$426.00**
Price: 917VSF, fluted barrel **$397.00**
Price: 917VS-CF, carbon fiber-patterned stock **$358.00**

MARLIN MODEL 915YN "LITTLE BUCKAROO"

Caliber: 22 S, L, LR, single shot. **Barrel:** 16.25" Micro-Groove. **Weight:** 4.25 lbs. **Length:** 33.25" overall. **Stock:** One-piece walnut-finished, press-checkered Maine birch with Monte Carlo; Mar-Shield finish. **Sights:** Ramp front, adjustable open rear. **Features:** Beginner's rifle with thumb safety, easy-load feed throat, red cocking indicator. Receiver grooved for scope mounting. Introduced 1989.

Price: **$203.00**
Price: 915YS (stainless steel with fire sights) **$227.00**

MARLIN 981TS

Bolt action rifle chambered in .22 S/L/LR. Features include tubular magazine (holds 25 Short, 19 Long or 17 Long Rifle cartridges; thumb safety; red cocking indicator; black fiberglass-filled synthetic stock with full pistol grip; molded-in checkering and swivel studs; 22-inch stainless steel barrel with Micro-Groove rifling (16 grooves). Adjustable semi-buckhorn folding rear sight, ramp front with high visibility, orange front sight post; cutaway Wide-Scan hood. Receiver grooved for scope mount; drilled and tapped for scope bases.

Price: . . . . **NA**

MARLIN MODEL 982 BOLT-ACTION RIFLE

Caliber: 22 WMR. **Barrel:** 22" Micro-Groove. **Weight:** 6 lbs. **Length:** 41" overall. **Stock:** Walnut Monte Carlo genuine American black walnut with swivel studs; full pistol grip; classic cut checkering; rubber rifle butt pad; tough Mar-Shield finish. **Sights:** Adjustable semi-buckhorn folding rear, ramp front sight with brass bead and Wide-Scan front sight hood. **Features:** 7-shot clip, thumb safety, red cocking indicator, receiver grooved for scope mount. 982S has stainless steel front breech bolt, barrel, receiver and bolt knob. All other parts are either stainless steel or nickel-plated. Has black Monte Carlo stock of fiberglass-filled polycarbonate with molded-in checkering, nickel-plated swivel studs. Introduced 2005. Made in U.S.A. by Marlin Firearms Co.

Price: 982VS (heavy stainless barrel, 7 lbs) **$309.00**
Price: 982VS-CF (carbon fiber stock) **$350.00**

Marlin Model 925M Bolt-Action Rifles

Similar to the Model 982 except chambered for 22 WMR. Has 7-shot clip magazine, 22" Micro-Groove barrel, checkered walnut-finished Maine birch stock. Introduced 1989.

Price: 925M **$234.00**
Price: 925RM, black fiberglass-filled synthetic stock **$220.95**

MARLIN MODEL 983 BOLT-ACTION RIFLE

Caliber: 22 WMR. **Barrel:** 22"; 1:16" twist. **Weight:** 6 lbs. **Length:** 41" overall. **Stock:** Walnut Monte Carlo with sling swivel studs, rubber buttpad. **Sights:** Ramp front with brass bead, removable hood; adjustable semi-buckhorn folding rear. **Features:** Thumb safety, red cocking indicator, receiver grooved for scope mount. 983S is same as the Model 983 except front breech bolt, striker knob, trigger stud, cartridge lifter stud and outer magazine tube are of stainless steel; other parts are nickel-plated. Introduced 1993. 983T has a black Monte Carlo fiberglass-filled synthetic stock with sling swivel studs. Introduced 2001.Made in U.S.A. by Marlin Firearms Co.

Price: 983 . . . . **$308.00**
Price: 983S (stainless barrel) **$337.00**
Price: 983T (fiberglass stock) **$245.00**

MEACHAM LOW-WALL RIFLE

Caliber: Any rimfire cartridge. **Barrel:** 26-34". **Weight:** 7-15 lbs. **Sights:** none. Tang drilled for Win. base, 3/8" dovetail slot front. **Stock:** Fancy eastern walnut with cheekpiece; ebony insert in forearm tip. Features; Exact copy of 1885 Winchester. With most Winchester factory options available including double set triggers. Introduced 1994. Made in U.S.A. by Meacham T&H Inc.

Price: From **$4,999.00**

MOSSBERG MODEL 817 VARMINT BOLT-ACTION RIFLE

Caliber: 17 HMR, 5-round magazine. **Barrel:** 21"; free-floating bull barrel, recessed muzzle crown. **Weight:** 4.9 lbs. (black synthetic), 5.2 lbs. (wood). **Stock:** Black synthetic or wood; length of pull, 14.25". **Sights:** Factory-installed Weaver-style scope bases. **Features:** Blued or brushed chrome metal finishes, crossbolt safety, gun lock. Introduced 2008. Made in U.S.A. by O.F. Mossberg & Sons, Inc.

Price: Black synthetic stock, chrome finish (2008) **$279.00**

MOSSBERG MODEL 801/802 BOLT RIFLES

Caliber: 22 LR, 10-round detachable magazine. **Barrel:** 18" free-floating. **Weight:** 4.1 to 4.6 lbs. **Sights:** Adjustable rifle. Receiver grooved for scope mount. **Stock:** Solid pink or pink marble finish synthetic. **Features:** Ergonomically placed magazine release and safety buttons, crossbolt safety, free gun lock. 801 Half Pint has 12.25" length of pull, 16" barrel, and weighs 4 lbs. Hardwood stock; removable magazine plug. Made in U.S.A. by O.F. Mossberg & Sons, Inc.

Price: Pink Plinkster (2008) **$199.00**
Price: Half Pint (2008) **$199.00**

NEW ENGLAND FIREARMS SPORTSTER SINGLE-SHOT RIFLES

Caliber: 22 LR, 22 WMR, 17 HMR, single-shot. **Barrel:** 20". **Weight:** 5.5 lbs. **Length:** 36.25" overall. **Stock:** Black polymer. **Sights:** None furnished; scope mount included. **Features:** Break open, side-lever release; automatic ejection; recoil pad; sling swivel studs; trigger locking system. Introduced 2001. Made in U.S.A. by New England Firearms.

Price: **$149.00**
Price: Youth model (20" barrel, 33" overall, weighs 5-1/3 lbs.) **$149.00**
Price: Sportster 17 HMR **$180.00**

NEW ULTRA LIGHT ARMS 20RF BOLT-ACTION RIFLE

Caliber: 22 LR, single shot or repeater. **Barrel:** Douglas, length to order. **Weight:** 5.25 lbs. **Length:** Varies. **Stock:** Kevlar/graphite composite, variety of finishes. **Sights:** None furnished; drilled and tapped for scope mount. **Features:** Timney trigger, hand-lapped action, button-rifled barrel, hand-bedded action, recoil pad, sling-swivel studs, optional Jewell trigger. Made in U.S.A. by New Ultra Light Arms.

Price: 20 RF single shot **$1,300.00**
Price: 20 RF repeater **$1,350.00**

REMINGTON MODEL FIVE SERIES

Caliber: 17 HMR, 22 LR, 22 WMR. **Barrel:** 16.5" (Youth), 22". **Barrel:** Carbon-steel, hammer-forged barrel, 1:16 twist, polished blue finish. **Weight:** 5.5 to 6.75 lbs. **Stock:** Hardwood, laminate, European Walnut. **Length:** 35.25" to 40.75" overall. **Features:** Detachable, steel magazine box with five-round capacity; steel trigger guard; chrome-plated bolt body; single stage trigger with manual two-position safety; buttplate; sling swivel studs (excluding Youth version); adjustable big game-style rifle sights; and dovetail-style receiver. Introduced 2006. Model Five Youth (22 LR) has 12.4-inch length of pull, 16.5-inch barrel, single-shot adapter. Model Five Laminate has weather-resistant brown laminate stock. Model Five European Walnut has classic satin-finish stock. Made in U.S.A. by Remington.

Price: Model Five Youth, 22 LR (2008). **$237.00**
Price: Model Five Laminate, 17 HMR (2008), 22 LR, 22 WMR **$363.00**
Price: Model Five European Walnut, 22 LR (2008) **$279.00**

ROSSI MATCHED PAIR SINGLE-SHOT RIFLE/SHOTGUN

Caliber: 17 HMR, 22 LR, 22 Mag. **Barrel:** 18.5" or 23". **Weight:** 6 lbs. **Stock:** Hardwood (brown or black finish). **Sights:** Fully adjustable front and rear. **Features:** Break-open breech, transfer-bar manual safety, includes matched 410-, 20 or 12 gauge shotgun barrel with bead front sight. Introduced 2001. Imported by BrazTech/Taurus.

Price: S121280RS **$160.00**
Price: S121780RS **$200.00**
Price: S122280RS **$160.00**
Price: S201780RS **$200.00**

RUGER K77/22 VARMINT RIFLE

Caliber: 22 LR, 10-shot, 22 WMR, 9-shot detachable rotary magazine. **Barrel:** 24", heavy. **Weight:** 7.25 lbs. **Length:** 43.25" overall. **Stock:** Laminated hardwood with rubber buttpad, quick-detachable swivel studs. **Sights:** None furnished. Comes with Ruger 1" scope rings. **Features:** Stainless steel or blued finish. Three-position safety, dual extractors. Stock has wide, flat forend. Introduced 1993.

Price: K77/22VBZ, 22 LR **$836.00**
Price: K77/22VMBZ, 22 WMR **$836.00**

RUGER 77/22 RIMFIRE BOLT-ACTION RIFLE

Caliber: 22 LR, 10-shot rotary magazine; 22 WMR, 9-shot rotary magazine. **Barrel:** 20". **Weight:** About 6 lbs. **Length:** 39.25" overall. **Stock:** Checkered American walnut, laminated hardwood, or synthetic stocks, stainless sling swivels. **Sights:** Plain barrel with 1" Ruger rings. **Features:** Mauser-type action uses Ruger's rotary magazine. Three-position safety, simplified bolt stop, patented bolt locking system. Uses the dual-screw barrel attachment system of the 10/22 rifle. Integral scope mounting system with 1" Ruger rings. Blued model introduced 1983. Stainless steel and blued with synthetic stock introduced 1989.

Price: 77/22R (no sights, rings, walnut stock). **$754.00**
Price: K77/22RP (stainless, no sights, rings, synthetic stock) . **$754.00**
Price: 77/22RM (22 WMR, blued, walnut stock) **$754.00**
Price: K77/22RMP (22 WMR, stainless, synthetic stock) **$754.00**

RUGER 77/17 RIMFIRE BOLT-ACTION RIFLE

Caliber: 17 HMR (9-shot rotary magazine. **Barrel:** 22" to 24". **Weight:** 6.5-7.5 lbs. **Length:** 41.25-43.25" overall. **Stock:** Checkered American walnut, laminated hardwood; stainless sling swivels. **Sights:** Plain barrel with 1" Ruger rings. **Features:** Mauser-type action uses Ruger's rotary magazine. Three-position safety, simplified bolt stop, patented bolt locking system. Uses the dual-screw barrel attachment system of the 10/22 rifle. Integral scope mounting system with 1" Ruger rings. Introduced 2002.

Price: 77/17-RM (no sights, rings, walnut stock) **$754.00**
Price: K77/17-VMBBZ (Target grey bbl, black laminate stock) **$836.00**

SAVAGE MARK I-G BOLT-ACTION RIFLE

Caliber: 22 LR, single shot. **Barrel:** 20.75". **Weight:** 5.5 lbs. **Length:** 39.5" overall. **Stock:** Walnut-finished hardwood with Monte Carlo-type comb, checkered grip and forend. **Sights:** Bead front, open adjustable rear. Receiver grooved for scope mounting. **Features:** Thumb-operated rotating safety. Blue finish. Rifled or smooth bore. Introduced 1990. Made in Canada, from Savage Arms Inc.

Price: Mark I-G, rifled or smooth bore, right- or left-handed . . . **$226.00**
Price: Mark I-GY (Youth), 19" barrel, 37" overall, 5 lbs. **$226.00**

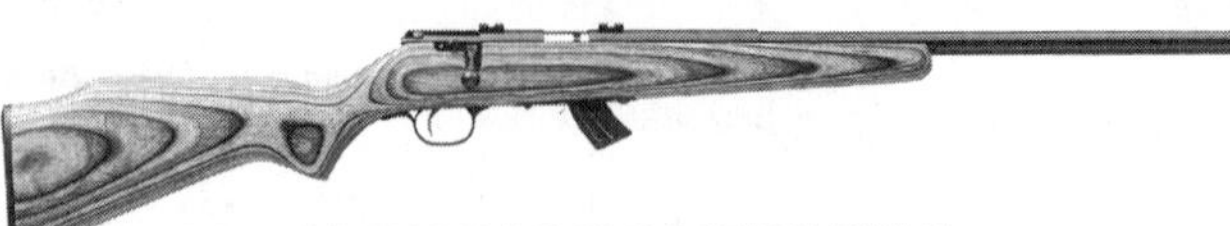

SAVAGE MARK II BOLT-ACTION RIFLE

Caliber: 22 LR, 10-shot magazine. **Barrel:** 20.5". **Weight:** 5.5 lbs. **Length:** 39.5" overall. **Stock:** Walnut-finished hardwood with Monte Carlo-type comb, checkered grip and forend. **Sights:** Bead front, open adjustable rear. Receiver grooved for scope mounting. **Features:** Thumb-operated rotating safety. Blue finish. Introduced 1990. Made in Canada, from Savage Arms, Inc.

Price: Mark II-BV. **$342.00**
Price: Mark II-GY (youth), 19" barrel, 37" overall, 5 lbs. **$226.00**
Price: Mark II-GL, left-hand **$226.00**
Price: Mark II-F, 17 HM2 . . . . **$202.00**
Price: Mark II XP Camo Scope Package (2008). **$400.00**
Price: Mark II Classic T, thumbhole walnut stock (2008) **$559.00**
Price: Mark II BTV: laminated thumbhole vent stock, AccuTrigger, blued receiver and bull barrel **$393.00**
Price: Mark II BVTS: stainless barrel/receiver; available in right- or left-hand (BTVLS) configuration . . . . **$393.00** (standard); **$441.00** (left hand)

Savage Mark II-FSS Stainless Rifle

Similar to the Mark II except has stainless steel barreled action and black synthetic stock with positive checkering, swivel studs, and 20.75" free-floating and button-rifled barrel with detachable magazine. Weighs 5.5 lbs. Introduced 1997. Imported from Canada by Savage Arms, Inc.

Price: **$273.00**

SAVAGE MODEL 93G MAGNUM BOLT-ACTION RIFLE

Caliber: 22 WMR, 5-shot magazine. **Barrel:** 20.75". **Weight:** 5.75 lbs. **Length:** 39.5" overall. **Stock:** Walnut-finished hardwood with Monte Carlo-type comb, checkered grip and forend. **Sights:** Bead front, adjustable open rear. Receiver grooved for scope mount. **Features:** Thumb-operated rotary safety. Blue finish. Introduced 1994. Made in Canada, from Savage Arms.

Price: Model 93G **$260.00**
Price: Model 93F (as above with black graphite/fiberglass stock) **$241.00**
Price: Model 93 Classic, American walnut stock (2008). **$566.00**
Price: Model 93 Classic T, American walnut thumbhole stock (2008) **$604.00**

Savage Model 93FSS Magnum Rifle

Similar to Model 93G except stainless steel barreled action and black synthetic stock with positive checkering. Weighs 5.5 lbs. Introduced 1997. Imported from Canada by Savage Arms, Inc.

Price: **$306.00**

Savage Model 93FVSS Magnum Rifle

Similar to Model 93FSS Magnum except 21" heavy barrel with recessed target-style crown, satin-finished stainless barreled action, black graphite/fiberglass stock. Drilled and tapped

 Prices given are believed to be accurate at time of publication however, many factors affect retail pricing so exact prices are not possible.

for scope mounting; comes with Weaver-style bases. Introduced 1998. Imported from Canada by Savage Arms, Inc.

Price: **$347.00**

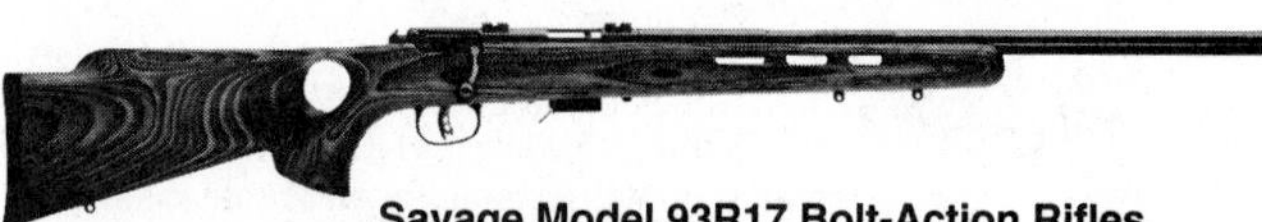

Savage Model 93R17 Bolt-Action Rifles

Similar to Model 93G Magnum but chambered in 17 HMR. Features include standard synthetic, hardwood or walnut stock or thumbhole stock with cheekpiece, 21" or 22" barrel, no sights, detachable box magazine.

Price: Model 93R17BTV: Laminted ventilated thumbhole stock, blued barrel/receiver **$393.00**
Price: Model 93R17BV: Standard brown laminate stock, heavy barrel **$342.00**
Price: Model 93R17GV: Checkered hardwood stock **$278.00**
Price: Model 93R17GLV: Left-hand configuration **$278.00**
Price: Model 93R17 Classic T: Checkered walnut thumbhole stock with unvented forend, blued barrel/receiver **$559.00**
Price: Model 93R17 Classic: Standard walnut stock **$559.00**
Price: Model 93R17BTVS: Laminated thumbhole vent stock, stainless steel barrel and receiver **$441.00**
Price: Model 93R17BLTVS: Left-hand **$441.00**
Price: Model 93R17BVSS: Similar to Model 93R17BTVS but with gray laminated non-thumbhole stock **$411.00**
Price: Model 93R17FVS: Black synthetic stock, AccuTrigger, blued or stainless heavy barrel **$347.00**

SAVAGE MODEL 30G STEVENS "FAVORITE"

Caliber: 22 LR, 22 WMR Model 30GM, 17 HMR Model 30R17. **Barrel:** 21". **Weight:** 4.25 lbs. **Length:** 36.75". **Stock:** Walnut, straight grip, Schnabel forend. **Sights:** Adjustable rear, bead post front. **Features:** Lever action falling block, inertia firing pin system, Model 30G half octagonal barrel, Model 30GM full octagonal barrel.

Price: Model 30G **$344.00**
Price: Model 30 Takedown **$360.00**

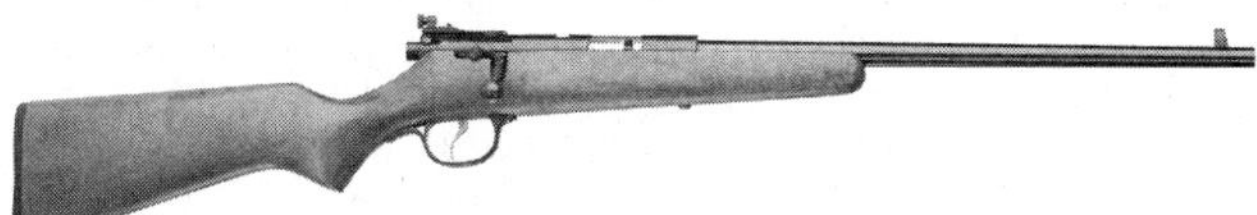

SAVAGE CUB T MINI YOUTH

Caliber: 22 S, L, LR; 17 Mach 2. **Barrel:** 16". **Weight:** 3.5 lbs. **Length:** 33". **Stock:** Walnut finished hardwood thumbhole stock. **Sights:** Bead post, front; peep, rear. **Features:** Mini single-shot bolt action, free-floating button-rifled barrel, blued finish. From Savage Arms.

Price: Cub T Thumbhole, walnut stained laminated **$266.00**
Price: Cub T Pink Thumbhole (2008) **$280.00**

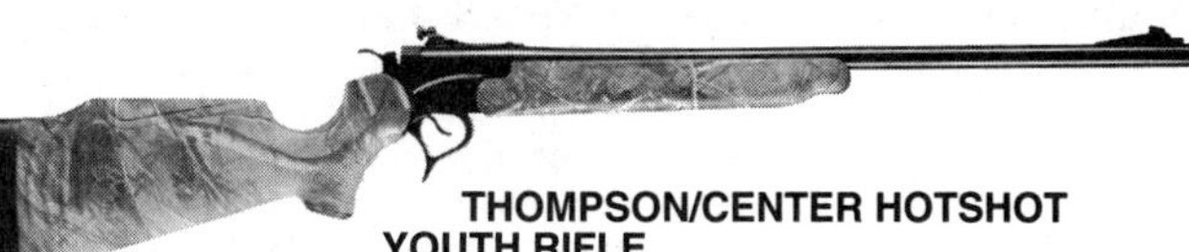

THOMPSON/CENTER HOTSHOT YOUTH RIFLE

Single-shot dropping-barrel rifle chambered in .22 Long Rifle. Features include a crowned 19-inch steel barrel, exposed hammer, synthetic forend and buttstock, peep sight (receiver drilled and tapped for optics), three stock pattern options (black, Realtree AP and pink AP). Overall weight 3 lbs., 11.5-inch length of pull.

Price: . . . . **$229.00 to $249.00**

WINCHESTER WILDCAT BOLT ACTION 22

Caliber: 22 S, L, LR; one 5-round and three 10-round magazines. **Barrel:** 21". **Weight:** 6.5 lbs. **Length:** 38-3/8". **Stock:** Checkered hardwood stock, checkered black synthetic Winchester buttplate, Schnabel fore-end. **Sights:** Bead post, front; buckhorn rear. **Features:** Steel sling swivel studs, blued finish. Wildcat Target/Varmint rifle has .866" diameter bull barrel. Receiver drilled, tapped, and grooved for bases. Adjustable trigger, dual front steel swivel studs. Reintroduced 2008. From Winchester Repeating Arms.

Price: **$259.00**
Price: Wildcat/Varmint **$309.00**

ANSCHUTZ 1903 MATCH RIFLE
Caliber: 22 LR, single shot. **Barrel:** 21.25". **Weight:** 8 lbs. **Length:** 43.75" overall. **Stock:** Walnut-finished hardwood with adjustable cheekpiece; stippled grip and forend. **Sights:** None furnished. **Features:** Uses Anschutz Match 64 action. A medium weight rifle for intermediate and advanced Junior Match competition. Available from Champion's Choice.
Price: Right-hand **$965.00**

ANSCHUTZ 64-MP R SILHOUETTE RIFLE
Caliber: 22 LR, 5-shot magazine. **Barrel:** 21.5", medium heavy; 7/8" diameter. **Weight:** 8 lbs. **Length:** 39.5" overall. **Stock:** Walnut-finished hardwood, silhouette-type. **Sights:** None furnished. **Features:** Uses Match 64 action. Designed for metallic silhouette competition. Stock has stippled checkering, contoured thumb groove with Wundhammer swell. Two-stage #5098 trigger. Slide safety locks sear and bolt. Introduced 1980. Available from Champion's Choice.
Price: 64-MP R **$950.00**
Price: 64-S BR Benchrest (2008) **$1,175.00**

Anschutz 2007 Match Rifle
Uses same action as the Model 2013, but has a lighter barrel. European walnut stock in right-hand, true left-hand or extra-short models. Sights optional. Available with 19.6" barrel with extension tube, or 26", both in stainless or blue. Introduced 1998. Available from Champion's Choice.
Price: Right-hand, blue, no sights **$2,410.90**

ANSCHUTZ 1827BT FORTNER BIATHLON RIFLE
Caliber: 22 LR, 5-shot magazine. **Barrel:** 21.7". **Weight:** 8.8 lbs. with sights. **Length:** 40.9" overall. **Stock:** European walnut with cheekpiece, stippled pistol grip and forend. **Sights:** Optional globe front specially designed for Biathlon shooting, micrometer rear with hinged snow cap. **Features:** Uses Super Match 54 action and nine-way adjustable trigger; adjustable wooden buttplate, biathlon butthook, adjustable hand-stop rail. Uses Anschutz/Fortner system straight-pull bolt action, blued or stainless steel barrel. Introduced 1982. Available from Champion's Choice.
Price: Nitride finish with sights, about **$2,895.00**

ANSCHUTZ SUPER MATCH SPECIAL MODEL 2013 RIFLE
Caliber: 22 LR, single shot. **Barrel:** 25.9". **Weight:** 13 lbs. **Length:** 41.7" to 42.9". **Stock:** Adjustable aluminum. **Sights:** None furnished. **Features:** 2313 aluminum-silver/blue stock, 500mm barrel, fast lock time, adjustable cheek piece, heavy action and muzzle tube, w/handstop and standing riser block. Introduced in 1997. Available from Champion's Choice.
Price: Right-hand **$3,195.00**

ANSCHUTZ 1912 SPORT RIFLE
Caliber: 22 LR. **Barrel:** 26" match. **Weight:** 11.4 lbs. **Length:** 41.7" overall. **Stock:** Non-stained thumbhole stock adjustable in length with adjustable butt plate and cheek piece adjustment. Flat forend raiser block 4856 adjustable in height. Hook butt plate. **Sights:** None furnished. **Features:** "Free rifle" for women. Smallbore model 1907 with 1912 **stock:** Match 54 action. Delivered with: Hand stop 6226, forend raiser block 4856, screw driver, instruction leaflet with test target. Available from Champion's Choice.
Price: **$2,595.00**

Anschutz 1913 Super Match Rifle
Same as the Model 1911 except European walnut International-type stock with adjustable cheekpiece, or color laminate, both available with straight or lowered forend, adjustable aluminum hook buttplate, adjustable hand stop, weighs 13 lbs., 46" overall. Stainless or blue barrel. Available from Champion's Choice.
Price: Right-hand, blue, no sights, walnut stock **$2,695.00**

Anschutz 1907 Standard Match Rifle
Same action as Model 1913 but with 7/8" diameter 26" barrel (stainless or blue). Length is 44.5" overall, weighs 10.5 lbs. Choice

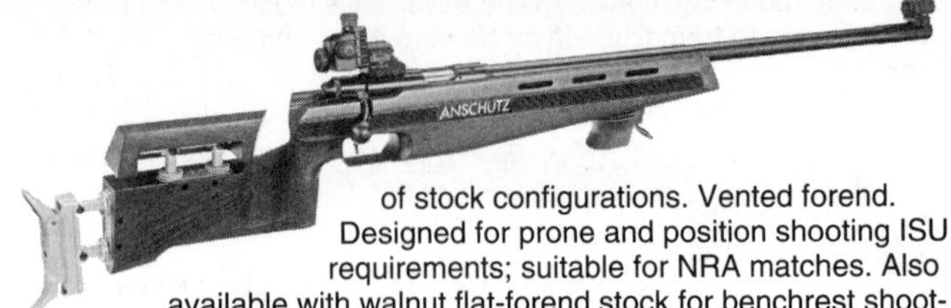

of stock configurations. Vented forend. Designed for prone and position shooting ISU requirements; suitable for NRA matches. Also available with walnut flat-forend stock for benchrest shooting. Available from Champion's Choice.
Price: Right-hand, blue, no sights **$1,655.00**

ARMALITE AR-10(T) RIFLE
Caliber: 308 Win., 10-shot magazine. **Barrel:** 24" target-weight Rock 5R custom. **Weight:** 10.4 lbs. **Length:** 43.5" overall. **Stock:** Green or black composition; N.M. fiberglass handguard tube. **Sights:** Detachable handle, front sight, or scope mount available. Comes with international-style flattop receiver with Picatinny rail. **Features:** National Match two-stage trigger. Forged upper receiver. Receivers hard-coat anodized. Introduced 1995. Made in U.S.A. by ArmaLite, Inc.
Price: Black **$1,912.00**
Price: AR-10, 338 Federal **$1,912.00**

ARMALITE M15A4(T) EAGLE EYE RIFLE
Caliber: 223 Rem., 10-round magazine. **Barrel:** 24" heavy stainless; 1:8" twist. **Weight:** 9.2 lbs. **Length:** 42-3/8" overall. **Stock:** Green or black butt, N.M. fiberglass handguard tube. **Sights:** One-piece international-style flattop receiver with Weaver-type rail, including case deflector. **Features:** Detachable carry handle, front sight and scope mount (30mm or 1") available. Upper and lower receivers have push-type pivot pin, hard coat anodized. Made in U.S.A. by ArmaLite, Inc.
Price: Green or black furniture **$1,296.00**

ARMALITE M15 A4 CARBINE 6.8 & 7.62X39
Caliber: 6.8 Rem, 7.62x39. **Barrel:** 16" chrome-lined with flash suppressor. **Weight:** 7 lbs. **Length:** 26.6". **Features:** Front and rear picatinny rails for mounting optics, two-stage tactical trigger, anodized aluminum/phosphate finish.
Price: **$1,107.00**

BLASER R93 LONG RANGE SPORTER 2 RIFLE
Caliber: 308 Win., 10-shot detachable box magazine. **Barrel:** 24". **Weight:** 10.4 lbs. **Length:** 44" overall. **Stock:** Aluminum with synthetic lining. **Sights:** None furnished; accepts detachable scope mount. **Features:** Straight-pull bolt action with adjustable trigger; fully adjustable stock; quick takedown; corrosion resistant finish. Introduced 1998. Imported from Germany by Blaser USA.
Price: **$3,848.00**

BUSHMASTER A2/A3 TARGET RIFLE
Caliber: 5.56mm, 223 Rem., 30-round magazine **Barrel:** 20", 24". **Weight:** 8.43 lbs. (A2); 8.78 lbs. (A3). **Length:** 39.5" overall (20" barrel). **Stock:** Black composition; A2 type. **Sights:** Adjustable post front, adjustable aperture rear.

Prices given are believed to be accurate at time of publication however, many factors affect retail pricing so exact prices are not possible.

Features: Patterned after Colt M-16A2. Chrome-lined barrel with manganese phosphate exterior. Available in stainless barrel. Made in U.S.A. by Bushmaster Firearms Co.
Price: (A3 type) $1,135.00

BUSHMASTER DCM-XR COMPETITION RIFLE

Caliber: 5.56mm, 223 Rem., 10-round magazine. **Barrel:** 20" extra-heavy (1" diameter) barrel with 1.8" twist for heavier competition bullets. **Weight:** About 12 lbs. with balance weights. **Length:** 38.5". **Stock:** NA. **Sights:** A2 rear sight. **Features:** Has special competition rear sight with interchangeable apertures, extra-fine 1/2- or 1/4-MOA windage and elevation adjustments; specially ground front sight post in choice of three widths. Full-length handguards over free-floater barrel tube. Introduced 1998. Made in U.S.A. by Bushmaster Firearms, Inc.
Price: A2. . . . . $1,150.00
Price: A3 . . . . $1,250.00

BUSHMASTER VARMINTER RIFLE

Caliber: 5.56mm. **Barrel:** 24", fluted. **Weight:** 8.4 lbs. **Length:** 42.25" overall. **Stock:** Black composition, A2 type. **Sights:** None furnished; upper receiver has integral scope mount base. **Features:** Chrome-lined .950" extra heavy barrel with counter-bored crown, manganese phosphate finish, free-floating aluminum handguard, forged aluminum receivers with push-pin takedown, hard anodized mil-spec finish. Competition trigger optional. Made in U.S.A. by Bushmaster Firearms, Inc.
Price: $1,360.00

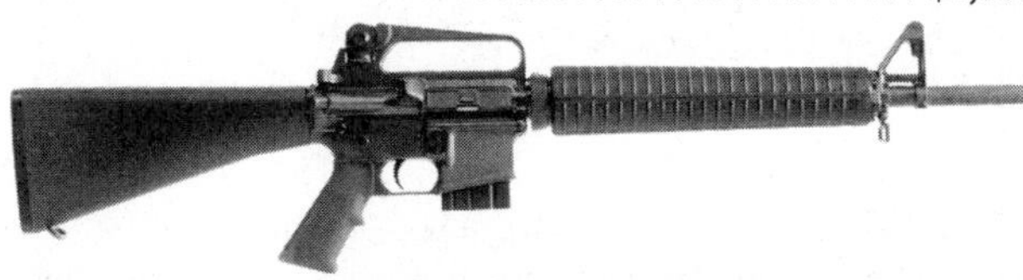

COLT MATCH TARGET HBAR & M4 RIFLES

Caliber: 223 Rem. **Barrel:** 20". **Weight:** 8 lbs. **Length:** 39" overall. **Stock:** Synthetic. **Sights:** Front: elevation adj. post; rear: 800-meter, aperture adj. for windage and elevation. **Features:** Heavy barrel, rate of rifling twist 1:7. Introduced 1991. Made in U.S.A. by Colt. M4 variant has 16.1" barrel.
Price: Model MT6601, MT6601C $1,183.00
Price: Model 6400C $1,289.00

Colt Match Target Competition HBAR Rifle

Similar to the Match Target except has removable carry handle for scope mounting, 1:9" rifling twist, 9-round magazine. Weighs 8.5 lbs. Introduced 1991.
Price: Model MT6700C $1,250.00

Colt Match Target Competition HBAR II Rifle

Similar to the Match Target Competition HBAR except has 16:1" barrel, overall length 34.5", and weighs 7.1 lbs. Introduced 1995.
Price: Model MT6731 . . . . $1,172.00

Colt Accurized Rifle

Similar to the Match Target Model except has 24" barrel. Features flat-top receiver for scope mounting, stainless steel heavy barrel, tubular handguard, and free-floating barrel. Matte black finish. Weighs 9.25 lbs. Made in U.S.A. by Colt's Mfg. Co., Inc.
Price: Model CR6724 . . . . $1,334.00

EAA/HW 660 MATCH RIFLE

Caliber: 22 LR. **Barrel:** 26". **Weight:** 10.7 lbs. **Length:** 45.3" overall. **Stock:** Match-type walnut with adjustable cheekpiece and buttplate. **Sights:** Globe front, match aperture rear. **Features:** Adjustable match trigger; stippled pistol grip and forend; forend accessory rail. Introduced 1991. Imported from Germany by European American Armory.
Price: About $999.00
Price: With laminate stock $1,159.00

ED BROWN MODEL 704, M40A2 MARINE SNIPER

Caliber: 308 Win., 30-06 Springfield. **Barrel:** Match-grade 24". **Weight:** 9.25 lbs. **Stock:** Hand bedded McMillan GP fiberglass tactical stock with recoil pad in special Woodland Camo molded-in colors. **Sights:** None furnished. Leupold Mark 4 30mm scope mounts with heavy-duty screws. **Features:** Steel trigger guard, hinged floor plate, three position safety.
Price: From. $3,695.00

OLYMPIC ARMS SM SERVICEMATCH AR15 RIFLES

Caliber: 223 Rem. minimum SAAMI spec, 30-shot magazine. **Barrel:** 20" broach-cut Ultramatch stainless steel 1x8 twist rate. **Weight:** 10 lbs. **Length:** 39.5" overall. **Stock:** A2 grip, A2 buttstock with trapdoor. **Sights:** A2 NM rear, elevation adjustable front post. **Features:** DCM-ready AR15, free-floating handguard looks standard, A2 upper, threaded muzzle, flash suppressor. Premium model adds pneumatic recoil buffer, Bob Jones interchangeable sights, two-stage trigger and Turner Saddlery sling. Made in U.S.A. by Olympic Arms, Inc.
Price: SM-1, 20" DCM ready $1,272.70
Price: SM-1P, Premium 20" DCM ready. $1,727.70

OLYMPIC ARMS UM ULTRAMATCH AR15 RIFLES

Caliber: 223 Rem. minimum SAAMI spec, 30-shot magazine. **Barrel:** 20" or 24" bull broach-cut Ultramatch stainless steel 1x10 twist rate. **Weight:** 8-10 lbs. **Length:** 38.25" overall. **Stock:** A2 grip, A2 buttstock with trapdoor. **Sights:** None, flat-top upper and gas block with rails. **Features:** Flat top upper, free floating tubular match handguard, Picatinny gas block, crowned muzzle, factory trigger job and "Ultramatch" pantograph. Premium model adds pneumatic recoil buffer, Harris S-series bipod, hand selected premium receivers and William Set Trigger. Made in U.S.A. by Olympic Arms, Inc.
Price: UM-1, 20" Ultramatch. $1,332.50
Price: UM-1P $1,805.70

OLYMPIC ARMS ML-1/ML-2 MULTIMATCH AR15 CARBINES

Caliber: 223 Rem. minimum SAAMI spec, 30-shot magazine. **Barrel:** 16" broach-cut Ultramatch stainless steel 1x10 twist rate. **Weight:** 7-8 lbs. **Length:** 34-36" overall. **Stock:** A2 grip and varying buttstock. **Sights:** None. **Features:** The ML-1 includes A2 upper

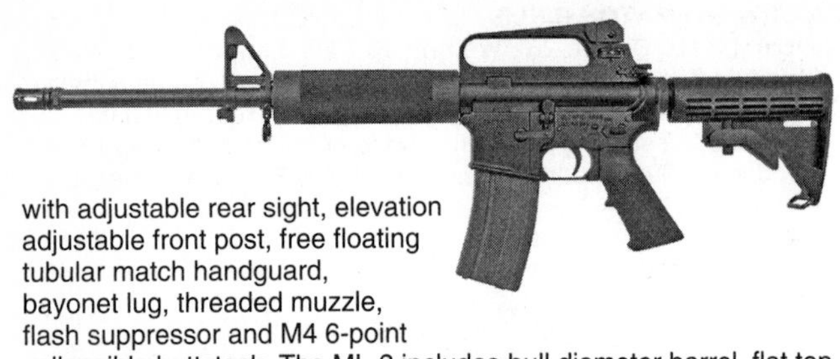

with adjustable rear sight, elevation adjustable front post, free floating tubular match handguard, bayonet lug, threaded muzzle, flash suppressor and M4 6-point collapsible buttstock. The ML-2 includes bull diameter barrel, flat top upper, free floating tubular match handguard, Picatinny gas block, crowned muzzle and A2 buttstock with trapdoor. Made in U.S.A. by Olympic Arms, Inc.

Price: ML-1 or ML-2 . . . . **$1,188.20**

OLYMPIC ARMS K8 TARGETMATCH AR15 RIFLES

Caliber: 5.56 NATO, 223 WSSM, 243 WSSM, .25 WSSM 30/7-shot magazine. **Barrel:** 20", 24" bull button-rifled stainless/chrome-moly steel 1x9/1x10 twist rate. **Weight:** 8-10 lbs. **Length:** 38"-42" overall. **Stock:** A2 grip, A2 buttstock with trapdoor. **Sights:** None. **Features:** Barrel has satin bead-blast finish; flat-top upper, free-floating tubular match handguard, Picatinny gas block, crowned muzzle and "Targetmatch" pantograph on lower receiver. K8-MAG model uses Winchester Super Short Magnum cartridges. Includes 24" bull chrome-moly barrel, flat-top upper, free-floating tubular match handguard, Picatinny gas block, crowned muzzle and 7-shot magazine. Made in U.S.A. by Olympic Arms, Inc.

Price: K8 . . . .**$908.70**
Price: K8-MAG **$1,363.70**

REMINGTON 40-XB RANGEMASTER TARGET CENTERFIRE

Caliber: 15 calibers from 220 Swift to 300 Win. Mag. **Barrel:** 27.25". **Weight:** 11.25 lbs. **Length:** 47" overall. **Stock:** American walnut, laminated thumbhole or Kevlar with high comb and beavertail forend stop. Rubber non-slip buttplate. **Sights:** None. Scope blocks installed. **Features:** Adjustable trigger. Stainless barrel and action. Receiver drilled and tapped for sights. Model 40-XB Tactical (2008) chambered in 308 Win., comes with guarantee of 0.75-inch maximum 5-shot groups at 100 yards. **Weight:** 10.25 lbs. Includes Teflon-coated stainless button-rifled barrel, 1:14 twist, 27.25 inch long, three longitudinal flutes. Bolt-action repeater, adjustable 40-X trigger and precision machined aluminum bedding block. Stock is H-S Precision Pro Series synthetic tactical stock, black with green web finish, vertical pistol grip. From Remington Custom Shop.

Price: 40-XB KS, aramid fiber stock, single shot **$2,780.00**
Price: 40-XB KS, aramid fiber stock, repeater **$2,634.00**
Price: 40-XB Tactical 308 Win. (2008) **$2,927.00**
Price: 40-XB Thumbhole Repeater. **$2,927.00**

REMINGTON 40-XBBR KS

Caliber: Five calibers from 22 BR to 308 Win. **Barrel:** 20" (light varmint class), 24" (heavy varmint class). **Weight:** 7.25 lbs. (light varmint class); 12 lbs. (heavy varmint class). **Length:** 38" (20" bbl.), 42" (24"bbl.). **Stock:** Aramid fiber. **Sights:** None. Supplied with scope blocks. **Features:** Unblued benchrest with stainless steel barrel, trigger adjustable from 1-1/2 lbs. to 3.5 lbs. Special two-oz. trigger extra cost. Scope and mounts extra.

Price: Single shot **$3,806.00**

REMINGTON 40-XC KS TARGET RIFLE

Caliber: 7.62 NATO, 5-shot. **Barrel:** 24", stainless steel. **Weight:** 11 lbs. without sights. **Length:** 43.5" overall. **Stock:** Aramid fiber. **Sights:** None furnished. **Features:** Designed to meet the needs of competitive shooters. Stainless steel barrel and action.

Price: **$3,000.00**

REMINGTON 40-XR CUSTOM SPORTER

Caliber: 22 LR, 22 WM. **Barrel:** 24" stainless steel, no sights. **Weight:** 9.75 lbs. **Length:** 40". **Features:** Model XR-40 Target rifle action. Many options available in stock, decoration or finish.

Price: Single shot **$4,391.00**

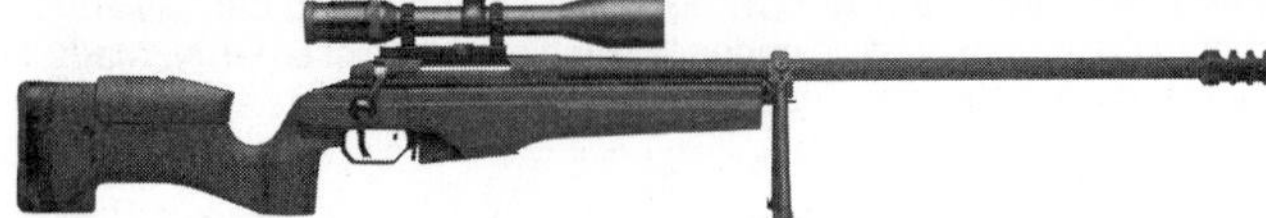

Price: 40-XRBR KS, bench rest 22 LR . **$2,927.00**

SAKO TRG-22 BOLT-ACTION RIFLE

Caliber: 308 Win., 10-shot magazine. **Barrel:** 26". **Weight:** 10.25 lbs. **Length:** 45.25" overall. **Stock:** Reinforced polyurethane with fully adjustable cheekpiece and buttplate. **Sights:** None furnished. Optional quick-detachable, one-piece scope mount base, 1" or 30mm rings. **Features:** Resistance-free bolt, free-floating heavy stainless barrel, 60-degree bolt lift. Two-stage trigger is adjustable for length, pull, horizontal or vertical pitch. Introduced 2000. Imported from Finland by Beretta USA.

Price: TRG-22 folding stock **$4,560.00**

SPRINGFIELD ARMORY M1A SUPER MATCH

Caliber: 308 Win. **Barrel:** 22", heavy Douglas Premium. **Weight:** About 11 lbs. **Length:** 44.31" overall. **Stock:** Heavy walnut competition stock with longer pistol grip, contoured area behind the rear sight, thicker butt and forend, glass bedded. **Sights:** National Match front and rear. **Features:** Has figure-eight-style operating rod guide. Introduced 1987. From Springfield Armory.

Price: About **$2,479.00**

Springfield Armory M1A/M-21 Tactical Model Rifle

Similar to M1A Super Match except special sniper stock with adjustable cheekpiece and rubber recoil pad. Weighs 11.6 lbs. From Springfield Armory.

Price: . . . .

$2,975.00

SPRINGFIELD ARMORY M-1 GARAND AMERICAN COMBAT RIFLES

Caliber: 30-06 Spfl., 308 Win., 8-shot. **Barrel:** 24". **Weight:** 9.5 lbs. **Length:** 43.6". **Stock:** American walnut. **Sights:** Military square post front, military aperture, MOA adjustable rear. **Features:** Limited production, certificate of authenticity, all new receiver, barrel and stock with remaining parts USGI mil-spec. Two-stage military trigger.

Price: About **$2,479.00**

STONER SR-15 MATCH RIFLE

Caliber: 223. **Barrel:** 20". **Weight:** 7.9 lbs. **Length:** 38" overall. **Stock:** Black synthetic. **Sights:** None furnished; flattop upper receiver for scope mounting. **Features:** Short Picatinny rail, two-stage match trigger. Introduced 1998. Made in U.S.A. by Knight's Mfg. Co.

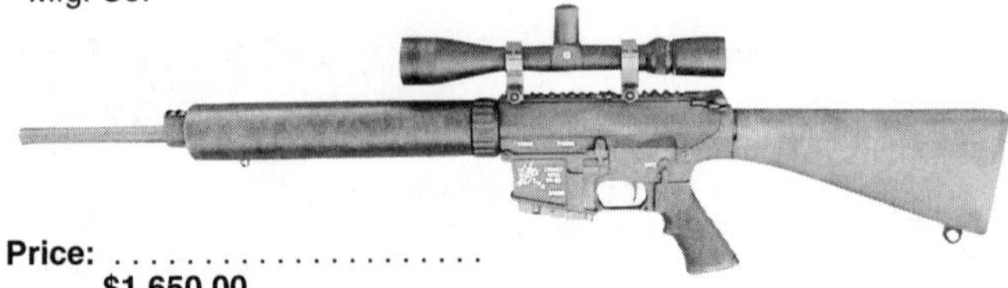

Price: . . . .
$1,650.00

Prices given are believed to be accurate at time of publication however, many factors affect retail pricing so exact prices are not possible.

STONER SR-25 MATCH RIFLE

Caliber: 7.62 NATO, 10-shot steel magazine, 5-shot optional. **Barrel:** 24" heavy match; 1:11.25" twist. **Weight:** 10.75 lbs. **Length:** 44" overall. **Stock:** Black synthetic AR-15A2 design. Full floating forend of mil-spec synthetic attaches to upper receiver at a single point. **Sights:** None furnished. Has integral Weaver-style rail. Rings and iron sights optional. **Features:** Improved AR-15 trigger, AR-15-style seven-lug rotating bolt. Introduced 1993. Made in U.S.A. by Knight's Mfg. Co.

Price: **$3,345.00**

Price: SR-25 Lightweight Match (20" medium match target contour barrel, 9.5 lbs., 40" overall) **$3,345.00**

TIME PRECISION 22 RF BENCH REST RIFLE

Caliber: 22 LR, single shot. **Barrel:** Shilen match-grade stainless. **Weight:** 10 lbs. with scope. **Length:** NA. **Stock:** Fiberglass. Pillar bedded. **Sights:** None furnished. **Features:** Shilen match trigger removable trigger bracket, full-length steel sleeve, aluminum receiver. Introduced 2008. Made in U.S.A. by Time Precision.

Price: **$2,200.00**

BENELLI LEGACY SHOTGUN

Gauge: 12, 20, 2-3/4" and 3" chamber. **Barrel:** 24", 26", 28" (Full, Mod., Imp. Cyl., Imp. Mod., cylinder choke tubes). Mid-bead sight. **Weight:** 5.8 to 7.4 lbs. **Length:** 49-5/8" overall (28" barrel). **Stock:** Select AA European walnut with satin finish. **Features:** Uses the rotating bolt inertia recoil operating system with a two-piece steel/aluminum etched receiver (bright on lower, blue upper). Drop adjustment kit allows the stock to be custom fitted without modifying the stock. Introduced 1998. Ultralight model has gloss-blued finish receiver. Weight is 6.0 lbs., 24" barrel, 45.5" overall length. WeatherCoat walnut stock. Introduced 2006. Imported from Italy by Benelli USA, Corp.

Price: Legacy **$1,689.00**
Price: Sport (2008) **$2,269.00**

BENELLI ULTRA LIGHT SHOTGUN

Gauge: 12, 20, 3" chamber. **Barrel:** 28". Mid-bead sight. **Weight:** 5.2 to 6 lbs. **Features:** Similar to Legacy line. Drop adjustment kit allows the stock to be custom fitted without modifying the stock. WeatherCoat walnut stock. Lightened receiver, shortened magazine tube, carbon-fiber rib and grip cap. Introduced 2008. Imported from Italy by Benelli USA, Corp.

Price: 12 gauge. **$1,539.00**

BENELLI M2 FIELD SHOTGUNS

Gauge: 20 ga., 12 ga., 3" chamber. **Barrel:** 21", 24", 26", 28". **Weight:** 5.4 to 7.2 lbs. **Length:** 42.5 to 49.5" overall. **Stock:** Synthetic, Advantage Max-4 HD, Advantage Timber HD, APG HD. **Sights:** Red bar. **Features:** Uses the Inertia Driven bolt mechanism. Vent rib. Comes with set of five choke tubes. Imported from Italy by Benelli USA.

Price: Synthetic ComforTech gel recoil pad **$1,319.00**
Price: Camo ComforTech gel recoil pad. **$1,335.00**
Price: Satin walnut **$1,229.00**
Price: Rifled slug synthetic **$1,380.00**
Price: Camo turkey model w/SteadyGrip stock **$1,429.00**
Price: Realtree APG HD ComforTech stock (2007) **$1,429.00**
Price: Realtree APG HD ComforTech 20 ga. (2007) **$1,429.00**
Price: Realtree APG HD LH ComforTech (2007) **$1,429.00**
Price: Realtree APG HD ComforTech Slug (2007). **$1,429.00**
Price: Realtree APG HD w/SteadyGrip stock (2007) **$1,429.00**
Price: Black Synthetic Grip Tight 20 ga. (2007) **$1,319.00**

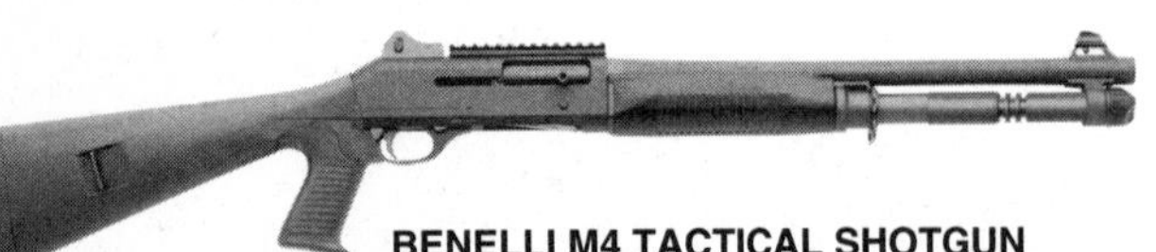

BENELLI M4 TACTICAL SHOTGUN

Gauge: 12 ga., 3" chamber. **Barrel:** 18.5". **Weight:** 7.8 lbs. **Length:** 40" overall. **Stock:** Synthetic. **Sights:** Ghost Ring rear, fixed blade front. **Features:** Auto-regulating gas-operated (ARGO) action, choke tube, Picatinny rail, standard and collapsible stocks available, optional LE tactical gun case. Introduced 2006. Imported from Italy by Benelli USA.

Price: Pistol grip stock, black synthetic. **$1,699.00**
Price: Desert camo pistol grip (2007) **$1,829.00**

BENELLI MONTEFELTRO SHOTGUNS

Gauge: 12 and 20 ga. Full, Imp. Mod, Mod., Imp. Cyl., Cyl. choke tubes. **Barrel:** 24", 26", 28". **Weight:** 5.3 to 7.1 lbs. **Stock:** Checkered walnut with satin finish. **Length:** 43.6 to 49.5" overall. **Features:** Uses the Inertia Driven rotating bolt system with a simple inertia recoil design. Finish is blue. Introduced 1987.

Price: 24", 26", 28" **$1,219.00**
Price: Left hand. **$1,229.00**
Price: 20 ga. **$1,219.00**
Price: 20 ga. short stock (LOP: 12.5") **$1,120.00**
Price: Silver (AA walnut; nickel-blue receiver) **$1,649.00**
Price: Silver 20 ga. **$1,649.00**

BENELLI SUPER BLACK EAGLE II SHOTGUNS

Gauge: 12, 3-1/2" chamber. **Barrel:** 24", 26", 28" (Cyl. Imp. Cyl., Mod., Imp. Mod., Full choke tubes). **Weight:** 7.1 to 7.3 lbs. **Length:** 45.6 to 49.6" overall. **Stock:** European walnut with satin finish, polymer, or camo. Adjustable for drop. **Sights:** Red bar front. **Features:** Uses Benelli inertia recoil bolt system. Vent rib. Advantage Max-4 HD, Advantage Timber HD camo patterns. Features ComforTech stock. Introduced 1991. Left-hand models available. Imported from Italy by Benelli USA.

Price: Satin walnut, non-ComforTech. **$1,549.00**
Price: Camo stock, ComforTech gel recoil pad **$1,759.00**
Price: Black Synthetic stock **$1,649.00**
Price: Max-4 HD Camo stock **$1,759.00**
Price: Timber HD turkey model w/SteadyGrip stock. **$1,680.00**
Price: Realtree APG HD w/ComforTech stock (2007) **$1,759.00**
Price: Realtree APG HD LH ComforTech stock (2007) **$1,759.00**
Price: Realtree APG HD Slug Gun (2007) **$1,730.00**

BENELLI CORDOBA SHOTGUN

Gauge: 20; 12; 3" chamber. **Barrel:** 28" and 30", ported, 10mm sporting rib. **Weight:** 7.2 to 7.3 lbs. **Length:** 49.6 to 51.6". **Features:** Designed for high-volume sporting clays and Argentina dove shooting. Inertia-driven action, Extended Sport CrioChokes, 4+1 capacity. Ported. Imported from Italy by Benelli USA.

Price: Black synthetic GripTight ComforTech stock **$1,869.00**
Price: Black synthetic GripTight ComforTech stock, 20 ga., (2007) **$1,869.00**
Price: Max-4 HD ComforTech stock (2007) **$2,039.00**

BENELLI SUPERSPORT & SPORT II SHOTGUNS

Gauge: 20; 12; 3" chamber. **Barrel:** 28" and 30", ported, 10mm sporting rib. **Weight:** 7.2 to 7.3 lbs. **Length:** 49.6 to 51.6". **Stock:** Carbon fiber, ComforTech (Supersport) or walnut (Sport II). **Sights:** Red bar front, metal midbead. Sport II is similar to the Legacy model except has nonengraved dual tone blue/silver receiver, ported wide-rib barrel, adjustable buttstock, and functions with all loads. Walnut stock with satin finish. Introduced 1997. **Features:** Designed for high-volume sporting clays. Inertia-driven action, Extended CrioChokes, 4+1 capacity. Ported. Imported from Italy by Benelli USA.

Price: Carbon fiber ComforTech stock **$1,979.00**
Price: Carbon fiber ComforTech stock, 20 ga. (2007) **$1,979.00**
Price: Sport II 20 ga. (2007) **$1,699.00**

BENELLI VINCI

Gas-operated semiauto shotgun chambered for 2-3/4- and 3-inch 12-gauge. Features include modular disassembly; interchangeable choke tubes; 24- to 28-inch ribbed barrel; black, MAX-4HD or APG HD finish; synthetic contoured stocks; optional Steady-Grip model;. Weight 6.7 to 6.9 lbs.

Price: . . . . **$1379.00 to $1599.00**

BENELLI LEGACY SPORT

Gas-operated semiauto shotgun chambered for 12, 20 (2-3/4- and 3-inch) gauge. Features include Inertia Driven system; sculptured lower receiver with classic game scene etchings; highly polished

 Prices given are believed to be accurate at time of publication however, many factors affect retail pricing so exact prices are not possible.

blued upper receiver; AA-Grade walnut stock; gel recoil pad; ported 24- or 26-inch barrel, Crio chokes. Weight 7.4 to 7.5 lbs.

Price: **$2,369.00**

BERETTA 3901 SHOTGUNS

Gauge: 12, 20 gauge; 3" chamber, semiauto. **Barrel:** 26", 28". **Weight:** 6.55 lbs. (20 ga.), 7.2 lbs. (12 ga.). **Length:** NA. **Stock:** Wood, X-tra wood (special process wood enhancement), and polymer. **Features:** Based on A390 shotgun introduced in 1996. Mobilchokes, removable trigger group. 3901 Target RL uses gas operating system; Sporting style flat rib with steel front bead and mid-bead, walnut stock and forearm, satin matte finish, adjustable LOP from 12P13", adjustable for cast on/off, Beretta's Memory System II to adjust the parallel comb. Weighs 7.2 lbs. 3901 Citizen has polymer stock. 3901 Statesman has basic wood and checkering treatment. 3901 Ambassador has X-tra wood stock and fore end; high-polished receiver with engraving, Gel-Tek recoil pad, optional TruGlo fiber-optic front sight. 3901 Rifled Slug Shotgun has black high-impact synthetic stock and fore end, 24" barrel,1:28 twist, Picatinny cantilever rail. Introduced 2006. Made in U.S. by Beretta USA.

Price: 3901 Target RL. **$900.00**
Price: 3901 Citizen, synthetic or wood, from **$750.00**
Price: 3901 Statesman **$900.00**
Price: 3901 Rifled Slug Shotgun. **$800.00**

BERETTA UGB25 XCEL SEMIAUTO SHOTGUN

Gauge: 12, 2-3/4" chambers. **Barrel:** 28", 30", 32"; competition-style interchangeable vent rib; Optima choke tubes. **Weight:** 7.7-9 lbs. **Stock:** High-grade walnut with oil finish; hand-checkered grip and forend, adjustable. **Features:** Break-open semiautomatic. High-resistance fiberglass-reinforced technopolymer trigger plate, self-lubricating firing mechanism. Rounded alloy receiver, polished sides, external cartridge carrier and feeding port, bottom eject. two technopolymer recoil dampers on breech bolt, double recoil dampers located in the receiver, Beretta Recoil Reduction System, recoil-absorbing Beretta Gel Tek recoil pad. Optima-Bore barrel with a lengthened forcing cone, Optimachoke and Extended Optimachoke tubes. Steel-shot capable, interchangeable aluminum alloy top rib. Introduced 2006. Imported from Italy by Beretta USA.

Price: **$3,875.00**

BERETTA A400 XPLOR UNICO SEMIAUTO SHOTGUN

Self-regulation gas-operated shotgun chambered to shoot all 12-ga, loads from 2-3/4 to 3.5 inches. Features include Kick-Off3 hydraulic damper; 26- or 28-inch "Steelium" barrel with interchangeable choke tubes; anodized aluminum receiver; sculpted, checkered walnut buttstock and forend.

Price: **$1625.00**

BERETTA AL391 TEKNYS SHOTGUNS

Gauge: 12, 20 gauge; 3" chamber, semiauto. **Barrel:** 26", 28". **Weight:** 5.9 lbs. (20 ga.), 7.3 lbs. (12 ga.). **Length:** NA. **Stock:** X-tra wood (special process wood enhancement). **Features:** Flat 1/4 rib, TruGlo Tru-Bead sight, recoil reducer, stock spacers, overbored bbls., flush choke tubes. Comes with fitted, lined case.

Price: From **$2,050.00**

BERETTA AL391 URIKA AND URIKA 2 AUTO SHOTGUNS

Gauge: 12, 20 gauge; 3" chamber. **Barrel:** 22", 24", 26", 28", 30"; five Mobilchoke choke tubes. **Weight:** 5.95 to 7.28 lbs. **Length:** Varies by model. **Stock:** Walnut, black or camo synthetic; shims, spacers and interchangeable recoil pads allow custom fit. **Features:** Self-

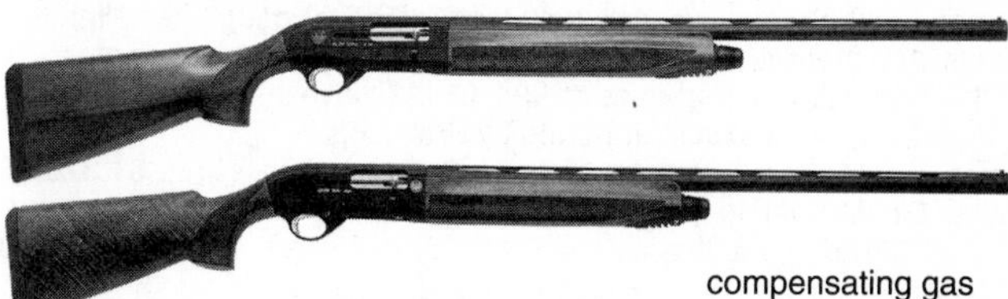

compensating gas operation handles full range of loads; recoil reducer in receiver; enlarged trigger guard; reduced-weight receiver, barrel and forend; hard-chromed bore. Introduced 2000. AL391 Urika 2 (2007) has self-cleaning action, X-Tra Grain stock finish. AL391 Urika 2 Gold has higher-grade select oil-finished wood stock, upgraded engraving (gold-filled gamebirds on field models, gold-filled laurel leaf on competition version). Kick-Off recoil reduction system available in Synthetic, Realtree Advantage Max-4 and AP models. Imported from Italy by Beretta USA.

Price: Urika 2 X-tra Grain, from **$1,400.00**
Price: Urika 2 Gold, from **$1,550.00**
Price: Urika 2 Synthetic **$975.00**
Price: Urika 2 Realtree AP Kick-Off,.................. **$1,350.00**

BERETTA A391 XTREMA2 3.5 AUTO SHOTGUNS

Gauge: 12 ga. 3.5" chamber. **Barrel:** 24", 26", 28". **Weight:** 7.8 lbs. **Stock:** Synthetic. **Features:** Semiauto goes with two-lug rotating bolt and self-compensating gas valve, extended tang, cross bolt safety, self-cleaning, with case.

Price: From **$1,250.00**

BREDA GRIZZLY

Gauge: 12, 3.5" chamber. **Barrel:** 28". **Weight:** 7.2 lbs. **Stock:** Black synthetic or Advantage Timber with matching metal parts. **Features:** Chokes tubes are Mod., IC, Full; inertia-type action, four-round magazine. Imported from Italy by Legacy Sports International.

Price: Blued/black (2008) **$1,826.00**
Price: Advantage Timber Camo (2008) **$2,121.00**

BREDA XANTHOS

Gauge: 12, 3" chamber. **Barrel:** 28". **Weight:** 6.5 lbs. **Stock:** High grade walnut. **Features:** Chokes tubes are Mod., IC, Full; inertia-type action, four-round magazine, spark engraving with hand-engraved details and hand-gilding figures on receiver. Blued, Grey or Chrome finishes. Imported from Italy by Legacy Sports International.

Price: Blued (2007)............................... **$2,309.00**
Price: Grey (2007) **$2,451.00**
Price: Chrome (2007)............................. **$3,406.00**

BREDA ECHO

Gauge: 12, 20. 3" chamber. **Barrel:** 28". **Weight:** 6.0-6.5 lbs. **Stock:** Walnut. **Features:** Chokes tubes are Mod., IC, Full; inertia-type action, four-round magazine, blue, grey or nickel finishes, modern engraving, fully checkered pistol grip. Imported from Italy by Legacy Sports International.

Price: Blued, 12 ga. (2008).......................... **$1,897.00**
Price: Grey, 12 ga. (2008) **$1,969.00**
Price: Nickel, 12 ga. (2008) **$2,214.00**
Price: Nickel, 20 ga. (2008) **$2,214.00**

BREDA ALTAIR

Gauge: 12, 20. 3" chamber. **Barrel:** 28". **Weight:** 5.7-6.1 lbs. **Stock:** Oil-rubbed walnut. **Features:** Chokes tubes are Mod., IC, Full; gas-actuated action, four-round magazine, blued finish, lightweight frame. Imported from Italy by Legacy Sports International.

Price: Blued, 12 ga. (2008).......................... **$1,320.00**
Price: Grey, 20 ga. (2008) **$1,320.00**

BROWNING GOLD AUTO SHOTGUNS

Gauge: 12, 3" or 3-1/2" chamber; 20, 3" chamber. **Barrel:** 12 ga.-26", 28", 30", Invector Plus choke tubes; 20 ga.-26", 30", Invector choke tubes. **Weight:** 7 lbs., 9 oz. (12 ga.), 6 lbs., 12 oz. (20 ga.). **Length:** 46.25" overall (20 ga., 26" barrel). **Stock:** 14"x1.5"x2-1/3"; select walnut with gloss finish; palm swell grip. **Features:** Self-regulating, self-cleaning gas system shoots all loads; lightweight receiver with special non-glare deep black finish; large reversible safety button;

large rounded trigger guard, gold trigger. The 20 gauge has slightly smaller dimensions; 12 gauge have back-bored barrels, Invector Plus tube system. Introduced 1994. Gold Evolve shotguns have new rib design, HiViz sights. Imported by Browning.

Price: Gold Evolve Sporting, 12 ga., 2-3/4" chamber **$1,326.00**
Price: Gold Superlite Hunter, 12 or 20 ga., 26" or 28" barrel, 6.6 lbs. **$1,161.00**

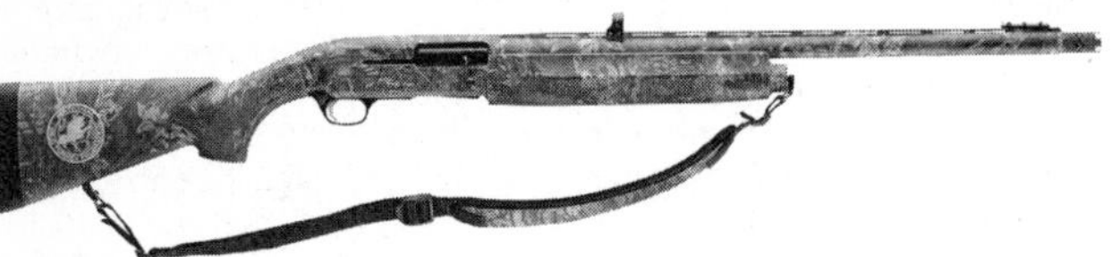

BROWNING GOLD NWTF TURKEY SERIES AND MOSSY OAK SHOTGUNS

Gauge: 12, 10, 3-1/2" chamber. Similar to the Gold Hunter except has specialized camouflage patterns, including National Wild Turkey Federation design. Includes extra-full choke tube and HiViz fiber-optic sights on some models and Dura-Touch coating. Camouflage patterns include Mossy Oak New Break-Up (NBU) or Mossy Oak New Shadow Grass (NSG). NWTF models include NWTF logo on stock. Introduced 2001. From Browning.

Price: NWFT Gold Ultimate Turkey, 24" barrel, 12 ga. 3-1/2" chamber **$1,513.00**
Price: NWFT Gold 10 Gauge, 24" barrel, 3-1/2" chamber . . **$1,639.00**

BROWNING GOLD GOLDEN CLAYS AUTO SHOTGUNS

Gauge: 12, 2-3/4" chamber. **Barrel:** 28", 30", Invector Plus choke tubes. **Weight:** about 7.75 lbs. **Length:** From 47.75 to 50.5". **Stock:** Select walnut with gloss finish; palm swell grip, shim adjustable. **Features:** Ported barrels, "Golden Clays" models feature gold inlays and engraving. Imported by Browning.

Price: Gold "Golden Clays" Sporting Clays, intr. 2005 . . . . . **$1,941.00**

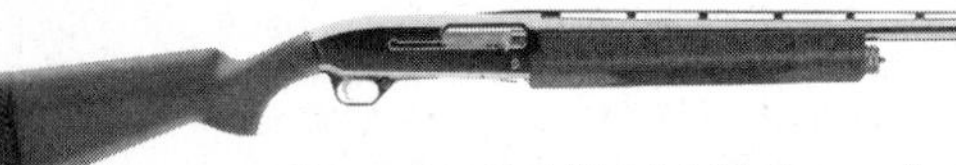

Browning Gold Light 10 Gauge Auto Shotgun

Similar to the Gold Hunter except has an alloy receiver that is 1 lb. lighter than standard model. Offered in 26" or 28" bbls. With Mossy Oak Break-Up or Shadow Grass coverage; 5-shot magazine. Weighs 9 lbs., 10 oz. (28" bbl.). Introduced 2001. Imported by Browning.

Price: Camo model only **$1,509.00**

BROWNING SILVER AUTO SHOTGUNS

Gauge: 12, 3" or 3-1/2" chamber; 20, 3" chamber. Barrel: 12 ga.-26", 28", 30", Invector Plus choke tubes. Weight: 7 lbs., 9 oz. (12 ga.), 6 lbs., 7 oz. (20 ga.). Stock: Satin finish walnut. Features: Active Valve gas system, semi-humpback receiver. Invector Plus tube system, three choke tubes. Imported by Browning.

Price: Silver Hunter, 12 ga., 3.5" chamber **$1,239.00**
Price: Silver Hunter, 20 ga., 3" chamber, intr. 2008 . . . . **$1,079.00**
Price: Silver Micro, 20 ga., 3" chamber, intr. 2008 . . . . **$1,079.00**
Price: Silver Sporting, 12 ga., 2-3/4" chamber, intr. 2009 . . . . **$1,199.00**
Price: Silver Sporting Micro, 12 ga., 2-3/4" chamber, intr. 2008. . . . . **$1,199.00**
Price: Silver Rifled Deer, Mossy Oak New Break-Up, 12 ga., 3" chamber, intr. 2008 . . . . **$1,319.00**
Price: Silver Rifled Deer Stalker, 12 ga., 3" chamber, intr. 2008. . . . . **$1,169.00**
Price: Silver Rifled Deer Satin, satin-finished aluminum alloy receiver and satin-finished walnut buttstock and forend **$1,229.00**
Price: Silver Stalker, black composite buttstock and forend **$1,179.00**

BROWNING MAXUS

Gauge: 12; 3" or 3.5" chambers. **Barrel:** 26" or 28". **Weight:** 6-7/8 lbs. **Length:** 47.25" to 49.25". **Stock:** Composite with close radius pistol grip. **Features:** Aluminum receiver, lightweight profile barrel with

vent rib, Vector Pro lengthened forcing cone, DuraTouch Armor Coating overall. Handles shorter shells interchangeably.

Price: Stalker, matte black finish overall, 3-1/2" **$1,379.00**
Price: Stalker, matte black finish overall, 3" **$1,199.00**
Price: Mossy Oak Duck Blind overall, 3-1/2" **$1,499.00**
Price: Mossy Oak Duck Blind overall, 3" **$1,339.00**

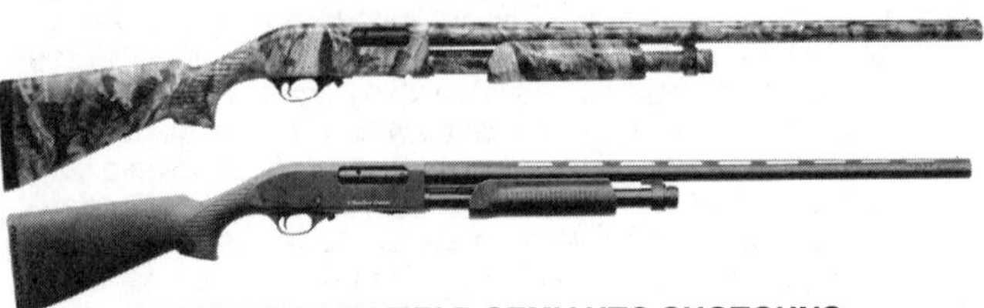

CHARLES DALY FIELD SEMIAUTO SHOTGUNS

Gauge: 12, 20, 28. **Barrel:** 22", 24", 26", 28" or 30". **Stock:** Synthetic black, Realtree Hardwoods or Advantage Timber. **Features:** Interchangeable barrels handle all loads including steel shot. Slug model has adjustable sights. Maxi-Mag is 3.5" chamber.

Price: Field Hunter, from. **$489.00**

CHARLES DALY SUPERIOR II SEMIAUTO SHOTGUNS

Gauge: 12, 20, 28. **Barrel:** 26", 28" or 30". **Stock:** Select Turkish walnut. **Features:** Factory ported interchangeable barrels; wide vent rib on Trap and Sport models; fluorescent red sights.

Price: Superior II Hunter, from **$649.00**
Price: Superior II Sport **$709.00**
Price: Superior II Trap. **$739.00**

ESCORT SEMIAUTO SHOTGUNS

Gauge: 12, 20; 3" or 3.5" chambers. **Barrel:** 22" (Youth), 26" and 28". **Weight:** 6.7-7.8 lbs. **Stock:** Polymer in black, Shadow Grass® or Obsession® camo finish, Turkish walnut, select walnut. **Sights:** Optional HiViz Spark front. **Features:** Black-chrome or dipped-camo metal parts, top of receiver dovetailed for sight mounts, gold plated trigger, trigger guard safety, magazine cut-off. Three choke tubes (IC, M, F) except the Waterfowl/Turkey Combo, which adds a .665 turkey choke to the standard three. Waterfowl/Turkey combo is two-barrel set, 24"/26" and 26"/28". Several models have Trio recoil pad. Models are: AS, AS Select, AS Youth, AS Youth Select, PS, PS Spark and Waterfowl/Turkey. Introduced 2002. Camo introduced 2003. Youth, Slug and Obsession camo introduced 2005. Imported from Turkey by Legacy Sports International.

Price: . . . . **$425.00 to $589.00**

FRANCHI INERTIA I-12 SHOTGUN

Gauge: 12, 3" chamber. **Barrel:** 24", 26", 28" (Cyl., IC, Mod., IM, F choke tubes). **Weight:** 7.5 to 7.7. lbs. **Length:** 45" to 49". **Stock:** 14-3.8" LOP, satin walnut with checkered grip and forend, synthetic, Advantage Timber HD or Max-4 camo patterns. **Features:** Inertia-Driven action. AA walnut stock. Red bar front sight, metal mid sight. Imported from Italy by Benelli USA.

Price: Synthetic. **$839.00**
Price: Camo **$949.00**
Price: Satin walnut **$949.00**

FRANCHI MODEL 720 SHOTGUNS

Gauge: 20, 3" chamber. **Barrel:** 24", 26", 28" w/(IC, Mod., F choke tubes). **Weight:** 5.9 to 6.1 lbs. **Length:** 43.25" to 49". **Stock:** WeatherCoat finish walnut, Max-4 and Timber HD camo. **Sights:** Front bead. **Features:** Made in Italy and imported by Benelli USA.

Price: **$1,049.00**
Price: Walnut, 12.5" LOP, 43.25" OAL **$999.00**

FRANCHI 48AL FIELD AND DELUXE SHOTGUNS

Gauge: 20 or 28, 2-3/4" chamber. **Barrel:** 24", 26", 28" (Full, Cyl., Mod., choke tubes). **Weight:** 5.4 to 5.7 lbs. **Length:** 42.25" to 48". **Stock:** Walnut with checkered grip and forend. **Features:** Long recoil-operated action. Chrome-lined bore; cross-bolt safety. Imported from Italy by Benelli USA.

Price: AL Field 20 ga. **$839.00**
Price: AL Deluxe 20 ga., A grade walnut **$1,099.00**
Price: AL Field 28 ga. **$999.00**

FRANCHI 720 COMPETITION SHOTGUN

Gauge: 20; 4+1. **Barrel:** 28" ported; tapered target rib and bead front sight. **Weight:** 6.2 lbs. **Stock:** Walnut with WeatherCoat. **Features:** Gas-operated, satin nickel receiver.

Price: **$1,149.00**

HARRINGTON & RICHARDSON EXCELL AUTO 5 SHOTGUNS

Gauge: 12, 3" chamber. **Barrel:** 22", 24", 28", four screw-in choke tubes (IC, M, IM, F). **Weight:** About 7 lbs. **Length:** 42.5" to 48.5" overall, depending on barrel length. **Stock:** American walnut with satin finish; cut checkering; ventilated buttpad. Synthetic stock or camo-finish. **Sights:** Metal bead front or fiber-optic front and rear. **Features:** Ventilated rib on all models except slug gun. Imported by H&R 1871, Inc.

Price: Synthetic, black, 28" barrel, 48.5" OAL **$415.00**
Price: Walnut, checkered grip/forend, 28" barrel, 48.5" OAL . . **$461.00**
Price: Waterfowl, camo finish **$521.00**
Price: Turkey, camo finish, 22" barrel, fiber optic sights. **$521.00**
Price: Combo, synthetic black stock, with slug barrel. **$583.00**

LANBER SEMIAUTOMATIC SHOTGUNS

Gauge: 12, 3". **Barrel:** 26", 28", chrome-moly alloy steel, welded, ventilated top and side ribs. **Weight:** 6.8 lbs. **Length:** 48-3/8". **Stock:** Walnut, oiled finish, laser checkering, rubber buttplate. **Sights:** Fiber-optic front. **Features:** Extractors or automatic ejectors, control and unblocking button. Rated for steel shot. Lanber Polichokes. Imported by Lanber USA.

Price: Model 2533. . . . . **$635.00**

MOSSBERG 930 AUTOLOADER

Gauge: 12, 3" chamber, 4-shot magazine. **Barrel:** 24", 26", 28", overbored to 10-gauge bore dimensions; factory ported, Accu-Choke tubes. **Weight:** 7.5 lbs. **Length:** 44.5" overall (28" barrel). **Stock:** Walnut or synthetic. Adjustable stock drop and cast spacer system. **Sights:** "Turkey Taker" fiber-optic, adjustable windage and elevation. Front bead fiber-optic front on waterfowl models. **Features:** Self-regulating gas system, dual gas-vent system and piston, EZ-Empty magazine button, cocking indicator. Interchangeable Accu-Choke tube set (IC, Mod, Full) for waterfowl and field models. XX-Full turkey Accu-Choke tube included with turkey models. Ambidextrous thumb-operated safety, Uni-line stock and receiver. Receiver drilled and tapped for scope base attachment, free gun lock. Introduced 2008. From O.F. Mossberg & Sons, Inc.

Price: Turkey, from **$545.00**
Price: Waterfowl, from **$545.00**
Price: Combo, from. **$604.00**
Price: Field, from. **$568.00**
Price: Slugster, from. **$539.00**
Price: Turkey Pistolgrip; full pistolgrip stock, matte black or Mossy Oak Obsession camo finish overall **$628.00**
Price: Tactical; 18.5" tactical barrel, black synthetic stock and matte black finish. **$653.00**
Price: Road Blocker; includes muzzle brake **$697.00**
Price: SPX; no muzzle brake, M16-style front sight, ghost ring rear sight, full pistolgrip stock, eight-round extended magazine **$667.00**
Price: SPX; conventional synthetic stock **$700.00**
Price: Home Security/Field Combo; 18.5" Cylinder bore barrel and 28" ported Field barrel; black synthetic stock and matte black finish **$604.00**

MOSSBERG MODEL 935 MAGNUM AUTOLOADING SHOTGUNS

Gauge: 12; 3" and 3.5" chamber, interchangeable. **Barrel:** 22", 24", 26", 28". **Weight:** 7.25 to 7.75 lbs. **Length:** 45" to 49" overall. **Stock:** Synthetic. **Features:** Gas-operated semiauto models in blued or camo finish. Fiber optics sights, drilled and tapped receiver, interchangeable Accu-Mag choke tubes.

Price: 935 Magnum Turkey: Realtree Hardwoods, Mossy Oak New Break-up or Mossy Oak Obsession camo overall, 24" barrel **$732.00**
Price: 935 Magnum Turkey Pistolgrip; full pistolgrip stock . . **$831.00**
Price: 935 Magnum Grand Slam: 22" barrel, Realtree Hardwoods or Mossy Oak New Break-up camo overall **$747.00**
Price: 935 Magnum Flyway: 28" barrel and Advantage Max-4 camo overall **$781.00**
Price: 935 Magnum Waterfowl: 26"or 28" barrel, matte black, Mossy Oak New Break-up, Advantage Max-4 or Mossy Oak Duck Blind cam overall . . . . . **$613.00 to $725.00**
Price: 935 Magnum Slugster: 24" fully rifled barrel, rifle sights, Realtree AP camo overall **$747.00**
Price: 935 Magnum Turkey/Deer Combo: interchangeable 24" Turkey barrel, Mossy Oak New Break-up camo overall **$807.00**
Price: 935 Magnum Waterfowl/Turkey Combo: 24" Turkey and 28" Waterfowl barrels, Mossy Oak New Break-up finish overall **$807.00**

REMINGTON MODEL 105 CTI SHOTGUN

Gauge: 12, 3" chamber, 4-shot magazine. **Barrel:** 26", 28" (IC, Mod., Full ProBore chokes). **Weight:** 7 lbs. **Length:** 46.25" overall (26" barrel). **Stock:** Walnut with satin finish. Checkered grip and forend. **Sights:** Front bead. **Features:** Aircraft-grade titanium receiver body, skeletonized receiver with carbon fiber shell. Bottom feed and eject, target grade trigger, R3 recoil pad, FAA-approved lockable hard case, .735" overbored barrel with lengthened forcing cones. TriNyte coating; carbon/aramid barrel rib. Introduced 2006.

Price: **$1,559.00**

REMINGTON MODEL SPR453 SHOTGUN

Gauge: 12; 3.5" chamber, 4+1 capacity. **Barrel:** 24", 26", 28" vent rib. **Weight:** 8 to 8.25 lbs. **Stock:** Black synthetic. **Features:** Matte finish, dual extractors, four extended screw-in SPR choke tubes (improved cylinder, modified, full and super-full turkey. Introduced 2006. From Remington Arms Co.

Price: Black synthetic **$497.00**

REMINGTON MODEL 11-87 SPORTSMAN SHOTGUNS

Gauge: 12, 20, 3" chamber. **Barrel:** 26", 28", RemChoke tubes. Standard contour, vent rib. **Weight:** About 7.75 to 8.25 lbs. **Length:** 46" to 48" overall. **Stock:** Black synthetic or Mossy Oak Break Up Mossy Oak Duck Blind, and Realtree Hardwoods HD and AP Green HD camo finishes. **Sights:** Single bead front. **Features:** Matte-black metal finish, magazine cap swivel studs. Sportsman Deer gun has 21-inch fully rifled barrel, cantilever scope mount.

Price: Sportsman Camo (2007), 12 or 20 ga. **$879.00**
Price: Sportsman black synthetic, 12 or 20 ga. **$772.00**
Price: Sportsman Deer FR Cantilever, 12 or 20 ga. **$892.00**
Price: Sportsman Youth Synthetic 20 ga., (2008). **$772.00**
Price: Sportsman Youth Camo 20 ga., (2008) **$879.00**
Price: Sportsman Super Magnum 12 ga., 28" barrel (2008). . . **$825.00**
Price: Sportsman Super Magnum Shurshot Turkey 12 ga., (2008) **$972.00**
Price: Sportsman Super Magnum Waterfowl 12 ga., (2008) . . **$959.00**
Price: Sportsman Compact Synthetic; black synthetic but with reduced overall dimensions **$772.00**

REMINGTON 11-87 SPORTSMAN FIELD

Semiauto shotgun chambered in 12 and 20 ga., 2-3/4- and 3-inch. Features include 26- (20) or 28-inch (12) barrel; vent rib; RemChokes (one supplied); satin-finished walnut stock and forend with fleur-de-lis pattern; dual sights; nickel-plated bolt and trigger.

Price: . . . . . **Starting at $845.00**

REMINGTON 11-87 SPORTSMAN SUPER MAG SYNTHETIC

Semiauto shotgun chambered in 12-ga. 3-1/2-inch. Features include black matte synthetic stock and forend; rubber overmolded grip panels on the stock and forend; black

padded sling; HiViz sights featuring interchangeable light pipe; 28-inch vent rib barrel; SuperCell recoil pad; RemChoke.
Price: $859.00

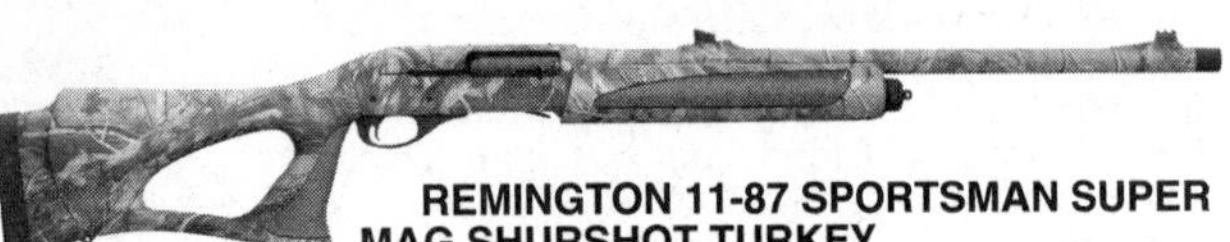

REMINGTON 11-87 SPORTSMAN SUPER MAG SHURSHOT TURKEY

Similar to 11-87 Sportsman Super Mag Synthetic but with ambidextrous ShurShot pistol-grip stock; full Realtree APG HD coverage; 23-inch barrel with fully adjustable TruGlo rifle sights. Wingmaster HD Turkey Choke included.
Price: $972.00

REMINGTON MODEL 1100 G3 SHOTGUN

Gauge: 20, 12; 3" chamber. **Barrel:** 26", 28". **Weight:** 6.75-7.6 lbs. **Stock:** Realwood semi-fancy carbon fiber laminate stock, high gloss finish, machine cut checkering. **Features:** Gas operating system, pressure compensated barrel, solid carbon-steel engraved receiver, titanium coating. Action bars, trigger and extended carrier release, action bar sleeve, action spring, locking block, hammer, sear and magazine tube have nickel-plated, Teflon coating. R3 recoil pad, overbored (.735" dia.) vent rib barrels, ProBore choke tubes. 20 gauge have Rem Chokes. Comes with lockable hard case. Introduced 2006.
Price: G3, 12 or 20 ga. $1,239.00
Price: G3 Left Hand, 12 ga. 28" barrel (2008) $1,329.00

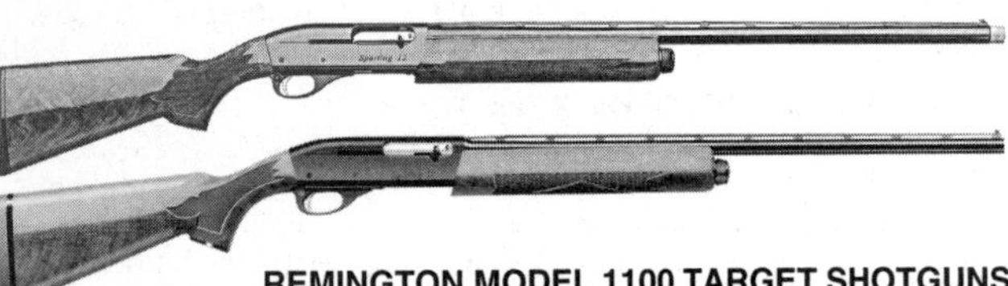

REMINGTON MODEL 1100 TARGET SHOTGUNS

Gauge: .410 bore, 28, 20, 12. **Barrel:** 26", 27", 28", 30" light target contoured vent rib barrel with twin bead target sights. **Stock:** Semi-fancy American walnut stock and forend, cut checkering, high gloss finish. **Features:** Gold-plated trigger. Four extended choke tubes: Skeet, Improved Cylinder, Light Modified and Modified. 1100 Tournament Skeet (20 and 12 gauge) receiver is roll-marked with "Tournament Skeet." 26" light contour, vent rib barrel has twin bead sights, Extended Target Choke Tubes (Skeet and Improved Cylinder). Model 1100 Premier Sporting (2008) has polished nickel receiver, gold accents, light target contoured vent rib Rem Choke barrels. Wood is semi-fancy American walnut stock and forend, high-gloss finish, cut checkering, sporting clays-style recoil pad. Gold trigger, available in 12, 20, 28 and .410 bore options, Briley extended choke tubes, Premier Sporting hard case. Competition model (12 gauge) has overbored (0.735" bore diameter) 30" barrel. **Weight:** 8 lbs. 10mm target-style rib with twin beads. Extended ProBore choke tubes in Skeet, Improved Cylinder, Light-Modified, Modified and Full. Semi-fancy American walnut stock and forend. Classic Trap model has polished blue receiver with scroll engraving, gold accents, 30" low-profile, light-target contoured vent rib barrel with standard .727" dimensions. Comes with specialized Rem Choke trap tubes: Singles (.027"), Mid Handicap (.034"), and Long Handicap (.041"). Monte Carlo stock of semi-fancy American walnut, deep-cut checkering, high-gloss finish.
Price: Sporting 12, 28" barrel, 8 lbs. $1,105.00
Price: Sporting 20, 28" barrel, 7 lbs. $1,105.00
Price: Sporting 28, 27" barrel, 6.75 lbs. $1,159.00
Price: Sporting 410, 27" barrel, 6.75 lbs. $1,159.00
Price: Classic Trap, 12 ga. 30" barrel $1,159.00
Price: Premier Sporting (2008), from $1,359.00
Price: Competition, standard stock, 12 ga. 30" barrel $1,692.00
Price: Competition, adjustable comb $1,692.00

Remington Model 1100 TAC-4

Similar to Model 1100 but with 18" or 22" barrel with ventilated rib; 12 gauge 2-3/4"only; standard black synthetic stock or Knoxx SpecOps SpeedFeed IV pistolgrip stock; RemChoke tactical choke tube; matte black finish overall. Length is 42-1/2" and weighs 7-3/4 lbs.
Price: $945.00

REMINGTON MODEL SP-10 MAGNUM SHOTGUN

Gauge: 10, 3-1/2" chamber, 2-shot magazine. **Barrel:** 23", 26", 30" (full and mod. RemChokes). **Weight:** 10.75 to 11 lbs. **Length:** 47.5" overall (26" barrel). **Stock:** Walnut with satin finish (30" barrel) or camo synthetic (26" barrel). Checkered grip and forend. **Sights:** Twin bead. **Features:** Stainless steel gas system with moving cylinder; 3/8" vent rib. Receiver and barrel have matte finish. Brown recoil pad. Comes with padded Cordura nylon sling. Introduced 1989. SP-10 Magnum Camo has buttstock, forend, receiver, barrel and magazine cap covered with Mossy Oak Duck Blind Obsession camo finish; bolt body and trigger guard have matte black finish. RemChoke tube, 26" vent rib barrel with mid-rib bead and Bradley-style front sight, swivel studs and quick-detachable swivels, non-slip Cordura carrying sling. Introduced 1993.
Price: SP-10 Magnum, satin finish walnut stock $1,772.00
Price: SP-10 Magnum Full Camo $1,932.00
Price: SP-10 Magnum Waterfowl $1,945.00

SAIGA AUTOLOADING SHOTGUN

Gauge: 12, 20, .410; 3" chamber. **Barrel:** 19", 24". **Weight:** 7.9 lbs. **Length: Stock:** Black synthetic. **Sights:** Fixed or adjustable leaf. **Features:** Magazine fed, 2- or 5-round capacity. Imported from Russia by Russian American Armory Co.
Price: $347.95

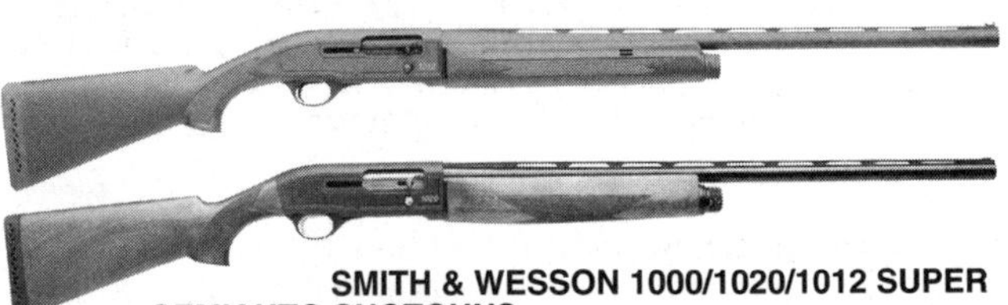

SMITH & WESSON 1000/1020/1012 SUPER SEMIAUTO SHOTGUNS

Gauge: 12, 20; 3" in 1000; 3-1/2" chamber in Super. **Barrel:** 24", 26", 28", 30". **Stock:** Walnut. Synthetic finishes are satin, black, Realtree MAX-4, Realtree APG. **Sights:** TruGlo fiber-optic. **Features:** 29 configurations. Gas operated, dual-piston action; chrome-lined barrels, five choke tubes, shim kit for adjusting stock. 20-ga. models are Model 1020 or Model 1020SS (short stock). Lifetime warranty. Introduced 2007. Imported from Turkey by Smith & Wesson.
Price: From $623.00

STOEGER MODEL 2000 SHOTGUNS

Gauge: 12, 3" chamber, set of five choke tubes (C, IC, M, F, XFT). **Barrel:** 24", 26", 28", 30". **Stock:** Walnut, synthetic, Timber HD, Max-4. **Sights:** Red bar front. **Features:** Inertia-recoil. Minimum recommended load: 3 dram, 1-1/8 oz. Imported by Benelli USA.
Price: Walnut $499.00
Price: Synthetic $499.00
Price: Max-4 .... $549.00
Price: Black synthetic pistol grip (2007) $499.00
Price: APG HD camo pistol grip (2007), 18.5" barrel $549.00

TRISTAR VIPER SEMIAUTOMATIC SHOTGUNS

Gauge: 12, 20; shoots 2-3/4" or 3" interchangeably. **Barrel:** 26", 28" barrels (carbon fiber only offered in 12-ga. 28" and 20-ga. 26"). **Stock:** Wood, black synthetic, Mossy Oak Duck Blind camouflage, faux carbon fiber finish (2008) with the new Comfort Touch technology. **Features:** Magazine cut-off, vent rib with matted sight plane, brass front bead (camo models have fiber-optic front sight), five round magazine-shot plug included, and 3 Beretta-style choke tubes (IC, M, F). Viper synthetic, Viper camo have swivel studs. Five-

year warranty. Viper Youth models have shortened length of pull and 24" barrel. Imported by Tristar Sporting Arms Ltd.
Price: From **$469.00**
Price: Camo models (2008), from **$569.00**

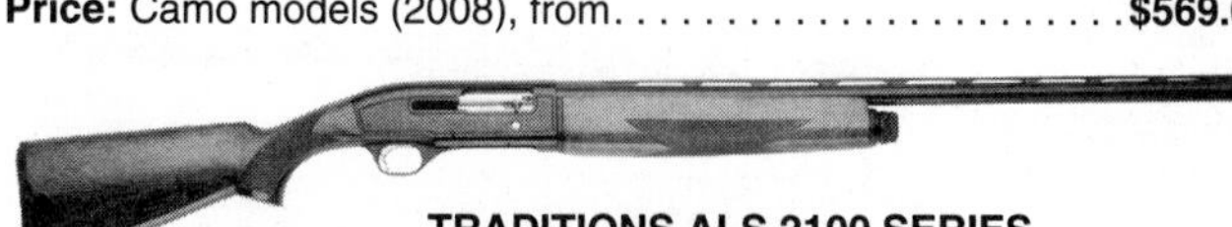

TRADITIONS ALS 2100 SERIES SEMIAUTOMATIC SHOTGUNS

Gauge: 12, 3" chamber; 20, 3" chamber. **Barrel:** 24", 26", 28" (Imp. Cyl., Mod. and Full choke tubes). **Weight:** 5 lbs., 10 oz. to 6 lbs., 5 oz. **Length:** 44" to 48" overall. **Stock:** Walnut or black composite. **Features:** Gas-operated; vent rib barrel with Beretta-style threaded muzzle. Introduced 2001 by Traditions.
Price: Field Model (12 or 20 ga., 26" or 28" bbl., walnut stock) **$479.00**
Price: Youth Model (12 or 20 ga., 24" bbl., walnut stock) **$479.00**
Price: (12 or 20 ga., 26" or 28" barrel, composite stock) **$459.00**

Traditions ALS 2100 Turkey Semiautomatic Shotgun
Similar to ALS 2100 Field Model except chambered in 12 gauge, 3" only with 26" barrel and Mossy Oak Break Up camo finish. Weighs 6 lbs.; 46" overall.
Price: **$519.00**

Traditions ALS 2100 Waterfowl Semiautomatic Shotgun
Similar to ALS 2100 Field Model except chambered in 12 gauge, 3" only with 28" barrel and Advantage Wetlands camo finish. Weighs 6.25 lbs.; 48" overall. Multi chokes.
Price: **$529.00**

Traditions ALS 2100 Hunter Combo
Similar to ALS 2100 Field Model except 2 barrels, 28" vent rib and 24" fully rifled deer. Weighs 6 to 6.5 lbs.; 48" overall. Choice TruGlo adj. sights or fixed cantilever mount on rifled barrel. Multi chokes.
Price: Walnut, rifle barrel **$609.00**
Price: Walnut, cantilever **$629.00**
Price: Synthetic **$579.00**

Traditions ALS 2100 Slug Hunter Shotgun
Similar to ALS 2100 Field Model, 12 ga., 24" barrel, overall length 44"; weighs 6.25 lbs. Designed specifically for the deer hunter. Rifled barrel has 1 in 36" twist. Fully adjustable fiber-optic sights.
Price: Walnut, rifle barrel **$529.00**
Price: Synthetic, rifle barrel **$499.00**
Price: Walnut, cantilever **$549.00**
Price: Synthetic, cantilever **$529.00**

Traditions ALS 2100 Home Security Shotgun
Similar to ALS 2100 Field Model, 12 ga., 20" barrel, overall length 40", weighs 6 lbs. Can be reloaded with one hand while shouldered and ontarget. Swivel studs installed in stock.
Price: **$399.00**

VERONA MODEL 401 SERIES SEMIAUTO SHOTGUNS
Gauge: 12. **Barrel:** 26", 28". **Weight:** 6.5 lbs. **Stock:** Walnut, black composite. **Sights:** Red dot. **Features:** Aluminum receivers, gas-operated, 2-3/4" or 3" Magnum shells without adj. or Mod., 4 screw-in chokes and wrench included. Sling swivels, gold trigger. Blued barrel. Imported from Italy by Legacy Sports International.
Price: **$1,199.00**
Price: 406 Series **$1,199.00**

WINCHESTER SUPER X3 SHOTGUNS

Gauge: 12, 3" and 3.5" chambers. **Barrel:** 26", 28", .742" back-bored; Invector Plus choke tubes. **Weight:** 7 to 7.25 lbs. **Stock:** Composite, 14.25"x1.75"x2". Mossy Oak New Break-Up camo with Dura-Touch Armor Coating. Pachmayr Decelerator buttpad with hard heel insert, customizable length of pull. **Features:** Alloy magazine tube, gunmetal grey Perma-Cote UT finish, self-adjusting Active Valve gas action, lightweight recoil spring system. Electroless nickel-plated bolt, three choke tubes, two length-of-pull stock spacers, drop and cast adjustment spacers, sling swivel studs. Introduced 2006. Made in Belgium, assembled in Portugal by U.S. Repeating Arms Co.
Price: Composite . . . . **$1,119.00 to $1.239.00**
Price: Cantilever Deer **$1,179.00**
Price: Waterfowl w/Mossy Oak Brush camo, intr. 2007 . . . . **$1,439.00**
Price: Field model, walnut stock, intr. 2007 . . . . **$1,439.00**
Price: Gray Shadow **$1,299.00**
Price: All-Purpose Field **$1,439.00**
Price: Classic Field **$1,159.00**
Price: NWTF Cantiliever Extreme Turkey **$1,499.00**

WINCHESTER SUPER X3 FLANIGUN EXHIBITION/SPORTING
Similar to X3 but .742" backbored barrel, red-toned receiver, black Dura-Touch Armor Coated synthetic stock.
Price: **$1,459.00**

WINCHESTER SUPER X2 AUTO SHOTGUNS

Gauge: 12, 3", 3-1/2" chamber. **Barrel:** Belgian, 24", 26", 28"; Invector Plus choke tubes. **Weight:** 7-1/4 to 7.5 lbs. **Stock:** 14.25"x1.75"x2". Walnut or black synthetic. **Features:** Gas-operated action shoots all loads without adjustment; vent rib barrels; 4-shot magazine. Introduced 1999. Assembled in Portugal by U.S. Repeating Arms Co.
Price: Universal Hunter T **$1,252.00**
Price: NWTF Turkey, 3-1/2", Mossy Oak Break-Up camo . . **$1,236.00**
Price: Universal Hunter Model **$1,252.00**

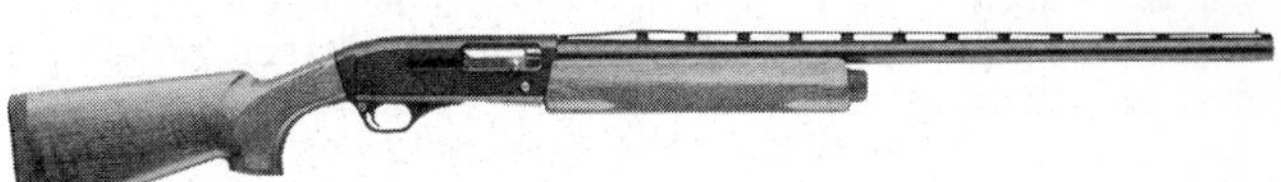

Winchester Super X2 Sporting Clays Auto Shotguns
Similar to the Super X2 except has two gas pistons (one for target loads, one for heavy 3" loads), adjustable comb system and high-post rib. Back-bored barrel with Invector Plus choke tubes. Offered in 28" and 30" barrels. Introduced 2001. From U.S. Repeating Arms Co.
Price: Super X2 sporting clays **$999.00**
Price: Signature red stock **$1,015.00**
Price: Practical MK I, composite stock, TruGlo sights **$1,116.00**

Prices given are believed to be accurate at time of publication however, many factors affect retail pricing so exact prices are not possible.

BENELLI SUPERNOVA PUMP SHOTGUNS

Gauge: 12; 3.5" chamber. **Barrel:** 24", 26", 28". **Length:** 45.5-49.5". **Stock:** Synthetic; Max-4 , Timber, APG HD (2007). **Sights:** Red bar front, metal midbead. **Features:** 2-3/4", 3" chamber (3-1/2" 12 ga. only). Montefeltro rotating bolt design with dual action bars, magazine cut-off, synthetic trigger assembly, adjustable combs, shim kit, choice of buttstocks. 4-shot magazine. Introduced 2006. Imported from Italy by Benelli USA.

Price: Synthetic ComforTech **$499.00**
Price: Camo ComforTech **$599.00**
Price: SteadyGrip . . . . **$599.00 to $619.00**
Price: Tactical, Ghost Ring sight. . . . . **$459.00 to $499.00**
Price: Rifled Slug ComforTech, synthetic stock (2007) **$670.00**
Price: Tactical desert camo pistol grip, 18" barrel (2007) **$589.00**

BENELLI NOVA PUMP SHOTGUNS

Gauge: 12, 20. **Barrel:** 24", 26", 28". **Stock:** Black synthetic, Max-4, Timber and APG HD. **Sights:** Red bar. **Features:** 2-3/ 4", 3" chamber (3-1/2" 12 ga. only). Montefeltro rotating bolt design with dual action bars, magazine cut-off, synthetic trigger assembly, 4-shot magazine. Introduced 1999. Field & Slug Combo has 24" barrel and rifled bore; open rifle sights; synthetic stock; weighs 8.1 lbs. Imported from Italy by Benelli USA.

PrPrice: Max-4 HD camo stock **$499.00**
Price: H$_2$0 model, black synthetic, matte nickel finish. **$599.00**
Price: APG HD stock , 20 ga. (2007) **$529.00**
Price: Tactical, 18.5" barrel, Ghost Ring sight **$429.00**
Price: Black synthetic youth stock, 20 ga. **$429.00**
Price: APG HD stock (2007), 20 ga.. . . . . **$529.00**

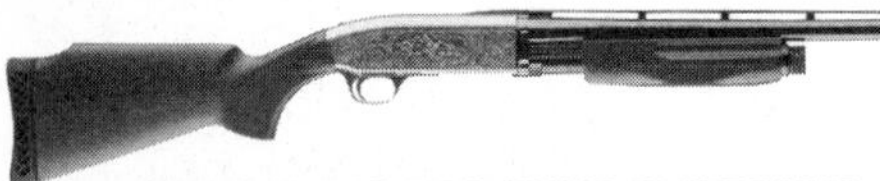

BROWNING BPS PUMP SHOTGUNS

Gauge: 10, 12, 3-1/2" chamber; 12, 16, or 20, 3" chamber (2-3/4" in target guns), 28, 2-3/4" chamber, 5-shot magazine, .410, 3" chamber. **Barrel:** 10 ga.-24" Buck Special, 28", 30", 32" Invector; 12, 20 ga.-22", 24", 26", 28", 30", 32" (Imp. Cyl., Mod. or Full), .410-26" barrel. (Imp. Cyl., Mod. and Full choke tubes.) Also available with Invector choke tubes, 12 or 20 ga.; Upland Special has 22" barrel with Invector tubes. BPS 3" and 3-1/2" have back-bored barrel. **Weight:** 7 lbs., 8 oz. (28" barrel). **Length:** 48.75" overall (28" barrel). **Stock:** 14.25"x1.5"x2.5". Select walnut, semi-beavertail forend, full pistol grip stock. **Features:** All 12 gauge 3" guns except Buck Special and game guns have back-bored barrels with Invector Plus choke tubes. Bottom feeding and ejection, receiver top safety, high post vent rib. Double action bars eliminate binding. Vent rib barrels only. All 12 and 20 gauge guns with 3" chamber available with fully engraved receiver flats at no extra cost. Each gauge has its own unique game scene. Introduced 1977. Stalker is same gun as the standard BPS except all exposed metal parts have a matte blued finish and the stock has a black finish with a black recoil pad. Available in 10 ga. (3-1/2") and 12 ga. with 3" or 3-1/2" chamber, 22", 28", 30" barrel with Invector choke system. Introduced 1987. Rifled Deer Hunter is similar to the standard BPS except has newly designed receiver/magazine tube/barrel mounting system to eliminate play, heavy 20.5" barrel with rifle-type sights with adjustable rear, solid receiver scope mount, "rifle" stock dimensions for scope or open sights, sling swivel studs. Gloss or matte finished wood with checkering, polished blue metal. Introduced 1992. Imported from Japan by Browning.

Price: Stalker (black syn. stock), 12 ga., from **$549.00**
Price: Rifled Deer Hunter (22" rifled bbl., cantilever mount), intr. 2007. . . . . **$699.00**
Price: Trap, intr. 2007 . . . . **$729.00**
Price: Hunter, 16 ga., intr. 2008 . . . . **$569.00**
Price: Upland Special, 16 ga., intr. 2008 . . . . **$569.00**
Price: Mossy Oak New Breakup, 3", 12 ga. only **$679.00**
Price: Mossy Oak New Breakup, 3-1/2", 12 ga. only **$799.00**

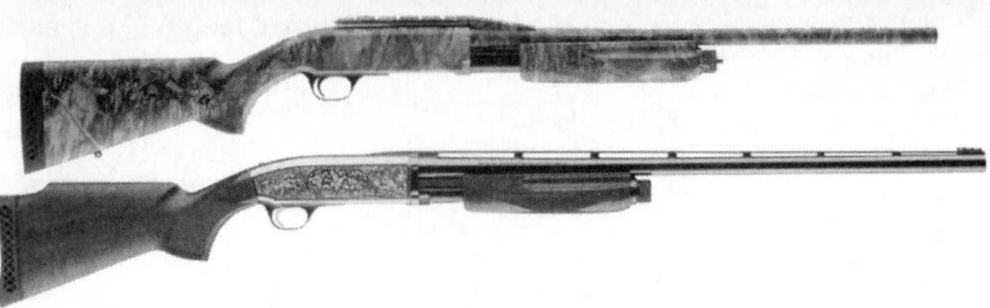

Price: Mossy Oak Duck Blind finish overall, 3" **$679.00**
Price: Mossy Oak Duck Blind finish overall, 3-1/2" **$799.00**
Price: Rifled Deer Mossy Oak New Break-Up, 12 ga. **$719.00**
Price: Rifled Deer Mossy Oak New Break-Up, 20 ga. **$839.00**
Price: Micro Trap, similar to BPS Trap but with compact dimensions (13-3/4" length of pull, 48-1/4" overall length), 12 gauge only **$729.00**

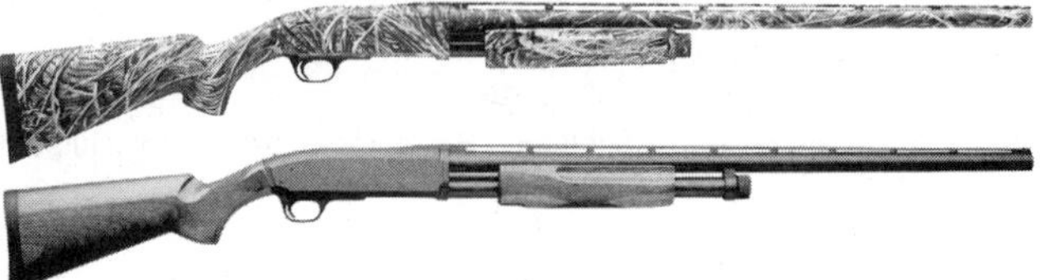

Browning BPS 10 Gauge Camo Pump Shotgun

Similar to the standard BPS except completely covered with Mossy Oak Shadow Grass camouflage. Available with 26" and 28" barrel. Introduced 1999. Imported by Browning

Price: **$799.00**

Browning BPS NWTF Turkey Series Pump Shotgun

Similar to the standard BPS except has full coverage Mossy Oak Break-Up camo finish on synthetic stock, forearm and exposed metal parts. Offered in 12 gauge, 3" or 3-1/2" chamber; 24" bbl. has extra-full choke tube and HiViz fiber-optic sights. Introduced 2001. From Browning.

Price: 12 ga., 3-1/2" chamber. **$859.00**
Price: 12 ga., 3" chamber **$709.00**

Browning BPS Micro Pump Shotgun

Similar to the BPS Stalker except 20 ga. only, 22" Invector barrel, stock has pistol grip with recoil pad. Length of pull is 13.25"; weighs 6 lbs., 12 oz. Introduced 1986.

Price: **$569.00**

CHARLES DALY FIELD PUMP SHOTGUNS

Gauge: 12, 20. **Barrel:** Interchangeable 18.5", 24", 26", 28", 30" multi-choked. **Weight:** NA. **Stock:** Synthetic, various finishes, recoil pad. Receiver: Machined aluminum. **Features:** Field Tactical and Slug models come with adustable sights; Youth models may be upgraded to full size. Imported from Turkey by K.B.I., Inc.

Price: Field Tactical **$274.00**
Price: Field Hunter **$499.00**
Price: Field Hunter, Realtree Hardwood. **$289.00**
Price: Field Hunter Advantage **$289.00**

CHARLES DALY MAXI-MAG PUMP SHOTGUNS

Gauge: 12 gauge, 3-1/2". **Barrel:** 24", 26", 28"; multi-choke system. **Weight:** NA. **Stock:** Synthetic black, Realtree Hardwoods, or Advantage Timber receiver, aluminum alloy. **Features:** Handles 2-3/4", 3" and 3-1/2" loads. Interchangeable ported barrels; Turkey package includes sling, HiViz sights, XX Full choke. Imported from Turkey by K.B.I., Inc.

Price: Field Hunter **$329.00**
Price: Field Hunter Advantage **$319.00**
Price: Field Hunter Hardwoods. **$319.00**
Price: Field Hunter Turkey **$434.00**

EMF OLD WEST PUMP (SLIDE ACTION) SHOTGUN

Gauge: 12. **Barrel:** 20". **Weight:** 7 lbs. **Length:** 39-1/2" overall. **Stock:** Smooth walnut with cushioned pad. **Sights:** Front bead. **Features:** Authentic reproduction of Winchester 1897 pump shotgun;

Prices given are believed to be accurate at time of publication however, many factors affect retail pricing so exact prices are not possible.

blue receiver and barrel; standard modified choke. Introduced 2006. Imported from China for EMF by TTN.
Price: **$449.90**

ESCORT PUMP SHOTGUNS
Gauge: 12, 20; 3" chamber. **Barrel:** 18" (AimGuard and MarineGuard), 22" (Youth Pump), 26", and 28" lengths. **Weight:** 6.7-7.0 lbs. **Stock:** Polymer in black, Shadow Grass® camo or Obsession® camo finish. Two adjusting spacers included. Youth model has Trio recoil pad. **Sights:** Bead or Spark front sights, depending on model. AimGuard and MarineGuard models have blade front sights. **Features:** Black-chrome or dipped camo metal parts, top of receiver dovetailed for sight mounts, gold plated trigger, trigger guard safety, magazine cut-off. Three choke tubes (IC, M, F) except AimGuard/MarineGuard which are cylinder bore. Models include: FH, FH Youth, AimGuard and Marine Guard. Introduced in 2003. Imported from Turkey by Legacy Sports International.
Price: . . . . **$389.00 to $469.00**

HARRINGTON & RICHARDSON PARDNER PUMP FIELD GUN FULL-DIP CAMO
Gauge: 12, 20; 3" chamber. **Barrel:** 28" fully rifled. **Weight:** 7.5 lbs. **Length:** 48-1/8" overall. **Stock:** Synthetic or hardwood. **Sights:** NA. **Features:** Steel receiver, double action bars, cross-bolt safety, easy takedown, vent rib, screw-in Modified choke tube. Ventilated recoil pad and grooved forend with Realtree APG-HDTM full camo dip finish.
Price: Full camo version **$278.00**

IAC MODEL 87W-1 LEVER-ACTION SHOTGUN
Gauge: 12; 2-3/4" chamber only. **Barrel:** 20" with fixed Cylinder choke. **Weight:** NA. **Length:** NA. **Stock:** American walnut. **Sights:** Bead front. **Features:** Modern replica of Winchester Model 1887 lever-action shotgun. Includes five-shot tubular magazine, pivoting split-lever design to meet modern safety requirements. Imported by Interstate Arms Corporation.
Price: **$429.95**

ITHACA GUN COMPANY DEERSLAYER III SLUG SHOTGUN
Gauge: 12, 20; 3" chamber. **Barrel:** 26" fully rifled, heavy fluted with 1:28 twist for 12 ga.; 1:24 for 20 ga. **Weight:** 8.14 lbs. to 9.5 lbs. with scope mounted. **Length:** 45.625" overall. **Stock:** Fancy black walnut stock and forend. **Sights:** NA. **Features:** Updated, slug-only version of the classic Model 37. Bottom ejection, blued barrel and receiver.
Price: **$1,189.00**

ITHACA GUN COMPANY MODEL 37 28 GAUGE SHOTGUN
Gauge: 28. **Barrel:** 26" or 28". **Weight:** NA. **Length**: NA. **Stock:** Black walnut stock and forend. **Sights:** NA. **Features:** Scaled down receiver with traditional Model 37 bottom ejection and easy takedown. Available in Fancy "A," Fancy "AA," and Fancy "AAA" grades with increasingly elaborate receiver engraving and decoration. Special order only.
Price: Fancy "A" grade **$999.00**

MOSSBERG MODEL 835 ULTI-MAG PUMP SHOTGUNS
Gauge: 12, 3-1/2" chamber. **Barrel:** Ported 24" rifled bore, 24", 28", Accu-Mag choke tubes for steel or lead shot. **Weight:** 7.75 lbs. **Length:** 48.5" overall. **Stock:** 14"x1.5"x2.5". Dual Comb. Cut-checkered hardwood or camo synthetic; both have recoil pad. **Sights:** White bead front, brass mid-bead; fiber-optic rear. **Features:** Shoots 2-3/4", 3" or 3-1/2" shells. Back-bored and ported barrel to reduce recoil, improve patterns. Ambidextrous thumb safety, twin extractors, dual slide bars. Mossberg Cablelock included. Introduced 1988.

Price: Thumbhole Turkey **$674.00**
Price: Tactical Turkey **$636.00**
Price: Synthetic Thumbhole Turkey, from **$493.00**
Price: Turkey, from **$487.00**
Price: Waterfowl, from **$437.00**
Price: Combo, from **$559.00**

MOSSBERG MODEL 500 JIC II
Takedown pump-action shotgun chambered in 3-inch 12 gauge. Similar to other 500 models but features pistol grip, matte black finish overall and comes packaged in black nylon zippered case.
Price: **$435.00**

MOSSBERG MODEL 500 SPORTING PUMP SHOTGUNS
Gauge: 12, 20, .410, 3" chamber. **Barrel:** 18.5" to 28" with fixed or Accu-Choke, plain or vent rib. **Weight:** 6-1/4 lbs. (.410), 7-1/4 lbs. (12). **Length:** 48" overall (28" barrel). **Stock:** 14"x1.5"x2.5". Walnut-stained hardwood, black synthetic, Mossy Oak Advantage camouflage. Cut-checkered grip and forend. **Sights:** White bead front, brass mid-bead; fiber-optic. **Features:** Ambidextrous thumb safety, twin extractors, disconnecting safety, dual action bars. Quiet Carry forend. Many barrels are ported. From Mossberg.
Price: Turkey. **$410.00**
Price: Waterfowl, from **$406.00**
Price: Combo, from. **$391.00**
Price: Field, from. **$354.00**
Price: Slugster, from **$354.00**

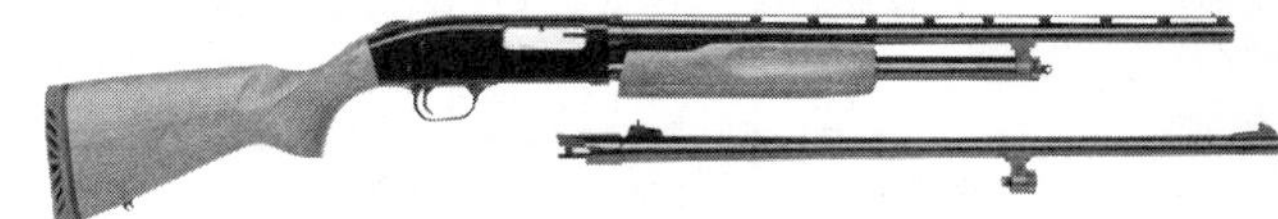

Mossberg Model 500 Bantam Pump Shotgun
Same as the Model 500 Sporting Pump except 12 or 20 gauge, 22" vent rib Accu-Choke barrel with choke tube set; has 1" shorter stock, reduced length from pistol grip to trigger, reduced forend reach. Introduced 1992.
Price: **$354.00**
Price: Super Bantam (2008), from **$338.00**

MOSSBERG 510 MINI BANTAM SHOTGUN
Compact pump-action shotgun based on Model 500 action, chambered in 3-inch 20 gauge and .410. Features include an 18.5-inch vent rib barrel with interchangeable (20) or fixed (.410) choke, black synthetic stock with removable inserts to adjust LOP from 12 to 14+ inches, 4-shot capacity. Weight 5 lbs.
Price: **$364.00**

NEW ENGLAND PARDNER PUMP SHOTGUN
Gauge: 12 ga., 3". **Barrel:** 28" vent rib, screw-in Modified choke tube. **Weight:** 7.5 lbs. **Length:** 48.5". **Stock:** American walnut,

grooved forend, ventilated recoil pad. **Sights:** Bead front. **Features:** Machined steel receiver, double action bars, five-shot magazine.
Price: **$200.00**

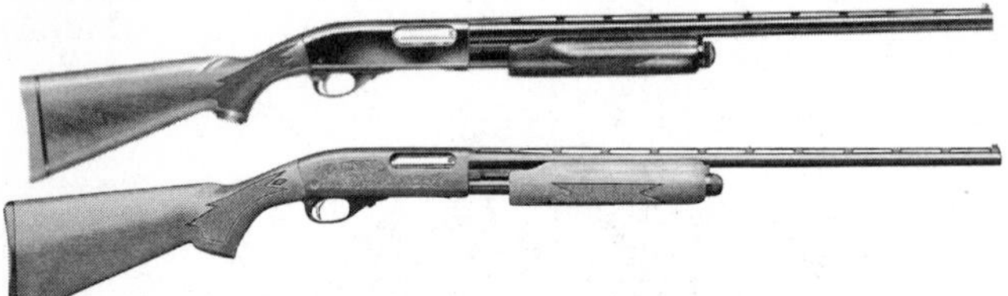

REMINGTON MODEL 870 WINGMASTER SHOTGUNS
Gauge: 12, 20, 28 ga., .410 bore. **Barrel:** 25", 26", 28", 30" (RemChokes). **Weight:** 7-1/4 lbs. **Length:** 46", 48". **Stock:** Walnut, hardwood. **Sights:** Single bead (Twin bead Wingmaster). **Features:** Light contour barrel. Double action bars, cross-bolt safety, blue finish. LW is 28 gauge and .410-bore only, 25" vent rib barrel with RemChoke tubes, high-gloss wood finish. Limited Edition Model 870 Wingmaster 100th Anniversary Commemorative Edition (2008 only) is 12 gauge with gold centennial logo, "100 Years of Remington Pump Shotguns" banner. Gold-plated trigger, American B Grade walnut stock and forend, high-gloss finish, fleur-de-lis checkering.
Price: Wingmaster, walnut, blued **$785.00**
Price: LW .410-bore **$839.00**
Price: 100th Anniversary (2008), 12 ga., 28" barrel **$1,035.00**

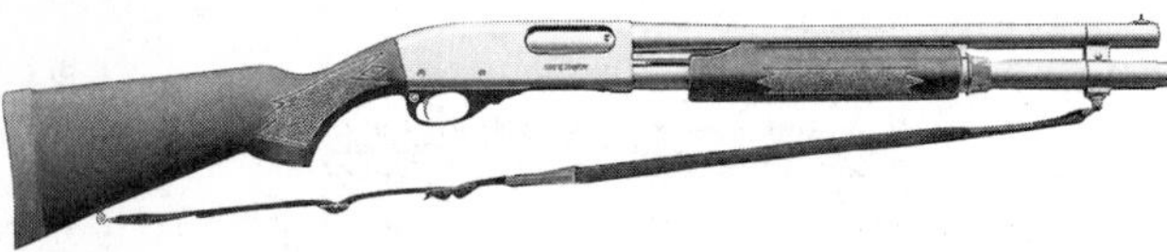

Remington Model 870 Marine Magnum Shotgun
Similar to 870 Wingmaster except all metal plated with electroless nickel, black synthetic stock and forend. Has 18" plain barrel (cyl.), bead front sight, 7-shot magazine. Introduced 1992. XCS version with TriNyte corrosion control introduced 2007.
Price: **$772.00**

REMINGTON MODEL 870 CLASSIC TRAP SHOTGUN
Similar to Model 870 Wingmaster except has 30" vent rib, light contour barrel, singles, mid- and long-handicap choke tubes, semi-fancy American walnut stock, high-polish blued receiver with engraving. Chamber 2.75". From Remington Arms Co.
Price: **$1,039.00**
Price: XCS (2007)................................. **$899.00**

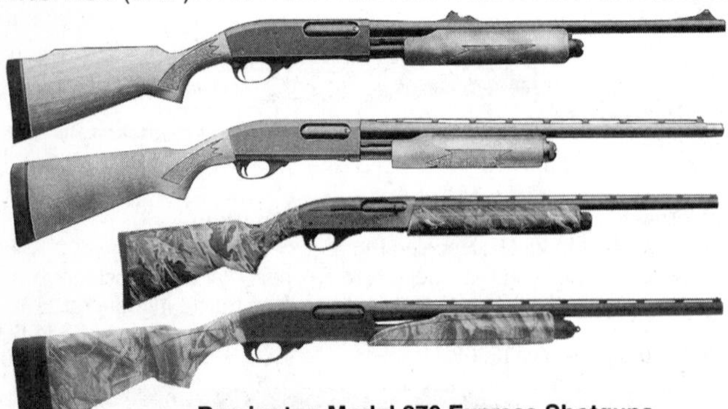

Remington Model 870 Express Shotguns
Similar to Model 870 Wingmaster except laminate, synthetic black, or camo stock with solid, black recoil pad and pressed checkering on grip and forend. Outside metal surfaces have black oxide finish. Comes with 26" or 28" vent rib barrel with mod. RemChoke tube. ShurShot Turkey (2008) has ShurShot synthetic pistol-grip thumbhole design, extended forend, Mossy Oak Obsession camouflage, matte black metal finish, 21" vent rib barrel, twin beads, Turkey Extra Full Rem Choke tube. Receiver drilled and tapped for mounting optics. ShurShot FR CL (Fully Rifled Cantilever, 2008) includes compact 23" fully-rifled barrel with integrated cantilever scope mount.
Price: 12 and 20 ga., laminate or synthetic right-hand stock . . **$383.00**
Price: 12 or 20 ga., laminate or synthetic left-hand stock..... **$409.00**
Price: Express Synthetic, 12 ga., 18" barrel (2007) **$383.00**
Price: Express Synthetic, 20 ga., 7 round capacity, from..... **$385.00**
Price: Express Synthetic Deer FR 12 ga., rifle sights **$425.00**
Price: Express Laminate Deer FR 12 ga., rifle sights **$416.00**
Price: Express Synthetic or Laminate Turkey 12 ga., 21" barrel **$388.00**
Price: Express Camo Turkey 12 ga., 21" barrel **$445.00**
Price: Express Combo Turkey/Deer Camo 12 ga. **$612.00**
Price: Express Synthetic Youth Combo 20 ga.............. **$543.00**
Price: Express Magnum ShurShot Turkey (2008) **$492.00**
Price: Express Magnum ShurShot FR CL (2008)........... **$500.00**
Price: Express ShurShot Synthetic Cantilever; 12 or 20 ga. with ShurShot stock and cantilever scope mount **$532.00**
Price: Express Compact Deer; 20 ga., similar to 870 Express Laminate Deer but with smaller dimensions **$395.00**
Price: Express Compact Pink Camo; 20 ga. **$429.00**
Price: Express Compact Synthetic; matte black synthetic stock **$383.00**
Price: Express Compact Camo; camo buttstock and forend . **$429.00**
Price: Express Compact Jr.; Shorter barrel and LOP **$383.00**

Remington Model 870 Express Super Magnum Shotgun
Similar to Model 870 Express except 28" vent rib barrel with 3-1/2" chamber, vented recoil pad. Introduced 1998. Model 870 Express Super Magnum Waterfowl (2008) is fully camouflaged with Mossy Oak Duck Blind pattern, 28-inch vent rib Rem Choke barrel, "Over Decoys" Choke tube (.007") fiber-optic HiViz single bead front sight; front and rear sling swivel studs, padded black sling.
Price: **$431.00**
Price: Super Magnum synthetic, 26" **$431.00**
Price: Super Magnum turkey camo (full-coverage RealTree Advantage camo), 23" **$564.00**
Price: Super Magnum combo (26" with Mod. RemChoke and 20" fully rifled deer barrel with 3" chamber and rifle sights; wood stock) **$577.00**
Price: Super Magnum Waterfowl (2008).................. **$577.00**

Remington Model 870 Special Purpose Shotguns (SPS)
Similar to the Model 870 Express synthetic, chambered for 12 ga. 3" and 3-1/2" shells, has Realtree Hardwoods HD or APG HD camo-synthetic stock and metal treatment, TruGlo fiber-optic sights. Introduced 2001. SPS Max Gobbler introduced 2007. Knoxx SpecOps adjustable stock, Williams Fire Sights fiber-optic sights, R3 recoil pad, Realtree APG HD camo. Drilled and tapped for Weaver-style rail
Price: SPS 12 ga. 3"................................ **$671.00**
Price: SPS Super Mag Max Gobbler (2007).............. **$819.00**
Price: SPS Super Mag Max Turkey ShurShot 3-1/2" (2008) . . **$644.00**
Price: SPS Synthetic ShurShot FR Cantilever 3" (2008) **$671.00**

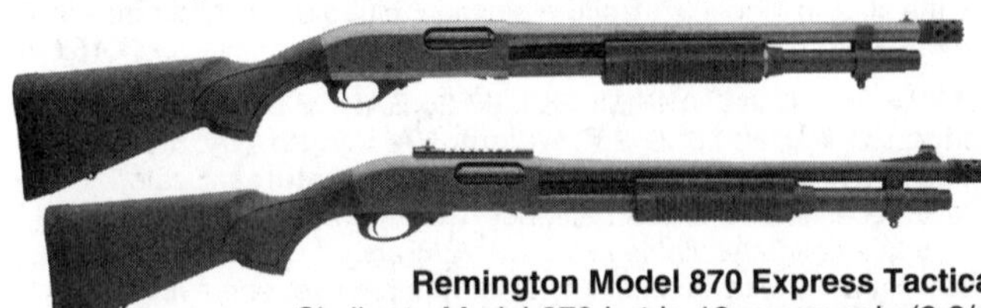

Remington Model 870 Express Tactical
Similar to Model 870 but in 12 gauge only (2-2/4" and 3" interchangeably) with 18.5" barrel, Tactical RemChoke extended/ported choke tube, black synthetic buttstock and forend, extended magazine tube, gray powdercoat finish overall. 38.5" overall length, weighs 7.5 lbs.
Price: **$372.00**
Price: Model 870 TAC Desert Recon; desert camo stock and sand-toned metal surfaces **$692.00**
Price: Model 870 Express Tactical with Ghost Ring Sights; Top-mounted accessories rail and XS ghost ring rear sight **$505.00**

REMINGTON MODEL 870 SPS SHURSHOT SYNTHETIC SUPER SLUG
Gauge: 12; 2-3/4" and 3" chamber, interchangeable. **Barrel:** 25.5" extra-heavy, fully rifled pinned to receiver. **Weight:** 7-7/8 lbs. **Length:** 47" overall. **Features:** Pump-action model based on 870 platform. SuperCell recoil pad. Drilled and tapped for scope mounts with Weaver rail included. Matte black metal surfaces, Mossy Oak Treestand Shurshot buttstock and forend.

Prices given are believed to be accurate at time of publication however, many factors affect retail pricing so exact prices are not possible.

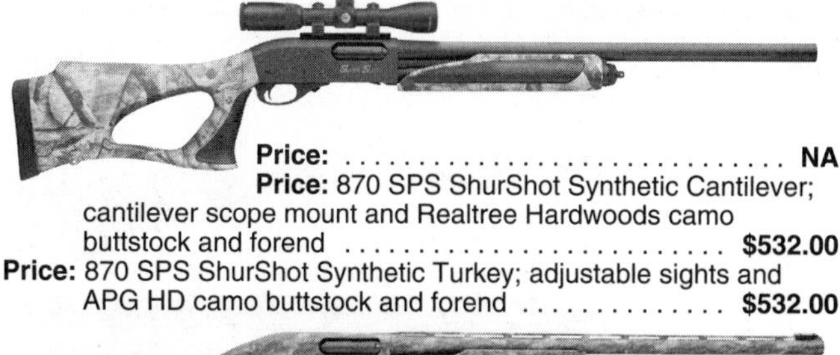

Price: .... NA
Price: 870 SPS ShurShot Synthetic Cantilever; cantilever scope mount and Realtree Hardwoods camo buttstock and forend $532.00
Price: 870 SPS ShurShot Synthetic Turkey; adjustable sights and APG HD camo buttstock and forend $532.00

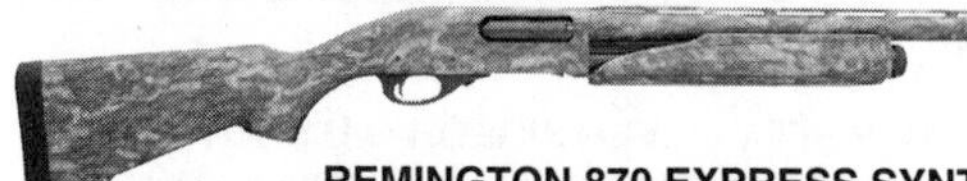

REMINGTON 870 EXPRESS SYNTHETIC SUPER MAG TURKEY-WATERFOWL CAMO

Pump action shotgun chambered in 12-ga., 2-3/4 to 3-1/2 inch. Features include full Mossy Oak Bottomland camo coverage; 26-inch barrel with HiViz fiber-optics sights; Wingmaster HD Waterfowl and Turkey Extra Full RemChokes; SuperCell recoil pad; drilled and tapped receiver.
Price: $601.00

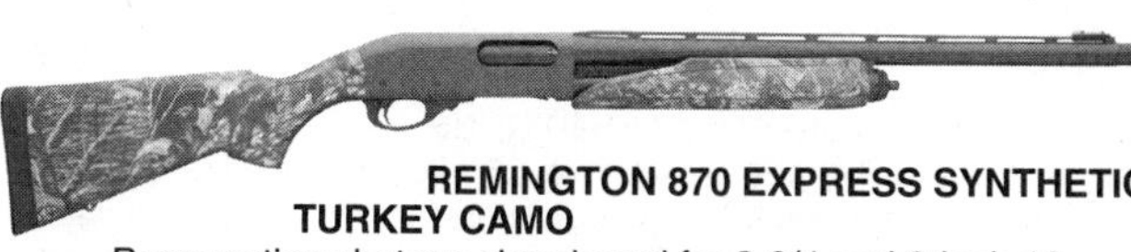

REMINGTON 870 EXPRESS SYNTHETIC TURKEY CAMO

Pump action shotgun chambered for 2-3/4 and 3-inch 12-ga. Features include 21-inch vent rib bead-sighted barrel; standard Express finish on barrel and receiver; Turkey Extra Full RemChoke; synthetic stock with integrated sling swivel attachment.
Price: $445.00

REMINGTON 870 SUPER MAG TURKEY-PREDATOR CAMO WITH SCOPE

Pump action shotgun chambered in 12-ga., 2-3/4 to 3-1/2 inch. Features include 20-inch barrel; TruGlo red/green selectable illuminated sight mounted on pre-installed Weaver-style rail; black padded sling; Wingmaster HD™ Turkey/Predator RemChoke; full Mossy Oak Obsession camo coverage; ShurShot pistol grip stock with black overmolded grip panels; TruGlo 30mm Red/Green Dot Scope pre-mounted.
Price: $679.00

REMINGTON MODEL 887 NITRO MAG PUMP SHOTGUN

Gauge: 12; 3.5", 3", and 2-3/4" chambers. **Barrel:** 28". **Features:** Pump-action model based on the Model 870. Interchangeable shells, black matte ArmoLokt rustproof coating throughout. SuperCell recoil pad. Solid rib and Hi-Viz front sight with interchangeable light tubes. Black synthetic stock with contoured grip panels.
Price: $399.00
Price: Model 887 Nitro Mag Waterfowl, Advantage Max-4 camo overall $532.00

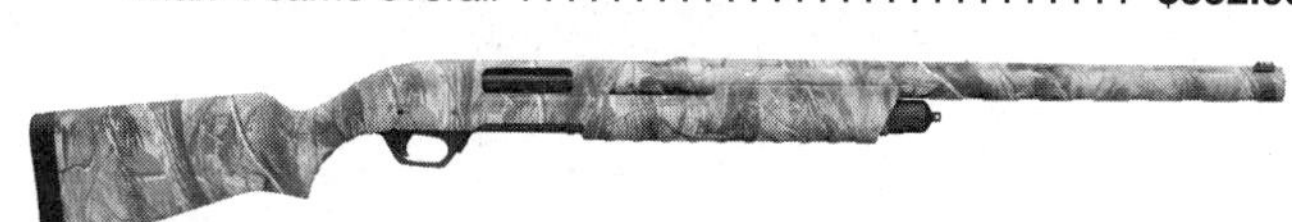

REMINGTON 887 BONECOLLECTOR EDITION

Pump action shotgun chambered in 12-ga., 2-3/4 to 3-1/2 inch. Features include ArmorLokt rustproof coating; synthetic stock and forend; 26-inch barrel; full camo finish; integral swivel studs; SuperCell recoil pad; solid rib and HiViz front sight. Bone Collector logo.
Price: $623.00

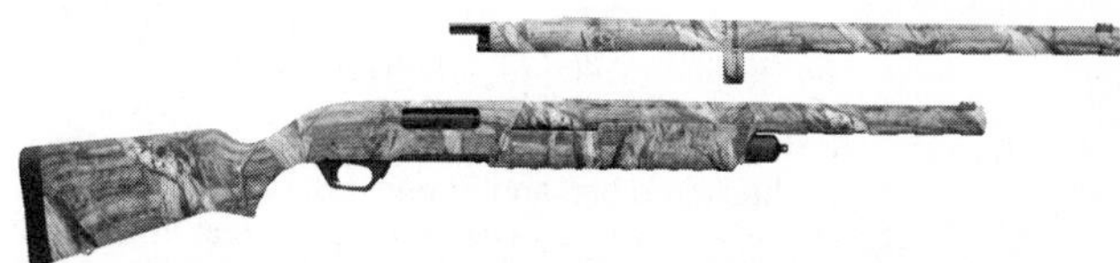

REMINGTON 887 NITRO MAG CAMO COMBO

Pump action shotgun chambered in 12-ga., 2-3/4 to 3-1/2 inch. Features include 22-inch turkey barrel with HiViz fiber-optic rifle sights and 28-inch waterfowl with a HiViz sight; extended Waterfowl and Super Full Turkey RemChokes are included; SuperCell recoil pad; synthetic stock and forend with specially contoured grip panels; full camo coverage.
Price: $693.00

STEVENS MODEL 350 PUMP SHOTGUN

Pump-action shotgun chambered for 2.5- and 3-inch 12-ga. Features include all-steel barrel and receiver; bottom-load and -eject design; black synthetic stock; 5+1 capacity.
Price: Field Model with 28-inch barrel, screw-in choke.......$267.00
Price: Security Model with 18-inch barrel, fixed choke.......$241.00
Price: Combo Model with Field and Security barrels $307.00
Price: Security Model with 18.25-inch barrel w/ghost ring rear sight....................................$254.00

STOEGER MODEL P350 SHOTGUNS

Gauge: 12, 3.5" chamber, set of five choke tubes (C, IC, M, IM, XF). **Barrel:** 18.5",24", 26", 28". **Stock:** Black synthetic, Timber HD, Max-4 HD, APG HD camos. **Sights:** Red bar front. **Features:** Inertia-recoil, mercury recoil reducer, pistol grip stocks. Imported by Benelli USA.
Price: Synthetic....................................$329.00
Price: Max-4, Timber HD $429.00
Price: Black synthetic pistol grip (2007) $329.00
Price: APG HD camo pistol grip (2007) $429.00

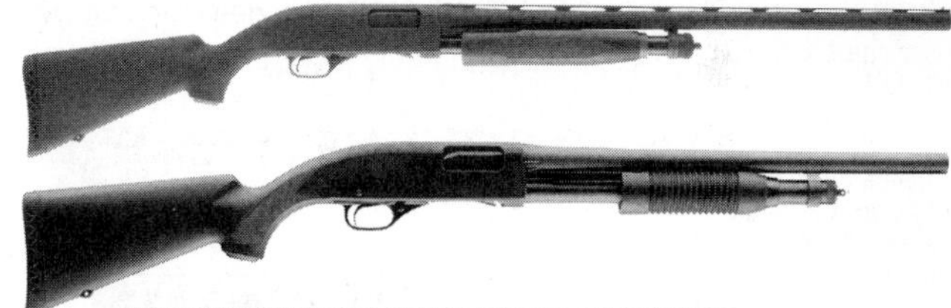

WINCHESTER SUPER X PUMP SHOTGUNS

Gauge: 12, 3" chambers. **Barrel:** 18"; 26" and 28" barrels are .742" back-bored, chrome plated; Invector Plus choke tubes. **Weight:** 7 lbs. **Stock:** Walnut or composite. **Features:** Rotary bolt, four lugs, dual steel action bars. Walnut Field has gloss-finished walnut stock and forearm, cut checkering. Black Shadow Field has composite stock and forearm, non-glare matte finish barrel and receiver. Speed Pump Defender has composite stock and forearm, chromed plated, 18" cylinder choked barrel, non-glare metal surfaces, five-shot magazine, grooved forearm. Weight, 6.5 lbs. Reintroduced 2008. Made in U.S.A. from Winchester Repeating Arms Co.
Price: Black Shadow Field $359.00
Price: Defender....................................$319.00

BERETTA DT10 TRIDENT SHOTGUNS

Gauge: 12, 2-3/4", 3" chambers. **Barrel:** 28", 30", 32", 34"; competition-style vent rib; fixed or Optima choke tubes. **Weight:** 7.9 to 9 lbs. **Stock:** High-grade walnut stock with oil finish; hand-checkered grip and forend, adjustable stocks available. **Features:** Detachable, adjustable trigger group, raised and thickened receiver, forend iron has adjustment nut to guarantee wood-to-metal fit. Introduced 2000. Imported from Italy by Beretta USA.

Price: DT10 Trident Trap, adjustable stock. **$7,400.00**
Price: DT10 Trident Skeet **$7,900.00**
Price: DT10 Trident Sporting, from. **$6,975.00**

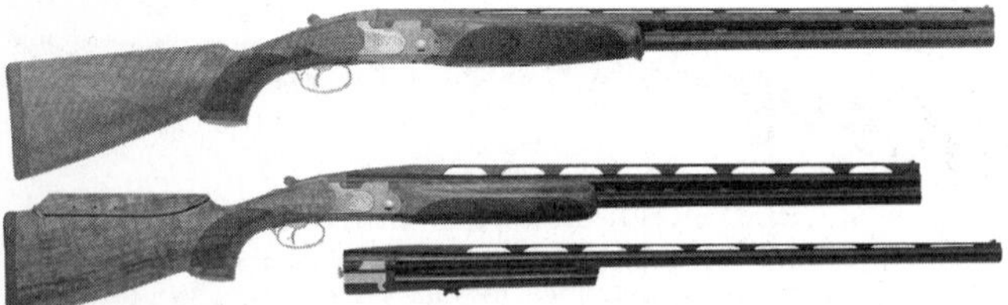

BERETTA SV10 PERENNIA O/U SHOTGUN

Gauge: 12, 3" chambers. **Barrel:** 26", 28", 30". Optima-Bore profile, polished blue. Bore diameter 18.6mm (0.73 in.) Self-adjusting dual conical longitudinal locking lugs, oversized monobloc bearing shoulders, replaceable hinge pins. Ventilated top rib, 6x6mm. Long guided extractors, automatic ejection or mechanical extraction. Optimachoke tubes. **Weight:** 7.3 lbs. **Stock:** Quick take-down stock with pistol grip or English straight stock. Kick-off recoil reduction system available on request on Q-Stock. **Length of pull:** 14.7", drop at comb, 1.5", drop at heel, 2.36" or 1.38"/2.17". Semibeavertail forend with elongated forend lever. New checkering pattern, matte oil finish, rubber pad. **Features:** Floral motifs and game scenes on side panels; nickel-based protective finish, arrowhead-shaped sideplates, solid steel alloy billet. Kick-Off recoil reduction mechanism available on select models. Fixed chokes on request, removable trigger group, titanium single selective trigger. Manual or automatic safety, newly designed safety and selector lever. Gel-Tek recoil pad available on request. Polypropylene case, 5 chokes with spanner, sling swivels, plastic pad, Beretta gun oil. Introduced 2008. Imported from Italy by Beretta USA.

Price: From. **$3,250.00**

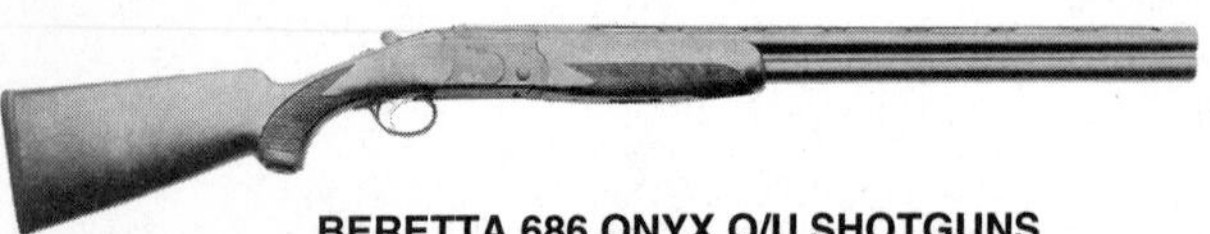

BERETTA SERIES 682 GOLD E SKEET, TRAP, SPORTING O/U SHOTGUNS

Gauge: 12, 2-3/4" chambers. **Barrel:** skeet-28"; trap-30" and 32", Imp. Mod. & Full and Mobilchoke; trap mono shotguns-32" and 34" Mobilchoke; trap top single guns-32" and 34" Full and Mobilchoke; trap combo sets-from 30" O/U, to 32" O/U, 34" top single. **Stock:** Close-grained walnut, hand checkered. **Sights:** White Bradley bead front sight and center bead. **Features:** Receiver has Greystone gunmetal gray finish with gold accents. Trap Monte Carlo stock has deluxe trap recoil pad. Various grades available. Imported from Italy by Beretta USA.

Price: 682 Gold E Trap with adjustable stock. **$4,425.00**
Price: 682 Gold E Trap Unsingle **$4,825.00**
Price: 682 Gold E Sporting. **$4,075.00**
Price: 682 Gold E Skeet, adjustable stock **$4,425.00**

BERETTA 686 ONYX O/U SHOTGUNS

Gauge: 12, 20, 28; 3", 3.5" chambers. **Barrel:** 26", 28" (Mobilchoke tubes). **Weight:** 6.8-6.9 lbs. **Stock:** Checkered American walnut. **Features:** Intended for the beginning sporting clays shooter. Has wide, vented target rib, radiused recoil pad. Polished black finish on receiver and barrels. Introduced 1993. Imported from Italy by Beretta U.S.A.

Price: White Onyx. **$1,975.00**
PPrice: White Onyx Sporting **$2,175.00**

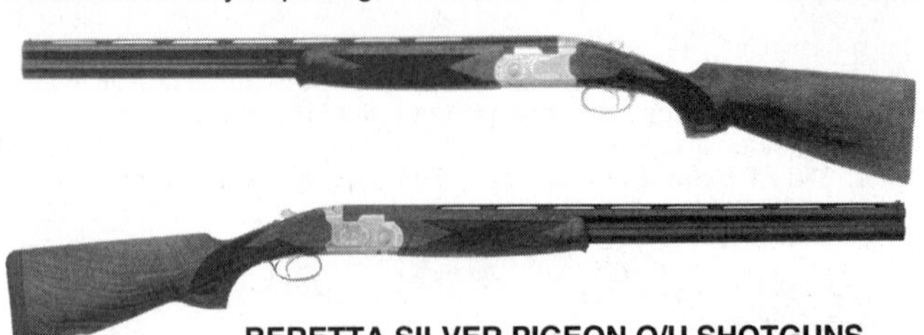

BERETTA SILVER PIGEON O/U SHOTGUNS

Gauge: 12, 20, 28, 3" chambers (2-3/4" 28 ga.). .410 bore, 3" chamber. **Barrel:** 26", 28". **Weight:** 6.8 lbs. **Stock:** Checkered walnut. **Features:** Interchangeable barrels (20 and 28 ga.), single selective gold-plated trigger, boxlock action, auto safety, Schnabel forend.

Price: Silver Pigeon S. **$2,400.00**
Price: Silver Pigeon II **$3,150.00**
Price: Silver Pigeon III **$3,275.00**
Price: Silver Pigeon IV **$3,200.00**
Price: Silver Pigeon V. **$3,675.00**

BERETTA ULTRALIGHT O/U SHOTGUNS

Gauge: 12, 2-3/4" chambers. **Barrel:** 26", 28", Mobilchoke tubes. **Weight:** About 5 lbs., 13 oz. **Stock:** Select American walnut with checkered grip and forend. **Features:** Low-profile aluminum alloy receiver with titanium breech face insert. Electroless nickel receiver with game scene engraving. Single selective trigger; automatic safety. Introduced 1992. Ultralight Deluxe except has matte electroless nickel finish receiver with gold game scene engraving; matte oil-finished, select walnut stock and forend. Imported from Italy by Beretta U.S.A.

Price: **$2,075.00**
Price: Ultralight Deluxe **$2,450.00**

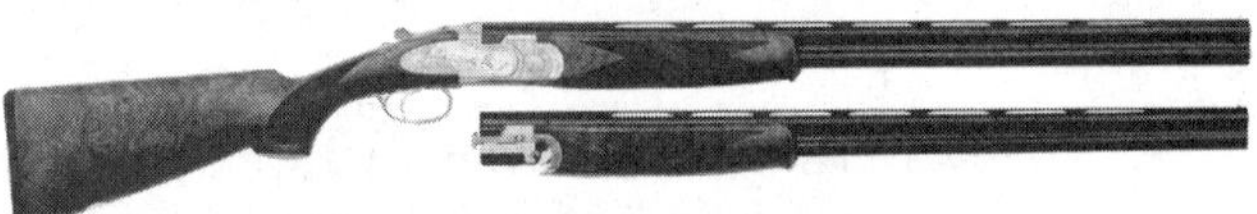

BERETTA COMPETITION SHOTGUNS

Gauge: 12, 20, 28, and .410 bore, 2-3/4", 3" and 3-1/2" chambers. **Barrel:** 26" and 28" (Mobilchoke tubes). **Stock:** Close-grained walnut. **Features:** Highly-figured, American walnut stocks and forends, and a unique, weather-resistant finish on barrels. Silver designates standard 686, 687 models with silver receivers; 686 Silver Pigeon has enhanced engraving pattern, Schnabel forend; Gold indicates higher grade 686EL, 687EL models with full sideplates. Imported from Italy by Beretta U.S.A.

Price: S687 EELL Gold Pigeon Sporting (D.R. engraving). . **$7,675.00**

BILL HANUS 16-GAUGE BROWNING CITORI M525 FIELD

Gauge: 16. **Barrel:** 26" and 28". **Weight:** 6-3/4 pounds. **Stock:** 1-1/2" x 2-3/8" x 14-1/4" and cast neutral. Adjusting for cast-on for left-handed shooters or cast-off for right-handed shooters, $300 extra. Oil finish. **Features:** Full pistol grip with a graceful Schnable forearm and built on a true 16-gauge frame. Factory supplies three Invector choke tubes: IC-M-F and Bill Hanus models come with two Briley-made skeet chokes for close work over dogs and clay-target games.

Price: **$1,795.00**

BROWNING CYNERGY O/U SHOTGUNS

Gauge: 12, 20, 28. **Barrel:** 26", 28", 30", 32". **Stock:** Walnut or composite. **Sights:** White bead front most models; HiViz Pro-Comp sight on some models; mid bead. **Features:** Mono-Lock hinge, recoil-reducing interchangeable Inflex recoil pad, silver nitride receiver; striker-based trigger, ported barrel option. Models include: Cynergy Sporting, Adjustable Comb; Cynergy Sporting Composite CF; Cynergy Field, Composite; Cynergy Classic

Prices given are believed to be accurate at time of publication however, many factors affect retail pricing so exact prices are not possible.

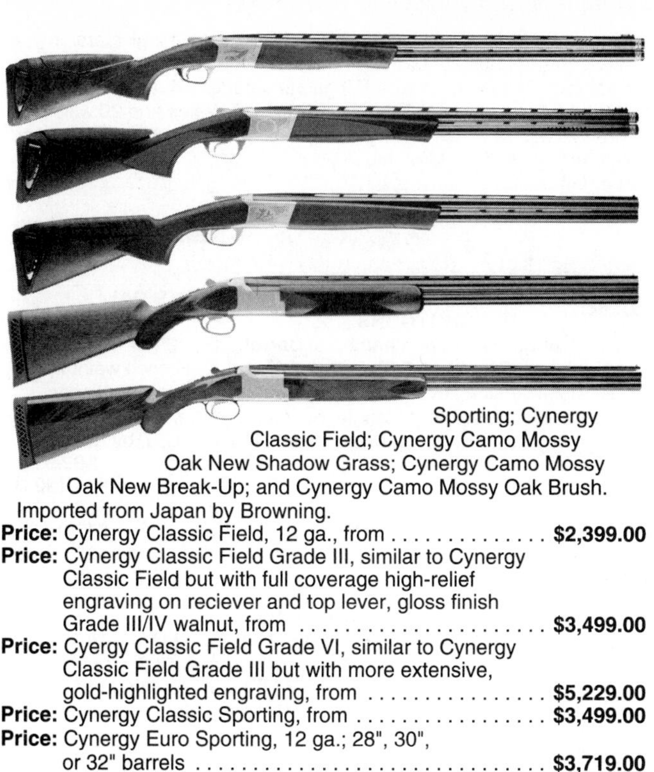

Sporting; Cynergy Classic Field; Cynergy Camo Mossy Oak New Shadow Grass; Cynergy Camo Mossy Oak New Break-Up; and Cynergy Camo Mossy Oak Brush. Imported from Japan by Browning.

Price: Cynergy Classic Field, 12 ga., from **$2,399.00**
Price: Cynergy Classic Field Grade III, similar to Cynergy Classic Field but with full coverage high-relief engraving on reciever and top lever, gloss finish Grade III/IV walnut, from **$3,499.00**
Price: Cyergy Classic Field Grade VI, similar to Cynergy Classic Field Grade III but with more extensive, gold-highlighted engraving, from **$5,229.00**
Price: Cynergy Classic Sporting, from **$3,499.00**
Price: Cynergy Euro Sporting, 12 ga.; 28", 30", or 32" barrels **$3,719.00**
Price: Cynergy Euro Sporting Composite 12 ga. **$3,499.00**
Price: Cynergy Euro Sporting, adjustable comb, intr. 2006 . **$4,079.00**
Price: Cynergy Feather, 12 ga. intr. 2007. . . . . **$2,579.00**
Price: Cynergy Feather, 20, 28 ga., .410, intr. 2008. . . . . . . **$2,599.00**
Price: Cynergy Euro Sporting, 20 ga., intr. 2008 . . . . **$3,739.00**
Price: Cynergy Euro Field, Invector Plus tubes in 12 and 20 gauge, standard Invector tubes on 28 gauge and 410 . . . . **$2,509.00**

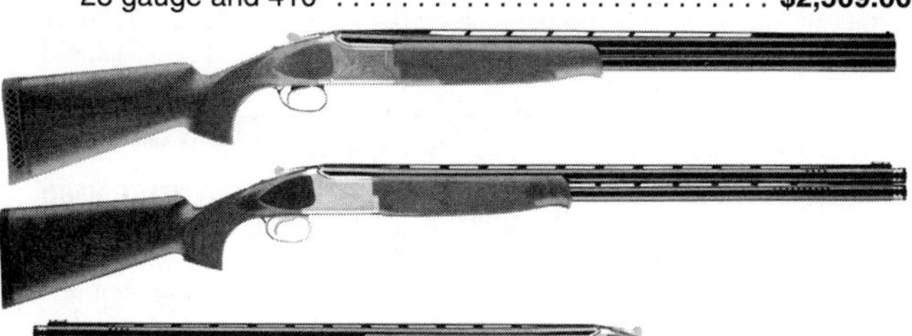

BROWNING CITORI O/U SHOTGUNS

Gauge: 12, 20, 28 and .410. **Barrel:** 26", 28" in 28 and .410. Offered with Invector choke tubes. All 12 and 20 gauge models have back-bored barrels and Invector Plus choke system. **Weight:** 6 lbs., 8 oz. (26" .410) to 7 lbs., 13 oz. (30" 12 ga.). **Length:** 43" overall (26" bbl.). **Stock:** Dense walnut, hand checkered, full pistol grip, beavertail forend. Field-type recoil pad on 12 ga. field guns and trap and skeet models. **Sights:** Medium raised beads, German nickel silver. **Features:** Barrel selector integral with safety, automatic ejectors, three-piece takedown. Citori 625 Field (intr. 2008) includes Vector Pro extended forcing cones, new wood checkering patterns, silver-nitride finish with high-relief engraving, gloss oil finish with Grade II/III walnut with radius pistol grip, Schnabel forearm, 12 gauge, three Invector Plus choke tubes. Citori 625 Sporting (intr. 2008) includes standard and adjustable combs, 32", 30", and 28" barrels, five Diamond Grade extended Invector Plus choke tubes. Triple Trigger System allows adjusting length of pull and choice of wide checkered, narrow smooth, and wide smooth canted trigger shoe. HiViz Pro-Comp fiber-optic front sights. Imported from Japan by Browning.

Price: Lightning, from **$1,763.00**
Price: White Lightning, from **$1,836.00**
Price: Superlight Feather **$2,098.00**
Price: Lightning Feather, combo 20 and 28 ga. **$1,869.00**
Price: 625 Field, 12, 20 or 28 ga. and 410. Weighs 6 lbs. 12 oz. to 7 lbs. 14 oz. **$2,339.00**
Price: 625 Sporting, 12, 20 or 28 ga. and 410, standard comb, intr. 2008. . . . . **$3,329.00**
Price: 625 Sporting, 12 ga., adj. comb, intr. 2008. . . . . **$3,639.00**

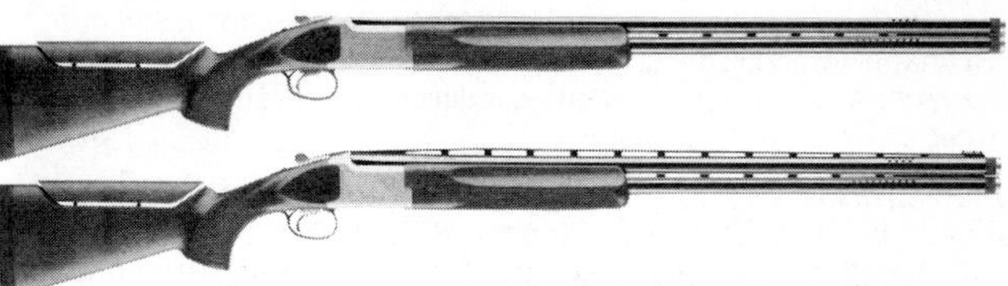

Browning Citori High Grade Shotguns

Similar to standard Citori except has engraved hunting scenes and gold inlays, high-grade, hand-oiled walnut stock and forearm. Introduced 2000. From Browning.

Price: Grade IV Lightning, engraved gray receiver, introduced 2005, from. **$2,999.00**
Price: Grade VII Lightning, engraved gray or blue receiver, introduced 2005, from. **$4,769.00**
Price: GTS High Grade, intr. 2007 . . . . **$4,309.00**

Browning Citori XS Sporting O/U Shotguns

Similar to the standard Citori except available in 12, 20, 28 or .410 with 28", 30", 32" ported barrels with various screw-in choke combinations: S (Skeet), C (Cylinder), IC (Improved Cylinder), M (Modified), and IM (Improved Modified). Has pistol grip stock, rounded or Schnabel forend. Weighs 7.1 lbs. to 8.75 lbs. Introduced 2004. Ultra XS Prestige (intr. 2008) has silver-nitride finish receiver with gold accented, high-relief Ultra XS Special engraving. Also, single selective trigger, hammer ejectors, gloss oil finish walnut stock with right-hand palm swell, adjustable comb, Schnabel forearm. Comes with five Invector-Plus Midas Grade choke tubes.

Price: XS Special, 12 ga.; 30", 32" barrels **$3,169.00**
Price: XS Skeet, 12 or 20 ga. **$2,829.00**
Price: XS Special High Post Rib, intr. 2007 . . . . **$3,169.00**
Price: Ultra XS Prestige, intr. 2008. **$4,759.00**

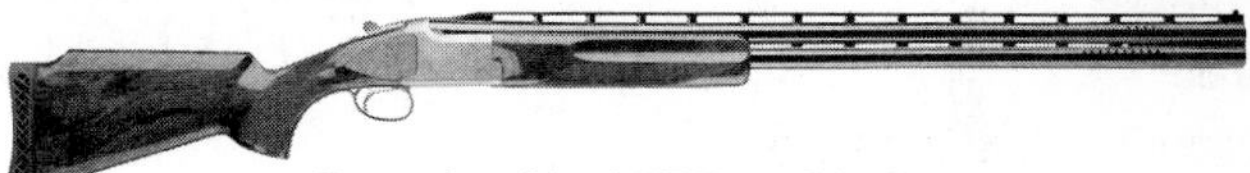

Browning Citori XT Trap O/U Shotgun

Similar to the Citori XS Special except has engraved silver nitride receiver with gold highlights, vented side barrel rib. Available in 12 gauge with 30" or 32" barrels, Invector-Plus choke tubes, adjustable comb and buttplate. Introduced 1999. Imported by Browning.

Price: XT Trap. **$2,639.00**
Price: XT Trap w/adjustable comb **$2,959.00**
Price: XT Trap Gold w/adjustable comb, introduced 2005 . . **$4,899.00**

CHARLES DALY MODEL 206 O/U SHOTGUN

Gauge: 12, 3" chambers. **Barrel:** 26", 28", 30", chrome-moly steel. **Weight:** 8 lbs. **Stock:** Checkered select Turkish walnut stocks. **Features:** Single selective trigger, extractors or selective automatic ejectors. Sporting model has 10mm ventilated rib and side ventilated ribs. Trap model comes with 10mm top rib and side ventilated ribs and includes a Monte Carlo Trap buttstock. Both competition ribs have mid-brass bead and front fluorescent sights. Five Multi-Choke tubes. Introduced 2008. Imported from Turkey by K.B.I., Inc.

Price: Field, 26" or 28", extractors **$759.00**
Price: Field, 26" or 28", auto-eject **$884.00**
Price: Sporting, 28" or 30" ported, ... **$999.00**
Price: Trap, 28" or 30" ported, ... **$1,064.00**

CZ SPORTING OVER/UNDER

Gauge: 12, 3" chambers. **Barrel:** 30", 32" chrome-lined, back-bored with extended forcing cones. **Weight:** 9 lbs. **Length:** NA. **Stock:** Neutral cast stock with an adjustable comb, trap style forend, pistol grip and ambidextrous palm swells. #3 grade Circassian walnut. At lowest position, drop at comb: 1-5/8"; drop at heel: 2-3/8"; length of pull: 14-1/2". **Features:** Designed for Sporting Clays and FITASC competition. Hand engraving, satin black-finished receiver. Tapered rib with center bead and a red fiber-optic front bead, 10 choke tubes with wrench, single selective trigger, automatic ejectors, thin rubber pad with slick plastic top. Introduced 2008. From CZ-USA.

Price: **$2,509.00**

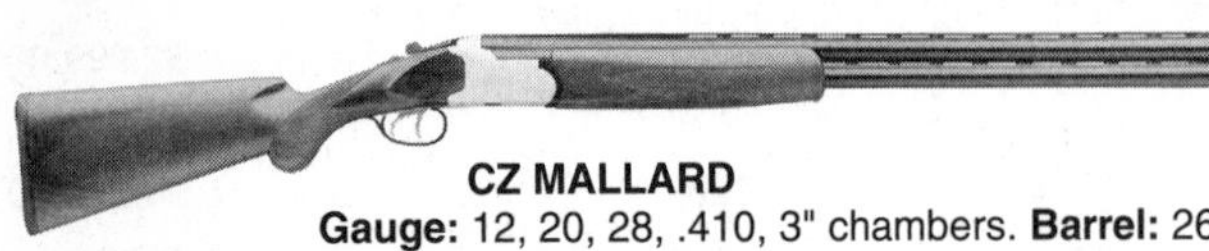

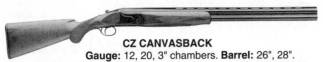

CZ CANVASBACK

Gauge: 12, 20, 3" chambers. **Barrel:** 26", 28". **Weight:** 7.3 lbs. **Length:** NA. **Stock:** Round-knob pistol grip, Schnabel forend, Turkish walnut. **Features:** Single selective trigger, set of 5 screw-in chokes, black chrome finished receiver. From CZ-USA.

Price: **$819.00**

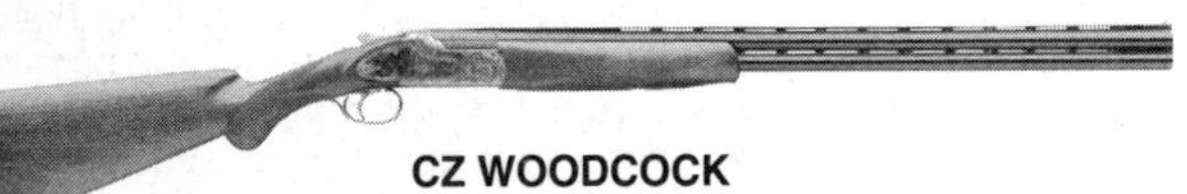

CZ MALLARD

Gauge: 12, 20, 28, .410, 3" chambers. **Barrel:** 26". **Weight:** 7.7 lbs. **Length:** NA. **Stock:** Round-knob pistol grip, Schnabel forend, Turkish walnut. **Features:** Double triggers and extractors, coin finished receiver, multi chokes. From CZ-USA.

Price: **$562.00**

CZ REDHEAD

Gauge: 12, 20, 3" chambers. **Barrel:** 28". **Weight:** 7.4 lbs. **Length:** NA. **Stock:** Round-knob pistol grip, Schnabel forend, Turkish walnut. **Features:** Single selective triggers and extractors (12 & 20 ga.), screw-in chokes (12, 20, 28 ga.) choked IC and Mod (.410), coin finished receiver, multi chokes. From CZ-USA.

Price: **$965.00**

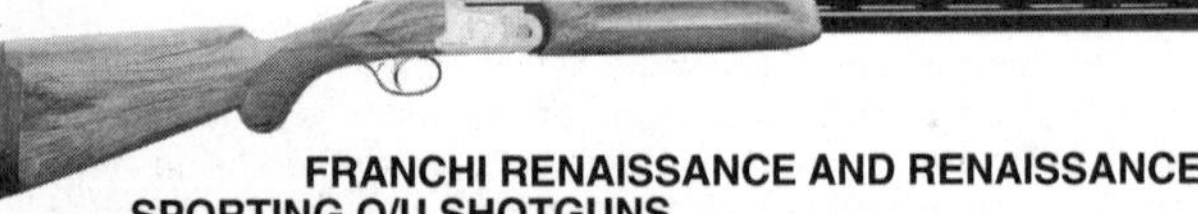

CZ WOODCOCK

Gauge: 12, 20, 28, .410, 3" chambers. **Barrel:** 26". **Weight:** 7.7 lbs. **Length:** NA. **Stock:** Round-knob pistol grip, Schnabel forend, Turkish walnut. **Features:** Single selective triggers and extractors (auto ejectors on 12 & 20 ga.), screw-in chokes (12, 20, 28 ga.) choked IC and Mod (.410), coin finished receiver, multi chokes. The sculptured frame incorporates a side plate, resembling a true side lock, embellished with hand engraving and finished with color casehardening. From CZ-USA.

Price: **$1,246.00**

ESCORT OVER/UNDER SHOTGUNS

Gauge: 12, 3" chamber. **Barrel:** 28". **Weight:** 7.4 lbs. **Stock:** Walnut or select walnut with Trio recoil pad; synthetic stock with adjustable comb. Three adjustment spacers. **Sights:** Bronze front bead. **Features:** Blued barrels, blued or nickel receiver. Trio recoil pad. Five interchangeable chokes (SK, IC, M, IM, F); extractors or ejectors (new, 2008), barrel selector. Hard case available. Introduced 2007. Imported from Turkey by Legacy Sports International.

Price: **$599.00**

FRANCHI RENAISSANCE AND RENAISSANCE SPORTING O/U SHOTGUNS

Gauge: 12, 20, 28, 3" chamber. **Barrel:** 26", 28". **Weight:** 5.0 to 6.0 lbs. **Length:** 42-5/8" to 44-5/8". **Stock:** 14.5" LOP, European oil-finished walnut with standard grade A grade, and AA grade choices. Prince of Wales grip. **Features:** TSA recoil pad, interchangeable chokes, hard case. Introduced 2006. ***Sporting model:*** **Gauge:** 12 , 3". **Barrel:** 30" ported. **Weight:** 7.9 lbs. **Length:** 46 5/8". **Stock:** 14.5" LOP, A-grade European oil-finished walnut. **Features:** TSA recoil pad, adjustable comb, lengthened forcing cones, extended choke tubes (C, IC, M and wrench), hard case. Introduced 2007. Imported from Italy by Benelli USA.

Price: Field **$1,729.00**
Price: Classic **$1,899.00**
Price: Elite. **$2,399.00**
Price: Sporting **$2,249.00**

KIMBER MARIAS O/U SHOTGUN

Gauge: 20, 16; 3". **Barrel:** 26", 28", 30". **Weight:** 6.5 lbs. **Length:** NA. **Stock:** Turkish walnut stocks, 24-lpi checkering, oil finish. **LOP:** 14.75". **Features:** Hand-detachable back-action sidelock, bone-charcoal case coloring. Hand-engraving on receiver and locks, Belgian rust blue barrels, chrome lined. Five thinwall choke tubes, automatic ejectors, ventilated rib. Gold line cocking indicators on locks. Grade I has 28" barrels, Prince of Wales stock in grade three Turkish walnut in either 12 or 20 gauge. Grade II shas grade four Turkish walnut stocks, 12 gauge in Prince of Wales and 20 with either Prince of Wales or English profiles. Introduced 2008. Imported from Italy by Kimber Mfg., Inc.

Price: Grade II. **$5,799.00**

KOLAR SPORTING CLAYS O/U SHOTGUNS

Gauge: 12, 2-3/4" chambers. **Barrel:** 30", 32", 34"; extended choke tubes. **Stock:** 14-5/8"x2.5"x1-7/8"x1-3/8". French walnut. Four stock versions available. **Features:** Single selective trigger, detachable, adjustable for length; overbored barrels with long forcing cones; flat tramline rib; matte blue finish. Made in U.S. by Kolar.

Price: Standard. **$9,595.00**
Price: Prestige **$14,190.00**
Price: Elite Gold **$16,590.00**
Price: Legend **$17,090.00**
Price: Select **$22,590.00**
Price: Custom. . . . . **Price on request**

Kolar AAA Competition Trap O/U Shotgun

Similar to the Sporting Clays gun except has 32" O/U /34" Unsingle or 30" O/U /34" Unsingle barrels as an over/under, unsingle, or combination set. Stock dimensions are 14.5"x2.5"x1.5"; American or French walnut; step parallel rib standard. Contact maker for full listings. Made in U.S.A. by Kolar.

Price: Over/under, choke tubes, standard **$9,595.00**
Price: Combo (30"/34", 32"/34"), standard **$12,595.00**

Kolar AAA Competition Skeet O/U Shotgun

Similar to the Sporting Clays gun except has 28" or 30" barrels with Kolarite AAA sub gauge tubes; stock of American or French walnut with matte finish; flat tramline rib; under barrel adjustable for point of impact. Many options available. Contact maker for complete listing. Made in U.S.A. by Kolar.

Price: Standard, choke tubes **$10,995.00**
Price: Standard, choke tubes, two-barrel set **$12,995.00**

KRIEGHOFF K-80 SPORTING CLAYS O/U SHOTGUN

Gauge: 12. **Barrel:** 28", 30", 32", 34" with choke tubes. **Weight:** About 8 lbs. **Stock:** #3 Sporting stock designed for gun-down shooting. **Features:** Standard receiver with satin nickel finish and classic scroll engraving. Selective mechanical trigger adjustable for position. Choice of tapered flat or 8mm parallel flat barrel rib. Free-floating barrels. Aluminum case. Imported from Germany by Krieghoff International, Inc.

Price: Standard grade with five choke tubes, from **$9,395.00**

KRIEGHOFF K-80 SKEET O/U SHOTGUNS

Gauge: 12, 2-3/4" chambers. **Barrel:** 28", 30", 32", (skeet & skeet), optional choke tubes). **Weight:** About 7.75 lbs. **Stock:** American skeet or straight skeet stocks, with palm-swell grips. Walnut. **Features:** Satin gray receiver finish. Selective mechanical trigger adjustable for position. Choice of ventilated 8mm parallel flat rib or ventilated 8-12mm tapered flat rib. Introduced 1980. Imported from Germany by Krieghoff International, Inc.

Price: Standard, skeet chokes **$8,375.00**
Price: Skeet Special (28", 30", 32" tapered flat rib, skeet & skeet choke tubes). **$9,100.00**

KRIEGHOFF K-80 TRAP O/U SHOTGUNS

Gauge: 12, 2-3/4" chambers. **Barrel:** 30", 32" (Imp. Mod. & Full or choke tubes). **Weight:** About 8.5 lbs. **Stock:** Four stock dimensions or adjustable stock available; all have palm-swell grips. Checkered European walnut. **Features:** Satin nickel receiver. Selective mechanical trigger, adjustable for position. Ventilated step rib. Introduced 1980. Imported from Germany by Krieghoff International, Inc.

Price: K-80 O/U (30", 32", Imp. Mod. & Full), from **$8,850.00**
Price: K-80 Unsingle (32", 34", Full), standard, from **$10,080.00**
Price: K-80 Combo (two-barrel set), standard, from. **$13,275.00**

Krieghoff K-20 O/U Shotgun

Similar to the K-80 except built on a 20-gauge frame. Designed for skeet, sporting clays and field use. Offered in 20, 28 and .410; 28", 30" and 32" barrels. Imported from Germany by Krieghoff International Inc.

Price: K-20, 20 gauge, from **$9,575.00**
Price: K-20, 28 gauge, from **$9,725.00**
Price: K-20, .410, from **$9,725.00**

LEBEAU-COURALLY BOSS-VEREES O/U SHOTGUN

Gauge: 12, 20, 2-3/4" chambers. **Barrel:** 25" to 32". **Weight:** To customer specifications. **Stock:** Exhibition-quality French walnut. **Features:** Boss-type sidelock with automatic ejectors; single or double triggers; chopper lump barrels. A custom gun built to customer specifications. Imported from Belgium by Wm. Larkin Moore.

Price: From **$96,000.00**

LJUTIC LM-6 SUPER DELUXE O/U SHOTGUNS

Gauge: 12. **Barrel:** 28" to 34", choked to customer specs for live birds, trap, international trap. **Weight:** To customer specs. **Stock:** To customer specs. Oil finish, hand checkered. **Features:** Custom-made gun. Hollow-milled rib, pull or release trigger, push-button opener in front of trigger guard. From Ljutic Industries.

Price: Super Deluxe LM-6 O/U **$19,995.00**
Price: Over/Under combo (interchangeable single barrel, two trigger guards, one for single trigger, one for doubles) **$27,995.00**
Price: Extra over/under barrel sets, 29"-32" **$6,995.00**

MARLIN L. C. SMITH O/U SHOTGUNS

Gauge: 12, 20. **Barrel:** 26", 28". **Stock:** Checkered walnut w/recoil pad. **Length:** 45". **Weight:** 7.25 lbs. **Features:** 3" chambers; 3 choke tubes (IC, Mod., Full), single selective trigger, selective automatic ejectors; vent rib; bead front sight. Imported from Italy by Marlin. Introduced 2005.

Price: LC12-OU (12 ga., 28" barrel) **$1,254.00**
Price: LC20-OU (20 ga., 26" barrel, 6.25 lbs., OAL 43") . . . **$1,254.00**

MERKEL MODEL 2001EL O/U SHOTGUN

Gauge: 12, 20, 3" chambers, 28, 2-3/4" chambers. **Barrel:** 12-28"; 20, 28 ga.-26.75". **Weight:** About 7 lbs. (12 ga.). **Stock:** Oil-finished walnut; English or pistol grip. **Features:** Self-cocking Blitz boxlock action with cocking indicators; Kersten double cross-bolt lock; silver-grayed receiver with engraved hunting scenes; coil spring ejectors; single selective or double triggers. Imported from Germany by Merkel USA.

Price: **$9,995.00**
Price: Model 2001EL Sporter; full pistol grip stock **$9,995.00**

Merkel Model 2000CL O/U Shotgun

Similar to Model 2001EL except scroll-engraved case-hardened receiver; 12, 20, 28 gauge. Imported from Germany by Merkel USA.

Price: **$8,495.00**
Price: Model 2016 CL; 16 gauge **$8,495.00**

PERAZZI MX8/MX8 SPECIAL TRAP, SKEET O/U SHOTGUNS

Gauge: 12, 2-3/4" chambers. **Barrel:** Trap: 29.5" (Imp. Mod. & Extra Full), 31.5" (Full & Extra Full). Choke tubes optional. Skeet: 27-5/8" (skeet & skeet). **Weight:** About 8.5 lbs. (trap); 7 lbs., 15 oz. (skeet). **Stock:** Interchangeable and custom made to customer specs. **Features:** Has detachable and interchangeable trigger group with flat V springs. Flat 7/16" vent rib. Many options available. Imported from Italy by Perazzi U.S.A., Inc.

Price: MX Trap Single **$10,934.00**

Perazzi MX8 Special Skeet O/U Shotgun

Similar to the MX8 Skeet except has adjustable four-position trigger, skeet stock dimensions. Imported from Italy by Perazzi U.S.A., Inc.

Price: From **$11,166.00**

PERAZZI MX8 O/U SHOTGUNS

Gauge: 12, 2-3/4" chambers. **Barrel:** 28-3/8" (Imp. Mod. & Extra Full), 29.5" (choke tubes). **Weight:** 7 lbs., 12 oz. **Stock:** Special specifications. **Features:** Has single selective trigger; flat 7/16" x 5/16" vent rib. Many options available. Imported from Italy by Perazzi U.S.A., Inc.

Price: Standard **$12,532.00**
Price: Sporting **$11,166.00**
Price: Trap Double Trap (removable trigger group) **$15,581.00**
Price: Skeet **$12,756.00**
Price: SC3 grade (variety of engraving patterns) . . . . **$23,000.00+**
Price: SCO grade (more intricate engraving, gold inlays). **$39,199.00+**

Perazzi MX8/20 O/U Shotgun

Similar to the MX8 except has smaller frame and has a removable trigger mechanism. Available in trap, skeet, sporting or game models with fixed chokes or choke tubes. Stock is made to customer specifications. Introduced 1993. Imported from Italy by Perazzi U.S.A., Inc.

Price: From **$11,731.00**

PERAZZI MX12 HUNTING O/U SHOTGUNS

Gauge: 12, 2-3/4" chambers. **Barrel:** 26.75", 27.5", 28-3/8", 29.5" (Mod. & Full); choke tubes available in 27-5/8", 29.5" only (MX12C). **Weight:** 7 lbs., 4 oz. **Stock:** To customer specs; interchangeable. **Features:** Single selective trigger; coil springs used in action; Schnabel forend tip. Imported from Italy by Perazzi U.S.A., Inc.

Price: From **$11,166.00**
Price: MX12C (with choke tubes). From **$11,960.00**

Perazzi MX20 Hunting O/U Shotguns

Similar to the MX12 except 20 ga. frame size. Non-removable trigger group. Available in 20, 28, .410 with 2-3/4" or 3" chambers. 26" standard, and choked Mod. & Full. Weight is 6 lbs., 6 oz. Imported from Italy by Perazzi U.S.A., Inc.

Price: From **$11,166.00**
Price: MX20C (as above, 20 ga. only, choke tubes). From **$11,960.00**

PERAZZI MX10 O/U SHOTGUN

Gauge: 12, 2-3/4" chambers. **Barrel:** 29.5", 31.5" (fixed chokes). **Weight:** NA. **Stock:** Walnut; cheekpiece adjustable for elevation and cast. **Features:** Adjustable rib; vent side rib. Externally selective trigger. Available in single barrel, combo, over/under trap, skeet, pigeon and sporting models. Introduced 1993. Imported from Italy by Perazzi U.S.A., Inc.

Price: MX200410 . . . . **$18,007.00**

PERAZZI MX28, MX410 GAME O/U SHOTGUN

Gauge: 28, 2-3/4" chambers, .410, 3" chambers. **Barrel:** 26" (Imp. Cyl. & Full). **Weight:** NA. **Stock:** To customer specifications. **Features:** Made on scaled-down frames proportioned to the gauge. Introduced 1993. Imported from Italy by Perazzi U.S.A., Inc.

Price: From **$22,332.00**

PIOTTI BOSS O/U SHOTGUN

Gauge: 12, 20. **Barrel:** 26" to 32", chokes as specified. **Weight:** 6.5 to 8 lbs. **Stock:** Dimensions to customer specs. Best quality figured walnut. **Features:** Essentially a custom-made gun with many options. Introduced 1993. Imported from Italy by Wm. Larkin Moore.

Price: From **$69,000.00**

POINTER OVER/UNDER SHOTGUN

Gauge: 12, 20, 28, .410, 3" chambers. **Barrel:** 28", blued. **Weight:** 6.1 to 7.6 lbs. **Stock:** Turkish Walnut. **Sights:** Fiber-optic front, bronze mid-bead. Choke: IC/M/F. **Features:** Engraved nickel receiver, automatic ejectors, fitted hard plastic case. Clays model has

oversized fiber-optic front sight and palm swell pistol grip. Introduced 2007. Imported from Turkey by Legacy Sports International.
Price: .... $1,299.00 to $1,499.00

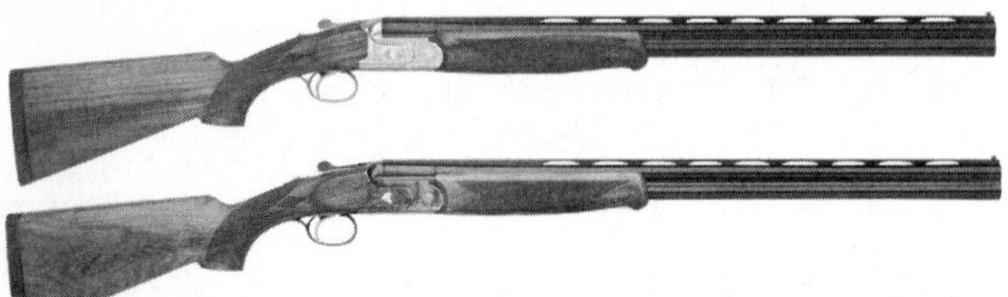

REMINGTON PREMIER OVER/UNDER SHOTGUNS

Gauge: 12, 20, 28, 3" chambers; 28, 2-3/4" chambers. **Barrel:** 26", 28", 30" in 12 gauge; overbored (.735), polished blue; 7mm vent rib. **Sights:** Ivory front bead, steel mid bead. **Weight:** 6.5 to 7.5 lbs. **Stock:** Walnut, cut checkering, Schnabel forends. Checkered pistol grip, checkered forend, satin finish, rubber butt pad. Right-hand palm swell. **Features:** Single selective mechanical trigger, selective automatic ejectors; serrated free-floating vent rib. Five flush mount ProBore choke tubes for 12s and 20s; 28-gauge equipped with 3 flush mount ProBore choke tubes. Hard case included. Introduced 2006. Made in Italy, imported by Remington Arms Co.
Price: Premier Field, nickel-finish receiver, from $2,086.00
Price: Premier Upland, case-colored receiver finish, from .. $2,226.00
Price: Premier Competition STS (2007) $2,540.00
Price: Premier Competition STS Adj. Comb (2007) $2,890.00

REMINGTON SPR310 OVER/UNDER SHOTGUNS

Gauge: 12, 20, 28, .410 bore, 3" chambers; 28, 2-3/4" chambers. **Barrel:** 26", 28", 29.5"; blued chrome-lined. **Weight:** 7.25 to 7.5 lbs. **Stock:** Checkered walnut stock and forend, 14.5" LOP; 1.5" drop at comb; 2.5" drop at heel. **Features:** Nickel finish or blued receiver. Single selective mechanical trigger, selective automatic ejectors; serrated free-floating vent rib. SC-4 choke tube set on most models. Sporting has ported barrels, right-hand palm swell, target forend, wide rib. Introduced 2008. Imported by Remington Arms Co.
Price: SPR310, from................................ $598.00
Price: SPR310 Sporting $770.00

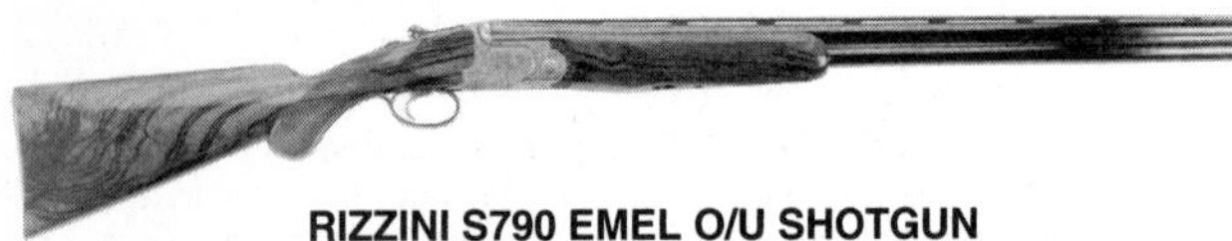

RIZZINI S790 EMEL O/U SHOTGUN

Gauge: 20, 28, .410. **Barrel:** 26", 27.5" (Imp. Cyl. & Imp. Mod.). **Weight:** About 6 lbs. **Stock:** 14"x1.5"x2-1/8". Extra fancy select walnut. **Features:** Boxlock action with profuse engraving; automatic ejectors; single selective trigger; silvered receiver. Comes with Nizzoli leather case. Introduced 1996. Imported from Italy by Wm. Larkin Moore & Co.
Price: From $14,600.00

Rizzini S792 EMEL O/U Shotgun

Similar to S790 EMEL except dummy sideplates with extensive engraving coverage. Nizzoli leather case. Introduced 1996. Imported from Italy by Wm. Larkin Moore & Co.
Price: From $15,500.00

RIZZINI UPLAND EL O/U SHOTGUN

Gauge: 12, 16, 20, 28, .410. **Barrel:** 26", 27.5", Mod. & Full, Imp. Cyl. & Imp. Mod. choke tubes. **Weight:** About 6.6 lbs. **Stock:** 14.5"x1-1/2"x2.25". **Features:** Boxlock action; single selective trigger; ejectors; profuse engraving on silvered receiver. Comes with fitted case. Introduced 1996. Imported from Italy by Wm. Larkin Moore & Co.
Price: From $5,200.00

Rizzini Artemis O/U Shotgun

Same as Upland EL model except dummy sideplates with extensive game scene engraving. Fancy European walnut stock. Fitted case. Introduced 1996. Imported from Italy by Wm. Larkin Moore & Co.
Price: From $3.260.00

RIZZINI S782 EMEL O/U SHOTGUN

Gauge: 12, 2-3/4" chambers. **Barrel:** 26", 27.5" (Imp. Cyl. & Imp. Mod.). **Weight:** About 6.75 lbs. **Stock:** 14.5"x1.5"x2.25". Extra fancy select walnut. **Features:** Boxlock action with dummy sideplates, extensive engraving with gold inlaid game birds, silvered receiver, automatic ejectors, single selective trigger. Nizzoli leather case. Introduced 1996. Imported from Italy by Wm. Larkin Moore & Co.
Price: From $18,800.00

RUGER RED LABEL O/U SHOTGUNS

Gauge: 12, 20, 3" chambers; 28 2-3/4" chambers. **Barrel:** 26", 28", 30" in 12 gauge. **Weight:** About 7 lbs. (20 ga.); 7.5 lbs. (12 ga.). **Length:** 43" overall (26" barrels). **Stock:** 14"x1.5"x2.5". Straight grain American walnut. Checkered pistol grip or straight grip, checkered forend, rubber butt pad. **Features:** Stainless steel receiver. Single selective mechanical trigger, selective automatic ejectors; serrated free-floating vent rib. Comes with two skeet, one Imp. Cyl., one Mod., one Full choke tube and wrench. Made in U.S. by Sturm, Ruger & Co.
Price: Red Label with pistol grip stock $1,956.00
Price: English Field with straight-grip stock $1,956.00
Price: Sporting clays (30" bbl.) $1,956.00

Ruger Engraved Red Label O/U Shotgun

Similar to Red Label except scroll engraved receiver with 24-carat gold game bird (pheasant in 12 gauge, grouse in 20 gauge, woodcock in 28 gauge). Introduced 2000.
Price: Engraved Red Label, pistol grip only $2,180.00

SAVAGE MILANO O/U SHOTGUNS

Gauge: 12, 20, 28, and 410, 2-3/4" (28 ga.) and 3" chambers. **Barrel:** 28"; chrome lined, elongated forcing cones, automatic ejectors. 12, 20, and 28 come with 3 Interchokes (F-M-IC); 410 has fixed chokes (M-IC). **Weight:** 12 ga., 7.5 lbs; 20, 28 gauge, .410, 6.25 lbs. **Length:** NA. **Stock:** Satin finish Turkish walnut stock with laser-engraved checkering, solid rubber recoil pad, Schnabel forend. **Features:** Single selective, mechanical set trigger, fiber-optic front sight with brass mid-rib bead. Introduced 2006. Imported from Italy by Savage Arms, Inc.
Price: $1,714.00

SKB MODEL GC7 O/U SHOTGUNS

Gauge: 12 or 20, 3"; 28, 2-3/4"; .410, 3". **Barrel:** 26", 28", Briley internal chokes. **Weight:** NA. **Length:** NA. **Stock:** Grade II and Grade III American black walnut, high-gloss finish, finger-groove forend. **Sights:** Top ventilated rib, sloped with matte surface (Game). **Features:** Low-profile boxlock action; Greener crossbolt locking action, silver-nitride finish; automatic ejectors, single selective trigger. Introduced 2008. Imported from Japan by SKB Shotguns, Inc.
Price: GC7 Game Bird Grade 1, from.................. $1,569.00
Price: GC7 Clays Grade 1, from...................... $1,679.00

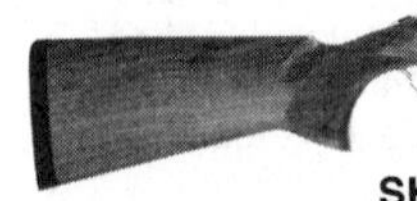

SKB MODEL 85TSS O/U SHOTGUNS

Gauge: 12, 20, .410: 3"; 28, 2-3/4". **Barrel:** Chrome lined 26", 28", 30", 32" (w/choke tubes). **Weight:** 7 lbs., 7 oz. to 8 lbs., 14 oz. **Stock:** Hand-checkered American walnut with matte finish, Schnabel or grooved forend. Target stocks available in various styles. **Sights:** HiViz competition sights. **Features:** Low profile boxlock action with Greener-style cross bolt; single selective trigger; manual safety. Back-bored barrels with lengthened forcing cones. Introduced 2004. Imported from Japan by SKB Shotguns, Inc.
Price: Sporting Clays, Skeet, fixed comb, from $2,199.00
Price: Sporting clays, Skeet, adjustable comb, from $2,429.00
Price: Trap, standard or Monte Carlo $2,329.00
Price: Trap adjustable comb......................... $2,529.00
Price: Trap Unsingle (2007) $2,799.00

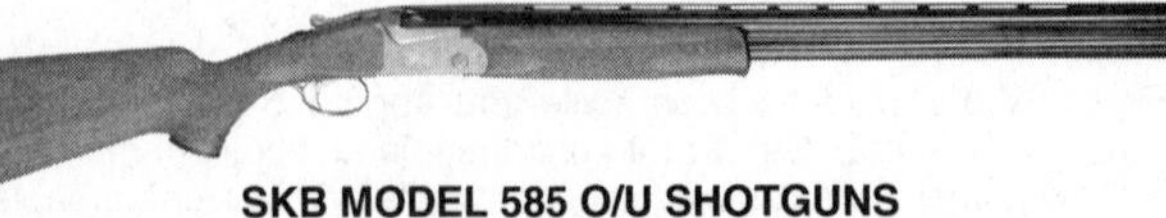

SKB MODEL 585 O/U SHOTGUNS

Gauge: 12 or 20, 3"; 28, 2-3/4"; .410, 3". **Barrel:** 12 ga.-26", 28", (InterChoke tubes); 20 ga.-26", 28" (InterChoke tubes); 28-26", 28" (InterChoke tubes); .410-26", 28" (InterChoke tubes). **Weight:** 6.6 to 8.5 lbs. **Length:** 43" to 51-3/8" overall. **Stock:** 14-1/8"x1.5"x2-3/16".

Prices given are believed to be accurate at time of publication however, many factors affect retail pricing so exact prices are not possible.

Hand checkered walnut with matte finish. **Sights:** Metal bead front (field). **Features:** Boxlock action; silver nitride finish; manual safety, automatic ejectors, single selective trigger. All 12-gauge barrels are back-bored, have lengthened forcing cones and longer choke tube system. Introduced 1992. Imported from Japan by SKB Shotguns, Inc.

Price: Field **$1,699.00**
Price: Two-barrel field set, 12 & 20. **$2,749.00**
Price: Two-barrel field set, 20 & 28 or 28 & .410 . . . . **$2,829.00**

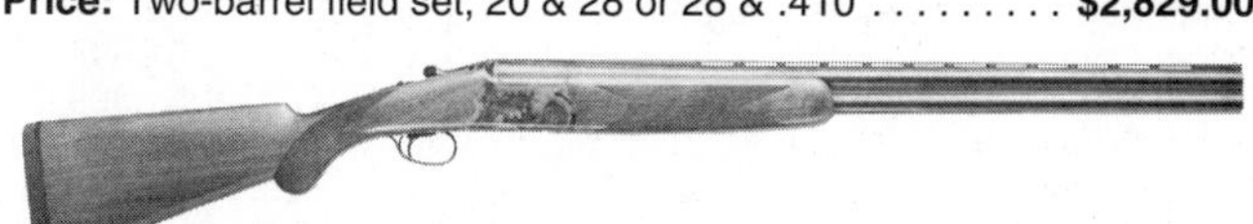

SMITH & WESSON ELITE SILVER SHOTGUNS

Gauge: 12, 3" chambers. **Barrel:** 26", 28", 30", rust-blued chopper-lump. **Weight:** 7.8 lbs. **Length:** 46-48". **Sights:** Ivory front bead, metal mid-bead. **Stock:** AAA (grade III) Turkish walnut stocks, hand-cut checkering, satin finish. **Features:** Smith & Wesson-designed trigger-plate action, hand-engraved receivers, bone-charcoal case hardening, lifetime warranty. Five choke tubes. Introduced 2007. Made in Turkey, imported by Smith & Wesson.

Price: **$2,380.00**

STEVENS MODEL 512 GOLD WING SHOTGUNS

Gauge: 12, 20, 28, .410; 2-3/4" and 3" chambers. **Barrel:** 26", 28". **Weight:** 6 to 8 lbs. **Sights:** NA. **Features:** Five screw-in choke tubes with 12, 20, and 28 gauge; .410 has fixed M/IC chokes. Black chrome, sculpted receiver with a raised gold pheasant, laser engraved trigger guard and forend latch. Turkish walnut stock finished in satin lacquer and beautifully laser engraved with fleur-de-lis checkering on the side panels, wrist and Schnabel forearm.

Price: **$649.00**

STOEGER CONDOR O/U SHOTGUNS

Gauge: 12, 20, 2-3/4" 3" chambers; 16, .410. Barrel: 22", 24", 26", 28", 30". Weight: 5.5 to 7.8 lbs. Sights: Brass bead. Features: IC, M, or F screw-in choke tubes with each gun. Oil finished hardwood with pistol grip and forend. Auto safety, single trigger, automatic extractors.

Price: Condor, 12, 20, 16 ga. or .410 . . . . **$399.00**
Price: Condor Supreme (w/mid bead), 12 or 20 ga. **$599.00**
Price: Condor Combo, 12 and 20 ga. Barrels, from **$549.00**
Price: Condor Youth, 20 ga. or .410 . . . . **$399.00**
Price: Condor Competition, 12 or 20 ga. **$599.00**
Price: Condor Combo, 12/20 ga., RH or LH (2007) **$829.00**
Price: Condor Outback, 12 or 20 ga., 20" barrel. **$369.00**

TRADITIONS CLASSIC SERIES O/U SHOTGUNS

Gauge: 12, 3"; 20, 3"; 16, 2-3/4"; 28, 2-3/4"; .410, 3". **Barrel:** 26" and 28". **Weight:** 6 lbs., 5 oz. to 7 lbs., 6 oz. **Length:** 43" to 45" overall. **Stock:** Walnut. **Features:** Single-selective trigger; chrome-lined barrels with screw-in choke tubes; extractors (Field Hunter and Field I models) or automatic ejectors (Field II and Field III models); rubber butt pad; top tang safety. Imported from Fausti of Italy by Traditions.

Price: Field Hunter: Blued receiver; 12 or 20 ga.; 26" bbl. has IC and Mod. tubes, 28" has mod. and full tubes **$669.00**
Price: Field I: Blued receiver; 12, 20, 28 ga. or .410; fixed chokes (26" has I.C. and mod., 28" has mod. and full). . **$619.00**
Price: Field II: Coin-finish receiver; 12, 16, 20, 28 ga. or .410; gold trigger; choke tubes **$789.00**
Price: Field III: Coin-finish receiver; gold engraving and trigger; 12 ga.; 26" or 28" bbl.; choke tubes **$999.00**
Price: Upland II: Blued receiver; 12 or 20 ga.; English-style straight walnut stock; choke tubes **$839.00**
Price: Upland III: Blued receiver, gold engraving; 20 ga.; high-grade pistol grip walnut stock; choke tubes **$1,059.00**
Price: Upland III: Blued, gold engraved receiver, 12 ga. Round pistol grip stock, choke tubes **$1,059.00**
Price: Sporting Clay II: Silver receiver; 12 ga.; ported barrels with skeet, i.c., mod. and full extended tubes. **$959.00**
Price: Sporting Clay III: Engraved receivers, 12 and 20 ga., walnut stock, vent rib, extended choke tubes. **$1,189.00**

TRADITIONS MAG 350 SERIES O/U SHOTGUNS

Gauge: 12, 3-1/2". **Barrel:** 24", 26" and 28". **Weight:** 7 lbs. to 7 lbs., 4 oz. **Length:** 41" to 45" overall. **Stock:** Walnut or composite with Mossy Oak Break-Up or Advantage Wetlands camouflage. **Features:** Black matte, engraved receiver; vent rib; automatic ejectors; single selective trigger; three screw-in choke tubes; rubber recoil pad; top tang safety. Imported from Fausti of Italy by Traditions.

Price: (Mag Hunter II: 28" black matte barrels, walnut stock, includes I.C., Mod. and Full tubes) **$799.00**
Price: (Turkey II: 24" or 26" camo barrels, Break-Up camo stock, includes Mod., Full and X-Full tubes) **$889.00**
Price: (Waterfowl II: 28" camo barrels, Advantage Wetlands camo stock, includes IC, Mod. and Full tubes) **$899.00**

TRISTAR HUNTER EX O/U SHOTGUN

Gauge: 12, 20, 28, .410. **Barrel:** 26", 28". **Weight:** 5.7 lbs. (.410); 6.0 lbs. (20, 28), 7.2-7.4 lbs. (12). Chrome-lined steel mono-block barrel, five Beretta-style choke tubes (SK, IC, M, IM, F). **Length:** NA. **Stock:** Walnut, cut checkering. 14.25"x1.5"x2-3/8". **Sights:** Brass front sight. **Features:** All have extractors, engraved receiver, sealed actions, self-adjusting locking bolts, single selective trigger, ventilated rib. 28 ga. and .410 built on true frames. Five-year warranty. Imported from Italy by Tristar Sporting Arms Ltd.

Price: From **$619.00**

VERONA 501 SERIES O/U SHOTGUNS

Gauge: 12, 20, 28, .410 (3" chambers). **Barrel:** 28". **Weight:** 6-7 lbs. **Stock:** Enhanced walnut with Scottish net type checkering and oiled finish. **Features:** Select fire single trigger, automatic ejectors, chromed barrels with X-CONE system to reduce felt recoil, and ventilated rubber butt pad. Introduced 1999. Imported from Italy by Legacy Sports International.

Price: Combos 20/28, 28/.410 . . . . **$1,599.00**

Verona 702 Series O/U Shotguns

Same as 501 series model except. with deluxe nickel receiver.

Price: **$1,699.00**

Verona LX692 Gold Hunting O/U Shotguns

Similar to Verona 501 except engraved, silvered receiver with false sideplates showing gold inlaid bird hunting scenes on three sides; Schnabel forend tip; hand-cut checkering; black rubber butt pad. Available in 12 and 20 gauge only, five Interchoke tubes. Introduced 1999. Imported from Italy by B.C. Outdoors.

Price: **$1,295.00**
Price: LX692G Combo 28/.410. . . . . **$2,192.40**

Verona LX680 Sporting O/U Shotgun

Similar to Verona 501 except engraved, silvered receiver; ventilated middle rib; beavertail forend; hand-cut checkering; available in 12 or 20 gauge only with 2-3/4" chambers. Introduced 1999. Imported from Italy by B.C. Outdoors.

Price: **$1,159.68**

Verona LX680 Skeet/Sporting/Trap O/U Shotgun

Similar to Verona 501 except skeet or trap stock dimensions; beavertail forend, palm swell on pistol grip; ventilated center barrel rib. Introduced 1999. Imported from Italy by B.C. Outdoors.

Price: **$1,736.96**

Verona LX692 Gold Sporting O/U Shotgun

Similar to Verona LX680 except false sideplates have gold-inlaid bird hunting scenes on three sides; red high-visibility front sight. Introduced 1999. Imported from Italy by B.C. Outdoors.

Price: Skeet/sporting. **$1,765.12**
Price: Trap (32" barrel, 7-7/8 lbs.) **$1,594.80**

VERONA LX680 COMPETITION TRAP O/U SHOTGUNS

Gauge: 12. **Barrel:** 30" O/U, 32" single bbl. **Weight:** 8-3/8 lbs. combo, 7 lbs. single. **Stock:** Walnut. **Sights:** White front, mid-rib bead.

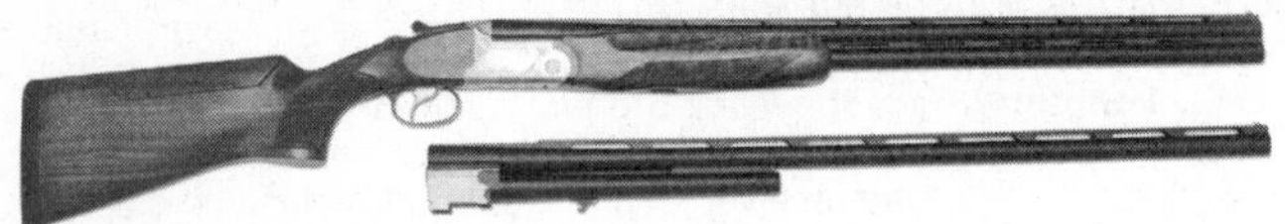

Features: Interchangeable barrels switch from OU to single configurations. 5 Briley chokes in combo, 4 in single bbl. extended forcing cones, ported barrels 32" with raised rib. By B.C. Outdoors.
Price: Trap Single (LX680TGTSB) **$1,736.96**
Price: Trap Combo (LX680TC). **$2,553.60**

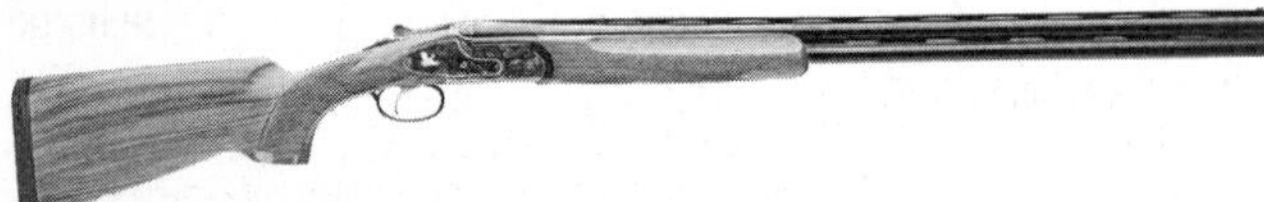

VERONA LX702 GOLD TRAP COMBO O/U SHOTGUNS

Gauge: 20/28, 2-3/4" chamber. **Barrel:** 30". **Weight:** 7 lbs. **Stock:** Turkish walnut with beavertail forearm. **Sights:** White front bead. **Features:** 2-barrel competition gun. Color case-hardened side plates and receiver with gold inlaid pheasant. Vent rib between barrels. 5 Interchokes. Imported from Italy by B.C. Outdoors.
Price: Combo **$2,467.84**
Price: 20 ga. **$1,829.12**

Verona LX702 Skeet/Trap O/U Shotguns

Similar to Verona LX702. Both are 12 gauge and 2-3/4" chamber. Skeet has 28" barrel and weighs 7.75 lbs. Trap has 32" barrel and weighs 7-7/8 lbs. By B.C. Outdoors.
Price: Skeet **$1,829.12**
Price: Trap **$1,829.12**

WEATHERBY ATHENA GRADE V AND GRADE III CLASSIC FIELD O/U SHOTGUNS

Gauge: Grade III and Grade IV: 12, 20, 3" chambers; 28, 2-3/4" chambers. Grade V: 12, 20, 3" chambers. **Barrel:** 26", 28" monobloc, IMC multi-choke tubes. Modified Greener crossbolt action. Matte ventilated top rib with brilliant front bead. **Weight:** 12 ga., 7.25 to 8 lbs.; 20 ga. 6.5 to 7.25 lbs. **Length:** 43" to 45". **Stock:** Rounded pistol grip, slender forend, Old English recoil pad. Grade V has oil-finished AAA American Claro walnut with 20-lpi checkering. Grade III has AA Claro walnut with oil finish, fine-line checkering. **Features:** Silver nitride/gray receivers; Grade III has hunting scene engraving. Grade IV has chrome-plated false sideplates featuring single game scene gold plate overlay. Grade V has rose and scroll engraving with gold-overlay upland game scenes. Top levers engraved with gold Weatherby flying "W". Introduced 1999. Imported from Japan by Weatherby.
Price: Grade III **$2,599.00**
Price: Grade IV **$2,799.00**
Price: Grade V **$3,999.00**

WEATHERBY ORION D'ITALIA O/U SHOTGUNS

Gauge: 12, 20, 3" chambers; 28, 2-3/4" chamber. **Barrel:** 26", 28", IMC multi-choke tubes. Matte ventilated top rib with brilliant bead front sight. **Weight:** 6-1/2 to 8 lbs. **Stock:** 14.25"x1.5"x2.5". American walnut, checkered grip and forend. Old English recoil pad. **Features:** All models have a triggerguard that features Weatherby's "Flying W" engraved with gold fill. D'Italia I available in 12 and 20 gauge, 26" and 28" barrels. Walnut stock with high lustre urethane finish. Metalwork is blued to high lustre finishand has a gold-plated trigger for corrosion protection. D'Italia II available in 12, 20 and 28 gauge with 26" and 28" barrels. Fancy grade walnut stock, hard chrome receiver with sculpted frameheads, elaborate game and floral engraving pattern, and matte vent mid & top rib with brilliant front bead sight. D'Italia III available in 12 and 20 gauge with 26" and 28" barrels. Hand-selected, oil-finished walnut stock wtih 20 LPI checkering, intricate engraving and gold plate game scene overlay, and damascened monobloc barrel and sculpted frameheads. D'Italia SC available in 12 gauge only with barrel lengths of 28", 30", and 32", weighs 8 lbs. Features satin, oil-finished walnut stock that is adjustable for cheek height with target-style pistol grip and Schnaubel forend, shallow receiver aligns hands for improved balance and pointability, ported barrels reduce muzzle jump, and fiber optic front sight for quick targer acquisition. Introduced 1998. Imported from Japan by Weatherby.
Price: D'Italia I **$1,699.00**
Price: D'Italia II **$1,899.00**
Price: D'Italia III **$2,199.00**
Price: D'Italia SC. **$2,599.00**

WINCHESTER SELECT MODEL 101 O/U SHOTGUNS

Gauge: 12, 2-3/4", 3" chambers. **Barrel:** 28", 30", 32", ported, Invector Plus choke system. **Weight:** 7 lbs. 6 oz. to 7 lbs. 12. oz. **Stock:** Checkered high-gloss grade II/III walnut stock, Pachmayr Decelerator sporting pad. **Features:** Chrome-plated chambers; back-bored barrels; tang barrel selector/safety; Signature extended choke tubes. Model 101 Field comes with solid brass bead front sight, three tubes, engraved receiver. Model 101 Sporting has adjustable trigger, 10mm runway rib, white mid-bead, Tru-Glo front sight, 30" and 32" barrels. Camo version of Model 101 Field comes with full-coverage Mossy Oak Duck Blind pattern. Model 101 Pigeon Grade Trap has 10mm steel runway rib, mid-bead sight, interchangeable fiber-optic front sight, porting and vented side ribs, adjustable trigger shoe, fixed raised comb or adjustable comb, Grade III/IV walnut, 30" or 32" barrels, molded ABS hard case. Reintroduced 2008. From Winchester Repeating Arms. Co.
Price: Model 101 Field **$1,739.00**
Price: Model 101 Deluxe Field **$1,659.00**
Price: Model 101 Sporting **$2,139.00**
Price: Model 101 Pigeon Grade Trap, intr. 2008 . . . . **$2,299.00**
Price: Model 101 Pigeon Grade Trap w/adj. comb, intr. 2008. . . . . **$2,429.00**
Price: Model 101 Light (2009) **$1,999.00**
Price: Model 101 Pigeon Sporting (2009) **$2,579.00**

ARRIETA SIDELOCK DOUBLE SHOTGUNS

Gauge: 12, 16, 20, 28, .410. **Barrel:** Length and chokes to customer specs. **Weight:** To customer specs. **Stock:** To customer specs. Straight English with checkered butt (standard), or pistol grip. Select European walnut with oil finish. **Features:** Essentially custom gun with myriad options. H&H pattern hand-detachable sidelocks, selective automatic ejectors, double triggers (hinged front) standard. Some have selfopening action. Finish and engraving to customer specs. Imported from Spain by Quality Arms, Inc.

Price: Model 557. . . . . **$4,500.00**
Price: Model 570. . . . . **$5,350.00**
Price: Model 578. . . . . **$5,880.00**
Price: Model 600 Imperial. **$7,995.00**
Price: Model 601 Imperial Tiro **$9,160.00**
Price: Model 801. . . . . **$14,275.00**
Price: Model 802. . . . . **$14,275.00**
Price: Model 803. . . . . **$9,550.00**
Price: Model 871. . . . . **$6,670.00**
Price: Model 872. . . . . **$17,850.00**
Price: Model 873. . . . . **$16,275.00**
Price: Model 874. . . . . **$13,125.00**
Price: Model 875. . . . . **$19,850.00**
Price: Model 931. . . . . **$20,895.00**

AYA MODEL 4/53 SHOTGUNS

Gauge: 12, 16, 20, 28, 410. **Barrel:** 26", 27", 28", 30". **Weight:** To customer specifications. **Length:** To customer specifications. **Features:** Hammerless boxlock action; double triggers; light scroll engraving; automatic safety; straight grip oil finish walnut stock; checkered butt. Made in Spain. Imported by New England Custom Gun Service, Lt.

Price: **$2,999.00**
Price: No. 2. . . . . **$4,799.00**
Price: No. 2 Rounded Action **$5,199.00**

BERETTA 471 SIDE-BY-SIDE SHOTGUNS

Gauge: 12, 20; 3" chamber. **Barrel:** 24", 26", 28"; 6mm rib. **Weight:** 6.5 lbs. **Stock:** English or pistol stock, straight butt for various types of recoil pads. Beavertail forend. English stock with recoil pad in red or black rubber, or in walnut and splinter forend. Select European walnut, checkered, oil finish. **Features:** Optima-Choke Extended Choke Tubes. Automatic ejection or mechanical extraction. Firing-pin block safety, manual or automatic, open top-lever safety. Introduced 2007. Imported from Italy by Beretta U.S.A.

Price: Silver Hawk. **$3,750.00**

BILL HANUS NOBILE III BY FABARM

Gauge: 20. **Barrel:** 28" Tribor® barrels with 3" chambers and extra-long 82mm (3-1/4") internal choke tubes. **Weight:** 5.75 lbs. **Stock:** Upgraded walnut 1-1/2"x2-1/4"x14-3/8", with 1/4" cast-off to a wood butt plate. Altering to 1/4" cast-on for left-handed shooters, $300 extra. **Features:** Tribor® barrels feature extra-long forcing cones along with over-boring, back-boring and extra-long (82mm vs 50mm) choke tubes which put more pellets in the target area. Paradox®-rifled choke tube for wider patterns at short-range targets. Adjustable for automatic ejectors or manual extraction. Adjustable opening tension. Fitted leather case.

Price: **$3,395.00**

CONNECTICUT SHOTGUN MANUFACTURING COMPANY RBL SIDE-BY-SIDE SHOTGUN

Gauge: 12, 16, 20, 28. **Barrel:** 26", 28", 30", 32". **Weight:** NA. **Length:** NA. **Stock:** NA. **Features:** Round-action SXS shotguns made in the USA. Scaled frames, five TruLock choke tubes. Deluxe fancy grade walnut buttstock and forend. Quick Change recoil pad in two lengths. Various dimensions and options available depending on gauge.

Price: 12 gauge **$2,950.00**
Price: 20 gauge **$2,799.00**
Price: 28 gauge **$3,650.00**

CZ BOBWHITE AND RINGNECK SHOTGUNS

Gauge: 12, 20, 28, .410. (5 screw-in chokes in 12 and 20 ga. and fixed chokes in IC and Mod in .410). **Barrel:** 20". **Weight:** 6.5 lbs.

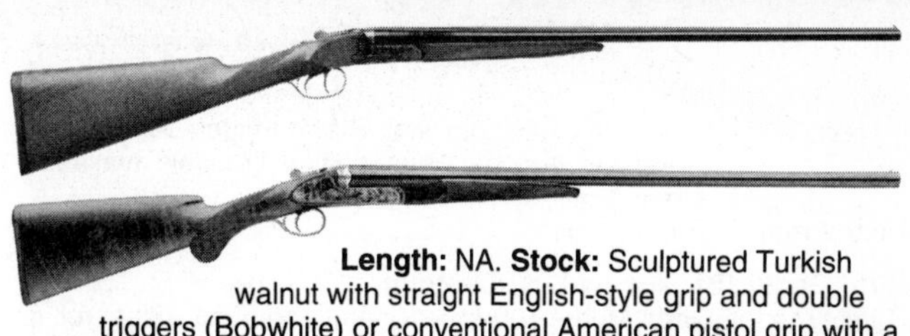

Length: NA. **Stock:** Sculptured Turkish walnut with straight English-style grip and double triggers (Bobwhite) or conventional American pistol grip with a single trigger (Ringneck). Both are hand checkered 20 lpi. **Features:** Both color case-hardened shotguns are hand engraved.

Price: Bobwhite. **$789.00**
Price: Ringneck. **$1,036.00**

CZ HAMMER COACH SHOTGUNS

Gauge: 12, 3" chambers. **Barrel:** 20". **Weight:** 6.7 lbs. **Length:** NA. **Stock:** NA. **Features:** Following in the tradition of the guns used by the stagecoach guards of the 1880's, this cowboy gun features double triggers, 19th century color case-hardening and fully functional external hammers.

Price: **$904.00**

DAKOTA PREMIER GRADE SHOTGUN

Gauge: 12, 16, 20, 28, .410. **Barrel:** 27". **Weight:** NA. **Length:** NA. **Stock:** Exhibition-grade English walnut, hand-rubbed oil finish with straight grip and splinter forend. **Features:** French grey finish; 50 percent coverage engraving; double triggers; selective ejectors. Finished to customer specifications. Made in U.S. by Dakota Arms.

Price: From **$14,950.00**

Dakota Legend Shotgun

Similar to Premier Grade except has special selection English walnut, full-coverage scroll engraving, oak and leather case. Made in U.S. by Dakota Arms.

Price: From **$19,000.00**

EMF OLD WEST HAMMER SHOTGUN

Gauge: 12. **Barrel:** 20". **Weight:** 8 lbs. **Length:** 37" overall. **Stock:** Smooth walnut with steel butt place. **Sights:** Large brass bead. **Features:** Colt-style exposed hammers rebounding type; blued receiver and barrels; cylinder bore. Introduced 2006. Imported from China for EMF by TTN.

Price: **$474.90**

FOX, A.H., SIDE-BY-SIDE SHOTGUNS

Gauge: 16, 20, 28, .410. **Barrel:** Length and chokes to customer specifications. Rust-blued Chromox or Krupp steel. **Weight:** 5-1/2 to 6.75 lbs. **Stock:** Dimensions to customer specifications. Hand-checkered Turkish Circassian walnut with hand-rubbed oil finish. Straight, semi or full pistol grip; splinter, Schnabel or beavertail forend; traditional pad, hard rubber buttplate or skeleton butt. **Features:** Boxlock action with automatic ejectors; double or Fox single selective trigger. Scalloped, rebated and color case-hardened receiver; hand finished and handengraved. Grades differ in engraving, inlays, grade of wood, amount of hand finishing. Introduced 1993. Made in U.S. by Connecticut Shotgun Mfg.

Price: CE Grade **$14,500.00**
Price: XE Grade **$16,000.00**
Price: DE Grade **$19,000.00**
Price: FE Grade **$24,000.00**
Price: 28/.410 CE Grade. **$16,500.00**
Price: 28/.410 XE Grade. **$18,000.00**
Price: 28/.410 DE Grade. **$21,000.00**
Price: 28/.410 FE Grade. **$26,000.00**

GARBI MODEL 100 DOUBLE SHOTGUN

Gauge: 12, 16, 20, 28. **Barrel:** 26", 28", choked to customer specs. **Weight:** 5-1/2 to 7.5 lbs. **Stock:** 14.5"x2.25"x1.5". European walnut. Straight grip, checkered butt, classic forend. **Features:** Sidelock action, automatic ejectors, double triggers standard. Color case-

hardened action, coin finish optional. Single trigger; beavertail forend, etc. optional. Five additional models available. Imported from Spain by Wm. Larkin Moore.
Price: From **$4,850.00**

Garbi Model 101 Side-by-Side Shotgun
Similar to the Garbi Model 100 except hand engraved with scroll engraving; select walnut stock; better overall quality than the Model 100. Imported from Spain by Wm. Larkin Moore.
Price: From **$6,250.00**

Garbi Model 103 A & B Side-by-Side Shotguns
Similar to the Garbi Model 100 except has Purdey-type fine scroll and rosette engraving. Better overall quality than the Model 101. Model 103B has nickel-chrome steel barrels, H&H-type easy opening mechanism; other mechanical details remain the same. Imported from Spain by Wm. Larkin Moore.
Price: Model 103A. From **$14,100.00**
Price: Model 103B. From **$21,600.00**

Garbi Model 200 Side-by-Side Shotgun
Similar to the Garbi Model 100 except has heavy-duty locks, magnum proofed. Very fine Continental-style floral and scroll engraving, well figured walnut stock. Other mechanical features remain the same. Imported from Spain by Wm. Larkin Moore.
Price: **$17,100.00**

KIMBER VALIER SIDE-BY-SIDE SHOTGUN
Gauge: 20, 16, 3" chambers. Barrels: 26" or 28", IC and M. **Weight:** 6 lbs. 8 oz. **Stock:** Turkish walnut, English style. **Features:** Sidelock design, double triggers, 50-percent engraving; 24 lpi checkering; auto-ejectors (extractors only on Grade I). Color case-hardened sidelocks, rust blue barrels. Imported from Turkey by Kimber Mfg., Inc.
Price: Grade II. **$4,999.00**

LEBEAU-COURALLY BOXLOCK SIDE-BY-SIDE SHOTGUN
Gauge: 12, 16, 20, 28, .410-bore. **Barrel:** 25" to 32". **Weight:** To customer specifications. **Stock:** French walnut. **Features:** Anson & Deely-type action with automatic ejectors; single or double triggers. Custom gun built to customer specifications. Imported from Belgium by Wm. Larkin Moore.
Price: From **$25,500.00**

LEBEAU-COURALLY SIDELOCK SIDE-BY-SIDE SHOTGUN
Gauge: 12, 16, 20, 28, .410-bore. **Barrel:** 25" to 32". **Weight:** To customer specifications. **Stock:** Fancy French walnut. **Features:** Holland & Holland-type action with automatic ejectors; single or double triggers. Custom gun built to customer specifications. Imported from Belgium by Wm. Larkin Moore.
Price: From **$56,000.00**

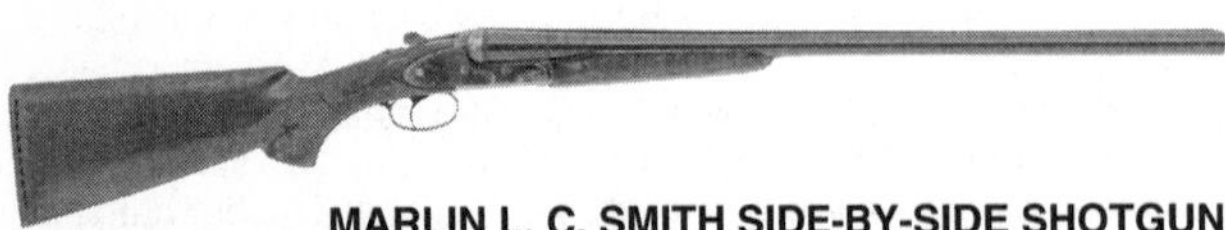

MARLIN L. C. SMITH SIDE-BY-SIDE SHOTGUN
Gauge: 12, 20, 28, .410. **Stock:** Checkered walnut w/recoil pad. **Features:** 3" chambers, single trigger, selective automatic ejectors; 3 choke tubes (IC, Mod., Full); solid rib, bead front sight. Imported from Italy by Marlin. Introduced 2005.
Price: LC12-DB (28" barrel, 43" OAL, 6.25 lbs) **$1,962.00**
Price: LC28-DB (26" barrel, 41" OAL, 6 lbs). **$1,484.00**

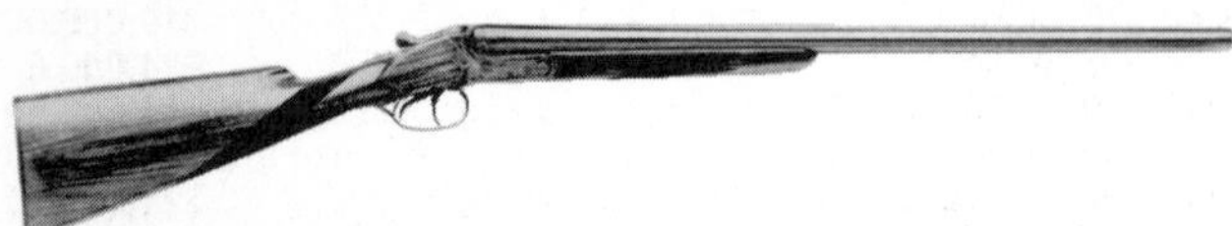

MERKEL MODEL 47E, 147E SIDE-BY-SIDE SHOTGUNS
Gauge: 12, 3" chambers, 16, 2.75" chambers, 20, 3" chambers. **Barrel:** 12, 16 ga.-28"; 20 ga.-26.75" (Imp. Cyl. & Mod., Mod. & Full). **Weight:** About 6.75 lbs. (12 ga.). **Stock:** Oil-finished walnut; straight English or pistol grip. **Features:** Anson & Deeley-type boxlock action with single selective or double triggers, automatic safety, cocking indicators. Color case-hardened receiver with standard arabesque engraving. Imported from Germany by Merkel USA.
Price: Model 47E (H&H ejectors) **$4,595.00**
Price: Model 147E (as above with ejectors) **$5,795.00**

Merkel Model 47EL, 147EL Side-by-Side Shotguns
Similar to Model 47E except H&H style sidelock action with cocking indicators, ejectors. Silver-grayed receiver and sideplates have arabesque engraving, engraved border and screws (Model 47E), or fine hunting scene engraving (Model 147E). Limited edition. Imported from Germany by Merkel USA.
Price: Model 47EL **$7,195.00**
Price: Model 147EL **$7,695.00**

Merkel Model 280EL, 360EL Shotguns
Similar to Model 47E except smaller frame. Greener cross bolt with double under-barrel locking lugs, fine engraved hunting scenes on silver-grayed receiver, luxury-grade wood, Anson and Deely boxlock action. H&H ejectors, single-selective or double triggers. Introduced 2000. Imported from Germany by Merkel USA.
Price: Model 280EL (28 gauge, 28" barrel, Imp. Cyl. and Mod. chokes) **$7,695.00**
Price: Model 360EL (.410, 28" barrel, Mod. and Full chokes) **$7,695.00**
Price: Model 280EL Combo **$11,195.00**

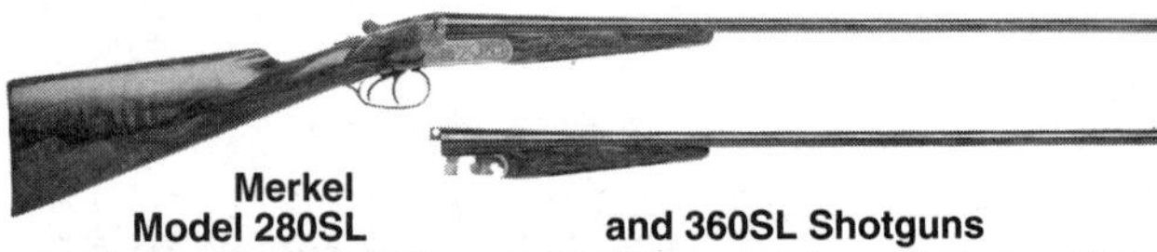

Merkel Model 280SL and 360SL Shotguns
Similar to Model 280EL and 360EL except has sidelock action, double triggers, English-style arabesque engraving. Introduced 2000. Imported from Germany by Merkel USA.
Price: Model 280SL (28 gauge, 28" barrel, Imp. Cyl. and Mod. chokes). **$10,995.00**
Price: Model 360SL (.410, 28" barrel, Mod. and Full chokes) **$10,995.00**

MERKEL MODEL 1620 SIDE-BY-SIDE SHOTGUN
Gauge: 16. Features: Greener crossbolt with double under-barrel locking lugs, scroll-engraved case-hardened receiver, Anson and Deely boxlock aciton, Holland & Holland ejectors, English-style stock, single selective or double triggers, or pistol grip stock with single selective trgger. Imported from Germany by Merkel USA.
Price: **$4,995.00**
Price: Model 1620E; silvered, engraved receiver **$5,995.00**
Price: Model 1620 Combo; 16- and 20-gauge two-barrel set **$7,695.00**
Price: Model 1620EL; upgraded wood **$7,695.00**
Price: Model 1620EL Combo; 16- and 20-gauge two-barrel set **$11,195.00**

PIOTTI KING NO. 1 SIDE-BY-SIDE SHOTGUN
Gauge: 12, 16, 20, 28, .410. **Barrel:** 25" to 30" (12 ga.), 25" to 28" (16, 20, 28, .410). To customer specs. Chokes as specified. **Weight:** 6.5 lbs. to 8 lbs. (12 ga. to customer specs.). **Stock:** Dimensions to customer specs. Finely figured walnut; straight grip with checkered butt with classic splinter forend and hand-rubbed oil finish standard. Pistol grip, beavertail forend. **Features:** Holland & Holland pattern sidelock action, automatic ejectors. Double trigger; non-selective single trigger optional. Coin finish standard; color case-hardened optional. Top rib; level, file-cut; concave, ventilated optional. Very fine, full coverage scroll engraving with small floral bouquets. Imported from Italy by Wm. Larkin Moore.
Price: From **$38,300.00**

Piotti Lunik Side-by-Side Shotgun
Similar to the Piotti King No. 1 in overall quality. Has Renaissance-style large scroll engraving in relief. Best quality Holland & Holland-pattern sidelock ejector double with

Prices given are believed to be accurate at time of publication however, many factors affect retail pricing so exact prices are not possible.

chopper lump (demi-bloc) barrels. Other mechanical specifications remain the same. Imported from Italy by Wm. Larkin Moore.
Price: From **$39,900.00**

PIOTTI PIUMA SIDE-BY-SIDE SHOTGUN
Gauge: 12, 16, 20, 28, .410. **Barrel:** 25" to 30" (12 ga.), 25" to 28" (16, 20, 28, .410). **Weight:** 5-1/2 to 6-1/4 lbs. (20 ga.). **Stock:** Dimensions to customer specs. Straight grip stock with walnut checkered butt, classic splinter forend, hand-rubbed oil finish are standard; pistol grip, beavertail forend, satin luster finish optional. **Features:** Anson & Deeley boxlock ejector double with chopper lump barrels. Level, file-cut rib, light scroll and rosette engraving, scalloped frame. Double triggers; single non-selective optional. Coin finish standard, color case-hardened optional. Imported from Italy by Wm. Larkin Moore.
Price: From **$19,200.00**

REMINGTON SPR210 SIDE-BY-SIDE SHOTGUNS
Gauge: 12, 20, 28, .410 bore, 3" chambers; 28, 2-3/4" chambers. **Barrel:** 26", 28", blued chrome-lined. **Weight:** 6.75 to 7 lbs. **Stock:** checkered walnut stock and forend, 14.5" LOP; 1.5" drop at comb; 2.5" drop at heel. **Features:** Nickel or blued receiver. Single selective mechanical trigger, selective automatic ejectors; SC-4 choke tube set on most models. Steel receiver/mono block, auto tang safety, rubber recoil pad. Introduced 2008. Imported by Remington Arms Co.
Price: SPR210, from **$479.00**

REMINGTON SPR220 SIDE-BY-SIDE SHOTGUNS
Gauge: 12, 20, 2-3/4" or 3" chambers. **Barrel:** 20", 26", blued chrome-lined. **Weight:** 6.25 to 7 lbs. Otherwise similar to SPR210 except has double trigger/extractors. Introduced 2008. Imported by Remington Arms Co.
Price: SPR220, from **$342.00**

RIZZINI SIDELOCK SIDE-BY-SIDE SHOTGUN
Gauge: 12, 16, 20, 28, .410. **Barrel:** 25" to 30" (12, 16, 20 ga.), 25" to 28" (28, .410). To customer specs. Chokes as specified. **Weight:** 6.5 lbs. to 8 lbs. (12 ga. to customer specs). **Stock:** Dimensions to customer specs. Finely figured walnut; straight grip with checkered butt with classic splinter forend and hand-rubbed oil finish standard. Pistol grip, beavertail forend. **Features:** Sidelock action, auto ejectors. Double triggers or non-selective single trigger standard. Coin finish standard. Imported from Italy by Wm. Larkin Moore.
Price: 12, 20 ga. From **$106,000.00**
Price: 28, .410 bore. From **$95,000.00**

RUGER GOLD LABEL SIDE-BY-SIDE SHOTGUN
Gauge: 12, 3" chambers. **Barrel:** 28" with skeet tubes. **Weight:** 6.5 lbs. **Length:** 45". **Stock:** American walnut straight or pistol grip. **Sights:** Gold bead front, full length rib, serrated top. **Features:** Spring-assisted break-open, SS trigger, auto eject. Five interchangeable screw-in choke tubes, combination safety/barrel selector with auto safety reset.
Price: **$3,226.00**

SMITH & WESSON ELITE GOLD SHOTGUNS
Gauge: 20, 3" chambers. **Barrel:** 26", 28", 30", rust-blued chopper-lump. **Weight:** 6.5 lbs. **Length:** 43.5-45.5". **Sights:** Ivory front bead, metal mid-bead. **Stock:** AAA (grade III) Turkish walnut stocks, hand-cut checkering, satin finish. English grip or pistol grip. **Features:** Smith & Wesson-designed trigger-plate action, hand-engraved receivers, bone-charcoal case hardening,lifetime warranty. Five choke tubes. Introduced 2007. Made in Turkey, imported by Smith & Wesson.
Price: **$2,380.00**

STOEGER UPLANDER SIDE-BY-SIDE SHOTGUNS
Gauge: 16, 28, 2-3/4 chambers. 12, 20, .410, 3" chambers. **Barrel:** 22", 24", 26", 28". **Weight:** 7.3 lbs. **Sights:** Brass bead. **Features:** Double trigger, IC & M fixed choke tubes with gun.
Price: With fixed or screw-in chokes. **$369.00**
Price: Supreme, screw-in chokes, 12 or 20 ga. **$489.00**
Price: Youth, 20 ga. or .410, 22" barrel, double trigger **$369.00**
Price: Combo, 20/28 ga. or 12/20 ga. **$649.00**

STOEGER COACH GUN SIDE-BY-SIDE SHOTGUNS
Gauge: 12, 20, 2-3/4", 3" chambers. **Barrel:** 20". **Weight:** 6.5 lbs. **Stock:** Brown hardwood, classic beavertail forend. **Sights:** Brass bead. **Features:** IC & M fixed chokes, tang auto safety, auto extractors, black plastic buttplate. Imported by Benelli USA.
Price: Supreme blued finish **$469.00**
Price: Supreme blued barrel, stainless receiver **$469.00**
Price: Silverado Coach Gun with English synthetic stock. **$469.00**

TRADITIONS ELITE SERIES SIDE-BY-SIDE SHOTGUNS
Gauge: 12, 3"; 20, 3"; 28, 2-3/4"; .410, 3". **Barrel:** 26". **Weight:** 5 lbs., 12 oz. to 6.5 lbs. **Length:** 43" overall. **Stock:** Walnut. **Features:** Chrome-lined barrels; fixed chokes (Elite Field III ST, Field I DT and Field I ST) or choke tubes (Elite Hunter ST); extractors (Hunter ST and Field I models) or automatic ejectors (Field III ST); top tang safety. Imported from Fausti of Italy by Traditions.
Price: Elite Field I DT C 12, 20, 28 ga. or .410; IC and Mod. fixed chokes (F and F on .410); double triggers . . **$789.00 to $969.00**
Price: Elite Field I ST C 12, 20, 28 ga. or .410; same as DT but with single trigger . . . . **$969.00 to $1,169.00**
Price: Elite Field III ST C 28 ga. or .410; gold-engraved receiver; high-grade walnut stock **$2,099.00**
Price: Elite Hunter ST C 12 or 20 ga.; blued receiver; IC and Mod. choke tubes **$999.00**

TRADITIONS UPLANDER SERIES SIDE-BY-SIDE SHOTGUNS
Gauge: 12, 3"; 20, 3". **Barrel:** 26", 28". **Weight:** 6-1/4 lbs. to 6.5 lbs. **Length:** 43" to 45" overall. **Stock:** Walnut. **Features:** Barrels threaded for choke tubes (Improved Cylinder, Modified and Full); top tang safety, extended trigger guard. Engraved silver receiver with side plates and lavish gold inlays. Imported from Fausti of Italy by Traditions.
Price: Uplander III Silver 12, 20 ga. **$2,699.00**
Price: Uplander V Silver 12, 20 ga. **$3,199.00**

TRISTAR BRITTANY CLASSIC SIDE-BY-SIDE SHOTGUN
Gauge: 12, 16, 20, 28, .410, 3" chambers. **Barrel:** 27", chrome lined, three Beretta-style choke tubes (IC, M, F). **Weight:** 6.3 to 6.7 lbs. **Stock:** Rounded pistol grip, satin oil finish. **Features:** Engraved case-colored one-piece frame, auto selective ejectors, single selective trigger, solid raised barrel rib, top tang safety. Imported from Spain by Tristar Sporting Arms Ltd.
Price: From **$1,419.00**

WEATHERBY SBS ATHENA D'ITALIA SIDE-BY-SIDE SHOTGUNS
Gauge: D'Italia: 12, 20, 2-3/4" or 3" chambers, 28, 2-3/4" chambers. **Barrel:** 26" on 20 and 28 gauges; 28" on 12 ga. Chrome-lined, lengthened forcing cones, backbored. **Weight:** 6.75 to 7.25 lbs. **Length:** 42.5" to 44.5". **Stock:** Walnut, 20-lpi laser cut checkering, "New Scottish" pattern. **Features:** All come with foam-lined take-down case. Machined steel receiver, hardened and chromed with coin finish, engraved triggerguard with roll-formed border. D'Italia has double triggers, brass front bead. PG is identical to D'Italia, except for rounded pistol grip and semi-beavertail forearm. Deluxe features sculpted frameheads, Bolino-style engraved game scene with floral engraving. AAA Fancy Turkish walnut, straight grip, 24-lpi hand checkering, hand-rubbed oil finish. Single mechanical trigger; right barrel fires first. Imported from Italy by Weatherby.
Price: SBS Athena D'Italia SBS **$3,129.00**
Price: SBS Athena D'Italia PG SBS **$3,799.00**

BERETTA DT10 TRIDENT TRAP TOP SINGLE SHOTGUN
Gauge: 12, 3" chamber. **Barrel:** 34"; five Optima Choke tubes (Full, Full, Imp. Modified, Mod. and Imp. Cyl.). **Weight:** 8.8 lbs. **Stock:** High-grade walnut; adjustable. **Features:** Detachable, adjustable trigger group; Optima Bore for improved shot pattern and reduced recoil; slim Optima Choke tubes; raised and thickened receiver for long life. Introduced 2000. Imported from Italy by Beretta USA.
Price: **$7,400.00**

BROWNING BT-99 TRAP O/U SHOTGUNS
Gauge: 12. **Barrel:** 30", 32", 34". **Stock:** Walnut; standard or adjustable. **Weight:** 7 lbs. 11 oz. to 9 lbs. **Features:** Back-bored single barrel; interchangeable chokes; beavertail forearm; extractor only; high rib.
Price: BT-99 w/conventional comb, 32" or 34" barrels **$1,529.00**
Price: BT-99 w/adjustable comb, 32" or 34" barrels **$1,839.00**
Price: BT-99 Golden Clays w/adjustable comb, 32" or 34" barrels **$3,989.00**
Price: BT-99 Grade III, 32" or 34" barrels, intr. 2008 ...... **$2,369.00**

HARRINGTON & RICHARDSON ULTRA SLUG HUNTER/TAMER SHOTGUNS
Gauge: 12, 20 ga., 3" chamber, .410. **Barrel:** 20" to 24" rifled. **Weight:** 6 to 9 lbs. **Length:** 34.5" to 40". **Stock:** Hardwood, laminate, or polymer with full pistol grip; semi-beavertail forend. **Sights:** Gold bead front. **Features:** Break-open action with side-lever release, automatic ejector. Introduced 1994. From H&R 1871, LLC.
Price: Ultra Slug Hunter, blued, hardwood **$273.00**
Price: Ultra Slug Hunter Youth, blued, hardwood, 13-1/8" LOP....................................... **$273.00**
Price: Ultra Slug Hunter Deluxe, blued, laminated **$273.00**
Price: Tamer .410 bore, stainless barrel, black polymer stock . **$173.00**

HARRINGTON & RICHARDSON ULTRA LITE SLUG HUNTER
Gauge: 12, 20 ga., 3" chamber. **Barrel:** 24" rifled. **Weight:** 5.25 lbs. **Length:** 40". **Stock:** Hardwood with walnut finish, full pistol grip, recoil pad, sling swivel studs. **Sights:** None; base included. **Features:** Youth Model, available in 20 ga. has 20" rifled barrel. Deluxe Model has checkered laminated stock and forend. From H&R 1871, LLC.
Price: **$194.00**

Harrington & Richardson Ultra Slug Hunter Thumbhole Stock
Similar to the Ultra Lite Slug Hunter but with laminated thumbhole stock and weighs 8.5 lbs.
Price: .... **NA**

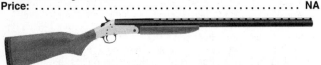

HARRINGTON & RICHARDSON TOPPER MODELS
Gauge: 12, 16, 20, .410, up to 3.5" chamber. **Barrel:** 22 to 28". **Weight:** 5-7 lbs. **Stock:** Polymer, hardwood, or black walnut. **Features:** Satin nickel frame, blued barrel. Reintroduced 1992. From H&R 1871, LLC.

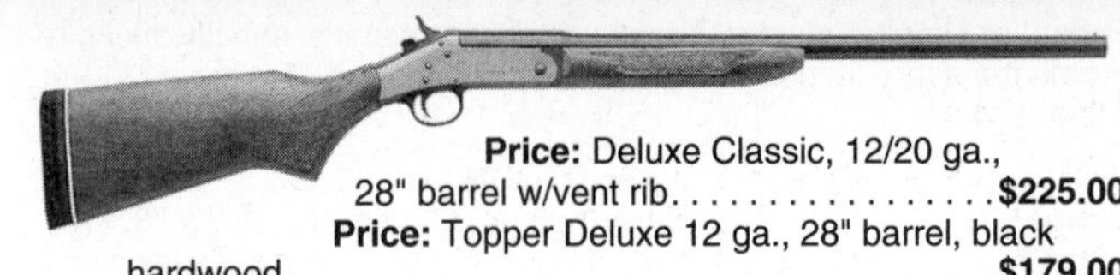

Price: Deluxe Classic, 12/20 ga., 28" barrel w/vent rib................ **$225.00**
Price: Topper Deluxe 12 ga., 28" barrel, black hardwood **$179.00**
Price: Topper 12, 16, 20 ga., .410, 26" to 28", black hardwood **$153.00**
Price: Topper Junior 20 ga., .410, 22" barrel, hardwood **$160.00**
Price: Topper Junior Classic, 20 ga., .410, checkered hardwood **$160.00**

Harrington & Richardson Topper Trap Gun
Similar to other Topper Models but with select checkered walnut stock and forend wtih fluted comb and full pistol grip; 30" barrel with two white beads and screw-in chokes (Improved Modified Extended included); deluxe Pachmayr trap recoil pad.
Price: **$360.00**

KRIEGHOFF K-80 SINGLE BARREL TRAP GUN
Gauge: 12, 2-3/4" chamber. **Barrel:** 32" or 34" Unsingle. Fixed Full or choke tubes. **Weight:** About 8-3/4 lbs. **Stock:** Four stock dimensions or adjustable stock available. All hand-checkered European walnut. **Features:** Satin nickel finish. Selective mechanical trigger adjustable for finger position. Tapered step vent rib. Adjustable point of impact.
Price: Standard grade Full Unsingle, from **$10,080.00**

KRIEGHOFF KX-5 TRAP GUN
Gauge: 12, 2-3/4" chamber. **Barrel:** 32", 34"; choke tubes. **Weight:** About 8.5 lbs. **Stock:** Factory adjustable stock. European walnut. **Features:** Ventilated tapered step rib. Adjustable position trigger, optional release trigger. Fully adjustable rib. Satin gray electroless nickel receiver. Fitted aluminum case. Imported from Germany by Krieghoff International, Inc.
Price: **$5,395.00**

LJUTIC MONO GUN SINGLE BARREL SHOTGUN
Gauge: 12 only. **Barrel:** 34", choked to customer specs; hollow-milled rib, 35.5" sight plane. **Weight:** Approx. 9 lbs. **Stock:** To customer specs. Oil finish, hand checkered. **Features:** Custom gun. Pull or release trigger; removable trigger guard contains trigger and hammer mechanism; Ljutic pushbutton opener on front of trigger guard. From Ljutic Industries.
Price: Std., med. or Olympic rib, custom bbls., fixed choke.. **$7,495.00**
Price: Stainless steel mono gun **$8,495.00**

Ljutic LTX Pro 3 Deluxe Mono Gun
Deluxe, lightweight version of the Mono gun with high quality wood, upgrade checkering, special rib height, screw-in chokes, ported and cased.
Price: **$8,995.00**
Price: Stainless steel model **$9,995.00**

NEW ENGLAND FIREARMS PARDNER AND TRACKER II SHOTGUNS
Gauge: 10, 12, 16, 20, 28, .410, up to 3.5" chamber for 10 and 12 ga. 16, 28, 2-3/4" chamber. **Barrel:** 24" to 30". **Weight:** Varies from 5 to 9.5 lbs. **Length:** Varies from 36" to 48". **Stock:** Walnut-finished hardwood with full pistol grip, synthetic, or camo finish. **Sights:** Bead front on most. **Features:** Transfer bar ignition; break-open action with side-lever release. Introduced 1987. From New England Firearms.
Price: Pardner, all gauges, hardwood stock, 26" to 32" blued barrel, Mod. or Full choke.................. **$140.00**
Price: Pardner Youth, hardwood stock, straight grip, 22" blued barrel **$149.00**
Price: Pardner Screw-In Choke model, intr. 2006 .... **$164.00**

Price: Turkey model, 10/12 ga., camo finish or black . . . . **$192.00 to $259.00**
Price: Youth Turkey, 20 ga., camo finish or black **$192.00**
Price: Waterfowl, 10 ga., camo finish or hardwood **$227.00**
Price: Tracker II slug gun, 12/20 ga., hardwood. **$196.00**

REMINGTON SPR100 SINGLE-SHOT SHOTGUNS
Gauge: 12, 20, .410 bore, 3" chambers. **Barrel:** 24", 26", 28", 29.5", blued chrome-lined. **Weight:** 6.25 to 6.5 lbs. **Stock:** Walnut stock and forend. **Features:** Nickel or blued receiver. Cross-bolt safety, cocking indicator, titanium-coated trigger, selectable ejector or extractor. Introduced 2008. Imported by Remington Arms Co.
Price: SPR100, from. **$479.00**

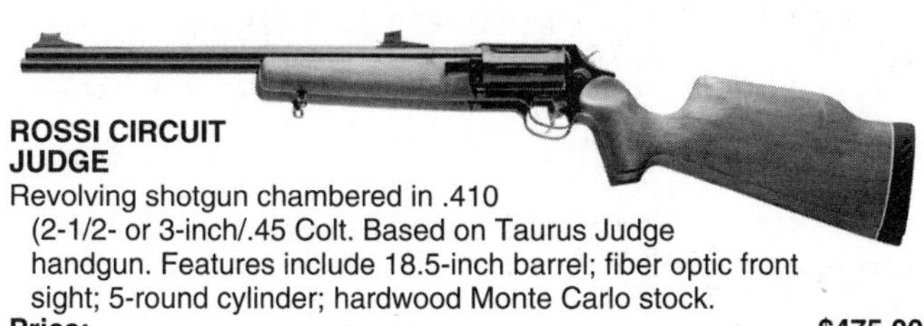

ROSSI CIRCUIT JUDGE
Revolving shotgun chambered in .410 (2-1/2- or 3-inch/.45 Colt. Based on Taurus Judge handgun. Features include 18.5-inch barrel; fiber optic front sight; 5-round cylinder; hardwood Monte Carlo stock.
Price: **$475.00**

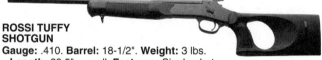

ROSSI SINGLE-SHOT SHOTGUNS
Gauge: 12, 20, .410. **Barrel:** 22" (Youth), 28". **Weight:** 3.75-5.25 lbs. **Stocks:** Wood. **Sights:** Bead front sight, fully adjustable fiber optic sight on Slug and Turkey. **Features:** Single-shot break open, 8 models available, positive ejection, internal transfer bar mechanism, trigger block system, Taurus Security System, blued finish, Rifle Slug has ported barrel.
Price: From **$117.00**

ROSSI TUFFY SHOTGUN
Gauge: .410. **Barrel:** 18-1/2". **Weight:** 3 lbs. **Length:** 29.5" overall. **Features:** Single-shot break-open model with black synthetic thumbhole stock in blued or stainless finish.
Price: . . . . **Appx. $150.00**

ROSSI MATCHED PAIRS
Gauge/Caliber: 12, 20, .410, .22 Mag, .22LR, .17HMR, .223 Rem, .243 Win, .270 Win, .30-06, .308 Win, .50 (black powder). **Barrel:** 23", 28". **Weight:** 5-6.3 lbs. **Stocks:** Wood or black synthetic. **Sights:** Bead front on shotgun barrel, fully adjustable front and rear on rifle barrel, drilled and tapped for scope, fully adjustable fiber optic sights (black powder). **Features:** Single-shot break open, 27 models available, internal transfer bar mechanism, manual external safety, blue finish, trigger block system, Taurus Security System, youth models available.
Price: Rimfire/Shotgun, from. **$160.00**
Price: Centerfire/Shotgun **$271.95**
Price: Black Powder Matched Pair, from **$262.00**

ROSSI MATCHED SET
Gauge/Caliber: 12, 20, .22 LR, .17 HMR, .243 Win, .270 Win, .50 (black powder). **Barrel:** 33.5". **Weight:** 6.25-6.3 lbs. **Stocks:** Wood. **Sights:** Bead front on shotgun barrel, fully adjustable front and rear on rifle barrel, drilled and tapped for scope, fully adjustable fiber optic sights (black powder). **Features:** Single-shot break open, 4 models available, internal transfer bar mechanism, manual external safety, blue finish, trigger block system, Taurus Security System, youth models available.
Price: From **$374.00**

TAR-HUNT RSG-12 PROFESSIONAL RIFLED SLUG GUN
Gauge: 12, 2-3/4" or 3" chamber, 1-shot magazine. **Barrel:** 23", fully rifled with muzzle brake. **Weight:** 7.75 lbs. **Length:** 41.5" overall. **Stock:** Matte black McMillan fiberglass with Pachmayr Decelerator pad. **Sights:** None furnished; comes with Leupold windage or Weaver bases. **Features:** Uses rifle-style action with two locking lugs; two-position safety; Shaw barrel; single-stage, trigger; muzzle brake. Many options available. All models have area-controlled feed action. Introduced 1991. Made in U.S. by Tar-Hunt Custom Rifles, Inc.
Price: 12 ga. Professional model **$2,585.00**
Price: Left-hand model add. **$110.00**

Tar-Hunt RSG-16 Elite Shotgun
Similar to RSG-12 Professional except 16 gauge; right- or left-hand versions.
Price: **$2,585.00**

Tar-Hunt RSG-20 Mountaineer Slug Gun
Simi- lar to the RSG-12 Professional except chambered for 20 gauge (2-3/4" and 3" shells); 23" Shaw rifled barrel, with muzzle brake; two-lug bolt; one-shot blind magazine; matte black finish; McMillan fiberglass stock with Pachmayr Decelerator pad; receiver drilled and tapped for Rem. 700 bases. Right- or left-hand versions. Weighs 6.5 lbs. Introduced 1997. Made in U.S. by Tar-Hunt Custom Rifles, Inc.
Price: **$2,585.00**

THOMPSON/CENTER ENCORE RIFLED SLUG GUN
Gauge: 20, 3" chamber. **Barrel:** 26", fully rifled. **Weight:** About 7 lbs. **Length:** 40.5" overall. **Stock:** Walnut with walnut forearm. **Sights:** Steel; click-adjustable rear and ramp-style front, both with fiber optics. **Features:** Encore system features a variety of rifle, shotgun and muzzle-loading rifle barrels interchangeable with the same frame. Break-open design operates by pulling up and back on trigger guard spur. Composite stock and forearm available. Introduced 2000.
Price: **$684.00**

THOMPSON/CENTER ENCORE TURKEY GUN
Gauge: 12 ga. **Barrel:** 24". **Features:** All-camo finish, high definition Realtree Hardwoods HD camo.
Price: **$763.00**

THOMPSON/CENTER ENCORE PROHUNTER TURKEY GUN
Contender-style break-action single shot shotgun chambered in 12 or 20 gauge 3-inch shells. Features include 24-inch barrel with interchangeable choke tubes (Extra Full supplied), composite buttstock and forend with non-slip inserts in cheekpiece, pistol grip and forend. Adjustable fiber optic sights, Sims recoil pad, AP camo finish overall. Overall length: 40.5 inches. Weight: 6-1/2 lbs.
Price: **$799.00**

BENELLI M3 CONVERTIBLE SHOTGUN

Gauge: 12, 2-3/4", 3" chambers, 5-shot magazine. **Barrel:** 19.75" (Cyl.). **Weight:** 7 lbs., 4oz. **Length:** 41" overall. **Stock:** High-impact polymer with sling loop in side of butt; rubberized pistol grip on stock. **Sights:** Open rifle, fully adjustable. Ghost ring and rifle type. **Features:** Combination pump/auto action. Alloy receiver with inertia recoil rotating locking lug bolt; matte finish; automatic shell release lever. Introduced 1989. Imported by Benelli USA. Price with pistol grip, open rifle sights.

Price: With ghost ring sights, pistol grip stock **$1,489.00**

BENELLI M2 TACTICAL SHOTGUN

Gauge: 12, 2-3/4", 3" chambers, 5-shot magazine. **Barrel:** 18.5" IC, M, F choke tubes. **Weight:** 6.7 lbs. **Length:** 39.75" overall. **Stock:** Black polymer. **Sights:** Rifle type ghost ring system, tritium night sights optional. **Features:** Semiauto intertia recoil action. Cross-bolt safety; bolt release button; matte-finish metal. Introduced 1993. Imported from Italy by Benelli USA.

Price: With rifle sights **$1,159.00**
Price: With ghost ring sights, standard stock **$1,269.00**
Price: With ghost ring sights, pistol grip stock **$1,269.00**
Price: With rifle sights, pistol grip stock **$1,159.00**
Price: ComforTech stock, rifle sights **$1,269.00**
Price: Comfortech Stock, Ghost Ring **$1,379.00**

BERETTA TX4 SEMIAUTO SHOTGUN

Gas-operated semiauto shotgun chambered for 3-inch 12-ga. shells. Features include 18-inch barrel with interchangeable choke tubes; adjustable ghost ring rear sight with military-style front sight; adjustable length of pull; integral picatinny rail on receiver; 5+1 capacity; soft rubber grip inlays in buttstock and forend.

Price: **$1450.00**

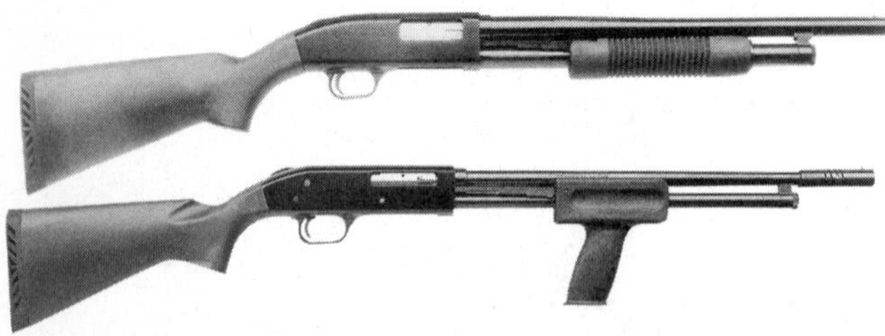

MOSSBERG MODEL 500 SPECIAL PURPOSE SHOTGUNS

Gauge: 12, 20, .410, 3" chamber. **Barrel:** 18.5", 20" (Cyl.). **Weight:** 7 lbs. **Stock:** Walnut-finished hardwood or black synthetic. **Sights:** Metal bead front. **Features:** Available in 6- or 8-shot models. Top-mounted safety, double action slide bars, swivel studs, rubber recoil pad. Blue, Parkerized, Marinecote finishes. Mossberg Cablelock included. From Mossberg. The HS410 Home Security model chambered for .410 with 3" chamber; has pistol grip forend, thick recoil pad, muzzle brake and has special spreader choke on the 18.5" barrel. Overall length is 37.5", weight is 6.25 lbs. Blue finish; synthetic field stock. Mossberg Cablelock and video included. Mariner model has Marinecote metal finish to resist rust and corrosion. Synthetic field stock; pistol grip kit included. 500 Tactical 6-shot has black synthetic tactical stock. Introduced 1990.

Price: Rolling Thunder, 6-shot **$471.00**
Price: Tactical Cruiser, 18.5" barrel **$434.00**
Price: Persuader/Cruiser, 6 shot, from **$394.00**
Price: Persuader/Cruiser, 8 shot, from **$394.00**
Price: HS410 Home Security **$404.00**
Price: Mariner 6 or 9 shot, from **$538.00**
Price: Tactical 6 shot, from **$509.00**

MOSSBERG MODEL 590 SPECIAL PURPOSE SHOTGUN

Gauge: 12, 3" chamber, 9 shot magazine. **Barrel:** 20" (Cyl.). **Weight:** 7.25 lbs. **Stock:** Synthetic field or Speedfeed. **Sights:** Metal bead front or Ghost Ring. **Features:** Top-mounted safety, double slide action bars. Comes with heat shield, bayonet lug, swivel studs, rubber recoil pad. Blue, Parkerized or Marinecote finish. Mossberg Cablelock included. From Mossberg.

Price: Synthetic stock, from **$471.00**
Price: Speedfeed stock, from **$552.00**

MOSSBERG 930 TACTICAL AUTOLOADER WITH HEAT SHIELD

Similar to Model 930 Tactical but with ventilated heat shield handguard.

Price: **$626.00**

REMINGTON MODEL 870 AND MODEL 1100 TACTICAL SHOTGUNS

Gauge: 870: 12, 2-3/4 or 3" chamber; 1100: 2-3/4". **Barrel:** 18", 20", 22" (Cyl or IC). **Weight:** 7.5-7.75 lbs. **Length:** 38.5-42.5" overall. **Stock:** Black synthetic, synthetic Speedfeed IV full pistol-grip stock, or Knoxx Industries SpecOps stock w/recoil-absorbing spring-loaded cam and adjustable length of pull (12" to 16", 870 only). **Sights:** Front post w/dot only on 870; rib and front dot on 1100. **Features:** R3 recoil pads, LimbSaver technology to reduce felt recoil, 2-, 3- or 4-shot extensions based on barrel length; matte-olive-drab barrels and receivers. Model 1100 Tactical is available with Speedfeed IV pistol grip stock or standard black synthetic stock and forend. Speedfeed IV model has an 18" barrel with two-shot extension. Standard synthetic-stocked version is equipped with 22" barrel and four-shot extension. Introduced 2006. From Remington Arms Co.

Price: 870, Speedfeed IV stock, 3" chamber, 38.5" overall, from **$587.00**
Price: 870, SpecOps stock, 3" chamber, 38.5" overall, from . . **$587.00**
Price: 1100, synthetic stock, 2-3/4" chamber, 42.5" overall . . . **$945.00**
Price: 870 TAC Desert Recon (2008), 18" barrel, 2-shot **$692.00**

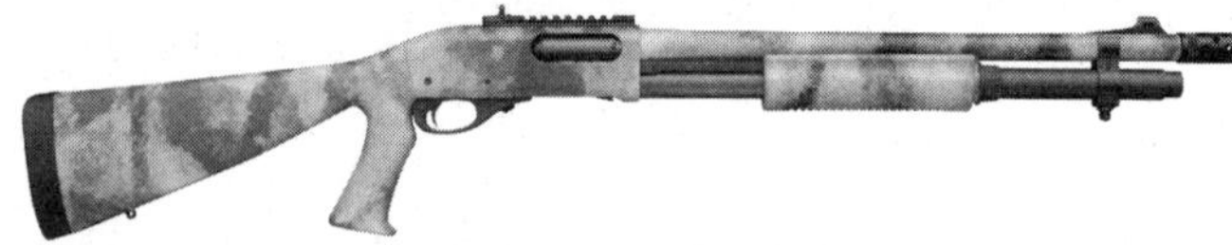

REMINGTON 870 EXPRESS TACTICAL A-TACS CAMO

Pump action shotgun chambered for 2-3/4- and 3-inch 12-ga. Features include full A-TACS digitized camo; 18-1/2-inch barrel; extended ported Tactical RemChoke; SpeedFeed IV pistol-grip stock with SuperCell recoil pad; fully adjustable XS® Ghost Ring Sight rail with removable white bead front sight; 7-round capacity with factory-installed 2-shot extension; drilled and tapped receiver; sling swivel stud.

Price: **$665.00**

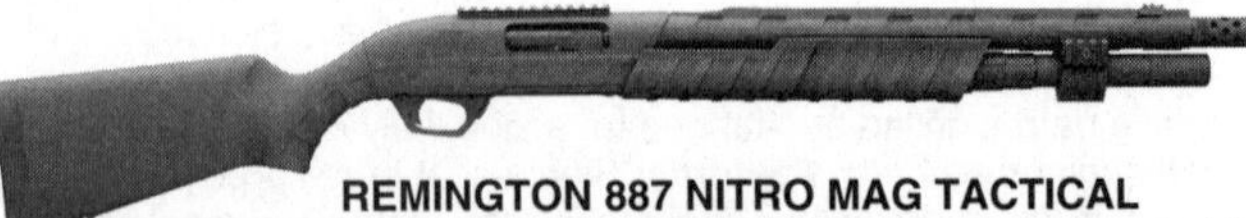

REMINGTON 887 NITRO MAG TACTICAL

Pump action shotgun chambered in 12-ga., 2-3/4 to 3-1/2 inch. Features include 18-1/2-inch barrel with ported, extended tactical RemChoke; 2-shot magazine extension; barrel clamp with integral Picatinny rails; ArmorLokt coating; synthetic stock and forend with specially contour grip panels.

Price: **$498.00**

TACTICAL RESPONSE TR-870 STANDARD MODEL SHOTGUNS

Gauge: 12, 3" chamber, 7-shot magazine. **Barrel:** 18" (Cyl.). **Weight:** 9 lbs. **Length:** 38" overall. **Stock:** Fiberglass-filled polypropolene with non-snag recoil absorbing butt pad. Nylon tactical forend houses flashlight. **Sights:** Trak-Lock ghost ring sight system. Front sight has Tritium insert. **Features:** Highly modified Remington 870P with

Prices given are believed to be accurate at time of publication however, many factors affect retail pricing so exact prices are not possible.

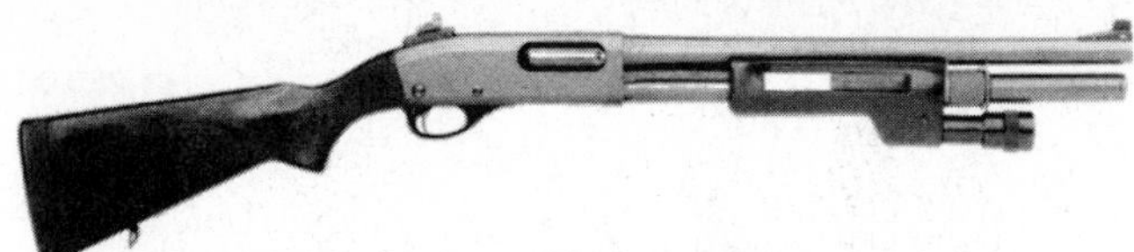

Parkerized finish. Comes with nylon three-way adjustable sling, high visibility non-binding follower, high performance magazine spring, Jumbo Head safety, and Side Saddle extended 6-shot shell carrier on left side of receiver. Introduced 1991. From Scattergun Technologies, Inc.
Price: Standard model **$1,050.00**
Price: Border Patrol model, from **$1,050.00**
Price: Professional model, from **$1,070.00**

TRISTAR COBRA PUMP
Gauge: 12, 3". **Barrel:** 28". **Weight:** 6.7 lbs. Three Beretta-style choke tubes (IC, M, F). **Length:** NA. **Stock:** Matte black synthetic stock and forearm. **Sights:** Vent rib with matted sight plane. **Features:** Five-year warranty. Cobra Tactical Pump Shotgun magazine holds 7, return spring in forearm, 20" barrel, Cylinder choke. Introduced 2008. Imported by Tristar Sporting Arms Ltd.
Price: Tactical **$349.00**

FRENCH-STYLE DUELING PISTOL
Caliber: 44. **Barrel:** 10". **Weight:** 35 oz. **Length:** 15.75" overall. **Stocks:** Carved walnut. **Sights:** Fixed. **Features:** Comes with velvet-lined case and accessories. Imported by Mandall Shooting Supplies.
Price: **$295.00**

HARPER'S FERRY 1805 PISTOL
Caliber: 58 (.570" round ball). **Barrel:** 10". **Weight:** 39 oz. **Length:** 16" overall. **Stocks:** Walnut. **Sights:** Fixed. **Features:** Case-hardened lock, brass-mounted German silver-colored barrel. Replica of the first U.S. gov't.-made flintlock pistol. Imported by Navy Arms, Dixie Gun Works.
Price: Dixie Gun Works RH0225 . . . . **$495.00**
Price: Dixie Kit FH0411. . . . . **$395.00**

KENTUCKY FLINTLOCK PISTOL
Caliber: 45, 50, 54. **Barrel:** 10.4". **Weight:** 37-40 oz. **Length:** 15.4" overall. **Stocks:** Walnut. **Sights:** Fixed. **Features:** Specifications, including caliber, weight and length may vary with importer. Case-hardened lock, blued barrel; available also as brass barrel flintlock Model 1821. Imported by The Armoury.
Price: Single cased set (Navy Arms) **$375.00**

KENTUCKY PERCUSSION PISTOL
Similar to Flint version but percussion lock. Imported by The Armoury, Navy Arms, CVA (50-cal.).
Price: . . . . **$129.95 to $225.00**
Price: Steel barrel (Armoury) **$179.00**
Price: Single cased set (Navy Arms) **$355.00**
Price: Double cased set (Navy Arms) **$600.00**

LE PAGE PERCUSSION DUELING PISTOL
Caliber: .45. **Barrel:** 10.25" octagon, rifled. **Weight:** 36-41 oz. **Length:** 16.9" overall. **Stocks:** Walnut, fluted butt. **Sights:** Blade front, open style rear. **Features:** Double set trigger. Bright barrel, brass furniture (silver plated). Imported by Dixie Gun Works
Price: PH0310 . . . . **$525.00**

LYMAN PLAINS PISTOL
Caliber: 50 or 54. **Barrel:** 8"; 1:30" twist, both calibers. **Weight:** 50 oz. **Length:** 15" overall. **Stocks:** Walnut half-stock. **Sights:** Blade front, square notch rear adjustable for windage. **Features:** Polished brass trigger guard and ramrod tip, color case-hardened coil spring lock, springloaded trigger, stainless steel nipple, blackened iron furniture. Hooked patent breech, detachable belt hook. Introduced 1981. From Lyman Products.
Price: Finished **$349.95**
Price: Kit **$289.95**

PEDERSOLI MANG TARGET PISTOL
Caliber: 38. **Barrel:** 10.5", octagonal; 1:15" twist, **Weight:** 2.5 lbs. **Length:** 17.25" overall. **Stocks:** Walnut with fluted grip. **Sights:** Blade front, open rear adjustable for windage. **Features:** Browned barrel, polished breech plug, remainder color case-hardened. Imported from Italy by Dixie Gun Works.
Price: PH0503. . . . . **$1,250.00**

QUEEN ANNE FLINTLOCK PISTOL
Caliber: 50 (.490" round ball). **Barrel:** 7.5", smoothbore. **Stocks:** Walnut. **Sights:** None. **Features:** German silver-colored steel barrel, fluted brass trigger guard, brass mask on butt. Lockplate left in the white. Made by Pedersoli in Italy. Introduced 1983. Imported by Dixie Gun Works.

Baby Dragoon 1848

Price: RH0211 . . . . **$375.00**
Price: Kit FH0421 . . . . **$295.00**

TRADITIONS KENTUCKY PISTOL
Caliber: 50. **Barrel:** 10"; octagon with 7/8" flats; 1:20" twist. **Weight:** 40 oz. **Length:** 15" overall. **Stocks:** Stained beech. **Sights:** Blade front, fixed rear. **Features:** Bird's-head grip; brass thimbles; color case-hardened lock. Percussion only. Introduced 1995. From Traditions.
Price: Finished **$209.00**
Price: Kit **$174.00**

TRADITIONS TRAPPER PISTOL
Caliber: 50. **Barrel:** 9.75"; 7/8" flats; 1:20" twist. **Weight:** 2.75 lbs. **Length:** 16" overall. **Stocks:** Beech. **Sights:** Blade front, adjustable rear. **Features:** Double-set triggers; brass buttcap, trigger guard, wedge plate, forend tip, thimble. From Traditions.
Price: Percussion **$286.00**
Price: Flintlock **$312.00**
Price: Kit **$149.00**

TRADITIONS VEST-POCKET DERRINGER
Caliber: 31. **Barrel:** 2.25"; brass. **Weight:** 8 oz. **Length:** 4.75" overall. **Stocks:** Simulated ivory. **Sights:** Bead front. **Features:** Replica of riverboat gamblers' derringer; authentic spur trigger. From Traditions.
Price: **$165.00**

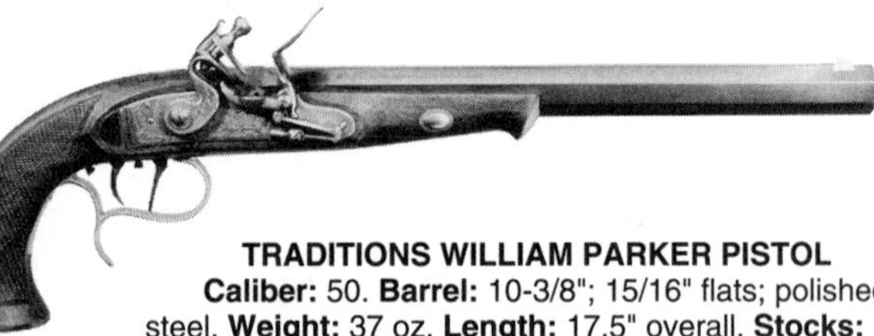

TRADITIONS WILLIAM PARKER PISTOL
Caliber: 50. **Barrel:** 10-3/8"; 15/16" flats; polished steel. **Weight:** 37 oz. **Length:** 17.5" overall. **Stocks:** Walnut with checkered grip. **Sights:** Brass blade front, fixed rear. **Features:** Replica dueling pistol with 1:20" twist, hooked breech. Brass wedge plate, trigger guard, cap guard; separate ramrod. Double-set triggers. Polished steel barrel, lock. Imported by Traditions.
Price: **$381.00**

 Prices given are believed to be accurate at time of publication however, many factors affect retail pricing so exact prices are not possible.

ARMY 1860 PERCUSSION REVOLVER

Caliber: 44, 6-shot. **Barrel:** 8". **Weight:** 40 oz. **Length:** 13-5/8" overall. **Stocks:** Walnut. **Sights:** Fixed. **Features:** Engraved Navy scene on cylinder; brass trigger guard; case-hardened frame, loading lever and hammer. Some importers supply pistol cut for detachable shoulder stock, have accessory stock available. Imported by Cabela's (1860 Lawman), EMF, Navy Arms, The Armoury, Cimarron, Dixie Gun Works (half-fluted cylinder, not roll engraved), Euroarms of America (brass or steel model), Armsport, Traditions (brass or steel), Uberti U.S.A. Inc., United States Patent Fire-Arms.

Price: Dixie Gun Works RH0125 . . . . **$240.00**
Price: Brass frame (EMF) **$215.00**
Price: Single cased set (Navy Arms) **$300.00**
Price: Double cased set (Navy Arms) **$490.00**
Price: 1861 Navy: Same as Army except 36-cal., 7.5" bbl., weighs 41 oz., cut for shoulder stock; round cylinder (fluted available), from Cabela's, CVA (brass frame, 44 cal.), United States Patent Fire-Arms . . . . **$99.95 to $385.00**
Price: Steel frame kit (EMF) **$240.00**
Price: Colt Army Police, fluted cyl., 5.5", 36-cal. (Cabela's) . **$229.99**
Price: With nickeled frame, barrel and backstrap, gold-tone fluted cylinder, trigger and hammer, simulated ivory grips (Traditions) **$199.00**

BABY DRAGOON 1848, 1849 POCKET, WELLS FARGO

Caliber: 31. **Barrel:** 3", 4", 5", 6"; seven-groove; RH twist. **Weight:** About 21 oz. **Stocks:** Varnished walnut. **Sights:** Brass pin front, hammer notch rear. **Features:** No loading lever on Baby Dragoon or Wells Fargo models. Unfluted cylinder with stagecoach holdup scene; cupped cylinder pin; no grease grooves; one safety pin on cylinder and slot in hammer face; straight (flat) mainspring. From Armsport, Cimarron F.A. Co., Dixie Gun Works, EMF, Uberti U.S.A. Inc.

Price: 5.5" barrel, 1849 Pocket with loading lever (Dixie). . . . **$250.00**
Price: 4" (Uberti USA Inc.) **$275.00**

DIXIE WYATT EARP REVOLVER

Caliber: 44. **Barrel:** 12", octagon. **Weight:** 46 oz. **Length:** 18" overall. **Stocks:** One-piece hardwood. **Sights:** Fixed. **Features:** Highly polished brass frame, backstrap and trigger guard; blued barrel and cylinder; case-hardened hammer, trigger and loading lever. Navy-size shoulder stock requires minor fitting. From Dixie Gun Works.

Price: RH0130 . . . . **$187.50**

LE MAT REVOLVER

Caliber: 44/20 ga. **Barrel:** 6.75" (revolver); 4-7/8" (single shot). **Weight:** 3 lbs., 7 oz. **Length:** 14" overall. **Stocks:** Hand-checkered walnut. **Sights:** Post front, hammer notch rear. **Features:** Exact reproduction with all-steel construction; 44-cal. 9-shot cylinder, 20-gauge single barrel; color case-hardened hammer with selector; spur trigger guard; ring at butt; lever-type barrel release. From Navy Arms.

Price: Cavalry model (lanyard ring, spur trigger guard) **$750.00**
Price: Army model (round trigger guard, pin-type barrel release). **$750.00**
Price: Naval-style (thumb selector on hammer) **$750.00**

NAVY MODEL 1851 PERCUSSION REVOLVER

Caliber: 36, 44, 6-shot. **Barrel:** 7.5". **Weight:** 44 oz. **Length:** 13" overall. **Stocks:** Walnut finish. **Sights:** Post front, hammer notch rear. **Features:** Brass backstrap and trigger guard; some have 1st Model squareback trigger guard, engraved cylinder with navy battle scene; case-hardened frame, hammer, loading lever. Imported by The Armoury, Cabela's, Cimarron F.A. Co., Navy Arms, EMF, Dixie Gun Works, Euroarms of America, Armsport, CVA (44-cal. only), Traditions (44 only), Uberti U.S.A. Inc., United States Patent Fire-Arms.

Price: Brass frame (Dixie Gun Works RH0100) **$275.00**
Price: Steel frame (Dixie Gun Works RH0210). **$200.00**
Price: Engraved model (Dixie Gun Works RH0110) **$275.00**
Price: Confederate Navy (Cabela's) **$139.99**
Price: Hartford model, steel frame, German silver trim, cartouche (EMF) **$190.00**
Price: Man With No Name Conversion (Cimarron, 2006) . . . **$480.00**

NEW MODEL 1858 ARMY PERCUSSION REVOLVER

Caliber: 36 or 44, 6-shot. **Barrel:** 6.5" or 8". **Weight:** 38 oz. **Length:** 13.5" overall. **Stocks:** Walnut. **Sights:** Blade front, groove-in-frame rear. **Features:** Replica of Remington Model 1858. Also available from some importers as Army Model Belt Revolver in 36-cal., a shortened and lightened version of the 44. Target Model (Uberti U.S.A. Inc., Navy Arms) has fully adjustable target rear sight, target front, 36 or 44. Imported by Cimarron F.A. Co., CVA (as 1858 Army, brass frame, 44 only), Navy Arms, The Armoury, EMF, Euroarms of America (engraved, stainless and plain), Armsport, Traditions (44 only), Uberti U.S.A. Inc.

Price: Steel frame, Dixie RH0220. . . . . **$315.00**
Price: Steel frame kit (Euroarms) . . . . **$115.95 to $150.00**
Price: Stainless steel Model 1858 (Euroarms, Uberti U.S.A. Inc., Navy Arms, Armsport, Traditions) . . . . **$169.95 to $380.00**
Price: Target Model, adjustable rear sight (Cabela's, Euroarms, Uberti U.S.A. Inc., Stone Mountain Arms) . . . . **$95.95 to $399.00**
Price: Brass frame (CVA, Cabela's, Traditions, Navy Arms) . . . . **$79.95 to $199.99**
Price: Buffalo model, 44-cal. (Cabela's) **$119.99**
Price: Hartford model, steel frame, cartouche (EMF) **$225.00**
Price: Improved Conversion (Cimarron) **$492.00**

NORTH AMERICAN COMPANION PERCUSSION REVOLVER

Caliber: 22. **Barrel:** 1-1/8". **Weight:** 5.1 oz. **Length:** 4.5" overall. **Stocks:** Laminated wood. **Sights:** Blade front, notch fixed rear. **Features:** All stainless steel construction. Uses standard #11 percussion caps. Comes with bullets, powder measure, bullet seater, leather clip holster, gun rag. Long Rifle or Magnum frame size. Introduced 1996. Made in U.S. by North American Arms.

Price: Long Rifle frame. **$215.00**

North American Super Companion Percussion Revolver

Similar to the Companion except has larger frame. Weighs 7.2 oz., has 1-5/8" barrel, measures 5-7/16" overall. Comes with bullets, pow-

der measure, bullet seater, leather clip holster, gun rag. Introduced 1996. Made in U.S. by North American Arms.
Price: **$230.00**

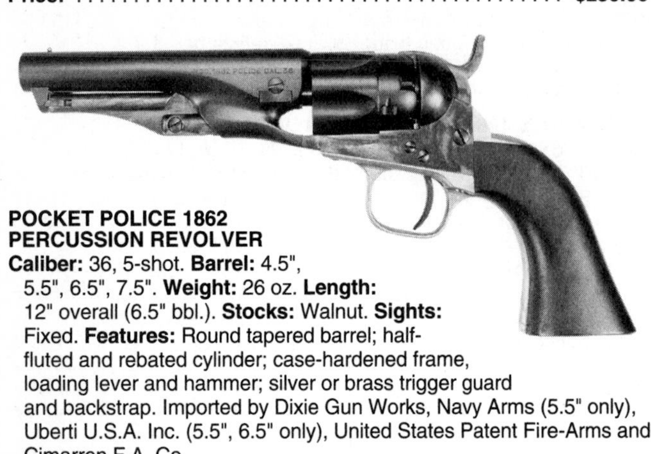

POCKET POLICE 1862 PERCUSSION REVOLVER
Caliber: 36, 5-shot. **Barrel:** 4.5", 5.5", 6.5", 7.5". **Weight:** 26 oz. **Length:** 12" overall (6.5" bbl.). **Stocks:** Walnut. **Sights:** Fixed. **Features:** Round tapered barrel; half-fluted and rebated cylinder; case-hardened frame, loading lever and hammer; silver or brass trigger guard and backstrap. Imported by Dixie Gun Works, Navy Arms (5.5" only), Uberti U.S.A. Inc. (5.5", 6.5" only), United States Patent Fire-Arms and Cimarron F.A. Co.
Price: Dixie Gun Works RH0422 .... **$315.00**
Price: Hartford model, steel frame, cartouche (EMF) **$300.00**

ROGERS & SPENCER PERCUSSION REVOLVER
Caliber: 44. **Barrel:** 7.5". **Weight:** 47 oz. **Length:** 13.75" overall. **Stocks:** Walnut. **Sights:** Cone front, integral groove in frame for rear. **Features:** Accurate reproduction of a Civil War design. Solid frame; extra large nipple cut-out on rear of cylinder; loading lever and cylinder easily removed for cleaning. From Dixie Gun Works, Euroarms of America (standard blue, engraved, burnished, target models), Navy Arms.
Price: Dixie Gun Works RH1320 .... **$425.00**
Price: Nickel-plated **$215.00**
Price: Engraved (Euroarms) **$430.00**
Price: Target version (Euroarms) .... **$239.00 to $270.00**
Price: Burnished London Gray (Euroarms) ..... **$245.00 to $370.00**

SHERIFF MODEL 1851 PERCUSSION REVOLVER
Caliber: 36, 44, 6-shot. **Barrel:** 5". **Weight:** 40 oz. **Length:** 10.5" overall. **Stocks:** Walnut. **Sights:** Fixed. **Features:** Brass backstrap and trigger guard; engraved navy scene; case-hardened frame, hammer, loading lever. Imported by EMF.
Price: Steel frame **$169.95**
Price: Brass frame **$140.00**

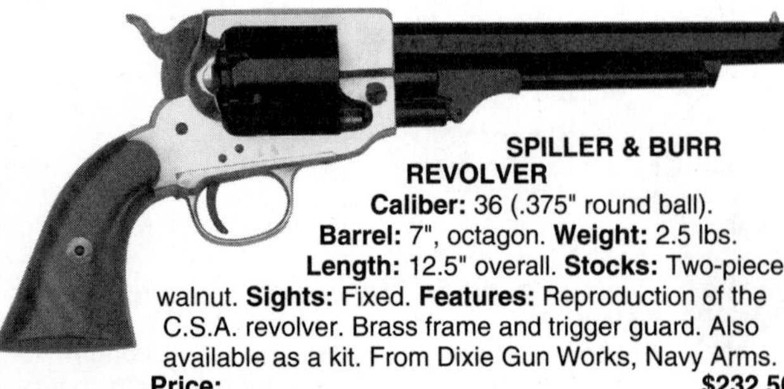

SPILLER & BURR REVOLVER
Caliber: 36 (.375" round ball). **Barrel:** 7", octagon. **Weight:** 2.5 lbs. **Length:** 12.5" overall. **Stocks:** Two-piece walnut. **Sights:** Fixed. **Features:** Reproduction of the C.S.A. revolver. Brass frame and trigger guard. Also available as a kit. From Dixie Gun Works, Navy Arms.
Price: **$232.50**

UBERTI 1847 WALKER REVOLVERS
Caliber: 44 6-shot engraved cylinder. **Barrel:** 9" 7 grooves. **Weight:** 4.5 lbs. **Length:** 15.7" overall. **Stocks:** One-piece hardwood. **Sights:** Fixed. **Features:** Copy of Sam Colt's first commercially-made revolving pistol, loading lever available, no trigger guard. Case-hardened hammer. Blued finish. Made in Italy by Uberti, imported by Benelli USA.
Price: **$429.00**

UBERTI 1848 DRAGOON AND POCKET REVOLVERS
Caliber: 44 6-shot engraved cylinder. **Barrel:** 7.5" 7 grooves. **Weight:** 4.1 lbs. **Stocks:** One-piece walnut. **Sights:** Fixed. **Features:** Copy of Eli Whitney's design for Colt using Walker parts. Blued barrel, backstrap, and trigger guard. Made in Italy by Uberti, imported by Benelli USA.
Price: 1848 Whitneyville Dragoon, 7.5" barrel ... **$429.00**
Price: 1848 Dragoon, 1st-3rd models, 7.5" barrel . **$409.00**
Price: 1848 Baby Dragoon, 4" barrel **$339.00**

UBERTI 1858 NEW ARMY REVOLVERS
Caliber: 44 6-shot engraved cylinder. **Barrel:** 8" 7 grooves. **Weight:** 2.7 lbs. **Length:** 13.6". **Stocks:** Two-piece walnut. **Sights:** Fixed. **Features:** Blued or stainless barrel, backstrap; brass trigger guard. Made in Italy by Uberti, imported by Benelli USA.
Price: 1858 New Army Stainless 8" barrel **$429.00**
Price: 1858 New Army 8" barrel **$349.00**
Price: 1858 Target Carbine 18" barrel **$549.00**
Price: 1862 Pocket Navy 5.5" barrel, 36 caliber **$349.00**
Price: 1862 Police 5.5" barrel, 36 caliber **$349.00**

UBERTI 1861 NAVY PERCUSSION REVOLVER
Caliber: 36, 6-shot. **Barrel:** 7.5", 7-groove, round. **Weight:** 2 lbs., 6 oz. **Length:** 13". **Stocks:** One-piece walnut. **Sights:** German silver blade front sight. **Features:** Rounded trigger guard, "creeping" loading lever, fluted or round cylinder, steel backstrap, trigger guard, cut for stock. Imported by Cimarron F.A. Co., Uberti U.S.A. Inc., Dixie Gun Works.
Price: Dixie RH0420 .... **$295.00**

1862 POCKET NAVY PERCUSSION REVOLVER
Caliber: 36, 5-shot. **Barrel:** 5.5", 6.5", octagonal, 7-groove, LH twist. **Weight:** 27 oz. (5.5" barrel). **Length:** 10.5" overall (5.5" bbl.). **Stocks:** One-piece varnished walnut. **Sights:** Brass pin front, hammer notch rear. **Features:** Rebated cylinder, hinged loading lever, brass or silver-plated backstrap and trigger guard, color-cased frame, hammer, loading lever, plunger and latch, rest blued. Has original-type markings. From Cimarron F.A. Co., Uberti U.S.A. Inc., Dixie Gun Works.
Price: With brass backstrap, trigger guard **$250.00**

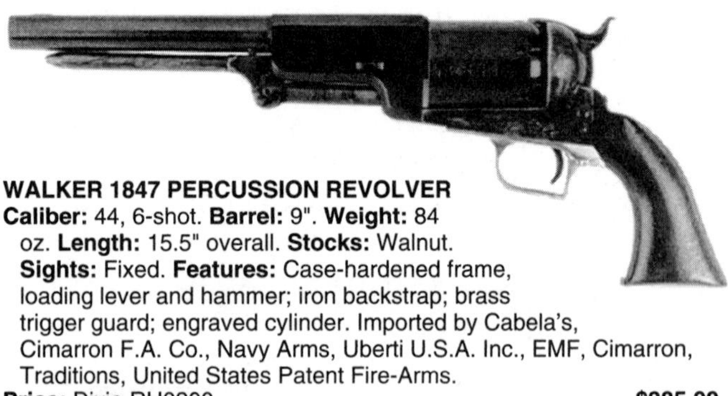

WALKER 1847 PERCUSSION REVOLVER
Caliber: 44, 6-shot. **Barrel:** 9". **Weight:** 84 oz. **Length:** 15.5" overall. **Stocks:** Walnut. **Sights:** Fixed. **Features:** Case-hardened frame, loading lever and hammer; iron backstrap; brass trigger guard; engraved cylinder. Imported by Cabela's, Cimarron F.A. Co., Navy Arms, Uberti U.S.A. Inc., EMF, Cimarron, Traditions, United States Patent Fire-Arms.
Price: Dixie RH0200 .... **$385.00**
Price: Dixie Kit RH0400 .... **$300.00**
Price: Hartford model, steel frame, cartouche (EMF) **$350.00**

ARMOURY R140 HAWKEN RIFLE

Caliber: 45, 50 or 54. **Barrel:** 29". **Weight:** 8.75 to 9 lbs. **Length:** 45.75" overall. **Stock:** Walnut, with cheekpiece. **Sights:** Dovetailed front, fully adjustable rear. **Features:** Octagon barrel, removable breech plug; double set triggers; blued barrel, brass stock fittings, color case-hardened percussion lock. From Armsport, The Armoury.

Price: . . . . **$225.00 to $245.00**

BOSTONIAN PERCUSSION RIFLE

Caliber: 45. **Barrel:** 30", octagonal. **Weight:** 7.25 lbs. **Length:** 46" overall. **Stock:** Walnut. **Sights:** Blade front, fixed notch rear. **Features:** Color case-hardened lock, brass trigger guard, buttplate, patchbox. Imported from Italy by EMF.

Price: **$285.00**

CABELA'S BLUE RIDGE RIFLE

Caliber: 32, 36, 45, 50, .54. **Barrel:** 39", octagonal. **Weight:** About 7.75 lbs. **Length:** 55" overall. **Stock:** American black walnut. **Sights:** Blade front, rear drift adjustable for windage. **Features:** Color case-hardened lockplate and cock/hammer, brass trigger guard and buttplate, double set, double-phased triggers. From Cabela's.

Price: Percussion **$569.99**
Price: Flintlock **$599.99**

CABELA'S TRADITIONAL HAWKEN

Caliber: 50, 54. **Barrel:** 29". **Weight:** About 9 lbs. **Stock:** Walnut. **Sights:** Blade front, open adjustable rear. **Features:** Flintlock or percussion. Adjustable double-set triggers. Polished brass furniture, color case-hardened lock. Imported by Cabela's.

Price: Percussion, right-hand or left-hand **$339.99**
Price: Flintlock, right-hand **$399.99**

CABELA'S KODIAK EXPRESS DOUBLE RIFLE

Caliber: 50, 54, 58, 72. **Barrel:** Length NA; 1:48" twist. **Weight:** 9.3 lbs. **Length:** 45.25" overall. **Stock:** European walnut, oil finish. **Sights:** Fully adjustable double folding-leaf rear, ramp front. **Features:** Percussion. Barrels regulated to point of aim at 75 yards; polished and engraved lock, top tang and trigger guard. From Cabela's.

Price: 50, 54, 58 calibers **$929.99**
Price: 72 caliber **$959.99**

COOK & BROTHER CONFEDERATE CARBINE

Caliber: 58. **Barrel:** 24". **Weight:** 7.5 lbs. **Length:** 40.5" overall. **Stock:** Select walnut. **Features:** Re-creation of the 1861 New Orleans-made artillery carbine. Color case-hardened lock, browned barrel. Buttplate, trigger guard, barrel bands, sling swivels and nosecap of polished brass. From Euroarms of America.

Price: **$563.00**
Price: Cook & Brother rifle (33" barrel) **$606.00**

CVA OPTIMA ELITE BREAK-ACTION RIFLE

Caliber: 45, 50. **Barrel:** 28" fluted. **Weight:** 8.8 lbs. **Stock:** Ambidextrous solid composite in standard or thumbhole. **Sights:** Adj. fiber-optic. **Features:** Break-action, stainless No. 209 breech plug, aluminum loading rod, cocking spur, lifetime warranty.

Price: CR4002 (50-cal., blued/Realtree HD) **$398.95**
Price: CR4002X (50-cal., stainless/Realtree HD) **$456.95**
Price: CR4003X (45-cal., stainless/Realtree HD) **$456.95**
Price: CR4000T (50-cal), blued/black fiber grip thumbhole) . **$366.95**
Price: CR4000 (50-cal., blued/black fiber grip **$345.95**
Price: CR4002T (50-cal., blued/Realtree HD thumbhole) . . . **$432.95**
Price: CR4002S (50-cal., stainless/Realtree HD thumbhole) **$422.95**
Price: CR4000X (50-cal., stainless/black fiber grip thumbhole) **$451.95**
Price: CR4000S (50-cal., stainless steel/black fiber grip) . . . **$400.95**

CVA Optima 209 Magnum Break-Action Rifle

Similar to Optima Elite but with 26" bbl., nickel or blue finish, 50 cal.

Price: PR2008N (nickel/Realtree HD thumbhole) **$345.95**
Price: PR2004N (nickel/Realtree) **$322.95**
Price: PR2000 (blued/black) **$229.95**
Price: PR2006N (nickel/black) **$273.95**

CVA Wolf 209 Magnum Break-Action Rifle

Similar to Optima 209 Mag but with 24 barrel, weighs 7 lbs, and in 50-cal. only.

Price: PR2101N (nickel/camo) **$253.95**
Price: PR2102 (blued/camo). **$231.95**
Price: PR2100 (blued/black) **$180.95**
Price: PR2100N (nickel/black) **$202.95**
Price: PR2100NS (nickel/black scoped package) **$277.95**
Price: PR2100S (blued/black scoped package) **$255.95**

CVA APEX

Caliber: 45, 50. **Barrel:** 27", 1:28 twist. **Weight:** 8 lbs. **Length:** 42". **Stock:** Synthetic. **Features:** Ambi stock with rubber grip panels in black or Realtree APG camo, crush-zone recoil pad, reversible hammer spur, quake claw sling, lifetime warranty.

Price: CR4010S (50-cal., stainless/black) **$576.95**
Price: CR4011S (45-cal., stainless/black) **$576.95**
Price: CR4012S (50-cal., stainless/Realtree HD) **$651.95**
Price: CR4013S (45-cal., stainless/Realtree HD) **$651.95**

CVA ACCURA

Similar to Apex but weighs 7.3 lbs., in stainless steel or matte blue finish, cocking spur.

Price: PR3106S (50-cal, stainless steel/Realtree APG thumbhole) **$495.95**
Price: PR3107S (45-cal., stainless steel/Realtree APG thumbhole) **$495.95**
Price: PR 3104S (50-cal., stainless steel/black fibergrip thumbhole) **$438.95**
Price: PR3100 (50-cal., blued/black fibergrip **$345.95**
Price: PR3100S (50-cal., stainless steel/black fibergrip **$403.95**
Price: PR3102S (50-cal., stainless steel/Realtree APG) **$460.95**

CVA BUCKHORN 209 MAGNUM

Caliber: 50. **Barrel:** 24". **Weight:** 6.3 lbs. **Sights:** Illuminator fiber-optic. **Features:** Grip-dot stock, thumb-actuated safety; drilled and tapped for scope mounts.

Price: Black stock, blue barrel **$145.00**

CVA KODIAK MAGNUM RIFLE

Caliber: 50. No. 209 primer ignition. **Barrel:** 28"; 1:28" twist. **Stock:** Ambidextrous black or Mossy Oak® camo. **Sights:** Fiber-optic. **Features:** Blue or nickel finish, recoil pad, lifetime warranty. From CVA.

Price: Mossy Oak® camo; nickel barrel **$300.00**
Price: Stainless steel/black fibergrip **$288.95**
Price: Blued/black fibergrip. **$229.95**

DIXIE EARLY AMERICAN JAEGER RIFLE

Caliber: 54. **Barrel:** 27.5" octagonal; 1:24" twist. **Weight:** 8.25 lbs. **Length:** 43.5" overall. **Stock:** American walnut; sliding wooden patchbox on butt. **Sights:** Notch rear, blade front. **Features:** Flintlock or percussion. Browned steel furniture. Imported from Italy by Dixie Gun Works.

Price: Flintlock FR0838. . . . . **$695.00**
Price: Percussion PR0835, case-hardened **$695.00**
Price: Kit **$775.00**

DIXIE DELUXE CUB RIFLE

Caliber: 32, 36, 40, 45. **Barrel:** 28" octagon. **Weight:** 6.25 lbs. **Length:** 44" overall. **Stock:** Walnut. **Sights:** Fixed. **Features:** Short rifle for small game and beginning shooters. Brass patchbox and furniture. Flint or percussion, finished or kit. From Dixie Gun Works

Price: Deluxe Cub (45-cal.) **$525.00**
Price: Deluxe Cub (flint) **$530.00**
Price: Super Cub (50-cal) **$530.00**
Price: Deluxe Cub (32-cal. flint) **$725.00**
Price: Deluxe Cub (36-cal. flint) **$725.00**
Price: Deluxe Cub kit (32-cal. percussion) **$550.00**
Price: Deluxe Cub kit (36-cal. percussion) **$550.00**
Price: Deluxe Cub (45-cal. percussion) **$675.00**
Price: Super Cub (percussion) **$450.00**
Price: Deluxe Cub (32-cal. percussion) **$675.00**
Price: Deluxe Cub (36-cal. percussion) **$675.00**

DIXIE PEDERSOLI 1857 MAUSER RIFLE

Caliber: 54. **Barrel:** 39-3/8". **Weight:** 9.5 lbs. **Length:** 54.75" overall. **Stock:** European walnut with oil finish, sling swivels. **Sights:** Fully adjustable rear, lug front. **Features:** Percussion (musket caps). Armory bright finish with color case-hardened lock and barrel tang, engraved lockplate, steel ramrod. Introduced 2000. Imported from Italy by Dixie Gun Works.

Price: PR1330. . . . . **$995.00**

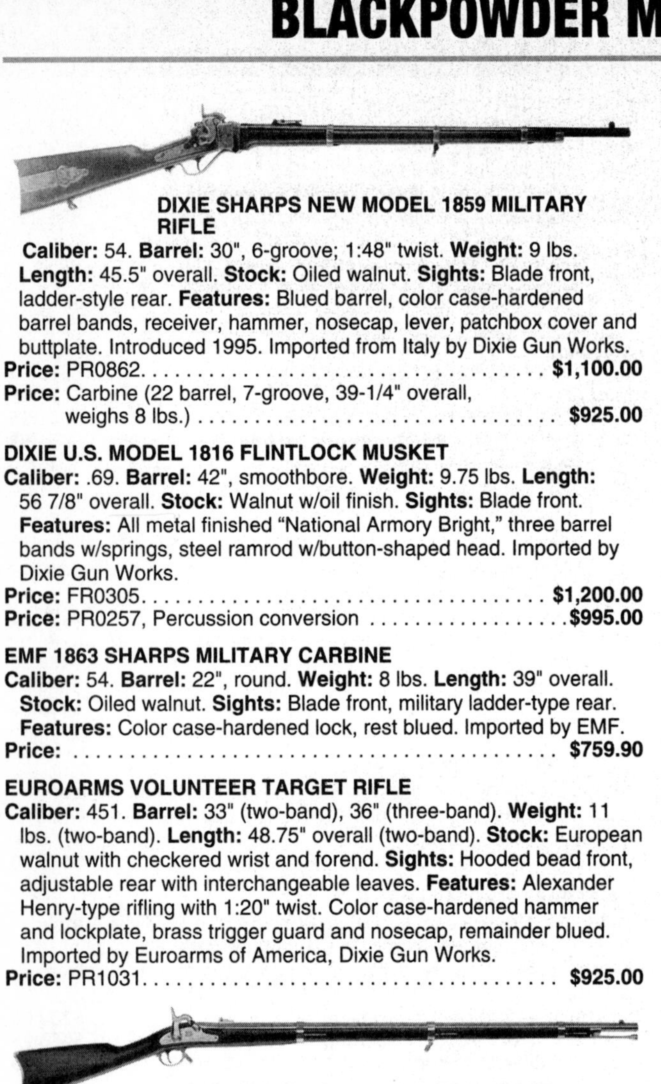

DIXIE SHARPS NEW MODEL 1859 MILITARY RIFLE

Caliber: 54. **Barrel:** 30", 6-groove; 1:48" twist. **Weight:** 9 lbs. **Length:** 45.5" overall. **Stock:** Oiled walnut. **Sights:** Blade front, ladder-style rear. **Features:** Blued barrel, color case-hardened barrel bands, receiver, hammer, nosecap, lever, patchbox cover and buttplate. Introduced 1995. Imported from Italy by Dixie Gun Works.

Price: PR0862. . . . . **$1,100.00**

Price: Carbine (22 barrel, 7-groove, 39-1/4" overall, weighs 8 lbs.) **$925.00**

DIXIE U.S. MODEL 1816 FLINTLOCK MUSKET

Caliber: .69. **Barrel:** 42", smoothbore. **Weight:** 9.75 lbs. **Length:** 56 7/8" overall. **Stock:** Walnut w/oil finish. **Sights:** Blade front. **Features:** All metal finished "National Armory Bright," three barrel bands w/springs, steel ramrod w/button-shaped head. Imported by Dixie Gun Works.

Price: FR0305. . . . . **$1,200.00**

Price: PR0257, Percussion conversion **$995.00**

EMF 1863 SHARPS MILITARY CARBINE

Caliber: 54. **Barrel:** 22", round. **Weight:** 8 lbs. **Length:** 39" overall. **Stock:** Oiled walnut. **Sights:** Blade front, military ladder-type rear. **Features:** Color case-hardened lock, rest blued. Imported by EMF.

Price: **$759.90**

EUROARMS VOLUNTEER TARGET RIFLE

Caliber: 451. **Barrel:** 33" (two-band), 36" (three-band). **Weight:** 11 lbs. (two-band). **Length:** 48.75" overall (two-band). **Stock:** European walnut with checkered wrist and forend. **Sights:** Hooded bead front, adjustable rear with interchangeable leaves. **Features:** Alexander Henry-type rifling with 1:20" twist. Color case-hardened hammer and lockplate, brass trigger guard and nosecap, remainder blued. Imported by Euroarms of America, Dixie Gun Works.

Price: PR1031. . . . . **$925.00**

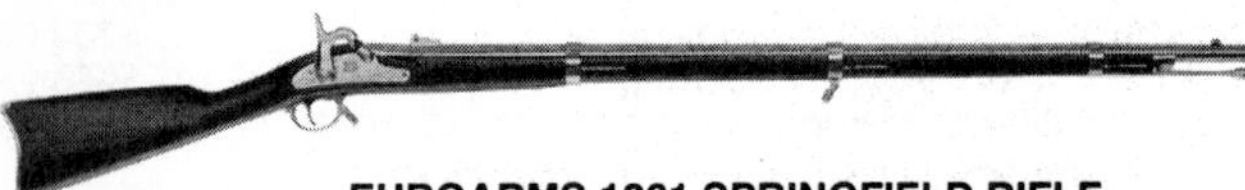

EUROARMS 1861 SPRINGFIELD RIFLE

Caliber: 58. **Barrel:** 40". **Weight:** About 10 lbs. **Length:** 55.5" overall. **Stock:** European walnut. **Sights:** Blade front, three-leaf military rear. **Features:** Reproduction of the original three-band rifle. Lockplate marked "1861" with eagle and "U.S. Springfield." White metal. Imported by Euroarms of America.

Price: **$730.00**

EUROARMS ZOUAVE RIFLE

Caliber: 54, 58 percussion. **Barrel:** 33". **Weight:** 9.5 lbs. Overall **length:** 49". **Features:** One-piece solid barrel and bolster. For 54 caliber, .535 R.B., .540 minnie. For 58 caliber, .575 R.B., .577 minnie. 1863 issue. Made in Italy. Imported by Euroarms of America.

Price: **$469.00**

EUROARMS HARPERS FERRY RIFLE

Caliber: 58 flintlock. **Barrel:** 35". **Weight:** 9 lbs. Overall **length:** 59.5". **Features:** Antique browned barrel. Barrel .575 RB. .577 minnie. 1803 issue. Made in Italy. Imported by Euroarms of America.

Price: **$735.00**

GONIC MODEL 93 M/L RIFLE

Caliber: 45, 50. **Barrel:** 26"; 1:24" twist. **Weight:** 6.5 to 7 lbs. **Length:** 43" overall. **Stock:** American hardwood with black finish. **Sights:** Adjustable or aperture rear, hooded post front. **Features:** Adjustable trigger with side safety; unbreakable ramrod; comes with A. Z. scope bases installed. Introduced 1993. Made in U.S. by Gonic Arms, Inc.

Price: Model 93 Standard (blued barrel). **$720.00**

Price: Model 93 Standard (stainless brl., 50 cal. only) **$782.00**

Gonic Model 93 Deluxe M/L Rifle

Similar to the Model 93 except has classic-style walnut or gray laminated wood stock. Introduced 1998. Made in U.S. by Gonic Arms, Inc.

Price: Blue barrel, sights, scope base, choice of stock. **$902.00**

Price: Stainless barrel, sights, scope base, choice of stock (50 cal. only) **$964.00**

Gonic Model 93 Mountain Thumbhole M/L Rifles

Similar to the Model 93 except has high-grade walnut or gray laminate stock with extensive hand-checkered panels, Monte Carlo cheekpiece and beavertail forend; integral muzzle brake. Introduced 1998. Made in U.S. by Gonic Arms, Inc.

Price: Blued or stainless **$2,700.00**

HARPER'S FERRY 1803 FLINTLOCK RIFLE

Caliber: 54 or 58. **Barrel:** 35". **Weight:** 9 lbs. **Length:** 59.5" overall. **Stock:** Walnut with cheekpiece. **Sights:** Brass blade front, fixed steel rear. **Features:** Brass trigger guard, sideplate, buttplate; steel patchbox. Imported by Euroarms of America, Navy Arms (54-cal. only), and Dixie Gun Works.

Price: 54-cal. (Navy Arms) **$625.00**

Price: 54-cal. (Dixie Gun Works), FR0171 . . . . **$995.00**

Price: 54-cal. (Euroarms) **$809.00**

HAWKEN RIFLE

Caliber: 45, 50, 54 or 58. **Barrel:** 28", blued, 6-groove rifling. **Weight:** 8.75 lbs. **Length:** 44" overall. **Stock:** Walnut with cheekpiece. **Sights:** Blade front, fully adjustable rear. **Features:** Coil mainspring, double-set triggers, polished brass furniture. From Armsport and EMF.

Price: . . . . **$220.00 to $345.00**

J.P. HENRY TRADE RIFLE

Caliber: 54. **Barrel:** 34"; 1" flats. **Weight:** 8.5 lbs. **Length:** 45" overall. **Stock:** Premium curly maple. **Sights:** Silver blade front, fixed buckhorn rear. **Features:** Brass buttplate, side plate, trigger guard and nosecap; browned barrel and lock; L&R Large English percussion lock; single trigger. Made in U.S. by J.P. Gunstocks, Inc.

Price: **$965.50**

J.P. MURRAY 1862-1864 CAVALRY CARBINE

Caliber: 58 (.577" Minie). **Barrel:** 23". **Weight:** 7 lbs., 9 oz. **Length:** 39" overall. **Stock:** Walnut. **Sights:** Blade front, rear drift adjustable for windage. **Features:** Blued barrel, color case-hardened lock, blued swivel and band springs, polished brass buttplate, trigger guard, barrel bands. From Dixie Gun Works.

Price: Dixie Gun Works PR0173 . . . . **$750.00**

KENTUCKY FLINTLOCK RIFLE

Caliber: 44, 45, or 50. **Barrel:** 35". **Weight:** 7 lbs. **Length:** 50" overall. **Stock:** Walnut stained, brass fittings. **Sights:** Fixed. **Features:** Available in carbine model also, 28" bbl. Some variations in detail, finish. Kits also available from some importers. Imported by The Armoury.

Price: About . . . . **$217.95 to $345.00**

Kentucky Percussion Rifle

Similar to Flintlock except percussion lock. Finish and features vary with importer. Imported by The Armoury and CVA.

Price: About **$259.95**

Price: 45 or 50 cal. (Navy Arms) **$425.00**

Price: Kit, 50 cal. (CVA) **$189.95**

KNIGHT SHADOW RIFLE

Caliber: 50. **Barrel:** 26". **Weight:** 7 lbs., 12 oz. **Length:** 42" overall. **Stock:** Checkered with recoil pad, swivel studs, Realtree APG HD. or black composite. **Sights:** Fully adjustable, metallic fiber-optic. **Features:** Bolt-action in-line system uses #209 shotshell primer for ignition; primer is held in plastic drop-in Primer Disc. Available in blued or stainless steel. Made in U.S. by Knight Rifles (Modern Muzzleloading).

Price: Blued/black. **$289.99**

Price: Stainless/black **$329.99**

Price: Realtree APG HD camo (2009) **$329.99**

Prices given are believed to be accurate at time of publication however, many factors affect retail pricing so exact prices are not possible.

KNIGHT ROLLING BLOCK RIFLE
Caliber: 50, 52. **Barrel:** 27"; 1:28" twist. **Weight:** 8 lbs. **Length:** 43.5" overall. **Stock:** Brown Sandstone laminate, checkered, recoil pad, sling swivel studs. **Sights:** Fully adjustable, metallic fiber-optic. **Features:** Uses #209 shotshell primer, comes in stainless steel or blued, with walnut or black composite stock. Made in U.S. by Knight Rifles (Modern Muzzleloading).
Price: 50 Stainless/black. **$419.99**
Price: 50 Blued/black **$329.99**
Price: 50 Stainless/Realtree (2009) **$459.99**
Price: 50 Stainless/Brown Sandstone (2009) **$438.88**
Price: 52 Stainless/Next G-1 . . . . **$459.99**

KNIGHT LONG RANGE HUNTER
Caliber: 50. **Barrel:** 27" custom fluted; 1:28" twist. **Weight:** 8 lbs. 6 oz. **Length:** 45.5" overall. **Stock:** Cast-off design thumbhole, checkered, recoil pad, sling swivel studs, in Forest Green or Sandstone. **Sights:** Fully-adjustable, metallic fiber-optic. **Features:** Full plastic jacket ignition system. Made in U.S. by Knight Rifles (Modern Muzzleloading).
Price: SS Forest Green. **$769.99**
Price: SS Forest Green Thumbhole **$799.99**

KNIGHT EXTREME
Caliber: 50, 52. **Barrel:** 26", fluted stainess, 1:28" twist. **Weight:** 7 lbs. 14 oz to 8 lbs. **Length:** 45" overall. **Stock:** Stainless steel laminate, blued walnut, black composite thumbhole with blued or SS, Realtree Hardwoods Green HD with thumbhole. **Sights:** Fully adjustable metallic fiber-optics. **Features:** Full plastic jacket ignition system. Made in U.S. by Knight Rifles (Modern Muzzleloading).
Price: 50 SS/Realtree (2009) **$529.99**
Price: 52 SS/black (2009) **$229.94**
Price: 50 SS/black **$459.99**
Price: 50 SS/black w/thumbhole **$489.99**
Price: 50 SS/brown **$569.99**

KNIGHT BIGHORN
Caliber: 50. **Barrel:** 26"; 1:28" twist. **Weight:** 7 lbs. 3 oz. **Length:** 44.5" overall. **Stock:** Realtree Advantage MAX-1 HD or black composite thumbhole, checkered with recoil pad, sling swivel studs. **Sights:** Fully adjustable metallic fiber-optic. **Features:** Uses 4 different ignition systems (included): #11 nipple, musket nipple, bare 208 shotgun primer and 209 Extreme shotgun primer system (Extreme weatherproof full plastic jacket system); one-piece removable hammer assembly. Made in U.S. by Knight Rifles (Modern Muzzleloading).
Price: Stainless/Realtree w/thumbhole (2009) **$459.99**
Price: Stainless/black **$419.99**
Price: Stainless/black w/thumbhole **$439.99**

KNIGHT 52 MODELS
Caliber: 52. **Barrel:** 26";1:26" twist (composite), 27" 1:28" twist (G-1 camo). **Weight:** 8 lbs. **Length:** 43.5" (G-1 camo); 45" (composite) overall. **Stock:** Standard black composite or Next G-1, checkered with recoil pad, sling swivel studs. **Sights:** Fully adjustable metallic fiber-optic. **Features:** PowerStem breech plug. Made in U.S. by Knight Rifles (Modern Muzzleloading).
Price: Stainless/black (2009) **$299.94**
Price: Stainless/Next G-1 . . . . **$459.99**

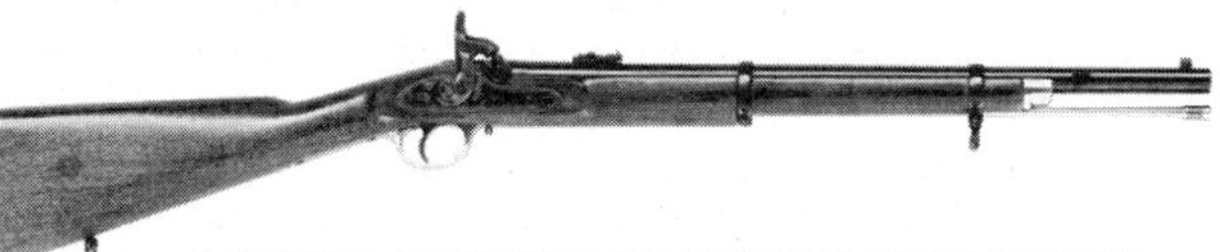

LONDON ARMORY 1861 ENFIELD MUSKETOON
Caliber: 58, Minie ball. **Barrel:** 24", round. **Weight:** 7 to 7.5 lbs. **Length:** 40.5" overall. **Stock:** Walnut, with sling swivels. **Sights:** Blade front, graduated military-leaf rear. **Features:** Brass trigger guard, nosecap, buttplate; blued barrel, bands, lockplate, swivels. Imported by Euroarms of America, Navy Arms.
Price: . . . . **$300.00 to $521.00**
Price: Kit . . . . **$365.00 to $402.00**

LONDON ARMORY 2-BAND 1858 ENFIELD
Caliber: .577" Minie, .575" round ball. **Barrel:** 33". **Weight:** 10 lbs. **Length:** 49" overall. **Stock:** Walnut. **Sights:** Folding leaf rear adjustable for elevation. **Features:** Blued barrel, color case-hardened lock and hammer, polished brass buttplate, trigger guard, nosecap. From Navy Arms, Euroarms of America, Dixie Gun Works.
Price: PR0330 . . . . **$650.00**

LONDON ARMORY 3-BAND 1853 ENFIELD
Caliber: 58 (.577" Minie, .575" round ball, .580" maxi ball). **Barrel:** 39". **Weight:** 9.5 lbs. **Length:** 54" overall. **Stock:** European walnut. **Sights:** Inverted "V" front, traditional Enfield folding ladder rear. **Features:** Re-creation of the famed London Armory Company Pattern 1853 Enfield Musket. One-piece walnut stock, brass buttplate, trigger guard and nosecap. Lockplate marked "London Armoury Co." and with a British crown. Blued Baddeley barrel bands. From Euroarms of America, Navy Arms.
Price: About . . . . **$350.00 to $606.00**

LYMAN TRADE RIFLE
Caliber: 50, 54. **Barrel:** 28" octagon;1:48" twist. **Weight:** 10.8 lbs. **Length:** 45" overall. **Stock:** European walnut. **Sights:** Blade front, open rear adjustable for windage or optional fixed sights. **Features:** Fast twist rifling for conical bullets. Polished brass furniture with blue steel parts, stainless steel nipple. Hook breech, single trigger, coil spring percussion lock. Steel barrel rib and ramrod ferrules. Introduced 1980. From Lyman.
Price: 50-cal. percussion **$474.95**
Price: 50-cal. flintlock **$499.95**
Price: 54-cal. percussion **$474.95**
Price: 54-cal. flintlock **$499.95**

LYMAN DEERSTALKER RIFLE
Caliber: 50, 54. **Barrel:** 24", octagonal; 1:48" rifling. **Weight:** 10.4 lbs. **Stock:** Walnut with black rubber buttpad. **Sights:** Lyman #37MA beaded front, fully adjustable fold-down Lyman #16A rear. **Features:** Stock has less drop for quick sighting. All metal parts are blackened, with color case-hardened lock; single trigger. Comes with sling and swivels. Available in flint or percussion. Introduced 1990. From Lyman.
Price: 50-cal. flintlock **$529.95**
Price: 50-, 54-cal., flintlock, left-hand **$569.95**
Price: 54 cal. flintlock **$529.95**
Price: 50-, 54 cal. percussion **$487.95**
Price: 50-, 54-cal. stainless steel **$609.95**

LYMAN GREAT PLAINS RIFLE
Caliber: 50, 54. **Barrel:** 32"; 1:60" twist. **Weight:** 11.6 lbs. **Stock:** Walnut. **Sights:** Steel blade front, buckhorn rear adjustable for windage and elevation and fixed notch primitive sight included. **Features:** Blued steel furniture. Stainless steel nipple. Coil spring lock, Hawken-style trigger guard and double-set triggers. Round thimbles recessed and sweated into rib. Steel wedge plates and toe plate. Introduced 1979. From Lyman.
Price: Percussion **$654.95**
Price: Flintlock **$699.95**
Price: Percussion kit **$519.95**
Price: Flintlock kit **$574.95**
Price: Left-hand percussion **$669.95**
Price: Left-hand flintlock **$709.95**

Lyman Great Plains Hunter Model
Similar to Great Plains model except 1:32" twist shallow-groove barrel and comes drilled and tapped for Lyman 57GPR peep sight.
Price: Percussion **$654.95**
Price: Flintlock **$699.95**
Price: Left-hand percussion **$669.95**

MARKESBERY KM BLACK BEAR M/L RIFLE
Caliber: 36, 45, 50, 54. **Barrel:** 24"; 1:26" twist. **Weight:** 6.5 lbs. **Length:** 38.5" overall. **Stock:** Two-piece American hardwood,

walnut, black laminate, green laminate, black composition, X-Tra or Mossy Oak® Break-up™ camouflage. **Sights:** Bead front, open fully adjustable rear. **Features:** Interchangeable barrels; exposed hammer; Outer-Line Magnum ignition system uses small rifle primer or standard No. 11 cap and nipple. Blue, black matte, or stainless. Made in U.S. by Markesbery Muzzle Loaders.

Price: American hardwood walnut, blue finish **$536.63**
Price: American hardwood walnut, stainless **$553.09**
Price: Black laminate, blue finish **$539.67**
Price: Black laminate, stainless **$556.27**
Price: Black composite, blue finish **$532.65**
Price: Black composite, stainless **$549.93**
Price: Green laminate, blue finish **$539.00**
Price: Green laminate, stainless **$556.27**

Markesbery KM Brown Bear Rifle

Similar to KM Black Bear except one-piece thumbhole stock with Monte Carlo comb. Stock in Crotch Walnut composite, green or black laminate, black composite or X-Tra or Mossy Oak® Break-Up™ camouflage. Made in U.S. by Markesbery Muzzle Loaders, Inc.

Price: Black composite, blue finish **$658.83**
Price: Crotch Walnut, blue finish **$658.83**
Price: Walnut wood **$662.81**
Price: Black wood **$662.81**
Price: Black laminated wood **$662.81**
Price: Green laminated wood **$662.81**
Price: Black composite, stainless **$676.11**
Price: Crotch Walnut composite, stainless **$676.11**
Price: Walnut wood, stainless **$680.07**
Price: Black wood, stainless **$680.07**
Price: Black laminated wood, stainless **$680.07**
Price: Green laminate, stainless **$680.07**

Markesbery KM Grizzly Bear Rifle

Similar to KM Black Bear except thumbhole buttstock with Monte Carlo comb. Stock in Crotch Walnut composite, green or black laminate, black composite or X-Tra or Mossy Oak® Break-Up camouflage. Made in U.S. by Markesbery Muzzle Loaders, Inc.

Price: Black composite, blue finish **$642.96**
Price: Crotch Walnut, blue finish **$642.96**
Price: Walnut wood **$646.93**
Price: Black wood **$646.93**
Price: Black laminate wood **$646.93**
Price: Green laminate wood **$646.93**
Price: Black composite, stainless **$660.98**
Price: Crotch Walnut composite, stainless **$660.98**
Price: Black laminate wood, stainless **$664.20**
Price: Green laminate, stainless **$664.20**
Price: Walnut wood, stainless **$664.20**
Price: Black wood, stainless **$664.20**

Markesbery KM Polar Bear Rifle

Similar to KM Black Bear except one-piece stock with Monte Carlo comb. Stock in American Hard-wood walnut, green or black laminate, black composite, or X-Tra or Mossy Oak® Break-Up™ camouflage. Interchangeable barrel system, Outer-Line ignition system, cross-bolt double safety. Available in 36, 45, 50, 54 caliber. Made in U.S. by Markesbery Muzzle Loaders, Inc.

Price: American Hardwood walnut, blue finish **$539.01**
Price: Black composite, blue finish **$536.63**
Price: Black laminate, blue finish **$541.17**
Price: Green laminate, blue finish **$541.17**
Price: American Hardwood walnut, stainless **$556.27**
Price: Black composite, stainless **$556.04**
Price: Black laminate, stainless **$570.56**
Price: Green laminate, stainless **$570.56**

MARKESBERY KM COLORADO ROCKY MOUNTAIN RIFLE

Caliber: 36, 45, 50, 54. **Barrel:** 24"; 1:26" twist. **Weight:** 6.5 lbs. **Length:** 38.5" overall. **Stock:** American hardwood walnut, green or black laminate. **Sights:** Firesight bead on ramp front, fully adjustable open rear. **Features:** Replicates Reed/Watson rifle of 1851. Straight grip stock with or without two barrel bands, rubber recoil pad, large-spur hammer. Made in U.S. by Markesbery Muzzle Loaders, Inc.

Price: American hardwood walnut, blue finish **$545.92**
Price: Black or green laminate, blue finish **$548.30**
Price: American hardwood walnut, stainless **$563.17**
Price: Black or green laminate, stainless **$566.34**

MDM BUCKWACKA IN-LINE RIFLES

Caliber: 45 Nitro Mag., 50. **Barrel:** 23", 25". **Weight:** 7 to 7.75 lbs. **Stock:** Black, walnut, laminated and camouflage finishes. **Sights:** Williams Fire Sight blade front, Williams fully adjustable rear with ghost-ring peep aperture. **Features:** Break-open action; Incinerating Ignition System incorporates 209 shotshell primer directly into breech plug; 50-caliber models handle up to 150 grains of Pyrodex; synthetic ramrod; transfer bar safety; stainless or blued finish. Made in U.S. by Millennium Designed Muzzleloaders Ltd.

Price: 45 Nitro, stainless steel, walnut stock **$399.95**
Price: 45 Nitro, stainless steel, Mossy Oak Break-up stock . **$465.95**
Price: 45 Nitro, blued action, walnut stock **$369.95**
Price: 45 Nitro, blued action, Mossy Oak Break-up stock . . . **$425.95**
Price: 50-cal., stainless steel, walnut stock **$399.95**
Price: 50-cal., stainless steel, Mossy Oak Break-up stock . . **$465.95**
Price: 50-cal., blued action, walnut stock **$369.95**
Price: 50-cal., blued action, Mossy Oak Break-up stock **$435.95**
Price: 50-cal., Youth-Ladies, blued action, walnut stock **$369.95**
Price: 50-cal., Youth-Ladies, stainless steel, walnut stock . . **$399.95**

MDM M2K In-Line Rifle

Similar to Buckwacka except adjustable trigger and double-safety mechanism designed to prevent misfires. Made in U.S. by Millennium Designed Muzzleloaders Ltd.

Price: . . . . **$529.00 to $549.00**

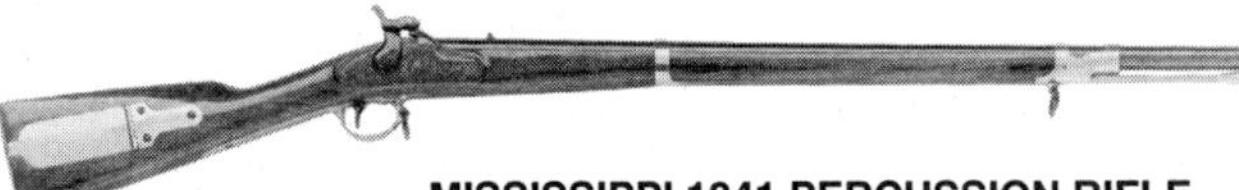

MISSISSIPPI 1841 PERCUSSION RIFLE

Caliber: 54, 58. **Barrel:** 33". **Weight:** 9.5 lbs. **Length:** 48-5/8" overall. **Stock:** One-piece European walnut full stock with satin finish. **Sights:** Brass blade front, fixed steel rear. **Features:** Case-hardened lockplate marked "U.S." surmounted by American eagle. Two barrel bands, sling swivels. Steel ramrod with brass end, browned barrel. From Navy Arms, Dixie Gun Works, Euroarms of America.

Price: Dixie Gun Works PR0870. . . . . **$825.00**

NAVY ARMS 1861 MUSKETOON

Caliber: 58. **Barrel:** 39". **Weight:** NA. **Length:** NA. **Stock:** NA. **Sights:** Front is blued steel base and blade, blued steel lip-up rear adjustable for elevation. **Features:** Brass nosecap, triggerguard, buttplate, blued steel barrel bands, color case-hardened lock with engraved lockplate marked "1861 Enfield" ahead of hammer & crown over "PH" on tail. Barrel is marked "Parker Hale LTD Birmingham England." Imported by Navy Arms.

Price: **$900.00**

NAVY ARMS PARKER-HALE 1853 THREE-BAND ENFIELD

Caliber: 58. **Barrel:** 39", tapered, round, blued. **Weight:** NA. **Length:** 55-1/4" overall. **Stock:** Walnut. **Sights:** Front is blued steel base and blade, blued steel lip-up rear adjustable for elevation. **Features:** Meticulously reproduced based on original gauges and patterns. Features brass nosecap, triggerguard, buttplate, blued steel barrel bands, color case-hardened lock with engraved lockplate marked "Parker-Hale" ahead of hammer & crown over "PH" on tail. Barrel is marked "Parker Hale LTD Birmingham England." From Navy Arms.

Price: Finished rifle **$1,050.00**

Navy Arms Parker-Hale 1858 Two-Band Enfield

Similar to the Three-band Enfield with 33" barrel, 49" overall length. Engraved lockplate marked "1858 Enfield" ahead of hammer & crown over "PH" on tail. Barrel is marked "Parker Hale LTD Birmingham England."

Price: **$1,050.00**

NAVY ARMS PARKER-HALE VOLUNTEER RIFLE

Caliber: 451. **Barrel:** 32", 1:20" twist. **Weight:** 9.5 lbs. **Length:** 49" overall. **Stock:** Walnut, checkered wrist and forend. **Sights:** Globe front, adjustable ladder-type rear. **Features:** Recreation of the type of gun issued to volunteer regiments during the 1860s. Rigby-pattern rifling, patent breech, detented lock. Stock is glass beaded for accuracy. Engfaved lockplate marked "Alex Henry" & crown on tail, barrel marked "Parker Hale LTD Birmingham England" and "Alexander Henry Rifling .451" Imported by Navy Arms.

Price: **$1,400.00**

NAVY ARMS PARKER-HALE WHITWORTH MILITARY TARGET RIFLE

Caliber: 45. **Barrel:** 36". **Weight:** 9.25 lbs. **Length:** 52.5" overall. **Stock:** Walnut. Checkered at wrist and forend. **Sights:** Hooded post front, open step-adjustable rear. **Features:** Faithful reproduction of Whitworth rifle. Trigger has detented lock, capable of fine adjustments without risk of the sear nose catching on the half-cock notch and damaging both parts. Engraved lockplate marked "Whitworth" ahead of hammer & crown on tail. Barrel marked "Parker Hale LTD Birmingham England" in one line on front of sight and "Sir Joseph Whitworth's Rifling .451" on left side. Introduced 1978. Imported by Navy Arms.

Price: **$1,550.00**

NAVY ARMS BROWN BESS MUSKET

Caliber: 75, smoothbore. **Barrel:** 41.8". **Weight:** 9 lbs., 5 oz. **Length:** 41.8" overall. **Features:** Brightly polished steel and brass, one-piece walnut stock. Signature of gunsmith William Grice and the date 1762, the crown and alphabetical letters GR (Georgius Rex). Barrel is made of steel, satin finish; the walnut stock is oil finished. From Navy Arms.

Price: **$1,100.00**

NAVY ARMS COUNTRY HUNTER

Caliber: 50. **Barrel:** 28.4", 6-groove, 1:34 twist. **Weight:** 6 lbs. **Length:** 44" overall. **Features:** Matte finished barrel. From Navy Arms.

Price: **$450.00**

NAVY ARMS PENNSYLVANIA RIFLE

Caliber: 32, 45. **Barrel:** 41.6". **Weight:** 7 lbs. 12 oz. to 8 lbs. 6 oz. **Length:** 56.1" overall. **Features:** Extra long rifle finished wtih rust brown color barrel and one-piece oil finished walnut stock. Adjustable double-set trigger. Vertically adjustable steel front and rear sights. From Navy Arms.

Price: **$675.00**

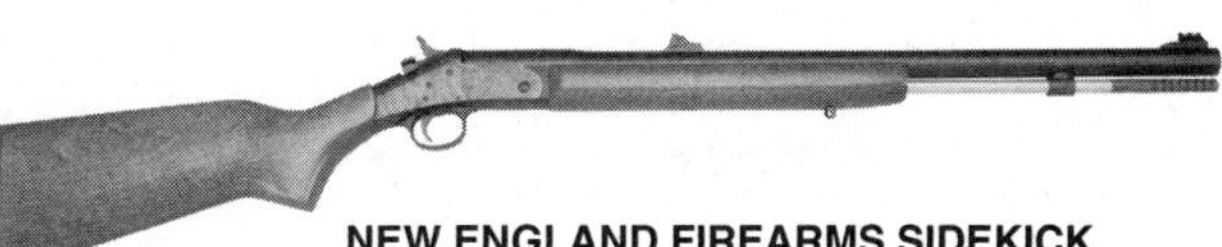

NEW ENGLAND FIREARMS SIDEKICK

Caliber: 50, 209 primer ignition. **Barrel:** 26" (magnum). **Weight:** 6.5 lbs. **Length:** 41.25". **Stock:** Black matte polymer or hardwood. **Sights:** Adjustable fiber-optic open, tapped for scope mounts. **Features:** Single-shot based on H&R break-open action. Uses No. 209 shotgun primer held in place by special primer carrier. Telescoping brass ramrod. Introduced 2004.

Price: Wood stock, blued frame, black-oxide barrel) **$216.00**
Price: Stainless barrel and frame, synthetic stock) **$310.00**

NEW ENGLAND FIREARMS HUNTSMAN

Caliber: 50, 209 primer ignition. **Barrel:** 22" to 26". **Weight:** 5.25 to 6.5 lbs. **Length:** 40" to 43". **Stock:** Black matte polymer or hardwood. **Sights:** Fiber-optic open sights, tapped for scope mounts. **Features:** Break-open action, transfer-bar safety system, breech plug removable for cleaning. Introduced 2004.

Price: Stainless Huntsman **$306.00**
Price: Huntsman **$212.00**
Price: Pardner Combo 12 ga./50 cal muzzleloader **$259.00**
Price: Tracker II Combo 12 ga. rifled slug barrel /50 cal. **$288.00**
Price: Handi-Rifle Combo 243/50 cal. **$405.00**

New England Firearms Stainless Huntsman

Similar to Huntsman, but with matte nickel finish receiver and stainless bbl. Introduced 2003. From New England Firearms.

Price: **$381.00**

PACIFIC RIFLE MODEL 1837 ZEPHYR

Caliber: 62. **Barrel:** 30", tapered octagon. **Weight:** 7.75 lbs. **Length:** NA. **Stock:** Oil-finished fancy walnut. **Sights:** German silver blade front, semi-buckhorn rear. Options available. **Features:** Improved underhammer action. First production rifle to offer Forsyth rifle, with narrow lands and shallow rifling with 1:14" pitch for high-velocity round balls. Metal finish is slow rust brown with nitre blue accents. Optional sights, finishes and integral muzzle brake available. Introduced 1995. Made in U.S. by Pacific Rifle Co.

Price: From **$995.00**

Pacific Rifle Big Bore African Rifles

Similar to the 1837 Zephyr except in 72-caliber and 8-bore. The 72-caliber is available in standard form with 28" barrel, or as the African with flat buttplate, checkered upgraded wood; weight is 9 lbs. The 8-bore African has dual-cap ignition, 24" barrel, weighs 12 lbs., checkered English walnut, engraving, gold inlays. Introduced 1998. Made in U.S. by Pacific Rifle Co.

Price: 72-caliber, from **$1,150.00**
Price: 8-bore, from **$2,500.00**

PEIFER MODEL TS-93 RIFLE

Caliber: 45, 50. **Barrel:** 24" Douglas premium; 1:20" twist in 45; 1:28" in 50. **Weight:** 7 lbs. **Length:** 43.25" overall. **Stock:** Bell & Carlson solid composite, with recoil pad, swivel studs. **Sights:** Williams bead front on ramp, fully adjustable open rear. Drilled and tapped for Weaver scope mounts with dovetail for rear peep. **Features:** In-line ignition uses #209 shotshell primer; fast lock time; fully enclosed breech; adjustable trigger; automatic safety; removable primer holder. Blue or stainless. Made in U.S. by Peifer Rifle Co. Introduced 1996.

Price: Blue, black stock. **$730.00**
Price: Blue, wood or camouflage composite stock, or stainless with black composite stock **$803.00**
Price: Stainless, wood or camouflage composite stock **$876.00**

PRAIRIE RIVER ARMS PRA BULLPUP RIFLE

Caliber: 50. **Barrel:** 28"; 1:28" twist. **Weight:** 7.5 lbs. **Length:** 31.5" overall. **Stock:** Hardwood or black all-weather. **Sights:** Blade front, open adjustable rear. **Features:** Bullpup design thumbhole stock. Patented internal percussion ignition system. Left-hand model available. Dovetailed for scope mount. Introduced 1995. Made in U.S. by Prairie River Arms, Ltd.

Price: 4140 alloy barrel, hardwood stock **$199.00**
Price: All Weather stock, alloy barrel **$205.00**

REMINGTON GENESIS MUZZLELOADER

Caliber: 50. **Barrel:** 28", 1-in-28" twist, blued, camo, or stainless fluted. **Weight:** 7.75 lbs. **Length:** NA. **Stock:** Black synthetic, Mossy Oak New Break-Up, Realtree Hardwoods HD. **Sights:** Williams fiber-optic sights, drilled and tapped for scope mounts. **Features:** TorchCam action, 209 primer, up to 150-grain charges. Over-travel hammer, crossbolt safety with ambidextrous HammerSpur (right- and left-handed operation). Buckmasters version has stainless fluted barrel with a Realtree Hardwoods HD camo stock, laser-engraved Buckmasters logo. Aluminum anodized ramrod with jag, front and rear swivel studs, removable 7/16" breech plug; optimized for use with Remington Kleanbore 209 Muzzleloading Primers. Introduced 2006. Made in U.S. by Remington Arms Co.

Price: Genesis ML, black synthetic, carbon matte blued **$237.00**
Price: Genesis MLS Overmold synthetic, stainless satin **$307.00**
Price: Genesis ML Camo Mossy Oak Break-Up full camo **$349.00**
Price: Genesis ML Camo Mossy Oak Break-Up matte blue **$293.00**
Price: Genesis MLS Camo, Mossy Oak Break-up, stainless satin **$342.00**
Price: Genesis ML SF Synthetic Thumbhole **$349.00**
Price: Genesis ML SF Synthetic Thumbhole, stainless satin **$405.00**

Price: Genesis ML SF Buckmasters (2007) **$363.00**
Price: Genesis ML SF laminate thumbhole, stainless satin . . **$538.00**

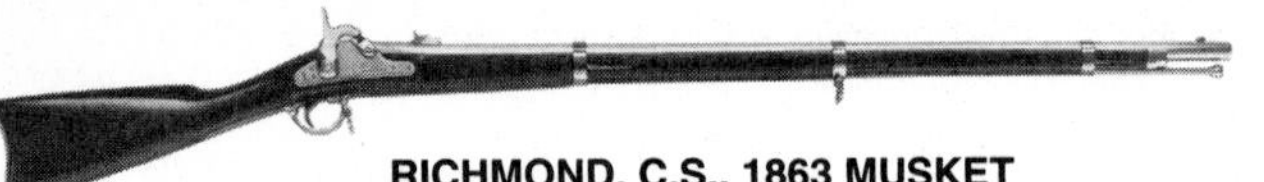

RICHMOND, C.S., 1863 MUSKET
Caliber: 58. **Barrel:** 40". **Weight:** 11 lbs. **Length:** 56.25" overall. **Stock:** European walnut with oil finish. **Sights:** Blade front, adjustable folding leaf rear. **Features:** Reproduction of the three-band Civil War musket. Sling swivels attached to trigger guard and middle barrel band. Lockplate marked "1863" and "C.S. Richmond." All white metal. Brass buttplate and forend cap. Imported by Euroarms of America, Navy Arms, and Dixie Gun Works.
Price: Euroarms **$730.00**
Price: Dixie Gun Works PR0846 . . . . **$1,050.00**
Price: Navy Arms **$1,005.00**

ROCKY MOUNTAIN HAWKEN
Caliber: NA. **Barrel:** 34-11/16". **Weight:** 10 lbs. **Length:** 52" overall. **Stock:** Walnut or maple. **Sights:** Blade front, drift adjustable rear. Fea-tures: Percussion, double set trigger, casehard-ened furniture, hook breech, brown barrel. Made by Pedersoli in Italy. Imported by Dixie Gun Works.
Price: Maple Stock PR3430 . . . .**$925.00**
Price: Walnut Stock PR3435 . . . .**$875.00**

ROSSI MUZZLELOADERS
Caliber: .50. **Barrel:** 20", 23". **Weight:** 5-6.3 lbs. **Stocks:** Wood. **Sights:** Fully adjustable fiber optic sights. **Features:** Black powder break open, 2 models available, manual external safety, Taurus Security System, blue or stainless finish, youth models available. From Rossi USA.
Price: **$209.00**
Price: Youth Size (2008). **$269.00**
Price: S50MB **$179.95**
Price: S50SM **$229.95**
Price: S45YBM (2009) **$195.95**
Price: S45YSM (2009) **$242.95**
Price: S50YBN (2009) **$195.95**
Price: S50YSM (2009) **$242.95**

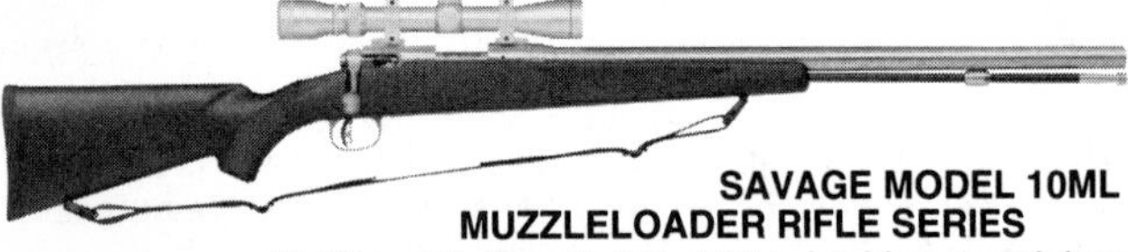

SAVAGE MODEL 10ML MUZZLELOADER RIFLE SERIES
Caliber: 50. **Barrel:** 24", 1:24 twist, blue or stainless. **Weight:** 7.75 lbs. **Stock:** Black synthetic, Realtree Hardwood JD Camo, brown laminate. **Sights:** Green adjustable rear, Red FiberOptic front. **Features:** XP Models scoped, no sights, designed for smokeless powder, #209 primer ignition. Removeable breech plug and vent liner.
Price: Model 10ML-II. **$531.00**
Price: Model 10ML-II Camo **$569.00**
Price: Model 10MLSS-II Camo **$628.00**
Price: Model 10MLBSS-II **$667.00**
Price: Model 10ML-IIXP **$569.00**
Price: Model 10MLSS-IIXP **$628.00**

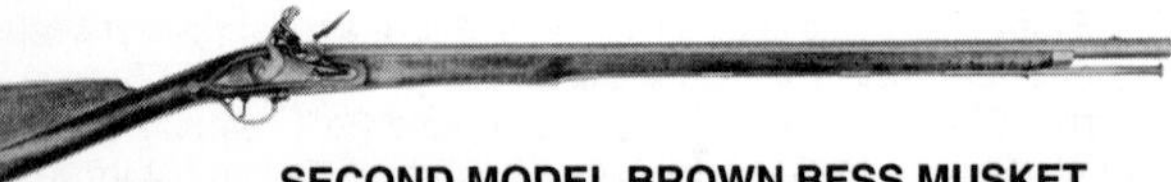

SECOND MODEL BROWN BESS MUSKET
Caliber: 75, uses .735" round ball. **Barrel:** 42", smoothbore. **Weight:** 9.5 lbs. **Length:** 59" overall. **Stock:** Walnut (Navy); walnut-stained hardwood (Dixie). **Sights:** Fixed. **Features:** Polished barrel and lock with brass trigger guard and buttplate. Bayonet and scabbard available. From Navy Arms, Dixie Gun Works.
Price: Finished . . . . **$475.00 to $950.00**
Price: Kit, Dixie Gun Works, FR0825 . . . .**$875.00**
Price: Carbine (Navy Arms) **$835.00**
Price: Dixie Gun Works FR0810 . . . . **$995.00**

THOMPSON/CENTER TRIUMPH MAGNUM MUZZLELOADER
Caliber: 50. **Barrel:** 28" Weather Shield coated. **Weight:** NA. **Length:** NA. **Stock:** Black composite or Realtree AP HD Camo. **Sights:** NA. **Features:** QLA 209 shotshell primer ignition. Introduced 2007. Made in U.S. by Thompson/Center Arms.
Price: **$457.00**

Thompson/Center Bone Collector
Similar to the Triumph Magnum but with added Flex Tech technology and Energy Burners to a shorter stock. Also added is Thompson/Center's premium fluted barrel with Weather Shield and their patented Power Rod.
Price: **$708.00**

THOMPSON/CENTER ENCORE 209X50 MAGNUM
Caliber: 50. **Barrel:** 26"; interchangeable with centerfire calibers. **Weight:** 7 lbs. **Length:** 40.5" overall. **Stock:** American walnut butt and forend, or black composite. **Sights:** TruGlo fiber-optic front and rear. **Features:** Blue or stainless steel. Uses the stock, frame and forend of the Encore centerfire pistol; break-open design using trigger guard spur; stainless steel universal breech plug; uses #209 shotshell primers. Introduced 1998. Made in U.S. by Thompson/Center Arms.
Price: Stainless with camo stock **$772.00**
Price: Blue, walnut stock and forend **$678.00**
Price: Blue, composite stock and forend **$637.00**
Price: Stainless, composite stock and forend **$713.00**
Price: All camo Realtree Hardwoods **$729.00**

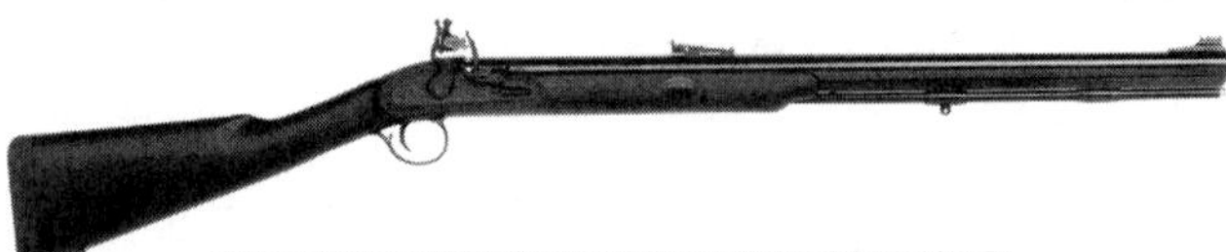

THOMPSON/CENTER FIRE STORM RIFLE
Caliber: 50. **Barrel:** 26"; 1:28" twist. **Weight:** 7 lbs. **Length:** 41.75" overall. **Stock:** Black synthetic with rubber recoil pad, swivel studs. **Sights:** Click-adjustable steel rear and ramp-style front, both with fiber-optic inserts. **Features:** Side hammer lock is the first designed for up to three 50-grain Pyrodex pellets; patented Pyrodex Pyramid breech directs ignition fire 360 degrees around base of pellet. Quick Load Accurizor Muzzle System; aluminum ramrod. Flintlock only. Introduced 2000. Made in U.S. by Thompson/Center Arms.
Price: Blue finish, flintlock model with 1:48" twist for round balls, conicals **$436.00**
Price: SST, flintlock **$488.00**

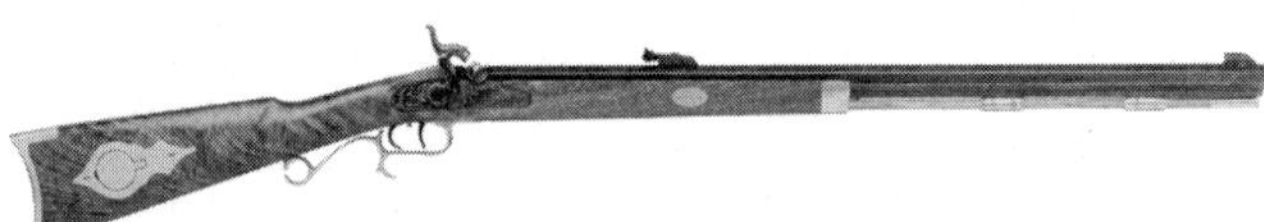

THOMPSON/CENTER HAWKEN RIFLE
Caliber: 50. **Barrel:** 28" octagon, hooked breech. **Stock:** American walnut. **Sights:** Blade front, rear adjustable for windage and elevation. **Features:** Solid brass furniture, double-set triggers, button rifled barrel, coil-type mainspring. From Thompson/Center Arms.
Price: Percussion model **$590.00**
Price: Flintlock model **$615.00**

THOMPSON/CENTER OMEGA
Caliber: 50". **Barrel:** 28", fluted. **Weight:** 7 lbs. **Length:** 42" overall. **Stock:** Composite or laminated. **Sights:** Adjustable metal rear sight with fiber-optics; metal ramp front sight with fiber-optics. **Features:** Drilled and tapped for scope mounts. Thumbhole stock, sling swivel studs. From T/C..
Price: **$777.00**

THOMPSON/CENTER IMPACT MUZZLELOADING RIFLE
50-caliber single shot rifle. Features include 209 primer ignition, sliding hood to expose removable breechplug, synthetic stock adjustable from 12.5 to 13.5 inches, 26-inch blued 1:28 rifled barrel, adjustable fiber optic sights, aluminum ramrod, camo composite stock, QLA muzzle system. Weight 6.5 lbs.
Price: . . . .**$249.00 to $269.00**

THOMPSON/CENTER NORTHWEST EXPLORER MUZZLELOADING RIFLE
50-caliber single shot rifle. Features include dropping block action, #11 percussion cap ignition, 28-inch blued or Weathershield 1:48 rifled barrel, adjustable fiber optic sights, aluminum ramrod, black or camo

Prices given are believed to be accurate at time of publication however, many factors affect retail pricing so exact prices are not possible.

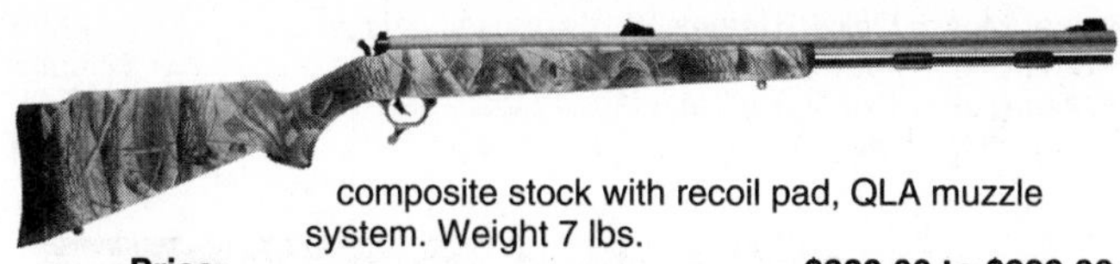

composite stock with recoil pad, QLA muzzle system. Weight 7 lbs.

Price: .... **$329.00 to $399.00**

TRADITIONS BUCKSKINNER CARBINE

Caliber: 50. **Barrel:** 21"; 15/16" flats, half octagon, half round; 1:20" or 1:66" twist. **Weight:** 6 lbs. **Length:** 37" overall. **Stock:** Beech or black laminated. **Sights:** Beaded blade front, fiber-optic open rear click adjustable for windage and elevation or fiber-optics. **Features:** Uses V-type mainspring, single trigger. Non-glare hardware; sling swivels. From Traditions.

Price: Flintlock **$249.00**
Price: Flintlock, laminated stock **$303.00**

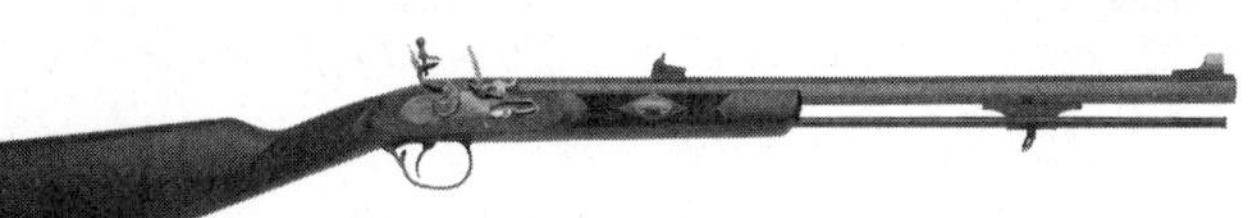

TRADITIONS DEERHUNTER RIFLE SERIES

Caliber: 32, 50 or 54. **Barrel:** 24", octagonal; 15/16" flats; 1:48" or 1:66" twist. **Weight:** 6 lbs. **Length:** 40" overall. **Stock:** Stained hardwood or All-Weather composite with rubber buttpad, sling swivels. **Sights:** Lite Optic blade front, adjustable rear fiber-optics. **Features:** Flint or percussion with color case-hardened lock. Hooked breech, oversized trigger guard, blackened furniture, PVC ramrod. All-Weather has composite stock and C-nickel barrel. Drilled and tapped for scope mounting. Imported by Traditions, Inc.

Price: Percussion, 50-cal.; blued barrel; 1:48" twist **$228.00**
Price: Flintlock, 50 caliber only; 1:48" twist **$278.00**
Price: 50-cal., synthetic/blued **$224.00**
Price: Flintlock, 50-cal., synthetic/blued **$256.00**
Price: Redi-Pak, 50 cal. flintlock **$308.00**
Price: Flintlock, left-handed hardwood, 50 cal. **$337.00**
Price: 50-cal., hardwood/blued **$264.00**

TRADITIONS PURSUIT BREAK-OPEN MUZZLELOADER

Caliber: 45, 54 and 12 gauge. **Barrel:** 28", tapered, fluted; blued, stainless or Hardwoods Green camo. **Weight:** 8.25 lbs. **Length:** 44" overall. **Stock:** Synthetic black or Hardwoods Green. **Sights:** Steel fiber-optic rear, bead front. Introduced 2004 by Traditions, Inc.

Price: Steel, blued, 45 or 50 cal., synthetic stock **$279.00**
Price: Steel, nickel, 45 or 50 cal., synthetic stock **$309.00**
Price: Steel, nickel w/Hardwoods Green stock **$359.00**
Price: Matte blued; 12 ga., synthetic stock **$369.00**
Price: Matte blued; 12 ga. w/Hardwoods Green stock **$439.00**
Price: Lightweight model, blued, synthetic stock **$199.00**
Price: Lightweight model, blued, Mossy Oak® Break-Up™ Camo stock **$239.00**
Price: Lightweight model, nickel, Mossy Oak® Break-Up™ Camo stock **$279.00**

TRADITIONS EVOLUTION LONG DISTANCE BOLT-ACTION BLACKPOWDER RIFLE

Caliber: 45, 50 percussion. **Barrel:** 26", fluted with porting. **Sights:** Steel fiber-optic. **Weight:** 7 to 7.25 lbs. **Length:** 45" overall. **Features:** Bolt-action, cocking indicator, thumb safety, aluminum ramrod, sling studs. Wide variety of stocks and metal finishes. Introduced 2004 by Traditions, Inc.

Price: 50-cal. synthetic stock **$314.00**
Price: 45-cal, synthetic stock **$259.00**
Price: 50-cal. AW/Adv. Timber HD **$370.00**
Price: 50-cal. synthetic black/blued **$293.00**

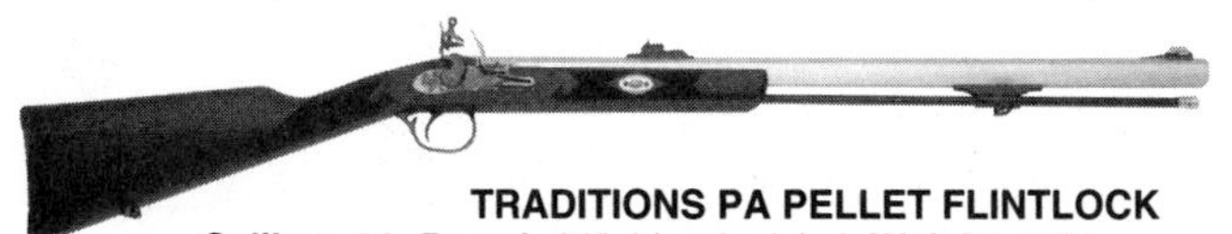

TRADITIONS PA PELLET FLINTLOCK

Caliber: 50. **Barrel:** 26", blued, nickel. **Weight:** 7 lbs. **Stock:** Hardwood, synthetic and synthetic break-up. **Sights:** Fiber-optic. **Features:** Removeable breech plug, left-hand model with hardwood stock. 1:48" twist.

Price: Hardwood, blued **$343.00**
Price: Hardwood left, blued **$378.00**

TRADITIONS HAWKEN WOODSMAN RIFLE

Caliber: 50. **Barrel:** 28"; 15/16" flats. **Weight:** 7 lbs., 11 oz. **Length:** 44.5" overall. **Stock:** Walnut-stained hardwood. **Sights:** Beaded blade front, hunting-style open rear adjustable for windage and elevation. **Features:** Percussion only. Brass patchbox and furniture. Double triggers. From Traditions.

Price: 50-cal. nickel/black laminate **$299.95**
Price: 50-cal Percussion **$396.00**
Price: 50-cal., left-hand **$415.00**
Price: 50-cal., flintlock **$434.00**

TRADITIONS KENTUCKY RIFLE

Caliber: 50. **Barrel:** 33.5"; 7/8" flats; 1:66" twist. **Weight:** 7 lbs. **Length:** 49" overall. **Stock:** Beech; inletted toe plate. **Sights:** Blade front, fixed rear. **Features:** Full-length, two-piece stock; brass furniture; color case-hardened lock. From Traditions.

Price: **$364.00**

TRADITIONS PENNSYLVANIA RIFLE

Caliber: 50. **Barrel:** 40.25"; 7/8" flats; 1:66" twist, octagon. **Weight:** 9 lbs. **Length:** 57.5" overall. **Stock:** Walnut. **Sights:** Blade front, adjustable rear. **Features:** Brass patchbox and ornamentation. Double-set triggers. From Traditions.

Price: Flintlock **$720.00**
Price: Percussion **$664.00**

TRADITIONS SHENANDOAH RIFLE

Caliber: 36, 50. **Barrel:** 33.5" octagon; 1:66" twist. **Weight:** 7 lbs., 3 oz. **Length:** 49.5" overall. **Stock:** Walnut. **Sights:** Blade front, buckhorn rear. **Features:** V-type mainspring; double-set trigger; solid brass buttplate, patchbox, nosecap, thimbles, trigger guard. Introduced 1996. From Traditions.

Price: Flintlock **$588.00**
Price: Percussion **$551.00**
Price: 36 cal. flintlock, 1:48" twist **$618.00**
Price: 36 cal. percussion, 1:48" twist **$558.00**

TRADITIONS TENNESSEE RIFLE

Caliber: 50. **Barrel:** 24", octagon; 15/16" flats; 1:66" twist. **Weight:** 6 lbs. **Length:** 40.5" overall. **Stock:** Stained beech. **Sights:** Blade front, fixed rear. **Features:** One-piece stock has inletted brass furniture, cheekpiece; double-set trigger; V-type mainspring. Flint or percussion. From Traditions.

Price: Flintlock **$484.00**
Price: Percussion **$439.00**

TRADITIONS TRACKER 209 IN-LINE RIFLES

Caliber: 45, 50. **Barrel:** 22" blued or C-nickel finish; 1:28" twist, 50 cal. 1:20" 45 cal. **Weight:** 6 lbs., 4 oz. **Length:** 41" overall. **Stock:** Black, Advantage Timber® composite, synthetic. **Sights:** Lite Optic blade front, adjustable rear. **Features:** Thumb safety; adjustable trigger; rubber butt pad and sling swivel studs; takes 150 grains of Pyrodex pellets; one-piece breech system takes 209 shotshell primers. Drilled and tapped for scope. From Traditions.

Price: (Black composite or synthetic stock, 22" blued barrel). **$161.00**
Price: (Black composite or synthetic stock, 22" C-nickel barrel) **$184.00**
Price: (Advantage Timber® stock, 22" C-nickel barrel) **$249.00**
Price: (Redi-Pak, black stock and blued barrel, powder flask, capper, ball starter, other accessories) **$219.00**
Price: (Redi-Pak, synthetic stock and blued barrel, with scope) **$265.00**

ULTRA LIGHT ARMS MODEL 209 MUZZLELOADER

Caliber: 45 or 50. **Barrel:** 24" button rifled; 1:32 twist. **Weight:** Under 5 lbs. **Stock:** Kevlar/Graphite. **Features:** Recoil pad, sling swivels

included. Some color options available. Adj. Timney trigger, positive primer extraction.
Price: **$1,300.00**

WHITE MODEL 97 WHITETAIL HUNTER RIFLE
Caliber: 45, 50. **Barrel:** 22", 1:20" twist (45 cal.); 1:24" twist (50 cal.). **Weight:** 7.7 lbs. **Length:** 40" overall. **Stock:** Black laminated or black composite. **Sights:** Marble TruGlo fully adjustable, steel rear with white diamond, red bead front with high-visibility inserts. **Features:** In-line ignition with FlashFire one-piece nipple and breech plug that uses standard or magnum No. 11 caps, fully adjustable trigger, double safety system, aluminum ramrod; drilled and tapped for scope. Hard case. Made in U.S.A. by Split Fire Sporting Goods.
Price: Whitetail w/laminated or composite stock........... **$499.95**
Price: Adventurer w/26" stainless barrel & thumbhole stock) **$699.95**
Price: Odyssey w/24" carbon fiber wrapped barrel & thumbhole stock **$1,299.95**

WHITE MODEL 98 ELITE HUNTER RIFLE
Caliber: 45, 50. **Barrel:** 24", 1:24" twist (50 cal). **Weight:** 8.6 lbs. **Length:** 43.5" overall. **Stock:** Black laminate wtih swivel studs. **Sights:** TruGlo fully adjustable, steel rear with white diamond, red bead front with high-visibility inserts. **Features:** In-line ignition with FlashFire one-piece nipple and breech plug that uses standard or magnum No. 11 caps, fully adjustable trigger, double safety system, aluminum ramrod, drilled and tapped for scope, hard gun case. Made in U.S.A. by Split Fire Sporting Goods.
Price: Composite or laminate wood stock................ **$499.95**

White Thunderbolt Rifle
Similar to the Elite Hunter but is designed to handle 209 shotgun primers only. Has 26" stainless steel barrel, weighs 9.3 lbs. and is 45.5" long. Composite or laminate stock. Made in U.S.A. by Split Fire Sporting Goods.
Price: **$599.95**

WHITE MODEL 2000 BLACKTAIL HUNTER RIFLE
Caliber: 50. **Barrel:** 22", 1:24" twist (50 cal.). **Weight:** 7.6 lbs. **Length:** 39-7/8" overall. **Stock:** Black laminated with swivel studs with laser engraved deer or elk scene. **Sights:** TruGlo fully adjustable, steel rear with white diamond, red bead front with high-visibility inserts. **Features:** Teflon finished barrel, in-line ignition with FlashFire one-piece nipple and breech plug that uses standard or magnum No. 11 caps, fully adjustable trigger, double safety system, aluminum ramrod, drilled and tapped for scope. Hard gun case. Made in U.S.A. by Split Fire Sporting Goods.
Price: Laminate wood stock, w/laser engraved game scene . **$599.95**

WHITE LIGHTNING II RIFLE
Caliber: 45 and 50 percussion. **Barrel:** 24", 1:32 twist. **Sights:** Adj. rear. **Stock:** Black polymer. **Weight:** 6 lbs. **Features:** In-line, 209 primer ignition system, blued or nickel-plated bbl., adj. trigger, Delrin ramrod, sling studs, recoil pad. Made in U.S.A. by Split Fire Sporting Goods.
Price: **$299.95**

WHITE ALPHA RIFLE
Caliber: 45, 50 percussion. **Barrel:** 27" tapered, stainless. **Sights:** Marble TruGlo rear, fiber-optic front. **Stock:** Laminated. **Features:** Lever action rotating block, hammerless; adj. trigger, positive safety. All stainless metal, including trigger. Made in U.S.A. by Split Fire Sporting Goods.
Price: **$449.95**

WINCHESTER APEX SWING-ACTION MAGNUM RIFLE
Caliber: 45, 50. **Barrel:** 28". **Stock:** Mossy Oak® Camo, Black Fleck. **Sights:** Adj. fiber-optic. **Weight:** 7 lbs., 12 oz. Overall **length:** 42". **Features:** Monte Carlo cheekpiece, swing-action design, external hammer.
Price: Mossy Oak®/stainless **$489.95**
Price: Black Fleck/stainless **$449.95**
Price: Full Mossy Oak® **$469.95**
Price: Black Fleck/blued **$364.95**

WINCHESTER X-150 BOLT-ACTION MAGNUM RIFLE
Caliber: 45, 50. **Barrel:** 26". **Stock:** Hardwoods or Timber HD, Black Fleck, Break-Up™. **Weight:** 8 lbs., 3 oz. **Sights:** Adj. fiber-optic. **Features:** No. 209 shotgun primer ignition, stainless steel bolt, stainless fluted bbl.
Price: Mossy Oak®, Timber, Hardwoods/stainless......... **$349.95**
Price: Black Fleck/stainless **$299.95**
Price: Mossy Oak®, Timber, Hardwoods/blued **$279.95**
Price: Black Fleck/blued **$229.95**

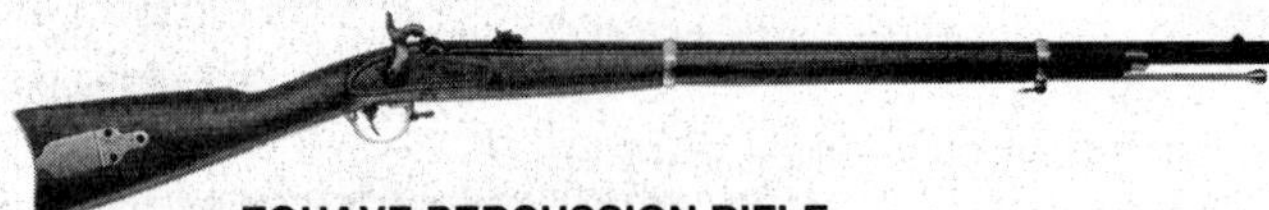

ZOUAVE PERCUSSION RIFLE
Caliber: 58, 59. **Barrel:** 32.5". **Weight:** 9.5 lbs. **Length:** 48.5" overall. **Stock:** Walnut finish, brass patchbox and buttplate. **Sights:** Fixed front, rear adjustable for elevation. **Features:** Color case-hardened lockplate, blued barrel. From Navy Arms, Dixie Gun Works, EMF, Euroarms of America.
Price: Dixie Gun Works PR0853 (58)................... **$525.00**

CABELA'S BLACKPOWDER SHOTGUNS

Gauge: 10, 12, 20. **Barrel:** 10-ga., 30"; 12-ga., 28.5" (Extra-Full, Mod., Imp. Cyl. choke tubes); 20-ga., 27.5" (Imp. Cyl. & Mod. fixed chokes). **Weight:** 6.5 to 7 lbs. **Length:** 45" overall (28.5" barrel). **Stock:** American walnut with checkered grip; 12- and 20-gauge have straight stock, 10-gauge has pistol grip. **Features:** Blued barrels, engraved, color case-hardened locks and hammers, brass ramrod tip. From Cabela's.

Price: 10-gauge **$849.99**
Price: 12-gauge **$719.99**
Price: 20-gauge **$659.99**

DIXIE MAGNUM PERCUSSION SHOTGUN

Gauge: 10, 12, 20. **Barrel:** 30" (Imp. Cyl. & Mod.) in 10-gauge; 28" in 12-gauge. **Weight:** 6.25 lbs. **Length:** 45" overall. **Stock:** Hand-checkered walnut, 14" pull. **Features:** Double triggers; light hand engraving; case-hardened locks in 12-gauge, polished steel in 10-gauge; sling swivels. From Dixie Gun Works.

Price: 12 ga. PS0930 .... **$825.00**
Price: 12-ga. Kit PS0940 .... **$725.00**
Price: 20-ga. PS0334 .... **$825.00**
Price: 10-ga. PS1030 .... **$900.00**
Price: 10-ga. kit PS1040 .... **$725.00**
Price: Coach Gun, 12 ga. 20" bbl PS0914 .... **$800.00**

KNIGHT TK2000 NEXT G-1 CAMO MUZZLELOADING SHOTGUN

Gauge: 12. **Barrel:** 26", extra-full choke tube. **Weight:** 7 lbs., 7 oz. **Length:** 45" overall. **Stock:** Synthetic black or Realtree Hardwoods; recoil pad; swivel studs. **Sights:** Fully adjustable rear, blade front with fiber-optics. **Features:** Receiver drilled and tapped for scope mount; in-line ignition; adjustable trigger; removable breech plug; double safety system; Imp. Cyl. choke tube available. Made in U.S. by Knight Rifles (Modern Muzzleloading)

Price: **$379.99**

NAVY ARMS SIDE-BY-SIDE SHOTGUN

Caliber: 12 smoothbore. **Barrel:** 28.5". **Weight:** 7 lbs. **Length:** 44.3" overall. **Features:** English model reproduction has checkered walnut stock, slightly choked and inside choked blued barrels, engraved locks. From Navy Arms.

Price: **$910.00**

WHITE TOMINATOR SHOTGUN

Caliber: 12. **Barrel:** 25" blue, straight, tapered stainless steel. **Weight:** NA. **Length:** NA. **Stock:** Black laminated or black wood. **Sights:** Drilled and tapped for easy scope mounting. **Features:** Internchangeable choke tubes. Custom vent rib with high visibility front bead. Double safeties. Fully adjustable custom trigger. Recoil pad and sling swivel studs. Made in U.S.A. by Split Fire Sporting Goods.

Price: **$349.95**

Prices given are believed to be accurate at time of publication however, many factors affect retail pricing so exact prices are not possible.

ARS HUNTING MASTER AR6 AIR PISTOL
Caliber: .22 (.177 + 20 special order). **Barrel:** 12" rifled. **Weight:** 3 lbs. **Length:** 18.25 overall. **Power:** NA. **Grips:** Indonesian walnut with checkered grip. **Sights:** Adjustable rear, blade front. **Features:** 6 shot repeater with rotary magazine, single or double action, receiver grooved for scope, hammer block and trigger block safeties.
Price: $659.00

BEEMAN P1 MAGNUM AIR PISTOL
Caliber: .177, 20. **Barrel:** 8.4". **Weight:** 2.5 lbs. **Length:** 11" overall. **Power:** Top lever cocking; spring-piston. **Grips:** Checkered walnut. **Sights:** Blade front, square notch rear with click micrometer adjustments for windage and elevation. Grooved for scope mounting. **Features:** Dual power for .177 and 20 cal.; low setting gives 350-400 fps; high setting 500-600 fps. All Colt 45 auto grips fit gun. Dry-firing feature for practice. Optional wood shoulder stock. Imported by Beeman.
Price: . . . . $499.95 to $525.95

BEEMAN P3 PNEUMATIC AIR PISTOL
Caliber: .177. **Barrel:** NA. **Weight:** 1.7 lbs. **Length:** 9.6" overall. **Power:** Single-stroke pneumatic; overlever barrel cocking. **Grips:** Reinforced polymer. **Sights:** Front and rear fiber-optic sights. **Features:** Velocity 410 fps. Polymer frame; automatic safety; two-stage trigger; built-in muzzle brake.
Price: $245.95
Price: With scope $335.95

BEEMAN/FEINWERKBAU P44
Caliber: .177, single shot. **Barrel:** 9.17". **Weight:** 2.10 lbs. **Length:** 16.54" overall. **Power:** Pre-charged pneumatic. **Grips:** Walnut grip. **Sights:** front and rear sights. **Features:** 500 fps, sighting line adjustable from 360 to 395mm, adjustable 3-d grip in 3 sizes, adjustable match trigger, delivered in special transport case.
Price: $2,575.95
Price: Left-hand model $2,655.95

BEEMAN/FEINWERKBAU P56
Caliber: .177, 5-shot magazine. **Barrel:** 8.81". **Weight:** 2.43 lbs. **Length:** 16.54" overall. **Power:** Pre-charged pneumatic. **Grips:** Walnut Morini grip. **Sights:** front and rear sights. **Features:** 500 fps, match-adjustable trigger, adjustable rear sight, front sight accepts interchangeable inserts, delivered in special transport case.
Price: $2,654.00

BEEMAN/FWB 103 AIR PISTOL
Caliber: .177. **Barrel:** 10.1", 12-groove rifling. **Weight:** 2.5 lbs. **Length:** 16.5" overall. **Power:** Single-stroke pneumatic, underlever cocking. **Grips:** Stippled walnut with adjustable palm shelf. **Sights:** Blade front, open rear adjustable for windage and elevation. Notch size adjustable for width. Interchangeable front blades. **Features:** Velocity 510 fps. Fully adjustable trigger. Cocking effort 2 lbs. Imported by Beeman.
Price: Right-hand $2,110.00
Price: Left-hand $2,350.00

BEEMAN HW70A AIR PISTOL
Caliber: .177. **Barrel:** 6-1/4", rifled. **Weight:** 38 oz. **Length:** 12-3/4" overall. **Power:** Spring, barrel cocking. **Grips:** Plastic, with thumbrest. **Sights:** Hooded post front, square notch rear adjustable for windage and elevation. Comes with scope base. **Features:** Adjustable trigger, 31-lb. cocking effort, 440 fps MV; automatic barrel safety. Imported by Beeman.
Price: $289.95

BENJAMIN & SHERIDAN CO2 PISTOLS
Caliber: .22, single shot. **Barrel:** 6-3/8", brass. **Weight:** 1 lb. 12 oz. **Length:** 9" overall. **Power:** 12-gram CO2 cylinder. **Grips:** American Hardwood. **Sights:** High ramp front, fully adjustable notched rear. **Features:** Velocity to 500 fps. Turnbolt action with cross-bolt safety. Gives about 40 shots per CO2 cylinder. Black or nickel finish. Made in U.S. by Crosman Corp.
Price: EB22 (.22) $118.59

BENJAMIN & SHERIDAN PNEUMATIC PELLET PISTOLS
Caliber: .177, .22, single shot. **Barrel:** 9-3/8", rifled brass. **Weight:** 2 lbs., 8 oz. **Length:**12.25" overall. **Power:** Underlever pnuematic, hand pumped. **Grips:** American Hardwood. **Sights:** High ramp front, fully adjustable notch rear. **Features:** Velocity to 525 fps (variable). Bolt action with cross-bolt safety. Choice of black or nickel finish. Made in U.S. by Crosman Corp.
Price: Black finish, HB17 (.177), HB22 (.22) $133.59

CROSMAN C11
Caliber: .177, 18-shot BB or pellet. **Weight:** 1.4 lbs. **Length:** 8.5". **Power:** 12g CO2. **Sights:** Fixed. **Features:** Compact semi-automatic BB pistol. Velocity up to 480 fps. Under barrel weaver style rail.
Price: $52.99

CROSMAN 2240
Caliber: .22. **Barrel:** Rifled steel. **Weight:** 1 lb. 13 oz. **Length:** 11.125". **Power:** CO2. **Grips:** NA. **Sights:** Blade front, rear adjustable. **Features:** Ergonomically designed ambidextrous grip fits the hand for perfect balance and comfort with checkering and a thumbrest on both grip panels. From Crosman.
Price: $57.83

CROSMAN 3576 REVOLVER
Caliber: .177, pellets. **Barrel:** Rifled steel. **Weight:** 2 lbs. **Length:** 11.38". **Power:** CO2. **Grips:** NA. **Sights:** Blade front, rear adjustable. **Features:** Semi-auto 10-shot with revolver styling and finger-molded grip design, 6" barrel for increased accuracy. From Crosman.
Price: $52.59

CROSMAN MODEL 1088 REPEAT AIR PISTOL
Caliber: .177, 8-shot pellet clip. **Barrel:** Rifled steel. **Weight:** 17 oz. **Length:** 7.75" overall. **Power:** CO2 Powerlet. **Grips:** Checkered black plastic. **Sights:** Fixed blade front, adjustable rear. **Features:** Velocity about 430 fps. Single or double semi-automatic action. From Crosman.
Price: $60.99

CROSMAN PRO77
Caliber: .177, 17-shot BB. **Weight:** 1.31 lbs. **Length:** 6.75". **Power:** 12g CO2. **Sights:** Fixed. **Features:** Compact pistol with realistic recoil. Under the barrel weaver style rail. Velocity up to 325 fps.
Price: Pro77CS $114.00

CROSMAN T4
Caliber: .177, 8-shot BB or pellet. **Weight:** 1.32 lbs. **Length:** 8.63". **Power:** 12g CO2. **Sights:** Fixed front, windage adjustable rear. **Features:** Shoots BBs or pellets. Easy patent-pending CO2 piercing mechanism. Under the barrel weaver style rail.
Price: T4CS $89.59
Price: T4OPS, includes adjustable Red Dot sight, barrel compensator, and pressure operated tactical flashlight. Comes in foam padeed, hard sided protective case $167.99

DAISY POWERLINE® MODEL 15XT AIR PISTOL
Caliber: .177 BB, 15-shot built-in magazine. **Barrel:** NA. **Weight:** NA. **Length:** 7.21". **Power:** CO2. **Grips:** NA. **Sights:** NA. **Features:** Velocity 425 fps. Made in the U.S.A. by Daisy Mfg. Co.
Price: $50.99
Price: With electronic point sight $64.99

DAISY MODEL 717 AIR PISTOL
Caliber: .177, single shot. **Weight:** 2.25 lbs. **Length:** 13-1/2" overall. **Grips:** Molded checkered woodgrain with contoured thumbrest. **Sights:** Blade and ramp front, open rear with windage and elevation adjustments. **Features:** Single pump pneumatic pistol. Rifled steel barrel. Crossbolt trigger block. Muzzle velocity 360 fps. From Daisy Mfg. Co.
Price: $220.94

DAISY MODEL 747 TRIUMPH AIR PISTOL
Caliber: .177, single shot. **Weight:** 2.35 lbs. **Length:** 13-1/2" overall.

Grips: Molded checkered woodgrain with contoured thumbrest. **Sights:** Blade and ramp front, open rear with windage and elevation adjustments. **Features:** Single pump pneumatic pistol. Lothar Walther rifled high-grade steel barrel; crowned 12 lands and grooves, right-hand twist. Precision bore sized for match pellets. Muzzle velocity 360 fps. From Daisy Mfg. Co.
Price: **$264.99**

DAISY POWERLINE® 201
Caliber: .177 BB or pellet. **Weight:** 1 lb. **Length:** 9.25" overall. **Sights:** Blade and ramp front, fixed open rear. **Features:** Spring-air action, trigger-block safety and smooth-bore steel barrel. Muzzle velocity 230 fps. From Daisy Mfg. Co.
Price: **$29.99**

DAISY POWERLINE® 693 AIR PISTOL
Caliber: .177, single shot. **Weight:** 1.10 lbs. **Length:** 7.9" overall. **Grips:** Molded checkered. **Sights:** Blade and ramp front, fixed open rear. **Features:** Semi-automoatic BB pistol with a nickel finish and smooth bore steel barrel. Muzzle veocity 400 fps. From Daisy Mfg. Co.
Price: **$76.99**

DAISY POWERLINE® 5170 CO2 PISTOL
Caliber: .177 BB. **Weight:** 1 lb. **Length:** 9.5" overall. **Sights:** Blade and ramp front, open rear. **Features:** CO2 semi-automatic action, manual trigger-block safety, upper and lower rails for mounting sights and other accessories and a smooth-bore steel barrel. Muzzle velocity 520 fps. From Daisy Mfg. Co.
Price: **$59.99**

DAISY POWERLINE® 5501 CO2 BLOWBACK PISTOL
Caliber: .177 BB. **Weight:** 1 lb. **Length:** 9.5" overall. **Sights:** Blade and ramp front, open rear. **Features:** CO2 semi-automatic blow-back action, manual trigger-block safety, and a smooth-bore steel barrel. Muzzle velocity 430 fps. From Daisy Mfg. Co.
Price: **$99.99**

EAA/BAIKAL IZH-M46 TARGET AIR PISTOL
Caliber: .177, single shot. **Barrel:** 10". **Weight:** 2.4 lbs. **Length:** 16.8" overall. **Power:** Underlever single-stroke pneumatic. **Grips:** Adjustable wooden target. **Sights:** Micrometer fully adjustable rear, blade front. **Features:** Velocity about 440 fps. Hammer-forged, rifled barrel. Imported from Russia by European American Armory.
Price: **$430.00**

GAMO P-23, P-23 LASER PISTOL
Caliber: .177, 12-shot. **Barrel:** 4.25". **Weight:** 1 lb. **Length:** 7.5". **Power:** CO2 cartridge, semi-automatic, 410 fps. **Grips:** Plastic. **Sights:** NA. **Features:** Walther PPK cartridge pistol copy, optional laser sight. Imported from Spain by Gamo.
Price: .... **$89.95**, (with laser) **$139.95**

GAMO PT-80, PT-80 LASER PISTOL
Caliber: .177, 8-shot. **Barrel:** 4.25". **Weight:** 1.2 lbs. **Length:** 7.2". **Power:** CO2 cartridge, semi-automatic, 410 fps. **Grips:** Plastic. **Sights:** 3-dot. **Features:** Optional laser sight and walnut grips available. Imported from Spain by Gamo.
Price: .... **$108.95**, (with laser) **$159.95**
Price: (with walnut grip) **$119.95**

HAMMERLI AP-40 AIR PISTOL
Caliber: .177. **Barrel:** 10". **Weight:** 2.2 lbs. **Length:** 15.5". **Power:** NA. **Grips:** Adjustable orthopedic. **Sights:** Fully adjustable micrometer. **Features:** Sleek, light, well balanced and accurate.
Price: **$1,400.00**

MAGNUM RESEARCH DESERT EAGLE
Caliber: .177, 8-shot pellet. 5.7" rifled. **Weight:** 2.5 lbs. 11" overall. **Power:** 12g CO2. **Sights:** Fixed front, adjustable rear. Velocity of 425 fps. 8-shot rotary clip. Double or single action. The first .177 caliber air pistol with BLOWBACK action. Big and weighty, designed in the likeness of the real Desert Eagle.
Price: **$172.31**

MAGNUM BABY DESERT
Caliber: .177, 15-shot BB. 4" **Weight:** 1.0 lbs. 8-1/4" overall. **Power:** 12g CO2. **Sights:** Fixed front and rear. Velocity of 420 fps. Double action BB repeater. Comes with bonus Picatinny top rail and built-in bottom rail.
Price: **$41.54**

MORINI CM 162 EL MATCH AIR PISTOLS
Caliber: .177, single shot. **Barrel:** 9.4". **Weight:** 32 oz. **Length:** 16.1" overall. **Power:** Scuba air. **Grips:** Adjustable match type. **Sights:** Interchangeable blade front, fully adjustable match-type rear. **Features:** Power mechanism shuts down when pressure drops to a preset level. Adjustable electronic trigger.
Price: **$1,075.00**

PARDINI K58 MATCH AIR PISTOLS
Caliber: .177, single shot. **Barrel:** 9". **Weight:** 37.7 oz. **Length:** 15.5" overall. **Power:** Precharged compressed air; single-stroke cocking. **Grips:** Adjustable match type; stippled walnut. **Sights:** Interchangeable post front, fully adjustable match rear. **Features:** Fully adjustable trigger. Short version K-2 available. Imported from Italy by Larry's Guns.
Price: **$819.00**

RWS 9B/9N AIR PISTOLS
Caliber: .177, single shot. **Barrel:** 8". **Weight:** 2.38 lbs. **Length:** 10.4". **Power:** 550 fps. **Grips:** Right hand with thumbrest. **Sights:** Adjustable. **Features:** Spring-piston powered. Black or nickel finish.
Price: 9B/9N **$150.00**

SMITH & WESSON 586
Caliber: .177, 10-shot pellet. Rifled. **Power:** 12g CO2. **Sights:** Fixed front, adjustable rear. 10-shot rotary clip. Double or single action. Replica revolvers that duplicate both weight and handling.
Price: 4" barrel, 2.5 lbs, 400 fps **$215.34**
Price: 6" barrel, 2.8 lbs, 425 fps **$231.49**
Price: 8" barrel, 3.0 lbs, 460 fps **$247.65**
Price: S&W 686 Nickel, 6" barrel, 2.8 lbs, 425 fps **$253.03**

STEYR LP10P MATCH AIR PISTOL
Caliber: .177, single shot. **Barrel:** 9". **Weight:** 38.7 oz. **Length:** 15.3" overall. **Power:** Scuba air. **Grips:** Adjustable Morini match, palm shelf, stippled walnut. **Sights:** Interchangeable blade in 4mm, 4.5mm or 5mm widths, adjustable open rear, interchangeable 3.5mm or 4mm leaves. **Features:** Velocity about 500 fps. Adjustable trigger, adjustable sight radius from 12.4" to 13.2". With compensator. Recoil elimination.
Price: **$1,400.00**

TECH FORCE SS2 OLYMPIC COMPETITION AIR PISTOL
Caliber: .177 pellet, single shot. **Barrel:** 7.4". **Weight:** 2.8 lbs. **Length:** 16.5" overall. **Power:** Spring piston, sidelever. **Grips:** Hardwood. **Sights:** Extended adjustable rear, blade front accepts inserts. **Features:** Velocity 520 fps. Recoilless design; adjustments allow duplication of a firearm's feel. Match-grade, adjustable trigger; includes carrying case. Imported from China by Compasseco, Inc.
Price: **$295.00**

TECH FORCE 35 AIR PISTOL
Caliber: .177 pellet, single shot. **Weight:** 2.86 lbs. **Length:** 14.9" overall. **Power:** Spring-piston, underlever. **Grips:** Hardwood. **Sights:** Micrometer adjustable rear, blade front. **Features:** Velocity 400 fps. Grooved for scope mount; trigger safety. Imported from China by Compasseco, Inc.
Price: **$39.95**

Tech Force S2-1 Air Pistol
Similar to Tech Force 8 except basic grips and sights for plinking.
Price: **$29.95**

WALTHER LP300 MATCH PISTOL
Caliber: .177. **Barrel:** 236mm. **Weight:** 1.018g. **Length:** NA. **Power:** NA. **Grips:** NA. **Sights:** Integrated front with three different widths, adjustable rear. **Features:** Adjustable grip and trigger.
Price: **$1,800.00**

WALTHER PPK/S
Caliber: .177, 15-shot steel BB. 3-1/2". **Weight:** 1.2 lbs. 6-1/4" overall. **Power:** 12g CO2. **Sights:** Fixed front and rear. Velocity of 295 fps. Lookalike of one of the world's most famous pistols. Realistic recoil. Heavyweight steel construction.
Price: **$71.92**
Price: With laser sight **$94.23**
Price: With BiColor pistol, targets, shooting glasses, BBs **$84.62**

WALTHER CP99 COMPACT
Caliber: .177, 17-shot steel BB semi-auto. 3". **Weight:** 1.7 lbs. 6-1/2" overall. **Power:** 12g CO2. **Sights:** Fixed front and rear. Velocity of 345 fps. Realistic recoil, blowback action. Heavyweight steel construction. Built-in Picatinny mount.
Price: **$83.08**

AIRFORCE CONDOR RIFLE
Caliber: .177, .22 single shot. **Barrel:** 24" rifled. **Weight:** 6.5 lbs. **Length:** 38.75" overall. **Power:** Pre-charged pneumatic. **Stock:** NA. **Sights:** Intended for scope use, fiber-optic open sights optional. **Features:** Lothar Walther match barrel, adjustable power levels from 600-1,300 fps. 3,000 psi fill pressure. Automatic safety. Air tank volume: 490cc. An integral extended scope rail allows easy mounting of the largest air-gun scopes. Operates on high-pressure air from scuba tank or hand pump. Manufactured in the U.S.A by AirForce Airguns.
Price: Gun only (.22 or .177) **$631.00**

AIRFORCE TALON AIR RIFLE
Caliber: .177, .22, single shot. **Barrel:** 18" rifled. **Weight:** 5.5 lbs. **Length:** 32.6". **Power:** Pre-charged pneumatic. **Stock:** NA. **Sights:** Intended for scope use, fiber-optic open sights optional. **Features:** Lothar Walther match barrel, adjustable power levels from 400-1,000 fps, 3,000 psi fill pressure. Automatic safety. Air tank volume: 490cc. Operates on high-pressure air from scuba tank or hand pump. Manufactured in the U.S.A. by AirForce Airguns.
Price: Gun only (.22 or .177). **$514.25**

AIRFORCE TALON SS AIR RIFLE
Caliber: .177, .22, single shot. **Barrel:** 12" rifled. **Weight:** 5.25 lbs. **Length:** 32.75". **Power:** Pre-charged pneumatic. **Stock:** NA. **Sights:** Intended for scope use, fiber-optic open sights optional. **Features:** Lothar Walther match barrel, adjustable power levels from 400-1,000 fps. 3,000 psi fill pressure. Automatic safety. Chamber in front of barrel strips away air turbulence, protects muzzle and reduces firing report. Air tank volume: 490cc. Operates on high-pressure air from scuba tank or hand pump. Manufactured in the U.S.A. by AirForce Airguns.
Price: Gun only (.22 or .177). **$535.50**

AIRROW MODEL A-8SRB STEALTH AIR RIFLE
Caliber: .177, .22, .25, 9-shot. **Barrel:** 20"; rifled. **Weight:** 6 lbs. **Length:** 34" overall. **Power:** CO2 or compressed air; variable power. **Stock:** Telescoping CAR-15-type. **Sights:** Variable 3.5-10x scope. **Features:** Velocity 1100 fps in all calibers. Pneumatic air trigger. All aircraft aluminum and stainless steel construction. Mil-spec materials and finishes. From Swivel Machine Works, Inc.
Price: About **$2,299.00**

AIRROW MODEL A-8S1P STEALTH AIR RIFLE
Caliber: #2512 16" arrow. **Barrel:** 16". **Weight:** 4.4 lbs. **Length:** 30.1" overall. **Power:** CO2 or compressed air; variable power. **Stock:** Telescoping CAR-15-type. **Sights:** Scope rings only. 7 oz. rechargeable cylinder and valve. **Features:** Velocity to 650 fps with 260-grain arrow. Pneumatic air trigger. Broadhead guard. All aircraft aluminum and stainless steel construction. Mil-spec materials and finishes. A-8S Models perform to 2,000 PSIG above or below water levels. Waterproof case. From Swivel Machine Works, Inc.
Price: **$1,699.00**

ARS HUNTING MASTER AR6 AIR RIFLE
Caliber: .22, 6-shot repeater. **Barrel:** 25-1/2". **Weight:** 7 lbs. **Length:** 41-1/4" overall. **Power:** Precompressed air from 3000 psi diving tank. **Stock:** Indonesian walnut with checkered grip; rubber buttpad. **Sights:** Blade front, adjustable peep rear. **Features:** Velocity over 1000 fps with 32-grain pellet. Receiver grooved for scope mounting. Has 6-shot rotary magazine. Imported by Air Rifle Specialists.
Price: **$580.00**

BEEMAN HW100
Caliber: .177 or .22, 14-shot magazine. **Barrel:** 21-1/2". **Weight:** 9 lbs. **Length:** 42.13" overall. **Power:** Pre-charged. **Stock:** Walnut Sporter checkering on the pistol grip & forend; walnut thumbhose with lateral finger grooves on the forend & stippling on the pistol grip. **Sights:** None. Grooved for scope mounting. **Features:** 1140 fps .177 caliber; 945 fps .22 caliber. 14-shot magazine, quick-fill cylinder. Two-stage adjustable match trigger and manual safety.
Price: .177 or .22 caliber Sport Stock **$1,649.95**
Price: .177 or .22 caliber Thumbhole Stock **$1,649.95**

BEEMAN R1 AIR RIFLE
Caliber: .177, .20 or .22, single shot. **Barrel:** 19.6", 12-groove rifling. **Weight:** 8.5 lbs. **Length:** 45.2" overall. **Power:** Spring-piston, barrel cocking. **Stock:** Walnut-stained beech; cut-checkered pistol grip; Monte Carlo comb and cheekpiece; rubber buttpad. **Sights:** Tunnel front with interchangeable inserts, open rear click-adjustable for windage and elevation. Grooved for scope mounting. **Features:** Velocity 940-1000 fps (.177), 860 fps (20), 800 fps (.22). Non-drying nylon piston and breech seals. Adjustable metal trigger. Milled steel safety. Right- or left-hand stock. Adjustable cheekpiece and buttplate at extra cost. Custom and Super Laser versions available. Imported by Beeman.
Price: Right-hand **$729.95**
Price: Left-hand **$789.95**

BEEMAN R7 AIR RIFLE
Caliber: .177, .20, single shot. **Barrel:** 17". **Weight:** 6.1 lbs. **Length:** 40.2" overall. **Power:** Spring-piston. **Stock:** Stained beech. **Sights:** Hooded front, fully adjustable micrometer click open rear. **Features:** Velocity to 700 fps (.177), 620 fps (20). Receiver grooved for scope mounting; double-jointed cocking lever; fully adjustable trigger; checkered grip. Imported by Beeman.
Price: .177. . . . . **$409.95**
Price: .20 . . . . **$429.95**

BEEMAN R9 AIR RIFLE
Caliber: .177, .20, single shot. **Barrel:** NA. **Weight:** 7.3 lbs. **Length:** 43" overall. **Power:** Spring-piston, barrel cocking. **Stock:** Stained hardwood. **Sights:** Tunnel post front, fully adjustable open rear. **Features:** Velocity to 1000 fps (.177), 800 fps (20). Adjustable Rekord trigger; automatic safety; receiver dovetailed for scope mounting. Imported from Germany by Beeman Precision Airguns.
Price: .177. . . . . **$499.95**
Price: .20 . . . . **$524.95**

BEEMAN R11 MKII AIR RIFLE
Caliber: .177, single shot. **Barrel:** 19.6". **Weight:** 8.6 lbs. **Length:** 43.5" overall. **Power:** Spring-piston, barrel cocking. **Stock:** Walnut-stained beech; adjustable buttplate and cheekpiece. **Sights:** None furnished. Has dovetail for scope mounting. **Features:** Velocity 910-940 fps. All-steel barrel sleeve. Imported by Beeman.
Price: **$679.95**

BEEMAN RX-2 GAS-SPRING MAGNUM AIR RIFLE
Caliber: .177, .20, .22, .25, single shot. **Barrel:** 19.6", 12-groove rifling. **Weight:** 8.8 lbs. **Power:** Gas-spring piston air; single stroke barrel cocking. **Stock:** Laminated wood stock. **Sights:** Tunnel front, click-adjustable rear. **Features:** Velocity adjustable to about 1200 fps. Imported by Beeman.
Price: .177, right-hand **$889.95**
Price: .20, right-hand **$909.95**
Price: .22, right-hand **$889.95**
Price: .25, right-hand **$909.95**

BEEMAN R1 CARBINE
Caliber: .177,. 20, .22 single shot. **Barrel:** 16.1". **Weight:** 8.6 lbs. **Length:** 41.7" overall. **Power:** Spring-piston, barrel cocking. **Stock:** Stained beech; Monte Carlo comb and checkpiece; cut checkered pistol grip; rubber buttpad. **Sights:** Tunnel front with interchangeable inserts, open adjustable rear; receiver grooved for scope mounting. **Features:** Velocity up to 1000 fps (.177). Non-drying nylon piston and breech seals. Adjustable metal trigger. Machined steel receiver end cap and safety. Right- or left-hand stock. Imported by Beeman.
Price: .177, 20, .22, right-hand **$749.95**

BEEMAN/FEINWERKBAU 700 P ALUMINUM OR WOOD STOCK
Caliber: .177, single shot. **Barrel:** 16.6". **Weight:** 10.8 lbs. Aluminum; 9.9 lbs. Wood. **Length:** 43.3-46.25" Aluminum; 43.7" Wood. **Power:** Pre-charged pneumatic. **Stock:** Aluminum stock P laminated hardwood. **Sights:** Tunnel front sight with interchangeable inserts, click micrometer match aperture rear sight. **Features:** Velocity 570 fps. Recoilless action. Anatomical grips can be tilted and pivoted to the barrel axis. Adjustable buttplate and cheekpiece.
Price: Aluminum 700, right, blue or silver. **$3,934.95**
Price: Aluminum 700, universal **$3,069.95**

BEEMAN/FEINWERKBAU P70 FIELD TARGET
Caliber: .177, single shot. **Barrel:** 24.6". **Weight:** 10.6 lbs. **Length:** 43.3" overall. **Power:** Pre-charged pneumatic. **Stock:** Aluminum stock (red or blue) anatomical grips, buttplate & cheekpiece. **Sights:**

None, receiver grooved for scope mounting. **Features:** 870 fps velocity. At 50 yards, this air rifle is capable of achieving 1/2-inch groups. Match adjustable trigger. 2001 US Field Target National Champion.
Price: P70FT, precharged, right (red or blue) **$3,819.95**
Price: P70FT, precharged, left (red or blue) **$3,964.95**

BEEMAN/HW 97 AIR RIFLE
Caliber: .177, .20, .22, single shot. **Barrel:** 17.75". **Weight:** 9.2 lbs. **Length:** 44.1" overall. **Power:** Spring-piston, underlever cocking. **Stock:** Walnut-stained beech; rubber buttpad. **Sights:** None. Receiver grooved for scope mounting. **Features:** Velocity 830 fps (.177). Fixed barrel with fully opening, direct loading breech. Adjustable trigger. Imported by Beeman Precision Airguns.
Price: .177. . . . . **$779.95**
Price: .20, .22 . . . . **$799.95**

BENJAMIN & SHERIDAN PNEUMATIC (PUMP-UP) AIR RIFLE
Caliber: .177 or .22, single shot. **Barrel:** 19-3/8", rifled brass. **Weight:** 5-1/2 lbs. **Length:** 36-1/4" overall. **Power:** Underlever pneumatic, hand pumped. **Stock:** American walnut stock and forend. **Sights:** High ramp front, fully adjustable notched rear. **Features:** Variable velocity to 800 fps. Bolt action with ambidextrous push-pull safety. Black or nickel finish. Made in the U.S. by Benjamin Sheridan Co.
Price: 392 or 397 . . . . **$249.40**

BERETTA CX4 STORM
Caliber: .177, 30-shot semi-auto. 17-1/2", rifled. **Weight:** 5.25 lbs. **Length:** 30.75" overall. **Power:** 88g CO2. **Stock:** Replica style. **Sights:** Adjustable front and rear. Blowback action. Velocity of 600 fps. Accessory rails.
Price: **$276.92**

BSA SUPERTEN MK3 AIR RIFLE
Caliber: .177, .22 10-shot repeater. **Barrel:** 17-1/2". **Weight:** 7 lbs., 8 oz. **Length:** 37" overall. **Power:** Precharged pneumatic via buddy bottle. **Stock:** Oil-finished hardwood; Monte Carlo with cheekpiece, cut checkered grip; adjustable recoil pad. **Sights:** No sights; intended for scope use. **Features:** Velocity 1000+ fps (.177), 1000+ fps (.22). Patented 10-shot indexing magazine, bolt-action loading. Left-hand version also available. Imported from U.K.
Price: **$599.95**

BSA SUPERTEN MK3 BULLBARREL
Caliber: .177, .22, .25, single shot. **Barrel:** 18-1/2". **Weight:** 8 lbs., 8 oz. **Length:** 43" overall. **Power:** Spring-air, underlever cocking. **Stock:** Oil-finished hardwood; Monte Carlo with cheekpiece, checkered at grip; recoil pad. **Sights:** Ramp front, micrometer adjustable rear. Maxi-Grip scope rail. **Features:** Velocity 950 fps (.177), 750 fps (.22), 600 fps (25). Patented rotating breech design. Maxi-Grip scope rail protects optics from recoil; automatic anti-beartrap plus manual safety. Imported from U.K.
Price: Rifle, MKII Carbine (14" barrel, 39-1/2" overall) **$349.95**

BSA MAGNUM SUPERSPORT AIR RIFLE, CARBINE
Caliber: .177, .22, .25, single shot. **Barrel:** 18-1/2". **Weight:** 6 lbs., 8 oz. **Length:** 41" overall. **Power:** Spring-air, barrel cocking. **Stock:** Oil-finished hardwood; Monte Carlo with cheekpiece, recoil pad. **Sights:** Ramp front, micrometer adjustable rear. Maxi-Grip scope rail. **Features:** Velocity 950 fps (.177), 750 fps (.22), 600 fps (25). Patented Maxi-Grip scope rail protects optics from recoil; automatic anti-beartrap plus manual tang safety. Muzzle brake standard. Imported for U.K.
Price: **$194.95**
Price: Carbine, 14" barrel, muzzle brake **$214.95**

BSA METEOR AIR RIFLE
Caliber: .177, .22, single shot. **Barrel:** 18-1/2". **Weight:** 6 lbs. **Length:** 41" overall. **Power:** Spring-air, barrel cocking. **Stock:** Oil-finished hardwood. **Sights:** Ramp front, micrometer adjustable rear. **Features:** Velocity 650 fps (.177), 500 fps (.22). Automatic anti-beartrap; manual tang safety. Receiver grooved for scope mounting. Imported from U.K.
Price: Rifle **$144.95**
Price: Carbine **$164.95**

CROSMAN MODEL POWERMASTER 664SB AIR RIFLES
Caliber: .177 (single shot pellet) or BB, 200-shot reservoir. **Barrel:** 20", rifled steel. **Weight:** 2 lbs. 15 oz. **Length:** 38-1/2" overall. **Power:** Pneumatic; hand-pumped. **Stock:** Wood-grained ABS plastic; checkered pistol grip and forend. **Sights:** Fiber-optic front, fully adjustable open rear. **Features:** Velocity about 645 fps. Bolt action, cross-bolt safety. From Crosman.
Price: **$105.50**

CROSMAN MODEL PUMPMASTER 760 AIR RIFLES
Caliber: .177 pellets (single shot) or BB (200-shot reservoir). **Barrel:** 19-1/2", rifled steel. **Weight:** 2 lbs., 12 oz. **Length:** 33.5" overall. **Power:** Pneumatic, hand-pump. **Stock:** Walnut-finished ABS plastic stock and forend. **Features:** Velocity to 590 fps (BBs, 10 pumps). Short stroke, power determined by number of strokes. Fiber-optic front sight and adjustable rear sight. Cross-bolt safety. From Crosman.
Price: Model 760 . . . . **$40.59**

CROSMAN MODEL REPEATAIR 1077 RIFLES
Caliber: .177 pellets, 12-shot clip. **Barrel:** 20.3", rifled steel. **Weight:** 3 lbs., 11 oz. **Length:** 38.8" overall. **Power:** CO2 Powerlet. **Stock:** Textured synthetic or hardwood. **Sights:** Blade front, fully adjustable rear. **Features:** Velocity 590 fps. Removable 12-shot clip. True semi-automatic action. From Crosman.
Price: **$73.99**

CROSMAN MODEL .2260 AIR RIFLE
Caliber: .22, single shot. **Barrel:** 24". **Weight:** 4 lbs., 12 oz. **Length:** 39.75" overall. **Power:** CO2 Powerlet. **Stock:** Hardwood. **Sights:** Blade front, adjustable rear open or peep. **Features:** Variable pump power; three pumps give 395 fps, six pumps 530 fps, 10 pumps 600 fps (average). Full-size adult air rifle. From Crosman.
Price: **$83.84**

CROSMAN MODEL CLASSIC 2100 AIR RIFLE
Caliber: .177 pellets (single shot), or BB (200-shot BB reservoir). **Barrel:** 21", rifled. **Weight:** 4 lbs., 13 oz. **Length:** 39-3/4" overall. **Power:** Pump-up, pneumatic. **Stock:** Wood-grained checkered ABS plastic. **Features:** Three pumps give about 450 fps, 10 pumps about 755 fps (BBs). Cross-bolt safety; concealed reservoir holds over 200 BBs. From Crosman.
Price: Model 2100B **$62.99**

DAISY 1938 RED RYDER AIR RIFLE
Caliber: BB, 650-shot repeating action. **Barrel:** Smoothbore steel with shroud. **Weight:** 2.2 lbs. **Length:** 35.4" overall. **Stock:** Wood stock burned with Red Ryder lariat signature. **Sights:** Post front, adjustable open rear. **Features:** Walnut forend. Saddle ring with leather thong. Lever cocking. Gravity feed. Controlled velocity. From Daisy Mfg. Co.
Price: **$55.99**

DAISY MODEL 840B GRIZZLY AIR RIFLE
Caliber: .177 pellet single shot; or BB 350-shot. **Barrel:** 19", smoothbore, steel. **Weight:** 2.25 lbs. **Length:** 36.8" overall. **Power:** Single pump pneumatic. **Stock:** Molded wood-grain stock and forend. **Sights:** Ramp front, open, adjustable rear. **Features:** Muzzle velocity 320 fps (BB), 300 fps (pellet). Steel buttplate; straight pull bolt action; cross-bolt safety. Forend forms pump lever. From Daisy Mfg. Co.
Price: **$60.99**
Price: (840C in Mossy Oak Breakup Camo) **$64.99**

DAISY MODEL 4841 GRIZZLY
Caliber: .177 pellet single shot. **Barrel:** NA. **Weight:** NA. **Length:** 36.8" overall. **Power:** Single pump pneumatic. **Stock:** Composite camo. **Sights:** Blade and ramp front. **Features:** Muzzle velocity 350 fps. Fixed Daisy Model 808 scope. From Daisy Mfg. Co.
Price: **$69.99**

DAISY MODEL 105 BUCK AIR RIFLE
Caliber: .177 or BB. **Barrel:** Smoothbore steel. **Weight:** 1.6 lbs. **Length:** 29.8" overall. **Power:** Lever cocking, spring air. **Stock:** Stained solid wood. **Sights:** TruGlo fiber-optic, open fixed rear.

Features: Velocity to 275. Crossbolt trigger block safety. From Daisy Mfg. Co.
Price: **$39.99**

DAISY AVANTI MODEL 888 MEDALIST
Caliber: .177, pellet. **Barrel:** Lothar Walther rifled high-grade steel, crowned, 12 lands and grooves, right-hand twist. Precision bore sized for match pellets. **Weight:** 6.9 lbs. **Length:** 38.5" overall. **Power:** CO2 single shot bolt. **Stock:** Sporter-style multicolored laminated hardwood. **Sights:** Hooded front with interchangeable aperture inserts; micrometer adjustable rear peep sight. **Features:** Velocity to 500. Crossbolt trigger block safety. From Daisy Mfg. Co.
Price: **$525.99**

DAISY AVANTI MODEL 887 GOLD MEDALIST
Caliber: 177, pellet. **Barrel:** Lothar Walther rifled high-grade steel, crowned, 12 lands and grooves, right hand twist. Precision bore sized for match pellets. **Weight:** 7.3 lbs. **Length:** 39.5" overall. **Power:** CO2 power single shot bolt. **Stock:** Laminated hardwood. **Sights:** Front globe sight with changeable aperture inserts: rear diopter sight with micrometer click adjustment for windage and elevation. **Features:** Velocity to 500. Crossbolt trigger block safety. Includes rail adapter. From Daisy Mfg. Co.
Price: **$599.99**

DAISY MODEL 853 LEGEND
Caliber: .177, pellet. **Barrel:** Lothar Walther rifled high-grade steel barrel, crowned, 12 lands and grooves, right-hand twist. Precision bore sized for match pellets. **Weight:** 5.5 lbs. **Length:** 38.5" overall. **Power:** Single-pump pneumatic, straight pull-bolt. **Stock:** Full-length, sporter-style hardwood with adjustable length. **Sights:** Hooded front with interchangeable aperture inserts; micrometer adjustable rear. **Features:** Velocity to 510. Crossbolt trigger block safety with red indicator. From Daisy Mfg. Co.
Price: **$432.00**
Price: Model 835 Legend EX; velocity to 490 . . . . . **$432.00**

DAISY MODEL 753 ELITE
Caliber: .177, pellet. **Barrel:** Lothar Walther rifled high-grade steel barrel, crowned, 12 lands and grooves, right-hand twist. Precision bore sized for match pellets. **Weight:** 6.4 lbs. **Length:** 39.75" overall. **Power:** Recoilless single pump pneumatic, straight pull bolt. **Stock:** Full length match-style hardwood stock with raised cheek piece and adjustable length. **Sights:** Front globe sight with changeable aperture inserts, diopter rear sight with micrometer adjustable rear. **Features:** Velocity to 510. Crossbolt trigger block safety with red indicator. From Daisy Mfg. Co.
Price: **$558.99**

DAISY MODEL 105 BUCK AIR RIFLE
Caliber: .177 or BB. **Barrel:** Smoothbore steel. **Weight:** 1.6 lbs. **Length:** 29.8" overall. **Power:** Lever cocking, spring air. **Stock:** Stained solid wood. **Sights:** TruGlo fiber-optic, open fixed rear. **Features:** Velocity to 275. Cross-bolt trigger block safety. From Daisy Mfg. Co.
Price: **$39.99**

DAISY POWERLINE® TARGETPRO 953 AIR RIFLE
Caliber: .177 pellets, single shot. **Weight:** 6.40 lbs. **Length:** 39.75" overall. **Power:** Pneumatic single-pump cocking lever; straight-pull bolt. **Stock:** Full-length, match-style black composite. **Sights:** Front and rear fiber optic. **Features:** Rifled high-grade steel barrel with 1:15 twist. Max. Muzzle Velocity of 560 fps. From Daisy Mfg. Co.
Price: **$29.99**

DAISY POWERLINE® 500 BREAK BARREL
Caliber: .177 pellet, single shot. **Barrel:** Rifled steel. **Weight:** 6.6 lbs. **Length:** 45.7" overall. **Stock:** Stained solid wood. **Sights:** Truglo® fiber-optic front, micro-adjustable open rear, adjustable 4x32 riflescope. **Features:** Auto rear-button safety. Velocity to 490 fps. Made in U.S.A. by Daisy Mfg. Co.
Price: **$120.99**

DAISY POWERLINE® 800 BREAK BARREL
Caliber: .177 pellet, single shot. **Barrel:** Rifled steel. **Weight:** 6.6 lbs. **Length:** 46.7" overall. **Stock:** Black composite. **Sights:** Truglo fiber-optic front, micro-adjustable open rear, adjustable 4x32 riflescope. **Features:** Auto rear-button safety. Velocity to 800 fps. Made in U.S.A. by Daisy Mfg. Co.
Price: **$120.99**

DAISY POWERLINE® 880 AIR RIFLE
Caliber: .177 pellet or BB, 50-shot BB magazine, single shot for pellets. **Barrel:** Rifled steel. **Weight:** 3.7 lbs. **Length:** 37.6" overall. **Power:** Multi-pump pneumatic. **Stock:** Molded wood grain; Monte Carlo comb. **Sights:** Hooded front, adjustable rear. **Features:** Velocity to 685 fps. (BB). Variable power (velocity, range) increase with pump strokes; resin receiver with dovetailed scope mount. Made in U.S.A. by Daisy Mfg. Co.
Price: **$71.99**

DAISY POWERLINE® 901 AIR RIFLE
Caliber: .177. **Barrel:** Rifled steel. **Weight:** 3.7 lbs. **Length:** 37.5" overall. **Power:** Multi-pump pneumatic. **Stock:** Advanced composite. **Sights:** Fiber-optic front, adjustable rear. **Features:** Velocity to 750 fps. (BB); advanced composite receiver with dovetailed mounts for optics. Made in U.S.A. by Daisy Mfg. Co.
Price: **$83.99**

DAISY POWERLINE® 1000 BREAK BARREL
Caliber: .177 pellet, single shot. **Barrel:** Rifled steel. **Weight:** 6.6 lbs. **Length:** 46.7" overall. **Stock:** Black composite. **Sights:** Truglo® fiber-optic front, micro-adjustable open rear, adjustable 4x32 riflescope. **Features:** Auto rear-button safety. Velocity to 750 fps (BB). Made in U.S.A. by Daisy Mfg. Co.
Price: **$231.99**

EAA/BAIKAL IZH61 AIR RIFLE
Caliber: .177 pellet, 5-shot magazine. **Barrel:** 17.8". **Weight:** 6.4 lbs. **Length:** 31" overall. **Power:** Spring-piston, side-cocking lever. **Stock:** Black plastic. **Sights:** Adjustable rear, fully hooded front. **Features:** Velocity 490 fps. Futuristic design with adjustable stock. Imported from Russia by European American Armory.
Price: **$122.65**

GAMO VIPER AIR RIFLE
Caliber: .177. **Barrel:** NA. **Weight:** 7.25 lbs. **Length:** 43.5". **Power:** Single-stroke pneumatic, 1200 fps. **Stock:** Synthetic. **Sights:** 3-9x40IR scope. **Features:** 30-pound cocking effort. Imported from Spain by Gamo.
Price: **319.95**

GAMO SHADOW AIR RIFLES
Caliber: .177. **Barrel:** 18", fluted polymer bull. **Weight:** 6.1 to 7.15 lbs. **Length:** 43" to 43.3". **Power:** Single-stroke pneumatic, 850-1,000 fps. **Stock:** Tough all-weather molded synthetic. **Sights:** NA. **Features:** Single shot, manual safety,
Price: Sport **$219.95**
Price: Hunter **$219.95**
Price: Big Cat 1200 . . . . **$169.95**
Price: Fox **$279.95**

GAMO HUNTER AIR RIFLES
Caliber: .177. **Barrel:** NA. **Weight:** 6.5 to 10.5 lbs. **Length:** 43.5-48.5". **Power:** Single-stroke pneumatic, 850-1,000 fps. **Stock:** Wood. **Sights:** Varies by model **Features:** Adjustable two-stage trigger, rifled barrel, raised scope ramp on receiver. Realtree camo model available.
Price: Sport **$219.95**
Price: Pro **$279.95**
Price: Extreme (.177), Extreme .22 . . . . **$529.95**

GAMO WHISPER AIR RIFLES
Caliber: .177, .22. **Barrel:** 18", fluted polymer bull. **Weight:** 5.28 to 7.4 lbs. **Length:** 45.7" to 46". **Stock:** Tough all-weather molded synthetic. **Sights:** Fiber-optic front with sight guard, adjustable rear.

 Prices given are believed to be accurate at time of publication however, many factors affect retail pricing so exact prices are not possible.

Features: Single shot, manual trigger safety. Non-removable noise dampener (with up to 52 percent reduction).
Price: Whisper **$279.95**
Price: Whisper Deluxe **$319.95**
Price: Whisper VH (Varmint Hunter/Whisper in one rifle).... **$329.95**
Price: Whisper .22 .... **$299.95**
Price: CSI Camo (.177) **$329.95**
Price: CSI Camo (.22) **$329.95**

HAMMERLI AR 50 AIR RIFLE
Caliber: .177. **Barrel:** 19.8". **Weight:** 10 lbs. **Length:** 43.2" overall. **Power:** Compressed-air. **Stock:** Anatomically-shaped universal and right-hand; match style; multi-colored laminated wood. **Sights:** Interchangeable element tunnel front, adjustable Hammerli peep rear. **Features:** Vibration-free firing release; adjustable match trigger and trigger stop; stainless air tank, built-in pressure gauge. Gives 270 shots per filling. Imported from Switzerland by SIG SAUER, Inc.
Price: **$1,653.00**

HAMMERLI MODEL 450 MATCH AIR RIFLE
Caliber: .177, single shot. **Barrel:** 19.5". **Weight:** 9.8 lbs. **Length:** 43.3" overall. **Power:** Pneumatic. **Stock:** Match style with stippled grip, rubber buttpad. Beech or walnut. **Sights:** Match tunnel front, Hammerli diopter rear. **Features:** Velocity about 560 fps. Removable sights; forend sling rail; adjustable trigger; adjustable comb. Imported from Switzerland by SIG SAUER, Inc.
Price: Beech stock **$1,355.00**
Price: Walnut stock............................... **$1,395.00**

HAMMERLI 850 AIR MAGNUM
Caliber: .177, .22, 8-shot repeater. 23-1/2", rifled. **Weight:** 5.8 lbs. 41" overall. **Power:** 88g CO2. **Stock:** All-weather polymer, Monte Carlo, textured grip and forearm. **Sights:** Hooded fiber optic front, fiber optic adjustable rear. Velocity of 760 fps (.177), 655 (22). Blue finish. Rubber buttpad. Bolt-action. Scope compatible.
Price: .177, .22 .... **$235.99**

HAMMERLI STORM ELITE
Caliber: .177, single shot. 19-1/2", rifled. **Weight:** 6.8 lbs. 45-1/2" overall. **Power:** Spring-air, break-barrel cocking. **Stock:** Synthetic, burled wood look, checkered grip and forearm, cheekpiece. **Sights:** Hooded fiber optic front, fiber optic adjustable rear. Velocity of 1000 fps. 24 lbs. cocking effort. Nickel finish. Rubber buttpad. Scope compatible.
Price: **$165.90**

HAMMERLI RAZOR
Caliber: .177, .22, single shot. **Barrel:** 19", rifled. **Weight:** 17.5 lbs. **Length:** 45-1/2" overall. **Power:** Spring-air, break-barrel cocking. **Stock:** Vaporized beech wood, checkered grip and forearm, cheekpiece. Sleek curves. **Sights:** Hooded fiber optic front, fiber optic adjustable rear. **Features:** Velocity of 1000 fps (.177), 820 (.22). 35 lbs. cocking effort. Blued finish. Rubber buttpad. Scope compatible.
Price: **$219.99**

HAMMERLI NOVA
Caliber: .177, single shot. 18", rifled. **Weight:** 7.8 lbs. 45-1/2" overall. **Power:** Spring-air, under-lever cocking. **Stock:** Vaporized beech wood competition, checkered grip and forearm, cheekpiece. **Sights:** Hooded fiber optic front, fiber optic adjustable rear. **Features:** Velocity of 1000 fps. 36 lbs. cocking effort. Blued finish. Rubber buttpad. Scope compatible.
Price: **$342.00**

HAMMERLI QUICK
Caliber: .177, single shot. 18-1/4", rifled. **Weight:** 5.5 lbs. 41" overall. **Power:** Spring-air, break-barrel cocking. **Stock:** Synthetic impact proof, checkered grip and forearm, cheekpiece. **Sights:** Hooded fiber optic front, fiber optic adjustable rear. Compact, lightweight. Velocity of 620 fps. 18 lbs. cocking effort. Blued finish. Rubber buttpad. Scope compatible. Automatic safety.
Price: **$120.00**

RWS 460 MAGNUM
Caliber: .177, .22, single shot. 18-7/16", rifled. **Weight:** 8.3 lbs. 45" overall. **Power:** Spring-air, underlever cocking. **Stock:** American Sporter, checkered grip and forearm. **Sights:** Ramp front, adjustable rear. Velocity of 1350 fps (.177), 1150 (.22). 36 lbs. cocking effort. Blue finish. Rubber buttpad. Top-side loading port. Scope compatible.
Price: .177, .22 .... **$630.99**

RWS MODEL 34
Caliber: .177, .22, single shot. **Barrel:** 19-1/2", rifled. **Weight:** 7.3 lbs. **Length:** 45" overall. **Power:** Spring-air, break-barrel cocking. **Stock:** Wood. **Sights:** Hooded front, adjustable rear. **Features:** Velocity of 1000 fps (.177), 800 (.22). 33 lbs. cocking effort. Blued finish. Scope compatible.
Price: .177, .22 .... **$202.00**

RWS 34 PANTHER
Caliber: .177, .22, single shot. 19-3/4", rifled. **Weight:** 7.7 lbs. 46" overall. **Power:** Spring-air, break-barrel cocking. **Stock:** Synthetic black. **Sights:** Ramp fiber optic front, adjustable fiber optic rear. Velocity of 1000 fps (.177), 800 (.22). 33 lbs. cocking effort. Blued finish. Scope compatible. Automatic safety.
Price: .177, .22 .... **$192.00**

RWS 48
Caliber: .177, .22, single shot. 17", rifled, fixed. **Weight:** 9.0 lbs. 42-1/2" overall. **Power:** Spring-air, side-lever cocking. **Stock:** Wood stock. **Sights:** Adjustable front, adjustable rear. Velocity of 1100 fps (.177), 900 (.22). 39 lbs. cocking effort. Blued finish. Scope compatible. Automatic safety.
Price: .177, .22 .... **$330.00**

TECH FORCE 6 AIR RIFLE
Caliber: .177 pellet, single shot. **Barrel:** 14". **Weight:** 6 lbs. **Length:** 35.5" overall. **Power:** Spring-piston, sidelever action. **Stock:** Paratrooper-style folding, full pistol grip. **Sights:** Adjustable rear, hooded front. **Features:** Velocity 800 fps. All-metal construction; grooved for scope mounting. Imported from China by Compasseco, Inc.
Price: **$69.95**

TECH FORCE 99 AIR RIFLE
Caliber: .177, .22, single shot. **Barrel:** 18", rifled. **Weight:** 8 lbs. **Length:** 44.5" overall. **Power:** Spring piston. **Stock:** Beech wood; raised cheek piece and checkering on pistol grip and forearm, plus soft rubber recoil pad. **Sights:** Insert type front. **Features:** Velocity 1,100 fps (.177; 900 fps: .22); fixed barrel design has an underlever cocking mechanism with an anti-beartrap lock and automatic safety. Imported from China by Compasseco, Inc.
Price:177 or .22 caliber **$152.96**

WALTHER LEVER ACTION
Caliber: .177, 8-shot lever action. **Barrel:** 19", rifled. **Weight:** 7.5 lbs. **Length:** 38" overall. **Power:** Two 12g CO2. **Stock:** Wood. **Sights:** Fixed front, adjustable rear. **Features:** Classic design. Velocity of 630 fps. Scope compatible.
Price: **$475.50**

WINCHESTER MODEL 1000SB
Caliber: .177, pellet, break-barrel spring air. **Barrel:** Rifled steel. **Weight:** 6.6 lbs. **Length:** 44.5" overall. **Stock:** Sporter style black composite. **Sights:** TRUGLO fiber optic with hooded front and micro adjustable rear. **Features:** Velocity of 1000 fps. 4 X 32 adjustable objective, fog proof/shockproof scope with crosshair reticle. From Daisy Mfg. Co.
Price: **$231.99**

WINCHESTER MODEL 1000B
Caliber: .177, pellet, break-barrel spring air. **Barrel:** Rifled steel, solid steel shroud. **Weight:** 6.6 lbs. **Length:** 44.5" overall. **Stock:** Black composite. **Sights:** TRUGLO fiber optic with hooded front and micro adjustable rear. **Features:** Velocity of 1000 fps. From Daisy Mfg. Co.
Price: **$184.99**

Prices given are believed to be accurate at time of publication however, many factors affect retail pricing so exact prices are not possible.

WINCHESTER MODEL 1000XS

Caliber: .177, pellet, break-barrel spring air. **Barrel:** Rifled steel, solid steel shroud. **Weight:** 6.6 lbs. **Length:** 46.7" overall. **Stock:** Walnut. **Sights:** Hooded front with blade and ramp, micro-adjustable rear. **Features:** Velocity of 1000 fps, uniquely designed 4 X 32 scope with adjustable objective. From Daisy Mfg. Co.

Price: **$269.99**

WINCHESTER MODEL 1000X

Caliber: .177, pellet, break-barrel spring air. **Barrel:** Rifled steel, solid steel shroud. **Weight:** 6.6 lbs. **Length:** 46.7" overall. **Stock:** Walnut. **Sights:** Hooded front with blade and ramp, micro-adjustable rear. **Features:** Velocity of 1000 fps. From Daisy Mfg. Co.

Price: **$228.99**

WINCHESTER MODEL 800XS

Caliber: .177, pellet, break-barrel spring air. **Barrel:** Rifled steel, solid steel shroud. **Weight:** 6.6 lbs. **Length:** 46.7" overall. **Stock:** Walnut. **Sights:** Hooded front with blade and ramp, micro-adjustable rear. **Features:** Velocity of 800 fps. Scope is fogproof and shockproof with fully adjustable windage and elevation and cross hair reticle. Also includes mounting rings. From Daisy Mfg. Co.

Price: **$201.99**

WINCHESTER MODEL 800X

Caliber: .177, pellet, break-barrel spring air. **Barrel:** Rifled steel, solid steel shroud. **Weight:** 6.6 lbs. **Length:** 46.7" overall. **Stock:** Walnut. **Sights:** Hooded front with blade and ramp, micro-adjustable rear. **Features:** Velocity of 800 fps. From Daisy Mfg. Co.

Price: **$164.99**

A

A. Uberti S.p.A., Via Artigiana 1, Gardone Val Trompia, Brescia 25063, ITALY, P: 011 390308341800, F: 011 390308341801, www.ubertireplicas.it
Firearms

A.R.M.S., Inc./Atlantic Research Marketing Systems, Inc., 230 W. Center St., West Bridgewater, MA 02379, P: 508-584-7816, F: 508-588-8045, www.armsmounts.com
Scopes, Sights and Accessories

AA & E Leathercraft, 107 W. Gonzales St., Yoakum, TX 77995, P: 800-331-9092, F: 361-293-9127, www.tandybrands.com
Bags & Equipment Cases; Custom Manufacturing; Hunting Accessories; Knives/Knife Cases; Leathergoods; Shooting Range Equipment; Sports Accessories

ACIGI / Fujiiryoki, 4399 Ingot St., Fremong, CA 94538, P: 888-816-0888, F: 510-651-6188, www.fujichair.com
Wholesaler/Distributor

ACR Electronics, Inc., 5757 Ravenswood Rd., Ft. Lauderdale, FL 33312, P: 800-432-0227, F: 954-983-5087, www.acrelectronics.com
Backpacking; Hunting Accessories; Lighting Products; Sports Accessories; Survival Kits/First Aid; Training and Safety Equipment

Accro-Met, Inc., 3406 Westwood Industrial Drive, Monroe, NC 28110, P: 800-543-4755, F: 704-283-2112, www.accromet.com
Gun Barrels; Wholesaler/Distributor

Accu-Fire, Inc., P.O. Box 121990, Arlington, TX 76012, P: 888-MUZZLEMATE, F: 817-303-4505
Firearms Maintenance Equipment

Accu-Shot/B&T Industries, LLC, P.O. Box 771071, Wichita, KS 67277, P: 316-721-3222, F: 316-721-1021, www.accu-shot.com
Gun Grips & Stocks; Hunting Accessories; Law Enforcement; Scopes, Sights & Accessories; Shooting Range Equipment; Sports Accessories; Training and Safety Equipment

Accuracy International North America, Inc., 35100 North State Highway, Mingus, TX 76463-6405, P: 907-440-4024, www.accuracyinternational.org
Firearms; Firearms Maintenance Equipment; Law Enforcement; Magazines, Cartridge; Scopes, Sights & Accessories; Wholesaler/Distributor

AccuSharp Knife Sharpeners/Fortune Products, Inc., 205 Hickory Creek Road, Marble Falls, TX 78654, P: 800-742-7797, F: 800-600-5373, www.accusharp.com
Archery; Camping; Cooking Equipment/Accessories; Cutlery; Hunting Accessories; Knives/Knife Cases; Sharpeners; Sports Accessories

Action Target, P.O. Box 636, Provo, UT 84603-0636, P: 888-377-8033, F: 801-377-8096, www.actiontarget.com
Law Enforcement; Shooting Range Equipment; Targets; Training & Safety Equipment

AcuSport Corp., One Hunter Place, Bellefontaine, OH 43311, P: 800-543-3150, www.acusport.com
Ammunition; Black Powder Accessories; Firearms; Hunting Accessories; Online Services; Retailer Services; Scopes, Sights & Accessories; Wholesaler/Distributor

Adams Arms/Retrofit Piston Systems, 255 Hedden Court, Palm Harbor, FL 34681, P: 727-853-0550, F: 727-353-0551, www.arisfix.com

ADCO Arms Co., Inc., 4 Draper St., Woburn, MA 01801, P: 800-775-3687, F: 781-935-1011, www.adcosales.com
Ammunition; Firearms; Paintball Accessories, Scopes, Sights & Accessories

ADS, Inc., Pinehurst Centre, 477 Viking Dr., Suite 350, Virginia Beach, VA 23452, P: 800-948-9433, F: 757-481-2039, www.adstactical.com

ADSTAR, Inc., 1390 Jerusalem Ave., North Merrick, NY 11566, P: 516-483-1800, F: 516-483-2590
Emblems & Decals; Outdoor Art, Jewelry, Sculpture

Advanced Armament Corp., 1434 Hillcrest Rd., Norcross, GA 30093, P: 770-925-9988, F: 770-925-9989, www.advanced-armament.com
Firearms; Hearing Protection; Law Enforcement

Advanced Engineered Systems, Inc., 14328 Commercial Parkway, South Beloit, IL 61080, P: 815-624-7797, F: 815-624-8198, www.advengsys.com
Ammunition; Custom Manufacturing

Advanced Technology International, 2733 W. Carmen Ave., Milwaukee, WI 53209, P: 800-925-2522, F: 414-664-3112, www.atigunstocks.com
Books/Industry Publications; Gun Grips & Stocks; Gun Parts/Gunsmithing; Hunting Accessories; Law Enforcement; Scopes, Sights & Accessories

Advanced Training Systems, 4524 Highway 61 North, St. Paul, MN 55110, P: 651-429-8091, F: 651-429-8702, www.duelatron.com
Law Enforcement; Shooting Range Equipment; Targets; Training & Safety Equipment

Advantage® Camouflage, P.O. Box 9638, Columbus, GA 31908, P: 800-992-9968, F: 706-569-9346, www.advantagecamo.com
Camouflage

Advantage Tactical Sight/WrenTech Industries, LLC, 7 Avenida Vista Grande B-7, Suite 510, Sante Fe, NM 87508, F: 310-316-6413 or 505-466-1811, F: 505-466-4735, www.advantagetactical.com
Scopes, Sights & Accessories

Adventure Action Gear/+VENTURE Heated Clothing, 5932 Bolsa Ave., Suite 103, Huntington Beach, CA 92649, P: 310-412-1070, F: 610-423-5257, www.ventureheat.com
Men & Women's Clothing; Export/Import Specialists; Footwear; Gloves, Mitts, Hats; Sports Accessories; Vehicles, Utility & Rec.; Wholesaler/Distributor

Adventure Lights, Inc., 444 Beaconsfield Blvd., Suite 201, Beaconsfield, Quebec H9W 4C1, CANADA, P: 514-694-8477, F: 514-694-2353

Adventure Medical Kits, P.O. Box 43309, Oakland, CA 94624, P: 800-324-3517, F: 510-261-7419, www.adventuremedicalkits.com
Backpacking; Books/Industry Publications; Camping; Custom Manufacturing; Hunting Accessories; Sports Accessories; Survival Kits/First Aid; Training & Safety Equipment

AE Light/Div. of Allsman Enterprises, LLC, P.O. Box 1869, Rogue River, OR 97537, P: 541-471-8988, F: 888-252-1473, www.aelight.com
Camping; Custom Manufacturing; Hunting Accessories; Law Enforcement; Lighting Products; Wholesale/Distributor

AES Optics, 201 Corporate Court, Senatobia, MS 38668, P: 800-416-0866, F: 662-301-4739, www.aesoutdoors.com
Eyewear

Aetco, Inc., 2825 Metropolitan Place, Pomona, CA 91767, P: 800-982-5258, F: 800-451-2434, www.aetcoinc.com
Firearms; Hearing Protection; Holsters; Law Enforcement; Leathergoods; Lighting Products; Training & Safety Equipment; Wholesaler/Distributor

Africa Sport Hunting Safaries, 11265 E. Edison St., Tucson, AZ 85749, P: 520-440-5384, F: 520-885-8032, www.africasporthuntingsafaris.com
Archery; Outdoor Art, Jewelry, Sculpture; Outfitter; Tours/Travel

AFTCO Bluewater/Al Agnew, 17351 Murphy Ave., Irvine, CA 92614, P: 949-660-8757, F: 949-660-7067, www.aftcobluewater.com

Aftermath Miami/Stunt Studios, 3911 Southwest 47th Ave., Suite 914, Davie, FL 33314, P: 954-581-5822, F: 954-581-3165, www.aftermathairsoft.com
Airsoft Guns & Accessories

Aguila Ammunition/Centurion Ordnance, Inc., 11614 Rainbow Ridge, Helotes, TX 78023, P: 210-695-4602, F: 210-695-4603, www.aguilaammo.com
Ammunition

Aimpoint, Inc., 14103 Mariah Court, Chantilly, VA 20151, 877-246-7646, F: 703-263-9463, www.aimpoint.com
Scopes, Sights & Accessories

AimShot/Osprey International, Inc., 25 Hawks Farm Rd., White, GA 30184, P: 888-448-3247, F: 770-387-0114, www.aimshot.com, www.miniosprey.com
Archery; Binoculars; Holsters; Hunting Accessories; Law Enforcement; Lighting Products; Scopes, Sights & Accessories; Wholesaler/Distributor

Aimtech Mount Systems, P.O. Box 223, Thomasville, GA 31799-0223, P: 229-226-4313, F: 229-227-0222, www.aimtech-mounts.com
Hunting Accessories; Scopes, Sights & Accessories

Air Gun, Inc., 9320 Harwin Dr., Houston, TX 77036, P: 800-456-0022, F: 713-780-4831, www.airrifle-china.com
Airguns; Ammunition; Hunting Accessories; Scopes, Sights & Accessories; Wholesaler/Distributor

AirForce Airguns, P.O. Box 2478, Fort Worth, TX 76113, P: 877-247-4867, F: 817-451-1613, www.airforceairguns.com
Airguns; Hunting Accessories; Law Enforcement; Scopes, Sights & Accessories

Aitec Co., Ltd., Export Dept., Rm. 817, Crystal Beach ok, Jung Dong Haeundae-Gu Busan, 612 010, SOUTH KOREA, P: 011 82517416497, F: 011 82517462194, www.aitec.co.kr
Lighting Products

Ajax Custom Grips, Inc./Ajax Shooter Supply, 9130 Viscount Row, Dallas, TX 75247, P: 800-527-7537, F: 214-630-4942, www.ajaxgrips.com
Gun Grips & Stocks; Gun Parts/Gunsmithing; Holsters; Law Enforcement; Lighting Products; Magazines, Cartridge; Wholesaler/Distributor

AKDAL/Ucyildiz Arms Ind./Blow & Voltran, Bostanci Cd. Uol Sk. No: 14/A, Y. Dudullu-Umraniye, Istanbul, 34775, TURKEY, P: 011-90 216527671011, F: 011-90 2165276705, www.akdalarms.com, www.voltranarms.com
Airguns; Firearms

Aker International Inc., 2248 Main St., Suite 6, Chula Vista, CA 91911, P: 800-645-AKER, F: 888-300-AKER, www.akerleather.com
Holsters; Hunting Accessories; Law Enforcement; Leathergoods

Al Mar Knives, P.O. Box 2295, Tualatin, OR 97062, P: 503-670-9080, www.almarknives.com
Custom Manufacturing, Knives/Knife Cases

Alexander Arms, U.S. Army Radford Arsenal, Radford, VA 24141, P: 540-639-8356, F: 540-639-8353, www.alexanderarms.com
Ammunition; Firearms; Magazine, Cartridges; Reloading

All-Star Apparel, 6722 Vista Del Mar Ave., Suite C. La Jolla, CA 92037, P: 858-205-7827, F: 858-225-3544, www.all-star.ws
Camouflage; Men & Women's Clothing; Gloves, Mitts, Hats

All Weather Outerwear, 34 35th St., Brooklym, NY 11232, P: 800-965-6550, F: 718-788-2205
Camouflage; Men's Clothing

AllClear, LLC dba Auspit Rotisserie BBQ's, 2050 Russett Way, Carson City, NV 89703, P: 775-468-5665, F: 775-546-6091, www.auspitbbq.com

Allen Company, 525 Burbank St., P.O. Box 445, Broomfield, CO 80020, P: 800-876-8600, F: 303-466-7437, www.allencompany.net
Archery; Black Powder Accessories; Eyewear; Gun Cases; Hearing Protection; Hunting Accessories; Scopes, Sights & Accessories; Shooting Range Equipment

Alliant Powder/ATK Commercial Products, Route 114, Building 229, P.O. Box 6, Radford, VA 24143, P: 800-276-9337, F: 540-639-8496, www.alliantpowder.com
Reloading

Alot Enterprise Company, Ltd., 1503 Eastwood Centre, 5 A Kung Ngam Village Rd., Shaukeiwan, HONG KONG, P: 011 85225199728, F: 011 85225190122, www.alothk.com
Binoculars; Compasses; Eyewear; Hunting Accessories; Photographic Equipment; Scopes, Sights, & Accessories; Sports Accessories; Telescopes

Alpen Outdoor Corp., 10329 Dorset St., Rancho Cucamonga, CA 91730, P: 877-987-8379, F: 909-987-8661, www.alpenoutdoor.com
Backpacking; Binoculars; Camping; Hunting Accessories; Scopes, Sights & Accessories; Shooting Range Equipment; Sports Accessories, Wholesaler/Distributor

Alpine Archery, P.O. Box 319, Lewiston, ID 83501, P: 208-746-4717, F: 208-746-1635

ALPS Mountaineering, 1 White Pine, New Haven, MO 63068, P: 800-344-2577, F: 573-459-2044, www.alpsouthdoorz.com
Backpacking; Camouflage; Camping; Hunting Accessories; Sports Accessories

ALS Technologies, Inc., 1103 Central Blvd., P.O. Box 525, Bull Shoals, AR 72619, P: 877-902-4257, F: 870-445-8746, www.alslesslethal.com
Ammunition; Firearms; Gun Parts/Gunsmithing; Law Enforcement; Training & Safety Equipment

Alta Industries, 1460 Cader Lane, Petaluma, CA 94954, P: 707-347-2900, F: 707-347-2950, www.altaindustries.com

Altama Footwear, 1200 Lake Hearn Dr., Suite 475, Atlanta, GA 30319, P: 800-437-9888, F: 404-260-2889, www.altama.com
Footwear; Law Enforcement

Altamont Co., 291 N. Church St., P.O. Box 309, Thomasboro, IL 61878, P: 800-626-5774, F: 217-643-7973, www.altamontco.com
Gun Grips & Stocks

AlumaGrips, 2851 N. 34th Place, Mesa, AZ 85213, P: 602-690-5459, F: 480-807-3955
Firearms Maintenance Equipment; Gun Grips & Stocks; Gun Parts/Gunsmithing; Law Enforcement

AmChar Wholesale, Inc., 100 Airpark Dr., Rochester, NY 14624, P: 585-328-3951, F: 585-328-3749, www.amchar.com

American COP Magazine/FMG Publications, 12345 World Trade Dr., San Diego, CA 92128, P: 800-537-3006, F: 858-605-0247, www.americancopmagazine.com
Books/Industry Publications; Law Enforcement; Videos

American Cord & Webbing Co., Inc., 88 Century Dr., Woonsocket, RI 02895, P: 401-762-5500, F: 401-762-5514, www.acw1.com
Archery; Backpacking; Bags & Equipment Cases; Custom Manufacturing; Law Enforcement; Pet Supplies

American Defense Systems, Inc., 230 Duffy Ave., Hicksville, NY 11801, P: 516-390-5300, F: 516-390-5308, www.adsiarmor.com
Custom Manufacturing; Shooting Range Equipment; Training & Safety Equipment

American Furniture Classics/Div. of Dawson Heritage Furniture, P.O. Box 111, Webb City, MO 64870, P: 888-673-9080, F: 417-673-9081, www.americanfurnitureclassics.com
Gun Cabinets/Racks/Safes; Gun Cases; Home Furnishings

American Gunsmithing Institute (AGI), 1325 Imola Ave. West, P.O. Box 504, Napa, CA 94559, P: 800-797-0867, F: 707-253-7149, www.americangunsmith.com
Books/Industry Publications; Computer Software; Firearms Maintenance Equipment; Gun Parts/Gunsmithing; Videos

American Pioneer Powder, Inc., 20423 State Road 7, Suite F6-268, Boca Raton, FL 33498, P: 888-756-7693, F: 888-766-7693, www.americanpioneerpowder.com
Black Powder/Smokeless Powder; Reloading

American Plastics/SEWIT, 1225 N. MacArthur Drive, Suite 200, Tracy, CA 95376, P: 209-834-0287, F: 209-834-0924, www.americanplastics.com
Backpacking; Bags & Equipment Cases; Export/Import Specialists; Gun Cases; Holsters; Hunting Accessories; Survival Kits/First Aid; Wholesaler/Distributor

American Security Products Co., 11925 Pacific Ave., Fontana, CA 92337, P: 800-421-6142, F: 951-685-9685, www.amsecusa.com
Gun Cabinets/Racks/Safes

American Tactical Imports, 100 Airpark Dr., Rochester, NY 14624, P: 585-328-3951, F: 585-328-3749

American Technologies Network, Corp./ATN, Corp., 1341 San Mateo Ave., South San Francisco, CA 94080, P: 800-910-2862, F: 650-875-0129, www.atncorp.com
Binoculars; Law Enforcement; Lighting Products; Photographic Equipment; Scopes, Sights & Accessories; Telescopes

Americase, Inc., 1610 E. Main St., Waxahachie, TX 75165, P: 800-972-2737, F: 972-937-8373, www.americase.com
Bags & Equipment Cases; Custom Manufacturing; Gun Cases; Hunting Accessories

AmeriGlo, 5579-B Chamblee Dunwoody Rd., Suite 214, Atlanta, GA 30338, P: 770-390-0554, F: 770-390-9781, www.ameriglo.com
Camping; Law Enforcement; Lighting Products; Scopes, Sights & Accessories; Survival Kits/First Aid; Training & Safety Equipment

Ameristep, 901 Tacoma Court, Clio, MI 48420, P: 800-374-7837, F: 810-686-7121, www.ameristep.com
Archery; Blinds; Hunting Accessories; Training & Safety Equipment; Treestands

Ammo-Loan Worldwide, 815 D, Lewiston, ID 83501, P: 208-746-7012, F: 208-746-1703

Ammo-Up, 10601 Theresa Dr., Jacksonville, FL 32246, P: 800-940-2688, F: 904-645-5918, www.ammoupusa.com
Shooting Range Equipment

AMT/Auto Mag Co./C.G., Inc., 5200 Mitchelldale, Suite E17, Houston, TX 77092, P: 713-686-3232, F: 713-681-5665

Anglers Book Supply/Hunters & Shooters Book & DVD Catalog, 1380 W. 2nd Ave., Eugene, OR 97402, P: 800-260-3869, F: 541-342-1785, www.anglersbooksupply.com
Books/Industry Publications; Computer Software; Videos; Wholesaler/Distributor

ANXO-Urban Body Armor Corp., 7359 Northwest 34 St., Miami, FL 33122, P: 866-514-ANXO, F: 305-593-5498, www.urbanbodyarmor.com
Men & Women's Clothing; Custom Manufacturing; Law Enforcement

Apple Creek Whitetails, 14109 Cty. Rd. VV, Gillett, WI 54124, P: 920-598-0154, F: 920-855-1773, www.applecreekwhitetails.com

ARC/ArcticShield, Inc./X-System, 1700 West Albany, Suite A, Broken Arrow, OK 74012, P: 877-974-4353, F: 918-258-8790, www.arcoutdoors.com
Footwear; Hunting Accessories; Scents & Lures; Sports Accessories

Arc'Teryx, 100-2155 Dollarton Hwy., North Vancouver, British Columbia V7H 3B2, CANADA, P: 604-960-3001, F: 604-904-3692, www.arcteryx.com
Backpacking; Camouflage; Men's Clothing; Custom Manufacturing; Gloves, Mitts, Hats; Law Enforcement; Outfitter

Arctic Adventures, 19950 Clark Graham, Baie D'urfe, Quebec H9X 3R8, CANADA, P: 800-465-9474, F: 514-457-9834, www.arcticadventures.ca
Outfitter

Ares Defense Systems, Inc., P.O. Box 10667, Blacksburg, VA 24062, P: 540-639-8633, F: 540-639-8634, www.aresdefense.com
Firearms; Gun Parts/Gunsmithing; Law Enforcement; Lighting Products; Magazines, Cartridge; Scopes, Sights & Accessories; Shooting Range Equipment; Survival Kits/First Aid

Argentina Ducks & Doves LLC, P.O. Box 129, Pittsview, AL 36871, P: 334-855-9474, F: 334-855-9474, www.argentinaducksanddoves.com
Outfitter; Tours/Travel

ArmaLite, Inc., 745 S. Hanford St., Geneseo, IL 61254, P: 309-944-6939, F: 309-944-6949, www.armalite.com
Firearms; Firearms Maintenance Equipment

Armament Technology, Inc./ELCAN Optical Technologies, 3045 Robie St., Suite 113, Halifax, Nova Scotia B3K 4P6, CANADA, P: 902-454-6384, F: 902-454-4641, www.armament.com
International Exhibitors; Law Enforcement; Scopes, Sights & Accessories; Telescopes; Wholesaler/Distributor

Armatix GmbH, Feringastrabe. 4, Unterfohring, D 85774, GERMANY, P: 011 498999228140, F: 011 498999228228, www.armatix.de

Armi Sport di Chiappa Silvia e C. SNC-Chiappa Firearms, Via Milano, 2, Azzano Mella (Bs), 25020, ITALY, P: 011-39 0309749065, F: 011-39 0309749232, www.chiappafirearms.com
Black Powder Accessories; Firearms; International Exhibitors

Armor Express, 1554 E. Torch Lake Dr., P.O. Box 21, Central Lake, MI 49622, P: 866-357-3845, F: 231-544-6734, www.armorexpress.com
Law Enforcement

Armorshield USA, LLC, 30 ArmorShield Dr., Stearns, KY 42647, P: 800-386-9455, F: 800-392-9455, www.armorshield.net
Law Enforcement

Arms Corp. of the Philippines/Armscor Precision International, Armscorp Ave., Bgy Fortune, Marikina City, 1800, PHILIPPINES, P: 011 6329416243, F: 011 6329420682, www.armscor.com.ph
Airguns; Ammunition; Bags & Equipment Cases; Custom Manufacturing; Firearms; Gun Barrels; Gun Parts/Gunsmithing; International Exhibitors

Arms Tech, Ltd., 5025 North Central Ave., Suite 459, Phoenix, AZ 85012, P: 602-272-9045, F: 602-272-1922, www.armstechltd.com
Firearms; Law Enforcement

Arno Bernard Custom Knives, 19 Duiker St., Bethlehem, 9700, SOUTH AFRICA, P: 011 27583033196, F: 011 27583033196

Arrieta, Morkaiko, 5, Elgoibar, (Guipuzcoa) 20870, SPAIN, P: 011-34 943743150, F: 011-34 943743154, www.arrietashotguns.com
Firearms

Arrow Precision, LLC, 2750 W. Gordon St., Allentown, PA 18104, P: 610-437-7138, F: 610-437-7139, www.arrow-precision.com
Archery; Crossbows & Accessories; Paintballs, Guns & Accessories

ARS Business Solutions, LLC, 940 Industrial Dr., Suite 107, Sauk Rapids, MN 56379, P: 800-547-7120, www.arss.com
Computer Software; Retailer Services

Arsenal, Inc., 3300 S. Decatur Blvd., Suite 10632, Las Vegas, NV 89102, P: 888-539-2220, F: 702-643-8860, www.arsenalinc.com
Firearms

Artistic Plating Co., 405 W. Cherry St., Milwaukee, WI 53212, P: 414-271-8138, F: 414-271-5541, www.artisticplating.net
Airguns; Ammunition; Archery; Cutlery; Firearms; Game Calls; Gun Barrels; Reloading

ARY, Inc., 10301 Hickman Mills Dr., Suite 110, Kansas City, MO 64137, P: 800-821-7849, F: 816-761-0055, www.aryinc.com
Cutlery; Knives/Knife Cases

ASAT Outdoors, LLC, 307 E. Park Ave., Suite 207A, Anaconda, MT 59711, P: 406-563-9336, F: 406-563-7315
Archery; Blinds; Camouflage; Men's Clothing; Gloves, Mitts, Hats; Hunting Accessories; Law Enforcement; Paintball Accessories

Ashbury International Group, Inc., P.O. Box 8024, Charlottesville, VA 22906, P: 434-296-8600, F: 434-296-9260, www.ashburyintlgroup.com
Camouflage; Firearms; Law Enforcement; Scopes, Sights & Accessories; Wholesaler/Distributor

Asociacion Armera, P. I Azitain, 2-J, P.O. Box 277, Eibar, Guipúzcoa 20600, SPAIN, P: 011 34943208493, F: 011 34943700966, www.a-armera.com
Associations/Agencies

ASP, Inc., 2511 E. Capitol Dr., Appleton, WI 54911, P: 800-236-6243, F: 800-236-8601, www.asp-usa.com
Law Enforcement; Lighting Products; Training & Safety Equipment

A-Square Company/A-Square of South Dakota, LLC, 302 Antelope Dr., Chamberlain, SD 57325, P: 605-234-0500, F: 605-234-0510, www.asquareco.com
Ammunition; Books/Industry Publications; Firearms; Reloading

Astra Radio Communications, 2238 N. Glassell St., Suite D., Orange, CA 92865, P: 714-637-2828, F: 714-637-2669, www.arcmics.com
Two-Way Radios

Atak Arms Ind., Co. Ltd., Imes San. Sit. A Blok 107, Sk. No: 70, Y. Dudullu, Umraniye, Istanbul, 34775 TURKEY, P: +902164203996, F: +902164203998, www.atakarms.com
Airguns; Firearms; Training & Safety Equipment

Atascosa Wildlife Supply, 1204 Zanderson Ave., Jourdanton, TX 78026, P: 830-769-9711, F: 830-769-1001

ATK/ATK Commercial Products, 900 Ehlen Dr., Anoka, MN 55303, P: 800-322-2342, F: 763-323-2506, www.atk.com
Ammunition; Binoculars; Clay Targets; Firearms Maintenance Equipment; Reloading; Scopes, Sights & Accessories; Shooting Range Equipment; Targets

ATK /ATK Law Enforcement, 2299 Snake River Ave., Lewiston, ID 83501, P: 800-627-3640, F: 208-798-3392, www.atk.com
Ammunition; Bags & Equipment Cases; Binoculars; Firearms Maintenance Equipment; Reloading; Scopes, Sights & Accessories

Atlanco, 1125 Hayes Industrial Dr., Marietta, GA 30062-2471, P: 800-241-9414, F: 770-427-9011, www.truspec.com
Camouflage; Men's Clothing; Custom Manufacturing; Law Enforcement; Wholesaler/Distributor

Atlanta Cutlery Corp., 2147 Gees Mill Rd., Conyers, GA 30013, P: 800-883-8838, F: 770-760-8993, www.atlantacutlery.com
Custom Manufacturing; Cutlery; Firearms; Holsters; Knives/Knife Cases; Leathergoods; Wholesaler/Distributor

Atlas Glove Consumer Products/LFS, Inc., 851 Coho Way, Bellingham, WA 98225, P: 800-426-8860, F: 888-571-8175, www.lfsinc.com/atlasoutdoor
Gloves, Mitts, Hats

Atsko, 2664 Russel St., Orangeburg, SC 29115, P: 800-845-2728, F: 803-531-2139, www.atsko.com
Archery; Backpacking; Camouflage; Camping; Custom Manufacturing; Hunting Accessories; Scents & Lures

AuctionArms.com, Inc., 3031 Alhambra Dr., Suite 101, Cameron Park, CA 95682, P: 877-GUN-AUCTION, F: 530-676-2497, www.auctionarms.com
Airguns; Archery; Black Powder Accessories; Black Powder/Smokeless Powder; Camping; Firearms; Online Services

Autumnwood Wool Outfitters, Inc., 828 Upper Pennsylvania Ave., Bangor, PA 18013, P: 610-588-5744, F: 610-588-4868, www.autumnwoodoutfitters.com

Avon Protection Systems, 1369 Brass Mill Rd., Suite A, Belcamp, MD 21017, P: 888-286-6440, F: 410-273-0126, www.avon-protection.com
Law Enforcement; Training & Safety Equipment

A-Way Hunting Products (MI), 3230 Calhoun Rd., P.O. Box 492, Beaverton, MI, 48612, P: 989-435-3879, F: 989-435-8960, www.awayhunting.com
Decoys; Game Calls; Scents & Lures; Videos

AWC Systems Technology, 1515 W. Deer Valley Rd., Suite A-105, Phoenix, AZ 85027, P: 623-780-1050, F: 800-897-5708, www.awcsystech.com

AyA-Aguirre Y Aranzabal, Avda. Otaola, 25-3a Planta, Eibar, (Guipúzcoa) 20600, SPAIN, P: 011-34-943-820437, F: 011-34-943-200133, www.aya-fineguns.com
Firearms

B

B-Square/Div. Armor Holdings, Inc., 8909 Forum Way, Fort Worth, TX 76140, P: 800-433-2909, F: 817-926-7012

BAM Wuxi Bam Co., Ltd., No 37 Zhongnan Rd., Wuxi, JiangSu 214024, CHINA, P: 011-86 51085432361, FL 011-86 51085401258, www.china-bam.com
Airguns; Gun Cases; Scopes, Sights & Accessories

BCS International, 1819 St. George St., Green Bay, WI 54302, P: 888-965-3700, F: 888-965-3701
Bags & Equipment Cases; Camouflage; Men & Women's Clothing; Export/Import Specialists; Leathergoods

B.E. Meyers, 14540 Northeast 91st St., Redmond, WA 98052, P: 800-327-5648, F: 425-867-1759, www.bemeyers.com
Custom Manufacturing; Law Enforcement

B & F System, Inc., The, 3920 S. Walton Walker Blvd., Dallas, TX 75236, P: 214-333-2111, F: 214-333-2137, www.bnfusa.com
Binoculars; Cooking Equipment/Accessories; Cutlery; Gloves, Mitts, Hats; Leathergoods; Scopes, Sights & Accessories; Telescopes; Wholesaler/Distributor

BOGgear, LLC, 111 W. Cedar Lane, Suite A, Payson, AZ 85541, P: 877-264-7637, F: 505-292-9130, www.boggear.com
Binoculars; Firearms; Hunting Accessories; Law Enforcement; Outfitter; Photographic Equipment; Shooting Range Equipment; Training & Safety Equipment

BSA Optics, 3911 S.W. 47th Ave., Suite 914, Ft. Lauderdale, FL 33314, P: 954-581-2144, F: 954-581-3165, www.bsaoptics.com
Binoculars; Scopes, Sights & Accessories; Sports Accessories; Telescopes

B.S.N. Technology Srl, Via Guido Rossa, 46/52, Cellatica (Bs), 25060, ITALY, P: 011 390302522436, F: 011 390302520946, www.bsn.it
Ammunition; Gun Barrels; Reloading

Bad Boy, Inc., 102 Industrial Dr., Batesville, AR 72501, P: 870-698-0090, F: 870-698-2123

Bad Boy Enterprises, LLC/Bad Boy Buggies, 2 River Terminal Rd., P.O. Box 19087, Natchez, MS 39122, P: 866-678-6701, F: 601-442-6707, www.badboybuggies.com
Vehicles, Utility & Rec

Badger Barrels, Inc., 8330 196 Ave., P.O. Box 417, Bristol, WI 53104, P: 262-857-6950, F: 262-857-6988, www.badgerbarrelsinc.com
Gun Barrels

Badger Ordnance, 1141 Swift St., North Kansas City, MO 64116, P: 816-421-4956, F: 816-421-4958, www.badgerordnance.com
Custom Manufacturing; Firearms; Firearms Maintenance Equipment; Gun Parts/Gunsmithing; Law Enforcement; Magazines, Cartridge; Scopes, Sights & Accessories; Telescopes

Badland Beauty, LLC, P.O. Box 151507, Lufkin, TX 75915, P: 936-875-5522, F: 936-875-5525, www.badlandbeauty.com
Women's Clothing

BAE Systems/Mobility & Protection Systems, 13386 International Parkway, Jacksonville, FL 32218, P: 904-741-5600, F: 904-741-9996, www.baesystems.com
Bags & Equipment Cases; Black Powder/Smokeless Powder; Gloves, Mitts, Hats; Holsters; Hunting Accessories; Law Enforcement; Scopes, Sights & Accessories; Training & Safety Equipment

Bandera/Cal-Bind, 1315 Fernbridge Dr., Fortuna, CA 95540, P: 866-226-3378, F: 707-725-1156, www.banderausa.com
Archery; Hunting Accessories; Leathergoods; Sports Accessories; Wholesaler/Distributor

Barbour, Inc., 55 Meadowbrook Dr., Milford, NH 03055-4613, P: 800-338-3474, F: 603-673-6510, www.barbour.com
Bags & Equipment Cases; Men & Women's Clothing; Footwear; Gloves, Mitts, Hats; Leathergoods

Bardin & Marsee Publishing, 1112 N. Shadesview Terrace, Birmingham, AL 35209, P: 205-453-4361, F: 404-474-3086, www.theoutdoorbible.com
Books/Industry Publications

Barnaul Cartridge Plant CJSC, 28 Kulagina St., Barnaul, 656002, RUSSIAN FEDERATION, P: 011 0073852774391, F: 011 0073852771608, www.ab.ru/~stanok
Ammunition

Barnes Bullets, Inc., P.O. Box 620, Mona, UT 84645, P: 801-756-4222, F: 801-756-2465, www.barnesbullets.com
Black Powder Accessories; Computer Software; Custom Manufacturing; Hunting Accessories; Law Enforcement; Recoil Protection Devices & Services; Reloading

Barnett Outdoors, LLC, 13447 Byrd Dr., P.O. Box 934, Odessa, FL 33556, P: 800-237-4507, F: 813-920-5400, www.barnettcrossbows.com
Archery; Crossbows & Accessories; Sports Accessories

Baron Technology, Inc./Baron Engraving, 62 Spring Hill Rd., Trumbull, CT 06611, P: 203-452-0515, F: 203-452-0663, www.baronengraving.com
Custom Manufacturing; Cutlery; Firearms; Gun Parts/Gunsmithing; Knives/Knife Cases; Law Enforcement; Outdoor Art, Jewelry, Sculpture; Sports Accessories

Barrett Firearms Mfg., Inc., P.O. Box 1077, Murfreesboro, TN 37133, P: 615-896-2938, F: 615-896-7313, www.barrettrifles.com
Firearms

Barska Optics, 1721 Wright Ave., La Verne, CA 91750, P: 909-445-8168, F: 909-445-8169, www.barska.com

Bates Footwear/Div. Wolverine World Wide, Inc., 9341 Courtland Dr., Rockford, MI 49351, P: 800-253-2184, F: 616-866-5658, www.batesfootwear.com
Footwear; Law Enforcement

Battenfeld Technologies, Inc., 5885 W. Van Horn Tavern Rd., Columbia, MO 65203, P: 877-509-9160, F: 573-446-6606, www.battenfeldtechnologies.com
Firearms Maintenance Equipment; Gun Grips & Stocks; Gun Parts/Gunsmithing; Hearing Protection; Recoil Protection Devices & Services; Reloading; Shooting Range Equipment; Targets

Battle Lake Outdoors, 203 W. Main, P.O. Box 548, Clarissa, MN 56440, P: 800-243-0465, F: 218-756-2426, www.battlelakeoutdoors.com
Archery; Backpacking; Bags & Equipment Cases; Black Powder Accessories; Camping; Gun Cases; Hunting Accessories; Law Enforcement

Batz Corp., 1524 Highway 291 North, P.O. Box 130, Prattsville, AR 72129, P: 800-637-7627, F: 870-699-4420, www.batzusa.com
Backpacking; Camping; Custom Manufacturing; Hunting Accessories; Knives/Knife Cases; Lighting Products; Pet Supplies; Retail Packaging

Bayco Products, Inc., 640 S. Sanden Blvd., Wylie, TX 75098, P: 800-233-2155, F: 469-326-9401, www.baycoproducts.com

Beamshot-Quarton USA, Inc., 5805 Callaghan Rd., Suite 102, San Antonio, TX 78228, P: 800-520-8435, F: 210-735-1326, www.beamshot.com
Airguns; Archery; Crossbows & Accessories; Hunting Accessories; Law Enforcement; Lighting Products; Paintball Accessories; Scopes, Sights & Accessories

Bear & Son Cutlery, Inc., 1111 Bear Blvd. SW, Jacksonville, AL 36265, P: 800-844-3034, F: 256-435-9348, www.bearandsoncutlery.com
Cutlery; Hunting Accessories; Knives/Knife Cases

Bear Valley Outfitters, P.O. Box 2294, Swan River, Manitoba R0L-1Z0 CANADA, P: 204-238-4342, F: 204-238-4342, www.bearvalleyoutfitters.com

Beeman Precision Airguns, 5454 Argosy Ave., Huntington Beach, CA 92649, P: 714-890-4800, F: 714-890-4808, www.beeman.com
Airguns; Ammunition; Gun Cases; Holsters; Lubricants; Scopes, Sights & Accessories; Targets

Beijing Defense Co., Ltd., 18 B, Unit One, No. 1 Building, Linghangguoji, Guangqumen Nanxiao St., Chongwen District, Beijing, 100061, CHINA, P: 011 861067153626, F: 011 861067152121, www.tacticalgear.com
Backpacking; Bags & Equipment Cases; Gun Cases; Holsters; Training & Safety Equipment

Bell and Carlson, Inc., 101 Allen Rd., Dodge City, KS 67801, P: 620-225-6688, F: 620-225-9095, www.bellandcarlson.com
Camouflage; Custom Manufacturing; Gun Grips & Stocks; Gun Parts/Gunsmithing; Hunting Accessories; Shooting Range Equipment

Bell-Ranger Outdoor Apparel, 1538 Crescent Dr., P.O. Box 14307, Augusta, GA, 30909, P: 800-241-7618, F: 706-738-3608, www.bellranger.com
Camouflage; Men & Women's Clothing; Hunting Accessories

Benchmade Knife Company, Inc., 300 Beavercreek Rd., Oregon City, OR 97045, P: 800-800-7427, F: 503-655-7922, www.benchmade.com
Knives/Knife Cases; Men's Clothing

Benelli Armi S.p.A./Benelli USA, 17603 Indian Head Hwy., Accokeek, MD 20607, P: 301-283-6981, F: 301-283-6986, www.benelli.it, www.benelliusa.com
Firearms

Beretta/Law Enforcement and Defense, 17601 Beretta Dr., Accokeek, MD 20607, P: 800-545-9567, F: 301-283-5111, www.berettale.com
Firearms; Gun Parts/Gunsmithing; Holsters; Law Enforcement; Lighting Products

Beretta U.S.A. Corp., 17601 Beretta Dr., Accokeek, MD 20607, P: 800-636-3420, F: 253-484-3775

Bergan, LLC, 27600 Hwy. 125, Monkey Island, OK 74331, P: 866-217-9606. F: 918-257-8950, www.berganexperience.com
Pet Products

Berger Bullets, 4275 N. Palm St., Fullerton, CA 92835, P: 714-447-5456, F: 714-447-5478, www.bergerbullets.com
Ammunition; Custom Manufacturing; Reloading

Berry's Manufacturing, Inc., 401 N. 3050 East, St. George, UT 84790, P: 800-269-7373, F: 435-634-1683, www.berrysmfg.com
Ammunition; Custom Manufacturing; Export/Import Specialists; Gun Cases; Reloading; Wholesaler/Distributor

Beta Company, The, 2137B Flintstone Dr., Tucker, GA 30084, P: 800-669-2382, F: 770-270-0599, www.betaco.com
Law Enforcement; Magazines, Cartridge

Beyond Clothing/Beyond Tactical, 1025 Conger St., Suite 8, Eugene, OR 97402, P: 800-775-2279, F: 703-997-6581, www.beyondtactical.com
Backpacking; Camouflage; Men & Women's Clothing; Custom Manufacturing; Law Enforcement

BFAST, LLC, 10 Roff Ave., Palasades Park, NJ 07650, P: 973-706-8210, F: 201-943-3546, www.firearmsafetynet.com
Law Enforcement; Shooting Range Equipment; Sports Accessories; Training & Safety Equipment

Bianchi International, 3120 E. Mission Blvd. Ontario, CA 91761, P: 800-347-1200, F: 800-366-1669, www.bianchi-intl.com
Backpacking; Bags & Equipment Cases; Gun Cases; Holsters; Hunting Accessories; Knives/Knife Cases; Leathergoods; Sports Accessories

Big Game Treestands, 1820 N. Redding Ave., P.O. Box 382, Windom, MN 56101, P: 800-268-5077, F: 507-831-4350, www.biggametreestands.com
Blinds; Hunting Accessories; Shooting Range Equipment; Treestands

Big Sky Carvers/Montana Silversmiths, 308 E. Main St., P.O. Box 507, Manhattan, MT 59741, P: 406-284-3193, F: 406-284-4028, www.bigskycarvers.com
Decoys; Home Furnishings; Lighting Products; Outdoor Art, Jewelry, Sculpture; Watches; Wholesaler/Distributor

Big Sky Racks, Inc., 25A Shawnee Way, Bozeman, MT 58715, P: 800-805-8716, F: 406-585-7378, www.bigskyracks.com
Gun Cabinets, Racks, Safes; Gun Locks; Hunting Accessories

BigFoot Bag/PortaQuip, 1215 S. Grant Ave., Loveland, CO 80537, P: 877-883-0200, F: 970-663-5415, www.bigfootbag.com
Bags & Equipment Cases; Camping; Hunting Accessories; Law Enforcement; Paintball Accessories; Sports Accessories; Tours & Travel

Bill's Sewing Machine Co., 301 Main Avenue East, Hildebran, NC 28637, P: 828-397-6941, F: 828-397-6193, www.billsewing.com

Bill Wiseman & Co., Inc., 18456 Hwy. 6 South, College Station, TX 77845, P: 979-690-3456, F: 979-690-0156, www.billwisemanandco.com
Firearms; Gun Barrels; Gun Parts/Gunsmithing

BioPlastics Co., 34655 Mills Rd., North Ridgeville, OH 44039, P: 440-327-0485, F: 440-327-3666, www.bioplastics.us

Birchwood Casey, 7900 Fuller Rd., Eden Prairie, MN 55344, P: 800-328-6156, F: 952-937-7979, www.birchwoodcasey.com
Black Powder Accessories; Camping; Firearms Maintenance Equipment; Gun Cases; Gun Parts/Gunsmithing; Hunting Accessories; Lubricants; Targets

Bison Designs, 735 S. Lincoln St., Longmont, CO 80501, P: 800-536-2476, F: 303-678-9988, www.bisondesigns.com
Backpacking; Men & Women's Clothing; Pet Supplies; Survival Kits/First Aid; Training & Safety Equipment; Wholesaler/Distributor

Black Hills Ammunition, P.O. Box 3090, Rapid City, SD 57709, P: 605-348-5150, F: 605-348-9827, www.black-hills.com
Ammunition

Black Hills Shooters Supply, Inc., 2875 Creek Dr., Rapid City, SD 57703, P: 800-289-2506, F: 800-289-4570, www.bhshooters.com
Reloading; Wholesaler/Distributor

Black Powder Products Group, 5988 Peachtree Corners East, Norcross, GA 30071, P: 800-320-8767, F: 770-242-8546, www.bpiguns.com
Black Powder Accessories; Firearms; Firearms Maintenance Equipment; Hunting Accessories; Scopes, Sights & Accessories

BlackHawk Products Group, 6160 Commander Pkwy., Norfolk, VA 23502, P: 800-694-5263, F: 757-436-3088, www.blackhawk.com
Bags & Equipment Cases; Men's Clothing; Gloves, Mitts, Hats; Holsters; Hunting Accessories; Knives/Knife Cases; Law Enforcement; Recoil Protection Devices & Services

Blackheart International, LLC, RR3, Box 115, Philippi, WV 26416, P: 877-244-8166, F: 304-457-1281, www.bhigear.com
Ammunition; Gun Parts/Gunsmithing; Holsters; Law Enforcement; Magazines, Cartridge; Scopes, Sights & Accessories; Survival Kits/First Aid; Training & Safety Equipment

Blackwater, P.O. Box 1029, Moyock, NC 27958, P: 252-435-2488, F: 252-435-6388, www.blackwaterusa.com
Bags & Equipment Cases; Men's Clothing; Custom Manufacturing; Gun Cases; Holsters; Law Enforcement; Targets; Training & Safety Equipment

Blade-Tech Industries, 2506 104th St. Court S, Suite A, Lakewood, WA 98499, P: 253-581-4347, F: 253-589-0282, www.blade-tech.com
Bags & Equipment Cases; Custom Manufacturing; Cutlery; Holsters; Hunting Accessories; Knives/Knife Cases; Law Enforcement; Sports Accessories

Blaser Jagdwaffen GmbH, Ziegelstadel 1, Isny, 88316, GERMANY, P: 011 4907562702348, F: 011 4907562702343, www.blaser.de
Firearms; Gun Barrels; Gun Cases; Gun Grips & Stocks; Hunting Accessories

Blauer Manufacturing Co. 20 Aberdeen St., Boston, MA 02215, P: 800-225-6715, www.blauer.com
Law Enforcement; Men & Women's Clothing

Blue Book Publications, Inc., 8009 34th Ave. S, Suite 175, Minneapolis, MN 55425, P: 800-877-4867, F: 952-853-1486, www.bluebookinc.com
Books/Industry Publications; Computer Software

Blue Force Gear, Inc., P.O. Box 853, Pooler, GA 31322, P: 877-430-2583, F: 912-964-7701, www.blueforcegear.com
Bags & Equipment Cases; Hunting Accessories; Law Enforcement; Scopes, Sights & Accessories; Sports Accessories

Blue Ridge Knives, 166 Adwolfe Rd., Marion, VA 24354, P: 276-783-6143, F: 276-783-9298, www.blueridgeknives.com
Binoculars; Cutlery; Export/Import Specialists; Knives/Knife Cases; Lighting Products; Scopes, Sights & Accessories; Sharpeners; Wholesaler/Distributor

Blue Stone Safety Products Co., Inc., 2950 W. 63rd St., Chicago, IL 60629, P: 773-776-9472, F: 773-776-9472, www.wolverineholsters.com
Holsters; Law Enforcement

Bluegrass Armory, 145 Orchard St., Richmond, KY 40475, P: 859-625-0874, F: 859-625-0874, www.bluegrassarmory.com
Firearms

Bluestar USA, Inc., 111 Commerce Center Drive, Suite 303, P.O. Box 2903, Huntersville, NC 28078, P: 877-948-7827, F: 704-875-6714, www.bluestar-hunting.com
Archery; Crossbows & Accessories; Hunting Accessories; Law Enforcement; Training & Safety Equipment; Wholesaler/Distributor

BlueWater Ropes/Yates Gear, Inc., 2608 Hartnell Ave., Suite 6, Redding, CA 96002, P: 800-YATES-16, F: 530-222-4640, www.yatesgear.com
Law Enforcement; Training & Safety Equipment; Wholesaler/Distributor

Bobster Eyewear, 12220 Parkway Centre Dr., Suite B, Poway, CA 92064, P: 800-603-2662, F: 858-715-0066, www.bobster.com
Eyewear; Hunting Accessories; Law Enforcement; Shooting Range Equipment; Sports Accessories; Training & Safety Equipment

Body Specs Sunglasses & Goggles, 22846 Industrial Place, Grass Valley, CA 95949, P: 800-824-5907, F: 530-268-1751, www.bodyspecs.com
Eyewear; Law Enforcement; Shooting Range Equipment; Training & Safety Equipment

Bogs Footwear/The Combs Co., 16 Oakway Center, Eugene, OR 97401, P: 800-485-2070, F: 541-484-1345, www.bogsfootwear.com or www.raftersfootwear.com
Footwear

Boker USA, Inc., 1550 Balsam St., Lakewood, CO 80214, P: 800-992-6537, F: 303-462-0668, www.bokerusa.com
Cutlery; Knives/Knife Cases

Border Crossing Scents, 8399 Bristol Rd., Davison, MI 48423, P: 888-653-2759, F: 810-653-2809, www.bordercrossingscents.com
Scents & Lures

Boss Buck, Inc., 210 S. Hwy. 175, Seagoville, TX 75159, P: 972-287-1216, F: 972-287-1892, www.bossbuck.com
Blinds; Feeder Equipment; Hunting Accessories; Scents & Lures; Treestands

Boston Leather, Inc., 1801 Eastwood Dr., P.O. Box 1213, Sterling, IL 61081, P: 800-733-1492, F: 800-856-1650, www.bostonleather.com
Bags & Equipment Cases; Custom Manufacturing; Gun Cases; Holsters; Knives/Knife Cases; Law Enforcement; Leathergoods; Pet Supplies

Boyds' Gunstock Industries, Inc., 25376 403rd Ave., Mitchell, SD 57301, P: 605-996-5011, F: 605-996-9878, www.boydsgunstocks.com
Custom Manufacturing; Firearms Maintentance Equipment; Gun Grips & Stocks; Gun Parts/Gunsmithing; Hunting Accessories; Shooting Range Equipment

Boyt Harness/Bob Allen Sportswear, 1 Boyt Dr., Osceola, IA 50213, P: 800-685-7020, www.boytharness.com
Gun Cases; Hunting Accessories; Law Enforcement; Men & Women's Clothing; Pet Supplies; Shooting Accessories

BraeVal, 23 E. Main St., Torrington, CT 06790, P: 860-482-7260, F: 860-482-7247, www.braeval.net
Men's Clothing

Brass Magnet, 5910 S. University Blvd., Suite C 18-330, Greenwood Village, CO 80121, P: 303-347-2636, F: 360-364-2636

Brazos Walking Sticks, 6408 Gholson Rd., Waco, TX 76705, P: 800-880-7119, F: 254-799-7199, www.brazos-walking-sticks.com
Canes; Walking Sticks

Breaching Technologies, Inc., P.O. Box 701468, San Antonio, TX 78270, P: 866-552-7427, F: 210-590-5193, www.breachingtechnologies.com
Law Enforcement; Training & Safety Equipment

Break-Free, 13386 International Parkway, Jacksonville, FL 32218, P: 800-433-2909, F: 800-588-0339, www.break-free.com
Law Enforcement; Lubricants

Brenneke™ of America, L.P., P.O. Box 1481, Clinton, IA 52733, P: 800-753-9733, F: 563-244-7421, www.brennekeusa.com
Ammunition

Brenzovich Firearms & Training Center/dba BFTC, 22301 Texas 20, Fort Hancock, TX 79839, P: 877-585-3775, F: 915-764-2030, www.brenzovich.com
Airguns; Ammunition; Archery; Black Powder Accessories; Export/Import Specialists; Firearms; Training & Safety Equipment; Wholesaler/Distributor

Brigade Quartermasters, Ltd., 1025 Cobb International Dr., Kennesaw, GA 30152, P: 770-428-1248, F: 720-426-7211

Briley Manufacturing, Inc., 1230 Lumpkin Rd., Houston, TX 77043, P: 800-331-5718, F: 713-932-1043
Chokes, Gun Accessories, Gunsmithing

Brite-Strike Technologies, 26 Wapping Rd., Jones River Industrial Park, Kingston, MA 02364, P: 781-585-5509, F: 781-585-5332, www.brite-strike.com
Law Enforcement; Lighting Products

Broco, Inc., 10868 Bell Ct., Rancho Cucamonga, CA 91730, P: 800-845-7259, F: 800-845-7259, www.brocoinc.com
Law Enforcement

Brookwood/Fine Uniform Co., 1125 E. Broadway, Suite 51, Glendale, CA 91205, P: 626-443-3736, F: 626-444-1551, www.brookwoodbags.com
Archery; Backpacking; Bags & Equipment Cases; Camping; Gun Cases; Hunting Accessories; Knives/Knife Cases; Shooting Range Equipment

Brookwood Companies, Inc., 25 W. 45th St., 11th Floor, New York, NY 10036, P: 800-426-5468, F: 646-472-0294, www.brookwoodcos.com

Brownells/Brownells MIL/LE Supply Group, 200 S. Front St., Montezuma, IA 50171, P: 800-741-0015, F: 800-264-3068, www.brownells.com
Export/Import Specialists; Firearms Maintenance Equipment; Gun Grips & Stocks; Gun Parts/Gunsmithing; Lubricants; Magazines, Cartridge; Scopes, Sights & Accessories; Wholesaler/Distributor

Browning, 1 Browning Place, Morgan, UT 84050, P: 801-876-2711, F: 801-876-3331, www.browning.com

Browning Archery, 2727 N. Fairview Ave., Tucson, AZ 85705, P: 520-838-2000, F: 520-838-2019, www.browning-archery.com
Archery

Browning Footwear, 107 Highland St., Martinsburg, PA 16662, P: 800-441-4319, F: 814-793-9272, www.browningfootwear.com
Footwear

Browning Hosiery/Carolina Hosiery, 2316 Tucker St., Burlington, NC 27215, P: 336-226-5581, F: 336-226-9721, www.browninghosiery.com
Men & Women's Clothing, Footwear

Browning Off Road/Polaris Industries, 2100 Hwy. 55, Medina, MN 55340, P: 763-542-0500, F: 763-542-2317, www.browning offroad.com
Vehicles, Utility & Rec

Browning Outdoor Health and Safety Products, 1 Pharmacal Way, Jackson, WI 53037, P: 800-558-6614, F: 262-677-9006, www.browningsupplies.com
Survival Kits/First Aid

Browning Signature Automotive/Signature Products Group, 2550 S. Decker Lake Blvd. Suite 1, Salt Lake City, UT 84119, P: 801-237-0184, F: 801-237-0118, www.spgcompany.com
Emblems & Decals

Bruce Foods/Cajun Injector, Inc., P.O. Box 1030, New Iberia, LA 70562, P: 337-365-8101, F: 337-364-3742, www.brucefoods.com
Camping; Cooking Equipment/Accessories; Food; Online Services

Brunton, 2255 Brunton Ct., Riverton, WY 82501, P: 307-857-4700, F: 307-857-4703, www.brunton.com
Backpacking, Binoculars, Camping, Scopes

Buck Gardner Calls, LLC, 2129 Troyer Ave., Building 249, Suite 104, Memphis, TN 38114, P: 901-946-2996, F: 901-946-8747, www.buckgardner.com
Duck Calls & Accessories; Cooking

Buck Knives, Inc., 660 S. Lochsa St., Post Falls, ID 83854, P: 800-326-2825, www.buckknives.com
Backpacking; Camping; Custom Manufacturing; Cutlery; Hunting Accessories; Knives/Knife Cases; Law Enforcement; Sharpeners

Buckaroo-Stoo/BVM Productions, 2253 Kingsland Ave., Bronx, NY 10469, P: 877-286-4599, F: 718-652-3014, www.buckaroostoo.com
Scents & Lures

Buck Stop Lure Company, Inc., 3600 Grow Rd., P.O. Box 636, Stanton, MI 48888, P: 800-477-2368, F: 989-762-5124, www.buckstopscents.com
Archery; Books/Industry Publications; Hunting Accessories; Pet Supplies; Scents & Lures; Videos

Buck Wear, Inc., 2900 Cowan Ave., Baltimore, MD 21223, P: 800-813-7708, F: 410-646-7700, www.buckwear.com
Men & Women's Clothing

Buffalo Tools/Sportsman Series, 1220 N. Price Rd., St. Louis, MO 63132, P: 800-568-6657, F: 636-537-1055, www.buffalotools.com
Cooking Equipment/Accessories; Export/Import Specialists; Wholesaler/Distributor

Buffer Technologies, P.O. Box 105047, Jefferson City, MO 65110, P: 877-628-3337, F: 573-634-8522, www.buffertech.com
Gun Parts/Gunsmithing; Law Enforcement; Magazines, Cartridge; Recoil Protection Devices & Services

Bug Band, 127 Riverside Dr., Cartersville, GA 30120, P: 800-473-9467, F: 678-721-9279, www.bugband.com
Archery; Backpacking; Camping; Hunting Accessories; Law Enforcement; Outfitter; Survival Kits/First Aid; Wholesaler/Distributor

Bul, Ltd., 10 Rival St., Tel Aviv, 67778, ISRAEL, P: 011 97236392911, F: 011 97236874853, www.bultransmark.com
Firearms; Gun Barrels; Gun Parts/Gunsmithing; Law Enforcement

Bulldog Barrels, LLC, 106 Isabella St., 4 North Shore Center, Suite 110, Pittsburgh, PA 15212, P: 866-992-8553, F: 412-322-1912, www.bulldogbarrels.com
Firearms; Gun Barrels; Gun Parts/Gunsmithing

Bulldog Cases, 830 Beauregard Ave., Danville, VA 24541, P: 800-843-3483, F: 434-793-7504
Bags & Equipment Cases; Camouflage; Gun Cases; Holsters

Bulldog Equipment, 3706 SW 30th Ave., Hollywood, FL 33312, P: 954-581-5510 or 954-448-5221, F: 954-581-4221, www.bulldogequipment.us
Backpacking; Bags & Equipment Cases; Custom Manufacturing; Gloves, Mitts, Hats; Gun Cases; Law Enforcement; Outfitter

Bulls and Beavers, LLC, P.O. Box 2870, Sun Valley, ID 83353, P: 208-726-8217, www.bullsandbeavers.com

Burn Machine, LLC, The, 26305 Glendale, Suite 200, Redford, MI 48239, P: 800-380-6527, F: 313-794-4355, www.theburnmachine.com
Sports Accessories; Training & Safety Equipment; Wholesaler/Distributor

Burris Company, Inc., 331 E. 8th St., Greeley, CO 80631, P: 970-356-1670, F: 970-356-8702, www.burrisoptics.com
Binoculars; Scopes, Sights & Accessories; Targets

Bushido Tactical, LLC, P.O. Box 721289, Orlando, FL 32972, P: 407-454-4256, F: 407-286-4416, www.bushidotactical.com
Law Enforcement; Training

Bushnell Law Enforcement/Bushnell Outdoor Products, 9200 Cody St., Overland Park, KS 66214, P: 800-423-3537, F: 800-548-0446, www.unclemikesle.com
Binoculars; Firearms Maintenance Equipment; Gloves, Mitts, Hats; Gun Cases; Holsters; Law Enforcement; Lubricants; Scopes, Sights & Accessories

Business Control Systems Corp., 1173 Green St., Iselin, NJ 08830, P: 800-233-5876, F: 732-283-1192, www.businesscontrol.com
Archery; Computer Software; Firearms; Law Enforcement; Retailer Services; Shooting Range Equipment; Wholesaler/Distributor

Butler Creek Corp./Bushnell Outdoor Accessories, 9200 Cody St., Overland Park, KS 66214, P: 800-423-3537, F: 800-548-0446, www.butlercreek.com
Firearms Maintenance Equipment; Gun Barrels; Gun Grips & Stocks; Hunting Accessories; Leathergoods; Scopes, Sights & Accessories

C

CAM Commerce Solutions, 17075 Newhope St., Fountain Valley, CA 92708, 866-840-4443, F: 702-564-3206, www.camcommerce.com
Computer Software

CASL Industries/Tanglefree/Remington, P.O. Box 1280, Clayton, CA 94517, P: 877-685-5055, F: 925-685-6055, www.tanglefree.com or www.caslindustries.com
Bags & Equipment Cases; Blinds; Camouflage; Decoys; Gun Cases; Hunting Accessories

CAS Hanwei, 650 Industrial Blvd., Sale Creek, TN 37373-9797, P: 800-635-9366, F: 423-332-7248, www.cashanwei.com
Custom Manufacturing; Cutlery; Knives/Knife Cases; Leathergoods; Wholesaler/Distributor

CCF Race Frames LLC, P.O. Box 29009, Richmond, VA 23242, P: 804-622-4277, F: 804-740-9599, www.ccfraceframes.com
Firearms; Firearms Maintenance Equipment; Gun Parts/Gunsmithing; Law Enforcement

CCI Ammunition/ATK Commercial Products, 2299 Snake River Ave., Lewiston, ID 83501, P: 800-256-8685, F: 208-798-3392, www.cci-ammunition.com
Ammunition

CGTech, 9000 Research Dr., Irvine, CA 92618, P: 949-753-1050, F: 949-753-1053, www.cgtech.com
Computer Software; Custom Manufacturing

CJ Weapons Accessories, 317 Danielle Ct., Jefferson City, MO 65109, P: 800-510-5919, F: 573-634-2355, www.cjweapons.com
Firearms Maintenance Equipment; Gun Parts/Gunsmithing; Hunting Accessories; Law Enforcement; Magazines, Cartridge; Shooting Range Equipment; Sports Accessories; Wholesaler/Distributor

CMMG, Inc., 620 County Rd. 118, P.O. Box 369, Fayette, MO 65248, P: 660-248-2293, F: 660-248-2290, www.cmmginc.com
Firearms; Law Enforcement; Magazines, Cartridge

CTI Industries Corp., 22160 N. Pepper Rd., Barrington, IL 60010, P: 866-382-1707, F: 800-333-1831, www.zipvac.com
Archery; Backpacking; Bags & Equipment Cases; Camping; Cooking Equipment/Accessories; Custom Manufacturing; Food; Hunting Accessories

CVA, 5988 Peachtree Corners East, Norcross, GA 30071, P: 800-320-8767, F: 770-242-8546
Black Powder Accessories; Firearms; Firearms Maintenance Equipment; Gun Barrels

CZ-USA/Dan Wesson, 3327 N. 7th St., Kansas city, KS 66115, P: 800-955-4486, F: 913-321-4901, www.cz-usa.com
Firearms

Cablz, 411 Meadowbrook Lane, Birmingham, AL 35213, P: 205-222-4477, F: 205-870-8847

Caesar Guerini USA, 700 Lake St., Cambridge, MD 21613, P: 866-901-1131, F: 410-901-1137, www.gueriniusa.com
Firearms

CALVI S.p.A., Via Iv Novembre, 2, Merate (LC), 23807, ITALY, P: 011 3903999851, F: 011 390399985240, www.calvi.it
Custom Manufacturing; Firearms; Gun Barrels; Gun Locks; Gun Parts/Gunsmithing

Camdex, Inc., 2330 Alger, Troy, MI 48083, P: 248-528-2300, F: 248-528-0989, www.camdexloader.com
Reloading

Camelbak Products, 2000 S. McDowell Blvd., Petaluma, CA 94954, P: 800-767-8725, F: 707-665-3844, www.camelbak.com
Backpacking; Bags & Equipment Cases; Gloves, Mitts, Hats; Holsters; Law Enforcement

Camerons Products/CM International, Inc., 2547 Durango Dr., P.O. Box 60220, Colorado Springs, CO 80960, P: 888-563-0227, F: 719-390-0946, www.cameronsproducts.com
Backpacking; Camping; Cooking Equipment/Accessories; Hunting Accessories; Retailer Services; Tours/Travel; Wholesaler/Distributor

Camfour, Inc., 65 Westfield Industrial Park Rd., Westfield, MA 01085, P: 800-FIREARM, F: 413-568-9663, www.camfour.com
Ammunition; Black Powder Accessories; Computer Software; Export/Import Specialists; Firearms; Hunting Accessories; Law Enforcement; Wholesaler/Distributor

Cammenga Corp., 100 Aniline Ave. N, Suite 258, Holland, MI 49424, P: 616-392-7999, F. 616-392-9432, www.cammenga.com
Magazines, Cartridge; Reloading; Training & Safety Equipment

Camo Unlimited, 1021 B Industrial Park Dr., Marietta, GA 30062, P: 866-448-CAMO, F: 770-420-2299, www.camounlimited.com
Blinds; Camouflage; Hunting Accessories; Paintball Accessories

C-More Systems, 7553 Gary Rd., P.O. Box 1750, Manassas, VA 20109, P: 888-265-8266, F: 703-361-5881, www.cmore.com
Airguns; Archery; Crossbows & Accessories; Custom Manufacturing; Firearms; Hunting Accessories; Law Enforcement; Scopes, Sights & Accessories; Shooting Range Equipment

CamoSpace.com, P.O. Box 125, Rhodesdale, MD 21659, P: 410-310-0380, F: 410-943-8849

Camouflage Face Paint, 2832 Southeast Loop 820, Fort Worth, TX 76140, P: 877-625-3879, F: 817-615-8670, www.camofacepaint.com
Archery; Camouflage; Custom Manufacturing; Export/Import Specialists; Hunting Accessories; Online Services; Paintball Accessories; Wholesaler/Distributor

Camowraps, 429 South St., Slidell, LA 70460, P: 866-CAMO-MAN, F: 985-661-1447, www.camowraps.com
Camouflage; Custom Manufacturing; Emblems & Decals; Printing Services

Camp Chef, 675 North 600 West, P.O. Box 4057, Logan, UT 84321, P: 800-783-8347, F: 435-752-1592, www.campchef.com
Cooking Equipment/Accessories

Camp Technologies, LLC/Div. DHS Technologies, LLC, 33 Kings Hwy., Orangeburg, NY 10962, P: 866-969-2400, F: 845-365-2114, www.camprtv.com
Backpacking; Camping; Hunting Accessories; Law Enforcement; Outfitter; Sports Accessories; Vehicles, Utility & Rec

CampCo/Smith & Wesson Watches HUMVEE/UZI, 4625 W. Jefferson Blvd., Los Angeles, CA 90016, P: 888-9-CAMPCO, F: 323-766-2424, www.campco.com
Backpacking; Binocular; Camping; Compasses; Knives/Knife Cases; Law Enforcement; Lighting Products; Wholesaler/Distributor

Canal Street Cutlery Co., 30 Canal St., Ellenville, NY 12428, P: 845-647-5900, F: 845-647-1456, www.canalstreetcutlery.com
Cutlery; Knives/Knife Cases

Cannon Safe, Inc., 216 S. 2nd Ave., Building 932, San Bernardino, CA 92408, P: 800-242-1055, F: 909-382-0707, www.cannonsafe.com
Gun Cabinets/Racks/Safes; Gun Locks

Careco Multimedia, Inc., 5717 Northwest Pkwy., Suite 104, San Antonio, TX 78249, P: 800-668-8081, F: 251-948-3011, www.americanaoutdoors.com, www.outdooraction.com, www.fishingandhuntingtexas.com
Online Services; Videos; Wholesaler/Distributor

Carl Zeiss Optronics GmbH, Gloelstr. 3-5, Wetzlar, 35576, GERMANY, P: 011 4964414040, F: 011 496441404510, www.zeiss.com/optronics
Law Enforcement; Scopes, Sights & Accessories; Shooting Range Equipment; Targets; Telescopes

Carl Zeiss Sports Optics/Zeiss, 13005 N. Kingston Ave., Chester, VA 23836, P: 800-441-3005, F: 804-530-8481, www.zeiss.com/sports
Binoculars; Scopes, Sights & Accessories

Carlson's Choke Tubes, 720 S. Second St., P.O. Box 162, Atwood, KS 67730, P: 785-626-3700, F: 785-626-3999, www.choketube.com
Custom Manufacturing; Firearms Maintenance Equipment; Game Calls; Gun Parts/Gunsmithing; Hunting Accessories; Scopes, Sights & Accessories; Shooting Range Equipment

Carson Optical, 35 Gilpin Ave., Hauppauge, NY 11788, P: 800-967-8427, F: 631-427-6749, www.carsonoptical.com
Binoculars; Export/Import Specialists; Scopes, Sights & Accessories; Telescopes

Cartuchos Saga, Pda. Caparrela s/n, Lleida, 25192, SPAIN, P: 011 34973275000, F: 011 34973275008
Ammunition

Case Cutlery (W.R. Case & Sons Cutlery Co.), Owens Way, Bradford, PA 16701, P: 800-523-6350, F: 814-358-1736, www.wrcase.com
Cutlery; Knives/Knife Cases; Sharpeners

Caspian Arms, Ltd., 75 Cal Foster Dr., Wolcott, VT 05680, P: 802-472-6454, F: 802-472-6709, www.caspianarms.com
Firearms; Gun Parts/Gunsmithing; Law Enforcement

Cass Creek International, LLC, 1881 Lyndon Blvd., Falconer, NY 14733, P: 800-778-0389, F: 716-665-6536, www.casscreek.com
Game Calls; Hunting Accessories

Cejay Engineering, LLC/InfraRed Combat Marking Beacons, 2129 Gen Booth Blvd., Suite 103-284, Virginia Beach, VA 23454, P: 603-880-8501, F: 603-880-8502, www.cejayeng.com
Lighting Products

Celestron, 2835 Columbia St., Torrance, CA 90503, P: 310-328-9560, F: 310-212-5835, www.celestron.com
Binoculars; Scopes, Sights & Accessories; Telescopes

Center Mass, Inc., 6845 Woonsocket, Canton, MI 48187, P: 800-794-1216, F: 734-416-0650, www.centermassinc.com
Bags & Equipment Cases; Emblems & Decals; Hunting Accessories; Law Enforcement; Men's Clothing; Shooting Range Equipment; Targets; Training & Safety Equipment

Century International Arms, Inc., 430 S. Congress Dr., Suite 1, DelRay Beach, FL 33445, P: 800-527-1252, F: 561-265-4520, www.centuryarms.com
Ammunition; Firearms; Firearms Maintenance Equipment; Gun Parts/Gunsmithing; Law Enforcement; Magazines, Cartridge; Scopes, Sights & Accessories; Wholesaler/Distributor

Cequre Composite Technologies, 5995 Shier-Rings Rd., Suite A, Dublin, OH 43016, P: 614-526-0095, F: 614-526-0098, www.wearmor.com
Custom Manufacturing; Law Enforcement; Shooting Range Equipment; Targets

Cerakote/NIC Industries, Inc., 7050 Sixth St., White City, OR 97503, P: 866-774-7628, F: 541-830-6518, www.nicindustries.com
Camouflage; Custom Manufacturing; Firearms; Firearms Maintenance Equipment; Knives/Knife Cases; Law Enforcement; Lubricants; Paintball Guns

Champion Traps and Targets/ATK Commercial Products, N5549 Cty. Trunk Z, Onalaska, WI 54650, P: 800-635-7656, F: 763-323-3890, www.championtargetr.com
Clay Targets; Hearing Protection; Shooting Range Equipment; Targets

Chapin International, P.O. Box 549, Batavia, NY 14020, P: 800-444-3140, F: 585-813-0118, www.chapinmfg.com
Feeder Equipment

Chapman Innovations, 343 W. 400 South, Salt Lake City, UT 84101, P: 801-415-0024, F: 801-415-2001, www.carbonx.com
Gloves, Mitts, Hats; Law Enforcement; Men & Women's Clothing

Charter Arms/MKS Supply, Inc., 8611A North Dixie Dr., Dayton, OH 45414, P: 866-769-4867, F: 937-454-0503, www.charterfirearms.com
Firearms

Cheddite France, 99 Route de Lyon, P.O. Box 112, Bourg-les-Valence, 26500, FRANCE, P: 011 33475564545, F: 011 33475563587, www.cheddite.com
Ammunition

Chengdu Lis Business, 4-3-9, 359 Shuhan Rd., Chengdu, SICH 610036, CHINA, P: 0110862887541867, F: 011 862887578686, www.lisoptics.com
Binoculars; Compasses; Cutlery; Lighting Products; Scopes, Sights & Accessories; Telescopes

CheyTac Associates, LLC, 363 Sunset Dr., Arco, ID 83213, P: 256-325-0622, F: 208-527-3328, www.cheytac.com
Ammunition; Computer Software; Custom Manufacturing; Firearms; Law Enforcement; Training & Safety Equipment

Chiappa Firearms-Armi Sport di Chiappa Silvia e C. SNC, Via Milano, 2, Azzano Mella (Bs), 25020, ITALY, P: 011 390309749065, F: 011 390309749232, www.chiappafirearms.com
Black Powder Accessories; Firearms

China Shenzhen Aimbond Enterprises Co., Ltd., 19D, Building No. 1, China Phoenix Building, No. 2008, Shennan Rd., Futian District, Shenzhen, Guangdong 518026, CHINA, P: 011 8675582522730812, F: 011 8675583760022, www.sino-optics.com
Binoculars; Eyewear; Firearms Maintenance Equipment; Hunting Accessories; Lighting Products; Scopes, Sights & Accessories; Telescopes

Chip McCormick Custom, LLC, 105 Sky King Dr., Spicewood, TX 78669, P: 800-328-2447, F: 830-693-4975, www.cmcmags.com
Gun Parts/Gunsmithing; Magazines, Cartridge

Choate Machine & Tool, 116 Lovers Lane, Bald Knob, AR 72010, P: 800-972-6390, F: 501-724-5873, www.riflestock.com
Gun Grips & Stocks; Law Enforcement

Chongqing Dontop Optics Co., Ltd., No. 5 Huangshan Ave. Middle Beibu New District, Chongqing, 401121, CHINA, P: 011 862386815057, F: 011 862386815100, www.dontop.com
Binoculars; Custom Manufacturing; Scopes, Sights & Accessories; Shooting Range Equipment; Telescopes

Chongqing Jizhou Enterprise Co., Ltd., Rm 8-1, Block A3, Jiazhou Garden, Chongqing, Yubei 401147, CHINA, P: 011 862367625115, F: 011 862367625121, www.cqjizhou.com
Binoculars; Compasses; Scopes, Sights & Accessories; Telescopes

Chonwoo Corp./Chonwoo Case & Cover (Tianjin) Co., Ltd., 4-6, SamJun-Dong Songpa-gu, Seoul, 138-837, SOUTH KOREA, P: 011 8224205094, F: 011 8224236154, www.chonwoo.co.kr
Backpacking; Bags & Equipment Cases; Gun Cases; Holsters; Hunting Accessories; Knives/Knife Cases; Leathergoods

Chris Reeve Knives, 2949 S. Victory View Way, Boise, ID 83709, P: 208-375-0367, F: 208-375-0368, www.chrisreeve.com
Backpacking; Camping; Cutlery; Hunting Accessories; Knives/Knife Cases; Law Enforcement; Sports Accessories

Christensen Arms, 192 E. 100 North, Fayette, UT 84630, P: 888-517-8855, F: 435-528-5773, www.christensenarms.com
Custom Manufacturing; Firearms; Gun Barrels

Christie & Christie Enterprises, Inc., 404 Bolivia Blvd., Bradenton, FL 34207, P: 440-413-0031, F: 440-428-5551
Gun Grips & Stocks; Gun Parts/Gunsmithing; Magazines, Cartridge; Scopes, Sights & Accessories; Wholesaler/Distributor

Cimarron Firearms Co., 105 Winding Oaks Rd., P.O. Box 906, Fredericksburg, TX 78624, P: 830-997-9090, F: 830-997-0802, www.cimarron-firearms.com
Black Powder Accessories; Firearms; Gun Cases; Gun Grips & Stocks; Gun Parts/Gunsmithing; Holsters; Leathergoods; Wholesaler/Distributor

Citadel (Cambodia) Pt., Ltd., Nr 5 Str 285 Tuol Kork, Phnom Penh, BP 440, CAMBODIA, P: 011 85512802676, F: 011 85523880015, www.citadel.com.kh
Cutlery

Clark Textile Co./ASF Group, 624 S. Grand Ave., San Pedro, CA 90731, P: 310-831-2334, F: 310-831-2335, www.asfgroup.com
Camouflage; Printing Services

Classic Accessories, 22640 68th Ave. S, Kent, WA 98032, P: 800-854-2315, F: 253-395-3991, www.classicaccessories.com
Bags & Equipment Cases; Camouflage; Gun Cases; Hunting Accessories; Pet Supplies; Wholesaler/Distributor

Classic Old West Styles, 1712 Texas Ave., El Paso, TX 79901, P: 800-595-COWS, F: 915-587-0616, www.cows.com
Custom Manfacturing; Holsters; Hunting Accessories; Leathergoods; Men's Clothing; Outfitter; Sports Accessories; Wholesaler/Distributor

Claude Dozorme Cutlery, Z.A. de Racine-B.P. 19, La Monnerie, 63650, FRANCE, P: 011 33473514106, F: 011 33473514851, www.dozorme-claude.fr
Cutlery

Claybuster Wads/Harvester Muzzleloading, 635 Bob Posey St., Henderson, KY 42420, P: 800-922-6287, F: 270-827-4972, www.claybusterwads.com
Black Powder Accessories; Reloading

Clever SRL, Via A. Da Legnago, 9/A, I-37141 Ponteflorio, Verona, ITALY, P: 011 390458840770, F: 011 390458840380, www.clevervr.com
Ammunition

Cliff Weil, Inc., 8043 Industrial Park Rd., Mechanicsville, VA 23116, P: 800-446-9345, F: 804-746-2595, www.cliffweil.com
Eyewear

Club Red, Inc./Bone Collector by Michael Waddell, 4645 Church Rd., Cumming, GA 30028, P: 888-428-1630, F: 678-947-1445, www.clubredinc.com
Emblems & Decals; Men & Women's Clothing

Clymer Precision, 1605 W. Hamlin Rd., Rochester Hills, MI 48309, P: 877-REAMERS, F: 248-853-1530, www.clymertool.com
Black Powder Accessories; Books/Industry Publications; Custom Manufacturing; Firearms Maintenance Equipment; Gun Parts/Gunsmithing; Law Enforcement; Reloading

CMere Deer®, 205 Fair Ave., P.O. Box 1336, Winnsboro, LA, 71295, P: 866-644-8600, F: 318-435-3885, www.cmeredeer.com
Scents & Lures

Coastal Boot Co., Inc. 2821 Center Port Circle, Pompano Beach, FL 33064, P: 954-782-3244, F: 954-782-4342, www.coastalboot.com
Footwear

Coast Products/LED Lenser, 8033 NE Holman St., Portland, OR 97218, P: 800-426-5858, F: 503-234-4422, www.coastportland.com
Camping; Compasses; Cutlery; Knives/Knife Cases; Law Enforcement; Lighting Products; Sharpeners

Cobra Enterprises of Utah, Inc., 1960 S. Milestone Dr., Suite F, Salt Lake City, UT 84104, P: 801-908-8300, F: 801-908-8301, www.cobrapistols.net
Firearms

Codet Newport Corp./Big Bill Work Wear, 924 Crawford Rd., Newport, VT 05855, P: 800-992-6338, F: 802-334-8268, www.bigbill.com
Backpacking; Bags & Equipment Cases; Camouflage; Camping; Footwear; Gloves, Mitts, Hats; Men's Clothing

Cold Steel Inc., 3036 Seaborg Ave., Suite A, Ventura, CA 93003, P: 800-255-4716, F: 805-642-9727, www.coldsteel.com
Cutlery; Knives/Knife Cases; Law Enforcement; Sports Accessories; Videos

Collector's Armoury, Ltd., P.O. Box 1050, Lorton, VA 22199, P: 800-336-4572, F: 703-493-9424, www.collectorsarmoury.com
Black Powder Accessories; Books/Industry Publications; Cutlery; Firearms; Holsters; Home Furnishings; Training & Safety Equipment; Wholesaler/Distributor

Colonial Arms, Inc. 1504 Hwy. 31 S, P.O. Box 250, Bay Minette, AL 36507, P: 800-949-8088, F: 251-580-5006, www.colonialarms.com
Firearms; Firearms Maintenance Equipment; Gun Barrels; Gun Parts/Gunsmithing; Hunting Accessories; Lubricants; Recoil Protection Devices & Services; Wholesaler/Distributor

Colt's Manufacturing Co., LLC, P.O. Box 1868, Hartford, CT 06144, P: 800-962-COLT, F: 860-244-1449, www.coltsmfg.com
Custom Manufacturing; Firearms; Gun Parts/Gunsmithing; Law Enforcement

Columbia River Knife and Tool, 18348 SW 126th Pl., Tualatin, OR 97062, P: 800-891-3100, F: 503-682-9680, www.crkt.com
Knives/Knife Cases; Sharpeners

Columbia Sportswear Co., 14375 NW Science Park Dr., Portland, OR 97229, P: 800-547-8066, F: 503-985-5800, www.columbia.com
Bags & Equipment Cases; Binoculars; Footwear; Gloves, Mitts, Hats; Men & Women's Clothing; Pet Supplies; Scopes, Sights & Accessories

Combined Tactical Systems, 388 Kinsman Rd., P.O. Box 506, Jamestown, PA 16134, P: 724-932-2177, F: 724-932-2166, www.less-lethal.com
Law Enforcement

Compass Industries, Inc., 104 E. 25th St., New York, NW 10010, P: 800-221-9904, F: 212-353-0826, www.compassindustries.com
Binoculars; Camping; Compasses; Cutlery; Export/Import Specialists; Eyewear; Hunting Accessories; Wholesaler/Distributor

Competition Electronics, 3469 Precision Dr., Rockford, IL 61109, P: 815-874-8001, F: 815-874-8181, www.competitionelectronics.com
Firearms Maintenance Equipment; Reloading; Shooting Range Equipment; Training & Safety Equipment

Condor Outdoor Products, 1866 Business Center Dr., Duarte, CA 91010, P: 800-552-2554, F: 626-303-3383, www.condoroutdoor.com
Backpacking; Bags & Equipment Cases; Camouflage; Footwear; Gun Cases; Holsters; Wholesaler/Distributor

Condor Tool & Knife, Inc., 6309 Marina Dr., Orlando, FL 32819, P: 407-876-0886, F: 407-876-0994, www.condortk.com
Archery; Camping; Custom Manufacturing; Cutlery; Gun Cases; Hunting Accessories; Knives/Knife Cases; Leathergoods

Connecticut Shotgun Mfg. Co., 100 Burritt St., New Britain, CT 06053, P: 800-515-4867, F: 860-832-8707, www.connecticutshotgun.com
Firearms; Firearms Maintenance Equipment; Gun Cabinets/Racks/Safes; Gun Cases; Gun Parts/Gunsmithing; Hunting Accessories; Knives/Knife Cases; Scopes, Sights & Accessories

Consorzio Armaioli Bresciani, Via Matteotti, 325, Gardone V.T., Brescia 25063, ITALY, P: 011 39030821752, F: 011 39030831425, www.armaiolibresciani.org
Firearms; Gun Parts/Gunsmithing; Videos

Consorzio Cortellinai Maniago SRL, Via Della Repubblica, 21, Maniago, PN 33085, ITALY, P: 011 39042771185, F: 011 390427700440, www.consorziocoltellinai.it
Camping; Cutlery; Hunting Accessories; Knives/Knife Cases; Law Enforcement

Convert-A-Ball Distributing, Inc., 955 Ball St., P.O. Box 199, Sidney, NE 69162, P: 800-543-1732, F: 308-254-7194, www.convert-a-ball.net
Camping; Vehicles, Utility & Rec

Cooper Firearms of MT, Inc./Cooper Arms, 4004 Hwy. 93 North, P.O. Box 114, Stevensville, MT 59870, P: 406-777-0373, F: 406-777-5228, www.cooperfirearms.com
Custom Manufacturing; Firearms

CopShoes.com/MetBoots.com, 6655 Poss Rd., San Antonio, TX 78238, P: 866-280-0400, F: 210-647-1401, www.copshoes.com
Footwear; Hunting Accessories; Law Enforcement

Cor-Bon/Glaser/Div. Dakota Ammo Inc., 1311 Industry Rd., P.O. Box 369, Sturgis, SD 57785, P: 605-347-4544, F: 605-347-5055, www.corbon.com
Ammunition

Cornell Hunting Products, 114 Woodside Dr., Honea Path, SC 29654, P: 864-369-9587, F: 864-369-9587, www.cornellhuntinproducts.com
Backpacking; Game Calls; Hunting Accessories; Wholesaler/Distributor

Corsivia, Poligono El Campillo, Calle Alemania, 59-61, Zuera, (Zaragoza) 50800, SPAIN, P: 011 34976680075, F: 011 34976680124, www.corsivia.com
Clay Targets

Counter Assault Pepper Sprays/Bear Deterrent, Law Enforcement & Personal Defense, 120 Industrial Court, Kalispell, MT 59901, P: 800-695-3394. F: 406-257-6674, www.counterassault.com
Archery; Backpacking; Camping; Hunting Accessories; Law Enforcement; Sports Accessories; Survival Kits/First Aid; Training & Safety Equipment

Crackshot Corp., 2623 E 36th St. N, Tulsa, OK 74110, P: 800-667-1753, F: 918-838-1271, www.crackshotcorp.com
Archery; Backpacking; Camping; Footwear; Hunting Accessories; Men & Women's Clothing; Training & Safety Equipment

Creative Castings/Les Douglas, 12789 Olympic View Rd. NW, Silverdale, WA 98383, P: 800-580-6516, F: 800-580-0495, www.wildlifepins.com
Custom Manufacturing; Emblems & Decals; Outdoor Art, Jewelry, Sculpture; Pet Supplies; Retailer Services; Watches; Wholesaler/Distributor

Creative Pet Products, P.O. Box 39, Spring Valley, WI 54767, P: 888-436-4566, F: 877-269-6911, www.petfirstaidkits.com
Gloves, Mitts, Hats; Pet Supplies; Survival Kits/First Aid; Training & Safety Equipment

Crest Ultrasonics Corp., P.O. Box 7266, Trenton, NJ 08628, P: 800-273-7822, F: 877-254-7939, www.crest-ultrasonics.com
Custom Manufacturing; Firearms Maintenance Equipment; Gun Parts/Gunsmithing; Law Enforcement; Lubricants; Shooting Range Equipment; Wholesaler/Distributor

Crimson Trace Holdings, LLC/Lasergrips, 9780 SW Freeman Dr., Wilsonville, OR 97070, P: 800-442-2406, F: 503-783-5334, www.crimsontrace.com
Firearms; Gun Grips & Stocks; Hunting Accessories; Law Enforcement; Scopes, Sights & Accessories; Training & Safety Equipment

Critter Cribs, P.O. Box 48545, Fort Worth, TX 76148, P: 877-611-2742, F: 866-351-3291, www.crittercribs.com
Camouflage; Hunting Accessories; Law Enforcement; Pet Supplies

Crooked Horn Outfitters, 26315 Trotter Dr., Tehachapi, CA 93561, P: 877-722-5872, F: 661-822-9100, www.crookedhorn.com
Archery; Bags & Equipment Cases; Binoculars; Hunting Accessories

Crosman Corp., Inc., Routes 5 and 20, East Bloomfield, NY 14443, P: 800-724-7486, F: 585-657-5405, www.crosman.com
Airguns; Airsoft; Ammunition; Archery; Crossbows & Accessories; Scopes, Sights & Accessories; Shooting Range Equipment; Targets

Crye Precision, LLC, 63 Flushing Ave., Suite 252, Brooklyn, NY 11205, P: 718-246-3838, F: 718-246-3833, www.cryeprecision.com
Bags & Equipment Cases; Camouflage; Custom Manufacturing; Law Enforcement; Men's Clothing

Cuppa, 3131 Morris St. N, St. Petersburg, FL 33713, P: 800-551-6541, F: 727-820-9212, www.cuppa.net
Custom Manufacturing; Emblems & Decals; Law Enforcement; Outdoor Art, Jewelry, Sculpture; Retailer Services

Custom Leather, 460 Bingemans Centre Dr., Kitchener, Ontario N2B 3X9, CANADA, P: 800-265-4504, F: 519-741-2072, www.customleather.com
Custom Manufacturing; Gun Cases; Hunting Accessories; Leathergoods

Cutting Edge Tactical, 166 Mariners Way, Moyock, NC 27958, P: 800-716-9425, F: 252-435-2284, www.cuttingedgetactical.com
Bags & Equipment Cases; Binoculars; Eyewear; Footwear; Gun Grips & Stocks; Law Enforcement; Lighting Products; Training & Safety Equipment

Cybrics, Ltd., No 68, Xing Yun Rd., Jin San Industrial Area, Yiwu, Zhejiang 322011, CHINA, P: 011 8657985556142, F: 011 8657985556210, www.cybrics.eu
Bags & Equipment Cases; Camouflage; Gloves, Mitts, Hats; Men & Women's Clothing

Cygnus Law Enforcement Group, 1233 Janesville Ave., Fort Atkinson, WI 53538, P: 800-547-7377, F: 303-322-0627, www.officer.com
Law Enforcement

Cylinder & Slide, Inc., 245 E. 4th St., Fremont, NE 68025, P: 800-448-1713, F: 402-721-0263, www.cylinder-slide.com
Firearms; Gun Barrels; Gun Grips & Stocks; Gun Parts/Gunsmithing; Magazines, Cartridge; Scopes, Sights & Accessories; Wholesaler/Distributor

D

DAC Technologies/GunMaster, 12120 Colonel Glenn Rd., Suite 6200, Little Rock, AR 72210, P: 800-920-0098, F: 501-661-9108, www.dactec.com
Black Powder Accessories; Camping; Cooking Equipment/Accessories; Firearms Maintenance Equipment; Gun Cabinets/Racks/Safes; Gun Locks; Hunting Accessories; Wholesaler/Distributor

DMT-Diamond Machine Technology, 84 Hayes Memorial Dr., Marlborough, MA 01752, P: 800-666-4368, F: 508-485-3924, www.dmtsharp.com
Archery; Cooking Equipment/Accessories; Cutlery; Hunting Accessories; Knives/Knife Cases; Sharpeners; Sports Accessories; Taxidermy

D & K Mfg., Co., Inc., 5180 US Hwy. 380, Bridgeport, TX 76426, P: 800-553-1028, F: 940-683-0248, www.d-k.net
Bags & Equipment Cases; Custom Manufacturing; Emblems & Decals; Law Enforcement; Leathergoods

D.S.A., Inc., 27 W. 990 Industrial Ave. (60010), P.O. Box 370, Lake Barrington, IL 60011, P: 847-277-7258, F: 847-277-7263, www.dsarms.com
Ammunition; Books/Industry Publications; Firearms; Gun Grips & Stocks; Gun Parts/Gunsmithing; Law Enforcement; Magazines, Cartridge; Scopes, Sights & Accessories

Daisy Manufacturing Co./Daisy Outdoors Products, 400 W. Stribling Dr., P.O. Box 220, Rogers, AR 72756, P: 800-643-3458, F: 479-636-0573, www.daisy.com
Airguns; Airsoft; Ammunition; Clay Targets; Eyewear; Scopes, Sights & Accessories; Targets; Training & Safety Equipment

Dakota Arms, Inc., 1310 Industry Rd., Sturgis, SD 57785, P: 605-347-4686, F: 605-347-4459, www.dakotaarms.com
Ammunition; Custom Manufacturing; Export/Import Specialists; Firearms; Gun Cases; Gun Grips & Stocks; Gun Parts/Gunsmithing; Reloading

Damascus Protective Gear, P.O. Box 543, Rutland, VT, 05702, P: 800-305-2417, F: 805-639-0610, www.damascusgear.com
Archery; Custom Manufacturing; Gloves, Mitts, Hats; Law Enforcement; Leathergoods

Danalco, Inc., 1020 Hamilton Rd., Suite G, Duarte, CA 91010, P: 800-868-2629, F: 800-216-9938, www.danalco.com
Footwear; Gloves, Mitts, Hats

Dan's Whetstone Co., Inc./Washita Mountain Whetstone Co., 418 Hilltop Rd., Pearcy, AR 71964, P: 501-767-1616, F: 501-767-9598, www.danswhetstone.com
Black Powder Accessories; Camping; Cutlery; Gun Parts/Gunsmithing; Hunting Accessories; Knives/Knife Cases; Sharpeners; Sports Accessories

Daniel Defense, Inc., 6002 Commerce Blvd., Suite 109, Savannah, GA 31408, P: 866-554-4867, F: 912-964-4237, www.danieldefense.com
Firearms

Danner, Inc., 17634 NE Airport Way, Portland, OR 97230, P: 800-345-0430, F: 503-251-1119
Footwear

Darkwoods Blind, LLC, 1209 SE 44th, Suite 2, Oklahoma City, OK 73129, P: 405-520-6754, F: 405-677-2262, www.darkwoodsblind.com
Archery; Blinds; Camouflage; Custom Manufacturing; Firearms; Hunting Accessories; Outfitter; Vehicles, Utility & Rec

Darn Tough Vermont, 364 Whetstone Dr., P.O. Box 307, Northfield, VT 05663, P: 877-DARNTUFF, F: 802-485-6140, www.darntough.com
Backpacking; Camping; Footwear; Hunting Accessories; Men & Women's Clothing

Davidson's, 6100 Wilkinson Dr., Prescott, AZ, 86301, P: 800-367-4867, F: 928-776-0344, www.galleryofguns.com
Ammunition; Firearms; Law Enforcement; Magazines, Cartridge; Online Services; Scopes, Sights & Accessories; Wholesaler/Distributor

Day Six Outdoors, 1150 Brookstone Centre Parkway, Columbus, GA 31904, P: 877-DAY-SIX0, F: 706-323-0178, www.day6outdoors.com
Feeder Equipment; Wildlife Management

Del Norte Outdoors, P.O. Box 5046, Santa Maria, CA 93456, P: 805-474-1793, F: 805-474-1793, www.delnorteoutdoors.com
Archery; Hunting Accessories; Sports Accessories

Del-Ton, Inc., 218B Aviation Pkwy., Elizabethtown, NC 28337, P: 910-645-2172, F: 910-645-2244, www.del-ton.com
Firearms; Gun Barrels; Gun Parts/Gunsmithing; Law Enforcement; Wholesaler/Distributor

DeLorme, Two DeLorme Dr., Yarmouth, ME 04096, P: 800-335-6763, F: 800-575-2244, www.delorme.com
Books/Industry Publications; Computer Software; Hunting Accessories; Sports Accessories; Tours/Travel

Demyan, 10, 2nd Donskoy Ln., Moscow, 119071, RUSSIAN FEDERATION, P: 011 74959847629, F: 011 74959847629, www.demyan.info
Airguns; Firearms

Dengta Sinpraise Weaving & Dressing Co., Ltd., Tai Zihe District, Wangshuitai Pangjiahe, Liao Yang, LiaoNing Province 111000, CHINA, P: 011 964193305888, F: 011 864193990566, www.sinpraise-hunting.com
Camouflage; Camping; Men & Women's Clothing; Sports Accessories

DeSantis Holster and Leather Goods Co., 431 Bayview Ave., Amityville, NY 11701, P: 800-424-1236, F: 631-841-6320, www.desantisholster.com
Bags & Equipment Cases; Gun Cases; Holsters; Hunting Accessories; Law Enforcement; Leathergoods

Desert Tactical Arms, P.O. Box 65816, Salt Lake City, UT 84165, P: 801-975-7272, F: 801-908-6425, www.deserttacticalarms.com
Firearms; Law Enforcement

Desiccare, Inc., 3400 Pomona Blvd., Pomona, CA 91768, P: 800-446-6650, F: 909-444-9045, www.desiccare.com
Food; Footwear; Gun Cabinets/Racks/Safes; Leathergoods; Scents & Lures

Diamondback Tactical, 23040 N. 11th Ave., Bldg. 1, Phoenix, AZ 85027, P: 800-735-7030, F: 623-583-0674, www.diamondbacktactical.com
Law Enforcement

Diana/Mayer & Grammelspacher GmbH & Co. KG, Karlstr, 34, Rastatt, 76437, GERMANY, P: 011 4972227620, F: 011 49722276278, www.diana-airguns.de
Airguns; Scopes, Sights & Accessories

Dillon Precision Products, Inc., 8009 E. Dillon's Way, Scottsdale, AZ 85260, P: 800-223-4570, F: 480-998-2786, www.dillonprecision.com
Bags & Equipment Cases; Feeder Equipment; Hearing Protection; Holsters; Hunting Accessories; Reloading

Dimension 3D Printing, 7655 Commerce Way, Eden Prairie, MN 55344, P: 888-480-3548, F: 952-294-3715, www.dimensionprinting.com
Computer Software; Custom Manufacturing; Gun Parts/Gunsmithing; Hunting Accessories; Scopes, Sights & Accessories

Ding Zing Chemical Products Co., Ltd., No. 8-1 Pei-Lin Rd., Hsiao-Kang Dist., Kaohsiung, 812, TAIWAN, P: 011 88678070166, F: 011 88678071616, www.dingzing.com
Backpacking; Bags & Equipment Cases; Camping; Custom Manufacturing; Footwear; Gloves, Mitts, Hats; Men & Women's Clothing; Sports Accessories

Directex, 304 S. Leighton Ave., Anniston, AL 36207, P: 800-845-3603, F: 256-235-2275, www/directex.net
Archery; Backpacking; Bags & Equipment Cases; Custom Manufacturing; Export/Import Specialists; Gun Cases; Holsters; Hunting Accessories

Dixie Gun Works, Inc., 1412 W. Reelfoot Ave., P.O. Box 130, Union City, TN 38281, P: 800-238-6785, F: 731-885-0440, www.dixiegunworks.com
Black Powder Accessories; Book/Industry Publications; Firearms; Gun Parts/Gunsmithing; Hunting Accessories; Knives/Knife Cases

DNZ Products, LLC/Game Reaper & Freedom Reaper Scope Mounts, 2710 Wilkins Dr., Sanford, NC 27330, P: 919-777-9608, F: 919-777-9609, www.dnzproducts.com
Black Powder Accessories; Custom Manufacturing; Gun Parts/Gunsmithing; Hunting Accessories; Scopes, Sights & Accessories

Do-All Traps, LLC/dba Do-All Outdoors, 216 19th Ave. N, Nashville, TN 37203, P: 800-252-9247, F: 800-633-3172, www.doalloutdoors.com
Clay Targets; Gun Cases; Hunting Accessories; Outdoor Art, Jewelry, Sculpture; Recoil Protection Devices & Services; Shooting Range Equipment; Targets; Taxidermy

Doc's Deer Farm and Scents, 2118 Niles-Cortland Rd., Cortland, OH 44420, P: 330-638-9507, F: 330-638-2772, www.docsdeerscents.com
Archery; Hunting Accessories; Scents & Lures

Docter Optic/Imported by Merkel USA, 7661 Commerce Lane, Trussville, AL 35173, P: 800-821-3021, F: 205-655-7078, www.merkel-usa.com
Binoculars; Scopes, Sights & Accessories

Dogtra Co., 22912 Lockness Ave., Torrance, CA, 90501, P: 888-811-9111, F: 310-534-9111, www.dogtra.com
Hunting Accessories; Pet Supplies; Training & Safety Equipment

Dokken Dog Supply, Inc., 4186 W. 85th St., Northfield, MN 55057, P: 507-744-2616, F: 507-744-5575, www.deadfowltrainer.com
Hunting Accessories; Pet Supplies; Scents & Lures; Training & Safety Equipment

DoubleStar/J&T Distributing, P.O. Box 430, Winchester, KY 40391, P: 888-736-7725, F: 859-745-4638, www.jtdistributing.com
Firearms; Firearms Maintenance Equipment; Gun Barrels; Gun Parts/Gunsmithing; Magazines, Cartridge; Wholesaler/Distributor

Down Range Mfg., LLC, 4170 N. Gun Powder Circle, Hastings, NE 68901, P: 402-463-3415, F: 402-463-3452, www.downrangemfg.com
Ammunition; Clay Targets; Custom Manufacturing; Reloading

Down Wind Scents, LLC, P.O. Box 549, Severna Park, MD 21146, P: 410-647-8451, F: 410-647-7828, www.downwindscents.com
Archery; Firearms Maintenance Equipment; Hunting Accessories; Lubricants; Scents & Lures

DPMS Firearms, LLC, 3312 12th St. SE, St. Cloud, MN 56304, P: 800-578-3767, F: 320-258-4449, www.dpmsinc.com
Firearms; Scopes, Sights & Accessories

Dri Duck Traders, 7007 College Blvd., Suite 700, Overland Park, KS 66221, P: 866-852-8222, F: 913-234-6280, www.driducktraders.com
Camouflage; Men & Women's Clothing

DriFire, LLC, 3151 Williams Rd., Suite E, Columbus, GA 31909, P: 866-266-4035, F: 706-507-7556, www.drifire.com
Camouflage; Men & Women's Clothing; Training & Safety Equipment

DryGuy, LLC, P.O. Box 1102, Mercer Island, WA 98040, P: 888-330-9452, F: 206-232-9830, www.maxxdry.com
Backpacking; Bags & Equipment Cases; Camping; Footwear; Gloves, Mitts, Hats; Hunting Accessories; Sports Accessories; Wholesaler/Distributor

Du-Lite Corp., 171 River Rd., Middletown, CT 06457, P: 860-347-2505, F: 860-344-9404, www.du-lite.com
Gunsmithing; Lubricants

Duck Commander Co., Inc./Buck Commander Co., Inc., 1978 Brownlee Rd., Calhoun, LA 71225, P: 318-396-1126, F: 318-396-1127, www.duckcommander.com, www.buckcommander.com
Camping; Emblems & Decals; Food; Game Calls; Gun Cases; Hunting Accessories, Men & Women's Clothing; Videos

Ducks Unlimited, Inc., One Waterfowl Way, Memphis, TN 38120, P: 800-45-DUCKS, F: 901-758-3850, www.ducks.org
Books/Industry Publications; Camouflage; Decoys; Firearms; Hunting Accessories; Outdoor Art, Jewelry, Sculpture; Wildlife Management

Duk-Inn-Blind, 49750 Alpine Dr., Macomb, MI 48044, P: 586-855-7494, F: 603-626-4672
Blinds; Camouflage; Hunting Accessories; Wholesaler/Distributor

Dummies Unlimited, Inc., 2435 Pine St., Pomona, CA 91767, P: 866-4DUMMIES, F: 909-392-7510, F: 909-392-7510, www.dummiesunlimited.com
Law Enforcement; Shooting Range Equipment; Targets; Training & Safety Equipment

Duostock Designs, Inc., P.O. Box 32, Welling, OK 74471, P: 866-386-7865, F: 918-431-3182, www.duostock.com
Firearms; Gun Grips & Stocks; Law Enforcement; Recoil Protection Devices & Services

Durasight Scope Mounting Systems, 5988 Peachtree Corners East, Norcross, GA 30071, P: 800-321-8767, F: 770-242-8546, www.durasight.com
Scopes, Sights & Accessories

Dynamic Research Technologies, LLC, 405 N. Lyon St., Grant City, MO 64456, P: 660-564-2331, F: 660-564-2103, www.drtammo.com
Ammunition; Reloading

E

E-Z Mount Corp., 1706 N. River Dr., San Angelo, TX 76902, P: 800-292-3756, F: 325-658-4951, www.ezmountcorp@zipnet.us
Gun Cabinets/Racks/Safes

E-Z Pull Trigger, 932 W. 5th St., Centralia, IL 62801, P: 618-532-6964, F: 618-532-5154, www.ezpulltriggerassist.com
Firearms; Gun Parts/Gunsmithing; Hunting Accessories

E.A.R., Inc./Insta-Mold Div., P.O. Box 18888, Boulder, CO 80303, P: 800-525-2690, F: 303-447-2637, www.earinc.com
Eyewear; Hearing Protection; Law Enforcement; Shooting Range Equipment; Wholesaler/Distributor

ER Shaw/Small Arms Mfg., 5312 Thoms Run Rd., Bridgeville, PA 15017, P: 412-221-4343, F: 412-221-4303, www.ershawbarrels.com
Custom Manufacturing; Firearms; Gun Barrels

ECS Composites, 3560 Rogue River Hwy., Grants Pass, OR 97527, P: 541-476-8871, F: 541-474-2479, www.transitcases.com
Custom Manufacturing; Gun Cases; Law Enforcement; Sports Accessories

EMCO Supply, Inc./Red Rock Outdoor Gear, 2601 Dutton Ave., Waco, TX 76711, P: 800-342-4654, F: 254-662-0045
Backpacking; Bags & Equipment Cases; Blinds; Camouflage; Compasses; Game Calls; Hunting Accessories; Law Enforcement

E.M.F. Co., Inc./Purveyors of Fine Firearms Since 1956, 1900 E. Warner Ave., Suite 1-D, Santa Ana, CA 92705, P: 800-430-1310, F: 800-508-1824, www.emf-company.com
Black Powder Accessories; Firearms; Gun Parts/Gunsmithing; Holsters; Leathergoods; Wholesaler/Distributor

EOTAC, 1940 Old Dunbar Rd., West Columbia, SC 29172, P: 803-744-9930, F: 803-744-9933, www.eotac.com
Tactical Clothing

ESS Goggles, P.O. Box 1017, Sun Valley, ID 83353, P: 877-726-4072, F: 208-726-4563
Eyewear; Hunting Accessories; Law Enforcement; Shooting Range Equipment; Training & Safety Equipment

ETL/Secure Logic, 2351 Tenaya Dr., Modesto, CA 95354, P: 800-344-3242, F: 209-529-3854, www.securelogiconline.com
Firearms; Gun Cabinets/Racks/Safes; Training & Safety Equipment

EZ 4473/American Firearms Software, 5955 Edmond St., Las Vegas, NV 89118, P: 702-364-9022, F: 702-364-9063, www.ez4473.com
Computer Software; Retailer Services

EZE-LAP® Diamond Products, 3572 Arrowhead Dr., Carson City, NV 89706, P: 800-843-4815, F: 775-888-9555, www.eze-lap.com
Camping; Cooking Equipment/Accessories; Cutlery; Gun Parts/Gunsmithing; Hunting Accessories; Sharpeners; Sports Accessories

Eagle Grips, Inc., 460 Randy Rd., Carol Stream, IL, 60188, P: 800-323-6144, F: 630-260-0486, www.eaglegrips.com
Gun Grips & Stocks

Eagle Imports, Inc., 1750 Brielle Ave., Suite B-1, Wanamassa, NJ 07712, P: 732-493-0333, F: 732-493-0301, www.bersafirearmsusa.com

Export/Import Specialists; Firearms; Holsters; Magazines, Cartridge; Wholesaler/Distributor

Eagle Industries Unlimited, Inc., 1000 Biltmore Dr., Fenton, MO 63026, P: 888-343-7547, F: 636-349-0321, www.eagleindustries.com
Backpacking; Bags & Equipment Cases; Camping; Gun Cases; Holsters; Hunting Accessories; Law Enforcement; Sports Accessories

Eagle Seed Co., 8496 Swan Pond Rd., P.O. Box 308, Weiner, AR 72479, P: 870-684-7377, F: 870-684-2225, www.eagleseed.com
Custom Manufacturing; Retail Packaging; Wholesaler/Distributor; Wildlife Management

Ear Phone Connection, 25139 Avenue Stanford, Valencia, CA 91355, P: 888-372-1888, F: 661-775-5622, www.earphoneconnect.com
Airsoft; Hearing Protection; Law Enforcement; Paintball Accessories; Two-Way Radios

EarHugger Safety Equipment, Inc., 1819 N. Main St., Suite 8, Spanish Fork, UT 84660, P: 800-236-1449, F: 801-371-8901, www.earhuggersafety.com
Law Enforcement

Easy Loop Lock, LLC, 8049 Monetary Dr., Suite D-4, Riviera Beach, FL 33404, P: 561-304-4990, F: 561-337-4655, www.ellock.com
Camping; Gun Locks; Hunting Accessories; Sports Accessories; Wholesaler/Distributor

E-Z Mount Corp., 1706 N. River Dr., San Angelo, TX 76902, P: 800-292-3756, F: 325-658-4951, www.ezmountcorp@zipnet.us
Gun Cabinets/Racks/Safes

E-Z Pull Trigger, 932 W. 5th St., Centralia, IL 62801, P: 618-532-6964, F: 618-532-5154, www.ezpulltriggerassist.com
Firearms; Gun Parts/Gunsmithing; Hunting Accessories

Eberlestock, P.O. Box 862, Boise, ID 83701, P: 877-866-3047, F: 240-526-2632, www.eberlestock.com
Archery; Backpacking; Bags & Equipment Cases; Gun Grips & Stocks; Hunting Accessories; Law Enforcement

Ed Brown Products, Inc., P.O. Box 492, Perry, MO 63462, P: 573-565-3261, F: 573-565-2791, www.edbrown.com
Computer Software; Custom Manufacturing; Firearms; Gun Barrels; Gun Parts/Gunsmithing; Magazines, Cartridge; Scopes, Sights & Accessories

EdgeCraft Corp./Chefs Choice, 825 Southwood Rd., Avondale, PA 19311, P: 800-342-3255, F: 610-268-3545, www.edgecraft.com
Cooking Equipment/Accessories; Custom Manufacturing; Cutlery; Export/Import Specialists; Hunting Accessories; Knives/Knife Cases; Sharpeners

Edgemaker Co., The/(formerly) The Jennex Co., 3902 Funston St., Toledo, OH 43612, P: 800-531-EDGE, F: 419-478-0833, www.edgemaker.com
Camping; Cutlery; Hunting Accessories; Sharpeners; Sports Accessories; Wholesaler/Distributor

El Paso Saddlery, 2025 E. Yandell, El Paso, TX 79903, P: 915-544-2233, F: 915-544-2535, www.epsaddlery.com
Holsters; Leathergoods

Elastic Products/Industrial Opportunities, Inc., 2586 Hwy. 19, P.O. Box 1649, Andrews, NC 28901, P: 800-872-4264, F: 828-321-4784, www.elasticproducts.com
Camouflage; Custom Manufacturing; Hunting Accessories; Men's Clothing

ELCAN Optical Technologies, 1601 N. Plano Rd., Richardson, TX 75081, P: 877-TXELCAN, F: 972-344-8260, www.elcan.com
Binoculars; Custom Manufacturing; Law Enforcement; Scopes, Sights & Accessories

Elder Hosiery Mills, Inc., 139 Homewood Ave., P.O. Box 2377, Burlington, NC 27217, P: 800-745-0267, F: 336-226-5846, www.elderhosiery.com
Footwear

Eley Limited/Eley Hawk Limited, Selco Way, First Ave., Minworth Industrial Estate, Minworth, Sutton Coldfield, West Midlands B76 1BA, UNITED KINGDOM, P: 011 4401213134567, F: 011-4401213134568, www.eleyammunition.com, www.eleyhawkltd.com
Ammunition

Elite First Aid, Inc., 700 E. Club Blvd., Durham, NC 27704, P: 800-556-2537, F: 919-220-6071, www.elite1staid.com
Backpacking; Camping; Cooking Equipment/Accessories; Hunting Accessories; Sports Accessories; Survival Kits/First Aid; Wholesaler/Distributor

Elite Iron, LLC, 1345 Thunders Trail, Bldg. D, Potomac, MT 59823, P: 406-244-0234, F: 406-244-0135, www.eliteiron.net
Law Enforcement; Scopes, Sights & Accessories

Elite Survival Systems, 310 W. 12th St., P.O. Box 245, Washington, MO 63090, P: 866-340-2778, F: 636-390-2977, www.elitesurvival.com
Backpacking; Bags & Equipment Cases; Custom Manufacturing; Footwear; Gun Cases; Holsters; Knives/Knife Cases; Law Enforcement

Ellett Brothers, 267 Columbia Ave., P.O. Box 128, Chapin, SC 29036, P: 800-845-3711, F: 800-323-3006, www.ellettbrothers.com
Ammunition; Archery; Black Powder Accessories; Firearms; Hunting Accessories; Leathergoods; Scopes, Sights & Accessories; Wholesaler/Distributor

Ellington-Rush, Inc./Cough Silencer/SlingStix, 170 Private Dr., Lula, GA 30554, P: 706-677-2394, F: 706-677-3425, www.coughsilencer.com, www.slingstix.com
Archery; Black Powder Accessories; Game Calls; Hunting Accessories; Law Enforcement; Shooting Range Equipment

Elvex Corp., 13 Trowbridge, Bethel, CT 06801, P: 800-888-6582, F: 203-791-2278, www.elvex.com
Eyewear; Hearing Protection; Hunting Accessories; Law Enforcement; Men's Clothing; Paintball Accessories

Emerson Knives, Inc., 2730 Monterey St., Suite 101, Torrance, CA 90503, P: 310-212-7455, F: 310-212-7289, www.emersonknives.com
Camping; Cutlery; Knives/Knife Cases; Men & Women's Clothing; Wholesaler/Distributor

Empire Pewter Manufacturing, P.O. Box 15, Amsterdam, NY 12010, P: 518-843-0048, F: 518-843-7050
Custom Manufacturing; Emblems & Decals; Outdoor Art, Jewelry, Sculpture

Energizer Holdings, 533 Maryville University Dr., St. Louis, MO 63141, P: 314-985-2000, F: 314-985-2207, www.energizer.com
Backpacking; Camping; Hunting Accessories; Law Enforcement; Lighting Products; Sports Accessories; Survival Kits/First Aid; Training & Safety Equipment

Enforcement Technology Group, Inc., 400 N. Broadway, 4th Floor, Milwaukee, WI 53202, P: 800-873-2872, F: 414-276-1533, www.etgi.us
Custom Manufacturing; Law Enforcement; Online Services; Shooting Range Equipment; Training & Safety Equipment; Wholesaler/Distributor

Entreprise Arms, Inc., 5321 Irwindale Ave., Irwindale, CA 91706-2025, P: 626-962-8712, F: 626-962-4692, www.entreprise.com
Firearms; Gun Parts/Gunsmithing

Environ-Metal, Inc./Hevishot®, 1307 Clark Mill Rd., P.O. Box 834, Sweet Home, OR 97386, P: 541-367-3522, F: 541-367-3552, www.hevishot.com
Ammunition; Law Enforcement; Reloading

EOTAC, 1940 Old Dunbar Rd., West Columbia, SC 29172, P: 888-672-0303, F: 803-744-9933, www.eotac.com
Gloves, Mitts, Hats; Men's Clothing

Epilog Laser, 16371 Table Mountain Pkwy., Golden, CO 80403, P: 303-277-1188, F: 303-277-9669, www.epiloglaser.com

Essential Gear, Inc./eGear, 171 Wells St., Greenfield, MA 01301, P: 800-582-3861, F: 413-772-8947, www.essentialgear.com
Backpacking; Camping; Hunting Accessories; Law Enforcement; Lighting Products; Sports Accessories; Survival Kits/First Aid; Training & Safety Equipment

European American Armory Corp., P.O. Box 560746, Rockledge, FL 32956, P: 321-639-4842, F: 321-639-7006, www.eaacorp.com
Airguns; Firearms

Evans Sports, Inc., 801 Industrial Dr., P.O. Box 20, Houston, MO 65483, P: 800-748-8318, F: 417-967-2819, www.evanssports.com
Ammunition; Bags & Equipment Cases; Camping; Custom Manufacturing; Gun Cabinets/Racks/Safes; Hunting Accessories; Retail Packaging; Sports Accessories

Evolved Habitats, 2261 Morganza Hwy., New Roads, LA 70760, P: 225-638-4016, F: 225-638-4009, www.evolved.com
Archery; Export/Import Specialists; Hunting Accessories; Pet Supplies; Scents & Lures; Wildlife Management

Extendo Bed Co., 223 Roedel Ave., Caldwell, ID 83605, P: 800-752-0706, F: 208-286-0925, www.extendobed.com
Law Enforcement; Training & Safety Equipment

Extreme Dimension Wildlife Calls, LLC, 208 Kennebec Rd., Hampden, ME 04444, P: 866-862-2825, F: 207-862-3925, www.phantomcalls.com
Game Calls

Extreme Shock USA, 182 Camp Jacob Rd., Clintwood, VA 24228, P: 877-337-6772, F: 276-926-6092, www.extremeshockusa.net
Ammunition; Law Enforcement; Lubricants; Reloading

ExtremeBeam Tactical, 2275 Huntington Dr., Suite 872, San Marino, CA 91108, P: 626-372-5898, F: 626-609-0640, www.extremebeamtactical.com
Camping; Law Enforcement; Lighting Products; Outfitter

Exxel Outdoors, Inc., 14214 Atlanta Dr., Laredo, TX 78045, P: 956-724-8933, F: 956-725-2516, www.prestigemfg.com
Camping; Export/Import Specialists; Men's Clothing

F

F&W Media/Krause Publications, 700 E. State St., Iola, WI 54990, P: 800-457-2873, F: 715-445-4087, www.krausebooks.com
Books/Industry Publications; Videos

F.A.I.R. Srl, Via Gitti, 41, Marcheno, 25060, ITALY, P: 011 39030861162, F: 011 390308610179, www.fair.it
Firearms; Gun Barrels; Gun Parts/Gunsmithing; Hunting Accessories

F.A.P. F. LLI Pietta SNC, Via Mandolossa, 102, Gussago, Brescia 25064, ITALY, P: 011 390303737098, F: 011 390303737100, www.pietta.it
Black Powder Accessories; Firearms; Gun Cases; Gun Grips & Stocks; Gun Parts/Gunsmithing; Holsters

F.I.A.V. L. Mazzacchera SPA, Via S. Faustino, 62, Milano, 20134, ITALY, P: 011 390221095411, F: 011 390221095530, www.flav.it
Gun Parts/Gunsmithing

FMG Publications/Shooting Industry Magazine, 12345 World Trade Dr., San Diego, CA 92128, P: 800-537-3006, F: 858-605-0247, www.shootingindustry.com
Books/Industry Publications; Videos

FNH USA, P.O. Box 697, McLean, VA 22101, P: 703-288-1292, F: 703-288-1730, www.fnhusa.com
Ammunition; Firearms; Law Enforcement; Training & Safety Equipment

F.T.C. (Friedheim Tool), 1433 Roosevelt Ave., National City, CA 91950, 619-474-3600, F: 619-474-1300, www.ftcsteamers.com
Firearms Maintenance Equipment

Fab Defense, 43 Yakov Olamy St., Moshav Mishmar Hashiva, 50297, ISRAEL, P: 011 972039603399, F: 011 972039603312, www.fab-defense.com
Gun Grips & Stocks; Law Enforcement; Targets

FailZero, 7825 SW Ellipse Way, Stuart, FL 34997, P: 772-223-6699, F: 772-223-9996
Gun Parts/Gunsmithing

Falcon Industries, P.O. Box 1690, Edgewood, NM 87015, P: 877-281-3783, F: 505-281-3991, www.ergogrips.net
Gun Grips & Stocks; Gun Parts/Gunsmithing; Law Enforcement; Scopes, Sights & Accessories; Sports Accessories

Fasnap® Corp., 3500 Reedy Dr., Elkhart, IN 46514, P: 800-624-2058, F: 574-264-0802, www.fasnap.com
Backpacking; Bags & Equipment Cases; Gun Cases; Holsters; Hunting Accessories; Knives/Knife Cases; Leathergoods; Wholesaler/Distributor

Faulk's Game Call Co., Inc., 616 18th St., Lake Charles, LA 70601, P: 337-436-9726, FL 337-494-7205, www.faulkcalls.com
Game Calls

Fausti Stefano s.r.l., Via Martiri dell'Indipendenza 70, Marcheno (BS), 25060, ITALY, P: 011 390308960220, F: 011 390308610155, www.faustistefanoarms.com
Firearms

Feather Flage "Ducks In A Row Camo"/B & D Garments, LLC, P.O. Box 5326, Lafayette, LA 70502, P: 866-DUK-CAMO, F: 337-896-8137, www.featherflage.com
Camouflage; Wholesaler/Distributor

Federal Premium Ammunition/ATK Commercial Products, 900 Ehlen Dr., Anoka, MN 55303, P: 800-322-2342, F: 763-323-2506, www.federalpremium.com
Ammunition

Feijuang International Corp., 4Fl-1/7, No. 177 Min-Sheng West Road, Taipei, TAIWAN, P: 011 886225520169, F: 011 886225578359
Blinds; Camping; Compasses; Eyewear; Hearing Protection; Hunting Accessories; Sports Accessories

Fenix Flashlights, LLC/4Sevens, LLC, 4896 N. Royal Atlanta Dr., Suite 305, Tucker, GA 30084, P: 866-471-0749, F: 866-323-9544, www.4sevens.com
Backpacking; Camping; Law Enforcement; Lighting Products

FenixLightUS/Casualhome Worldwide, Inc., 29 William St., Amityville, NY 11701, P: 877-FENIXUS, F: 631-789-2970, www.fenixlightus.com
Camping; Law Enforcement; Lighting Products; Scopes, Sights & Accessories; Shooting Range Equipment; Wholesaler/Distributor

Field & Stream Watches, 12481 NW 44th St., Coral Springs, FL 33065, P: 954-509-1476, F: 954-509-1479, www.tfg24gold.com
Camping; Hunting Accessories; Outfitter; Sports Accessories; Watches; Wholesaler/Distributor

Filson, 1555 4th Ave. S, Seattle, WA 98134, P: 800-297-1897, F: 206-624-4539, www.filson.com
Bags & Equipment Cases; Footwear; Gloves, Mitts, Hats; Gun Cases; Hunting Accessories; Leathergoods; Men & Women's Clothing

Final Approach/Bushnell Outdoor Accessories, 9200 Cody, Overland Park, KS 66214, P: 800-423-3537, F: 913-752-3539, www.kolpin-outdoors.com
Bags & Equipment Cases; Blinds; Decoys; Gun Cases; Hunting Accessories; Videos

Fiocchi of America, Inc., 6930 N. Fremont Rd., Ozark, MO 65721, P: 800-721-AMMO, 417-725-1039, www.fiocciusa.com
Ammunition; Reloading

First Choice Armor & Equipment, Inc., 209 Yelton St., Spindale, NC 28160, P: 800-88-ARMOR, F: 866-481-4929, www.firstchoicearmor.com
Law Enforcement; Training & Safety Equipment

First-Light USA, LLC, 320 Cty. Rd. 1100 North, Seymour, IL 61875, P: 877-454-4450, F: 877-454-4420, www.first-light-usa.com
Backpacking; Camping; Firearms; Law Enforcement; Lighting Products; Survival Kits/First Aid; Training & Safety Equipment

Flambeau, Inc., P.O. Box 97, Middlefield, OH 44062, P: 440-632-1631, F: 440-632-1581, www.flambeauoutdoors.com
Bags & Equipment Cases; Crossbows & Accessories; Custom Manufacturing; Decoys; Game Calls; Gun Cases

Fleming & Clark, Ltd., 3013 Honeysuckle Dr., Spring Hill, TN 37174, P: 800-373-6710, F: 931-487-9972, www.flemingandclark.com
Bags & Equipment Cases; Footwear; Gun Cases; Hunting Accessories; Knives/Knife Cases; Leathergoods; Men's Clothing; Wholesaler/Distributor

Flitz International, Ltd., 821 Mohr Ave., Waterford, WI 53185, P: 800-558-8611, F: 262-534-2991, www.flitz.com
Black Powder Accessories; Firearms Maintenance Equipment; Gun Barrels; Gun Grips & Stocks; Gun Parts/Gunsmithing; Knives/Knife Cases; Lubricants; Scopes, Sights & Accessories

Fobus Holsters/CAA-Command Arms Accessories, 780 Haunted Lane, Bensalem, PA 19020, P: 267-803-1517, F: 267-803-1002, www.fobusholsters.com, www.commandarms.com
Bags & Equipment Cases; Firearms; Gun Cases; Gun Grips & Stocks; Gun Parts/Gunsmithing; Holsters; Law Enforcement; Scopes, Sights & Accessories

Foiles Migrators, Inc., 101 N. Industrial Park Dr., Pittsfield, IL 62363, P: 866-83-GEESE, F: 217-285-5995, www.foilesstraitmeat.com
Game Calls; Hunting Accessories

FoodSaver/Jarden Consumer Solutions, 24 Latour Ln., Little Rock, AR 72223, P: 501-821-0138, F: 501-821-0139, www.foodsaver.com
Backpacking; Camping; Cooking Equipment/Accessories; Food; Hunting Accessories

Force One, LLC, 520 Commercial Dr., Fairfield, OH 45014, P: 800-462-7880, F: 513-939-1166, www.forceonearmor.com
Custom Manufacturing; Law Enforcement

Forster Products, Inc., 310 E. Lanark Ave., Lanark, IL 61046, P: 815-493-6360, F: 815-493-2371, www.forsterproducts.com
Black Powder Accessories; Custom Manufacturing; Firearms Maintenance Equipment; Gun Parts/Gunsmithing; Lubricants; Reloading; Scopes, Sights & Accessories

Fort Knox Security Products, 993 N. Industrial Park Rd., Orem, UT 84057, P: 800-821-5216, F: 801-226-5493, www.ftknox.com
Custom Manufacturing; Gun Cabinets/Racks/Safes; Home Furnishings; Hunting Accessories

Foshan City Nanhai Weihong Mold Products Co., Ltd./Xinwei Photo Electricity Industrial Co., Ltd., Da Wo District, Dan Zhao Town, Nanhai, Foshan City, GuangZhou, 528216, CHINA, P: 011 8675785444666, F: 011 8675785444111, www.weihongmj.net
Binoculars; Scopes, Sights & Accessories

Fox Knives Oreste Frati SNC, Via La Mola, 4, Maniago, Pordenone 33085, ITALY, P: 011 39042771814, F: 011 390427700514, www.foxcutlery.com
Camouflage; Camping; Cutlery; Hunting Accessories; Knives/Knife Cases; Law Enforcement; Wholesaler/Distributor

Fox Outdoor Products, 2040 N. 15th Ave., Melrose Park, IL 60160, P: 800-523-4332, F: 708-338-9210, www.foxoutdoor.com
Bags & Equipment Cases; Camouflage; Eyewear; Gun Cases; Holsters; Law Enforcement; Men's Clothing; Wholesaler/Distributor

FoxFury Personal Lighting Solutions, 2091 Elevado Hill Dr., Vista, CA 92084, P: 760-945-4231, F: 760-758-6283, www.foxfury.com
Backpacking; Camping; Hunting Accessories; Law Enforcement; Lighting Products; Paintball Accessories; Sports Accessories; Training & Safety Equipment

FOXPRO, Inc., 14 Fox Hollow Dr., Lewistown, PA 17044, P: 866-463-6977, F: 717-247-3594, www.gofoxpro.com
Archery; Decoys; Game Calls; Hunting Accessories

Foxy Huntress, 17 Windsor Ridge, Frisco, TX 75034, P: 866-370-1343, F: 972-370-1343, www.foxyhuntress.com
Camouflage; Women's Clothing

Franchi, 17603 Indian Head Hwy., Accokeek, MD 20607, P: 800-264-4962, www.franchiusa.com
Firearms

Franklin Sports, Inc./Uniforce Tactical Division, 17 Campanelli Pkwy., Stoughton, MA 02072, P: 800-225-8647, F: 781-341-3220, www.uniforcetactical.com
Camouflage; Eyewear; Gloves, Mitts, Hats; Law Enforcement; Leathergoods; Men's Clothing; Wholesaler/Distributor

Franzen Security Products, Inc., 680 Flinn Ave., Suite 35, Moorpark, CA 93021, P: 800-922-7656, F: 805-529-0446, www.securecase.com
Bags & Equipment Cases; Custom Manufacturing; Gun Cases; Gun Locks; Hunting Accessories; Law Enforcement; Shooting Range Equipment; Training & Safety Equipment

Fraternal Blue Line, P.O. Box 260199, Boston, MA 02126, P: 617-212-1288, F: 617-249-0857, www.fraternalblueline.org
Custom Manufacturing; Emblems & Decals; Law Enforcement; Men & Women's Clothing; Wholesaler/Distributor

Freedom Arms, Inc., 314 Hwy. 239, Freedom, WY 83120, P: 800-833-4432, F: 800-252-4867, www.freedomarms.com
Firearms; Gun Cases; Holsters; Scopes, Sights & Accessories

Freelinc, 266 W. Center St., Orem, UT 84057, P: 866-467-1199, F: 801-672-3003, www.freelinc.com
Law Enforcement

Frogg Toggs, 131 Sundown Drive NW, P.O. Box 609, Arab, AL 35016, P: 800-349-1835, F: 256-931-1585, www.froggtoggs.com
Backpacking; Camouflage; Footwear; Hunting Accessories; Men & Women's Clothing

Front Line/Army Equipment, Ltd., 6 Platin St., Rishon-Le-Zion, 75653, ISRAEL, P: 011 97239519460, F: 011 97239519463, www.front-line.co.il
Bags & Equipment Cases; Gun Cases; Holsters

Frost Cutlery Co., 6861 Mountain View Rd., Ooltewah, TN 37363, P: 800-251-7768, F: 423-894-9576, www.frostcutlery.com
Camping; Cooking Equipment/Accessories; Cutlery; Hunting Accessories; Knives/Knife Cases; Retail Packaging; Sharpeners; Wholesaler/Distributor

Fujinon, Inc., 10 High Point Dr., Wayne, NJ 07470, P: 973-633-5600, F: 973-694-8299, www.fujinon.jp.com
Binoculars; Scopes, Sights & Accessories

Fusion Tactical, 4200 Chino Hills Pkwy., Suite 820-143, Chino Hills, CA 91709, P: 909-393-9450, F: 909-606-6834
Custom Manufacturing; Retail Packaging; Sports Accessories; Training & Safety Equipment

G

G24 Innovations, Ltd., Solar Power, Westloog Environmental Centre, Cardiff, CF3 2EE, UNITED KINGDON, 011 442920837340, F: 011 443930837341, www.g24i.com
Bags & Equipment Cases; Camping; Custom Manufacturing; Lighting Products

G96 Products Co., Inc., 85-5th Ave., Bldg. 6, P.O. Box 1684, Paterson, NJ 07544, P: 877-332-0035, F: 973-684-3848, www.g96.com
Black Powder Accessories; Firearms Maintenance Equipment; Lubricants

GG&G, 3602 E. 42nd Stravenue, Tucson, AZ 85713, P: 800-380-2540, F: 520-748-7583, www.gggaz.com
Custom Manufacturing; Firearms; Gun Barrels; Gun Grips & Stocks, Gun Parts/Gunsmithing; Law Enforcement; Lighting Products; Scopes, Sights & Accessories

G.A. Precision, 1141 Swift St., N. Kansas City, MO 64116, P: 816-221-1844, F: 816-421-4958, www.gaprecision.net
Firearms

G.G. Telecom, Inc./Spypoint, 555 78 Rd., Suite 353, Swanton, VT 05488, CANADA, P: 888-SPYPOINT, F: 819-604-1644, www.spy-point.com
Hunting Accessories; Photographic Equipment

G-LOX, 520 Sampson St., Houston, TX 77003, P: 713-228-8944, F: 713-228-8947, www.g-lox.com
Archery; Gun Cabinets/Racks/Safes; Gun Locks; Hunting Accessories; Shooting Range Equipment

GSM Products/Walker Game Ear, 3385 Roy Orr Blvd., Grand Prairie, TX 75050, P: 877-269-8490, F: 760-450-1014, www.gsmoutdoors.com
Archery; Feeder Equipment; Hearing Protection; Hunting Accessories; Lighting Products; Scopes, Sights & Accessories; Wildlife Management

GT Industrial Products, 10650 Irma Dr., Suite 1, Northglenn, CO 80233, P: 303-280-5777, F: 303-280-5778, www.gt-ind.com
Camping; Hunting Accessories; Lighting Products; Survival Kits/First Aid

Galati Gear/Galati International, 616 Burley Ridge Rd., P.O. Box 10, Wesco, MO 65586, P: 877-425-2847, F: 573-775-4308, www.galatigear.com, www.galatiinternational.com
Bags & Equipment Cases; Cutlery; Gun Cases; Holsters; Knives/Knife Cases; Law Enforcement; Sports Accessories

Galileo, 13872 SW 119th Ave., Miami, FL 33186, P: 800-548-3537, F: 305-234-8510, www.galileosplace.com
Binoculars; Photographic Equipment; Scopes, Sights & Accessories; Telescopes

Gamebore Cartridge Co., Ltd., Great Union St., Hull, HU9 1AR, UNITED KINGDOM, P: 011 441482223707, F: 011 4414823252225, www.gamebore.com
Ammunition; Cartridges

Gamehide–Core Resources, 12257C Nicollet Ave. S, Burnsville, MN 55337, P: 888-267-3591, F: 952-895-8845, www.gamehide.com
Archery; Camouflage; Custom Manufacturing; Export/Import Specialists; Gloves, Mitts, Hats; Hunting Accessories; Men & Women's Clothing

Gamo USA Corp., 3911 SW 47th Ave., Suite 914, Fort Lauderdale, FL 33314, P: 954-581-5822, F: 954-581-3165, www.gamousa.com
Airguns; Ammunition; Hunting Accessories; Online Services; Scopes, Sights & Accessories; Targets

Garmin International, 1200 E. 151st St., Olathe, KS 66062, P: 913-397-8200, F: 913-397-8282, www.garmin.com
Backpacking; Camping; Compasses; Computer Software; Hunting Accessories; Sports Accessories; Two-Way Radios; Vehicles, Utility & Rec

Garrett Metal Detectors, 1881 W. State St., Garland, TX 75042, P: 972-494-6151, F: 972-494-1881, www.garrett.com
Law Enforcement; Sports Accessories

Geissele Automatics, LLC, 1920 W. Marshall St., Norristown, PA 19403, P: 610-272-2060, F: 610-272-2069, www.ar15trigger.com
Firearms; Gun Parts/Gunsmithing

Gemstar Manufacturing, 1515 N. 5th St., Cannon Falls, MN 55009, P: 800-533-3631, F: 507-263-3129
Bags & Equipment Cases; Crossbows & Accessories; Custom Manufacturing; Gun Cases; Law Enforcement; Paintball Accessories; Sports Accessories; Survival Kits/First Aid

Gemtech, P.O. Box 140618, Boise, ID 83714, P: 208-939-7222, www.gem-tech.com
Firearms; Hearing Protection; Law Enforcement; Training & Safety Equipment; Wildlife Management

General Inspection, LLC, 10585 Enterprise Dr., Davisburg, MI 48350, P: 888-817-6314, F: 248-625-0789, www.geninsp.com
Ammunition; Custom Manufacturing

General Starlight Co., 250 Harding Blvd. W, P.O. Box 32154, Richmond Hill, Ontario L4C 9S3, CANADA, P: 905-850-0990, www.electrooptic.com
Binoculars; Law Enforcement; Photographic Equipment; Scopes, Sights & Accessories; Telescopes; Training & Safety Equipment; Wholesaler/Distributor

Generation Guns–(G2) ICS, No. 6, Lane 205, Dongihou Rd., Shengang Township, Taichung County, 429, TAIWAN, P: 011 886425256461, F: 011 886425256484, www.icsbb.com
Airsoft; Sports Accessories

Gerber Legendary Blades, 14200 SW 72nd Ave., Portland, OR 97224, P: 800-443-4871, F: 307-857-4702, www.gerbergear.com
Knives/Knife Cases; Law Enforcement; Lighting Products

Gerstner & Sons, Inc., 20 Gerstner Way, Dayton, OH 45402, P: 937-228-1662, F: 937-228-8557, www.gerstnerusa.com
Bags & Equipment Cases; Custom Manufacturing; Gun Cabinets/Racks/Safes; Gun Cases; Home Furnishings; Knives/Knife Cases; Shooting Range Equipment

GH Armor Systems, 1 Sentry Dr., Dover, TN 37058, P: 866-920-5940, F: 866-920-5941, www.gharmorsystems.com
Custom Manufacturing; Law Enforcement; Men & Women's Clothing

Giant International/Motorola Consumer Products, 3495 Piedmont Rd., Suite 920, Bldg. Ten, Atlanta, GA 30305, P: 800-638-5119, F: 678-904-6030, www.giantintl.com
Backpacking; Camouflage; Camping; Hunting Accessories; Training & Safety Equipment; Two-Way Radios

Ginsu Outdoors, 118 E. Douglas Rd., Walnut Ridge, AR 72476, P: 800-982-5233, F: 870-886-9142, www.ginsuoutdoors.com
Cutlery; Hunting Accessories; Knives/Knife Cases

Girsan–Yavuz 16, Batlama Deresi Mevkii Sunta Sok. No 19, Giresun, 28200, TURKEY, P: 011 905332160201, F: 011 904542153928, www.yavuz16.com
Firearms; Gun Parts/Gunsmithing

Glacier Glove, 4890 Aircenter Circle, Suite 210, Reno, NV 89502, P: 800-728-8235, F: 775-825-6544, www.glacierglove.com
Gloves, Mitts, Hats; Hunting Accessories; Men's Clothing

Glendo Corp./GRS Tools, 900 Overlander Rd., P.O. Box 1153, Emporia, KS 66801, P: 800-835-3519, F: 620-343-9640, www.glendo.com
Books/Industry Publications; Custom Manufacturing; Lighting Products; Scopes, Sights & Accessories; Videos; Wholesaler/Distributor

Glock, Inc., 6000 Highlands Pkwy., Smyrna, GA 30082, P: 770-432-1202, F: 770-433-8719, www.glock.com, www.teamglock.com, www.glocktraining.com, www.gssfonline.com
Firearms; Gun Parts/Gunsmithing; Holsters; Knives/Knife Cases; Law Enforcement; Men & Women's Clothing; Retailer Services

Goex, Inc., P.O. Box 659, Doyline, LA 71023, P: 318-382-9300, F: 318-382-9303, www.goexpowder.com
Ammunition; Black Powder/Smokeless Powder

Gold House Hardware (China), Ltd., Rm 12/H, 445 Tian He Bei Rd., Guangzhou, 510620, CHINA, P: 011 862038801911, F: 011 862038808485, www.ghhtools.com
Camping; Cutlery; Gun Cases; Hunting Accessories; Knives/Knife Cases; Scopes, Sights & Accessories; Targets

Goldenrod Dehumidifiers, 3600 S. Harbor Blvd., Oxnard, CA 93035, P: 800-451-6797, F: 805-985-1534, www.goldenroddehumidifiers.com
Gun Cabinets/Racks/Safes

Golight, Inc., 37146 Old Hwy. 17, Culbertson, NE 69024, P: 800-557-0098, F: 308-278-2525, www.golight.com
Camping; Hunting Accessories; Law Enforcement; Lighting Products; Vehicles, Utility & Rec

Gore & Associates, Inc., W.L., 295 Blue Ball Rd., Elkton, MD 21921, P: 800-431-GORE, F: 410-392-9057, www.gore-tex.com
Footwear; Gloves, Mitts, Hats; Law Enforcement; Men & Women's Clothing

Gould & Goodrich, Inc., 709 E. McNeil St., Lillington, NC, 27546, P: 800-277-0732, FL 910-893-4742, www.gouldusa.com
Holsters; Law Enforcement; Leathergoods

Grabber/MPI Outdoors, 5760 N. Hawkeye Ct. SW, Grand Rapids, MI 49509, P: 800-423-1233, F: 616-940-7718, www.warmers.com
Archery; Backpacking; Camouflage; Camping; Footwear; Gloves, Mitts, Hats; Hunting Accessories; Survival Kits/First Aid

Gradient Lens Corp., 207 Tremont St., Rochester, NY 14608, P: 800-536-0790, F: 585-235-6645, www.gradientlens.com
Firearms Maintenance Equipment; Gun Barrels; Gun Parts/Gunsmithing; Scopes, Sights & Accessories; Shooting Range Equipment

Grand View Media Group, 200 Croft St., Suite 1, Birmingham, AL 35242, P: 888-431-2877, F: 205-408-3798, www.gvmg.com
Books/Industry Publications

Granite Security Products, Inc., 4801 Esco Dr., Fort Worth, TX 76140, P: 817-561-9095, F: 817-478-3056, www.winchestersafes.com
Gun Cabinets/Racks/Safes

Gransfors Bruks, Inc., P.O. Box 818, Summerville, SC 29484. P: 843-875-0240, F: 843-821-2285
Custom Manufacturing; Law Enforcement; Men's Clothing; Wholesaler/Distributor

Grant Adventures Int'l., 9815 25th St. E, Parrish, FL 34219, P: 941-776-3029, F: 941-776-1092
Archery; Outfitter

Grauer Systems, 38 Forster Ave., Mount Vernon, NY 10552, P: 415-902-4721, www.grauerbarrel.com
Firearms; Gun Barrels; Gun Grips & Stocks; Law Enforcement; Lighting Products; Scopes, Sights & Accessories

Graves Recoil Systems, LLC/Mallardtone, LLC, 9115 Crows Nest Dr., Pine Bluff, AR 71603, P: 870-534-3000, F: 870-534-3000, www.stockabsorber.com
Black Powder Accessories; Firearms; Game Calls; Hunting Accessories; Recoil Protection Devices & Services; Wholesaler/Distributor

Great American Tool Co., Inc./Gatco Sharpeners/Timberline Knives, 665 Hertel Ave., Buffalo, NY 14207, P: 800-548-7427, F: 716-877-2591, www.gatcosharpeners.com
Cutlery; Knives/Knife Cases; Sharpeners

Green Supply, Inc., 3059 Audrain Rd., Suite 581, Vandalia, MO 63382, P: 800-424-4867, F: 573-594-2211, www.greensupply.com
Ammunition; Camping; Computer Software; Firearms; Hunting Accessories; Online Services; Retailer Services; Scopes, Sights & Accessories; Wholesaler/Distributor

Grip On Tools, 4628 Amash Industrial Dr., Wayland, MI 49348, P: 616-877-0000, F: 616-877-4346

Grizzly Industrial, 1821 Valencia St., Bellingham, WA 98229, P: 800-523-4777, F: 800-438-5901, www.grizzly.com
Firearms Maintenance Equipment; Gun Cabinets/Racks/Safes; Gun Parts/Gunsmithing

Grohmann Knives, Ltd., 116 Water St., P.O. Box 40, Pictou, Nova Scotia B0K 1H0, CANADA, P: 888-7-KNIVES, F: 902-485-5872, www.grohmannknives.com
Backpacking; Camping; Cooking Equipment/Accessories; Custom Manufacturing; Cutlery; Hunting Accessories; Knives/Knife Cases; Sharpeners

GrovTec US, Inc., 16071 SE 98t Ave., Clackamas, OR, 97015, P: 503-557-4689, F: 503-557-4936, www.grovtec.com
Custom Manufacturing; Firearms Maintenance Equipment; Gun Parts/Gunsmithing; Holsters

Guay Guay Trading Co., Ltd., 11F-3, No. 27, Lane 169, Kangning St., Shijr City, Taipei County 221, TAIWAN, P: 011 886226922000, F: 011 886226924000, www.guay2.com
Airsoft

Gun Grabber Products, Inc., 3417 E. 54th St., Texarkana, AR 71854, P: 877-486-4722, F: 870-774-2111, www.gungrab.com
Gun Cabinets/Racks/Safes; Hunting Accessories

Gun Video, 4585 Murphy Canyon Rd., San Diego, CA 92123, P: 800-942-8273, F: 858-569-0505, www.gunvideo.com
Books/Industry Publications; Gun Parts/Gunsmithing; Law Enforcement; Training & Safety Equipment; Videos

GunBroker.com, P.O. Box 2511, Kennesaw, GA 30156, P: 720-223-2083, F: 720-223-0164, www.gunbroker.com
Airguns; Computer Software; Firearms; Gun Parts/Gunsmithing; Hunting Accessories; Online Services; Reloading; Retailer Services

GunMate Products/Bushnell Outdoor Accessories, 9200 Cody, Overland Park, KS 66214, P: 800-423-3537, F: 800-548-0446, www.unclemikes.com
Gun Cases; Holsters; Hunting Accessories; Leathergoods

Gunslick Gun Care/ATK Commercial Products, N5549 Cty. Trunk Z, Onalaska, WI 54650, P: 800-635-7656, F: 763-323-3890, www.gunslick.com
Firearms Maintenance Equipment; Lubricants

GunVault, Inc., 216 S. 2nd Ave., Bldg. 932, San Bernardino, CA 92408, P: 800-222-1055, F: 909-382-2042, www.gunvault.com
Gun Cabinets/Racks/Safes; Gun Cases; Gun Locks

H

HKS Products, Inc., 7841 Foundation Dr., Florence, KY 41042, P: 800-354-9814, F: 859-342-5865, www.hksspeedloaders.com
Hunting Accessories; Law Enforcement

H & C Headware/Capco Sportswear, 5945 Shiloh Rd., Alpharetta, GA 30005, P: 800-381-3331, F: 800-525-2613, www.kccaps.com
Camouflage

H & M Metal Processing, 1850 Front St., Cuyanoga Falls, OH 44221, P: 330-928-9021, F: 330-928-5472, www.handmmetal.com
Airguns; Archery; Black Powder Accessories; Custom Manufacturing; Firearms Maintenance Equipment; Gun Barrels; Gun Parts/Gunsmithing

Haas Outdoors, Inc./Mossy Oak, P.O. Box 757, West Point, MS 39773, P: 662-494-8859, F: 662-509-9397

H-S Precision, Inc., 1301 Turbine Dr., Rapid City, SD 57703, P: 605-341-3006, F: 605-342-8964, www.hsprecision.com
Firearms; Gun Barrels; Gun Grips & Stocks; Law Enforcement; Magazines, Cartridge; Shooting Range Equipment

Haix®-Schuhe Produktions-u. Vertriebs GmbH, Aufhofstrasse 10, Mainburg, Bavaria 84048, GERMANY, P: 011 49875186250, F: 011 498751862525, www.haix.com
Footwear; Law Enforcement; Leathergoods

Haix North America, Inc., 157 Venture Ct., Suite 11, Lexington, KY 40511, P: 866-344-4249, F: 859-281-0113, www.haix.com
Footwear; Law Enforcement; Leathergoods

Haley Vines Outdoor Collection Badland Beauty, P.O. Box 150308, Lufkin, TX 75915, P: 936-875-5522, F: 936-875-5525, www.haleyvines.com
Bags & Equipment Cases; Gloves, Mitts, Hats; Wholesaler/Distributor; Women's Clothing

Hallmark Dog Training Supplies, 3054 Beechwood Industrial Ct., P.O. Box 97, Hubertus, WI 53033, P: 800-OK4DOGS, F: 262-628-4434, www.hallmarkdogsupplies.com
Custom Manufacturing; Hunting Accessories; Pet Supplies; Scents & Lures; Videos; Wholesaler/Distributor

Halys, 1205 W. Cumberland, Corbin, KY 40701, P: 606-528-7490, F: 606-528-7497, www.halysgear.com
Custom Manufacturing; Men & Women's Clothing; Wholesaler/Distributor

Hammerhead Ind./Gear Keeper, 1501 Goodyear Ave., Ventura, CA 93003, P: 888-588-9981, F: 805-658-8833, www.gearkeeper.com
Backpacking; Camping; Compasses; Game Calls; Hunting Accessories; Law Enforcement; Lighting Products; Sports Accessories

HangZhou Fujie Outdoor Products, Inc., Qinyuanyashe, Shenghuoguan, Suite 1108, 163# Jichang Rd., Hanzhou, ZHJG 310004, CHINA, P: 011 8657181635196, F: 011 8657187718232, www.hangzhou-outdoor.com
Footwear; Gloves, Mitts, Hats; Gun Cases; Men & Women's Clothing

Hardigg Storm Case, 147 N. Main St., South Deerfield, MA 01373, P: 800-542-7344, F: 413-665-8330
Bags & Equipment Cases; Gun Cases

Harris Engineering, Inc., 999 Broadway, Barlow, KY 42024, P: 270-334-3633, F: 270-334-3000
Hunting Accessories; Shooting Range Equipment; Sports Accessories

Harris Publications, Inc./Harris Tactical Group, 1115 Broadway, 8th Floor, New York, NY 10010, P: 212-807-7100, F: 212-807-1479, www.tactical-life.com
Airguns; Books/Industry Publications; Cutlery; Firearms; Knives/Knife Cases; Law Enforcement; Paintball Guns; Retailer Services

Hastings, 717 4th St., P.O. Box 135, Clay Center, KS 67432, P: 785-632-3169, F: 785-632-6554, www.hastingsammunition.com
Ammunition; Firearms; Gun Barrels

Hatsan Arms Co., Izmir-Ankara Karayolu 26. Km. No. 289, OSB Kemalpasa, Izmir, 35170, TURKEY, P: 011 902328789100, F: 011 902328789723, www.hatsan.com.tr
Airguns; Firearms; Scopes, Sights & Accessories

Havalon Knives/Havels Inc., 3726 Lonsdale St., Cincinnati, OH 45227, P: 800-638-4770, F: 513-271-4714, www.havalon.com
Hunting Accessories; Knives/Knife Cases

Havaser Turizm, Ltd., Nargileci Sokak No. 4, Mercan, Eminonu, 34450, TURKEY, P: 011 90212135452, F: 011 902125128079
Firearms

Hawke Sport Optics, 6015 Highview Dr., Suite G, Fort Wayne, IN 46818, P: 877-429-5347, F: 260-918-3443, www.hawkeoptics.com
Airguns; Binoculars; Computer Software; Crossbows & Accessories; Scopes, Sights & Accessories

Haydel's Game Calls, 5018 Hazel Jones Rd., Bossier City, LA 71111, P: 800-HAYDELS, F: 888-310-3711, www.haydels.com
Archery; Emblems & Decals; Game Calls; Gun Parts/Gunsmithing; Hunting Accessories; Videos

Health Enterprises, 90 George Leven Dr., N. Attleboro, MA 02760, P: 800-633-4243, F: 508-695-3061, www.healthenterprises.com
Hearing Protection

Heat Factory, Inc., 2390 Oak Ridge Way, Vista, CA 92081, P: 800-993-4328, F: 760-727-8721, www.heatfactory.com
Archery; Backpacking; Camping; Footwear; Gloves, Mitts, Hats; Hunting Accessories, Men & Women's Clothing

Heatmax, Inc., 505 Hill Rd., Dalton, GA 30721, P: 800-432-8629, F: 706-226-2195, www.heatmax.com
Archery; Backpacking; Camping; Footwear; Hunting Accessories; Law Enforcement; Pet Supplies; Sports Accessories

Heckler & Koch, Inc., 5675 Transport Blvd., Columbus, GA 31907, P: 706-568-1906, F: 706-568-9151, www.hk-usa.com
Firearms

Helly Hansen Pro (US), Inc., 3703 I St. NW, Auburn, WA 98001, P: 866-435-5902, F: 253-333-8359, www.hellyhansen.com
Men's Clothing

Hen & Rooster Cutlery, 6861 Mountain View Rd., Ooltewah, TN 37363, P: 800-251-7768, F: 423-894-9576, www.henandrooster.com
Camping; Cooking Equipment/Accessories; Cutlery; Hunting Accessories; Retail Packaging; Wholesaler/Distributor

Hendon Publishing Co./Law and Order/Tactical Response Magazines, 130 Waukegan Rd., Suite 202, Deerfield, IL 60015, P: 800-843-9764, F: 847-444-3333, www.hendonpub.com
Books/Industry Publications; Law Enforcement

Heritage Manufacturing, Inc., 4600 NW 135th St., Opa Locka, FL 33054, P: 305-685-5966, F: 305-687-6721, www.heritagemfg.com
Firearms

Heros Pride, P.O. Box 10033, Van Nuys, CA 91410, P: 888-492-9122, F: 888-492-9133, www.herospride.com
Custom Manufacturing; Emblems & Decals; Law Enforcement; Men & Women's Clothing; Wholesaler/Distributor

Hi-Point Firearms/MKS Supply, Inc., 8611-A N. Dixie Dr., Dayton, OH 45414, P: 877-425-4867, F: 937-454-0503, www.hi-pointfirearms.com
Firearms; Holsters; Law Enforcement; Magazines, Cartridge

Hiatt Thompson Corp., 7200 W. 66th St., Bedford Park, IL 60638, P: 708-496-8585, F: 708-496-8618, www.handcuffsusa.com
Law Enforcement

HideAway/Remington Packs/Cerf Bros. Bag Co., 2360 Chaffee Dr., St. Louis, MO 63146, P: 800-237-3224, F: 314-291-5588, www.cerfbag.com
Backpacking; Bags & Equipment Cases; Camouflage; Camping; Gun Cases; Wholesaler/Distributor

High Standard Mfg., Co./F.I., Inc. ATM–AutoMag, 5200 Mitchelldale, Suite E17, Houston, TX 77092, P: 800-272-7816, F: 713-681-5665, www.highstandard.com
Firearms; Gun Barrels; Gun Grips & Stocks; Gun Parts/Gunsmithing; Lubricants; Magazines, Cartridge

Highgear/Highgear USA, Inc., 145 Cane Creek Industrial Park Rd., Suite 200, Fletcher, NC 28732, P: 888-295-4949, F: 828-681-5320, www.highgear.com
Camping; Compasses; Hunting Accessories; Lighting Products; Sports Accessories; Survival Kits/First Aid

Hillman Ltd., No. 62, Tzar Samuil St., Sofia, Sofia 1000, BULGARIA, P: 011 35929882981, F: 011 35929882981, www.hillman.bg
Backpacking; Camouflage; Footwear; Gloves, Mitts, Hats; Gun Cases; Hunting Accessories; Men & Women's Clothing

HitchSafe Key Vault, 18424 Hwy. 99, Lynnwood, WA 98037, P: 800-654-1786, F: 206-523-9876, www.hitchsafe.com
Gun Cabinets/Racks/Safes; Gun Locks; Hunting Accessories; Outfitter; Sports Accessories; Vehicles, Utility & Rec

HiViz Shooting Systems/North Pass, Ltd., 1941 Heath Pkwy., Suite 1, Fort Collins, CO 80524, P: 800-589-4315, F: 970-416-1208, www.hivizsights.com
Black Powder Accessories; Gun Parts/Gunsmithing; Hunting Accessories; Paintball Accessories; Recoil Protection Devices & Services; Scopes, Sights & Accessories; Sports Accessories

Hobie Cat Co./Hobie Fishing/Hobie Kayaks, 4925 Oceanside Blvd., Oceanside, CA 92056, P: 760-758-9100, F: 760-758-1841, www.hobiecat.com
Bags & Equipment Cases; Camping; Hunting Accessories; Sports Accessories; Tours/Travel

Hodgdon Powder Co., 6231 Robinson, Shawnee Mission, KS 66202, P: 913-362-9455, F: 913-362-1307, www.hodgdon.com
Black Powder/Smokeless Powder; Books/Industry Publications; Reloading

Hog Wild, LLC, 221 SE Main St., Portland, OR 97214, P: 888-231-6465, F: 503-233-0960, www.hogwildtoys.com
Sports Accessories; Watches

Hogue, Inc., 550 Linne Rd., Paso Robles, CA 93447, P: 805-239-1440, F: 805-239-2553, www.hogueinc.com
Gun Grips & Stocks; Holsters

Homak Manufacturing Co., Inc., 1605 Old Rt. 18, Suite 4-36, Wampum, PA 16157, P: 800-874-6625, F: 724-535-1081, www.homak.com
Custom Manufacturing; Gun Cabinets/Racks/Safes; Gun Cases; Gun Locks; Hunting Accessories; Reloading; Retail Packaging

HongKong Meike Digital Technology Co., Ltd., No. 12 Jiaye Rd. Pinghu St., Longgang District, Shenzhen, GNGD 518111, CHINA, P: 011 8613424151607, F: 011 8675528494339, www.mkgrip.com
Scopes, Sights & Accessories

Hope Global, 50 Martin St., Cumberland, RI 02864, P: 401-333-8990, F: 401-334-6442, www.hopeglobal.com
Custom Manufacturing; Footwear; Hunting Accessories; Law Enforcement; Pet Supplies; Scopes, Sights & Accessories; Shooting Range Equipment; Sports Accessories

Hoppe's/Bushnell Outdoor Accessories, 9200 Cody, Overland Park, KS 66214, P: 800-221-9035, F: 800-548-0446, www.hoppes.com
Black Powder Accessories; Firearms Maintenance Equipment; Hearing Protection; Law Enforcement; Lubricants; Shooting Range Equipment

Horizon Manufacturing Ent., Inc./RackEm Racks, P.O. Box 7174, Buffalo Grove, IL 60089, P: 877-722-5369 (877-RACKEM-9), F: 866-782-1550, www.rackems.com
Airguns; Custom Manufacturing; Firearms; Firearms Maintenance Equipment; Footwear; Gloves, Mitts, Hats; Gun Cabinets/Racks/Safes; Holsters; Hunting Accessories; Law Enforcement; Shooting Range Equipment

Hornady Manufacturing Co., 3625 Old Potash Hwy., P.O. Box 1848, Grand Island, NE 68803, P: 308-382-1390, F: 308-382-5761, www.hornady.com
Ammunition; Black Powder Accessories; Lubricants; Reloading

Horus Vision, LLC, 659 Huntington Ave., San Bruno, CA 94066, P: 650-588-8862, F: 650-588-6264, www.horusvision.com
Computer Software; Law Enforcement; Scopes, Sights & Accessories; Targets; Watches

Howard Leight by Sperian, 900 Douglas Pike, Smithfield, RI 02917, P: 866-786-2353, F: 401-233-7641, www.howardleightshootingsports.com, www.sperianprotection.com
Eyewear; Hearing Protection; Hunting Accessories; Sports Accessories; Training & Safety Equipment

Huanic Corp., No. 67 Jinye Rd., Hi-tech Zone, Xi'an, SHNX 710077, CHINA, P: 011 862981881001, F: 011 862981881011, www.huanic.com
Hunting Accessories; Scopes, Sights & Accessories; Shooting Range Equipment; Targets

Hubertus Solingen Cutlery, 147 Wuppertaler Strasse, Solingen, D-42653, GERMANY, P: 011 49212591994, F: 011 49212591992, www.hubertus-solingen.de
Custom Manufacturing; Cutlery; Knives/Knife Cases; Survival Kits/First Aid

Hunter Co., Inc./Hunter Wicked Optics, 3300 W. 71st Ave., Westminster, CO 80030, P: 800-676-4868, F: 303-428-3980, www.huntercompany.com
Binoculars; Custom Manufacturing; Gun Cases; Holsters; Hunting Accessories; Knives/Knife Cases; Leathergoods; Scopes, Sights & Accessories

Hunter Dan, 64 N. US 231, P.O. Box 103, Greencastle, IN 46135, P: 888-241-4868, F: 765-655-1440, www.hunterdan.com
Archery; Home Furnishings; Hunting Accessories; Outdoor Art, Jewelry, Sculpture; Sports Accessories; Training & Safety Equipment

Hunter's Edge, LLC, 270 Whigham Dairy Rd., Bainbridge, GA 39817, P: 888-455-0970, F: 912-248-6219, www.hunters-edge.com
Archery; Camouflage; Decoys; Game Calls; Gloves, Mitts, Hats; Hunting Accessories; Men's Clothing; Scents & Lures

Hunter's Specialties, 6000 Huntington Ct. NE, Cedar Rapids, IA 52402, P: 800-728-0321, F: 319-395-0326, www.hunterspec.com
Archery; Blinds; Camouflage; Game Calls; Gloves, Mitts, Hats; Hunting Accessories; Scents & Lures; Videos

Hunterbid.com/Chiron, Inc., 38 Crosby Rd., Dover, NH 03820, P: 603-433-8908, F: 603-431-4072, www.hunterbid.com
Gun Grips & Stocks; Gun Parts/Gunsmithing

Hunting's-A-Drag, 42 Maple St., Rifton, NY 12471, P: 845-658-8557, F: 845-658-8569, www.gamesled.com
Hunting Accessories

Huntington Die Specialties, 601 Oro Dam Blvd., P.O. Box 991, Oroville, CA 95965, P: 866-RELOADS, F: 530-534-1212, huntingtons.com
Black Powder Accessories; Books/Industry Publications; Reloading; Wholesaler/Distributor

HyperBeam, 1504 Sheepshead Bay Rd., Suite 300, Brooklyn, NY 11236, P: 888-272-4620, F: 718-272-1797, www.nightdetective.com
Binoculars; Hunting Accessories; Law Enforcement; Lighting Products; Photographic Equipment; Scopes, Sights & Accessories; Shooting Range Equipment; Telescopes

Hyskore/Power Aisle, Inc., 193 West Hills Rd., Huntington Station, NY 11746, P: 631-673-5975, F: 631-673-5976, www.hyskore.com
Custom Manufacturing; Export/Import Specialists; Eyewear; Firearms Maintenance Equipment; Gun Cabinets/Racks/Safes; Hearing Protection; Shooting Range Equipment

I

I.C.E., 68 Route 125, Kingston, NH 03848, P: 603-347-3005, F: 603-642-9291, www.icesigns.com
Retailer Services

ICS, No. 6, Lane 205, Dongzou Rd., Taichung, Shangang 429, TAIWAN, P: 011-88 6425256461, F: 011-88 6425256484, icsbb.com
Airguns; Sports Accessories; Training & Safety Equipment

IHC, Inc., 12400 Burt Rd., Detroit, MI 48228, P: 800-661-4642, F: 313-535-3220, www.ihccorp.com
Archery; Backpacking; Camping; Crossbows & Accessories; Firearms; Lighting Products; Magazines, Cartridge; Scopes, Sights & Accessories

i-SHOT/S.E.R.T. System, 16135 Kennedy St., Woodbridge, VA 22191, P: 703-670-8001, F: 703-940-9148, www.ishot-inc.com
Bags & Equipment Cases; Custom Manufacturing; Firearms; Law Enforcement; Training & Safety Equipment; Wholesaler/Distributor

Icebreaker, Inc., P.O. Box 236, Clarkesville, GA 30523, P: 800-343-BOOT, F: 706-754-0423, www.icebreakerinc.com
Camouflage; Footwear; Gloves, Mitts, Hats; Hunting Accessories

Impact Gel Sports, P.O. Box 128, Melrose, WI 54642, P: 608-488-3630, F: 608-488-3633, www.impactgel.com
Footwear

Import Merchandiser's Inc./MasterVision Cap Lights, N-11254 Industrial Lane, P.O. Box 337, Elcho, WI 54428, P: 715-275-5132, F: 715-275-5176, www.mastervisionlight.com
Camping; Custom Manufacturing; Gloves, Mitts, Hats; Hunting Accessories; Lighting Products; Sports Accessories

IMR Powder Co., 6231 Robinson, Shawnee Mission, KS 66202, P: 913-362-9455, F: 913-362-1307, www.imrpowder.com
Black Powder/Smokeless Powder; Reloading

Indo-US Mim Tec. Pvt., Ltd., 315 Eisenhower Pkwy., Suite 211, Ann Arbor, MI 48108, P: 734-327-9842, F: 734-327-9873, www.mimindia.com
Airguns; Archery; Crossbows & Accessories; Gun Locks; Gun Parts/Gunsmithing; Knives/Knife Cases; Paintball Guns; Scopes, Sights & Accessories

Industrial Revolution/Light My Fire USA, 9225 151st Ave. NE, Redmond, WA 98052, P: 888-297-6062, F: 425-883-0036, www.industrialrev.com
Camping; Cooking Equipment/Accessories; Cutlery; Knives/Knife Cases; Lighting Products; Photographic Equipment; Survival Kits/First Aid; Wholesaler/Distributor

Indusys Techologies Belgium SPRL (UFA–Belgium), 22 Pas Bayard, Tavier, Liege B-4163, BELGIUM, P: 011 3243835234, F: 011 3243835189, www.indusys.be
Ammunition; Reloading; Shooting Range Equipment; Training & Safety Equipment

Innovative Plastech, Inc., 1260 Kingsland Dr., Batavia, IL 60510, P: 630-232-1808, F: 630-232-1978
Custom Manufacturing; Retail Packaging; Sports Accessories

INOVA/Emissive Energy Corp., 135 Circuit Dr., North Kingstown, RI 02852, P: 401-294-2030, F: 401-294-2050, www.inovalight.com
Backpacking; Camping; Hunting Accessories; Law Enforcement; Lighting Products; Sports Accessories; Survival Kits/First Aid; Training & Safety Equipment

Insight Tech-Gear, 23 Industrial Dr., Londonderry, NH 03053, P: 877-744-4802, F: 603-668-1084, www.insighttechgear.com
Hunting Accessories; Law Enforcement; Lighting Products; Paintball Accessories; Scopes, Sights & Accessories; Training & Safety Equipment

Instant Armor, Inc., 350 E. Easy St., Suite 1, Simi Valley, CA 93065, P: 805-526-3046, F: 805-526-9213, www.instantarmor.com
Law Enforcement

Instrument Technology, Inc., P.O. Box 381, Westfield, MA 10186, P: 413-562-3606, F: 413-568-9809, www.scopes.com
Law Enforcement

InterMedia Outdoors, Inc., 512 7th Ave., 11th Floor, New York, NY 10018, P: 212-852-6600, F: 212-302-4472, www.imoutdoorsmedia.com
Books/Industry Publications

International Cartridge Corp., 2273 Route 310, Reynoldsville, PA 15851, P: 877-422-5332, F: 814-938-6821, www.iccammo.com
Ammunition; Law Enforcement; Reloading; Shooting Range Equipment; Training & Safety Equipment

International Supplies/Seahorse Protective Cases, 945 W. Hyde Park, Inglewood, CA 90302, P: 800-999-1984, F: 310-673-5988, www.internationalsupplies.com
Bags & Equipment Cases; Export/Import Specialists; Eyewear; Gun Cases; Lighting Products; Photographic Equipment; Retailer Services; Wholesaler/Distributor

Interstate Arms Corp., 6 Dunham Rd., Billerica, MA 01821, P: 800-243-3006, F: 978-671-0023, www.interstatearms.com
Firearms

Iosso Products, 1485 Lively Blvd., Elk Grove, IL 60007, P: 888-747-4332, F: 847-437-8478, www.iosso.com
Black Powder Accessories; Crossbows & Accessories; Firearms Maintenance Equipment; Gun Parts/Gunsmithing; Hunting Accessories; Law Enforcement; Lubricants; Reloading

Iowa Rotocast Plastics, Inc., 1712 Moellers Dr., P.O. Box 320, Decorah, IA 52101, P: 800-553-0050, F: 563-382-3016, www.irpoutdoors.com
Backpacking; Blinds; Camping; Custom Manufacturing; Emblems & Decals; Printing Services; Sports Accessories; Wholesaler/Distributor

Irish Setter, 314 Main St., Red Wing, MN 55066, P: 888-SETTER-O, www.irishsetterboots.com
Footwear; Men's Clothing

Ironclad Performance Wear, 2201 Park Place, Suite 101, El Segundo, CA 90245, P: 888-314-3197, F: 310-643-0300
Camouflage; Gloves, Mitts, Hats; Hunting Accessories; Leathergoods; Men & Women's Clothing; Sports Accessories

Itasca by C.O. Lynch Enterprises, 2655 Fairview Ave. N, Roseville, MN 55113, P: 800-225-2565, F: 651-633-9095, www.itascacol.com
Footwear

Ithaca Gun Co., LLC, 420 N. Warpole St., Upper Sandusky, OH 43351, P: 877-648-4222, F: 419-294-3230, www.ithacagun.com
Firearms

ITT, 7635 Plantation Rd., Roanoke, VA 24019, P: 800-448-8678, F: 540-366-9015, www.nightvision.com
Binoculars; Scopes, Sights & Accessories

ITW Military Products, 195 E. Algonquin Rd., Des Plaines, IL 60016, P: 203-240-7110, F: 847-390-8727, www.itwmilitaryproducts.com
Backpacking; Bags & Equipment Cases; Camouflage; Cooking Equipment/Accessories; Custom Manufacturing; Law Enforcement

Iver Johnson Arms Inc./Manufacturing Research, 1840 Baldwin St., Suite 10, Rockledge, FL 32955, P: 321-636-3377, F: 321-632-7745, www.iverjohnsonarms.com
Firearms; Gun Parts/Gunsmithing; Training & Safety Equipment

J

J.F. Griffin Publishing, LLC, 430 Main St., Suite 5, Williamstown, MA 01267, P: 413-884-1001, F: 413-884-1039, www.jfgriffin.com
Books/Industry Publications

JBP Holsters/Masters Holsters, 10100 Old Bon Air Pl., Richmond, VA 23235, P: 804-320-5653, F: 804-320-5653, www.jbpholsters.com
Gun Cases; Holsters; Hunting Accessories; Law Enforcement; Leathergoods; Sports Accessories; Training & Safety Equipment; Wholesaler/Distributor

JGS Precision Tool Mfg., LLC, 60819 Selander Rd., Coos Bay, OR 97420, P: 541-267-4331, F: 541-267-5996, www.jgstools.com
Firearms Maintenance Equipment; Gun Parts/Gunsmithing

J & J Armory/Dragon Skin/Pinnacle Armor, 1344 E. Edinger Ave., Santa Ana, CA 92705, P: 866-9-ARMORY, F: 714-558-4817, www.jandjarmory.com
Firearms; Law Enforcement; Training & Safety Equipment

J & J Products Co., 9134 Independence Ave., Chatsworth, CA 91311, P: 626-571-8084, F: 626-571-8704, www.jandjproducts.com
Custom Manufacturing; Hunting Accessories; Recoil Protection Devices & Services; Reloading; Retail Packaging; Sports Accessories

J & K Outdoor Products, Inc., 3864 Cty. Rd. Q, Wisconsin Rapids, WI 54495, P: 715-424-5757, F: 715-424-5757, www.jkoutdoorproducts.com
Archery; Hunting Accessories; Law Enforcement; Paintball Accessories; Scopes, Sights & Accessories

J-Tech (Steady Flying Enterprise Co., Ltd.), 1F, No. 235 Ta You Rd., Sung Shang, Taipei, 105, TAIWAN, P: 011 886227663986, F: 011 886287874836, www.tacticaljtech.com
Backpacking; Custom Manufacturing; Gloves, Mitts, Hats; Gun Cases; Holsters; Law Enforcement; Lighting Products; Wholesaler/Distributor

Jaccard Corp., 3421 N. Benzing Rd., Orchard Park, NY 14127, P: 866-478-7373, F: 716-825-5319, www.jaccard.com
Cooking Equipment/Accessories

Jack Brittingham's World of Hunting Adventure, 609-A E. Clinton Ave., Athens, TX 75751, P: 800-440-4515, F: 903-677-2126, www.jackbrittingham.com
Hunting Accessories; Training & Safety Equipment; Videos; Wildlife Management

Jack Link's Beef Jerky, One Snackfood Ln., P.O. Box 397, Minong, WI 54859, P: 800-346-6896, F: 715-466-5986, www.linksnacks.com
Custom Manufacturing

Jackite, Inc., 2868 W. Landing Rd., Virginia Beach, VA 23456, P: 877-JACKITE, F: 877-JACKFAX, www.jackite.com
Decoys; Hunting Accessories; Outdoor Art, Jewelry, Sculpture; Wholesaler/Distributor

Jackson Rifles X-Treme Shooting Products, LLC, Glenswinton, Parton, Castle Douglas, SCOTLAND DG7 3NL, P: 011 441644470223, F: 011 441644470227, www.jacksonrifles.com
Firearms; Gun Barrels; Gun Parts/Gunsmithing; Wholesaler/Distributor

Jacob Ash Holdings, Inc., 301 Munson Ave., McKees Rocks, PA 15136, P: 800-245-6111, F: 412-331-6347, www.jacobash.com
Camouflage; Gloves, Mitts, Hats; Hunting Accessories; Law Enforcement; Leathergoods; Men & Women's Clothing; Sports Accessories

James River Manufacturing, Inc./James River Armory, 3601 Commerce Dr., Suite 110, Baltimore, MD 21227, P: 410-242-6991, F: 410-242-6995, www.jamesriverarmory.com
Firearms

Japan Optics, Ltd., 2-11-29, Ukima, Kita-ku, Tokyo, 115-0051, JAPAN, P: 011 81359146680, F: 011 81353722232
Scopes, Sights & Accessories

Jeff's Outfitters, 599 Cty. Rd. 206, Cape Girardeau, MO 63701, P: 573-651-3200, F: 573-651-3207, www.jeffsoutfitters.com
Bags & Equipment Cases; Custom Manufacturing; Gun Cases; Hunting Accessories; Knives/Knife Cases; Leathergoods; Scopes, Sights & Accessories

Jest Textiles, Inc./Bucksuede, 13 Mountainside Ave., Mahwah, NJ 07430, P: 800-778-7918, F: 866-899-4951, www.jesttex.com
Bags & Equipment Cases; Camouflage; Custom Manufacturing; Export/Import Specialists; Gloves, Mitts, Hats; Home Furnishings; Men & Women's Clothing

John Marshall Design, LLC, P.O. Box 46105, Baton Rouge, LA 70895, P: 800-697-2698, F: 225-275-5900
Camouflage; Home Furnishings; Men & Women's Clothing

John's Guns/A Dark Horse Arms Co., 1041 FM 1274, Coleman, TX 76834.P: 325-382-4885, F: 325-382-4887, www.darkhorsearms.com
Custom Manufacturing; Firearms; Hearing Protection; Law Enforcement

Johnston Brothers, 623 Meeting St., Bldg. B, P.O. Box 21810, Charleston, SC 29413, P: 800-257-2595, F: 800-257-2534
Bags & Equipment Cases; Firearms Maintenance Equipment; Gun Cases

Jonathan Arthur Ciener, Inc., 8700 Commerce St., Cap Canaveral, FL 32920, P: 321-868-2200, F: 321-868-2201, www.22lrconversions.com
Firearms; Gun Barrels; Gun Parts/Gunsmithing; Hunting Accessories; Magazines, Cartridge; Recoil Protection Devices & Services; Shooting Range Equipment; Training & Safety Equipment

Jordan Outdoor Enterprises, Ltd., P.O. Box 9638, Columbus, GA 31908, P: 800-992-9968, F: 706-569-9346, www.realtree.com
Camouflage; Videos

Joseph Chiarello & Co., Inc./NSSF Endorsed Insurance Program, 31 Parker Rd., Elizabeth, NJ 07208, P: 800-526-2199, F: 908-352-8512, www.guninsurance.com
Insurance; Retailer Services

Joy Enterprises, 1862 Dr., ML King Jr. Blvd., Port Commerce Center III, Riviera Beach, FL 33404, P: 800-500-FURY, F: 561-863-3277, www.joyenterprises.com
Binoculars; Camping; Compasses; Cutlery; Knives/Knife Cases; Law Enforcement; Sharpeners; Sports Accessories

JP Enterprises, Inc., P.O. Box 378, Hugo, NN 55038, P: 651-426-9196, F: 651-426-2472, www.jprifles.com
Firearms; Gun Parts/Gunsmithing; Recoil Protection Devices & Services; Scopes, Sights & Accessories

JS Products, Inc./Snap-on, 5440 S. Procyon Ave., Las Vegas, NV 89118, P: 702-362-7011, F: 702-362-5084
Lighting Products

K

KA Display Solutions, Inc., P.O. Box 99, 512 Blackman Blvd. W, Wartrace, TN 37183, P: 800-227-9540, F: 931-389-6686, www.kadsi.com
Custom Manufacturing; Gun Cabinets/Racks/Safes; Gun Cases; Home Furnishings; Knives/Knife Cases; Retailer Services; Scopes, Sights & Accessories

K.B.I., Inc./Charles Daly, P.O. Box 6625, Harrisburg, PA 17112, P: 866-325-9486, F: 717-540-8567, www.charlesdaly.com
Ammunition; Export/Import Specialists; Firearms; Hunting Accessories; Law Enforcement; Scopes, Sights & Accessories

Ka-Bar Knives, Inc., 200 Homer St., Olean, NY 14760, P: 800-282-0130, FL 716-790-7188, www.ka-bar.com
Knives/Knife Cases; Law Enforcement

KDF, Inc., 2485 St. Hwy. 46 N, Seguin, TX 78155, P: 800-KDF-GUNS, F: 830-379-8144
Firearms; Gun Grips & Stocks; Recoil Protection Devices & Services; Scopes, Sights & Accessories

KDH Defense Systems, Inc., 401 Broad St., Johnstown, PA 15906, P: 814-536-7701, F: 814-536-7716, www.kdhdefensesystems.com
Law Enforcement

KNJ Manufacturing, LLC, 757 N. Golden Key, Suite D, Gilbert, AZ 85233, P: 800-424-6606, F: 480-497-8480, www.knjmfg.com
Bags & Equipment Cases; Custom Manufacturing; Gun Cases; Holsters; Hunting Accessories; Law Enforcement; Wholesaler/Distributor

KNS Precision, Inc., 112 Marschall Creek Rd., Fredericksburg, TN 78624, P: 830-997-0000, F: 830-997-1443, www.knsprecisioninc.com
Firearms; Gun Grips & Stocks; Gun Parts/Gunsmithing; Law Enforcement; Lighting Products; Scopes, Sights & Accessories; Training & Safety Equipment; Wholesaler/Distributor

KP Industries, Inc., 3038 Industry St., Suite 108, Oceanside, CA 92054, P: 800-956-3377, F: 760-722-9884, www.kpindustries.com
Export/Import Specialists; Law Enforcement; Outfitter; Paintball Accessories; Shooting Range Equipment; Sports Accessories; Training & Safety Equipment

K-VAR Corp., 3300 S. Decatur Blvd., Suite 10601, Las Vegas, NV 89102, P: 702-364-8880, F: 702-307-2303, www.k-var.com
Firearms Maintenance Equipment; Gun Barrels; Gun Grips & Stocks; Magazines, Cartridge; Scopes, Sights & Accessories

Kahr Arms, 130 Goddard Memorial Dr., Worcester, MA 01603, P: 508-795-3919, FL 508-795-7046, www.kahr.com
Firearms; Holsters; Law Enforcement

Kakadu Traders Australia, 12832 NE Airport Way, Portland, OR 97230, P: 800-852-5288, F: 503-255-7819, www.kakaduaustralia.com
Bags & Equipment Cases; Camouflage; Men & Women's Clothing; Wholesaler/Distributor

Kalispel Case Line/Cortona Shotguns, 418641 SR 20, P.O. Box 267, Cusick, WA 99119, P: 509-445-1121, F: 509-445-1082, www.kalispelcaseline.com
Archery; Bags & Equipment Cases; Export/Import Specialists; Firearms; Gun Cases; Law Enforcement; Wholesaler/Distributor

Katz Knives, 10924 Mukilteo Speedway, Suite 287, Mukilteo, WA 98275, P: 800-848-7084, F: 480-786-9338, www.katzknives.com
Backpacking; Camping; Custom Manufacturing; Cutlery; Knives/Knife Cases; Sharpeners; Wholesaler/Distributor

Kel-Tec CNC Ind., Inc., 1475 Cox Rd., Cocoa, FL 32926, P: 321-631-0068, F: 321-631-1169, www.kel-tec-cnc.com
Firearms

Kelbly's, Inc., 7222 Dalton Fox Lk. Rd., North Lawrence, OH 44666, P: 330-683-4674, F: 330-682-7349, www.kelbly.com
Firearms; Scopes, Sights & Accessories

Kenetrek Boots, 237 Quail Run Rd., Suite A, Bozeman, MT, 59718, P: 800-232-6064, F: 406-585-5548, www.kenetrek.com
Footwear; Men's Clothing

Keng's Firearms Specialty, Inc./Versa-Pod/Champion Gun Sights, 875 Wharton Dr. SW, P.O. Box 44405, Atlanta, GA 30336, P: 800-848-4671, F: 404-505-8445, www.versapod.com
Gun Grips & Stocks; Hunting Accessories; Scopes, Sights & Accessories

KenMar Products, 411 Cameron Rd., Mattawa, Ontario P0H 1V0, CANADA, P: 866-456-5959, F: 705-744-6540, www.kenmarproducts.com
Camouflage; Gun Cases; Hunting Accessories; Leathergoods; Men's Clothing; Scents & Lures; Sports Accessories

Kent Cartridge, 727 Hite Rd., P.O. Box 849, Kearneysville, WV, 25430, P: 888-311-5368, F: 304-725-0454, www.kentgamebore.com
Ammunition

Kenyon Consumer Products/KCP Acquisition, LLC, 141 Fairgrounds Rd., West Kingston, RI 02892, P: 800-537-0024, F: 401-782-4870, www.kenyonconsumer.com
Backpacking; Camping; Law Enforcement; Men & Women's Clothing

Kernel Game Call, 13231 Champion Forest Dr., Suite 201, Houston, TX 77069, P: 830-928-2140, F: 830-792-6215
Feeder Equipment; Game Calls

Kershaw Knives, 18600 SW Teton Ave., Tualatin, OR 97062, P: 800-325-2891, F: 503-682-7168, www.kershawknives.com
Cutlery; Knives/Knife Cases

Kestrel Pocket Weather Meters, 21 Creek Circle, Boothwyn, PA 19061, P: 800-784-4221, F: 610-447-1577, www.kestrelweather.com
Backpacking; Camping; Crossbows & Accessories; Hunting Accessories; Law Enforcement; Shooting Range Equipment; Sports Accessories; Training & Safety Equipment

Keyes Hunting Gear, P.O. Box 1047, Pagosa Springs, CO 81147, P: 317-442-8132, F: 317-770-2127, www.keyeshuntinggear.com
Archery; Backpacking; Bags & Equipment Cases; Camouflage; Camping; Hunting Accessories; Men & Women's Clothing

Keystone Sporting Arms, LLC, 155 Sodom Rd., Milton, PA 17847, P: 800-742-0455, F: 570-742-1455, www.crickett.com
Airsoft; Books/Industry Publications; Firearms; Gun Grips & Stocks; Hunting Accessories; Shooting Range Equipment; Targets; Training & Safety Equipment

KG Industries, LLC, 16790 US Hwy. 63 S, Bldg. 2, Hayward, WI 54843, P: 800-348-9558, F: 715-934-3570, www.kgcoatings.com

Camouflage; Custom Manufacturing; Firearms; Firearms Maintenance Equipment; Gun Barrels; Knives/Knife Cases; Law Enforcement; Lubricants

Kick-EEZ Products, 1819 Schurman Way, Suite 106, Woodland, WA 98674, P: 877-KICKEEZ, F: 360-225-9702, www.kickeezproducts.com
Black Powder Accessories; Clay Targets; Gun Grips & Stocks; Gun Parts/Gunsmithing; Hunting Accessories; Recoil Protection Devices & Services; Targets

Kiesler Distributor of Lewis Machine & Tool Co., 2802 Sable Mill Rd., Jeffersonville, IN 47130, P: 800-444-2950, F: 812-284-6651, www.kiesler.com
Firearms

Kilgore Flares Co., LLC, 155 Kilgore Dr., Toone, TN 38381, P; 731-228-5371, F: 731-228-4173, www.kilgoreflares.com
Ammunition

Kimar Srl/Chaippa Firearms, Via Milano, 2, Azzano Mella, 25020, ITALY, P: 011 390309749065, F: 011 390309749232, www.kimar.com
Airguns; Firearms; Pet Supplies; Training & Safety Equipment

Kimber Mfg., Inc./Meprolight, Inc., One Lawton St., Yonkers, NY 10705, P: 888-243-4522, F: 406-758-2223
Firearms; Law Enforcement

Kingman Training/Kingman Group, 14010 Live Oak Ave., Baldwin Park, CA 91706, P: 888-KINGMAN, F: 626-851-8530, www.kingmantraining.com
Bags & Equipment Cases; Eyewear; Gun Cases; Men's Clothing; Paintball Accessories, Guns & Paintballs

Kingport Industries, LLC, 1303 Shermer Rd., Northbrook, IL 60062, P: 866-303-5463, F: 847-446-5663, www.kingportindustries.com
Bags & Equipment Cases; Custom Manufacturing; Export/Import Specialists; Leathergoods; Wholesaler/Distributor

King's Outdoor World, 1450 S. Blackhawk Blvd., P.O. Box 307, Mt. Pleasant, UT 84647, P: 800-447-6897, F: 435-462-7436, www.kingoutdoorworld.com
Camouflage; Custom Manufacturing; Hunting Accessories; Men's Clothing; Wholesaler/Distributor

Kitasho Co., Ltd./Kanetsune, 5-1-11 Sakae-Machi, Seki-City, Gifu-Pref, 501 3253 JAPAN, P: 11 81575241211, FL 011 81575241210, www.kanetsune.com
Knives/Knife Cases

Knight Rifles/Div. Modern Muzzleloading, 715B Summit Dr., Decatur, AL 52544, P: 800-696-1703, F: 256-260-8951, www.knightrifles.com
Firearms

Knight's Manufacturing Co., 701 Columbia Blvd., Titusville, FL 32780, P: 321-607-9900, F: 321-383-2143, www.knightarmco.com
Firearms; Scopes, Sights & Accessories

Kolpin Outdoors/Bushness Outdoor Accessories, 9200 Cody, Overland Park, KS 66214, P: 800-423-3537, F: 800-548-0446, www.kolpin-outdoors.com
Firearms Maintenance Equipment; Gun Cases; Hunting Accessories

Konus USA Corp., 7530 NW 79th St., Miami, FL 33166, P: 305-884-7618, F: 305-884-7620, www.konususa.com
Binoculars; Compasses; Eyewear; Scopes, Sights & Accessories; Sports Accessories; Telescopes; Watches

Kowa Optimed, Inc., 20001 S. Vermont Ave., Torrance CA 90502, P: 800-966-5692, F: 310-327-4177, www.kowa-usa.com
Binoculars; Scopes, Sights & Accessories; Telescopes

Krause Publications/F&W Media, 700 E. State St., Iola, WI 54990, P: 888-457-2873, F: 715-445-4087, www.krausebooks.com
Books/Industry Publications; Videos

Krieger Barrels, Inc., 2024 Mayfield Rd., Richfield, WI 53076, P: 262-628-8558, F: 262-628-8748, www.kriegerbarrels.com
Gun Barrels

Kriss-TDI, 2697 International Dr., Pkwy. 4, 140, Virginia Beach, VA 23452, P: 202-821-1089, F: 202-821-1094, www.kriss-tdi.com
Firearms; Law Enforcement; Magazines, Cartridge

Kroll International, 51360 Danview Tech Ct., Shelby TWP, MI 48315, P: 800-359-6912, F: 800-359-9721, www.krollcorp.com
Bags & Equipment Cases; Footwear; Gloves, Mitts, Hats; Holsters; Hunting Accessories; Knives/Knife Cases; Law Enforcement; Wholesaler/Distributor

Kruger Optical, LLC, 141 E. Cascade Ave., Suite 208, P.O. Box 532, Sisters, OR 97759, P: 541-549-0770, F: 541-549-0769, www.krugeroptical.com
Binoculars; Scopes, Sights & Accessories

Kunming Yuanda Optical Co., Ltd./Norin Optech Co. Ltd., 9/F Huihua Bldg. No. 80 Xianlie, Zhong Rd., Guangzhou, 51007, CHINA, P: 011 862037616375, F: 011 862037619210, www.norin-optech.com
Binoculars; Compasses; Scopes, Sights & Accessories; Sports Accessories; Telescopes

Kutmaster/Div. Utica Cutlery Co., 820 Noyes St., Utica, NY 13503, P: 800-888-4223, F: 315-733-6602, www.kutmaster.com
Backpacking; Camping; Cooking Equipment & Accessories; Cutlery; Hunting Accessories; Knives/Knife Cases; Sports Accessories; Survival Kits/First Aid

Kwik-Site Co./Ironsighter Co., 5555 Treadwell, Wayne, MI 48184, P: 734-326-1500, F: 734-326-4120, www.kwiksitecorp.com
Black Powder Accessories; Firearms Maintenance Equipment; Hunting Accessories; Scopes, Sights & Accessories; Sporting Accessories

L

L.P.A. Srl di Ghilardi, Via Vittorio Alfieri, 26, Gardone V.T., 25063, ITALY, P: 011 390308911481, F: 011 390308910951, www.lpasights.com
Black Powder Accessories; Gun Parts/Gunsmithing; Scopes, Sights & Accessories

L-3 Communications-Eotech, 1201 E. Ellsworth Rd., Ann Arbor, MI 48108, P: 734-741-8868, F: 734-741-8221, www.l-3com.com/eotech
Law Enforcement; Scopes, Sights & Accessories

L-3 Electro-Optical Systems, 3414 Herrmann Dr., Garland, TX 75041, P: 866-483-9972, F: 972-271-2195, www.l3nightvision.com
Law Enforcement; Scopes, Sights & Accessories

L.A. Lighter, Inc./Viclight, 19805 Harrison Ave., City of Industry, CA 91789, P: 800-499-4708, F: 909-468-1859, www.lalighter.com
Camping; Cooking Equipment/Accessories; Lighting Products; Sports Accessories; Training & Safety Equipment; Wholesaler/Distributor

L.A.R. Manufacturing, 4133 W. Farm Rd., West Jordan, UT 84088, P: 801-280-3505, F: 801-280-1972, www.largrizzly.com
Firearms

La Crosse Technology, Ltd., 2809 Losey Blvd. S, La Crosse, WI 54601, P: 800-346-9544, F: 608-796-1020, www.lacrossetechnology.com
Sports Accessories; Wholesaler/Distributor

LEM Products, 109 May Dr., Harrison, OH 45030, P: 513-202-1188, F: 513-202-9494, www.lemproducts.com
Books/Industry Publications; Cooking Equipment/Accessories; Cutlery; Knives/Knife Cases; Sharpeners; Videos; Wholesaler/Distributor

L&R Ultrasonics, 577 Elm St., Kearny, NJ 07032, P: 201-991-5330, F: 201-991-5870, www.lrultrasonics.com
Decoys; Firearms; Firearms Maintenance Equipment; Gun Parts/Gunsmithing; Lubricants; Reloading; Shooting Range Equipment

LRB Arms, 96 Cherry Lane, Floral Park, NY 11001, P: 516-327-9061, F: 516-327-0246, www.lrbarms.com
Firearms; Wholesaler/Distributor

LRI–Photon Micro Light, 20448 Hwy. 36, Blachly, OR 97412, P: 541-925-3741, F: 541-925-3751, www.laughingrabbitinc.com
Backpacking; Camping; Hunting Accessories; Law Enforcement; Lighting Products; Sports Accessories; Survival Kits/First Aid; Training & Safety Equipment

Lachausee/New Lachaussée, UFA Belgium, Rue de Tige, 13, Herstal, Liège B 4040, BELGIUM, P: 011 3242488811, F: 011 3242488800, www.lachaussee.com
Ammunition; Firearms Maintenance Equipment; Reloading; Shooting Range Equipment

Lakeside Machine, LLC, 1213 Industrial St., Horseshoe Bend, AR 72512, P: 870-670-4999, F: 870-670-4998, www.lakesideguns.com
Custom Manufacturing; Firearms; Hunting Accessories; Law Enforcement

Lanber, Zubiaurre 3, P.O. Box 3, Zaldibar, (Vizcaya) 48250, SPAIN, P: 011 34946827702, F: 011 34946827999, www.lanber.com
Firearms

Lancer Systems, 7566 Morris Ct., Suite 300, Allentown, PA, 18106, P: 610-973-2614, F: 610-973-2615, www.lancer-systems.com
Custom Manufacturing; Gun Parts/Gunsmithing; Magazines, Cartridge

Landmark Outdoors/Yukon Advanced Optics/Sightmark/Mobile Hunter/Trophy Score/Amacker, 201 Regency Pkwy., Mansfield, TX 76063, P: 877-431-3579, F: 817-453-8770, www.landmarkoutdoors.com
Airsoft; Binoculars; Custom Manufacturing; Feeder Equipment; Hunting Accessories; Law Enforcement; Paintball Accessories; Scopes, Sights & Accessories; Shooting Range Equipment; Treestands; Wholesaler/Distributor

Lanigan Performance Products/KG Industries, 10320 Riverburn Dr., Tampa, FL 33467, P: 813-651-5400, F: 813-991-6156, www.thesacskit.com
Gun Parts/Gunsmithing

Lansky Sharpeners, P.O. Box 50830, Henderson, NV 89016, P: 716-877-7511, F: 716-877-6955, www.lansky.com
Archery; Camping; Cooking Equipment/Accessories; Cutlery; Hunting Accessories; Knives/Knife Cases; Law Enforcement; Sharpeners

Lapua/Vihtavuori, 123 Winchester Dr., Sedalia, MO 65301, P: 660-826-3232, F: 660-826-3232, www.lapua.com
Ammunition; Books/Industry Publications; Reloading; Videos

LaRue Tactical, 850 CR 177, Leander, TX 78641, P: 512-259-1585, F: 512-259-1588, www.laruetactical.com
Custom Manufacturing; Scopes, Sights & Accessories; Targets

Laser Ammo, Ltd., #7 Bar Kochva St., Rishon Lezion, 75353, ISRAEL, P: 682-286-3311, www.laser-ammo.com
Ammunition; Firearms; Law Enforcement; Scopes, Sights & Accessories; Shooting Range Equipment; Training & Safety Equipment

Laser Devices, Inc., 2 Harris Ct., Suite A-4, Monterey, CA 93940, P: 800-235-2162, F: 831-373-0903, www.laserdevices.com
Holsters; Law Enforcement; Lighting Products; Scopes, Sights & Accessories; Shooting Range Equipment; Sports Accessories; Targets; Training & Safety Equipment

Laser Shot, Inc., 4214 Bluebonnet Dr., Stafford, TX 77477, P: 281-240-8241, F: 281-240-8241
Law Enforcement; Training & Safety Equipment

LaserLyte, 101 Airpark Rd., Cottonwood, AZ 86326, P: 928-649-3201, F: 928-649-3970, www.laserlyte.com
Hunting Accessories; Scopes, Sights & Accessories

LaserMax, Inc., 3495 Winton Place Bldg. B, Rochester, NY 14623, P: 800-527-3703, F: 585-272-5427, www.lasermax.com
Airsoft; Crossbows & Accessories; Firearms; Law Enforcement; Paintball Accessories; Scopes, Sights & Accessories; Shooting Range Equipment; Training & Safety Equipment

Lauer Custom Weaponry/Duracoat Products, 3601 129th St., Chippewa Falls, WI 54729, P: 800-830-6677, F: 715-723-2950, www.lauerweaponry.com
Camouflage; Custom Manufacturing; Firearms; Hunting Accessories; Law Enforcement; Lubricants; Magazines, Cartridge; Scopes, Sights & Accessories

Law Enforcement Targets, Inc., 8802 W. 35 W. Service Dr. NE, Blaine, MN 55449, P: 800-779-0182, F: 651-645-5360, www.letargets.com
Eyewear; Gun Cabinets/Racks/Safes; Gun Grips & Stocks; Hearing Protection; Law Enforcement; Targets; Training & Safety Equipment

Law Officer Magazine/Div. Elsevier Public Safety/Elsevier, 525 B St., Suite 1900, San Diego, CA 92101, P: 800-266-5367, F: 619-699-6396, www.lawofficer.com
Books/Industry Publications; Law Enforcement

Lawman Leather Goods, P.O. Box 30115, Las Vegas, NV 89173, P: 877-44LAWMAN, F: 702-227-0036, www.lawmanleathergoods.com
Black Powder Accessories; Books/Industry Publications; Holsters; Law Enforcement; Leathergoods; Wholesaler/Distributor

Lazzeroni Arms Co., 1415 S. Cherry Ave., Tuscon, AZ 85713, P: 888-4-WARBIRD, F: 520-624-6202, www.lazzeroni.com
Ammunition; Firearms

Leapers, Inc., 32700 Capitol St., Livonia, MI 48150, P: 734-542-1500, F: 734-542-7095, www.leapers.com
Airguns; Airsoft; Bags & Equipment Cases; Gun Cases; Holsters; Law Enforcement; Lighting Products; Scopes, Sights & Accessories

Leatherman Tool Group, Inc., 12106 NE Ainsworth Circle, Portland, OR 97220, P: 800-847-8665, F: 503-253-7830, www.leatherman.com
Backpacking; Hunting Accessories; Knives/Knife Cases; Lighting Products; Sports Accessories

Leatherwood/Hi-Lux Optics/Hi-Lux, Inc., 3135 Kashiwa St., Torrance, CA 90505, P: 888-445-8912, F: 310-257-8096, www.hi-luxoptics.com
Binoculars; Scopes, Sights & Accessories; Telescopes

Legacy Sports International, 4750 Longley Lane, Suite 208, Reno, NV 89502, P: 775-828-0555, F: 775-828-0565, www.legacysports.com
Firearms; Gun Cabinets/Racks/Safes; Gun Cases; Scopes, Sights & Accessories

Leica Sport Optics/Leica Camera Inc., 1 Peart Ct., Unit A, Allendale, NJ 07401, P: 800-222-0118, F: 201-955-1686, www.leica-camera.com/usa
Binoculars; Photographic Equipment; Scopes, Sights & Accessories

LensPen–Parkside Optical, 650-375 Water St., Vancouver, British Columbia V6B 5C6, CANADA, P: 877-608-0868, F: 604-681-6194, www.lenspens.com
Binoculars; Hunting Accessories; Law Enforcement; Photographic Equipment; Scopes, Sights & Accessories; Sports Accessories; Telescopes

Les Baer Custom, Inc., 1804 Iowa Dr., Leclaire, IA 52753, P: 563-289-2126, F: 563-289-2132, www.lesbaer.com
Custom Manufacturing; Export/Import Specialists; Firearms; Gun Barrels; Gun Parts/Gunsmithing

Leupold & Stevens, Inc., 14400 NW Greenbriar Pkwy. 9700, P.O. Box 688, Beaverton, OR 97006, P: 503-646-9171, F: 503-526-1478, www.leupold.com
Binoculars; Lighting Products; Scopes, Sights & Accessories

Level Lok Shooting System/Div. Brutis Enterprises Inc., 105 S. 12th St., Pittsburgh, PA 15203, P: 888-461-7468, F: 412-488-5440, www.levellok.com
Binoculars; Firearms; Gun Grips & Stocks; Hunting Accessories; Photographic Equipment; Scopes, Sights & Accessories; Shooting Range Equipment; Sports Accessories

Levy's Leathers Limited, 190 Disraeli Freeway, Winnipeg, Manitoba R3B 2Z4, CANADA, P: 800-565-0203, F: 888-329-5389, www.levysleathers.com
Archery; Bags & Equipment Cases; Hunting Accessories; Knives/Knife Cases; Leathergoods

Lew Horton Distributing Co., Inc., 15 Walkup Dr., P.O. Box 5023, Westboro, MA 01581, P: 800-446-7866, F: 508-366-5332, www.lewhorton.com
Ammunition; Firearms; Hunting Accessories; Knives/Knife Cases; Law Enforcement; Magazines, Cartridge; Scopes, Sights & Accessories; Wholesaler/Distributor

Lewis Machine & Tool, 1305 11th St. W, Milan, IL 61264, P: 309-787-7151, F: 309-787-7193, www.lewismachine.net
Firearms

Liberty Mountain, 4375 W. 1980 S, Suite 100, Salt Lake City, UT 84104, P: 800-366-2666, F: 801-954-0766, www.libertymountain.com
Backpacking; Camping; Cooking Equipment/Accessories; Gloves, Mitts, Hats; Knives/Knife Cases; Lighting Products; Survival Kits/First Aid; Wholesaler/Distributor

Liberty Safe & Security Products, Inc., 1199 W. Utah Ave., Payson, UT 84651, P: 800-247-5625, F: 801-465-5880, www.libertysafe.com
Firearms Maintenance Equipment; Gun Cabinets/Racks/Safes; Gun Locks; Home Furnishings; Hunting Accessories; Law Enforcement; Sports Accessories; Training & Safety Equipment

Light My Fire USA, 9225 151st Ave. NE, Redmond, WA 98052, P: 888-297-6062, F: 425-883-0036
Camping; Cooking Equipment/Accessories; Knives/Knife Cases; Survival Kits/First Aid

Lightfield Ammunition Corp., P.O. Box 162, Adelphia, NJ 07710, P: 732-462-9200, F: 732-780-2437, www.lightfieldslugs.com
Ammunition

LightForce USA, Inc/NightForce Optics, 1040 Hazen Ln., Orofino, ID 83544, P: 800-732-9824, F: 208-476-9817, www.nightforceoptics.com
Law Enforcement; Lighting Products; Scopes, Sights & Accessories; Telescopes

LimbSaver, 50 W. Rose Nye Way, Shelton, WA 98584, P: 877-257-2761, F: 360-427-4025, www.limbsaver.com
Archery; Crossbows & Accessories; Hunting Accessories; Men's Clothing; Paintball Accessories; Recoil Protection Devices & Services; Scopes, Sights & Accessories

Linton Cutlery Co., Ltd., 7F, No. 332, Yongji Rd., Sinyi District, Taipei, 110, TAIWAN, P: 011 886227090905, F: 011 886227003978, www.linton-cutlery.com
Cutlery; Export/Import Specialists; Hunting Accessories; Law Enforcement; Sports Accessories; Wholesaler/Distributor

Linville Knife and Tool Co., P.O. Box 71, Bethania, NC 27010, P: 336-923-2062
Cutlery; Gun Grips & Stocks; Knives/Knife Cases

Lipseys, P.O. Box 83280, Baton Rouge, LA 70884, P: 800-666-1333, FL 225-755-3333, www.lipseys.com
Black Powder Accessories; Firearms; Holsters; Hunting Accessories; Magazines, Cartridge; Online Services; Scopes, Sights & Accessories; Wholesaler/Distributor

Little Giant Ladders, 1198 N. Spring Creek Pl., Springville, UT 84663, P: 800-453-1192, F: 801-489-1130, www.littlegiantladders.com
Law Enforcement; Training & Safety Equipment

Little Sportsman, Inc., 315 N. 400 W, P.O. Box 715, Fillmore, UT 84631, P: 435-743-4400, F: 435-846-2132, www.littlesportsman.com
Books/Industry Publications

LockSAF/VMR Capital Group, 2 Gold St., Suite 903, New York, NY 10038, P: 877-568-5625, F: 877-893-4502, www.locksaf.com
Gun Cabinets/Racks/Safes

Loksak, Inc. (formerly Watchful Eye), P.O. Box 980007, Park City, UT 84098, P: 800-355-1126, F: 435-940-0956, www.loksak.com
Bags & Equipment Cases

Lone Wolf Distributors, Inc., 57 Shepard Rd., P.O. Box 3549, Oldtown, ID 83822, P: 888-279-2077, F: 208-437-1098, www.lonewolfdist.com
Books/Industry Publications; Firearms Maintenance Equipment; Gun Barrels; Gun Parts/Gunsmithing; Holsters; Scopes, Sights & Accessories; Videos; Wholesaler/Distributor

Lone Wolf Knives, 9373 SW Barber St., Suite A, Wilsonville, OR 97070, P: 503-431-6777, F: 503-431-6776, www.lonewolfknives.com
Archery; Backpacking; Camouflage; Camping; Cutlery; Hunting Accessories; Knives/Knife Cases; Law Enforcement

Long Perng Co., Ltd., #16, Hejiang Rd., Chung Li Industrial Zone, Chung Li City, Taoyuan Hsien, 320, TAIWAN, P: 011 88634632468, F: 011 88634631948, www.longperng.com.tw
Binoculars; Scopes, Sights & Accessories; Telescopes

Longleaf Camo, 1505 Airport Rd., Flowood, MS 39232, P: 866-751-2266, F: 601-719-0713, www.longleafcamo.com
Camouflage; Footwear; Gloves, Mitts, Hats; Men & Women's Clothing

Loon Lake Decoy Co., Inc., 170 Industrial Ct., Wabasha, MN 55981, P: 800-555-2696, F: 612-565-4871, www.loonlakedecoycompany.com
Custom Manufacturing; Decoys; Home Furnishings; Hunting Accessories; Lighting Products; Outdoor Art, Jewelry, Sculpture; Wholesaler/Distributor

Lorpen North America, Inc., 100 Ironside Crescent, Suite 8, Toronto, Ontario M1X 1M9, CANADA, P: 888-224-9781, F: 416-335-8201, www.lorpen.com
Footwear

Lothar Walther Precision Tools, Inc., 3425 Hutchinson Rd., Cumming, GA 30040, P: 770-889-9998, F: 770-889-4919, www.lothar-walther.com
Custom Manufacturing; Export/Import Specialists; Gun Barrels

Lou's Police Distributor, 7815 W. 4th Ave., Hialeah, FL 33014, P: 305-822-5362, F: 305-822-9603, www.louspolice.com
Ammunition; Firearms; Gun Grips & Stocks; Hearing Protection; Holsters; Law Enforcement; Scopes, Sights & Accessories; Wholesaler/Distributor

LouderThanWords.US/Heirloom Precision, LLC, 2118 E. 5th St., Tempe, AZ 85281, P: 480-804-1911, www.louderthanwords.us
Firearms; Gun Parts/Gunsmithing; Holsters

Lowa Boots, 86 Viaduct Rd., Stamford, CT 06907, P: 888-335-5692, F: 203-353-0311, www.lowaboots.com
Footwear; Men & Women's Clothing

Lowrance–Navico, Eagle–Navico, 12000 E. Skelly Dr., Tulsa, OK 74128, P: 800-352-1356, F: 918-234-1707, www.lowrance.com
Archery; Backpacking; Camping; Hunting Accessories; Law Enforcement; Sports Accessories; Survival Kits/First Aid; Vehicles, Utility & Rec

Lowy Enterprises, Inc., 1970 E. Gladwick St., Rancho Dominguez, CA 90220, P: 310-763-1111, F: 310-763-1112, www.lowyusa.com
Backpacking; Bags & Equipment Cases; Custom Manufacturing; Law Enforcement; Outfitter; Paintball Accessories; Sports Accessories; Wholesaler/Distributor

Luggage-USA, Inc./L A Luggage, 710 Ducommun St., Los Angeles, CA 90012, P: 888-laluggage, F: 213-626-0800, www.luggage-usa.com
Backpacking; Bags & Equipment Cases; Camouflage; Camping; Export/Import Specialists; Gun Cases; Leathergoods; Wholesaler/Distributor

Lumberjack Tools, 9304 Wolf Pack Terrace, Colorado Springs, CO 80920, P: 719-282-3043, F: 719-282-3046, www.lumberjacktools.com
Camping; Crossbows & Accessories; Firearms; Home Furnishings; Hunting Accessories; Taxidermy; Treestands; Wholesaler/Distributor

Luminox Watch Co., 2301 Kerner Blvd., Suite A, San Rafael, CA 94901, P: 415-455-9500, F: 415-482-8215, www.luminox.com
Backpacking; Camping; Custom Manufacturing; Hunting Accessories; Law Enforcement, Outdoor Art, Jewelry, Sculpture; Sports Accessories; Watches

LWRC International, LLC, 815 Chesapeake Dr., Cambridge, MD 21613, P: 410-901-1348, F: 410-228-1799, www.lwrifles.com
Ammunition; Custom Manufacturing; Firearms; Firearms Maintenance Equipment; Gun Barrels; Gun Parts/Gunsmithing; Law Enforcement; Magazines, Cartridge

Lyalvale Express Limited, Express Estate, Whittington, Lichfield, WS13 8XA, UNITED KINGDOM, P: 011-44 1543434400, F: 011-44 1543434420, www.lyalvaleexpress.com
Ammunition

Lyman-Pachmayr-Trius Products/TacStar-A-Zoom-Butchs-Uni-Dot, 475 Smith St., Middletown, CT 06457, P: 800-225-9626, F: 860-632-1699, www.lymanproducts.com
Black Powder Accessories; Books/Industry Publications; Firearms; Firearms Maintenance Equipment; Gun Parts/Gunsmithing; Reloading; Scopes, Sights & Accessories; Shooting Range Equipment

Lyons Press, 246 Goose Ln., Guilford, CT 06437, P: 800-243-0495, F: 800-820-2329, www.glovepequot.com
Books/Industry Publications; Wholesaler/Distributor

M

MDM/Millennium Designed Muzzleloaders, Ltd., RR 1, Box 405, Maidstone, VT 05905, P: 802-676-331, F: 802-676-3322, www.mdm-muzzleloaders.com
Ammunition; Black Powder Accessories; Black Powder/Smokeless Powder; Custom Manufacturing; Firearms Maintenance Equipment; Gun Barrels; Gun Cases; Scopes, Sights & Accessories

MDS Inc., 3429 Stearns Rd., Valrico, FL 33596, P: 800-435-9352, F: 813-684-5953, www.mdsincorporated.com
Firearms Maintenance Equipment; Gun Parts/Gunsmithing; Law Enforcement

MFI, 563 San Miguel, Liberty, KY 42539, P: 606-787-0022, F: 606-787-0059, www.mfiap.com
Custom Manufacturing; Export/Import Specialists; Firearms; Gun Grips & Stocks; Gun Parts/Gunsmithing; Scopes, Sights & Accessories; Sports Accessories; Wholesaler/Distributor

MGI, 102 Cottage St., Bangor, ME 04401, P: 207-945-5441, F: 207-945-4010, www.mgimilitary.com
Firearms; Gun Barrels; Law Enforcement

MGM–Mike Gibson Manufacturing, 17891 Karcher Rd., Caldwell, ID 83607, P: 888-767-7371, F: 208-454-0666, www.mgmtargets.com
Clay Targets; Custom Manufacturing; Firearms; Gun Cabinets/Racks/Safes; Shooting Range Equipment; Targets; Training & Safety Equipment

MG Arms, Inc., 6030 Treaschwig Rd., Spring, TX 77373, P: 281-821-8282, F: 281-821-6387, www.mgarmsinc.com
Ammunition; Custom Manufacturing; Firearms; Gun Grips & Stocks; Wholesaler/Distributor

MPI Outdoors/Grabber, 5760 N. Hawkeye Ct., Grand Rapids, MI 49509, P: 800-423-1233, F: 616-977-7718, www.warmers.com
Backpacking; Camouflage; Camping; Cooking Equipment/Accessories; Gloves, Mitts, Hats; Hunting Accessories; Lighting Products; Survival Kits/First Aid

MPRI, 10220 Old Columbia Rd., Suites A & B, Columbia, MD 21046, P: 800-232-6448, F: 410-309-1506, www.mpri.com
Ammunition; Gun Barrels; Law Enforcement; Shooting Range Equipment; Targets; Training & Safety Equipment

MPT Industries, 6-B Hamilton Business Park, 85 Franklin Rd., Dover, NJ 07801, P: 973-989-9220, F: 973-989-9234, www.mptindustries.com
Airguns; Camping; Firearms; Firearms Maintenance Equipment; Lubricants; Paintball Guns; Sports Accessories

M-Pro 7 Gun Care/Bushnell Outdoor Accessories, 9200 Cody, Overland Park, KS 66214, P: 800-845-2444, F: 800-548-0446, www.mpro7.com
Black Powder Accessories; Firearms Maintenance Equipment; Gun Parts/Gunsmithing; Hunting Accessories; Law Enforcement; Lubricants

M-Pro 7 Gun Care, 225 W. Deer Valley Rd., Suite 4, Phoenix, AZ 85027, P: 888-YES-4MP7, F: 623-516-0414, www.mpro7.com
Black Powder Accessories; Firearms Maintenance Equipment; Gun Parts/Gunsmithing; Hunting Accessories; Law Enforcement; Lubricants

MSA, 121 Gamma Dr., Pittsburgh, PA 15238, P: 800-672-2222, F: 412-967-3373
Bags & Equipment Cases; Eyewear; Hearing Protection; Law Enforcement; Survival Kits/First Aid; Training & Safety Equipment

MSA Safety Works, 121 Gamma Dr., Pittsburgh, PA 15238, P: 800-969-7562, F: 800-969-7563, www.msasafetyworks.com
Eyewear; Hearing Protection; Shooting Range Equipment; Training & Safety Equipment

MT2, LLC/Metals Treatment Technologies, 14045 W. 66th Ave., Arvada, CO 80004, P: 888-435-6645, F: 303-456-5998, www.mt2.com
Firearms Maintenance Equipment; Shooting Range Equipment

MTM Case-Gard Co., P.O. Box 13117, Dayton, OH 45413, P: 800-543-0548, F: 937-890-1747, www.mtmcase-gard.com
Bags & Equipment Cases; Black Powder Accessories; Camping; Firearms Maintenance Equipment; Gun Cases; Hunting Accessories; Reloading; Targets

Mace Security International, 160 Benmont Ave., Bennington, VT 05201, P: 800-255-2634, F: 802-753-1209, www.mace.com

Archery; Camping; Hunting Accessories; Law Enforcement; Sports Accessories; Training & Safety Equipment

Mag Instrument, Inc./Maglite, 2001 S. Hellman Ave., Ontario, CA 91761, P: 800-289-6241, F: 775-719-4586, www.maglite.com
Backpacking; Camping; Hunting Accessories; Lighting Products; Sports Accessories; Survival Kits/First Aid; Training & Safety Equipment

Magellan Navigation, 471 El Camino Real, Santa Clara, CA 94050, P: 408-615-5100, F: 408-615-5200, www.magellangps.com
Backpacking; Camping; Compasses; Computer Software; Hunting Accessories; Sports Accessories; Vehicles, Utility & Rec

Maglula, Ltd., P.O. Box 302, Rosh Ha'ayin, 48103, ISRAEL, P: 011 97239030902, F: 011 97239030902, www.maglula.com
Firearms Maintenance Equipment; Gun Parts/Gunsmithing; Magazines, Cartridge; Shooting Range Equipment

Magnum USA, 4801 Stoddard Rd., Modesto, CA 95356, P: 800-521-1698, F: 209-545-2079, www.magnumboots.com
Footwear; Law Enforcement; Men's Clothing

Magnum Research, Inc., 7110 University Ave. NE, Minneapolis, MN 55432, P: 800-772-6168, F: 763-574-0109, www.magnumresearch.com
Firearms

Magnum Tents, P.O. Box 18127, Missoula, MT 59808, P: 877-836-8226, F: 877-836-8226, www.magnumtents.com
Camping; Hunting Accessories

Magpul Industries Corp., P.O. Box 17697, Boulder, CO 80308, P: 877-462-4785, F: 303-828-3469, www.magpul.com
Firearms; Gun Grips & Stocks; Gun Parts/Gunsmithing; Law Enforcement; Videos

Magtech Ammunition Co., Inc., 248 Apollo Dr., Suite 180, Lino Lakes, MN 55014, P: 800-466-7191, F: 763-235-4004, www.magtechammunition.com
Ammunition; Export/Import Specialists; Law Enforcement; Reloading; Shooting Range Equipment; Wholesaler/Distributor

Mahco, Inc., 1202 Melissa Dr., Bentonville, AR 72712, P: 479-273-0052, F: 479-271-9248
Bags & Equipment Cases; Binoculars; Camouflage; Camping; Hunting Accessories; Knives/Knife Cases; Scopes, Scopes, Sights & Accessories

Majestic Arms, Ltd., 101-A Ellis St., Staten Island, NY 10307, P: 718-356-6765, F: 718-356-6835, www.majesticarms.com
Firearms; Gun Barrels; Gun Parts/Gunsmithing

Mako Group, 74 Rome St., Farmingdale, NY 11735, P: 631-880-3396, F: 631-880-3397, www.themakogroup.com
Custom Manufacturing; Gun Grips & Stocks; Law Enforcement; Lighting Products; Scopes, Sights & Accessories; Targets; Training & Safety Equipment; Wholesaler/Distributor

Mancom Manufacturing Inc., 1335 Osprey Dr., Ancaster, Ontario L9G 4V5, CANADA, P: 888-762-6266, F: 905-304-6137, www.mancom.ca
Custom Manufacturing; Law Enforcement; Shooting Range Equipment; Training & Safety Equipment

Manners Composite Stocks, 1209 Swift, North Kansas City, MO 64116, P: 816-283-3334, www.mannerstock.com
Custom Manufacturing; Firearms Maintenance Equipment; Gun Grips & Stocks; Law Enforcement; Shooting Range Equipment

Dave Manson Precision Reamers/Div. Loon Lake Precision, Inc., 8200 Embury Rd., Grand Blanc, MI 48439, P: 810-953-0732, F: 810-953-0735, www.mansonreamers.com
Black Powder Accessories; Custom Manufacturing; Firearms Maintenance Equipment; Gun Barrels; Gun Parts/Gunsmithing; Recoil Protection Devices & Services; Reloading

Mantis Knives/Famous Trails, 1580 N. Harmony Circle, Anaheim, CA 92807, P: 877-97-SCOPE, F: 714-701-9672, www.mantisknives.com
Binoculars; Camping; Hunting Accessories; Knives/Knife Cases; Law Enforcement; Photographic Equipment; Scopes, Sights & Accessories; Wholesaler/Distributor

Manzella Productions, 80 Sonwil Dr., Buffalo, NY 14225, P: 716-681-8880, F: 716-681-6888
Hunting Accessories; Law Enforcement

Marbles, 420 Industrial Park, Gladstone, MI 49837, P: 906-428-3710, F: 906-428-3711, www.marblescutlery.com
Compasses; Cutlery; Scopes, Sights & Accessories; Sharpeners

Marlin Firearms/H&R, 100 Kenna Dr., P.O. Box 248, North Haven, CT 06473, P: 888-261-1179, F: 336-548-8736, www.marlinfirearms.com
Firearms

Marvel Precision, LLC, P.O. Box 127, Cortland, NE 68331, P: 800-295-1987, F: 402-791-2246, www.marvelprecision.com
Firearms; Wholesaler/Distributor

Masen Co., Inc., John, 1305 Jelmak St., Grand Prairie, TX 75050, P: 972-970-3691, F: 972-970-3691, www.johnmasen.com
Firearms Maintenance Equipment; Gun Grips & Stocks; Gun Parts/Gunsmithing; Magazines, Cartridge; Online Services; Scopes, Sights & Accessories; Wholesaler/Distributor

Maserin Coltellerie SNC, Via dei Fabbri, 19, Maniago, 33085, ITALY, P: 011 39042771335, F: 011 390427700690, www.maserin.com
Cutlery; Hunting Accessories; Knives/Knife Cases; Law Enforcement; Sports Accessories

Master Cutlery, Inc., 700 Penhorn Ave., Secausus, NJ 07094, P: 888-271-7228, F: 888-271-7228, www.mastercutlery.com
Airsoft; Crossbows & Accessories; Custom Manufacturing; Cutlery

Masterbuilt Manufacturing, Inc., 1 Masterbuilt Ct., Columbus, GA 31907, P: 800-489-1581, F: 706-327-5632, www.masterbuilt.com
Camping; Cooking Equipment/Accessories; Hunting Accessories; Vehicles, Utility & Rec

Matterhorn Footwear/Cove Shoe Co., HH Brown Work & Outdoor Group, 107 Highland St., Martinsburg, PA 16662, P: 800-441-4319, F: 814-793-9272, www.matterhornboot.com
Footwear; Law Enforcement; Training & Safety Equipment

Matz Abrasives/Stagecoach, 1209 W. Chestnut St., Burbank, CA 91506, P: 818-840-8042, F: 818-840-8340, www.matzrubber.com
Black Powder Accessories; Custom Manufacturing; Firearms; Firearms Maintenance Equipment; Gun Grips & Stocks; Gun Parts/Gunsmithing; Hunting Accessories; Recoil Protection Devices & Services

Maurice Sporting Goods, Inc., 1910 Techny Rd., Northbrook, IL 60065, P: 866-477-3474, F: 847-715-1419, www.maurice.net
Archery; Camping; Firearms Maintenance Equipment; Game Calls; Gloves, Mitts, Hats; Hunting Accessories; Sports Accessories; Wholesaler/Distributor

Maxit Designs, Inc., P.O. Box 1052, Carmichael, CA 95609, P: 800-556-2948, F: 916-489-7031, www.maxit-inc.com
Footwear; Gloves, Mitts, Hats; Men & Women's Clothing

Maxpedition Hard-Use Gear/Edgygear, Inc., P.O. Box 5008, Palos Verdes, CA 90274, P: 877-629-5556, F: 310-515-5950, www.maxpedition.com
Backpacking; Bags & Equipment Cases; Gun Cases; Holsters; Hunting Accessories; Knives/Knife Cases; Law Enforcement; Sports Accessories

MaxPro Police & Armor, 4181 W. 5800 N, Mountain Green, UT 84050, P: 801-876-3616, F: 801-876-2746, www.maxpropolice.com
Training & Safety Equipment

Mayville Engineering Co. (MEC), 800 Horicon St., Suite 1, Mayville, WI 53050, P: 800-797-4MEC, F: 920-387-5802, www.mecreloaders.com
Reloading

McConkey, Inc./ATV Backpacker Cart, P.O. Box 1362, Seeley Lake, MT 59868, P: 308-641-1085, F: 866-758-9896, www.atvbackpackercart.com
Ammunition; Backpacking; Camping; Hunting Accessories; Sports Accessories; Vehicles, Utility & Rec; Wholesaler/Distributor

McGowan Manufacturing Co., 4854 N. Shamrock Pl., Suite 100, Tucson, AZ 85705, P: 800-342-4810, F: 520-219-9759, www.mcgowanmfg.com
Archery; Camping; Cooking Equipment/Accessories; Crossbows & Accessories; Cutlery; Hunting Accessories; Knives/Knife Cases; Sharpeners

McKeon Products, Inc./Mack's Hearing Protection, 25460 Guenther, Warren, MI 48091, P: 586-427-7560, F: 586-427-7204, www.macksearplugs.com
Camping; Hearing Protection; Hunting Accessories; Sports Accessories; Training & Safety Equipment

McMillan Fiberglass Stocks, 1638 W. Knudsen Dr., Suite A, Phoenix, AZ 85027, P: 877-365-6148, F: 623-581-3825, www.mcmillanusa.com
Firearms; Gun Grips & Stocks

McNett Corp., 1411 Meador Ave., Bellingham, WA 98229, P: 360-671-2227, F: 360-671-4521, www.mcnett.com
Backpacking; Camouflage; Camping; Hunting Accessories; Knives/Knife Cases; Lubricants; Paintball Accessories; Sports Accessories

Mcusta Knives/Mcusta Knives USA, P.O. Box 22901, Portland, OR 97269, P: 877-714-5487, F: 503-344-4631, www.mcustausa.com
Cooking Equipment/Accessories; Cutlery; Hunting Accessories; Knives/Knife Cases; Law Enforcement; Sports Accessories; Wholesaler/Distributor

Mead Industries, Inc., 411 Walnut St., P.O. Box 402, Wood River, NE 68883, P: 308-583-2875, F: 308-583-2002
Ammunition

MEC-GAR SRL, Via Mandolossa, 102/a, Gussago, Brescia, 25064, ITALY, P: 011 390303735413, F: 011 390303733687, www.mec-gar.it
Gun Parts/Gunsmithing; Law Enforcement; Magazine, Cartridge

Medalist/Performance Sports Apparel, 1047 Macarthur Rd., Reading PA, 19605, P: 800-543-8952, F: 610-373-5400, www.medalist.com
Camouflage; Hunting Accessories; Men & Women's Clothing

Meggitt Training Systems/Caswell, 296 Brogdon Rd., Suwanee, GA 30024, P: 800-813-9046, F: 678-288-1515, www.meggitttrainingsystems.com
Custom Manufacturing; Law Enforcement; Shooting Range Equipment; Targets; Training & Safety Equipment

Meissenberg Designs, 7583 MT Hwy. 35, Bigfork, MT 59911, P: 877-974-7446, F: 866-336-2571, www.oldwoodsigns.com
Home Furnishings; Printing Services

Medota Products, Inc., 120 Bridgepoint Way, Suite B, South St. Paul, MN 55075, P: 800-224-1121, F: 651-457-9085, www.mendotaproducts.com
Custom Manufacturing; Hunting Accessories; Pet Supplies; Training & Safety Equipment

Meopta USA, Inc., 50 Davids Dr., Hauppauge, NY, 11788, P: 800-828-8928, F: 631-436-5920, www.meopta.com
Binoculars; Scopes, Sights & Accessories; Telescopes

Meprolight, 2590 Montana Hwy. 35, Suite B, Kalispell, MT 59901, P: 406-758-2222, F: 406-758-2223
Scopes, Sights & Accessories

Meprolight, Ltd., 58 Hazait St., Or-Akiva Industrial Park, Or-Akiva, 30600, ISRAEL, P: 011 97246244111, F: 011 97246244123, www.meprolight.com
Binoculars; Firearms; Gun Parts/Gunsmithing; Hunting Accessories; Law Enforcement; Lighting Products; Scopes, Sights & Accessories; Telescopes

Mercury Luggage Mfg. Co./Code Alpha Tactical Gear, 4843 Victory St., Jacksonville, FL 32207, P: 800-874-1885, F: 904-733-9671, www.mercuryluggage.com
Bags & Equipment Cases; Camouflage; Custom Manufacturing; Export/Import Specialists; Law Enforcement

Merkel USA, 7661 Commerce Ln., Trussville, AL 35173, P: 800-821-3021, F: 205-655-7078, www.merkel-usa.com
Binoculars; Firearms; Scopes, Sights & Accessories

Mesa Tactical, 1760 Monrovia Ave., Suite A14, Costa Mesa, CA 92627, P: 949-642-3337, F: 949-642-3339, www.mesatactical.com
Gun Grips & Stocks; Law Enforcement; Scopes, Sights & Accessories

Metal Ware Corp./Open Country, 1700 Monroe St., P.O. Box 237, Two Rivers, WI 54241, P: 800-624-2949, F: 920-794-3161, www.opencountrycampware.com
Backpacking; Camping; Cooking Equipment/Accessories; Sports Accessories

Meyerco, 4481 Exchange Service Dr., Dallas, TX 75236, P: 214-467-8949, F: 214-467-9241, www.meyercousa.com
Bags & Equipment Cases; Camping; Cutlery; Gun Cases; Hunting Accessories; Knives/Knife Cases; Law Enforcement; Sharpeners

Mick Lacy Game Calls, 628 W. Main St., Princeville, IL 61559, P: 800-681-1070, F: 309-385-1068, www.micklacygamecalls.com
Game Calls; Hunting Accessories

Microsonic, 2960 Duss Ave., Ambridge, PA 15003, P: 724-266-9480, F: 724-266-9482, www.microsonic-inc.com
Hearing Protection

Microtech Knives, Inc./Microtech Small Arms Research, Inc., 300 Chestnut St., Bradford, PA 16701, P: 814-363-9260, F: 814-363-9284, www.msarinc.com
Custom Manufacturing; Cutlery; Firearms; Knives/Knife Cases; Law Enforcement; Sports Accessories

Midland Radio Corp., 5900 Parretta Dr., Kansas City, MO, 64120, P: 816-241-8500, F: 816-241-5713, www.midlandradio.com
Hunting Accessories; Sports Accessories; Training & Safety Equipment; Two-Way Radios

Midwest Industries, Inc., 828 Philip Dr., Suite 2, Waukesha, WI 53186, P: 262-896-6780, F: 262-896-6756, www.midwestindustriesinc.com
Gun Cases; Gun Parts/Gunsmithing; Law Enforcement; Lubricants; Magazines, Cartridge; Scopes, Sights & Accessories

Midwest Quality Gloves, Inc., 835 Industrial Rd., P.O. Box 260, Chillicothe, MO 64601, P: 800-821-3028, F: 660-646-6933, www.midwestglove.com
Archery; Camouflage; Gloves, Mitts, Hats; Hunting Accessories; Men's Clothing

Mil-Comm Products Co., Inc., 2 Carlton Ave., East Rutherford, NJ 07073, P: 888-947-3273, F: 201-935-6059, www.mil-comm.com
Black Powder Accessories; Firearms Maintenance Equipment; Gun Cabinets/Racks/Safes; Gun

Locks; Gun Parts/Gunsmithing; Law Enforcement; Lubricants; Paintball Guns

Mil-Spec Plus/Voodoo Tactical, 435 W. Alondra Blvd., Gardena, CA 90248, P: 310-324-8855, F: 310-324-6909, www.majorsurplus.com
Bags & Equipment Cases; Eyewear; Footwear; Gloves, Mitts, Hats; Gun Cases; Law Enforcement

Mil-Tac Knives & Tools, P.O. Box 642, Wylie, TX 75098, P: 877-MIL-TAC6, F: 972-412-2208, www.mil-tac.com
Cutlery; Eyewear; Gloves, Mitts, Hats; Gun Parts/Gunsmithing; Hunting Accessories; Knives/Knife Cases; Law Enforcement; Survival Kits/First Aid

Militaria, Inc., Rt. 2, P.O. Box 166, Collins, GA 30421, P: 912-693-6411, F: 912-693-2060
Books/Industry Publications; Emblems & Decals; Firearms Maintenance Equipment; Lubricants; Wholesaler/Distributor

Military Outdoor Clothing, Inc., 1917 Stanford St., Greenville, TX 75401, P: 800-662-6430, F: 903-454-2433, www.militaryoutdoorclothing.com
Bags & Equipment Cases; Camouflage; Gloves, Mitts, Hats; Law Enforcement; Men & Women's Clothing

Milkor USA, Inc., 3735 N. Romero Rd., Suite 2M, Tucson, AZ 85705, P: 520-888-0103, F: 520-888-0122, www.milkorusainc.com
Firearms

Millett Sights/Bushnell Outdoor Products, 6200 Cody, Overland Park, KS 66214, P: 888-276-5945, F: 800-548-0446, www.millettsights.com
Black Powder Accessories; Gun Parts/Gunsmithing; Hunting Accessories; Law Enforcement; Scopes, Sights & Accessories

Minox USA, 438 Willow Brook Rd., Merdien, NH 03770, P: 866-469-3080, F: 603-469-3471, www.minox.com
Binoculars

Mocean, 1635 Monrovia Ave., Costa Mesa, CA 92627, P: 949-646-1701, F: 949-646-1590, www.mocean.net
Custom Manufacturing; Law Enforcement; Men & Women's Clothing; Wholesaler/Distributor

MOJO Outdoors, 2984 New Monroe Rd., P.O. Box 8460, Monroe, LA 71211, P: 318-283-7777, F: 318-283-1127, www.mojooutdoors.com
Decoys

Molehill Mt. Equipment, Inc., 416 Laskspur St., Suite A, Ponderay, ID 83852, P: 800-804-0820, F: 208-263-3056, www.molehillmtn.com
Camouflage; Camping; Footwear; Gloves, Mitts, Hats; Men & Women's Clothing

Montana Canvas, 110 Pipkin Way, Belgrade, MT 59714, P: 800-235-6518, F: 406-388-1039, www.montanacanvas.com
Camping; Hunting Accessories

Montana Decoys, P.O. Box 2377, Colstrip, MT 59323, P: 888-332-6998, F: 406-748-3471, www.montantadecoy.com
Decoys

Montana Rifle Co./Montana Rifleman, Inc., 3172 Montana Hwy. 35, Kalispell, MT 59901, P: 406-755-4867, F: 406-755-9449, www.montanarifle.com
Custom Manufacturing; Firearms; Gun Barrels; Gun Parts/Gunsmithing

Moore Texas Hunting, 108 S. Ranch House Rd., Suite 800, Aledo, TX 76008, P: 817-688-1774, F: 817-441-1606, www.mooretexashunting.com
Custom Manufacturing; Hunting Accessories; Sports Accessories; Wholesaler/Distributor

Morovision Night Vision, Inc., P.O. Box 342, Dana Point, CA 92629, P: 800-424-8222, F: 949-488-3361, www.morovision.com
Binoculars; Camping; Hunting Accessories; Law Enforcement; Lighting Products; Photographic Equipment; Scopes, Sights & Accessories; Wholesaler/Distributor

Morton Enterprises, 35 Pilot Ln., Great Cacapon, WV, 25422, P: 877-819-7280, www.uniquecases.com
Bags & Equipment Cases; Custom Manufacturing; Gun Cases; Hunting Accessories; Law Enforcement; Sports Accessories

Mossy Oak, P.O. Box 757, West Point, MS 39773, P: 662-494-8859, F: 662-494-8837, www.mossyoak.com
Books; Camouflage; Home Furnishings; Hunting Accessories; Men & Women's Clothing; Videos

Mostly Signs, 12993 Los Nietos Rd., Sante Fe Springs, CA 90670, P: 888-667-8595, F: 800-906-9855, www.mostlysigns.com
Home Furnishings; Wholesaler/Distributor

Moteng, Inc., 12220 Parkway Centre Dr., Poway, CA 92064, P: 800-367-5900, F: 800-367-5903, www.moteng.com
Camping; Cutlery; Knives/Knife Cases; Law Enforcement; Lighting Products; Online Services; Training & Safety Equipment; Wholesaler/Distributor

Mothwing Camo/Gameday Camo, P.O. Box 2019, Calhoun, GA 30703, P: 800-668-4946, F: 706-625-2484, www.mothwing.com
Camouflage; Men & Women's Clothing; Vehicles, Utility & Rec

Moultrie Products, LLC, 150 Industrial Rd., Alabaster, AL 35007, P: 800-653-3334, F: 205-664-6706, www.moultriefeeders.com
Feeder Equipment; Photographic Equipment; Wildlife Management

Mountain Corp./Mountain Life, 59 Optical Ave., P.O. Box 686, Keene, NH 03431, P: 800-545-9684, F: 603-355-3702, www.themountain.com
Law Enforcement; Men & Women's Clothing; Outfitter; Retail Packaging; Wholesaler/Distributor

Mountain House/Oregon Freeze Dry, 525 25th SW, Albany, OR 97321, P: 800-547-0244, F: 541-812-6601, www.mountainhouse.com
Backpacking; Camping; Hunting Accessories

Mounting Solutions Plus, 10655 SW 185 Terrace, Miami, FL 33157, P: 800-428-9394, F: 305-232-1247, www.mountsplus.com
Scopes, Sights & Accessories; Wholesaler/Distributor

MTM-Multi Time Machine, Inc., 1225 S. Grand Ave., Los Angeles, CA 90015, P: 213-741-0808, F: 213-741-0840, www.specialopswatch.com
Archery; Backpacking; Camouflage; Hunting Accessories; Law Enforcement; Sports Accessories; Watches

Mud River Dog Products, 355 E. Hwy. 264, Suite D, Bethel Heights, AR 72764, P: 479-927-2447, F: 479-927-2667, www.mudriverdogproducts.com
Bags & Equipment Cases; Blinds; Camping; Custom Manufacturing; Hunting Accessories; Men's Clothing; Pet Supplies, Vehicles, Utility & Rec

Muela, Ctra. N-420, KM 165, 500, Argamasilla De Calatrava, (Ciudad Real) 13440, SPAIN, P: 011 34926477093, F: 011 34926477237, www.mmuela.com
Knives/Knife Cases

Muller Prinsloo Knives, P.O. Box 2263, Bethlehem, 9700, SOUTH AFRICA, P: 011 27824663885, F: 011 27583037111
Knives/Knife Cases

Mystery Ranch, 34156 E. Frontage Rd., Bozeman, MT 59715, P: 406-585-1428, F: 406-585-1792, www.mysteryranch.com
Backpacking; Bags & Equipment Cases; Camping; Law Enforcement; Photographic Equipment

N

Nantong Universal Optical Instruments Co., Ltd., No. 1 Pingchao Industrial Garden, Nantong, Jiangsu 226361, CHINA, P: 011 8651386726888, F: 011 8651386718158, www.zoscn.com
Airguns; Binoculars; Gun Cases; Gun Locks; Scopes, Sights & Accessories; Wholesaler/Distributor

National Emblem, Inc., 17036 S. Avalon Blvd., Carson, CA 90746, P: 800-877-6185, F: 310-515-5966, www.nationalemblem.com
Custom Manufacturing; Emblems & Decals; Gloves, Mitts, Hats

National Geographic Maps, P.O. Box 4357, Evergreen, CO 80437, P: 800-962-1643, F: 800-626-8676, www.nationalgeographic.com/map
Archery; Backpacking; Books/Industry Publications; Camping; Compasses; Computer Software; Sports Accessories

National Muzzle Loading Rifle Association, P.O. Box 67, Friendship, IN 47021, P: 812-667-5131, F: 812-667-5137, www.nmlra.com

National Rifle Association, 11250 Waples Mill Rd., Fairfax, VA 22030, P: 800-672-3888, F: 703-267-3810, www.nra.org

National Wild Turkey Federation, 770 Augusta Rd., P.O. Box 530, Edgefield, SC 29824, P: 800-843-6983, F: 803-637-0034, www.nwtf.org

Nation's Best Sports, 4216 Hahn Blvd., Fort Worth, TX 76117, P: 817-788-0034, F: 817-788-8542, www.nationsbestsports.com
Retailer Services

Nature Coast Laser Creations, 9185 Mercedes Terrace N, Crystal River, FL 34428, P: 352-564-0794, www.laserautotags.com
Custom Manufacturing; Emblems & Decals; Hunting Accessories; Outdoor Art, Jewelry, Sculpture; Paintball Accessories; Sports Accessories; Vehicles, Utility & Rec

N-Vision Optics, 220 Reservior St., Suite 26, Neenham, MA 02494, P: 781-505-8360, F: 781-998-5656, www.nvisionoptics.com
Binoculars; Law Enforcement; Scopes, Sights & Accessories

Navy Arms Co./Forgett Militaria, 219 Lawn St., Martinsburg, WV 25405, P: 304-262-1651, F: 304-262-1658, www.navyarms.com
Firearms

Nester Hosiery, Inc., 1400 Carter St., Mount Airy, NC 27030, P: 888-871-1507, F: 336-789-0626, www.nesteroutdoorsocks.com
Backpacking; Camping; Custom Manufacturing; Footwear; Hunting Accessories; Men & Women's Clothing; Sports Accessories

New Century Science & Tech, Inc., 10302 Olney St., El Monte, CA 91731, P: 866-627-8278, F: 626-575-2478, www.ncstar.com
Binoculars; Crossbows & Accessories; Custom Manufacturing; Export/Import Specialists; Firearms Maintenance Equipment; Gun Cases; Lighting Products; Scopes, Sights & Accessories

New Ultra Light Arms, 214 Price St., P.O. Box 340, Granville, WV 26534, P: 304-292-0600, FL 304-292-9662, www.newultralight.com
Firearms

Newcon Optik, 105 Sparks Ave., Toronto M2H 2S5, CANADA, P: 877-368-6666, F: 416-663-9065, www.newcon-optik.com
Binoculars; Hunting Accessories; Law Enforcement; Paintballs; Photographic Equipment; Scopes, Sights & Accessories; Shooting Range Equipment

Nextorch, Inc., 2401 Viewcrest Ave., Everett, WA 98203, P: 425-290-3092, www.nextorch.com
Hunting Accessories; Knives/Knife Cases; Lighting Products

Night Optics USA, Inc., 5122 Bolsa Ave., Suite 101, Huntington Beach, CA 92649, P: 800-30-NIGHT, F: 714-899-4485, www.nightoptics.com
Binoculars; Camping; Hunting Accessories; Law Enforcement; Scopes, Sights & Accessories; Training & Safety Equipment; Wholesaler/Distributor; Wildlife Management

Night Owl Optics/Bounty Hunter/Fisher Research Labs, 1465-H Henry Brennan, El Paso, TX 79936, P: 800-444-5994, F: 915-633-8529, www.nightowloptics.com
Binoculars; Camping; Hunting Accessories; Law Enforcement; Photographic Equipment; Scopes, Sights & Accessories; Sports Accessories; Telescopes

Night Vision Depot, P.O. Box 3415, Allentown, PA 18106, P: 610-395-9743, F: 610-395-9744, www.nvdepot.com
Binoculars; Hunting Accessories; Law Enforcement; Lighting Products; Scopes, Sights & Accessories; Wholesaler/Distributor

Night Vision Systems (NVS), 542 Kemmerer Ln., Allentown, PA 18104, P: 800-797-2849, F: 610-391-9220, www.nighvisionsystems.com
Law Enforcement; Scopes, Sights & Accessories

Nighthawk Custom, 1306 W. Trimble, Berryville, AR 72616, P: 877-268-4867, F: 870-423-4230, www.nighthawkcustom.com
Firearms; Gun Grips & Stocks; Gun Parts/Gunsmithing; Hearing Protection; Holsters

Nikon, Inc., 1300 Walt Whitman Rd., Melville, NY 11747, P: 631-547-4200, FL 631-547-4040, www.nikonhunting.com
Binoculars; Hunting Accessories; Scopes, Sights & Accessories

Ningbo Electric and Consumer Goods I/E. Corp., 17/F, Lingqiao Plaza, 31 Yaohang Street, Ningbo, Zhejiang, 315000 CHINA P: 011 8657487194807; F: 011 8657487296214

Nite Ize, Inc., 5660 Central Ave., Boulder, CO 80301, P: 800-678-6483, F: 303-449-2013, www.niteize.com
Bags & Equipment Cases; Camping; Custom Manufacturing; Holsters; Lighting Products; Pet Supplies

Nite Lite Co., 3801 Woodland Heights Rd., Suite 100, Little Rock, AR 72212, P: 800-648-5483, F: 501-227-4892, www.huntsmart.com
Game Calls; Hunting Accessories; Lighting Products; Men's Clothing; Pet Supplies; Scents & Lures; Scopes, Sights & Accessories; Training & Safety Equipment

Nitrex Optics/ATK Commercial Products, N5549 Cty. Tk. Z, Onalaska, WI 54650, P: 800-635-7656, F: 763-323-3890, www.nitrexoptics.com
Binoculars; Scopes, Sights & Accessories

NiViSys Industries LLC, 400 S. Clark Dr., Suite 105, Tempe, AZ 85281, P: 480-970-3222, F: 480-970-3555, www.nivisys.com
Binoculars; Law Enforcement; Lighting Products; Photographic Equipment; Scopes, Sights & Accessories; Wholesaler/Distributor

Norica Laurona, Avda. Otaola, 16, Eibar, (Guipúzcoa) 20600, P: 011 34943207445, F: 011 34943207449, www.norica.es, www.laurona.com
Airguns; Ammunition; Firearms; Hearing Protection; Hunting Accessories; Knives/Knife Cases; Scopes, Sights & Accessories

Norma Precision AB/RUAG Ammotec, Jagargatan, Amotfors, S-67040, SWEDEN, P: 044-46-571-31500, F: 011-46-571-31540, www.norma.cc
Ammunition; Custom Manufacturing; Reloading

North American Arms, Inc., 2150 S. 950 E, Provo, UT 84606, P: 800-821-5783, F: 801-374-9998, www.northamericanarms.com
Firearms

North American Hunter, 12301 Whitewater Dr., Minnetonka, MN 55343, P: 800-688-7611, F: 952-936-9169, www.huntingclub.com
Books/Industry Publications

Northern Lights Tactical, P.O. 10272, Prescott, AZ 86304, P: 310-376-4266, F: 310-798-9278, www.northernlightstactical.com
Archery; Hunting Accessories; Law Enforcement; Paintball Accessories; Shooting Range Equipment; Targets; Training & Safety Equipment; Vehicles, Utility & Rec

Northridge International, Inc., 23679 Calabasas Rd., Suit 406, Calabasas, CA 91302, P: 661-269-2269, www.northridgeinc.com
Camouflage; Compasses; Cutlery; Firearms; Firearms Maintenance Equipment; Gun Barrels; Gun Cases; Survival Kits/First Aid

Northwest Territorial Mint, P.O. Box 2148, Auburn, WA 98071, P: 800-344-6468, F: 253-735-2210, www.nwtmint.com
Custom Manufacturing; Emblems & Decals; Knives/Knife Cases; Outdoor Art, Jewelry, Sculpture

Northwest Tracker, Inc., 6205 NE 63rd St., Vancouver, WA 98661, P: 360-213-0363, F: 360-693-2212, www.trackeroutpost.com
Gun Cabinets/Racks/Safes; Gun Cases; Hunting Accessories; Treestands

Nosler, Inc., 107 SW Columbia, P.O. Box 671, Bend, OR 97709, P: 800-285-3701, F: 800-766-7537, www.nosler.com
Ammunition; Black Powder Accessories; Books/Industry Publications; Firearms; Reloading

Not Your Daddy's, 7916 High Heath, Knoxville, TN 37919, P: 865-806-8496, F: 865-690-4555
Gun Cases

Nova Silah Sanayi, Ltd., Merkez Mah. Kultur Cad. No: 22/14, Duzce, TURKEY, P: 011-90 2125140279, F: 011-90 2125111999
Firearms

Novatac, Inc., 300 Carlsbad Village Dr., Suite 108A-100, Carlsbad, CA 92008, P: 760-730-7370, FL 760-730-7375, www.novatac.com
Backpacking; Camping; Hunting Accessories; Law Enforcement; Lighting Products; Survival Kits/First Aid; Training & Safety Equipment

NRA FUD, 11250 Waples Mill Rd., Fairfax, VA 22030, P: 703-267-1300, F: 703-267-3800, www.nrafud.com
Decoys; Hunting Accessories; Wholesaler/Distributor

NTA Enterprise, Inc./Huntworth/Thermologic, R J Casey Industrial Park, Columbus Ave., Pittsburgh, PA 15233, P: 877-945-6837, F: 412-325-7865, www.thermologicgear.com
Archery; Backpacking; Camouflage; Gloves, Mitts, Hats; Hunting Accessories; Men & Women's Clothing; Sports Accessories

Numrich Gun Parts Corp./Gun Parts Corp., 226 Williams Ln., P.O. Box 299, West Hurley, NY 12491, P: 866-686-7424, F: 877-GUN-PART, www.e-gunparts.com
Firearms Maintenance Equipment; Gun Barrels; Gun Cases; Gun Grips & Stocks; Gun Parts/Gunsmithing; Hunting Accessories; Magazines, Cartridge; Scopes, Sights & Accessories

Nutri-Vet, LLC, 495 N. Dupont Ave., Boise, ID 83713, P: 877-728-8668, F: 208-377-1941, www.nutri-vet.com
Pet Supplies

Nuwai International Co., Ltd./Nuwai LED Flashlight, 11 FL., 110 Li Gong St., Bei, Tou Taipei, 11261, TAIWAN, P: 011 886228930199, F: 011 886228930198, www.nuwai.com
Camping; Lighting Products; Outfitter

Nylok Corp., 15260 Hallmark Dr., Macomb, MI 48042, P: 586-786-0100, FL 810-780-0598
Custom Manufacturing; Gun Parts/Gunsmithing; Lubricants

O

O'Keeffe's Co., 251 W. Barclay Dr., P.O. Box 338, Sisters, OR 97759, P: 800-275-2718, F: 541-549-1486, www.okeeffescompany.com
Archery; Backpacking; Camping; Footwear; Outfitter; Sports Accessories; Survival Kits/First Aid

O.F. Mossberg & Sons, Inc., 7 Grasso Ave., North Haven, CT 06473, P: 203-230-5300, F: 203-230-5420, www.mossberg.com
Firearms; Gun Barrels; Hunting Accesories; Law Enforcement

Oakley, Inc., One Icon, Foothill Ranch, CA 92610, P: 800-525-4334, F: 858-459-4336, www.usstandardissue.com
Eyewear; Footwear

Odyssey Automotive Specialty, 317 Richard Mine Rd., Wharton, MJ 07885, P: 800-535-9441, F: 973-328-2601, www.odysseyauto.com
Custom Manufacturing; Gun Cabinets/Racks/Safes; Gun Cases; Law Enforcement; Vehicles, Utility & Rec

Oehler Research, Inc., P.O. Box 9135, Austin, TX 78766, P: 800-531-5125, F: 512-327-6903, www.oehler-research.com
Ammunition; Computer Software; Hunting Accessories; Reloading; Shooting Range Equipment; Targets

Oklahoma Leather Products/Don Hume Leathergoods, 500 26th NW, Miami, OK 74354, P: 918-542-6651, F: 918-542-6653, www.oklahomaleatherproducts.com
Black Powder Accessories; Custom Manufacturing; Cutlery; Holsters; Hunting Accessories; Knives/Knife Cases; Law Enforcement; Leathergoods

Old Western Scrounger, Inc., 50 Industrial Pkwy., Carson City, NV 89706, P: 800-UPS-AMMO, F: 775-246-2095, www.ows-ammunition.com
Ammunition; Reloading

Olivon Manufacturing Co., Ltd./Olivon-Worldwide, 600 Tung Pu Rd., Shanghai, China, Shanghai, Jiangsu, CHINA, P: 604-764-7731, F: 604-909-4951, www.olivonmanufacturing.com
Bag & Equipment Cases; Binoculars; Gun Cabinets/Racks/Safes; Gun Cases; Hunting Accessories; Scopes, Sights & Accessories; Telescopes

Olympic Arms, Inc., 624 Old Pacific Hwy. SE, Olympia, WA 98513, P: 800-228-3471, F: 360-491-3447, www.olyarms.com
Firearms; Gun Barrels; Gun Grips & Stocks; Gun Parts/Gunsmithing; Law Enforcement; Training & Safety Equipment

On-Target Productions, Inc., 6722 River Walk Dr., Valley City, OH 44280, P: 330-483-6183, F: 330-483-6183, www.ontargetdvds.com
Videos

On Time Wildlife Feeders, 110 E. Railroad Ave., Ruston, LA 71270, P:318-225-1834, F: 315-225-1101

One Shot, 6871 Main St., Newtown, OH 45244, P: 513-233-0885, F: 513-233-0887

Ontario Knife Co./Queen Cutlery Co./Ontario Knife Co., 26 Empire St., P.O. Box 145, Franklinville, NY 14737, P: 800-222-5233, F: 800-299-2618, www.ontarioknife.com
Camping; Custom Manufacturing; Cutlery; Hunting Accessories; Knives/Knife Cases; Law Enforcement; Training & Safety Equipment

Op. Electronics Co., Ltd., 53 Shing-Ping Rd. 5/F, Chungli, 320, TAIWAN, P: 011 88634515131, F: 011 88634615130, www.digi-opto.com
Scopes, Sights & Accessories; Training & Safety Equipment

Opti-Logic Corp., 201 Montclair St., P.O. Box 2002, Tullahoma, TN 37388, P: 888-678-4567, F: 931-455-1229, www.opti-logic.com
Archery; Binoculars; Crossbows & Accessories; Hunting Accessories; Law Enforcement; Scopes, Sights & Accessories

Optisan Corp., Taipei World Trade Center 4B06, 5, Hsin Yi Rd., Section 5, Taipei, 110, TAIWAN, P: 011 8675785799936, F: 011 862081117707
Bags & Equipment Cases; Binoculars; Lighting Products; Photographic Equipment; Scopes, Sights & Accessories; Telescopes

Optolyth/Sill Optics GmbH & Co KG, Johann-Höllfritsch-Straße 13, Wendelstein, 90530, GERMANY, P: 011 499129902352, F: 011 499129902323, www.optolyth.de
Binoculars; Scopes, Sights & Accessories

Original Footwear Co., 4213 Technology Dr., Modesto, CA 95356, P: 888-476-7700, F: 209-545-2739, www.originalswat.com
Footwear; Law Enforcement; Wholesaler/Distributor

Original Muck Boot Co., 1136 2nd St., Rock Island, IL 61201, P: 800-790-9296, F: 800-267-6809, www.muckbootcompany.com
Footwear

Osprey International Inc./AimShot, 25 Hawks Farm Rd., White, GA 30184, P: 888-448-3247, F: 770-387-0114, www.osprey-optics.com
Binoculars; Hunting Accessories; Law Enforcement; Lighting Products; Scopes, Sights & Accessories; Wholesaler/Distributor

Otis Technology, Inc., 6987 Laura St., P.O. Box 582, Lyon Falls, NY 13368, P: 800-OTISGUN, F: 315-348-4332, www.otisgun.com
Black Powder Accessories; Firearms Maintenance Equipment; Gun Parts/Gunsmithing; Hunting Accessories; Lubricants; Paintball Accessories; Scopes, Sights & Accessories; Training & Safety Equipment

Otte Gear, 332 Bleecker St., Suite E10, New York, NY 10014, P: 212-604-0304, F: 773-439-5237, www.ottegear.com
Backpacking; Camouflage; Camping; Gloves, Mitts, Hats; Men's Clothing

Otter Outdoors, 411 W. Congress, Maple Lake, MN 55358, P: 877-466-8837, F: 320-963-6192, www.otteroutdoors.com
Blinds; Custom Manufacturing; Hunting Accessories; Sports Accessories; Vehicles, Utility & Rec

Outdoor Cap Co., 1200 Melissa Ln., P.O. Box 210, Bentonville, AR 72712, P: 800-279-3216, F: 800-200-0329, www.outdoorcap.com
Camouflage; Custom Manufacturing; Gloves, Mitts, Hats; Hunting Accessories; Men & Women's Clothing

Outdoor Connection, 424 Neosho, Burlington, NS 66839, P: 888-548-0636, F: 620-364-5563, www.outdoor-connection.com
Outfitter; Tours/Travel

Outdoor Connection, Inc., 7901 Panther Way, Waco, TX 76712, P: 800-533-6076, F: 866-533-6076, www.outdoorconnection.com
Bags & Equipment Cases; Camouflage; Gun Cases; Gun Parts/Gunsmithing; Hunting Accessories; Retail Packaging; Shooting Range Equipment; Sports Accessories

Outdoor Edge Cutlery Corp., 4699 Nautilus Ct. S, Suite 503, Boulder, CO 80301, P: 800-447-3343, F: 303-530-7020, www.outdooredge.com
Cutlery; Hunting Accessories; Sharpeners

Outdoor Kids Club Magazine, P.O. Box 35, Greenville, OH 45331, P: 937-417-0903, www.outdoorkidsclub.com
Books/Industry Publications

Outdoor Research, 2203 First Ave. S, Seattle, WA 98134, P: 888-467-4327, F: 206-467-0374, www.outdoorresearch.com/gov
Gloves, Mitts, Hats; Law Enforcement

OutdoorSportsMarketingCenter.com, 95 Old Stratton Chase, Atlanta, GA 30328, P: 256-653-5087, F: 404-943-1634, www.outdoorsportsmarketingcenter.com
Books/Industry Publications; Computer Software; Emblems & Decals; Online Services; Printing Services; Retail Packaging; Retailer Services

Outers Gun Care/ATK Commercial Products, N5549 Cty. Tk. Z, Onalaska, WI 54650, P: 800-635-7656, F: 763-323-3890, www.outers-guncare.com
Firearms Maintenance Equipment; Lubricants

Over The Hill Outfitters/Adventures Beyond, 4140 Cty. Rd. 234, Durango, CO 81301, P: 970-385-7656, www.overthehilloutfitters.com
Outfitter

Ozonics, 107A This Way, P.O. Box 598, Lake Jackson, TX 77566, P: 979-285-2400, F: 979-297-7744, www.ozonicshunting.com
Scents & Lures

P

PMC/Poongsan, 60-1, Chungmoro - 3ka, Chung-Gu, Seoul 100-705, C.P.O. Box 3537, Seoul, SOUTH KOREA, P: 011 92234065628, F: 011 92234065415, www.pmcammo.com
Ammunition; Law Enforcement

PSC, Pendleton Safe Co., 139 Lee Byrd Rd., Loganville, GA 30052, P: 770-466-6661, F: 678-990-7888
Gun Safes

PSI, LLC, 2 Klarides Village Dr., Suite 336, Seymour, CT 06483, P: 203-262-6484, F: 203-262-6562, www.precisionsalesintl.com
Gun Parts/Gunsmithing; Law Enforcement; Magazines, Cartridge; Scopes, Sights & Accessories

P.S. Products, Inc./Personal Security Products, 414 S. Pulaski St., Suite 1, Little Rock, AR 72201, P: 877-374-7900, F: 501-374-7800, www.psproducts.com
Custom Manufacturing; Export/Import Specialists; Holsters; Law Enforcement; Sports Accessories; Wholesaler/Distributor

Pacific Solution, 14225 Telephone Ave., Suite D, Chino, CA 91710, P: 909-465-9858, F: 909-465-9878
Cutlery; Hunting Accessories; Knives/Knife Cases; Wholesaler/Distributor

Pacific Sun Marketing, 14505 N. 5th St., Bellevue, WA 98007, P: 425-653-3900, F: 425-653-3908
Home Furnishings; Hunting Accessories; Outdoor Art, Jewelry, Sculpture

Pacific Tool & Gauge, Inc., 598 Avenue C, P.O. Box 2549, White City, OR 97503, P: 541-826-5808, F: 541-826-5304, www.pacifictoolandgauge.com
Black Powder Accessories; Books/Industry Publications; Custom Manufacturing; Firearms Maintenance Equipment; Gun Parts/Gunsmithing; Law Enforcement; Reloading

Palco Sports Airsoft, 8575 Monticello Ln. N, Maple Grove, MN 55369-4546, P: 800-882-4656, F: 763-559-2286, www.palcosports.com
Airguns; Airsoft; Crossbows & Accessories; Paintball Guns & Accessories; Sports Accessories

Panthera Outdoors, LLC, 1555 Wedgefield Dr., Rock Hill, SC 29732, P: 276-673-5278

Para USA, Inc., 10620 Southern Loop Blvd., Charlotte, NC 28134-7381, P: 866-661-1911, www.para-usa.com
Firearms

Paragon Luggage, 1111-A Bell Ave., Tustin, CA 92780, P: 714-258-8698, F: 714-258-0018

Paramount Apparel, Inc., 1 Paramount Dr., P.O. Box 98, Bourbon, MO 65441, P: 800-255-4287, F: 800-428-0215, www.paramountoutdoors.com
Camouflage; Custom Manufacturing; Gloves, Mitts, Hats; Hunting Accessories; Men & Women's Clothing; Retailer Services; Sports Accessories

Parker-Hale, Bedford Rd., Petersfield, Hampshire GU32 3XA, UNITED KINGDOM, P: 011-44 1730268011, F: 011-44 1730260074, www.parker-hale.co.uk
Firearms Maintenance Equipment; Law Enforcement; Lubricants

Parmatech Corp., 2221 Pine View Way, Petaluma, CA 94954, P: 800-709-1555, F: 707-778-2262, www.parmatech.com
Custom Manufacturing; Gun Parts/Gunsmithing

Parris Manufacturing, 1825 Pickwick St., P.O. Box 338, Savannah, TN 38372, P: 800-530-7308, F: 731-925-1139, www.parrismfgco.com
Airguns; Archery; Binoculars; Camouflage; Crossbows & Accessories; Wholesaler/Distributor

Passport Sports, Inc., 3545 N. Courtenay Pkwy., P.O. Box 540638, Merritt Island, FL 32953, P: 321-459-0005, F: 321-459-3482, www.passport-holsters.com
Bags & Equipment Cases; Custom Manufacturing; Gun Cases; Holsters; Leathergoods

Patriot3, Inc., P.O. Box 278, Quantico, VA 22134, P: 888-288-0911, F: 540-891-5654, www.patriot3.com
Law Enforcement

Patriot Ordnance Factory, 23623 N. 67th Ave., Glendale, AZ 85310, P: 623-561-9572, F: 623-321-1680, www.pof-usa.com
Custom Manufacturing; Firearms; Gun Barrels; Gun Parts/Gunsmithing; Hunting Accessories; Law Enforcement

PBC, 444 Caribbean Dr., Lakeland, FL 33803, P: 954-304-5948, www.pbccutlery.com
Cutlery; Knives/Knife Cases

Peacekeeper International, 2435 Pine St., Pomona, CA 91767, P: 909-596-6699, F: 909-596-8899, www.peacekeeperproducts.com
Holsters; Law Enforcement; Leathergoods; Targets; Training & Safety Equipment

Peak Beam Systems, Inc., 3938 Miller Rd., P.O. Box 1127, Edgemont, PA 19028, P: 610-353-8505, F: 610-353-8411, www.peakbeam.com
Law Enforcement; Lighting Products

Peca Products, Inc., 471 Burton St., Beloit, WI 53511, P: 608-299-1615, F: 608-229-1827, www.pecaproducts.com
Custom Manufacturing; Firearms Maintenance Equipment; Hunting Accessories; Law Enforcement; Photographic Equipment; Scopes, Sights & Accessories; Sports Accessories; Wholesaler/Distributor

Pedersoli 2 SRL, Via Artigiani, 13, Gardone V.T., 25063, ITALY, P: 011 390308915000, F: 011 390308911019, www.davide-pedersoli.com
Black Powder Accessories; Firearms; Gun Grips & Stocks

Pedersoli Davide & C. SNC, Via Artigiani, 57, Gardone V.T., Brescia 25063, ITALY, P: 011 39308915000, F: 011 39308911019, www.davide-pedersoli.com
Black Powder Accessories; Cutlery; Firearms; Knives/Knife Cases

Peerless Handcuff Co., 95 State St., Springfield, MA 01103, P: 800-732-3705, F: 413-734-5467, www.peerless.net
Law Enforcement

Peet Shoe Dryer, Inc./Peet Dryer, 919 St. Maries River Rd., P.O. Box 618, St. Maries, ID 83861, 800-222-PEET (7338), F: 800-307-4582, www.peetdryer.com
Footwear; Gloves, Mitts, Hats; Hunting Accessories

Pelican Products, Inc., 23215 Early Ave., Torrance, CA 90505, P: 800-473-5422, F: 310-326-3311
Archery; Backpacking; Bags & Equipment Cases; Camping; Crossbows & Accessories; Gun Cases; Hunting Accessories; Paintball Accessories

Peltor, 5457 W. 79th St., Indianapolis, IN 46268, P: 800-327-3431, F: 800-488-8007, www.aosafety.com
Eyewear; Hearing Protection; Shooting Range Equipment; Two-Way Radios

PentagonLight, 151 Mitchell Ave., San Francisco, CA 94080, P: 800-PENTA-15, F: 650-877-9555, www.pentagonlight.com
Holsters; Hunting Accessories; Law Enforcement; Lighting Products; Sports Accessories; Survival Kits/First Aid; Wholesaler/Distributor

Pentax Imaging Co., 600 12th St., Suite 300, Golden, CO 80401, P: 800-877-0155, F: 303-460-1628, www.pentaxsportoptics.com
Binoculars; Photographic Equipment; Scopes, Sights & Accessories

Perazzi U.S.A., Inc., 1010 W. Tenth St., Azusa, CA 91702, P: 626-334-1234, F: 626-334-0344
Firearms

Perfect Fit, 39 Stetson Rd., Ruite 222, P.O. Box 439, Corinna, ME 04928, P: 800-634-9208, F: 800-222-0417, www.perfectfitusa.com
Custom Manufacturing; Emblems & Decals; Law Enforcement; Leathergoods; Training & Safety Equipment; Wholesaler/Distibutor

Permalight (Asia) Co., Ltd./Pila Flashlights, 4/F, Waga Commercial Centre, 99 Wellington St., Central HONG KONG, P: 011 85228150616, F: 011 85225423269, www.pilatorch.com
Camping; Firearms; Hunting Accessories; Law Enforcement; Lighting Products; Training & Safety Equipment; Wholesaler/Distributor

Pete Rickard Co., 115 Walsh Rd., Cobleskill, NY 12043, P: 518-234-2731, F: 518-234-2454, www.peterickard.com
Archery; Game Calls; Hunting Accessories; Leathergoods; Lubricants; Pet Supplies; Scents & Lures; Shooting Range Equipment

Petzl America, Freeport Center M-7, P.O. Box 160447, Clearfield, UT 84016, P: 877-807-3805, F: 801-926-1501, www.petzl.com
Gloves, Mitts, Hats; Law Enforcement; Lighting Products; Training & Safety Equipment

Phalanx Corp., 4501 N. Dixie Hwy., Boca Raton, FL 33431, P: 954-360-0000, F: 561-417-0500, www.smartholster.com
Gun Locks; Holsters; Law Enforcement; Training & Safety Equipment

Phillips Plastics, 1201 Hanley Rd., Hudson, WI 54016, P: 877-508-0252, F: 715-381-3291, www.phillipsplastics.com
Custom Manufacturing

Phoebus Tactical Flashlights/Phoebus Manufacturing, 2800 Third St., San Francisco, CA 94107, P: 415-550-0770, F: 415-550-2655, www.phoebus.com
Lighting Products

Photop Suwtech, Inc., 2F, Building 65, 421 Hong Cao Rd., Shanghai, 200233, CHINA, P: 011 862164853978, F: 011 862164850389, www.photoptech.com
Law Enforcement; Lighting Products; Scopes, Sights & Accessories

Pine Harbor Holding Co., Inc., P.O. Box 336, Chippewa Falls, WI 54729, P: 715-726-8714, F: 715-726-8739
Blinds; Camouflage; Decoys; Hunting Accessories

Pinnacle Ammunition Co., 111 W. Port Plaza, Suite 600, St. Louis, MO 63146, P: 888-702-2660, F: 314-293-1943, www.pinnacleammo.com
Ammunition

PistolCam, Inc., 1512 Front St., Keeseville, NY 12944, P: 518-834-7093, F: 518-834-7061, www.pistolcam.com
Firearms; Gun Parts/Gunsmithing; Law Enforcement; Photographic Equipment; Scopes, Sights & Accessories; Videos

Plano Molding Co., 431 E. South St., Plano, IL 60545, P: 800-226-9868, F: 630-552-9737, www.planomolding.com
Archery; Bags & Equipment Cases; Firearms Maintenance Equipment; Gun Cases; Hunting Accessories

Plotmaster Systems, Ltd., 111 Industrial Blvd., P.O. Box 111, Wrightsville, GA 31096, P: 888-629-4263, F: 478-864-9109, www.theplotmaster.com
Feeder Equipment; Wholesaler/Distributor; Wildlife Management

PlotSpike Wildlife Seeds/Ragan and Massey, Inc., 100 Ponchatoula Pkwy., Ponchatoula, LA 70454, P: 800-264-5281, F: 985-386-5565, www.plotspike.com
Scents & Lures; Wildlife Management

Plymouth Engineered Shapes, 201 Commerce Ct., Hopkinsville, KY 42240, P: 800-718-7590, F: 270-886-6662, www.plymouth.com/engshapes.aspx
Crossbows & Accessories; Firearms; Gun Barrels; Gun Parts/Gunsmithing

Point Blank Body Armor/PACA Body Armor, 2102 SW 2 St., Pompano Beach, FL 33069, P: 800-413-5155, F: 954-414-8118, www.pointblankarmor.com, www.pacabodyarmor.com
Law Enforcement

Point Tech, Inc., 160 Gregg St., Suite 1, Lodi, NJ 07644, P: 201-368-0711, F: 201-368-0133
Firearms; Gun Barrels; Gun Parts/Gunsmithing

Polaris USA, Inc./Signal Mobile USA, 4511 N. O'Connor Rd., Suite 1150, Irving, TX 75062, P: 817-719-1086, F: 817-887-0807, www.polarisvision.com, www.ezsignal.com

Police and Security News, 1208 Juniper St., Quakertown, PA 18951, P: 215-538-1240, F: 215-538-1208, www.policeandsecuritynews.com
Books/Industry Publications; Law Enforcement

Police Magazine/Police Recruit Magazine, 3520 Challenger St., Torrance, CA 90503, P: 480-367-1101, F: 480-367-1102, www.policemag.com
Books/Industry Publications; Law Enforcement

PoliceOne.com, 200 Green St., Second Floor, San Francisco, CA 94111, P: 800-717-1199, F: 480-854-7079, www.policeone.com
Law Enforcement

Port-A-Cool, 709 Southview Circle, P.O. Box 2167, Center, TX 75935, P: 800-695-2942, F: 936-598-8901
Camouflage; Custom Manufacturing; Sports Accessories; Training & Safety Equipment

Portman Security Systems Ltd., 330 W. Cummings Park, Woburn, MA 01801, P: 781-935-9288, F: 781-935-9188, www.portmansecurity.com
Custom Manufacturing; Firearms Maintenance Equipment; Gun Parts/Gunsmithing; Law Enforcement; Pet Supplies; Scopes, Sights & Accessories; Vehicles, Utility & Rec

PowerBelt Bullets, 5988 Peachtree Corners E, Norcross, GA 30071, P: 800-320-8767, F: 770-242-8546, www.powerbeltbullets.com
Ammunition; Black Powder Accessories

PowerFlare, 6489 Camden Ave., Suite 108, San Jose, CA 95120, P: 877-256-6907, F: 408-268-5431, www.powerflare.com
Lighting Products; Survival Kits/First Aid; Training & Safety Equipment; Wholesaler/Distributor

PowerTech, Inc./Smith & Wesson Flashlights, 360 E. South St., Collierville, TN 38017, P: 901-850-9393, F: 901-850-9797, www.powertechinc.com
Camping; Hunting Accessories; Law Enforcement; Lighting Products; Sports Accessories

Practical Air Rifle Training Systems, LLC, P.O. Box 174, Pacific, MO 63069, P: 314-271-8465, F: 636-271-8465, www.smallarms.com
Airguns; Custom Manufacturing; Law Enforcement; Shooting Range Equipment; Targets; Training & Safety Equipment

Precision Ammunition, LLC, 5402 E. Diana St., Tampa, FL 33610, P: 888-393-0694, F: 813-626-0078, www.precisionammo.com
Ammunition; Law Enforcement; Reloading

Precision Metalsmiths, Inc., 1081 E. 200th St., Cleveland, OH 44117, P: 216-481-8900, F: 216-481-8903, www.precisionmetalsmiths.com
Archery; Custom Manufacturing; Firearms; Gun Barrels; Gun Locks; Gun Parts/Gunsmithing; Knives/Knife Cases; Scopes, Sights & Accessories

Precision Reflex, Inc., 710 Streine Dr., P.O. Box 95, New Bremen, OH 45869, P: 419-629-2603, F: 419-629-2173, www.pri-mounts.com
Custom Manufacturing; Firearms; Gun Barrels; Law Enforcement; Magazines, Cartridge; Scopes, Sights & Accessories

Predator, Inc., 2605 Coulee Ave., La Crosse, WI 54601, P: 800-430-3305, F: 608-787-0667, www.predatorcamo.com
Archery; Backpacking; Blinds; Camouflage; Men's Clothing

Predator International, 4401 S. Broadway, Suite 201, Englewood, CO 80113, P: 877-480-1636, F: 303-482-2987, www.predatorpellets.com
Airguns; Airsoft; Ammunition

Predator Sniper Products, 102 W. Washington St., P.O. Box 743, St. Francis, KS 67756, P: 785-332-2731, F: 785-332-8943, www.predatorsniperstyx.com
Custom Manufacturing; Game Calls; Hunting Accessories; Shooting Range Equipment; Wholesaler/Distributor

Predator Trailcams LLC, 10609 W. Old Hwy. 10 R.D., Saxon, WI 54559, P: 715-893-5001, F: 715-893-5005, www.predatortrailcams.com
Archery; Firearms; Hunting Accessories; Outfitter; Photographic Equipment; Sports Accessories; Wildlife Management

Premier Reticles, 175 Commonwealth Ct., Winchester, VA 22602, P: 540-868-2044, F: 540-868-2045 www.premierreticles.com
Scopes, Sights & Accessories; Telescopes

Premierlight, 35 Revenge Rd., Unit 9, Lordswood, Kent ME5 8DW, UNITED KINGDOM, P: 011-44-1634-201284, F: 011-44-1634-201286, www.premierlight-uk.com
Backpacking; Camping; Hunting Accessories; Law Enforcement; Lighting Products; Sports Accessories; Training & Safety Equipment; Wholesaler/Distributor

Prestige Apparel Mfg. Co./Exxel Outdoors, 300 American Blvd., Haleyville, AL 35565, P: 800-221-7452, F: 205-486-9882, www.exxel.com
Camouflage; Camping; Custom Manufacturing; Export/Import Specialists; Gloves, Mitts, Hats; Men's Clothing; Wholesaler/Distributor

Primary Weapons Systems, 800 E. Citation Ct., Suite C, Boise, ID 83716, P: 208-344-5217, F: 208-344-5395, www.primaryweapons.com
Firearms; Firearms Maintenance Equipment; Gun Parts/Gunsmithing; Law Enforcement; Recoil Protection Devices & Services

Primax Hunting Gear Ltd., Rm. 309, 3/F Jiali Mansion, 39-5#, Xingning Rd., Ningbo, Zhejiang 315040, CHINA, P: 011 8657487894016, F: 011 8657487894017, www.primax-hunting.com
Backpacking; Bags & Equipment Cases; Blinds; Camping; Compasses; Gun Cases; Hunting Accessories; Scopes, Sights & Accessories

Primos Hunting Calls, 604 First St., Flora, MS 39071, P: 800-523-2395, F: 601-879-9324, www.primos.com
Archery; Blinds; Camouflage; Decoys; Game Calls; Hunting Accessories; Scents & Lures; Videos

Princeton Tec, P.O. Box 8057, Trenton, NJ 08650, P: 800-257-9080, FL 609-298-9601, www.princetontec.com
Backpacking; Camping; Cooking Equipment/ Accessories; Lighting Products; Photographic Equipment; Sports Accessories; Training & Safety Equipment

Pro-Iroda Industries, Inc., No. 68, 32nd Rd., Taichung Industrial Park, Taichung, 407, TAIWAN, P: 888-66-IRODA, F: 440-247-4630, www.pro-iroda.com
Archery; Camping; Cooking Equipment/Accessories; Custom Manufacturing

Pro-Shot Products, P.O. Box 763, Taylorville, IL 62568, P: 217-824-9133, F: 217-824-8861, www.proshotproducts.com
Black Powder Accessories; Firearms Maintenance Equipment; Lubricants

Pro-Systems Spa, Via al Corbé 63, ITALY, P: 011 390331576887, F: 011 390331576295, www.pro-systems.it, www.pro-systems.us
Law Enforcement

Pro Ears/Benchmaster, 101 Ridgeline Dr., Westcliffe, CO 81252, P: 800-891-3660, F: 719-783-4162, www.pro-ears.com
Crossbows & Accessories; Custom Manufacturing; Hearing Protection; Hunting Accessories; Law Enforcement; Shooting Range Equipment; Sports Accessories; Training & Safety Equipment

Pro Line Manufacturing Co., 186 Parish Dr., Wayne, NJ 07470, P: 800-334-4612, F: 973-692-0999, www.prolineboots.com
Camouflage; Footwear; Leathergoods; Wholesaler/ Distributor

Professionals Choice/G&A Investments, Inc., 2615 Fruitland Ave., Vernon, CA 90058, P: 323-589-2775, F: 323-589-3511, www.theprofessionalschoice.net
Firearms Maintenance Equipment; Gun Parts/ Gunsmithing; Lubricants; Wholesaler/Distributor

Proforce Equipment, Inc./Snugpak USA, 2201 NW 102nd Place, Suite 1, Miami, FL 33172, P: 800-259-5962, F: 800-664-5095, www.proforceequipment.com
Backpacking; Camping; Hunting Accessories; Knives/Knife Cases; Law Enforcement; Men's Clothing; Survival Kits/First Aid; Watches

Prois Hunting Apparel for Women, 28000B W. Hwy. 50, Gunnison, CO 81230, P: 970-641-3355, F: 970-641-6602, www.proishunting.com
Camouflage; Hunting Accessories; Women's Clothing

ProMag Industries, Inc./Archangel Manufacturing, LLC, 10654 S. Garfield Ave., South Gate, CA 90280, P: 800-438-2547, F: 562-861-6377, www.promagindustries.com
Gun Grips & Stocks; Gun Parts/Gunsmithing; Law Enforcement; Magazines, Cartridge; Retail Packaging; Scopes, Sights & Accessories

Promatic, Inc., 7803 W. Hwy. 116, Gower, MO 64454, UNITED KINGDOM, P: 888-767-2529, F: 816-539-0257, www.promatic.biz
Airguns; Clay Targets; Shooting Range Equipment; Targets; Training & Safety Equipment

Propper International Sales, 520 Huber Park Ct., St. Charles, MO 63304, P: 800-296-9690, F: 877-296-9690, www.propper.com
Camouflage; Law Enforcement; Men's Clothing

Protective Products International, 1649 NW 136th Ave., Sunrise, FL 33323, P: 800-509-9111, F: 954-846-0555, www.body-armor.com
Custom Manufacturing; Export/Import Specialists; Law Enforcement; Men & Women's Clothing; Training & Safety Equipment; Vehicles, Utility & Rec

Pumo GmbH IP Solingen, An den Eichen 20-22, Solingen, HMBG 42699, GERMANY, P: 011 492851589655, F: 011 492851589660, www.pumaknives.de
Custom Manufacturing; Cutlery; Hunting Accessories; Knives/Knife Cases; Sharpeners

Pyramex Safety Products, 281 Moore Lane, Collierville, TN 38017, P: 800-736-8673, F: 877-797-2639, www.pyramexsafety.com
Eyewear; Hearing Protection; Training & Safety Equipment

Pyramyd Air, 26800 Fargo Ave., Suite L, Bedford, OH 44146, P: 888-262-4867, F: 216-896-0896, www.pyramydair.com
Airguns, Airsoft

Q

Quail Unlimited, 31 Quail Run, Edgefield, SC 29824, P: 803-637-5731, F: 803-637-5303, www.qu.org
Books/Industry Publications; Firearms; Hunting Accessories; Men & Women's Clothing; Outdoor Art, Jewelry, Sculpture; Wildlife Management

Quake Industries, Inc., 732 Cruiser Ln., Belgrade, MT 59714, P: 770-449-4687, F: 406-388-8810, www.quakeinc.com
Archery; Crossbows & Accessories; Custom Manufacturing; Hunting Accessories; Scopes, Sights & Accessories; Sports Accessories; Treestands

Quaker Boy, Inc., 5455 Webster Rd., Orchard Park, NY 14127, P: 800-544-1600, F: 716-662-9426, www.quakerboy.com
Camouflage; Game Calls; Gloves, Mitts, Hats; Hunting Accessories; Targets; Videos

Quality Cartridge, P.O. Box 445, Hollywood, MD 20636, P: 301-373-3719, F: 301-373-3719, www.qual-cart.com
Ammunition; Custom Manufacturing; Reloading

Quality Deer Management Assoc., 170 Whitetail Way, P.O. Box 160, Bogart, GA 30622, P: 800-209-3337, F: 706-353-0223, www.qdma.com
Books/Industry Publications; Men & Women's Clothing; Videos; Wholesaler/Distributor; Wildlife Management

Quantico Tactical Supply, 109 N. Main St., Raeford, NC 28376, P: 910-875-1672, F: 910-875-3797, www.quanticotactical.com
Eyewear; Firearms; Footwear; Holsters; Knives/Knife Cases; Law Enforcement; Survival Kits/First Aid

Quayside Publishing Group, 400 1st Ave. N, Suite 300, Minneapolis, MN 55401, P: 800-328-0590, F: 612-344-8691, www.creativepub.com
Books/Industry Publications

Quiqlite, Inc., 6464 Hollister Ave., Suite 4, Goleta, CA 93117, P: 866-496-2606, F: 800-910-5711, www.quiqlite.com
Backpacking; Camping; Hunting Accessories; Law Enforcement; Lighting Products; Reloading; Training & Safety Equipment

R

R & R Racing, Inc., 45823 Oak St., Lyons, OR 97358, P: 503-551-7283, F: 503-859-4711, www.randrracingonline.com
Custom Manufacturing; Hearing Protection; Shooting Range Equipment; Targets; Training & Safety Equipment; Wholesaler/Distributor

R & W Rope Warehouse, 39 Tarkiln Pl., P.O. Box 50420, New Bedford, MA 02745, P: 800-260-8599, F: 508-995-1114, www.rwrope.com
Backpacking; Camouflage; Camping; Custom Manufacturing; Hunting Accessories; Law Enforcement; Pet Supplies; Training & Safety Equipment

Rackulator, Inc., P.O. Box 248, Golden Valley, ND 58541, P: 888-791-4213, F: 701-983-4625, www.rackulator.com
Hunting Accessories

Radians, 7580 Bartlett Corp. Dr., Bartlett, TN 38133, P: 877-723-4267, F: 901-266-2558, www.radiansinc.com
Camouflage; Eyewear; Footwear; Gloves, Mitts, Hats; Hearing Protection; Hunting Accessories; Sports Accessories; Training & Safety Equipment

Raine, Inc., 6401 S. Madison Ave., Anderson, IN 46013, P: 800-826-5354, F: 765-622-7691, www.raineinc.com
Bags & Equipment Cases; Camping; Custom Manufacturing; Holsters; Knives/Knife Cases; Law Enforcement; Two-Way Radios

Rainer Ballistics, 4500 15th St. E, Tacoma, WA 98424, P: 800-638-8722, F: 253-922-7854, www.rainierballistics.com
Ammunition; Reloading; Wholesaler/Distributor

Ram Mounting Systems, 8410 Dallas Ave. S, Seattle, WA 98108, P: 206-763-8361, F: 206-763-9615, www.ram-mount.com
Hunting Accessories; Law Enforcement; Sports Accessories; Vehicles, Utility & Rec

Ramba, Via Giorgio La Pira, 20 Flero (Bs), Brescia 25020, ITALY, P: 011 390302548522, F: 011 390302549749, www.ramba.it
Ammunition; Reloading

Ranch Products, P.O. Box 145, Malinta, OH 43535, P: 419-966-2881, F: 313-565-8536, www.ranchproducts.com
Gun Parts/Gunsmithing; Scopes, Sights & Accessories

Rancho Trinidad, 4803 Fountainhead, Houston, TX 77066, P: 210-487-1640, F: 210-487-1640, www.ranchotrinidad.com
Outfitter; Tours/Travel

Randolph Engineering, Inc., 26 Thomas Patten Dr., Randolph, MA 02368, P: 800-541-1405, F: 781-986-0337, www.randolphusa.com
Eyewear

Range Systems, 5121 Winnetka Ave. N, Suite 150, New Hope, MN 55428, P: 888-999-1217, F: 763-537-6657, www.range-systems.com
Eyewear; Law Enforcement; Shooting Range Equipment; Targets; Training & Safety Equipment

Ranger/Xtratuf/NEOS Footwear, 1136 2nd St., Rock Island, IL 61201, P: 800-790-9296, F: 800-267-6809, www.npsusa.com
Footwear

Rapid Dominance Corp., 2121 S. Wilmington Ave., Compton, CA 90220, P: 800-719-5260, F: 310-608-3648, www.rapiddominance.com
Bags & Equipment Cases; Gloves, Mitts, Hats; Men's Clothing; Wholesaler/Distributor

Rat Cutlery Co., 60 Randall Rd., Gallant, AL 35972, P: 865-933-8436, F: 256-570-0175, www.ratcutlery.com
Backpacking; Camping; Cutlery; Knives/Knife Cases; Law Enforcement; Survival Kits/First Aid; Tours/ Travel; Training & Safety Equipment

Rattlers Brand/Boyt Harness Co., One Boyt Dr., Osceola, IA 50213, P: 800-550-2698, F: 641-342-2703, www.rattlersbrand.com
Camouflage; Sports Accessories

Raza Khalid & Co., 14/8, Haji Pura, P.O. Box 1632, Sailkot, Punjab 51310, PAKISTAN, P: 011 92523264232, F: 011 92523254932, www.razakhalid.com
Bags & Equipment Cases; Gloves, Mitts, Hats; Gun Cases; Hunting Accessories; Law Enforcement; Paintball Accessories; Pet Supplies; Shooting Range Equipment

RBR Tactical Armor, Inc., 3113 Aspen Ave., Richmond, VA 23228, P: 800-672-7667, F: 804-726-6027, www.rbrtactical.com
Custom Manufacturing; Law Enforcement

RCBS/ATK Commercial Products, 605 Oro Dam Blvd., Oroville, CA 95965, P: 800-533-5000, F: 530-533-1647, www.rcbs.com
Reloading

Real Geese/Webfoot-LSP, 130 Cherry St., P.O. Box 675, Bradner, OH 43406, P: 419-800-8104, F: 888-642-6369, www.realgeese.com
Bags & Equipment Cases; Custom Manufacturing; Decoys; Emblems & Decals; Home Furnishings; Hunting Accessories; Printing Services; Retail Packaging

Realtree® Camouflage, P.O. Box 9638, Columbus, GA 31908, P: 800-992-9968, F: 706-569-9346, www.realtree.com
Camouflage; Videos

Recknagel, Landwehr 4, Bergrheinfeld, 97493, GERMANY, P: 011 49972184366, F: 011 49972182969, www.recknagel.de
Gun Parts/Gunsmithing; Scopes, Sights & Accessories

Recognition Services, 8577 Zionsville Rd., Indianapolis, IN 46268, P: 877-808-9400, F: 877-808-3565, www.we-belong.com
Custom Manufacturing; Emblems & Decals; Law Enforcement; Outfitter

ReconRobotics, Inc., 770 W. 78th St., Edina, MN 55439, P: 952-935-5515, F: 952-935-5508, www.reconrobotics.com
Law Enforcement

Redding Reloading Equipment, 1089 Starr Rd., Cortland, NY 13045, P: 607-753-3331, F: 607-756-8445, www.redding-reloading.com
Lubricants; Reloading

Redman Training Gear, 10045 102nd Terrace, Sebastian, FL 32958, P: 800-865-7840, F: 800-459-2598, www.redmangear.com
Law Enforcement; Training & Safety Equipment

Redwolf Airsoft Specialist, 7A-C, V GA Building, 532 Castle Peak Rd., Cheung Sha Wan, HONG KONG, P: 011 85228577665, F: 011 85229758305, www.redwolfairsoft.com
Airsoft

Reel Wings Decoy Co., Inc., 1122 Main Ave., Fargo, ND 58103, P: 866-55DECOY, F: 701-293-8234, www.reelwings.com
Camouflage; Decoys; Wholesaler/Distributor

Reflective Art, Inc., 403 Eastern Ave. SE, Grand Rapids, MI 49508, P: 800-332-1075, F: 616-452-2112, www.reflectiveartinc.com
Home Furnishings

Reliable of Milwaukee, P.O. Box 563, Milwaukee, WI 53201, P: 800-336-6876, F: 414-272-6443, www.reliableofmilwaukee.com
Archery; Bags & Equipment Cases; Camouflage; Footwear; Gloves, Mitts, Hats; Hunting Accessories; Men & Women's Clothing

Reminton Apparel/The Brinkmann Corp., 4215 McEwen Rd., Dallas, TX 75244, P: 877-525-9070, F: 800-780-0109, www.brinkmann.net
Camouflage; Gloves, Mitts, Hats; Hunting Accessories; Men's Clothing

Remington Arms Co., Inc., 870 Remington Dr., P.O. Box 700, Madison, NC 27025, P: 800-243-9700
Ammunition; Cutlery; Firearms; Footwear; Gun Parts/ Gunsmithing; Hunting Accessories

Repel Products, P.O. Box 348, Marion, IA 52302, P: 866-921-1810, F: 319-447-0967, www.repelproducts.com
Archery; Hunting Accessories; Sports Accessories; Wildlife Management

Rescomp Handgun Technologies/CR Speed, P.O. Box 11786, Queenswood, 0186, SOUTH AFRICA, P: 011 27123334768, F: 011 27123332112, www.crspeed.co.za
Bags & Equipment Cases; Custom Manufacturing; Holsters; Law Enforcement; Scopes, Sights & Accessories; Sports Accessories; Wholesaler/ Distributor

Revision Eyewear, Ltd., 7 Corporate Dr., Essex Junction, VT 05452, CANADA, P: 802-879-7002, F: 802-879-7224, www.revisionready.com
Eyewear; Hunting Accessories; Law Enforcement; Paintball Accessories; Shooting Range Equipment; Sports Accessories; Training & Safety Equipment

Rich-Mar Sports, North 7125 1280 St., River Falls, WI 54022, P: 952-881-6796, F: 952-884-4878, www.richmarsports.com
Cooking Equipment/Accessories; Hunting Accessories; Law Enforcement; Sports Accessories; Training & Safety Equipment

Ridge Outdoors U.S.A., Inc./Ridge Footwear, P.O. Box 389, Eustis, FL 32727-0389, P: 800-508-2668, F: 866-584-2042, www.ridgeoutdoors.com
Footwear; Law Enforcement; Men & Women's Clothing; Sports Accessories

Ring's Manufacturing, 99 East Dr., Melbourne, FL 32904, P: 800-537-7464, F: 321-951-0017, www.blueguns.com
Custom Manufacturing; Law Enforcement; Training & Safety Equipment

Rio Ammunition, Fountainview, Suite 207, Houston, TX 77057, P: 713-266-3091, F: 713-266-3092, www.rioammo.com, www.ueec.es
Ammunition; Black Powder/Smokeless Powder; Law Enforcement

Rio Bonito Ranch, 5309 Rio Bonito Ranch Rd., Junction, TX 76849, P: 800-864-4303, F: 325-446-3859, www.riobonito.com
Outfitter

Rite In The Rain, 2614 Pacific Hwy. E, Tacoma, WA 98424, P: 253-922-5000, F: 253-922-5300, www.riteintherain.com
Archery; Backpacking; Camping; Custom Manufacturing; Law Enforcement; Printing Services; Sports Accessories; Targets

River Oak Outdoors, Inc., 705 E. Market, Warrensburg, MO 64093, P: 660-580-0256, F: 816-222-0427, www.riveroakoutdoors.com
Custom Manufacturing; Game Calls; Gun Cabinets/Racks/Safes; Home Furnishings; Hunting Accessories; Sports Accessories

River Rock Designs, Inc., 900 RR 620 S, Suite C101-223, Austin, TX 78734, P: 512-263-6985, F: 512-263-1277, www.riverrockledlights.com
Backpacking; Camping; Hunting Accessories; Law Enforcement; Lighting Products; Sports Accessories; Training & Safety Equipment

River's Edge Treestands, Inc./Ardisam, Inc./Yukon Tracks, 1690 Elm St., Cumberland, WI 54829, P: 800-450-3343, F: 715-822-2124, www.huntriversedge.com, www.ardisam.com
Archery; Blinds; Camouflage; Gloves, Mitts, Hats; Hunting Accessories; Treestands

Rivers Edge Products, One Rivers Edge Ct., St. Clair, MO 63077, P: 888-326-6200, F: 636-629-7557, www.riversedgeproducts.com
Camouflage; Camping; Home Furnishings; Knives/Knife Cases; Leathergoods; Lighting Products; Pet Supplies; Wholesaler/Distributor

Rivers West/H2P Waterproof System, 2900 4th Ave. S, Seattle, WA 98134, P: 800-683-0887, F: 206-682-8691, www.riverswest.com
Camouflage; Law Enforcement; Men & Women's Clothing

RM Equipment, 6975 NW 43rd St., Miami, FL 33166, P: 305-477-9312, F: 305-477-9620, www.40mm.com
Firearms; Gun Grips & Stocks; Law Enforcement

RNT Calls, Inc./Buckwild Hunting Products and Quackhead Calls, 2315 Hwy. 63 N, P.O. Box 1026, Stuttgart, AR 72160, P: 877-993-4868, F: 601-829-4072, www.rntcalls.com
Custom Manufacturing; Emblems & Decals; Game Calls; Gloves, Mitts, Hats; Hunting Accessories; Scents & Lures; Videos

Robert Louis Company, Inc., 31 Shepard Hill Rd., Newtown, CT 06470, P: 800-979-9156, F: 203-270-3881, www.shotguncombogauge.com
Gun Parts/Gunsmithing; Shooting Range Equipment; Training & Safety Equipment

Rock Creek Barrels, Inc., 101 Ogden Ave., Albany, WI 53502, P: 608-862-2357, F: 608-862-2356, www.rockcreekbarrels.com
Gun Barrels

Rock River Arms, Inc., 1042 Cleveland Rd., Colona, IL 61241, P: 866-980-7625, F: 309-792-5781, www.rockriverarms.com
Custom Manufacturing; Firearms; Gun Barrels; Gun Grips & Stocks; Gun Parts/Gunsmithing; Law Enforcement; Magazines, Cartridge; Scopes, Sights & Accessories

Rockpoint Apparel, 9925 Aldine Westfield Rd., Houston, TX 77093, P: 713-699-9896, F: 713-699-9856, www.rockpoint-apparel.com
Camouflage; Custom Manufacturing; Export/Import Specialists; Gloves, Mitts, Hats; Men & Women's Clothing

Rocky Brands, 39 E. Canal St., Nelsonville, OH 45764, P: 740-753-9100, F: 740-753-7240, www.rockybrands.com
Footwear

Rocky Mountain Elk Foundation, 5705 Grant Creek Rd., P.O. Box 8249, Missoula, MT 59808, P: 800-CALL-ELK, F: 406-523-4550, www.elkfoundation.org
Books/Industry Publications; Wildlife Management

Rohrbaugh Firearms Corp., P.o. Box 785, Bayport, NY 11705, P: 800-803-2233, F: 631-242-3183, www.rohrbaughfirearms.com
Firearms

ROKON, 50 Railroad Ave., Rochester, NH 03839, P: 800-593-2369, F: 603-335-4400, www.rokon.com
Export/Import Specialists; Hunting Accessories; Sports Accessories; Vehicles, Utility & Rec

ROK Straps, 162 Locust Hill Dr., Rochester, NY 14618, P: 585-244-6451, F: 570-694-0773, www.rokstraps.com
Backpacking; Camouflage; Camping; Hunting Accessories; Pet Supplies; Sports Accessories

Rose Garden, The, 1855 Griffin Rd., Suite C370, Dania Beach, FL 33004, P: 954-927-9590, F: 954-927-9591, www.therosegardendb.com
Export/Import Specialists; Home Furnishings; Outdoor Art, Jewelry, Sculpture; Wholesaler/Distributor

Rose Plastic USA, LP, 525 Technology Dr., P.O. Box 698, California, PA 15419, P: 724-938-8530, F: 724-938-8532, www.rose-plastic.us
Bags & Equipment Cases; Custom Manufacturing; Gun Cases; Retail Packaging

Rossi/BrazTech, 16175 NW 49th Ave., Miami, FL 33014, P: 800-948-8029, F: 305-623-7506, www.rossiusa.com
Black Powder Accessories; Firearms

Rothco, 3015 Veterans Memorial Hwy., P.O. Box 1220, Ronkonkoma, NY 11779, P: 800-645-5195, F: 631-585-9447, www.rothco.com
Bags & Equipment Cases; Camouflage; Hunting Accessories; Knives/Knife Cases; Law Enforcement; Men & Women's Clothing; Survival Kits/First Aid; Wholesaler/Distributor

RPM, Inc./Drymate, 6665 W. Hwy. 13, Savage, MN 55378, P: 800-872-8201, F: 952-808-2277, www.drymate.com
Blinds; Camping; Custom Manufacturing; Firearms Maintenance Equipment; Home Furnishings; Hunting Accessories; Pet Supplies; Sports Accessories; Vehicles, Utility & Rec

RSR Group, Inc., 4405 Metric Dr., Winter Park, FL 32792, P: 800-541-4867, F: 407-677-4489, www.rsrgroup.com
Airguns; Ammunition; Cutlery; Firearms; Gun Cases; Holsters; Scopes, Sights & Accessories; Wholesaler/Distributor

RS International Industry/Hong Kong Co., Ltd., Room 1109, 11F, WingHing Industrial Bldg., Chai Wan Kok St., Tsuen Wan N.T., HONG KONG, P: 011 85224021381, F: 011 85224021385, www.realsword.com.hk
Airsoft

RTZ Distribution/HallMark Cutlery, 4436B Middlebrook Pike, Knoxville, TN 37921, P: 866-583-3912, F: 865-588-0425, www.hallmarkcutlery.com
Cutlery; Knifes/Knife Cases; Law Enforcement; Sharpeners

RUAG Ammotec, Uttigenstrasse 67, Thun, 3602, SWITZERLAND, P: 011 41332282879, F: 011 41332282644, www.ruag.com
Ammunition; Law Enforcement

Ruffed Grouse Society, Inc., 451 McCormick Rd., Coraopolis, PA 15108, P: 888-564-6747, F: 412-262-9207, www.ruffedgrousesociety.org
Wildlife Management

Ruger Firearms, 1 Lacey Pl., Southport, CT 06890, P: 203-259-7843, F: 203-256-3367, www.ruger.com
Firearms

Ruko, LLC, P.O. Box 38, Buffalo, NY 14207, P: 716-874-2707, F: 905-826-1353, www.rukoproducts.com
Camping; Compasses; Custom Manufacturing; Cutlery; Export/Import Specialists; Hunting Accessories; Knives/Knife Cases; Sharpeners

Russ Fields Safaris, Gameston, Alicedale Rd., P.O. Box 100, Grahamstown, East Cape, 6140, SOUTH AFRICA, P: 011 27834449753, F: 011 27466225837, www.southafricanhunting.com
Outfitter

Russian American Armory Co., 677 S. Cardinal Ln., Suite A, Scottsburg, IN 47170, P: 877-752-2894, F: 812-752-7683, www.raacfirearms.com
Firearms; Knives/Knife Cases; Magazines, Cartridge

RVJ International/Happy Feet, 6130 W. Flamingo Rd., PMB 460, Las Vegas, NV 89103, P: 702-871-6377, F: 702-222-1212, www.happyfeet.com
Books/Industry Publications; Footwear; Hunting Accessories; Men & Women's Clothing; Sports Accessories

S

S&K Industries, Inc., S. Hwy. 13, Lexington, MO 64067, P: 660-259-4691, F: 660-259-2081, www.sandkgunstocks.com
Custom Manufacturing; Gun Grips & Stocks

Saab Barracuda, LLC, 608 McNeill St., Lillington, NC 27546, P: 910-893-2094, F: 910-893-8807, www.saabgroup.com
Camouflage; Law Enforcement

Sabre Defence Industries, LLC, 450 Allied Dr., Nashville, TN 37211, P: 615-333-0077, F: 615-333-6229, www.sabredefence.com
Firearms; Gun Barrels

Sack-Ups, 1611 Jamestown Rd., Morganton, NC 28655, P: 877-213-6333, F: 828-584-6326, www.sackups.com
Archery; Black Powder Accessories; Firearms Maintenance Equipment; Gun Cases; Hunting Accessories; Knives/Knife Cases; Sports Accessories

Safari Club International, 4800 W. Gates Pass Rd., Tucson, AZ 85745, P: 520-620-1220, F: 520-618-3528, www.safariclub.org
Books/Industry Publications

Safari Nordik, 639 Labelle Blvd., Blainville, Quebec J7C 1V8, CANADA, P: 800-361-3748, F: 450-971-1771, www.safarinordik.com
Outfitter; Tours/Travel

Safari Press, 15621 Chemical Ln., Huntington Beach, CA 92649, P: 714-894-9080, F: 714-894-4949, www.safaripress.com
Books/Industry Publications

Safari Sunsets, 9735 Slater Ln., Overland Park, KS 66212, P: 877-894-1671, F: 913-894-1686, www.safarisunsets.com
Men's Clothing

Safe Guy/Gun Storage Solutions, 18317 N. 2600 East Rd., Cooksville, IL 61730, P: 309-275-1220, www.storemoreguns.com
Gun Cabinets/Racks/Safes

Safety Bullet, Inc., P.O. Box 007, Panama City, FL 32444, P: 850-866-0190, www.safetybullet.com
Gun Locks

Safety Harbor Firearms, Inc., 915 Harbor Lake Dr., Suite D, Safety Harbor, FL 34695, P: 727-725-4700, F: 727-724-1872, www.safetyharborfirearms.com
Firearms

Sage Control Ordnance, Inc./Sage International, Ltd., 3391 E. Eberhardt St., Oscoda, MI 48750, P: 989-739-7000, F: 989-739-7098, www.sageinternationalltd.com
Ammunition; Firearms; Gun Grips & Stocks; Gun Locks; Law Enforcement; Reloading

Salt River Tactical, LLC/Ost-Kraft, LLC, P.O. Box 20397, Mesa, AZ 85277, P: 480-656-2683, www.saltrivertactical.com
Bags & Equipment Cases; Firearms Maintenance Equipment; Hunting Accessories; Law Enforcement; Scopes, Sights & Accessories; Shooting Range Equipment; Wholesaler/Distributor

SAM Medical Products, P.O. Box 3270, Tualatin, OR 97062, P: 800-818-4726, F: 503-639-5425, www.sammedical.com
Backpacking; Camping; Law Enforcement; Outfitter; Shooting Range Equipment; Survival Kits/First Aid; Training & Safety Equipment

Samco Global Arms, Inc., 6995 NW 43rd St., Miami, FL 33166, P: 800-554-1618, F: 305-593-1014, www.samcoglobal.com
Ammunition; Firearms; Sports Accessories

Samson Mfg. Corp., 110 Christian Ln., Whately, MA 01373, P: 888-665-4370, F: 413-665-1163, www.samson-mfg.com
Firearms; Gun Parts/Gunsmithing; Law Enforcement; Scopes, Sights & Accessories

San Angelo/Rio Brands, 10981 Decatur Rd., Philadelphia, PA 19154, P: 800-531-7230, F: 830-393-7621, www.riobrands.com
Backpacking; Blinds; Camping; Cooking Equipment/Accessories; Gun Cabinets/Racks/Safes; Hunting Accessories; Taxidermy

Sandhurst Safaris, P.O. Box 57, Tosca, 8618, SOUTH AFRICA, P: 011 27824535683, F: 011 27539331002, www.sandhurstsafaris.com
Tours/Travel

Sandpiper of California, 687 Anita St., Suite A, Chula Vista, CA 91911, P: 866-424-6622, F: 619-423-9599, www.pipergear.com
Backpacking; Bags & Equipment Cases; Camouflage; Custom Manufacturing; Law Enforcement

Sandviper, 1611 Jamestown Rd., Morganton, NC 28655, P: 800-873-7225, F: 828-584-6326
Law Enforcement

Sante Fe Stone Works, Inc., 3790 Cerillos Rd., Sante Fe, NM 87507, P: 800-257-7625, F: 505-471-0036, www.santefestoneworks.com
Cutlery

Sargent & Greenleaf, Inc., One Security Dr., Nicholasville, KY 40356, P: 800-826-7652, F: 859-887-2057, www.sargentandgreenleaf.com
Gun Cabinets/Racks/Safes

Sarsilmaz Silah San. A.S, Nargileci Sokak, No. 4, Sarsilmaz Is Merkezi, Mercan, Eminonu, Istanbul, 34116, TURKEY, P: 011 902125133507, F: 011 902125111999, www.sarsilmaz.com
Firearms

Savage Arms, Inc., 118 Mountain Rd., Suffield, CT 06078, P: 866-233-4776, F: 860-668-2168, www.savagearms.com

Black Powder/Smokeless Powder; Firearms; Knives/Knife Cases; Law Enforcement; Shooting Range Equipment

Savannah Luggage Works, 3428 Hwy. 297 N, Vidalia, GA 30474, P: 800-673-6341, F: 912-537-4492, www.savannahluggage.com
Backpacking; Bags & Equipment Cases; Custom Manufacturing; Holsters; Law Enforcement; Training & Safety Equipment

SBR Ammunition, 1118 Glynn Park Rd., Suite E, Brunswick, GA 31525, P: 912-264-5822, F: 912-264-5888, www.sbrammunition.com
Ammunition; Firearms; Law Enforcement

Sceery Outdoors, LLC, P.O. Box 6520, Sante Fe, NM 87502; P: 800-327-4322 or 505-471-9110; F: 505-471-3476; www.sceeryoutdoors.net
Decoys; Game Calls; Hunting Accessories

Scent-Lok Technologies, 1731 Wierengo Dr., Muskegon, MI 49442, P: 800-315-5799, F: 231-767-2824, www.scentlok.com
Bags & Equipment Cases; Camouflage; Gloves, Mitts, Hats; Men & Women's Clothing; Videos

SCENTite Blinds, P.O. Box 36635, Birmingham, AL 35236, P: 800-828-1554, F: 205-424-4799, www.fargasonoutdoors.com
Archery; Backpacking; Blinds; Crossbows & Accessories; Hunting Accessories; Photographic Equipment; Scents & Lures; Treestands

Scentote, 1221 Keating, Grand Rapids, MI 49503, P: 616-742-0946, F: 616-742-0978, www.scentote.com
Archery; Hunting Accessories; Men's Clothing; Scents & Lures

Scharch Mfg., Inc/Top Brass, 10325 Cty. Rd. 120, Salida, CO 81201, P: 800-836-4683, F: 719-539-3021, www.scharch.com
Ammunition; Magazines, Cartridge; Reloading; Retail Packaging; Shooting Range Equipment

Scherer Supplies, Inc., 205 Four Mile Creek Rd., Tazewell, TN 37879, P: 423-733-2615, F: 423-733-2073
Custom Manufacturing; Magazines, Cartridge; Wholesaler/Distributor

Schmidt & Bender GmbH, Am Grossacker 42, Biebertal, Hessen 35444, GERMANY, P: 011 496409811570, US: 800-468-3450, F: ++49-6409811511, www.schmidt-bender.de, www.schmidtbender.com
Hunting Accessories; Law Enforcement; Scopes, Sights & Accessories; Sports Accessories; Telescopes

Schott Performance Fabrics, Inc., 2850 Gilchrist Rd., Akron, OH 44305, P: 800-321-2178, F: 330-734-0665, www.schottfabrics.com
Camouflage; Export/Import Specialists; Hunting Accessories; Men's Clothing

Scopecoat by Devtron Diversified, 3001 E. Cholla St., Phoenix, AZ 85028, P: 877-726-7328, F: 602-224-9351, www.scopecoat.com
Scopes, Sights & Accessories

SDG Seber Design Group, Inc. 2438 Cades Way, Vista, CA 92081, P: 760-727-5555, F: 760-727-5551, www.severdesigngroup.com
Camping; Cutlery; Knives/Knife Cases; Law Enforcement

Seasonal Marketing, Inc., P.O. Box 1410, La Pine, OR 97739, P: 972-540-1656, www.caddiswadingsysstems.net
Footwear; Hunting Accessories

Second Amendment Foundation, 12500 NE Tenth Pl., Bellevue, WA 98005, P: 425-454-7012, F: 425-451-3959, www.saf.org
Books/Industry Publications

SecuRam Systems, Inc., 350 N. Lantana St., Suite 211, Camarillo, CA 93010, P: 805-388-2058, F: 805-383-1728, www.securamsys.com
Gun Cabinets/Racks/Safes

Secure Firearm Products, 213 S. Main, P.O. Box 177, Carl Junction, MO 64834, P: 800-257-8744, F: 417-649-7278, www.securefirearmproducts.com
Bags & Equipment Cases; Custom Manufacturing; Gun Cases; Shooting Range Equipment; Targets

Secure Vault/Boyt Harness Co., One Boyt Dr., Osceola, IA 50213, P: 800-550-2698, F: 641-342-2703
Gun Cabinets/Racks/Safes

Security Equipment Corp., 747 Sun Park Dr., Fenton, MO 63026, P: 800-325-9568, F: 636-343-1318, www.sabrered.com
Backpacking; Camping; Custom Manufacturing; Law Enforcement; Training & Safety Equipment

Seldon Technologies, Inc., P.O. Box 710, Windsor, VT 05089, P: 802-674-2444, F: 802-674-2544, www.seldontech.com
Backpacking; Camping; Hunting Accessories

Self Defense Supply, Inc., 1819 Firman Dr., Suite 101, Richardson, TX 75081, P: 800-211-4186, F: 942-644-6980, www.selfdefensesupply.com
Airguns; Airsoft; Binoculars; Camping; Crossbows & Accessories; Cutlery; Lighting Products; Wholesaler/Distributor

Sellier & Bellot, USA, Inc., P.O. Box 7307, Shawnee Mission, KS 66207, P: 913-664-5933, F: 913-664-5938, www.sb-usa.com
Ammunition; Law Enforcement

Sentry Group, 900 Linden Ave., Rochester, NY 14625, P: 800-828-1438, F: 585-381-8559, www.sentrysafe.com
Gun Cabinets/Racks/Safes; Home Furnishings; Hunting Accessories; Law Enforcement

Sentry Solutions, Ltd., 5 Souhegan St., P.O. Box 214, Wilton, NH 03086, P: 800-546-8049, F: 603-654-3003, www.sentrysolutions.com
Firearms Maintenance Equipment; Gun Parts/Gunsmithing; Hunting Accessories; Lubricants; Sharpeners; Sports Accessories

Serbu Firearms, Inc., 6001 Johns Rd., Suite 144, Tampa, FL 33634, P: 813-243-8899, F: 813-243-8899, www.serbu.com
Firearms; Law Enforcement

Sharp Shoot R Precision, Inc., P.O. Box 171, Paola, KS 66071, P: 785-883-4444, F: 785-883-2525, www.sharpshootr.com
Black Powder Accessories; Custom Manufacturing; Firearms Maintenance Equipment; Lubricants; Reloading; Sports Accessories

Shasta Wear, 4320 Mountain Lakes Blvd., Redding, CAR 96003, P: 800-553-2466, F: 530-243-3274, www.shastawear.com
Emblems & Decals; Export/Import Specialists; Gloves, Mitts, Hats; Men & Women's Clothing; Outdoor Art, Jewelry, Sculpture; Retailer Services; Wholesaler/Distributor

SHE Safari, LLC, 15535 W. Hardy, Suite 102, Houston, TX 77060, P: 281-448-4860, F: 281-448-4118, www.shesafari.com
Camouflage; Women's Clothing

Sheffield Equipment, 4569 Mission Gorge Pl., San Diego, CA 92120, P: 619-280-0278, F: 619-280-0011, www.sheffieldcuttingequip.com
Bags & Equipment Cases; Camouflage; Custom Manufacturing; Holsters; Leathergoods; Men & Women's Clothing

Sheffield Tools/GreatLITE Flashlights, 165 E. 2nd St., P.O. Box 3, Mineola, NY 11501, P: 800-457-0600, F: 516-746-5366, www.sheffield-tools.com
Backpacking; Camping; Cutlery; Hunting Accessories; Knives/Knife Cases; Lighting Products

Shelterlogic, 150 Callender Rd., Watertown, CT 06795, P: 800-932-9344, F: 860-274-9306, www.shelterlogic.com
Camouflage; Camping; Custom Manufacturing; Hunting Accessories; Law Enforcement; Pet Supplies; Sports Accessories

Shenzhen Champion Industry Co., Ltd., Longqin Rd. No. 13, Shahu, Pingshan, Longgang Shenzhen City, GNGD 518118, CHINA, P: 011 8675589785877, F: 011 8675589785875, www.championcase.com
Bags & Equipment Cases; Cutlery; Gun Cabinets/Racks/Safes; Gun Cases; Gun Locks; Gun Parts/Gunsmithing; Home Furnishings; Knives/Knife Cases

Shepherd Enterprises, Inc., P.O. Box 189, Waterloo, NE 68069, P: 402-779-2424, F: 402-779-4010, www.shepherdscopes.com
Scopes, Sights & Accessories

Sherluk Marketing, Law Enforcement & Military, P.O. Box 156, Delta, OH 43615, P: 419-923-8011, F: 419-923-8120, www.sherluk.com
Firearms; Firearms Maintenance Equipment; Gun Grips & Stocks; Gun Parts/Gunsmithing; Law Enforcement; Wholesaler/Distributor

Shiloh Rifle Manufacturing, 201 Centennial Dr., P.O. Box 279, Big Timber, MT 59011, P: 406-932-4454, F: 406-932-5627, www.shilohrifle.com
Black Powder Accessories; Firearms

Shirstone Optics/Shinei Group, Inc., Komagome-Spancrete Bldg. 8F, Honkomagome 5-4-7, Bunkyo-Ku, Toyko, 113-0021, JAPAN, P: 011 81339439550, F: 011 81339430695, www.shirstone.com
Binoculars; Firearms; Scopes, Sights & Accessories

Shocknife, Inc., 20 Railway St., Winnipeg, Manitoba R2X 2P9, CANADA, P: 866-353-5055, F: 204-586-2049, www.shocknife.com
Knives/Knife Cases; Law Enforcement; Training & Safety Equipment

Shooter's Choice Gun Care/Ventco, Inc., 15050 Berkshire Industrial Pkwy., Middlefield, OH 44062, P: 440-834-8888, F: 440-834-3388, www.shooters-choice.com
Firearms Maintenance Equipment; Gun Parts/Gunsmithing; Law Enforcement; Lubricants

Shooters Depot, 5526 Leopard St., Corpus Christi, TX 78408, P: 361-299-1299, F: 361-289-9906, www.shootersdepot.com
Firearms; Gun Barrels

Shooters Ridge/ATK Commercial Products, N5549 Cty. Tk. Z, Onalaska, WI 54650, P: 800-635-7656, F: 763-323-3890, www.shootersridge.com
Bags & Equipment Cases; Gun Cabinets/Racks/Safes; Hunting Accessories; Magazines, Cartridge; Sports Accessories

Shooting Chrony, Inc., 2446 Cawthra Rd., Bldg. 1, Suite 10, Mississauga, Ontario L5A 3K6, CANADA, P: 800-385-3161, F: 905-276-6295, www.shootingchrony.com
Archery; Black Powder Accessories; Computer Software; Hunting Accessories; Lighting Products; Reloading; Shooting Range Equipment; Sports Accessories

Shooting Ranges International, Inc./Advanced Interactive Systems, 3885 Rockbottom St., North Las Vegas, NV 89030, P: 702-362-3623, F: 702-310-6978, www.shootingrangeintl.com
Firearms; Law Enforcement; Shooting Range Equipment

Shooting Sports Retailer, 255 W. 36th St., Suite 1202, New York, NY 10018, P: 212-840-0660, F: 212-944-1884, www.shootingsportsretailer.com
Books/Industry Publications

Sierra Bullets, 1400 W. Henry St., Sedalia, MO 65301, P: 888-223-3006, F: 660-827-4999, www.sierrabullets.com
Books/Industry Publications; Computer Software; Reloading; Videos

SIG SAUER, 18 Industrial Dr., Exeter, NH 03833, P: 603-772-2302, F: 603-772-9082, www.sigsauer.com
Bags & Equipment Cases; Firearms; Holsters; Knives/Knife Cases; Law Enforcement; Training & Safety Equipment

Sightron, Inc., 100 Jeffrey Way, Suite A, Youngville, NC 27596, P: 800-867-7512, F: 919-556-0157, www.sightron.com
Binoculars; Scopes, Sights & Accessories

Silencio/Jackson Safety, 1859 Bowles Ave., Suite 200, Fenton, MO 63026, P: 800-237-4192, F: 636-717-6820, www.jacksonsafety.com
Eyewear; Hearing Protection; Law Enforcement

Silma SRL, Via I Maggio, 74, Zanano Di Sarezzo, Brescia 25068, ITALY, P: 011 390308900505, F: 011 390308900712, www.silma.net
Firearms

Silver Stag, 328 Martin St., Blaine, WA 98230, P: 888-233-7824, F: 360-332-4390, www.silverstag.com
Black Powder Accessories; Camping; Crossbows & Accessories; Custom Manufacturing; Cutlery; Hunting Accessories; Knives/Knife Cases; Outdoor Art, Jewelry, Sculpture

Silver State Armory, LLC, P.O. Box 2902, Pahrump, NV 89041, P: 775-537-1118, F: 775-537-1119
Ammunition; Firearms

Simmons, 9200 Cody St., Overland Park, KS 66214, P: 913-782-3131, F: 913-782-4189
Binoculars; Hunting Accessories; Law Enforcement; Scopes, Sights & Accessories

Simunition Operations, General Dynamics Ordnance & Tactical Systems, 5 Montée des Arsenaux, Le Gardeur, Quebec J5Z 2P4, CANADA, P: 800-465-8255, F: 450-581-0231, www.simunition.com
Ammunition; Gun Barrels; Law Enforcement; Magazines, Cartridge, Training & Safety Equipment

Sinclair International, 2330 Wayne Haven St., Fort Wayne, IN 46803, P: 800-717-8211, F: 260-493-2530, www.sinclairintl.com
Ammunition; Bags & Equipment Cases; Books; Cleaning Products; Reloading; Scopes, Sights & Accessories; Software; Targets, Videos

SISCO, 2835 Ana St., Rancho Dominguez, CA 90221, P: 800-832-5834, F: 310-638-6489, www.honeywellsafes.com
Gun Cabinets/Racks/Safes; Hunting Accessories

Sitka, Inc., 870 Napa Valley Corporate Way, Suite N, Napa, CA 94558, P: 877-SITKA MG, F: 707-253-1121, www.sitkagear.com
Men's Clothing

SKB Corp., 1607 N. O'Donnell Way, Orange, CA 92867, P: 800-654-5992, F: 714-283-0425, www.skbcases.com
Archery; Bags & Equipment Cases; Gun Cases; Hunting Accessories; Knives/Knife Cases; Law Enforcement; Sports Accessories

SKB Shotguns, 4441 S. 134th St., Omaha, NE 68137, P: 800-752-2767, P: 402-330-8040, www.skbshotguns.com
Firearms

Smith & Warren, 127 Oakley Ave., White Plains, NY 10601, P: 800-53-BADGE, F: 914-948-1627, www.smithwarren.com
Custom Manufacturing; Law Enforcement

Smith & Wesson, 2100 Roosevelt Ave., Springfield, MA 01104, P: 800-331-0852, F: 413-747-3317, www.smith-wesson.com
Firearms; Law Enforcement

Smith Optics Elite Division, 280 Northwood Way, P.O. Box 2999, Ketchum, ID 83340, P: 208-726-4477, F: 208-727-6598, www.elite.smithoptics.com
Eyewear; Law Enforcement; Shooting Range Equipment; Training & Safety Equipment

Smith's, 1700 Sleepy Valley Rd., Hot Springs, AR 71901, P: 800-221-4156, F: 501-321-9232, www.smithsedge.com
Backpacking; Camping; Cutlery; Hunting Accessories; Sharpeners

Smith Security Safes, Inc., P.O. Box 185, Tontogany, OH 43565, P: 800-521-0335, F: 419-823-1505, www.smithsecuritysafes.com
Gun Cabinets/Racks/Safes

Sniper's Hide.com/Snipers Hide, LLC, 3205 Fenton St., Wheat Ridge, CO 80212, P: 203-530-3301, F: 203-622-7331, www.snipershide.com
Books/Industry Publications; Firearms; Law Enforcement; Online Services; Training & Safety Equipment

Snow Peak USA, Inc., P.O. Box 2002, Clackamas, OR 97015, P: 503-697-3330, F: 503-699-1396, www.snowpeak.com
Backpacking; Camping; Cooking Equipment/Accessories; Cutlery

Soft Air USA Inc./Cybergun, 1452 Hughes Rd., Suite 100, Grapevine, TX 76051, P: 480-330-3358, F: 925-906-1360, www.softairusa.com
Airguns; Airsoft; Paintball Guns & Accessories

Sog Armory, Inc., 11707 S. Sam Houston Pkwy. W, Suite R, Houston, TX 77031, P: 281-568-5685, F: 285-568-9191, www.sogarmory.com
Firearms; Firearms Maintenance Equipment; Gun Barrels; Gun Grips & Stocks; Law Enforcement; Scopes, Sights & Accessories; Wholesaler/Distributor

SOG Specialty Knives, 6521 212th St. SW, Lynnwood, WA 98036, P: 888-405-6433, F: 425-771-7689, www.sogknives.com
Cutlery; Hunting Accessories; Knives/Knife Cases; Law Enforcement

Sohn Mfg., Inc., 544 Sohn Dr., Elkhart Lake, WI 53020, P: 920-876-3361, F: 920-876-2952, www.sohnmanufacturing.com
Emblems & Decals; Printing Services

Solkoa, Inc., 3107 W. Colorado Ave., Suite 256, Colorado Springs, CO 80904, P: 719-685-1072, F: 719-623-0067, www.solkoa.com
Bags & Equipment Cases; Compasses; Hunting Accessories; Law Enforcement; Survival Kits/First Aid; Training & Safety Equipment; Wholesaler/Distributor

Sona Enterprises, 7825 Somerset Blvd., Suite D, Paramount, CA 90723, P: 562-633-3002, F: 562-633-3583
Binoculars; Camouflage; Camping; Compasses; Lighting Products; Survival Kits/First Aid; Wholesaler/Distributor

SOTech/Special Operations Technologies, 206 Star of India Ln., Carson, CA 90746, P: 800-615-9007, F: 310-202-0880, www.specopstech.com
Backpacking; Bags & Equipment Cases; Custom Manufacturing; Gun Cases; Holsters; Law Enforcement; Shooting Range Equipment; Survival Kits/First Aid

Source One Distributors, 3125 Fortune Way, Suite 1, Wellington, FL 33414, P: 866-768-4327, F: 561-514-1021, www.buysourceone.com
Bags & Equipment Cases; Binoculars; Eyewear; Firearms; Knives/Knife Cases; Men's Clothing; Scopes, Sights & Accessories; Wholesaler/Distributor

Southern Belle Brass, P.O. Box 36, Memphis, TN 38101, P: 800-478-3016, F: 901-947-1924, www.southernbellebrass.com
Firearms Maintenance Equipment; Holsters; Law Enforcement; Men's Clothing; Paintball Guns; Targets; Training & Safety Equipment; Wholesaler/Distributor

Southern Bloomer Mfg. Co. & Muzzleloader Originals, 1215 Fifth St., P.O. Box 1621, Bristol, TN 37621, P: 800-655-0342, F: 423-878-8761, www.southernbloomer.com
Ammunition; Black Powder Accessories; Firearms Maintenance Equipment; Gun Parts/Gunsmithing; Hunting Accessories; Law Enforcement; Reloading; Shooting Range Equipment

SPA Defense, 3409 NW 9th Ave., Suite 1104, Ft. Lauderdale, FL 33309, P: 954-568-7690, F: 954-630-4159, www.spa-defense.com
Firearms; Law Enforcement; Scopes, Sights & Accessories; Tactical Equipment

Spartan Imports, 213 Lawrence Ave., San Francisco, CA 94080, P: 650-589-5501, F: 650-589-5552, www.spartanimports.com
Airguns; Firearms; Law Enforcement; Paintball Guns; Scopes, Sights & Accessories; Training & Safety Equipment; Wholesaler/Distributor

Spec.-Ops. Brands, 1601 W. 15th St., Monahans, TX 79756, P: 866-773-2677, F: 432-943-5565, www.specopsbrand.com
Bags & Equipment Cases; Custom Manufacturing; Holsters; Knives/Knife Cases; Law Enforcement; Shooting Range Equipment; Sports Accessories; Training & Safety Equipment

Specialty Bar Products Co., 4 N. Shore Center, Suite 110, 106 Isabella St., Pittsburgh, PA 15212, P: 412-322-2747, F: 412-322-1912, www.specialty-bar.com
Firearms; Gun Barrels; Gun Parts/Gunsmithing

Specter Gear, Inc., 1107 E. Douglas Ave., Visalia, CA 93292, P: 800-987-3605, F: 559-553-8835, www.spectergear.com
Bags & Equipment Cases; Gun Cases; Holsters; Law Enforcement

Speer Ammunition/ATK Commercial Products, 2299 Snake River Ave., Lewiston, ID 83501, P: 800-256-8685, F: 208-746-3904, www.speer-bullets.com
Ammunition; Reloading

Spiewak/Timberland Pro Valor, 463 Seventh Ave., 11th Floor, New York, NY 10018, P: 800-223-6850, F: 212-629-4803, www.spiewak.com
Footwear; Law Enforcement

Spitfire, Ltd., 8868 Research Blvd., Suite 203, Austin, TX 78758, P: 800-774-8347, F: 512-453-7504, www.spitfire.us
Backpacking; Camping; Sporting Range Equipment; Sports Accessories; Training & Safety Equipment

SportDOG Brand, 10427 Electric Ave., Knoxville, TN 37932, P: 800-732-0144, F: 865-777-4815, www.sportdog.com
Hunting Accessories; Pet Supplies; Training & Safety Equipment; Videos

SportEAR/HarrisQuest Outdoor Products, 528 E. 800 N, Orem, UT 84097, P: 800-530-0090, F: 801-224-5660, www.harrisquest.com
Clay Targets; Hearing Protection; Hunting Accessories; Law Enforcement; Scopes, Sights & Accessories; Shooting Range Equipment; Sports Accessories; Training & Safety Equipment

SportHill, 725 McKinley St., Eugene, OR 97402, P: 541-345-9623, F: 541-343-7261, www.sporthillhunting.com
Archery; Camouflage; Gloves, Mitts, Hats; Men & Women's Clothing; Sports Accessories

Sporting Clays Magazine, 317 S. Washington Ave., Suite 201, Titusville, FL 32796, P: 321-268-5010, F: 321-267-7216, www.sportingclays.net
Books/Industry Publications

Sporting Supplies International, Inc.®, P.O. Box 757, Placentia, CA 92871, P: 888-757-WOLF (9653), F: 714-632-9232, www.wolfammo.com
Ammunition

Sports Afield Magazine, 15621 Chemical Ln., Huntington Beach, CA 92649, P: 714-894-9080, F: 714-894-4949, www.sportsafield.com
Books/Industry Publications

Sports South, LLC, 1039 Kay Ln., P.O. Box 51367, Shreveport, LA 71115, 800-388-3845, www.internetguncatalog.com
Ammunition; Binoculars; Black Powder Accessories; Firearms; Hunting Accessories; Reloading; Scopes, Sights & Accessories; Wholesaler/Distributor

Spot, Inc., 461 S. Milpitas Blvd., Milpitas, CA 95035, F: 408-933-4543, F: 408-933-4954, www.findmespot.com
Backpacking; Camping; Outfitter; Sports Accessories; Survival Kits/First Aid; Training & Safety Equipment

Springboard Engineering, 6520 Platt Ave., Suite 818, West Hills, CA 91307, P: 818-346-4647, F: 818-346-4647
Backpacking; Law Enforcement; Lighting Products; Sports Accessories; Survival Kits/First Aid; Training & Safety Equipment; Wholesaler/Distributor

Springfield Armory, 420 W. Main St., Geneseo, IL 61254, P: 800-680-6866, F: 309-944-3676, www.springfield-armory.com
Firearms

Spyder Paintball/Kingman Group, 14010 Live Oak Ave., Baldwin Park, CA 91706, P: 888-KINGMAN, F: 626-851-8530, www.spyder.tv
Bags & Equipment Cases; Eyewear; Gun Cases; Men's Clothing; Paintball Guns & Accessories

Spyderco, Inc., 820 Spyderco Way, Golden, CO 80403, P: 800-525-7770, F: 303-278-2229, www.spyderco.com
Knives/Knife Cases

SRT Supply, 4450 60th Ave. N, St. Petersburg, FL 33714, P: 727-526-5451, F: 727-527-6893, www.srtsupply.com
Ammunition; Export/Import Specialists; Firearms; Law Enforcement; Wholesaler/Distributor

Stack-On Products Co., 1360 N. Old Rand Rd., P.O. Box 489, Wauconda, IL 60084, P: 800-323-9601, F: 847-526-6599, www.stack-on.com
Bags & Equipment Cases; Gun Cabinets/Racks/Safes; Gun Cases; Hunting Accessories; Shooting Range Equipment; Sports Accessories; Training & Safety Equipment

Stackpole Books, Inc., 5067 Ritter Rd., Mechanicsburg, PA 17055, P: 800-732-3669, F: 717-796-0412, www.stackpolebooks.com
Books/Industry Publications

Stag Arms, 515 John Downey Dr., New Britain, CT 06051, P: 860-229-9994, F: 860-229-3738, www.stagarms.com
Firearms; Law Enforcement

Stallion Leather/Helios Systems, 1104 Carroll Ave., South Milwaukee, WI 53172, P: 414-764-7126, F: 414-764-2878, www.helios-sys.com
Bags & Equipment Cases; Holsters; Knives/Knife Cases; Law Enforcement; Leathergoods; Sports Accessories

Stansport, 2801 E. 12th St., Los Angeles, CA 90023, P: 800-421-6131, F: 323-269-2761, www.stansport.com
Backpacking; Bags & Equipment Cases; Camping; Compasses; Cooking Equipment/Accessories; Hunting Accessories; Lighting Products; Survival Kits/First Aid

Stark Equipment Corp., 55 S. Commercial St., 4th Floor, Manchester, NH 03101, P: 603-556-7772, F: 603-556-7344, www.starkequipment.com
Gun Grips & Stocks; Hunting Accessories; Law Enforcement

Starlight Cases™, 2180 Hwy. 70-A E, Pine Level, NC 27568, P: 877-782-7544, F: 919-965-9177, www.starlightcases.com
Bags & Equipment Cases; Custom Manufacturing; Gun Cabinets/Racks/Safes; Gun Cases; Hunting Accessories; Law Enforcement; Scopes, Sights & Accessories; Shooting Range Equipment

Steiner Binoculars, 97 Foster Rd., Suite 5, Moorestown, NJ 08057, P: 800-257-7742, F: 856-866-8615, www.steiner-binoculars.com
Binoculars

SteriPEN/Hydro-Photon, Inc., 262 Ellsworth Rd., Blue Hill, ME 04614, P: 888-783-7473, F: 207-374-5100, www.steripen.com
Backpacking; Camping; Cooking Equipment/Accessories; Law Enforcement; Sports Accessories; Survival Kits/First Aid; Training & Safety Equipment

Sterling Sharpener, P.O. Box 620547, Woodside, CA 94062, P: 800-297-4277, F: 650-851-1434, www.sterlingsharpener.com
Backpacking; Camping; Cooking Equipment/Accessories; Hunting Accessories; Knives/Knife Cases; Law Enforcement; Sharpeners; Survival Kits/First Aid

Stewart EFI, LLC, 45 Old Waterbury Rd., Thomaston, CT 06787, P: 800-228-2509, F: 860-283-3174, www.stewartefi.com
Ammunition; Backpacking; Custom Manufacturing; Firearms Hearing Protection; Law Enforcement; Lighting Products; Magazines, Cartridge

Steyr Arms, Inc., P.O. Box 840, Trussville, GA 35173, P: 205-467-6544, F: 205-467-3015, www.steyrarms.com
Firearms; Law Enforcement

STI International, 114 Halmar Cove, Georgetown, TX 78628, P: 512-819-0656, F: 512-819-0465, www.stiguns.com
Firearms; Gun Barrels; Gun Parts/Gunsmithing

Stil Crin SNC, Via Per Gottolengo, 12A, Pavone Mella, Brescia 25020, ITALY, P: 011-390309599496, F: 011-390309959544, www.stilcrin.it
Firearms Maintenance Equipment; Gun Cases; Gun Locks; Lubricants

Stoeger Industries, 17603 Indian Head Hwy., Accokeek, MD 20607, P: 800-264-4962, F: 301-283-6988, www.stoegerindustries.com
Airguns; Firearms

Stoney-Wolf Productions, 130 Columbia Court W, Chaska, MN 55318, P: 800-237-7583, F: 952-361-4217, www.stoneywolf.com
Books/Industry Publications; Computer Software; Food; Videos

Stoney Point Products, Inc., 9200 Cody, Overland Park, KS 66214, P: 800-221-9035, F: 800-548-0446, www.stoneypoint.com
Backpacking; Hearing Protection; Hunting Accessories; Shooting Range Equipment; Sports Accessories

Stormy Kromer Mercantile, 1238 Wall St., Ironwood, MI 49938, P: 888-455-2253, F: 906-932-1579, www.stormykromer.com
Camouflage; Gloves, Mitts, Hats; Men's Clothing

Strangler Chokes, Inc., 7958 US Hwy. 167 S, Winnfield, LA 71483, P: 318-201-3474, F: 318-473-0982
Custom Manufacturing; Firearms; Gun Barrels; Gun Parts/Gunsmithing; Hunting Accessories; Scopes, Sights & Accessories

Streamlight, Inc., 30 Eagleville Rd., Eagleville, PA 19403, P: 800-523-7488, F: 800-220-7007, www.streamlight.com
Hunting Accessories; Law Enforcement; Lighting Products; Training & Safety Equipment

Streamworks, Inc., 3233 Lance Dr., Suite B, Stockton, CA 92505, P: 209-337-3307, F: 209-337-3342, www.hattail.com
Hearing Protection

Streetwise Security Products/Cutting Edge Products, Inc., 235-F Forlines Rd., Winterville, NC 28590, P: 800-497-0539, F: 252-830-5542, www.streetwisesecurity.net
Law Enforcement

Strider Knives, Inc., 120 N. Pacific St., Suite L7, San Marcos, CA 92069, P: 760-471-8275, F: 503-218-7069, www.striderknives.com
Backpacking; Custom Manufacturing; Cutlery; Hunting Accessories; Knives/Knife Cases; Law Enforcement; Training & Safety Equipment

Strike-Hold/MPH System Specialties, Inc., P.O. Box 1923, Dawsonville, GA 30534, P: 866-331-0572, F: 325-204-2550, www.strikehold.com

Black Powder Accessories; Export/Import Specialists; Firearms Maintenance Equipment; Hunting Accessories; Law Enforcement; Lubricants; Paintball Accessories; Wholesaler/Distributor

Strong Leather Co., 39 Grove St., P.O. Box 1195, Gloucester, MA 01930, P: 800-225-0724, F: 866-316-3666, www.strongbadgecase.com
Bags & Equipment Cases; Holsters; Law Enforcement; Leathergoods

Sturm, 430 S. Erwin St., Cartersville, GA 30120, P: 800-441-7367, F: 770-386-6654, www.sturm-miltec.com
Camouflage; Camping; Firearms; Gun Grips & Stocks; Magazines, Cartridge; Men's Clothing; Scopes, Sights & Accessories

Sun Optics USA, 1312 S. Briar Oaks Rd., Cleburne, TX 76031, P: 817-447-9047, F: 817-717-8461
Binoculars; Custom Manufacturer; Gun Parts/Gunsmithing; Hunting Accessories; Scopes, Sights & Accessories

Sunbuster/Gustbuster, 1966-B Broadhollow Rd., Farmingdale, NY 11735, P: 888-487-8287, F: 631-777-4320, www.sunbuster.info
Clay Targets; Custom Manufacturing; Eyewear; Hunting Accessories; Law Enforcement; Shooting Range Equipment; Sports Accessories; Wholesaler/Distributor

Sunlite Science & Technology, Inc., 345 N. Iowa St., Lawrence, KS 66044, P: 785-832-8818, F: 913-273-1888, www.powerledlighting.com
Camping; Hunting Accessories; Law Enforcement; Lighting Products; Sports Accessories; Survival Kits/First Aid; Tours/Travel; Training & Safety Equipment

Sunny Hill Enterprises, Inc., W. 1015 Cty. HHH, Chilton, WI 53014, P: 920-898-4707, F: 920-898-4749, www.sunny-hill.com
Custom Manufacturing; Firearms; Gun Barrels; Gun Parts/Gunsmithing; Law Enforcement; Magazines, Cartridge

Super Seer Corp., P.O. Box 700, Evergreen, CO 80437, P: 800-645-1285, F: 303-674-8540, www.superseer.com
Law Enforcement

Super Six Classic, LLC, 635 Hilltop Trail W, Fort Atkinson, WI 53538, P: 920-568-8299, F: 920-568-8259
Firearms

Superior Arms. 836 Weaver Blvd., Wapello, IA 52653, P: 319-523-2016, F: 319-527-0188, www.superiorarms.com
Firearms

Superior Concepts, Inc., 10791 Oak St., P.O. Box 465, Donald, OR 97020, P: 503-922-0488, F: 503-922-2236, www.laserstock.com
Gun Grips & Stocks; Gun Parts/Gunsmithing; Hunting Accessories; Magazines, Cartridge; Scopes, Sights & Accessories

Sure Site, Inc., 351 Dion St., P.O. Box 335, Emmett, ID 83617, P: 800-627-1576, F: 208-365-6944, www.suresiteinc.com
Shooting Range Equipment; Targets

SureFire, LLC, 18300 Mount Baldy Circle, Fountain Valley, CA 92708, P: 800-828-8809, F: 714-545-9537, www.surefire.com
Knives/Knife Cases; Lighting Products; Scopes, Sights & Accessories

Surgeon Rifles, 48955 Moccasin Trail Rd., Prague, OK 74864, P: 405-567-0183, F: 405-567-0250, www.surgeonrifles.com
Firearms; Gun Parts/Gunsmithing; Law Enforcement

Survival Armor, Inc., 13881 Plantation Rd., International Center I, Suite 8, Ft. Myers, FL 33912, P: 866-868-5001, F: 239-210-0898, www.survivalarmor.com
Law Enforcement; Training & Safety Equipment

Survival Corps, Ltd., Ostashkovskoe Shosse, house 48a, Borodino, Moscow Obl, Mitishinski Region, 141031, RUSSIAN FEDERATION, P: 011 74952257985, F: 011 74952257986, www.survivalcorps.ru
Bags & Equipment Cases; Camouflage; Holsters; Law Enforcement; Outfitter

Swany America Corp., 115 Corporate Dr., Johnstown, NY 12095, P: 518-725-3333, F: 518-725-2026, www.swanyhunting.com
Gloves, Mitts, Hats

Swarovski Optik North America, 2 Slater Rd., Cranston, RI 02920, P: 800-426-3089, F: 401-734-5888, www.swarovskioptik.com
Bags & Equipment Cases; Binoculars; Knives/Knife Cases; Scopes, Sights & Accessories; Telescopes; Wholesaler/Distributor

SWAT Magazine, 5011 N. Ocean Blvd., Suite 5, Ocean Ridge, FL 33435, P: 800-665-7928, F: 561-276-0895, www.swatmag.com
Books/Industry Publications; Law Enforcement; Online Services; Retailer Services; Training & Safety Equipment

Swift Bullet Co., 201 Main St., P.O. Box 27, Quinter, KS 67752, P: 785-754-3959, F: 785-754-2359, www.swiftbullets.com
Ammunition

Switch Pack, LLC, 302 NW 4th St., Grants Pass, OR 97526, P: 541-479-3919, F: 541-474-4573
Backpacking; Blinds; Hunting Accessories; Retailer Services; Sports Accessories; Wholesaler/Distributor

SWR Manufacturing, LLC, P.O. Box 841, Pickens, SC 29671, P: 864-850-3579, F: 864-751-2823, www.swrmfg.com
Firearms; Hearing Protection; Law Enforcement; Recoil Protection Devices & Services; Training & Safety Equipment

Sylvansport, 10771 Greenville Hwy., Cedar Mountain, NC 28718, P: 828-883-4292, F: 828-883-4817, www.sylvansport.com
Backpacking; Camping; Hunting Accessories; Sports Accessories; Tours/Travel; Vehicles, Utility & Rec

Systema Co., 5542 S. Integrity Ln., Fort Mohave, AZ 86426, P: 877-884-0909, F: 267-222-4787, www.systema-engineering.com
Airguns; Airsoft; Law Enforcement; Training & Safety Equipment

Szco Supplies, Inc., 2713 Merchant Dr., P.O. Box 6353, Baltimore, MD 21230, P: 800-232-6998, F: 410-368-9366, www.szco.com
Camping; Custom Manufacturing; Cutlery; Hunting Accessories; Knives/Knife Cases; Pet Supplies; Sharpeners; Wholesaler/Distributor

T

T.Z. Case, 1786 Curtiss Ct., La Verne, CA 91750, P: 888-892-2737, F: 909-392-8406, www.tzcase.com
Airguns; Archery; Custom Manufacturing; Firearms; Gun Cases; Hunting Accessories

Tac Force, 8653 Garvey Ave., Suite 202, Rosemead, CA 91733, P: 626-453-8377, F: 626-453-8378, www.tac-force.com
Backpacking; Bags & Equipment Cases; Gloves, Mitts, Hats; Gun Cases; Holsters; Law Enforcement; Paintball Accessories

Tac Wear, Inc., 700 Progress Ave., Suite 7, Toronto, Ontario M1H 2Z7, CANADA, P: 866-TAC-WEAR, F: 416-289-1522, www.tacwear.com
Gloves, Mitts, Hats; Hunting Accessories; Law Enforcement; Men & Women's Clothing; Sports Accessories; Training & Safety Equipment

Tactical & Survival Specialties, Inc. (TSSI), 3900 Early Rd., P.O. Box 1890, Harrisonburg, VA 22801, P: 877-535-8774, F: 540-434-7796, www.tacsurv.com
Bags & Equipment Cases; Custom Manufacturing; Knives/Knife Cases; Law Enforcement; Men & Women's Clothing; Survival Kits/First Aid; Training & Safety Equipment; Wholesaler/Distributor

Tactical Assault Gear (TAG), 1330 30th St., Suite A, San Diego, CA 92154, P: 888-899-1199, F: 619-628-0126, www.tacticalassaultgear.com
Bags & Equipment Cases; Holsters; Men's Clothing

Tactical Command Industries, Inc., 2101 W. Tenth St., Suite G, Antioch, CA 94509, P: 888-990-1600, F: 925-756-7977, www.tacticalcommand.com
Custom Manufacturing; Hearing Protection; Law Enforcement; Training & Safety Equipment; Two-Way Radios

Tactical Electronics/SPA Defense, P.O. Box 152, Broken Arrow, OK 74013, P: 866-541-7996, F: 918-249-8328, www.tacticalelectronics.com
Photographic Equipment

Tactical Innovations, Inc., 345 Sunrise Rd., Bonners Ferry, ID 83805, P: 208-267-1585, F: 208-267-1597, www.tacticalinc.com
Firearms; Gun Barrels; Gun Grips & Stocks; Holsters; Law Enforcement; Magazines, Cartridge; Wholesaler/Distributor

Tactical Medical Solutions, Inc., 614 Pinehollow Dr., Anderson, SC 29621, P: 888-TACMED1, F: 864-224-0064
Law Enforcement; Survival Kits/First Aid; Training & Safety Equipment

Tactical Operations Products, 20972 SW Meadow Way, Tualatin, OR 97062, P: 503-638-9873, F: 503-638-0524, www.tacoproducts.com
Airsoft; Backpacking; Bags & Equipment Cases; Camping; Law Enforcement; Lighting Products; Paintball Accessories

Tactical Products Group, Inc., 755 NW 17th Ave., Suite 108, Delray Beach, FL 33445, P: 866-9-TACPRO, F: 561-265-4061, www.tacprogroup.com
Export/Import Specialists; Footwear; Gun Cases; Holsters; Knives/Knife Cases; Law Enforcement; Men's Clothing; Wholesaler/Distributor

Tactical Rifles, 19250 Hwy. 301, Dade City, FL 33523, P: 352-999-0599, F: 352-567-9825, www.tacticalrifles.net
Firearms

Tactical Solutions, 2181 Commerce Ave., Boise, ID 83705, P: 866-333-9901, F: 208-333-9909, www.tacticalsol.com
Firearms; Gun Barrels; Gun Grips & Stocks; Gun Parts/Gunsmithing; Scopes, Sights & Accessories; Wholesaler/Distributor

TacticalTECH1, 251 Beulah Church Rd., Carrollton, GA 30117, P: 800-334-3368, F: 770-832-1676
Bags & Equipment Cases; Eyewear; Law Enforcement; Lighting Products; Training & Safety Equipment

TAG Safari Clothes, 1022 Wirt Rd., Suite 302, Houston, TX 77055, P: 800-TAG-2703, F: 713-688-6806, www.tagsafari.com
Camping; Footwear; Gun Cases; Leathergoods; Men & Women's Clothing; Online Services; Wholesaler/Distributor

Tagua Gun Leather, 3750 NW 28th St., Miami, FL 33142, P: 866-678-2482, F: 866-678-2482, www.taguagunleather.com
Firearms; Holsters; Hunting Accessories; Law Enforcement; Leathergoods; Wholesaler/Distributor

Talley Manufacturing, Inc., 9183 Old Number Six Hwy., P.O. Box 369, Santee, SC 29142, P: 803-854-5700, F: 803-854-9315, www.talleyrings.com
Black Powder Accessories; Custom Manufacturing; Gun Parts/Gunsmithing; Hunting Accessories; Scopes, Sights & Accessories; Sports Accessories

Tandy Brands Outdoors, 107 W. Gonzales St., Yoakum, TX 77995, P: 800-331-9092, F: 361-293-9127, www.tandybrands.com
Bags & Equipment Cases; Custom Manufacturing; Hunting Accessories; Knives/Knife Cases; Leathergoods; Shooting Range Equipment; Sports Accessories

TangoDown, Inc., 1588 Arrow Hwy., Unit F, La Verne, CA 91750-5334, P: 909-392-4757, F: 909-392-4802, www.tangodown.com
Gun Grips & Stocks; Law Enforcement; Lighting Products; Magazines, Cartridge; Scopes, Sights & Accessories; Targets

TAPCO, Inc.,3615 Kennesaw N. Industrial Pkwy., P.O. Box 2408, Kennesaw, GA 30156-9138, P: 800-554-1445, F: 800-226-1662, www.tapco.com
Custom Manufacturing; Firearms Maintenance Equipment; Gun Grips & Stocks; Gun Parts/Gunsmithing; Law Enforcement; Magazines, Cartridge; Recoil Protection Devices & Services; Wholesaler/Distributor

Target Shooting, Inc., 1110 First Ave. SE, Watertown, SD 57201, P: 800-611-2164, F: 605-882-8840, www.targetshooting.com
Scopes, Sights & Accessories; Shooting Range Equipment

Tasco/Bushnell Outdoor Products, 9400 Cody, Overland Park, KS 66214, P: 800-221-9035, F: 800-548-0446, www.tasco.com
Binoculars; Scopes, Sights & Accessories; Telescopes

Taser International, 1700 N. 85th St., Scottsdale, AZ 85255, P: 800-978-2737, F: 480-991-0791, www.taser.com
Law Enforcement

Task Holsters, 2520 SW 22nd St., Suite 2-186, Miami, FL 33145, P: 305-335-8647, F: 305-858-9618, www.taskholsters.com
Bags & Equipment Cases; Export/Import Specialists; Gun Cases; Holsters; Hunting Accessories; Law Enforcement; Leathergoods; Wholesaler/Distributor

Taurus International Manufacturing, Inc., 16175 NW 49th Ave., Miami, FL 33014, P: 800-327-3776, F: 305-623-7506, www.taurususa.com
Firearms

Taylor Brands, LLC/Imperial Schrade & Smith & Wesson Cutting Tools, 1043 Fordtown Rd., Kingsport, TN 37663, P: 800-251-0254, F: 423-247-5371, www.taylorbrandsllc.com
Backpacking; Camping; Cutlery; Hunting Accessories; Knives/Knife Cases; Law Enforcement

Taylor's & Co., Inc., 304 Lenoir Dr., Winchester, VA 22603, P: 800-655-5814, F: 540-722-2018, www.taylorsfirearms.com
Black Powder Accessories; Firearms; Firearms Maintenance Equipment; Gun Parts/Gunsmithing; Wholesaler/Distributor

Team Realtree®, P.O. Box 9638, Columbus, GA 31908, P: 800-992-9968, F: 706-569-9346, www.realtree.com
Camouflage; Men & Women's Clothing

Team SD/TSD Sports, 901 S. Fremont Ave., Suite 218, Alhambra, CA 91803, P: 626-281-0979, F: 626-281-0323, www.airsoftsd.com
Airguns; Airsoft; Paintball Guns & Accessories; Scopes, Sights & Accessories; Sports Accessories; Training & Safety Equipment; Wholesaler/Distributor

Team Wendy, 17000 St. Clair Ave., Bldg. 1, Cleveland, OH 44110, P: 877-700-5544, F: 216-738-2510, www.teamwendy.com
Custom Manufacturing; Hunting Accessories; Law Enforcement; Sports Accessories; Training & Safety Equipment

TEARepair, Inc., 2200 Knight Rd., Bldg. 2, P.O. Box 1879, Land O'Lakes, FL 34639, P: 800-937-3716, F: 813-996-4523, www.tear-aid.com

Camping; Hunting Accessories; Retail Packaging; Sports Accessories; Survival Kits/First Aid; Wholesaler/Distributor

Tech Mix, Inc., 740 Bowman St., Stewart, MN 55385, P: 877-466-6455, F: 320-562-2125, www.techmixinc.com
Pet Supplies

Technoframes, Via Aldo Moro 6, Scanzorosciate Bergamo, 24020, ITALY, P: 866-246-1095, F: 011 39035668328, www.technoframes.com
Ammunition; Bags & Equipment Cases; Gun Cases; Hunting Accessories; Magazines, Cartridge; Reloading; Shooting Range Equipment

Tecomate Seed, 33477 Hwy. 99E, Tangent, OR 97389, P: 800-547-4101, F: 541-926-9435, www.tecomateseed.com
Wildlife Management

Teijin Aramid USA, Inc., 801-F Blacklawn Rd., Conyers, GA 30012, P: 800-451-6586, F: 770-929-8138, www.teijinaramid.com
Law Enforcement

Television Equipment Associates, Inc., 16 Mount Ebo Rd. S, P.O. Box 404, Brewster, NY 10509, P: 310-457-7401, F: 310-457-0023, www.swatheadsets.com
Law Enforcement

Temco Communications, Inc., 13 Chipping Campden Dr., South Barrington, IL 60010, P: 847-359-3277, F: 847-359-3743, www.temcom.net
Hearing Protection; Law Enforcement; Two-Way Radios

Ten-X Ammunition, Inc., 5650 Arrow Hwy., Montclair, CA 91763, P: 909-605-1617, F: 909-605-2844, www.tenxammo.com
Ammunition; Custom Manufacturing; Law Enforcement; Reloading; Training & Safety Equipment; Wholesaler/Distributor

TenPoint Crossbow Technologies, 1325 Waterloo Rd., Suffield, OH 44260, P: 800-548-6837, F: 330-628-0999, www.tenpointcrossbows.com
Archery; Crossbows & Accessories

Teton Grill Co., 865 Xenium Lane N, Plymouth, MN 55441, P: 877-838-6643, F: 763-249-6385, www.tetongrills.com
Cooking Equipment/Accessories; Custom Manufacturing; Cutlery; Knives/Knife Cases

Tetra® Gun Care, 8 Vreeland Rd., Florham Park, NJ 07932, P: 973-443-0004, F: 973-443-0263, www.tetraguncare.com
Firearms Maintenance Equipment; Gun Parts/Gunsmithing; Lubricants

Texas Hunt Co., P.O. Box 10, Monahans, TX 79756, P: 888-894-8682, F: 432-943-5565, www.texashuntco.com
Bags & Equipment Cases; Hunting Accessories; Knives/Knife Cases; Vehicles, Utility & Rec; Wholesaler/Distributor

Texsport, P.O. Box 55326, Houston, TX 77255, P: 800-231-1402, F: 713-468-1535, www.texsport.com
Backpacking; Bags & Equipment Cases; Camouflage; Camping; Compasses; Cooking Equipment/Accessories; Lighting Products; Wholesaler/Distributor

Thermacell/The Schawbel Corp., 100 Crosby Dr., Suite 102, Bedford, MA 01730, P: 866-753-3837, F: 781-541-6007, www.thermacell.com
Archery; Backpacking; Camouflage; Camping; Crossbows & Accessories; Holsters; Hunting Accessories; Scents & Lures

Thermore, 6124 Shady Lane SE, Olympia, WA 98503, P: 800-871-6563, www.thermore.com
Gloves, Mitts, Hats; Men & Women's Clothing; Pet Supplies

Thompson/Center Arms, A Smith & Wesson Co., P.O. Box 5002, Rochester, NH 01104, P: 603-332-2333, F: 603-332-5133, www.tcarms.com
Black Powder Accessories; Black Powder/Smokeless Powder; Firearms; Gun Barrels; Hunting Accessories

Thorogood Shoes, 108 S. Polk St., Merrill, WI 54452, P: 800-826-0002, F: 800-569-6817, www.weinbrennerusa.com
Footwear; Law Enforcement; Leathergoods; Men & Women's Clothing

Thunderbolt Customs, Inc., 7296 S. Section Line Rd., Delaware, OH 43015, P: 740-917-9135, www.thunderboltcustoms.com
Backpacking; Black Powder Accessories; Camping; Firearms; Hunting Accessories; Pet Supplies; Scopes, Sights & Accessories; Shooting Range Accessories

Tiberius Arms, 2717 W. Ferguson Rd., Fort Wayne, IN 46809, P: 888-982-2842, F: 260-572-2210, www.tiberiusarms.com
Airguns; Law Enforcement; Paintball Guns & Accessories; Training & Safety Equipment

Tiger-Vac, Inc., 73 SW 12 Ave., Bldg. 1, Suite 7, Dania, FL 33004, P: 800-668-4437, F: 954-925-3626, www.tiger-vac.com
Shooting Range Equipment; Training & Safety Equipment

Timney Manufacturing, Inc., 3940 W. Clarendon Ave., Phoenix, AZ 85019, P: 866-4TIMNEY, F: 602-241-0361, www.timneytriggers.com
Firearms Maintenance Equipment; Gun Locks; Gun Parts/Gunsmithing

Tinks, 10157 Industrial Dr., Covington, GA 30014, P: 800-624-5988, F: 678-342-9973, www.tinks69.com
Archery; Hunting Accessories; Scents & Lures; Videos

Tisas-Trabzon Gun Industry Corp., Degol Cad. No: 13-1 Tandogan Ankara, 06580, TURKEY, P: 011 903122137509, F: 011 903122138570, www.trabzonsilah.com
Firearms; Gun Barrels

TMB Designs, Unit 11, Highgrove Farm Ind Est Pinvin, Pershore, Worchestershire WR10 2LF, UNITED KINGDOM, P: 011 441905840022, F: 011 441905850022, www.cartridgedisplays.com
Ammunition; Custom Manufacturing; Emblems & Decals; Hunting Accessories; Outdoor Art, Jewelry, Sculpture; Sports Accessories

Toadbak, Inc., P.O. Box 18097, Knoxville, TN 37928-8097, P: 865-548-1283
Camouflage; Men's Clothing

Tony's Custom Uppers & Parts, P.O. Box 252, Delta, OH 43515, P: 419-822-9578, F: 419-822-9578
Custom Manufacturing; Gun Barrels; Gun Parts/Gunsmithing; Wholesaler/Distributor

Tool Logic, Inc., 2290 Eastman Ave., Suite 109, Ventura, CA 93003, P: 800-483-8422, F: 805-339-9712, www.toollogic.com
Backpacking; Compasses; Cutlery; Knives/Knife Cases; Lighting Products; Sports Accessories; Survival Kits/First Aid

Top Brass Tackle/dba Cypress Knees Publishing, P.O. Box 209, Starkville, MS 39760, P: 662-323-1559, F: 662-323-7466, www.outdooryouthadventures.com
Books/Industry Publications

TOPS Knives, P.O. Box 2544, Idaho Falls, ID 82403, P: 208-542-0113, F: 208-552-2945, www.topsknives.com
Backpacking; Custom Manufacturing; Hunting Accessories; Knives/Knife Cases; Law Enforcement; Leathergoods; Men's Clothing; Survival Kits/First Aid

Torel, 107 W. Gonzales St., Yoakum, TX 77995, P: 800-331-9092, F: 361-293-9127, www.tandybrands.com
Bags & Equipment Cases; Custom Manufacturing; Hunting Accessories; Knives/Knife Cases; Leathergoods; Shooting Range Equipment; Sports Accessories

Torrey Pines Logic, Inc., 12651 High Bluff Dr., Suite 100, San Diego, CA 92130, P: 858-755-4549, F: 858-350-0007, www.tplogic.com
Binoculars; Law Enforcement; Scopes, Sights & Accessories; Telescopes

Traditions Performance Firearms, 1375 Boston Post Rd., P.O. Box 776, Old Saybrook, CT 06475-0776, P: 800-526-9556, F: 860-388-4657, www.traditionsfirearms.com
Black Powder Accessories; Firearms; Hunting Accessories; Scopes, Sights & Accessories

Transarms Handels GmbH & Co. KG, 6 Im Winkel, Worms, Rheinland Pfalz 67547, GERMANY, P: 011 490624197770, F: 011 4906241977777
Ammunition; Export/Import Specialists; Firearms; Firearms Maintenance Equipment; Gun Barrels; Gun Parts/Gunsmithing; Law Enforcement; Magazines, Cartridge

Traser H3 Watches, 2930 Domingo Ave., Suite 159, Berkeley, CA 94705, P: 510-479-7523, F: 510-479-7532, www.traserusa.com
Custom Manufacturing; Export/Import Specialists; Law Enforcement; Lighting Products; Men's Clothing; Training & Safety Equipment; Wholesaler/Distributor

Tree Talon, 148 Main St., P.O. Box 1370, Bucksport, ME 04416, P: 207-469-1900, F: 207-469-6121, www.treetalon.com
Hunting Accessories

Tri-Tronics, Inc., 1705 S. Research Loop, Tucson, AZ 85710, P: 800-765-2275, F: 800-320-3538, www.tritronics.com
Hunting Accessories; Pet Supplies; Sports Accessories

Trijicon, Inc., 49385 Shafer Ave., P.O. Box 930059, Wixom, MI 48393, P: 800-338-0563, F: 248-960-7725, www.trijicon.com
Scopes, Sights & Accessories

Triple K Manufacturing Co., Inc., 2222 Commercial St., San Diego, CA 92113, P: 800-521-5062, F: 877-486-6247, www.triplek.com
Black Powder Accessories; Gun Parts/Gunsmithing; Holsters; Hunting Accessories; Law Enforcement; Leathergoods; Magazines, Cartridge; Pet Supplies

Tristar Sporting Arms, Ltd., 1816 Linn St., North Kansas City, MO 64116, P: 816-421-1400, F: 816-421-4182, www.tristarsporting.com
Export/Import Specialists; Firearms

Trophy Animal Health Care, 1217 W. 12th St., Kansas City, MO 64101, P: 800-821-7925, F: 816-474-0462, www.trophyanimalcare.com
Pet Supplies

Troy Industries, Inc., 128 Myron St., West Springfield, MA 01089, P: 866-788-6412, F: 413-383-0339, www.troyind.com
Firearms; Gun Grips & Stocks; Gun Parts/Gunsmithing; Law Enforcement; Scopes, Sights & Accessories

Tru Hone Corp., 1721 NE 19th Ave., Ocala, FL 34470, P: 800-237-4663, F: 352-622-9180, www.truhone.com
Sharpeners

TruckVault, Inc., 211 Township St., P.O. Box 734, Sedro Woolley, WA 98284, P: 800-967-8107, F: 800-621-4287, www.truckvault.com
Custom Manufacturing; Gun Cabinets/Racks/Safes; Hunting Accessories; Law Enforcement; Pet Supplies; Sports Accessories; Training & Safety Equipment

True North Tactical, 500 N. Birdneck Rd., Suite 200, Virginia Beach, VA 23451, P: 800-TNT-1478, F: 757-491-9652, www.truenorthtactical.com
Backpacking; Bags & Equipment Cases; Gun Cases; Holsters; Law Enforcement; Wholesaler/Distributor

TrueTimber Outdoors, 150 Accurate Way, Inman, SC 29349, P: 864-472-1720, F: 864-472-1834, www.truetimber.com
Bags & Equipment Cases; Blinds; Camouflage; Footwear; Gloves, Mitts, Hats; Hunting Accessories; Men & Women's Clothing

Truglo, Inc., 710 Presidential Dr., Richardson, TX 75081, P: 888-8-TRUGLO, F: 972-774-0323, www.truglo.com
Archery; Binoculars; Black Powder Accessories; Crossbows & Accessories; Hunting Accessories; Law Enforcement; Scopes, Sights & Accessories; Watches

Trulock Tool, 113 Drayton St. NW, P.O. Box 530, Whigham, GA 39897, P: 800-293-9402, F: 229-762-4050, www.trulockchokes.com
Ammunition; Custom Manufacturing; Firearms Maintenance Equipment; Gun Parts/Gunsmithing; Hunting Accessories; Recoil Protection Devices & Services; Sports Accessories; Wholesaler/Distributor

Trumark Mfg. Co., Inc., 1835 38th St., Boulder, CO 80301, P: 800-878-6272, F: 303-442-1380, www.slingshots.com
Archery; Backpacking; Crossbows & Accessories; Hunting Accessories; Sports Accessories

Tuff-N-Lite, 325 Spencer Rd., Conover, NC 28613, P: 877-883-3654, F: 828-322-7881, www.tuffnlite.com
Gloves, Mitts, Hats; Men & Women's Clothing

TufForce, 1734 Ranier Blvd., Canton, MI 48187, P: 800-382-7989, F: 888-686-0373, www.tufforce.com
Bags & Equipment Cases; Gun Cases; Gun Grips & Stocks; Holsters; Hunting Accessories; Law Enforcement; Scopes, Sights & Accessories; Wholesaler/Distributor

Tunilik Adventure, 11600 Philippe Panneton, Montreal, Quebec H1E 4G4, CANADA, P: 866-648-1595, F: 514-648-1431, www.adventuretunilik.com
Outfitter

TurtleSkin Protective Products, 301 Turnpike Rd., New Ipswich, NH 03071, P: 888-477-4675, F: 603-291-1119, www.turtleskin.com
Gloves, Mitts, Hats; Hunting Accessories; Law Enforcement; Men & Women's Clothing; Sports Accessories

U

U.S. Armament Corp., 121 Valley View Dr., Ephrata, PA 17522, P: 717-721-4570, F: 717-738-4890, www.usarmamentcorp.com
Firearms

U.S. Armor Corp., 16433 Valley View Ave., Cerritos, CA 90703, P: 800-443-9798, F: 562-207-4238, www.usarmor.com
Law Enforcement; Training & Safety Equipment

U.S. Explosive Storage, LLC, 355 Industrial Park Dr., Boone, NC 28607, P: 877-233-1481, F: 800-295-1653, www.usexplosive.com
Custom Manufacturing; Firearms Maintenance Equipment; Gun Cabinets/Racks/Safes; Law Enforcement; Magazines, Cartridge; Training & Safety Equipment

U.S. Fire-Arms Mfg. Co., Inc., P.O. Box 1901, Hartford, CT 06144-1901, P: 860-296-7441, F: 860-296-7688, www.usfirearms.com
Firearms; Gun Parts/Gunsmithing

U.S. Optics, Inc., 150 Arovista Circle, Brea, CA 92821, P: 714-582-1956, F: 714-582-1959, www.usoptics.com
Custom Manufacturing; Law Enforcement; Scopes, Sights & Accessories

U.S. Tactical Supply, Inc., 939 Pacific Blvd. SE, Albany, OR 97321, P: 877-928-8645, F: 541-791-2965, www.ustacticalsupply.com
Bags & Equipment Cases; Gun Parts/Gunsmithing; Holsters; Hunting Accessories; Knives/Knife Cases; Law Enforcement; Scopes, Sights & Accessories; Wholesaler/Distributor

Uberti, A., 17603 Indian Head Hwy., Accokeek, MD 20607-2501, P: 800-264-4962, F: 301-283-6988, www.uberti.com

Firearms

Ultimate Hunter, Inc., 610 Prather, P.O. Box 542, Maryville, MO 64468, P: 660-562-3838, F: 660-582-4377, www.ambushlures.com
Decoys

Ultimate Survival Technologies, LLC, 14428 167th Ave. SE, Monroe, WA 98272, P: 866-479-7994, F: 206-965-9659, www.ultimatesurvival.com
Backpacking; Bags & Equipment Cases; Camping; Hunting Accessories; Law Enforcement; Men's Clothing; Sports Accessories; Survival Kits/First Aid

Ultra Dot Distribution, 6304 Riverside Dr., P.O. Box 362, Yankeetown, FL, 34498, P: 352-447-2255, F: 352-447-2266, www.ultradotusa.com
Scopes, Sights & Accessories

Ultra Lift Corp., 475 Stockton Ave., Unit E, San Jose, CA 95126, P: 800-346-3057, F: 408-297-1199, www.ultralift.com/safes.html
Custom Manufacturing; Gun Cabinets/Racks/Safes; Gun Cases; Retailer Services; Sports Accessories; Training & Safety Equipment

Ultra Paws, 12324 Little Pine Rd. SW, Brainerd, MN 56401, P: 800-355-5575, F: 218-855-6977, www.ultrapaws.com
Backpacking; Hunting Accessories; Law Enforcement; Outfitter; Pet Supplies; Survival Kits/First Aid; Training & Safety Equipment; Wholesaler/Distributor

Ultramax Ammunition/Wideview Scope Mount, 2112 Elk Vale Rd., Rapid City, SD 57701, P: 800-345-5852, F: 605-342-8727, www.ultramaxammunition.com
Ammunition

Ultrec Engineered Products, LLC, 860 Maple Ridge Ln., Brookfield, WI 53045, P: 262-821-2023, F: 262-821-1156, www.ultrec.com
Backpacking; Binoculars; Firearms; Hunting Accessories; Law Enforcement; Photographic Equipment; Shooting Range Equipment; Training & Safety Equipment

Umarex/Umarex, USA/RAM–Real Action Marker, 6007 S. 29th St., Fort Smith, AR 72908, P: 479-646-4210, F: 479-646-4206, www.umarexusa.com, www.trainingumarexusa.com
Airguns; Airsoft; Ammunition; Firearms; Law Enforcement; Paintball Guns; Scopes, Sights & Accessories; Training & Safety Equipment

Uncle Mike's/Bushnell Outdoor Accessories, 9200 Cody St., Overland Park, KS 66214, P: 800-423-3537, F: 800-548-0446, www.unclemikes.com
Bags & Equipment Cases; Gloves, Mitts, Hats; Gun Cases; Holsters; Hunting Accessories

Under Armour Performance, 1020 Hull St., Third Floor, Baltimore, MD 21230, P: 888-427-6687, F: 410-234-1027, www.underarmour.com
Bags & Equipment Cases; Camouflage; Gloves, Mitts, Hats; Law Enforcement; Men & Women's Clothing; Outfitter; Sports Accessories

United Cutlery Corp., 201 Plantation Oak Dr., Thomasville, GA 31792, P: 800-548-0835, F: 229-551-0182, www.unitedcutlery.com
Camping; Compasses; Custom Manufacturing; Cutlery; Knives/Knife Cases; Law Enforcement; Sharpeners; Wholesaler/Distributor

United Shield International, 1606 Barlow St., Suite 1, Traverse City, MI 49686, P: 800-705-9153, F: 231-933-5368, www.unitedshield.net
Law Enforcement

United Weavers of America, Inc., 3562 Dug Gap Rd. SW, Dalton, GA 30721, P: 800-241-5754, F: 706-226-8844, www.unitedweavers.net
Home Furnishings

Universal Power Group, 1720 Hayden, Carrollton, TX 75006, P: 866-892-1122, F: 469-892-1123, www.upgi.com, www.deerfeeder.com
Blinds; Camping; Decoys; Export/Import Specialists; Feeder Equipment; Hunting Accessories; Lighting Products; Wholesaler/Distributor

Urban–E.R.T. Slings, LLC, P.O. Box 429, Clayton, IN 46118, P: 317-223-6509, F: 317-539-2710, www.urbanertslings.com
Firearms; Hunting Accessories; Law Enforcement; Paintball Accessories

US Night Vision Corp., 3845 Atherton Rd., Suite 9, Rocklin, CA 95765, P: 800-500-4020, F: 916-663-5986, www.usnightvision.com
Binoculars; Hunting Accessories; Law Enforcement; Paintball Accessories; Scopes, Sights & Accessories; Sports Accessories; Training & Safety Equipment; Wholesaler/Distributor

US Peacekeeper Products, Inc., W245, N5570 Corporate Circle, Sussex, WI 53089, P: 800-428-0800, F: 262-246-4845, uspeacekeeper.com
Bags & Equipment Cases; Gloves, Mitts, Hats; Hunting Accessories; Men & Women's Clothing

Uselton Arms, 390 Southwinds Dr., Franklin, TN 37064, P: 615-595-2255, F: 615-595-2254, www.useltonarms.com
Custom Manufacturing; Firearms; Gun Barrels; Gun Grips & Stocks; Gun Parts/Gunsmithing; Law Enforcement

V

V.H. Blackinton & Co., Inc., 221 John Dietsch Blvd., P.O. Box 1300, Attleboro Falls, MA 02763, P: 800-699-4436, F: 508-695-5349, www.blackinton.com
Custom Manfucturing; Emblems & Decals; Law Enforcement

V-Line Industries, 370 Easy St., Simi Valley, CA 93065, P: 805-520-4987, F: 805-520-6470, www.vlineind.com
Gun Cabinets; Racks/Safes; Gun Cases

Valdada Optics, P.O. Box 270095, Littleton, CO 80127, P: 303-979-4578, F: 303-979-0256, www.valdada.com
Binoculars; Compasses; Custom Manufacturing; Law Enforcement; Photographic Equipment; Scopes, Sights & Accessories; Telescopes; Wholesaler/Distributor

Valiant Armoury, 3000 Grapevine Mills Pkwy., Suite 101, Grapevine, TX 76051, P: 877-796-7374, F: 972-539-9351, www.valliantarmouryswords.com
Wholesaler/Distributor

Valley Operational Wear, LLC/OP Wear Armor, P.O. Box 9415, Knoxville, TN 37940, P: 865-259-6248, F: 865-259-6255
Law Enforcement

Valley Outdoors, P.O. Box 108, Fort Valley, GA 31030, P: 478-397-0531, F: 478-825-3398, www.valleyoutdoors.us
Outfitter

Valor Corp., 1001 Sawgrass Corporate Pkwy., Sunrise, FL 33323, P: 800-899-VALOR, F: 866-248-9594, www.valorcorp.com
Airguns; Ammunition; Cutlery; Firearms; Knives/Knife Cases; Law Enforcement; Magazines, Cartridge; Wholesaler/Distributor

Vang Comp Systems, 400 W. Butterfield Rd., Chino Valley, AZ 86323, P: 928-636-8455, F: 928-636-1538, www.vangcomp.com
Firearms; Gun Barrels; Gun Parts/Gunsmithing

Vanguard USA, Inc., 9157 E. M-36, Whitmore Lake, MI 48189, P: 800-875-3322, F: 888-426-7008, www.vanguardworld.com
Archery; Bags & Equipment Cases; Binoculars; Gun Cases; Hunting Accessories; Photographic Equipment; Scopes, Sights & Accessories; Shooting Range Equipment

Vector Optics, 3964 Callan Blvd., South San Francisco, CA 94080, P: 415-632-7089, CHINA, P: 011 862154040649, www.vectoroptics.com
Scopes, Sights & Accessories; Sports Accessories; Wholesaler/Distributor

Vega Holster srl, Via Di Mezzo 31 Z.I., Calcinaia (PI), 56031, ITALY, P: 011 390587489190, F: 011 390587489901, www.vegaholster.com
Bags & Equipment Cases; Gun Cases; Holsters; Hunting Accessories; Law Enforcement; Leathergoods; Shooting Range Equipment

Vega Silah Sanayi, Ltd., Tigcilar Sokak No. 1 Mercan, Eminonu, Istanbul, 34450, TURKEY, P: 011 902125200103, F: 011 902125120879
Firearms

Verney-Carron SA, 54 Blvd. Thiers, Boite Postale 72, St. Etienne Cedex 1, 42002, FRANCE, P: 011 33477791500, F: 011 33477790702, www.verney-carron.com
Custom Manufacturing; Firearms; Gun Barrels; Law Enforcement; Wholesaler/Distibutor

Versatile Rack Co., 5232 Alcoa Ave., Vernon, CA 90058, P: 323-588-0137, F: 323-588-5067, www.versatilegunrack.com
Firearms Maintenance Equipment; Gun Cabinets/Racks/Safes; Gun Cases; Gun Locks; Hunting Accessories; Reloading; Shooting Range Equipment; Sports Accessories

VibraShine, Inc./Leaf River Outdoor Products, 113 Fellowship Rd., P.O. Box 557, Taylorsville, MS 39168, P: 601-785-9854, F: 601-785-9874, www.myleafriver.com
Firearms Maintenance Equipment; Hunting Accessories; Photographic Equipment; Reloading

Victorinox Swiss Army, 7 Victoria Dr., Monroe, CT 06468, P: 800-243-4032, F: 800-243-4006, www.swissarmy.com
Camping; Cutlery; Hunting Accessories; Knives/Knife Cases; Lighting Products; Sports Accessories

Vintage Editions, Inc., 88 Buff Ln., Taylorsville, NC 28681, P: 800-662-8965, F: 828-632-4187, www.vintageeditions.com
Custom Manufacturing; Home Furnishings; Hunting Accessories; Pet Supplies; Sports Accessories

Virginia Blade, 5177 Boonsboro Rd., Lynchburg, VA 24503, P: 434-384-1282, F: 434-384-4541

Viridian Green Laser Sights/Laser Aiming Systems Corp., 12637 Sable Dr., Burnsville, MN 55337, P: 800-990-9390, F: 952-882-6227, www.viridiangreenlaser.com
Holsters; Law Enforcement; Lighting Products; Scopes, Sights & Accessories

Vixen Optics, 1010 Calle Cordillera, Suite 106, San Clemente, CA 92673, P: 949-429-6363, F: 949-429-6826, www.vixenoptics.com
Binoculars; Scopes, Sights & Accessories; Telescopes; Wholesaler/Distributor

Vltor Weapon Systems, 3735 N. Romero Rd., Tucson, AZ 85705, P: 866-468-5867, F: 520-293-8807, www.vltor.com
Firearms; Gun Grips & Stocks; Gun Parts/Gunsmithing; Law Enforcement; Recoil Protection Devices & Services

Volquartsen Custom, 24276 240th St., P.O. Box 397, Carroll, IA 51401, P: 712-792-4238, F: 712-792-2542, www.volquartsen.com
Custom Manufacturing; Firearms; Gun Barrels; Gun Grips/Stocks; Gun Parts/Gunsmithing

Vortex Optics, 2120 W. Greenview Dr., Middleton, WI 53562, P: 800-426-0048, F: 608-662-7454
Binoculars; Scopes, Sights & Accessories

Vyse-Gelatin Innovations, 5024 N. Rose St., Schiller Park, IL 60176, P: 800-533-2152, F: 800-533-2152, www.vyse.com
Airguns; Ammunition; Firearms; Law Enforcement; Magazines, Cartridge; Paintball Guns & Accessories; Shooting Range Equipment

Vytek, 195 Industrial Rd., Fitchburg, MA 01420, P: 978-342-9800, F: 978-342-0606, www.vy-tek.com
Custom Manufacturing; Emblems & Decals; Retailer Services; Sports Accessories

W

W.R. Case & Sons Cutlery Co., Owens Way, Bradford, PA 16701, P: 800-523-6350, F: 814-368-1736, www.wrcase.com
Cutlery; Knives/Knife Cases; Sharpeners

Walls Industries, Inc., 1905 N. Main, Cleburne, TX 76033, P: 800-433-1765, F: 817-645-8544, www.wallsoutdoors.com
Camouflage; Gloves, Mitts, Hats; Men's Clothing

Walther USA, 2100 Roosevelt Ave., Springfield, MA 01104, P: 800-372-6454, F: 413-747-3317, www.waltheramerica.com
Bags & Equipment Cases; Firearms; Knives/Knife Cases; Law Enforcement; Lighting Products

Warson Group, Inc., 121 Hunter Ave., Suite 204, St. Louis, MO 63124, P: 877-753-2426, F: 314-721-0569, www.warson-group.com
Footwear

Watershed Drybags, 2000 Riverside Dr., Asheville, NC 28804, P: 828-252-7111, F: 828-252-7107, www.drybags.com
Backpacking; Bags & Equipment Cases; Camping; Gun Cases; Hunting Accessories; Law Enforcement; Survival Kits/First Aid; Training & Safety Equipment

WD-40 Co., 1061 Cudahy Pl., San Diego, CA 92110, P: 800-448-9340, F: 619-275-5823, www.wd40.com
Lubricants

Weatherby, Inc., 1605 Commerce Way, Paso Robles, CA 93446, P: 800-227-2016, F: 805-237-0427, www.weatherby.com
Ammunition; Custom Manufacturing; Firearms

Weaver Optics/ATK Commercial Products, N5549 Cty. Tk. Z, Onalaska, WI 54650, P: 800-635-7656, F: 763-323-3890, www.weaveroptics.com
Binoculars; Scopes, Sights & Accessories

Weber's Camo Leather Goods/Wilderness Dreams Lingerie & Swimwear, 615 Nokomis St., Suite 400, Alexandria, MN 56308, P: 320-762-2816, F: 320-763-9762, www.webersleather.com
Bags & Equipment Cases; Camouflage; Footwear; Home Furnishings; Hunting Accessories; Leathergoods; Men & Women's Clothing

Wellco Enterprises, 150 Westwood Circle, P.O. Box 188, Waynesville, NC 28786, P: 800-840-3155, F: 828-456-3547, www.wellco.com
Footwear; Law Enforcement

Wells Creek Outfitters, 803-12 SW 12th St., Bentonville, AR, 72712, P: 479-273-1174, F: 479-273-0137
Camouflage; Hunting Accessories; Men's Clothing

Wenger N.A./Wenger, Maker of the Genuine Swiss Army Knife, 15 Corporate Dr., Orangeburg, NY 10962, P: 800-431-2996, F: 845-425-4700, www.wengerna.com
Backpacking; Camping; Cutlery; Footwear; Hunting Accessories; Knives/Knife Cases; Watches

Western Powders, Inc., P.O. Box 158, Miles City, MT 59301, P: 800-497-1007, F: 406-234-0430, www.blackhorn209.com
Black Powder/Smokeless Powder; Firearms Maintenance Equipment; Lubricants; Reloading; Wholesaler/Distributor

Western Rivers, Inc., 1582 N. Broad St., Lexington, TN 38351, P: 800-967-0998, F: 731-967-1243, www.western-rivers.com
Decoys; Game Calls; Hunting Accessories; Lighting Products; Pet Supplies; Scents & Lures; Scopes, Sights & Accessories

Westfield Outdoor, Inc., 1593 Esprit Dr., Westfield, IN 46074, P: 317-569-0679, F: 317-580-1834, www.westfieldoutdoor.com
Backpacking; Camping

White Flyer Targets/Div. Reagent Chemical & Research, Inc., 115 Route 202/31 S, Ringoes, NJ 08851, P: 800-322-7855, F: 908-284-2113, www.whiteflyer.com
Clay Targets; Firearms; Shooting Range Equipment; Targets

Whites Boots, E. 4002 Ferry Ave., Spokane, WA 99202, P: 509-535-2422, F: 509-535-2423, www.whitesboots.com
Footwear

Whitetails Unlimited, 2100 Michigan St., Sturgeon Bay, WI 54235, P: 920-743-6777, F: 920-743-4658, www.whitetailsunlimited.com
Online Services; Outdoor Art, Jewelry, Sculpture; Videos; Wildlife Management

Wilcox Industries Corp., 25 Piscataque Dr., Newington, NH 03801, P: 603-431-1331, F: 603-431-1221, www.wilcoxind.com
Law Enforcement; Scopes, Sights & Accessories

Wild West Guns, LLC, 7100 Homer Dr., Anchorage, AK 99518-3229, P: 800-992-4570, F: 907-344-4005, www.wildwestguns.com
Custom Manufacturing; Firearms; Gun Parts/Gunsmithing; Outfitter; Recoil Protection Devices & Services; Scopes, Sights & Accessories; Wholesaler/Distributor

Wild Wings, LLC, 2101 S. Hwy. 61, P.O. Box 451, Lake City, MN 55041, P: 800-445-6413, F: 651-345-2981, www.wildwings.com
Decoys; Home Furnishings; Outdoor Art, Jewelry, Sculpture; Wholesaler/Distributor

Wilderness Calls, 12118 Capur St., Orlando, FL 38837, P: 407-620-8833, F: 407-620-8853

Wilderness Mint, P.O. Box 1866, Orting, WA 98360, P: 800-294-9600, F: 360-893-4400, www.wildernessmint.com
Emblems & Decals; Hunting Accessories; Outdoor Art, Jewelry, Sculpture; Watches

Wildfowler Outfitter/Tundra Quest, LLC, 5047 Walnut Grove, San Gabriel, CA 91776, P: 877-436-7177, F: 626-286-9918
Archery; Blinds, Custom Manufacturing; Export/Import Specialists; Feeder Equipment; Men's Clothing; Outfitter; Treestands

Wildlife Research Center, Inc., 14485 Azurite St. NW, Ramsey, MN 55303, P: 800-873-5873, F: 763-427-8354, www.wildlife.com
Scents & Lures

Wildsteer, 9 Avenue Eugene Brisson, Bourges, F-18000, FRANCE, P: 011 33248211380, F: 011 33248211380, www.wildsteer.com
Archery; Knives/Knife Cases; Leathergoods

Wiley X., Inc., 7491 Longard Rd., Livermore, CA 94551, P: 800-776-7842, F: 925-455-8860, www.wileyx.com
Eye Protection

William Henry Studio, 3200 NE Rivergate St., McMinnville, OR 97128, P: 888-563-4500, F: 503-434-9704, www.williamhenrystudio.com
Cutlery; Knives/Knife Cases

Williams Gun Sight Co., 7389 Lapeer Rd., Davison, MI 48423, P: 800-530-9028, F: 810-658-2140, www.williamsgunsight.com
Black Powder Accessories; Books/Industry Publications; Compasses; Gun Parts/Gunsmithing; Hunting Accessories; Scopes, Sights & Accessories

Wilson Arms Co., 97 Leetes Island Rd., Branford, CT 06405, P: 203-488-7297, F: 203-488-0135, www.wilsonarms.com
Custom Manufacturing; Firearms; Gun Barrels

Winchester Ammunition/Div. Olin Corp., 427 N. Shamrock St., East Alton, IL 62024, P: 618-258-2365, F: 618-258-3609, www.winchester.com
Ammunition

Winchester Repeating Arms, 275 Winchester Ave., Morgan, UT 84050, P: 801-876-3440, F: 801-876-3737, www.winchesterguns.com
Firearms

Winchester Safes/Granite Security Products, Inc., 4801 Esco Dr., Fort Worth, TX 76140, P: 817-561-9095, F: 817-478-3056, www.winchestersafes.com
Gun Cabinets/Racks/Safes

Winchester Smokeless Propellant, 6231 Robinson, Shawnee Mission, KS 66202, P: 913-362-9455, F: 913-362-1307
Black Powder/Smokeless Powder; Reloading

Winfield Galleries, LLC, 2 Ladue Acres, Ladue, MO 63124, P: 314-645-7636, F: 314-781-0224, www.winfieldgalleries.com
Computer Software; Outdoor Art, Jewelry, Sculpture

Wing-Sun Trading, Inc., 15501 Heron Ave., La Mirada, CA 90638, P: 866-944-1068, F: 714-522-6417
Backpacking; Binoculars; Camping; Compasses; Lighting Products; Photographic Equipment; Scopes, Sights & Accessories; Wholesaler/Distributor

Witz Sport Cases, 11282 Pyrites Way, Gold River, CA 95670, P: 800-499-1568, F: 916-638-1250, www.witzprod.com
Bags & Equipment Cases

Wolf Peak International, 1221 Marshall Way, Layton, UT 84041, P: 866-953-7325, F: 801-444-9353, www.wolfpeak.net
Airguns; Airsoft; Backpacking; Camouflage; Eyewear; Hunting Accessories; Law Enforcement; Shooting Range Equipment

Wolfe Publishing Co., 2625 Stearman Rd., Suite A, Prescott, AZ 86301, P: 800-899-7810, F: 928-778-5124, www.riflemagazine.com
Books/Industry Publications; Footwear; Gun Cabinets/Racks/Safes; Online Services; Outdoor Art, Jewelry, Sculpture

Wolverine, 9341 Courtland Dr., Rockford, MI 49351, P: 800-253-2184, F: 616-866-5666, www.wolverine.com
Footwear; Gloves, Mitts, Hats; Men's Clothing

Woods Outfitting, P.O. Box 3037, Palmer, AK 99645, P: 907-746-2534, F: 907-745-6283, www.woods-outfitting.com
Outfitter

Woods Wise Products, P.O. Box 681552, Franklin, TN 37068, P: 800-735-8182, F: 931-364-7925, www.woodswise.com
Blinds; Custom Manufacturing; Decoys; Game Calls; Hunting Accessories; Scents & Lures; Videos

Woolrich, Inc./Elite Series Tactical, 1 Mill St., Woolrich, PA 17779, P: 800-996-2299, F: 570-769-7662, www.woolrich.com, www.woolricheliteseriestactical.com
Footwear; Gloves, Mitts, Hats; Home Furnishings; Law Enforcement; Men & Women's Clothing; Wholesaler/Distributor

World Famous Sports, 3625 Dalbergia St., Suite A, San Diego, CA 92113, P: 800-848-9848, F: 619-231-1717, www.worldfamoussports.com
Bags & Equipment Cases; Camouflage; Camping; Gloves, Mitts, Hats; Hunting Accessories; Men & Women's Clothing

Wrangler Rugged Wear/Wrangler ProGear, 400 N. Elm St., Greensboro, NC 27401, P: 336-332-3977, F: 336-332-3518, www.wrangler.com
Men's Clothing

Wycon Safari Inc. (WY)/Wynn Condict, P.O. Box 1126, Saratoga, MY 82331, P: 307-327-5502, F: 307-327-5332, www.wyconsafariinc.com
Outfitter

X

X-Caliber Accuracy Systems, 1837 First St., Bay City, MI 48708, P: 989-893-3961, F: 989-893-0241, www.xcaliberaccuracy.com
Hunting Accessories

X-Caliber Tactical, 1111 Winding Creek Pl., Round Rock, TX 78664, P: 512-524-2621, www.xcalibertactical.com
Airguns; Airsoft; Custom Manufacturing; Export/Import Specialists; Law Enforcement; Wholesaler/Distributor

Xenonics Holdings, Inc., 2236 Rutherford Rd., Suite 123, Carlsbad, CA 92008, P: 760-448-9700, FL 760-929-7571, www.xenonics.com
Law Enforcement; Lighting Products

XGO/Polarmax, 5417 N.C. 211, P.O. Box 968, West End, NC 27376, P: 800-552-8585, F: 910-673-3875, www.xgotech.com
Men & Women's Clothing

Xisico USA, Inc./Rex Optics USA, Inc., 16802 Barker Springs, Suite 550, Houston, TX 77084, P: 281-647-9130, F: 208-979-2848, www.xisicousa.com
Airguns; Ammunition; Binoculars; Scopes, Sights & Accessories

XS Sight Systems, 2401 Ludella St., Fort Worth, TX 76105, P: 888-744-4880, F: 800-734-7939, www.xssights.com
Gun Parts/Gunsmithing; Law Enforcement; Scopes, Sights & Accessories

Y

Yaktrax, 9221 Globe Center Dr., Morrisville, NC 27560, P: 800-446-7587, F: 919-544-0975, www.yaktrax.com
Backpacking; Camping; Footwear; Sports Accessories

Yamaha Motor Corp., U.S.A., 6555 Katella Ave., Cypress, CA 90630, P: 714-761-7300, F: 714-503-7184
Vehicles, Utility & Rec

Yankee Hill Machine Co., Inc., 20 Ladd Ave., Suite 1, Florence, MA 01062, P: 877-892-6533, F: 413-586-1326, www.yhm.net
Firearms; Gun Barrels; Gun Cases; Gun Parts/Gunsmithing; Law Enforcement; Scopes, Sights & Accessories

Yukon Advanced Optics, 201 Regency Pkwy., Mansfield, TX 76063, P: 817-453-9966, F: 817-453-8770
Archery; Backpacking; Binoculars; Camping; Custom Manufacturing; Hunting Accessories; Scopes, Sights & Accessories; Wholesaler/Distributor

Z

Z-Blade, Inc., 28280 Alta Vista Ave., Valencia, CA 91355, P: 800-734-5424, F: 661-295-2615, www.pfimold.com
Custom Manufacturing; Hunting Accessories; Knives/Knife Cases

Zak Tool, 319 San Luis Rey Rd., Arcadia, CA 91007, P: 615-504-4456, F: 931-381-2568, www.zaktool.com
Law Enforcement; Training & Safety Equipment

Zanotti USA, 7907 High Knoll Ln., Houston, TX 77095, P: 281-414-2184, www.zanottiusa.com
Custom Manufacturing; Firearms

Zarc International, Inc., P.O. Box 108, Minonk, IL 61760, P: 800-882-7011, F: 309-432-3490, www.zarc.com
Law Enforcement; Retail Packaging

Zephyr Graf-x, 5443 Earhart Rd., Loveland, CO 80538, P: 970-663-3242, F: 970-663-7695, www.zhats.com
Camouflage; Custom Manufacturing; Gloves, Mitts, Hats; Men & Women's Clothing; Retailer Services

Zero Tolerance Knives, 18600 SW Tetaon Ave., Tualatin, OR 97062, P: 800-325-2891, F: 503-682-7168, www.ztknives.com
Knives/Knife Cases; Law Enforcement

Ziegel Engineering Working Designs, Jackass Field Carts, 2108 Lomina Ave., Long Beach, CA 90815, P: 562-596-9481, F: 562-598-4734, www.ziegeleng.com
Archery; Bags & Equipment Cases; Black Powder Accessories; Custom Manufacturing; Gun Cabinets/Racks/Safes; Gun Cases; Law Enforcement; Shooting Range Equipment

Zippo Manufacturing Co., 33 Barbour St., Bradford, PA 16701, P: 814-368-2700, F: 814-362-1350, www.zippo.com
Camping; Knives/Knife Cases; Lighting Products; Sports Accessories

Zistos Corp., 1736 Church St., Holbrook, NY 11741, P: 631-434-1370, F: 631-434-9104, www.zistos.com
Law Enforcement

Zodi Outback Gear, P.O. Box 4687, Park City, UT 84060, P: 800-589-2849, F: 800-861-8228
Archery; Backpacking; Camping; Cooking Equipment/Accessories; Hunting Accessories; Pet Supplies; Sports Accessories; Training & Safety Equipment

ZOLL Medical Corp., 269 Mill Rd., Chelmsford, MA 01824, P: 800-348-9011, F: 978-421-0025, www.zoll.com
Law Enforcement; Survival Kits/First Aid; Training & Safety Equipment

NUMBERS

10 Minute Deer Skinner, P.O. Box 158, Stillwater, OK 74076; P: 405-377-2222, F: 405-624-6060, www.tenminutedeerskinner.com
Cooking Equipment/Accessories; Hunting Accessories; Outfitter, Videos

32north Corp - STABILicers, 6 Arctic Circle, Buddeford, ME 04005, P: 800-782-2423, F: 207-284-5015, www.32north.com
Backpacking; Footwear; Hunting Accessories; Law Enforcement; Sports Accessories

3M Thinsulate™ Insulation / 3M Scotchgard™ Protector, 3M Center Building 235-2F-06, St. Paul, MN 55144-1000, P: 800-364-3577, F: 651-737-7659, www.thinsulate.com
Men & Women's Clothing; Footwear; Gloves, Mitts, Hats

3Point5.com, 224 South 200 West, Suite 230, Salt Lake City, UT 84101, P: 801-456-6900/2007, F: 801-485-5039, www.3point5.com

5.11 Tactical Series, 4300 Spyres Way, Modesto, CA 95356, P: 866-451-1726/348, F: 209-548-5348, www.511tactical.com
Bags & Equipment Cases; Men & Women's Clothing; Eyewear; Footwear; Gloves, Mitts, Hats; Law Enforcement; Watches

5-Hour Energy, 46570 Humboldt Drive, Novi, MI 48377, P: 248-960-1700/209, F: 248-960-1980, www.fivehour.com
Food; Hunting Accessories; Law Enforcement; Outfitter; Sports Accessories; Wholesaler/Distributor